D1604847

Minnesota Place Names

Minnesota Place Names

A Geographical Encyclopedia

Third Edition, Revised and Enlarged

WARREN UPHAM

MINNESOTA HISTORICAL SOCIETY PRESS

Publication of this book was supported in part by the Elmer L. and Eleanor J. Andersen Publications Endowment Fund of the Minnesota Historical Society.

www.mnhs.org/mhspress

Manufactured in the United States of America

10 9 8 7 6 5 4 3 2 1

International Standard Book Number
0-87351-396-7

♾ The paper used in this publication meets the minimum requirements of the American National Standard for Information Sciences—Permanence for Printed Library Materials, ANSI Z39.48-1984.

Library of Congress
Cataloging-in-Publication Data

Upham, Warren, 1850–1934.
    Minnesota place names : a geographical encyclopedia / Warren Upham.—3rd ed., rev. and enl.
        p. cm.
    Rev. ed. of: Minnesota geographic names. 1979.
    Includes index.
    ISBN 0-87351-396-7 (hc. : alk. paper)
    1. Names, Geographical—Minnesota.
    2. Minnesota—History, Local.
    I. Upham, Warren, 1850–1934. Minnesota geographic names.
    II. Title.

F604.U66 2001
977.6—dc21
                                        00-048207

Minnesota Place Names

━━━━━━━━━━

Counties

Introduction to the Third Edition

For decades, *Minnesota Place Names* has settled arguments, delighted browsers, enriched road trips, satisfied curiosity, located ancestors, and launched research projects. No matter what their questions, people have found in this book the stories behind the names, those miniature history lessons that capture the lost lore of familiar places and reveal the history woven through everyday life. This revised third edition significantly expands the astonishing wealth of information collected by Warren Upham and makes it available to a new generation.

Revising this classic has presented a considerable challenge. The first edition, published in 1920 as *Minnesota Geographic Names*, included about 15,000 names. The 1969 edition reproduced the original text and, in three separate lists, added 1,400 names and corrections. This completely revised and updated third edition, with more than 20,000 names, incorporates those lists as well as more names of new and old places. Research was carried out by Patricia C. Harpole, who had recently retired as the society's reference librarian. Consulting various federal, state, and local authorities, reading numerous local histories, digging into little-known sources, she tirelessly updated and added thousands of entries.

Users of this comprehensive resource will still hear the idiosyncratic and antiquarian voice of its compiler, Warren Upham, who collected Minnesota place names for forty years. While fans of earlier editions will be pleased to meet an old friend again, newer readers may be surprised by Upham's distinctly nineteenth-century voice. But that voice is appropriate: the work still reflects the obsession of its creator. The biographical sketch "Warren Upham and Minnesota's Place Names" on page viii helps explain how and why.

This volume will not remain accurate for long. New cities are incorporated as suburbs grow into the countryside—and even their names do not remain unchanged. The city of Ventura, incorporated in May 2000, was named for the state's world-famous governor by city leaders who hoped to win publicity and support for the incorporation. Residents voted six months later to rename the city St. Augusta, the name carried by the township since 1863. Place names may change for other reasons. In 1995 the Minnesota legislature mandated that all nineteen of the state's geographic features using the name "squaw" be renamed, because the word is believed to be a French corruption of an Iroquois word for female genitalia. And places may be invented. While there is no Lake Wobegon in Minnesota, in 1998 a bicycle trail in Stearns County was named the Lake Wobegon Trail. It winds past the towns that inspired Garrison Keillor's creation of the community.

Minnesota Place Names offers readers more than an amusing list of stories from the past. It suggests a personal connection to history. Naming a place is a way of connecting to it, of making it more familiar, of taking ownership of it—of developing a true sense of place. These names help communities establish identity, honor those who came before them, both Indian and white, and sometimes even reveal the namers' dreams for the future. By knowing those stories, we share in that honoring and in those dreams. It is the way we say, "This is our home."

Warren Upham
and Minnesota's Place Names

Warren Upham was a compulsive collector of minutiae. A geologist, archaeologist, and librarian, a pedantic precisionist and a formalist of infinite Old World courtesy, he amassed an astonishing compendium in this volume. At its first publication in 1920, *Minnesota Geographic Names* was a pioneering, pace-setting effort in place-name literature. It also reflected its author's personality and passions. Upham's distinctive voice inspires curiosity about the man himself and the process by which he wrote the book.

Upham, one of ten children, was born in 1850 on a farm near Amherst, New Hampshire. He was a graduate of Dartmouth College, class of 1871. From 1874 to 1878 he served as an assistant on the geological survey of New Hampshire, and he held the same position on the geological survey of Minnesota from 1879 to 1885 under state geologist Newton H. Winchell. During his first three years in Minnesota, Upham was engaged in field work, traveling (as the *St. Paul Daily Globe* reported on October 20, 1895) "11,000 miles, driving with horse about twenty-five miles daily, and thus thoroughly examining fifty of the . . . counties of Minnesota." He spent another two years—1893 and 1894—painstakingly surveying Aitkin and Cass Counties, the area around Duluth, and northern St. Louis County.

Upham put the knowledge gained in his travels to good use, becoming a prolific writer in the field of geology. He contributed articles to periodicals such as the *American Geologist* and the Minnesota Academy of Science *Bulletin*; his books include *The Geology of Lake Agassiz* (1887) and *Geologic and Archaeologic Time* (1915). In all, he published 321 books, papers, articles, and addresses.

An interruption in his Minnesota residency occurred in 1895 when he spent part of a year as archaeologist and librarian at the Western Reserve Historical Society in Cleveland. On January 1, 1896, Upham returned to Minnesota to succeed J. Fletcher Williams as superintendent and librarian of the Minnesota Historical Society, a dual post that he held until 1914; from then until 1934 he served as the society's archaeologist.

Although Upham's early notebooks and diaries are filled with place-name references carefully recorded in his minuscule handwriting, the first official indication of his interest in this subject appeared in the society's minute books on May 8, 1899. Before a meeting of the institution's executive council on that date Upham "read a part of a paper prepared by him, entitled 'Origin of Minnesota Geographic Names.'" The minutes recorded that "the Council voted its thanks, and referred this paper to the Publication Committee." The society, however, made no further attempt to publish it at that time.

In 1901 Upham, anxious to get on with his place-name study under the society's sponsorship, argued that "the value and utility [of such research] can hardly be overestimated." By 1903 the society's *Biennial Report* recorded that plans were definitely afoot for a volume "giving the origin, meaning, and date, so far as can be ascertained, of all our proper names, as of the state, its counties and townships, cities, villages, railway stations, post offices, creeks, rivers and lakes, hills and mountains, and the streets and parks in cities." In that year, Upham began serious work on the subject, a task that was not to be completed until seventeen years later. Progress was no doubt slowed by his work with Rose Dunlap on *Minnesota Biographies*, an 891-page compendium of more than 14,000 brief sketches of Minnesotans, published in 1912 as volume fourteen of the *Collections of the Minnesota Historical Society.*

Research on the projected place-name volume was taking up most of his time by 1916. That summer was spent on what he called "considerable journeys" to the eighty-six county seats (Lake of the Woods County was established in 1922). During the winter of 1916, Upham returned to desk research and was "chiefly occupied in gathering such information from published county histories of this state, early books and pamphlets and maps of the first and later explorers, descriptions by travelers, U.S. exploring expeditions, books relating to our Indian tribes, the series of the Society's publications, early newspaper files, and all other published sources of such information in this Society's Library or elsewhere in St. Paul and Minneapolis."

The actual writing consumed about three years, and on January 23, 1919, Upham reported to his successor, the society's new superintendent, Solon J. Buck, that the manuscript was "fully ready for printing." Buck gave his "cordial approval," and by mid-1920 the finished work made its appearance in an edition of fifteen hundred copies as volume seventeen of the *Collections of the Minnesota Historical Society.*

In the 1910s the study of place names in this country had not reached anything like the high point of acceptability it enjoyed in Europe, especially in England. The Upham volume, therefore, made hardly a ripple on the ocean of historical publications. It garnered only a listing in *Writings on American History for 1920* and brief notices in the *Iowa Journal of History and Politics,* which called it a "distinct contribution," and the *Michigan History Magazine,* which saw it as a "model piece of workmanship," and (with tongue in cheek?) "prime material for the coming epic poet of the Gopher State." The only serious review of the book appeared, naturally enough, in the *Minnesota History Bulletin.* Melvin R. Gilmore, ethnobotanist and then curator of the State Historical Society of North Dakota, wrote, "Whoever undertakes and faithfully carries out the task of compiling the place names of a state, with their derivation and significance, performs a praiseworthy accomplishment and does a distinct public service. . . . This is . . . a most noteworthy work, the result of a vast amount of diligent, persistent, and painstaking labor. . . . It is to be wished that every state might have wrought out for it as good and full an account of its place names as this which has been written for Minnesota."

Upham's interest in place names did not flag with the publication of his book. The library of the Minnesota Historical Society possesses the author's own copy, copiously and carefully annotated in his spidery handwriting. His notes include amplifications, additions, corrections, and peripheral information that he considered germane or that simply interested him. Several notes, for instance, reflect the growing use of the state's nickname, "Land of Ten Thousand Lakes," which came into general use after the book's publication. In 1917 Upham himself had called Lake Minnetonka in Hennepin County "the Kohinoor of Minnesota's ten thousand lakes." In his annotated copy, the author expanded in several places on the origin of that inspired publicity catch phrase—from its first mention by Henry R. Schoolcraft in 1851 to its use in the Minnesota *Legislative Manual* of 1881. He called attention to volume one of *The Geology of Minnesota* (1884) in which N. H. Winchell stated: "The number of lakes in Minnesota is about ten thousand," and he recorded the appearance of the slogan "the country of ten thousand lakes" in the *St. Paul Dispatch and Pioneer Press Almanac and Year-Book for 1916.* Still another annotation recalled the organization late in 1917 of the Ten Thousand Lakes of Minnesota Association, which from 1919 through 1922 expended a total of $102,000 appropriated by the state legislature for the promotion of tourism. (In 2001 the state's Department of Natural Resources counted 11,842 bodies of water over ten acres in size.)

Upham died in 1934. He was eulogized by the *St. Paul Pioneer Press* as a member of "that distinguished group of pioneer Minnesota scientists who made the first survey of the state's geology." *Minnesota History* magazine remembered him as "a careful student, patient and industrious in assembling data, persevering in effort, willing to face large tasks, a representative of the old school of scholar and gentleman." He left his engineering level, rod, and other survey instruments to the Minnesota Historical Society's collections. And he left to all Minnesotans his great work on place names, which continues to contribute to the understanding of the state's history.

Introduction
to the Original Edition

During sixteen years, from 1879 to 1894, of service for the geological surveys of Minnesota, the United States, and Canada, in travel over large areas of this state, the Dakotas, and Manitoba, my attention was often attracted to the origins of their names of places, partly received directly from the Indian languages, and in many other instances translated from the aboriginal names. Frequently our geographic names note remarkable topographic features or are derived from the fauna and flora. Perhaps a greater number commemorate pioneer white explorers, early fur traders, and agricultural settlers.

Later work for the Minnesota Historical Society, since 1895, has permitted and even required more detailed consideration and record in this field. Many memorials of our territorial and state history are preserved in geographic names, and each nationality contributing to the settlement has its share in this nomenclature. As the first immigrants of the state along the Atlantic and Gulf Coast brought many place names from England, France, Holland, and Spain, so in Minnesota many geographic names have come from beyond the sea. Here the influence of a large proportion of immigration from Germany is shown by such names as New Ulm, New Trier, Hamburg, Cologne, and New Munich. Old Bohemia is brought to mind by the city of New Prague. Sweden, Norway, and Denmark are well represented by Stockholm, Malmo, Bergen, Trondhjem, Denmark, and many other township and village names. In the early eastern and southern states, Plymouth, Boston, Portsmouth, Bangor, New York, Charleston, St. Augustine, and New Orleans recalled tender memories of the Old World.

Likewise, these German and Bohemian and Scandinavian names have a great meaning to the immigrants from those countries who have made their new homes here.

To illustrate how this subject is like a garden of flowers, or like an epic poem, reference may be made to the names of the eighty-six [eighty-seven] Minnesota counties. Fifteen came directly, or through translation, from the Dakota or Sioux language, eight being retained as Sioux words, Anoka, Dakota, Isanti, Kandiyohi, Wabasha, Waseca, Watonwan, and Winona. Six are translated into English, namely, Big Stone, Blue Earth, Cottonwood, Redwood, Traverse, and Yellow Medicine; and one is received in its French translation, Lac qui Parle. Twelve counties bear names of Ojibwe origin; but only five, Chisago, Kanabec, Koochiching, Mahnomen, and Wadena, are Indian words, and the first was made by a white man's coinage. The seven others are Chippewa (the anglicized form of Ojibwe), Clearwater, Crow Wing, Mille Lacs (a translation in French), Otter Tail, Red Lake, and Roseau (another French translation).

Fifty-two counties have received personal names, which may be arranged in four lists. The early explorers of this area are commemorated by seven counties; the fur traders of the early half of the last century, by four; citizens of Minnesota as a territory and state have been honored by the names of twenty-six counties; and citizens of other parts of the United States are similarly honored in fifteen counties. First enumerating the seven county names from explorers, we have Beltrami, Carver, Cass, Hennepin, Le Sueur, Nicollet, and Pope. The four named for early fur traders are Aitkin, Faribault, Morrison, and Renville. The twenty-six counties named for Minnesota citizens are Becker, Brown, Carlton, Cook, Freeborn, Goodhue, Hubbard, Jackson, Kittson, Marshall, McLeod, Meeker, Mower, Murray, Nobles, Olmsted, Pennington, Ramsey, Rice, Sherburne, Sibley, Stearns, Steele, Swift, Todd, and Wilkin Counties. Among the fifteen counties named for citizens of this country outside of Minnesota, five are in honor of presidents of the United States, these being Washington, Polk, Fillmore, Lincoln, and Grant. The ten others in this list are Benton, Clay, Dodge, Douglas, Houston, Lyon, Martin, Scott, Stevens, and Wright.

Six of our counties have names given by white men for natural features, in addition to the larger number so derived from the Indian languages. These are Itasca, taking the name of the lake, formed of two Latin words; Lake County, named for Lake Superior; Pine County, so named for its extensive pine forests; Pipestone County, for the Indian pipestone quarry there; Rock County, for the very prominent rock outcrop near Luverne; and St. Louis County, for its river of that name [also Lake of the Woods County, which became the eighty-seventh county]. One county received its name, Norman, in honor of its large number of immigrants from Norway.

The earliest systematic endeavor to trace the origins of Minnesota county names was published by John Fletcher Williams, secretary of the Minnesota Historical Society, as an article in the *St. Paul Pioneer*, March 13, 1870. Another contribution to this subject, by Return I. Holcombe of St. Paul, was in the *Pioneer Press Almanac*, 1896. Both these lists have been consulted, with much advantage, for the present volume.

In ascertaining derivations and meanings of Dakota and Ojibwe names, very valuable aid has been obtained from a paper, "Minnesota Geographical Names Derived from the Dakota Language, with some that are Obsolete," by Prof. Andrew W. Williamson, of Augustana College, Rock Island, Ill., published in the Thirteenth Annual Report of the Geological and Natural History Survey of Minnesota, for 1884, pages 104–112; and from another paper, in the Fifteenth Report of the same survey, for 1886, pages 451–477, "Minnesota Geographical Names Derived from the Chippewa Language," by Rev. Joseph A. Gilfillan of White Earth, who also supplied in later letters

many further notes of Ojibwe names. These two papers are the most important sources of information on Minnesota geographic terms of Indian origin, supplementing the frequent references to origins of names by Hennepin, Carver, Mackenzie, Thompson, Pike, Long and Keating, Beltrami, Schoolcraft, Allen, Featherstonhaugh, Catlin, Lea, Nicollet, and other explorers of the area which is now Minnesota.

The narratives of these discoverers and explorers, and many later books, pamphlets, newspapers, atlases, and maps, have been examined in the library of the Minnesota Historical Society. Special acknowledgments are due to the following books and authors:

Grammar and Dictionary of the Dakota Language, edited by Rev. Stephen R. Riggs, published by the Smithsonian Institution, Washington, 1852; and a revised edition of the greater part, a *Dakota-English Dictionary*, issued in 1890 as volume 7, "Contributions to North American Ethnology."

An English-Dakota Dictionary, compiled by John P. Williamson, printed by the American Tract Society, 1902.

A Grammar of the Otchipwe [Ojibwe] *Language*, 1878; *A Dictionary of the Otchipwe Language*, Part 1, *English-Otchipwe*, 1878; and Part 2, *Otchipwe-English*, 1880. These are editions published in Montreal, of volumes by Bishop Frederic Baraga, the *Grammar* having been first published in Detroit, 1850, and the *Dictionary* in Cincinnati, 1853.

A Glossary of Chippewa Indian Names of Rivers, Lakes, and Villages by Rev. Chrysostom Verwyst of Bayfield, Wis., in *Acta et dicta . . . of the Catholic Church in the Northwest*, published in St, Paul, volume 4, pages 253–274, July 1916.

Handbook of American Indians North of Mexico, edited by Frederick W. Hodge, published by the Smithsonian Institution as Bulletin 30, Bureau of American Ethnology, two volumes, 1907, 1910.

The Geological and Natural History Survey of Minnesota, 1872–1901, by Prof. N. H. Winchell, state geologist, and assistants: Annual Reports, 24 volumes; Bulletins, 10 volumes, treating partly of the mammals, birds, fishes, and the flora; Final Reports, 6 volumes, having chapters for all the counties and for the iron ore ranges.

Memoirs of Explorations in the Basin of the Mississippi by Hon. J. V. Brower of St. Paul, 8 volumes, 1898–1905. Four of these volumes relate to parts of this state, being vol. 3, Mille Lac, 1900; vol. 4, Kathio, 1901; vol. 5, Kakabikansing, 1902; and vol. 6, Minnesota, 1903.

Minnesota Historical Society Collections, 15 volumes, 1850–1915. Biographic references for places bearing names of personal derivation have been supplied in the greater part by the fourteenth volume, *Minnesota Biographies, 1655–1912.*

The Aborigines of Minnesota, a Report Based on the Collections of Jacob V. Brower, and on the Field Surveys and Notes of Alfred J. Hill and Theodore H. Lewis, Collated, Augmented and Described by N. H. Winchell, published by the Minnesota Historical Society, St. Paul, 1911.

The Origin of Certain Place Names in the United States, second edition, by Henry Gannett, published in 1905 as Bulletin 258 of the U.S. Geological Survey.

Complete Pronouncing Gazetteer or Geographical Dictionary of the World, published by the J. B. Lippincott Company, 1911, two volumes.

A History of the Origin of the Place Names Connected with the Chicago & Northwestern and Chicago, St. Paul, Minneapolis & Omaha Railways, . . . compiled by one [W. H. Stennett] *who for more than 34 years has been an officer in the employ of the system,* Chicago, 1908.

In the early progress of this research, a paper by the author, "Origin of Minnesota Geographic Names," including quite full notes for each county name, was read at a monthly meeting of the executive council of the Minnesota Historical Society, May 8, 1899; and a second address, entitled "The Origin and Meaning of Minnesota Names of Rivers, Lakes, Counties, Townships, and Cities," was presented at an annual meeting of this society, January 11, 1904. These papers were mainly published in a series of articles in the *Office Blotter,* a Minneapolis journal issued chiefly for the interest of Minnesota county officers, April to August, 1904; and they were again published with slight changes and additions in the *Magazine of History,* New York, volume 8, September to November, 1908. More condensed and somewhat revised, they were embodied in a newspaper article, "Whence Came the Names of Minnesota's Counties," in the *St. Paul Pioneer Press,* November 19, 1911. After further revision, notes of origins of the county names were published in numerous Minnesota daily newspapers, usually one

county each day in alphabetic order, in the spring and summer of 1916.

For interviews with county officers, pioneer settlers, and others, twenty counties of northern Minnesota were visited by the author in the autumn of 1909; and in the year 1916, from April to October, all the eighty-six counties were visited. Such personal interviews, to some extent followed by correspondence, have been the chief sources of information for most parts of this work, except for the considerable list of counties having published histories. Dates of organization of townships and villages are noted mainly from the county histories, so that comparatively few dates are given under other counties.

Published and personal sources consulted for each county are stated at the beginning of its catalogue of townships. To the many citizens who have contributed notes of the origins of place names, the author and the people of Minnesota are enduringly indebted. Within the lifetime of pioneers who shared in the first settlement and in all the development of this commonwealth, a careful record has been made of a very significant portion of its history.

The first chapter of the book treats of general features, as districts bearing topographic names, the state name and sobriquets, and the larger lakes and rivers. Eighty-six [eighty-seven] chapters treat of the place names of the counties in alphabetic order. The name of each county is first somewhat fully noticed; next the townships and villages are listed in their alphabetic series, preceded by the due mention of books and persons supplying information for the county; and last are records of lakes and steams, hills, prairies, and, in some of the counties, Indian reservations, iron ore ranges, state and national forests, state parks, glacial lakes, beaches, and moraines. Localities of exceptional historic interest are found in nearly every county.

To find notations of any city, township, village, lake, river or creek, hills and prairies, iron ranges, etc., the reader will consult the index, which is the key to all its contents. An explanation of abbreviations used in the index is given on its first page.

WARREN UPHAM

Minnesota Historical Society
St. Paul

Minnesota Place Names

General Features

The most conspicuous geographic features of this state are its large rivers and lakes, including the Minnesota River, whence the state is named, the Mississippi, largest of this continent, which here has its source and a great part of its course, the Red River, the Rainy, the St. Louis, and the St. Croix Rivers, Lake Superior, adjoining Minnesota by 150 miles of its northwest shore, Rainy Lake and Lake of the Woods, Red Lake, Winnibigoshish and Leech Lakes, and Mille Lacs, each requiring mention as belonging partly to two or more counties. Likewise the origins and meaning of the names of many smaller rivers and lakes need to be given in this chapter, to which reference may be made under their several counties, unless their names, borne by counties, townships, or villages, are thus fully noticed.

Districts Bearing Topographic Names

Only limited areas of Minnesota have low mountains or even any noteworthy hills that have received names. Such are hilly or somewhat mountainous tracts on the Vermilion and Mesabi Ranges, names that designate belts having immense deposits of iron ores, noted under Itasca, St. Louis, Lake, and Cook Counties. The first of these ranges was named from the Vermilion Lake and River in St. Louis County. The second has an Ojibwe name, spelled "Missabay Heights" by Joseph N. Nicollet, translated as Giant Mountain by Rev. Joseph A. Gilfillan. It is spelled Missabe, pronounced in three syllables, by Frederic Baraga's *Dictionary of the Ojibway Language,* which defines it as "Giant; also, a very big stout man."

The third and more southern belt of iron ores, latest discovered but now having many and large mines, was named the Cuyuna Range by its discoverer, Cuyler Adams, from his own name and from his dog, Una, who accompanied him on many prospecting trips. This iron range has no prominently hilly tract.

From Duluth to the northeast corner of this state, the land rises generally 500 to 800 feet or more above Lake Superior within a few miles of its shore, forming the southern margin of a high wooded area that reaches to the international boundary and is diversified by mostly low ridges and hills. Seen from passing boats, the eroded front of this highland for about 30 miles in Cook County, from Carlton Peak to Grand Marais, presents a peculiarly serrate profile and is therefore commonly called the Sawtooth Mountains, more definitely noted for that county.

Morainic hills of the glacial drift, amassed along the borders of the continental ice sheet, are traced in 12 successive belts across this state. The most noteworthy development of these hills is found in Otter Tail County, where the eighth and ninth moraines are merged to form the Leaf Hills, called "mountains" by the settlers in contrast with the lower hills in other parts of the state, rising in steep slopes to heights of 200 to 350 feet along an extent of about 20 miles. Their name, more fully considered in the county chapter, is translated from the Ojibwe name, which was thence applied by the Ojibwe to the Leaf Lakes and River and by the white people to Leaf Mountain Township.

An important contrast is exhibited by the vegetation in different parts of Minnesota. Forest covers its northeastern two-thirds approximately, while about one-third, lying at the south and southwest and reaching in the Red River Valley to the Canadian line as also the part of this valley north to Lake Winnipeg, is prairie. Half of the state, on the northeast, had originally extensive tracts of very valuable white pine and red pine, which have been mostly cut down by lumbermen. Interspersed with these and other evergreen species, as the spruces, balsam fir, and arbor vitae, were tracts of maple, elm, bass, oak, ash, and other deciduous trees. The Big Woods, a translation from the early French name, Grand Bois, occupied a large area west of the Mississippi, including Wright, Carver, Scott, and Le Sueur Counties, with parts of adjacent counties. Until its timber was cleared off for cultivation of the land in farms, this area was heavily wooded with the deciduous forest, shedding its leaves before winter, lying south of the geographic range of the pines and their allies.

In the great prairie region of southwestern Minnesota and extending northward into the northeast part of South Dakota, a large elevated district is enclosed by the contour line of 1,500 feet above the sea. This area comprises Pipestone County and the greater parts of Lincoln, Murray, Nobles, and Rock Counties in this state, having an entire length in the two states of about 160 miles. It was named by the early French voyageurs and explorers the Coteau des Prairies, as on Nicollet's map, meaning the Highland of the Prairies.

The many beautiful lakes of Alexandria and its vicinity, the adjoining country southward to Glenwood and northwest to Fergus Falls and their landscapes of alternating woods and small openings of prairies, have given the name Park Region to that district, lying between the unbroken northeastern forest and the limitless prairie on the west.

Another area of many lakes and streams, having somewhat similar features as the foregoing but with a mainly less rolling and diversified contour, excepting the valleys and enclosing bluffs of its rivers, was named by Nicollet the Undine Region, comprising the country of the Blue Earth River and its tributaries, as noticed in the chapter of Blue Earth County.

The Name of the State

Minnesota received its name from the largest river that lies wholly within its area, excepting only that its sources above Big Stone Lake are in South Dakota. During 150 years, up to the time of the organization of Minnesota Territory in 1849, the name St. Pierre or St. Peter had been generally applied to this river by French and English explorers and writers. March 6, 1852, the territorial legislature adopted a memorial to the president of the United States, requesting that this name should be discontinued and that only the aboriginal name should be used for the river, the same as for the territory, by the different government departments; and this was so decreed on June 19 of the same year by an act of Congress.

The old name, St. Peter's River, of French derivation, seems probably to have been given in commemoration of its first exploration by Pierre Charles Le Sueur. If so, however, his first journey up the Minnesota River was more than ten years before his expedition upon it in the year 1700 when he mined what he supposed to be an ore of copper in the bluffs of the Blue Earth River near the site of Mankato; for the St. Peter and St. Croix Rivers are mentioned by these names in Nicolas Perrot's proclamation at his Fort St. Antoine on Lake Pepin, taking possession of this region for France, dated May 8, 1689.

The Dakota, or Sioux, name Minnesota means sky-tinted water (*Minne*, water, and *sota*, somewhat clouded), as Rev. Edward D. Neill translated it on the authority of Rev. Gideon H. Pond. The river at its stages of flood becomes whitishly turbid. An illustration of the meaning of the words was told to the present writer by Mrs. Moses N. Adams, the widow of the well-known missionary of the Dakotas. She stated that at various times the Dakota women explained it to her by dropping a little milk into water and calling the whitishly clouded water "Minne sota."

Maj. Stephen H. Long in 1817 wrote that the Mississippi above the St. Croix had a name meaning Clear River, and Dr. William W. Folwell in 1919 concluded that the Minnesota means this, contrasted with the very muddy Missouri.

In the years 1846–48, Hon. Henry H. Sibley and Hon. Morgan L. Martin, the delegate in Congress from Wisconsin, proposed this name for the new territory, which thus followed the example of Wisconsin in adopting the title of a large stream within its borders. During the next few years, it displaced the name St. Peter as applied in common usage by the white people to the river, whose euphonious Dakota title will continue to be borne by the river and the state.

Gen. James H. Baker, in an address on the history of Lake Superior before the Minnesota Historical Society at its annual meeting in 1879 and published in the third volume of its Collections (1880, pp. 333–55), directed attention, as follows, to a somewhat comparable Ojibwe name for the wooded northern part of this state. "In one of my expeditions upon the north shore, being accompanied by an intelligent Chippewa chief, I found the shrub, Balm of Gilead, a small tree of medicinal virtue, in great abundance. He gave me its Chippewa name as *Mah-nu-sa-tia,* and said it was the name given by their people to all that country west of the great lake, because it was the country yielding the Mah-nu-sa-tia. In conversing with other intelligent Chippewas, I found this statement was invariably confirmed. They claim it as the traditional name of the land to the west of the lake." This Ojibwe word, however, had no influence upon the selection of our territorial and state name. Indeed, it was generally unknown to the white people here until more than 20 years after the Dakota name was chosen.

The name Itasca, devised in 1832 by Henry R. Schoolcraft with the aid of Rev. William T. Boutwell for the lake at the head of the Mississippi, was urged by Boutwell for the territory. Other names were suggested in the discussions of Congress: Chippeway, Jackson, and Washington. Final choice of the name Minnesota was virtually decided in the convention held at Stillwater on August 26, 1848, which petitioned to Congress for territorial organization.

Jonathan Carver, who wintered with the Dakota on the Minnesota River in 1766–67, was the earliest author to record its Dakota name. He spelled it Menesotor in his *Travels through the Interior Parts of North America* and Menesoter on the accompanying map. It was spelled Menesota by Long and William H. Keating; Menisothé by Giacomo C. Beltrami; Minisotah by Nicollet; Minnay sotor by George W. Featherstonhaugh; Minesota by Hon. M. L. Martin and Hon. Stephen A. Douglas in bills introduced by them respectively in the House and Senate for organization of the territory; and Minnesota by Hon. H. H. Sibley at the Stillwater convention.

Sobriquets of Minnesota

Like Michigan, which is frequently called the Wolverine state, and Wisconsin, the Badger state, Minnesota has a favorite sobriquet or nickname, the Gopher state. Its origin has been given by the late Judge Charles E. Flandrau, who, in his *History of Minnesota,* says that the beaver, as well as the gopher, was advocated to give such a popular title. The latter gained the ascendancy, soon after the admission of Minnesota to statehood, on account of the famous "Gopher cartoon," published in derision of the Five Million Loan bill, which was passed by the first state legislature to encourage the building of railroads. The striped gopher, common throughout our prairie region, is the species depicted by the cartoon (*Minnesota in Three Centuries,* 1908, vol. I, pp. 75–76).

Minnesota is also often called the North Star state, in allusion to the motto "L'Etoile du Nord," chosen by Governor Sibley for the state seal in 1858. Another epithet for our fertile commonwealth more recently came into use from the Pan-American Exposition at Buffalo, N.Y., in 1901, where the superior exhibits of wheat, flour, and dairy products of Minnesota caused her to be called "the Bread and Butter state."

The Mississippi

The chief river of Minnesota, and indeed of North America, bears for all time the Algonquian name that it received from the Ojibwe who paddled their birch canoes on its head stream, within the area of this state, and on the lakes at its sources. This name, Mississippi, means simply the Great River. Such it is, being the second among the great rivers of the world, surpassed only by the Amazon.

Jean Nicolet, the first white explorer of Wisconsin, in the winter of 1634–35 went from Lake Michigan and Green Bay to Lake Winnebago and the upper Fox River and learned there from the Indians that the sea, as he understood them to say, was within three days' travel farther to the southwest. What he heard of was the Mississippi River.

It was first made known by name to Europeans in the *Jesuit Relations* of 1666–67, published in Paris in 1668, which mentions "the great river named Messipi." The *Relations* of 1670–71 gave a more definite description as follows: "It is a Southward course that is taken by the great river called by the natives Missisipi, which must empty somewhere in the region of the Florida sea, more than four hundred leagues hence (from the upper Great Lakes). . . . Some Savages have assured us that this is so noble a river that, at more than three hundred leagues' distance from its mouth, it is larger than the one flowing before Quebec; for they declare that it is more than a league wide [referring probably to its expansion in Lake Pepin]. They also state that all this vast stretch of country consists of nothing but treeless prairies."

Earlier names had been given by the Spaniards to this river in its lower part, seen on their expeditions. Thus, on the map resulting from Álonzo Álvarez de Pineda's exploration of the Gulf coast in 1519, the Mississippi is named Rio del Espiritu Santo (River of the Holy Spirit), and it continued to be commonly or frequently mapped under that name until its present Algonquian designation was generally adopted.

Father Jacques Marquette, writing of his canoe voyage on this river in 1673 with Louis Joliet, called it the Missisipi, but his map named it "R. de la Conception."

Father Louis Hennepin, in the first edition of his travels published in Paris in 1683, called the Mississippi the River Colbert, for the great French statesman who died that year, and so mapped it; but later editions named and mapped it as "Le Grand Fleuve Meschasipi."

Robert Cavalier, sieur de la Salle, writing August 22, 1682, designated it as "the river Colbert, named by the Iroquois Gastacha, and by the Ottawas the Mississipy." Elsewhere, however, in the same and other writings, La Salle and his companions more commonly used only the latter name, spelling it Mississipi.

Nicolas Perrot, after spending many years on the upper part of this river, in his Mémoire written in 1718 or within two or three years later, spoke of "the Micissypy, which is now named the Louisianne"; and a French map published in 1718 gave the name as "the Missisipi or St. Louis."

Carver, who traveled into the area of Minnesota in 1766, described and mapped this river with its present spelling, Mississippi, which was followed by Zebulon M. Pike, Gen. Lewis Cass and Schoolcraft, Long and Keating, Beltrami, and all later writers. Before this form became fully established, the name, as printed in books and maps, had many variations, which, according to an estimate by Dr. Elliott Coues, numbered probably 30 or more.

The first part of the name, *Missi*, means Great, being akin to the modern Ojibwe word, *Kitchi*, great, or *Gitche*, as it is spelled by Longfellow in "The Song of Hiawatha"; and the second part, *sippi*, otherwise spelled *sipi* or *sebe* or *zibi*, is the common Algonquian or Ojibwe word for a river. This name, received from the Ojibwe and other Algonquins by the earliest French missionaries and traders in the upper Mississippi region, though used by these Indians only for the upper part of the river as known to them, was extended by Marquette and Joliet and by La Salle to its entire course, displacing the numerous former Indian names that had been applied to its lower part.

Gilfillan wrote: "Below the junction of Leech

Lake river, it is called Kitchi-zibi, or Great river. I cannot find by inquiry that the Chippewas have ever called it Missizibi (Mississippi) or Missazibi. But I consider it very probable that in remote times they did, for Missa-zibi (Mississippi) would express the same idea in their language, and would be proper, as witness Missa-sagaiigun (Mille Lacs), meaning Great Lake. It so exactly corresponds with their language that it must have been taken from it."

Endeavoring to translate more fully the aboriginal significance of *Missi*, Henry Gannett says that Mississippi means "great water" or "gathering in of all the waters" and "an almost endless river spread out."

The phrase "Father of Waters," popularly given to this river, has no warrant in the Algonquian name. In 1854 Schoolcraft wrote: "The prefixed word Missi is an adjective denoting all, and, when applied to various waters, means the collected or assembled mass of them. . . . It is only symbolically that it can be called the Father of American rivers, unless such sense occurs in the other Indian tongues."

The United State Congress recognized the significance of the river in 1988 by creating the Mississippi National River and Recreational Area as part of the National Park system. Stretching along 76 miles through the Twin Cities to the river's junction with the St. Croix River, this area encompasses 54,000 acres, of which 43 acres are owned by the National Park Service.

Red Lake and River

Red Lake is translated from its Ojibwe name, which, like Vermilion Lake, refers to the red and vermilion hues of the smooth water surface reflecting the color of the sky at sunset on calm evenings in summer, as noted in the chapters of Red Lake County and St. Louis County. The Red River, named from the lake, is the boundary of Minnesota at the west side of six counties, flowing thence to Lake Winnipeg. Its more distinctive name, Red River of the North, was used by Nicollet to distinguish it from the Red River tributary to the lower Mississippi.

An exceedingly flat plain adjoins the Red River, having an imperceptible descent northward, as also from each side to its central line. Along the axial depression the river has cut a channel 20 to 60 feet deep. It is bordered by only a few and narrow areas of bottomland, instead of which its banks usually rise steeply on one side and by moderate slopes on the other to the broad valley plain that thence reaches nearly level 10 to 25 miles from the river. This vast plain, lying half in Minnesota and half in North Dakota, with continuation into Manitoba and so stretching from Lake Traverse and Breckenridge north to Lake Winnipeg, a distance of 300 miles, is the widely famed Red River valley, one of the most productive wheat-raising districts of the world.

Glacial Lake Agassiz and River Warren

The farmers and other residents of this fertile plain are well aware that they live on the area once occupied by a great lake, for its beaches, having the form of smoothly rounded ridges of gravel and sand, a few feet high, with a width of several rods, are observable extending horizontally long distances upon each of the slopes that rise east and west of the valley plain. Hundreds of farmers have located their buildings on the beach ridges as the most dry and sightly spots on their land, affording opportunity for perfectly drained cellars even in the most wet spring seasons and also yielding to wells, dug through this sand and gravel, better water than is usually obtainable in wells on the adjacent clay areas.

Numerous explorers of this region, from Long and Keating in 1823, to Gen. Gouverneur K. Warren in 1868 and Prof. Newton. H. Winchell in 1872, observed the lacustrine features of the valley, and the last named geologist first gave what is now generally accepted as the true explanation of the lake's existence, namely, that it was produced in the closing stage of the glacial period by the dam of the continental ice sheet at the time of its final melting away. As the border of the ice sheet retreated northward along the valley, drainage from it could not flow as now freely to the north through Lake Winnipeg and into the ocean at

Hudson Bay but was turned southward by the ice barrier to the lowest place on the watershed dividing this basin from that of the Mississippi. The lowest point is found at Browns Valley, on the western boundary of Minnesota, where an ancient watercourse, about 125 feet deep and a mile to a mile and a half wide, extends from Lake Traverse at the head of the Bois des Sioux, a tributary of the Red River, to Big Stone Lake, through which the head stream of the Minnesota River passes in its course to the Mississippi and the Gulf of Mexico.

Detailed exploration of the shorelines and area of this lake was begun by the present writer for the Minnesota Geological Survey in the years 1879–81 under the direction of Professor Winchell, the state geologist. In subsequent years I was employed in tracing the lakeshores through North Dakota for the U.S. Geological Survey and through southern Manitoba to the distance of 100 miles north from the international boundary to Riding Mountain for the Geological Survey of Canada. For the last named survey, also, J. B. Tyrrell extended the exploration of the shorelines more or less completely for 200 miles farther north, along the Riding and Duck Mountains and the Porcupine and Pasquia Hills, west of Lakes Manitoba and Winnipegosis, to the Saskatchewan River.

This glacial lake was named in the eighth annual report of the Minnesota Geological Survey, for the year 1879, in honor of Louis Agassiz, the first prominent advocate of the theory of the formation of the drift by land ice. The outflowing river, whose channel is now occupied by Lakes Traverse and Big Stone and Brown's Valley, was named, in a paper read before the American Association for the Advancement of Science at its Minneapolis meeting in 1883, the River Warren in commemoration of Gen. Warren's admirable work in the U.S. Engineering Corps in publishing maps and reports of the Minnesota and Mississippi River surveys. Descriptions of Lake Agassiz and the River Warren were partly given in the eighth and eleventh annual reports of the Minnesota Geological Survey and in the first, second,

and fourth volumes of its final report. Monograph 25 of the U.S. Geological Survey, "The Glacial Lake Agassiz," published in 1896, treats of its entire explored extent (658 pp., with many maps). Its area exceeded that of the state of Minnesota, being about 110,000 square miles or more than the united areas of the five Great Lakes that outflow to the St. Lawrence River.

Lake Superior and Other Lakes and Rivers

The name of Lake County refers to its adjoining the Grand Lac of Samuel de Champlain's map in 1632, which was mapped under its present name, Lake Superior, by Marquette in 1673. Its being the greatest lake in the series flowing to the St. Lawrence, or even the greatest freshwater lake in the world by surface area, was noted in the name used by Champlain in translation from Kitchigumi of the Ojibwe. Superior means simply the Upper Lake in that series.

Rainy Lake and River are likewise translations from their aboriginal and early French names. From the narration of a French voyageur Jacques de Noyon, who was there in 1688 or within a year or two earlier or later, we have the name Ouchichiq or Koochiching, given by the Crees to this river and adopted by the Ojibwe. Joseph la France, traveling there in 1740, noted the derivation of the name Lac de la Pluie, meaning in English the Lake of the Rain, from the mist of the falls of Rainy River at the present city named International Falls. Further consideration of these names is given for Koochiching County.

On the sketch map drawn in 1730 by an Assiniboine named Ochagach for Verendrye, the Lake of the Woods is unnamed, but the country at its north side is shown as inhabited by the Cree. In 1737 and 1754 it was mapped as Lac des Bois, from which the English name is translated.

La France in 1740 recorded its aboriginal names, in translation, as "Lake Du Bois, or Des Isles," that is, the Lake of the Woods or of the Islands. It is entirely surrounded by woods, though the border of the great prairie region is not far westward, and its second name was given for the multitude of islands in its northern part. The

Ojibwe name of its broad southern part, adjoining Beltrami and Roseau Counties as noted by Gilfillan and Chrysostom Verwyst, refers to the sand dunes of Oak Point and Sable Island at the mouth of the Rainy River, whence this part was frequently called Sand Hill Lake by the early fur traders.

The St. Louis River is duly noticed for the county named from it, with mention of its earlier French name as the river of Fond du Lac, so called because there the series of falls and rapids along its last 15 miles descends to the level of Lake Superior. The Ojibwe name it Kitchigumi zibi, Lake Superior River.

Cass Lake early known as Red Cedar Lake in translation from the Ojibwe was renamed in honor of Gen. Lewis Cass, who, with Schoolcraft as historian of his expedition, visited it in 1820, regarding it as the chief source of the Mississippi. He is also commemorated by Cass County, for which the names of this lake and of Winnibigoshish and Leech Lakes are fully noticed.

Thief River lying mostly in Marshall County and having its source in Thief Lake is translated from the Ojibwe name, which is explained for the city at its mouth, Thief River Falls in Pennington County.

Clearwater River lying in three counties, one of which bears this name, is again a translation from the Ojibwe like Eau Claire of the same meaning, which designates a river, a county, and its city and county seat in Wisconsin.

The Wild Rice River and the lakes so named near its source are translations from Manomin or Mahnomen, the native grain much used and highly prized by the Ojibwe people as a staple part of their food, noted more in detail for Mahnomen County.

Crow Wing River and the county named from it present another translation from these Indians, for the outline of an island at the junction of this river with the Mississippi, which they fancifully compared with the wing of a raven. Farther south, on the boundary between Wright and Hennepin Counties, they applied to the Crow River a different name, correctly designating our American crow, the marauder of newly planted cornfields. These names, with the Ojibwe words from which they were translated, are again noticed in the chapter of Crow Wing County.

Sauk River in Todd and Stearns Counties, Osakis Lake at its source, lying partly in Douglas County, and the villages and cities of Osakis, Sauk Centre, and Sauk Rapids, the last being on the east side of the Mississippi opposite the mouth of the Sauk River, derived their names from a small party of Sac or Sauk Indians, who came as refugees from their own country in Wisconsin and lived near Osakis Lake, as related for the township and village of Sauk Rapids in Benton County.

Mille Lacs, as named by the French meaning "a thousand lakes," bore a Dakota name, Mde Wakan, nearly like Mini Wakan, their equivalent name which is translated Spirit Lake in Iowa. Its Ojibwe name is Minsi or Missi sagaigon, as spelled respectively by Nicollet in 1843 and De L'Isle in 1703, meaning Great Lake, just as the Mississippi is the Great River. These names are more elaborately reviewed in the chapter for Mille Lacs County, which also notes the origin of the name Rum River the outlet of this lake.

Kettle River in Carlton and Pine Counties is noticed for the latter in explanation of the name of Kettle River Township.

The Pine Lakes and River and the Ojibwe village of Chengwatana, meaning Pine Village, gave the names of Pine County and Pine City, its county seat.

Snake River is translated from the Ojibwe name, Kanabec sibi, which has several other spellings. Kanabec, retained as the designation of a county, with its accent on the second syllable, is widely different in both pronunciation and meaning from the Kennebec River in Maine.

St. Croix River, which, with the expansion of its lowest 20 miles in Lake St. Croix, forms the boundary of this state on the east side of Pine, Chisago, and Washington Counties, was called the River du Tombeau (Tomb or Grave River) by Hennepin in 1680, "R. de la Magdeleine" on Jean Baptiste Louis Franquelin's map in 1688, and the River St. Croix (Holy Cross) by Perrot's proclamation in 1689 and by the *Relation* of André Pénicaut in 1700. A cross had been set at its mouth, as noted by Pénicaut, probably to mark the grave of some French trader or voyageur. La Harpe, writing of Le Sueur's expedition in 1700, which was the theme of Pénicaut's *Relation*, described this stream as "a great river called St. Croix, because a Frenchman of that name was wrecked at its mouth."

Lake Pepin bears this name on De L'Isle's map of Canada or New France published in 1703. It may have been chosen, as stated by Gannett, in honor of Pepin le Bref, king of the Franks, who was born in 714 and died in 768. He was a son of Charles Martel and was the father of Charlemagne. Very probably the name was placed on the map by De L'Isle under request of his patron, the king of France. Pepin was an infrequent personal surname among the French settlers of Canada, whence many explorers and traders came to this region, but history has failed to record for whom and why this large lake of the Mississippi was so named. Hennepin, in his narration and map, had called it Lac des Pleurs (Lake of Tears) because there, as he wrote, some of the Dakota by whom he had been taken captive, with his companions, "wept the whole night, to induce the others to consent to our death." Pénicaut named it Lac Bon Secours, meaning Lake Good Help, apparently in allusion to the abundance of buffalo and other game found in its vicinity. This name, Bon Secours, and another, River des Boeufs, that is, River of Buffaloes, were early applied to the Chippewa River in Wisconsin, which was the geologic cause of Lake Pepin, by bringing much alluvium into the valley of the Mississippi below the lake. Its origin was thus like that of Lake St. Croix and like Lac qui Parle on the Minnesota River.

Cannon River joining the Mississippi at the head of Lake Pepin, is changed from its earlier French name, River aux Canots, meaning Canoe River, which alluded to canoes frequently left in concealment near its mouth by Indians and by French traders, especially when going on the hunt for buffalo in the adjoining prairie country. The present erroneous name, losing its original sig-

nificance, comes from the narratives of Pike's expedition in 1805–6 and of Long's expeditions in 1817 and 1823. Pike used both names, Canoe River when telling of his voyage up the Mississippi and Cannon River in the journal of his return. Nicollet, in his report and map published in 1843, called it Lahontan River and also Cannon River, supposing it to be identifiable as the Long River of Baron Louis A. Lahontan's *New Voyages to North-America*, which purported to relate his travel here in the winter of 1688–89. That stream, however, with later knowledge seems instead to be entirely fictitious (*Minnesota in Three Centuries*, 1908, vol. I, pp. 239–41).

According to Nicollet, the name given by the Dakota to Cannon River was Inyan bosndata, in translation Standing Rock. It referred to the unequally eroded rock column or spire called by the white settlers Castle Rock, whence a township and railway station near this river in Dakota County are named.

Zumbro River bears a name more remarkably changed from its original form than the Cannon River, being derived from the early French name, River des Embarras, meaning River of Difficulties. Its surface in its lower course and on the Mississippi bottomland was obstructed by driftwood, as noted by Albert Lea in the expedition with Stephen W. Kearny in 1835. This burden and embarrassment prevented or hindered its navigation by the canoes of the French voyageurs for the fur trade. Two villages on the river are named Zumbrota and Zumbro Falls, respectively in Goodhue and Wabasha Counties, for which these names are more fully considered. In St. Louis County, the large river whence it is named receives two tributaries that were likewise each named River des Embarras by the French, because of their burden of driftwood, the upper one being now the Embarrass River and the lower now called Floodwood River. Thomas Forsyth in 1819 noted this stream as Driftwood River.

Beside the Zumbro in Goodhue County, the township and village of Pine Island recall its Dakota name, Wazi Oju, as the river is called on Nicollet's map, signifying Pines Planted, in allusion to the grove of large white pines adjoining this village.

Root River, the most southeastern large tributary to the Mississippi in this state, rising in Mower County and flowing through Olmsted, Fillmore, and Houston Counties, was called Racine River by Pike, Root River by Long in 1817, and both its Dakota name, Hokah, and the English translation, Root, are used in Keating's *Narrative* of Long's expedition in 1823. With more strictly accurate spelling and pronunciation, the Dakota word is *hutkan*, meaning Racine in the French language and Root in English, while the Dakota word *hokah* means a heron. Racine Township and railway village in Mower County and Hokah, similarly the name of a township and village in Houston County, were derived from the river.

Tributaries of the Minnesota River to be mentioned here are the Pomme de Terre and Chippewa Rivers from the north; the Lac qui Parle River, having the French name of a lake through which the Minnesota flows, and the Yellow Medicine, Redwood, Cottonwood, and Blue Earth Rivers from the southwest and south; and Watonwan and Le Sueur Rivers, which flow into the Blue Earth. Each of these streams, excepting the first, is most fully noticed for a county bearing its name, and the Pomme de Terre Lake and River, translated by the French from the Dakota, are noticed for a township so named in Grant County. It is noteworthy that our names of all these rivers, excepting Le Sueur, which commemorates the early French explorer, were originally received from the Dakota people, who had long inhabited this part of Minnesota when the first explorers and settlers came. Only Watonwan, however, retains its form as a Dakota word.

Four streams that have their sources in this state and flow into Iowa, namely, the Rock, Des Moines, Cedar, and Upper Iowa Rivers, will complete this list. Rock River, translated from its Dakota name, refers to the prominent rock hill, commonly now called "the Mound," which rises precipitously west of this river in Mound Township of Rock County, the most southwestern in Minnesota. Both the township and county, like the river, were named for this high outcrop of red quartzite. The same rock formation, continuing north in Pipestone County, includes the renowned Pipestone Quarry, whence came the names of that county, its county seat, and the creek that flows past the quarry.

The Des Moines River flows through Murray, Cottonwood, and Jackson Counties, thence crosses Iowa, gives its name to the capital of that state, and joins the Mississippi at its southeast corner. Franquelin in 1688 and De L'Isle in 1703 mapped it as "R. des Moingona," the name being taken from an Indian village, Moingona, shown by Franquelin not far from the site of the present village of this name in Boone County near the center of Iowa. The name was spelled by Pike as De Moyen and Des Moyan; Long called it De Moyen; and Beltrami, Le Moine and Monk River. It has three names on Nicollet's map: "Inyan Shasha of the Sioux," meaning Red Stone, in allusion to its flowing through a gorge of red sandstone in Marion County, Iowa; "Moingonan of the Algonkins," from the early maps; and "Des Moines of the French," meaning the River of the Monks. The third name, which has been too long in use to be changed, is an erroneous translation by the early traders, based merely on the pronunciation of the old Algonquian name. An interesting paper on its origin by Dr. Charles R. Keyes is in the *Annals of Iowa* (third series, vol. 3, pp. 554–59, with three maps, Oct. 1898).

Cedar River, flowing from Dodge and Mower Counties in this state, is the longest stream of northeastern Iowa. Like the Missouri River, which exceeds the upper Mississippi in length, it is tributary to a shorter stream, the Iowa River, about 25 miles above the junction of the latter with the Mississippi. Red cedar trees, whose fragrant red wood is much esteemed for chests and other furniture, growing in many places along the bluffs of this river, supplied its aboriginal name, translated by Nicollet and on present maps as Red Cedar River. Its upper part, in this state, is more commonly called simply Cedar River, and its two chief cities in Iowa are named Cedar Rapids and Cedar Falls. The same name, Red Cedar, was derived in translation from the Ojibwe for the lake of the upper Mississippi, renamed as Cass Lake, and for the present Cedar Lake in Aitkin County, besides numerous other relatively small lakes, streams, and islands in various parts of Minnesota. Far northward the full name Red Cedar was used in distinction from the arbor vitae, which often is called white cedar, having similarly durable wood of a light color.

Upper Iowa River begins in Mower County, runs meanderingly along parts of the south line of Fillmore County, and passes southeast and east in Iowa to the Mississippi near the northeast corner of that state, which is named from the larger Iowa River flowing past Iowa Falls and Iowa City. The application of the name to a district west of the Mississippi and later to the territory and state, as first used for the district by Lieut. Albert M. Lea

in 1836, has been well told by Prof. Benjamin F. Shambaugh in the volume of *Annals of Iowa* before cited for the Des Moines River (third series, 3, 641–44, Jan. 1899), with 14 references to preceding papers and books that treat of the origin of the state name. It was originally the name of a Siouan tribe living there, whose hunting grounds extended north to the Blue Earth and Minnesota Rivers at the time of Le Sueur's expedition in 1700–1. Their tribal name, spelled in many ways, was translated "sleepy ones" by Riggs, being analogous with the name of the Dakota chief Sleepy Eye, who is commemorated by a city in Brown County. *The Handbook of American Indians* gives more than 75 variations in the former spelling of the name that now is established in common use as Iowa (Part 1, 1907, p. 614).

Aitkin County

This county, established May 23, 1857, and organized June 30, 1871, was named for William Alexander Aitkin, a fur trader with the Ojibwe Indians. Aitkin's name is properly spelled with an "e" (Aitken), although in a letter written in 1898 to the Minnesota Historical Society from his son, Roger, it was always spelled with an "i." He was born in Scotland in 1785, came from Edinburgh to America in his boyhood, and about the year 1802 came to the Northwest, being in the service of a trader named John Drew. Aitkin married into an influential Indian family, was soon a trader on his own account, and rapidly advanced until in 1831 he took charge of the Fond du Lac department of the American Fur Company, under John Jacob Astor, with headquarters at Sandy Lake in this county, adjoining the east side of the Mississippi River. He died September 16, 1851, and is buried on the east bank of the Mississippi, opposite the mouth of the Swan River in Morrison County, where he had a trading post during his last nine years, after 1842.

The name of Aitkin County was at first erroneously spelled Aiken, with which it is identical in pronunciation, and it was changed to its present spelling in 1872 by an act of the legislature.

Information on the origins of township names was received from Thomas R. Foley, Jr., real estate and insurance agent, and Carl E. Taylor, court commissioner, both of Aitkin, during a visit there in May 1916.

AITKIN TOWNSHIP bears the same name as the county. Its village, also bearing this name, was founded on September 13, 1870, as a station of the Northern Pacific Railroad, which in that year was built through the county, when Nathaniel Tibbetts, then with a surveying party, selected a claim of 160 acres in sections 23 to 26 to which he brought his family in 1871. The next year, in the county organization, it was made the county seat; it was incorporated on August 19, 1889, and reincorporated on March 16, 1915. Its post office was established in 1872, with Tibbetts as first postmaster; see also LANKIAGUN.

ARTHYDE a village in Millward Township, section 34, established on land donated by Guy Thomsen, Arthur Hutchins, and Clyde Hutchins; its post office was called Millward, 1898–1909, Charles Millward, postmaster; in 1909 the name was changed to honor the Hutchins brothers, Arthur and Clyde; the post office closed in 1954.

ATTICA a post office, 1889–1911, located in Nordland Township.

AXTELL a former railroad stop of the Soo Line in Jevne Township, section 15, was named for a construction worker who drowned in Round Lake.

BAIN TOWNSHIP is named in honor of William Bain, the hotel owner, who was one of the proprietors of the railway station site of the same name.

The township dissolved in 1939 and became part of Unorganized Territory of Northwest Aitkin. Bain, a settlement in Bain Township, section 26, had a post office, 1911–44.

BALL BLUFF TOWNSHIP should be Bald Bluff, being for the conspicuous morainic drift hill so named, having a bald grassy top without trees, in section 32 of this township at the east side of the Mississippi. There was a village of this name in section 29.

BALSAM TOWNSHIP is from two species of trees that are common or frequent in this county, the balsam fir and the balsam poplar. A settlement of the same name in section 19 was first developed by the Prairie River Lumber Company, which had a sawmill; its post office operated 1905–37.

BEAVER was named for beavers and their dams found by the earliest settlers on the head streams of Split Rock River in the south part of this township.

BENNETTVILLE a settlement in Hazelton Township, had a country post office, 1898–1937, located variously in sections 4 and 10; the site had a box manufacturing company and sawmill.

BILLINGS a post office, 1896–1907, also known as Cedar Lake Station, was in Aitkin Township. It was named for D. W. Billings, owner of the sawmill and general store; the name changed to Cedar Lake in 1907.

BLOEMENDAL a post office, 1901–14, in Wagner Township, located in various sections over the years; established in the log home of Lucas H. C. Bloemendal, who volunteered its use when a post office was needed in the area between McGrath and Finlayson.

BLUEBERRY CROSSING a site in Jevne Township, section 34, where the Northern Pacific Railroad installed a crossing and small siding; named for the Blueberry Trail, on which Indians had maintained a small building as a summer campsite for the berry pickers.

BOOT LAKE a post office, 1914–35, located in Cornish Township; had a semi-weekly stage to Jacobson.

BOSTON see SEAVEY.

BOYERS a locality in Macville Township on the Hixson county map, 1930.

BRAUER a station of the Hill City Railway in Quadna Township, sections 28–29.

BRIDGE PARK see JACOBSON.

CAYO a post office, 1918–20, Turner Township, 14 miles northwest of Tamarack, with Percy A. Cayo, postmaster.

CEDAR LAKE a station of the Northern Pacific Railroad in Aitkin Township, section 31, had a post office, 1907–16; formerly named Billings, 1896–1907.

CLARK TOWNSHIP had early settlers of this name, one being Frank Clark, who removed to McGregor.

CORNISH was named for Charles E. and Milo F. Cornish, settlers in section 34 of this township, coming from southern Minnesota.

DADS CORNER a locality in Rice River Township.

DARINA a station of the Minneapolis, St. Paul and Sault Ste. Marie Railroad (Soo Line), Kimberly Township, section 22; platted in 1909 by the Soo Line and named West Lake, but the post office disapproved of the name so the railroad changed it; the post office was not established, and the site was never developed.

DAVIDSON is for A. D. Davidson, senior partner in the Davidson and McRae Stock Farm Company of Duluth and later of Winnipeg, owners of numerous tracts of land in this township. He died in Rochester, Minn., April 1916. The township organized in 1904 and dissolved in 1951.

DICK TOWNSHIP was named in honor of Mildred Dick, assistant in the office of the county auditor; dissolved in 1933 and became part of Unorganized Territory of Southeast Aitkin.

DORRIS a post office, 1896–1912, Farm Island Township, section 17, had a church, school, and two sawmills.

EAST LAKE Spalding Township, was named for its location east of Wild Rice Lake. Anthony Spicola, its first settler, owned a general store and provided post office service for four months at his own expense, delivering the mail on foot; after the postal route was approved, he ran it out of his store for 42 years. The village had a sawmill and a Soo Line station in section 20.

EASTWOOD a post office, 1898–1917, Lakeside Township, sections 27 and 34.

ELMWOOD a post office, 1903–8, Idun Township, which was transferred to McGrath.

ERICK a post office, 1900–14, on the border of Nordland and Glen Townships, serving the north half of Glen Township; named for Magnus Erickson, the first postmaster.

ESQUAGAMAH TOWNSHIP derived its name from Esquagamah Lake, crossed by its east side. This is an Ojibwe name, meaning the last lake, given to it as the last and most western in a series of three lakes lying mainly in Waukenabo Township, which is named for the most eastern of these lakes. The township had a post office, 1900–10, and became part of Unorganized Territory of Northwest Aitkin in 1942.

FARM ISLAND TOWNSHIP is from its lake of this name, having an island of 29 acres, on which the Ojibwe formerly had large cultivated fields.

FLEMING LAKE a post office, 1909–30, in Fleming Township, sections 11 and 14, had a church and sawmill.

FLEMING TOWNSHIP has Fleming Lake, in section 22, named for an early settler there.

FRIDHEM a locality with a Swedish name in Davidson Township.

GERTRUDE a post office authorized on February 18, 1903, George Jewett, postmaster, and again on May 25, 1903, John H. Payne, postmaster, but not put into operation; location not known.

GIESE a logging and farming settlement in Wagner Township, section 15; named for George F. Giese, who owned the local store and was the first postmaster; referred to by local people as " Henkle Town" because so many people named Henkel lived there; a post office operated 1918–53.

GLEN an unincorporated village, in Glen Township, section 33, and Malmo Township, section 4, bears a euphonious name selected by its settlers at the time of the township organization; a post office operated 1899–1954.

GLORY a post office, 1901–13, in Nordland Township, section 35. Erick O. Swanson, owner of the general store, was asked to set up a post office but choosing the name was difficult, as Swanson submitted many names, the name finally coming from the song "Glory, Glory Hallelujah"; Swanson operated his store until his death in 1948.

GRASS TWINE SPUR a station of the Northern Pacific Railroad, McGregor Township, section 34.

GRAYLING a logging and farming settlement, McGregor Township, section 24; not platted or incorporated; its post office operated 1897–1929; had a station of the Northern Pacific Railroad; the area was also referred to as Sandy River Crossing or Sandy River Bridge.

HASSMAN a community platted in Morrison Township, section 35. During the late 1800s to early 1900s, logging companies sent logs down the Mississippi River to a spot near this prospective town; development of a community did not take place although a post office existed 1914–15. Many of the first families to settle the area were of French descent from Quebec.

HAUGEN TOWNSHIP is named in honor of Christopher G. Haugen, former sheriff of this county. The township had a post office, 1904–5, with Andrew E. Haugen, postmaster.

HAYPOINT a post office, 1900–19, Macville Township, with a triweekly stage to Hill City.

HAZELTON TOWNSHIP is for Cutler J. Hazelton, a former county commissioner whose homestead was on Pine Lake in this township. Cutler post office, 1894–1924, on the south side of this lake, was also named for him.

Nichols post office, beside Mille Lacs in the southwest corner of Hazelton, was named for Austin R. Nichols, its postmaster, who settled there in 1879. A biographic sketch is given under the city of Austin, Mower County, also named in his honor. The site was also called Nichols' Place and Nichols Farm but was never platted as a village although several businesses were located there.

HEBRON a post office, 1911–13 and 1915–17, in Hebron Township.

HEBRON TOWNSHIP was doubtless named by settlers coming from a town of this name in some eastern state. The original Hebron is an ancient town in Palestine. The township (T. 50, R. 25) dissolved in 1937 and became part of Unorganized Territory of Northwest Aitkin.

HENKLE TOWN see GIESE.

HIAWATHA see JACOBSON.

HICKORY a post office, 1884–86 and 1888–1906, Farm Island Township, section 23.

HILL CITY a city in Hill Lake Township, section 14; incorporated on February 19, 1910, and separated from the township on March 22, 1911; its post office began in 1901. The early settlement had a station of the Hill City Railway, three hotels, a woodenware factory, and a number of other businesses; the major industries were shipping cooperage stock, forest products, and produce.

HILL LAKE TOWNSHIP and its village, named Hill City, as also its Hill Lake are all so designated from the prominent hill of morainic drift in section 25. This is the culminating point of a very knolly and broken tract of the same moraine extending into the adjoining sections, to which locality, and especially to its highest part, the Ojibwe applied the name Pikwadina (or Piquadinaw), "it is hilly." Hence came the common name "Poquodenaw mountain," used by the lumbermen and given to this hill on the map of Aitkin County in the Minnesota Geological Survey.

IDUN TOWNSHIP was named by Tolleif George Thomsen who came to the area in 1893, for a Scandinavian Asir's (a deity) daughter, Idun, meaning youth and beauty.

INDIAN POINT an Indian village, Davidson Township, abandoned by 1897 and completely razed in 1939 when work was begun on a wildlife refuge.

JACOBSON a village, Ball Bluff Township, section 9; named for longtime area pioneer and first postmaster, Paul Jacobson, and made up of several earlier communities: Mississippi (or Mississippi Landing), which was the Swan River Logging Company's main headquarters and terminus for unloading logs to be floated down the Mississippi River, and a station of the Duluth, Mississippi River, and Northern Railroad from 1892 to 1900 in section 4; Hiawatha, an 1894 platted town site east of Mississippi Landing, which had a post office authorized on May 24, 1893, but not established; and a 1928 town site called Bridge Park, a name retained by a subdivision of the community; the post office was established in 1901.

JEVNE TOWNSHIP bears the surname of a Scandinavian family settling there.

JEWETT TOWNSHIP honors D. M. Jewett, a pioneer in section 20. The township had a post office, 1905–9, and was dissolved in 1937.

KANSANI a post office authorized on April 28, 1905, with Erik Autio, postmaster, but not established; no location noted.

KIMBERLY TOWNSHIP was named from its station established when the Northern Pacific Railroad was built in 1870, in honor of Moses C. Kimberly of St. Paul. He was born in Sandisfield, Mass., December 1, 1845; came to Minnesota in 1870 as a surveyor and engineer for this railroad; was during many years its general superintendent. The township had a post office, 1879–1974, in section 14.

LAKESIDE TOWNSHIP is at the east side of Mille Lacs.

LANKIAGUN a Sandy Lake Indian village, was the county seat when Aitkin County was created; located in Aitkin Township, section 24, near the mouth of the Repple River (or Mud River); in 1870 the village of Aitkin was founded, and the site was again designated as the county seat.

LANSFORD a post office, Jevne Township, section 33; first named Ude, 1904–7, for a German hunter and trapper named Uhde, who had settled nearby; the *h* in the name was dropped by the railroad when the Northern Pacific flag station in section 35 was created; this station eliminated the stop in section 32 called Portage Crossing; the post office name was changed in 1907 to Lansford, and the railroad followed suit; the post office closed in 1925.

LAWLER a village in Salo Township, section 19; developed as a sawmill town; in 1910 the Soo Line came through as one connecting point between the Crosby iron mines and Duluth, with Lawler Junction in section 24. On October 12, 1918, sparks from a train smokestack just west of Lawler started a fire, which winds spread to Moose Lake and Cloquet, and destroyed all of the village except for Charlie Spicola's store and the Lawler Hotel. A post office operated 1909–64.

LEE TOWNSHIP was named in honor of Olaf Lee, a pioneer Norwegian farmer in section 18.

LE MAY TOWNSHIP was named for Frank Le May, one of the first settlers. The township became part of Unorganized Territory of Northwest Aitkin in 1932.

LIBBY an unincorporated village, Turner Township; the American Fur Company had a post here in 1832; the site was first known as Palmburg; its post office operated 1891–1953.

LIBBY TOWNSHIP is for Mark Libby, who long ago was a fur trader there on the outlet of Sandy Lake.

LOGAN TOWNSHIP was named for the long and narrow lakes, often shaped like a horseshoe or oxbow, which lie in abandoned parts of the old channels of the Mississippi, occurring frequently in this and other townships. For these lakes of the alluvial land adjoining the river the name "logans" has been in common use in Aitkin County during the 50 years or more since the region was first invaded by lumbermen (*Geology of Minnesota*, vol. IV, pp. 26–27).

LONGFELLOW see WHITEPINE.

MACVILLE TOWNSHIP is for pioneer Scottish settlers there named McAninch and McPheters.

MALMO TOWNSHIP is named for the large city of Malmo in southern Sweden, on the sound opposite Copenhagen. Malmo, an unincorporated community in Malmo Township, sections 5 and 32, was settled in the early 1880s; the major industries were logging, farming, hoop making, and a creamery; the post office was established in the Nyquist store, 1889–1954.

MAPLEHURST a flag stop of the Soo Line in Davidson Township, sections 21 and 22, established in 1909; probably named by railroad officials for the many maple trees at the site; no depot or other development other than the Davidson-McRae stock ranch, where the stop was located, took place.

McGRATH a city in Williams Township, section 5; incorporated as a village on March 23, 1923, and separated from the township on August 8, 1923. James E. McGrath, who had 17 logging camps on the Snake River and Chesley Brook, began work in the area about 1895, and in 1907 donated 40 acres for a town site, which the Patterson Land Company platted as Elmwood; renamed McGrath at the time the post office was established in 1908.

McGREGOR a city in McGregor Township, sections 30 and 31; incorporated on August 27, 1903, and separated from the township on March 24, 1919; named either for a hunter and trapper named McGregor who came from New York or for Maj. John G. MacGregor of Minneapolis; the post office was established in 1890.

McGREGOR TOWNSHIP was named after the station and village of the Northern Pacific Railroad in section 31, which also became a station and junction of the Soo Line.

MEDARY a site in Morrison Township, section 2, on the bank of the Mississippi River near Mille Lacs Lake; named for Gov. Samuel Medary; incorporated May 19, 1857; no trace remains.

MILLWARD see ARTHYDE

MILLWARD TOWNSHIP was named for one of its early settlers. The township dissolved in 1935, became part of Unorganized Territory of Southeast Aitkin, and reorganized in 1987.

MINNEWAWA a locality in Shamrock Township, section 29, on the lake of the same name.

MISSISSIPPI (MISSISSIPPI LANDING) see JACOBSON.

MORRISON TOWNSHIP was named for Edward Morrison, one of its pioneer farmers.

NICHOLS see HAZELTON TOWNSHIP.

NORDLAND TOWNSHIP bears the name of a large district in northern Norway.

OJIBWAY a paper town in Aitkin Township, sections 25 and 26, across the Repple River from Aitkin; the owners platted a town site and sold shares at high prices, but the venture collapsed and no development occurred.

OPSTEAD a stage route opened in 1892 between Aitkin and Opstead, and after 1900 a mail route opened from Opstead to section 6 of Williams Township.

OSTLUN a post office, 1901–17, Seavey Township, section 29.

PALISADE a city in Logan Township, section 22; incorporated as a village on July 7, 1922, and separated from the township on September 19, 1922; named by an official of the Soo Line for the high embankment on either side of the Mississippi River; its post office began in 1910.

PALMBURG see LIBBY.

PIERCEVILLE a station of the Hill City Railway, Ruth Township, section 18.

PINE KNOLL (Pineknoll), a settlement in Aitkin Township, section 9; shown on most maps as two words. Among the earliest settlers in the area were Christopher Welton and his sons, in 1882, at whose home the post office was established, 1900–15.

PLINY TOWNSHIP has the name of a celebrated naturalist of ancient Rome; it had a post office, 1903–8, in section 3.

PORTAGE a shipping point on the Mississippi River located on the border of Libby and Workman Townships; the first settler, Patrick Sanders, an Irish-Canadian lumberman who homesteaded the site, established the post office, 1889–1911, in his general store.

PORTAGE CROSSING see LANSFORD.

QUADNA (each syllable having the sound of *a* in fall) is shortened from the earlier name Piquadinaw, first given to this township on account of its tracts of knolly and hilly drift extending eastward from the high hill so named by the Ojibwe, as before mentioned, in Hill Lake Township. The township dissolved in 1933.

RABEY an unincorporated village, Ruth Township, section 10; had a station of the Hill City Railway, a post office, 1913–41, a major farm development company, and a large mercantile store.

REDTOP (Red Top), a town site located in Idun

Township, section 29; the Soo Line acquired land in May 1908 from Richard J. Lewis and platted a town site, which was never incorporated; the post office operated 1909–54. The origin of the name is either from the nickname of a local red-haired girl or from the redtop field grass that grows in the area.

RICE RIVER a post office, 1908–11, in Morrison Township, section 36; the site had a general store.

RICE RIVER TOWNSHIP received its name from its being crossed by the head streams of the Rice River, named, like the large Rice Lake from wild rice (*Zizania aquatica*), which was harvested by the Indians as a valuable natural food supply.

RONALD a post office, 1894–1926, in Beaver Township.

ROSSBURG an unincorporated village, Spencer Township, section 24; had a station of the Northern Pacific Railroad; settlement began as early as the 1880s; the post office, 1901–37, was first located in postmaster Luigi Digiovanni's store.

RUTH TOWNSHIP (T. 52, R. 24) became part of Unorganized Territory of Northwest Aitkin in 1937.

SALO TOWNSHIP was named by its Finn settlers for a town in southwestern Finland.

SALTVIK a post office authorized on April 28, 1905, with John G. Jacobson, postmaster, but not established; location not noted.

SANDY RIVER CROSSING see **GRAYLING**.

SEAVER a village in Ball Bluff Township, section 8, which had a station of the Hill City Railway in section 6.

SEAVEY TOWNSHIP was named for a family residing in Aitkin, one of whom, Frank E. Seavey, was during many years the clerk of the county court. Two post offices located in Seavey Township existed by the name of Seavey: the first was named Tripp, 1895–96, changed to Seavey, 1896–98, with Loring G. Seavey, postmaster, and again changed in 1898 to Waldeck; the second was named Boston, 1899–1904, became Seavey in 1904, and was discontinued in 1938.

SHAMROCK TOWNSHIP was named by Irish settlers for the trifoliate plant long ago chosen as the national emblem of Ireland.

SHESHEBEE a summer resort area, Shamrock Township, section 27, which had a post office, 1918–33.

SHOVEL LAKE TOWNSHIP and its railway station were named for Shovel Lake, crossed by the south line of the township. The township had a post office, 1910–52, in section 34. It was dissolved in 1943 and became part of Unorganized Territory of Northwest Aitkin.

SILVER STAR was a planned community near McGrath, created following World War I with inexpensive land sales through a McGrath banker; at one time about 20 families were in the area.

SOLANA a community in Dick Township (T. 44, R. 22), section 5, which existed because of railroad and lumber camps and slowly disappeared as the timber did. The community was named by a surveyor from Salinas, Kans., who changed the spelling; or more picturesquely for a lumber camp cook who did everything "slow," that is, "slow" Anna; or for the county in California, whose Spanish pronunciation is "so lah´ no," while this community's pronunciation is "so lay no"; its post office, 1910–38, was originally misspelled Solano.

SPALDING TOWNSHIP was named in honor of John L. Spalding, former treasurer of this county.

SPENCER TOWNSHIP is for William Spencer, who was a druggist in Aitkin, but removed to Texas.

STROLE a post office, 1904–09, Glen Township.

SWATARA a post office, 1903–8, and since 1911, Macville Township, section 20; it had a station on the Soo Line.

TAMARACK is a village of the Northern Pacific Railroad in Clark Township; incorporated as a village on July 26, 1921, and separated from the township on October 18, 1921; grew up out of the extensive peat- and tamarack-covered bogs when the Northern Pacific laid track from Duluth to Brainerd. The first families arrived in the area about 1874; although the community suffered great damage during the Hinckley fire of 1894 and the 1918 fire, a land boom followed; its post office began in 1898.

THOR a community made up the entire township of Lee and the northeastern portion of Glen Township was incorporated in 1904; a post office was located in section 18, 1904–37.

TRIPP see **SEAVEY**.

TRONNES a community in Pliny Township, section 20, was named for the home of Peter and Grace Anderson, who came to the area about 1900, and operated the post office in their house, 1901–10.

TURNER TOWNSHIP is for L. E. Turner, formerly a county commissioner.

UDE see LANSFORD.

UNORGANIZED TERRITORY OF NORTHEAST AITKIN includes formerly unnamed townships T. 51, R. 22 and T. 52, R. 22.

UNORGANIZED TERRITORY OF NORTHWEST AITKIN includes the former townships Shovel Lake, LeMay, White Elk, Bain, Hebron, Quadna, and formerly unnamed T. 51, R. 25.

UNORGANIZED TERRITORY OF SOUTHEAST AITKIN includes the former townships of Dick and Millward.

VALENTINE a post office, 1901–2, located 16 miles east of Aitkin.

VALPARAISO a post office, 1909–18, Nordland Township, section 11, was established at Nicola Wladmarif's home, later at Wehmanen's place, then the Zuelke place, until 1918 when it became part of a rural route.

VERDON TOWNSHIP and post office, 1901–35, were named for Verdon Wells, son of E. B. Wells, the postmaster.

VETERANSVILLE a locality in White Pine Township, where in 1922 disabled World War I veterans purchased 80-acre lots of farmland, renaming the area. Only a few families remained by the late 1920s, after finding the land mostly rocks and stumps; a post office was located there 1922–27; see also WHITEPINE.

WAGNER TOWNSHIP was named for a former assistant in the office of the county register of deeds, Bessie Wagner, who became Mrs. Hammond, and moved to Montana.

WALDECK a locality in Morrison Township, section 2, 1898–1927, with Grace Waldeck as first postmaster; this shipping point on the Mississippi River had a sawmill and blacksmith.

WASHBURN a railroad station of the Hill City Railway in Quadna Township, section 24.

WAUKENABO TOWNSHIP (accented on the syllable next to the last, with the sound of ah) has the Ojibwe name of the eastern one of its series of three lakes. Rev. Joseph A. Gilfillan wrote it with a somewhat different spelling: "Wakonabo sagaiigun, the lake of the broth of wakwug or fish milt, or eggs-broth lake; or Broth-of-moss-growing-on-rocks-or-trees lake. The Indians use the latter in case of starvation. Both the above explanations are given by different Indians." A post office,

1902–16, was located in sections 10, 11, and 33 at various times.

WEALTHWOOD is a name proposed by Mrs. Daniel J. Knox of Aitkin, for the lakeside summer resort platted in section 20 of this fractional township, which previously was a part of Nordland; had a post office, 1891–1925, Jessie C. Knox, first postmaster. Daniel J. Knox developed a stock farm on the shore of Mille Lacs Lake, which he named Wealthwood.

WHITE ELK TOWNSHIP bears the name of the lake crossed by its east line, translated from its Ojibwe name. The township dissolved, became part of Unorganized Territory of Northwest Aitkin.

WHITEOAK a post office, 1901–11, four miles southeast of Aitkin, in Nordland Township.

WHITEPINE a village on the Soo Line, located in White Pine Township, section 35, formerly named Longfellow, 1903–9. James E. McGrath Lumber Co., of Stillwater, purchased land along the Snake River, and by 1909 the company had constructed a large sawmill complex including shops, post office, 1909–21, and school, and had an estimated 1,000 workers living in this community or in Stillwater; the land eventually was sold to become Veteransville.

WILLIAMS TOWNSHIP was named in honor of George T. Williams of Aitkin, who during many years was the county judge of probate.

WILLOW RIVER a post office, 1874–80, Waukenabo Township, section 35.

WORKMAN TOWNSHIP is thought to be named for a pioneer settler there, who later removed from the county.

Lakes and Streams

Joseph N. Nicollet's map, published in 1843, gives the following names of lakes and streams partly or wholly within the area of Aitkin County, as they have since continued in use: the Mississippi River, Willow and Little Willow Rivers, West and East Savanna Rivers, Aitkin Lake, Sandy Lake, and Mille Lacs.

Other names which survive with slight changes from that map are Prairie River, tributary to the West Savanna, called Little Prairie River by Nicollet; Mud Lake and River, tributary to the Mississippi at Aitkin, which were called Muddy Lake and River; and Cedar Lake, Nicollet's Red Cedar

Lake, which Zebulon M. Pike in 1805–6 called the Lower Red Cedar Lake (to distinguish it from the Upper Red Cedar Lake, far up the Mississippi, renamed in 1820 Lake Cassina, now Cass Lake).

The very elaborate "Historico-Geographical Chart of the Upper Mississippi River," published by Dr. Elliott Coues in 1895 with his annotated edition of Pike's expeditions, includes interesting notes of successive geographic names and their dates in Aitkin County.

Willow River was called Alder River by Henry R. Schoolcraft in 1820 and likewise in 1855. It flows through a nearly level and largely swampy area, which bears abundant willows and alders. Its Ojibwe name is translated Willow River by Gilfillan.

West Savanna River was so called in 1820 by Schoolcraft. The Savanna Rivers, West and East, retain these names as given by the early French voyageurs; but this word, nearly equivalent to prairie, was originally of American origin. It was a Carib word and was introduced into European languages by Spanish writers near the middle of the sixteenth century. By the Ojibwe the East Savanna River was named Mushki-gonigumi sibi, "the marsh-portage river," having reference to the very marshy portage made on this much used canoe route in passing to the West Savanna River and Sandy Lake. The portage and stretches of both rivers were set aside as Savanna State Park in 1961.

The early French name of Sandy Lake was Lac au Sable or du Sable. The French and English alike translated it from the Ojibwe name, recorded by both Gilfillan and Chrysostom Verwyst as Ga-mitawangagumag Sagaiigun, "the-place-of-bare-sand lake." The North West Company established a trading post on the west shore of this lake in 1794, which was visited by David Thompson in 1798 and by Pike in January 1806, but before the time of Aitkin's taking charge there in 1831, the old post had been abandoned for a new site at the mouth of the outlet of Sandy Lake on the narrow point between the outlet and the Mississippi River.

Rice River and its tributary Rice Lake (named Lake Dodge by Nicollet, probably for Governor Henry Dodge of Wisconsin), also another Rice Lake of very irregular outline, lying close south of Sandy Lake, received their names as before noted in connection with Rice River Township from their large and valuable supplies of the excellent native grain called wild rice. The Ojibwe name of the wild rice, Manomin, is applied to this stream on Nicollet's map in the common form of its spelling as given in Frederic Baraga's *Dictionary of the Ojibway Language*. Another form is Mahnomen, given to a county of this state. Its French translation is Folle Avoine, meaning in our language "false or fool oat," nearly like the name, "Wild Oats River," used for this Rice River by Giacomo C. Beltrami in 1823.

White Elk Brook or Creek like the township of this name, is so called, in the Ojibwe usage, for the lake of its source.

Moose River, tributary to Willow River, is translated from its Ojibwe name, given by Gilfillan as Moz-oshtigwani sibi, Moosehead River. It receives the outflow of several small lakes of which the most eastern, called Moose Lake in Macville, has been mainly drained.

Little Willow River is named, like the larger stream that often is called Big Willow River, for its plentiful willows.

Sisabagama Lake (accented on the middle syllable, with the long vowel sound) and the outflowing creek or river of the same name, close east of Aitkin, have had various spellings. Gilfillan spelled and defined this Ojibwe name as Sesabeguma Lake "Every-which-way lake, or the lake which has arms running in all directions"; but such description is not applicable to this lake unless it be considered to include the group of several neighboring lakes that together are tributary to this stream.

Snake and Little Snake Rivers, having their sources in the southeast part of Aitkin County and flowing south into Kanabec County, are translations from their Ojibwe names, as is noted in the chapter on that county, which bears the aboriginal name of the Snake River.

Cowan's Brook, in Williams Township, tributary to the Snake River was named for an early lumberman there.

Pine Lake and Big Pine Lake in Wagner, the latter extending east into Pine County, gave their name to the outflowing Pine River. These lakes and great areas around them, in both Aitkin and Pine Counties, originally had majestic white pine forests.

Dam Lake and Brook, in Kimberly, received this name from the low, ice-formed ridges of gravel and sand on the shores of this lake, especially at its mouth.

Sandy River, flowing west and then north into the lake of this name and outflowing by a very crooked course of more than two miles, though its junction with the Mississippi is only about a half mile from the lake, follows the Indian rule of nomenclature, that a lake gives its name to the stream flowing through it or from it.

Prairie River, like the West Savanna River, which unites with it, received its name from its small open spaces of grassy and bushy land without trees in this generally wooded region.

Savanna Lake, adjoining the old portage of the fur traders, and the Lower Savanna Lake, through which their canoes passed to Sandy Lake, also have reference to such small savannas, which are more commonly called prairies excepting in the southern states.

Tamarack River, flowing into Prairie River, was named for its plentiful growth of the tamarack, a graceful species of our coniferous trees (the only one that is not evergreen).

Aitkin Lake, in sections 19 and 20 of Turner, was named like this county for William A. Aitkin, the fur trader, who very probably often fished and hunted there.

Bald Bluff Lake lies at the southern base of the hill of this name.

Birch Lake, in section 19 of Hazelton, is named for its yellow and paper birches, the latter being the species used for bark canoes.

Blind Lake, in T. 48, R. 27, is mainly enclosed by a large swamp and has no outlet, as its name implies.

Cedar Lake, before mentioned, was named from the red cedars that in scanty numbers are found on its hilly shores and islands.

Clear Lake, in sections 28 and 33, Glen, is exceptionally beautiful, with very clear water and enclosed by high shores.

Elm Island Lake, at the center of Nordland, has a small island bearing elm trees.

Farm Island Lake gave its name to that township, in allusion to the farming by the Ojibwe. The outflowing Mud River passes in the next two miles through Pine, Hickory, and Spirit Lakes, which in the atlas are shown to be connected by straits, so that they might be termed a series of three bays continuous with the first named large lake.

Fleming, French, Jenkins, and Wilkins Lakes in Fleming Township are probably named for early settlers, trappers and hunters, or lumbermen. A larger lake of this group, named Gun Lake, was formerly called Lake Manomin (i.e., Wild Rice).

Hanging Kettle Lake, translated from its Ojibwe name, in sections 13 and 14, Farm Island Township, is connected eastward by straits with Diamond and Mud Lakes.

Horseshoe Lake, in sections 23 and 24 of Shamrock, is named for its curved shape.

Island Lake, in sections 11 to 14 of Turner, has a large central island.

Lone Lake, in sections 29 and 30 of Nordland, has no visible outlet, but it probably supplies the water of large chalybeate springs that issue close south of the road near the middle of the south side of Mud Lake.

Mallard Lake, in section 2 of Hazelton, formerly called Rice lake, is named for its mallard ducks.

Nelson and Douglas Lakes, section 23 of Clark, now drained away, were named for M. Nelson and E. Douglas, owners of adjoining lands.

The name of Nord Lake in Nordland is of similar origin with the township name, meaning north and given by Norwegian settlers.

Pine Lake, named for its pine woods in Hazelton Township, was earlier known as Hazelton Lake or Echo Lake.

Portage Lake, section 6 of Davidson, was at the end of a portage on a former canoe route.

Rabbit Lake in Glen Township has high shores of irregular outlines, an excellent hunting ground.

Rat Lake in Workman and Rat House Lake in sections 26 and 35, Cornish, are named for their muskrats.

Sugar Lake in Malmo is named for its sugar maple trees, this species having been much used by the Ojibwe for sugar-making.

Twenty Lake in Malmo is named from the number of its section.

Vladimirof Lake, mainly in section 10 of Nordland, was formerly known as Section Ten Lake but has been renamed for a settler who owned lands close north and east of the lake.

This county also has the following names of lakes, which are of frequent occurrence elsewhere.

Bass Lake in section 28 of Aitkin, another of this name in section 10 of Farm Island (lately renamed as Hammal Lake), and a third Bass Lake in section 19 of Turner.

Long Lake in Glen Township.

Mud Lake in Nordland, another in the north part of Logan, and a third and fourth in section 10 of McGregor and sections 14 and 23 of White Elk.

Otter Lake in section 34 of LeMay, and another in section 9 of Logan.

Pickerel Lake in section 27 of Aitkin.

Round Lake in section 31 of Hazelton, another in Jevne, a third, crossed by the line between Haugen and Shamrock, and a fourth between Waukenabo and Esquagamah Lakes.

Glacial Lake Aitkin

In the village of Aitkin and westward, a beach ridge of gravel and sand, having a height of three to five feet, marks the south shore of a glacial lake, which existed during a geologically very short time in the broad and shallow depression of this part of the Mississippi Valley. It was first described and mapped by the present writer in Volume IV of the *Final Report of the Geological Survey of Minnesota*, published in 1899, being then known to extend from the edge of Crow Wing County eastward and northward in Aitkin, Spencer, and Morrison Townships.

Later and more detailed examinations, by Frank Leverett and Frederick William Sardeson, show that this glacial lake reached northward along the Mississippi to the mouth of Swan River, in the north edge of Aitkin County (Bulletin no. 13, Minnesota Geological Survey, published in 1917). The length of Glacial Lake Aitkin was about 50 miles, but it had only a slight depth of water, nowhere exceeding 20 feet, above the Mississippi, Willow, and Rice Rivers, and above the Sandy River and Lake.

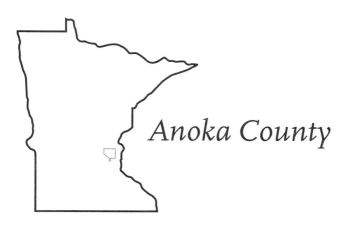

Anoka County

The name of this county, established May 23, 1857, was taken from the town of Anoka, which was first settled in 1851–52 and was named in 1853. It is a Dakota word meaning, as Prof. A. W. Williamson wrote, "on both sides; applied by founders to the city laid out on both sides of Rum River, and since applied to the county," of which this city is the county seat. Rev. Moses N. Adams, who came as a missionary to the Dakota in 1848 and learned their language, stated that as a Dakota word, Anoka means "the other side, or both sides."

According to the late Return I. Holcombe and others, including Albert M. Goodrich, the historian of this county, the Ojibwe also sometimes used a name of nearly the same sound for the Rum River and for the site of Anoka near its mouth meaning "where they work," on account of the extensive early lumbering and log driving on this stream. The Ojibwe verb "I work" is *anoki*, as given in Frederic Baraga's *Dictionary of the Ojibway Language*, with many inflected forms and compound words from this root, all referring to work in some way as their central thought.

But the selection of the name Anoka had reference only to its use by the Dakota people, whose language is wholly unlike that of the Ojibwe. A newspaper article on this subject written in 1873 by L. M. Ford is quoted by Goodrich as follows: "The name for the new town was a topic of no little interest, and the writer had something to do in its selection. It was decided to give it an Indian name. The Dakota Lexicon, just published, and of which I was the owner of a copy, was not infrequently consulted and at length the euphonious name Anoka was decided upon. . . . It was said to mean 'on both sides,' when rendered into less musical English, and to this day the name is by no means inappropriate, as the town is growing up and extending on either side of the beautiful but badly named river."

━━━━━━

Information for this county has been gathered from the History of the Upper Mississippi Valley, *1881, in which Anoka County and its civil divisions are treated in pages 222–93; from the* History of Anoka County and the Towns of Champlin and Dayton in Hennepin County, *320 pages, 1905, by Albert M. Goodrich; and from Charles W. Lenfest, county treasurer, Frank Hart, clerk of the court, and Clarence D. Green, real estate agent, during a visit to Anoka in October 1916.*

ANDOVER a city located in Grow Township, section 26; incorporated November 12, 1974; had a station of the Great Northern Railway.

ANOKA was founded in 1850 by Orrin W. Rice, Neal D. Shaw, and others, by whom its name was adopted in May 1853; also known as Rum River by some local residents before 1853; the post office was established while part of Benton County as Decorri, 1852–54, changing its name in 1854. The "City of Anoka" was incorporated by the state legislature July 29, 1858, and later the "Borough of Anoka," March 5, 1869, but both these acts failed of acceptance by the vote of the township. Finally, under a legislative act of March 2, 1878, this city was set off from the township of the same name, the first city election being held on March 12.

BELT LINE a station of the Great Northern and Northern Pacific Railroads, Fridley Township, section 10.

BERLIN a station of the Northern Pacific Railroad in Fridley Township, section 24.

BETHEL a city in St. Francis Township, was first settled in 1856 by Quakers and was organized the next year; it was established as a post office in 1865 at a site known as Bethel Corners, incorporated as a village in 1902 and reincorporated in 1913. Its name is from ancient Palestine, meaning "House of God," and was selected for this township by Moses Twitchell, who settled here as an immigrant from Bethel, Maine.

BLAINE a city in Ramsey County incorporated January 29, 1954; the site in section 32 of Blaine Township was originally named Villas City but was abandoned by 1887; it was part of the city of Anoka until 1877.

BLAINE GARDENS a locality in Blaine Township, sections 21 and 28, circa 1914–32.

BLAINE TOWNSHIP settled in 1862, was the east part of Anoka until 1877, when it was separately organized and was named in honor of James Gillespie Blaine, a prominent Republican statesman of Maine. He was born in Pennsylvania, January 31, 1830, and died in Washington, D.C., January 27, 1893; was a member of Congress from Maine, 1863–76, being the speaker in 1869–75; U.S. senator, 1876–81; and secretary of state, March to December 1881, and 1889–92. In the presidential campaign of 1884 he was an unsuccessful candidate. He wrote *Twenty Years of Congress*, published in 1884–86.

BREEZY SHORE a village, Columbus Township, section 30, on the southeast shore of Coon Lake, circa 1932.

BRIGHTON JUNCTION a station of the Minnesota Transfer Railway Co. in Fridley Township, one mile north of Fridley, circa 1937.

BRYAN a station of the Minneapolis, Anoka and Cuyuna Railroad, Anoka Township, section 26.

BURNS see NOWTHEN.

BURNS TOWNSHIP settled in 1854 or earlier, was a part of St. Francis until 1869, being then organized and named, probably, for the celebrated poet. This name was adopted on the suggestion of James Kelsey, who was elected the first township treasurer.

CEDAR an unincorporated village in Oak Grove Township, section 26; its post office was established as Snapp, 1899–1900, the name changing to Cedar in 1900; the early site had a station of the Great Northern Railway and a cheese factory.

CEDAR VALLEY a post office, 1856–59; location not known.

CENTERVILLE settled in 1850–52, was organized in 1857 and incorporated on September 27, 1910. Its village of this name, thence given to the township, was platted in the spring of 1854, having a central situation between the Mississippi and St. Croix Rivers. The settlers in the village and vicinity were mostly French, and this came to be known as the French settlement, while numerous German settlers in the western part of the township caused that to be called the German settlement. The post office was named Columbus, 1856–63, and then Centreville, 1863–93, before its current spelling, and was discontinued in 1905. The first sawmill in the county was built here in 1854 by Charles Peltier. In 1971 a number of streets were renamed to reflect its history; see also Columbus Township.

CIRCLE PINES a city incorporated April 13, 1950, southeast of Blaine on Baldwin Lake in what was formerly Blaine Township; a post office was established in 1948.

CLOUGH a community in Blaine Township, section 32; first settled in 1897 and had a post office, 1897–1902.

CLOUTIER'S ISLAND an island in Ramsey Township located on the Mississippi River opposite the town of Ramsey; a campsite was established there in 1849 by John R. Bean and John Simpson.

COLD SPRINGS a station of the Minneapolis, Anoka and Cuyuna Railroad in Fridley Township, section 27, shown on maps, 1918–38.

COLEMAN a station of the Minneapolis, Anoka and Cuyuna Railroad in Fridley Township, section 3; named for Thomas Coleman, born in Ireland in 1848, who came to this township in 1866 and purchased a farm in sections 3 and 4.

COLUMBIA HEIGHTS a suburb of Minneapolis in

the south edge of the former Fridley Township, was platted and named by the late Thomas Lowry of that city and was incorporated in 1921. It began as a dairy farm owned by Al Davies, was a golf course in 1921, and then developed into a community of homes in 1947; it surrounds the present city of Hilltop.

COLUMBUS TOWNSHIP settled in 1855 and organized in 1857, was named for Christopher Columbus. It had a post office, which was originally established in Ramsey County and reestablished in Anoka County, 1864–66. James Starkey, who owned the Columbus Hotel and the sawmill, platted a townsite in 1856 and served as general land agent, surveyor, and postmaster; Starkey built the first church building, which also held the first school. The community vanished when the post office was transferred to Centerville.

CONSTANCE an unincorporated village in Grow Township, section 13; its post office operated 1897–1955; a Burlington Northern Railroad station was in section 14.

COON CREEK a post office in Anoka Township, section 26, established in 1869 in the farmhouse of the Caswell family, both father and son serving as postmaster, followed by several others postmasters who rented the farmhouse until the building was sold in 1893. The name was changed to Cooncreek in 1895 and discontinued in 1905. The area was first settled in 1855 and had a station used by both the Great Northern and Northern Pacific Railroads. Major industries were a condensed peat factory and a pressed-brick and terra-cotta works.

COON LAKE BEACH a settlement in Bethel Township, section 26.

COON RAPIDS a city formed when Anoka Township was incorporated on October 20, 1952, its name changing to Coon Rapids; had a station of the Minneapolis, Anoka and Cuyuna Railroad.

COOPER'S CORNER a site in St. Francis Township. When the Great Northern Railway completed its line through the area in 1898 and the Bethel post office, established in 1863, was moved to a new townsite two miles west becoming the present Bethel, the old site, which had a general store run by James Cooper, became known as Cooper's Corner.

COTTAGE GROVE a village in Linwood Township, section 4, on the southeast shore of Martin Lake, circa 1932.

DAYTON see RAMSEY.

DECORRI see ANOKA.

DEMAREST a post office, 1897–1902, in Ramsey Township, section 3. Daniel M. Demarest, postmaster, named for his father, Franklin Demarest, was born in New York in 1831, settled in Burns Township in 1855, and moved to Ramsey Township during the winter of 1860–61.

EAST BETHEL a city that encompasses the former Bethel Township (T. 33, R. 23), incorporated as a village on June 7, 1957.

EDGEWATER a village in Fridley Township, three miles south of Fridley, with a station of the Minneapolis, Anoka and Cuyuna Railroad.

FAIRVIEW a village in Fridley Township, section 1, circa 1932.

FOLEY a station of the Minneapolis, Anoka and Cuyuna Railroad in Anoka Township, section 26.

FRENCHY CORNER a village in Anoka Township, section 4, south of Crooked Lake.

FRIDLEY a fractional township comprising only about 16 square miles, was established by legislative act as Manomin County (meaning Wild Rice) on the same date, May 23, 1857, with the establishment of Anoka County. "John Banfil settled in what is now Fridley in 1847, and kept a stopping place for the accommodation of travelers. Two years later Henry M. Rice acquired considerable land and built a country residence at Cold Springs, giving his name to the creek which flows through the town. . . . A ferry across the Mississippi River was established about 1854" (Goodrich, pp. 162–63). This small county continued nearly 13 years, until in 1869–70 it was united with Anoka County as Manomin Township. The name was changed to Fridley in 1879, and it was incorporated as a village June 18, 1949.

Abram McCormick Fridley, in whose honor this township received its name was born in Steuben County, N.Y., May 1, 1817. He came to Long Prairie, Minnesota, in 1851 as agent for the Winnebago Indians, was afterward a farmer in this township, and in 1869 opened a large farm in Becker, Sherburne County. He was a representative in the legislature in 1855, 1869–71, and 1879. He died in Fridley Township, March 1888.

GERMAN SETTLEMENT an area of Centerville Township where many German settlers made claims in 1885.

GLASTENBURY a townsite of Bethel Township

(T. 34, R. 23), which was incorporated on May 23, 1857; no trace remains.

GLEN CARY a village in Ham Lake Township, southwest of the lake of the same name. It began with seven or eight shanties built in 1856 along with a school and was platted in 1857; the site burned that same year and was not rebuilt, reverting to farmland.

GROW TOWNSHIP settled about 1853, was organized in 1857 with the name Round Lake, which in 1859 was changed to Grow in honor of Galusha Aaron Grow of Pennsylvania. He was born in 1823 and died in 1907, was a member of Congress in 1851–63 and again in 1894–1902, and was the Speaker of the House, 1861–63. "For ten years, at the beginning of each Congress, he introduced in the House a free homestead bill, until it became a law in 1862." This grand public service caused him to be remembered gratefully by millions of homesteaders.

HAM LAKE TOWNSHIP settled in 1857, was attached to Grow Township until 1871 when it was separately organized. It had been previously called Glengarry, a name from Scotland, which its Swedish settlers found difficult to pronounce. The county commissioners therefore named the new township Ham Lake from its lake in sections 16 and 17, which had acquired this name on account of its form. Ham Lake, a city in Ham Lake Township, was incorporated November 13, 1973.

HAMLAKE see LAKENETTA.

HANSON a station of the Minneapolis, Anoka and Cuyuna Railroad in Anoka Township, section 22, and of the Minneapolis and Northern Railroad in section 21.

HEIGHTS a post office authorized on January 20, 1896, with Albert Dollenmayer, postmaster, but not established; location not known.

HEWSON a station of the Minneapolis, Anoka and Cuyuna railroad; location not known.

HILLCREST a village in Fridley Township, section 10, circa 1932.

HILLTOP a city incorporated May 4, 1956, which is located within the center of the city of Columbia Heights.

HYDE PARK a village in Fridley Township, section 23, circa 1932.

ITASKA the first post office in Anoka County, 1852–79, located in Ramsey Township; it was originally established and discontinued in Benton County, and spelled Itasca from 1852 to 1854; it was laid out as a community in 1852 near a trading post, which ceased to exist with the removal of the Indians in 1856. Buildings begun in 1852 included a hotel, saloon, garage, and steamboat landing, and later a St. Paul and Pacific Railroad station.

JESPERSON see LAKENETTA.

JOHNSVILLE a locality in Blaine Township, section 8.

LAKE VIEW POINT a village in Bethel Township, section 35, on the west shore of Coon Lake, circa 1932.

LAKENETTA a village in Ham Lake Township, section 10; located on the eastern shore of Lake Netta, the site is also seen on maps as Lake Netta. Its post office began as Hamlake, 1895–1900; then Jesperson, 1900–4; and last Lakenette, 1904–5. The townsite had a creamery, several stores, a cattle dealer, garage and blacksmith shop, and several churches.

LEXINGTON a city incorporated May 12, 1950; originally a paper town laid out on the Rum River about 1855 in sections 26 and 35 of what was then Blaine Township (T. 31, R. 23) and not developed at that time.

LINO LAKES a city in Centerville Township, section 9, incorporated May 11, 1955; earlier it had a farmers post office called Lino, 1894–1904, located in Vernum B. Parks's general store, as well as a Catholic church and a creamery.

LINWOOD TOWNSHIP first settled in 1855 and organized in 1871, received its name from Linwood Lake, the largest and most attractive one in a series or chain of ten or more lakes extending from northeast to southwest through this township and onward to Ham Lake. The name doubtless refers to the lin tree or linden. Our American species (*Tilia americana*), usually called basswood, is abundant here and is common or frequent through nearly all this state. The township had a post office, 1865–1903, in section 8, as well as a number of small businesses, a general store, and a Methodist church.

LUNDAHLS POINT a village in Bethel Township, section 35, on the north shore of Coon Lake, circa 1932.

MANCHESTER a paper town laid out on the Rum River above St. Francis about 1855.

MANOMIN (Manomine) see FRIDLEY.

MITCHELL CORNER a settlement in Burns Township at the corner of sections 2, 3, 10, and 11.

MORT a post office in Bethel Township, section 11, established in 1897 in the home of John Purmort, the postmaster, and continued until 1904, serving settlers around Coon Lake; Hudson Guy, the first mail carrier, ate dinner and changed horses each day at the Purmorts.

MYERS a station of the Minneapolis, Anoka and Cuyuna Railroad in Fridley Township, section 10.

NEAPOLIS a post office, 1880–83; site not known.

NELSON a station of the Minneapolis and Northern Railroad in Fridley Township, section 22.

NEW DAYTON a station on the Minneapolis, Anoka and Cuyuna Railroad, Ramsey Township.

NORTHTOWN a station of the Great Northern and Northern Pacific railroads, Fridley Township, section 34.

NOWTHEN a community in Burns Township, sections 21 and 28; its post office was first called Burns, 1876–94. The site had two churches and two schools, and the principal occupations were carpentry and livestock. The name was changed to Nowthen in 1894 and discontinued in 1905; the site is almost abandoned.

OAK GROVE TOWNSHIP settled in 1855, was organized in 1857. "The name is derived from the profuse growth of oak trees, which are about equally distributed over the township" (*History of the Upper Mississippi Valley*, p. 285). Oak Grove a village in section 18, located on the Rum River, was first settled in 1854, had a post office, 1857–1901, and was incorporated in 1993.

OAK LEAF a post office, 1884; site not known.

OAK PARK a locality in Blaine Township.

OAK SPRINGS a post office in Oak Grove Township, spelled Oak Spring, 1865–67, and Oak Springs, 1868–81.

OAKLAND a station of the Minneapolis, Anoka and Cuyuna Railroad in Anoka Township, section 16.

OLD JONATHAN see st. francis.

ONAWAY PARK a station in Fridley Township, section 10, of the Minneapolis and Northern Railroad.

OSBORNE a village in Fridley Township, which had a station of the Minneapolis, Anoka and Cuyuna Railroad.

OTONA see st. francis.

PINE RIDGE a village in Columbus Township, section 30, on the southeast shore of Coon Lake, circa 1932.

PINEHURST a village in Bethel Township, section 25, circa 1932.

PLEASANTVIEW a village in Fridley Township, section 26, circa 1932; see also Hennepin County.

PLYMOUTH a village in Fridley Township, section 26, circa 1914–32; see also Hennepin County.

POWERS a station of the Great Northern Railway in Anoka Township, section 26.

RAMSEY first permanently settled in 1850, was organized in 1857, being then named Watertown; but in November 1858, this township was renamed in honor of Alexander Ramsey, the first governor of Minnesota Territory, 1849–53, and later the second governor of this state, 1850–63. The city was incorporated on November 12, 1974.

Itasca was the name given by Governor Ramsey and others to a townsite platted in 1852 on sections 19 and 30 in this township near an Indian trading post, and the first post office of Anoka County was established there and named Itasca in May of that year. The name was copied from Lake Itasca at the head of the Mississippi, which had been so named by Schoolcraft in 1832. It was later applied during many years, after the building of the Northern Pacific Railroad through this county, to its station near the former Itasca village site. Both the village and the railway station were abandoned, but a new station named Dayton, for the village of Dayton at the opposite side of the Mississippi, was established on the Northern Pacific and Great Northern railroads about a mile southeast from the former Itasca station. This old village name is now retained here only by the neighboring Lake Itasca, of small size, scarcely exceeding a half mile in diameter.

REPUBLIC a village in Columbus Township; settled in 1885, the site had a sorghum mill, shoemaker, blacksmith, hotel, a livery, and a post office, 1891–1902, in Cyrus C. Grubbs's general store.

RESERVOIR HILLS a village in Fridley Township, section 36, circa 1932.

RICE LAKE a community in the former Columbus Township, settled in the 1890s and now part of Lino Lakes.

RIEDEL a village in Fridley Township, section 27, circa 1909–37; it had a station of the Minneapolis and Northern Railroad.

RIVERSIDE a paper town in Fridley Township, sections 1 and 2, laid out about 1855 on the Rum River above St. Francis.

RIVERVIEW a station of the Minneapolis, Anoka and Cuyuna Railroad, location not known.

ST. FRANCIS TOWNSHIP settled in 1855 and organized in 1857, bears the name given by Father Louis Hennepin in 1680 to the Rum River. It was transferred by Jonathan Carver in 1766 to the Elk River and now is borne by the chief northern tributary of that river. The name is in commemoration of St. Francis of Assisi in Italy, who was born in 1181 or 1182 and died in 1226, founder of the Franciscan order, to which Hennepin belonged. St. Francis, a city incorporated on May 16, 1962, was first settled in 1855 on the Rum River, which furnished power to extensive roller mills. Businesses included flour mills, general stores, corn canning, and potato starch factories. A post office was established in 1857, former names being Old Jonathan, St. Jonathan (1857 in Ramsey County), and Otona.

ST. JONATHAN see ST. FRANCIS.

SHADY OAKS a village in Oak Grove Township, sections 10 and 15, circa 1932.

SNAPP see CEDAR.

SODERVILLE a post office established in Ham Lake Township, section 5, in 1955 and later operating as a community postal station and commercial district.

SONORA a village in Fridley Township, with a station of the Minneapolis, Anoka and Cuyuna Railroad.

SOUTH BEND a village in Fridley Township, circa 1937.

SPRING LAKE PARK a city incorporated (with Ramsey County) on December 31, 1953.

STERLING a paper town platted on the southeast shore of Mille Lacs Lake.

SUNSET SHORE a village in Ham Lake Township, sections 16 and 21, on the east shore of Ham Lake, circa 1932.

THOMPSON PARK a rural branch post office, 1958–63; location not known.

THOMPSON RIVERVIEW TERRACE a locality in Coon Rapids Township.

TRAVERS a post office, 1865–66; location not found.

TUTHILL a post office, 1897–1904, in Blaine Township, section 6, Charles D. Tuthill, postmaster.

VALLEYVIEW a village in Fridley Township, section 26, circa 1932.

VILLAS CITY see BLAINE.

WASHINGTON a village in Columbus Township, section 35, circa 1932.

WENTZTOWN a post office, 1859–61; location not found.

WHITTLOCKS a village in Centerville Township, sections 34 and 35, circa 1932.

WORTH a station of the Northern Pacific Railroad; location not found.

Lakes and Streams

The Mississippi has been considered in the first chapter, and the origin of the name Rum River, outflowing from Mille Lacs, is noted for Mille Lacs County.

A noteworthy series of lakes extends through Columbus and Centerville, including, in their order from northeast to southwest, Mud, Howard, Columbia, Tamarack, Randeau, Peltier, Centerville, George Watch, Marshan, Rice (or Traverse), Reshanau, Baldwin, and Golden Lakes. The second to the fifth of these lakes are now much lowered or wholly drained away.

Peltier Lake was named for early settlers Charles, Paul, and Oliver Peltier, the first of whom built a sawmill.

Rice Lake probably received its name from its wild rice, but Rice Creek, flowing through this series of lakes, was named for Hon. Henry M. Rice of St. Paul, U.S. senator, who was an early resident in Fridley Township, as before noted. This Rice Lake has been also known as Traverse Lake for F. W. Traverse living at its northwest side.

Golden Lake, the most southwestern in the series, lying in sections 25 and 36, Blaine, was named for John Golden owner of land adjoining it, who was one of three brothers, early immigrants to this county from Ireland.

Another series of lakes, tributary in its northern part to the Sunrise River and at the south to Coon Creek, lies in Linwood, Bethel, and Ham Lake Townships. This series includes from northeast to southwest Typo Lake and Lake Martin; Island Lake, named for its island; Linwood Lake, giving its name to the township; Boot Lake, named from its outline; Rice Lake, having wild rice; Coon Lake and Little Coon Lake, named, like the creek, for raccoons, formerly much hunted here; and Lake Netta and Ham Lake, the latter, as before noted, being named from its form and giving name also to its township.

Cedar Creek and the adjoining Cedar station and village of the Great Northern Railway are named for the white cedar, or arbor vitae, growing there in swamps.

Seeley, Trott, and Ford Brooks on the west side of Rum River are named for their early settlers.

In Burns Township, Norris Lake in section 1 was likewise named for Grafton Norris; and Hare Lake in section 21, now drained, for James U. Hare, who was formerly postmaster of Nowthen post office, now discontinued, near this lake. (It is said that the name of this post office was recommended by Mr. Hare's neighbors from his common use of it, "Now then," in conversation).

Other lakes named for pioneer settlers are Minard Lake and Jones Lake in Bethel, the latter (now drained) having been also known as Lone Pine Lake; Lake George in Oak Grove Township;

Bunker Lake in section 36, Grow Township, named for Kendall Bunker, a homesteader there; and Lake Amelia in section 35, Centerville.

The following lakes bear names that occur somewhat frequently in many other counties:

Cedar Lake, in sections 33 and 34, Centerville.

Crooked Lake, in section 33, Grow, and section 4, Anoka.

Deer Lake, sections 15 and 22, Bethel.

Fish Lake, in the north part of Bethel.

Goose Lake, now drained, sections 15 and 16, Burns.

Grass Lake, section 11, Oak Grove.

Mud Lake, in section 16, Bethel; and another in section 13, Columbus.

Otter Lake, sections 35 and 36, Centerville.

Pickerel Lake, mostly drained, section 22, Burns.

The two Rice Lakes, occurring in the series before noted.

Round Lake, sections 20 and 29, Grow.

Swan Lake, now drained, in section 25, Oak Grove.

Twin Lake, section 19, Burns.

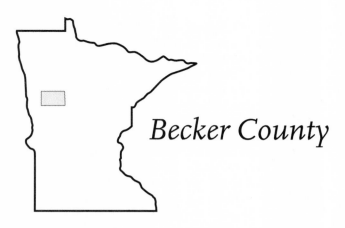

Becker County

This county, established March 18, 1858, but not organized until 13 years later by a legislative act approved March 1, 1871, was named in honor of George Loomis Becker of St. Paul. He was born in Locke, Cayuga County, N.Y., February 4, 1829, was graduated at the University of Michigan in 1846, studied law, came to Minnesota in 1849, and began law practice in St. Paul. He was mayor of this city in 1856, was Democratic candidate for governor of Minnesota in 1859, and was a state senator, 1868–71. He was commonly called Gen. Becker, having been appointed by Gov. Henry H. Sibley to his military staff in 1858 with the rank of brigadier general. In 1862 he became land commissioner of the St. Paul and Pacific Railroad and was ever afterward occupied in advancing the railroad interests of Minnesota, being a member of the state railroad and warehouse commission from 1885 to 1901. He died in St. Paul, January 6, 1904.

On October 13, 1857, Becker was elected as one of three members of Congress, to which number it was thought that the new state would be entitled. It was afterward decided, however, that the state could have only two representatives, and in casting lots for these two, Becker was unsuccessful. His generous acquiescence was in part rewarded by this county name.

Information has been gathered from A Pioneer History of Becker County by Alvin H. Wilcox (1907, 757 pages); from H. S. Dahlen, county auditor; George D. Hamilton, editor of the Detroit Record; and Charles G. Sturtevant, formerly county surveyor, all interviewed during a visit to Detroit in August 1909; and from maps in the office of J. A. Narum, county auditor, examined during a second visit in September 1916.

ANGOLA a post office, 1880–82, and flag stop of the Northern Pacific Railroad, located in Audubon Township, section 24.

ATLANTA TOWNSHIP settled in 1871, was organized January 25, 1879, being then named Martin, perhaps for Martin Hanson, one of the first settlers. Two months afterward it was renamed Atlanta, "from the resemblance its undulating surface bears to the Atlantic ocean."

AUDUBON TOWNSHIP was organized August 19, 1871, but was named successively Windom Colfax, and Oak Lake, holding the last of these names from 1872 until 1881. The Northern Pacific station and village established here, also the small lake adjoining the village site, had received the name Audubon in August 1871 in honor of John James Audubon (1780–1851), the great American ornithologist celebrated for his pictures of birds. This name was proposed by his niece, a member of a party of tourists who "camped where the Audubon depot now stands." In January 1881 the township name was changed to Audubon, and on

February 23 of that year the village was incorporated.

BAXTER see CALLAWAY.

BIRCH HILL a locality in Lake View Township, section 19, circa 1929.

BRAGER a country post office, 1903–34, Shell Lake Township. George W. N. Brager was the first postmaster and operated a hotel; his wife, Anna C. Brager, ran a general store.

BUCKS MILL a post office, 1886–1905, Lake View Township, section 31; Simeon S. Buck, who owned the general store, feed mill, and blacksmith shop, was the first postmaster.

BURLINGTON organized August 26, 1872, "was so named from the city of Burlington in the state of Vermont, by Mrs. E. L. Wright, a Vermonter, whose husband took a leading part in the organization of the township."

CALLAWAY TOWNSHIP organized March 30, 1906, is named for William R. Callaway of Minneapolis, general passenger agent of the Minneapolis, St. Paul and Sault Ste. Marie Railroad (hereafter cited as Soo Line), which had previously established a station and village of this name in section 32. The village, formerly known as Baxter, was incorporated on April 30, 1907, and separated from the township on March 19, 1912; its post office began in 1904. The early settlement had a feed mill, several hotels, and grain elevators; its main exports were grain, livestock, hay, and potatoes.

CARSON see OSAGE.

CARSONVILLE TOWNSHIP organized September 20, 1881, was named by Alvin H. Wilcox, then county treasurer, in honor of George M. Carson, a prominent pioneer, who in June 1879 took a homestead in section 18, Osage (the east part of Carsonville till its separate organization in 1891).

CHAPIN a post office, 1890–91, location not found.

CLIFFORD a country post office, 1888–1911, Spruce Grove Township, section 20. Carroll H. Clifford was first postmaster as well as justice of the peace; in 1900 his wife, Delia A. Clifford, was postmaster. Local businesses included sawmills, general stores, and a photographic studio; had a station of the Great Northern Railway.

CORMORANT TOWNSHIP organized February 26, 1872, received this name from its Big Cormorant and Upper Cormorant Lakes, which are translated from the Ojibwe names. Our species is the double-crested cormorant, which nests plentifully about these lakes. Cormorant, a village in sections 35 and 36, was first settled in 1876, with a country post office called Cormorant Mills, 1878–81, then changed to Cormorant and discontinued in 1933. A grist mill, built in 1880, was by 1890 a first-class roller flouring mill. The village also had a sawmill run by water power, two hotels, and a school.

CUBA organized in the winter of 1871–72, was named for Cuba, Allegany County, N.Y., the native place of Charles W. Smith, who came as one of the first settlers of this township in 1871.

DAHL a country post office, 1901–11, in Grand Park Township, section 18, with Peter O. Dahl its postmaster; the area's major industry was a sawmill.

DETROIT LAKES a city and the county seat, in Detroit Township from its organization in 1871; incorporated as a village in 1880 and as a city in 1900; located in a popular summer resort area on Detroit Lake and the Pelican River; the latter provided power for a flour mill. The post office was called Detroit City (1871–1906) and Detroit (1906–26) before changing to its present name by a vote of its citizens on September 7, 1926. The early settlement had a station of the Northern Pacific Railroad in section 27 and exported wheat, furs, butter, and snakeroot. An area in section 34, absorbed by the city, was called Tyler Town when settled about 1871 near the Pelican River, then renamed Johnstonville for Col. George H. Johnston, who sold real estate and was a miller in the community.

DETROIT TOWNSHIP settled in 1868 and organized July 29, 1871, derived its name from Detroit Lake which, according to the history of Becker County, had been so named by a French traveler here who was a Catholic missionary. Having camped for a night on the north shore of the lake in full view of the long bar that stretches nearly across it and leaves a strait (*detroit*, in French) between its two parts, he thence applied this name to the lake. It appeared on our state maps in 1860. The Ojibwe name of this lake refers also to its strait, being translated by Rev. Joseph A. Gilfillan as "the lake in which there is crossing on the sandy place."

DIX a post office, 1884–86, with Charles E. Mollen as the postmaster in his general store; the community also had a district school, a church, and steam- and water-power sawmills, according to the business gazetteer of the period, but the location was not given.

DREWES a country post office, 1904–10, Toad Lake Township; grocer Henry Drewes was the postmaster.

ELBOW LAKE a locality in Round Lake Township, section 6.

ELM GROVE a village in Lake View Township, section 20, located on Lake Melissa, circa 1916–29.

ELSIE a farmers post office, 1905–6, located in Evergreen Township.

ENGLEWOOD a village in Detroit Township, section 9, circa 1929.

ERIE TOWNSHIP first settled in 1872–73 and organized August 18, 1878, was named for Erie County in New York by settlers who came from the city of Buffalo, which is in that county. A post office was located there, 1884–93.

EUNICE see LAKE EUNICE.

EVERGREEN organized January 4, 1888, was named for its abundant evergreen trees, including the pines, spruce, balsam fir, and the red and white cedars. It is estimated that in 1880 this township had "about five million feet of standing white pine." Evergreen was a locality in Evergreen Township, section 23, circa 1937.

FINN a country post office, 1906–17, in Toad Lake Township, on the southeast end of the lake.

FOREST TOWNSHIP T. 142N, R. 37W, formerly part of Round Lake Township, on the White Earth Reservation.

FRAZEE a city in Burlington Township on the Otter Tail River, sections 26 and 35, was first settled in 1870, platted in 1873, and incorporated in 1891; had a station of the Northern Pacific Railroad in section 35. The village was named in honor of Randolph L. Frazee, owner of its lumber mill, flour mill, and general store. He was born at Hamden Junction, Ohio, July 3, 1841; came to Minnesota in 1866 and to this place in 1872; was a representative in the legislature in 1875; removed in 1890 to Pelican Rapids; and died there June 4, 1906. The post office was named Frazee City from 1874 to 1892, with Frazee the first postmaster; the name was shortened to Frazee in 1892. The early settlement had one of the largest sawmills in the state.

GLEN a village in Atlanta Township near Eddy Lake.

GOLDENROD a post office in Savannah Township, 1904–25, with Joseph Schmitt as postmaster; John Schmitt owned the general store; industries in the community were sawmills and flour mills.

GRAND PARK TOWNSHIP organized July 31, 1892, was so named for its beautiful scenery of rolling and hilly woodland, interspersed with lakes and traversed by the headstream of the Red River.

GREEN VALLEY organized May 3, 1886, received this name from the valley of Shell River, which crosses the northeast part of this township.

HAMDEN TOWNSHIP organized September 19, 1871, was named for Hamden in one of the eastern states, this being a town or village name in Connecticut, New York, New Jersey, and Ohio; had a post office, 1874–75.

HEIGHT OF LAND TOWNSHIP organized January 26, 1886, bears the name of the large lake crossed by its north boundary. The Red or Otter Tail River flows through this lake, from which a former canoe route led eastward to Shell Lake and River, tributary by the Crow Wing River to the Mississippi. Gilfillan translated the Ojibwe name, "Ajawewesitagun sagaiigun, the lake where the portage is across a divide separating water which runs different ways, or Height of Land Lake."

HITTERDAL a village in Atlanta Township, circa 1916.

HOLMESVILLE TOWNSHIP which received its first settlers in 1871 and 1873, was organized March 19, 1889, as East Richwood but this was soon changed to the present name in honor of Elon G. Holmes. He was born in Madison County, N.Y., in 1841, served in the Twenty-sixth New York Regiment in the Civil War, came to Minnesota in 1865, settled in Detroit in 1872 and was president of the First National Bank there, and was a state senator, 1887–89.

JARVIS a post office, 1884–86, in Height of Land Township, section 10, with Daniel O. Jarvis, postmaster.

JOHNSTONVILLE see DETROIT LAKES.

LABELLE a station of the Northern Pacific Railroad in Lake Park Township, section 2, with a small settlement in section 35 of Cuba Township.

LAKE CENTER a locality in Lake Eunice Township, section 4, platted as a resort community about 1911, also known as Maple Lodge.

LAKE EUNICE TOWNSHIP settled in 1870 and organized September 3, 1872, "was named by the

United States surveyors in honor of Eunice McClelland, who was the first white woman to settle near the lake. She was the wife of John McClelland." He was elected the first clerk of this township and was also the first register of deeds of the county, holding the latter office six years. The post office, in section 26, first named Eunice, 1880–92, was discontinued in 1900. The community had a saw and planing mill and a general store.

LAKE PARK TOWNSHIP settled in 1870, was organized September 19, 1871, being then named Liberty, which was changed to the present name in 1876. Its many lakes were collectively named by the Ojibwe, as translated by Gilfillan, "the lakes where there are streams, groves, prairies, and a beautiful diversified park country." Lake Park, a city in sections 2 and 3, was incorporated on February 25, 1881, as a village; a station on the Northern Pacific Railroad was built in 1871, unofficially called Lakeside. A post office was established as Loring, 1872–73, the name changing to Lake Park in 1873.

LAKE VIEW a village in Lake View Township, section 2, circa 1929.

LAKE VIEW TOWNSHIP was settled in 1870–71 and organized March 12, 1872. The name was suggested by Mrs. Charles H. Sturtevant, "as there were so many lakes in the township and so many pretty views from them."

LINDEN LAWN a village in Lake View Township, section 19, on Lake Melissa, also known as Linden Park, circa 1916–29.

LINNELL a farmers post office, 1883–1912, Carsonville Township, section 10; Mrs. Abby M. Linnell, first postmaster, came here with her two sons and opened a store.

LOCAL a post office, 1899–1931, in Height of Land Township, section 11.

LONNROT a village in Wolf Lake Township, section 28, with a commemorative Finnish name, first settled in 1888 on Wolf Lake; had a station of the Northern Pacific Railroad and a post office, 1898–1914; the first postmaster, William Isola, was also the township clerk.

LORING see LAKE PARK.

MANY POINT a post office, 1947–51, in Toad Lake Township.

MAPLE GROVE TOWNSHIP T. 142N, R. 39–40W, part of the White Earth Reservation.

MAPLE LODGE see LAKE CENTER.

McHUGH a village in Burlington Township, section 18, first settled in 1870; its post office operated 1887–1918; had a station of the Northern Pacific Railroad, and its major industry was manufacturing fence rails and wood ties.

MIDWAY a village in Runeberg Township, section 8, circa 1934–38.

OAK CITY see OAK LAKE.

OAK GROVE a village in Lake View Township, section 7, circa 1929.

OAK LAKE a village located in Audubon Township, section 24, which had a station of the Northern Pacific Railroad in section 19 of Detroit Township but was virtually abandoned in 1872 when the railroad built a station at Audubon; also known as Oak Lake Cut and Oak City.

OAK PARK a post office, 1872–74; location not found.

OAKLAWN a village in Lake View Township, section 18, located on Lake Sallie, circa 1916–29.

OGEMA (with accent on the initial long *o*, *g* as in get, and *a* like ah), meaning in the Ojibwe language "a chief," a city in White Earth Township, sections 18 and 19; incorporated as a village on October 28, 1907, and separated from the township on March 18, 1908; had a station of the Soo Line in section 19; its post office began in 1906 with Theodore Thoennes as postmaster and owner of the feed store.

OSAGE TOWNSHIP settled in 1879, was united in township government with Carsonville until May 4, 1891, when it was separately organized, deriving this name from Osage, the county seat of Mitchell County, Iowa. It is also a geographic name in Arkansas, Missouri, Kansas, and Oklahoma, but originally it was adopted for the Osage tribe of Indians, "the most important southern Siouan tribe of the western division" (F. W. Hodge, *Handbook of American Indians*). The post office was named Carson 1881–83, and reestablished as Osage in 1885. The Straight River provided power for the sawmill and feed mill; Squire S. McKinley, the postmaster of Carson and then Osage, platted the townsite, located across the river from his dam and sawmill.

PEBBLE BEACH a village in Lake View Township, section 18, on Lake Sallie, circa 1916–29.

PINE LAKE see PINE POINT (TOWNSHIP).

PINE POINT a locality in Pine Point Township,

sections 27, 28, 33, and 34, formerly the site of an Indian agency.

PINE POINT TOWNSHIP T. 141N, R. 37W, shown on 1930s map as Pine Lake Township.

PINE SPRINGS a village in Osage Township on the north end of Straight Lake, circa 1939.

PLUMB a country post office, 1902–19, located in Shell Lake Township, section 26.

POKEGAMA BEACH a village in Lake View Township, section 1, on Detroit Lake, circa 1916–29.

PONSFORD a village in Carsonville Township, section 5; settled about 1880 and named for Orville D. Ponsford, an early settler; the post office was established in 1892.

RAVENSWOOD a village in Lake View Township, section 23, circa 1929.

RICEVILLE organized in 1912, derived its name from the south branch of the Wild Rice River, which flows through the northwest part of this township.

RICHWOOD TOWNSHIP organized June 23, 1871, was named from Richwood in the Province of Ontario, Canada, the native town of W. W. McLeod, who settled on the site of Richwood village on the Buffalo River in May 1871, being one of the owners of a sawmill there. The village was incorporated in 1877, although it is not presently incorporated; its post office was established in 1872, changing to a community post office for the surrounding area in 1975.

ROCHERT a country post office in Holmesville Township, section 33, established in 1902.

ROUND LAKE TOWNSHIP T. 142N, R. 37–38W and T. 141N, R. 38W, on the White Earth Reservation.

RUNEBERG TOWNSHIP settled in 1882 and organized May 24, 1887, was named in honor of Johan Ludwig Runeberg, the great Swedish poet. He was born at Jakobstad in Finland, February 5, 1804, and died at Borga, near Helsingfors, May 6, 1877. A country post office was located in the township, 1888–1906; a small community was settled here in 1882, with a sawmill and general store.

SAND BEACH SANITARIUM a station of the Northern Pacific Railroad, Audubon Township, section 7.

SAVANNAH TOWNSHIP organized October 12, 1901, was named for its several tracts of grassy meadowland along stream courses, "made in an early day by the backwater from the dams of the beavers." (The American origin of this word has been noted for the West Savanna River in Aitkin County.) A country post office was located on Boot Lake, 1902–25.

SENJEN a country post office, 1896–1918, in Height of Land Township on Height of Land Lake; had a general store and sawmill.

SHADY BEACH a village in Lake View Township, sections 17 and 20, located on Lake Sallie, circa 1916–29.

SHELL LAKE TOWNSHIP first settled in 1881 and organized December 7, 1897, bears the name of its large lake, the source of the Shell River. These English names were derived probably from the shells found along the shore of the lake. The Ojibwe name means, as translated by Gilfillan, "the lake lying near the mountain," having reference to the portage thence across the water divide to Height of Land Lake. A post office operated 1886–1907.

SHIPMAN a post office, 1900–4, located in Green Valley Township, afterward being on a rural free delivery route from Park Rapids.

SHOREHAM a community in Lake View Township, section 20; bears the name of a seaport in Sussex, England; the county commissioners rejected its petition for incorporation as a village in 1941. Located in a popular summer resort area, the village, platted in 1904, had a station of the Soo Line and a post office, 1895–1907, which became a rural branch until 1955. Around 1900 the Pelican Valley Navigation Company had three daily boat trips from Detroit City.

SILVER LEAF settled in 1882–83, was organized March 3, 1888, receiving its name "from the silvery appearance of the leaves of the poplar, with which the township abounds."

SNELLMAN a village and post office, 1912–19, with a commemorative Finnish name, located in Wolf Lake Township, section 6.

SPANGELO a farmers post office, 1881–90, which was originally misspelled and corrected from Spanglo in 1881, located in Atlanta Township on the south branch of the Wild Rice River.

SPENCEDELL a post office authorized on October 14, 1904, with Ella H. Mills, postmaster, but not established; location not found.

SPRING CREEK TOWNSHIP organized in 1912, is named for its small creeks and many springs, headwaters of the south branch of the Wild Rice River.

SPRUCE GROVE TOWNSHIP settled in 1880, was organized January 19, 1889. "As the predominant timber in the town was evergreens, it was called Spruce Grove. The township was heavily timbered with pine (five million feet), spruce, balsam, oak, poplar, birch, elm, basswood, ironwood, and tamarack."

SPRUCEDELL a country post office, 1904–21, located in Grand Park Township.

SPRY a post office authorized on September 14, 1904, with Joseph T. Porter, postmaster, but not established; location not found.

SUGAR BUSH TOWNSHIP T. 141N, R. 39–40W, on the White Earth Reservation.

TEGNEER a country post office, 1890–1906, whose name may be of Finnish origin, located in Spruce Grove Township.

TOAD LAKE TOWNSHIP settled in 1887 and organized January 5, 1892, received this name from its large lake, a translation from the Ojibwe name *Mukuki* (or *Omakaki*) *sagaiigun*. Thence also came the name of the outflowing Toad River and of the prominent morainic drift hill in section 8, on the west side of this lake, called "Toad mountain," which commands an extensive view of the surrounding country. Toad Lake, a settlement in the township, had two general stores in 1920.

TWO INLETS settled in 1881 and organized September 20, 1898, was named from Two Inlets Lake in the east part of this township. It receives two inflowing streams close together at its north end, the larger one being the Fish Hook River, which flows through this lake. A country post office was located in section 3, 1900–9, with a sawmill and flour mill.

TYLER TOWN see **DETROIT LAKES**.

VELZORA a post office, 1904, later on a rural free delivery route from Park Rapids; location not found.

VOSS a country post office, 1896–1907, located in Atlanta Township.

WALWORTH TOWNSHIP settled in 1879 and organized April 3, 1883, was named by Albert E. Higbie, one of its first pioneers, for Walworth County, Wis. He came from the adjoining Jefferson County in that state. A post office operated in the township, 1890–91.

WAWEACUMIG a post office, 1911–14, whose first postmaster was Margaret C. Jourdan; location not found.

WEST SHORE a village in Lake View Township, section 4, on Detroit Lake, circa 1916–29.

WEST SHORHAM a village in Lake View Township, section 30, circa 1929.

WESTBURY a village in Richwood Township, section 30; had a post office, 1904–42, a station of the Soo Line, a lumber company, creamery, and several general stores; the first post office was located in the Farmers Mercantile Company, with Ole Thompson as postmaster.

WHITE EARTH TOWNSHIP organized March 30, 1906, was named for its village of White Earth, the location of the U.S. government agency of the White Earth Reservation, which lies in three counties, Becker, Mahnomen, and Clearwater. The removal of the Ojibwe to this reservation began in 1868, the first party coming to the site of the agency on June 14, which is celebrated there each year as a great anniversary day.

The reservation and its agency were named from White Earth Lake, the most beautiful one of the many fine lakes in the reservation, lying about five miles northeast of the agency. Its Ojibwe name is given by Gilfillan, "Ga-wababigunikag sagaiigun, the-place-of-white-clay-lake, so called from the white clay which crops out in places at the shore of the lake."

The village of White Earth, in section 23, on the White Earth Reservation, had a number of businesses and a post office from 1871, and was the site of a U.S. Indian school.

WOLF LAKE TOWNSHIP first settled in 1888 by immigrants from Finland, was organized April 4, 1896, receiving this name from its large lake, which was so named by the settlers on account of its form. Many wolves, bears, and deer were killed here during the first years of settlement. The city of Wolf Lake, in section 33, was incorporated as a village on May 12, 1949; had a country post office, 1909–11, under the name Wolf, and was reestablished as Wolf Lake in 1947.

WOODLAND a settlement in Evergreen Township, section 28; had a post office established in 1888 in Corliss Township, Otter Tail County, which was transferred to Becker County in 1901 and became a rural branch, 1910–21.

Lakes and Streams

The Otter Tail or Red River, traversing this county, received its name from the large Otter Tail Lake in the next county on the south, which is named from that lake and the river, as noted in its chapter. Pelican River, flowing through the Detroit series of lakes to Otter Tail River, is noted in the same chapter for Pelican Township and the village of Pelican Rapids, named like this river in translation of the Ojibwe name for Lake Lida, which adjoins it and is tributary to it in Otter Tail County.

The origins of the names of several lakes of Becker County are noticed in the foregoing list of its townships. These are the Cormorant Lakes in the township of this name, to which may be added Little Cormorant Lake in Audubon and Lake Eunice Townships, Detroit Lake, Height of Land Lake, Lake Eunice, the many little lakes in Lake Park Township, Shell Lake, Toad Lake, Two Inlets Lake, White Earth Lake, and Wolf Lake.

Elbow Lake, the most northern in the series through which the Red or Otter Tail River flows, is noted by Gilfillan as a translation of its Ojibwe name, having reference to its sharply bent form. The next lake in this series is Little Bemidji Lake, a mile long, this Ojibwe word signifying a lake that is crossed by a stream.

Many Point Lake is translated from the aboriginal name, referring to the many bays and intervening points of the shore. Round Lake, likewise from the Ojibwe name, requires no explanation, being one of our most common lake names throughout the state. The Upper and Lower Egg Lakes, west of Round Lake, and the outflowing Egg River are again translations, referring to nests and eggs of water-loving birds.

Flat Lake is another name of Indian origin, which perhaps should be better translated as Shallow Lake. Below the junction of the Round Lake and Shallow Lake Rivers, as they are named by the Ojibwe, the Red River passes through a small lake in section 16, Grand Park, which Gilfillan translated as "the-blackbird-place-of-wild-rice lake." It has been more simply anglicized as Blackbird Lake.

West of Height of Land Lake are Pine, Tamarack, and Cotton Lakes, the last probably named for a pioneer.

Other lakes whose Ojibwe names are translated include Fish Hook Lake (close west of White Earth Lake), Big Rat Lake, Big Rush Lake, Ice Cracking, Green Water and Pine Point Lakes, Basswood Lake, Juggler Lake, Lake of the Valley, Strawberry Lake, the Big and Little Sugar Bush Lakes (so named for maple trees and the making of maple sugar by the Indians), and Tulaby Lake (named for a species of whitefish, the tullibee), these being in the White Earth Reservation. Straight Lake and River are likewise translations from the aboriginal names.

The Buffalo River received its name from the white people for a tributary having its sources in Audubon, which was called by the Ojibwe, as translated, "Buffalo River, from the fact that buffaloes were always found wintering there." The present Buffalo Lake, in the nomenclature of these Indians, is "the lake where it keeps crumbling away from the gnawing of beavers," and they apply the same name, as stated by Gilfillan, to what we call Buffalo River, flowing into the Red River. In a word, therefore, the Ojibwe name in translation would be Beaver Lake and River.

Boot Lake in Savannah, and Moon Lake in sections 2 and 11, Richwood, are so named for their outlines. Mission Lake in White Earth is named for the adjoining Catholic mission and church.

The following lakes, in the alphabetic order of their townships, were named for settlers on or near them: Balke Lake and Lake Tilde in Atlanta; Homstad, McKinstry, Marshall, and Reep Lakes in Audubon; Chilton and Pearce Lakes in Burlington; Anderson and Fairbanks Lakes in Callaway; Floyd and Little Floyd Lakes in Detroit; Howe Lake in Erie; Collett Lake in Evergreen Township; Momb's Lake in Holmesville; Boyer Lake, Lake Labelle, and Stakke Lake in Lake Park Township; Lake Abbey, Curfman, Monson, Reeves, and Sauer's Lakes in Lake View; Campbell, Houg, and Sands Lakes in Richwood; Bisson and Trotochaud Lakes in Riceville; Lake Clarence in Spring Creek Township; and Du Forte and Morrison Lakes in White Earth.

Several lakes in the southwest part of this county were named for the wives or daughters of pioneer settlers, as Lakes Sallie and Melissa, through which the Pelican River flows below Detroit Lake, Lake Eunice (giving name to its township), Lake Maud, and Lake Ida. Excepting Lake

Eunice, before noticed as named for Mrs. John McClelland, only one other of these has been identified with its surname, this being for Melissa Swetland, one of three daughters in the family of a pioneer from Canada, well remembered by Miss Nellie C. Childs, assistant county superintendent of schools.

This county has other lakes, bearing the following names, for which their origin and significance have not been ascertained: Acorn and Eagle Lakes in Burlington; Brandy Lake and St. Clair Lake in Detroit, and another St. Clair Lake in sections 13 and 14, Callaway; Pearl Lake in Lake Eunice Township; Lake Forget-me-not in Lake Park; Dead Lake and Hungry Lake in Silver Leaf Township; Chippewa Lake in Grand Park; and Rock Lake in Holmesville.

Common lake names that need no explanation, occurring here, are two Bass Lakes in the White Earth Reservation; Long Lake in Detroit; Oak Lake, the locality of an early settlement, between Detroit and Audubon; Loon Lake in section 24, Lake Eunice Township; Fox Lake in section 7, Lake View; Pickerel Lake and Perch Lake in Erie; Island Lake in Shell Lake Township; Mud Lake, south of Toad Lake, another a mile west of Little Toad Lake, and a third in section 2, Silver Leaf; four Rice Lakes, in Detroit, Erie, Grand Park, and Holmesville; Round Lake, before noted, in the White Earth Reservation, and another in Holmesville; Turtle Lake in section 7, Cormorant; and Twin Lakes in sections 11 to 13, Height of Land.

Hills

In this large county wholly overspread by the glacial and modified drift deposits, with no outcrop of the underlying rock formations, most of the surface is only moderately undulating or rolling and in certain belts knolly and hilly, while other tracts in the northwest and southeast parts of the county have gentle and uniform slopes or are nearly level.

Two marginal moraine hills of exceptional height, though rising only about 150 or 200 feet above the lowest depressions near them, are popularly named Detroit Mountain, about three miles east from the city of Detroit, and Toad Mountain, west of Toad Lake. The former was called by the Ojibwe, as noted by Gilfillan, "Ashiwabiwin, Looking out, from the Sioux having been always there on top of the mountain looking out for the Chippeways."

Smoky Hill in the north edge of section 15, Carsonville, is a steep hill of gravel and sand, about 200 feet above the mainly level surrounding country. It would be called by glacial geologists a kame, having been amassed where a drift-laden stream descended from the border of the melting and departing ice sheet.

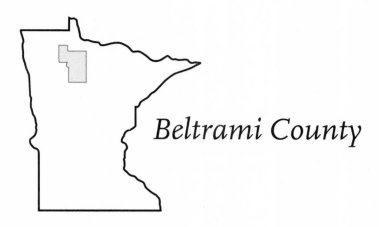

Beltrami County

Thirty years intervened between the establishment of Beltrami County, February 28, 1866, and its organization, when its county seat and earliest settlement, Bemidji, received incorporation as a village, May 20, 1896.

The county name was adopted in honor of Giacomo Costantino Beltrami, the Italian explorer in 1823 of the most northern sources of the Mississippi River, near the center of the part of this county lying south of Red Lake. Anglicized, his name was James Constantine, and on the title page of his published works, relating his travels, it is given by initials as J. C. Beltrami. Except David Thompson in 1798, he was the first explorer to supply descriptions of Red and Turtle Lakes, though undoubtedly they had been previously visited by roving traders and their canoe voyagers.

Beltrami was born at Bergamo, Italy, in 1779. His father advised him to enter the law profession, and he held numerous official positions as a chancellor and a judge, but in 1821, being accused of implication in plots to establish an Italian republic, he was exiled.

After traveling in France, Germany, and England, Beltrami sailed from Liverpool to Philadelphia and arrived there February 21, 1823. About a month later he reached Pittsburgh, there made the acquaintance of Lawrence Taliaferro, the Indian agent at the new Fort St. Anthony (two years afterward renamed Fort Snelling), and traveled with him by steamboat down the Ohio and up the Mississippi, coming on May 10 to the fort.

From July 9 to August 7, Beltrami traveled to Pembina with the exploring expedition of Maj. Stephen H. Long, to whom he had been commended by William Joseph Snelling and Taliaferro. He left that expedition at Pembina and went southeastward along an Indian trail, with two Ojibwe and a mixed-blood interpreter, to the junction of the Thief and Red Lake Rivers, whence his journey was by canoe up the latter river to Red Lake. From an Ojibwe village near the mouth of the lake, Beltrami traveled with a canoe along its southwestern shore to the Little Rock or Gravel River, where he stopped at the hut of a mixed-blood man, who became his guide. August 26 and 27 were spent in making long portages with the guide and an another Ojibwe, leaving the south shore of Red Lake a short distance east from the site of the agency and going south, passing small lakes and coming at last by a few miles of canoeing to Lake Puposky, now also called Mud Lake. Proceeding still southward the next morning, Beltrami soon came to a lake named by him for a deceased friend, Lake Julia, which he thought to have no visible outlet but to send its waters by filtration through the swampy ground both northward and southward, being thus a source both of the Red Lake River, called by him Bloody River, and of the Turtle River, the most northern affluent of the Mississippi. The narrative of Beltrami shows that he arrived at Lake Julia by a short portage, but on the map of the U.S. land surveys it is shown as having an outlet into Mud Lake, thus belonging to the Red River basin.

On September 4 Beltrami reached Red Cedar Lake, since known as Cass Lake, and during the next three days he voyaged down the Mississippi to the mouth of Leech Lake River. Thence he went up that stream to Leech Lake, where he made the acquaintance of Cloudy Weather, a leader in the band of the Pillager Ojibwe, by whom he was accompanied in the long canoe voyage of return to the Mississippi and down this river to Fort St. Anthony.

The next winter was spent by Beltrami in New Orleans, where he published his narration in 1824, written in French, bearing a title that in English would be "The Discovery of the Sources of the Mississippi and of the Bloody River." In 1828 he published in London his most celebrated work, entitled *A Pilgrimage in Europe and America, leading to the Discovery of the Sources of the Mississippi and Bloody River; with a Description of the Whole Course of the former and of the Ohio.* This work of two volumes is cast in the form of a series of letters addressed to an Italian countess. Eight letters, in pages 126 to 491 of Vol. 2, contain the account of his travels in Minnesota.

During his later years, until 1850, Beltrami resided in various cities of France, Germany, Austria, and Italy, and his last five years were spent on his estate at Filotrano, near Macerata, Italy, where he died in February 1855.

The city of Bergamo, his birthplace, in 1865 published a volume of 134 pages commemorating his life and work, dedicated to the Minnesota Historical Society. In translation from this book, Alfred J. Hill presented in the second volume of this society's Historical Collections a biographic sketch of Beltrami, together with a communication from Maj. Taliaferro giving reminiscences of him.

Information was received from John Wilmann, county auditor, during a visit to Bemidji in September 1909, and from H. W. Alsop, deputy auditor, in a second visit there, August 1916.

ALASKA TOWNSHIP was named by settlers who had traveled to Alaska.

ALGOMA PARK a village in Northern Township, section 33, circa 1916–23.

ANDERSON a post office, 1914–17, Birch Island Township, which changed its name to Heulin, which see.

ANDERSON a siding of the Minneapolis, Red Lake and Manitoba Railroad, Northern Township, section 31.

ANDRUSIA a locality in Ten Lakes Township, near the lake of the same name.

ANGLIN a post office authorized on July 7, 1887, with Ford W. Benedict as postmaster; it operated until February 9, 1888; no location found.

ASPELIN a post office, 1910–23, in Big Grass Township, section 30, with August O. Aspelin, postmaster.

AURE a country post office, 1903–19, located in Roosevelt Township, section 3; the Aure school was consolidated with the Debs school.

BARTIN a post office, 1917–26, located in Yale Township, section 7.

BATTLE TOWNSHIP is named for Battle River, flowing through this township into the east end of the south half of Red Lake. The stream was so named by the Ojibwe on account of their having fought here with the Dakota.

BATTLERIVER a country post office, 1901–19, located in Battle Township, section 15, which postmaster Joseph Jerome operated in his general store.

BELLE a post office, 1914–19, located in Birch Lake Township, section 24.

BEMIDJI BEACH a village in Northern Township, section 15, on the north end of Lake Bemidji, circa 1916.

BEMIDJI TOWNSHIP and city were named for an Ojibwe leader whose band of about 50 people had their homes on and near the south end of Lake Bemidji and around Lake Irving, including the site where white settlers founded this town. The chief died in April 1904 at the age of 85 years. His name was taken from the older Ojibwe name of this lake, crossed by the Mississippi. Rev. Joseph A. Gilfillan translated it as "the lake where the current flows directly across the water, referring to the river flowing squarely out of the lake on the east side, cutting it in two as it were, very briefly Cross lake." The city was settled in 1866. Its post office was spelled Bermidji 1894–98, when it was changed to its present spelling and incorporated as a village. During the city's early settlement, there were three sawmills, two planing mills, four churches, three schools, a number of small businesses, the Bemidji Opera House, and the Band of Bemidji.

BENVILLE TOWNSHIP was probably named for a pioneer settler.

BERGQUIST a post office, 1913–14, with Mary Bergquist, postmaster; location not found.

BIG GRASS TOWNSHIP T. 158N, R. 38W, dissolved and became part of the Unorganized Township of North Beltrami. It was named from the South Branch of Roseau River, which has its sources in the north edge of this township. This French name, *Roseau*, translated from the Ojibwe name of Roseau Lake and River, means the very coarse grass or reed (*Phragmites communis*), which is common or frequent in the edges of lakes and slow streams throughout this northwestern part of Minnesota.

BIRCH ISLAND TOWNSHIP T. 155N, R. 32W, became part of Unorganized Territory of Upper Red Lake. Located on the north side of the north half of Red Lake, it was named for its having a well-wooded tract of canoe birch, elm, oak, ash, basswood, and other trees along and near the lakeshore between the Two Rivers and for a mile eastward. This was a heavily timbered island, as it was called, rising 10 to 25 feet above the lake, in remarkable contrast with nearly all other parts of the north shore, which are a very extensive tamarack swamp only a few feet above the lake and reaching thence north 10 to 15 miles or more.

BIRCH TOWNSHIP has valuable timber of the paper or canoe birch and also of the yellow or gray birch, the former species being greatly used by the Indians for making their birch-bark canoes.

BIRCHMONT a village in Northern Township, section 21.

BLACK DUCK TOWNSHIP received its name from its large Black Duck Lake, the source of the river of the same name tributary to Red Lake. The name derives from the cormorant, which in Ojibwe means "black." The species popularly known by this name is, according to Dr. Thomas S. Roberts, the ring-necked duck (*Marila collaris*), frequent or common throughout the state.

BLACKDUCK a city located on the border of Hines and Summit Townships, was incorporated as a village on May 7, 1901; the townsite was homesteaded by Nichola Jansen in 1900 and purchased that same year by Marcus D. Stoner, who surveyed and platted the townsite with the help of Cass Thompson, a sawmill owner in Langor Township, who purchased the first 21 lots and moved his mill into Blackduck. The post office was established in 1900. The main exports were lumber, livestock, produce, potatoes, and butter. It had a station of the Northern Pacific Railroad in section 18 of Hines Township.

BROOK LAKE TOWNSHIP T. 146N, R. 30W, dissolved and became the Unorganized Territory of Brook Lake. The most southeastern of this county, it was named from a small lake in section 27, Moose Lake Township, adjoining this on the north, and a brook flows from it into section 3 of this township.

BUENA VISTA a community, 1896–1912, in Turtle Lake Township; its first post office was located in the Summit Hotel with John W. Speelman as postmaster, who named the town for Buena Vista ("good view" in Spanish), Oregon, where his wife had been born. The community was the site of the first county fair and had several stores, a hotel, a box factory, and a sawmill.

BUZZLE TOWNSHIP and Buzzle Lake, in its section 21, were named in honor of an early settler beside the lake. A country post office was located in the township, 1900–1905.

CARMEL a post office, 1901–17, located in Lee Township, section 2; Olaf Hawkins, owner of the general store, served as postmaster; there was also a sawmill and feed company and a photo studio operated by the Hawkins brothers.

CARR LAKE a small community south of Bemidji comprised of 25 sections of land in Bemidji and Grant Valley Townships in Beltrami County and overlapping into Hubbard County; there are no stores or a post office; the school is the community center. The community is closely associated with Bemidji; the first homesteaders in 1896 included Robert H. Carr, for whom the lake and community are named.

CHAUTAUQUA BEACH a village in Northern Township, section 21, circa 1916.

CORMANT is shortened from the Cormorant River, which flows through this township, named by Beltrami (in translation of the Ojibwe name) for the double-crested cormorant, frequent in many parts of Minnesota. The full form of the name had been earlier applied to a township of Becker County, preventing its use elsewhere in this state; with the abridged spelling, however, it was admitted again into the list of our township names.

CORMANTVALLEY a country post office, 1909–12, located in Cormant Township.

CORMENT see INEZ.

CROSS LAKE see PONEMAH.

DEBS a post office, 1916–25, located in Roosevelt Township, section 10, with close economic ties to the community of Aure; it was possibly named for Eugene V. Debs, as was Eugene Township in Lake of the Woods County.

DELPHINE a post office, 1900–1901, in Hagali Township.

DOMAAS see JED.

DURAND TOWNSHIP is in honor of Charles Durand, a homesteader on the northeast side of Lake Puposky.

DYSART a country post office, 1898–1905, in Hines Township; the area was first settled in 1896 and had a sawmill nearby.

ECKLES see WILTON.

ECKLES TOWNSHIP bears the name of an early landholder interested in the building of a branch of the Great Northern Railway. A country post office was located in section 16, 1908–10.

ELAND TOWNSHIP T. 153N, R. 30W, dissolved and became part of Unorganized Territory of Upper Red Lake. It was named by the early settlers, perhaps for the eland of South Africa, a large species of antelope or elk formerly found there in immense herds.

FARLEY a community in Port Hope Township, section 28, was founded in 1902 by early lumbermen William Blakely and Ed Farley, who tossed a coin to see whose name would be given to the township and its post office, 1902–15; both men built the hotel and named it for Blakely; it had a station of the Minnesota and International Railway.

FIRMAN a post office, 1904–12, was located in section 34 of Woodrow Township.

FOUR TOWN a post office, 1919–35, located in section 36 of Spruce Grove Township, which Ole E. Wiseth, first postmaster, operated in his general store.

FOWLDS a logging community in Maple Ridge Township, sections 22 and 27, was settled about 1896, with a post office, 1906–11, and named for its postmaster, John Fowlds; a station of the Minnesota and International Railway was in section 23.

FOY a post office, 1903–18, located in Battle Township, section 6.

FROHN was named for a district of Gudbrandsdalen, Norway, , the former home of immigrants in this township.

FUNKLEY a city in Hornet Township, section 25, was incorporated as a village on January 14, 1904; it was also known earlier as Hovey Junction for the Minnesota and International Railway station. The townsite was requested by Matt Fisher, established in 1903, and named for Henry Funkley, a county attorney; its post office operated 1903–67.

FUNSTON a post office, 1900–1901; location not found.

GATES CORNER a locality in Pine Island State Forest, also listed in Koochiching County.

GRANT VALLEY TOWNSHIP and its Grant Lake, in section 4, with Grant Creek its outlet, were named for an early settler or lumberman.

GULL LAKE see RALPH.

HAGALI was named for an early Norwegian settler of this township.

HAMRE TOWNSHIP derived its name from a small district in Norway, whence some of its settlers came. A country post office was in section 10, 1904–7.

HEULIN a post office in Birch Lake Township, section 26, 1917–36, which began as Anderson, 1914–17, with general store owner Frank O. Heulin as postmaster; the name changed to Heulin in 1917, Heulin continuing as postmaster.

HINES a community in Hines Township, section 28, was established in 1904 with its post office, located one mile east of an earlier site settled in 1892 on the south shore of Blackduck Lake by William Hines, who operated a farm and sawmill, and named for the Hines family; it had a station of the Minnesota and International Railway. A railway station in Black Duck Township was also named for William Hines.

HORNET TOWNSHIP was originally named Murray, a duplication of an older Minnesota township name, and the change and selection of the present name caused much contention. A post office called Hornet was authorized on August 6, 1902, with James H. Van Nett as postmaster, but not established; no location noted but probably in Hornet Township.

HOVEY JUNCTION see FUNKLEY.

ILAG a post office, 1913–34, located in Big Grass Township, section 23.

INEZ a community in Cormant Township, on Perry Creek, first settled in 1901; its post office was named Corment, 1902–5, and Inez, 1905–19.

ISLAND LAKE a village in section 28 of Alaska Township, at the end of a lumber railway branch, was named for the adjoining Island Lake, which has a small island close to this village. It had a post office, 1906–22.

JED a post office in Washkish Township, first called Domaas, 1907–15, and discontinued in 1936.

JELLE a post office, 1903–38, in Hamre Township, section 29, named for its first postmaster, Louis Jelle.

JONES TOWNSHIP was named for a pioneer there.

KEATING a post office authorized on August 18, 1903, with Edward J. Keating as postmaster, but not established; location not found.

KELLIHER TOWNSHIP and its city at the end of a branch railway built for lumbering, were named for A. O. Kelliher, a former agent here for lumber companies. The city was incorporated as a village on October 3, 1903, the year its post office was established; in 1892 Ulysses (Jess) and John Freestone filed stone and timber claims, and it is Jess's claim that became the site of Kelliher; in 1897 the claim was sold to a Weyerhaeuser man, who in turn sold the land to the Crookston Lumber Company, a large landholder in the Bullhead Lake area. The city was platted by A. O. Kelliher for George S. Eddy of the Crookston Lumber Company. It had a station of the Minnesota and International Railway.

KITCHI a post office, 1909–13, Moose Lake Township, section 29; Stephen M. Schaak, postmaster, was the owner of the general store and a sawmill.

KONIG TOWNSHIP T. 155N, R. 30W, became part of Unorganized Territory of Upper Red Lake; it was named for a settler there from Germany.

LAKESIDE a village in Northern Township, section 25, circa 1916–23.

LAMMERS was named for the Lammers Brothers (George A. and Albert J.) of Stillwater, who engaged in real estate and lumber business in this township.

LANGOR TOWNSHIP received its name in honor of Henry A. Langord (the final letter being omitted), a settler of Norwegian descent coming here from Wisconsin. A post office was located in the township, 1896–07, with Langord as postmaster; he also owned the general store and sawmill.

LAVINIA a post office in Northern Township, section 25, established in 1906, discontinued in 1907, reestablished as Northern, 1915–16, and again named Lavinia, 1916–39; it had a station of the Minnesota and International Railway, which was also known as Mississippi.

LEE TOWNSHIP was named for settlers from Norway, their original name having been changed to this spelling.

LEMLOH a village in T. 149N, R. 33W (Nebish and Durand), with a station of the Minneapolis, Red Lake and Manitoba Railroad.

LIBERTY TOWNSHIP received this name in accordance with the petition of its settlers.

LOUIS a post office, 1904–33, in Moose Lake Township, section 4.

LUDLOW a post office, 1914–15, located in unnamed township T. 156N, R. 31W, section 36.

LYNX a country post office, 1901–8, located in Liberty Township, section 14; it had a station of the Minneapolis, Red Lake and Manitoba Railroad.

MALCOLM a post office, 1904–44, located in Minnie Township, section 19; the name was suggested by a group of early settlers from Sweden for their homeland post office of Malkom, but the spelling was altered by the U.S. Post Office Department.

MALTBY a post office, 1899–1914, in Grant Valley Township, was originally established in Hubbard County, with Milo S. Maltby the first postmaster.

MAPLE RIDGE TOWNSHIP was named for its sugar maple trees and for its situation at the sources of streams descending north to Red Lake. Sugar Bush Township is also named for the maple trees and sugar making, to be more fully noted in a later page.

MARSH SIDING a village in Northern Township, section 7, with a station of the Minneapolis, Red Lake and Manitoba Railroad.

McPHAIL a country post office, 1903–8; location not found.

MINNIE TOWNSHIP has the feminine name derived from the name of this state, perhaps chosen in honor of the wife or daughter of one of its pioneers.

MISSISSIPPI see LAVINIA.

MOOSE a post office, 1917–18, located in Moose Lake Township; also listed as Moosenberg.

MOOSE LAKE TOWNSHIP is named for its Moose Lake and Little Moose Lake, which are probably translated from their Ojibwe names.

MYRAN a country post office, 1902–10, located in Benville Township, section 28, which Franz B. Gustafson, postmaster, operated in his general store.

NEBISH TOWNSHIP and its lake of this name are from the Ojibwe word *anibish*, tea, the much relished drink alike of the white settlers and the Indians. The village in section 35 was established in 1898 on the northeast shore of Nebish Lake by Haaversen and Richards, lumbermen who contracted to log for the Crookston Lumber Company; when a spur railroad line was built to Whitefish Lake, a new town was created called Whitefish Junction; in 1905 that line was extended to Bemidji, and in 1913, the site was platted and became the new Nebish. The post office operated 1898–1959 and as a rural branch until 1963; a station of the Minneapolis, Red Lake and Manitoba Railroad was in section 27.

NEELEY'S SIDING a village in T. 149N, R. 33W, with a station of the Minneapolis, Red Lake and Manitoba Railroad.

NEWHAVEN a country post office, 1905–9, in Liberty Township, section 11; it had a station of the Northern Pacific Railroad.

NORTH BEMIDJI a village in Bemidji Township, section 15, with a station of the Northern Pacific Railroad.

NORTH POLE a proposed village in Bemidji Township, just north of the city on the shore of Lake Bemidji; a post office was created in November 1940 by the county board of commissioners to take ad-

vantage of the holiday; however, Gov. Joseph A. A. Burnquist said there was no valid reason to incorporate such a village, as there was no business except a summer resort hotel and a store; the edict was upheld by the District Court on April 8, 1941; the name does appear on a state highway tourist map of 1941.

NORTH WOOD TOWNSHIP T. 157N, R. 38W, became part of Unorganized Territory of North Beltrami; it was named for its timber and its situation in the north part of this county.

NORTHERN see LAVINIA.

NORTHERN TOWNSHIP received this name because it includes the north part of Lake Bemidji.

NYMORE a village on the Mississippi River in Bemidji Township, section 16, was named for Martin Nye, a Bemidji pioneer, who was a veteran of the Civil War. It had a post office, 1904–23, and a railroad station also known as South Bemidji. The village is presently within the Bemidji city limits.

OAKDALE PARK a village in Northern Township, section 35, on Lake Bemidji, circa 1916–23.

OAKWOOD a post office, 1900–1907, located in Hagali Township.

OAKWOOD PARK a village in Northern Township, section 24, circa 1916–40.

O'BRIEN TOWNSHIP was named for a lumberman there, William O'Brien, from Stillwater, Minnesota.

ORHEIM a country post office, 1904–14, located in Spruce Grove Township, section 27; Rasmus Orheim, for whom the site was named, was the first postmaster.

OTTO see SHOTLEY.

PENNINGTON an unincorporated village in Brook Lake Township, section 4; its post office was established in 1911.

PIKE a post office authorized on July 28, 1896, with Patrick LeMay as postmaster, but not established; location not found.

PINE BEACH PARK a village in Northern Township, section 25, circa 1916–23.

PINEWOOD a logging community in Buzzle Township, section 33, was first settled in 1879 and named by the early settlers for the pine timber of the area; it had a hotel, a sawmill, a general store, a livery, and a station of the Minneapolis, St. Paul and Sault Ste. Marie Railroad (Soo Line); its post office began in 1910.

PLEASANT HARBOR a village in Northern Township, section 16, circa 1916.

PONEMAH a village on the north shore of the southern half of Red Lake, having a U.S. government school for the Ojibwe children, bears a name used by Henry W. Longfellow in *The Song of Hiawatha*. Minnehaha in dying, and afterward Hiawatha, depart

> *To the Islands of the Blessed,*
> *To the Kingdom of Ponemah,*
> *To the Land of the Hereafter.*

The village is the oldest on the Red Lake Reservation; it was known as Cross Lake until 1901 when the post office was established as Ponemah with John G. Morrison as first postmaster.

PORT HOPE TOWNSHIP was named by one of its first settlers, Capt. William Wetzel, a veteran of the Mexican War and the Civil War, probably for Port Hope, Canada, on the north shore of Lake Ontario.

PUPOSKY is a village in section 23 of Durand Township on Lake Puposky, an Ojibwe name recorded and translated by Beltrami signifying "the end of the shaking lands," that is, swamps whose surface is shaken and sinks when walked on. It has been also translated as Mud Lake, with Mud River outflowing from it. The village was founded in 1904 when the Minneapolis, Red Lake and Manitoba Railroad came; its post office began in 1905.

QUIRING TOWNSHIP had a post office, 1900–1936, in section 23; its name was supposedly derived during the township's organizational meeting, when several names to honor early settlers were proposed, and an argument ensued until one of the organizers shouted, "Let us be quiet and stop quarreling," causing another of the organizers to coin the name from quiet and quarreling.

RALPH a country post office, 1898–1902, also known as Gull Lake, located in Port Hope Township.

REBEDEW a post office, 1904–7, in Birch Township.

RED LAKE TOWNSHIP T. 155N, R. 31W, dissolved and became part of Unorganized Territory of Upper Red Lake.

REDBY an unincorporated village located on the south shore of Red Lake, on the Red Lake Reservation in T. 151N, R. 33W, section 20, received its name from the lake; its post office was established in 1907. It is the only community within the reservation that has taxable land under private ownership; industries include the Red Lake Indian Mills and the Red Lake Fisheries Association. The North West Fur Company had a trading post at the site.

REDLAKE a village in T. 151N, R. 34W, section 21, on the Red Lake Reservation, was the site of the first post office in the county, established in 1852 in what was then part of Pembina County; St. Mary's Mission located here in 1858.

RIVERSIDE a village in Bemidji Township, sections 1 and 2, had a station of the Minnesota and International Railway.

ROBERG a post office authorized on November 28, 1911, with Eugene Rossgard as postmaster, but not established; location not found.

ROOSEVELT TOWNSHIP including the greater part of Clearwater Lake, crossed by the west line of this county, was named in honor of Theodore Roosevelt, president of the United States, 1901–9.

ROSBY a locality east of the city of Bemidji, in Bemidji Township.

ROYAL BEACH a village in Northern Township, section 28, circa 1916–23.

SAUM a village located in Battle Township, section 24; it has had a post office since 1904 and is the site of a restored one-room log school, which stands next to the Saum school built in 1912, the first consolidated school in Minnesota and the third in the United States.

SCRIBNER a station on the Soo Line in Eckles Township, section 20.

SELKCE see WILTON.

SHILLING a village in T. 156N, R. 35W, section 6; the post office, 1917–35, was located in the mercantile store of postmaster Walter C. Schilling.

SHOOKS TOWNSHIP was named for Edward Shooks, an early lumberman who secured a railroad spur line at the site that came to be called Shook's Siding. The village in section 24 had a station of the Minnesota and International Railway and a post office, 1911–66.

SHOTLEY TOWNSHIP has Shotley Brook, here flowing into the north half of Red Lake. A platted townsite in section 10 had a hotel, a saloon, and stores; its name is a corrupted spelling of Joseph Shillette's name; he was an early trapper of the area. Several post offices existed by the name: Shotly 1903–13; a second Shotly, 1913–17, which had been named Otto, 1908–13, named for Otto B. Habedark, the first postmaster at his general store; and Shotley, 1923–35, formerly named Stanley, 1914–23; the present named Shotley Brook is a crossroads with a store and church.

SMITHPORT a post office, 1914–16, in Birch Island Township, section 32.

SOLWAY a city in section 28 of Lammers Township, and the Solway Lumber Company, which formerly worked in its vicinity, were named after Solway Firth, the wide inlet from the Irish Sea between England and Scotland. The post office began in 1898, the school was built in 1899, and by 1900 there were seven saloons, two hotels, two livery barns, several restaurants and stores, a weekly newspaper, a blacksmith, a feed store, a jail, a sawmill, and a hall, many of which burned in fires between 1905 and 1910; it had a station of the Great Northern Railway.

SOUTH BEMIDJI a village in Bemidji Township, with a Soo Line station.

SPAULDING a post office, 1897–1908, and Northern Pacific Railroad station in Liberty Township, section 34; the major industry was the sawmill.

SPRUCE GROVE TOWNSHIP was named for its spruce timber, abundant on many tracts throughout northern Minnesota.

SPUR a post office, 1910–21, in Port Hope Township.

STANLEY see SHOTLEY.

STEENERSON TOWNSHIP was named for Hon. Halvor Steenerson of Crookston, representative in Congress, 1903–23.

SUGAR BUSH TOWNSHIP was named, like Maple Ridge Township also in this county, for its maple trees used by both the Indians and white people for sugar making. Beltrami wrote of the Ojibwe process of making maple sugar, as follows (in his *Pilgrimage*, vol. II, p. 402): "The whole of this territory abounds with innumerable maple or sugar trees, which the Indians divide into various *sugaries*. The sap of the trees flows through incisions made in them by the Indians in spring at the foot of the trunk. It is received in buckets of birch bark and conveyed to the laboratory of each respective sugary, where it is boiled in large cauldrons till the watery parts are evaporated. The dregs descend, and the saccharine matter remains adhering to the sides of the vessel. When this process is completed the sugar is made."

SUMMIT TOWNSHIP has the highest land crossed by the Minnesota and International Railway, called therefore a "summit" by its surveyors. The village in section 19 had a station of the railway.

TAYLOR TOWNSHIP T. 148N, R. 31W, dissolved and became Unorganized Territory of Taylor; it was named in honor of James Taylor, an early homesteader there, then a merchant at Tenstrike, the village on the west border of this township.

TEN LAKES TOWNSHIP T. 146N, R. 31W.

TENSTRIKE a city on the border of Port Hope and Taylor Townships, was incorporated as a village on March 11, 1901; the original site, located one mile west of the present site, was platted and may have been named in 1899 as Tenstrike Center by Almon A. White of St. Paul, alluding to the completely successful bowling that with the first ball knocks down all the ten pins. Other stories about the origin of the name exist, one centering on a remark by M. R. Brown, owner of a prospering trading post on the townsite, who exclaimed, "I sure made a tenstrike here." The post office began in 1899, and it had a station of the Minnesota and International Railway.

THORHULT a post office, 1906–35, in Steenerson Township, section 23, is named for a place in Sweden.

TURTLE LAKE TOWNSHIP bears the name of its large lake, translated, as also the outflowing Turtle River, from the Ojibwe name. David Thompson, who traveled here in 1798, wrote of this lake that "its many small bays give it the rude form of a turtle."

TURTLE RIVER TOWNSHIP likewise is named for its Turtle River Lake and for the river so named flowing through this lake, the most northern tributary of the Mississippi. A boom lumber village in the township began on land on Turtle River Lake purchased in 1899 by Fred DeSilver, who built a hotel and several stores; when the 1901 survey for the Minnesota and International Railway extension passed through the present site, merchants and residents removed their buildings to the 1898 homestead claim of Simon E. Bright. The post office operated 1899–1944, with Nels Otterstad as the first postmaster; he was also a land surveyor and timber cruiser. By 1910, two large fires had destroyed most buildings on the main street.

UNORGANIZED TERRITORY OF BROOK LAKE formerly Brook Lake Township, T. 146N, R. 30W.

UNORGANIZED TERRITORY OF LOWER RED LAKE includes unnamed townships T. 156N, R. 30–35W; and T. 157N, R. 36–37W.

UNORGANIZED TERRITORY OF NORTH BELTRAMI includes Big Grass, North Wood, Winner, and Yale Townships and unnamed townships T. 150N, R. 34–35W.

UNORGANIZED TERRITORY OF TAYLOR formerly Taylor Township, T. 148N, R. 31W.

UNORGANIZED TERRITORY OF UPPER RED LAKE includes Birch Lake, Eland, Konig, Red Lake, and Washkish Townships and unnamed townships T. 152N, R. 33–34W; T. 153N, R. 32–38W; T. 154N, R. 33–38W; and T. 155N, R. 33–35W.

WASKISH a community in Washkish Township, section 8; the post office was established in 1910, with Frank Lyons as first postmaster; Lyons erected the first building in 1902, a small log cabin that was a store, home, and eventually the post office, and he named the site Wahwaushkayshe, shortened to Washkish, and again to Waskish. This was a popular summer fishing area; the entire townsite was purchased by the state in 1934 because the Department of Conservation needed a portion of land where the Tamarack River empties into the lake for the purpose of netting pike and stripping spawn when the fish start their spring run.

WASHKISH TOWNSHIP T. 154N, R. 30W, dissolved and became part of Unorganized Territory of Upper Red Lake; the name is from the Ojibwe word *wawashkeshi*, the deer.

WAVILLE a village in Northern Township, section 35.

WERNER a settlement in Turtle Lake Township, section 19, on the Minneapolis, Red Lake and Manitoba Railroad.

WILTON a city in sections 33 and 34 of Eckles Township, incorporated on May 26, 1906, was named for some one of the 15 or more villages and towns of this name in the eastern states, Canada, and England. The post office was first named Selkce, 1900–1903 (Eckles spelled backwards), and then changed to its present name; the site is also shown as Eckles and Eckels on various maps. The Great Northern Railway had a station in section 33, and the Soo Line had a station in section 34.

WINNER TOWNSHIP T. 158N, R. 37W, dissolved and became part of Unorganized Territory of North Beltrami.

WOODROW TOWNSHIP was in honor of Woodrow Wilson, president of the United States, 1913–21.

WYNNE a post office, 1912–14, in Alaska Township; James B. Wynne was the postmaster.

YALE TOWNSHIP T. 158N, R. 36W, became part of Unorganized Territory of North Beltrami.

———

Lakes and Streams

The names of the Mississippi River and Cass Lake have been considered in the first chapter of this work, and Red Lake will be later noticed in connection with Red Lake County.

In the preceding list of townships, sufficient mention is made of several lakes, rivers, and creeks, these being Battle River, Lake Bemidji, Black Duck Lake and River, Brook Lake, Buzzle Lake, Cormorant River, Grant Lake and Creek, Moose Lake and Little Moose Lake, Nebish Lake, Lake Puposky or Mud Lake and the outflowing Mud River, Shotley Brook, Turtle Lake and River and the Turtle River Lake.

The longest southern tributary of Red Lake on the canoe route of Beltrami is Mud River, the outlet of Lake Puposky or Mud Lake, which he called "the river of Great Portage." This name, as he wrote, was given by the Indians, "because a dreadful storm that occurred on it blew down a vast number of forest trees on its banks, which encumber its channel, and so impede its navigation as to make an extensive or great portage in order to reach it." In accordance with the recommendation of Beltrami, it is sometimes called Red Lake River, indicating it to be the upper part of the river that outflows from Red Lake.

Lake Julia, before noted as the highest source of this stream, was thought by Beltrami to send its waters partly southward, so that it supplied to him the title of "the Julian sources of Bloody River and the Mississippi."

Henry R. Schoolcraft, in the *Narrative* of his expedition to Lake Itasca in 1832 (published in 1834), wrote the name of Lake Bemidji as "Pamitchi Gumaug or Lac Travers." On Joseph N. Nicollet's map, 1843, it is "Pemidji L."

Lake Irving, closely connected with Lake Bemidji by a strait and forming the south boundary of the city of Bemidji, was named by Schoolcraft for Washington Irving, the eminent American author (1783–1859). It was frequently called Little

Bemidji Lake by the early settlers, which name has passed out of use.

Lake Marquette, in sections 29 to 31, Bemidji, was also named by Schoolcraft for the zealous French missionary and explorer of the Mississippi (1637–75). It is on the Plantagenian or South Fork of the Mississippi, which Schoolcraft ascended on his way to Lake Itasca, now named Schoolcraft River (or Yellow Head River, for his Ojibwe guide), more fully noticed in the chapter of Hubbard County.

The Mississippi for about six miles next below Lake Bemidji has a series of rapids, which were ascended in 1832 by Schoolcraft and were described by him as follows in his *Narrative* (published in 1855). "Boulders of the geological drift period are frequently encountered in ascending them, and the river spreads itself over so considerable a surface that it became necessary for the bowsmen and steersman to get out into the shallows and lead up the canoes. These canoes were but of two fathoms length, drew but a few inches of water, and would not bear more than three persons. . . . There were ten of these rapids encountered before we reached the summit or plateau of Lake Pemidjegumaug, which is the Lac Traverse of the French. These were called the Metoswa rapids, from the Indian numeral for ten" (*Midasswi* in Frederic Baraga's *A Dictionary of the Ojibway Language*).

A few miles below these rapids, the Mississippi in the southeast corner of Frohn Township flows through Wolf Lake, which was called Pamitascodiac by the Ojibwe. It was thought by Schoolcraft to be so named for a tract of prairie adjoining it, "from pemidj, across, muscoda, a prairie, and ackee, land."

One to two miles farther east the Mississippi passes through the south end of Lake Andrusia, named by Schoolcraft in 1832 for Andrew Jackson, who was president of the United States, 1829–37.

For the next two miles the course of this river is occupied by Allen's Bay, which is connected with Cass Lake by a short and narrow strait. This body of water was named also by Schoolcraft, for Lieut. James Allen, a member of the expedition of 1832, "who, on his return down the Mississippi, was the first to explore it." Allen was born in Ohio, 1806; was graduated at the U.S. Military Acade-

my, 1829; was promoted to be captain, First Dragoons, 1837; conducted an expedition to the sources of the Des Moines and Blue Earth Rivers in 1844; and died at Fort Leavenworth, Kans., August 23, 1846. He was author of a report to the government on each of these two Minnesota expeditions.

The following lakes bear names of early settlers: Campbell Lake, Lake Erick, and Peterson Lake (also called Mud Lake), in Liberty Township; Myrtle Lake, in sections 4 and 9, Roosevelt; Buzzle and Funkley Lakes, in Buzzle Township; Movil Lake, in Turtle Lake and Northern Townships; Robideau and Gilsted Lakes, in Birch Township; and Swenson and Grace Lakes, in Frohn Township.

Pimushe Lake, in Moose Lake Township, which we receive from Nicollet's map, bears an Ojibwe name, but it has not been identified in Baraga's *Dictionary*.

Kichi Lake, on the south line of the same township, also mapped with this name by Nicollet, now spelled Kitihi Lake, means in the Ojibwe language Big Lake. Its approved form is *Kitchi*, in Baraga's *Dictionary*, or *Gitche*, in Longfellow's *Song of Hiawatha*. It is thus of exactly the same meaning as a second Big Lake three miles distant on the west in Sugar Bush Township.

Nearly all the other lakes of this county, not already noted, chiefly occurring only in its southern third part, have names of common or frequent use and evident origin, many indeed being translations of the aboriginal names. These include Moose and Turtle Lakes, in Alaska Township; Bass Lake, in Nebish, also Bass and Little Bass Lakes, in Turtle River Township; Clearwater Lake and River, to be more fully noticed for Clearwater County; two White Fish Lakes, in Hagali and Buzzle Townships; Loon Lake and Medicine Lake, in Hagali, the latter of Ojibwe origin; Gull Lake, in Hagali and Port Hope; Deer, Pony, and Long Lakes, in Liberty Township, and another Long Lake in Turtle River Township; Black Lake, Fox, Gnat, and Three Island Lakes, in Turtle Lake Township; Twin Lakes, in Taylor; Grass Lake, on the line between Eckles and Grant Valley; Rice Lake, on the east line of Sugar Bush, and another in Jones Township, the latter more commonly known by its Ojibwe name, Manomin Lake, each referring to the luxuriant growths of wild rice; Boot and Fern Lakes, in Grant Valley, the former named for its outline; and School Lake, in Frohn, lying partly in the school section 16.

Tributaries and Points of Red Lake

In September 1885, the present writer made a canoe trip for geologic observations along the entire shoreline of Red Lake, starting east from the agency. The journey, more than 100 miles in extent and occupying six days, was wholly within the Red Lake Reservation, which has since been greatly reduced in its area. My canoemen were two Ojibwe, Roderick McKenzie and William Sayers, each of whom had received a fair education and could converse well in English. McKenzie, by his acquaintance with the Indians about the lake, was specially serviceable in obtaining information of the names applied by them to streams and points of land along the shore, and the translations of these are given in my report, published by the Geological and Natural History Survey of Minnesota (vol. 4, 1899, pp. 155–65). A sketch map of Red Lake and its vicinity drawn during this travel and published by the U.S. Geological Survey is Plate 12 in Monograph 25, 1896, "The Glacial Lake Agassiz." Much abridged from the report cited, the following are my notes of translations of the Ojibwe names then in use.

The stream at the agency is Pike Creek, rendered Gold Fish Creek by Beltrami, but by the English residents it is more commonly called Mill Creek. A saw- and gristmill, having ten feet head, is built on this stream about a quarter of a mile from its mouth. Its sources, according to Rev. F. W. Smith, are a series of three or four lakelets, the lowest of which, lying on the southwest side of the road to Cass Lake, is called by the Indians Little Lake but by the white men Ten Mile Lake, being about ten miles distant from the agency. The highest, named Cranberry Lake, has quite irregular outlines, lying mostly in sections 34 and 35, T. 150, R. 34, in the east part of Alaska Township.

Near the village, about five miles east of the agency, is a slightly projecting point, called the Chief's Point. It rises steeply 25 to 30 feet above the lake. Indian cornfields were seen on its top in small clearings of the forest.

Mud River, called the Red Lake River on former maps, and Great Portage River by Beltrami, enters the lake about a half mile east of the Chief's Point. This is larger than Pike Creek but smaller than Sandy River and Blackduck River. Its head stream passes through Lake Puposky, named on the township plats Mud Lake, and through two lower small lakes called Wild Rice Lakes.

Big Point, a broad swell of the shore, standing out perhaps an eighth of a mile beyond the general outline westward but little from that eastward, is nearly a mile east of Mud River.

In the distance of six miles from Big Point to Blackduck River, four small creeks enter the lake, bordered by tracts of marsh grass along the lower part of their course. On these meadows we saw many stacks of hay that had been put up by the Indians, and the name Hay Creek is applied to one of these streams. Hay is also cut by the Indians on the meadows of nearly all the streams about Red Lake.

Blackduck River flows into the most southeast part of the southern half of the lake. It is called Cakakisciou River on Beltrami's map, and Cormorant River on Nicollet's and later maps, but it is known to the English-speaking residents only by the name of Blackduck River. Its principal tributary, coming in from the northeast, is now named the Cormorant River.

Battle River, from which a township is named, enters the lake about four miles farther north. It is of nearly the same size as Big Rock Creek and Mud River.

In canoeing thence to the Narrows, only one small tributary was seen, called Sucker Creek. About three miles west of this creek is Elm Point, and nearly two miles beyond this we passed the more conspicuous Uninhabited Point, so named by the Indians because of ancient clearings along the shore for a mile to the east, where in some former time, probably a century or longer ago, the Ojibwe had a village and cultivated fields. Their bark lodges and more permanent log houses, with patches of corn and potatoes, were seen here and there all along this shore from its most eastern portion to the Narrows.

Beyond the Uninhabited Point the shore trends west-northwest past Pelican, Halfway, and Rabbit Points, successively about three-fourths of a mile apart. About a mile northwestward from Rabbit Point is Sand Cliff Point. The base of this is the usual wall of boulders, derived from erosion of glacial drift; but its upper part, rising steeply from near the lake level to a height of 75 or 80 feet, is levelly bedded sand and fine gravel.

Next to the northwest a plain of sand and gravel, bearing no forest and perhaps in part natural prairie, about 25 feet above the lake, extends two-thirds of a mile or more, diminishing from a third to an eighth of a mile in width. On this tract, about a mile south of the Narrows, is the principal Ojibwe village of Red Lake, consisting in 1885 of 40 or 50 lodges. This village was represented on Nicollet's map (1843), which was of so early date that it does not show St. Paul, Minneapolis, nor any other city or town in Minnesota.

A later note should be added, that, according to Frances Densmore of Red Wing, Minn., who has visited these Indians to write of their music, this village is called by them "Wabacing (where the wind blows from both sides)." The name refers to the exposed situation between the south and north parts of the lake.

Big Sand Bar Creek of 1885 is now named Shotley Brook. At its mouth it has deposited a delta of sand and fine gravel, which projects 15 rods into the lake. About three miles farther northeast is Little Sand Bar Creek, also called Dumas Creek, in section 31, Washkish.

Tamarack River, called Sturgeon or Amenikaning River on Beltrami's map, comes in at the extreme east end of the lake. It is 50 to 100 feet wide near its mouth and is bordered by shores of alluvial sand only 3 or 4 feet high.

Poplar Creek, 15 to 20 feet wide and 2 or 3 feet deep, comes in about ten miles from the east end of the lake, and three miles farther west the Two Rivers, each 30 feet wide and 3 or 4 feet deep, have their mouths about a half mile apart.

Some 50 rods west from the west one of the Two Rivers is the beginning of the "winter road" to the Lake of the Woods, a trail used by the Indians in winter, when the vast swamps of the intervening country are frozen.

Wild Rice River (Manomin Creek of the Ojibwe) joins the lake at the extreme northwestern portion of this north half, where the shore turns in a graceful curve to the south. This is a large stream, 40 to 50 feet wide and 5 to 7 feet deep for a distance of at least 50 rods from its mouth. Wild rice grows along its banks for a width of 6 to 10 feet. About a mile southwest from its mouth this river flows through the north end of a shallow lake, called Wild Rice Lake from its rank growth of this useful grain, which supplies a large part of the winter food of the Indians.

From the West Narrows Point, the north shore of the south half of Red Lake trends west and southwest about four miles to Starting Point, so named by the Indians because they gather there for starting in company in canoe trips to the outlet and down the Red Lake River.

Oak Creek, about ten feet wide, comes in some six miles north of the outlet, deriving its name from the occurrence of several large oaks on the beach near its mouth. A marsh, destitute of trees but with tamarack and spruce swamp beyond it westward, borders the lake thence about two miles to Last Creek, which is of similar small size, being the last tributary passed in approaching the outlet.

Red Lake River receives no tributary, excepting recent drainage ditches, till it reaches the mouth of Thief River, 45 miles distant by a straight line from this lake.

Sandy River, which comes in at the most southwestern portion of the lake, is about 35 feet wide and 4 feet deep.

Big Rock Creek, flowing into Red Lake next eastward, is also called Shell Creek for Shell Lake from which it issues, where it is crossed by the road from the Red Lake Agency to White Earth. It takes the former name from two large boulders, each about eight feet in diameter, which lie some five rods apart on the lakeshore, one on each side of the mouth of this stream.

About four and a half miles farther east we passed Little Rock Point and Creek, a third of a mile apart, so called because of the beach of many little boulders, one to two feet in diameter, which extends an eighth of a mile each way from the mouth of the creek. It was called Gravel River by Beltrami, who visited and named a series of eight small lakes tributary to it. These lakes, which cannot now be exactly identified, he named for the children of a family endeared to him in friendship, Alexander, Lavinius, Everard, Frederica, Adela, Magdalena, Virginia, and Eleonora.

Red Water Creek, very small, probably named thus in allusion to the bog iron ore of its springs, enters the lake between the Little Rock Creek and the agency. A pretty lake tributary to this creek, beside the road to White Earth, is called Green Lake, probably from its reflection of the foliage of the surrounding woods.

It has been suggested that the Ojibwe name translated Red Lake may have been taken from this Red Water Creek, or from other inflowing streams and springs whose beds are made reddish and yellow by the rust-colored bog ore of iron. Beltrami imaginatively translated it as Bloody Lake, attributing it to bloodshed in Indian wars. More reliably, Rev. Joseph A. Gilfillan, through inquiries among the Indians, as noted for Red Lake County, learned that the aboriginal name was from the redness of the lake and sky reflected at evening from the bright red, vermilion, and golden hues of the sunset.

Beltrami Island of Lake Agassiz

The only large island of the Glacial Lake Agassiz was between Red Lake and the Lake of the Woods in Beltrami, Lake of the Woods, and Roseau Counties. The highest parts of that island, which was named in 1893 for Beltrami, are about 130 feet above Red Lake and 1,310 feet above the sea. When the glacial lake had fallen to the contour line of 1,200 feet, the higher Beltrami Island had an area of about 1,160 square miles (*Journal of Geology*, vol. 23, pp. 780–84, Nov.-Dec., 1915).

State Parks and National Forests

In a move to conserve a stand of virgin red pine, the state created Lake Bemidji State Park in 1923. The area included the beach and lake shore on the north end of Lake Bemidji. Later additions incorporated a bog area containing several unusual plant species. In the spring of 2000 the state made further efforts to preserve bog areas by establishing the Big Bog State Recreation Area on the north side of Upper Red Lake. The county shares Chippewa National Forest with Cass and Itasca Counties.

Red Lake Reservation

Red Lake Reservation was created for the Red Lake band of Ojibwe by treaties in 1863, 1889, and 1904. It consists of about 640 square miles of land in Beltrami and Clearwater Counties and seven other counties in the northwest part of the state, including the Northwest Angle. It also has about 360 square miles of surface water, mainly in Lower and Upper Red Lakes. This is a closed reservation; land is held by the band, which is sovereign and self-governing.

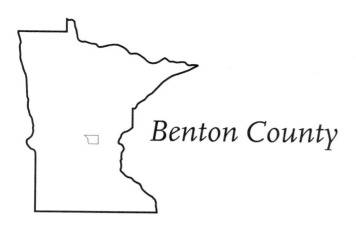

Benton County

This county, one of the first established in Minnesota Territory, October 27, 1849, and organized January 7, 1850, was named for Thomas Hart Benton, who was U.S. senator from Missouri during 30 years, 1821 to 1851. He was born near Hillsborough, N.C., March 14, 1782, and died in Washington, April 10, 1858. He studied law and was admitted to the bar in Nashville in 1811, was an aide-de-camp of Gen. Andrew Jackson in the War of 1812 and also raised a regiment of volunteers, removed to St. Louis in 1815 and established a newspaper that vigorously advocated the admission of Missouri to the Union, and in 1820 he was elected as one of the senators of the new state. In Congress his work for the original enactment of homestead land laws, in 1824–28, won the gratitude of pioneer settlers throughout the West. He is also honored by Benton Township in Carver County and by the name of Lake Benton in Lincoln County, applied by Joseph N. Nicollet in his expedition of 1838. Seven other states have counties named for him, and 20 states have cities, villages, and post offices of this name. In 1899 his statue was placed in the National Statuary Hall at the Capitol, Washington, D.C., as one of the two representing Missouri.

Benton was the author of *Thirty Years' View: History of the American Government, 1820–1850*, published in two volumes, 1854 and 1856. During the last two years of his life, with singular literary industry, he prepared the manuscript of his *Abridgment of the Debates of Congress, from 1789 to 1856*, which was published in 16 volumes, 1857 to 1863. Several biographies of him have been issued, one by Theodore Roosevelt in 1887 being in the "American Statesmen" series.

Information for this county was gathered from the History of the Upper Mississippi Valley, *1881, pages 340–69; from records in the office of J. E. Kasner, county auditor, at Foley, in a visit there in May 1916; from William H. Fletcher of Sauk Rapids, chairman of the board of county commissioners; and from Hon. Charles A. Gilman of St. Cloud, who was a prominent pioneer of Benton County.*

ALBERTA TOWNSHIP organized in 1868, was named for one of its early settlers, a farmer whose first name was Albert.

BRENNYVILLE an unincorporated village in Alberta Township, section 13.

BUJARSKI a village in Granite Ledge Township, section 3.

BUSHVILLE a village in Gilmanton Township, sections 7 and 8.

CLEAR LAKE see SHERBURNE COUNTY.

COATES a village in Minden Township, section 29.

DUELM a hamlet in section 34, St. George Township, was named by its German settlers; had a post office, 1870–1909, a general store, and a creamery; the community exported wheat and stock.

EAST ST. CLOUD in this county, is a part of the city of St. Cloud, which is mainly in Stearns County, west of the Mississippi, but also reaches east of the river into Benton and Sherburne Counties; it had a station of the Great Northern and Northern Pacific Railroads in section 36.

ESTEVILLE see **ESTES BROOK**, Mille Lacs County.

FOLEY a railway village and the county seat, located in Gilmanton Township, was named for John Foley, its founder, one of five brothers who came to this state from Lanark County, Ontario. Its post office was established in 1883. When this line of the Great Northern Railway was built, in 1882–84, John and others of the brothers were contractors, camping on the site of this village, and he acquired lands here. Later he led in the effort, 1901–2, of transferring the county seat from Sauk Rapids to this place. He died in St. Paul, August 11, 1908. In 1890, the Foley brothers operated a lumber and general store, and Thomas Foley, son of John, was postmaster; the townsite had a steam-power saw, a planing mill, creameries, a grain elevator, and a pickle factory.

FRUITVILLE a village in Mayhew Lake Township, section 9.

GILMAN a city in Alberta Township, sections 33 and 34; incorporated as a village on February 11, 1959; its post office began in 1885, with George Pappenfus as first postmaster, in the general store and saloon owned by the Pappenfus brothers; it had a creamery and cheese factory.

GILMANTON TOWNSHIP organized in 1866, was named in honor of Charles Andrew Gilman, who was born in Gilmanton, N.H., February 9, 1833, came to Sauk Rapids, Minnesota, in 1855, and removed to St. Cloud in 1861. He was receiver and afterward register of the U.S. land office in St. Cloud for several years; was a member of the state senate, 1868–69, and of the house, 1875–79, being speaker the last two years, and again was a member of the house in 1915; was lieutenant governor, 1880–87; and state librarian, 1894–99. During about 30 years he was much engaged in lumbering in Benton and Morrison Counties, and he located many permanent settlers in this township.

GLENDORADO TOWNSHIP organized September 20, 1868, received this name (partly Spanish, meaning "the golden glen") by petition of its settlers; had a post office, 1898–1906, located in section 25.

GRAHAM TOWNSHIP was named for one of its pioneer farmers.

GRANITE LEDGE TOWNSHIP was named for its granite rock outcrops in sections 17, 18, 20, and 24, the last being on the West branch of the Rum River.

HOBERT a village in Minden Township, section 22, with a siding station of the Great Northern Railway.

JAKEVILLE a village in Alberta Township, section 29.

LANGOLA TOWNSHIP organized July 12, 1858, has a unique name, unknown elsewhere, proposed by its petitioners for organization. The village Langola, in section 11, had a post office, which had been established in 1854 as Royalton in Morrison County and was transferred to Langola; it operated 1857–78, at which time the name was changed back to Royalton, and returned to Morrison County.

MAYHEW LAKE TOWNSHIP and also its lake and creek of this name, are in honor of George V. Mayhew, who was born in St. Lawrence County, N.Y., February 18, 1824; served in the Mexican War; came to Minnesota in 1854 and settled in the present Minden Township of this county beside the creek named for him; was a representative in the legislature in 1861; and served in the Seventh Minnesota Regiment in the Civil War, becoming a first lieutenant. A country post office was in section 8, 1898–1901; postmaster Louis Esselman operated the general store and farm implement dealership with his brother.

MAYWOOD TOWNSHIP organized in 1867, received this euphonious name on the request of its settlers. New Jersey, Kentucky, Indiana, Illinois, Missouri, and Nebraska also have villages so named. The village of Maywood in section 31 had a sawmill, sled and wagon timber factory, and a post office, 1868–1901.

MINDEN TOWNSHIP organized in 1858, received its name from an eastern state, or more probably it was given by immigrants from Germany for the ancient city of Minden in Prussia; it had a post office, 1869–71.

NORTH BENTON a village in Alberta Township, section 21, also known as Tadych Store.

OAK PARK a railway village in Maywood, section 15, first settled in 1882, is named for the oak groves of its vicinity. Its post office began in 1883; it had a flag station of the Great Northern Railway, a general store, several mills, a hotel, and a creamery.

OSAUKA a section of Sauk Rapids located in Sauk Rapids Township on the Mississippi River.

PARENT a small railway village in St. George Township, section 8, was named for Auguste Parent and others of his family there, farmers of French descent; it had a rural post office, 1889–1937; its first postmaster was John Marshall, a coal and wood dealer.

POPPLE CREEK a village in Mayhew Lake Township, section 25; it had a country post office called Raether, 1896–1901 and 1904, located in postmaster Frederick C. Raether's general store.

PREBISH a village in Granite Ledge Township, section 6, circa 1935.

PULARSKI a village in Graham Township, section 29, circa 1935.

RAETHER see **POPPLE CREEK.**

RICE a railway village in Langola in section 29, is in honor of George T. Rice, who kept a hotel about three-fourths of a mile farther west for the stage travel previous to the building of this railway. His name was also given to an extensive prairie that includes the western two-thirds of Langola and the northwest part of Watab Township. The village was first settled in 1877 on the Little Rock River and was sometimes called Langola for the township; its post office began in 1878 as Rices, changing to Rice in 1889; it had a station of the Northern Pacific Railroad, several mills and elevators, a creamery and cheese factory, plus a variety of other businesses.

RONNEBY another railway village, in sections 19 and 20, Maywood Township, was named from a town near Karlskrona in southern Sweden, on the River Ronneby near its mouth in the Baltic Sea. The village was incorporated on August 31, 1899, and was originally named St. Francis but changed when the post office was established in 1897 because that name was already in use; the post office discontinued in 1973.

ST. CLOUD a city with Sherburne and Stearns Counties; see Stearns County.

ST. FRANCIS see **RONNEBY.**

ST. GEORGE TOWNSHIP organized September 27, 1858, was named in compliment to three promi-

nent early settlers of the south part of this county, George V. Mayhew, George McIntyre, and another who had the same first name.

SARTELL a railway village, organized in November 1907, adjoining the Mississippi in Sauk Rapids Township, with extension west of the river in Le Sauk, Stearns County, was named for Joseph B. Sartell, who was the first settler of the west side, coming in 1854 as a farmer. Later he built and operated sawmills. He resided there, with seven sons, until his death, January 27, 1913, at the age of 86 years.

SAUK RAPIDS TOWNSHIP was organized in 1854, and the village was platted in that year but was not separately organized until 1881. The village was known as Washington in 1850 when J. C. Ramsey and Henry Jackson laid out a townsite at the foot of the Sauk Rapids; it had a station of the Northern Pacific and Great Northern Railroads in section 23, two flour mills, a cheese factory, a brewery, several hotels, a number of general and specialty stores, and two weekly newspapers. This village was the county seat from the organization of the county in 1850 until 1902, when the county offices were removed to Foley, as before noted. The village separated from the township in 1927. Sauk Rapids derived its name from the adjoining rapids of the Mississippi, called Grand Rapids by Zebulon Pike in 1805 and mapped by him as Big Falls, falling about 20 feet in the first mile below the mouth of the Sauk River, mapped by Pike as Sack River, which comes in from Stearns County.

The origin of the names of Sauk River and of Osakis Lake and village at its source, in Todd and Douglas Counties, as also of the Sauk Lakes and Little Sauk Township in Todd County, of Sauk Centre and Le Sauk Townships in Stearns County, of Sauk Rapids, and of Osauka, an addition platted at the northwest edge of this village, was from refugee Sauk, or Sac, Indians, who came to Osakis Lake from the home of this tribe, allied with the Fox Indians, in Wisconsin. This was told in a historical paper by the late judge Loren W. Collins as follows: "Five Sacs, refugees from their own tribe on account of murder which they had committed, made their way up to the lake [Osakis] and settled near the outlet upon the east side. . . . On one of the excursions made by some of the Pillager bands of Chippewas to the asylum of the O-zau-kees, it was found that all had been killed, supposedly by the Sioux" (*History of Stearns County*, 1915, vol. 1, p. 24).

SKAJA a village in Graham Township, section 23, which had a general store.

TADYCH STORE see **NORTH BENTON**.

WASHINGTON see **SAUK RAPIDS**.

WATAB TOWNSHIP organized in 1858, like its Indian trading post, which had been established ten years earlier, was named for the Watab River called Little Sack River by Pike, tributary to the Mississippi from the west about five miles north of St. Cloud. This is the Ojibwe word for the long and very slender roots of both the tamarack and jack pine, which were dug by the Indians, split, and used as threads in sewing their birch-bark canoes. Both these coniferous trees grow on or near the lower part of the Watab River.

Rev. F. W. Smith, an Ojibwe pastor, of Red Lake Agency, informed the present writer in 1885 during my visit there that in northern Minnesota the Ojibwe principally use the roots of the jack pine as watab, although the roots of both tamarack and arbor vitae are also somewhat used (*Minn. Geol. and Nat. Hist. Survey*, Bulletin No. 3, 1887, p. 53). The name of this river and township doubtless refers to the jack pines there, this being at the southwest limit of that species, whereas the geographic range of the tamarack extends considerably farther south and west.

The village named Watab was about two miles and a half north from the mouth of this river and on the opposite or eastern side of the Mississippi, in section 34. During about ten years following its establishment in 1848, Watab was the most important commercial place in Minnesota Territory northwestward from St. Paul, but later it was superseded by Sauk Rapids and St. Cloud. The village was the county seat for a short time about 1853, when it was platted; it had a post office, 1852–85, with David Gilman, postmaster, and was reestablished, 1891–1914.

WILLIAMSVILLE a post office, 1873–77, located in Gilmanton Township, section 8.

Lakes and Streams

The name of the Mississippi was fully noticed in the first chapter; the Elk and St. Francis Rivers are considered in the chapter for Sherburne and Anoka Counties, which respectively have the village and township of Elk River and St. Francis Township; and a preceding page gives the origin of the name of Mayhew Lake and Creek.

Donovan Lake, in section 34, Minden, named for John Donovan, a farmer near it, was formerly called Minden Lake.

Halfway Brook, tributary to the Mississippi close north of Sartell, received this name for its being nearly midway between Sauk Rapids and Watab.

The southern two-thirds of Watab Township has many outcrops of granite and syenite, continuing from their much quarried area in Sauk Rapids and East St. Cloud. At each side of the river road, in the vicinity of the Watab railway station, small hills and knobs of these rocks rise about 40 feet above the road and 75 to 90 feet above the river. One of these hills of rough, bald rock, called by Henry R. Schoolcraft the Peace Rock, rises directly from the river's edge about a half mile south from the mouth of Little Rock Creek, which, with its Little Rock Lake, was thence so named. It is a translation of the Ojibwe name, signifying, as more elaborately stated by Rev. Joseph A. Gilfillan, "where the little rocky hills project out every once in a while, here and there." Pike noted the large prairie here and northward as favorite grazing for elk, and he therefore mapped these as Elk Lake and Lake River.

Peace Rock was named for its marking, with the Watab River, a part of the old line of boundary between the Ojibwe and the Dakota, to which agreement was made by their leaders in the Treaty of 1825 at Prairie du Chien.

Big Stone County

This county, established February 20, 1862, and organized April 13, 1874, derived its name from Big Stone Lake, through which the Minnesota River flows on the west boundary of the county and state. It is a translation of the Dakota name, alluding to the conspicuous outcrops of granite and gneiss, extensively quarried, which occur in the Minnesota valley from a half mile to three miles below the foot of the lake. The city and county building in Minneapolis is constructed of the stone from these quarries, which also supplied four massive columns of the state capitol rotunda, on its north and south sides. The Dakota name, poorly pronounced and indistinctly heard, was written *Eatakeka* by William H. Keating in his *Narrative* of Stephen H. Long's expedition in 1823, but Prof. A. W. Williamson more correctly spelled it in two words, *Inyan tankinyanyan*, the first meaning "stone," the second "very great," as shown by the repetition of the first word and duplication of its final syllable.

Guillaume de L'Isle's map of Canada, or New France, in 1703 calls this the Lake of the Tintons, that is, the Prairie Sioux. The same name is given by the maps of Philippe Buache, 1754, and Jacques N. Bellin, 1755. Jonathan Carver, who was on the Minnesota River in 1766–67, mapped this lake but left it unnamed. Long's expedition gave its earliest correct delineation, with its present name and the older equivalent Dakota and French names.

Big Stone Lake extends in a somewhat crooked course from northwest to southeast 26 miles; its width is 1 mile to 1.5 miles, and its greatest depth is reported to be from 15 to 30 feet. More than a thousand acres along the north shore was set aside as the Big Stone State Park in 1961. The park consists of two areas—Meadowbrook, which has public facilities, and Bonanza, which contains rare glacial till hill prairie.

Information has been gathered from History of the Minnesota Valley, *1882, pages 973–86; and from Hayden French of Ortonville, clerk of the court for this county, and Martin Irwin Matthews, who for many years was one of the county commissioners and later was the municipal judge in Ortonville, each being interviewed during a visit there in September 1916.*

ADELAIDE a village and country post office, 1879–1906, in Otrey Township, section 12.

AKRON TOWNSHIP first settled in 1872 and organized July 25, 1881, was named for Akron, Ohio, whence some of its pioneers came.

ALMOND TOWNSHIP organized March 29, 1880, was named for the township and village of this name in Allegany County, N.Y., or for Almond Township and village in Portage County, Wis.

ARTICHOKE TOWNSHIP whose first settler came in May 1869, received its name from the former Artichoke Lake, now drained, which was five miles long, stretching from section 11 south to section 36. This name was probably translated from the Dakota name of the lake, referring to the edible tuber roots of a species of sunflower (*Helianthus tuberosus*), which was much used by the Indians as food, called *pangi* by the Dakota, abundant here and common or frequent throughout this state. The village Artichoke, in section 11, had a post office, known as Artichoke Lake, 1876–1913; Nels Johnson was the first postmaster and also the town treasurer.

BARRY a railway village in Toqua Township, was named in honor of the Barry brothers, homesteading farmers there, who came from Lowell, Mass. Incorporated as a village in 1900, it was located on the land claim of Edmond Barry, who with his brother William came in 1879 to the area following their brother James and William Nash. First called Lowell, the name was changed when the post office was established in 1881 with Miss Maria M. Barry as first postmaster in the Barry farmhouse. Her brother James owned the general store and lumber dealership; the blacksmith shop and general store were built in 1880, the coal and wood yard in 1885, and the elevator and bowling alley by the Barry brothers in 1891; it had a station of the Great Northern Railway in section 9.

BATAVIA STATION see CLINTON.

BEARDSLEY the railway village of Browns Valley Township, sections 8 and 17, was named for W. W. Beardsley, who platted it in November 1880. He was born in Schuyler County, N.Y., in 1852, removed to Pennsylvania at the age of 21 years and to Wisconsin in 1875, came to Minnesota in 1878, homesteading the farm that included the site of this village. It had a station of the Great Northern Railway in section 8; the first building erected was the coal and lumber business of Henry Stonebraker; the post office was established in 1881. The village was incorporated in 1891.

BIG STONE CENTER a locality in Akron Township.

BIG STONE TOWNSHIP organized October 4, 1879, received its name, like the county, from the adjoining lake. A country post office was located in the township in section 24, 1878–1906; it had a general store and two or three houses; blacksmith William B. Dow was the postmaster.

BONANZA GROVE a locality on Big Stone Lake in Foster Township, section 18, also known as Bonanza Beach.

BROWNS VALLEY TOWNSHIP first settled in 1875 and organized April 5, 1880, was named by Thomas Bailey, a homesteader there who came from Tennessee. The name was taken from the very remarkable valley between lakes Big Stone and Traverse, in which a trading post and the village of this name had been established by Hon. Joseph R. Brown, situated in the southwest corner of Traverse County. Brown County was named for him, and biographic notes are given in its chapter.

CENTRAL see CLINTON.

CLINTON a railway village at the center of Almond Township, in section 16, was named probably for one of the many villages, towns, and counties bearing this name, which are found in our eastern and southern states. The village was settled about 1877 as Central, an agricultural community exporting wheat, barley, oats, and potatoes, with a post office of that name from 1878 to 1885. The name changed to Clinton in 1885 and the village was platted, and although the Chicago, Milwaukee and St. Paul Railroad station was moved to the village, the railroad insisted on calling it Batavia until the village was incorporated in 1890. The railroad loading platform, named Rupert, two miles south of the village, was also moved in 1890 to the village. Erickson's Addition, now the main business part of the city, was platted in 1886 and incorporated into the village in 1888. The first store, the post office, and the lumberyard were built by Peter McCormick, the first postmaster. The village had feed mills, a plow factory, four grain elevators, a creamery, and several general stores; the first county fair was held there in 1907.

COLD SPRINGS GRANITE CO. a station of the Minneapolis, St. Paul and Sault Ste. Marie Railroad (Soo Line) in Ortonville Township, section 22.

CORRELL a city, located in Akron Township, sections 3 and 4, was originally a way station of the Chicago, Milwaukee and St. Paul Railroad, platted in 1879 by D. N. Correll, a public surveyor from St. Paul, for whom the city was named, and recorded by the Hastings and Dakota Railway in 1881. The post office began in 1880, with farmer Henry L. Holmes as postmaster. The Thomas F. Koch Land Company purchased the townsite in

1890 and sold it to Charles F. Woods, who in turn developed the Farmers Elevator in 1893.

CUSTER a country post office, 1877–1903, located in Prior Township, section 30.

FOSTER a village of summer residences on the shore of Big Stone Lake in Prior Township, was platted in 1880 on the preemption claim of M. I. Matthews, who settled there in 1872. It was named for Foster L. Balch of Minneapolis, president of the Big Stone Lake Navigation and Improvement Company. The village had a post office, 1879–85.

GRACEVILLE TOWNSHIP and its village, which was founded by Catholic colonists in 1877–78, were named in honor of Thomas Langdon Grace, who during 25 years was the bishop of St. Paul, 1859 to 1884. He was born in Charleston, S.C., November 15, 1814, and died in St. Paul, February 22, 1897. Another version of the naming of the city is that it is for Grace, the first white child born there and daughter of M. J. McDonald, who built the first house in 1878. The village was incorporated on February 18, 1881; it was formerly called Lake Tokna for the post office, 1871–79, which was established in Traverse County. Bishop John Ireland purchased 80 acres for the townsite and 120 acres adjacent for a farm colony in 1878. The village had a Catholic convent, a Catholic academy, elevators, flour and roller mills, horse and livestock breeders, and a station of the Great Northern Railway in section 4.

HILO a village in Toqua Township, sections 9 and 10, with a post office, 1879–83.

HOLMLIE a post office in Browns Valley Township, 1877–80, with Arnt J. Holmlie, postmaster; the name was changed to Phillips in 1880–81, with Charles Phillips, postmaster. Located on Big Stone Lake, its exports were wheat, livestock, fish, and butter.

JOHNSON a city in Moonshine Township, sections 3 and 10, settled about 1880. It was named in honor of a section foreman who worked on the Great Northern Railway. Its post office was first established 1883–87 and reestablished in 1891; it was incorporated as a village in 1903. The village once had a bank, a cream station, several stores, a hotel, a school, a lumber company, a livery stable, three grain elevators, and a blacksmith, and a station of the Great Northern Railway in section 3.

KINGSBURY a post office, 1879, located in Akron Township.

LAKE TOKNA see GRACEVILLE.

LOVGREN'S WOOD LOT a family farm and community located in Prior Township on the shores of Big Stone Lake. The first settler, Gustav Lindholm, emigrated from Sweden in the late 1860s, homesteaded in 1869, and brought his family to the United States in 1890. Oscar Lovgren arrived from Småland and began work for Lindholm, married Lindholm's daughter in 1909, and managed Lindholm's farm until his death in 1931; a fourth-generation Lovgren still resides on the farm.

LOWELL a post office, 1879–81, with Phebe White as postmaster; location not found.

MALTA TOWNSHIP organized February 14, 1880, was at first named Clarksville for David K. J. Clark, its first settler, who came in June 1876. It was renamed, after a town of New York and villages in Ohio and Illinois, for the island of Malta in the Mediterranean Sea.

MAUD a farmers post office, 1886–1907, in Prior Township, section 33, at the time of settlement; the area is now Foster Township. The site had a hotel and general store.

MOONSHINE TOWNSHIP took its name from its Moonshine Lake, which was named by David K. J. Clark, mentioned as a settler in Malta. On his first coming here in 1876 from Wabasha County, his first camp was beside this lake, which he then named, intending to call it Moon Lake for the surname of his wife, Mrs. Mary A. Moon Clark; but in the evening the bright moonlight caused the name to be thus changed.

ODESSA TOWNSHIP first settled in June 1870, was named for the city of Odessa in southern Russia, whence seed wheat used in this vicinity was brought. The railway village of Odessa was platted in 1879 in section 29 when the Chicago, Milwaukee and St. Paul Railroad was being built and incorporated as a village in 1895. The village had grain elevators and flour mills; the post office began in 1879; the postmaster and first settler, A. D. Beardsley, was also an express and railroad agent at the depot, lumber dealer, and general store owner; the flour mill burned down shortly after World War I. The popularly accepted story of the origin of the village's name is that it was named for Beardsley's daughter, Dessa, who died of diphtheria at age three.

ORTONVILLE TOWNSHIP received its first settlers

in 1871, and in September of the next year its village was platted by Cornelius Knute Orton, for
whom the village and township were named. He
was of Norwegian descent and was born in Dane
County, Wis., in 1846, came to Minnesota in 1857,
settled on a land claim here in 1871, engaged in
real estate business, and was a banker, merchant,
and a member of the board of county commissioners. He died in Ortonville, December 24,
1890. The village was established as the county
seat of the as yet unorganized county and was organized as a city on January 28, 1881.

A steamer line made regular trips on Big
Stone Lake, making the area a popular summer
resort. The village had a station of the Soo Line in
section 16, also known as Stateline, grain elevators, a flour mill, a stone quarry, and a mineral
spring, which gave rise to a brewing industry until the county went dry in 1915. O. M. Osen built
The Greenhouse in 1912 and supplied plants all
over the country until his retirement in 1946. The
Big Stone Canning Company was founded in
1902; during World War II, a prisoner-of-war
camp was built at the company, where in
1944–45, 360 prisoners worked in the warehouse
during corn-canning seasons or in crews shock-
ing grain for area farmers.

OTREY TOWNSHIP first settled by Thomas and
William Otrey from Illinois in June 1859, was organized February 14, 1880. It was then named
Trenton but later was renamed in honor of these
brothers, who had served in the Civil War.

PETERSBURG a village in Big Stone Township, section 32, circa 1913.

PHILLIPS see HOLMLIE.

PRIOR TOWNSHIP settled in 1870 and organized
in 1879, was named in honor of Charles H. Prior
of Minneapolis, superintendent of the Hastings
and Dakota division of the Chicago, Milwaukee
and St. Paul Railroad. He had large land interests
in this township and in Ortonville.

RUPERT see CLINTON.

SARDIS a post office, 1884–1903, located in Prior
Township, section 34.

SAUK RAPIDS a city in Sauk Rapids Township. The
site was originally occupied as an Indian trading
post by the traders who followed the Winnebago
on their removal from Iowa in 1848; the Winnebago becoming established at Long Prairie and
Watab in 1849, the traders abandoned the post.

In the fall of 1850, attorney George W. Sweet purchased the claim on which the trading houses
were standing and in November 1851 fitted one of
the buildings for a dwelling. From that time may
be dated the first permanent settlement. The
townsite was laid out in July 1854, the first store
was built in October 1854 by George W. Sweet,
and the first hotel was built of logs in 1855. The
town had a station of the Great Northern and
Northern Pacific Railroads in section 23.

STEPNEY a post office, 1879–83; location not
found.

TOKUA STATION a village in Graceville Township,
section 5 and 8.

TOQUA TOWNSHIP (formerly spelled Tokua), first
settled in 1877 and organized March 16, 1880, received its name from the two Tokua Lakes in
Graceville and the similar pair of lakes in this
township, which latter were called by the Dakota, as translated, the Tokua Brothers Lakes. This
aboriginal name is spelled Ta Kara on Joseph N.
Nicollet's map, 1843, *Ta* being the Dakota word
for the moose, while *Kara* doubtless refers to the
Kahra band of the Dakota.

William H. Keating, the historian of Stephen
H. Long's expedition in 1823, wrote as follows (in
his vol. I, p. 403), describing this band. "KAHRA
(Wild Rice). These Indians dwell in very large and
fine skin lodges. The skins are well prepared and
handsomely painted. They have no permanent
residence, but frequently visit Lake Travers. Their
hunting grounds are on Red River. They follow
Tatankanaje (the Standing Buffalo), who is a chief
by hereditary right, and who has acquired distinction as a warrior."

Nicollet also used the word *Kara* as the final
part of other names, Plan Kara and Manstitsa
Kara, given on his map to two points or hillocks
of the valley bluff east of the northern end of Lake
Traverse. Stephen R. Riggs, however, in his Dakota dictionary published in 1852, rejected all use of
the letter *r* in that language, so that the name
Kahra or *Kara* may not be identifiable in that
work. Tokua (or Toqua) was the white men's endeavor to spell the Dakota name for these pairs of
lakes, which Nicollet spelled as Ta Kara.

Samuel J. Brown, of the village of Browns Valley, stated that this name "was taken from a picture
carved on a tree, meaning probably some animal
so pictured." This accords well with the meaning

of the name given by Nicollet, as the moose of the Kara or Kahra band of Dakota, perhaps a family totem or the mystic patron of the clan.

———

Lakes and Streams

Since the first coming of the homestead farmers nearly 50 years ago, the area of this county has witnessed the drying up of many of its former shallow lakes, partly because plowing and cultivation of the soil permit the rains and the water from the melting of the winter snows to sink in larger proportion into the ground, not running off to the hollows. In recent years, others of the lakes have been drained by ditches, the lake beds being allotted fractionally to the adjoining landowners. The map of Big Stone County published by the Minnesota Geological Survey (vol. 1, 1884, ch. XXI) has more than 50 lakes; but the 1916 atlas of Minnesota showed only 4 or 5 yet remaining, these being unnamed.

Artichoke and Moonshine Lakes, and the Tokua Lakes and Tokua Brothers Lakes, noted in the foregoing list of townships, have disappeared by drainage.

Only a few streams of noteworthy size and bearing names flow here into the Minnesota River and Big Stone Lake. These include Five Mile Creek, so named for its distance west of the Pomme de Terre River and the village of Appleton, in the adjoining Swift County; Stony Run, in Big Stone and Odessa Townships, named for the plentiful boulders along parts of this stream; and Fish Creek, tributary to Big Stone Lake at the northwest corner of Prior.

The Glacial River Warren

Big Stone Lake, flowing south in the Minnesota River, and Lake Traverse, flowing north in the Bois des Sioux and Red Rivers, are on the opposite sides of a continental water divide, one of these lakes sending its outflow to the Gulf of Mexico, the other to Hudson Bay. But they lie in a continuous valley, one to two miles wide, which was evidently channeled by a great river formerly flowing southward. The part of the ancient watercourse between these lakes, a distance of nearly five miles, is widely known as Browns Valley. As noticed in the first chapter, the former river here outflowing from the Glacial Lake Agassiz in the Red River basin has been named the River Warren in honor of Gen. Gouverneur K. Warren.

Fifteen miles below Big Stone Lake, the Minnesota River flows through Marsh Lake, on the south side of Akron, now mainly drained, which formerly was four miles long and about a mile wide. It was so named from its being shallow and full of reeds and grass.

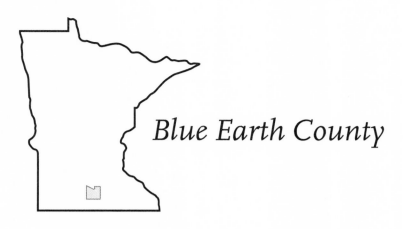

Blue Earth County

This county was established March 5, 1853, and took its name from the Blue Earth River, for a bluish green earth that was used by the Sisseton Dakota as a pigment, found in a shaley layer of the rock bluff of this stream about three miles from its mouth.

The blue earth was the incentive and cause of a very interesting chapter of our earliest history. Pierre Charles Le Sueur, the French explorer, before his first return to France in 1695, had discovered the locality whence the Indians procured this blue and green paint, which he thought to be an ore of copper, and he then took some of it to Paris, submitted it to L'Huillier, one of the king's assayers, and secured the royal commission to work the mines. But disasters and obstacles deterred him from this project until four years later, when having come from a third visit in France with 30 miners to Biloxi, near the mouth of the Mississippi, he ascended this river in the year 1700, using a sailing and rowing vessel and two canoes. Coming forward along the Minnesota River, he reached the mouth of the Blue Earth River on the last day in September or the first in October.

Le Sueur spent the ensuing year on this river, having built a camp or post named Fort L'Huillier, and in the spring mined a large quantity of the supposed copper ore. Taking a selected portion of the ore, amounting to two tons, and leaving a garrison at the fort, Le Sueur again navigated nearly the whole length of the Mississippi and arrived at the Gulf of Mexico in February 1702. Thence with

Pierre Le Moyne, Sieur d'Iberville, the founder and first governor of Louisiana, who was a cousin of Le Sueur's wife, he sailed for France in the latter part of April, carrying the ore or blue earth, of which, however, nothing more is known.

Thomas Hughes of Mankato, historian of the city and county, identified in 1904 the sites of Fort L'Huillier and the mine of the blue or green earth, which are described in a paper contributed to the Minnesota Historical Society Collections (vol. XII, pp. 283–85).

André Pénicaut's *Relation* of Le Sueur's expedition was translated by Alfred J. Hill in the Minnesota Historical Society Collections (vol. III, 1880, pp. 1–12), and a map showing the locations of the fort and mine, ascertained by Hughes, was published in 1911 by Newton H. Winchell, on p. 493, *The Aborigines of Minnesota* (1911). From that expedition and the mine, we have the name of the Blue Earth River and of this county, and also of the township and city of Blue Earth in Faribault County.

This name was probably received by Le Sueur and his party from that earlier given to the river by the Dakota. The *Relation* of Pénicaut, however, might be thought to indicate otherwise, as follows: "We called this Green river, because it is of that color by reason of a green earth which, loosening itself from the copper mines, becomes dissolved in it and makes it green." In the language of the Dakota the same word, *to*, is used both for blue and green, and their name of the Blue Earth River is Makato (*maka*, earth; *to*, blue or green).

William H. Keating wrote in the *Narrative* of Stephen H. Long's expedition, 1823: "By the Dacotas it is called Makato Osa Watapa, which signifies 'the river where blue earth is gathered.'"

The Dakota name is retained, with slight change, by the township and city of Mankato. On the earliest map of Minnesota Territory, in 1850, it appeared as Mahkahta for one of its original nine counties, reaching from the Mississippi above the Crow Wing west to the Missouri.

———

Information of the origins of the local names has been gathered from History of the Minnesota Valley, *1882, pp. 532–637; from* The Standard Historical and Pictorial Atlas and Gazetteer of Blue Earth County, *1895, 147 pages; from the* History of Blue Earth County, *by Thomas Hughes, 1909, 622 pages; and from Evan Hughes, judge of probate, Andrew G. Johnson, county treasurer, Thomas Hughes, and Judge Lorin Cray, during my visits in Mankato in July and October 1916.*

AMBOY the railway village of Shelby Township, in section 23, was platted October 31, 1879, laid out on land formerly owned by George Quiggle, and incorporated on June 15, 1887. It was named by Robert Richardson, its first postmaster and merchant, for the town of his former home in Illinois; the name is an Indian word meaning "hollow inside" or "like a bowl." The village had a station of the Chicago, St. Paul, Minneapolis and Omaha Railway, grist, feed and flour mills, five elevators, a creamery, and a sorghum factory. The community exported grain, flax, livestock, and produce.

BEAUFORD TOWNSHIP was originally established under the name of Winneshiek (the Winnebago chief for whom a county of Iowa is named), April 16, 1858, when it was in the Winnebago Reservation. It was organized March 13, 1866, with the present name, suggested by Albert Gates "after a town in the east, from which some of the settlers had come." (The U.S. Postal Guide formerly had one post office of this name, this being in Floyd County, Virginia, but it was discontinued several years ago. Beaufort, nearly the same, is a frequent geographic name.) The village of Beauford, in section 16, also known as Beauford Heights, had a post office, 1867–75 and 1882–1904, a general store, and a blacksmith shop.

BELLEVIEW a rural settlement with a post office, 1873–79, located in McPherson Township, section 31.

BENNING a locality in Lime Township, section 29, which had a station of the Chicago, St. Paul, Minneapolis and Omaha Railway.

BLAINE see WATONWAN.

BRADLEY railway station, in Lime Township, section 20, five miles north of Mankato, was named for the Bradley crossing of the Minnesota River, established by the Bradley family, on whose farm this station was located (William H. Stennett, *Origins of the Place Names of the Chicago and Northwestern Railways*, p. 169).

BURDETTE a station on the Chicago and Northwestern Railway, Lime Township.

BUTTERNUT a post office, 1894–1904, in Butternut Valley Township, section 20, had two general stores, a blacksmith, and a creamery.

BUTTERNUT VALLEY see CAMBRIA.

BUTTERNUT VALLEY TOWNSHIP established January 6, 1857, organized in May 1858, was named in accordance with the suggestion of Col. Samuel D. Shaw, who had come from the town of Butternuts in Otsego County, N.Y. The butternut tree is common or frequent, especially in river valleys, through the southeastern part of Minnesota.

CAMBRIA TOWNSHIP first settled in 1855, organized June 3, 1867, was named by Robert H. Hughes, a pioneer homesteader, who had come from Cambria, Wis. This was the ancient Latin name of Wales, the native land of nearly all the settlers here or of their parents. Cambria, a locality in the township, formerly named Butternut Valley, a portion of the farm owned by William Edwards, was purchased by the Chicago and Northwestern Railway and platted in 1895 by the Western Town Lot Company. The first building was the general store owned by Ernest Hughes; the post office, first called Butternut Valley, 1857–80, was located in Butternut Valley Township, section 19, in the home of Samuel D. Shaw, moved several times, changed its name to Cambria, 1881–82, and was reestablished in 1901–67.

CARNEY a village in Lime Township, section 32, with a station of the Chicago, St. Paul, Minneapolis and Omaha Railway.

CASTLE GARDEN a post office, 1869–75, in Rapidan Township, section 15.

CAZNOVIA a place name in Decoria Township, circa 1930.

CERESCO TOWNSHIP established July 8, 1857, organized May 11, 1858, was named by Isaac Slocum for his former hometown in Wisconsin. A farmers post office was located in the township, section 14, 1857–59 and 1888–1900.

CHAMPION MILLS a community in Shelby Township, section 16, had flour and feed mills run by power from the Blue Earth River; a post office operated 1878–80.

COBB RIVER a post office, 1860–61; location not found.

CRAY a railway station, in Judson Township, section 23, eight miles west of Mankato, was named for Judge Lorin Cray, who during many years was the Mankato attorney of the Chicago, St. Paul, Minneapolis and Omaha Railway company.

CREAM a community of Medo Township, section 12, whose original buildings were in Waseca County until George Blaisdell built the first store just across the county line from his farm home. Blaisdell became the first postmaster, the post office operating 1895–1903. The origin of the name is lost in history but may have related to the several creameries and cheese factories in the area; a creamery, a feed mill, and a general store were the main businesses in 1900; however, during the early 1900s most of the businesses and buildings (including the Modern Woodman Hall) were moved, many to Pemberton.

CRISPS STORE a post office, 1861–65, located in postmaster Anthony J. Crisp's store; location not found.

CRYSTAL LAKE CITY a platted townsite in Garden City Township, which was vacated by the county board in 1863.

DANVILLE TOWNSHIP established April 6, 1858, was then named Jackson but because an earlier township of Minnesota had that name, it was changed October 14, 1858, in compliment to Lucius Dyer, a settler who had come from Danville,

Vt. The village of Danville, in section 1, had three churches, a district school, a creamery, and a farmers post office, 1876–99.

DECORIA TOWNSHIP named April 6, 1858, was in the Winnebago reservation, and it remained without organization till October 8, 1867, being the latest organized township of this county. The name is in commemoration of a Winnebago chief called "One-Eyed Dekora," having lost an eye. This chief and the tribe aided the whites during the Black Hawk War of 1832, in which he displayed great ability and courage. He lived through the removals of the Winnebago from Wisconsin to northeastern Iowa in 1837–38, from Iowa to Long Prairie, Minnesota, in 1848, thence to Blue Earth County in 1855, next to a reservation in Dakota Territory, 1863, and last to Nebraska in 1866. He was a renowned orator, and from his prowess in war and influence in council was known among his own people as Waukon Decorah, meaning in translation "Wonderful Decorah." Two important towns of Iowa, Waukon and Decorah, which are the county seats of its most northeast counties on the border of Minnesota, were named for him. This name, variously spelled also as De Kaury, Day Kauray, Day Korah, De Corrah, etc., belonged to a Winnebago family of hereditary chiefs through four generations or more, who had descended from a French army officer, Sabrevoir De Carrie (Frederick W. Hodge, *Handbook of American Indians*, vol. I, 1907, p. 384; Charles H. Sparks, *History of Winneshiek County*, Iowa, 1877; W. E. Alexander, *History of Winneshiek and Allamakee Counties*, Iowa, 1882).

A post office was located in section 28 of the township in the home of postmaster John S. Larkin, 1868–69, then in the section 34 in the home of George Todd until discontinued in 1875.

EAGLE LAKE a railway village in sections 7 and 18, Le Ray Township, received its name from the neighboring lake, which had been so named by the U.S. land surveyors because many bald eagles had nests in high trees on the lakeshore. It was platted in November 1872 by Freeman A. Cate on a portion of his farm in section 18, and in 1874 James Steward and Walter L. Breckenridge platted another site just east of the original one. It was incorporated as a village on July 14, 1902. The village was the principal center of wood and lumber businesses in the county in 1870s; it had a station of the Chicago and Northwestern Railway in section 18, mills, and elevators; and exported wheat, pork, hoop poles, and wood. Its post office was known as Spirer, 1870–73, the name a form of Speir, Germany, as suggested by J. Beirlis. Over the years the city has seen a gradual change from an industrial village to a residential site.

EDGEWOOD see **VERNON CENTER.**

FORT JUDSON built in 1863 as protection against Indians; made of sod walls, which eventually eroded; a marker was placed there by the Blue Earth County Historical Society.

GARDEN CITY TOWNSHIP was established April 6, 1858, but was then named Watonwan for the river. The village, section 27, had been platted in June 1856, being named Fremont for John C. Frémont, the Republican candidate for president in the campaign of that year. In October 1858, it was replatted by Simeon P. Folsom, who renamed it Garden City, having reference to the native floral charms of the place. Stennett wrote of it, "Even to this day, in the spring the surrounding country is like a garden of wild flowers." In February 1864, the township was changed to Garden City by an act of the state legislature. The name here antedates it on Long Island, N.Y., where the only town so named in the eastern states was founded in 1869 by A. T. Stewart, the multimillionaire merchant. The village had a station on a branch of the St. Paul and Sioux City Railroad, and its post office began in 1857. The first mill was built by Samuel M. Folsom, and with other mills in the area, the village became the mill town of the county, with the Watonwan River providing power. The village also had a sorghum factory, a patent medicine factory, elevators, a stone quarry, and several butter and cheese companies.

GARDEN PRAIRIE a post office, 1867–75, located in Mapleton Township, section 12.

GARRETT a post office, 1888, with Lewis B. Garrett, postmaster; location not found.

GOOD THUNDER the railway village of Lyra Township, platted in April 1871, and incorporated March 2, 1893, was named for a chief of the Winnebago, whose village was close east of this site. The ford of the Maple River here had been previously called Good Thunder's ford. He was a friend of the white people, and in 1862 refused the overtures of the Dakota for the Winnebago to join in their war against the white settlers. He died several years later on the Missouri River, after the removal of his tribe to Dakota.

This was also the name of a Dakota, Wa-kin-yan-was-te, in translation Good Thunder, who likewise was friendly to the whites, becoming Gen. Henry H. Sibley's chief of scouts during his expeditions against the Dakota. He was converted to be a Christian in 1861 and was the first Dakota baptized by Bishop Henry B. Whipple, receiving then the name Andrew. He lived as a farmer at the mission of Birch Cooley, and during many years was the warden of its Dakota church. In 1889 he was a guest of the village of Good Thunder at its celebration of the Fourth of July, when he and many of its people thought the name of the village to have been given in his honor. To make it more sure, by the speeches of that day it was so rechristened (*Good Thunder Herald*, Feb. 21, 1901). He died at the Lower Agency near Redwood Falls, February 15, 1901. Portraits of this Good Thunder and his wife are given in *The Aborigines of Minnesota* (p. 509), but he is there erroneously called a Winnebago, and another portrait of him is in Whipple's *Lights and Shadows of a Long Episcopate* (p. 128).

It seems most probable that when this name was first chosen for the village, although the greater number of those naming it had in mind the Winnebago chief, others of them and many in the county supposed it to be for the Dakota scout, the exemplary Christian convert. Both these Indians certainly were very well known by the people of this township and county.

In 1987 the Good Thunder Development Corporation began the Good Thunder Elevator Mural project. A St. Paul muralist, Ta-Coumba Aiken, was commissioned to paint the 72-foot-high elevator and four surrounding 60-foot storage bins, depicting the town's past. The face of Good Thunder, the Dakota scout, is visible from nearly two miles away.

HAWKINS see **MAPLETON.**

HILTON see **ST. CLAIR.**

HOPE a post office, 1874–96, established in Antrim Township, Watonwan County, and transferred to Pleasant Mound Township, Blue Earth County, section 30, in 1886; it had a church and a general store.

ICELAND see **PERTH.**

JAMESTOWN half of a government township, first

settled in 1856 and organized May 11, 1858, then including also Le Ray Township, was named by Enoch G. Barkhurst, "in honor of the first English colony of Virginia." The name there was given to honor James I, king of England in 1603–25.

JUDSON TOWNSHIP organized May 11, 1858, was "named by Robert Patterson, in honor of the great Baptist missionary." Adoniram Judson was born in Malden, Mass., August 9, 1788, and died at sea, April 12, 1850. He went to Burma as a missionary in 1812, completed the translation of the Bible into Burmese in 1833, and completed a Burmese-English dictionary in 1849. Patterson had earlier platted and named Judson village, December 10, 1856, on the Minnesota River in section 33. The village was first settled by Patterson and John Goodwin, who built a public landing in the town and a steamboat landing upriver, with ferry service across the Minnesota River to Eureka in Nicollet County. The village had a sawmill, a gristmill, and several stores. A branch of the Chicago and Northwestern Railway was laid south of the village, and a new townsite platted by the Western Town Lot Company in 1900 near the station, named for its oldest settler. The post office operated 1857–1973.

KAMMRATH a post office, 1889–90, Frederick Kammrath, postmaster; location not found.

LAKE CRYSTAL a railway village and junction, platted in May 1869, incorporated by the legislature February 24, 1870, was named by Gen. Judson W. Bishop of St. Paul, engineer of the survey and construction of this railway, for the adjoining lake, which, according to Stennett, "was named by John C. Fremont and J. N. Nicollet, who explored the country around it in 1838, because of the unusual brilliancy and crystal purity of its waters." (This lake and the others near are unnamed on Joseph N. Nicollet's map, 1843.) The village was known as Loon Lake when its post office was established in 1867, the name changing in 1869.

LEHILLIER a village in South Bend Township, section 14. A townsite was laid out a short distance above the mouth of the Blue Earth River in September 1857, and a hotel was built but not used; the site did not develop.

LEHILLIER CITY a locality in Mankato Township, section 14.

LE RAY TOWNSHIP first settled in 1856, organized in 1860, was at first named Lake and was re-named Tivoli but on September 5, 1860, received its present name. The only use of this name elsewhere is for a township of Jefferson County, N.Y., whence probably some of the settlers here had come.

LIBERTY a post office, 1856–69, in Liberty Township.

LIME TOWNSHIP organized May 11, 1858, was named by George Stannard for its extensive outcrops of limestone, which have since been much quarried. The village of Lime, in section 2, had a station of the Chicago and Northwestern Railway.

LINCOLN TOWNSHIP settled in 1856, was at first named Richfield, April 6, 1858, but it remained without separate organization until September 26, 1865, when it was renamed for the martyred war president.

LINDEN SETTLEMENT see BROWN COUNTY, LINDEN.

LITTLE COBB a country post office in Medo Township, section 25, 1875–1904.

LOON LAKE see LAKE CRYSTAL.

LORTZ a farmers post office, 1889–1902, in Decoria Township, section 29; Henry Lortz was the postmaster.

LOWELL a townsite in Garden City Township, section 13, surveyed in December 1865; had a grist mill, a blacksmith shop, and a few homes; after several changes in ownership, the mill was moved and the townsite abandoned.

LYRA TOWNSHIP at first named Tecumseh, April 16, 1858, was renamed Winneshiek in May 1866, but at the time of its organization, September 22, 1866, it was finally named Lyra, as proposed by Rev. J. M. Thurston, "after a town he had come from in the east." (It appears in our eastern states only as a post office in Scioto County, Ohio.) "It comes to us from ancient mythology and was originally used to designate a northern constellation . . . as it was supposed to represent the lyre carried by Apollo."

MADISON LAKE a city in Jamestown Township, section 34, was named for the adjoining lake, which had been so named by the government surveyors in honor of James Madison, fourth president of the United States, 1809–17. The village was first settled in 1885 and had a station of the Minneapolis and St. Louis Railroad and several mills; a post office began in 1885 with George Washington Allyn as the first postmaster. The village was incorporated on December 15, 1891.

Located on Madison Lake, the village and surrounding area were touted as picturesque and flourishing, inviting a summer tourist trade for rowing, fishing, and sailing, and by 1900 the community had a well-developed resort trade. Point Pleasant, a townsite first settled about 1871 and platted in 1885, was included as part of the village at the time of incorporation.

MANKATO JUNCTION a station of the Chicago and Northwestern Railway, Lime Township, named from its nearness and relationship to Mankato.

MANKATO SPRINGS a village in Le Ray Township, section 29, circa 1895–1930; also known as Mankato Mineral Springs for its mineral springs.

MANKATO TOWNSHIP was established April 6, 1858, and was organized in connection with the present city of Mankato, May 11, 1858. The city charter was adopted March 24, 1868, and the first election of the township, separate from the city, was held April 7, 1868. The first settlement of Mankato and of this county was in February 1852 by Parsons King Johnson, and on the 14th of that month the Blue Earth Settlement Claim Association was organized in St. Paul by Henry Jackson, P. K. Johnson, Col. D. A. Robertson, Justus C. Ramsey, brother of the governor of the territory, and others. Hughes writes of their choice of the name for the settlement to be founded, as follows: "The honor of christening the new city was accorded to Mrs. P. K. Johnson and Mrs. Henry Jackson, who selected the name 'Mankato,' upon the suggestion of Col. Robertson. He had taken the name from Nicollet's book, in which the French explorer compared the 'Mahkato' or Blue Earth River, with all its tributaries, to the water nymphs and their uncle in the German legend of 'Undine.' . . . No more appropriate name could be given the new city, than that of the noble river at whose mouth it is located."

Growth of the community was attributed to transportation, as four railroads met in Mankato. In 1880 the city was fourth in size in the state, with a population of 5,500, and supported a number of industries: machine shops, flour, feed, and planing mills, a woolen mill, linseed oil works, several carriage and wagon factories, four breweries, a pottery and brick yards, three newspapers, and fourteen churches. The community is the site of Bethany Lutheran College, founded in 1927; and Minnesota State University—Mankato, which

began as a normal school, 1867–1921, teachers college, 1921–57, state college, 1957–75, and state university since 1975.

MAPLE RIVER a post office, 1867–72; location not found.

MAPLETON first settled in April 1856, was named Sherman in 1858 for Isaac Sherman, an old settler of Danville, or perhaps for Asa P. Sherman of this township. It was organized, with its first town meeting, April 2, 1861, taking its present name from the Maple River, which received this name from the government surveyors in 1854 for its plentiful maple trees. The site of the city of Mapleton, in section 4, was first settled in 1856 by a colony named the Minnesota Settlement Association from New York. The first townsite was platted in section 7 in 1858 but was soon superseded by a new townsite, platted January 21, 1871, on land owned by David Smith in section 4. The city was incorporated on February 23, 1878. The city had a station of the Southern Minnesota Railroad; its post office, begun in 1857, was called Mapleton, Old Mapleton, Hawkins (Sylvester Hawkins being postmaster, 1863–66), and then Mapleton Station until 1888, when it was reestablished as Mapleton.

McPHERSON was at first named Rice Lake Township August 21, 1855; was renamed McClellan for Gen. George B. McClellan September 2, 1863; and received its present name by an act of the state legislature in February 1865 in honor of Gen. James B. McPherson. He was born in Sandusky, Ohio, November 14, 1828; was graduated at West Point, 1853; was appointed a major general in 1862; served with distinction in the siege and capture of Vicksburg; became commander of the Army of the Tennessee in the spring of 1864; and was killed near Atlanta, Ga., July 22, 1864.

MEDO a township of the Winnebago reservation, was named by the county commissioners April 16, 1858, but it was not organized until September 2, 1863. This is a Dakota word meaning a species of plant (*Apios tuberosa*), which has roots that bear small tubers much used by the Indians as food. It is common or frequent through the south half of this state, extending north to the upper Mississippi River. Dr. Charles C. Parry, with David D. Owen's geological survey in 1848, wrote of it as "Pomme de Terre of the French voyageurs; Mdo, or wild potato, of the Sioux Indians." It is also called ground-nut because its nutlike tubers grow in a series along the root. Medo, a village in section 9, had a post office, 1866–1904, a sawmill, a feed mill, a wagon maker, two general stores, and a hotel.

MINNEOPA a village in South Bend Township, section 20, was settled in 1876 and named from the falls nearby in the Minneopa River. The name is a contraction of a Dakota word meaning "follows the water, two waterfalls." A station of the Chicago, St. Paul, Minneapolis and Omaha Railway was in section 21.

MINNESOTA LAKE see FARIBAULT COUNTY.

MONTEVIDEO a post office, 1857–59, located in Montevideo Township, section 23; an effort was made to create a village in 1857, but the site was not platted.

MYRNA a village in Vernon Center Township, settled in 1870. A country post office, 1873–1900, was first in section 30 in the home of Thomas L. Perkins, then moved in 1878 to section 19 in the home of E. D. Cornish.

PARK a post office, 1880–86, in Le Ray Township, section 3, located in the resort run by Chauncey H. Austin, a shoe-store owner in Mankato. George Washington Allyn desired a post office at Madison Lake, and because of a conflict in the number of post offices allowed, convinced Austin to discontinue the post office.

PEMBERTON a city located in Medo Township, section 1, was named for a Chicago and Northwestern Railway official. The village was platted in 1907, and the post office began in 1908; it was incorporated on April 26, 1946. Many of the businesses and buildings, including the Modern Woodman Hall, were moved to this site from Cream.

PERCH LAKE a village in Beauford Township, section 25; the post office operated 1868–71 in the home of postmaster Albert J. Gates, and 1871–1875 in the home of Henry Mately.

PERTH a village in Lincoln Township, section 7, was named in 1905 from the city in Scotland. It had formerly been called Iceland, 1867–71, for the native island of some of its immigrants. The village had a station of the Chicago, St. Paul, Minneapolis and Omaha Railway.

PLEASANT MOUND TOWNSHIP was first named Otsego April 6, 1858, but on October 14 of that year it was renamed Willow Creek, "probably an eastern name familiar to some old settler." There is a creek of this name in the east part of the township, flowing northeast into the Blue Earth River. A village named Pleasant Mound, first settled in 1857 in section 26, had a post office established in 1863 at the home of F. O. Marks, near a series of hills of drift gravel, called kames, in section 25, which then was moved to section 26 in the home of John S. Parks. The Dakota name of these hills, according to Hughes, was Ichokse or Repah Kichakse, meaning "to cut in the middle, perhaps from the fact that the ridge is divided into a number of mounds, or it may mean 'thrown down or dumped in heaps,' as the spelling is uncertain." September 6, 1865, this township was organized and was given its present name, on the suggestions of Marks and Parks, taken like that of the post office from the knolly gravel ridge.

POINT PLEASANT see MADISON LAKE.

PRION a post office, 1899–1900; location not found.

RAPIDAN MILLS a country post office, 1891–1900, located in Rapidan Township two miles west of Rapidan on the Rapidan River; also had a gristmill, a feed mill, a blacksmith shop, and a general store.

RAPIDAN TOWNSHIP which was in the Winnebago reservation, was at first named De Soto, April 16, 1858, but at its organization, April 15, 1865, it received the present name, suggested by C. P. Cook, from the Civil War for the Rapidan River of Virginia. This name is also given to rapids and a dam of the Blue Earth River in the northwest part of this township, about two miles west of Rapidan village on the railway. The unincorporated village, in section 9, was first settled in 1863, with a railroad station of the Chicago, St. Paul, Minneapolis and Omaha Railway; its post office operated 1875–1964, when it was changed to a rural branch. The village had a grist mill, a general store, and a cooperative creamery, 1897–1967. The Rapidan Dam built by Northern States Power Company in 1910 brought the first electricity. In 1922 four school districts consolidated, and a school building was erected, being one of the first consolidated schools in the county.

ST. CLAIR a city located on the Le Sueur River, section 8, in McPherson Township, was a railway terminal village, on the site of the old Winnebago Agency, where after the removal of the Indians, a village named Hilton was platted on land of Aaron Hilton in 1865. Its name was changed to St. Clair by officers of the Chicago, Milwaukee and St. Paul Railroad. The post office was formerly named Winnebago Agency from 1856 to 1886, when it was changed to St. Clair. Hilton had a sawmill there until 1884; the village had a railroad station, a grain elevator, and a steam flour mill, exporting flour and wheat. The village was incorporated in 1907.

SCHOSTAG MILL located in Danville Township and built by Gottlieb Schostag in 1861. The Dutch-type wind-powered flour and grist mill stood on a rise of the west bank of Minnesota Lake. The mill ceased operation with Schostag's death in 1906, and for the next 33 years, although deteriorating, it was considered a landmark of historical interest, being the only mill of that design in the entire northwest; the mill was destroyed by fire in 1939.

SEPPMANN WINDMILL located in Minneopa State Park.

SEYMOUR a village laid out on the north shore of Crystal Lake, Judson Township; no plat was filed because of a dispute among the owners, and the site was not developed.

SHELBY TOWNSHIP established by the county commissioners April 6, 1858, was then named Liberty but was renamed on October 14 of that year. Isaac Shelby, whose name is borne by nine counties in our central and southern states and also by numerous towns and villages, with several other cities and villages named Shelbyville, was born in Maryland, December 11, 1750, and died near Stanford, Ky., July 18, 1826. He served very honorably in the Revolutionary War and again in the War of 1812; was the first governor of Kentucky, 1792–96, and also in 1812–16; returned from each period of his governorship to the cultivation of his farm; was six times a presidential elector but declined other public service.

SHELBYVILLE a village in Shelby Township, section 35, was platted in April 1856, but was superseded by the more centrally located railway village of Amboy, platted in 1879, so that the Shelbyville post office was discontinued in 1881. This village name was given by Rev. John W. Powell, who came here in October 1855 from Shelbyville, Ind. The village was the site of the county fair in the early 1860s.

SHERMAN a farmhouse post office, 1866–97,

Danville Township, section 20; began with first postmaster George W. Blake and moved to the home of James McBroom, breeder of Norman horses, Merino sheep, and Durham cattle.

SKYLINE a city in South Bend Township, section 22, incorporated January 8, 1957.

SMITHS MILL a settlement in Le Ray Township, section 25, which began when Peter P. Smith built a sawmill across the county line in Waseca County in 1873; when the railroad switching station of a Chicago and Northwestern Railway branch line was established opposite that site in Blue Earth County, the station took the name, and a depot was built in 1883. Several steam sawmills using native lumber were located on the site; it had a post office from around 1898, which was then transferred to Waseca County, where it remained under various forms of the name until 1967.

SOUTH BEND TOWNSHIP "derived its name from the fact that the Minnesota river makes its great southern bend on its northern boundary." This name was proposed by David C. Evans by whom, with Capt. Samuel Humbertson and others, the village of South Bend was founded in the summer of 1853 as a rival of Mankato. Its plat was recorded September 22, 1854. The township was organized May 11, 1858. The village was incorporated on March 20, 1858, but the incorporation was discontinued. It had a station on the St. Paul and Sioux City Railroad, a grist mill, and a stone yard. Sometimes called South Bend City, its post office operated 1856–1900. By 1909 only the schoolhouse, the Welsh Congregational Church (removed to Pemberton in 1930), the Eckstrom general store, and a few homes remained.

SPEIR see EAGLE LAKE.

SPIRER see EAGLE LAKE.

STERLING TOWNSHIP first settled in 1855, was organized in April and May 1858, then being named Mapleton, but on January 3, 1860, the county commissioners granted the petition of the settlers in this township to rename it Sterling. It was so organized, separate from the present Mapleton, April 3, 1860. Robert Taylor proposed the name for the city and county in Scotland, spelled Stirling, but as Hughes writes, "William Russell contended for the name 'Sterling,' as more appropriate and expressive of the quality of the soil and people, and the majority sided with him." The village of Sterling, in section 16, had a post office, which was called Sterling, 1862–68; Sterling Centre, 1868–93; and Sterling Center, 1893–1904.

STONE a railway station three miles north of Mankato, "was originally called Quarry, owing to stone quarries in the vicinity. In 1902 the name was changed to Stone, and came from the same 'stone quarries' that had given it the earlier name" (Stennett, *Origin of the Place Names of the Chicago and Northwestern Railways*).

TIVOLI a village in Mankato Township, section 25; surveyed in April 1858 on land owned by Moses Bennett and others; Bennett built a sawmill at the site. The plat was vacated in 1870. It had a post office, 1859–1900, and saw and flour mills, fruit growers, and carpet weavers as the main industries.

UPTON a farmers post office, 1886–1900, located in Pleasant Mound Township, section 3.

VERNON CENTER TOWNSHIP settled in 1855, was at first named Montevideo by the county commissioners, April 6, 1858, but ten days later they renamed it Vernon, and on October 14 of the same year they changed this to the present name. A village had been platted here in June 1857 by proprietors who came from Mount Vernon, Ohio, two of whom, Col. Benjamin F. Smith and Benjamin McCracken, gave to it the name Vernon. The many villages and cities of the United States that bear this name, including the home of Washington in Virginia, received it primarily in honor of the distinguished English admiral Edward Vernon (1684–1757), the hero of the expeditions capturing Porto Bello in 1739 and attacking Cartagena in 1741. When the Chicago, St. Paul, Minneapolis and Omaha Railway was built through this township in 1879, the first name given to the station here was Edgewood, for its being at the edge of a grove, but it was renamed in 1885 for the township, although neither the township nor the station is quite centrally situated. The city of Vernon Center, in section 26, was incorporated as a village in 1899; the post office was established in 1858. Early businesses were flour mills, a sorghum factory, elevators, lumber dealers, a creamery, the Barnes Opera House and the Vernon Center Opera House, and several general stores.

VOLKSVILLE a business settlement in Jamestown Township, section 20. About 1867 brothers W. and R. Volk built Volks Hall, which had a cooper shop on the first floor and a meeting hall upstairs; a mill pond; and a sawmill for shingles and planing. Fred Volk built a furniture factory in 1869, and later a gristmill was added; the factory had major fire damage in 1880, was rebuilt, and was torn down in 1902. Because the plants and mills were so extensive, the site became known as Volksville.

WATONWAN a post office established in 1858. A paper village in Garden City Township named Watonwan City was laid out in August 1857 following the first sawmill built on the Watonwan River in 1856 in section 32; the Butterfield Mills and Watonwan City did not succeed, and in 1863 the plat was vacated. In 1882 the name of the post office was changed to Blaine and was discontinued in 1889, although a community still existed until 1908.

WATTERS a station on the Chicago Great Western Railroad in Mankato Township, section 34, with a post office, 1890–91.

WAVERLY a post office, 1858–59; location not found.

WEST MANKATO a paper town in South Bend Township, circa 1868.

WILLOW CREEK a village in Pleasant Mound Township, section 13; it had a post office, 1863–1902, a flour mill, and a general store.

WINNEBAGO AGENCY see ST. CLAIR.

━━━━━

Lakes and Streams

Minneopa Creek, its falls, and the state park are noted in a later part of the present chapter.

In the foregoing notes of townships and villages, other streams and lakes have been noticed, namely, Maple River, Willow Creek in Pleasant Mound Township, Lake Crystal, and Eagle and Madison Lakes.

The U.S. surveyors named Washington, Jefferson, and Madison Lakes in commemoration of the early presidents. These are notably large in a group of many lakes, the first and second being in the south edge of Le Sueur County, adjoining Jamestown, and the third in Jamestown and Le Ray. Hughes records the Dakota name of Lake Washington as Okapah, meaning the Choke Cherry Lake, and of Lake Madison as Wakonseche, that is, the Evil Spirit, or Abundant Mystery, or the Sacred Shade.

Government surveyors also named the Maple

River, which the Dakota called the Tewapa-Tankiyan River (meaning big water-lily root), and the Big Cobb River, which bore a Dakota name, Tewapadan (little lily root). The names used by the Indians, copied thus from Nicollet's map (1843), referred to the roots that they dug for food in the shallow water of these streams and their tributary lakes. On the township plats the Big Cobb and Little Cobb Rivers were spelled without their final letter, though probably named for some member or acquaintance of the surveying party.

Lake Lura is said to have been so designated by one of the early settlers from the name "Lura" found carved on a tree upon its shore, and thence it was given to a neighboring township in Faribault County. It had two Dakota names, Tewapa (water lily) and Ata'kinyan or Ksanksan (crooked or irregular).

Jackson Lake, on the east line of Shelby, named for Norman L. Jackson, the first settler of that township, who located on its shore, had the Dakota name Sinkpe (muskrat). Hughes writes: "The southern half of its bed, being shallow, was thickly populated by these animals, whose rush-built homes literally covered that portion of the lake. The spot was noted among both the Indians and pioneers for trapping these furbearing rats."

Wita Lake, in Lime Township, retains its Dakota name, meaning Island Lake, for its two islands.

The aborigines are also commemorated by two Indian Lakes, in Le Ray and South Bend Townships.

Names of pioneer settlers are borne by Ballantyne Lake in Jamestown for James Ballantyne, a schoolteacher and homesteader; Gilfillin Lake in Jamestown and Le Ray for Joseph Gilfillin, who left his home near this take to join the Ninth Minnesota Regiment, Company E, and was killed only two weeks later in service against the Dakota near New Ulm, September 3, 1862; Kilby Lake on the line of Judson and Butternut Valley for Benjamin E. Kilby; Armstrong, Dackins, Lieberg, Solberg, and Strom Lakes in Butternut Valley, for John Armstrong, Edward Dackins, Ole P. Lieberg, Olens Solberg, and Andrew Strom, the largest of these, Solberg Lake, and also Dackins Lake, having been recently drained by ditches; Mills Lake in Garden City Township for Titus Mills, whose farm bordered on this lake; Morgan Creek in Cambria for Richard Morgan, also sometimes otherwise named for others of the settlers

along its course; Rogers Lake in sections 7 and 18, Danville, for John E., Robert H., and Josiah Rogers, early settlers on its shore; Albert and George Lakes in Jamestown; and Lake Alice in Le Ray, and Ida Lake in Shelby, each probably named for the wife or daughter of a pioneer.

Other names are of obvious significance, as Cottonwood Lake in Medo; Duck Lake and also Long and Mud Lakes in Jamestown; another Mud Lake in Le Ray; Fox Lake in South Bend; Perch Lake and Perch Creek; Lily and Loon Lakes adjoining Lake Crystal, the first very shallow and filled with lilies, water grasses, and rushes; Rice Lake in McPherson, named for its wild rice, like many other lakes throughout this state; and Rush Lake in Judson.

The Undine Region

Nicollet in 1841 gave to the area of Blue Earth County, with parts of other counties adjoining it, "the name of *Undine Region* . . . derived from that of an interesting and romantic German tale, the heroine of which belonged to the extensive race of water-spirits living in the brooks and rivers and lakes, whose father was a mighty prince. She was moreover the niece of a great brook (the Mankato), who lived in the midst of forests, and was beloved by all the many great streams of the surrounding country."

The author of *Undine*, entitled for its heroine, published in 1811, was Friedrich Fouqué, who was born at Brandenburg, Prussia, in 1777, and died at Berlin in 1843. Her name is from the Latin *unda*, a wave, whence we derive several common words, as undulation and inundate, and speak of undulating prairies, where they have a broadly wavy surface.

On Nicollet's map the Undine Region extends from the Redwood River east to the upper part of Cannon River, and from the Minnesota River south to the north edge of Iowa.

Minneopa State Park

The state legislature in 1905 provided for the purchase of land containing the Minneopa Falls on the creek of this name in South Bend Township, about four miles west of Mankato, for public use as a state park. Its area is about 60 acres, comprising the falls, two near together, of 60 feet descent, with the gorge below. The railway station and townsite, named Minneopa, close to the falls, were platted in September 1870. This name is contracted from Dakota words, *minne-hinhe-nonpa*, which mean "water falling twice" or "two waterfalls." An early name of this stream was Lyons Creek, for a pioneer. It flows from Strom, Lily, and Crystal Lakes.

The Winnebago Reservation

Green Bay of Lake Michigan was known to the French in Pierre E. Radisson's time as the Bay of the Puants, or Winnebago, an outlying tribe of the Siouan stock, mainly surrounded by Algonquian tribes. Their name, meaning the People of the Stinking Water, that is, of the Sea, or of muddy and ill-smelling lakes roiled by winds, was adopted by the French from its use among the Algonquins. In 1832 the Winnebago ceded their country south and east of the Fox and Wisconsin Rivers to the United States, and afterward many of the tribe were removed to northeastern Iowa. Thence, in 1848, they were removed to Long Prairie in the central part of what is now Minnesota, and in 1855 they were again removed, to a reservation in Blue Earth and Waseca Counties of this state. In 1863, after the Dakota War, they were removed to a reservation in Dakota Territory, and in 1866 to a more suitable reservation in Nebraska.

The reservation that was provided here for this tribe by a treaty made at Washington on February 27, 1855, included in Blue Earth County the townships of Rapidan, Decoria, McPherson, Lyra, Beauford, and Medo, and it continued six miles east in Waseca County, there including Alton and Freedom Townships. By a later treaty at Washington, April 15, 1859, the Winnebago relinquished the west half of this reservation, "to be sold by the United States in trust for their benefit," and by an act of Congress, February 21, 1863, the east half, comprising McPherson, Medo, Alton, and Freedom, was directed to be similarly sold, another reservation having been provided in Dakota.

Glacial Lake Minnesota

In the basins of the Blue Earth and Minnesota Rivers, flowing northward from the edge of Iowa to the Mississippi at Fort Snelling, a glacial lake was held by the barrier of the departing continental glacier during its final melting. This temporary lake was mapped and named in my work for the U.S. Geological Survey (Monograph XXV, "The Glacial Lake Agassiz," 1896, pls. III and XI-II; pp. 254 and 264). To the later and reduced condition of this glacial lake, when it outflowed to the Cannon River, Prof. Newton H. Winchell in 1901 gave the name of Lake Undine ("Glacial Lakes of Minnesota," Bulletin of the Geol. Society of America, vol. 12, pp. 109–28, with a map).

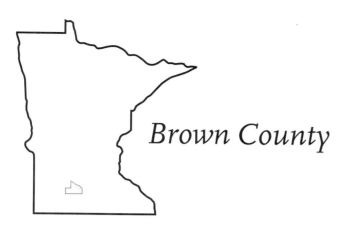

Brown County

Established by legislative act February 20, 1855, and organized February 11, 1856, this county was named in honor of Joseph Renshaw Brown, one of the most prominent pioneers of this state. He was born in Harford County, Md., January 5, 1805, and died in New York City, November 9, 1870.

In his boyhood he ran away from an apprenticeship for the printing business at Lancaster, Pa., enlisted in the army as a drummer boy, and at the age of 14 years came to the area of Minnesota, with the troops who built Fort St. Anthony (in 1825 renamed Fort Snelling). In May 1822, with William Joseph Snelling, son of the commandant, he explored the creek and lake since named Minnehaha and Minnetonka.

John Fletcher Williams, secretary of the Minnesota Historical Society, wrote in 1871, as follows, of Brown's varied life work and of his personal qualities.

"On leaving the army, somewhere about 1825, he resided at Mendota, Saint Croix, and other points in the State, and engaged in the Indian trade, lumbering, and other occupations. His energy, industry and ability soon made him a prominent character on the frontier, and no man in the Northwest was better known. He acquired a very perfect acquaintance with the Dakota tongue, and attained an influence among that nation (being allied to them by marriage), which continued unabated to his death. He held, at different times during his life, a number of civil offices, which he filled with credit and ability.... He was also a leading member of the famous 'Stillwater Conven-

tion' of citizens held in August, 1848, to take steps to secure a Territorial organization for what is now Minnesota. He was the Secretary of the Territorial Councils of 1849 and 1851, and Chief Clerk of the House of Representatives in 1853, a member of the Council in 1854 and '55 and House in 1857, and Territorial Printer in 1853 and '54. He was also a member from Sibley county in the Constitutional Convention ('Democratic Wing') of 1857, and took a very prominent part in the formation of our present State Constitution.... He shaped much of the legislation of our early territorial days, and chiefly dictated the policy of his party, of whose conventions he was always a prominent member....

"But it is as a journalist and publisher I desire principally to speak of him here. His first regular entrance into the printing business in Minnesota was in the year 1852, though he had before written considerable for the press. Shortly after the death of James M. Goodhue, which occurred in August of that year, Major Brown purchased the 'Minnesota Pioneer,' and edited and published it under his own name for nearly two years. In the spring of 1854, he transferred the establishment to Col. E. S. Goodrich. During the period of his connection with the paper, he established a reputation as one of the most sagacious, successful and able political editors in the Territory, and as a sharp, interesting and sensible writer.

"In 1857 he established at Henderson, which town had been founded and laid out by him a short time before, a journal called the 'Henderson

Democrat,' which soon became a prominent political organ, and was continued with much ability and success until 1860 or '61."

Joseph A. Wheelock wrote in the *St. Paul Press*, November 12, 1870: "A drummer boy, soldier, Indian trader, lumberman, pioneer, speculator, founder of cities, legislator, politician, editor, inventor, his career—though it hardly commenced till half his life had been wasted in the obscure solitudes of this far Northwestern wilderness—

has been a very remarkable and characteristic one, not so much for what he has achieved, as for the extraordinary versatility and capacity which he has displayed in every new situation."

The village of Browns Valley in Traverse County, founded by Joseph R. Brown and others, was the place of his trading post and home during his last four years, and an adjoining township of Big Stone County also bears this name.

Information has been gathered from History of the Minnesota Valley, *1882, pp. 698–762, and* History of Brown County, *L. A. Fritsche, M.D., editor, two volumes, 1916, pp. 519, 568; from Benedict Juni, Richard Pfefferle, and August Schwerdtfeger, each of New Ulm; and from the county offices of the register of deeds, judge of probate, and clerk of the court during a visit at New Ulm in July 1916.*

ALBIN settled in 1866, was organized June 23, 1870. "The preliminary meeting for the organization of the town was held at the house of S. Rima; a name for the town could not be agreed upon, and Albin was suggested by Mrs. Rima" (*History of the Minnesota Valley*, p. 758). A post office operated in the township, 1890–96.

BACKSVILLE a post office, 1866–77; location not found.

BAD TRACK a post office, 1857; location not found.

BASHAW TOWNSHIP organized in April 1874, was named for Joseph Baschor (or Pascher), a Bohemian, who was the first settler, coming in the spring of 1869. The name was changed in spelling to give a more easy English pronunciation.

BEDFORD see **DOTSON**.

BLAIR a post office, 1862–65; location not found.

BURNS see **SPRINGFIELD**.

BURNSTOWN first settled in 1857, was named for J. F. Burns, one of the early settlers, who came in 1858. This township was organized October 14, 1871. "In 1877 the village of Burns was surveyed . . . on the line of the Winona and St. Peter railroad. . . . February 21, 1881, it was incorporated under the name of Springfield."

COBDEN a city in Prairieville and Leavenworth

Townships, was originally named North Branch, from its location near Sleepy Eye Creek, the principal north branch of the Cottonwood River, but in 1886 it was changed to Cobden, for the English statesman. The village was platted February 16, 1901, was incorporated on April 7, 1905, and separated from the township on April 24, 1906; its post office operated 1886–1972. The village had two elevators and two creameries, and a station of the Chicago and North Western Railroad in section 31 of Prairieville Township. Richard Cobden was born in Sussex, England, June 3, 1804, and died in London, April 2, 1865. He entered parliament in 1841, visited the United States in 1854, and was especially noted as an advocate of free trade and of peace. During our Civil War he was a supporter of the cause of the North.

COMFREY a city on the south line of Bashaw Township, sections 34 and 35, also associated with Cottonwood County. It was incorporated as a village on February 19, 1900, and platted in 1902 by the Western Town Lot Company, taking its name from a nearby post office, which had been established in 1877. That had been so named "by A. W. Pederson, the first postmaster, from the plant, comfrey . . . that he had met with in his reading" (William H. Stennett, *Origin of Place Names of the Chicago and Northwestern Railways*). The hotel was built in 1899 and razed in 1940; a large creamery operated from 1899 to 1955. W. R. Hodges, the first newspaper publisher, built a two-story building, the second floor becoming known as Hodges Hall, providing stage entertainment.

COTEAU PERCE a post office, 1857; location not found.

COTTONWOOD TOWNSHIP first settled in 1855, organized October 24, 1858, was named for the Cottonwood River on its north edge, and the Little Cottonwood River, flowing through its center, their names being translations from the Dakota, as noted more fully in the chapter for Cottonwood County. A post office operated in the township at various times between 1859 and 1874.

DOTSON railway station, in Stately Township, section 12, established in 1899, was named for Enoch Dotson, an early settler of the neighboring village of Sanborn in Redwood County. A post office was located in the station, 1901–5. The area was laid out in 1899 under the name of Bedford, for a town in Massachusetts, but was changed when the post office was established.

EDEN TOWNSHIP which was a part of the Dakota reservation till 1863, was first settled by white immigrants in December 1864 and was organized April 2, 1867. Its name was chosen by the settlers because of the beauty of its scenery and fertility of the soil. Lone Tree post office was established in Eden Township in 1869, being named for the neighboring lake, which had received this name from a large lone cottonwood tree, once a famous landmark.

ESSIG the railway village in Milford, section 19, "was named by C. C. Wheeler, then an officer of the Chicago and Northwestern Railway, to honor one of the Brothers Essig, who erected the first business building in the place" (Stennett, *Origin of Place Names of the Chicago and Northwestern Railways*). The name is for John Essig, a farmer here since 1882, who was born in Will County, Ill., May 29, 1851. He came to Minnesota in 1866 with his parents, who settled on a farm in Milford. His father, John F. Essig, who was born in Germany, lived in Milford till 1886 and later in Springfield, where he died in 1896. The village was platted in 1885, at which time it was known as Siding No. 1 for its railway station; settlement began in 1886, and its post office was established with John Essig as first postmaster. The Milford Fish Pond and Look Out Point (1894–1900) was established by Alfred and Louis Vogel of New Ulm on ten acres of land nearby as a recreational center for business people of New Ulm, with picnic areas, fishing, and boating. A flash flood in 1900 washed away the fish pond; restoration was begun in 1977.

EVAN a railway village in section 8, Prairieville, was first platted as Hanson station in May 1887 by Nels Hanson and became an incorporated village March 22, 1904. A post office was established in 1886, named Evan by the first postmaster, Martin Norseth, for his wife, Eva, and its name was transferred to this village.

GODAHL a locality in Albin Township, sections 35 and 36, which extends into Watonwan County, Nelson Township, sections 1 and 2.

GOLDEN GATE a village in Home Township, section 30, located less than a mile from Sleepy Eye, was begun about 1864, flourished for a period, and disappeared by 1920; it had a post office, 1868–1900. Some local pioneers said the name was too high-toned and nicknamed the village Podunk, a name that clung until the village died; some called it Hell's Half Acre because of the rough element imbibing in local saloons, forcing the community to endorse strict prohibition. Spring Creek, a tributary of the Mississippi River, supplied power to a flour mill built by John Heimerdinger, and his home is one of the few remaining structures.

GOSHEN a village in Cottonwood Township, section 36, circa 1913.

HANSKA a city in the east edge of Lake Hanska Township, section 24, bears as its name, like the township, the common Dakota word meaning "long" or "tall," which these Indians gave to the remarkably long and narrow lake in this township and Albin. The village was platted October 9, 1899, and was incorporated on May 1, 1901; its post office began in 1890. The village had a creamery, three grain elevators, a roller mill, and a station on the Minneapolis and St. Louis Railroad.

HOME the largest township of this county, settled in 1857, organized June 30, 1866, was so named in accordance with the petition of its settlers. According to a local story, three supervisors of the township at their first meeting had to select a name. The hour was late, and one impatiently said, "Let's go home!" to which another answered, "Let's call it Home Township!" A post office operated, 1868–1900.

IBERIA a small hamlet near the center of Stark Township, section 16, bears the ancient name of the Spanish and Portuguese peninsula. The post office of this name was established February 1, 1870, and was discontinued February 24, 1893.

The first settlers were Frederick Benham and his family in 1864. During the community's existence there was a grist mill powered by the Big Cottonwood River, three saloons with dance halls, two blacksmiths, two stores, a mill built in 1872 and closed in 1882, and a few residences and other buildings.

LAKE HANSKA TOWNSHIP first settled in 1857, organized June 21, 1870, was named for its long lake, as before noted for its village of Hanska.

LEAVENWORTH TOWNSHIP was organized April 16, 1859. It was probably named in honor of Henry Leavenworth, commander of the troops who came in 1819 to found the fort at first called Fort St. Anthony, renamed as Fort Snelling in 1825. Speculators platted a community in 1857 in sections 22 and 27, and a log dwelling was built on the site for John B. Calkins, left to protect the land. A post office opened in 1858 with Calkins as postmaster. Almost abandoned during the Dakota War, the site regained settlers, growing with stores, blacksmiths, a mill, and a school. Growth stopped when the railroad bypassed the village, and by the mid-1880s only a saloon and a mill existed, the latter burning down shortly thereafter; the post office operated at various times between 1858 and 1902.

LINDEN TOWNSHIP settled in 1856, organized in 1859, was named for its groves of the American linden, usually called basswood. The largest groves here bordered Lake Linden, which had been earlier so named. The village of Linden, in section 11, had a post office, 1869–1904, and a general store and a creamery. The Linden Settlement, settled in the 1850s mainly by Norwegians, with some Danes and Swedes, began about 12 miles west of Mankato, extending through the western corner of Blue Earth County, and 18 miles into Brown and Watonwan Counties, taking in six townships in three counties

LONE TREE a village located in Eden Township, sections 9 and 14, had a country post office, called Lone Tree Lake, 1869–94, and Lone Tree, 1894–1905, and a church and a school.

McCLEARY a post office, 1896–1903, located in Mulligan Township, section 28.

MILFORD TOWNSHIP first settled in 1853, set apart by the county board for organization on June 28, 1858, was named from a sawmill built in 1854–55 on a small creek, tributary to the Minnesota River where it was crossed by a ford. This was the first sawmill in the upper Minnesota valley. A post office, in section 8, 1861–63 and 1866–99, operated with a Chicago and North Western station called Milford Siding in section 13; the Milford State Monument commemorating the Dakota War was donated for the Junior Pioneers in 1913.

MULLIGAN TOWNSHIP settled in 1865, organized April 26, 1871, was named for an early pioneer, probably from Ireland. A post office operated in the township, 1883–88.

NEW ULM the county seat, founded in 1854–55 by German colonists coming from Chicago and Cincinnati, was named for Ulm in Germany, near the village of Erbach, which was, according to the late Hon. William Pfaender, the place of emigration of 20 of the 32 persons in the first company of pioneer settlers, who came in the autumn of 1854. The post office opened in 1856. It was incorporated as a town by an act of the legislature, March 6, 1857; as a borough, February 19, 1870; and as a city, February 24, 1876. It received its present charter on March 1, 1887. Early businesses were, in addition to flour and planing mills, five breweries, notably Augustus Schell's, potteries, cigar and soda water factories, elevators, brickyards, a vinegar factory, a U.S. land office, a pipe organ factory, five creameries, two stone quarries, several weekly newspapers, numerous stores and artisans workshops, including that of Anton Gag, notable photographer and artist, a Lutheran Society college, and the Sisters of Charity Music School and their St. Alexander Hospital. The city was the center of a large trade in farm products and had stations of the Minneapolis and St. Louis Railroad in section 28 and 30 of Milford Township, the latter also known as the Aufderheide spur station.

NILE a post office, 1871–76; location not found.

NORTH BRANCH see **COBDEN**.

NORTH STAR TOWNSHIP first settled in 1858, set apart for organization on January 9, 1873, received its name in allusion to the French motto "L'Etoile du Nord," on our state seal, whence Minnesota is often called the North Star State.

PITSON a village in Stately Township, section 5, circa 1930.

PRAIRIEVILLE TOWNSHIP whose first settlers came in 1866, was organized in March 1870, taking this name because it consists almost wholly of prairie land. See also SLEEPY EYE.

RED STONE a village in Cottonwood Township, two miles below New Ulm on the Minnesota River, existing about 1857.

REDWOOD JUNCTION a railroad station of the Chicago and North Western Railroad, in Prairieville Township, section 36.

REDWOOD MILLS a post office, 1857; location not found.

SEARLES a railway village in Cottonwood Township, section 21, was platted October 10, 1899, being named by officials of the Minneapolis and St. Louis Railroad company. Its post office was called Sperl, 1900–2, and Searles since 1902. A station of the Minneapolis and St. Louis Railroad was in section 22.

SIGEL TOWNSHIP settled in 1856, organized April 28, 1862, was named in honor of Franz Sigel, a general in the Civil War. He was born at Sinsheim, Baden, Germany, November 18, 1824; died in New York City, August 21, 1902. He came to the United States in 1852; settled in St. Louis, 1858, as a teacher in a German institute; organized a regiment of U.S. volunteers, 1861, of which he became colonel; won the battle of Carthage, Mo., July 5, 1861; was promoted to the rank of major general, March 1862, and took command of a wing of the Army of Virginia; was appointed to the command of the Department of West Virginia in February 1864; was U.S. pension agent in New York City, 1885–89. About the year 1873 Gen. Sigel visited New Ulm and this township.

SLEEPY EYE the city and railway junction in Home Township, platted by Thomas Allison and Walter Brackenridge as Sleepy Eye Lake, September 18, 1872, incorporated as a village February 14, 1878, and as a city in 1903, was named, like the adjoining lake, for a chief of the Sisseton Dakota. The post office was called Prairieville, 1871–72, when it was changed to Sleepy Eye. Businesses included a brewery, marble works, grain elevators, creameries, and mills; a Catholic seminary was located there, and a station of the Chicago and North Western was in section 32; a plant for canning peas and corn began operation in 1930.

Sleepy Eyes's favorite home and village during some parts of many years were beside this lake. He was born near the site of Mankato; became a chief between 1822 and 1825; signed the treaties of Prairie du Chien, 1825 and 1830, of St. Peter's in 1836, and Traverse des Sioux, 1851. Doane Robinson wrote: "Sleepy Eyes died in Roberts county, South Dakota, but many years after his death his remains were disinterred and removed to Sleepy Eye, Minn., where they were buried under a monument erected by the citizens" (Hodge, *Handbook of American Indians*, Part II, 1910). The monument, close to the railway station, bears this inscription beneath the portrait of the chief in bas-relief sculpture: "Ish-tak-ha-ba, Sleepy Eye, Always a Friend of the Whites. Died 1860."

An interesting biographic sketch of "Sleepy Eyes, or Ish-ta-hba, which is very literally translated," by Rev. Stephen R. Riggs in the *Minnesota Free Press*, St. Peter, January 27, 1858, is reprinted in the *Minnesota History Bulletin*, vol. 2, no. 8, pp. 484–95, November 1918.

SOUDE a post office, 1877–82; location not found.

SPERL see SEARLES.

SPRINGFIELD the railway village in Burnstown, platted in 1877, was then named Burns, but at its incorporation, February 21, 1881, received its present name. This is said by Stennett to be derived from the city of Springfield, Mass., but Juni refers its origin to a very large spring there, on the north side of the Cottonwood River and high above it. The earlier name of Burns Station and the name of the township were for brothers, John and Dan Burns; when Michael Gamble built the first store in 1872, he chose a new name, Springfield, and became the first postmaster when the office opened in 1873. The Opera House was built in 1892 and was the site of traveling shows, medicine shows, Turner Club men's gymnastics, dances, school entertainment, sports, graduations, and political and suffrage rallies. The village, built principally of brick, had five grain elevators, brick and tile works, a flour mill, and a creamery. The Potter Stockyard began in 1930 on land Reuben Potter had purchased in 1919 from his father, former Senator L. E. Potter, and was renamed Springfield Stockyard in 1976 when Merlin Fredin and his sons became owners.

STARK TOWNSHIP settled in 1858, organized April 7, 1868, was named for August Starck, a German pioneer farmer there.

STATELY settled in 1873, was the last township organized in this county, April 7, 1879. The origin of its name has not been ascertained, but as an

English word, of frequent use, it means "having a grand and impressive appearance, lofty, dignified." The west part of the south line of Stately crosses the highest land of this county, commanding a far prospect northward and eastward. A post office was located in the township 1883–1900.

———————

Lakes and Streams

Cottonwood and Little Cottonwood Rivers are noticed in connection with Cottonwood Township, and most fully in the chapter on the county of that name. Lone Tree Lake is mentioned under Eden Township, and Lakes Hanska and Linden with the townships so named. Sleepy Eye Lake and Creek received their names, like the city, from the Dakota chief.

Only a few other names of streams remain to be noticed. Big Spring Creek, also called Spring Branch Creek, in Eden and Home Townships, takes its name from its large springs; Mine Creek in North Star Township refers doubtless to prospecting or mining there; and Mound Creek in Stately may have been named, as also this township, in allusion to the highland on its upper course.

The following lakes bear names of early pioneers, whose homes were usually beside them or in their vicinity: George Lake, named for Captain Sylvester A. George, and Rose Lake, for Fred Rose, in Home Township, the former having been earlier called Cross Lake in allusion to its four bays having somewhat the outline of a cross; Kruger Lake in Prairieville for Louis Kruger, a German farmer; Lake Hummel, also named Clear Lake, in Sigel; Lake Emerson, now drained, on the south line of Linden; Broome and Omsrud Lakes in Lake Hanska Township; and Lake Altermatt in Leavenworth for John B. Altermatt, a Swiss farmer.

Lake Juni in section 26, Sigel, is named in honor of Benedict Juni of New Ulm. He was born in Switzerland, January 12, 1852, and came to the United States when five years old with his parents, who settled on a farm in Milford. In 1862 he was a captive of the Dakota from August 18 to the surrender of the prisoners at Camp Release, as narrated by him in the *History of Brown County* (vol. I, pp. 111–22). During more than 30 years he was a teacher in the public schools of this county.

School Lake, also in Sigel, received this name from its lying mainly in the school section 16.

Dane Lake in Linden was named for its several Dane settlers in a mainly Norwegian township.

Bachelor Lake in Stark was named for a lone homesteader there, unmarried; and Rice Lake mostly in section 29 of the same township, for its wild rice, a name that formerly was also applied to the present Lake Altermatt.

The origin of the name of Boy's Lake in Leavenworth was not learned.

Reed Lake in section 6, Bashaw, was named for its abundant growth of reeds; and Wood Lake crossed by the south line of Mulligan and lying mainly in Watonwan County, for its adjoining groves, the source of firewood used by the early settlers.

State Park

In 1937 land along the Cottonwood River near New Ulm was set aside for Cottonwood State Park. Through the 1930s WPA workers built several stone buildings, which remain in use. The Civilian Conservation Corps dammed the river to create a reservoir; subsequent flooding in 1947, 1965, and 1969 damaged the dam, which was finally removed in 1995, restoring the river to its natural flow. During World War II the park became a German prisoner-of-war camp. In 1945 the park was renamed Flandrau State Park in recognition of the contributions of Charles E. Flandrau to the state.

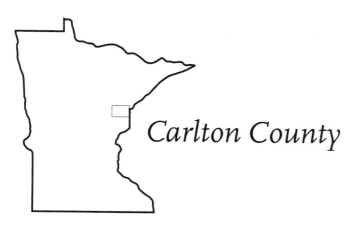

Carlton County

This county, established May 23, 1857, with a further legislative act of February 18, 1870, and organized September 26, 1870, was named in honor of Reuben B. Carlton, one of the first settlers of Fond du Lac, at the head of lake navigation on the St. Louis River, near the line between St. Louis and Carlton Counties. He was born in Onondaga County, N.Y., March 4, 1812; came to Fond du Lac in 1847 as a farmer and blacksmith for the Ojibwe; was one of the proprietors of the townsite of Fond du Lac, being a trustee under the act of its incorporation in 1857; and was a member of the first state senate, 1858. He owned about 80 acres adjoining that village and the river, on which he resided until his death, December 6, 1863.

The village of Carlton, the county seat of this county since 1886, was also named for him, and he is further commemorated by Carlton's Peak, near Tofte in Cook County, the most prominent point on the north shore of Lake Superior in Minnesota, forming the western end of the Sawtooth Range.

Fifty years after Carlton's death, James Bardon of Superior, Wis., wrote the following personal remembrance and estimate of him to Henry Oldenburg of Carlton, dated September 10, 1913.

"'Colonel' Carlton, as he was called, was a man of large frame, fully six feet in height, a strong personality, of good looks and pleasing manners, a man of much intelligence. He became associated with the bright and enterprising men who laid out and established Superior, Duluth, and other places about the head of Lake Superior. An avenue here in Superior was named after him. . . . Colonel Carlton was more prominently identified with the westerly part of St. Louis county, now Carlton county, in the early days, than any other man; and when the new county was projected it is likely that all men agreed that Carlton was the appropriate name for it . . . a really noble character."

For the origins and significance of local names in this county, information was gathered from F. A. Watkins, judge of probate, visited at Carlton in September 1909, and again in August 1916; and also from Hon. Spencer J. Searls, in the second of these visits.

ATKINSON TOWNSHIP was named for John Atkinson, an early settler there, who during many years was employed as a land examiner for the St. Paul and Duluth Railroad company. The village of Atkinson in section 25 had a station of the Northern Pacific Railroad, a post office, 1894–1956, a sawmill, a hotel, and a general store.

AUTOMBA was named after the railway station of the Minneapolis, St. Paul and Sault Ste. Marie Railroad (Soo Line) in this township, but the origin of this name remains to be ascertained. The village in section 32 had a post office, 1914–54; its first general store was built in 1910 by Henry Maunula, who had moved from Moose Lake, where he had the first blacksmith shop.

BARKER a village in Silver Brook Township, section 35; its post office began as Lalone, 1891–99, Olive La Lone, postmaster, changing to Barker, 1899–1910, its postmaster being John L. Lallen, a market gardener. The village had a station of the Northern Pacific Railroad.

BARNUM TOWNSHIP received its name in honor of George G. Barnum, a resident of Duluth, who was paymaster of the Lake Superior and Mississippi Railroad (later named the St. Paul and Duluth) when it was being built. The city of Barnum, section 1, was incorporated as a village in 1967; had a station of the Northern Pacific and a post office from 1872.

BESEMANN TOWNSHIP was named for a former German landowner there, Ernst Besemann, who removed to Chaska.

BLACK HOOF was named for the creek that flows circuitously through this township to the Nemadji River. It is translated from the Ojibwe name of the creek. A station of the Soo Line with a post office, 1921–24, was in section 23.

BROWNELL a station of the Northern Pacific Railroad located in Thomson Township, section 2.

CARLTON a city and the county seat in Twin Lakes Township, took its name, like the county, in honor of Reuben B. Carlton. From the building of the Northern Pacific Railroad in 1870 to 1891, this place was called Northern Pacific Junction, being at the junction of that transcontinental line with the older Lake Superior and Mississippi line. The city began as a lumbering community, with power supplied by the St. Louis River and Otter Creek for a planing mill; the St. Joseph and Mary log cabin church was built in the early 1800s west of the city.

CHUB LAKE a station of the Burlington Northern located in Twin Lakes Township.

CLOQUET (retaining the French pronunciation of its last syllable, as in *bouquet* and *sobriquet*), incorporated as a city, was named for the Cloquet River from which, and from other tributaries of the St. Louis River, came the logs of its lumber manufacturing. The map of Stephen H. Long's expedition, in 1823, shows that stream as Rapid River, and it is unnamed on the map by David Thompson in 1826 for the proposed routes of the international boundary; but on Joseph N. Nicollet's map, published in 1843, it has the present title, Cloquet River. It is not used outside of Minnesota as a geographic name, and here was probably derived from some fur trader. It is applied also to an island of the Mississippi in section 10, Dayton Township, Hennepin County.

The city begun as a lumber town in Knife Falls Township in 1878 and was known as Knife Falls until 1886; it was platted in 1882; the post office was called Knife Falls in 1879, changing to Cloquet in 1880; a site called Dunlap was annexed in 1884. Nearly all of the town was leveled by the forest fire of October 12, 1918. Industries include Northwest Paper Company, founded by Weyerhaeuser interests in 1898; Wood Conversion Company, started by Weyerhaeuser in 1921; Diamond Match Company, founded in 1929; and USG Acoustical Products Company. It is also the site of the University of Minnesota Cloquet Forestry Center.

CORONA the Latin word meaning "a crown," was first given to a station of the Northern Pacific Railway, perhaps because it is near the highest land crossed between Lake Superior and the Mississippi, and thence it was given to the township, in accordance with the petition of the settlers. The village of Corona in section 5 had a post office, 1910–21, and a general store.

CROMWELL a city in the south edge of Red Clover Township, section 33, was organized January 17, 1891, receiving its name from the Northern Pacific Railroad company. It was incorporated as a village in 1903; the post office was established in 1882.

DUESLER a village in Blackhoof Township, section 33; had a station on the Soo Line, and a post office, 1925–35, Charles W. Carlson, postmaster, at Carlson general store.

DUNLAP see CLOQUET.

EAGLE TOWNSHIP was named for its Eagle Lake. Our common species is the bald eagle, so called for its white head, found throughout Minnesota, nesting in large trees, preferably on lakeshores or islands.

ELKTON a locality in T. 46, R. 19, circa 1874–87.

ESKO a community in Thomson Township, sections 21, 22, 27, and 28, with a post office since 1935; it has a Finnish personal name.

FINLAND see KETTLE RIVER.

FOXBORO a village in Holyoke Township, section 1, circa 1892–94, near the Nemadji dam.

FROGNER a station on the Soo Line in Wrenshall Township, section 13.

GREELY a station of the Northern Pacific Railroad, located in Thomson Township (T. 48, R. 16), section 11.

HARNEY a community in Thomson Township, section 14; first settled in 1896 with a flour mill and a station on the Duluth Winnipeg and Pacific Railway; its post office operated 1896–1904 and 1920–54.

HOLYOKE TOWNSHIP organized in 1903, received its name from the earlier railway station, where it was given by the Great Northern Railway company. The logging village in section 17 had a hotel, a general store, and a post office established in 1894.

HOWELL a village in Thomson Township (T. 48, R. 16), section 2.

HUSON a station of the Great Northern Railway located in Silver Brook Township, section 22.

IVERSON a village in Twin Lakes Township, section 5, had a station of the Northern Pacific Railroad and a post office, 1909–27, operated by postmaster, Joseph P. Pfeifer, in his general store. The station was named by the Northern Pacific Railroad company for Ole Iverson, a pioneer settler there.

JUNCTION see CARLTON.

KALEVALA a post office, 1901–13, in Automba Township, section 26; Matt Johnson was postmaster at his homestead; next Herman Lampel became postmaster on his farm near Kettle River until the post office was absorbed by Kettle River.

KALEVALA TOWNSHIP has many Finnish settlers, by whom it was given this name of the national epic poem of Finland, meaning "the abode or land of heroes." English translations of it were published in 1888 and in 1907. "The elements of the poem are ancient popular songs.... The poem owes its present coherent form to Elias Lönnrot (1802–84), who during years of assiduous labor collected the material in Finland proper, but principally in Russian Karelia eastward to the White Sea.... The Kalevala is written in eight-syllabled trochaic verse, with alliteration, but without rime. The whole is divided into fifty cantos or runes. Its subject matter is mythical, with a few Christian elements. Its central hero is

Wainamoinen, the god of poetry and music. It is the prototype, in form and contents, of Longfellow's 'Hiawatha'" (*Century Cyclopedia of Names*).

KETTLE RIVER a city in Silver Township, section 9, is named for the river, a translation of its Ojibwe name, Akiko sibi. The original townsite plat was called Finland; the Finnish word *Kattilajoki* means "kettle river city." Its post office was established in 1910, with Joseph Winquist postmaster in his general store; it absorbed the Kalevala post office in 1913. The store was destroyed in the 1918 forest fire. The city had a station of the Great Northern and Soo Line Railroads.

KNIFE FALLS see CLOQUET.

KNIFE FALLS TOWNSHIP is named for the falls of the St. Louis River, falling 16 feet, in the west part of section 13, east of Cloquet. On the canoe route used by fur traders during 100 years, these falls were passed by a portage about a mile long on the south side of the river, of which Prof. Newton H. Winchell wrote: "It is well named Knife portage, because where it starts, and for some distance, the slates are thin, perpendicular, and sharp like knives."

KOMOKA a village in Twin Lakes Township, section 2.

LAKE VIEW TOWNSHIP having Tamarack Lake, nearly two miles long, adjoining tamarack woods, and several other lakes of small size, received this name by vote of the settlers.

LALONE see BARKER.

LINDSAY a station of the Northern Pacific Railroad in Knife Falls Township, section 36.

MAHTOWA TOWNSHIP has a name formed from the Dakota *mahto* and the last syllable of the Ojibwe *makwa*, each meaning "a bear"; sometimes seen as Mah-to-wa. The village of Mahtowa, section 9, was settled in 1875 with a station of the Northern Pacific Railroad and a post office, established in 1898.

MOOSE LAKE TOWNSHIP has reference to its Moose Lake and Moose Head Lake, each probably translated from their original Ojibwe names. The city of Moose Lake had a station of the Northern Pacific and Soo Line Railroads in section 20; its first house was built by John Coutia about 1869. Frank Duquette was the first merchant, moving there after Little Moose Station on the old military road closed, and served as first postmaster in 1872. Cornelius McCabe built the first full-service store, with a hall upstairs for meetings, known as McCabe Hall. One hundred ninety-eight persons from Moose Lake perished in the forest fire of October 12, 1918.

N.P. JUNCTION see CARLTON.

NEMADJI the Soo Line station in Barnum Township, received this Ojibwe name from the Nemadji River meaning Left Hand River. The name refers to its being next on the left hand when one passes from Lake Superior into the St. Louis River. The village of Nemadji, in section 11, had a post office, 1912–53; Erick Lind was the first postmaster, and later his wife, I. C. Lind, was postmaster in their general store.

NORMAN a village in Sawyer Township, section 4, with a flag stop of the Northern Pacific Railroad.

NORTH END a village in Twin Lakes Township, section 10, with a station of the Great Northern Railway.

OTTER CREEK a village in Silver Brook Township, section 19, with a station of the Northern Pacific Railroad in section 20.

PERCH LAKE TOWNSHIP is named for its Perch Lake, which is somewhat larger than its adjacent Big Lake, each being very probably translations of the aboriginal names.

PICKERING a village in Mahtowa Township, section 18.

PINE GROVE a village in Twin Lakes Township, sections 5 and 8.

PLEASANT VALLEY a village in Wrenshall Township, section 21, with a station of the Soo Line and a general store.

PROGRESS has a euphonious and auspicious name, selected by the petitioners for the township organization.

RED CLOVER TOWNSHIP was named similarly with the last noted. This beautiful and highly valued species of clover is of Old World origin, but it is nearly everywhere cultivated with grasses in the sowing of lands for hay.

RHODES MILL a station of the Great Northern Railway; location not found.

SALO a settlement in Kalevala Township, section 8, with a general store and post office, 1903–35; its post office building was one of the few buildings remaining as of 1970. Its name is of Finnish derivation.

SAWYER a railway station in Atkinson Township,

was named by the officers of the Northern Pacific Railroad company; the station was first named Zebulon. The village, in section 4, had a post office, established in 1891, and a sawmill, a hotel, and a general store.

SCANLON the lumber manufacturing village in Thomson Township, sections 19 and 30, between Cloquet and Carlton, was named for M. Joseph Scanlon, president of the Brooks-Scanlon Company, Minneapolis. He was born in Lyndon, Wis., August 24, 1861, settled in Minneapolis in 1889, and engaged in many large enterprises of logging, the manufacture of lumber, and building and operating railroads to supply logs. In addition to his company's very large lumber interests at this village, he conducted similar lumbering and sawmills at Cass Lake, and also in Oregon, Louisiana, and Florida. The community was incorporated as a village in 1902. It was served by the Great Northern, Northern Pacific, and Milwaukee Railroads; its post office, located in the general store, operated 1901–54.

SILVER TOWNSHIP has a euphonious name chosen by its settlers for the Silver Creek there tributary to the Kettle River.

SKELTON TOWNSHIP was named for two brothers, John and Harry E. Skelton, who lived in the village of Barnum. The former was the county surveyor in 1897–1901, and the latter was judge of probate for the county, 1901–4, dying in office.

SPLIT ROCK TOWNSHIP was named for the small river flowing through it, on which ledges of slates and schists have been deeply channeled near its mouth, the rocks of the opposite banks appearing therefore as if split apart.

STATE LINE a station of the Northern Pacific Railroad in Wrenshall Township, nine miles southeast of Carlton.

SUMMIT a village in Thomson Township (T. 49, R. 16), sections 23 to 26.

SUOMI a post office, 1894–95; location not found.

THOMSON TOWNSHIP received its name from the station and village of the St. Paul and Duluth and Northern Pacific Railroads, built in 1870. This village was the county seat from that date until 1886 and was incorporated as a village in 1891; it had a post office, 1870–1955. The name was given by officers of the former line in honor of David Thompson, the Canadian explorer and geographer, but it has been generally spelled as if for

James Thomson (1700–1748), the Scottish poet, author of "The Seasons." Articles in the St. Paul newspapers of 1869 and 1870, however, spelled the name Thompson and stated it was named for J. Edgar Thompson, president of the Pennsylvania Central Railroad.

David Thompson was born in Westminster (now a part of London), England, April 30, 1770, and died in Longueuil, near Montreal, February 10, 1857. He was in the service of the Hudson Bay Company, 1784–97, and of the North West Company the next 18 years. In the spring of 1798 he traveled from the mouth of the Assiniboine River, the site of the city of Winnipeg, to Pembina, thence to the trading house of the North West Company on the site of Red Lake Falls, thence by the Clearwater and Red Lake Rivers to Red Lake, thence by Turtle Lake and River to Red Cedar Lake (now Cass Lake), thence down the Mississippi to the North West trading post on Sandy Lake, thence by the Savanna Rivers and portage to the St. Louis River, and down this river, past the site of Thomson, to the trading post at Fond du Lac, and thence along the south shore of Lake Superior to Sault Ste. Marie. Thompson's account of this journey through northern Minnesota, with descriptions of the rivers and lakes and the country traversed, forms chapters XVI to XIX in his *Narrative of Explorations in Western America, 1784–1812*, edited by J. B. Tyrrell, published in 1916 as volume XII (pp. xcviii, 582, with maps and sketches), Publications of the Champlain Society. This work is reviewed, with a biographic sketch of Thompson, in the *Minnesota History Bulletin* (vol. 1, pp. 522–27, November 1916).

TWIN LAKES TOWNSHIP was named for its two small lakes in section 36, on the first road laid out from St. Paul, through Chisago and Pine Counties, to the head of Lake Superior. A map of Minnesota in 1856 by Silas Chapman shows this road with a small settlement named Twin Lakes, which was the only locality indicated as having inhabitants in Carlton County. Its nearest railroad point was Blackhoof. It was nominally the county seat until Thomson was so designated by the legislative act of February 18, 1870. The settlement had a post office, 1856–70.

WINGATE a station of the Northern Pacific and Great Northern Railroads, located in Silver Brook Township, section 21.

WOODBURY a locality in Red Clover Township, section 31, on Woodbury Lake.

WRENSHALL a city in Silver Brook Township, sections 20, 21, 28, and 29; incorporated as a village on March 17, 1926. The post office was established in 1893 with John Habhegger as first postmaster in his general store; it had a station of the Northern Pacific and Milwaukee Railroads in section 28.

WRENSHALL TOWNSHIP was named from the railway station and village, which received this name from the Northern Pacific Railroad company. It is for C. C. Wrenshall, who during several years was in charge of maintenance and repairs of bridges for this railway.

WRIGHT a city in Lake View Township, sections 3 and 4, recalls the work of George Burdick Wright, who during many years was engaged in land examinations and locating new settlers in northern and western Minnesota. He was born in Williston, Vt., June 21, 1835, and died in Fergus Falls, Minn., April 29, 1882. He came to Minnesota in 1856 and first settled in Minneapolis; was the principal founder of Fergus Falls, in 1871; and secured the building of a branch of the Northern Pacific Railroad in 1881–82 from Wadena to Fergus Falls and Breckenridge.

The name also had a second and equal reason for being chosen, to commemorate Charles Barstow Wright of Philadelphia, Pa., who was a director of the Northern Pacific Railroad company, 1870–74, and was its president from 1875 for four years, during a period of restoration of business credit and prosperity after the great financial panic and depression of 1873. For Minnesota, in 1877–78 he directed the construction of the Western Railroad, a line between St. Paul and Brainerd, which became a part of the Northern Pacific system. The village had a Northern Pacific Railroad station, and its post office began in 1894.

ZEBULON see **SAWYER**.

Lakes and Streams

The preceding list has sufficiently referred to Black Hoof Creek, Cloquet River (north of Carlton County), Eagle Lake, Knife Falls and portage of the St. Louis River, Tamarack Lake, Moose and Moose Head Lakes, Nemadji River, Perch Lake and Big Lake, Split Rock River, and the Twin Lakes.

West and East Net Rivers (or Creeks) in Holyoke are probably translated from their Ojibwe names, referring to nets for catching fish.

Skunk, Deer, Mud, and Clear Creeks, flowing into Nemadji River, need no explanations, and the same may be said of Otter Creek at Carlton, probably an Ojibwe name translated, and of Midway and Hay Creeks in Thomson, the former being midway between Thomson and Fond du Lac.

Stony Brook, the outlet of Perch Lake; Tamarack River flowing west from Tamarack Lake; Moose Horn and Dead Moose Rivers and Otter Brook (now called Silver Creek), each flowing from the west into the Kettle River; and Moose River, its tributary from the east, are likewise of obvious or simple derivations, some or all of them being translations of the Ojibwe names.

Portage River, an eastern branch of Moose River, refers to the portage from it to the head stream of Nemadji River, being an ancient aboriginal and French name.

Gillespie Brook in Silver Township bears probably the name of an early lumberman or trapper.

This county has two Silver Creeks, one flowing to the Kettle River in Silver Township, the other a smaller stream heading about a mile south of Carlton and flowing three miles east to the St. Louis River.

In Ahkeek Lake, Corona, lately called Kettle Lake, we have the Ojibwe name and its English translation, this lake being near the most northern sources of the Kettle River.

Other names of lakes in this county, some being translations, and nearly all being of evident origin or meaning, include Dead Fish Lake in section 12, Progress; White Fish Lake (lately called Big Lake), one to two miles south of Barnum village; Bear Lake close east of Barnum, and another Bear Lake in section 4, Black Hoof; Coffee, Echo, and Sand Lakes in the south part of Moose Lake Township; Chub and Hay Lakes in Twin Lakes Township; Rocky Lake (now called Park Lake) in Atkinson; and Island Lake on the Northern Pacific Railroad, whence the early name of its station there was Island Lake, later changed to Cromwell.

Cole Lake in sections 7 and 8, Lake View, was named for James Cole, a Civil War veteran, who was a homesteader there; and Woodbury Lake section 31, Red Clover, similarly commemorates an early settler.

Hanging Horn Lake, crossed by the west line of section 7, Barnum, translates its Ojibwe name, as also probably Horn Lake in section 3, Atkinson.

Moran Lake in section 8, Atkinson, was named for Henry P. Moran, an early Irish homesteader and trapper.

Venoah Lake (formerly called Mink Lake), three miles south of Carlton, received its present name in compliment to the daughters, Winona and Marie, of Judge F. A. Watkins, who kindly supplied much information for this chapter. The lake name was coined from their pet names as children about 20 years ago.

State Parks

In 1915 and 1916, Minnesota received by donation from the estate of Jay Cooke more than 2,000 acres of land, bordering each side of the St. Louis River through its winding course of about ten miles, from the Northern Pacific Railroad at Carlton and Thomson, along its rapids and falls descending 395 feet in crossing Range 16, to the east line of the county and state. With additional adjoining lands of equal or greater area, expected to be obtained by further donations and by purchases, a large state park was planned, to preserve these Dalles of the St. Louis for the enjoyment and recreation of the people.

Jay Cooke was born in Sandusky, Ohio, August 10, 1821, and died at Ogontz, near Philadelphia, Pa., February 16, 1905. In 1861 he founded in Philadelphia the banking house of Jay Cooke and Company, and during the next four years of the Civil War he was the principal financial agent of the federal government, negotiating loans for the war expenses to a value of about $2 billion. In 1873 his house failed, on account of too heavy investments in the Northern Pacific bonds.

"Before the financial crash of 1873, Mr. Cooke regarded himself as one of the richest men of the country. He built in the beautiful suburbs of Philadelphia a palace which, for size and costliness, had scarcely an equal on this side of the Atlantic. In this palace, called 'Ogontz,' he dispensed a lavish hospitality. He had also a summer residence named 'Gibraltar,' on a rocky cape at the entrance of Sandusky Bay on Lake Erie. . . . After the crash came he lived for a long time in retirement in a little cottage, in the country, near Philadelphia, to all appearances a broken man. But after getting through the bankruptcy courts, he reappeared in business circles in Philadelphia, occupied his old office on South Third street, and began to build up a second fortune.... His career offers the rare instance of a man losing one fortune and making another when past the meridian of life" (Eugene V. Smalley, *History of the Northern Pacific Railroad*, 1883).

Sixteen years later than the writing here cited, his wealth "was estimated to be as large as at any period of his life." He was a generous patron of education, of churches, and of charities, and in his later years spent much of his time in the recreations of hunting and fishing. An excellent biography, *Jay Cooke, Financier of the Civil War*, by Ellis Paxson Oberholtzer, was published in 1907 (two vols., pp. 658, 590, with portraits and many other illustrations).

The county gained a second state park in 1971. The state turned 965 acres from the Moose Lake State Hospital farm over to the Department of Natural Resources for Moose Lake State Park. The park, off Interstate 35, includes Moosehead and Echo Lakes, both formed by melting ice when the glaciers retreated. The surrounding area is glacial till.

Fond du Lac Reservation

The reservation for the Fond du Lac band of the Lake Superior Ojibwe, established by a treaty at La Pointe, Wis., September 30, 1854, comprises the present Knife Falls and Perch Lake Townships, with the edges of the adjoining townships in this county, and thence reaches north to the St. Louis River, thus including a tract in St. Louis County equivalent to about two townships. The name Fond du Lac, meaning the farther end or head of the lake, was applied by the early French traders and voyageurs to their trading post on the north side of the St. Louis River, where its strong current is slackened by coming nearly to the level of Lake Superior, which, in its extension of St. Louis Bay, is about two miles away. The same name was given also to this river, called "R. du Fond du Lac" on Jean Baptiste Louis Franquelin's map, 1688, renamed St. Louis by Gilles Robert de Vaugondy's map in 1755.

Glacial Lakes St. Louis, Nemadji, and Duluth

Prof. N. H. Winchell, in the fourth volume (published in 1899) of the *Final Report of the Geological Survey of Minnesota*, gave the names St. Louis and Nemadji to two early and relatively small glacial lakes in Carlton County, which successively outflowed to the Moose and Kettle Rivers by channels in Mahtowa and Barnum Townships, respectively about 1,125 and 1,070 feet above the sea. They were followed by the slightly lower Glacial Lake Duluth, named by Frank B. Taylor of the U.S. Geological Survey, which in its maximum stage occupied a large area of the Lake Superior basin, with outlet at the head of the Brulé River in Douglas County, Wis., to the Upper St. Croix Lake and River.

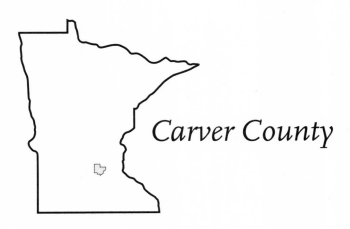

Carver County

This county, established February 20, 1855, was named for Capt. Jonathan Carver, explorer and author, who was born in Wyemouth, Massachusetts, on April 13, 1710, and died in London, England, January 31, 1780. He commanded a company in the French war, and in 1763, when the treaty of peace was declared, he resolved to explore the newly acquired possessions of Great Britain in the Northwest. In 1766 he traveled from Boston to the upper Mississippi River and spent the ensuing winter with the Dakota on the Minnesota River in the vicinity of the site of New Ulm. On his return, according to statements published after his death, he negotiated a treaty, May 1, 1767, at Carver's Cave, in the east edge of the present city of St. Paul, by which the Dakota granted to him a large tract of land on the east side of the Mississippi. Carver continued his explorations by a canoe journey along the north and east shore of Lake Superior. He returned to Boston in October 1768, soon sailed to England, and spent the remainder of his life in London.

Carver's *Travels through the Interior Parts of North America*, a volume of 543 pp., with two maps, was published in London in 1778, and new editions were issued the next year in London and in Dublin. After the author's death, his friend Dr. John C. Lettsom contributed to the third London edition, in 1781, a biographic account of Capt. Carver, in 22 pp., including the first publication of the deed or grant of land obtained by Carver from the Dakota.

Several American editions of this work, with abridgment and changes, were published during the years 1784 to 1838, and translations of it into German, French, and Dutch were published respectively in 1780, 1784, and 1796.

The Minnesota River is noted on Carver's map of his *Travels* as "River St. Pierre, call'd by the Natives Wadapawmenesoter," this being one of the earliest records of the Dakota name of this river and state. At its north side, nearly opposite to the site of New Ulm, three Dakota teepees are pictured, with the statement that "About here the Author Winter'd in 1766."

Numerous endeavors made by heirs of Capt. Carver and by others to whom their rights were assigned for establishing their claims and ownership of the large tract deeded to him by the Dakota have been narrated by Rev. John Mattocks in his address at the Carver centenary celebration in 1867, published in vol. 2 of the Minnesota Historical Society Collections; by John Fletcher Williams in his *History of the City of St. Paul and of the County of Ramsey*, forming vol. 4 in the same series, published in 1876; and most fully, with many documents submitted to the U.S. Congress relating to the Carver claims, in an article by Daniel S. Durrie, to which Lyman C. Draper added important footnotes, in vol. 6, pp. 220–70, of the Wisconsin Historical Society Collections, published in 1872.

Between 40 and 45 years after Carver's death, the supposed rights of his heirs under the deed were denied and annulled in Congress by the Committees on Public Lands and on Private Land

Claims. One of the grounds for this decision was that no citizens, but only the state, whether Great Britain, as in 1767, or the United States after the treaty of 1783, could so receive ownership of lands from the aborigines.

———

Information of origins and meanings of geographic names in this county has been gathered from History of the Minnesota Valley, *1882, pp. 352–410; from* Compendium of History and Biography of Carver and Hennepin Counties, *R. I. Holcombe, historical editor, 1915, pp. 187–342; and from John Glaeser, judge of probate; Albert Meyer, register of deeds; and Hon. Frederick E. Du Toit, Sr., each of Chaska, interviewed during a visit there in July 1916.*

ASSUMPTION a village in section 18, Hancock, received its name from the Catholic church there, referring to the ascent of the Virgin Mary into heaven and its anniversary, celebrated on August 15. Its post office operated 1881–1906, after being established in Sibley County.

AUGUSTA a railway station in section 3, Dahlgren, was named in honor of the wives of two settlers, each having this name and having come from Augusta in Eau Claire County, Wis. The village Augusta, on the border of Dahlgren and Laketown Townships, had a post office, beginning in 1861 as Oberles Corners, Frederick Oberle, postmaster, changing in 1883 when it moved to the Ernst Poppizt general store.

BAVARIA LAKE SETTLEMENT a Dutch colony near Bavaria Lake in Chanhassen and Laketown Townships, circa 1852–53.

BENTON JUNCTION a station of the Minneapolis, St. Paul and Sault Ste. Marie Railroad (Soo Line) in Dahlgren Township, section 8.

BENTON TOWNSHIP first settled in May 1855, organized May 11, 1858, was named, like Benton County, in honor of the distinguished U.S. Senator Thomas Hart Benton, whose life and public services are more fully noted in the chapter for that county. He died April 10, 1858, a month before this township was organized and named. The village of Benton, on the northeast shore of the little Lake Benton and a half mile north of Cologne, platted in June 1880, was incorporated in March 1881; it had a post office, 1861–83.

BEVENS CREEK a village in Benton Township, section 24, named for two St. Paul brothers, Corydon D. and Henry L. Bevens; it had a post office from April to May in 1873, when it was transferred to East Union.

BONGARD a village in Benton Township, section 17; its post office operated at various times, 1872–1976, with Gerhard Bongard as first postmaster; it had a station of the Soo Line, a creamery, a grain elevator, and a feed mill.

CAMDEN TOWNSHIP settled in July 1856, had a village platted and a post office established in the same year, but this township was not organized until the spring of 1859. It was named doubtless for some one of the 18 villages and cities of this name in the older eastern and southern states, of which the largest is the city of Camden, N.J., on the Delaware River, opposite to Philadelphia.

CARVER a very small fractional township bordering on the Minnesota River, was named, like this county, in honor of Jonathan Carver. The first settlers came in 1851–52, and the township was organized May 11, 1858. Carver Creek named by Capt. Carver for himself, the outlet of Clearwater or Waconia Lake and numerous other lakes of smaller size, here joins the Minnesota River. On Joseph N. Nicollet's map it is "Odowan R.," which is the Dakota word for a song or hymn. The city of Carver, located at the intersection of several railroads, was platted in February 1857 and was incorporated February 17, 1877, comprising all the township. Carver Creek supplied power for an early flour mill; the village also had a wool carding mill, a grist mill, and a feed mill; its post office was established in 1856. In the 1930s a large dance pavilion was built, financed by stock sales; about 1969 an organization called Carver-on-the-Mississippi, Inc., began restoring homes and buildings.

CARVER BEACH an area of Chanhassen.

CHANHASSEN TOWNSHIP received its earliest settlers in June 1852 and was organized May 11, 1858.

The name, adopted on the suggestion of Rev. Henry M. Nichols, means the "sugar maple," being formed of two Dakota words, *chan* (tree) and *hassen* (for *hasan*, from *haza* or *hah-zah*, the huckleberry or blueberry), thus signifying "the tree of sweet juice." The township merged on May 8, 1967, with the village of Watertown. The city of Chanhassen, sections 12 and 13, and extending into Hennepin County, was incorporated as a village on April 25, 1896; its post office, 1854–63, began in Hennepin County and transferred to Carver County in 1857. The village was permanently settled in 1881, and a post office was reestablished in 1882.

CHASKA TOWNSHIP and city, the county seat, have, unlike the preceding name, the French sound of *ch* like *sh*. This was the name generally given in a Dakota family to the first-born child if a son, as Winona was the general name of a first-born daughter. This word is pronounced by the Dakota, and by Rev. Stephen R. Riggs's dictionary, with the English sound of *ch* (as in charm), and with the long vowel sound in the last syllable, as if spelled *kay*, but common usage of the white people has given erroneously the French pronunciation (*ch* as in charade), with the last syllable short, like Alaska.

The earliest permanent settlers came in 1853, and the date of the township organization was May 11, 1858. The village was founded in June 1854 by the Shaska Company "(the name was thus misspelled in the act of incorporation of the company)." March 6, 1871, it was incorporated as a village, and on March 3, 1891, as a city ; its post office was established in 1854 in Hennepin County and transferred to Carver County in 1855. One of its first industries was the manufacture of brick, and by 1900 there were ten brick yards employing about 600 men and making 60 million bricks annually; later businesses were the Samels Bros. and White Canning Company, W. A. Gedney Co., pickle packers, and the Minnesota Sugar Company. The Beyrer Brewery is listed on the historical register as the county's last surviving brewer with original equipment in operable condition, and the Crystal Sugar Plant is the oldest surviving sugar beet processing plant in Minnesota. A small lake at the southwest side of the city is named Chaska Lake, and a creek here tributary to the Minnesota River is likewise called Chaska Creek. See also JONATHAN.

COLOGNE a city in Benton Township, section 13, platted in August 1880, incorporated as a village on February 9, 1881, and reincorporated on October 29, 1913, was named by German settlers for the large and ancient city of Cologne (the German Köln) on the Rhine. The post office began in 1879, with Peter Wirt as first postmaster in his hardware store. The village had a station served by several railroads.

CONEY ISLAND a railway hamlet and summer resort at the north side of Clearwater Lake, in Waconia Township, section 2, was named from the island of 37 acres in the southern part of the lake near Waconia village. The island was named for the popular Coney Island beach of Long Island near New York City. The adoption of this name, however, was suggested by its similarity in sound with Waconia. The island was purchased in 1884 by Lambert Naegele, who had it surveyed and platted, and then cleared the land and built a pavilion in the island's center and the Coney Island Hotel in 1886, the latter a two-story building of the stick style of architecture. Also in 1884 the Tivoli beer garden was opened by Peter Lindner. The community existed from 1884 to 1900; it had a flag station of the Great Northern Railway in section 1.

DAHLGREN TOWNSHIP settled in 1854, organized April 5, 1864, was named Liberty in 1863. "May 9, 1864, the name of the town was changed . . . to Dahlgren, at the suggestion of the state auditor, in honor of our distinguished admiral, because the name Liberty had already been appropriated by another town in the state" (*History of the Minnesota Valley*). John Adolphus Bernard Dahlgren, of Swedish parentage, was born in Philadelphia, November 13, 1809, and died in the city of Washington, July 12, 1870. He became a lieutenant in the U.S. Navy in 1837, was assigned to ordnance duty in Washington, 1847, and introduced important improvements in naval armament, including the Dahlgren gun, which he invented. He was appointed chief of the bureau of ordnance, July 18, 1862, became a rear admiral, February 7, 1863, and gained renown for his service through the Civil War. His biography, by his widow, was published in 1882 (660 pp., with two portraits).

The village of Dahlgren, in sections 10 and 15, had a station of the Chicago, Milwaukee and St. Paul Railroad; a post office, 1872–86, John Lorfield being first postmaster at his hotel; a flour mill; and a sash and door factory.

EAST HAMBURG a village in Young America Township, section 28, circa 1927.

EAST UNION a village in Dahlgren Township, section 34, settled in 1853 by Swedish immigrants, most being from Vara and Herrljunga parishes in Västergötland, who named the community Oscar's Settlement or King Oscar's Settlement in honor of Oscar I, who was then king of Sweden and Norway. In 1858 they established a Swedish Lutheran congregation named Union with about 100 families, which later that year was divided into two areas, one part called East Union, which eventually became the name of the entire community. The post office, 1873–1903, was briefly called Bevens Creek; the community had a cooperative creamery, a sorghum mill, and a grist mill.

ELM GROVE a post office, 1858–60; location not found.

GÖTAHOLM a Swedish Lutheran congregation settlement near Watertown, established in 1858; the name combines Göta as in Götaland, Sweden, the home area of most of the settlers, and Holm, an abbreviation of the Latin Holmiensis (from Stockholm) associated with Johannes Campanius, a Swedish missionary to the Indians of the New Sweden colony.

GOTHA a village in sections 1 and 2, Hancock, was named for the ancient city of Gotha, in central Germany; it had a post office, 1884–1902, with Vitalis Ahlen, postmaster in his general store, a creamery, and a windmill factory.

HAMBURG a city in sections 28 and 33, Young America, was named for the great German city and port of Hamburg, on the River Elbe, which was founded and fortified by Charlemagne about the beginning of the ninth century. It was incorporated as a village on May 1, 1900; the post office was spelled Hamburgh from 1881 to 1892, at which time it changed to the present spelling. The village had a sawmill, two creameries, a grain elevator, and a station of the Chicago and North Western Railroad.

HANCOCK TOWNSHIP settled in the spring of 1856, organized March 23, 1868, was named in honor of Winfield Scott Hancock. He was born at Montgomery Square, Pa., February 14, 1824; died at Governor's Island, N.Y., February 9, 1886. After graduation at West Point, 1844, he served as lieutenant in the Mexican War, was a general during the Civil War, and was commander of the military department of the Atlantic, 1872–86. In the presidential campaign of 1880, he was the unsuccessful Democratic candidate.

HAZELTINE a locality in Chanhassen Township, section 20, which had a station of the Chicago, Milwaukee and St. Paul Railway; now the site of a golf course.

HAZELTON a station in Hollywood Township, section 10, on the Luce Electric Line and other railroads, five miles north of New Germany.

HELVETIA a small village near the southeast corner of Hollywood Township, was platted in the autumn of 1856 and named Helvetia by John Buhler, an immigrant from Switzerland, of which this was the ancient Latin name. A post office with the same name was in Hollywood Township, section 31, 1875–88, at which time it was transferred to Mayer; the first postmaster was Jacob Lahr, who owned flour mills and sawmills.

HOLLYWOOD TOWNSHIP was settled in 1856 and organized April 3, 1860. Matthew Kelly, an Irish settler, proposed the township name, saying that he had seen the shrub named holly, which is common in Ireland, growing here in the woods. After the name had been adopted, it was ascertained that the European holly does not occur in this country, but Minnesota has two species of this family, found rarely on bluffs of Lake Pepin, the St. Croix River, and northward. The township had a post office, 1869–70 and 1882–98, in section 14.

HYDES LAKE a village in Waconia Township, near the city of Waconia, circa 1940.

JONATHAN a planned community in Chaska Township, now part of the city of Chaska, based on plans of Henry Turney McKnight, a Minnesota state senator, who died in 1972, and named after Jonathan Carver. The community, begun in 1969 on 2,200 of a proposed 5,000-acre site, comprised five villages, an industrial park, and a town center, completed in 1987. Each village consisted of a mix of single family units, rental and condominium apartments, and row houses; schools; churches; recreation facilities and parks;

and a supermarket. The Y-shaped town center contained stores, offices, theaters, and restaurants. The community had a station of the Chicago, Milwaukee and St. Paul Railroad in section 21. The Hazeltine Golf Course was designed as part of the community.

KING OSCAR'S SETTLEMENT see EAST UNION.

LA BELLE a post office, 1856–57; location not found.

LAKE AUBURN a village in Laketown Township, section 11, circa 1927–40.

LAKETOWN so named on the suggestion of John Salter for its ten small lakes and the large Clearwater Lake on its west boundary, was first settled in April 1853 and was organized May 11, 1858. It was at first called Liberty but was renamed as now on June 12, 1858, a month after the organization. The Swedish community on the east side of Clearwater Lake has been often called Scandia, the ancient Roman name for the southern part of Sweden. See also VICTORIA.

MAPLE a station on the Great Northern Railway, Waconia Township, section 3, with a creamery nearby.

MASSES a village in Laketown Township, section 4, with a station of the Great Northern Railway.

MAYER a city on the line between Camden and Waconia Townships, was named by officers of the Great Northern Railway company. It was incorporated as a village on August 28, 1900; the post office was at Helvetia before being transferred here in 1888. The community had several sawmills and flour mills, a sorghum mill, and a creamery. A station of the Great Northern Railway was in section 1 of Camden Township.

MINNETONKA HEIGHTS a village in Laketown Township, section 1, circa 1898.

MINNEWASHTA a village mainly of summer homes on the northeast end of the largest lake in Chanhassen, received its name from the lake. It consists of two Dakota words, *minne*, water, and *washta*, good.

MOTORDALE see NEW GERMANY.

MUDCURA a townsite mentioned in the *Norwood Times*, December 2, 1938, in regard to a group of residents meeting to vote on the organization of a new village.

MURPHY a village in Watertown Township, on the Minneapolis and St. Louis Railroad.

MURRAY HILL a village in Chanhassen Township, section 3, circa 1898–1928.

NAVAHO HEIGHTS a village in Waconia Township, section 6, circa 1927.

NEW GERMANY a city in sections 4 and 5, Camden, was named in compliment to the many German settlers in its vicinity. During World War I, this name was changed to Motordale, on account of popular indignation against Germany. It was incorporated as a village in 1901; its post office was established in 1886 as Purity and changed to New Germany in 1902 to match its railroad station. The community had feed, saw, and sorghum mills, a canning factory, and several grain elevators.

NORWOOD a city in sections 14 and 15, Young America, platted in 1872 and incorporated in 1881, is said to have been "named by Mr. [James] Slocum, an early banker there, for an eastern relative or friend of his wife." Fifteen villages and post offices in eastern and southern states have this name. The post office began in 1873, with Slocum as first postmaster. The community had a number of general and specialty stores, artisans, workshops, and lumber dealers, and a station of the Chicago and North Western and Soo Line railroads in section 14. In January 1997 the town merged with Young America to become Norwood Young America.

OBERLES CORNERS see AUGUSTA.

PAULBERT a post office, 1917–18, on the Luce Electric Line, with a general store, a grain elevator, and a lumber company; location not found.

PLEASANT VIEW a village and summer resort in section 1, Chanhassen, at the north end of Long Lake, circa 1913–27, was thus euphoniously named by its proprietors.

PURITY see NEW GERMANY.

RED CEDAR POINT a village in Chanhassen Township, sections 5 and 8, circa 1927.

REDFIELD a post office, 1863–72; location not found.

ROCKY RUN a post office, 1860–74, established in McLeod County, transferring to Carver County in 1870; location not found.

ST. CLAIR a village in Camden Township, incorporated on May 19, 1857, and first called Hiawatha; had a post office, 1856–58; no trace of the site remains.

SAN FRANCISCO a fractional township beside the Minnesota River, settled in 1854 and organized May 11, 1858, was named by William Foster, who in 1854 platted and so named a village site on his claim, taking this name from the metropolis of California. The village flourished only about ten years, and its site then reverted to be farming land. It had a post office, 1856–58 and 1861–62.

SCANDIA a village in Laketown Township, was first settled in the mid-1850s, when seven Swedish families arrived, and incorporated on May 19, 1857. The village had a postal station, 1856–66, with Andrew Bergquist, first postmaster, located near Gotaholm on Clear Water Lake (now called Waconia Lake); no trace remains.

SHADY POINT a village on the border of Chanhassen and Laketown Townships, circa 1927.

SUMMIT SIDING a village in Chanhassen Township, section 35, with a station of the Minneapolis and St. Louis Railroad.

SUNNYSIDE a village in Waconia Township, section 20, circa 1898.

THORNTON a station of the Great Northern Railway in Waconia Township.

UNION see EAST UNION.

VEDUM a post office, 1882–83; location not found.

VICTORIA a city in Chanhassen and Laketown Townships, was named in honor of the queen of England. It began as a station of the Minneapolis and St. Louis Railroad in Laketown Township, section 13, was incorporated as a village on December 30, 1915, and separated from the township on March 28, 1916. Its post office in section 15 of Laketown Township was called Laketown, 1860–83, at which time the name was changed to the present. See also LAKETOWN.

VINLAND a hamlet of summer homes in section 2, Chanhassen, at the south end of Christmas Lake, circa 1898–1928, was named for the region of temporary Norse settlement about the beginning of the eleventh century on the northeast coast of North America. The name is Icelandic, meaning "wine-land," because grapes were found there.

WACONIA TOWNSHIP settled in 1855, organized May 11, 1858, bears the Dakota name of its large lake, meaning a "fountain or spring." The village of Waconia was platted and named by Roswell P. Russell in March 1857. This lake is also called Clearwater Lake. "It has about 18 miles of shore, most of which is high with a gravelly beach. The water is very clear, hence its name, and well stocked with fish."

The city of Waconia was incorporated on November 2, 1881, and reincorporated on July 1, 1910, at which time it separated from the township. Its post office began in 1860. The city developed around the gristmills and sawmills of the area and the station of the Minneapolis and St. Louis Railroad, adding grain elevators, flour and sorghum mills, creameries, and hotels.

WATERTOWN first settled in 1856, organized April 13, 1858, received this name "because of the township's large water supply," by five or six lakes and the South fork of the Crow River. The city of Watertown, located on the Crow River, platted in 1858, was incorporated February 26, 1877. It merged with Chanhassen Township on May 8, 1967. A number of industries developed there, including sorghum, saw, and flour mills, plow works, hotels, a creamery, and a brewery; it had a station of the Electric Short Line. Its post office was established in Hennepin County in 1856 and moved to Carver County in 1857.

WELCOME HEIGHTS a village in Waconia Township, section 20, circa 1898.

YOUNG AMERICA TOWNSHIP had a village of this name, which was platted in section 11 in the fall of 1856 and was incorporated March 4, 1879. The same name is also given to a small lake there. At the organization of the township in 1858, it was first named Farmington, but later in that year was renamed Florence, and in 1863 it was again changed to the present name, like its village. This name is a familiar expression for the vigor and progressiveness of the young people of the United States. Its only use elsewhere as a geographic name is for a village in Cass County, Ind. The community had a station of the Minneapolis and St. Louis Railroad, a flour mill, a creamery, and grain elevators; its post office began in 1856. In January 1997 the town merged with Norwood to become Norwood Young America.

ZUMBRA HEIGHTS a station of the Chicago and North Western Railroad, located in Laketown Township, section 7.

Lakes and Streams

At the Little Rapids of the Minnesota River, adjoining the southeast quarter of section 31, Carver, a ledge of the Jordan sandstone running across the riverbed causes a fall of two feet, and again about a quarter of a mile up the river its bed is similarly crossed by this sandstone, having there a fall of slightly more than one foot. In the stage of low water, these very slight falls prevent the passage of boats, but at a fuller stage the river wholly covers the ledges, with no perceptible rapid descent, being then freely navigable. Fur trading posts were located there during many years. A lake there, close west of the river, is named Rapids Lake.

In the list of townships and villages, the origins and meanings of the names of several lakes and streams have been noted, including Lake Benton, Carver Creek, Chaska Lake and Creek, Clearwater or Waconia Lake and its Coney Island, Lake Minnewashta, Long Lake in Chanhassen, and Young America Lake.

Names given in honor of early settlers, mostly having taken homesteads on or near the lake or stream so designated, include Bevins Creek, flowing through San Francisco to the Minnesota River; Lakes Lucy, Ann, and Susan in Chanhassen, the first and second being named respectively for the wives of Burritt S. and William S. Judd, and the third for Susan Hazeltine, who taught the first school in Carver County and is also commemorated here, with her father, by Hazeltine Lake; Virginia Lake in section 6, and Bradford Lake in sections 24 and 25, Chanhassen, and Bavaria Lake, crossed by the west line of that township, named for the native land of settlers near it; Pierson, Reitz, Schutz (or Goldschmidt), Stieger (or Herman), and Watermann's Lakes in Laketown, commemorating John Pierson, Frederick Reitz, Matthias Schuetz, Carl Stieger, and Michael Wassermann, settlers near these several lakes; Buran's Lake for a German farmer adjoining it, Adolph Burandt; Lake Donders, and Hyde, Patterson, and Rutz Lakes in Waconia, the last three being for Ernst Heyd, the first county surveyor, who owned land there, William Patterson, one of the earliest settlers, and Peter Rutz; Berliner Lake in section 12, Camden, for a German settler from Berlin; Campbell Lake, section 18, Hollywood, for Patrick Campbell and his two brothers, Irish settlers; Miller's Lake in section 8, Dahlgren, for Herman

Mueller; Grüenhagen's, Heyer's, Hoeffken's, Maria, and Winkler's Lakes in Benton, the first for H. F. Grüenhagen, the second for Louis Heyer, the third for Henry Hoeffken, and the last for Ignatz Winkler; and Barnes, Brandt and Frederick's Lakes in Young America, respectively for William Barnes, the earliest homesteader there, Leroy Brandt, and Frederick Ohland.

Eagle Lake in section 34, Camden, was named for an eagle's nest there, in a very great cottonwood tree.

For Lake Auburn and Parley and Zumbra Lakes in Laketown, no information of the origin of their names has been learned.

Swede Lake in Watertown was named for its several Swedish settlers by the earliest of them, Daniel Justus, in August 1856. This neighborhood was known as Götaholm (Göta, a river of southern Sweden, *holm*, a grove). The same name, Swede Lake, was also formerly borne by the present Maria Lake, section 36, Benton.

Tiger Lake in Young America has reference to a "mountain lion," also named the cougar or puma, seen there by the first settlers. This species, very rare in Minnesota, more frequent in the region of the Rocky Mountains, was mentioned by Carver in the narration of his *Travels* as "the Tyger of America," one having been seen by him on an island of the Chippewa River, Wis. Tiger Lake was so named in May 1855 by Martin McLeod on a journey with John H. Stevens and others. "On the evening of the 20th," wrote Stevens, "we camped on a lake, and wild animals prowled around us all night long, in consequence of which Mr. McLeod called the place of our discomfort Tiger Lake" (*Personal Recollections of Minnesota*, 1890).

Several other lakes of this county have names of frequent occurrence and evident significance, as Rice Lake on the north line of Benton, and a second Rice Lake, section 36, Chanhassen, both named from their wild rice; Marsh Lake in section 26, Laketown; Mud and Oak Lakes, Watertown; and Goose and Swan Lakes in Waconia.

Cass County

Established September 1, 1851, but having remained without organization till 1897, this county commemorates the distinguished statesman Lewis Cass, who in 1820 commanded an exploring expedition that started from Detroit, passed through Lakes Huron and Superior, and thence advanced by way of Sandy Lake and the upper Mississippi as far as to the upper Red Cedar Lake. This name, a translation from the Ojibwe name, was changed by Henry R. Schoolcraft, the narrator of the expedition, to be Cassina or Cass Lake, in honor of its commander. He was born in Exeter, N.H., October 9, 1782, and died in Detroit, Mich., June 17, 1866. At the age of 18 years he came to Marietta, the first town founded in southern Ohio, and studied law there; was admitted to the bar in 1803 and began practice at Zanesville, Ohio; and was colonel and later brigadier general in the War of 1812. He was governor of Michigan Territory, 1813 to 1831; negotiated 22 treaties with Indian tribes; was secretary of war in the cabinet of President Andrew Jackson, 1831–36, including the time of the Black Hawk War; was minister to France, 1836–42; U.S. senator, 1845–48; Democratic candidate for the presidency in the campaign of 1848; again U.S. senator, 1849–57; and secretary of state in the cabinet of President James Buchanan, 1857–60.

To voyage along the upper Mississippi River and to describe and map its principal source were the motives for the expedition undertaken in 1820 by Cass. At this time Michigan Territory, of which he was governor, included the northeastern third of Minnesota, east of the Mississippi, and Missouri Territory extended across the present state of Iowa and western two-thirds of Minnesota.

The report of this expedition, published the next year, is titled *Narrative Journal of Travels from Detroit Northwest through the Great Chain of American Lakes to the Sources of the Mississippi River in the Year 1820, by Henry R. Schoolcraft . . . 1821* (424 pp., with a map and eight copper-plate engravings). This title page is engraved and is followed by another in print, which states that the author was "a member of the Expedition under Governor Cass." The explorations of the upper Mississippi by Cass and Schoolcraft, of whom the latter visited and named Lake Itasca in 1832, are related in a chapter of *Minnesota in Three Centuries* (1908, vol. I, pp. 347–56, with their portraits).

Several extended biographies of Gen. Cass were published during his lifetime, in 1848, 1852, and 1856, the years of successive presidential campaigns. In 1889 a marble statue of him was contributed by the state of Michigan as one of its two statues for the National Statuary Hall at the Capitol in Washington, and the proceedings and addresses in Congress upon the acceptance of the statue were published in a volume of 106 pages. Two years afterward, in 1891, a mature study of his biography, titled *Lewis Cass, by Andrew C. McLaughlin, Assistant Professor of History in the University of Michigan* (363 pp.), was published in the "American Statesmen" series.

For the origins and meanings of these names, information was gathered in October 1909 from Iver P. Byhre, county auditor, and in September 1916 from Nathan J. Palmer, clerk of the court, Mack Kennedy, sheriff, James S. Scribner, former county attorney, and M. S. Morical, all of Walker, the county seat, during my visits there.

AH-GWAH-CHING a village in Shingobee Township, sections 34 and 35; formerly named State Sanatorium with a post office of that name, 1908–22, at which time it changed to the present name, which means "outside" in Ojibwe, representing a treatment for the tuberculosis sanatorium here opened in 1907. The village had a station of the Northern Pacific Railroad.

ANSEL TOWNSHIP received the name of an earlier post office, operated 1895–1918, which was given by its postmaster Myron Smith, this being the first or christening name of one of the pioneers there.

ARTHURS POINT a summer resort in Powers Township, with a post office, 1916–30, and a station of the Minnesota and International Railway.

BACKUS a city in Powers Township, sections 30 and 31, was named in honor of Edward W. Backus of Minneapolis, lumberman, president of the Backus-Brooks Company and of the International Falls Lumber Company. It was incorporated as a village on December 17, 1902, and reincorporated on August 6, 1910, when separated from the township. The village was a terminus for several railroads and had grain elevators, a creamery, and a number of mills, including the tow mill of the American Grass Twine Company. It has had a post office since 1896.

BARCLAY TOWNSHIP bears the surname of one of its pioneers.

BECKER TOWNSHIP was named for J. A. Becker, an early settler there.

BENA a city, adjoining the most southern bay of Lake Winnibigoshish, in T. 145N, R. 28W, sections 26, 27, and 34, on the Leech Lake Reservation; incorporated as a village on November 14, 1906. It had a station of the Great Northern Railway in section 27, and its post office was established in 1898, with Ernest Flemming, owner of the hotel and dealer in general merchandise and heavy hauling, as postmaster. Its name is the Ojibwe word meaning "a partridge," spelled *biné* in Fred-

eric Baraga's *Dictionary of the Ojibway Language.* This game bird species, formerly common throughout the wooded region of this state, is the ruffed grouse, called the "partridge" in New England and in Minnesota, but less correctly known as the "pheasant" in the middle and southern states. Henry W. Longfellow used this word in his *Song of Hiawatha*: "Heard the pheasant, Bena, drumming."

BEULAH TOWNSHIP received its name in honor of Beulah Olds, the wife of an early homesteader there, this being her first name, a Hebrew word meaning "married."

BIGSWAMP a post office, 1896–1902, located in McKinley Township, section 18, with hunter and trapper Ernest Fleming as first postmaster and postal clerk Jesse Watson helping out during hunting season; a sawmill was on the site.

BIRCH LAKE TOWNSHIP was named for its lake adjoining Hackensack village. It is translated, as noted by Rev. Joseph A. Gilfillan, from the Ojibwe "Ga-wig-wasensikag sagaiigun, the-place-of-little-birches lake." On the map of the Minnesota Geological Survey it is called Fourteen Mile Lake, indicating its distance by the road south from the Leech Lake Agency.

BLIND LAKE TOWNSHIP T. 139N, R. 28W, formerly unnamed.

BOORN a post office, 1912; location not found.

BOY LAKE and **BOY RIVER TOWNSHIPS** were named from their large lake and river, which are translations of the Ojibwe names. Gilfillan wrote that Woman Lake and Boy Lake "are so called from women and boys, respectively, they having been killed in those lakes by the Sioux during an irruption made by them." The date and origin of the name of Boy Lake, whence by Ojibwe usage the outflowing river was likewise named, are stated by William W. Warren in his *History of the Ojibway People* (MHS Collections 5: 222–32) to have been about the year 1768, within a few years after the Ojibwe had driven the Dakota southward from Mille Lacs. A war party of Dakota invaded the upper Mississippi region by way of the Crow Wing and Gull Rivers and by a canoe route, with portages, through White Fish, Wabedo, and the Little Boy and Boy Lakes, to Leech Lake. At Boy Lake they "killed three little boys, while engaged in gathering wild rice. . . . From this circumstance, this large and beautiful sheet of water has derived its Ojibway name of Que-wis-ans (Little Boy)." Warren's narration shows that this attack was on the lower one of the two Boy Lakes, lying partly in the township named for it. Gilfillan's list of Ojibwe names and translations has exactly the same Ojibwe name for this lake, on the lower part of Boy River, and for the lake about ten miles south on the upper part of the river, which our maps name Little Boy Lake.

Joseph N. Nicollet mapped the lower Boy Lake under the name of Lake Hassler, in honor of Ferdinand Rudolph Hassler (b. in Switzerland, 1770, d. in Philadelphia, 1843), who was superintendent of the U.S. Coast Survey.

BOY RIVER a city of Boy River Township, sections 29 and 32; incorporated as a village on April 7, 1922; the post office was established in 1910. The village had a station of the Minneapolis, St. Paul and Sault Ste. Marie Railroad (Soo Line) and several hotels and general stores.

BREVIK a post office in Boy Lake Township, section 30, 1914–54, with Ole Brevik as first postmaster.

BRIDGEMAN a country post office, 1899–1911, located in May Township, section 27.

BULL MOOSE TOWNSHIP was named in compliment to the Progressive, or "Bull Moose," division of the Republican Party, which supported former President Theodore Roosevelt as its candidate in the presidential campaign of 1912.

BUNGO TOWNSHIP was named for descendants of an African American, Jean Bonga, who, according to Dr. Edward D. Neill, was brought from the West Indies and was a slave of Capt. Daniel Robertson, British commandant at Mackinaw from 1782 to 1787. His family intermarried with the Ojibwe, and the name became changed to Bungo. George Bonga was an interpreter for Governor Cass in 1820 at Fond du Lac, and he or another of this family was an interpreter for the Ojibwe treaty in 1837 at Fort Snelling. This township has a Bungo Brook, which was earlier so named, flowing out at its northeast corner. The village of Bungo in section 26 was first settled in 1894 as a farmers community, with a post office, 1896–1923.

BYRON was named for Byron Powell, the first white boy born in this township, son of Philo Powell, who later removed to northwestern Canada.

CASINO a village in May Township, section 12; had a blacksmith shop, a stone cutter, and several carpenters; its post office was called Cass, 1895–99, and Casino, 1899–1914.

CASS see CASINO.

CASS LAKE a city in Pike Bay Township, on the Leech Lake Reservation, received its name from the adjoining lake, which, as before noted, was named, like this county, in honor of Gen. Cass. Established in 1898, the city was a fast-growing tourist area because of its proximity to Cass Lake, Pike Bay, and the numerous other lakes of the area; it had ten hotels by 1920 and a station of the Great Northern Railway. Most of its residents were employed in the chief industry of lumbering. The post office was named Tuller in 1898, changing to Cass Lake in 1899; an earlier post office by this name was established and discontinued in that part of the county that was formerly Pembina County, 1852–57.

CHICKAMAW BEACH a city in Barclay Township, sections 19, 20, and 27; incorporated as a village on November 20, 1950.

CHIPPEWA a post office, 1861–68; location not found.

CLOVERDALE a post office authorized on September 6, 1907, with Henry Frisbey to be postmaster, but not established; location not found.

CREEK a post office, 1910–19; location not found.

CROOKED LAKE TOWNSHIP took this name from its Crooked Lake, half of which extends into Crow Wing County. It is a translation of the aboriginal name *Wewagigumag sagaiigun*. By a resolution of the state legislature, March 6, 1919, this lake was renamed Lake Roosevelt in honor of President Theodore Roosevelt, who two months previously, on January 6, died at his home, Oyster Bay, N.Y.

CUBA a Great Northern Railway village in T. 145N, R. 30W, section 17, in the Chippewa National Forest. Its station commemorates the Spanish-American War of 1898.

CYPHERS a railway station of the Minnesota and International Railway located five miles south of Walker in Shingobee Township, section 13, was named for a former resident, who removed into Hubbard County. A post office operated there, 1909–33, with Andrew Watt, first postmaster.

DEERFIELD TOWNSHIP was named, on request of its people, for the plentiful deer there, but it also is a common geographic name, borne by townships, villages, and post offices in 14 other states.

EAST GULL LAKE TOWNSHIP was named for its comprising the greater part of the northeast end of Gull Lake, with its continuation north to Upper Gull Lake. The city of East Gull Lake was incorporated as a village on May 8, 1947.

ELLIS a village in Byron Township, sections 10, 11, 14, and 15, with a country post office, 1890–1926, a blacksmith shop, and a general store.

ELWELLS CORNER a village in McKinley Township, circa 1939, located on Highway 64, 16 miles southwest of Backus and 14 miles west of Pine River.

ESTERDY a country post office, 1895–1910, in Byron Township, section 28, with a sawmill.

ESTHERVILLE see WABEDO.

FAIRVIEW TOWNSHIP received this euphonious name in accordance with the petition of its people for organization.

FEDERAL DAM is a city in Gould Township, sections 2 and 3, at the reservoir dam built by the U.S. government on Leech Lake River. It was incorporated as a village on October 30, 1911, and separated from the township on April 23, 1912; it had a station of the Soo Line and a post office since 1910.

FLEMING SPUR a station of the Great Northern Railway; location not found.

GLADIOLA a post office in Meadow Brook Township, section 31, 1903–14.

GLADSTONE a post office, 1886–87; location not found.

GOULD a post office in Boy River Township, section 8, 1902–11.

GOULD TOWNSHIP was named for M. I. Gould, a logger and farmer, who owned hay meadows there.

GRAFF a post office, 1902–35, in Moose Lake Township, section 26, with Englebert H. Flategraff as postmaster.

GRANT a post office, 1905–25, found in Moose Lake Township, section 3.

GULL RIVER station of the Northern Pacific Railroad, formerly a place of great importance for its lumber manufacturing, was named for the Gull Lake and River, each a translation of the name given by the Ojibwe, the latter, in accordance with their general rule, being supplied from the name of the lake. This aboriginal name is noted by Gilfillan as "Gagaiashkonzikag sagaiigun, the-place-of-young-gulls lake." Gull River was also a trading post of Clement H. Beaulieu in Sylvan Township, section 17; it had a post office, 1880–95, which transferred to Sylvan.

HACKENSACK a city in Birch Lake Township, section 19, was named for an earlier post office there established in 1888, which derived its name from the town of Hackensack in New Jersey, on the Hackensack River, given by James Curo, who was the first postmaster, ranchman, and merchant there. It was incorporated as a village on June 5, 1903, and separated from the township on May 18, 1911; it had a station of the Minnesota and International Railway; it was also the home of Lucette Diana Kensack, Paul Bunyan's girlfriend.

HIRAM TOWNSHIP was named by the petition for organization in honor of Hiram Wilson, an early settler.

HOME BROOK TOWNSHIP received the name of a post office earlier established, which had taken the name of the brook given by lumbermen. (*Brook* and *creek* have the same meaning in this state, the latter being the more common, or the only term in use, through the greater part of the state, but lumbermen and settlers coming from Maine and others of the eastern states have in many cases named the small streams as brooks, especially in the wooded northeastern third of Minnesota.)

HOMEBROOK a post office in Home Brook Township, section 31, 1902–13.

HORSESHOE a post office authorized on May 12, 1906, with Reuben C. Spence to be postmaster, but not established; location not found.

HULDA see MINNIE.

IMLAC a post office authorized on December 13, 1899, with Valentine C. Marx to be postmaster, but not established; location not found.

INGUADONA TOWNSHIP has a name of probably aboriginal derivation, but its significance has not been learned. It was given to the township from its lake so named. If it is of the Ojibwe language, its original form and pronunciation may have been so changed as to be now unidentifiable. Gilfillan gave the name of this lake as "Manominiganjiki, or The-rice-field." It was called Lake Gauss on Nicollet's map, for the celebrated German mathematician Carl Friedrich Gauss (1777–1855). A post office operated in the township, 1916–35.

ISLAND LAKE a station of the Northern Pacific Railroad, Powers Township, section 18.

KEGO the name of a township here, is a common Ojibwe word, meaning "a fish," used as a general term for any fish species. This is spelled *Gigo* in Baraga's *Dictionary*.

LAKE ALICE a post office, 1903–10, located in Shingobee Township.

LAKE SHORE a city in Lake Shore Township, section 19; incorporated as a village on March 19, 1947.

LAKE SHORE TOWNSHIP T. 135N, R. 29W.

LATHROP a post office, 1894–1901, where Dr. William J. Bain was postmaster, physician, general store owner, and lumbermen's supply dealer; location not found.

LEADER a village in Meadow Brook Township, section 6; had a creamery, a sawmill, and a general store, whose post office operated 1903–66, at which time it changed to a rural community branch.

LEAF CITY a post office, 1857–60; location not found.

LEECH a village on the Leech Lake Reservation, which had two churches, a school, a general store, and a post office, 1895–1905.

LEECH LAKE TOWNSHIP was named for the lake, translated from the Ojibwe name, noted by Gilfillan as "Ga-sagasquadjimekag sagaiigun, the-place-of-the-leech-lake; from the tradition that on first coming to it, the Chippeways saw an enormous leech swimming in it." Nicollet wrote that this aboriginal name "implies . . . that its waters contain a remarkable number of leeches." A post office was in section 32, 1858–59, established in Pembina County; reestablished, 1868–94, and again, 1915–30; it had a station serving the Great Northern and the Park Rapids and Leech Lake Railroads.

LIMA TOWNSHIP (pronounced here with the long English sound of *i*, unlike Lima in Peru) was named probably for the city of Lima in Ohio, where the pronunciation has been thus anglicized. Ten other states have towns and villages of this name. A post office operated 1911–14; its Soo Line station was named Pine Tree Spur for the logging company, Pine Tree Manufacturing Company.

LONGVILLE a city in Kego Township, section 34; incorporated as a village on March 1, 1941; the post office was established in 1904.

LOON LAKE TOWNSHIP was named for its lake in section 20. This large water bird was formerly frequent or common throughout this state and is yet common in its wooded northeast part.

LOTHROP a station of the Northern Pacific Railroad located in Turtle Lake Township, section 31.

MAE a post office, 1907–18, located in Beulah Township, section 32.

MAPLE TOWNSHIP received this name on the petition of its people for organization, referring to its plentiful sugar maple trees, a species that is common or abundant throughout Minnesota, excepting near its west side. The sap is much used for sugar-making, in the early spring, both by the Indians and the white people. Warren wrote of this Ojibwe work about Leech Lake: "The shores of the lake are covered with maple which yields to the industry of the hunters' women, each spring, quantities of sap which they manufacture into sugar."

MARCUS see WILKINSON.

MAY TOWNSHIP was named in honor of May Griffith, daughter of a former county auditor, Charles Griffith, in whose office she was an assistant. Lake May, formerly called Lake Frances, in the southwest edge of Walker village, is also named for her.

McKINLEY TOWNSHIP was named in honor of our third martyr president, William McKinley, who was born in Niles, Ohio, January 29, 1843, and died in Buffalo, N.Y., September 14, 1901, assassinated by an anarchist. He was president of the United States, 1897–1901.

MEADOW BROOK TOWNSHIP took its name from a brook where a schoolhouse was built and so named before the township was organized.

MEADOWBROOK a post office, 1905, in Meadow Brook Township.

MERNA a post office, 1907–11; location not found.

MILDRED a small railway village in Pine River Township, section 22, was named in honor of Mrs. Mildred Scofield, first postmaster and wife of the merchant there, who, with her husband, removed to the West. The post office operated 1899–1954; it had a station of the Northern Pacific Railroad.

MINNIE a post office, first called Hulda in 1904–5, then Minnie, 1905–7; location not found.

MOOSE LAKE TOWNSHIP was named for its small lake in sections 10 and 15.

MOTLEY a city under joint jurisdiction with Morrison County.

MUD LAKE TOWNSHIP was named for its Mud Lake, mostly shallow with a muddy bed and having much wild rice, through which the Leech Lake River flows. The Ojibwe name is translated by Gilfillan, "meaning shallow-mud-bottomed lake." Nicollet mapped it as Lake Bessel in honor of Friedrich Wilhelm Bessel (1784–1846), a distinguished Prussian astronomer.

NICHOLSON a post office, 1881–82; location not found.

NUSHKA a Great Northern Railway station on the Leech Lake Reservation, is an Ojibwe word of exclamation, meaning "Look!" It is used by Longfellow in *The Song of Hiawatha*.

ODANAH see ONIGUM.

OJIBWAY a village in Sylvan Township, at the mouth of the Crow Wing River, where a U.S. land office, under the act of 1856, was located.

OLEON a settlement about 1856; location not found.

ONIGUM a post office in Shingobee Township (T. 142–31), section 13, 1900–29, briefly named Odanah, and located on the Leech Lake Reservation, with a trading post and general store; it was formerly an Indian agency but was abandoned as such in 1919 when agencies consolidated at Cass Lake. The name means "across the bay."

OSHAWA a post office, 1916–44, located eight miles west of Backus in Deerfield Township, section 31.

OTTER TAIL PENINSULA a township.

OUTING a post office in Crooked Lake Township, section 27, since 1936; located in Crow Wing County, 1908–36, at which time it transferred to Cass County; it developed as a summer resort area with a general store and hotel.

PIKE BAY TOWNSHIP includes the large Pike Bay, more properly a separate lake, which is connected on the north with Cass Lake by a very narrow strait or thoroughfare. The name commemorates Zebulon Montgomery Pike, the commander of the expedition sent to the upper Mississippi in 1805–6 by the U.S. War Department. Pike came to Cass Lake (then known as the upper Red Cedar Lake) on February 12, 1806, by a land march from Leech Lake and across Pike Bay; spent a day at the North West Company's trading post there; and returned on the 14th by the same route. His biography is presented in the chapter of Morrison County, where he is honored by the names of a creek, a township, and rapids of the Mississippi, beside the site of his winter stockade camp.

PILLAGER a city in Sylvan Township, the adjoining Pillager Creek, and the lake of this name at its source are derived from the term *Pillagers*, applied to the Ojibwe of this vicinity and of the Leech Lake Reservation. According to the accounts given by Schoolcraft and his associate Dr. Douglass Houghton in the *Narrative* of the expedition in 1832 to Itasca Lake (pp. 111, 112, 254), this name, Mukkundwais or Pillagers, originated in the fall of 1767 or 1768, when a trader named Berti, who had a trading post at the mouth of Crow Wing River, was robbed of his goods.

Warren gave in the *History of the Ojibway People*, written in 1852, a more detailed narration of the robbery, or pillage, referring it erroneously to the year 1781. The name *Pillagers*, given to the Leech Lake band of the Ojibwe, had come into use as early as 1775, when the elder Alexander Henry found some of them at the Lake of the Woods.

Pillager was first settled in 1886 with a station of the Northern Pacific Railroad, a general store, a hotel, and a blacksmith; it incorporated as a village on September 4, 1900; its post office was established in 1886.

PINE LAKE TOWNSHIP bordering the most southern part of the shore of Leech Lake, contains eight lakes, with others crossed by its boundaries. It had abundant white pine timber, and thence came this name of its lakes, in sections 17 and 18, later given to the township. Its largest lake, in sections 28, 32, and 33, is called Boot Lake, from its outline.

PINE RIVER TOWNSHIP is on the upper part of Pine River, which flows eastward through White Fish Lake and joins the Mississippi near the center of Crow Wing County. This township has near Mildred station a second but smaller Boot Lake, named for its having a bootlike shape.

The city of Pine River on the corner of Barclay and Pine River Townships was incorporated as a village in 1901. It began as an outlet for agricultural and lumber products and had a grain elevator, a creamery, and a pickle factory. Its post office began in 1877 with trader and lumberman George A. Barclay as first postmaster.

PINE TREE SPUR see LIMA.

POKAGAMON FALLS a post office, 1857–60, which was established in Pembina County.

PONTO LAKE TOWNSHIP has a lake of this name in sections 3, 9, and 10, and an adjoining post office is named Pontoria. These are unique names, not in use elsewhere, and their derivation and significance remain to be learned.

PONTORIA a village in Ponto Lake Township, sections 15 and 16, with a post office, 1903–19; the name is no doubt taken from its township's name.

POPLAR TOWNSHIP had an earlier post office of this name in section 16, 1897–1954, referring to the plentiful poplar groves.

PORT VIEW a village in Home Brook Township, section 19, with a post office, 1901–15, whose original spelling was Portrew.

PORTAGE LAKE a station of the Soo Line, in the Chippewa National Forest, T. 144 N, R. 28 W, and the lake of this name, a half mile distant to the north, as also the neighboring Portage Bay of the large north arm of Leech Lake, refer to the canoe portage there between the waters of Leech and Winnibigoshish Lakes. On Nicollet's map this Portage Lake is named in honor of Peter Stephen Duponceau (b. in France, 1760, d. in Philadelphia, 1844), author of a *Memoir on the Indian Languages of North America*, published in 1835; and the Portage Bay bears the name of Pickering Bay on this map, for an American writer of another work on the same subject, published in 1836.

POWERS TOWNSHIP was named in honor of Gorham Powers of Granite Falls, who was a landowner there, having a summer home on Sanborn Lake in section 27. He was born in Pittsfield, Maine, September 14, 1840; served in the Civil War, 1862–65; was graduated at the Albany law school, 1866, and in the same year came to Minnesota, settling in Minneapolis; removed in 1868 to Granite Falls; was county attorney of Yellow Medicine County, 1872–77 and 1884–86; was a representative in the state legislature, 1879; and was judge in the Twelfth judicial district from 1890 until his death, at Granite Falls, April 15, 1915.

RABOIN a post office, 1911–36, in Wilkinson Township, section 17, with Joseph M. Raboin first postmaster; it had a station of the Park Rapids and Leech Lake Railroad.

REMER TOWNSHIP and the earlier Remer post office and railway village, were named in honor of E. N. and William P. Remer, brothers, of whom the former was treasurer and manager of the Reishus-Remer Land Company of Grand Rapids, and the latter was the first postmaster here. The city of Remer, sections 1 and 2, was incorporated as a village on January 12, 1912, and separated from the township on June 23, 1914. The post office began in 1904, along with a sawmill and several stores, and a station of the Soo Line Railroad.

ROGERS was named in honor of William A. Rogers, who had a homestead in this township, coming, as also his brothers Nathan and Frank, from St. John, N.B. He engaged in logging as a contractor, resided in Walker, and was killed by an elevator accident in Duluth. His son, Edward L. Rogers, was a county attorney of Cass County.

RUSH BROOK a post office, 1915–16, in Fairview Township, section 9; the site also had a school.

SALEM was named by its settlers in their petition for township organization. It is the name of townships, cities, villages, and post offices in 32 states of our Union.

SANTIAGO a village in T. 145 N, R. 30 W, Chippewa National Forest, with a station of the Great Northern Railway.

SCHLEY a Great Northern Railway station, was named in honor of Winfield Scott Schley, rear admiral of the U.S. Navy. He was born in Frederick County, Md., October 9, 1839; was graduated at the U.S. Naval Academy in 1860 and was an instructor there after the Civil War; commanded the "Flying Squadron" in the Spanish-American War, 1898, and directed the naval battle off Santiago, Cuba; author of an autobiography, *Forty-five Years under the Flag* (1904, 439 pp.); died in New York City, October 2, 1911.

Three successive stations and sidings of this railway in the north edge of Cass County, established in 1898–99, are commemorative of our short and decisive war with Spain, named Schley, Santiago, and Cuba. The village had a post office, 1931–68.

SHINGOBEE TOWNSHIP received this name from its Shingobee Creek, being the general Ojibwe word for the spruce, balsam fir, and arbor vitae, species of evergreen trees that are common or abundant through northern Minnesota, excepting the Red River Valley. It is spelled *jingob* in Baraga's *Dictionary*.

SHINGOBEE WINTER PLAYGROUND a sports center constructed by the U.S. Forest Service in a natural setting six miles south of Walker, which opened in 1939.

SLATER TOWNSHIP was named for David H. Slater, a homestead farmer in section 6.

SMITH'S a village in Shingobee Township, section 8, with a station of the Great Northern Railway.

SMOKY HOLLOW was named by Levi Morrow, a settler who came from Missouri, in remembrance of his former home in the state of New York, near a locality so named (or perhaps for Sleepy Hollow, a quiet valley near Tarrytown, on the Hudson, of which Washington Irving wrote in *The Sketch Book*). This township has in part a surface of marginal morainic drift, remarkably diversified with knolls, ridges, and hollows.

SNOWBALL a post office, 1907–17, in Thunder Lake Township, section 6.

STATE SANATORIUM see AH-GWAH-CHING.

STONYBROOK a village in Maple Township, sections 33 and 34, and Home Brook Township, sections 3 and 4, with a post office, 1895–1908 and 1910–11.

SYLVAN TOWNSHIP is named for its Sylvan Lake, which refers to the woods or groves on its shores. The Ojibwe name, noted by Gilfillan, means Fish Trap Lake. A lumbering community was in section 13, with a post office located about a mile distant called Gull River, 1880–95, then moving to Sylvan and discontinuing in 1929; it had a station of the Northern Pacific Railroad.

TEN MILE LAKE a village in Turtle Lake Township, section 31, with a station of the Minnesota and International Railway.

THELMA a post office authorized on May 3, 1899, with Mary E. Shelley to be postmaster, but not established; location not found.

THUNDER LAKE TOWNSHIP is derived likewise from its lake of this name, which is probably a translation of the aboriginal name.

TOBIQUE a village in Rogers Township, section 13, with a post office, 1912–54, and a station of the Soo Line.

TORREY TOWNSHIP was formerly part of Wahnena Township, T. 143N, R. 25W.

TRELIPE TOWNSHIP (pronounced in three syllables, with accent on the first, and with the short sound of each) is named, with variation of spelling, for the tullibee, a very common fish in the lakes of northern Minnesota, having a wide geographic range from New York to northwestern Canada. This species, *Argyrosomus tullibee*, closely resembles the common whitefish. The word was adopted, as noted by Richardson, from the Cree language. Tulaby Lake, crossed by the line between Becker and Mahnomen Counties, was also named for this fish, supplying another way of its spelling.

TULLER see CASS LAKE.

TURTLE LAKE TOWNSHIP is named for its two lakes in sections 22, 23, 26, and 27, called by the Ojibwe, as recorded by Gilfillan, "Mikinakosagaiigunun, or Turtle lakes."

UNORGANIZED TERRITORY OF EAST CASS formerly unnamed; T. 142N, R. 25W.

UNORGANIZED TERRITORY OF NORTH CASS part of the Chippewa National Forest.

WABEDO TOWNSHIP (accenting the first syllable) received its name from its Wabedo Lake. Warren, writing in 1852 in his *History of the Ojibway People*, related that an invading war party of the Dakota, about the year 1768, came "into Wab-ud-ow lake, where they spilt the first Ojibway blood, killing a hunter named Wab-ud-ow (White Gore), from which circumstance the lake is named to this day by the Ojibways." The same party, advancing northward, killed three boys gathering rice, whence Boy Lake and River received their name, as noted on a preceding page. Gilfillan spelled Wabedo Lake as "Wabuto sagaiigun, or Mushroom lake." A post office was located on the border of Wabedo and Blind Lake Townships, 1906–35, which was earlier named Estherville, 1904–6, with Esther M. Madson, postmaster.

WADENA a post office, 1857–60; location not found.

WAHNENA (with accent on the second syllable) was named for an Ojibwe leader who died about the year 1895. It became the name of T. 144N, R. 25W, part of the Chippewa National Forest, and was the name of T. 143N, R. 25W, which became Torrey Township.

WALDEN TOWNSHIP bears the name of a pond near Concord, Mass., beside which Henry D. Thoreau, the author, built a hut and lived about two years, 1845–47, as told in his book *Walden, or*

Life in the Woods, published in 1854. This is also the name of a town in northern Vermont and of a large manufacturing village in Orange County, N.Y.

WALKER a city and the county seat, located on Leech Lake, Shingobee Township, sections 21 and 22, was named in honor of Thomas Barlow Walker, who had large lumbering and land interests in Cass County and in several other counties of northern Minnesota. He was born in Xenia, Ohio, February 1, 1840, came to Minnesota in 1862 and was the surveyor of parts of the St. Paul and Duluth Railway line, commenced in 1868 the purchase of great tracts of pine lands, and later built and operated, in Crookston and elsewhere, many large lumber mills. He resided in Minneapolis and maintained a very valuable and choice art gallery to which the public were freely welcomed. An autobiographic paper by Mr. Walker is published in the MHS Collections ([1915] 15: 455–78, with his portrait).

The city was incorporated as a village on March 10, 1896, and its post office also opened in 1896. In its early development, the site was a resort community with abundant hunting and fishing in very scenic surroundings. In 1900 Fort Walker was at this location with Lieut. A. B. Downworth, commander. The village had a station of the Great Northern Railway in section 22.

WENDT a post office, 1904–7; location not found.

WHEELOCK a station of the Northern Pacific Railroad in May Township, section 22.

WHIPHOLT a village in Pine Lake Township, section 8, with a post office since 1925.

WHITE CITY a village in Shingobee Township, section 8, with a station of the Great Northern Railway.

WICKLOW a country post office, 1902–9, in McKinley Township, with a sawmill and a church.

WILKINSON TOWNSHIP commemorates Maj. Melville Cary Wilkinson, who was killed in a skirmish with the Bear Island band of the Pillager Indians at Sugar Point on Leech Lake, October 5, 1898. He was born in New York, November 14, 1835, served as a volunteer in the Civil War, and in 1866 entered the regular army. The "battle of Sugar point" and dealings with these Ojibwe preceding and following it are narrated in Charles E. Flandrau's *History of Minnesota* (1900, pp. 229–34), and more fully by Return I. Holcombe in *Minnesota*

in Three Centuries (1908, vol. IV, pp. 245–54). A post office in section 32 was first named Marcus, 1904–10, and was discontinued in 1954; it had a station of the Great Northern Railway.

WILSON TOWNSHIP T. 137N, R. 29W; residents of the settlement of houses and commercial properties along Highway 371 in the township voted in 1988 to create the city of Wilson.

WOODROW TOWNSHIP received its name, by petition of its citizens for the township organization, in honor of President Woodrow Wilson. He was born in Staunton, Va., December 28, 1856; was graduated at Princeton University, 1879; was professor there, of finance and political economy, 1890–1902, and president, 1902–10; author of several books on U.S. history and politics; was governor of New Jersey, 1911–13, and president of the United States, 1913–21.

ZUZU a post office, 1898–1900, with lumber dealer and general store owner Lewis S. Card as postmaster; location not found.

Bays, Points, and Islands of Leech Lake

The origin of the name of Leech Lake has been noted for the township so named. It was translated from the Ojibwe name, the French translation being Lac Sangsue (which in English is a bloodsucker, that is, a leech).

This lake has a very irregular outline, with numerous bays and projecting points, and it contains several islands. On the east is Boy River Bay, named for its inflowing river, with Sugar Point at its west entrance, named for its sugar maples, the site of the battle in 1898, when Maj. Wilkinson lost his life, as noted for the township of his name. Bear Island stretches three miles from north to south, lying in front of this bay and of Rice Bay at the southeast, and Pelican Island lies far out in the southern central part of the broad lake, these names being translations from those given by the Ojibwe.

Big Point and Otter Tail Point, respectively on the southwest and northwest borders of the main lake, guard the entrance to the more irregular western part. The peninsula juts into that part from the south, having itself a small Peninsula Lake, and bounded on the southeast by Agency Bay and on the west by the south arm and West Bay. At the south end of the Peninsula, a passage called the Narrows leads from the south arm to Agency Bay, and on the north the Peninsula is separated from the main shore by the North Narrows, and it terminates northeastward in Pine Point. Nearly all these names are self-explanatory, having an obvious significance. The Otter Tail Point, at the end of a tapering tract of land about five miles long, is a translation of the Ojibwe name, referring to its outline, which resembles an otter's tail, similarly as the large lake and county of this name have reference to a tapering point of land adjoining the eastern end of that lake.

On the north end of the Peninsula, at the North Narrows, was the village of Eshkebuge-coshe (Flat Mouth, b. 1774, d. about 1860), the very intelligent, friendly, and respected chief of the Pillager Ojibwe; and close east of this village, at the time of Schoolcraft's visit there in 1832, was the trading house of the American Fur Company. In the time of Pike's visit, 1806, the North West Company's trading post was about two miles distant to the northeast from the North Narrows, being opposite to Goose Island.

West Bay in its north part branches westward to the Northwest arm, entered by a very narrow and short strait, and opens northward, opposite to the North Narrows, into Duck Bay, which is entered with Prairie Point on the right, and with Aitkin Point, succeeded westward by the small Aitkin Bay on the left. Proceeding five miles up the Duck Bay, past Duck Island (sometimes called Minnesota Island), one comes at the northwest corner of this bay to the mouth of the Steamboat River "fringed with extensive fields of wild rice," whence a canoe route through several little lakes, with portages, leads to Pike Bay of Cass Lake.

Four years after the southward journey of Schoolcraft through Leech Lake in 1832, Rev. William T. Boutwell, his companion of that travel, who a year later had established a mission here for the Ojibwe, befriended Nicollet on his exploration of the upper Mississippi country in his relations with these Indians. Nicollet spent a week on Leech Lake in the middle of August 1836, having his camping place generally on Otter Tail Point. Boutwell's mission house was on or near the isthmus that connects the Peninsula with the mainland of the present Leech Lake Agency. On Nicollet's return from Lake Itasca, by way of the Mississippi and Cass Lake, he again camped on Otter Tail Point during the first week of September, visited with Boutwell, and had long interviews with Flat Mouth.

Sucker Bay lies west and north of Otter Tail Point and receives Sucker Brook at its north end. Flea Point, called Sugar Point on Schoolcraft's map of Leech Lake, juts into the southern part of the western side of the bay; the present Sucker Brook is designated on that map by the nearly equivalent name of Carp River. The Sucker Family of fishes, Catostomidae, includes "some 15 genera and more than 70 species," wholly limited in geographic range to the fresh waters of North America, excepting that two species occur in eastern Asia. Ulysses O. Cox, in his *Preliminary Report on the Fishes of Minnesota*, published in 1897, wrote of this family that "five genera and eleven species" were then known in this state. Our most plentiful species, known as the "common sucker," found in nearly all large lakes of Minnesota, "attains a length of 18 inches or more, . . . a food-fish of considerable importance."

On the northwest side of the northern part of the main lake are the Two Points and Noon Day Point, and this part ends in the little Portage Bay, called Rush Bay on Schoolcraft's map, whence this map notes the "Route to L. Winnipeg" (that is, Winnibigoshish). The present name of the bay, refers, as before mentioned, to that canoe route and its portage. Nicollet named this most northern bay of Leech Lake as Pickering Bay, in honor of John Pickering (1777–1846), of Massachusetts, a philologist, who in 1836 published *Remarks on the Indian Languages of North America*. This is the only name connected with Leech Lake, as mapped in much crude detail by Schoolcraft and Nicollet, that they bestowed otherwise than by translation of the Ojibwe names.

Islands of Cass Lake

Of the Ojibwe name of this lake, with its translation, Gilfillan wrote: "Cass lake is Ga-misqua-wakokag sagaiigun, or The-place-of-red-cedars lake, from some red cedars growing on the island; more briefly, Red Cedar lake." The same name was given also by these Indians to Cedar Lake in Aitkin County, as noted in the chapter for that county. Until the adoption of the new name, Cassina or Cass Lake, these were discriminated respectively as the Upper and Lower Red Cedar Lakes.

Gilfillan further wrote: "The large island in the lake was anciently called Gamisquawako miniss, or the island of red cedars. It is now called Kitchi miniss, or Great island." Schoolcraft in 1832 described and mapped it as "Colcaspi or Grand island," having coined the former word from parts of the names of its three explorers, Schoolcraft, Cass, and Pike. "The town of Ozawindib" (Yellow Head, who was the guide of Schoolcraft and his party in their expedition to Lake Itasca) was on this island, being a village of 157 people, with "small fields of corn and potatoes, cultivated by the women." It is now commonly called Star Island, and it has a small lake, about three-fourths of a mile long, which is called Lake Helen, this name having been given in honor of Miss Helen Gould, of New York City, on the occasion of her visit here about the year 1900.

Having set aside the Ojibwe name of Red Cedar Island for the new name, Colcaspi, Schoolcraft gave the name "R. Cedar I." on his map to a small island on the southeast. Garden and Elm Islands of Allen's Bay, in Beltrami County, each of very small area, are also mentioned by Schoolcraft, the former doubtless so named for its having been cultivated by the Indians.

Lake Winnibigoshish

David Thompson in 1798 gave this name as Lake Winepegoos in his *Narrative of Explorations in Western America*, published under editorial care of J. B. Tyrrell in 1916, but on Thompson's map, reproduced in facsimile in that work, it is Winnipeg Lake.

Schoolcraft's narrative journal of the expedition in 1820 under Gen. Cass, published in 1821, called it Lake Winnipec in the text, while the map spelled it Lake Winnepec. An island of boulders in its western part, not shown on maps but probably lying off a narrow projecting point, had large numbers of various species of waterfowl, one of which, a pelican found dead, caused it to be named Pelican Island.

The map in the *Narrative* of Stephen H. Long's expedition, 1823, notes it as "Lit. Winnepeek L."; Beltrami in the same year called it Lake Winnepec; and Lieut. James Allen, in 1832, spelled this name Lake Winnipeg, the same as the lake in Manitoba. Warren, writing in 1852 in his *History of the Ojibway People*, called it Lake Winnepeg.

In Nicollet's *Report*, from his exploration in 1836 published in 1843, it appears both in the text and on the map as Lake Winebigoshish. In the current accepted spelling of Winnibigoshish, the accent is placed on the syllable next to the last, with the long *o* sound. By the Ojibwe of that region, however, this lake name is generally pronounced like the etymologically cognate name of the Winnebago Indians and Lake Winnebago in Wisconsin (which is accented on the next before the final syllable and has the English long sound of the *a*), with addition of another syllable, shish. Gilfillan followed the orthography introduced to cartographers by Nicollet and defined the meaning as "miserable-wretched-dirty-water (Winni, filthy; bi, water; osh, bad, an expression of contempt; ish, an additional expression of contempt, meaning miserable, wretched)." The whole lake is shallow, with a mostly muddy bed at a depth probably nowhere exceeding 20 or 25 feet, so that the large waves of storms stir up the mud and sand of the lake bottom and shores, roiling the water upward to the surface upon nearly or quite all its area.

Similar shallowness and general muddiness of Lakes Winnipeg and Winnipegosis in Manitoba also caused them to receive these Ojibwe names, the former meaning "muddy water," as noted by Stephen W. Keating in 1823 (vol. II, p. 77), and the latter meaning "Little Winnipeg," according to Henry Youle Hind's *Narrative of the Canadian Exploring Expeditions* (vol. II, p. 42).

The spelling received from Nicollet, mispronounced by our white people, has been corrected, in accordance with the Ojibwe usage, to Winnebagoshish, by treaties of the United States with the Ojibwe under dates of May 7, 1864, and March 19, 1867, and in an executive order of President Ulysses S. Grant, May 26, 1874. Rev. S. R. Riggs, in a paper written in 1880, spelled the name as "Lake Winnebagooshish or Winnipeg" (MHS Collections 6: 157, 158). The orthography in the treaties here cited was also used by the present writer in the U.S. Geological Survey Monograph XXV ("The Glacial Lake Agassiz"), published in 1896, and was recommended by me in 1899 for general adoption (*Final Report of the Minn. Geol. Survey*, vol. IV, p. 57). It still seems to me desirable that the corrected spelling and pronunciation be adopted by Minnesota writers and speakers. The U.S. Geographic Board subsequently standardized the spelling as Winnibigoshish (Sixth Report, 1933).

Other Lakes and Streams

The list of townships and villages has included sufficient mention of numerous lakes and streams, including Birch Lake, Woman Lake, the Boy Lakes and River, Cass Lake, Crooked Lake, Gull River and Lake, Home Brook, Inguadona Lake, Leech Lake, Loon Lake, Lake May, Meadow Brook, Moose Lake (in the township of this name), Mud Lake and the Leech Lake River, Pike Bay of Cass Lake, Pillager Creek and Lake, Pine and Boot Lakes (in Pine Lake Township), Pine River, with the second Boot Lake in Pine River Township, Ponto Lake, Portage Lake, Shingobee Creek, Sylvan Lake, Thunder Lake, the Turtle Lakes in the township named for them, and Wabedo Lake.

On the canoe route from Cass Lake and Pike Bay to Leech Lake, Schoolcraft named the first lake, in sections 2 and 3, Wilkinson, Moss Lake, for the mosslike water plants seen growing in large masses on the lake bottom, which the canoemen "brought up on their paddles." Thence they made a portage of about two miles southwest into a lake at the center of this township, which Schoolcraft named Lake Shiba, spelled by the Latin form of "the initials of the names of the five gentlemen of the party, Schoolcraft, Houghton, Johnston, Boutwell, Allen." About a mile farther southwest, they came into "a river of handsome magnitude, broad and deep but without strong current," since named Steamboat River because it is ascended by steamboats from Duck Bay of Leech Lake, some three miles distant. Steamboat Lake, crossed by the west line of this county, lies a quarter of a mile west from the junction of the outlet of Lake Shiba with this river.

Going from Leech Lake southwest to the Crow Wing River, Schoolcraft took a somewhat frequented canoe route, starting from West Bay near the site of Walker and first portaging to the present Lake May (formerly called Lake Frances), then named the Warpool by the Ojibwe, who there began their war expeditions to the country of the Dakota. Next and very near was the Little Long Lake, in sections 33 and 34, May, and section 4, Shingobee. Thence they passed up a little inlet, through its four lakelets, and by portages through a series of three small lakes, each without outlet, coming next to the Long Water Lake in Hubbard County, at the head of the Crow Wing, beginning its series of eleven lakes. Schoolcraft's Lake of the Mountain and Lake of the Island, passed on this route before coming to the Long Water, remain unnamed on later maps.

Distances of travel south from the Leech Lake Agency, on the road to Hackensack and Brainerd, are noted by Three Mile Lake, Four Mile Lake, Six Mile Lake, Ten Mile Lake, Fourteen Mile Lake at Hackensack (called now Birch Lake, translated from its Ojibwe name), with the outflowing Fourteen Mile Creek, the head of Boy River, and Twenty-four Mile Creek, which outflows from Pine Mountain Lake, being the head stream of Pine River. These names are recognized as given by white pioneers, being unlike the majority derived by translations.

Gilfillan wrote that the long lake of the northwest part of t. 144, r. 27, in the Leech Lake Reservation, between Leech Lake River and Lake Winnibigoshish, is named "Kitchi-bugwudjiwi sagaiigun, meaning big-lake-in-the-wilderness or big-wilderness lake."

Bear River (also called Mud River), in Salem, flowing into the south end of Mud Lake, and Grave Lake at its head, in sections 10, 14, and 15, Slater, may be aboriginal names translated, but they are not identified in Gilfillan's list. Little Sand Lake section 28, Slater, and its larger companion, Sand Lake, crossed by the south line of this township, probably originated as white men's names, for Gilfillan gave the Ojibwe name of this Sand Lake as "Mikinako sagaiigun, Turtle lake." Its outlet is noted on the map of the Minnesota Geological Survey as Swift River, flowing northwest through the long and very narrow Swift Lake, which the Ojibwe name "Ningitawonan sagaiigun, Separating-canoe-route lake."

Big and Little Vermilion Lakes, the Upper Vermilion Lakes, and the larger Sugar Lake (noted on some maps as Little Sugar Lake), and the Vermilion River outflowing from them to the Mississippi, are translations from their Ojibwe names.

Willow River, Birch Brook and Lake in Lima Township, Big Rice Lake Thunder Little Thunder, and Turtle Lakes, and the long and narrow Blind Lake in Smoky Hollow Township are partly or all of Ojibwe derivation.

Lakes George and Washburn, Lawrence, Leavitt, and Morrison, in Crooked Lake and Beulah Townships, also the Washburn Brook, were named for lumbermen who formerly cut pine logs in these originally well-forested townships.

Little Norway Lake, named for its red or Norway pines, lying five miles south of Wabedo Lake, outflows westward to Ada Brook and Pine River. This brook and Lakes Ada and Hattie, also Mitten Lake and Lake Laura, outflowing by Laura Brook to Lake Inguadona, need further inquiries for the origins of their names.

Mule Lake, a mile west of Wabedo Lake, is said to have been named by the lumbermen for its outline, resembling a mule's head. Goose Lake, next on the west, was named for the wild geese.

Girl Lake in sections 33 and 34, Kego, and Baby Lake in sections 13, 14, 23, and 24, Powers, are names suggested probably by Woman and Boy Lakes, which latter are of Ojibwe origin, referring to persons of that tribe slain by the Dakota, as noted in the foregoing list of townships.

Whitefish and Little Whitefish Lakes, on the Fourteen Mile Creek near Hackensack, are named, like the larger Whitefish Lake on the Pine River in Crow Wing County, for their highly valued fish of this species, common or abundant in many lakes of northern Minnesota. The Ojibwe fisheries of Leech Lake are mentioned by Warren as follows: "The waters of the lake abound in fish of the finest quality, its whitefish equalling in size and flavor those of Lake Superior, and they are easily caught at all seasons of the year when the lake is free of ice, in gill-nets made and managed also by the women."

The Jack Pine Lakes, two of small size near together, in sections 28, 32, and 33, Hiram, the outflowing Pine Lake Brook, the large Pine Mountain Lake, which receives this brook, and its outlet, called Twenty-four Mile Creek or Norway Brook, flowing through Norway Lake, are lumbermen's names of the headwaters of Pine River.

On the west side of section 31, Bull Moose, is Township Corner Lake, so named from its location, and on the west line of sections 18 and 19, Bungo, is Spider Lake, named from its irregular and branching shape.

Stony Creek, flowing into the eastern end of Wabedo Lake, Stony Brook, tributary to the Upper Gull Lake, and Mosquito Brook and Swan Creek, respectively emptying into Crow Wing River about 7 and 14 miles west of Pillager, are names that need no explanations for their significance.

A few other names of lakes remain to be noted, including Lake Kilpatrick, through which Home Brook flows, probably named for a former lumberman there; War Club Lake in sections 9 and 16, Deerfield, named for its shape; Island Lake in section 7, Powers; Portage Lake in section 28, Shingobee, smaller than the other Portage Lake near Lake Winnibigoshish; Bass Lake in sections 24 and 25, Shingobee; Duck or Swamp Lake, a mile west from the north end of Duck Bay of Leech Lake; and Long Lake in the east half of Kego Township.

Schoolcraft State Park

In 1959 the state recognized the contribution of Henry R. Schoolcraft to the exploration of the Northwest by creating a park named for him. Situated along the Mississippi River near the outflow of the Vermilion River, the area probably was once a campsite of the expedition. Visitors to the 295-acre recreation area still find remnants of the logging enterprise that took place here.

Chippewa National Forest

By an act of Congress approved May 23, 1908, the Minnesota National Forest was established, comprising an area of about 14 government survey townships. It became the Chippewa National Forest on June 22, 1928. It lies mainly in the north part of Cass County, north of Leech Lake and River, extending to Cass Lake, and including Lake Winnibigoshish, with about four townships at its north and northwest sides in Itasca County. This large tract covers the Leech Lake Reservation, which had been long previously established. The text of the law for this national forest, fully safeguarding the rights of the Indians to whom it had been reserved, is published in the *Thirteenth Annual Report of the Forestry Commissioner of Minnesota*, Gen. C. C. Andrews, for the year 1907.

Leech Lake Reservation

Cass County has the Leech Lake Reservation (formerly called the Chippewa Indian Reservation). It is one of seven reservations in this state that have been set apart for bands of the Ojibwe (Chippewa). The reservation adjoins the north side of Leech Lake and its outlet, the Leech Lake River, extending thence north to the Mississippi, Cass Lake, and Lake Winnibigoshish, and it also extends east across the Mississippi to include a tract equal to about four townships in Itasca County. It was set apart for the Ojibwe of the Mississippi in a treaty at Washington, March 19, 1867.

The reservation continues along the south and east shores of Leech Lake, between Shingobee Creek and Boy River. It includes the village of Leech Lake Agency at the east side of Agency Bay. This part of the reservation, another at the north side of Lake Winnibigoshish, and a third part on the north side of Cass Lake, and including all its islands, were set apart for the Pillager and Winnibigoshish bands of the Ojibwe by a treaty at Washington, February 22, 1855; their areas were enlarged by executive orders of the president in 1873 and 1874.

Boutwell wrote of the Pillager band at Leech Lake in 1832 during the expedition with Schoolcraft to Lake Itasca: "This band is the largest and perhaps the most warlike in the whole Ojibway nation. It numbers 706, exclusive of a small band, probably 100, on Bear Island, one of the numerous islands in the lake" (MHS Collections 5: 481).

Chippewa County

This county, established February 20, 1862, and organized March 5, 1868, is named for the Chippewa River, which here joins the Minnesota. The river was called Manya Wakan ("of remarkable or wonderful bluffs") by the Dakota. Its present name was also given by the Dakota, because the country of their enemies, the Ojibwe or Chippewa Indians, extended southwestward to the headwaters of this stream, at Chippewa Lake in Douglas County. As the Chippewa River of Wisconsin received its name from war parties of this tribe descending it to the Mississippi, likewise the river in Minnesota was named for this tribe, whose warriors sometimes made it a part of their "war road" to the Minnesota valley, coming with their canoes from Leech Lake and Mille Lacs by the Crow Wing, Long Prairie, and Chippewa Rivers. The earliest publication of the name Chippewa River was by William H. Keating and Joseph N. Nicollet, though only the other Dakota name, Manya Wakan, is given on Nicollet's map. Ojibwe is more accurately the aboriginal tribal title, which is often anglicized as Chippewa, with the final vowel long. The form Ojibwe has been used in nearly all the publications of the Minnesota Historical Society. It is asserted by William W. Warren, the Ojibwe historian, that this name means "to roast till puckered up," referring to the torture of prisoners taken in war.

By the early French voyageurs and writers, the Ojibwe were commonly called Saulteurs, from their once living in large numbers about the Sault Ste. Marie. Their area, however, also comprised a great part of the shores of Lakes Huron and Superior, with the adjoining country to variable distances inland. During the eighteenth century they much extended their range southwestward, driving the Dakota from the wooded part of Minnesota, and also spreading across the Red River valley to the Turtle Mountain on the boundary between North Dakota and Manitoba.

William W. Warren, whose mother was Ojibwe, prepared, in 1851–53, an extended and very valuable *History of the Ojibway People*, chiefly relating to its part in Minnesota and Wisconsin, which was published in 1885 as Volume V of the Minnesota Historical Society Collections. In Volume IX of the same series, published in 1901, Rev. Joseph A. Gilfillan, who during 25 years was a very devoted missionary among the Ojibwe in the White Earth Reservation and other large parts of northern Minnesota, contributed a paper (74 pp.) vividly portraying the habits and mode of life of this people, their customs and usages in intercourse with each other and with the white people, their diverse types of physical and mental development and characteristics, and much of their recent history. The next paper in the same volume is by Bishop Henry B. Whipple, titled "Civilization and Christianization of the Ojibways in Minnesota" (14 pp.).

Information of the derivations and meanings of names in this county has been gathered from History of the Minnesota Valley, *1882, in pages 913–37; from* History of Chippewa and Lac qui Parle Counties, *by Lycurgus R. Moyer and O. G. Dale, joint editors, two volumes, 1916; and from Frank E. Bentley, judge of probate, J. J. Stennes, county auditor, and Elias Jacobson, clerk of the court, also much from the late Lycurgus R. Moyer, court commissioner and editor of the recently published county history, each of these being interviewed during my visit to Montevideo in July 1916.*

AGGIE a country post office, 1895–1902, in Grace Township, section 30, named for postmaster A. B. Stewart's wife, Agnes.

ASBURY a Great Northern Railway station in Granite Falls Township, section 3, was named, like the villages and post offices of this name in nine other states, in honor of Francis Asbury, the first Methodist Episcopal bishop in the United States, who was born in England, 1745, and died in Virginia, 1816. He was sent by John Wesley as a missionary to the American colonies in 1771.

BIG BEND CITY a village of Big Bend Township, section 2. The village had a general store, a roller mill, and a creamery.

BIG BEND TOWNSHIP first settled in July 1867, organized April 7, 1874, received its name for the bend of the Chippewa River in the north part of this township.

BUNDE a village of Clara City Township. W. D. Ammerman from Bunde, Rheiderland, Germany, tried to give this name to the township with no success; however, he gave the name to the Bunde Christian Reform Church and the small village he established.

CHIPPEWA CITY see MONTEVIDEO.

CLARA CITY a railway village on the line of Rheiderland and Stoneham, founded in 1887, was named in honor of the wife of Theodor F. Koch, one of the managers for a Holland syndicate buying farmlands and establishing colonies here. The railroad route in 1881 brought a depot, a water tank, and a windmill; the post office opened in postmaster Jacob Meyering's store. It was incorporated as a village on September 2, 1891.

CRATE TOWNSHIP was at first named Willow Lake for the lake, now drained, that was crossed by its south boundary. That name, however, could not be accepted by the state auditor because it had been previously given to another township of this state. The present name was selected by the citizens on July 23, 1888, in compliment to Fanning L. Beasley, an early homesteader in section 4, this being a nickname by which he was generally known. It had reference to his middle name, Lucretius.

EAST GRANITE FALLS a city that is part of Granite Falls, Yellow Medicine County. Henry Hill made a claim, laid out a townsite, and built a log house in 1870, followed by a gristmill and a water power system in 1871, which became the source of electricity for the power plant of greater Granite Falls. John Humphrey, grandfather of Vice-president Hubert H. Humphrey, had a sawmill and provided ferry service until a bridge was built in 1876. A post office operated 1880–90, with Aaron B. Register, postmaster; the Weaver House built by J. A. Weaver, a railroad man, is on the National Register of Historic Places.

GLITNER a country post office in section 15 of Mandt Township, 1891–1905; as Mandt Township never had a village; this post office, the general store nearby, and the Central Creamery built in 1899 were the only buildings forming a small community; also shown on maps as Glittner, Glentner, and Giltner.

GLUEK a village in Crate Township, section 31, developed in 1927 as a result of promises of becoming a railroad center; the Minnesota Western Railroad wanted the new town to be called Wesota because it was a Minnesota line serving the western part of the state; however, the name Gluek was attached to the community because Gluek Brewing Company financed the finishing of the line. A post office operated 1928–56, at which time it became a rural branch.

GRACE TOWNSHIP first settled in October 1869, and organized August 9, 1880, was named in honor of Grace Whittemore, daughter of Augustus A. Whittemore, a homesteader in section 8, who was the contractor and builder of the courthouse in Montevideo.

GRACELOCK a post office, 1901–3, located in Havelock Township, section 5.

GRANITE FALLS see YELLOW MEDICINE COUNTY.

GRANITE FALLS TOWNSHIP settled in 1866 and set apart for organization March 9, 1880, received its name from the rock outcrops and falls of the

Minnesota River here. This name is also borne by the adjoining city of Granite Falls, which is the county seat of Yellow Medicine County, and which extends across the river to include a part of section 34 in this township.

HAGAN in Big Bend Township was first settled in 1869 in section 3, with N. K. Hagen as first treasurer of the township and postmaster in his home, 1872–81, the postal department misspelling the name. The post office transferred to Swift County, 1881–83, returning to Chippewa County until 1907.

HAVELOCK TOWNSHIP settled in June 1872, organized October 6, 1873, was named by John C. and Aaron J. Mullin, brothers, and other settlers from the eastern provinces of Canada, in honor of the English general Sir Henry Havelock (1795–1857), the hero who in 1857 relieved the siege of Lucknow, India. The village of Havelock, in section 5, had a post office in section 20, 1881 and 1892–1901, until rural routes took over.

HAWK CREEK a post office, 1868–71, transferred to Jeanettville, Renville County.

HILL a post office, 1883–88; location not found.

KALMIA a post office, 1880–83, in Big Bend Township, formerly named Unadilla, 1872–80, with a gristmill at the site.

KRAGERO first permanently settled in 1867–68, organized April 7, 1873, was named for Hans H. Kragero, a pioneer farmer here, whose surname was taken from his native town, the seaport of Kragero in southern Norway, on an inlet of the Skagerrak. He was born June 17, 1841; was a sailor, and afterward lived in Chicago, 1866–69; and came to Minnesota in 1870, settling in section 12 of the south part of this township. The township had a post office, 1875–78.

LAC QUI PARLE MISSION the trading post of Joseph Renville, and the early Presbyterian mission for the Dakota conducted by Dr. Thomas S. Williamson and Stephen R. Riggs, 1835–54, were in what is now section 13 in the southern corner of Kragero, nearly opposite the mouth of the Lac qui Parle River and southeast from the foot of the lake. The site of the old mission station is marked by a granite block, inscribed "Lac qui Parle Mission, 1835." The mission is also the site of the first church building in the state, erected in 1841 on the bluff overlooking the Minnesota River near Lac qui Parle Lake; the mission is managed as a historic site by the Chippewa County Historical Society.

LEENTHROP TOWNSHIP settled in 1870, organized January 20, 1872, has probably a Swedish name, anglicized in spelling.

LONE TREE TOWNSHIP organized August 5, 1878, received its name for a lone and tall cottonwood tree near the west end of Bad Water or Lone Tree Lake, which tree was a landmark for the first immigrants.

LOURISTON settled in 1867, organized September 18, 1877, was named in compliment for Laura Armstrong, daughter of Henry Armstrong, who was a homesteader on section 8, and who was elected in the first township meeting as one of its justices and a member of its board of supervisors. The village of Louriston, section 6, had a post office, 1874–1909, located in the store owned by Henry Armstrong, with John S. Barnett first postmaster; the Donner Store was built in section 28 of the township, and when the Armstrong store closed, the post office was moved there; the Donner store closed in 1982.

MANDT first settled in 1869 and organized June 13, 1876, was named in honor of Engelbreth T. Mandt, an early settler in section 30, at whose house the first town meeting was held, in which also he taught the first school in the spring of 1875. The township had a rural branch post office, 1905–10.

MAYNARD a city in Stoneham Township, sections 29 to 32, was platted in 1887 by John M. Spicer of Willmar, superintendent of this division of the Great Northern Railway, and was named "in honor of his sister's husband." The city was built on a townsite owned by J. V. H. Bailey and L. D. Ruddock and laid out by county surveyor Lycurgus Moyer; it was incorporated on January 8, 1897; its post office began in 1889. The city had five elevators, blacksmiths, hardware stores, grocery stores, banks, livery barns, and professional offices.

MILAN a city in Kragero Township, was settled in 1870, was laid out as a village in 1880 by the Chicago, Milwaukee and St. Paul Railroad, was platted December 1, 1880, and was incorporated February 23, 1893. This name of the great city in northern Italy is borne also by villages in twelve other states of our Union. Thorbjorn Anderson provided postal service beginning in 1879 at his Anderson Department Store, which was sold to

A. Anderson, who enlarged it, claiming it to be the largest between Minneapolis and Aberdeen, S.Dak.; in 1891 Thorbjorn Anderson established the bank.

MINNESOTA FALLS a railway station of the Minneapolis, St. Paul and Sault Ste. Marie Railroad (Soo Line) located in Granite Falls Township, section 1, established in 1879, bears the name of a township and former village in Yellow Medicine County, on the opposite side of the Minnesota River, where on a fall or rapids of the river a dam and a sawmill and a flouring mill were built in 1871–72.

MONTEVIDEO the county seat, was platted May 25, 1870, was incorporated as a village March 4, 1879, and as a city June 30, 1908. This Latin name, signifying "from the mountain I see," or "Mount of Vision," was selected, according to the late L. R. Moyer, by Cornelius J. Nelson, a settler who came here in 1870 from the state of New York, platted additions to the village in 1876 and 1878, and was its president in 1881 and 1885–87. The village and future city "was given its high-sounding appellation by its romantic founders, who were so delighted by the wonderful view gained from the heights overlooking the interlocking valleys of the Minnesota and Chippewa Rivers at that point, that they translated their feeling into good, mouth-filling Latin." But this name, while very appropriate on account of the view here, was derived by Nelson from the large South American city that is the capital of Uruguay, whence the mayor of that Montevideo about the year 1905 presented the Uruguayan flag to this municipality.

Another good reason for the choice of this name, in allusion to the grand prospect seen from the river bluffs, may have been found in the aboriginal Dakota name of the Chippewa River, before noted as Manya Wakan (meaning "wonderful bluffs"), quite probably so named by these observing people in their admiration, like our own, for the beautiful and noble panorama here spread around them.

An earlier settlement on the opposite side of the Chippewa River was platted and named Chippewa City in the autumn of 1868, and the county seat was there until 1870, when it was changed to the new town of Montevideo by an act of the state legislature. The first permanent settler was

Daniel S. Wilkins, who arrived in Sparta Township in 1865, organized Chippewa City, and was its first postmaster, 1868–70, at his log cabin; the post office name changed to Montevideo in 1870, with George W. Frink, postmaster, who had made the first claim in 1867 across the river from where Chippewa City already existed, built a log cabin on what is now Main Street, and made additions to his cabin creating the first inn and tavern; his claim later became the site of the first community cemetery, and when the residential area was laid out in 1870, Frink built a large home in Frink's Addition.

MOOSEVILLE a village in Grace Township, 15 miles south of Benson, Swift County, on Highway 40; it had two stores, two cafés, and two filling stations. Its name was the most popular for the location, but it was also known as Dead Man Corner because of a 1930s automobile accident there, which killed four people.

MYERS see WEGDAHL.

PALMER CREEK see YELLOW MEDICINE COUNTY.

PIERSON a village in Rheiderland Township, section 14, in the 1930s.

PROSPERITY a post office, 1900–3, in Louriston Township, section 20.

REESOR a farming settlement in Tunsberg Township, section 12; it had a flour mill and a post office, 1870–80, located in postmaster Ole Thorgeson's log cabin.

RHEIDERLAND TOWNSHIP organized August 15, 1887, was named by early settlers from Holland, probably taking this name from Rheydt or Rheidt, a city of Rhenish Prussia, about 12 miles east of the Holland boundary.

ROSEWOOD first settled in 1869, organized September 2, 1871, was named for a village in Ohio, whence several German settlers of this township came.

ROSSLYN a post office, 1878–81, in Lone Tree Township, with Nancy Ross, postmaster; the area was first settled in 1870.

SANNGREN a post office, 1881–83; location not found.

SARON a village of the 1940s near Montevideo.

SIX MILE GROVE a post office, 1867–68; location not found.

SPARTA settled in 1868–69, organized March 22, 1870, was earliest called Chippewa, for the river; was renamed by petition of its people, several of whom had come from Sparta in Wisconsin. The name belonged to a renowned city of ancient Greece, extremely heroic in wars, and it is retained by a modern city partly on the same site. This township "received the first permanent white settlement in the county, it being within its limits that Chippewa City was situated, and a little later Montevideo."

STONEHAM organized August 9, 1880, was so named on the suggestion of a settler who came from the town of Stoneham, Mass., near Boston. A further motive for adoption of this name was to honor another of its citizens, Hammet Stone.

TUNSBERG first settled in the spring of 1865, organized March 21, 1870, is thought to have been named for a locality or a farm in Norway.

UNADILLA see KALMIA

WATSON a city in Tunsberg Township, sections 21 and 28, platted in August 1879 and incorporated as a village on May 24, 1883, was named by officers of the Chicago, Milwaukee and St. Paul Railroad company and was developed when a branch of the railroad came through the village; the station was first named Myers. The Watson Farmers Elevator was built in 1886, possibly the first co-operative elevator in the United States; it was deemed unsafe in 1993 and removed in a controlled burn by the Watson Fire Department. Rasmus Adamson, a blacksmith, was the first resident; the post office opened in 1879, at which time the post offices of Reesor and Wren were closed; Watson's Municipal Liquor Store was organized in 1940 when the county went "wet" and became a main attraction of the town.

WEGDAHL a railway village in section 2 of Sparta Township, was named in honor of the pioneer farmer on whose land it was platted, Hemming Arntzen Wegdahl, who was the first postmaster there. His surname was probably derived from the farm of his native place in Norway. The village began as Myers for the Myers Creamery but was changed to Wegdahl when the post office was established in 1871 at Weghdahl's general store, where it remained until discontinued in 1957, becoming a rural route until 1959. The Sambo Grocery store was built five feet higher than Main Street and had a cement sidewalk in front of it that became the stage for home talent and other shows.

WILLOW CREEK a village in Rosewood Township, section 28.

WILLOW GROVE a post office, 1874–76, in Crate Township.

WOODS TOWNSHIP settled in 1876, was organized in 1879. "Most of the odd sections were sold to a land syndicate headed by judge William W. Woods, of Ohio. It was for him that the township was named" (*History of Chippewa County*, vol. I, p. 214).

WREN a post office, 1871–81, in Tunsberg Township, section 6; the settlement also had a flour mill.

Streams and Lakes

The origin and significance of the name of the Minnesota River, adopted by the state, are presented in the first chapter; the lake of this river, named Lac qui Parle, will be considered in the chapter for the county of that name; and the Chippewa River, giving its name to this county, is fully noticed at the beginning of the present chapter.

Hawk Creek is translated from the Dakota name "Chetambe R.," given on Nicollet's map.

Palmer Creek was named for Frank Palmer, one of the first settlers there in 1866, and Brofee's Creek was likewise named for an early settler, these being tributary to the Minnesota River between Granite Falls and Montevideo.

Spring Creek, Dry Weather Creek, and Cottonwood Creek, flowing into the Chippewa River, need no explanation.

Shakopee Creek and Lake in the north part of Louriston, flowing to the Chippewa River in Swift County, received their name, the Dakota word meaning "six," from the Six Mile grove, which borders the river along that distance and reaches from the mouth of Shakopee Creek northward into Six Mile Grove Township at the center of that county. Another name of the Shakopee Lake, in somewhat common use, is Buffalo Lake.

Black Oak Lake, which was mostly in section 12, Sparta, four miles east of Montevideo, has been drained. It was mapped by Nicollet with its equivalent Dakota and English names, "Hutuhu Sapah, or Black Oak L." A grove of about 40 acres bordered it, as stated by the late L. R. Moyer, comprising many large bur oaks, but no black oaks, although the latter is generally a common or abundant species of southeastern Minnesota.

Willow Lake, previously mentioned in connection with Crate Township, as now drained, was named for its willows, of which eight species or more are found frequent or common throughout the state, ranging in size from low shrubs to small trees. Three shrubby willow species and one of tree size are listed in chapter 3 of the *History of Chippewa County*, by the late L. R. Moyer, titled "The Prairie Flora of Southwestern Minnesota."

Lone Tree Lake, which gave its name to a township, as before noted, has also been known as Bad Water Lake, being somewhat alkaline.

Epple Lake in sections 20 and 29, Woods, and Norberg Lake in section 26, Stoneham, bear the names of adjacent pioneer settlers.

Chisago County

Established September 1, 1851, and organized October 14 of that year, this county bears a name proposed by William H. C. Folsom of Taylors Falls, who wrote of its organization and the derivation of the name as follows (*Fifty Years in the Northwest*, 1888, pp. 298–99 and 306):

"The county takes the name of its largest and most beautiful lake. In its original, or rather aboriginal form, it was Ki-chi-sago, from two Chippewa words meaning 'kichi,' large and 'saga,' fair or lovely. For euphonic considerations the first syllable was dropped.

"This lake is conspicuous for its size, the clearness of its waters, its winding shore and islands, its bays, peninsulas, capes, and promontories. It has fully fifty miles of meandering shore line. Its shores and islands are well timbered with maple and other hard woods. It has no waste swamps, or marsh borders. When the writer first came to Taylor's Falls, this beautiful lake was unknown to fame. No one had seen it or could point out its location. Indians brought fish and maple sugar from a lake which they called Kichi-saga sagiagan, or 'large and lovely lake.' This lake, they said, abounded with 'kego,' fish. . . .

"The movement for the organization of a new county from the northern part of Washington commenced in the winter of 1851–52. A formidable petition to the legislature to make such organization, drawn up and circulated by Hon. Ansel Smith, of Franconia, and the writer, was duly forwarded, presented and acquiesced in by that body. The writer had been selected to visit the capital in the interest of the petitioners. Some difficulty arose as to the name. The writer had proposed 'Chi-sa-ga.' This Indian name was ridiculed, and Hamilton, Jackson, Franklin, and Jefferson, were in turn proposed. The committee of the whole finally reported in favor of the name, Chisaga, but the legislature, in passing the bill for our county organization, by clerical or typographical error changed the last 'a' in 'saga' to 'o,' which, having become the law, has not been changed."

In Frederic Baraga's *A Dictionary of the Ojibway Language* the second of the two Ojibwe words, *saga*, used by Folsom to form this name, is spelled *sasega*, or *sasegamagad*, being defined, "It is fair, it is ornamented, splendid." In pronunciation, this name Chisago has the English sound of *Ch*, and it accents the second syllable, preferably with *a* as in father (but in prevailing use taking the broad sound as in fall).

The sources of information for this county have been Fifty Years in the Northwest, *by William H. C. Folsom, 1888, pages 298–354; and Edward W. Stark, judge of probate, Alfred P. Stolberg, county attorney, and John A. Johnson, sheriff, interviewed during my visit at Center City, the county seat, in May 1916.*

ALMELUND a hamlet in the south part of Amador Township, section 25, founded about 1887, means in the Swedish language "Elm Valley." Most of the settlers were from Småland, Sweden. The first name suggested was Church Hill, until the post office was established in 1887. The name was adopted in compliment to the first postmaster there, John Almquist, whose name means an "elm twig or branch." Almquist, regarded as the founder of the community, was born in 1857 in Småland, emigrated to the United States in 1871 and to Chisago County in 1880, and died in Almelund in 1929. The post office discontinued in 1903 and was reestablished in 1927.

AMADOR settled in 1846, organized in 1858, bears a name that means in the Spanish language "a lover, a sweetheart." It is the name of a county and a village in central California, whence it was adopted here by settlers of this township who had previously visited California. In the same way, probably, came also this name as applied to small villages in Iowa, Kansas, and Michigan. The township had a post office, 1856–62 and 1883–93, in section 2. In 1889–90 the St. Croix Dam and Boom Company built the Nevers Dam in section 9, the world's largest pile-driven dam until it gave way to flood waters in 1954.

BRANCH named from the North Branch of the Sunrise River flowing through this township, "was set off from Sunrise and organized in 1872." The city of Branch in the township was incorporated as a village on March 1, 1961. See **NORTH BRANCH.**

CEDAR CREEK a post office, 1856–57, with Samuel Alyatt, postmaster; location not found.

CENTER CITY a city in Chisago Lake Township, was platted in May 1857 and has been the county seat since 1875. Its name refers to its central position between Chisago City and Taylors Falls. It is the state's oldest continuously inhabited Swedish settlement. It was incorporated as a village on November 10, 1903, and separated from the township on March 16, 1915. The first post of-fice, located in section 26 about one mile east of the present city, was named Centre City, 1858–63, then Chisago Lake, 1863–77, and then again Centre City, until 1893 when the present spelling was established.

CHIPPEWA a rural post office, 1856–58, in Sunrise Township; a townsite was platted in March 1856.

CHISAGO CITY a city in Chisago, Lake, and Wyoming Townships, was platted in 1855, taking its name from the lake. It was incorporated as a village on August 10, 1906. It had a station of the St. Paul and Duluth Railroad in section 6 of Chisago Township and a post office established in 1856.

CHISAGO LAKE see **CENTER CITY.**

CHISAGO LAKE TOWNSHIP likewise named for the beautiful lake, was settled in 1851 and was organized in 1858. This name, given to the county, has been fully noticed on a preceding page.

COON LAKE BEACH a rural branch post office, 1957–58, in Wyoming Township.

DALE a village in Fish Lake Township, section 17, about one mile southeast of Dalstrop, that existed about 1874; its name may be a derivation of Dalstrop or related to the fact that most of the immigrants were from Dalecarlia, Sweden.

DALSTROP a village in Fish Lake Township, section 7, with a farmers post office, 1890–1901.

DANEWOOD a village in Nessel Township, section 4; it began in 1870 with a sawmill, two creameries, and a post office, 1882–1902, with Sophus Albert Nebel, postmaster, general store owner, justice, and secretary of the telephone company.

DEER GARDEN a village in Wyoming Township, section 1, platted in October 1856; had a station of the St. Paul and Duluth Railroad.

DRONDTHEIM a townsite in Sunrise Township, section 1, platted in 1856 by C. C. P. Mayer on land he received in exchange for platting Chisago City; also known as Trontjheim. There is no indication that any buildings were erected.

FISH LAKE TOWNSHIP organized in 1868, having formerly been a part of Sunrise, is named for its lake in section 25 and the outflowing creek, both of which are translated from their Ojibwe names. The village of Fish Lake was located in the township about 1868.

FRANCONIA TOWNSHIP organized in 1858, received its name from the earlier village. The first settler was Ansel Smith, a teacher in St. Croix Falls, who built a home here in 1852, and is said to have named the village for his hometown in the White Mountains of New Hampshire, although others say it was named for his son, Francis, who died shortly before Smith came to Minnesota. Smith operated a trading post and served in the state legislature. This is also an ancient name of a large district in Germany. The lumber village of Franconia, section 3, was platted in 1858 and incorporated as a village in 1884; it is currently unincorporated. The site began developing with houses built along St. Lawrence Creek and on the hillside north of a business area. The tracks of the St. Paul and Duluth Railroad were laid in 1878, with a depot about a mile distant from the community, in section 2. Also arriving in 1852 were Henry and Lawrence Day, who began a factory making plugs for log raft construction, giving rise to the village nickname, Plugtown; three brothers, James, Rufus, and Charles Clark, came in 1855 and built a sawmill in 1856 and a stave mill in 1864. The post office was first located on E. S. White's farm, about one mile from the village, then moved in 1872 to the general store of Jonas Lindall, closing in 1898.

GENTLE PINES a commune near Taylors Falls, circa 1970, in what was once a lake lodge.

HANLEY a post office, 1856–57, John Hanley, postmaster; location not found.

HARRIS a city in Fish Lake Township, sections 21 and 28; first settled in 1870 and incorporated as a village on July 22, 1884. It had a hotel, a livery, and several stores, and a station of the Northern Pacific Railroad in section 28; a post office was established in 1874.

HARRIS TOWNSHIP first settled in 1856 and organized in 1884, received its name from its earlier railway village, which was platted in May 1873 and was incorporated in 1882, being named in honor of Philip S. Harris, a prominent officer of the St. Paul and Duluth Railroad company.

KOST a small village in Sunrise Township, section 29, was named in honor of Ferdinand A. Kost, who built a flouring mill there in 1883. At its height the village had saw, flour, and feed mills, a general store, a blacksmith, a creamery, and a school. It had a post office, 1884–1903, with Kost as first postmaster.

LENT TOWNSHIP organized in 1872, was named in honor of Harvey Lent, one of its first settlers, who came in 1855.

LINDSTROM a city in Chisago Lake Township, section 33, platted in 1880 on the central part of Chisago Lake, including many summer homes of city residents, was named for Daniel Lindstrom, a pioneer farmer. He was born in Helsingland, Sweden, in 1825; came to the United States, settling here; sold the greater part of his farm in 1878, which became the village site; and continued to reside here until his death in 1895. The city was incorporated as a village on August 28, 1894, and reincorporated on April 9, 1908; it has had a city charter since 1950. Its post office was established in 1880. The village had a station of the St. Paul and Duluth Railroad, three newspapers, including a Swedish weekly, two hotels, and a flour mill and grain elevator.

MARTINS a village in Rusheba Township, section 13, about 1916.

MIDDLE BRANCH two post offices by this name: the first, 1858–62, was transferred to Wyoming; the second operated 1864–65; exact locations not found.

MUSKOOTINK a post office, 1858–70, George L. Blood, postmaster; location not found.

NASHUA a village in Sunrise Township, sections 33 and 34, platted in July 1857.

NELSON'S BEACH a village in Chisago Lake Township, sections 28 and 33, about 1914–16.

NESSEL set off from Rushseba and organized in 1870, bears the name of its earliest pioneer farmer, Robert Nessel, who was born in Germany, 1834, came to the United States in 1847 and to Minnesota in 1854, and settled here in 1856.

NORTH BRANCH a city in Branch Township, sections 16, 17, 20, and 21, named for the North Branch of the Sunrise River and platted in January 1870; incorporated as a village on November 19, 1881, and included all of Branch Township until 1901 when reincorporation gave North Branch an area of one square mile and Branch Township was reestablished. Branch and North Branch merged in November 1994 to become North Branch. The first settler was John Elmgren, a Swedish farmer and railroad man, who came in the late 1860s; the community had G. M. Flanders's store, built in 1868, which was the start of the community and the site of the first post office in 1889; a station of the St. Paul and Duluth Railroad; J. F. Swanson's saloon and his flour mill, built in 1874 and burned in 1878; and the North

Branch Milling Company, organized in 1899. Lem Quillan came with a circus in 1877 and stayed to operate a store and the opera hall.

PALMDALE a village in Shafer Township, section 9, whose name was formed from a combination of the names of Frank Palmquist, an 1881 settler, and his wife, Ogda Emelia Elmdahl. Its post office operated 1899–1903; at the turn of the century, the community had a store, a creamery, a blacksmith, and a meeting and dance hall.

PANOLA a country post office, 1889–1901, located in Chisago Lake Township, with two feed mills and a sawmill nearby.

RUSH CITY a city of Rushseba Township; incorporated on March 8, 1873, and reincorporated on February 16, 1909. It had a station on the St. Paul and Duluth Railroad, lumber and flour mills, elevators, and a post office established in 1870; it was briefly called Rush in 1895. The city received this record by Folsom: "In 1868, at the completion of the St. Paul and Duluth railroad, a depot was built and a station established at the crossing of Rush river, around which rapidly grew up the village of Rush City. It was surveyed and platted by Benjamin W. Brunson, surveyor, in January, 1870."

RUSH POINT a village located in Rushseba Township, section 28; settled in 1870, with a steam sawmill, general stores, several churches, and a post office, 1879–1903, at which time it was absorbed by Rush City.

RUSHEBY a rural post office, 1856–70, with George B. Folsom first postmaster; location not found.

RUSHSEBA TOWNSHIP organized in 1858, is in its second part an Ojibwe name, *seba* or *sippi*, meaning "a river." Both Rush Lake in Nessel Township and its outflowing Rush River are translated from the aboriginal name. Several species of bulrushes and other rushes are common throughout this state, one of which (*Scirpus lacustris*), abundant in the shallow borders of lakes, was "in common use among the Indians for making mats."

ST. CROIX RIVER a village in Rushseba Township, section 8, with a Northern Pacific Railroad station of this name in Franconia Township, section 2. The station was named for the river crossed there, of which an extended notice in respect to the origin of the name has been given in the first chapter.

SHAFER TOWNSHIP is noticed as follows by Folsom: "A Swedish colony settled here in 1853. . . . The town organized first as Taylor's Falls but the name was changed to Shafer in 1873. . . . A railroad station . . . bears the name of Shafer, derived, together with the name of the township, from Jacob Shafer, who, as early as 1847, cut hay in sections 4 and 5. He seems to have been in no sense worthy of the honor conferred upon him, as he was but a transient inhabitant and disappeared in 1849. No one knows of his subsequent career. The honor ought to have been given to some of the hardy Swedes, who were the first real pioneers, and the first to make substantial improvements." The city of Shafer in section 32 was settled in 1881, and a post office was established the same year; incorporated as a village on March 14, 1922.

SNAKE RIVER DAM a post office, 1856, on the Pine County border and transferred to Alhambra in Pine County.

STACY a city in Lent Township, sections 29 and 32, first settled in 1870 and established in 1875, was named in honor of Dr. Stacy B. Collins, an early resident. The post office was established in 1873, and the village had a station of the St. Paul and Duluth Railroad; it was incorporated as a village on April 13, 1923.

STARK a small village in section 26, Fish Lake Township, was named in honor of Lars Johan Stark, who was the first postmaster there. He was born in Westergotland, Sweden, July 29, 1826, and died in Harris, Minn., May 5, 1910. He came to the United States in 1850 and settled at Chisago Lake, Minn., engaged in mercantile business and farming, and was a representative in the state legislature in 1865 and 1875. His son, Edward W. Stark, born in Fish Lake Township, December 5, 1869, was a merchant at Harris, 1890–1905; was a representative in the legislature in 1901–3; and was a judge of probate for this county after 1905. The village had a post office, 1868–1904.

SUNRISE TOWNSHIP organized October 26, 1858, had earlier a village of this name on the Sunrise prairie, where in 1853 a hotel and store were built by William Holmes. The name is received from the lake and river, whose Ojibwe name, Memokage (pronounced in four syllables), is translated by Gilfillan as "Sun-keep-rising." The village in sections 4 and 5, on the Sunrise River, began as a trading post for fur traders, lumberjacks, and occasionally Indians; the original townsite consisted of 19 blocks surveyed for proprietor John A. Brown by W. P. Payte in 1856; a second plat was done in 1857 with an addition and again in 1887 with additions. The first store was Brown's in 1853 (burned in 1944); the community had a few stores, a hotel, and a dance hall. The post office began as Sunrise City in 1856, changed to Sunrise in 1894, and discontinued in 1954.

TAYLORS FALLS a city at the head of the Dalles of the St. Croix River, in Shafer Township, platted in 1850–51, incorporated July 15, 1858, during many years the county seat, was named for Jesse Taylor, who came in 1838, and Joshua L. Taylor, to whom the former sold his claim in 1846. Jesse Taylor, pioneer, was born in Kentucky; was employed as a stone mason at Fort Snelling; was the first settler here, in 1838, and owned a sawmill; removed to Stillwater in 1846 and resided there until 1853; and was a representative in the territorial legislature, 1851–52. Joshua Lovejoy Taylor was born in Sanbornton, N.H., in 1816, and died in Ashland, Wis., April 27, 1901. He came to Minnesota in 1840, settling at Taylors Falls; engaged in lumbering; preempted a part of the site of this village; lived in California, 1849–56; returned here in 1856; and removed to Ashland in 1896. The city was reincorporated on November 14, 1901, and March 14, 1913, at which time it separated from the township. The city was earlier known as Baker's Falls when a company of that name was located here, then Taylor Place when platted; the post office was established in 1851, while still part of Washington County, Nathan C. D. Taylor, first postmaster. The community is the access point to the Dalles of the St. Croix River and Interstate Park.

Folsom wrote of this village and the adjacent part of the river at the Interstate bridge: "Many of the later residents query as to why it was ever called Taylor's Falls. It takes a keen eye to discover any fall in the river at the point named. The falls indeed were once far more conspicuous than they are now, owing to the fact that a large rock rose above the water at the ordinary stage, around which the crowded waters roared and swirled. That rock, never visible in later days, was called Death Rock, because three hapless mariners in a skiff were hurled against it by the swift current and drowned."

TRONTJHEIM see **DRONDTHEIM**.

WASHINGTON a village in Branch Township, sections 25 and 26, which was laid out in August 1856 by J. Y. Caldwell.

WILD RIVER JUNCTION a settlement founded by Sanford Brink near Taylors Falls, designed as a recreational center; existed circa 1950–70.

WOODLAWN BEACH a village in T. 33N, R. 20W, section 8, about 1914–20.

WYOMING TOWNSHIP organized in 1858, derived its name from the Wyoming Valley in Luzerne County, Pa., which is traversed by the North Branch of the Susquehanna River. A colony from that region settled in the western part of this township in 1855, and the eastern part had been earlier settled by Swedes. The city of Wyoming, sections 17 to 20, located on West Branch of the Sunrise River, was platted in 1869, the next year after the completion of the St. Paul and Duluth Railroad, and ten years later the branch from Wyoming to Taylors Falls was built. The post office was established in 1856; the Tombler Hotel built in 1855 burned in 1876 and was rebuilt; other early businesses included a patent medicine manufacturer.

This name, given also to the Territory of Wyoming, organized in 1868 and admitted to the Union as a state in 1890, is from the language of the Delaware or Lenape Indians, formerly a large branch of the Algonquian stock, signifying "large plains," "extensive meadows."

Lakes and Streams

In the preceding pages attention has been given to the names of several lakes and streams, including Chisago Lake, the Sunrise River and its North Branch, Fish Lake, and the Rush Lake and River. The St. Croix River, belonging to several counties, is considered in the first chapter with the large rivers of this state.

Names commemorating pioneer settlers include four in Fish Lake Township. These are Alexis Lake in sections 5 and 8, for John P. Alexis; Mandall Lake in the northwest quarter of section 15, for Lars Mandall; Molberg Lake in the northwest quarter of section 22, for Erick Molberg; and Neander Lake, section 11, named for Nels P. Neander. All of these settlers came as farmers, themselves or their parents being immigrants from Sweden.

Browning Creek in Harris was named for John W. Browning, a pioneer farmer from the eastern states and of English descent.

Colby Lake, about a mile northwest of Taylors Falls, was named for an early farmer who likewise came from the eastern states.

Bloom's Lake in section 7, Franconia, was named in honor of Gustaf Bloom, from Sweden, whose son, David Bloom, became county register of deeds in 1909; and Ogren's Lake in section 12 of this township, for Andrew Ogren, who was a soldier in the Civil War.

Linn Lake, adjoining the south end of the eastern body of Chisago Lake, was named for a family living at its west side.

Lake Comfort in sections 22 and 27, Wyoming, bears the name of Dr. John W. Comfort, a physician who lived there and had a wide country practice. It is also very frequently called "the Doctor's lake."

Heim's Lake in sections 29 and 30, Wyoming, mostly drained, received its name for families living there, especially for Conrad Heim, the pioneer.

Martha and Ellen Lakes, beside the railway in sections 1 and 12, Wyoming, and nearly adjoining the north end of Green Lake, are also commemorative of early pioneers, but inquiries have failed to supply their surnames.

Other lakes and creeks in this county, mostly bearing names that scarcely need explanations of their derivation, are Asp Lake in the northwest quarter of section 21, Fish Lake Township, having aspen or poplar groves; Pine Lake in sections 23 and 26, Nessel, for its white pines; another Pine Lake, about a mile south from the most southwestern arm of Chisago Lake, situated, like the foregoing, near the southwestern limit of the geographic range of our pines; Grass Lake, about two miles northeast of Harris, shallow and having much marsh grass on its borders; the Little Duck Lake in section 19, Franconia; the much larger Goose Lake and Goose Creek, flowing thence eastward to the St. Croix River; Spring Creek, tributary to the St. Croix three miles farther north; Rock Creek, flowing through the northeast part of Rushseba, named for the conspicuous rock outcrops on the St. Croix River about a half mile northeast from its mouth; Dry Creek in section 2, Shafer; Hay Creek, flowing into the Sunrise River three miles from its mouth; the Middle,

West, and South branches of the Sunrise River; Leech Lake, sections 35 and 36, Nessel, named, like the great Leech Lake in Cass County, for its plentiful leeches; Horseshoe and Little Horseshoe Lakes, respectively in sections 23 and 22, Fish Lake Township, named for their form; Horseshoe Creek, their outlet; Chain Lake in section 6, Branch, named for its form or outline, and for the small lakes connected with it southward in a chainlike series; Mud Lake in section 28, Lent, shallow, with muddy shores and bottom; School Lake in the school section 36, Lent; Spring Lake, one to two miles west of Lindstrom; Little Lake, a misnomer as it is nearly a mile long, lying a mile and a half northeast from Center City; Ice Lake in section 30, Franconia; Swamp Lake, sections 14 and 23, Franconia; Spider Lake, named for its branched outline, in section 27, near the south end of Chisago Lake Township; First, Second, and Third Lakes, consecutive in an east to west series, in sections 34 to 32, about a mile south and southwest of Spider Lake; Green Lake, after Chisago Lake the second in size in this county, named for the clearness and beauty of its water, reflecting the verdure of the grass and trees on its banks; and White Stone Lake in sections 11 and 14, Wyoming, named for its white pebbles or boulders.

Interstate Park at the Dalles of the St. Croix

The Legislative Manual of Minnesota, for 1907 and ensuing sessions, gives the following statement of the origin of this public park:

"In 1895 the State of Minnesota, by a legislative act, set aside a tract of about 110 acres in the town of Taylor's Falls, Chisago county, as a public park, to be called the State Park of the Dalles of the St. Croix. An act was also passed by the Wisconsin legislature of the same year, which provided a commission to ascertain the probable cost of acquiring a larger tract for a state park on the opposite side of the St. Croix River; and in 1899 and 1901 the State of Wisconsin passed acts for the purchase of lands there, amounting to about 600 acres. The original park on the Minnesota side of the river has been extended to an area of about 150 acres, and plans are under consideration for further extension to a total of about 500 acres in Minnesota. The two states have thus established an Interstate Park, including the grand and picturesque rock gorge called the Upper Dalles of the St. Croix, where the river for a distance of two-thirds of a mile, at and just south of the village of Taylor's Falls, flows through a chasm walled by cliffs of rock 75 to 150 feet high.

"The first suggestion for devoting this tract of remarkable natural beauty to such public use was made by George H. Hazzard, a pioneer of Minnesota Territory, to members of the Minnesota legislature in 1893. His idea was welcomed with enthusiasm by newspapers, commercial bodies, and the people of the State."

The name *Dalles,* applied by the early French voyageurs to rock-walled gorges of the Wisconsin River, the St. Croix and St. Louis Rivers in Minnesota, and the Columbia River on the boundary between Oregon and Washington, came from the French word *dalle,* meaning "a flagstone or slab of rock," referring in this name to the vertical and jointed rock cliffs enclosing the rivers at the localities so named, where in most instances (though not in the case of the St. Croix) the river flows through its gorge in rapids and falls.

In the Upper Dalles, at Taylors Falls, and again in the Lower Dalles, situated two miles farther down the river and reaching a third of a mile, close above the village of Franconia, the rock walls of trap, Keweenawan diabase, rise almost or quite perpendicularly on each side of the river, enclosing it at each place by a very picturesque gorge.

A paper titled "Giants' Kettles Eroded by Moulin Torrents," contributed by the present writer to the *Bulletin of the Geological Society of America* (vol. 12, 1900, pp. 25–44, with a map), was partly quoted as follows by the *Legislative Manual* in 1907 and 1909:

"To nearly every visitor the most interesting and wonderful feature of the Interstate Park consists in many large and small waterworn potholes, which are also, in their large examples, often called 'wells.' The languages of Germany, Sweden, and Norway, give the name 'giants' kettles' to such cylindric or caldron-shaped holes of stream erosion, which are everywhere characteristic of waterfalls and rapids, especially in crystalline rocks. These potholes, occurring most numerously near the steamboat landing of Taylor's Falls, at the central part of the Upper Dalles, and within a distance of fifty rods northward, are unsurpassed by any other known locality in the world, in respect to their variety of forms and grouping, their great number, the extraordinary irregularity of contour of the much jointed diabase in which they are eroded, and the difficulty of explanation of the conditions of their origin."

Like the giants' kettles of the Glacier Garden at Lucerne, Switzerland, these larger and deeper potholes are ascribed "to erosion by torrents of water falling through crevasses and vertical tunnels, called moulins, of an ice-sheet during some stage of the Glacial period. In this park they seem referable to the stage of final melting and departure of the ice-sheet from this area."

Wild River State Park

In 1968 the upper St. Croix River was added to the National Wild and Scenic Rivers System. With this impetus, the state proceeded to create a Wild River State Park. At the same time, the Northern States Power Company followed through with plans to donate 4,497 acres from a strip of land along the river in northern Chisago County to the state for use as a park. In 1973 the state had its fifth park on the St. Croix, but legislation for this one specified environmental rather than recreational uses. The park contains the remains of two fur trading posts and the town of Amador, along with the remnants of the dam site.

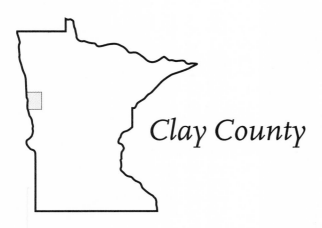

Clay County

This county, established March 8, 1862, and organized April 14, 1872, was named for the greatly admired statesman Henry Clay, of Lexington, Ky. He was born in Hanover County, Va., April 12, 1777; died in Washington, D.C., June 29, 1852. He began to study law in 1796, and in the next year, being admitted to practice, he removed to Kentucky; was U.S. senator, 1806–7 and 1810–11; was a member of Congress, 1811–21 and 1823–25, serving as speaker in 1811–14, 1815–20, and 1823–25; was peace commissioner at Ghent in 1814; was candidate for the presidency in 1824; secretary of state, 1825–29; again U.S. senator, 1831–42 and 1849–52; was Whig candidate for the presidency in 1832 and 1844; was the chief designer of the "Missouri Compromise," 1820, and of the compromise of 1850; was the author of the compromise tariff of 1833; said in a speech in 1850, "I would rather be right than be President."

Among the numerous biographies of Henry Clay, the most extended is by Rev. Calvin Colton, six volumes, containing speeches and correspondence, published in 1846–57; its revised edition, 1864; and its republication in 1904, ten volumes, with an introduction by Thomas B. Reed, and a "History of Tariff Legislation, 1812–96," by William McKinley.

Carl Schurz, on the final page of his *Life of Henry Clay*, published in 1887 (two volumes, in the "American Statesmen" series), pointed to his greatest political motive: "It was a just judgment which he pronounced upon himself when he wrote, 'If any one desires to know the leading and paramount object of my public life, the preservation of this Union will furnish the key.'" Near the end of the dark first year of the Civil War, and nearly ten years after Clay had died, this county was named. Minnesota had then raised four regiments for the defense of the Union.

Information of the origins and meanings of names in this county has been received from History of the Red River Valley, *two vols., 1909, pp. 798–830; from Hon. Solomon G. Comstock, of Moorhead, and Andrew O. Houglum, county auditor, interviewed during my visit in Moorhead in September 1916; and from Nathan Butler of Minneapolis, who was formerly a resident in Barnesville during twenty years, 1883–1903.*

ALLIANCE TOWNSHIP was named for the Farmers' Alliance, a political party of considerable prominence in Minnesota during the campaign of 1890. Hon. George N. Lamphere, in a paper titled "History of Wheat Raising in the Red River Valley" (MHS Collections 10: 1–33), stated that the agitation for lower railroad freight rates, which was the cause of the formation of the Farmers' Alliance, began in 1883–84 in Clay County, spread thence throughout the wheat-raising districts of this state and developed into the People's or Populist Party.

AMRUM a post office, 1902–3, with Jurgen P. Schnoor, postmaster; location not found.

AVERILL a railway village in Moland Township, section 1, platted in 1901 by county surveyor C. P. Jones for Emmett L. and Kate Dykeman, was named in honor of Gen. John Thomas Averill, who was born in Alma, Maine, March 1, 1825, and died in St. Paul, Minn., October 3, 1889. He was graduated at Wesleyan College; settled in Lake City, Minn., 1857; served during the Civil War in the Sixth Minnesota Regiment, becoming its colonel in 1864, and was brevetted a brigadier general in 1865. After the war he founded and conducted a wholesale paper house in St. Paul under the name of Averill, Carpenter and Co. In 1858–60 he was a state senator and in 1872–75 represented his district in Congress. The village had a grain elevator, a general store, a station of the Great Northern Railway, and a post office, 1899–1969.

BAKER a railway village in section 1, Alliance, was named for Lester H. Baker, a farmer there, who removed to the state of Washington. The village was first settled in 1879, the Great Northern Railway coming in 1880, and the first building was erected in 1883 by John Erickson to store grain; the post office was established as Navan in 1894 in Baker's store, the railroad requesting the name change in 1903 to Baker in his honor.

BARNES a village in Glyndon Township, with a station of the Northern Pacific Railroad.

BARNESVILLE TOWNSHIP was named after its railway village, which was established in 1874 by George S. Barnes, a farmer and wheat merchant, who owned and managed a very large farm near Glyndon and died there about the year 1910. Barnes built the first store, became president of North Pacific Grain Company, organized the Northern Pacific Elevator Company, and was responsible for construction of grain elevators along the Northern Pacific Railroad from St. Paul to Tacoma, Washington. The village was incorporated November 4, 1881, and received its charter as a city April 4, 1889; the post office began in 1877, and the village was platted in 1882. Hostile feelings among some settlers created a New Barnesville in 1883, formally organized in 1886, but reunited with Barnesville in 1889; the com-

munity served as an important agricultural market for the southern part of the county.

BONA a post office, 1902–4, in Alliance Township, section 20.

BORUP a post office, 1880–81, H. B. Jacobs, postmaster; location not found.

BURBANKTON a village in Kurtz Township, seven miles south of Moorhead at the mouth of Wild Rice River, which had a Catholic mission.

BURLINGTON a village in Kurtz Township, near Rustad, which had a Catholic church.

CARLETON a village in Moorhead Township, north of Moorhead, named for the well-known correspondent of the *Boston Journal* Charles Carleton Coffin.

COMSTOCK a city in Holy Cross Township, sections 21 and 28, was named in honor of Solomon Gilman Comstock of Moorhead, for whom also a township in Marshall County was named. He was born in Argyle, Maine, May 9, 1842; came to Minnesota in 1869, settling in Moorhead; was admitted to the bar in 1871; was a representative in the state legislature, 1876–77 and 1879–81; was a state senator, 1883–87; and was a representative in Congress, 1889–91. The city was incorporated on November 7, 1921, and separated from the township on March 18, 1926; it began in 1889 when David Askegaard moved his grain warehouse to the Comstock Siding in section 21; he built his home in 1890 and the first store in 1891; Askegaard also had a lumberyard, a creamery, and a potato warehouse, and served as postmaster when the post office was established in 1890.

CRAWFORD a station of the Great Northern Railway in Riverton Township, section 30.

CROMWELL TOWNSHIP settled partly by immigrants from England, was named in accordance with the petition of its citizens for Oliver Cromwell (1599–1658).

DAKOTA CITY a village in Georgetown Township, not developed; Henry Black was keeping the townsite for Pierre Bottineau and others.

DALE a village of Highland Grove Township, section 34, established in 1910 when Andrew L. Selsing moved Ole Gol's saloon from Winnipeg Junction and started a store, where he was depot agent and the first postmaster; the post office discontinued in 1971. The village had a hall, a jail, an elevator, and a number of houses.

DILWORTH a city in Moorhead Township, incorporated as a village on August 17, 1911; the community began in 1883 as a railroad siding, called Richardson for a few months, then renamed to honor coffee importer Joseph Dilworth, one of the original stockholders and a director of the Northern Pacific Railroad, residing in Pittsburgh, Pa., who purchased 4,000 acres in the vicinity and became one of the largest landholders along the railroad. It was the largest railroad village in western Minnesota when the Northern Pacific Railroad built its depot in section 11 in 1906. The townsite was platted in 1906, and the post office began in 1907. The village was often called Little Italy for the large Italian immigrant group who settled here.

DOUGLAS a Great Northern Railway station two miles south of Georgetown, in Kragnes Township, section 5, was named in honor of James Douglas, one of the first settlers of Moorhead. He was born in Scotland, March 13, 1821; came with his parents to the United States in 1832; came to Minnesota in 1871, settling in Moorhead, where he was a merchant, built the steamboats *Manitoba* and *Minnesota* in 1875 for the Red River trade, and secured the building of a flouring mill.

DOWNER the railway village of Elkton Township, section 21, was named by officers of the Great Northern Railway company. The first permanent settlers of the township were the Charles Lamb family, who came from Scotland in 1872 and to Clay County in 1878, moving to Downer later. The village was platted by Thomas S. and M. A. Roberts in 1902, at which time there was a Presbyterian church, a general store, a lumber company, a hotel, an implement dealer, and a blacksmith; it had a post office, 1886–1954, changing to a rural branch, 1954–60.

EGLON TOWNSHIP bears the name of a city of ancient Palestine, also of post offices in West Virginia, Kentucky, and Washington. Another version of the name's origin comes from the fact that Ole Overson called the area Ek Land when he settled here in 1871 because the woodland was mostly oak trees, the name meaning "oak land" in Norwegian but pronounced Egland, which the local inhabitants shortened to Eglon.

ELKTON TOWNSHIP refers to the elk formerly common or frequent here and in many parts of Minnesota. The original name, chosen on April 15,

1880, was Madison, which changed to Garfield on December 20, 1880, and to Elkton on January 4, 1881.

ELMWOOD TOWNSHIP received this euphonious name in accordance with its petition for organization, alluding to its abundant elm trees along the south fork of the Buffalo River.

FELTON TOWNSHIP was named, after its railway station, in honor of Samuel Morse Felton by the officers of the Great Northern Railway company. The city of Felton, in sections 27, 28, 33, and 34, was incorporated as a village on March 7, 1901, and separated from the township on October 2, 1922. Some accounts say the village was named for William Felton, state representative from the 41st district in the 15th Minnesota Legislature. The first settlers in 1879 were from Augusta, Wis.; the post office was established that year, with Michael Shea, postmaster; in 1880, eight years after the track was laid through the area, the St. Paul and Duluth Railroad platted the village in section 10, a mile and a half south of the present location; the village moved in 1883, and Flint W. Mills became postmaster in his store.

FINKLE a railway station four miles south of Moorhead, in section 33 of Moorhead Township, was named in honor of Henry G. Finkle, an early pioneer, of the firm of Bruns and Finkle, merchants in Moorhead.

FLOWING TOWNSHIP has chiefly Scandinavian settlers, by whom this name was adopted, but its significance remains to be ascertained, unless it refers to artesian or flowing wells. The many flowing wells in the Red River valley, of which Clay County and this township have a good number, are the subject of a chapter in "The Glacial Lake Agassiz" (Monograph 25, U.S. Geological Survey, 1896, pp. 523–81, with a map).

GARFIELD TOWNSHIP see ELKTON TOWNSHIP.

GEORGETOWN a city in George Township, was incorporated as a village on March 10, 1904. Old Georgetown, when it was established as a trading post of the Hudson's Bay Company in 1859, was first named Selkirk, in honor of Lord Selkirk, and renamed in honor of Sir George Simpson, governor of Hudson's Bay Company; it was abandoned in September 1862 during the Dakota War and was reestablished in 1864. The village consisted of several sheds for defense, a warehouse, a hotel, a dwelling house, a traders' store, and a guard-house, the site becoming a stock farm in 1873 and abandoned by 1875. Although mail was distributed earlier by the trading post manager, the first post office in the county was established at Old Georgetown in 1864 with Randolph M. Probstfield as postmaster. The present Georgetown, established in 1883 two miles southeast by the Moorhead Northern Railroad, had 640 acres platted by Soloman G. Comstock and Almond A. White, with the post office in C. B. Hill's store; Hill was county sheriff from 1891 to 1895. The township received its name from the trading post.

GLYNDON a city in Glyndon Township, section 2, was platted as a railway village in the spring of 1872, being named by officers of the Northern Pacific Railroad company, and thence the township was named. It is also the name of small villages in Pennsylvania and Maryland. The village was organized in 1875, incorporated as a village on February 14, 1881, and reincorporated on April 6, 1908. The oldest village in the county began as a tent village, with houses later built over the tent structures. It was named for a popular writer of *Atlantic Hearth and Home*, Laura Catherine Redden Searing, who used the name Howard Glyndon as a nom de plume. The post office began in 1872, first located in S. Campbell's store with Stiles R. Nettleton, postmaster; four hotels were built in the first year of settlement.

GOOSE PRAIRIE TOWNSHIP was named for the wild geese plentiful in its lakes and sloughs.

HAGEN TOWNSHIP commemorates Ole Hagen, an early Norwegian settler. A large manufacturing city in western Germany bears this name. The township was incorporated in 1883.

HAWLEY a city of Hawley Township, sections 1, 2, and 12, settled by an English colony in 1871, incorporated February 5, 1884, and its township, at first called Bethel, were renamed in honor of Gen. Joseph Roswell Hawley of Connecticut, one of the original stockholders of the Northern Pacific Railroad company. He was born in Stewartsville, N.C., October 31, 1826; died in Washington, D.C., March 17, 1905. He was graduated at Hamilton College, 1847; was admitted to practice law, 1850; became editor of the *Evening Press*, Hartford, Conn., 1857; served as a brigade and division commander in the Union army during the Civil War, and was brevetted major general in 1865; was president of the U.S. Centennial Commission,

1873–77; was a member of Congress, 1872–75 and 1879–81; was U.S. senator, 1881–1905.

The first permanent settler, Dan O'Donnell, built a saloon and hotel in 1871. From 1871 to 1872, the community was known by several other names: Reno's Camp, Buffalo Crossing, First Crossing of the Buffalo, Bethel, New Bethel, and Muskoday (Indian word for buffalo); the post office was opened on January 6, 1873, but renamed Yeovil briefly, April 18, 1873, to January 8, 1874, because of the arrival of colonists from Yeovil, Somerset, England, who had planned to build a city of that name on the site of present Muskoda but upon arrival in Hawley found that their land had been taken by claim jumpers; the Yeovil colonists remained in Hawley although the name was changed back.

HIGHLAND GROVE TOWNSHIP received its name for its location on the high ascent eastward from the Red River valley and for the groves beside its lakes and on the Buffalo River, the surface all about being mainly prairie.

HITTERDAL a city in Goose Prairie and Highland Grove Townships, incorporated as a village on April 1, 1918, and separated from the townships on May 3, 1919. It is named for a valley and lake in southern Norway. Among the first settlers were several people named Hitterdal. The town was named for Bendt O. Hitterdal, the original town proprietor. The post office began in 1887; M. J. Solum built a hardware and implement store on the first lot after the townsite was platted in 1896.

HOLY CROSS TOWNSHIP was named for a conspicuous wooden cross set on the prairie by Father Geniun at a cemetery about a half mile west of the Red River, in North Dakota, amid a Catholic community of French Canadian farmers. This township on the Minnesota side was settled by Norwegian farmers, who were Lutherans, and both sides of the river were comprised in the "Holy Cross neighborhood." Also this was the name of a mission site on the border of Holy Cross and Kurtz Townships, established in 1861 by missionaries from St. Boniface, Manitoba, with a post office begun in 1869 at the John Corneliussen farm, with Father Geniun, postmaster until 1871; the post office was discontinued in 1874 and was reestablished 1878–89.

HUMBOLDT TOWNSHIP settled by a German colony, is named in honor of the celebrated

German scientist, traveler, and author Alexander von Humboldt (1769–1859). In the years 1799 to 1804 he traveled in South America and Mexico, and later he published many books on his observations of natural sciences, history, and political affairs of this continent.

KEENE TOWNSHIP was named for a homesteader there, who was a veteran of the Civil War, or may have been named by Jacob Burrill, who came in 1879, for his hometown in New Hampshire. The township had a post office, 1898–1904, in section 26.

KRAGNES a village in Kragnes Township, section 34, was named in honor of Aanund Ole Kraaknes, who changed his name to Andrew O. Kragnes, a prominent Norwegian farmer, one of the first settlers of that township, who came from Houston County in 1872. He was born in Norway and came to the United States in 1852 with his parents, who two years later settled in Houston County. He helped establish the community, building an elevator, a lumberyard, a store, and a machinery agency. The village had a post office, 1884–1935, and a station of the Great Northern Railway.

KURTZ TOWNSHIP was named for Thomas C. Kurtz, formerly cashier of the Merchants' Bank, Moorhead, who removed to Portland, Ore. He is a son of Col. John D. Kurtz, of the U.S. Engineer Corps, who served with distinction during the Civil War, and later was superintendent of the engineering works of Delaware Bay and River. See also RUSTAD.

LA FAYETTE a village, first the site of a Hudson's Bay trading post incorporated as Shayenne City, May 23, 1857. A group of capitalists laid out a townsite in 1859 as La Fayette, advertising from 1859 to 1861 to encourage settlers and offering free land. In 1859, Randolph M. Probstfield began acquiring land near the trading post, and ten years later he disposed of his holdings, which included the townsite of La Fayette.

LAMBS a Great Northern Railway station in Oakport, section 16, was named for John and Patrick H. Lamb, brothers from Ireland, who were early settlers and engaged extensively in farming, brickmaking, railroad construction, and banking.

LUND a post office, 1879–81, Peterson Hansom, postmaster; location not found.

MADISON see ELKTON TOWNSHIP.

MANITOBA JUNCTION a village in Highland Grove Township, section 28. Its post office was in a community located one mile south, Winnipeg Junction, 1887–1910, changing to Manitoba Junction, 1910–11. It had a station of the Northern Pacific Railroad, two general stores, two restaurants, two hotels, one being the railroad hotel, a blacksmith shop, a saloon, a jail, a church, and a school.

MOLAND TOWNSHIP was named by Norwegian settler Olaf Thortvedt for his home parish in Norway.

MOORHEAD first settled in 1871, when the building of the Northern Pacific Railroad reached its site, was named in honor of William G. Moorhead of Pennsylvania, who was a director of that railroad company. He was a partner of Jay Cooke, the Northern Pacific financial agent, and his first wife was a sister of Cooke. He was president of the Philadelphia and Erie Railroad, and his brother, Gen. James Kennedy Moorhead, was likewise much interested in railway development, especially in the Northern Pacific finances. Moorhead was incorporated as a village February 25, 1875, and as a city February 24, 1881, and the township also bears this name.

The first building, in 1860, was the office of the Northwestern Stage Company, owned by J. C. Burbank of St. Paul; the post office was established and the first merchants were Henry A. Bruns and H. G. Finkle, with part of the building used as a hotel run by J. B. Chapin, later mayor of Fargo, N.Dak. When the inhabitants of Oakport Farm settlement begun by Andrew Holes on Randolph M. Probstfield's farm, with a tent community named Oshkosh by Probstfield, discovered in 1871 that the Northern Pacific Railroad was to be located south of them instead of through the farm, the entire settlement moved overnight to the site of Moorhead, creating a new tent city until replaced with frame buildings. Probstfield was a state senator, 1891–93.

The adjoining city of Fargo, in North Dakota, was named for William George Fargo (1818–81), of Buffalo, N.Y., founder of the Wells, Fargo Express Company and prominent as a Northern Pacific director.

Cass County, N.Dak., adjoining Clay County, and also its city of Casselton are named for Gen. George W. Cass of Pennsylvania, who was president of the Northern Pacific Railroad company in 1872–75. He was born in Ohio and was a nephew of Gov. Lewis Cass of Michigan; was graduated at the U.S. Military Academy, West Point, in 1832; was president during 25 years of the Pittsburg, Fort Wayne and Chicago Railroad company; purchased a large tract adjoining the Northern Pacific line between 15 and 20 miles west of Fargo, and employing Oliver Dalrymple as farm superintendent, was the first to demonstrate in 1876 the high agricultural value of the Red River valley lands for wheat raising on a large scale.

MORKEN TOWNSHIP was named in honor of Torgrim O. Morken, its first homesteader, who came here from Houston County in 1875. Morken served as first township clerk, and his farm was designated as the Wrodahl post office, 1881–82, to serve the surrounding community.

MUSKODA a former station of the Northern Pacific Railroad in the east edge of section 7, Hawley, had an Ojibwe name, meaning a meadow or tract of grassland, a large prairie. It is spelled *Muskoday* in Henry W. Longfellow's *Song of Hiawatha*, with accent on the first syllable. In Frederic Baraga's *Dictionary of the Ojibway Language* it is spelled *mashkode*, to be pronounced in three syllables nearly as by Longfellow. A few miles east of Clay County, the traveler on the Northern Pacific line passes out from the northeast forest region, and thence crosses an expanse of prairie and plain, mainly treeless, for 800 miles to the Rocky Mountains. (By a relocation of the railroad to secure an easier grade in the next seven miles west of Hawley, the site of Muskoda is left now about two-thirds of a mile distant at the north.) Large quantities of sand and gravel from two sand companies were shipped from the station; the village had a general store, a grain elevator, a large potato warehouse, and a post office, 1873–1930.

NADA a station of the Northern Pacific Railroad in Highland Grove Township, section 21.

NAVAN see BAKER.

OAKPORT TOWNSHIP has many oaks in the narrow fringe of timber along the navigable Red River. Oakport was also the name of a tent village in the township, three miles north of Moorhead, which lasted only a few months.

ONELAND/ONLAND see ULEN.

PARKE TOWNSHIP was named probably in honor of a pioneer settler, but three versions of the name ing exist. One is that it was first named Oak Grove until a man in one of the eastern states sent $50 to put a shingle on the school if they would rename the township in his honor; a second is that it was named Park because of its parklike beauty and then a man from one of the eastern states sent $50 for a shingle on the school and asked if they would add an *e* to the name in his honor; the third is that the original name was Parktown, and a man named Parke gave $100 and asked that the name be changed. A county in western Indiana bears this name.

REAL a post office, 1897–1908, in Viding Township, sections 27 and 28, Clifton Riel being the first postmaster and from whom the name was probably derived.

RICHARDSON see DILWORTH.

RIVERTON TOWNSHIP has reference to the Buffalo River, which flows across its northern part.

ROLLAG a village in Parke Township, section 27; settled primarily by Norwegians and Yankees and named for a place in Norway. It had a post office, 1880–1929; site of the yearly Western Minnesota Steam Threshers Reunion since 1954.

RUSTAD a railway village in Kurtz Township, section 28, was named in honor of Samuel Rustad, a Norwegian merchant there. The village was originally platted as Kurtz, and its post office was so named, 1891–1907; Rasmus Kirkhorn was the postmaster in his general store, 1891–1929; the post office closed in 1954.

RUTHRUFF a Great Northern Railway station in section 36, Moorhead, was named for a settler.

SABIN a city in Elmwood, sections 7 and 8, is in honor of Dwight May Sabin, who was born in Manlius, Ill., April 25, 1844, and died in Chicago, December 23, 1902. He came to Minnesota in 1867, and the next year settled in Stillwater, where he engaged in the lumber business and in the manufacture of machinery, engines, and cars. He was a state senator, 1871–73, and a U.S. senator, 1883–89. The city was platted in 1929 and incorporated as a village on August 15, 1929; its post office was established in 1881; a station of the Great Northern Railway was in section 8.

SARSFIELD a village of Georgetown Township, section 30, incorporated on May 23, 1857; no trace remains.

SITOMANEE a village in Kurtz Township, incorporated on May 23, 1857; no trace remains.

SKREE was named for Mikkel Skree, a Norwegian farmer, who was the first settler of this township.

SPRING PRAIRIE TOWNSHIP a euphonious name selected in the petition for organization, refers to its springs and rivulets.

STOCKWOOD a post office of Riverton Township, section 9, 1895–1921, located in the general store, with a school, a boardinghouse, and a depot of the Northern Pacific Railroad.

TANSEM TOWNSHIP earlier named Lund, was named for John O. Tansem, one of its pioneer farmers, a highly respected citizen. He was born in Eidsvold, Norway, in 1842, came to the United States in 1861, and settled here in the most southeastern township of this county in 1862. The township had a post office operating at various times between 1883 and 1905 in various sections of the township, usually located in a general store.

ULEN TOWNSHIP was named in honor of Ole Ulen, its first settler. He was born in Norway, April 18, 1818, and died in Ulen village, January 19, 1891. He came to the United States in 1851 and to Minnesota in 1853, settling in Houston County; was a farmer there until 1867; and removed to this county in 1872. The city of Ulen, sections 27, 28, 33, and 34, was established on part of Ulen's homestead and was incorporated as a village on November 12, 1896. The post office was established in 1884, its name changing to Odneland in 1885 for Ole Odneland (Tallak Aaneland), postmaster and general store owner, although it was sometimes spelled Oneland and Onland. When the railroad came in 1886, Odneland's (Aaneland's) store was in the path of the rails, so it was moved to the east side of the tracks on the northwest corner of Regelstad's farm. Ole Asleson platted a townsite, and the name was changed to Ulen with Odneland remaining as postmaster until the post office was reorganized in 1887 and Ole Christian Melbye became postmaster in his grocery store; Melbye moved into the first house built in village limits in 1887.

VIDING TOWNSHIP was named for a Swedish settler there.

WATT SIDING a station of the Northern Pacific Railroad in Glyndon Township, section 7, where potato warehouses and a fertilizer plant had been built.

WILLARDTON a post office, 1892–94; location not found.

WINNIPEG JUNCTION a village in Highland Grove Township, section 22, established in 1885 when the Northern Pacific Railroad came. It originally had a church, three stores, three saloons, two restaurants, two hotels, a bakery, a grain elevator, a school, three livery stables, and a post office, 1887–1910. In 1909, when the railroad moved its tracks one mile north, the community died, and the post office, the depot, and several stores were moved to Manitoba Junction.

WITHEROW a village in Riverton Township, section 12, which had a station of the Northern Pacific Railroad.

WRODAHL see MORKEN TOWNSHIP.

YEOVIL see HAWLEY.

Lakes and Streams

Buffalo River is translated from the Ojibwe name of its southern tributary flowing from lakes in and near Audubon in Becker County, of which Rev. Joseph A. Gilfillan wrote that it "is called Pijikiwizibi, or Buffalo River, from the fact that buffaloes were always found wintering there." Hence the white people have erroneously called the whole river Buffalo River. On Joseph N. Nicollet's map it is named "Pijihi or Buffalo R." The name used by the Ojibwe for our Buffalo Lake in Becker County and for the Buffalo River, flowing thence to the Red River, would be correctly translated as Beaver Lake and Beaver River.

Near the middle of the west side of Kragnes Township, on the Red River opposite to the mouth of the Sheyenne, a townsite named La Fayette was surveyed in March 1859, and there in April of that year, "the first steamboat on the Red river was built . . . the materials for which were transported across the country from Crow Wing on the Mississippi, where the steamer North Star was broken up for that purpose. The new boat was named the Anson Northup" (Lamphere, MHS Collections 10: 16, 17; *History of the Red River Valley*, 1909, pp. 569–72).

The Sheyenne River (here spelled unlike the Cheyenne River of South Dakota and the city Cheyenne, capital of Wyoming), flowing into the Red River from North Dakota, received this name, given by Nicollet as "Shayenn-oju R.," from the Dakota, designating it as the river of the Cheyenne tribe, meaning "people who speak a strange language." Rev. T. S. Williamson wrote (MHS Collections 1: 295–301) that when the Dakota first came to the Falls of St. Anthony, the Iowas occupied the country about the mouth of the Minnesota River, and the Cheyenne had their villages and cultivated fields "on the Minnesota between Blue Earth and Lac qui Parle, whence they moved to a western branch of Red river of the North, which still bears their name." David Thompson recorded the narration in 1798 by an Ojibwe chief of an Ojibwe war party who attacked and destroyed the Cheyenne village west of the Red River, probably about 1775 or 1780, but perhaps five or ten years later (Thompson's *Narrative of His Explorations in Western America, 1784–1812*, ed. J. B. Tyrrell [Toronto, 1916], pp. 236, 261–63). Next this tribe removed to a second Cheyenne River, west of the Missouri in South Dakota, and yet later they migrated farther across the plains to the west and south.

Wild Rice River, whose south branch runs through Ulen and Hagen, and the river of the same name in North Dakota, tributary to the Red River nine miles south of Fargo and Moorhead, are translated from the Ojibwe names, referring to their valued native grain, the wild rice, much harvested for food. It also gave the name of Mahnomen County, and is more fully noticed in the chapter for that county.

No explanations seem needed for the names of Hay Creek, tributary to the Buffalo River in section 33, Highland Grove, and a second Hay Creek in Skree and Elkton; Spring Creek, tributary to the last and joining it two miles southeast of Downer; and Stony and Willow Creeks, flowing through Barnesville Township to the South Branch of the Buffalo River. Each of the two creeks last named has been sometimes called Whiskey Creek, in allusion to a great spree of the railway graders when the former railway line from Breckenridge to Barnesville was completed. Another name for Stony Creek, crossed by the railway two miles north of the city of Barnesville, is Sieber's Creek, for Rudolph Sieber, who had a dairy farm at its north side.

Deerhorn Creek in Alliance Township, flowing northwestward from Wilkin County to the South Branch of the Buffalo River, received its name from antlers shed by deer and found by the pioneer settlers.

The east margin of Clay County, above the Glacial Lake Agassiz, has numerous small lakes. Among them are Silver Lake in section 26, Hawley, in allusion to its placid and shining surface; Moe Lake in sections 2, 11, and 12, Eglon, for Nels R. Moe, a farmer on its west side; Sand Lake in the east half of section 12, Eglon, for its sandy shore; Solum Lake in the southwest quarter of the same section for H. H. Solum, whose farm adjoins it; Lee Lake in sections 9 and 16, and Perch Lake in section 17, Eglon; Turtle Lake, crossed by the east line of section 12, Parke; and Grove Lake, partly in section 36, Tansem, lying mostly in Otter Tail County.

Buffalo Delta of Lake Agassiz

Where the Buffalo River enters the area of the Glacial Lake Agassiz, a delta of stratified gravel and sand was deposited during the earliest and highest stage of the ancient lake. The Herman or first beach and the east edge of the delta were crossed by the Northern Pacific Railroad at Muskoda, and the extent of the delta from north to south, on both sides of the river, is seven miles, with a width from two to three and a half miles (U.S. Geological Survey, Monograph 25, 1896, pp. 290–92, with map and section).

Buffalo River State Park

Part of the lake bottom of Glacial Lake Agassiz was preserved through the efforts of the Moorhead Rod and Gun Club when the state created Buffalo River State Park in 1937. The park is notable for the gravel ridges or "beach lines" that were part of the lake bottom. Numerous species of prairie wildflowers and grasses are abundant in the park.

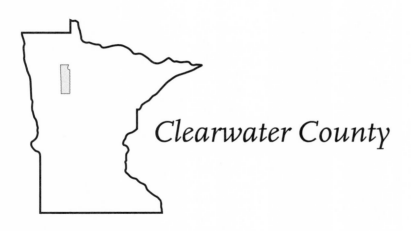

Clearwater County

This county, established December 20, 1902, received its name from the Clearwater River and Lake, which lie partly within its area. For the formerly great industry of pine lumbering, this was a very important river, the logs being floated down from the headstream and its tributaries into Clearwater Lake and thence to the Red Lake River and the sawmills at Crookston. Another Clearwater River, likewise flowing through a lake of the same name, empties into the Mississippi at the town of Clearwater in Wright County. Both of these rivers, with their lakes, and also the Eau Claire or Clearwater River in Wisconsin, derive their names by translation from those given by the Ojibwe and other Indian tribes long before the coming of white men. According to Rev. Joseph A. Gilfillan, the Ojibwe name of this river and the county, meaning Clearwater, is Gawakomitigweia. The name Clear Water River was used by David Thompson in 1798 and on Joseph N. Nicollet's map, 1843. It was called Clear River on the map of Stephen H. Long's expedition, 1823.

The quality denoted by this term, Clearwater, is in contrast with the more or less muddy and silty waters of the Missouri, Minnesota, and most other rivers, especially when they are in high flood stages, caused by the melting of winter snows at the return of spring or by exceptionally heavy rains, the inflowing drainage having washed down much mud, clay, and sand.

Another very remarkable contrast to clearness in river and lake waters is surprisingly shown by other streams of the northern woods and swamps, colored dark and yellowish by the drainage to them from decaying leaves, fallen branches and trunks of dead trees, and peaty soil, but most of all where extensive peat swamps and bogs supply water in any time of considerable drought, long saturated with the peat and decaying vegetation. In some cases, as the Rat Root River and Black or Rat Root Bay of Rainy Lake, in Koochiching County, seen during my travel in August 1916, the very dark water, nearly or quite stagnant, although containing almost no mud or silty matter, is yet the antithesis of clearness or transparency, being too dark for one to see into it even to a depth of only two or three feet. From frequent acquaintance with similar peat-stained streams, the observant Ojibwe were wont to distinguish other streams of opposite character by naming them for their crystal clearness.

Information of the origins and meanings of names was gathered from F. A. Norquist, county treasurer, Frederick S. Kalberg, editor of the Clearwater Crystal, *and Albert Kaiser, banker, of Bagley, during my visit in September 1909; from T. L. Tweite, county treasurer, in my second visit, September 1916; and for the Itasca State Park, lying mostly in this county, from vols. 7 and 11, Minnesota Historical Society Collections, 1893 and 1905, by the late Hon. Jacob V. Brower.*

Parts of Clearwater County include sections of the Red Lake and White Earth Reservations. For fuller treatments of these reservations see Beltrami County and Mahnomen County, respectively.

ALIDA (accented on the second syllable, with the long English sound of its vowel), a village in section 10, Bear Creek, with a post office in section 15, 1898–1945, was named by Gov. John Lind. Indiana and Kansas also have post offices of this name.

BAGLEY the city and county seat, Copley Township, sections 29 and 30, was named in honor of Sumner C. Bagley, an early lumberman of this part of the Clearwater River, who removed to Fosston in 1885 and died there in 1915. It was first settled in 1894 as a logging camp and grew when the Great Northern Railway came in 1898, the year the first store was built and its post office established; it was incorporated on January 4, 1899.

BEAR CREEK TOWNSHIP is named for its Bear Creek, flowing into the Mississippi River in section 26.

BEARD the Beard Store and post office was owned by Ole and Daisy Beard, 1900–13, and located in Leon Township, section 13.

BERNER a village in Winsor Township, section 24, with a general store post office, 1906–14, a creamery, and a blacksmith.

BLIX a post office, 1904–7, with Albert N. Blix, postmaster, in Nora Township.

CHURNES a former post office in section 35, Greenwood, was named for its postmaster, Alexander Churnes, a Norwegian pioneer farmer.

CLEARBROOK a city in Leon Township, section 29, took its name from the brook there. It began in 1907 as a community named Shanty Town, with a creamery, a blacksmith, a school, a store, and tent residences; the land sites of Shanty Town and Clearbrook were purchased from Peter Peterson,

who had homesteaded in 1896 and erected the first store; the village of Clearbrook developed in 1910 when the Minneapolis, St. Paul and Sault Ste. Marie Railroad (Soo Line) came, absorbing the Shanty Town site. The post office was established in 1901, located for one year in a log cabin on Henry Olberg's homestead four miles northeast of Clearbrook in section 22 and named Olberg in his honor. Albert Anderson purchased the log cabin in 1902, moving it to Clearbrook and becoming the postmaster and newspaper publisher; the name changed to Clearbrook in 1910. It was incorporated as a village on June 15, 1918.

CLOVER TOWNSHIP organized in 1914, received this name on the suggestion of James N. Vail, an early settler.

COPLEY TOWNSHIP was named in honor of Lafayette Copley, one of its first pioneers, who removed in 1916 to western Oregon. He came from Massachusetts and was the builder of five dams on the upper Clearwater River, used by Thomas B. Walker for log-driving. A post office was located there, 1895–99.

DOUGLAS LODGE a village in State Park Township, section 24, about 1916.

DUDLEY was named in honor of Frank E. Dudley, who was a county commissioner of Beltrami County when this township was organized, before the establishment of Clearwater County. He was born in Geauga County, Ohio, came to Minnesota in 1881, and was mayor of Bemidji, 1900–1902.

DUNOWEN a post office, 1906–13, in Clover Township, section 36.

EBRO a Great Northern Railway station and post office, 1898–1975, seven miles west of Bagley, section 6, Falk Township, has the name of a river in northeastern Spain.

EDDY TOWNSHIP was named in honor of Frank M. Eddy of Sauk Centre, Minn. He was born in Pleasant Grove, Minn., April 1, 1856; was a school teacher and later a land examiner for the Northern Pacific Railroad company; was clerk of the district court of Pope County, 1884–94; and was a representative in Congress, 1895–1903.

FALK TOWNSHIP T. 148N, R. 38W of the White Earth Reservation, was named for Erick Falk, newspaper publisher, who was a leader in formation of the county and a member of the first county board.

FLETCHER JUNCTION a village in Shevlin Township, three miles east of Shevlin village, with a station of the Great Northern Railway.

GONVICK a city in Pine Lake Township, sections 9 and 10, was incorporated as a village on August 1, 1917. It developed when an area of the Red Lake Reservation opened for prospective homesteaders on May 15, 1896. One version of the name's origin is that when a group of local men got together to change the name from Wildwood, they decided to name it for the oldest man present, Martin Gonvick, born in 1863. The other story is that it was named for Emma Gonvick Monsrud, first wife of Peter Monsrud, who built a sawmill on land Emma homesteaded in 1896; she died in 1899; the sawmill closed in 1929. The post office, established in Beltrami County, began in 1900, with storekeeper Nels Fredensberg, postmaster. The Soo Line came in 1910 and in addition to local construction, businesses from Wildwood moved there.

GREENWOOD TOWNSHIP was so named in its petition for organization, probably in allusion to the verdure of its woods.

GUNDER a post office, 1905–14, in Hangaard Township, section 19, Gunder G. Hangaard, postmaster in his home.

HANGAARD TOWNSHIP was named for Gunder G. Hangaard, its first homesteader, who came from Norway.

HOLST TOWNSHIP received its name in honor of Hans J. Holst, a Norwegian pioneer farmer there, who was sheriff of this county in 1904–8 and clerk of the township. A post office was located there, 1902–6.

ITASCA see LAKE ITASCA.

ITASCA TOWNSHIP lies next north of Itasca Lake and the state park.

KOLB a post office, 1904–7; location not found.

LAKE ITASCA a post office in Itasca Township, section 26, located at the north end of Itasca State Park, first called Itasca from 1897 to 1903, when changed to the present name.

LA PRAIRIE TOWNSHIP T. 143N–T. 145N, R. 38W of White Earth Reservation, was named for Scotty La Prairie, a leader among the Ojibwe.

LEON TOWNSHIP is for Leon Dickinson, the first white child born there, son of Daniel S. Dickinson, who later removed to Montana. The township was one of 52 townships of the Red Lake

Reservation opened for settlement on May 15, 1896. A post office was located in section 8, 1897–1910.

LEONARD a city in Dudley Township, sections 8 and 9, was named for Leonard French, first child of an early settler, George H. French, who became a merchant of this village. It was incorporated as a village on June 12, 1922; French had a log house trading post store with the post office, which began in 1899, on the shore of Four-legged Lake. The Soo Line established a station there in 1911.

LITTLE CHICAGO a trading post or country store in Greenwood Township near Clearwater River Crossing so named because it was an area famous for bootleg liquor.

MALLARD a village in sections 5 and 8, Itasca, received its name for the adjoining lake, having many mallard ducks. It was incorporated as a village on December 30, 1902, and is currently unincorporated; it had a post office, 1902–24.

MEADOWS a post office in section 7, Greenwood, 1902–7, was named for the wide natural meadows of the Clearwater River. The post office was in the store owned by Emma J. P. Campbell, postmaster.

MINERVA TOWNSHIP was named for the Roman goddess of wisdom by Frederick S. Kalberg, owner of the Pinehurst Farm on the southeast side of Lake Minerva, section 13.

MOONLIGHT a post office in Eddy Township, 1902–10. Henry Olberg carried the mail from Bagley, and his wife, Carrie Quam Olberg, was postmaster until 1905; Petra Henderson was postmaster until it discontinued. The name, to the delight of the community, was taken from the moon since mail service is as good in the night as in daylight.

MOOSE a post office, 1892–1908, in Moose Creek Township, with John H. McCallum, postmaster.

MOOSE CREEK TOWNSHIP has the small creek so named, flowing from section 21 to the northeast and east.

MURRAY a community in the vicinity of Ebro, circa 1907.

NEVING a post office, 1900–20, near the mouth of Clearwater Lake in Sinclair Township, section 14, was named for a lumberman and farmer there, Robert Neving, who removed to Saskatchewan about the year 1910.

NORA TOWNSHIP was named in honor of Knut

Nora, a Norwegian pioneer farmer there, who was a member of the first board of county commissioners.

OLBERG a former small village in the north edge of section 22, Leon, named for Anton Olberg, a pioneer from Norway, was superseded by Clearbrook when the railway was built there.

OSWALD see STARLIGHT.

PINE CENTER a crossroads community in Rice Township, section 9, on Highways 92 and 31, formerly named Zerkel, which had a post office, 1904–31.

PINE LAKE TOWNSHIP has the large lake of this name, outflowing by Pine River, a tributary of Lost River. The original wealth of this region consisted in its timber of the white and Norway pines, but the timber lands are now largely changed into farms or other uses.

PINELAKE a post office, 1897–1903; location not found.

POPPLE TOWNSHIP was named for its plentiful poplar woods, misspelled and mispronounced, by quite common usage, in this name. A post office was located in the township, 1890–93 and 1895–98, established and discontinued while part of Beltrami County.

REGINA a settlement south of Wheelock, possibly in Itasca Township, which existed about 1903; location not found.

RICE TOWNSHIP refers to the headwaters of the Wild Rice River, with the Rice Lakes. This river flows through the northwest corner of this township.

RUSTEN a country post office, 1903–6, located in section 24 of Eddy Township, with John Rusten, postmaster.

ST. JEFFERSON a settlement of the early 1920s just north of Gonvick in Pine Lake Township.

SCHLIEFVIEW a post office, 1909–11, with Nancy J. Schlief, postmaster; location not found.

SEELEY a post office authorized on March 29, 1906, with V. L. Ellis to be postmaster, but not established; location not found.

SHEVLIN TOWNSHIP and city were named in honor of the late Thomas Henry Shevlin of Minneapolis. He was born in Albany, N.Y., January 3, 1852; died in Pasadena, Calif., January 15, 1912. He came to Minnesota in 1886, settling in Minneapolis, and was president of several logging and lumber manufacturing companies, cutting

much pine timber in this county. He was donor of the Alice A. Shevlin Hall, University of Minnesota, built in 1906. The city was incorporated as a village in 1898, the same year the townsite was platted on 160 acres of land originally owned by Peter Burstad, and the post office was established, with Andrew L. Gordon, postmaster in his store, the first building in the community.

SINCLAIR TOWNSHIP received its name in honor of an early land surveyor, who possibly was John Sinclair, first clerk of the townsite.

STARLIGHT a post office, 1903–7, in Sinclair Township, section 21; a proposed change to rename as Oswald was authorized on October 2, 1907, but not done.

STATE PARK TOWNSHIP T. 143N, R. 36W, became part of Unorganized Territory of South Clearwater.

TECKLA a post office of Pine Lake Township, 1897–1910; the name was submitted by Mrs. Anna (Erik) Gunelius because she thought it sounded pretty, she being the postmaster on the Gunelius farm.

UNORGANIZED TERRITORY OF SOUTH CLEARWATER includes White Earth Reservation townships, former State Park Township (T. 143N, R. 36W) and unnamed T. 143N, R. 37W.

VANDA a post office authorized on June 2, 1904, with Ole Christenson to be postmaster, but not established; location not found.

VERN a rural post office, 1900–20, in Itasca Township, section 11.

WEME (pronounced in two syllables), a small hamlet in section 18, Eddy, was named for Hans Weme, a Norwegian merchant, who was its first postmaster. The post office, 1902–12, was located in Weme's store; a creamery was organized in 1907.

WHEELOCK a settlement at the northern end of the Walker and Akeley Logging Railroad, probably in Bear Creek Township.

WILDWOOD a village that became part of Gonvick, having a sawmill and the homestead of P. A. Monsrud, built in 1896 on Lost River. The Pine Lake Creamery Association was organized in 1907; the blacksmith shop had a hall on the second floor for dances, meetings, and magic lantern shows. The community had a number of other businesses until its demise in 1910, when the Soo Line went through Gonvick and businesses moved up the hill to be closer to the railroad.

WILLBORG a village in Eddy Township, with a post office, 1897–1909, was named for Swedish farmer Martin E. Willborg, born in Sweden in 1870 and died in 1949, who settled in this community in 1896, becoming the first postmaster; he was the county judge of probate, 1904–9.

WINSOR TOWNSHIP is in honor of Hans C. Widness, a Norwegian farmer. The name of the post office and township was anglicized in accordance with his suggestion. The community of Winsor in section 28, also known as Winsor Crossing, had a post office, 1896–1910, with Widness, postmaster in his store. His daughter, Stella, was the first white child born there in 1897. Several other stores, a hotel, a school, and three sawmills were built; the demise of the community came in 1910 when the Soo Line was built through Gonvick.

ZERKEL see **PINE CENTER**.

Lakes and Streams

In the foregoing list of townships and villages, attention has been given to Bear Creek, Clear Brook, Mallard Lake, Moose Creek, and the Pine Lake and River.

Rice Lake and the Upper Rice Lake and the Wild Rice River have probably borne these names in four successive languages, the Dakota , the Ojibwe, French, and English. The oldest printed reference is in the narrative of Joseph La France, a French and Ojibwe parentage, who in 1740–42 traveled and hunted with the Indians of a large region in northwestern Minnesota and in Canada northward to Lakes Winnipeg and Manitoba and Hudson Bay. In the story of his wandering, given by Arthur Dobbs in *An Account of the Countries adjoining to Hudson's Bay*, published in London in 1744, La France described the Upper Rice Lake, in Bear Creek and Minerva Townships of this county, as follows: "The Lake Du Siens is but small, being not above 3 Leagues in Circuit; but all around its Banks, in the shallow Water and Marshes, grows a kind of wild Oat, of the Nature of Rice; the outward Husk is black, but the Grain within is white and clear like Rice; this the Indians beat off into their Canoes, and use it for Food" (*Minnesota in Three Centuries*, 1908, vol. 1, pp. 299–302). This French name, Du Siens, seems probably to be from the Dakota word *psin*, meaning "wild rice."

Gilfillan gave the present Ojibwe name of this Upper Rice Lake as "Ajawewesitagun sagaiigun, meaning the lake where there is a portage from water running one way to waters running the opposite way, or briefly, Height-of-land lake." The portage was from the Mississippi River through this lake into the Wild Rice River.

Seven miles distant westward, lying on the course of the Wild Rice River, is the larger Rice Lake, in T. 145N, R. 38W, of this county, where our names of both the river and lake are received from the Ojibwe name, noted by Gilfillan as "Gamanominiganjikawi zibi, The river where wild rice stalk or plant is growing; so called from the last lake through which it flowed." According to the prevalent usage of the Ojibwe, they gave to the river their name of the lake whence it flows.

Nearly all the area of this lower Rice Lake has only shallow water, one to five feet deep, so that the lake is filled with a luxuriant growth of wild rice. It presents in the late summer, when viewed from a distance, the appearance of a grassy marsh. The greater part of this valuable grain gathered for food by the Indians of the White Earth Reservation is obtained from this lake and the Upper Rice Lake.

Thompson's map, from his field notes in 1798, has Wild Rice River; Long's map, 1823, has this name, and also Rice Lake; and Nicollet's map, 1843, has "Manomin R. or Wild Rice R." and "Rice L."

Four-legged Lake, in Dudley, is a translation of its Ojibwe name, given by Gilfillan as "Nio-gade (pronounced in four syllables) . . . from an old Indian of that name who lived there." Its outlet flows west into Ruffee Creek, called by the Ojibwe Four-legged Creek, which flows north to the Clearwater River. Our name of this creek is in honor of Charles A. Ruffee of Brainerd, who was appointed in 1874 by Gov. Cushman K. Davis to make inquiries and report on "the condition of the several bands of Chippewa Indians of Minnesota," with recommendations for state legislation toward their "ultimately becoming citizens of the State" (*Aborigines of Minnesota*, 1911, pp. 671–73).

Lost River, flowing from Holst and Eddy northwest and west to join the Clearwater River in Red Lake County, received its name for its formerly passing in section 17, Winsor, and for several miles onward, beneath a floating bog in a spruce swamp; but its course has been opened by a state ditch, with reclamation of adjoining lands for agriculture.

Peterson Lake in sections 4 and 5, Holst, was named for Nels M. Peterson, owner of the land on its south side.

Popple Township has Minnow Lake, named for its little fishes, in section 22, near the sources of Clearwater River; and Sabe Lake, a name whose origin was not ascertained, on the south side of section 24.

Lake Lomond, adjoining the north end of Bagley village, was named by Randolph A. Wilkinson of St. Paul, general solicitor of the Great Northern Railway company, for the "bonny Loch Lomond" of Scotland, the largest and most beautiful lake in Great Britain.

Walker Brook, flowing into the Clearwater River at the southeast corner of Bagley village, was named for Thomas B. Walker of Minneapolis, who engaged extensively during many years in lumbering on the Clearwater River and its branches. He is also honored by the name of the county seat of Cass County, as noted, with a biographic sketch, in its chapter.

Nora Township has Walker Brook Lake in section 1; Mud Lake, crossed by the east side of sections 25 and 36; and Mosquito Creek, flowing west and southwest, tributary to Rice Lake.

Little Mississippi River, beginning in the north part of Shevlin, on a nearly level tract within a mile south of the Clearwater River, runs south and southeast to Manomin or Rice Lake and the Mississippi in the southeast part of Jones Township, Beltrami County. It was called Piniddiwin River by Henry R. Schoolcraft in 1832, an abbreviation of the Ojibwe name, meaning "the place of violent deaths, in allusion to an inroad and murder committed at this place, in former times, by the Sioux" (that is, at or near the mouth of this stream).

Tamarack Lake, in sections 26 and 35, T. 146N, R. 38W, is named for the enclosing woods, consisting largely of the tamarack, our American larch.

Long Lake in section 24, Rice, extending southeast into Itasca Township, and Heart Lake in section 25, Rice, are named from their shape.

Gill and Sucker Lakes in sections 20 and 29,

Itasca, are named for their species of fish, caught in gill nets.

Big La Salle Lake is crossed by the east line of sections 12 and 13, Itasca, lying partly in Hubbard County. It is tributary, with the smaller La Salle Lake, a mile and a half farther north in that county, to the Mississippi by a short stream flowing north, which was named La Salle River by Capt. Willard Glazier in 1881. These recent names were adopted to preserve in this region one of the historic names used by Schoolcraft and Nicollet, who described and mapped a Lake Marquette and a Lake La Salle on the Schoolcraft or Yellow Head River, two to three miles south of the site of Bemidji. Only one lake is there, although nearly divided into two by a strait, and both parts are now named together as Lake Marquette.

Itasca State Park

Lake Itasca, the head of the Mississippi, and the greater part of the state park enclosing this lake lie in Clearwater County; small parts are in Becker and Hubbard Counties. Oldest of our state parks, its place at the source of the greatest river of North America gives to it national significance and value, geographic, historic, and educational.

The first expedition seeking to reach the head of the Mississippi was that of Gen. Lewis Cass in 1820, penetrating the northern forest to Cass Lake, which seems to have been regarded for some years afterward as the principal source of the river. A few years later, in 1823, Giacomo Costantino Beltrami traversed the country between the Red River valley and the upper Mississippi, crossing Red Lake and entering the Mississippi basin above Cass Lake by way of the Turtle Lake and River, which, from his giving the name Lake Julia to a little lake at the water divide, are called the Julian sources of the Mississippi. But another stream, somewhat larger than the Turtle River, was known to come from the west and southwest, and in 1832 Schoolcraft, under instructions from the government, conducted an expedition up that stream, which has ever since been rightly considered the main Mississippi, to the lake at its head, which the Ojibwe called Omushkos, that is, Elk Lake. Schoolcraft then named it Itasca, from the Latin words *veritas*, truth, and *caput*, head, supplied to him by William T. Boutwell, the name being made by writing the words together and cutting off, like Procrustes, the first and last syllables. Four years later, in 1836, Nicollet more fully explored this lake and claimed that its largest tributary, the creek or brook flowing into the extremity of its southwest arm, is "truly the infant Mississippi."

Here the question rested until Capt. Willard Glazier in 1881, six years after the government sectional survey of that area, made his expedition to Itasca and to the lake in section 22, T. 143N, R. 36W, called by the government survey plats Elk Lake, lying close southeast of the southwestern arm of Itasca, and thence voyaged in a canoe to the mouths of the Mississippi. His ridiculous renaming of Elk Lake for himself, with assertion that it should be regarded as the main source of this river, in his subsequently published books and maps, directed the attention of geographers anew to the determination of the source of the Great River.

Willard Glazier was born in Fowler, N.Y., August 22, 1841, and died in Albany, N.Y., in 1905. He served in New York regiments in the Civil War, attaining the rank of captain, and published several books on the history of the war. His biography, titled *Sword and Pen*, by John Algernon Owens (written in large part by Glazier), was published in 1884, 516 pp., including 80 pages on his expedition in the summer and autumn of 1881 by the canoe route from Leech Lake to Lake Itasca and Elk Lake and thence down the Mississippi, with a map of the sources of this river. His later books on the Mississippi are *Down the Great River*, 1887 (443 pp.), with the map redrawn, several names on it being changed; and *Headwaters of the Mississippi*, 1893 (527 pp.), with six maps, including the narrative of Glazier's second expedition, going again in 1891, with a large party, to the head of the river for reinforcement of the claims that Lake Glazier as named in 1881, is the geographic head and chief source. In this expedition the route, both in going and returning, was by the wagon road from Park Rapids to Lake Itasca.

On account of the claims of Glazier and his friends for Elk Lake, renamed Lake Glazier, to be regarded as the head of the Mississippi, Hopewell Clarke, of Minneapolis and later of St. Paul, made in October 1886, for Ivison, Blakeman, Taylor and Co., publishers, New York, a reconnaissance of Lake Itasca and its basin. His report, which appeared in *Science* for December 24, 1886, fully sustained the work and conclusion of Nicollet, before noted.

The Minnesota Historical Society next took up an investigation of the sources of this river, and the report of its committee, presented by Gen. James H. Baker at a meeting on February 8, 1887, repudiated Glazier's claims and refused the substitution of his name for Elk Lake. But a good result from this controversy was the great increase of public interest in the geography and history of the Itasca region, which brought within a few years the establishment of this state park. In October 1888, Hon. J. V. Brower began his explorations and surveys of Lake Itasca and its environs, which continued through four years, being commissioned in February 1889 to this work by the historical society; and he was the chief factor in securing the establishment of the park by an act of the state legislature, April 20, 1891, followed by an act of Congress, August 3, 1892, which granted to the state for this park all undisposed lands of the United States within its area.

The earliest printed proposal for the Itasca Park was a letter of Alfred J. Hill in the *St. Paul Dispatch*, March 28, 1889. Throughout the work of Brower in examination and surveys of the park area, Hill was a collaborator with him concerning the history of the early Spanish and French explorers of the whole extent of the Mississippi, contributing much of his excellent vol. 7 of the Minnesota Historical Society Collections, titled *The Mississippi River and its Source* (1893, pp. xv, 360).

The claims of Glazier are effectually cancelled by Brower in this work, Emile Levasseur in France, and N. H. Winchell, state geologist of Minnesota, followed with papers endorsing Brower's conclusion, that Nicollet's "infant Mississippi . . . a cradled Hercules," in the southern part of the state park, above Lake Itasca, is the veritable, highest, and farthest source of this river (MHS Collections, vol. 8: pt. 2, pp. 213–31, published December 1, 1896).

Jacob Vradenberg Brower, archaeologist and author, was born in York, Mich., January 21, 1844, and died in St. Cloud, Minn., June 1, 1905. He came to Long Prairie, Minn., in 1860; served in the First Minnesota Cavalry, 1862–63; served in the U.S. Navy, 1864–65; studied law and was admitted to the bar in 1873; was a representative in the legislature, 1873; was register of the U.S. land office in St. Cloud, 1874–79; was the first commissioner of Itasca Park, 1891–95; explored and mapped many aboriginal mounds. He was author of vol. 7, MHS Collections, before cited; vol. 11 in the same series, titled *Itasca State Park, an Illustrated History* (1905, 285 pp.); *Prehistoric Man at the Headwater Basin of the Mississippi* (1895, 77 pp.); *The Missouri River and its Utmost Source* (1896, 150 pp., and a second ed., 1897, 206 pp.); Memoirs of Explorations in the Basin of the Mississippi, a series of eight quarto vols.: 1. *Quivira* (1898, 96 pp.); 2. *Harahey* (1899, 133 pp.); 3. *Mille Lac* (1900, 140 pp.); 4. *Kathio* (1901, 136 pp.); 5. *Kakabikansing* (1902, 126 pp.); 6. *Minnesota, Discovery of Its Area* (1903, 127 pp.); 7. *Kansas, Monumental Perpetuation of its Earliest History, 1541–1896* (1903, 119 pp.); 8. *Mandan* (1904, 158 pp.). Biographic sketches and portraits of Brower and his associates in archaeology Alfred J. Hill and Theodore H. Lewis are given by Prof. N. H. Winchell in *The Aborigines of Minnesota*, (1911, pp. vi–xiv).

The people of this state will forever remember Brower with gratitude as the founder of Itasca State Park and its defender and guardian, amidst many difficulties and discouragements, through his last years. His heavy cares and efforts for truthfulness of the river history and to protect the park and lake against ruthless damage by lumbermen are shown throughout his latest book, the MHS Collections vol. 11, but in the darkest hour, when the biennial session of the state legislature in 1893 adjourned without providing for the maintenance of the park, with unfailing courage he exclaimed, "Itasca State Park shall live forever!"

The Itasca Moraine

Another subject of much interest is presented by the admirable development of a belt of marginal moraine hills, knolls, and short ridges, traversing the south and west edges of the park. This is part of a very extensive course of such irregularly hilly deposits of glacial and modified drift crossing Minnesota, named the Itasca or Tenth Moraine. It is one of twelve similar marginal moraines traced in this state by the present writer, formed at stages of temporary halt or readvance during the general recession and departure of the continental ice sheet.

Nomenclature of the Park

Most of the information for this list is from Brower's MHS vols. 7 and 11, supplemented with various details from other sources.

The Ojibwe call Itasca Lake Omushkos, as before noted, meaning Elk Lake, which also is their name of the river thence to Lake Bemidji, as similarly they call it Bemidji River thence to Cass Lake. In translation of the Ojibwe name, the early French fur traders called Itasca Lac La Biche, and Beltrami in like manner named it "Doe lake, west source of the Mississippi." Boutwell wrote in his *Journal*, 1832: "This is a small but beautiful body of water.... Its form is exceedingly irregular, from which the Indians gave it the name of Elk, in reference to its branching horns" (MHS Collections: 1). Brower wrote in vol. 7 (p. 119): "The topographical formation of the locality in its physical features—the shape of an elk's head with the horns representing the east and west arms—no doubt gave it the name 'Elk.'"

Gen. James H. Baker, surveyor general for Minnesota, transferred the name Elk Lake on the plats of the government survey, in 1875–76, to the lake at the east side of the southwest arm of Itasca, designated by the Ojibwe, as noted by Gilfillan, "Pekegumag sagaiigun, the water which juts off from another water." The same name was also used by the Ojibwe, and is retained without translation by the white people, for a lake and falls of the Mississippi in Itasca County, and for a lake and Indian battleground in Pine County, being for those places commonly spelled Pokegama.

This lake had been visited by Julius Chambers in 1872, who then called it "Dolly Varden" from the name of his canoe, and in 1881 Capt. Glazier's party applied to it his name, which he endeavored strenuously but unavailingly to maintain, as related in preceding pages. A short time previous to Glazier's visit, Rev. Joseph A. Gilfillan, going there in May 1881, had named it "Breck lake, in honor of the distinguished first missionary of the American [Episcopal] church to St. Paul and vicinity, who was afterwards first missionary of the church to the Chippewa Indians around the sources of the Mississippi."

Although worthily renamed for James Lloyd Breck (1818–76), the name Elk Lake is yet more desirably retained, because it preserves in translation the aboriginal title that was superseded by Schoolcraft's Itasca.

The only island of Itasca was named for Schoolcraft by his party, 1832. The three branches or arms of Itasca are called by Brower the north, east, and west arms, but the latter two are also known as the southeast and southwest arms.

The largest affluent, Nicollet's "infant Mississippi," is mapped by Brower as "Mississippi River" in "Nicollet Valley." This stream is also often called Nicollet Creek, as by Winchell, in 1896, and the map of the Mississippi River Commission, 1900. Three lakelets noted there by Nicollet, 1836, are "Nicollet's Lower, Middle, and Upper lakes." The headstream flowing into the Upper Lake rises from the "Mississippi Springs," above which, with underground drainage to them, is Floating Moss Lake; and close above and flowing into it from the south is Whipple Lake, at the head of the visible surface drainage. This last name was given by Gilfillan in 1881 to honor Bishop Henry B. Whipple (1822–1901), renowned for his interest in missions for both the Ojibwe and Dakota of this state.

Southward from Whipple Lake, and ensconced in hollows among the low hills and ridges of the Itasca Moraine, are the three little Triplet Lakes; the much larger Morrison Lake, named by Brower in honor of William Morrison, the early trader who was at Elk Lake (since named Itasca) in 1804; Little Elk Lake; Groseilliers and Radisson Lakes, named by Brower for the first white men in Minnesota, whose travels here, in 1655–56 and again in 1660, are the theme of a paper by the present writer (MHS Collections, vol. 10, pt. 2, 1905, pp. 449–594, with a map); the Picard Lakes, named for Anthony Auguelle, "called the Pickard du Gay," a companion of Father Louis Hennepin, 1680; Mikenna Lake, named by Alfred J. Hill, of undetermined meaning; and the large Lake Hernando de Soto, commemorating the Spanish discoverer of the Mississippi, 1541, with its Brower Island, named in honor of J. V. Brower by a committee of the Minnesota Historical Society. These many lakes of the morainic belt in the southwest part of the park, with several smaller lakelets, are believed to send seeping waters northward to

springs, rivulets, and creeks, which are tributary to the Mississippi above the west arm of Itasca and to Elk Lake. For this reason their area is named on Brower's maps as "the Greater Ultimate Reservoir Bowl at the source of the Mississippi river."

Elk Lake receives four small streams. At the west is Siegfried Creek, named by Brower for A. H. Siegfried, a representative of the *Louisville Courier-Journal*, who with others made a recreational expedition to Itasca and Elk Lakes in July 1879. Hall Lake, on the upper part of this creek, was also named by Brower in honor of Edwin S. Hall, the U.S. surveyor in 1875 for several townships here, including the park area. These names displace the Eagle Creek and Lake Alice, names given in 1881 by Glazier, the latter being for his daughter, who ten years afterward, in 1891, was a member of the second Glazier expedition.

The three other tributaries of Elk Lake are from the south, namely, Elk Creek, on the southwest; Clarke Creek, commemorating Hopewell Clarke, before mentioned as a surveyor here in 1886, with its mouth at the head of Chambers Bay; and Gay-gued-o-say Creek, named for Nicollet's Ojibwe guide to Itasca in 1836. Clarke Lake and Deer Park Lake flow into the last of these creeks at stages of high water.

Chambers Bay on the south side of Elk Lake, and Chambers Creek, its short outlet to Lake Itasca, honor Julius Chambers, the journalist and author, whose expedition here in 1872, before noted, probably became a chief incentive for his publication of a historical and descriptive book in 1910, titled *The Mississippi River and Its Wonderful Valley* (308 pp., with 80 illustrations and maps).

At the south end of the east arm of Itasca, Mary Creek brings the inflow from a series of lakes. The lowest, Mary Lake, is named like the creek, in honor of the wife of Peter Turnbull, a land surveyor and civil engineer from Canada, who opened the northern part of the road from Park Rapids to Itasca in 1883 and resided during the next two years on the east side of its east arm. In 1885 they removed to Park Rapids, where Mary Turnbull died in May 1889.

The higher lakes of Mary Valley, in their order from north to south, are the small Twin Lakes; Danger Lake, so named by Turnbull on account of water "flooding the ice surface in winter at its south shore," renamed Deming Lake for Hon. Portius C. Deming of Minneapolis, a friend and promoter of the interests of Itasca Park, who later was the president of the Minneapolis Board of Park Commissioners; Ako Lake, named for one of Hennepin's companions, 1680, whose name is also spelled Accault; and Josephine Lake, in honor of a daughter of Commissioner Brower, who was a teacher in the State Normal School at St. Cloud, and in the public schools of Minneapolis. The upper part of Mary Valley, holding these lakes, was called by Brower "the Lesser Ultimate Reservoir Bowl." This valley, excepting its mouth and west border, lies, with all its lakes, in the edge of Hubbard County, into which the Itasca Park extends a mile along its east side.

South and southwest of Josephine Lake, and beyond the water divide, several small lakes lie in the southeast corner of the park, mostly having no surface outlets but tributary by underground seepage to the basin of Crow Wing River. These include Sibilant Lake, named for its form resembling the letter *S*; Ni-e-ma-da Lake, of which Brower stated that "the name is composite in form, not of Indian origin"; a narrow northern arm of Little Man Trap Lake, so named, like the larger Man Trap Lake a dozen miles eastward, because many peninsulas and the tamarack swamps at the head of its bays baffled the hunter, or in former times the "cruiser" in search for pine lands, when attempting to pass around it; Gilfillan Lake, in honor of Rev. Joseph A. Gilfillan (1838–1913), Episcopal missionary to the Ojibwe in northern Minnesota during 25 years; and Frazier Lake, named for a homesteader whose cabin was beside it.

Other streams flowing into Lake Itasca include Island Creek, tributary to the west side of the north arm, opposite to Schoolcraft Island; French Creek, between Island Creek and Hill Point, named for George H. French, of the survey for the Mississippi River Commission, 1900; Boutwell Creek, named for Rev. William Thurston Boutwell (1803–90), who accompanied the Schoolcraft expedition in 1832; Sha-wun-uk-u-mig Creek, commemorating the Ojibwe guide of Rev. J. A. Gilfillan in his visit to the Itasca basin in 1881; and Floating Bog Creek, emptying into the bay of this name about a half mile east of the island.

Tributaries from the west to the Mississippi

River above Lake Itasca are Demaray Creek, named in honor of Georgiana Demaray, daughter of William Morrison, Spring Ridge Creek, and Howard Creek, named for Jane Schoolcraft Howard, daughter of the explorer and author Henry Rowe Schoolcraft.

Named points and bays of the Itasca shore, especially observed in canoeing, are Bear Point, at the west side of Floating Bog Bay; Turnbull Point, on the west side of the east arm, commemorating Peter Turnbull, before mentioned; Comber Bay and Point, next on the north, for W. G. Comber, assistant in the survey of the park area for the Mississippi River Commission, 1900; O'Neil Point, a little farther northwest, for Hon. John H. O'Neil of Park Rapids; Chaney Bay and Point, next south of Turnbull Point, in honor of Josiah B. Chaney (1828–1908), newspaper librarian of the Minnesota Historical Society, who visited the Itasca Park in 1901 and 1903; Ray's Bay and Point, nearly a half mile farther south, for Fred G. Ray, of the Mississippi River Commission survey, 1900; Ozawindib or Yellow Head Point, at the entrance to the west arm, for the Ojibwe guide of Schoolcraft's party in 1832; Tamarack Point, a quarter of a mile southwest from the last; Garrison Point, on the west side of the west arm, commemorating Oscar E. Garrison (1825–86), who examined the Lake Itasca region and the river below in 1880 for the Forestry Department of the U.S. Census; and Hill Point, on the west side of the north arm, named in honor of Alfred J. Hill (1823–95), the archaeologist, who, as before noted, was the first to propose the establishment of this state park.

Several additional names of lakes are to be noted: Bohall Lake for Henry Bohall, an assistant with Brower in 1889; Hays Lake for an assistant in 1891; Kirk Lake for Thomas H. Kirk, author of an *Illustrated History of Minnesota* (1887, 244 pp.), who visited Itasca and Elk Lakes in 1887; Lyendecker Lake for a comrade of Brower in his first visit to Itasca, 1888; Allen Lake for Lieut. James Allen (1806–46), who accompanied Schoolcraft's expedition in 1832, and whose very interesting report of it was published 28 years afterward in the American State Papers (vol. 5, Military Affairs, 1860, pp. 312–44, with a map); Budd Lake "after an Ohio family name"; McKay Lake for Rev. Stanley A. McKay of Owatonna, Minn., "who in the month of June, 1891, celebrated the ceremonies of baptism at Itasca lake"; Green Lake, west of Chaney Bay; Iron Corner Lake, near the iron post that marks the northeast corner of Becker County; and Augusta, Powder Horn, and Musquash Lakes, named by the Mississippi River Commission, 1900, adjoining the southwest side of Morrison Lake. The last of these lakes, Musquash, has the Algonquian name of the muskrat, a furbearer whose houses dot many of our shallow lakes.

Crescent Springs, Elk Springs, Nicollet Springs, Mississippi Springs, and Ocano Springs, the last bearing a name "found in Schoolcraft's Narrative," are shown on Brower's maps of the park.

Rhodes Hill was named for D. C. Rhodes of Verndale, Minn., photographer of the Brower survey; Morrison Hill, like Morrison Lake for the first recorded white visitor at Itasca; Morrow Heights in honor of A. T. Morrow, director of the survey of the Itasca basin for the Mississippi River Commission, 1900; Ockerson Heights for J. A. Ockerson, also a surveyor for that commission; Aiton Heights after Prof. George B. Aiton, of Minneapolis and later of Grand Rapids, who made botanic examinations of the park in 1891; and Comber Island in Morrison Lake for W. G. Comber, who has thus threefold honors, of this island and of a point and a bay on the Itasca shore.

The Lind Saddle Trail was named in honor of Gov. John Lind, who visited Itasca in 1899, then ordering this trail to be cut through the woods, as his personal donation for the improvement of the park.

North of the park limits, Division Creek (also called Sucker Creek) flows into the Mississippi from the heights on the west, "which divide the waters flowing to Hudson's Bay and the Gulf of Mexico."

McMullen Lake (formerly known as Squaw Lake), close outside the park at the northwest, was named by Brower in honor of William McMullen, the first permanent settler at Itasca Lake, in 1889, on the east side of the north arm.

Kakabikans Rapids, noted by Schoolcraft in 1855 as a name from the Ojibwe language meaning "little falls or rapids," are formed by very abundant glacial boulders in the channel of the Mississippi a few miles below Itasca Lake.

Several names that had their origin from the expedition of Glazier in 1881 are retained by popular use in Hubbard County, but only one has been so retained within the limits of the Itasca Park, this being La Salle River, in the northeast corner, named, with the lakes on its course to the north, in honor of the renowned early French explorer. It was called Andrus Creek by Brower in 1892, "after the treasurer of the Minnesota Game and Fish Commission." Schoolcraft in 1832 had mapped it as "Cano R.," and on the map of his "Summary Narrative," published in 1855, it was called "De Witt Clinton's R.," but in the text it is named "Chemaun or Ocano." The former word, *Chemaun*, is Ojibwe for a birch canoe, as used in Henry W. Longfellow's *Song of Hiawatha*, and the latter word, *Ocano*, is from the French "aux canots," that is, "at or of canoes," which was the ancient and original form that became anglicized into the name of the Cannon River in southeastern Minnesota.

A glacial lake was held temporarily in the Itasca basin by the barrier of the departing ice sheet at the end of the Ice Age, with an area "several times the present size of Itasca lake," named by Brower in vol. 11 Winchell Lake in honor of Prof. N. H. Winchell. This may be preferably called Glacial Lake Winchell, to distinguish it from Winchell Lake in Cook County.

Newton Horace Winchell was born in Northeast, Dutchess County, N.Y., December 17, 1839, and died in Minneapolis, May 2, 1914. Coming to Minnesota in 1872 and residing in Minneapolis, he was state geologist 28 years, 1872–1900; was editor of the *American Geologist*, 1888–1905; and was the archaeologist of the Minnesota Historical Society, 1906–14. His contribution to the Itasca Park literature, titled "The Source of the Mississippi," is in the MHS vol. 8 (pp. 226–31); a biographic memorial of him, in vol. 15 (pp. 824–830, with a portrait); and a more full memorial, in the *Bulletin of the Minnesota Academy of Science* (vol. 5, pp. 73–116).

Like the majestic progress of an epic poem or a grand drama, the history of the gradual discovery of the Mississippi River runs through four centuries. Begun when Amerigo Vespucci in 1498 mapped the delta and mouths of this mighty stream on the north shore of the Gulf of Mexico, it continued till Brower in 1889–92 mapped the shores and islands of Lake Hernando de Soto in the south edge of Itasca State Park. The moving picture of this history is portrayed in words and in maps by the volumes of the MHS Collections. In the nomenclature of the park, a good number of the great explorers of the river are recalled, De Soto, Groseilliers and Radisson, La Salle, Schoolcraft, Nicollet. The vain endeavors of Glazier to link his name with those heroes aroused the just indignation of geographers and the officers of the Minnesota Historical Society. During a decade or longer a great strife raged concerning the true head of the Mississippi and the rightful name of Elk Lake. In 1905 Glazier and Brower, chief opponents in the strife, died, but the Itasca State Park, which grew from it, "shall live forever."

Cook County

This county, established March 9, 1874, was named in honor of Maj. Michael Cook of Faribault, a prominent citizen and a brave soldier in the Civil War. He was born in Morris County, N.J., March 17, 1828; came to Minnesota, settling in Faribault, in 1855, and being a carpenter, aided in building some of the first frame houses there; and was a territorial and state senator, 1857 to 1862. In September 1862, he was mustered into the Tenth Minnesota Regiment, in which he was appointed major, and served until he fell mortally wounded in the battle of Nashville, December 16, 1864, his death occurring 11 days later.

Col. Charles H. Graves, the state senator from Duluth, introduced the bill to establish this county and to name it in honor of Pierre Gaultier de Varennes, sieur de la Vérendrye, the pioneer of exploration on the northern boundary of Minnesota, but the name was changed before the bill was enacted as a law. It has been thought by some that the name adopted was in commemoration of John Cook, who was killed by the Ojibwe, as also his entire family, in 1872, his house at Audubon, Minn., being burned to conceal the deed. Col. Graves has stated in a letter that this name was selected to honor Maj. Cook.

It may well be hoped that some county, yet to be formed adjoining the north line of Minnesota, will receive the name Vérendrye in historic commemoration of the explorations, hardships, and sacrifices of this patriotic and truly noble French explorer. He was the founder of the fur trade in northern Minnesota, Manitoba, and the Saskatchewan region, where it greatly flourished during the next hundred years, and two of his sons were the first white men to see the Rocky Mountains, or at least some eastern range or outpost group of the great Cordilleran mountain belt.

Information of the origins of geographic names in Cook County was gathered during my visit in August 1916 at Grand Marais, the county seat, from Thomas I. Carter, the county auditor; Axel E. Berglund, county surveyor; George Leng, clerk of the court; William J. Clinch, superintendent of schools; and John Drourillard and George Mayhew of Grand Marais.

Each of the organized townships in this county comprises several government survey townships, and Grand Marais and Rosebush are very irregular in their outlines, stretching from areas adjoining Lake Superior to areas on the international boundary, with narrow strips connecting their southern and northern parts.

All townships in Cook County dissolved in 1950; Schroeder and Tofte were reorganized. Three unorganized territories were formed: West Cook includes former Grand Marais, Lutson, and part of Rosebush; East Cook includes Colville, Hoveland, Maple Hill, and part of Rosebush; Grand Portage includes Grand Portage Reservation.

CASCADE a locality in Grand Marais Township (T. 60, R. 2), section 1, on the shore of Lake Superior.

CASCADE CAMP a station on the Northwest Paper Company railroad on the border of Grand Marais and Rosebush Townships (T. 62, R. 2).

CHICAGO BAY see HOVLAND.

CHIPPEWA CITY a community in the 1890s of Ojibwe, located about a half mile east of Grand Marais, the center of which was St. Francis Xavier Catholic Church, built in 1895.

COLVILLE TOWNSHIP organized in 1906, was named in honor of Col. William Colvill, to whose name a silent *e* is added for the township. He was born in Forestville, N.Y., April 5, 1830, and died in Minneapolis, June 12, 1905. He came to Red Wing, Minn., in 1854, and the next year established the *Red Wing Sentinel*, a Democratic newspaper. He served as captain and colonel of the First Minnesota Regiment, 1861–64, was colonel of the First Minnesota Heavy Artillery, 1865, and was brevetted brigadier general. He was a representative in the legislature in 1865 and again in 1878 and was attorney general of the state, 1866–68. In the battle of Gettysburg on July 2, 1863, he led his regiment in a famous charge, one of the noblest sacrifices to duty in all the annals of warfare. In his later years, Col. Colvill homesteaded a claim on the Lake Superior shore in this township (section 9, T. 61N, R. 2E), but his home previously, and also afterward, was near Red Wing. In 1909 his statue in bronze was placed in the rotunda of the state capitol.

CROFTVILLE a settlement in the early 1900s located east of Grand Marais, established by Peter Olsen and brothers Charles and Joe Croft, who had come to the area in 1894 and were known as herring-chokers.

FORT CHARLOTTE a fort established by the North West Company, prior to 1793, at T. 64N, R. 5E, section 29, at a site of a previous trading post erected in 1676–78 by Daniel Greysolon, sieur Du Luth, the first post built in Minnesota at the entrance of the Pigeon River on the north shore of Lake Superior. The fort was named for Queen Charlotte (1744–1818), the wife of George III of England.

FOX FORK a village in T. 62N, R. 1E, section 30, about 1924.

GOOD HARBOR HILL a small settlement on the hill and bay of the same name in Maple Hill Township (T. 61N, R. 1W), which began in the late 1890s as summer homes for many in Hovland and Grand Marais, developing into a farming and logging community; called Terrace Hill by some.

GRAND MARAIS TOWNSHIP received this French name, meaning a great marsh, in the early fur-trading times, referring to a marsh, 20 acres or less in area, nearly at the level of Lake Superior, situated at the head of the little bay and harbor that led to the settlement of the village there. Another small bay on the east, less protected from storms, is separated from the harbor by a slight projecting point and a short beach. In allusion to the two bays, the Ojibwe name the bay of Grand Marais as "Kitchi-bitobig, the great duplicate water; a parallel or double body of water like a bayou" (Gilfillan).

The city of Grand Marais in Rosebush Township (T. 61N, R. 1E), sections 20 and 21, was incorporated on April 21, 1903, and separated from the township on March 27, 1906. Ed. W. Wakelin purchased the first piece of property on the bay in 1872; by the end of 1873, Wakelin, Henry Mayhew and Samuel F. Howenstein owned all the land comprising the original village and lands along West and East Bays and retained control until the early 1900s in spite of buildings, docks, warehouses, railroad rights-of-way, and ore docks. The Mayhew brothers, Henry and Thomas W., had a store on the point made by the bays that served as a trading post; Joseph E. Mayhew was the first lighthouse keeper in 1886. The post office was established in Superior County, Wis., 1856–57, changed its name to Hiawatha, 1857–58, and became Grand Marais in 1873.

GRAND PORTAGE a village and formerly an important trading place, at the head of the bay of this name, and at the southeast end of the Grand Portage, nine miles long, to the Pigeon River above its principal falls, has the distinction of being the most eastern and oldest settlement of white men in the area of Minnesota. Probably during the period of Vérendrye's explorations, this place became the chief point for landing goods from the large canoes used in the navigation of the Great Lakes and for their being dispatched onward, from the end of this long portage, in smaller canoes to the many trading posts of all the rich fur country northwest of Lake Superior. In 1767, when Jonathan Carver went there in the hope of purchasing goods, Grand Portage was an important rendezvous and trading post. At the time of the Revolutionary War, as Gen. James H. Baker has well said, it was the "commercial emporium" of the northwestern fur trade. A post office called Grand Portage in Hovland Township, section 4, was first established in Superior County, Wis., 1856–64, and reestablished in Minnesota, 1864–71.

GUN FLINT CITY a proposed community in T. 65N, R. 4W, on the Port Arthur, Duluth and Western Railroad, promoted with prospects of mining explorations. A plat map was circulated in 1893 by the American Realty Company of Minneapolis, but the site was never developed.

GUN FLINT MINE a station of the Canadian Northern Railway; location not found.

GUNFLINT TRAIL a post office, 1950–53; specific location not found.

HIAWATHA See GRAND MARAIS.

HOVLAND the oldest organized township of this county, is in compliment to a pioneer settler named Brunes for his native place in Norway. The village is located in section 20. In 1888 Ole Brunes and Nels Ludwig Eliasen, two Norwegian carpenters from Duluth, built a log cabin on Brunes's homestead, the two families living together until Eliasen finished a cabin on the adjoining homestead, and other settlers followed. Fishing, logging, and trapping were the principal occupations. Until the post office was established in 1889, the community was called Chicago for the bay on which it is located, that name being used primarily by the Booth Packing Company as their ship's regular stop to pick up fishermen's boxes and barrels. The name was rejected by local residents because it was a corruption of the Ojibwe word *Shikag/Jikag*, meaning "skunk"; the name Hovland was submitted by Anna Brunes, taken from her grandfather's estate in Norway.

LAKE SAGUNAC/SAGINAGA an Indian village about 1800 that had a canoe factory, according to Alexander Henry the Younger; possibly a French post or Hudson's Bay post.

LOCKPORT a village in Lutsen Township (T. 60N, R. 3W), section 26, about 1937.

LUTSEN TOWNSHIP was named by its most prominent citizen, Carl A. A. Nelson, for a town in Prussian Saxony, made memorable by the battle there, 1632, in which the renowned Gustavus Adolphus, king of Sweden, lost his life. The village in section 33 has had a post office since 1890. It is known for it resorts and ski lodges.

MAPLE HILL TOWNSHIP has extensive sugar maple woods on the highland five to ten miles back from Lake Superior. The village of Maple Hill platted in 1896, is located north of Grand Marais and southeast of Devil Track Lake. Mineral prospecting and homesteading brought the first settlers; lumbering and farming were pursued later. The village had a town hall in 1900, a church in 1902, a cemetery, and a log school.

MEREDITH a railroad station in Schroeder Township, section 24.

MINERAL CENTER a post office, 1918–36, located in T. 63N, R. 5E, section 14, on the Grand Portage Reservation.

PAGE a railroad station in Schroeder Township (T. 60N, R. 5W), section 3.

PARKERVILLE a very early settlement at the mouth of the Pigeon River, T. 64N, R. 7E, which had two or three buildings and is now entirely gone.

PIGEON RIVER a village in T. 64N, R. 6E, section 20, about 1937.

REDMYER a village at Cross River with a post office, 1888–91, named for Henry J. Redmyer, fisherman, boatbuilder, and adventurer, who came from Hammerfest, Norway, about 1880; his son, Hendley E. Redmyer, applied for a post office and was postmaster; the post office closed because Lutsen, opened in 1890, was a better location to receive mail.

ROSEBUSH TOWNSHIP organized in 1907, took its name from Rosebush Creek, in translation of its Ojibwe name, Oginekan, though called "Fall river" on maps, in the east edge of T. 61N, R. 1W. The creek a mile farther west was mapped as "Rose Bush river."

ROVE LAKE now a ghost town, was a Catholic Indian Mission built in 1875 on Rove Lake, supposedly serving nearly 100 Indians, traders, and silver prospectors. A post office, also known as Rose Lake, existed 1877–78, with James H. Caldwell, postmaster.

SCHROEDER TOWNSHIP and village are in honor of John Schroeder, president of a lumber company having offices in Ashland and Milwaukee, Wis., for whom pine logs were cut and rafted away from the neighboring Temperance, Cross, and Two Island Rivers. The village, in section 1, had a post office, 1901–17, reestablished in 1924.

TEMPERANCE RIVER a village in Schroeder Township (T. 59N, R. 4E), sections 31 and 32, about 1916.

TERRACE HILL see GOOD HARBOR HILL.

TOFTE likewise the name of a township and village, section 21, founded in 1898, is in honor of settlers having this surname, derived from their former home in the district of Bergen, Norway. John Tofte, his twin brother, Andrew, and brothers Torger and Hans O. Engelsen came in 1893; they selected Carlton as the name because the settlement was on the lower slope of Carlton Peak, but the name was in use; thus they named the community for their home in Norway. Edward Toftey came in 1899, opening the first mill and employing over 25 men. Most of the town was destroyed in a forest fire in 1910 and rebuilt; its post office opened in 1897 with Hans Engelsen, postmaster.

TOMSONITE a post office, 1905–6, located in Grand Marais Township (T. 60N, R. 2W).

Lakes and Streams

Rev. Joseph A. Gilfillan, in his list of *Minnesota Geographical Names Derived from the Chippewa Language*, wrote: "Pigeon river is Omimi-zibi, Omimi meaning pigeon, and zibi . . . river." The accent of *Omimi* is on the second syllable, and *i* has the sound of the English long *e*. *The Song of Hiawatha* correctly anglicizes it,

"Cooed the pigeon, the Omemee."

Until 1870 or later, the passenger pigeon was common or abundant throughout Minnesota, coming early in April, breeding here, and returning southward in October and November. During the next 30 years they became scarce, and about the year 1900 they perished utterly from all that great region, eastern North America, where from time immemorial they had been very abundant. The species, once represented by countless millions, is extinct.

This river, which is the boundary between the United States and Canada, was delineated on "the oldest map of the region west of Lake Superior, . . . traced by a chief of the Assiniboines, named Ochagach, for Verendrye, in 1730," which is published in the *Final Report of the Geology of Minnesota* (vol. 1, 1884, pp. 18, 19). A series of 12 lakes is

shown by this map on the canoe route from the mouth of Pigeon River to "Lac Sesakinaga" (Saganaga), the fourth and eighth being named respectively "Lac Long" and "Lac Plat." Hence came the name "Long lake," given to the lower part of Pigeon River on the map of John Mitchell, 1755, which was used by the British and American commissioners in the Treaty of Paris, 1783, providing that the international boundary should run "through the middle of the said Long lake and the water communication between it and the Lake of the Woods, to the said Lake of the Woods; thence through the said lake to the most northwestern point thereof" (MHS Collections 15: 379–92 [1915], with map).

In 1775 this stream was called "the river Aux Groseilles," that is, Gooseberry River, by Alexander Henry the elder.

Pigeon Falls, 70 feet high, on the Pigeon River about two miles from its mouth, are pictured in the *Geology of Minnesota* (vol. 4, 1899, pl. PP, also p. 509). About a mile up from these falls, the river has a sharp angle in its course, pointing northward, called "The Horn."

In Split Rock Canyon, noted on the map of Cook County by Jewett and Son, 1911, about a half mile to one mile below (northeast from) the western end of the Grand Portage road, Pigeon River has "Falls, 144 feet." These falls were called "the Great Cascades" by Joseph G. Norwood in 1852, who stated in his report for the Owen Geological Survey that the river there descends 144 feet in a distance of 400 yards, through a narrow gorge formed by perpendicular walls of rock, varying from 40 to 120 feet in height.

Partridge Falls, an upper fall 30 feet high, and a lower fall, very close below, falling 10 feet, are on this river about two miles westward, by the zigzag course of the stream, from the end of the Grand Portage. The height of these falls was exaggerated by Alexander Mackenzie in his *Voyages from Montreal*, published in 1801, to be 120 feet, probably confounding the Partridge Falls with the much higher falls last mentioned. Dr. Alexander Winchell in 1887 called these falls "the Minnehaha of the boundary."

Fowl Portage, and the South and North Fowl Lakes, lowest in the series of lakes on the Pigeon River, are translated from their early French name, Outarde (a bustard, here in the usage of the voyageurs applied to the Canadian goose, *Branta canadensis*, our most common wild species), which was probably a translation from the aboriginal Ojibwe name. More definitely, therefore, these would be Goose Portage and Lakes.

Next are Moose Portage and Moose Lake, which Mackenzie called Elk Portage and Lake, but which David Thompson mapped, on the survey for the international boundary, 1826, as "Moose lake, d'Original." Both the English and French names came from the Ojibwe, "Mozo sagaiigun" (Gilfillan).

Big Cherry Portage, named for the wild cherries growing there, the Lower and Upper Lily Lakes, "where there is plenty of water lilies," and the Little Cherry Portage, translated from the French names used by Mackenzie, lead to Mountain Lake called Hill Lake by Norwood, translated from its Ojibwe name, given by Gilfillan as "Gatchigudjiwegumag sagaiigun, the lake lying close by the mountain." This refers to Moose Mountain, shown on the Jewett map, at the south side of the east end of this lake.

"The small new portage" of Mackenzie, next west of Mountain Lake, was called Watap Portage by Thompson, on account of the growth of jack pines, which also are referred to in the names of Watab River and Township (previously noted in the chapter for Benton County).

Rove Lake, called Watab Lake by Norwood and by Dr. Elliott Coues, through which the canoes next passed, was called by Mackenzie "a narrow line of water," and it was so mapped later by Thompson, very narrow and somewhat crooked, whence probably came the name, to rove or wander; but it is erroneously mapped as a rather broad lake in *Geology of Minnesota* (vol. 4, pls. 69 and 83), which error was retained on later maps of Cook County. The Ojibwe name of this lake means "the lake lying in the burnt wood country."

A very rugged and difficult portage, about a mile and a half in length, called by Mackenzie "the new Grande Portage" (on the Geol. Survey map, "Great New Portage"), leads to Rose or Mud Lake, which outflows eastward into Arrow Lake and River in Canada, being thus tributary to the Pigeon River. In the language of the Ojibwe, "Rose lake is Ga-bagwadjiskiwagag sagaiigun, or the shallow lake with mud bottom."

From Rose Lake westward two short portages, named Marten and Perch Portages, with an intervening "mud pond covered with white lilies," as noted by Mackenzie, lead to South Lake, as it was named by Thompson, where, wrote Mackenzie, "the waters of the Dove or Pigeon river terminate, and which is one of the sources of the great St. Lawrence in this direction."

North Lake, the first in the series flowing west to the Lake of the Woods, was so named by Thompson, his South and North Lakes having that relationship to the portage across the continental water divide. Mackenzie called North Lake "the lake of Hauteur de Terre" (Height of Land), and by Norwood it was named "Mountain lake."

Thence the canoes went down the outflowing stream into Gunflint Lake, named from flint or chert obtained in its rocks, also occurring abundantly as pebbles of its beaches, sometimes used for the flintlock guns that long preceded the invention of percussion caps. The English name is translated from the earlier Ojibwe and French names.

Northward in a distance of ten miles from the mouth of Gunflint Lake to Saganaga Falls and Lake, the international boundary has Magnetic Lake, Pine or Clove Lake, Granite Bay, Gneiss Lake, and Maraboeuf Lake, with intervening stretches of the stream, broken by frequent rapids and low falls, past which portages were made. The varying characters of the outcropping rocks supply a majority of these lake names. The most northern is a Canadian French name, used by Mackenzie, 1801, and on maps of Cook County (1911 and 1916), apparently for "marsh deer or buffalo" if it were anglicized; but this name, Maraboeuf, is not found in dictionaries. Thompson in 1826 mapped it, with no name, as a narrow and quite irregularly branched lake, nearly four miles long from south to north, its jagged eastern shoreline in Canada being wholly unlike its representation in our Cook County maps.

Maraboeuf Lake was called Banks' Pine Lake by Prof. N. H. Winchell in 1880 (*Ninth Annual Report*, p. 84), for its forest of jack pine (*Pinus banksiana*), but in the later reports of the Minnesota Geological Survey it is mapped as Granite Lake, for its lying within the area of Saganaga granite.

Mackenzie wrote that Lake Saganaga "takes its name from its numerous islands." Thompson mapped it as "Kaseiganagah lake." Gilfillan wrote, "Saganaga lake is Ga-sasuganagag sagaiigun, the lake surrounded by thick forests." (The pronunciation places the principal accent on the first syllable, and a secondary accent on the last.)

Winchell, from information given by the Ojibwe, wrote in the report before cited: "The word Saganaga signifies islands, or many islands, and seems to be the plural of Saginaw." Chrysostom Verwyst, however, defined Saginaw in Michigan (the river, bay, city, and county) as from an Ojibwe word, "Saging or Saginang, at the mouth of a river." According to Henry Gannett, *Saginaw* means "Sauk place," referring to the Sauk or Sac Indians. The Michigan name and our Saganaga, therefore, are probably not alike in their origin and meaning.

Three miles from Grand Portage village and bay, the Grand Portage Road crosses Poplar River, tributary to Pigeon River.

Dutchman Lake lies two miles west of Grand Portage, and Teal Lake is two miles northeast of that village.

"Mesqua-tawangewi zibi, or Red Sand river," as it was called by Gilfillan, and a lake of the same name, form the greater part of the west boundary of the Grand Portage Reservation. This stream is also called Reservation River, and the lake is named Swamp Lake on the maps of 1911 and 1916. In the treaty of September 30, 1854, which established the reservation, this stream is mentioned as "called by the Indians Maw-ske-gwaw-caw-maw-se-be, or Cranberry Marsh river."

Tom Lake, near the center of T. 63N, R. 3E, is at the head of Kamesh-keg River, meaning Swamp River, which flows north to Pigeon River.

Devil Fish and Otter Lakes outflow by the next tributary of Pigeon River, called Portage Brook, and a mile farther northwest it receives Stump River. Greenwood Lake, west of the Devil Fish, flows south to Brule River.

West of the Fowl Lakes, the northern tiers of townships in this county have a multitude of lakes, mostly narrow and much elongated from east to west, lying in eroded hollows of the bedrocks. These include Royal Lake, John Lake, McFarland Lake, the East and West Pike Lakes, Pine Lake, Long Lake, and Lakes Fanny and Marinda; Crocodile, East Bear Skin, Caribou, and Clearwater Lakes, in T. 64 and 65N, R. 1E, lying

south of Rove Lake; Morgan Lake, Misquah (Red) Lake, Cross, Horseshoe, and Swamp Lakes, Aspen and Flour Lakes, Hungry Jack Lake, Leo Lake, Poplar Lake, tributary by Poplar River to the North Branch of Brule River, Daniels Lake, Birch or West Bear Skin Lake, Duncan's, Moss, and Partridge Lakes, in T. 64 and 65N, R. 1W, lying south of Rose Lake; Winchell Lake, Gaskan and Johnson Lakes, Henson Lake, Pittsburg Lake, Stray Lake, another Caribou Lake, Meeds Lake, Moon Lake, Rush, Lum, and Portage Lakes, No Name or Birch Lake, Dunn Lake, Iron and Mayhew Lakes, Pope Lake, Crab Lake, and Lakes Emma and Louise, in T. 64 and 65N, R. 2W, lying south of the South and North Lakes; Kiskadinna or Colby Lake, Nebogigig or Onega Lake, Davis Lake, Trap and Cliff Lakes, Ida, Jay, and Ash Lakes, Long Island Lake, Finn Lake, Banadad or Banner Lake, Ross, George, and Karl Lakes, Tucker Lake and River, and Loon Lake, in T. 64 and 65N, R. 3W, being south of Gunflint Lake; Frost, Irish, Don, Tuscarora, Snipe, and Copper Lakes, in T. 64N, R. 4W, and Ham, Round or Bear, Brant or Charley, Cloud, Dingoshick, Akeley, Chub, Arc, and Larch Lakes, in T. 65N, R. 4W, south of Maraboeuf Lake; Hub or Mesabi, East and West, Crooked or Greenwood Island, Bullis or Gill's, Little Saganaga, Rattle, and Fern Lakes, in T. 64N, R. 5W, and Gabimichigama, Howard, Peter or Clothespin, French or Kakigo, Bat or Muscovado Lakes, Fay or Paulson Lake and Chub River outflowing from it, Jap Lake, Ray, Jasper or Frog Rock, Alpine or West Sea Gull, and Red Rock Lakes, and the large and very irregularly outlined Sea Gull Lake, with many islands, the largest being named Cucumber Island, in T. 65N, R. 5W, south of Lake Saganaga.

Many of the names of lakes in this list are of obvious derivations, as from the fish in them, the animals and birds and trees adjoining them, or from their outlines, as long, round, crooked, or having the form of a horseshoe, the crescent moon, or an arc.

The origins of only a few of the personal names borne by others of these lakes, as next noted, have been ascertained by the present writer.

Hungry Jack Lake refers to an assistant on the government surveys, Andrew Jackson Scott, a veteran of the Civil War, who for some time at this lake was reduced to very scanty food supplies.

Winchell Lake was named for Prof. N. H.

Winchell, state geologist, who is also honored by the Glacial Lake Winchell in Itasca State Park.

Meeds Lake was named in honor of Alonzo D. Meeds of Minneapolis, who was an assistant in the Minnesota Geological Survey.

Mayhew Lake is for the late Henry Mayhew of Grand Marais, who aided this survey in Cook County.

Charley Lake and Bashitanequeb Lake, the latter renamed on recent maps as Bullis or Gill's Lake, are for an Ojibwe, "Bashitanequeb (Charley Sucker), Indian guide, cook, and canoeman," in this survey (*Geology of Minnesota*, Final Report, vol. 4, 1899, p. 522, with his portrait).

Howard Lake was named for one of the Howard brothers, mining prospectors, of Duluth, and Paulson Lake for the owner of iron mines near it, on the Port Arthur, Duluth and Western Railroad, a branch of the Canadian Northern Railway.

Gilfillan recorded the following Ojibwe names for several of these lakes, which have been translated to their present names.

"Pine lake, Shingwako sagaiigun . . . Shingwak is a pine; o, a connective vowel; sagaiigun, lake."

"Near Rove lake is Ga-wakomitigweiag sagaiigun, or Clearwater lake."

"Iron lake is Biwabiko sagaiigun," the same with the town of Biwabik on the Mesabi Iron Range in St. Louis County.

"Ushkakweagumag sagaiigun, or Greenwood lake," has been sometimes called East Greenwood Lake, to distinguish it from another of this name in Lake County.

"Muko-waiani sagaiigun, or Bear-skin lake."

Frederic Baraga's *Dictionary* has "Kishkadina . . . there is a very steep hill, very steep ascent." This name, with slight change of spelling, is applied on recent maps to a lake that was not named by the maps of the Minnesota Geological Survey, and the lake called Kiskadinna by that survey is now Long Island Lake.

The two Caribou Lakes have the Canadian French name of the American reindeer, changed from *kalibu* of the Micmac Indians, meaning "'pawer or scratcher,' the animal being so called from its habit of shoveling the snow with its forelegs to find the food, covered by snow." The reindeer was formerly common in the north half of Minnesota.

Flour Lake, which received its name on ac-count of a cache of flour placed there during the government surveys, is erroneously spelled Flower on some published maps. The Ojibwe call this lake Pakwe-jigan (Bread or Flour), in allusion to this cache.

Sea Gull Lake, like the Gull Lake in Cass County, is a translation from the Ojibwe name, referring to the American herring gull and three other species, which frequent the large lakes throughout this state.

Turning to the streams and lakes tributary to Lake Superior from Cook County, in their order from southwest to northeast, we have first the Two Island River, named for Gull and Bear Islands, near its mouth.

Cross River, at Schroeder, was so called by Thomas Clark, assistant state geologist, in 1864 but later was named Baraga's River by Col. Charles Whittlesey in 1866. It had previously been named by the Ojibwe, as Gilfillan relates, "Tchibaiatigo zibi, i. e., wood-of-the-soul-or-spirit river; they calling the Cross wood of the soul, or disembodied spirit." The origin of this name was from a cross of wood erected by Father Baraga, who, as Verwyst relates, "landed here after a perilous voyage in a small fishing boat, across Lake Superior, 1845–6." Whittlesey, in his report of explorations, published in 1866, wrote: "At the mouth of this creek there was in 1848 a rough, weather-beaten cross nailed to the tall stump of a tree, on which was written in pencil the following words: 'In commemoration of the goodness of Almighty God in granting to the Reverend F. R. Baraga, Missionary, a safe traverse from La Pointe to this place, August, 1843.' . . . I have endeavored to perpetuate this incident, and the memory of Father Baraga, by naming the stream after him." Bishop Frederic Baraga was born in Slovenia, June 29, 1797, and died in Marquette, Mich., January 19, 1868. He was a Catholic missionary to the Indians in northern Michigan and Wisconsin and northeastern Minnesota, 1835–68; author of an Ojibwe grammar and dictionary, often quoted in this book, and of various religious works.

Temperance River was called Kawimbash River by Norwood, of David D. Owen's geological survey, 1848–52, and it retained that name, meaning "deep hollow," in Whittlesey's report, 1866, but it had received its present name in Clark's geological report, 1864, and was so mapped in 1871.

Clark explained the origin of the name Temperance as follows: "Most of the streams entering the lake on this shore, excepting when their volumes are swollen by spring or heavy rain floods, are nearly or quite closed at their mouths by gravel, called the *bar*, thrown up by the lake's waves; this stream, never having a 'bar' at its entrance, to incommode and baffle the weary voyageur in securing a safe landing, is called no *bar* or Temperance river." Its sources include Temperance Lake, close west of Brule Lake, which has two outlets, the larger flowing east to Brule River, and the other flowing west to Temperance Lake and River; Cherokee Lake, as it is named on recent maps, called Ida Belle Lake by the Minnesota Geological Survey, in honor of a daughter of Prof. Alexander Winchell, who became the wife of Horace V. Winchell; Saw Bill Lake, named for a species of duck; and Alton, Kelso, and Little Saw Bill Lakes.

Below Temperance Lake, the river of this name flows through Jack, Kelly, Peterson, and Baker Lakes. Other lakes near its course and tributary to it include Vern Lake, Pipe Lake, named for its outline, Moore, Marsh, and Anderson Lakes, on the east, and Clam Lake, Odd, Java, Smoke, and Burnt Lakes, on the west.

Near the west side of the county, and ranging from the northern watershed down the general slope toward Lake Superior, are Mesabi Lake, Dent, Bug, Poe, Wind, Duck, and Pie Lakes; Grace, Ella, Beth, and Phoebe Lakes; and Frear, Elbow, Whitefish, Twohey, Four Mile, and Cedar Lakes.

Gilfillan wrote that in the Ojibwe language, "Poplar river is Ga-manazadika zibi, i.e., place-of-poplars river." Clark in 1864 definitely translated it as "Balm of Gilead," a variety of the balsam poplar, common or frequent along rivers in northeastern Minnesota. Lakes tributary to this river include Gust Lake, named for Gust Hagberg, a Swedish homesteader near it; Long, Beaver, Pine, Rice, Haberstead, and Barker Lakes; Elbow or Tait Lake; and Lake Clara, Big, and Sucker Lakes, the last renamed Lake Christine in honor of the daughter of William J. Clinch, county superintendent of schools, who had a homestead there. East of Poplar River, mostly tributary to it, are the Twin Lakes, Mark, Pike, Trout, Bigsby, and Caribou Lakes, and Lake Agnes.

Small streams next eastward, flowing into Lake Superior, are named False Poplar, Spruce, and Indian Camp Rivers.

Cascade River, named from its series of beautiful waterfalls near its mouth, has Cascade and Little Cascade Lakes, Swamp Lake, Eagle and Zoo Lakes, and the large Island Lake. About six miles above its mouth, it receives an eastern tributary named Bally Creek in honor of Samuel Bally, a member of the board of county commissioners, who had a homestead there.

Cut Face and Fall Rivers and Rosebush Creek, small streams between Cascade River and Grand Marais, have no considerable lakes.

"Devil Track river," wrote Gilfillan, "is Manido bimadagakowini zibi, meaning the spirits (or God) walking-place-on-the-ice river." The Ojibwe applied this name primarily to Devil Track Lake, and thence, according to their custom, to the outflowing river. The name implies mystery or something supernatural about the lake and its winter covering of ice, but without the supremely evil idea that is given in the white men's translation. The wild rock gorge of the river below this lake may have suggested the aboriginal name, which was used by Norwood in 1851 and Clark in 1864. Its translation, as now used, dates from the settlement of Grand Marais by Henry Mayhew and others in 1871.

Tributary to Devil Track Lake and River are Swamp Lake and Creek, Clearwater Lake, Elbow Lake, named like numerous others, from its outline, and Monker Lake, named for Claus C. Monker, a Norwegian homesteader on its south side, who was later a fisherman, living in Grand Marais.

Next eastward are Durfee and Kimball Creeks, the latter having Kimball and Pickerel Lakes. Durfee Creek was named in honor of George H. Durfee, judge of probate of this county. Kimball Creek was named by Clark, in the geological exploration of 1864, for Charles G. Kimball, a number of the party, who lost his life near this stream by drowning in Lake Superior.

Diarrhoea River, which receives the outflow of Trout Lake, has this name on Norwood's map in the Owen survey, 1851, referring to illness thought due to drinking its water, and it is so named by Jewett's map, 1911. The maps of the Minnesota Geological Survey call it Greenwood River.

Brule River, called Wisacod by Norwood, is

given by Gilfillan as "Wissakode zibi or Half-burnt-wood river." Its largest lake, at the source of its South Branch, is Brule Lake, which, as before mentioned, has another outlet to Temperance River. One of the islands of Brule Lake is called Tamarack Island, for an old Ojibwe, John Tamarack, who lived on it. (*Brulé*, the French word meaning "burnt," has two syllables, the second having the English sound of lay. Brule as a place name has been anglicized and is pronounced as one syllable.)

Juno, Homer, Axe, and Star Lakes, the last probably named for its radiating arms, lie close south of Brule Lake.

The South Branch flows through Brule Bay, which is a separate small lake, Vernon, Swan, and Lower Trout Lakes. It receives from the north the outflow of Echo, Vance, and Little Trout Lakes, and on the south are Abita, Keno or Clubfoot, Pine, and Twin Lakes. Abita Lake, on the southern slope from Brule Mountain, has the distinction of being the highest lake in Minnesota, 2,048 feet above the sea.

The North Branch of Brule River receives the outflow from Poplar, Winchell, and Meeds Lakes, and a large number more, in the list of lakes before noted for the most northern townships of the county.

Below the junction of its South and North Branches, Brule River flows through Elephant Lake, as it is named on our maps, more commonly known by the people of the region as Northern Light Lake; and it receives Greenwood River, the outlet of Greenwood Lake.

Little Brule River is tributary to Lake Superior about a mile west of the large Brule River.

Between Brule and Pigeon Rivers, only small streams enter Lake Superior, including, in order from west to east, Flute Reed River, Swamp River, Red Sand or Reservation River, and Hollow Rock Creek.

Points, Bays, and Islands of Lake Superior

Sugar Loaf Point is two miles northeast from the southwest corner of this county.

Gull and Bear Islands gave the name of Two Island River, as before noted. At the mouth of this river the village of Saxton was platted by Commodore Saxton, Lyle Hutchins, and others in Au-

gust 1856, but was abandoned two years later, as related by Robert B. McLean of Duluth.

Between Poplar and Devil Track Rivers are Caribou Point, Black Point, Lover's Point and Bay, Terrace Point and Good Harbor Bay, and the two bays at Grand Marais.

Cow Tongue Point, as named in the Minnesota Geological Survey, a half mile southwest of Kimball Creek, is more commonly known as Scott's Point, for Andrew Jackson Scott who is commemorated also by Hungry Jack Lake in this county, before noted.

Fishhook Point is about two miles and a half southwest of the mouth of Brule River.

Chicago Bay, into which the Flute Reed River flows at Hovland village, was called Sickle Bay in the Geological Survey.

Thence northeastward are Horseshoe and Double Bays, Cannon Ball Bay, Red Rock Bay, Red Point, and Deronda Bay. The last was named by Prof. N. H. Winchell in 1880 from George Eliot's novel *Daniel Deronda*, published in 1876, read partly in camp there.

Two small unnamed islands lie about a half mile and one mile east of Cannon Ball Bay, and Arch Island is off the southwest point enclosing Deronda Bay.

Between Red Rock Bay and Red Point, a craggy part of the shore is called the East Palisades.

Grand Portage Island, which lies in front of the bay of this name, is now often called Ganon Island for Peter Ganon, who had a supply store on its northern point.

Hat Point, in front of Mt. Josephine, projects into the lake between Grand Portage Bay and Waus-wau-goning Bay. The name of the latter bay, considerably changed from its proper Ojibwe form, was translated by Gilfillan as "making-a-light-by torches," having reference to the spearing of fish at night, whence Clark in 1864 called it "Spear-fish bay," a more free translation.

East of this bay, within about three miles, Clark enumerated 12 islands, which he compared, in beauty of scenery and attractiveness for sportsmen, with the Apostle Islands near La Pointe, Wis. The largest was named Governor's Island by Dr. Augustus H. Hanchett of New York City, state geologist of Minnesota in 1864, in honor of Gov. Stephen Miller, and this name is retained by maps, but it is more commonly known as Susie Island, a name used by the later state geologist, Prof. N. H. Winchell, in 1880. The next in size, which rises highest, named by Clark as High Island, was called Lucille Island by Winchell. Others of this group were named Magnet and Syenite Islands by Clark, and Birch, Belle Rose, Little Brick, and Porcupine Islands by Winchell.

Northeast of these islands are Morrison and Clark Bays, the latter named by Hanchett in honor of his assistant, Thomas Clark, author of valuable reports on the geology of parts of Minnesota, published in 1861 and 1865. Clark was born in Le Ray, Jefferson County, N.Y., January 6, 1814; removed to Ohio about 1835, settling in Maumee; removed to Toledo in 1851; was a civil engineer, and came to Superior, Wis., in 1854; surveyed the original site of that city; later surveyed and settled at Beaver Bay, Minn., his home when a state senator, 1859–60; died in Superior, Wis., December 20, 1878.

Pigeon Point and Bay, named from the river, are the most eastern part of this state.

Mountains and Hills

In voyaging along the north side of Lake Superior, the highland in Cook County within one to two or three miles back from the shore is seen as a succession of serrate hills and low mountains, the peaks being generally about two miles apart for distances of many miles. The visible crest line thus presents a remarkable profile, resembling the teeth of an immense saw. Between Temperance River and Grand Marais, through nearly 30 miles, a somewhat regular series of these sharp outlines on the verge of the interior plateau has received the name of Sawtooth Mountains.

The most conspicuous and highest summit of this range, at its west end close back from the village of Tofte, was named Carlton Peak in 1848 by Col. Charles Whittlesey in honor of Reuben B. Carlton, of Fond du Lac, Minn., who in that year ascended this mountain with Whittlesey, for the geological survey of this region by David Dale Owen. He is likewise honored by the name of Carlton County. Another peak is called Good Harbor Hill, rising about a mile west of the bay so named.

Farquhar Peak, similarly situated near the lakeshore two miles west of Reservation River, was named in honor of an officer of the U.S. Survey of the Great Lakes.

Mt. Josephine, at the east side of Grand Portage Bay, was named for a daughter of John Godfrey of Detroit, Mich., who had a trading post at Grand Marais during several years, up to 1858. With a party of young people, she walked from Grand Portage to the top of this mountain about the year 1853.

Mountain Lake, on the international boundary, has Moose Mountain close south of its east end, and Mt. Reunion a mile west of its west end, the latter being a name given for its being a place of meeting for parties on the Minnesota Geological Survey.

Brule Mountain is the summit of the highland close south of Lower Trout Lake on the Brule River.

Eagle Mountain is about five miles southwest of Brule Mountain and a mile east of Eagle Lake.

Prospect Mountain is between the west ends of Gunflint and Loon Lakes.

The highest lands of Minnesota are the Misquah Hills, an east to west range south of Cross and Winchell Lakes, whose hilltops within four miles east and seven miles west of Misquah Lake are about 2,200 feet above the sea, the highest being 2,230 feet. The name of the Misquah Lake and Hills is the Ojibwe word meaning "red," in allusion to their red granite rocks that are exposed in extensive outcrops. Prof. N. H. Winchell wrote in 1881: "Misquah lake is flanked on the northeast and east by high brick-red hills, some of them being 500 or 600 feet high. The trees, being nearly all fire-killed and even consumed, allow a perfect view of the rock."

In the west edge of this county, the Mesabi Lake marks the eastern extension of the Mesabi Iron Range, which passes by Little Saganaga Lake and northeast to Gunflint Lake. This Ojibwe name was given on Joseph N. Nicollet's map in 1843 as "Missabay Heights." It has been spelled in several ways, Mesabi being its form in the reports and maps of the Minnesota Geological Survey. Gilfillan translated it as "Giant mountain," with an additional note: "Missabe is a giant of immense size and a cannibal. This is his mountain, consequently the highest, biggest mountain."

Winchell wrote of it, "The Chippewas at Grand Portage represent Missabe as entombed in the hills near there, the various hills representing different members of his body." Gunflint and North Lakes lie in the course of continuation of the Mesabi Range, about ten miles north from the range of the Misquah Hills, with which it is parallel.

Superior National Forest

Large tracts in Cook, Lake, and St. Louis Counties, exceeding a million acres, deemed chiefly valuable for forestry, were set apart by the U.S. government as a public reservation and named the Superior National Forest, in a proclamation of President Roosevelt, February 13, 1909, to which subsequent additions through similar proclamations have been since made. The initial recommendation for forestry reservation of these Minnesota lands was addressed to the commissioner of the U.S. General Land Office by Gen. C. C. Andrews, chief forest fire warden of this state, in 1902, and the authority for such national reservations had been vested in the president of the United States by an act of Congress in 1891.

Additional congressional action designated part of the Superior National Forest as a wilderness recreation area in 1926. After lengthy, heated struggle to avoid overuse and development, supporters of the area succeeded when Congress included the land under the National Wilderness Preservation Act of 1964. The area gained further protection in 1978 under the Boundary Waters Canoe Area Wilderness Area Wilderness Act, which limited logging, mining, and motorboat and snowmobile use. The BWCAW includes land in Cook, Lake, and St. Louis Counties along the United States–Canada border.

Grand Portage Reservation

An area of about 65 square miles, including the trading post and village of Grand Portage, the portage road to Pigeon River, and the tract southward to the lakeshore and west to Cranberry Marsh or Red Sand River, now commonly known as Reservation River, was set apart in a treaty with the Ojibwe at La Pointe, Wis., September 30, 1854, for the Grand Portage band of Lake Superior Ojibwe.

Glacial Lakes Duluth and Omimi

The great glacial lake that was held by the barrier of the departing ice sheet in the western part of the basin of Lake Superior, forming beach lines at Duluth 535 and 475 feet above Lake Superior, was named by the present writer in 1893 as the "Western Superior glacial lake." In 1897 and 1898, respectively, this cumbersome name was changed by Frank B. Taylor and Arthur H. Elftman to be Glacial Lake Duluth. The heights of its strand lines on Mt. Josephine were determined by leveling in 1891 by Prof. Andrew C. Lawson as 607 and 587 feet above Lake Superior, which is 602 feet above the sea.

A somewhat higher and much smaller glacial lake, existing for a relatively short time in the Pigeon River basin in eastern Cook County and extending slightly into Canada, was described and named Lake Omimi by Elftman, as follows (*Am. Geologist*, vol. 21, p. 104, Feb. 1898): "Before the ice had receded beyond mount Josephine it retained a lake of about 40 square miles in area lying in the upper valley of the present Pigeon river. The lake bed has an altitude of 1,255 to 1,360 feet above the sea. Its lowest point is thus about 50 feet higher than the upper stage of Lake Duluth. . . . When the ice receded from the vicinity of Grand Portage, Lake Omimi disappeared. The name Omimi is taken from the Chippewa name for Pigeon river."

State Parks

The year 1957 was a banner year for state parks in Cook County; the state created three of them. Temperance River State Park includes about 500 acres at the mouth of the Temperance River. A main feature of the park is the extensive potholes scoured out by sand and gravel in the river as it rushed through the deep, narrow gorge. Farther up the North Shore is Cascade River State Park, which began in the 1930s as a Civilian Conservation Corps camp. Most of the park land is in a narrow strip along the lake. The falls of the Cascade River, which descends 900 feet within three miles, are a principal attraction for tourists.

The third of these three parks also had beginnings in the 1930s as unemployed men undertook public works improvements to a recreation area. In 1957 a small area was set aside as the Bois

Brule State Park. The name was changed in 1963 to honor Judge Clarence R. Magney who had campaigned to preserve North Shore lands. Magney was a lawyer in Duluth, mayor of that city, and a Minnesota Supreme Court justice; he died May 14, 1962. The park is notable for the Brule River, its three waterfalls, and the plant life that occurs in the microcosm formed by the mist from the falls.

The state added a fourth park along the shore in 1989 with the creation of Grand Portage State Park. Like the other parks of the county, it has as its focus a cascading river, in this case the Pigeon River and its High Falls. Unlike the other parks, the state does not own the land, which is wholly within the Grand Portage Reservation. Instead, the state and the Grand Portage band cooperated to develop the area, but the land remains in trust with the band and the Bureau of Indian Affairs.

Grand Portage National Monument

By early in the twentieth century, the site of the fur trading post and trail at Grand Portage were decaying and disappearing. After a lengthy campaign to preserve and restore the site, the Grand Portage band agreed to transfer the land to the federal government, and in 1960 the site was designated Grand Portage National Monument. Following extensive archaeological excavation, the National Park Service began re-creating the buildings of the post and restoring the portage trail to the Pigeon River.

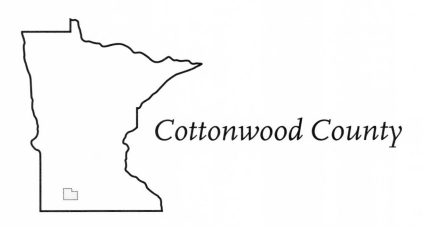

Cottonwood County

This county, established May 23, 1857, organized July 29, 1870, derived its name from the Cottonwood River, which touches the northeast corner of Germantown in this county and to which its northwest townships send their drainage by several small streams flowing northward. It is a translation of *Waraju*, the Dakota name, noted by William H. Keating and by Joseph N. Nicollet's report and map. Keating wrote that the river was so named "from the abundance of this tree on its banks," and Nicollet stated that the most important village of the Sisseton Dakota was on its north bank near its junction with the Minnesota River. The cottonwood, also called the necklace poplar, is a fast-growing, tall tree, common or frequent through the south half of this state and along the Red River valley but reaches its northeastern limit on the headwaters of the St. Croix

and the Mississippi. It is extensively planted for shade, as a shelter from winds, and for fuel, but at its time of shedding the seed from its tassels, which is in the spring, "the cotton from the seeds proves a source of much annoyance to the tidy housewife."

The Canadian French traders and voyageurs gave to the cottonwood the name *Liard*, meaning "a farthing," perhaps in allusion to the nearly worthless quality of its lumber for constructive uses. Their translation of this Dakota name was "Rivière aux Liards," as recorded by Keating in 1823. In the *Journal* of the younger Alexander Henry, published in 1897 as edited by Dr. Elliott Coues, Henry wrote in 1803–4 of another Rivière aux Liards, a tributary of Red Lake River, probably the Clearwater River, which also has given its name to a county of Minnesota.

The information of origins and meanings of geographic names in this county was received from History of Cottonwood and Watonwan Counties, *John A. Brown, editor (2 vols., 1916); from* A History of the Origin of the Place Names Connected with the Chicago and Northwestern and Chicago, St. Paul, Minneapolis and Omaha Railways, *by W. H. Stennett (202 pp., 1908); from S. A. Brown, county auditor, S. J. Fering, register of deeds, and A. W. Annes, judge of probate, during a visit in Windom, July 1916; and from E. C. Huntington of St.*

Paul, who for 36 years, 1871–1907, was editor of the Windom Reporter.

AMBOY TOWNSHIP organized October 10, 1872, was named by settlers from the eastern states. Townships or villages of this name are in Ohio, Indiana, Illinois, Michigan, New Jersey, and New York.

AMO TOWNSHIP organized March 4, 1873, was named by W. H. Benbow, then clerk of court for the county, to inculcate the principle of friendship, the meaning of the name in Latin being "I love." A post office was located there, 1873–76, with William W. Barlow, postmaster, and later, 1897–1907, was located in the Amo Store, built in 1896 and attached to the John F. Johnson home.

ANN TOWNSHIP organized in 1876, was named in honor of the wife of Hogan Anderson, then a member of the board of county commissioners, who was a homestead farmer in this township, wagonmaker, and merchant.

BAINBRIDGE a post office, 1882–88, located in farmer Charles Baxter's colonial-style home, which he enlarged to a stagecoach inn, named Bainbridge for his home place in New York; location not found.

BIG BEND a village in Great Bend Township and the first county seat. A railroad survey indicated that tracks would be laid through this site, but Charlie Chamberlain, who owned much of the land, wanted such a high price that the railroad resurveyed and followed the river into what is now Windom. The first township meeting was held at the home of Chamberlain, and the name chosen for the township was Big Bend, later changed to Great Bend. Post offices existed at the site, 1870–74 and 1879–1903.

BINGHAM LAKE a city in Lakeside Township, sections 9 and 16, platted July 28, 1875, incorporated February 26, 1900, and separated from the township, "was named from a nearby lake. The lake was named by the United States surveyor, for Senator K. S. Bingham, of Michigan." Kinsley Scott Bingham was born at Camillus, N.Y., December 16, 1808; removed to Michigan in 1833 and engaged in farming; was a representative in the state legislature, 1836–40; was a member of Congress, 1847–51; governor of Michigan, 1855–59; and a U.S. senator, 1859–61, until his death at Oak Grove, Mich., October 5, 1861. The first permanent settler was Daniel C. Davis, who with Rufus P. Mathews established all the corners of the townsite. Davis opened the general store; the post office began in 1871 with Mathews, first postmaster. The village had a station of the Chicago, St. Paul, Minneapolis and Omaha Railroad.

CARSON TOWNSHIP organized in July 1871, bears the name of the widely known frontiersman, trapper, guide, soldier, and Indian agent Christopher (commonly called Kit) Carson (1809–68), for

whom Carson City, the capital of Nevada, was named.

CASSEL a post office, 1878–79; location not found.

COMFREY a city in Selma Township, with Brown County.

COPENHAGEN a village in Storden Township started in 1893 with a creamery and several businesses; when the railroad went through Storden in 1899, many of the businesses moved there. It is not known why the village has the same name as the capital of Denmark.

DALE TOWNSHIP was organized March 30, 1872, having a name suggested by its valley and lakes. "When first discovered, there was a beautiful chain of lakes in the central eastern portion of this township. These were filled in their season with wild fowls, and many fish abounded in their waters. With the settlement of the country, several of these lakes have been drained out and are now utilized for pasture and field purposes by the farmers who own the property. Some of the lakes are still intact and are highly prized by the citizens of the county." A post office, 1878–95, was located first in the dugout home of Hosea Eastgate, known as Hosea's Cave; there is some question as to whether this was in Dale or Germantown Township.

DELFT in Carson Township, section 18, established as a railway station of the Chicago, St. Paul, Minneapolis and Omaha Railroad in 1892 and platted as a village June 18, 1902, "was named for the city in Holland by John Bartsch and Henry Wieb. Previous to adopting this name the village was called Wilhelmine, a female name common in Holland." The village had a general store built in 1903 by the Harder brothers, Jacob S. Harder being first postmaster when the office was established in 1903.

DELTON TOWNSHIP organized September 17, 1872, bears the same name with villages in Virginia, Michigan, and Wisconsin. A post office named Delton existed 1878–79, with John Yale, postmaster; location not found but probably in Delton Township.

GERMANTOWN organized January 24, 1874, received its name from its many German settlers, who were a large majority of the early homesteaders in this township.

GREAT BEND TOWNSHIP organized August 27,

1870, "derives its name from the big bend in the Des Moines River within its borders." More exactly the apex of this bend or angle of the river is in the extreme southeast corner of Amo Township.

HIGHWATER organized January 24, 1874, is named for Highwater Creek, which crosses the east half of this township, so called by the pioneer settlers "on account of its quick rising after a rain storm." See also **WESTBROOK**.

HOYT a village of Highwater Township, section 26, began with a cooperative creamery built in 1866. The post office was established in 1897, with Soren A. Berg as first postmaster in his home until building a store in 1898, named the Hoyt Store because most of the goods came from the Hoyt Merchandise Company of Chicago. The post office closed in 1903 and the store in 1920.

HUNTINGTON a post office of Lakeside Township, 1875–87, Eliza C. Huntington, first postmaster.

JEFFERS a city in Amboy Township, section 20, incorporated as a village on May 9, 1900, was named in honor of George Jeffers, a wealthy landowner, from whose homestead a part of the site of this railway village was purchased. The village was surveyed by the Chicago, Milwaukee and St. Paul Railroad in 1899, its first depot located in a boxcar. The townsite of 20 blocks, 4 blocks south and 5 blocks west of block 1, was platted by Frank H. Peavey, president of Interstate Land Co., and all streets were named after employees of the Peavey Elevator. The post office opened in 1900 in the Faust store, Albert A. Faust, first postmaster.

KEMI a post office, 1890–1900, in Rose Hill Township, section 16, whose name was given by the U.S. Post Office Department because it was short and different. John J. Hubin, postmaster, had pigeon-hole boxes in a lean-to attached to his house; the post office discontinued when Westbrook was established. No buildings are left, and a historical marker was placed at the site in 1949.

LAKESIDE TOWNSHIP organized August 1870, received its name for its several fine lakes, including Bingham, Clear, Cottonwood, Fish, and Wolf Lakes, of which the third and fifth nearly adjoin the village of Windom. Fish Lake has been renamed Willow Lake.

MIDWAY TOWNSHIP was organized March 16, 1895, having previously been a part of Mountain Lake Township. Its name refers to its situation on the railway, equidistant between St. Paul and Sioux City.

MOUNTAIN LAKE TOWNSHIP organized May 6, 1871, derived its name from its former large lake, in which a mountainlike island rose with steep shores and nearly flat top about 40 feet above the lake, having similar outlines to those of the surrounding bluffs and general upland. "The upper part of the island was covered with trees, which could be seen for many miles. This spot served as a landmark and a guide for many of the early settlers. . . . The lake, as known to pioneers, is no more; it has long since been drained, and grains and grasses grow in its old bed." The city of Mountain Lake, of Midway and Mountain Lake Townships, was platted May 25, 1872. The post office was established in 1871, first located in Paul Seegers's general store. The village had a flour mill and grain elevators and a station of the Chicago, St. Paul, Minneapolis and Omaha Railroad in section 30. The village grew with an influx of Dutch-German Mennonites from southern Russia until about 1910.

ODELL a post office, 1880–93, formerly named Warren in 1879–80; location not found.

RED ROCK DELLS a recreational area located in the northeast quarter of section 36, Germantown Township, a designated school land site. The land was first sold to Fred W. Willmert, who sold it immediately to John Paulson of Windom, owner until his death in 1938. It was then sold to Anton Schenk and his son, Alfred; seven acres at the site of the falls were purchased in 1968 by the county to create a park, picnic, and recreational site, the area having long been popular as a gathering place for young people.

REDROCK a post office, 1878–1900; location not found.

ROSE HILL TOWNSHIP organized April 5, 1879, received its name for its plentiful wild prairie roses and its low ridges and hills of morainic drift. A post office with this name existed, 1879–82, Heinrich Siemund, postmaster; location not found but probably in Rose Hill Township.

SELMA TOWNSHIP organized April 4, 1874, bears a Scandinavian feminine Christian name, given to the first child born there. The village in section 8 had a post office, 1882–1900, first located in Silas Blackmun's home; while he served two terms in the Minnesota legislature, 1884–88, his brother, Alonzo, was postmaster.

SOUTHBROOK the most southwestern township of this county, was organized in July 1871. It is crossed by the Des Moines River, to which this township sends small brooks and rivulets from springs in the river bluffs.

SPRINGFIELD organized August 27, 1870, was named by settlers from eastern states, many of which have townships, villages, and cities of this name.

STORDEN TOWNSHIP organized March 30, 1875, was known as Westbrook Township until 1872, and then named Town of Norsk for its many Norwegian pioneers but later was renamed in honor of its first settler, Nels Storden, an immigrant from Norway; the name was proposed by John Fitcha. The city of Storden, sections 29 and 30, was platted July 8, 1903, and was incorporated as a village on June 7, 1921. The post office was begun in 1875 with Ole Christopherson, postmaster, on his farm. The post office moved in 1903 to Copenhagen, located one mile north and west of Storden; eventually Copenhagen was absorbed into Storden; it had a station of the Chicago, St. Paul, Minneapolis and Omaha Railway.

TOWN OF NORSK see STORDEN TOWNSHIP.

WARREN see ODELL.

WESTBROOK organized September 17, 1870, was named for the west branch of Highwater Creek, which flows across the southeast part of this township. The city of Westbrook, sections 29 and 30, was incorporated as a village on February 16, 1901, and platted June 8, 1900, by Interstate Land Co. The first building was a boardinghouse built by Sivert Noreem, who later built the Commercial Hotel. The general store of Ole A. Pederson became the site of the post office in 1888. An earlier post office, West Brook, 1873–87, with Frithsof Riis as postmaster, changed its name to Highwater until 1888, when the new post office organized at Westbrook. The village had a station of the Chicago, St. Paul, Minneapolis and Omaha Railway.

WILDER a postal station near Windom.

WINDOM the county seat, was platted June 20, 1871, about a dozen lots at $100 each being sold the first day. By August of that year a number of stores were open for business, all buildings of wooden frame construction: a hardware store, a saloon, two bakeries, a grocery, two dry goods stores, a meat market, a print shop, a hotel, and a general store, a number of them owned by women; the post office began in 1871 with Samuel M. Espey, postmaster. It was incorporated as a village in the spring of 1875, the first ordinance of the village council being passed April 15, and was reincorporated September 9, 1884. It was named by Gen. Judson W. Bishop of St. Paul, chief engineer for construction of the railway, in honor of the distinguished statesman, William Windom of Winona. He was born in Belmont County, Ohio, May 10, 1827, and died in New York City, January 29, 1891. He received an academic education and studied law; came to Winona, Minn., in 1855; was a representative in Congress, 1859–69, and U.S. senator, 1871–81; was a member of the cabinet of President Garfield, in 1881, as secretary of the treasury but retired on the accession of President Arthur; was again U.S. senator, 1881–83. On the inauguration of President Harrison, in 1889, Windom was reappointed secretary of the treasury and held the office till his death, which was very sudden, from heart failure, just after making an address at a banquet of the New York Board of Trade. A volume titled *Memorial Tributes to the Character and Public Services of William Windom, Together with His Last Address* (161 pp.) was printed in 1891.

Lakes and Streams

Little Cottonwood River, and several streams flowing to the Cottonwood, namely, Mound, Dry, and Highwater Creeks, and Dutch Charley's Creek, receive the drainage of the northern part of this county. Mound Creek was named in allusion to the massive ridge of quartzite, mainly overspread with the glacial drift, whence it derives its highest springs; Dry Creek, because it becomes very small, or is wholly dried up, in severe droughts; Highwater Creek, as before noted, for its sudden rise after heavy rains; and Dutch Charley's Creek, for the earliest settler of Cottonwood County, Charles Zierke, whom the government surveyors found living beside that creek when they first came. Several lakes have been sufficiently noticed in the foregoing list of townships, including Mountain Lake, Bingham Lake, and others in Lakeside.

The former Glen and Summit Lakes, about two miles east of Windom, are now dry.

Bartsch, Eagle, Long, Maiden, and Rat Lakes are in Carson, the first named for Jacob Bartsch, a farmer there, and the last named for its muskrats.

Swan, Lenhart's, and Wilson's Lakes in Dale have been drained. The latter two, named respectively for John F. Lenhart and Samuel Wilson, settlers adjoining them, and a third, named Harder's Lake, were formerly called "the Three lakes." Arnold's Lake, close north of these, was named for a settler who came from Owatonna.

Lake Augusta was named in honor of the wife of a pioneer homesteader adjoining it. The outlet, Harvey Creek, flowing south to the Des Moines, commemorates Harvey Carey, like the lake to be later mentioned.

Hurricane Lake, now drained, had reference to a tornado that prostrated trees on its shore.

Bean Lake was named for an early settler, Joseph F. Bean, who had remarkable talent of memorizing what he read.

Double Lakes, a mile south of the last, are separated only by space for a road.

Berry and Carey Lakes were named for settlers near them, the latter for the brothers Harvey, John, and Ralph Carey.

Long Lake, a half mile west of Carey Lake, was formerly called the Twin Lakes.

Oaks Lake may have been so called by the early surveyors to preserve the name "Lake of the Oaks," which Lieut. James Allen in 1844 applied to Lake Shetek, 16 miles distant up the Des Moines River.

The two String Lakes, in the southwest part of the Great Bend Township, are named for their lying in a single winding stringlike course, scarcely separated.

Clear Lake, crossed by the south line of Southbrook, like another Clear Lake before mentioned in Lakeside, refers to the clearness of its deep water, not covered by grass and water plants as many shallow lakes.

Talcott Lake, through which the Des Moines River flows in Southbrook, is one of the names placed by Nicollet on his map, published in 1843, to commemorate friends and prominent men of science. His generous use of such names in the upper Mississippi region has been noticed in the chapter of Cass County. On and near the upper Des Moines River, he has Lakes Talcott and Graham, of which the latter is preserved as the name of two lakes and a township in Nobles County. These names are in honor of Andrew Talcott and James D. Graham, who, with James Renwick, were commissioners in 1840–43 to survey the disputed northeastern boundary of the United States. Andrew Talcott was born in Glastonbury, Conn., April 20, 1797, and died in Richmond, Va., April 22, 1883. He was graduated at the U.S. Military Academy, West Point, 1818; was engineer on many government works; was astronomer in surveys of the boundary between Ohio and Michigan, 1828–35; was chief engineer of railway work in Mexico during the Civil War.

The upper Des Moines River and adjoining region explored in 1844 by Lieut. James Allen and a company of dragoons, of which he presented a report and journal, published by Congress in 1846. Morainic drift hills along the southwest side of the Des Moines, two to five miles northwest of Windom, were noted by Allen as "high bluffs, . . . 150 or 200 feet above the general level of the country." These are named Blue Mounds in the description and map of this county by the Minnesota Geological Survey (vol. 1, 1884, ch. 16).

Crow Wing County

This county, established May 23, 1857, organized March 3, 1870, was named for the Crow Wing River, translated from the Ojibwe name, spelled Kagiwigwan on Joseph N. Nicollet's map, and Gagagiwigwuni by Rev. Joseph A. Gilfillan, who would preferably translate it, following Henry R. Schoolcraft, as "Raven Feather river."

Zebulon Pike in 1805 and Schoolcraft in 1820 and 1832 used the French name of this river, de Corbeau, meaning "of the Raven," but its more complete name in French was rivière à l'Aile de Corbeau, river of the Wing of the Raven, as translated by the voyageurs and traders from the Ojibwe name. In the *Summary Narrative of an Exploratory Expedition to the Sources of the Mississippi River in 1820*, published in 1855, Schoolcraft referred to the somewhat erroneous English translation, Crow Wing River, as follows: "The Indian name of this river is Kagiwegwon, or Raven's-wing or Quill, which is accurately translated by the term Aile de Corbeau, but it is improperly called Crow-wing. The Chippewa term for crow is andaig, and the French, corneille,—terms which are appropriately applied to another stream, nearer St. Anthony's Falls."

Mrs. E. Steele Peake, widow of an early missionary in 1856–61 to the Ojibwe at the mission stations of Gull Lake and Crow Wing, wrote in a letter of her reminiscences in the *Brainerd Dispatch*, September 22, 1911, concerning the aboriginal name of Crow Wing River: "Where the river joins the Mississippi was an island in the shape of a crow's wing, which gave the name to the river and the town."

The North American crow, common or frequent throughout the United States, has been confounded in this name with "his regal cousin, the raven," a larger bird, not addicted like the crow to uprooting and eating newly planted corn. Our American variety of the raven inhabits the country "from Arctic regions to Guatemala, but local and not common east of the Mississippi river." Dr. P. L. Hatch, in *Notes on the Birds of Minnesota*, 1892, wrote of ravens, "they are rarely seen in the vicinity of Minneapolis and St. Paul, but from Big Stone Lake to the British Possessions they seem to become increasingly common." Probably because the early English-speaking travelers and employees in the fur trade came from the eastern states, where the raven is practically unknown, they anglicized this name as Crow Wing, used only once by Schoolcraft in his *Narrative* of 1832, and criticized by him in 1855, as before cited.

After the adoption of the English name of the river, and 20 years or more before the county was outlined and named, the important Crow Wing trading post was established on the east side of the Mississippi opposite to the mouth of the Crow Wing River north of its island and was surrounded by a village of the Ojibwe and white men.

The earliest record of a trader near this site is in the list of licenses granted in 1826 by Lawrence Taliaferro, as Indian agent, one of these being for "Benjamin F. Baker, Crow Island, Upper

Mississippi," in the service of the American Fur Company (*Minnesota in Three Centuries*, 1908, vol. 2, p. 54). Among the traders licensed in 1833–34, none is mentioned for that post, which seems to have been abandoned.

There was again a station of the fur traders at Crow Wing, facing the northern mouth of the Crow Wing River, "about the year 1837," and it became a few years later "the center of Indian trading for all the upper country, the general supply store being located at this place. . . . In 1866, the settlement and village contained seven families of whites, and about twenty-three of half-breeds and Chippewas, with a large transient population. . . . The entire population was, from reliable estimates, about six hundred. Crow Wing, as a business point, has passed away, most of the buildings having been removed to Brainerd, and the remaining ones destroyed" (*History of the Upper Mississippi Valley*, 1881, pp. 637–38).

The village and post became the nucleus of the Crow Wing State Park, established in 1959. The whole park encompasses the intersection of the Mississippi and Crow Wing Rivers and includes parts of Morrison and Cass County, as well as Crow Wing County. A section of the trail connecting St. Paul with the Red River valley is preserved, and the house of trader Clement Beaulieu was moved back to its original site. The entire park was added to the National Register of Historic Places in 1970.

By an act of the legislature, February 18, 1887, which was ratified by the vote of the people of the county at the next general election, the part of Crow Wing County west of the Mississippi River, previously belonging to Cass County, was annexed to this county, somewhat more than doubling its former area.

Information for this county was gathered from History of the Upper Mississippi Valley *(1881, pp. 637–59); from Anton Mahlum, city clerk of Brainerd, Samuel R. Adair, county treasurer, and William H. Andrews, during my visit in Brainerd, May 1916; and by correspondence from John F. Smart, former county auditor, now of Fairhope, Ala.*

ALLEN TOWNSHIP was named for its first settler, a pioneer from the eastern states.

BALSAM see **LOERCH**.

BARROWS the mining village in Crow Wing Township, sections 9 and 16, and the Barrows Mine, five miles southwest from Brainerd, are named for Walter A. Barrows, Jr., of Brainerd, a miner who helped promote the Barrow Mine. The village was platted by the Iron Range Townsite Company and registered on April 4, 1911. It had a station of the Northern Pacific Railroad in section 16, and a post office, 1911–18, and 1921–24.

BAXTER TOWNSHIP commemorates the late Luther Loren Baxter of Fergus Falls, who during many years was an attorney for the Northern Pa-

cific company. He was born in Cornwall, Vt., in 1832; was admitted to practice law, 1854, and soon afterward settled in Minnesota; enlisted in the Fourth Minnesota Regiment, served at first as captain and was promoted to the rank of colonel; was a state senator in 1865–68 and 1870–76, and a representative in the legislature in 1869 and 1877–82; was judge in the Seventh judicial district, 1885–1911. He died at his home in Fergus Falls, May 22, 1915. The city of Baxter, section 12, incorporated as a village on May 25, 1939; it had a station of the Northern Pacific Railroad.

BAY LAKE TOWNSHIP received its name from its large lake, which was so named for its irregular outline, with many bays, projecting points, and islands. Its Ojibwe name, like that of another lake of similar form in Aitkin County, was Sisabagama (accented on the third syllable), meaning, according to Gilfillan, "Every-which-way lake, or the lake which has arms running in all directions." A post office was in section 4, 1884–85 and 1892–1904.

BORUZAK a townsite in Smiley Township, section 13, platted on August 14, 1909, by Leon and

Martha Boruzak of Chicago on a lake of the same name. The site had a silk goods manufacturer; the site was not developed.

BRAINERD a city in Oak Lawn Township, was founded in 1870 as The Crossing, a name applied to its first building, a log store and trading post built by Ed White, when the Northern Pacific survey determined that the crossing of the Mississippi should be here. The post office was established in 1870, and by early 1873 there were 21 stores, 18 hotels, boardinghouses, and lodging houses, 15 saloons, 5 churches, and a station of the Northern Pacific Railroad. It was organized as a city March 6, 1873, but an act of the legislature, January 11, 1876, substituted a township government. It again became a city on November 19, 1881. "The name first suggested for this place was 'Ogemaqua,' in honor of Emma Beaulieu, a woman of rare personal beauty, to whom the Indians gave the name mentioned, meaning Queen, or Chief Woman. The present name was chosen in honor of the wife of J. Gregory Smith, first president of the Northern Pacific Railroad Company, Mrs. Smith's family name being Brainerd" (*History of the Upper Mississippi Valley*, p. 640).

Mrs. Ann Eliza (Brainerd) Smith was a daughter of Hon. Lawrence Brainerd of St. Albans, Vt. Her husband, John Gregory Smith (1818–91), also a resident of St. Albans, honored by the name of Gregory Park or Square in Brainerd and by Gregory station and village in Morrison County, was governor of Vermont, 1863–65; was president of the Northern Pacific, 1866–72; and later was president of the Vermont Central Railroad until his death. Mrs. Smith was author of novels, books of travel, and other works. Her father, Lawrence Brainerd (1794–1870), was a director of the St. Albans Steamboat Company, a builder and officer of railroads in northern Vermont, a noted abolitionist, and was a U.S. senator, 1854–55.

Portraits of Mrs. Smith, for whom Brainerd was named, and her father, with extended biographic notices, are in *The Genealogy of the Brainerd-Brainard Family in America* (3 vols., 1908). The biographic sketch of her is in vol. 2, pp. 162–63, from which the following is quoted: "She was president of the board of managers for the Vermont woman's exhibit at the Centennial Exposition of 1876, at Philadelphia, and was frequently chosen in similar capacities as a representative Vermont woman. Her patriotic feeling was shown in the Civil War, at the rebel raid on St. Albans and the plunder of the banks, Oct. 19, 1864, and a commission as Lieutenant-Colonel was issued to her for gallantry and efficient service on that occasion by Adjutant-General P. T. Washburn." She was born in St. Albans, Vt., October 7, 1819, and died at her home there, January 6, 1905.

The Northern Pacific Railroad ran its first train to Brainerd, a special train, on March 11, 1871, and its regular passenger service began the next September. The first passenger train from the Twin Cities, by way of Sauk Rapids, came November 1, 1877. Crow Wing, the former trading post, was soon superseded by Brainerd, which the Ojibwe named "Oski-odena, New Town." It is known as the capital of Paul Bunyan's Playground, having many resorts and 500 lakes.

BREEZY POINT a city in Pelican Township, also known as Pelican Lakes, incorporated in 1939. It had a railroad station and postal services, 1928–65, sometimes as rural routes. The city is known for its many resorts.

BURNETTS a locality in Long Lake Township, section 27, circa 1874.

CALAIS a townsite in Long Lake Township, section 27, at the south end of Long Lake, platted for Elijah Dunphy in 1858 but not developed.

CEDAR LAKE JUNCTION a station of the Northern Pacific Railroad in Rabbit Lake Township, section 36.

CENTER TOWNSHIP formerly the unnamed T. 153N, R. 37W.

COOK'S CORNER a locality in Nokay Lake Township, about 1930.

CROSBY a city in Irondale and Deerwood Townships, was named in honor of George H. Crosby of Duluth, manager of iron mines. It was platted for George and Charlotte V. Crosby and registered on October 5, 1909, was incorporated on July 6, 1910, and separated from the township on May 19, 1911. The post office began in 1910. The village had a station of the Northern Pacific Railroad and Minneapolis, St. Paul and Sault Ste. Marie Railroad (Soo Line).

CROSSLAKE a city in Watertown Township, section 21, incorporated on August 12, 1959, located on the east shore of Cross Lake. It has had a post office since 1894; consolidated with North Cross Lake in 1972.

CROW WING TOWNSHIP was named for the site of the early Indian village and trading post of this name. The first development in the village, in section 20, was mainly a stopping-off place on route from St. Anthony to Red River, with traders' stores and warehouses, saloons, and blacksmith shops. It was incorporated as a village on May 23, 1857, and abandoned when the Northern Pacific Railroad tracks were built across the Mississippi River at Brainerd. It had a post office, 1856–76, first established in Benton County and reestablished, 1879–1930, during a period of redevelopment; and a station of the Northern Pacific and Soo Line railroads.

CRYSTAL SPRINGS a village in Dean Lake Township, sections 2 and 3.

CUYUNA a mining village in Rabbit Lake Township, and the iron ore range on which it is situated were named by and for Cuyler Adams of Deerwood, prospector, discoverer, and mine owner of this range, and for his dog, Una, who accompanied him in many lone prospecting trips, so that he affirmed that the discovery of workable ore deposits here should be credited jointly to himself and the valuable aid of Una. The village was incorporated on July 7, 1910, and separated from the township on March 3, 1911; the post office operated 1908–54; it had a station of the Soo Line. This iron range is more fully noticed at the end of this chapter.

DAGGETT BROOK TOWNSHIP was named for the brook flowing through it meanderingly to the Nokasippi River, which brook commemorates Benjamin F. Daggett, an early lumberman who cut much pine timber there. He was born in Wiscasset, Maine, September 31, 1821, and died in Sauk Rapids, Minn., August 31, 1901. He came to Minnesota in 1855, settling at Elk River, and engaged in lumbering, afterward residing at Little Falls and Sauk Rapids. (Another Daggett Brook, likewise named for this lumberman, is in the north part of this county, outflowing from Crooked Lake, through Mitchell, Eagle, Daggett, and Pine Lakes, to Cross Lake.) The township had a rural post office, 1887–90.

DAVENPORT TOWNSHIP has the name given by Nicollet to Cross Lake on the Pine River in honor of Col. William Davenport of the U.S. Army. He was a captain in the War of 1812; was promoted to the rank of lieutenant colonel, 1832, and colonel,

1842; was brevetted colonel in 1838 for meritorious service in Florida; resigned from the army, 1850; died April 12, 1858. He was commandant of Fort Snelling in the summer of 1836 and there became acquainted with Nicollet.

DEAN LAKE TOWNSHIP with its Dean Lake and Brook and the Upper Dean Lake, bears the name of a pioneer lumberman, Joseph Dean of Minneapolis, who cut its pine timber.

DEERWOOD a city of Deerwood Township, platted on February 1, 1892, and incorporated as a village on October 8, 1909. It was at first called Withington, "after the maiden name of the wife of one of the railway officials," was renamed for the plentiful deer in its woods, the name being thence given to the township. This change was made to avoid confusion with Worthington, Nobles County. Another version of the name's origin is that it was first known as Withington for J. S. Withington, a member of the first board of directors of the Northern Pacific Railroad. The village had a station of the Northern Pacific, and the post office was established in 1882.

DYKEMAN a post office, 1904–25, located in Garrison Township, section 18, named for David Dykeman, a pioneer settler.

EDON a village in Deerwood Township.

EMILY TOWNSHIP was named from Emily Lake, one of its group of four lakes having feminine names, Anna, Emily, Mary, and Ruth, but whether they were of one family, or what was the surname of any of them, has not been ascertained. Probably they were the daughters or wives of early lumbermen. The city of Emily, section 34, on the west shore of Lake Emily, was platted on November 22, 1905, by John and Amelia Lambert and incorporated on March 7, 1957; its post office began in 1900.

ESDON a post office, 1898–1909, in Bay Lake Township, section 31; a family name of postmaster John Walker.

FAIRFIELD TOWNSHIP has a euphonious name, perhaps derived from the township and large manufacturing village of this name in Maine. It is the name of counties, villages, and cities in many states.

FIFTY LAKES a city of Allen Township, section 26, incorporated May 10, 1949, with a post office since 1926.

FLAK a post office, 1894–1926, in Maple Grove

Township, section 3, named for birthplace in Norway of its first postmaster, Peter Alberts.

FORT GAINES see FORT RIPLEY.

FORT RIPLEY a city in Fort Ripley Township, incorporated March 19, 1927, near the east bank of the Mississippi, bears the name of the fort formerly on the opposite bank of this river, from 1849 to 1878, named in honor of Gen. Eleazar W. Ripley, more fully noticed in the chapter for Morrison County. Its post office was called Fort Gaines, 1849–51, when established in Todd County, with postmaster John H. McKinney; the name was changed in 1851, with Charles H. Oakes, postmaster.

FORT RIPLEY TOWNSHIP formerly the unnamed T. 137N, R. 32W.

FREDERICK a proposed townsite in Wolford Township, section 34, surveyed by owners Fred E. Wheaton of Minneapolis and W. J. Pilkey of St. Paul about 1917, which was not accepted by the county commissioners.

GABITAWIGAMA an early Lutheran mission in Smiley Township, near Gull Lake, about 1857.

GAIL LAKE TOWNSHIP formerly the unnamed T. 138N, R. 29W.

GARRISON TOWNSHIP was named in honor of Oscar E. Garrison, a land surveyor and civil engineer, who was born at Fort Ann, N.Y., July 21, 1825, and died on his farm in this township, April 2, 1886. He came to Minnesota in 1850, explored Lake Minnetonka and platted the village of Wayzata in 1854, removed to St. Cloud in 1860, served in the Northern Rangers against the Dakota, 1862, was agent of the U.S. Census, Department of Forestry, 1880, examining the region of the Upper Mississippi, on which his observations were published (49 pp.) in the Ninth Annual Report of the Minnesota Geological Survey. He took his homestead claim here in 1882. The city and resort community, sections 13 and 14, with over 200 lakes within a 20-mile radius, was settled in 1880 with Garrison platting the townsite first known as Rowe; it was incorporated on May 3, 1937. The post office opened in 1884; Mary J. Garrison, wife of Oscar, became postmaster and the name was changed. Section 13 of the township was platted as Midland in the early 1900s and is part of the present Garrison. A major sawmill was built there in 1895.

GORSTVILLE a settlement around John Gorst's mill in St. Mathias Township, section 33. Gorst was born in New Brunswick in 1838, came to Minnesota in 1855, served with Maine during the Civil War, returning to the area in October 1880, where he built the mill for manufacturing lumber.

GREATER CROSS LAKE area encompasses the recreational communities of Crosslake, Manhattan Beach, and North Cross Lake, with restaurants, night clubs, shops and stores, resorts, motels, and hotels.

HELLENSBURG a post office, 1900–8, located in Watertown Township, section 32, with George Frost, postmaster, and named for his daughter, Hellen.

HOMECROFT a village in Irondale (Klondike) Township, section 21, about 1913.

HUBERT see LAKE HUBERT.

IDEAL TOWNSHIP a fancy name, was originally called White Fish for the large lake of that name comprised almost wholly in this township.

IRON HUB a post office, 1910–14, located in Rabbit Lake Township, section 26; it had a station of the Soo Line.

IRON MOUNTAIN a mining village in Wolford Township, section 33.

IRONDALE TOWNSHIP formerly named Klondike Township, the name being changed February 5, 1918. Both names refer to the bed of iron ore discovered by Cuyler Adams in 1895 as the result of magnetic surveys, several of the best mining locations being in this township. A post office was located in the township, 1897–1907, section 26, with a station of the Northern Pacific Railroad.

IRONTON a city in Irondale (Klondike) Township, sections 9–11, platted on September 6, 1910, by Agnes Lamb and Carrie and John Hill, incorporated on June 5, 1911, and separated from the township on March 22, 1912. The post office was established in 1910; it had a Northern Pacific Railroad station.

JENKINS railway village and township were named for George W. Jenkins, a lumberman, who platted this village. The city of Jenkins was incorporated in 1969; the post office was established in 1895; it had a station of the Northern Pacific Railroad.

JESSIE a post office authorized on August 5, 1908, with Effie McKiddy to be postmaster, that may have operated for a few months; location not found.

JONESVILLE a village in Brainerd Township, section 11, which was a flag stop of the Northern Pacific Railroad.

JULESBURG a village in Irondale (Klondike) Township, section 14, which was platted for Jules Jamieson of Brainerd and registered on May 7, 1912; it a station of the Cuyuna Iron Range Railroad.

KATRINE a post office, 1898–1909, of Bay Lake Township, section 21, with Katie E. Young, first postmaster, who named it for Loch Katrine in Scotland.

KLONDIKE TOWNSHIP was named from the Klondike placer-gold region in the Yukon district, Canada, discovered in 1896, which took its name from the Klondike River (Indian, "Throndiuk, river full of fish"). This name was adopted in allusion to the large and valuable deposits of iron ore in the Cuyuna Iron Range. The name changed to Irondale, February 5, 1918.

LAKE a post office, 1901–6; location not found.

LAKE EDWARD TOWNSHIP bears the name of the largest one of its numerous lakes, given at the time of the government survey, probably in honor of a member of the surveying party.

LAKE HUBERT a railway village on the northeast end of the lake of this name, established in 1897 as Hubert, changing to the present name in 1928.

LAKE WOOD PARK a village in Lake Edward Township, section 7, and Smiley Township, section 12, about 1913.

LEAKS a station of the Minnesota and International Railway in Lake Edward Township, section 23, about three miles north of Brainerd, was named for John Leaks, a locomotive engineer of that railway; also known as Leaks Station and Leaks Lake.

LENOX a post office, 1889–90, located in Fort Ripley Township, section 2, with a station of the Northern Pacific Railroad.

LINDEN PARK a village in Bay Lake Township, section 20, circa 1913.

LITTLE PINE TOWNSHIP received its name for its lake and river of this name, tributary to the Pine River.

LITTLEPINE a post office of Little Pine Township, 1906–22, section 20.

LOERCH a post office, 1904–7, of Oak Lawn Township, section 1, named for John C. Loerch, postmaster and landowner; it was officially called Balsam during the period August to October 1904.

LONG LAKE TOWNSHIP received its name from its Long Lake, through which the Nokay River flows. Our name of this lake is a direct translation of its Ojibwe name, "Gaginogumag sagaiigun."

MANGANESE a mining village in Wolford Township, sections 23 and 28, has reference to its manganiferous iron ores, which have from 1 to 25 percent of manganese. These mines are on the northern border of this Cuyuna district. It was incorporated on November 10, 1913, but later unincorporated; it had a post office, 1912–24, and a station of the Soo Line.

MANHATTAN BEACH a city located north of Crosslake on Ox Lake in Watertown Township, incorporated on June 24, 1941; its post office began in 1939.

MAPLE GROVE TOWNSHIP has groves of sugar maple, interspersed with the other timber of its general forest.

MENAKEN a village about 1884; no location found.

MERRIFIELD a railway village seven miles north of Brainerd, bears the name W. D. Merrifield, an early settler in section 26. The village was platted on May 9, 1912, by Martha and Grant Bronson. A post office has existed since 1899, located in Lake Edward Township, section 35.

MIDLAND see GARRISON.

MISSION TOWNSHIP and its two Mission Lakes were named for an early missionary station there for the Ojibwe. A rural post office was located in section 25, 1901–42.

MOFFATT a post office, 1894–1907, of Fort Ripley Township, section 1, with Jacob C. Moffatt, postmaster.

NEUTRAL a post office, 1899–1911, in Garrison Township, section 4, so named because it was halfway between the east and west neighborhoods of the township.

NISSWA a city in Smiley Township, section 11, incorporated on December 4, 1946, bears an Ojibwe name, probably related to *nassawaii*, meaning "in the middle." The townsite was platted for Leon E. Lum, an attorney in Brainerd, and first known as Smiley with a post office of that name, 1898–1908. Thirteen bodies of water are within its corporate boundaries, the many small shops and various entertainment centers making it an attractive tourist area.

NOKAY LAKE TOWNSHIP has the lake of this name on the upper course and near the head of the Nokasippi or Nokay River, as it is spelled on Nicollet's map. This was the name of an Ojibwe leader and noted hunter, whom the *Handbook of American Indians* (pt. 2, 1910) mentions as follows: "A chief of the western Chippewa in the latter half of the 18th century, who attained some celebrity as a leader and hunter. The chief incident of his life relates to the war between the Mdewakanton [Dakota] and the Chippewa for possession of the banks of the upper Mississippi. In 1769, the year following the battle of Crow Wing, Minn., where the Chippewa, though maintaining their ground, were hampered by inferior numbers, they determined to renew the attack on the Mdewakanton with a larger force. This war party, under the leadership of Noka, referred to as 'Old Noka' evidently on account of his advanced age, attacked Shakopee's village on Minnesota River, the result being a drawn battle, the Chippewa retiring to their own territory without inflicting material damage on their enemy." William W. Warren, the historian of the Ojibwe, wrote of Nokay's skill in hunting (MHS Collections 5: 266). A post office was located in the township, 1857–58 and 1903–5.

NORTH CROSS LAKE a city in Watertown Township, incorporated as a city on December 9, 1964, and consolidated with Cross Lake on September 12, 1972.

OAK LAWN TOWNSHIP was named for its "oak openings," tracts occupied by scattered oak trees with small grassed spaces, somewhat like a prairie, interrupting the general woodland.

OGEMAQUE SEE BRAINERD.

OREFIELD a village in Rabbit Lake Township, section 19, about 1913.

ORELAND a mining village of Deerwood Township, sections 19 and 30, platted on January 20, 1912, by Oscar and Jennie Carlson; it had a post office, 1913–20, and a station of the Northern Pacific Railroad.

OSSIPEE a post office, 1897–1919, located in Center Township, section 6, named by Jacob V. Brower, who did a great deal of excavation in that area, for the river and lake of that name in New Hampshire.

OUTING a village in Emily Township, section 4,

on the southeastern shore of Crooked Lake, was platted on November 14, 1908, and registered on January 2, 1909, by William H. Andrews as a place for "outings" or short visits of city people and sportsmen in summer. See also CASS County.

PARKER STATION a station of the Minnesota and International Railway in T. 134N, R. 28W, section 2, named for F. S. Parker of Parkersville.

PELICAN LAKES a city in Pelican Township, section 8, incorporated as a city, June 30, 1939.

PELICAN TOWNSHIP was named for its large Pelican Lake, which was first mapped by the U.S. government surveys, about the year 1860. The remarkably fine group of large lakes in this county between Gull and White Fish Lakes was represented on earlier maps only by several quite small lakes, one of which is named Lake Taliaferro on Nicollet's map in honor of the Indian agent at Mendota. As Pelican Lake is the largest in this group, it may be thought to be the one so designated. It is translated from the Ojibwe name, given by Gilfillan as "Shede sagaiigun, Pelican lake." Henry W. Longfellow's *Song of Hiawatha* spells this Ojibwe word *Shada*, which has the long *a* sound in both syllables. The pelican, our largest bird species of Minnesota, was formerly common or frequent here, as attested by its name given to rivers, lakes, and islands.

PEQUOT a railway village in Sibley Township, bears the name of a former tribe of Algonquian Indians in eastern Connecticut. This village is the sole instance of its use as a geographic name.

PEQUOT LAKES a city in Sibley Township, sections 10 and 15, platted on March 10, 1900, by Walter and Flora Brown. The city had been called Sibley for an early logger and was renamed by a postal official for the first Indian-sounding name he thought of, which is the name of a former tribe of Algonquian Indians in eastern Connecticut. The post office has been operating since 1896; it had a Northern Pacific Railroad station.

PERRY LAKE TOWNSHIP and its lake of this name probably commemorate an early lumberman.

PERSHING a village platted by the Northern Minnesota Ore Co., on October 5, 1918; location not found.

PINE CENTER a village in Roosevelt Township, section 7.

PINE GROVE a post office, 1885; location not found.

PLATE LAKE TOWNSHIP received its name from

the lake at its southeast corner, the central and largest one of a group of several lakes forming the headwaters of Platte River. This is a French word, meaning "flat." The translation of the Ojibwe name of this lake, according to Gilfillan, is "Hump-as-made-by-a-man-lying-on-his-hands-and-knees."

RABBIT a post office authorized on May 9, 1908, with Rainerd Olson to be postmaster, but not established; location not found.

RABBIT LAKE TOWNSHIP similarly took the name of its Rabbit Lake, the head of Rabbit River, a short tributary of the Mississippi. The Ojibwe name of the lake, given by Gilfillan, is "Wabozo-wakaiiguni sagaiigun, Rabbit's-House lake."

RIVERTON is a city of the Cuyuna Iron Range in Irondale (Klondike) Township, sections 17 to 20, beside Little Rabbit Lake, through which Rabbit River flows just before joining the Mississippi. It was incorporated on January 5, 1912. It had a post office, 1913–65, and a station of the Northern Pacific Railroad in section 18.

ROCK a station of the Soo Line in T. 47N, R. 28W.

ROHRER a post office authorized on April 20, 1908, for Mission Township, with Melvin Bailey, who lived in section 30, to be postmaster, but not established.

ROOSEVELT TOWNSHIP was named in honor of Theodore Roosevelt, then president of the United States.

ROSS LAKE TOWNSHIP and its lake of this name are in honor of a pioneer lumberman there.

ROWE see GARRISON.

ST. COLUMBA MISSION a mission established by James Lloyd Breck on the east shore of Gull Lake, about 11 miles north of Fort Ripley.

ST. MATHIAS TOWNSHIP was named from its Catholic church, dedicated to Christ's disciple who was chosen by lot to be one of the 12 apostles, in the place of Judas. A rural post office was located in section 12, 1888–1908.

SCHWITZ a post office, 1912–13, in Roosevelt Township, section 18.

SEWELL a post office, 1903–5, with Justus T. Sewell, postmaster, located in Roosevelt Township, section 12.

SHEPHARD a post office, 1898–1905, in Daggett Brook Township, section 15.

SIBLEY LANDING a village near Pequot Lake named for an early logger; no location found.

SIBLEY TOWNSHIP was named from its Lake Sibley, a name given by Nicollet on his map, published in 1843, in honor of Henry Hastings Sibley, for whom also Sibley County was named.

SMILEY see NISSWA.

SMILEY TOWNSHIP having a common English or American surname, remains of undetermined derivation.

SWANBURG a village in Timothy Township, section 25, north of Big Trout Lake. Because of rumors of planned railroad construction in the area, a Swede from Pine River, Cass County, named Swan P. Hanson acquired land in the 1900s for the purpose of creating a community. Although the station of the Northern Pacific Railroad was built in Allen Township, section 30, a group of Norwegians settled at the site. Hanson never lived in the community, remaining in Pine River; however, the townsite was named for him, adding *burg* to his first name. The village had a post office, 1904–11 and 1914–19.

TIMOTHY TOWNSHIP at first called Clover, received the popular name of a European species of grass, much cultivated in Europe and America for hay, more commonly called "herd's grass" in New England. The seed of this grass was carried from New England to Maryland about the year 1720 by Timothy Hanson, whence came its prevalent American name. It grows very luxuriantly under cultivation in Minnesota and frequently is adventive by roadsides and about logging camps.

TROMMALD a mining city in Wolford Township, named for A. G. Trommald, county registrar of deeds, 1904–30. It was incorporated on August 9, 1917. The community had a post office, 1917–67, and a station of the Northern Pacific Railroad.

WATERTOWN has many lakes and the Pine River. In the central part of the west half of this township, the river flows into the west side of Cross Lake and out from its east side, whence the lake received this name. It is translated from the Ojibwe name, meaning the same as Lake Bemidji, "the lake which the river flows directly across." This lake was named Lake Davenport on Nicollet's map in honor of Col. William Davenport, of the U.S. Army, for whom also a township in this county is named.

WEST CROW WING TOWNSHIP formerly the unnamed T. 134N, R. 28–29W.

WOLFORD TOWNSHIP comprising the mining villages of Manganese and Iron Mountain, at the north edge of the Cuyuna Range, was named in honor of Robert Wolford, a pioneer farmer there. The village of Wolford, in section 22, was platted on March 21, 1913, by Richard and Rebecca Wolford. It had a post office, 1913–19, with Wilbert F. Wolford, postmaster.

WOODROW a village located in Oak Lawn Township, sections 12 and 13, was platted on March 6, 1914, by Paul and Marguerite Hale, and named for President Woodrow Wilson. It had a post office, 1915–31, and a Northern Pacific Railroad station.

WOODS a rural post office, 1907–13, located in Irondale (Klondike) Township, section 21.

WORKWATER a post office authorized on January 5, 1894, with George O. Sanborn to be postmaster, but not established; location not found.

Lakes and Streams

The preceding pages have noticed a number of the lakes and streams, including several given by Nicollet's map. Other names thus applied by Nicollet are Lake Plympton, now called Rush Lake, crossed by the Pine River between White Fish and Cross Lakes, in honor of Capt. Joseph Plympton (1787–1860), who was commandant of Fort Snelling in the years 1837–41; Lake Gratiot, now Upper Hay Lake, a mile east of Jenkins village, named in honor of Gen. Charles Gratiot (1788–1855), in charge of the U.S. engineer bureau and inspector of West Point; Manido River, the Ojibwe name for Spirit River, outflowing from Lake Gratiot to White Fish Lake; Lake Stewart, in Timothy Township, for the gallant U.S. naval officer Charles Stewart (1778–1869), famous for his services in the War of 1812; and Lakes Enke and Chanche, now respectively Lakes Washburn and Roosevelt, the former wholly and the latter partly in Cass County, tributary by the northern Daggett Brook to Cross Lake.

White Fish Lake is called Kadikomeg Lake on Nicollet's map, an attempt to record the aboriginal name, which Gilfillan noted more fully, "Ga-atikumegokag, the place of white fish." Another lake of this name, much smaller, is crossed by the east line of Roosevelt, lying partly in Mille Lacs County. The next lake across which Pine River passes below White Fish, named Lake Plympton by Nicollet, now known as Rush Lake, is called by the Ojibwe "Shingwakosagibid sagaiigun, the lake of the pine sticking up out of the water." Their name of the Pine River, which we retain in translation, is "Shingwako zibi," and Serpent Lake is translated from "Newe sagaiigun, Blow-Snake lake." Pike or Borden Lake, named for David S. Borden, a settler, in sections 10, 11, and 14, Garrison, is called "Wijiwi sagaiigun, the lake full of muskrat houses or beavers," as noted by Gilfillan; and the aboriginal name for Round Lake, through which the Nokay River flows in sections 11 and 14, St. Mathias, is Nokay Lake.

The larger Round Lake, in Smiley Township, is translated from "Ga-wawiiegumag," and the Ojibwe name of Lake Hubert, recorded by Gilfillan, is "Ga-manominiganjikag sagaiigun, Wild Rice lake." Gull Lake, a translation from the Ojibwe, has been more fully noticed in the chapter on Cass County.

In this region of plentiful game, finny, furred, and feathered, Lake Hubert, and the adjoining village of this name, may well have been so designated in honor of St. Hubert, the patron saint of huntsmen.

An enumeration of other lakes and streams in this county, not previously noticed, is as follows, taking first the part southeast of the Mississippi, in the order of townships from south to north, and of ranges from east to west, and next, in the same order, taking the northwest part of the county. Personal names, applied to many of these lakes, are nearly all commemorative of early settlers.

Camp or Crooked Lake, Erskine, Mud, Bass, Rock, and Bull Dog Lakes in Roosevelt Township.

Sebie, Mud, and Crow Wing (or Thunder) Lakes in Fort Ripley Township.

Clearwater, Miller, Barber, and Holt Lakes in Garrison.

Chrysler Lake in Maple Grove Township.

Russell Lake in Long Lake Township, named for T. P. Russell, a settler there at its north side.

Buffalo Creek in Crow Wing Township, named for buffalo frequenting its oak openings and small tracts of prairie.

A second and larger Clearwater Lake, Crooked, Hanks, Portage, Rice, and Birch Lakes, and a small Long Lake in section 1, Bay Lake Township.

Eagle, Pointon, Perch, and Grave Lakes in Nokay Lake Township.

Sand and Whitely Creeks, and Rice or White-ly Lake in Oak Lawn Township.

Agate and Black Lakes, Cedar Creek and Lake, Shine or Shirt Lake, and Hamlet, Portage, Rice, and Reno Lakes in Deerwood. The last was named in honor of Gen. Jesse Lee Reno, who served in the Mexican and Civil Wars, and was killed in the battle of South Mountain, Md., September 14, 1862.

Manomin, Portage, Blackhoof, Little Rabbit, Rice, Crocker, and Wolf Lakes in Irondale (Klondike).

Black Bear Lake in Wolford.

Little Sand or Perch Lake, White Sand, Red Sand, and Whipple Lakes in Baxter, the first township northwest of the Mississippi. The last is in honor of the eminent Bishop Henry B. Whipple, under whose direction and care were many missions for the Ojibwe and Dakota in Minnesota, including the Ojibwe mission of St. Columba at Gull Lake in the adjoining edge of Cass County.

Long Lake, Love Lake, Bass, Carp (or Mud), Gilbert, and Hartley Lakes in T. 134N, R. 28w and the east half of R. 29w.

The two Mission Lakes, named for an early Ojibwe mission near them, and Perch, Silver, Bass, Fawn, Spider, and Camel Lakes in T. 135N, R. 27w.

Markee and Twin Lakes, Garden, Rice, Clark, Hubert and Little Hubert, Gladstone, Mollie, and Crystal Lakes in Lake Edward Township.

Cullen, Fawn, Fish Trap (or Marsh), Roy, and Mud Lakes in Smiley.

Nelson Lake in Dean Lake Township, named for H. M. Nelson, the first settler having a family in that township.

Bass Lake, Fool's Lake, and Indian Jack Lake in Perry Lake Township.

Lizard, Sandbar or Horseshoe, and Bass Lakes, and the northern Mission Lake in Mission Township.

Long, Schaffer, and Upper Cullen Lakes in Pelican.

Twin Lakes in Sibley.

Island, Mud, and Rogers Lakes, Upper Dean Lake, Twin Lakes, and Stark Lake in Ross Lake Township.

Grass, Pickerel, and Trout Lakes, Dolney's Lake, Mud, Bass, and Adney Lakes in Fairfield.

Ox, Island, Hen, Rush, Daggett, Bass, Goodrich, O'Brien, Phelps, Big Bird, and Greer Lakes in Watertown, with two Pine Lakes, one in the northeast part of this township and the other in sections 32 to 34.

Big Trout, Mud, Bertha, Pig, Star, Bass, Kimball, Long, and Clear Lakes in White Fish Township.

The Upper and Lower Hay Lakes and Nelson Lake in Jenkins.

Little Pine Lake, Low's, Duck, Moulton, Bass, and Birchdale Lakes in Little Pine Township.

Papoose, Butterfield, and Dahler Lakes in Emily Township.

Mitchell, Eagle, East Fox, West Fox, and Kego Lakes in Allen, the last an Ojibwe name meaning Fish Lake.

Jale, Big Rice, and Swede Lakes in the east half of T. 138N, R. 29w, the most northwestern in this county.

The Mississippi has "an island in the mouth of Pine river, well timbered with pine, elm, and maple," as described by Schoolcraft in 1820; French Rapids, shown on Nicollet's map, about three miles north of Brainerd; Whitely Island, close below these rapids; three or four other small islands between this and the Crow Wing River; and at the mouth of that river, Crow Wing Island. Another name sometimes given to the last is McArthur's Island, as on the map accompanying the chapter for this county by the Minnesota Geological Survey, having reference to a Scottish trader named McArthur.

In the vicinity of the Buffalo Creek and the mouth of Crow Wing River, as Schoolcraft wrote in 1820, "the Buffalo Plains commence and continue downward, on both banks of the river, to the falls of St. Anthony. These plains are elevated about sixty feet above the summer level of the water, and consist of a sandy alluvion covered with rank grass and occasional clumps of the dwarf black oak."

Ahrens Hill

A remarkable series of gravel knolls and ridges, called kames and eskers, borders the Mississippi on its northwest side at Brainerd and for a distance of about three miles up the river. Its culmination and northern end is a hill that rises about 175 feet above both the river on its east side and Gilbert Lake on the west, being 100 feet higher than the mainly level sand and gravel plain of the river valley. This high and short esker was named Ahrens Hill in the *Geological Survey* (vol. 4, 1899, p. 73) for Charles Ahrens, the farmer of its southern and western slopes.

Cuyuna Iron Range

The origin of the name of this belt of iron ore deposits has been noted for the village of Cuyuna, in the preceding list, and the date of discovery of these beds of ore by Cuyler Adams, in 1895, was mentioned in the notice of Irondale Township. Mining and shipments of ore from the Cuyuna Range were begun in the years 1910 to 1912, and its production in 1915 was 1,137,043 tons. The explored extent of this iron ore district, extending from Randall in Morrison County, through Crow Wing County, and into central Aitkin County, has no prominent hills or highlands, and only very scanty outcrops of the bedrocks, which, with the ore deposits, are deeply covered by the glacial and modified drift. Shipment from the range reached its peak in 1953 at 3,714,000 tons; by 1977 production had ceased. Local efforts to find some use for the area resulted in the creation of Cuyuna Country State Recreation Area in 1993. In addition to including 15 mining pits, now filled with water, and rock piles, the area contains six lakes and several bogs.

Dakota County

This county, established October 27, 1849, was named for the Dakota people, meaning an alliance or league. Under this name are comprised a large number of allied and affiliated Indian tribes, who originally occupied large parts of Minnesota and adjoining states. The Dakota called themselves collectively by this name, but they have been frequently termed Sioux, this being a contraction from the appellation Nadouesioux, given with various spellings by Pierre E. Radisson, Father Louis Hennepin, and Robert Cavalier, sieur de la Salle , a term evidently of Algonquian origin, adopted by the early French explorers and traders.

Radisson says (*Voyages*, p. 154) that the first part of the Algonquian name for the Dakota, spelled, in the translation of his manuscript, Nadoneceronons, means an enemy. Rev. Moses N. Adams informed me that the Dakota dislike to be called Sioux and much prefer their own collective name, borne by this county, which implies friendship or even brotherly love.

For the origins and meanings of the names of townships, villages, post offices, lakes, creeks, etc., in this county, we are mainly indebted to its three published histories: Dakota County, Its Past and Present, Geographical, Statistical, and Historical, *by W. H. Mitchell, 1868 (162 pp.);* History of Dakota County, *by George E. Warner and Charles M. Foote, 1881 (551 pp.); and* History of Dakota and Goodhue Counties, *edited by Franklyn Curtiss-Wedge, 1910, two vols., the first (662 pp.) being for this county. Especial acknowledgment is due to the excellent contribution by the late Judge Francis M. Crosby of Hastings, titled "Origin of Names," in the third of these histories (pp. 131–33).*

ANTLER PARK a summer resort in Lakeville Township, section 30, with an amusement park constructed and operated by Marion W. Savage's company located on Lake Marion. It may have been named because of nearby Buck Hill, an area where Indians watched for deer. The resort had a station of the Minneapolis, Northfield and Southern Railroad in section 19.

APPLE VALLEY a city that was Lebanon Township until the village incorporated on January 1, 1969. The name was chosen by the major developer, Orrin Thompson, for Apple Valley, Calif., the Minnesota River valley, and the apple trees planted at each home in his development. The Minnesota Zoological Garden opened there in 1978.

ARGONNE a station of the Minneapolis, Northfield and Southern Railroad in Lakeville Township, section 12; also known as Argonne Farms.

ATHENS a post office, 1854–59, formerly called Pine Bend, and located in Inver Grove Township.

AUBURN a farming village of Vermillion Township, section 30, circa 1874–87.

BALACLAGUE a station of the Minneapolis, Northfield and Southern Railroad, about 1937; location not found.

BELLWOOD a settlement, 1854–60, in what was then Bellwood Township, now Marshan Township.

BIRCH LAKE a village in Inver Grove Township, section 28, on the St. Paul and Southern Electric Railroad line, about 1928–38.

BLACK DOG VILLAGE a Dakota Indian village, 1837–52, in Eagan Township, section 18; also known as Danoska; the current site of the Black Dog Power Plant.

BLACKBIRD JUNCTION a station of the Chicago, Milwaukee, St. Paul and Pacific Railroad in Ravenna Township, section 8.

BOHRER a station of the St. Paul and Southern Electric Railroad in Inver Grove Township, section 11, about 1928–38.

BREMER a station of the St. Paul and Southern Electric Railroad in Nininger Township, section 26, about 1928–38.

BROWNS a station of the St. Paul and Southern Electric Railroad in Rosemount Township, section 28, about 1928–38; also known as Browns Crossing.

BURNSVILLE a city incorporated as a village in June 1964, absorbing Burnsville Township and the northwest corner of Lebanon Township; incorporated as a city, June 18, 1969. Burnsville Township, originally named Union when established April 6, 1858, but changed before it was organized May 11, 1858, was named for its first settlers, "William Burns and family, consisting of his wife and five sons, who emigrated from Canada the same year [1853]. He settled in the northwest corner of the town, near the mouth of Credit river." The name is often found in records as Byrnesville, and the original spelling of the name of the first settlers was Byrne.

CARLISLE see PINE BEND.

CASCADE a locality of Randolph Township, section 7, about 1916–28.

CASTLE ROCK TOWNSHIP organized April 6, 1858, was named, on the suggestion of Peter Ayotte, an early settler, for a former well-known landmark, a pillar or towerlike remnant, spared by erosion and weathering, of "a sandstone rock which stands alone on a prairie in that town. This geologic formation, before its partial disintegration which left it in ruins, closely resembled a castle." Nicollet's *Report*, in 1843, gives its Dakota name, Inyan bosndata, Standing Rock, which, he adds,

on the authority of Pierre Charles Le Sueur in the year 1700, was the Dakota name also of the Cannon River. Prof. N. H. Winchell's "Final Report of the Geology of Minnesota," in vol. 2, 1888, has a good description and historical notice of Castle Rock in chapter 3 (pp. 76–79), "The Geology of Dakota County," with three pictures of it from photographs. Its height was 44 feet above the ground at its base, and 70 feet above an adjoining hollow, but the slender pillar, 19 feet high, forming its upper part, fell in about 1900. The village of Castle Rock, section 31, had a post office, first named Vermillion in 1855, changing to Castle Rock in 1858–95; it had a station of the Chicago, Milwaukee, St. Paul and Pacific Railroad.

CENTRALIA see PINE BEND.

CHRISTIANA a post office in Eureka Township, section 28, 1858–1902.

CLIFF a station of the Chicago, Milwaukee, St. Paul and Omaha Railroad in Mendota Township, section 23; its name, for the nearby cliffs, adopted in 1902, was suggested by F. L. Slaker, superintendent of the railroad; earlier it was also called East Connection.

COATES a city, which began in section 8 of Vermillion Township and was incorporated as a village on April 7, 1953, including portions of Rosemount, Vermillion, and Empire Townships; a post office was located there, 1904–20; named for G. A. Coates, an early settler.

DEER PARK a station of the Minneapolis, Northfield and Southern Railroad in Lakeville Township, section 2.

DOUGLAS TOWNSHIP established April 6, 1858, "was named for Stephen A. Douglas, the statesman." Its earliest spelling, Douglass, by the petitioners and county commissioners, though differing from that of the great politician and orator, was continued until 1911. He is also commemorated by the name of Douglas County.

EAGAN originally called Montgomery, was incorporated on October 19, 1972, absorbing Eagan Township. The township, established by legislative act in 1861, was named for Patrick Eagan, one of the first settlers, coming in 1853. An early post office was called Eagantown, 1860–62.

EAST CASTLE ROCK a post office in Castle Rock Township, first called South Hampton, 1861–65, changing to East Castle Rock, and discontinuing in 1897.

EAST CONNECTION see CLIFF.

ELLISON a station on the Minneapolis, Northfield and Southern Railroad, in Greenvale Township.

EMPIRE was named "for Empire, N.Y., the native place of Mrs. A. J. Irving, wife of one of the early settlers." This township was organized and named May 11, 1858.

EMPIRE CITY a settlement and a post office, 1856–1919, of Vermillion Township, section 29, and station of the Chicago Great Western Railroad.

ERENFIGHT a station of the St. Paul and Southern Electric Railroad in Inver Grove Township.

ETTER a village in Ravenna Township, section 21, had a post office, 1871–1927, and a station of the Chicago, Milwaukee and St. Paul Railroad on land owned by Alexander W. Etter and named for him. Etter opened a general store in 1873. The tracks were moved in 1928–29 to Prairie Island, and the depot built in 1871 was sold.

EUREKA CENTER a station of the Minneapolis, Northfield and Southern Railroad in Eureka Township, section 22.

EUREKA TOWNSHIP organized May 11, 1858, has for its name a Greek word, meaning "I have found it!" This was the exclamation of members of its "Indiana settlement," when they first arrived in 1854. A post office was located there, 1860–63.

FAIRFIELD see LAKEVILLE.

FARMINGTON an important railway town, "received its name from its situation in a district exclusively devoted to farming." The village was incorporated on February 12, 1872, created from a section of Empire Township, section 31, which later annexed more acreage from Empire Township as well as part of Castle Rock and Lakeville Townships. A post office was established in 1856. The village had a station serving several railroad lines.

FEATHERSTONE a village in Hastings Township, section 29, named for J. F. Featherstone, who owned land adjoining about 1928.

FISCHERVILLE a locality in Mendota Heights in Mendota Township, named for Frank Fischer, who opened a general store on Dodd Road near Highway 100 in 1924; the store was sold in 1961.

FORSTROM a station of the Minneapolis, Northfield and Southern Railroad in Eureka Township, section 27.

GLENTORO a place name of Inver Grove Township.

GREENVALE organized May 11, 1858, "probably received its name from the name given to a Sunday School in the southern part of the township. The name was doubtless inspired by the picturesque surroundings." The village, in section 2, had a station of the Minneapolis, St. Paul and Sault Ste. Marie Railroad (Soo Line).

HAMPTON TOWNSHIP established April 6, 1858, was named for "a place of that name in Connecticut. This appellation was suggested by Nathaniel Martin in honor of his birthplace." The city of Hampton, sections 8 and 9, was incorporated as a village on July 23, 1896; its post office was established in 1856; it had a station of the Chicago Great Western Railroad.

HANNA a station on the St. Paul and Southern Electric Railway, in Nininger Township, section 27.

HASTINGS the county seat, platted as a village in 1853 and incorporated as a city March 7, 1857, was named in drawing lots by its several proprietors, this second name of Henry Hastings Sibley, later governor and general, having been the winner's preference. "Judge Solomon Sibley, of Detroit, Mich., studied law in Massachusetts with Judge Hastings, whom he greatly admired, and gave this name to his son." The post office was established in 1854, and the village became a city with Washington County following the annexing of 262 acres from that county at the end of the Mississippi River bridge in 1905; other acreage was annexed from Nininger and Marshan Townships. The city was the site of the spiral bridge over the Mississippi River, which was dismantled in 1951.

Before the platting and naming of Hastings, this locality had been known during 33 years as Oliver's Grove, often ignorantly changed to "Olive Grove." The origin of this early name is told by John H. Case in vol. 15 of the MHS Collections (p. 377), as follows: "The site of the city of Hastings was earlier called Oliver's Grove, after Lieut. William G. Oliver, who was ascending the Mississippi with one or more keel boats in the autumn of 1819, but was prevented from going farther by a gorge of ice in the bend of the river opposite to this city. The boat or boats were probably run up to the outlet of Lake Rebecca, to be out of the way of the ice when the river broke up in the spring of 1820. Lieutenant Oliver was on his way from Fort Crawford at Prairie du Chien with supplies for the soldiers at St. Peter's camp, now Fort

Snelling, among whom was the first settler of Hastings, Joe Brown, the drummer boy, then about fourteen years of age."

HIGH ROCK ISLAND located in Mendota Township, is the site of a former sandstone quarry now part of Fort Snelling State Park. An 1879 map shows it in Slater Lake (named for James Slater, who at one time owned 647 acres nearby); the lake decreased with changes in the river channel, and the name was changed to Gun Club Lake.

HIGHLAND a station in Rosemount Township, section 18, on the St. Paul Electric Railroad.

IDELLA a post office, 1898–1905; location not found.

INVER GROVE HEIGHTS a city, which absorbed the village of Inver Grove and Inver Grove Township; the village of Inver Grove was incorporated on July 12, 1909, and the new village of Inver Grove Heights was incorporated on March 11, 1965. Its post office began in 1886; it had a station of the Chicago Great Western Railroad in section 2.

INVER GROVE TOWNSHIP T. 27N, R. 22W, was organized May 11, 1858. "The town was named by John McGroarty, the name Inver Grove being given in recollection of a place in Ireland from which many of the settlers came." The township was incorporated on March 11, 1965, as Inver Grove Heights.

JUDD a post office, 1881–90, located at Crystal Lake in Burnsville Township, with Esther E. Judd, postmaster.

KANES CROSSING a station in Rosemount Township, section 20, on the St. Paul Electric Railroad.

KAPOSIA a post office, 1853–54, located in West St. Paul Township, at the site of an Dakota village that was in existence about 1839–52; also known as Riverside in 1868.

LAKE AVALON a village in Lakeville Township, section 2, about 1916–28.

LAKE MARION a village in Lakeville Township, about 1937.

LAKEVILLE named like the township, received its first settlers in 1855. When the Hastings and Dakota Railway was built there, in 1869, a new village site was chosen, at first called Fairfield. This village superseded the older Lakeville and adopted that name in its act of incorporation, March 28, 1878. The city's post office began in 1854; it had a station of the Chicago, Milwaukee, St. Paul and Pacific Railroad.

LAKEVILLE TOWNSHIP established April 6, 1858, was named for Prairie Lake, which was renamed Lake Marion, as is further noted in the list of lakes of this county. The village merged with the township in 1867 and reincorporated on January 20, 1903; the township then dissolved February 20, 1967, when it merged with the village; it reorganized in 1969, separating from the village, and again merged in 1971.

LEBANON received its name "from Lebanon, N.H., from whence came Charles and H. J. Verrill, early settlers." It was organized May 11, 1858.

LEWISTON a milling area of Sciota Township, section 15, platted by Charles Lewis; prices for the lots were so high that a village never fully developed, although it had a post office, 1856–71, and a station of the Chicago Great Western Railroad.

LILYDALE a city of Mendota Township, section 4, platted as Lilly Dale (one of several variant forms of the name); addition in 1886 was named for the many lilies that flourished in nearby Pickerel Lake. It incorporated as a village, 1901–7, at which time it became part of the township, and reincorporated as a village on September 13, 1951.

LINCOLN PARK a station on the Chicago Great Western Railroad in T. 28N, R. 22W, section 34.

LIVINGSTON a station of the Minneapolis, Northfield and Southern Railroad in Eureka Township.

MADART a locality in Inver Grove Township, section 29, about 1937.

MANHART a station of the Minneapolis, Northfield and Southern Railroad in Greenvale Township, section 11.

MARCOTT a transit station in Inver Grove Township, section 21.

MARION HEIGHTS a locality of Lakeville Township, section 25, about 1916–28.

MARSHAN CITY a post office in Marshan Township in 1857, with Michael (Mehal) Marsh as postmaster, for whom the township was named.

MARSHAN TOWNSHIP "was named for Michael Marsh and his wife, Ann." Previous to its organization, May 11, 1858, it was known as Bellwood, for Joseph Bell, who took a claim there in 1854. It then had a small village, called Bellwood, with the first hotel of the township and a Catholic church, but the site "soon was abandoned."

MENDOTA a city of Mendota Township, was the first Euro-American settlement in Minnesota. The village began as a fur trading post in 1812;

permanent settlers came about 1822, at which time it was called St. Peter's. The name Mendota, adopted about the year 1837, is a Dakota name meaning "the mouth of a river," because here the Minnesota River joins the Mississippi. It was the county seat, 1854–57; was incorporated on March 5, 1853; became a village on July 6, 1887; and had a post office, 1854–1972, at which time it was changed to a branch of St. Paul. The township was established in April 1858.

MENDOTA HEIGHTS a city incorporated on February 21, 1956, as a village, absorbing Mendota Township.

MERRIMACK a post office, 1857–58, in Inver Grove Township, with a sawmill built in 1858 by Theophilus Cushing, a lumber dealer from Maine. He could not develop the site, and thus sold it and returned to Maine.

MIESVILLE a city in Douglas Township, section 14, was named for John Mies, by whom this little village was founded in 1874. The village was incorporated August 1, 1951, and had a post office, 1884–1903, which was first called Trout Brook, 1878–84.

MONTGOMERY see EAGAN.

MUNSON a station on the St. Paul Electric Railroad in Inver Grove Township, section 27.

NEW HOLAND a locality of Burnsville Township, section 14.

NEW TRIER a village in Hampton Township, sections 11 to 14, was "named for Trier, Germany, the native place of some of the early settlers in this vicinity." It was incorporated March 3, 1874; a post office was located there, 1867–1933.

NICOLS a station of the Chicago, Milwaukee and St. Paul Railroad, in Eagan Township, section 18, was named for John Nicols of St. Paul, the former owner of its site; sometimes referred to as Nichols Station.

NININGER TOWNSHIP established April 6, 1858, was named from its earlier "city of Nininger," section 18, which was platted in the summer of 1856 by John Nininger, for whom it was named. He resided in Pennsylvania and was a brother-in-law of Gov. Alexander Ramsey. In the winter of 1857–58 an act of incorporation of this city was passed by the legislature. In the spring of 1858, when it reached the height of its progress, Nininger "numbered nearly, if not quite, 1,000 inhabitants, and cast a vote of over 200." It had a

post office, 1856–89; no trace of the community remains.

NORTHFIELD a city with Rice County.

OAKLAND a station of the Chicago Great Western Railroad in Inver Grove Township, section 27, a site first settled about 1858.

ORCHARD GARDENS a settlement in Burnsville Township, section 35. About 1915, Marion W. Savage purchased several thousand acres of farmland, subdividing it into five- and ten-acre tracts to be sold to Twin Cities residents; the land had been platted for R. H. Benham Investment Company of Minneapolis about 1910 and designed into orchards, gardens, and small farms. From 1920 to 1926 the area was incorporated as a village, unincorporating in 1926. A flag-stop railroad depot was built in 1920 by the Minneapolis, Northfield and Southern Railroad for commuters, who used the Dan Patch line as their link to Minneapolis. The building was placed on the National Register of Historic Places in 1981.

OVERHEAD a station of the St. Paul and Southern Railroad, in section 27 of Inver Grove Township.

PINE BEND on the Mississippi River, includes the site of the village of a Dakota leader, Medicine Bottle, who seceded from the Kaposia village. "It is named from the fact that pine trees stand on the banks where the river makes a decided turn or bend." This was also the name of a station, on the upland, of the new St. Paul and Southern Electric Railway. The village in Inver Grove Township, sections 34 and 35, was platted in 1857 and incorporated on May 19, 1857. It had a post office in 1854, which was moved to Athens; another post office, which was Carlisle, 1852–54; then Centralia, 1856–57; and then Pine Bend, 1857–1904.

RADIO CENTER see WESCOTT.

RANDOLPH TOWNSHIP established April 20, 1858, was then named Richmond, "in honor of John Richmond, the first settler within its limits." This name was rejected September 18, 1858, because there was another Richmond in the state, and the township was called Wheatland until October 30, 1858, when it was renamed Randolph. "D. B. Hulburt, an admirer of the Virginia statesman, John Randolph, suggested that his distinguished surname be given to the town." This was "Randolph of Roanoke," as he was generally known, who was born in 1773 and died in 1833. The city of Randolph, in sections 5 to 8, was incorporated as a village on May 23, 1857, and again on November 15, 1904; it had a station of the Chicago Great Western Railroad, and its post office was established in 1886.

RAVENNA TOWNSHIP separated from the city of Hastings on June 5, 1860, was named by Albert T. Norton for Ravenna, Ohio where his wife had taught school.

REGAN a village of Burnsville Township, section 34, which was merged into Burnsville.

RICH VALLEY a village in Rosemount Township, section 34, was named "from its location in a valley of very fertile soil." It had a post office, 1858–1935, and a station of the Chicago Great Western Railroad.

RICHLAND a village in Nininger Township, section 25, about 1928–38.

RIVERSIDE a station of the Chicago Great Western Railroad in T. 28N, R. 22W, section 27; this name was also used for Kaposia in 1868.

ROSEMOUNT TOWNSHIP established April 6, 1858, "was named by Andrew Keegan and Hugh Derham, from the picturesque village of that name in Ireland." The city of Rosemount began in 1866 and incorporated as a village February 16, 1875, and again on October 23, 1908; it separated from the township on April 26, 1917, and merged with the township on January 21, 1971. Its post office was established in 1855, and it had a station serving several rail lines.

ST. PAUL PARK a station of the Chicago Great Western Railroad in section 11 of Inver Grove Township; see also Washington County.

SCHWARTZ a station on the St. Paul Electric Railroad in section 34 of Inver Grove Township.

SCIOTA TOWNSHIP organized May 11, 1858, "was named from Sciota, Ohio," as related by Judge Loren W. Collins.

SHUMWAY a station of the Minneapolis, Northfield and Southern Railroad in Greenvale Township, section 25; also known as the Shumway Ellison station.

SOUTH HAMPTON see EAST CASTLE ROCK.

SOUTH PARK a post office, 1887–1925, of T. 28N, R. 22W, section 16, which became part of South St. Paul.

SOUTH ST. PAUL organized as West St. Paul Township on May 11, 1858, and incorporated as a city, but returned to township status in 1862; it reincorporated on March 2, 1887, absorbing West

St. Paul Township until February 1889, when the city of West St. Paul was incorporated from the western portion of South St. Paul. In 1889, Inver Grove Township annexed the southern part of South St. Paul; it reincorporated as a city on January 20, 1906, and in the 1960s annexed acreage from Inver Grove Township. Its post office was established in 1888.

SPRING LAKE a village in Nininger Township, section 23, about 1928–38.

SPRING PARK a station of Chicago Great Western Railroad in T. 28N, R. 22W, section 34.

SUNFISH LAKE a city in Inver Grove Township; incorporated as a village on June 12, 1958.

TROUT BROOK see MIESVILLE.

UNION TOWNSHIP see BURNSVILLE TOWNSHIP.

VERMILLION TOWNSHIP organized April 5, 1858, was named for the Vermillion River, which bears a translation of its Dakota name, as more fully noted on an ensuing page. The city of Vermillion, in sections 15 and 22, incorporated as a village on February 23, 1881, and had an early post office, 1855–58, which changed to Castle Rock; a second post office began in 1874.

VROOMAN a station on the Minneapolis, Northfield and Southern Railroad; location not found.

WALLACE a farming village of West St. Paul Township, section 18, which had a post office, 1886–1907, with Thomas W. Wallace as first postmaster.

WATERFORD TOWNSHIP established April 20, 1858, "received its name from the fact that there was a ford across Cannon River within its limits. This ford was on the old trail from St. Paul to Faribault." The village, in section 30, had a sawmill and post office, 1854–1904.

WEICHSELBAUM a station of the Chicago, Milwaukee, St. Paul and Pacific Railroad in Lakeville Township, section 30.

WESCOTT a station of several rail lines, including the Minnesota Central Railroad, in Inver Grove Township, section 18, usually spelled Westcott, was named for a prominent pioneer, James Wescott, who settled there in 1854. He served in the First Minnesota Heavy Artillery in the Civil War, was treasurer of this county in 1860–62, and died on his farm near this station, May 4, 1910. The station was also known as Wescott Station and Radio Center.

WEST ST. PAUL incorporated as a city on February

23, 1889, when organized from several northwest sections of South St. Paul; an earlier city of West St. Paul in West St. Paul Township reverted to township status in 1862 and was annexed to St. Paul in 1874. When the city of South St. Paul was incorporated in 1887, it included all of West St. Paul Township; a post office was located there 1857–79, when it became part of the St. Paul postal system. The township was organized May 11, 1858, and by an act of the legislature approved March 9, 1874.

WESTCALL a post office, 1881–83; possibly same as Wescott.

WESTWOOD a station of the Chicago, Milwaukee and St. Paul Railroad, in Empire Township, section 27.

WHEATLAND TOWNSHIP see RANDOLPH TOWNSHIP.

WILSON a village in Nininger Township, section 30, about 1928–38.

Lakes and Streams

Three small lakes lying within about a mile south of the village of Mendota were named Lakes Charlotte, Lucy, and Abigail, on the earliest map of the vicinity of Fort St. Anthony, which in 1825 was renamed Fort Snelling. These names were given respectively in honor of the wives of Nathan Clark, Capt. George Gooding, and Col. Josiah Snelling. None of these names was retained. The most northeastern and largest of these lakes, known earlier as Duncan's Lake, now bears the name Lake Augusta, which was given to it in honor of the eldest daughter of Gen. Henry Hastings Sibley, who later was married to Capt. Douglas Pope. It is the lake that was named at first for Abigail Snelling.

Alimagnet Lake in Lebanon Township was named for Alice McQuillan, Maggie Davis, and Nettie Judd, local young women.

For Gun Club Lake and Slater Lake, see HIGH ROCK ISLAND.

Chub Lake and Chub Creek (or River) are named for the well-known species of fish, being quite probably a translation of their Dakota name.

Of Crystal Lake it is said that "when the government survey was made, its clear shining surface led to the adoption of its present name."

Black Dog Lake, four miles long, lying in the bottomland of the Minnesota River and occupying a deserted river course, was named for a Dakota, Black Dog, whose village was near the northeast end of the lake.

For the Big Foot Creek and Black Hawk Lake, apparently translations of Dakota names, no definite information has been obtained.

Lake Farquhar was named for John Farquhar, a pioneer who took a land claim near it.

Lake Isabelle, adjoining the east edge of the city of Hastings, was stated by the late Gen. William G. Le Duc to be named in honor of a daughter of Alexis Bailly, one of the original proprietors of this city. The Dakota name of this lake was Mahto-waukan, Spirit Bear.

Keegan Lake was named for Andrew Keegan, owner of a farm there.

Le May Lake commemorates settlers who lived near it.

Lake Earley was named for "William Earley, who settled on its western shore in 1854."

Orchard Lake, formerly called Round Lake, is named for the native crabapple trees and wild plum trees in the woods of its vicinity.

Lake Marion, formerly Prairie Lake, was renamed in honor of the late Marion W. Savage, owner of the famous trotting stallion Dan Patch and president of the Minneapolis, St. Paul, Rochester and Dubuque Electric Traction Company, whose railway line (commonly called the Dan Patch line) passed by the east side of this lake. At its southeast end were summer homes and pavilions for picnics and for boating, fishing, and hunting parties, this station being named Antlers Park, in allusion to the former abundance of deer in this region. For the village named Savage, beside the Minnesota River in Scott County, a biographic sketch of Mr. Savage is presented, with a note of the ownership of this electric railway.

Rice Lake, on the west line of Eureka and crossed by the line dividing Dakota and Scott Counties, was named for its wild rice.

Lake Rebecca, nearly two miles long, lying close northwest of Hastings, occupying a deserted channel of the Mississippi, was named, as told by Gen. Le Duc, for Rebecca Allison, daughter of a pioneer settler, who, after a few years residence here, returned to the East.

Spring Lake, on the southwest edge of the Mississippi bottomland, is named for its contiguous springs issuing from the base of the river bluffs.

Sunfish Lake, originally known as Lake Thereau, is named for this species of fish; and Pickerel Lake, similarly, for its large and abundant pickerel.

Rogers Lake commemorates E. G. Rogers, who owned a farm on its southeast side.

Vermillion Lake, quite small, in section 18, Eureka, and the Vermillion River, which lies wholly in this county, are a translation, first published by Nicollet's map in 1843, of the Dakota name. Its origin was probably from the very bright red and orange-colored ocher obtained by the Dakota in seams of Chimney Rock in Marshan, more fully noted on an ensuing page, and of other outcrops of the St. Peter sandstone beside or near the course of this river.

The lower parts of the Vermillion River, after it reaches the Mississippi bottomland, there flowing in two streams northwestward and southeastward to the great river, are named the Vermillion Slough. Four miles southeast of Hastings, this slough or river is joined by the Truedell Slough, named for a pioneer settler, by which it is connected with the Mississippi. Thence southeastward these two rivers, the Vermillion and the Mississippi, enclose Prairie Island, ten miles long, lying mostly in Goodhue County, under which its name and history are again noticed. The name is a translation of its earliest French name, Isle Pelée, called by Radisson "the first landing isle" (MHS Collections 10, pt. 2: 462–73, with a map of this island).

Dudley Island, in the Mississippi between one and two miles east of Hastings, belonging to Ravenna Township, was named, as stated by Irving Todd, Sr., for John Dudley of Prescott, Wis., owner of sawmills adjoining the mouth of the St. Croix River.

Belanger Island, in Nininger, south of the main channel of the Mississippi, bears the name of the first settler in this township, a French Canadian, whose cabin was on the bank of Spring Lake.

Pike Island, at the mouth of the Minnesota River and adjoining Mendota, is named for Lieut. (later Gen.) Zebulon M. Pike, who in 1805 on the west end of this island made a treaty with the Dakota for the tract on which Fort St. Anthony,

later named Fort Snelling, was built in the years 1820–24.

Kaposia, the village of the successive hereditary Dakota leaders, named Little Crow, was situated from 1837 to 1862 on a part of the site of South Park, a suburb of South St. Paul. Previously, in the time of the expeditions of Pike, Cass, and Long, this movable Indian village had been located on the eastern side of the Mississippi, as noted for Ramsey County. In 1820 and till 1833 or later, it was on the upper side of Dayton's bluff, within the area of St. Paul, but earlier, during a dozen years or more, in 1805 and in 1817, it was at the Grand Marais, one to two miles south of that bluff. Concerning the name, William H. Keating wrote: "The Indians designate this band by the name of Kapoja, which implies that they are deemed lighter and more active than the rest of the nation" (*Minnesota in Three Centuries*, vol. 1, pp. 366–68).

Hills and Rocks

The hilly tracts or belts of Dakota County consist of morainic glacial drift, amassed in abundant knolls, short ridges, and small hills, of which only a few rise to such prominence that they are named.

The most conspicuous hill, rising to about 1,175 feet above the sea, being about a hundred feet above any point in the view around it, is Buck Hill, near Crystal Lake, described as follows in the history of this county published in 1881: "At the west end of the lake is a high hill, . . . called by the early settlers 'Buck Hill.' From the top of this high eminence the Indians would watch the deer as they came to drink from the cool waters of the lake."

Another conspicuous height, near Mendota, is commonly called Pilot Knob, but on the oldest map of the vicinity of Fort Snelling, before mentioned, it is more properly named Pilot Hill.

In section 1, Marshan, are two prominent drift hills, which have been long known as "the Mounds."

Besides the Castle Rock, in the township so named, this county has several other somewhat similar castlelike or columnar rock masses. One of these, about ten miles north of the Castle Rock, is called Castle Hill on Nicollet's map, but since the settlement of the county it is named Lone Rock. About a mile and a half east of this is a Chimney Rock.

Again, about eight miles distant east-southeast from the last, there is another and more remarkable Chimney Rock. This is in the east edge of section 31, Marshan, about seven miles south of Hastings. As described in 1905 by the present writer (*Bulletin of the Minnesota Academy of Sci-* ences, vol. 4, p. 302, with a view from a photograph which well shows the reason for its name), this Chimney Rock "is the most picturesque and perfect example of columnar rock weathering in Minnesota. . . . It is a vertical pillar, measuring 34 feet in height and about 6 and 12 feet in its less and greater diameters, being no thicker near the base than in its upper part."

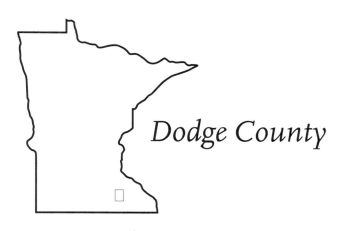

Dodge County

Established February 20, 1855, this county received its name in honor of Henry Dodge, governor of Wisconsin, and his son, Augustus C. Dodge, of Iowa. Henry Dodge was born in Vincennes, Ind., October 12, 1782, and died in Burlington, Iowa, June 19, 1867. He served in the War of 1812; was a colonel of volunteers in the Black Hawk War, 1832; commanded an expedition to the Rocky Mountains in 1835; was governor of Wisconsin Territory and superintendent of Indian affairs, 1836–41; delegate in Congress for Wisconsin, 1842–46; again governor of that territory, 1845–48; and was one of the first U.S. senators from the state of Wisconsin, 1848–57.

Governor Dodge on July 29, 1837, at Fort Snelling, then in Wisconsin, made a treaty with the Ojibwe, by which they ceded to the United States all their pine lands and agricultural lands on the upper part of the St. Croix River and its tributaries in the present states of Wisconsin and Minnesota. The tract ceded also reached west to include the upper part of the basin of Rum River and onward to the Mississippi between Sauk Rapids and the mouth of Crow Wing River. In September of the same year, under direction of Governor Dodge, about 20 Dakota men went with the Major Taliaferro, the Indian agent, to the city of Washington and there made a treaty ceding all their lands east of the Mississippi, together with the islands in this river. By these treaties a large tract of eastern Minnesota (then a part of Wisconsin), including the sites of St. Paul and St. Anthony, was opened to white settlement.

Augustus Caesar Dodge was born in St. Genevieve, Mo., January 12, 1812, and died in Burlington, Iowa, November 20, 1883. He was the delegate in Congress for Iowa Territory, 1840–47; was one of the first U.S. senators of Iowa, 1848–55, his father being also a senator at the same time; and was minister representing this country in Spain during four years, 1855–59. Biographies of both the father and son, with their portraits, by Louis Pelzer, have been published, respectively in 1911 and 1908, by the State Historical Society of Iowa in its Iowa Biographical Series.

For the origins and meanings of the geographic names of this county, information has been gathered from An Historical Sketch of Dodge County, *by W. H. Mitchell and U. Curtis, 1870 (125 pp.);* History of Winona, Olmsted, and Dodge Counties, *1884 (this county having pp. 769–1266);* Atlas of Dodge County, *by R. L. Polk and Co., 1905 (having pp. 61–129 of* text, historical and biographic, with illustrations*); and from the offices of George L. Taylor, county auditor, and George H. Slocum, editor of the* Mantorville Express, *visited in April 1916.*

ASHLAND TOWNSHIP first settled in May 1854, organized June 15, 1858, was named from its original village plat in 1855 by William Windom, Thomas Wilson, and Daniel S. Norton of Winona, with others. Each of the three proprietors here noted, then new immigrants to this territory, afterward attained great prominence in Minnesota history. This name, applied to townships, villages, cities, and counties, occurs in 26 other states of our Union. The township had a farming community named Ashland, with a post office, 1856–72.

AVON a post office, 1856–60 and 1862–66; location not found.

BERNE a village in Milton Township, section 17. The townsite was laid out in 1856 by Rudolph Smith and Jacob Klossner near their mill and was named Buchanan for the presidential candidate; the name being already in use, it was changed to Berne because a number of the township families had come from Berne, Switzerland. It had a post office first called Hector in 1857, changing to Buchanan and then Berne before discontinuing in 1902.

BUCHANAN formerly a small village having a sawmill, on the North Middle Branch of the Zumbro River, was named in honor of James Buchanan, elected in 1856 to the presidency of the United States. See also **BERNE**.

CANISTEO TOWNSHIP settled in 1854 and organized in 1858, was named by its numerous immigrants from Canisteo, a village and a township in Steuben County, N.Y., on the Canisteo River, which is about 60 miles long, flowing to the Tioga and Chemung Rivers, the latter a tributary of the Susquehanna. An early village there of the Delaware Indians was called Canisteo, being the origin of this name, said to mean "board on the water." This Indian village was described as "the largest of the Delaware towns, consisting of sixty good houses with three or four fire-places in each" (Roberts, *Historical Gazetteer of Steuben County*, 1891, pp. 15–17). A post office was located in the township, 1876–85.

CHENEY the post office at Eden railway station in Wasioja, 1886–1924, was named in honor of B. P. Cheney, a farmer there.

CLAREMONT TOWNSHIP first settled in September 1854, organized May 11, 1858, was named for the town of Claremont, N.H., whence several of its settlers came, including George Hitchcock, its first postmaster. The city of Claremont in section

28 was incorporated on March 22, 1878, and again on June 11, 1898, separating from the township on May 15, 1914. It had a station of the Chicago and Northwestern Railway and a post office from 1856.

CONCORD TOWNSHIP settled in April 1854, organized May 11, 1858, was named in like manner for the city of Concord, N.H., the capital of that state. The village plat was recorded June 7, 1856. The village in section 23 was settled about 1854, with a post office, 1856–1906.

DODGE CENTER a city of Wasioja Township, sections 33 and 34, founded in 1866, was platted in July 1869, and was incorporated February 29, 1872. This name was proposed by D. C. Fairbank on account of the location at the center of the county. A bill was submitted to the legislature in 1870 requesting the name be changed to Silas; however the bill was tabled, and the name remained. The city was reincorporated on June 7, 1907, and separated from the township on March 19, 1918. The post office was established in 1867. The first passenger train arrived here on the Winona and St. Peter Railroad, July 13, 1866; it had a station of the Chicago Great Western Railroad.

EAST CLAREMONT a post office, 1872–79, in Claremont Township, section 12.

EDEN the railway station and village in Wasioja Township, section 8, having Cheney post office, was named by officers of the Chicago Great Western Railroad company.

ELLINGTON TOWNSHIP settled in July 1855, organized May 11, 1858, had been at first named Pleasant Grove but was renamed for the town of Ellington in Connecticut. Mrs. John Van Buren, who proposed this change of name, "wrote the votes by which the matter was decided." The township had a post office, 1858–1902, in section 1.

HALLOWELL an early farming and lumbering village of Wasioja Township platted in 1856, with a post office, 1857–60; little remained by 1868.

HAYFIELD TOWNSHIP was organized March 30, 1872, having previously been a part of Vernon. Its name was adopted from a township of Crawford County in northwestern Pennsylvania. The city of Hayfield, sections 15 and 22, was incorporated January 7, 1896; it had a station of the Chicago Great Western Railroad, and the post office was established in 1885; the Vernon Co-operative

Creamery near Hayfield is the oldest farmer-owned creamery in the state.

KASSON a city in Mantorville Township, sections 32 and 33, was named in honor of Jabez Hyde Kasson, owner of the original town site. He was born in Springville, Pa., January 17, 1820, and came to Minnesota in 1856, settling on a farm in this township. When the Winona and St. Peter Railroad reached this place in the fall of 1865, this village was laid out by Kasson and others, the plat being recorded October 13, 1865, and in November the first passenger train came. The village was incorporated on February 24, 1870, and again on April 22, 1916, separating from the township on March 21, 1917. It had a station of the Chicago and Northwestern Railway, and its post office opened in 1866.

MANTOR JUNCTION a station on the Chicago and Northwestern Railway, one mile west of Kasson.

MANTORVILLE TOWNSHIP was first settled in April 1854, was incorporated under legislative acts of 1854 and 1857, and was organized under the state government, May 11, 1858. The village was platted March 26, 1856, by Peter Mantor, H. A. Pratt, and others, and in 1857 it was designated by a vote of the county to be the county seat. This name was adopted in honor of three brothers, Peter, Riley, and Frank Mantor, who came here in 1853 and 1854 from Linesville, Crawford County, Pa. Peter Mantor, the oldest of these brothers and the leader in founding this town, was born in Albany County, N.Y., December 15, 1815; settled on the site of the village of Mantorville, April 19, 1854, and built a sawmill and gristmill there; was a representative in the legislature, 1859–60; was captain of Company C, Second Minnesota Regiment, 1861; removed to Bismarck, N.Dak., in 1874, where he was register of the U.S. land office until 1880; died in Mantorville, September 23, 1888. The oldest settlement in the county, Mantorville was incorporated on May 19, 1857, and again on September 8, 1924, separating from the township on February 10, 1926; the post office was established in 1855; it had a station of the Chicago and Northwestern Railway.

MILTON TOWNSHIP settled in May 1854, organized May 20, 1858, had been successively called Watkins, Buchanan, and Berne. Georgia has a Milton County, and 30 other states have townships, villages, and cities of this name, honoring the grand poet and patriot of England (1608–74). A post office was located there, 1865–67.

OSLO a hamlet at the center of Vernon Township, section 21, was made a post office in 1879, discontinued in 1902. This name is now borne by a village of the Minneapolis, St. Paul and Sault Ste. Marie Railroad (Soo Line) in the southwest corner of Marshall County. It was the name of the original city founded in 1048 by Harald Sigurdsson near the site of Christiania, the capital of Norway. Oslo (or Opslo) became the chief city of Norway, but it was built mainly of wood, and after a great conflagration the city was refounded on the present site by the king, Christian IV, who gave his name to it in 1624.

OTHELLO a post office in Milton Township, section 36, with Olmsted County, New Haven Township, section 31.

RICE LAKE a village in the northwest corner of Claremont Township, section 6, received its name from the neighboring lake, crossed by the west line of this county. It refers to the growth of wild rice in this shallow lake, which was used as an important food supply by the Indians. The village was thriving by 1855 and was platted in 1857. Stephen L. Wilson opened the first store in 1857 and became the first postmaster; a number of businesses developed until 1865 when the railroad chose a path several miles away, causing the village to stop growing and eventually disappear; the only remaining building is the Rice Lake Church.

RIPLEY TOWNSHIP first settled in September 1854, organized May 14, 1858, may have been named for some eastern township or village, as in Maine, New York, Ohio, Indiana, Illinois, or West Virginia, in each of which states this name is found.

SACRAMENTO was a village platted in the fall of 1855 on the Zumbro River in the west edge of Mantorville, sections 18 and 19, against which it was a rival for election as the county seat, but it was defeated by the popular vote in 1857. A post office was located there, 1857–60. Within the next decade its buildings were removed, and its site reverted to farm use. The name, from California, had reference to scanty occurrence of placer gold in the drift of some localities on branches of the Zumbro and Root Rivers, as noted in reports of the Minnesota Geological Survey. One of the places of ill-repaid gold washing by the early settlers was near the site occupied a few years by this "deserted village."

THOE a farming community, which had a post office, 1881–86; location not found.

UNION SPRING a farming community of Canisteo Township, named for the 15 to 20 springs nearby, which all unite into one stream; it had a post office, 1858–73.

VENTURE a farming community of Ripley Township, section 35, with a post office, 1899–1906.

VERNON TOWNSHIP settled in October 1855, organized March 4, 1858, was named from Mount Vernon, Va., the home of George Washington, for Adm. Edward Vernon (1684–1757) of the British navy. A post office was located in section 4, 1867–82 and 1884; one of Minnesota's first cooperative creameries was established there about 1889.

VLASATY a railway station in Ashland, section 22, with a post office, 1896–1906, was named by officers of the Chicago Great Western Railroad.

WASIOJA TOWNSHIP settled in October 1854, organized in 1858, bears the Dakota name of the Zumbro River, spelled Wazi Oju on Joseph N. Nicollet's map in 1843. It is translated as "Pine river" by Nicollet and is defined as meaning "pine clad." Large white pines, far west of their general geographic range, grow on the Zumbro bluffs in the east part of this township, as also in Mantorville, and at Pine Island in Goodhue County. The village of Wasioja, section 13, was platted May 24, 1856. It had a station of the Chicago Great Western Railroad and a post office, 1856–1911.

WEST CONCORD a city in Concord Township, sections 17 to 20, which was settled in 1885, platted June 1, 1885, and incorporated as a village on February 19, 1894. It had a station of the Chicago

Great Western Railroad, and its post office was established in 1885.

WESTFIELD CENTRE a post office, 1875–93, in Westfield Township.

WESTFIELD TOWNSHIP settled in 1855, organized March 22, 1866, probably commemorates an eastern village or township whence some of its settlers had come. The name is so used in a dozen eastern states, and it is also borne by a river in Massachusetts.

Lakes and Streams

The North Middle Branch of Zumbro River, its South Middle Branch, and its South Branch, gather their head streams in this county; and from Hayfield and Westfield the Cedar River, a long and large stream of Iowa, receives its highest sources, its East, Middle, and West Forks.

Milliken and Harkcom Creeks, in Concord and Milton, flowing into the North Middle Zumbro, were named for pioneer settlers, as also Maston's Branch, flowing northeastward past Kasson to the South Middle Fork.

La Due's bluff, the site of the quarries in Mantorville, was named for Hon. A. D. La Due, a prominent early citizen, who died at Mantorville on January 12, 1899.

On the South Branch of the Zumbro, in the southwest quarter of section 12, Vernon, was the Indian Grove, named for a large number of Dakota who had their camp there in the winter of 1856–57.

Hammond or Manchester Lake and Prince Lake, in Ripley, were named for nearby farmers.

The origins of the names of Zumbro and Cedar Rivers are noticed in the first chapter, treating of the large rivers of this state.

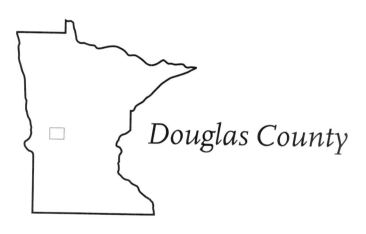

Douglas County

This county, established March 8, 1858, and organized June 15, 1866, was named in honor of Stephen Arnold Douglas, statesman and leader in the Democratic Party, eminent in his patriotic loyalty to the Union at the beginning of the Civil War. He was born in Brandon, Vt., April 23, 1813, and died in Chicago, June 3, 1861. He lived in Vermont to the age of 17 years; studied law and was admitted to practice in Illinois in 1834; was elected to the state legislature in 1835 and won there the sobriquet of "the Little Giant," by which he was ever afterward well known; was elected a judge of the state supreme court in 1841; was a member of Congress, 1843–47; and U.S. senator, 1847–61. On the application of Minnesota to be admitted as a state in 1857–58, Douglas earnestly advocated it, being then chairman of the Senate Committee on Territories.

In a series of debates in Illinois in 1858 with Abraham Lincoln, his Republican opponent, nominated for the U.S. senate, Douglas defended his view that Congress had no authority for exclusion of slavery from territories not yet received into the Union as states. Each of these great political leaders then aroused extraordinary interest throughout the nation, and two years later they were opposing candidates for the presidency; Lincoln was elected. The southern states seceded, and in 1861 the great Civil War began.

Several biographies of Douglas have been published, in the presidential campaign of 1860, again new editions of one of these in the midst of the Civil War and at its close, and more complete and dispassionate studies in recent years. The influence of his loyalty for preservation of the Union was an inestimable contribution to the making of history and the welfare of the world.

―――――――――――

Information for this county was gathered from the History of Douglas and Grant Counties, *Constant Larson, editor, 1916 (2 vols., 509, 693 pp.); Plat Book of Douglas County, 1886 (82 pp.), including a "Historical Sketch" in four pages; and from George P. Craig, judge of probate, Gustav A. Kortsch, president of the Douglas County Bank, R. C. Bondurant, local editor of the* Alexandria Post News, *Mrs. Charles F. Canfield, and Mrs. James H. Van Dyke, interviewed during a visit at Alexandria, the county seat, in May 1916.*

ALEXANDRIA settled in 1858, established as a township June 15, 1866, was named in honor of Alexander Kinkead, because he and his brother William were its first settlers, coming from Maryland. The form of the name follows that of the large city in Egypt, which was founded in the year 332 B.C. by Alexander the Great. Fifteen other states have villages or cities of this name. The village of Alexandria was incorporated February 20, 1877, its charter as a city was adopted in 1908, and it was incorporated as a city in 1909. It was surveyed in 1866 and purchased in 1868 by W. E. Hicks, who established a mill, a hotel, a store, and the first newspaper, also donating property for a courthouse, a jail, and Methodist and Congregational churches; he served as first postmaster when the office was established in 1858. The first passenger train on the railroad reached this place November 5, 1878. The village was known as a summer resort during the 1870s.

Alexander Kinkead removed to California. William Kinkead was born in Elkton, Md., December 3, 1835; came to Minnesota in 1856; served in the Second Minnesota Battery, 1862–63; was afterward chief clerk in the hospital at Washington for returned prisoners of war; died in St. Cloud, Minn., May 22, 1868.

BELLE RIVER TOWNSHIP settled in 1865, was established March 8, 1870, being then named Riverdale. January 4, 1871, the present name was chosen by vote of the people. Each of these names was suggested by the Long Prairie River, which flows meanderingly through the north half of this township, on its way toward the Long Prairie that borders it in Todd County, being what the French first word of the township name signifies, beautiful. A post office was located in section 8, 1885–1906.

BRANDON settled in 1860, was established as a township September 3, 1867, and was then called Chippewa, for its lakes and river of that name, used as a "road of war" by the Ojibwe in their forays to the Dakota country. Previously it had a station, also named Chippewa, of the Burbank stage route from St. Cloud to the Red River at the home and hotel of Henry Gager, on a low hill about two miles north of the present railway village, which received its name of Brandon for the birthplace of Stephen A. Douglas in Vermont, as laid out in August 1879. The township was also renamed. The city of Brandon was incorporated November 22, 1881. It was laid out by its owner, Lt. George A. Freudenreich. Its post office was named Chippewa Lake, 1861–69, before its present name.

CARLOS first settled in 1863, was made a township May 1, 1868. The city of Carlos was incorporated August 25, 1904, and had a station on the Minneapolis, St. Paul and Sault Ste. Marie Railroad (Soo Line) in section 23, and a post office, 1881–82 and since 1905. The name was adopted from the beautiful, large, and deep Lake Carlos,

which had received it before 1860, given by Glendy King, a homesteader near Alexandria, who had been a student at West Point. Lakes Carlos and Le Homme Dieu were named by him for two of his friends in the eastern states.

CHIPPEWA LAKE see **BRANDON**.

DENT see **NELSON**.

EVANSVILLE permanently settled in 1865, established as a township January 7, 1868, commemorates the first mail carrier, named Albert Evans, of the route opened in 1859 from St. Cloud to Fort Abercrombie, who had a log cabin there for staying overnight. He was killed in the Dakota War of 1862. The village of Evansville was platted in the fall of 1879, in anticipation of the Great Northern Railway's arrival, and was incorporated on February 18, 1881. Inn and saloon owner Jacob Shanar was the first postmaster in 1868.

FORADA a city in Hudson Township, section 20, platted in July 1903 by Cyrus A. Campbell of Parker's Prairie, Otter Tail County, incorporated July 20, 1905, has the first name of Mrs. Campbell, Ada; but that name was already widely known as the county seat of Norman County, and therefore it received the prefixed syllable. The city had a station of the Soo Line and a post office, 1904–54.

FRYKSENDE a community of Evansville Township during the 1870s.

GARFIELD a city of Ida Township, section 32, platted February 17, 1882, incorporated August 28, 1905, was named in honor of President James A. Garfield, who was shot July 2, 1881, by the assassin Charles J. Guiteau, and died at Elberon, N.J., our second martyred president, September 19, a few months before this village was founded. The post office began in 1880; it had a station of the Great Northern Railway.

GENEVA BEACH a village of summer homes at the south end of Lake Geneva in Alexandria Township, section 21, received its name from this lake, which, as also the adjoining Lake Victoria, was named by Walter Scott Shotwell. The former name was derived from the lake and historic city in Switzerland; the latter is in honor of Queen Victoria. The sponsor of these names was a son of Daniel Shotwell from New Jersey, whose homestead claim, taken in 1859, was between these lakes. The village had a station of the Great Northern Railway.

HOLMES CITY settled in 1858, established as a

township October 4, 1866, was named in honor of Thomas Andrew Holmes, leader of its first group of settlers. He was born in Bergerstown, Pa., March 4, 1804, and died in Cullman, Ala., July 2, 1888. He established an Indian trading post in 1839 at Fountain City, Wis., and in 1849 removed to Sauk Rapids, Minn.; was a member of the first territorial legislature; founded the towns of Shakopee and Chaska in 1851. Before engaging in the Indian trade, he had been one of the founders of Janesville, Wis., in 1836. Following the receding frontier, he went to Montana in 1862 and there participated in founding Bannack City, at an early locality of placer gold mining, which became the first capital of Montana Territory. The village of Holmes City, in section 2, was incorporated on June 24, 1858.

HUDSON TOWNSHIP first settled in 1864, organized April 16, 1869, was named from Hudson, Wis., whence some families of its pioneers came, including Mrs. Sam B. Childs, who proposed this name. The township had several earlier names: Maple Lake in 1867, Maple Town in 1868, and Roslyn, 1869–73. A post office was located in the township, 1872–83.

IDA TOWNSHIP settled in 1863, organized April 7, 1868, received the name of its large Lake Ida, which had been so named by Myron Coloney, one of its first settlers, for a friend, probably residing in an eastern state. A post office was located in the township, 1869–70.

INTERLACHEN PARK a summer village in Carlos Township, sections 32 and 33, bordering the north shore of Lake Le Homme Dieu and having its western end beside Lake Carlos, derived this name, with a slight change of spelling, from Interlaken, Switzerland, much visited by tourists, between Lakes Thun and Brienz. It means "between the lakes."

KENSINGTON a city of Solem Township, sections 27 and 28, was platted by Hon. William D. Washburn in March 1887, was incorporated August 28, 1891, and separated from the township on October 1, 1906. This is the name of a western section of the city of London, and it is also borne by villages and townships in seven other states. The city had a station on the Soo Line, and its post office began in 1887. On the farm of Olof Ohman, about three miles northeast from this village, the famous Kensington runestone was found in No-

vember 1898. It is described in the MHS Collections 15: 221–86, with illustrations and maps.

KRON a country post office, 1884–1907, in Lund Township, section 11, located in the general store of Anders Gustaf Johnson, postmaster, who also owned the general store in Melby.

LA GRAND TOWNSHIP first settled in 1860, was organized September 23, 1873, being then called West Alexandria, but in December of that year it was changed to La Grand, taking the name of an early resident of Alexandria.

LAKE MARY TOWNSHIP settled in 1863, established September 3, 1867, was named for its large lake, which commemorates Mary A. Kinkead, a homesteader of 1861 in section 24, La Grand, sister of Alexander and William Kinkead, before mentioned as the first settlers in Alexandria. Her homestead adjoined Lake Winona, which she probably named.

LEAF VALLEY to which the first settler came in 1866, was established as a township November 23, 1867. Its name refers to its situation at the southern border of the Leaf Hills, commonly called "mountains," which rise conspicuously in the adjoining edge of Otter Tail County. The township had a country post office, 1871–1905, in section 22.

LUND first settled in 1866, made a township March 1, 1872, is named for the very ancient city of Lund in southern Sweden, which has a famous university founded in 1666. In pagan times Lund attained great importance, and during a long period of the Middle Ages it was the seat of an archbishopric and was the largest city of Scandinavia.

MELBY the unincorporated village of Lund, section 17, was platted in April 1902, being named probably for a farming locality in Sweden, whence some of the settlers came, receiving from it their own personal surnames. The village had a station of the Great Northern Railway in section 20 and a post office from 1888.

MILL SITE a post office, 1871–72; location not found.

MILLERVILLE established as a township November 23, 1867, was named for John Miller, an early and prominent German settler. The city of Millerville was incorporated on September 2, 1903; the post office operated 1869–1907.

MILTONA TOWNSHIP was established December 19, 1871, receiving its name from the large Lake

Miltona, which occupies more than a sixth part of its area. The lake was named for Mrs. Florence Miltona Roadruck, wife of Benjamin Franklin Roadruck, who had a homestead in section 22, Leaf Valley, at the west end of this lake. In 1877 they returned to their former home in Indiana. (Letter from George L. Treat, of Alexandria.) Tradition tells that her family washing was often done on the lakeshore.

The city of Miltona, sections 25 and 26, was incorporated on March 31, 1930. It began as a station of the Soo Line on the northeast end of Lake Irene and was relocated to its present site when founder John Hintzen purchased land there during construction of the depot in the early 1900s. Although some sources say the city was named for the lake, others sources say it was named for an Indian chief who once lived in the area. Its post office operated, 1873–85, 1891–1905, and from 1911.

MOE settled in 1863, was established as a township September 3, 1867, being at first called Adkinsville in honor of Thomas Adkins, one of the first settlers. "Later the name was changed to Moe, in memory of a district in Norway, from which a number of the pioneers came." A post office was located in section 29, 1869–83 and 1895–1906.

NELSON a city of Alexandria Township, section 24, founded about the year 1875, was incorporated August 31, 1905. It had a station of the Great Northern Railway and a post office from 1881. The post office and village were at first named Dent in honor of Richard Dent, who settled at Alexandria in 1868 and died in Spokane, Wash., May 19, 1915. The name was changed to Nelson after 1881 in honor of Sen. Knute Nelson, the most eminent citizen of this county. He was born in Vossvangen, Norway, February 2, 1842; came to the United States when seven years old with his mother; served in the Fourth Wisconsin Regiment, 1861–64; was admitted to the bar in 1867; came to Minnesota in 1871 and settled on a farm near Alexandria; practiced law in Alexandria after 1872; was a state senator, 1875–78; representative in Congress, 1883–89; governor of Minnesota, 1893–95; and resigned to accept the office of U.S. senator, which position he filled with very distinguished ability and grand loyalty to this state and the nation. His biography is in *Lives of the Gover-*

nors of Minnesota, by Gen. James H. Baker (MHS Collections 13: 327–55 [1908], with portrait).

ORANGE was settled in 1863–64 and was established as a township January 7, 1868. It is said to be named for William of Orange. Eight states have counties of this name, and it is borne in 20 states by cities, villages, and townships.

OSAKIS first settled in 1859, was established June 15, 1866, this and Alexandria being the oldest townships of the county. The name was received from Osakis Lake, which, as also the Sauk River outflowing from it, has reference to Sauk Indians formerly living here, as narrated in connection with Sauk Rapids in the chapter on Benton County. In 1859 the stages running to Fort Abercrombie had a station on the site of Osakis village, and the earliest settlers took claims, but the Dakota War in 1862 caused these claims to be abandoned. The city, section 25, with Todd County, was founded in 1866 and was incorporated February 18, 1881, and again on January 5, 1887. It had a station serving both the Great Northern Railway and the Northern Pacific Railroad, and its post office began in 1864. The date of the first passenger train was November 1, 1878.

OSCAR LAKE a post office, 1874–87, in Holmes City Township, section 19.

ROSE CITY a populated place in Spruce Hill Township, section 14.

ROSE HILL a locality with a general store built after 1930; location not found.

SCRIVEN a post office, 1885–1905, in Spruce Hill Township, section 20.

SOLEM settled in 1866, was established as a township March 10, 1870. "The township takes its name from a district in Norway, from which place many of the pioneers came."

SPRUCE CENTER a village of Spruce Hill Township, which began in the 1880s with a store and blacksmith.

SPRUCE HILL TOWNSHIP the latest established in this county, was organized March 9, 1875. Its low timbered hills of morainic drift bear the black spruce, balsam fir, white pine, paper or canoe birch, balsam poplar, and blueberries, with other trees and shrubs, the several species thus named reaching here the southwestern limits of their geographic range. The village in section 33 was first settled about 1869, when a Mr. Gordon built a dam and sawmill on the site. It was considered a boom town in the 1880s. Its post office operated 1870–94. By 1900 the dam was gone, and community died, the last building being removed in 1928.

URNESS first settled in 1862–63, was established as a township, March 22, 1869, to be called Red Rock, from its lake of that name, referring to reddish boulders on its shore, one being especially noteworthy on the northeast shore of the main lake. On February 7, 1871, the commissioners received a petition requesting that the name of the township be changed to Urness, "in memory of a certain district in Norway." Two of its pioneer farmers, Andrew J. and Ole J. Urness, respectively in sections 24 and 12, coming in 1865, were immigrants from that district. The village of Urness, section 16, had two stores, a creamery, and the Good Templers Hall; the post office operated, 1877–1904, in the homes of the postmasters.

VAN a post office, 1884–95, in Holmes City Township, section 24.

———

Lakes and Streams

The foregoing list of the names of townships has included sufficient references to several rivers and lakes.

Only a few other names of streams are to be noticed, as Spruce and Stormy Creeks in Spruce Hill Township, and Calamus Creek named for its growth of the calamus, or sweet flag (*Acorus calamus*), in Osakis and Belle River Townships. More recently the last has been named Fairfield Creek in honor of Edwin, George, and Lloyd D. Fairfield, early settlers in Osakis and Orange, having homesteads near the farthest sources of this stream.

But there remains a multitude of lakes, unsurpassed in beauty and diversity. Some of these are named for pioneers whose homes adjoined the lakes; others for their outlines, as Horseshoe Lake, Moon Lake, two Crooked Lakes, Lobster Lake, and several Long Lakes; and others for their trees and animals, as Maple, Elk, and Turtle Lakes.

The complex and recurving series or chain of lakes, large and small, through which the headstream of Long Prairie River takes its course, consists in descending order of Lake Irene, earlier called Reservation Lake; Lakes Miltona and Ida,

respectively the largest and the next in size in this series; Lakes Charlie and Louise, named for a son and a daughter of Charles Cook, who settled in Alexandria in 1858, had been a fur merchant in London and a member of the Hudson's Bay Company, was the first postmaster of Alexandria, and after a few years returned to the eastern states and later to London, where he spent the remainder of his life; Union Lake, where this series receives an important inflowing stream from another large series of lakes at the west and south; Stone and Lottie Lakes; Lake Cowdry, named for Samuel B. Cowdry, a pioneer farmer in Alexandria, who removed in 1862, later attended the Seabury Divinity School, Faribault, and became an Episcopal rector in southern Minnesota; Lake Darling, commemorative of Andrew Darling, a pioneer who settled on the shore of this lake in 1860, an exceptionally successful farmer; and Lake Carlos, lowest of this series, sounded by Rev. C. M. Terry and found to have in some places a depth of 150 feet, being the deepest lake of this state. The area along the north shore of Lake Carlos was set aside as Lake Carlos State Park in 1937, thereby preserving timber land and making more of the state's Lake Region available to tourists.

Lake Irene in sections 14, 22, and 23, Miltona, is in honor of Irene Roadruck, for whose mother Lake Miltona is named, as noted for this township.

A second series, mentioned as tributary to Union Lake of the preceding series, has, in like descending order, Lake Andrews, named probably in honor of the first physician of Alexandria; Lake Mary, largest in this series, named for Mary Kinkead, wife of Alexander Kinkead; Mill and Lobster Lakes, the latter having numerous arms or claws; and Lake Mina, Berglin's Lake, and Fish Lake (the last formerly called Mill Lake).

A third series of lakes, tributary to Lake Carlos, includes another and smaller Union Lake, covering parts of four sections in Hudson; Burgan's Lake, named for William P. Burgan, a farmer who settled near its southwest shore in 1869; and Lakes Victoria, Geneva, and Le Homme Dieu, each having many summer homes along the shores.

To the eastern arm of Lake Victoria a fourth series sends its outflow, comprising Lover's Lake, Childs Lake, and Lake Jessie, the second being for

Edwin R. Childs, who came there as a homesteader in 1867.

Many lakes yet remain, not herein before noticed. In the order of townships from south to north, and of ranges from east to west, these are listed as follows.

Swims or Clifford Lake, Myer's, Owings, and English Grove Lakes in Orange, the last named for its grove on the homestead of William T. English, who settled there in 1863. These lakes were shallow and have been drained.

Maple Lake in Hudson.

Turtle, Long, and Mud Lakes in Lake Mary Township, the last drained.

Van Loon's Lake, Grubb Lake, Lake Rachel, Echo Lake, Grant's and Blackwell Lakes, Holmes City Lake, Oscar Lake, South Oscar Lake, and Freeborn, Mattson, and Olaf Lakes in Holmes City Township. Early settlers commemorated in these names include Noah Grant, who settled on section 2 in 1858; George Blackwell, on section 3, 1868; Miner Van Loon, section 24, 1865; John Freeborn, section 30, 1868; and John Mattson, section 32, 1868. (For the origin of the name of Lake Oscar, see the end of this chapter.)

Long Lake, Eng, Hegg, and Roland Lakes in Solem. Among the pioneer settlers in this township were Erick Pehrson Eng, Erick Hegg, and John Roland, for whom these lakes were named.

Lake Smith, Bird Lake, Crooked and Hanford Lakes in Osakis Township, the last two drained.

Lakes Agnes and Henry, north of the city of Alexandria, the former named for the eastern "lady love" of William Kinkead by Mrs. Caroline Cook, wife of Charles Cook, the merchant pioneer from London, and the latter for one of their children, brother of Charlie and Louise Cook (for whom other small lakes, previously noted, are named), and of Fanny Cook, who became the wife of James Henry Van Dyke, first merchant of Alexandria; Lake Winona, at the west side of Alexandria and extending into La Grand, for which lake and for this county the first white child born here was named Winona Douglas James, daughter of Joseph A. James, a settler who came from Philadelphia in 1858; Lake Conie, at the southeast edge of the city, and Shadow Lake in section 23, these all being in Alexandria Township.

Lake Alvin, Lake Latoka (origin and meaning not ascertained), Nelson Lake (for O. W. Nelson, a nearby farmer), and Lake Cook in Le Grand, the last being in honor of Charles Cook.

Elk Lake, Lakes Elizabeth, Gilbert, and William, Crooked Lake, Lake Brandon (named for John Brandon, a farmer whose home is at its east side), Thorstad and Minister Lakes in Moe, the last being near a Norwegian Lutheran church.

Amos Lake for Amos Johnson, Thorson Lake, Barsness Lake for Albert and Oscar Barsness, Holleque Lake, Quam Lake for P. J. Quam, and Lake Venus, with the much larger Red Rock Lake, before noticed, in Urness.

Mud Lake at the corner of sections 27, 28, 33, and 34, Carlos.

Baumbach, Hunt, Stowe's, and Grassy Lakes, Long and Moon Lakes, Lakes Aldrich and Nelson, Burrows, Whiskey, and Devil's Lakes in Brandon. The first was named in honor of Frederick von Baumbach, who was born in Prussia, August 30, 1838, and died at his home in Alexandria, Minn., November 30, 1917. He came to the United States with his father in 1848; served in the Fifth and Thirty-fifth Wisconsin Regiments during the Civil War, attaining the rank of major; came to Minnesota, settling at Alexandria, in 1867; was auditor of this county, 1872–78, and again in 1889–98; secretary of state of Minnesota, 1880–87; and internal revenue collector for this state, 1898–1914. Lake Mina, before noted in the second series tributary to Long Prairie River, was named for his mother.

Others of these Brandon Lakes were named for Joseph Hunt, homesteader on section 6 in 1867; Martin Stowe, section 18 in 1862; John D. Aldrich, section 23, 1868; and John Nelson, section 26, 1865.

Another Long Lake, Jennie, Erwin, Alberts, Solberg, Hubred, Davidson, Mahla, and Fanny Lakes in Evansville. Farmers commemorated by these names include George Erwin, Ole Alberts, A. H. Solberg, Oliver Hubred, D. J. Davidson, and M. H. Mahla.

Vermont and Wood Lakes in Miltona, the former named by settlers from that state.

Spring and Kelly's Lakes in Leaf Valley, the latter in honor of Patrick Kelly, an Irish homesteader at its east side in 1873.

Lakes Moses and Aaron, Lorsung, Wilken, Stockhaven, and Stockhousen Lakes in Millerville. The first two were named for the great Hebrew lawgiver and his brother, deliverers of their nation from Egyptian bondage and leaders toward the promised land of Palestine. The third and fourth of these lakes, named for Joseph Lorsung and John and William Wilken, have been drained, the bed of each being subdivided to the adjoining farms. The last was named, with change of spelling, in honor of Hans G. von Stackhausen, who took a homestead claim there in 1870.

Lund, the most northwestern township, has the large but shallow Lake Christina, the small Lakes Anka and Ina, bordering the south shore of that large lake, and Horseshoe Lake and Lake Sina. The last, in section 25, bears on early maps this name of Mount Sinai (called Sina in the seventh chapter of the Acts), where the Decalogue and other laws were received, the name being suggested by Lakes Moses and Aaron, a few miles distant.

Lake Christina and its companion, the large Pelican Lake in the adjoining corner of Grant County, appear, though with inaccurate outlines, on an early map of this state, dated January 1, 1860, their names being given as Lakes Christina and Ellenora. They were named in 1859 by James W. Taylor and Russell Blakeley in honor of Ellenora and Christina Sterling of Scotland. The name of Lake Oscar in Holmes City Township, though a common christening name, was quite surely not adopted to honor any settler there, but for Oscar I, the king of Sweden and Norway in 1844–59, father of Oscar II, who was the king in 1872–1907.

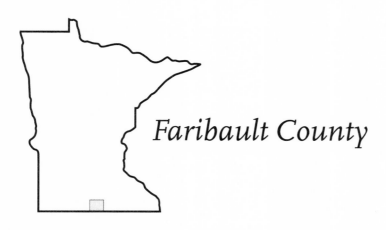

Faribault County

This county was established February 20, 1855, being named in honor of Jean Baptiste Faribault, who was engaged during the greater part of his long life as a trader among the Dakota, at first for the North West Company. He was born at L'Ile Dupas, Quebec, on October 29, 1775, and came to the Northwest in 1798, taking charge of a trading post on the Kankakee River near the south end of Lake Michigan. During the years 1799 to 1802, he was stationed at the Redwood post, situated on the Des Moines River, "about two hundred miles above its mouth," being in what is now the central part of Iowa. Coming to Minnesota in 1803, he took charge of a post at Little Rapids, on the Minnesota River a few miles above the present sites of Chaska and Carver, where he remained several years. Afterward he was a trader on his own account at Prairie du Chien, Wis., whence he removed to Pike Island, at the mouth of the Minnesota River, in the spring of 1820, having been promised military protection by Col. Henry Leavenworth, who had come there with troops in the preceding August for building the fort, which in 1825 was named Fort Snelling. Faribault and his family lived from 1826 to 1852 in Mendota, where he built a substantial stone house in 1838, the first in Minnesota, and in the winters during many years he traded with the Dakota at Little Rapids. His influence with the Indians west of the Mississippi, from the Missouri to the Red River, was very great. He endeavored to teach them agriculture and was the first white settler to cultivate the soil in this state. He spent his last years in the town of Faribault, in Rice County, founded at first as an Indian trading post by his eldest son, Alexander Faribault, for whom it was named. He died at the home of his daughter there, August 20, 1860.

An appreciative memoir of him by Gen. Henry H. Sibley, in the MHS Collections (3: 168–79), closes with these words: "Among the pioneers of Minnesota, there are none whose memory and whose name better deserve to be respected and perpetuated."

Information of the origins and meanings of the geographic names in this county was received from The History of Faribault County . . . to the close of the year 1879, *by Judge J. A. Kiester (1896, 687 pp.); and from John Siverson, register of deeds, and Henry P. Constans, proprietor of the Constans Hotel, interviewed at Blue Earth during my visit there in July 1916.*

ALTON a post office, 1876–94, of Brush Creek Township, first located in the home of John J. Northness, postmaster, and later moved to a store, which closed in 1894 when mail was transferred to Clayton; no trace of the community remains.

BANKS two villages in Foster Township. The first settlement located on the north end of East Rice Lake, in section 8, had a post office, a store, and a hotel in one building, a blacksmith shop, a church, a school, and several dwellings; only the church remained as of 1977. The second settlement, on the south end of the lake in section 17, was organized around a creamery, with a post office moving to a store there; no trace of the second settlement remains; the post office operated 1862–1904.

BARBER TOWNSHIP settled in June 1857, established September 27, 1858, and organized June 10, 1864, was named in honor of Chauncey Barber, whom the commissioners supposed to be a resident of this township. He came from Pennsylvania to Wisconsin, and in 1856 to this county, settling in Minnesota Lake Township, was its first hotel keeper, and platted its railway village on his lands in 1866. About 12 or 15 years later he removed to Oregon. See also **WESNER'S GROVE**.

BARODA a village in Clark Township, sections 13, 14, 23, and 24, which had a station of the Chicago, Milwaukee and St. Paul Railroad in section 13.

BASS LAKE a village in Delavan Township, section 9, established in 1859 on the east side of Bass Lake, for which it was named, in an oak grove often called " Camp Comfort"; settled primarily by Scottish immigrants. The village had a church, a school, and a post office, 1858–75.

BLAINE a village in section 1 of Rome Township, which had a blacksmith shop, a creamery, a general store, and a post office, 1895–1900.

BLUE EARTH TOWNSHIP first settled in May 1855, organized October 20, 1858, derived its name from its village, called Blue Earth, which had been platted in July 1856, and has ever since been the county seat. The village was named from the river, which the Dakota called Mahkahto, meaning green or blue earth, as more fully noticed in the chapter of Blue Earth County. The site was laid out by H. P. Carstans and J. B. Wakefield, was incorporated on May 19, 1857, became a village in 1879, and incorporated as a city on April 8, 1899; it had a station of the Chicago, St. Paul, Minneapolis and Omaha Railroad in section 17, and its post office began in 1856.

BRICELYN a city in Seely Township, sections 10 and 15, was named for John Brice, who owned and platted it. It was incorporated on July 15, 1903, and separated from the township on March 30, 1912; the post office began in 1899. The village

had a station of the Chicago and North Western Railway in section 10.

BRUSH CREEK TOWNSHIP settled in May 1856 and established September 27, 1858, received the name of its small creek, which joins the East Fork of Blue Earth River in section 26. The reason for the application of this name to the creek was "the thick growth of small trees, thickets and brush along its banks." The village of Brush Creek, sections 9 and 16, had a post office, 1873–82.

CLARK TOWNSHIP settled in June 1862, and organized September 7, 1869, had been named Cobb by the county commissioners in 1858 from their erroneous supposition that the Cobb River (of Blue Earth County) received a portion of its headwaters in this township. At its organization, in 1869, the name was changed to Thompson, in honor of Clark W. Thompson, "the largest land owner of the town and county." Because that name, however, was already in use for another township in Minnesota, it was renamed Clark, March 24, 1870, taking his first name. He was born near Jordan, Canada, July 23, 1825, and died at Wells, the railway village of this township, October 11, 1885. He came to Minnesota in 1853; engaged in milling in Houston County until 1861; was Indian agent, by appointment of President Lincoln, 1861–65; built the Southern Minnesota Railroad from the Mississippi River to Winnebago City, and afterward owned an extensive farm at Wells; was a representative in the territorial legislature, 1855; member of the state constitutional convention, 1857; a state senator, 1871; and president of the State Agricultural Society, 1880–85.

CLAYTON a village in Seely Township, section 4. The post office, 1860–99, began with David Pratt as postmaster and was locally called Prattsville. As the businesses diminished, buildings were moved to Bricelyn, and only the cemetery remained in 1977.

COLFAX a post office, 1861–65, of Winnebago Township, section 24; transferred to Center Creek Township in Martin County and renamed Center Creek.

CORNET a village in section 3 of Winnebago City Township; it had a mill, a blacksmith, and a post office, 1874–97. The village was better known locally as Woodland, and its bridge across the Blue Earth River is called the Woodland Bridge. Only stones at the mill's dam site remain.

DELAVAN settled in May 1856, organized October 20, 1858, was at first named Guthrie in honor of Sterrit Guthrie, one of the pioneer settlers. On May 1, 1872, the name was changed to Delavan to agree with that of the railway village, which had been platted October 11, 1870, in section 36. The proprietors of the village were Henry W. Holley, chief engineer of the Southern Minnesota Railroad, and Oren Delavan Brown, in whose honor the village name was suggested by Mrs. Holley. He was born in Jefferson County, N.Y., in 1837; came to Minnesota in 1856 with his father, Orville Brown, a prominent newspaper editor; was an engineer on the surveys for the Southern Minnesota Railroad, 1865–75, and later for the St. Paul and Sioux City Railroad; afterward resided in Luverne, Minn. The first passenger train arrived there December 19, 1870. The village was incorporated February 7, 1877, and separated from the township on May 9, 1917; the post office began as Delavan Station in 1870, shortening the name in 1885.

DELL a village in Emerald Township, section 23, with a post office, 1883–1904.

DUNBAR settled in 1856, organized April 3, 1866, was named Douglas by the county commissioners September 27, 1858, in honor of Stephen A. Douglas, for whom also Douglas County had been earlier named in the same year. But this name had been previously given to another Minnesota township, hence it was changed January 4, 1859, to be in honor of William Franklin Dunbar, then the state auditor. He was born in Westerly, R.I., November 10, 1820; and died in Caledonia, Minn. He came to Minnesota in 1854, settling in Caledonia, and opened a farm near that town; was a member of the territorial legislature, 1856; and was the first state auditor of Minnesota, 1858–60.

DUSTIN a farmers post office, 1893–96, 12 miles southeast of Blue Earth and 7 miles from Elmore, probably in Elmore Township.

EASTON a city in Lura Township, sections 35 and 36, platted in September 1873, incorporated March 9, 1874, and reincorporated on January 27, 1909, was named for Jason Clark Easton, one of the original proprietors. He was born in West Martinsburg, N.Y., May 12, 1823, and died in La Crosse, Wis., April 25, 1901. He came to Minnesota in 1856 and settled at Chatfield. There and in several other towns of southern Minnesota he

had extensive interests in banking, farmlands, and railways. He removed to La Crosse in 1883. The post office began in 1874.

EDEN a country post office, 1868–73, in Jo Daviess Township, five miles west of Blue Earth.

ELMORE first settled in November 1855 and organized in 1858, was then named Dobson in honor of James Dobson, who came from Indiana, settling here as a homesteader in April 1856. This name was changed to Elmore in 1862, commemorating Andrew E. Elmore, a prominent citizen of Wisconsin, who numbered among his friends several early settlers of this township. He was born in Ulster County, N.Y., May 8, 1814, and died at Fort Howard, Wis., January 13, 1906. He came to Wisconsin in 1839, settling in Mukwonago, Waukesha County, where he was a merchant during 25 years. In 1864 he removed to Green Bay, and after 1868 he resided at Fort Howard, near Green Bay. He was a member of the Wisconsin territorial legislature, 1842–44; of the first constitutional convention, 1846; the state legislature, 1859–60; and was during many years president of the state board of charities and reform. He was commonly called "the Sage of Mukwonago."

The city of Elmore, sections 32 and 33, was incorporated on November 24, 1891, and separated from the township on November 24, 1918. It had a station of the Chicago, St. Paul, Minneapolis and Omaha Railroad, and the post office was established in 1863.

EMERALD settled in 1856, organized April 3, 1866, was named by the county commissioners for Ireland, the "Emerald Isle," supposing erroneously that it had Irish settlers. A post office was located in the township in section 13, 1873–95 and 1897–1901.

EWALD a post office in section 30, Emerald Township, 1865–82, with Henry Ewald the first postmaster.

FOSTER settled in June 1856, organized September 24, 1864, was named in honor of Dr. Reuben R. Foster, one of the earliest settlers of the county. He was born in Jefferson County, N.Y., in 1808; came to Minnesota in 1856, settling in Walnut Grove Township; removed in 1858 to Blue Earth, and was its first resident physician; removed to Jackson, Minn., in 1869, and to St. Paul about 1880, where he died.

FOUNTAIN BROOK a post office, 1873–78, in section 6 of Lura Township.

FRANKLINTOWN see MINNESOTA LAKE.

FROST a city in Rome Township, sections 2 and 3, "was named for Charles S. Frost, an architect of Chicago" (Stennett, *Place Names of the Chicago and Northwestern Railways*, 1908). It was platted in 1899, incorporated as a village November 28, 1903, and again on July 6, 1916, separating from the township on February 24, 1914. The majority of early settlers came from Norway. The village had a station of the Minnesota and North Western Railway, and its post office began in 1899.

GRANT a post office in Pilot Grove Township, first called Long Lake, 1867–69, and discontinuing in 1876.

GRAPELAND a post office, 1857–94, of Lura Township, section 3, named by postmaster Ozias C. Healy for the wild grapes growing along the Maple River, which ran through his farm. The only other building was a blacksmith shop.

GUCKEEN a village in Jo Daviess Township, section 8, was first settled about 1900; it was named Derby, but the postal department refused the name as too close to other names, so it was named for Patrick Guckeen, on whose land the townsite was located. Its post office operated 1901–73, and it had a station of the Minnesota and North Western Railway.

HOMEDAHL a village in Seely Township, sections 29 and 30. The first settlers were the Osul Haaland family of Norway about 1860s; Rasmus O. Haaland requested a post office in his home, becoming first postmaster. The neighbors decided on the name, remembering a location in Norway. The post office operated 1877–1904; it had a station of the Chicago, Rock Island and Pacific Railroad.

HUNTLEY a railway village in Verona, section 7, first settled in 1875 and platted in August 1879 on land selected by Patrick Murphy, is named for Hon. Henry M. Huntington, a pioneer farmer. He was born in Yates County, N.Y., in 1835; came to Minnesota in 1857, settling in this township; served in the Sixth Minnesota Regiment during the Civil War; was a representative in the legislature in 1872; removed to his old home in New York in 1879, but returned in 1892, and afterward resided in Winnebago City. Because the name Huntington was previously in use in Minnesota, this shorter form was adopted. The post office opened in 1879.

JERUSALEM a site in the area of Winnebago City Township before the county was established.

JO DAVIESS TOWNSHIP (pronounced as Davis), settled in 1855, organized January 26, 1864, was named Johnson in 1858 by the county commissioners in honor of James and Alexander Johnson, who were early settlers of the county. It was found, however, that this name had been before given to another Minnesota township, and it was accordingly changed, the present name being adopted January 4, 1859, on the suggestion of James L. McCrery, one of the commissioners and the first settler in this township, a native of Kentucky. It is the name of the most northwestern county of Illinois, and Kentucky, Indiana, and Missouri have each a county named Daviess. It commemorates Joseph Hamilton Daviess, a brave soldier and an able lawyer and orator, who "in the early days of Kentucky ranked with her most gifted and honored names." He was born in Bedford County, Va., March 4, 1774, and was killed in the battle of Tippecanoe, November 7, 1811.

KIESTER TOWNSHIP settled in May 1866, organized in January 1872, was named Lake by the county commissioners in 1858 from their supposition that it had a number of lakes. Because another Minnesota township had previously received this name, it was changed January 4, 1859, in honor of Jacob Armel Kiester, who later became the historian of this county. He was born at Mount Pleasant, Pa., April 29, 1832, and died in Blue Earth, December 13, 1904. He was a student in Mt. Pleasant and Dickinson Colleges, Pa.; studied law, and was admitted to practice, 1855; came to Minnesota in 1857, settling in Blue Earth, which ever afterward was his home; was a representative in the legislature in 1865, and during many years was an officer of this county, being successively county surveyor, register of deeds, county attorney, and from 1869 to 1890 was judge of probate; was a state senator, 1891–93. He collected materials during more than 20 years for *The History of Faribault County*, before mentioned as the source of much information for this chapter; and he also wrote a continuation of that work, from 1880 to 1904 inclusive, of which typewritten copies (717 pp.) are in the library, Blue Earth, and the library of the Minnesota Historical Society,

St. Paul. The city of Kiester, sections 21 and 22, was platted in 1899 and incorporated as a village on November 19, 1900. It had a station of the Minnesota and North Western Railway and a post office from 1882.

LONG LAKE see **GRANT**.

LURA settled in May 1856, organized September 7, 1864, derived its name from Lake Lura, crossed by the north line of the county about a mile west from the northwest corner of this township. Its name is said to have been given "by one of the early settlers, from the name 'Lura' being carved on a tree upon its shore." In the chapter of Blue Earth County, its Dakota names are also noted. A post office was located in the township, 1858–61 and 1874.

MARENGO a planned village of Walnut Lake Township, incorporated on May 23, 1857, which was never developed.

MARNA a village in Emerald Township, section 30, which had a station of the Chicago and Northwestern Railway, whose railroad officials chose the name, a corruption of Marne, the French province and river. A post office operated 1901–11.

MINNESOTA LAKE TOWNSHIP settled in 1856, was organized in 1858, and was then named Marples by the commissioners in honor of Charles Marples, an early settler. He was an Englishman and had served seven years in the British army. After long residence here, he removed to Missouri. This township name was changed February 23, 1866, to Minnesota Lake for the former large lake, which has been drained and apportioned to the adjoining farms. It is a name received from the Dakota, meaning slightly whitish water, which they also applied to the Minnesota River, thence adopted by this state.

The city of Minnesota Lake, which extends into Danville Township, Blue Earth County, was platted in October 1866 and was incorporated February 14, 1876; it separated from the townships on August 6, 1911. The post office was first called Franklintown and operated in Blue Earth County beginning in 1857; it changed to Minnesota Lake in 1858. The village had a station of the Chicago, Milwaukee, St. Paul and Pacific Railroad.

OLESON a post office, 1896–1901, located in the same area as Brush Creek post office, Brush Creek Township, with Harvey L. Oleson as postmaster in his general store.

PILOT GROVE TOWNSHIP first settled in June 1856, organized in January 1864, "was so named because of the fine grove of native timber on the northern boundary of the town; and this grove was named Pilot Grove because in the early days, before roads were established, this grove was a sort of landmark, on the wide prairies, by which the immigrant was piloted on his way westward. It may be added, too, that this grove, with its fine lake of sparkling waters and rich grasses surrounding it, was, in the days of immigrants, a sort of capacious inn, or caravansary, or camping ground" (Kiester, *The History of Faribault County*). Pilot Grove Lake has been wholly drained away.

A post office was located in the township, 1866–1907; the site was never platted, although a store and lumberyard were built.

PRESCOTT settled in September 1855, organized September 16, 1861, received its name in 1858 for a settler who soon afterward moved away. "All that has been ascertained of him is, that he was a carpenter by trade, and that he was known by the name of 'Old Honesty.' " A post office operated there, 1863–68.

ROME TOWNSHIP settled in March 1863, organized in 1868, was named Campbell by the commissioners in 1858 for James Campbell, one of the first settlers in Elmore Township. At its organization, it was renamed Grant in honor of Gen. Ulysses S. Grant, who later in that year was elected president of the United States. This name, however, had been earlier given to another Minnesota township, wherefore it was again changed in March 1868, the present name being adopted for the city of Rome, N.Y., on the suggestion of Fred Everton, the second settler in this township, who during many years was chairman of its board of supervisors.

SEELY settled in June 1856, organized in 1858, commemorates Philander C. Seely, one of its earliest settlers. He was born in Cayuga County, N.Y., in 1823; came to Minnesota and to this county in 1857; was elected sheriff in 1861, receiving every vote polled; served in the Civil War; resided several years in this township and later in Blue Earth. A post office operated in the township, 1882–1900, first located in a store on postmaster John Reed's farm about two miles south of Bricelyn; a school was the only other building, and it was later moved to Bricelyn.

SHERIDAN a village begun when Andrew Elvebak built a general store on the Seely-Kiester Township line; the post office was located on postmaster Rasmus Havnen's farm, 1894–1900.

SWAN LAKE see **WESNER'S GROVE**.

VERONA settled in June 1855, organized in October 1858, was named after its post office, established in 1856 at the home of Henry T. Stoddard, with Newell Dewey as postmaster, in the southeast quarter of section 11, the name having been proposed by A. B. Cornell of Owatonna for this terminus of the mail route. It is the name of an important province in northern Italy and of its chief city, whence came the title of the Shakespeare drama "Two Gentlemen of Verona." Seventeen other states of our Union have villages or townships of this name. The post office, which operated until 1865, later moved above Henry Maxson's blacksmith shop until rural delivery came from Winnebago.

WALNUT LAKE TOWNSHIP settled in June 1856, organized in 1861, bears the name of its large lake, referring to its butternut trees, also called oil-nut and white walnut. It is translated from the Dakota name Tazuka. The village of Walnut Lake, section 27, on the northwest side of Walnut Lake, flourished with hotels, a post office, a school, several stores, dwellings, and a blacksmith shop. Its first post office operated 1860–69, when it was transferred to Wells; a second post office operated 1870–82. The village was a popular stage stop for persons hunting lands to the west.

WALTERS a city of Foster Township, section 26, was built on land owned by Thomas H. Brown, who filed a plat on August 15, 1900, and was incorporated as a village on August 18, 1903. The first business was a general store; the post office began in 1901. The name was chosen by officials of the Burlington, Cedar Rapids and Northern Railway.

WELLS a city in Clark Township, sections 4, 5, 8, and 9, was founded and named July 1, 1869, receiving the maiden surname of Mrs. Clark W. Thompson. The Southern Minnesota Railroad was completed to this place in January 1870 and the railroad from Mankato to Wells in 1874. This village was incorporated March 6, 1871. Within the next few years numerous flowing wells, 20 or more, were obtained in and near this village by boring through the glacial drift to depths of 110 to 120 feet, securing excellent water, which rises from the bottom to a height of 5 to 15 feet above the surface. These are the most remarkable wells of a large region in southern Minnesota, but the presence of artesian water here was unknown when the village was named. Clark W. Thompson built the first mill, a creamery, a cheese factory, a barrel factory, and a vinegar factory; donated a park site; and paid for a railroad to be built from La Crosse, Wis., the station later serving several lines. The post office was named Walnut Lake, 1860–69, and Well, 1869–72, at which time it was changed to Wells.

WESNER'S GROVE a village in Barber Township, which had a store, a post office called Swan Lake, 1864–66, and Barber, 1866–78, a Catholic church with a parsonage, a cemetery, and a number of houses. The site is named for Andrew Wesner, who operated an inn and stage stop, having come from Switzerland to Minnesota in 1856. The settlement disappeared after Easton was developed on the railroad three miles away.

WINNEBAGO TOWNSHIP settled in June 1855, organized in October 1858, was then named Winnebago City after the village of this name that was founded here by Andrew C. Dunn and others in September 1856. The townsite, in Winnebago City and Verona Townships, was platted in January 1857 and incorporated on February 19, 1857, being named for the Winnebago Indians, whose reservation during the years 1855 to 1863 was in the adjoining Blue Earth County. It was named "City" for discrimination from the Winnebago Agency near Mankato, but this part of the name was discontinued in 1905. The town became a village on March 8, 1873, was reincorporated on July 8, 1907, and was separated from the townships on May 17, 1918. The post office was first called Winnebago City, 1857–1905, when it was changed to the present name. The village had a station of the Chicago, St. Paul, Minneapolis and Omaha Railroad.

Lakes and Streams

In the preceding list, sufficient mention has been made for the Blue Earth River, Brush Creek, Cobb River (flowing through the northeast corner of this county), Lura Lake, Minnesota Lake, and Pilot Grove and Walnut Lakes.

Maple River, named for the maple trees along its course, flowing northward into Blue Earth County, gave the name there of Mapleton Township and village. Rice Lake in Delavan, near the head of the west branch of this river, was named Maple Lake on the state map of 1860. Its present name refers to its wild rice, like another Rice Lake in Foster.

Bass Lake in section 9, Delavan, was named for the well-known fish.

Hart Lake in section 28, Delavan, commemorates John and George Hart, who were pioneer farmers there.

Gorman's Lake, now drained, in section 17, Jo Daviess, was named in honor of Patrick Gorman, an early Irish settler beside it.

Goose and Swan Lakes were in sections 11 and 14, Brush Creek Township, but have been drained. Another Swan Lake, in section 15, Barber, was called Lake Kanta in 1860, a Dakota name, meaning Plum Lake, for its wild plum trees.

The two largest lakes of this county, Minnesota Lake, before noticed, and Ozahtanka Lake in Barber and Emerald Townships, have been drained, their beds being now cultivated farmlands. Both these names are on the map of 1860, each being the Dakota language. *Tanka*, like *tonka*, means "great," but *Ozah* is not defined in Stephen R. Riggs's *Dictionary*.

The former Mud Lake in section 23, Lura, is now traversed by a ditch and drained.

Jones Creek in Foster commemorates a settler or a trapper.

Coon Creek, tributary to the Blue Earth River from the east, and Badger Creek from the west, are named for furbearers, the first formerly common here but the latter rare in Minnesota, though common in parts of Wisconsin, giving its name as the sobriquet of that state.

Elm, Center, and South Creeks in Verona, flowing to the Blue Earth River from Martin County, are to be noticed in the chapter for that county.

The Kiester Moraine and Glacial Lake Minnesota

The fourth in the series of 12 terminal and marginal moraines formed in Minnesota by the continental ice sheet during its wavering departure, at the close of the glacial period, is called the Kiester Moraine from its prominent Kiester Hills in the township of this name. These marginal drift hills and the continuation of their morainic belt northwesterly in this county and onward through the state, probably passing into South Dakota in the vicinity of Big Stone Lake, were noted in vol. 1 of the Final Reports of the Minnesota Geological Survey, published in 1884.

At the time of formation of the Kiester Moraine, the Glacial Lake Minnesota, described in the chapter of Blue Earth County, overspread the greater part of Faribault County, reaching thence northwestward along its ice border, and outflowing south by the Union Slough in Iowa, at the head of the Blue Earth River, being thence tributary to the Des Moines River.

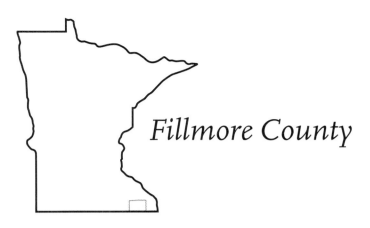

Fillmore County

This county, established March 5, 1853, was named for Millard Fillmore, who was president of the United States, 1850 to 1853, retiring from office on the day previous to the approval of the act creating this county. He was born at Summer Hill, Cayuga County, N.Y., February 7, 1800, and died at Buffalo, N.Y., March 8, 1874. He studied law and was admitted to practice in 1823; was a member of Congress, 1833–35 and 1837–43; was comptroller of the state of New York, 1847–49; was elected vice president on the Whig ticket headed by Zachary Taylor, 1848; and succeeded to the presidency by the death of Taylor, July 9, 1850.

Fillmore visited St. Paul in a large excursion of eastern people, June 8, 1854, as noted in the MHS Collections (8: 395–400).

Biographies of Fillmore were published in 1856, when he was nominated as presidential candidate of the American Party; and in 1915 Rev. William Elliot Griffis published a memorial review of his life and character (159 pp.), titled *Millard Fillmore, Constructive Statesman, Defender of the Constitution, President of the United States*. He is also commemorated by Fillmore County in Nebraska, by Millard County in Utah, and by villages named Fillmore in a dozen states.

Information of these names has been gathered from History of Fillmore County, *by Ellis C. Turner and others (1882, 626 pp.); the later history of this county, compiled by Franklyn Curtiss-Wedge (1912, 2 vols., continuously paged, 1,170 pp.); and from Archibald D. Gray and Andrew W. Thompson of Preston, and Calvin E. Huntley of Spring Valley, interviewed in April 1916.*

ALBA a farming community of Beaver Township, section 21, which flourished about 1855–1904, and had a post office, 1858–85. It was called Alba, meaning white, because the name was "short, eastern, and ancient."

ALXBRIDGE a village in Bristol Township, section 32, named in honor of England, New England, and other places where this kind of "bridge" ex-

ists. The village had a post office in 1855, which moved to Granger in 1857.

AMHERST settled in 1853, organized May 11, 1858, was named by one of its pioneer colonists, E. P. Eddy, "in honor of the place in which his wife was born." This was Amherst in Lorain County, Ohio, where her father, Henry Onstine, leader of these colonists, formerly lived. The settlers of the Ohio township came from New England, where towns of New Hampshire and Massachusetts had been named Amherst in honor of Gen. Jeffery Amherst, the English commander and hero of the siege and capture of Louisburg from the French in 1758. The village of Amherst, in section 27, was first called Strung Out Town because settlers built houses along the road in the ravine, later shortened to Stringtown; the post office operated 1870–1902.

ARENDAHL first settled in 1854, organized April 1, 1860, was named by Isaac Jackson, a Norwegian immigrant, who had lived 12 years in Dane County, Wis., and came to this township in 1856, the name being for the seaport city of Arendal on the southeast coast of Norway. "He named the town in remembrance of old associations, secured a post office, and was the first postmaster." The farming community of Arendahl, section 9, developed from 1854 to 1926 and had a post office, 1860–1905.

BEAR CREEK see IDAY.

BEAVER settled in 1854, organized May 11, 1858, received its name from the Beaver Creek (doubtless a home of beavers), which flows through this township, joining the Upper Iowa River in section 34.

BELDENA a locality in Spring Valley Township, section 9, which was surveyed and platted by its owner, Dr. W. P. Belden, but not recorded and not developed.

BELLVILLE a former village in Newburg Township, was founded in 1853 by two brothers, Edmund and Henry Bell. See also MABEL.

BERGEN a post office, 1858–65; location not found.

BIG SPRING a land speculation settlement in Harmony Township, section 6, first settled by James P. Tebbetts, who had the land platted and recorded as Big Springs. The village did not grow, but it had a post office, 1855–80.

BLOOMFIELD first settled in 1854, was organized May 11, 1858. Eighteen other states have villages or cities of this "spring reminding name."

BOOMER see CANTON.

BRATSBERG a hamlet in the southeast corner of section 10, Norway, bears the name of a district in southern Norway, comprising an area of about 5,500 square miles. The farming community in section 11 began about 1859. Its first post office, 1862, was in Ole Johnson's shanty one-half mile north of the hamlet, later moving to the Bratsberg Store, with Ole Hendrickson as postmaster; the post office changed to a rural branch in 1907, closing in 1909.

BRISTOL settled in July 1853, organized May 11, 1858, has the name of a large city in England, near the head of the Bristol Channel. It is also the name of counties in Massachusetts and Rhode Island and of villages and townships in 20 other states of our Union. It had a post office, 1872–1904, in section 16.

BRISTOL CENTRE a post office, 1861–67, formerly known as Vailville, 1857–61, located in Bristol Township, section 8.

CANFIELD a hamlet on the east line of section 21, York, was named for Sylvester B. Canfield, who established a store there in 1876. See also YORK.

CANTON first settled in March 1851, was organized May 11, 1858. "There was a spirited contest over the name, and quite a number were suggested, but the struggle was finally narrowed down to two names, 'Elyria,' suggested by E. P. Eddy, and that of 'Canton,' proposed by Fred Flor. The vote declared, in favor of Canton, but the Elyria party gave up reluctantly. . . . On the records up to 1860, the name Elyria is carried along in the town books, when it dropped out of sight." These are names of cities in northeastern Ohio, near the former homes of many settlers in this township. Canton is a large and very ancient city of southeastern China, and thence 23 states of our Union have given this name to villages, cities, and townships. The city of Canton was platted in 1879 and incorporated as a village on May 9, 1887; the post office was called Boomer, 1879–82, for its "booming" existence as suggested by John Manuel, the first postmaster, changing to Canton in 1882, with James Manuel as postmaster.

CARIMONA first settled in 1852, organized May 11, 1858, has the village of this name, in section 4, founded in 1853–54, which was the county seat in 1855–56, being succeeded by Preston. Its post office operated as Warpeton in 1854 and 1855, changing to Carimona in 1855 and closing in 1902. This village was an important stop on the stage line between Winona and Chatfield, and during several years it was a busy station of the stage route from Galena and Dubuque to St. Paul, as shown by the hotel register of the Carimona House, 1855–59, presented to the library of the Minnesota Historical Society. This was the name of a prominent leader of the Winnebago, who signed by his mark seven successive treaties of the United States, in 1816, 1825, 1827, 1828, 1829, 1832, and 1837. His name, borne also by his son, had a variety of spellings and is translated as "Walking Turtle." Dr. L. C. Draper wrote of him: "Naw-Kaw, or Car-a-mau-nee, or The Walking Turtle, went on a mission with Tecumseh in 1809 to the New York Indians, and served with that chief during the campaign of 1813, and was present at his death at the Thames." (See Wisconsin Historical Society Collections, vols. 2, 3, 5, 7, and 8; MHS Collections, vol. 4, J. Fletcher Williams's *History of St. Paul*, p. 256; and "Waubun, the 'Early Day' in the North-West," by Mrs. John H. Kinzie, 1856, p. 89.)

At a grand council held by Gov. Alexander Ramsey in St. Paul, March 14, 1850, with Winnebago leaders who had come from their reservation at Long Prairie, Carimona was one of the seven chiefs whose names are given by Williams. This man, doubtless a son of the older Carimona, removed from Wisconsin to Iowa, later to Minnesota, and died, after 1850, on the Yellow River in Allamakee County, Iowa. For him this village and township were named.

CARROLTON settled in the spring of 1854, organized May 11, 1858, received its name in honor of Charles Carrol of Carrolton in Maryland, the last survivor of the signers of the Declaration of Independence. He was born in Annapolis, Md., September 20, 1737, and died in Baltimore, November 14, 1832. A country post office was located in the township, 1867–70.

CHATFIELD TOWNSHIP settled in 1853, organized in 1858, was named in honor of Judge Andrew Gould Chatfield, who presided at the first court held at Winona, June 27, 1853. He was born in Butternuts, Otsego County, N.Y., January 27, 1810, and died in Belle Plaine, Minn., October 3, 1875. He was an associate justice of the supreme court of Minnesota Territory, 1853–57; was one of the founders of the town of Belle Plaine and practiced law there, 1857–71; was judge of the Eighth judicial district, 1871–75. The village of Chatfield, platted in the spring of 1854 and incorporated in 1857, was the first county seat for two years but was succeeded in 1855 by Carimona and by Preston since 1856. This village was incorporated as a city by the legislature, February 19, 1887. Its post office began in 1854.

CHERRY GROVE a village in Forestville Township, whose post office opened in 1857, moved to York Township, section 4, in 1869, and returned to section 33 of Forestville Township in February 1882. The village is the site of the Cherry Grove Garage, built by Bernard Pietenpol, widely acclaimed for his airplane designs, particularly one called the

Air Camper. He was born in Vermont in 1814, came to Minnesota in 1855, and died in 1893. The garage is on the National Register of Historic Places.

CHICKENTOWN a scenic valley in the hills of Preble Township named for the chickens found at every home. The last landmark, a log cabin, was torn down in 1973.

CHOICE a settlement located in a valley of the South Fork of Root River, Preble Township, section 3. The first store was built by Melgard and Lucason and sold to Sven Thompson in 1886, the latter becoming first postmaster; the post office operated 1887–1905.

CLEAR GRIT a former hamlet on the South Fork of Root River, in section 21, Carrolton, took the name given by John Kaercher to a flouring mill operated there by him with much success, 1872–81, retrieving ill fortune and losses that he had experienced through panics, fire, and flood from 1857 onward in Preston, Chatfield, Fillmore, and so on (MHS Collections 10: 42). The village had a post office, 1878–82.

DEER CREEK a post office, 1856–65, in Spring Valley Township, section 17.

DONALD SWITCH a station of the Chicago, Milwaukee, St. Paul and Pacific Railroad in Newburg Township, section 31.

ELKHORN see HAMILTON.

ELLIOTA a former village in section 32, Canton, was laid out in 1853 by Capt. Julius W. Elliott, its earliest settler and first postmaster and blacksmith. He was born in Vermont in 1822 and came to this county from Moline, Illinois, in 1853, bringing thence a company of the first settlers. In 1871 he removed to Missouri, where he died in 1876. The post office operated 1854–82.

ETNA a hamlet in section 25, Bloomfield, was platted as Tefton but received its name, from several that were suggested, by drawing lots when its post office, 1856–1901, called Etna, was established. This name of the lofty volcano in Sicily is borne by villages and post offices in 16 other states. The village also had a mill, a general store, a blacksmith shop, and a church, and was the site of iron ore mining development by Evergreen Mining Company, which in 1942 and 1943 produced 250,000 tons of low-grade ore.

ETTAVILLE a post office, 1858–69, of Beaver Township, section 36.

FAIRVIEW a post office, 1856–70, in Forestville Township, section 6.

FARMERS GROVE a post office, 1857–63 and 1865–71, in the north-central part of the county, four miles north of Isinours, probably in Carrolton.

FILLMORE TOWNSHIP settled in August 1854, organized May 11, 1858, was named, like the county, in honor of President Fillmore, taking this name from its village in section 3, which had been founded in 1853. It was platted in 1854 by Paul Jones and had a post office, 1855–1905.

FORESTVILLE TOWNSHIP first settled in 1852 and organized in 1855, received its name in honor of Forest Henry, the first probate judge of the county, who settled here in 1854 and in the next year was the first postmaster here. He was also one of the proprietors of the village of Forestville, section 13, platted in 1854 by Henry, R. M. Foster, and William Winslow in 1854 and incorporated in 1891. The post office operated 1855–1902.

FOUNTAIN settled in 1853, organized May 11, 1858, was named for its large "Fountain Spring" in section 4, whence the railway village of Fountain, platted when the railway was built, in 1870, derives its water supply. The village was incorporated, by an act of the legislature, on March 3, 1876. It had a station of the Chicago, Milwaukee, St. Paul and Pacific Railroad in section 10 and a post office from 1870.

FREE SOIL PRAIRIE SEE WYKOFF.

GRANGER a village in the south edge of Bristol, section 34, was platted in 1857 by C. H. Lewis and Brownell Granger of Boston, Mass., who also built a mill and opened its first store, where Granger was first postmaster. The post office was formerly at Arnoldsville, Iowa, moving to the Minnesota in 1857.

GREENFIELD a village in Harmony Township, section 23, first settled by Knud Peterson in 1856; for a time it thrived, but no trace remains.

GREENLEAFTON a little hamlet in section 1, York, "was named in honor of Miss Mary Greenleaf, of Philadelphia, who generously gave three thousand five hundred dollars to build the Dutch Reformed Church edifice." A post office operated there 1874–1905.

HAMILTON a small village in section 6 of Spring Valley Township and section 31 of Sumner, was platted in 1855 and named by early settlers from Hamilton, Ontario, Canada. A number of businesses developed until 1890, when the railroad went through Racine instead of Hamilton, causing the village to diminish. Its post office operated as Elkhorn, 1855–63, changing to Hamilton and closing in 1904. Ten states have Hamilton counties, and 26 states have townships, villages, or cities of this name, mostly in honor of Alexander Hamilton, patriot in the American Revolution and first secretary of the treasury of the United States, 1789–95.

HARMONY TOWNSHIP settled in the fall of 1852, was organized, May 11, 1858. This name is borne by villages and townships in 15 states of our Union. The city of Harmony was founded in 1880, incorporated on January 8, 1896, and reincorporated on March 19, 1908. The post office was first at Peterson and then transferred to Harmony in 1862 as Windom for Senator William Windom; the name changed to Harmony in 1865.

HAZEL PRAIRIE a post office, 1860–66; location not found.

HEALY a post office circa 1900, in Carimona Township.

HENRYTOWN a hamlet in Amherst, section 32, was platted in 1854 on Michael H. Onstine's farm, who named the townsite for his father, Henry Onstine, who was the leader in the settlement of that township, as before noted. The first post office, 1854–67, was named Richland and was located in the home of C. C. Onstine, with Elijah Austin as postmaster; the Henrytown post office operated 1883–84 and 1891–1902.

HIGHLAND a hamlet in sections 35 and 36, Holt, received the name of its former post office, referring to its elevation, which gives broad views over the valleys on the north and south. Early settlers were Norman A. Graves and Andrew Shattuck, who encouraged development of the community. The post office operated 1857–1902, with Graves as first postmaster in his farm home.

HOLT settled in the spring of 1854, organized May 11, 1858, was at first called Douglas in honor of the statesman Stephen A. Douglas, for whom a county of this state is named. Because that name had been applied to another Minnesota township, it was changed to Holt in 1862, honoring Gilbert Holt, a pioneer farmer in section 30, who "early in the seventies" removed to Dakota.

HURDAL a small village southwest of Ostrander

in Bloomfield Township; its first post office, 1880–91, was moved to Ostrander; a second post office operated 1892–99.

HUTTON a post office, 1892–1905, located in Preston Township, section 21, which had a station of the Chicago, Milwaukee and St. Paul Railroad.

IDAY a post office known as Bear Creek, 1861–64, and Iday, 1864–65, located in Jordan Township, section 16; named for its postmaster I. Day.

ISINOURS a village in Carrolton, section 20, established about 1870, was named, with a change of spelling, for George Isenhour, on whose land it was located. It had a station of the Chicago, Milwaukee, St. Paul and Pacific Railroad and a school; the tracks were removed to create part of the Root River Recreational Trail. The post office was called Preston Station, 1871–72, and closed in 1904.

JORDAN TOWNSHIP settled in 1853, organized May 11, 1858, was named for its North and South Jordan Creeks, which unite and flow into the Middle Branch of Root River. The name was given to these small streams by John Maine, one of the first settlers, who came from New England, fancifully deriving it from the River Jordan in Palestine. A post office operated in section 29, 1855–58.

KEDRON a post office, 1867–75, located in Sumner Township, section 16. The name was changed briefly to Summer Centre, and renamed Kedron, 1876–79.

LANESBORO a city in Carrolton and Holt, was platted in the spring of 1868, incorporated as a village on March 3, 1869, and reincorporated on May 4, 1907. Some of its early settlers came from Lanesboro Township in Berkshire County, Mass., and F. A. Lane was one of the stockholders in the townsite company. The post office was spelled Lanesborough, 1868–83, when it changed to the present form. The city is the site of the trailhead for the 35-mile-long Root River Recreational Trail.

LENORA a village in sections 2 and 11, Canton, was founded in 1855 by Rev. John L. Dyer. It was named by him for one of his family or for a friend. The first post office in 1856 was at Elijah Austin's home, who earlier was the postmaster of Richland, with Charles B. Milford, postmaster; later the post office was in the general store until discontinued in 1905.

LIBERTY a township platted in Spring Valley Township, section 24, by Henry Kibler on his farm, but no village developed.

LIME CITY a village in Spring Valley Township, section 4, named for the lime burned there; it had a sawmill as early as 1854.

LOOKING GLASS a post office, 1856–65, in Canton Township.

MABEL a railway village in Newburg, was platted by Frank Adams, chief engineer of this railway, giving it the name of his little daughter who had died. It was incorporated as a village in 1893; the post office was first called Bellville, 1855–80, with Wilson Bell as postmaster.

NEWBURG first settled in 1851, was organized May 11, 1858, taking the name of its village in section 8, which had been founded and named in 1853 by Hans Valder, a native of Norway, who with others came to this place from LaSalle County, Ill. Eighteen states of our Union have villages and post offices of this name. A post office was located in section 8, 1855–1902, with a station of the Chicago, Milwaukee, St. Paul and Pacific Railroad.

NORWAY settled in 1854, was organized April 3, 1860. "The name of the town is said to have been suggested by John Semmen, in honor of the native country of almost every inhabitant of the township."

ODESSA a post office, 1856–66, located in the south-central part of the county, 11 miles south of Preston, probably in Harmony Township.

OSTRANDER a city in Bloomfield, platted in 1890, was named for William and Charles Ostrander, who gave to the railway company parts of the village site. William Ostrander was born in the state of New York in 1819 and came to Minnesota in 1857, settling here as a farmer. The post office moved there from Hurdal in 1891. The city was incorporated as a village in 1918. It had a station of the Chicago Great Western Railroad and was the site of a low-grade iron mining operation during World War II and several years following.

PEKIN see PILOT MOUND.

PETERSON a city in Rushford Township, sections 19, 29 and 30, was founded in 1867, when the railway was built, on land donated for this use by Peter Peterson Haslerud, who settled here in July 1853. It was incorporated in April 20, 1909. He was born in Norway, July 21, 1828; came to the United States in 1843; was a representative in the legislature, 1862; died September 23, 1880. The first post office, 1855–62, with Knud Peterson, postmaster, transferred to Windom; the current post office began in 1870. The city had a station of the Chicago, Milwaukee, St. Paul and Pacific Railroad.

PILOT MOUND TOWNSHIP settled in 1854, organized May 11, 1858, is named for a flat-topped limestone hill in the southwest part of section 11. "It forms a prominent and striking object in the landscape, and formerly guided many a weary traveler as he wended his way toward the West." The village in section 10 had a post office, 1856–1905; the community was also known as Pekin.

PRAIRIE QUEEN a country post office, 1890–1902, in Bristol Township, section 4, ten miles southwest of Preston.

PREBLE settled in 1853–54, organized May 11, 1858, was named in honor of Edward Preble (1761–1807), of the United States Navy, commander of the expedition against Morocco and Tripoli in 1803–4. A post office operated 1876–1905 in section 24.

PRESTON STATION see ISINOURS.

PRESTON TOWNSHIP first settled in 1853, organized May 11, 1858, received the name that had been given to its village, platted in the spring of 1855, by John Kaercher, its founder and mill owner, "in honor of his millwright, Luther Preston." In 1856 a post office bearing this name was established, and Preston was appointed the first postmaster. Preston was convicted of theft in 1859. This village, situated at the center of the county, at the corner of Carimona, Fountain, Preston, and Carrolton Townships, has been the county seat since 1856. It was incorporated March 4, 1871, and separated from the townships on May 12, 1911. It had a station of the Chicago, Milwaukee, St. Paul and Pacific Railroad.

PROSPER a village in Canton Township, section 36, had a post office beginning in 1866, receiving its name from Eli B. Clark, who was postmaster in his home; as the village lies on the Iowa-Minnesota border, the post office moved 11 times between the two states, depending on the postmaster appointed.

RICHLAND a country post office, 1854–67, in Canton Township, section 11, begun at the home of Elijah Austin until the family moved to Lenora.

RUD a post office, 1894–1902, located in section 6 of Norway Township.

RUSHFORD settled in July 1853, organized May 11, 1858, was named on Christmas Day, 1854, by unanimous vote of the pioneer settlers, taking the name from Rush Creek here tributary to the Root River. The men and women so voting numbered nine, these being all the settlers at that date. "Rush creek was so called on account of the tall rushes that grew along its banks, where cattle and ponies could obtain a subsistence all winter." The city of Rushford, sections 11–14, founded in 1854, was named at the same time with the township. It was incorporated as a city on March 3, 1868, and often was called "the Trail City, on account of the intersection of several Indian foot paths." It has had a post office since 1856 and had a station of the Chicago, Milwaukee, St. Paul and Pacific Railroad.

SCOTLAND a post office of sections 27 and 34 of Preston Township, 1874–86, with a church and a school. The first postmaster was Duncan Stuart, and later blacksmith and machinist W. B. Mitchell was postmaster.

SOLAND a post office in Amherst Township, section 8, 1890–1902, located in postmaster Gilbert T. Soland's general store.

SPRING VALLEY TOWNSHIP settled in 1852, organized May 11, 1858, was named for its several very large springs, one being about a mile east of the village and two nearly as large within the townsite limits, one of these being walled up and used as a pumping supply for the waterworks. The township was the site of low-grade iron ore mining, 1942–67, by Hanna Mining Company. The city of Spring Valley was founded in 1855, incorporated on February 29, 1872, and reincorporated on April 28, 1919, when it separated from the township; its post office began in 1855.

STRINGTOWN village, begun in 1860, in section 27, Amherst, has its name "from the fact that all the settlers built their houses along the road in the ravine in which the would be village is located, thus stringing it out for some distance." See also AMHERST.

SUMMER CENTRE see KEDRON.

SUMNER settled in May 1853, organized May 11, 1858, was named by the earliest settlers in honor of the statesman Charles Sumner (1811–74), U.S. senator for Massachusetts from 1851 till his death, an uncompromising opponent of slavery, and during and after the Civil War chairman of the Senate committee on foreign affairs, 1861–71.

SYFORD'S a village in Canton Township; the

Dubuque and St. Paul stage line passed through there stopping at Mr. Syford's hotel.

TAWNEY a village in Preble Township, section 28, named for Senator James A. Tawney of Winona, who was traveling by as Tollef Halvorson was building his general store in 1894. The post office operated 1898–1905.

TEFTON see ETNA.

TRAIL CITY see RUSHFORD.

TRIBENS a post office, 1855–56, with William K. Triben, postmaster; location not found.

UXBRIDGE a post office, 1855–57; location not found.

VAILVILLE see BRISTOL CENTRE.

VOGEN a village in Rushford Township with a post office, 1892–95.

WARPETON see CARIMONA.

WASHINGTON a country post office, 1856–1903, of Sumner Township, section 36, which began in postmaster James H. Tedman's home, later moving to the general store, with Mrs. P. J. Palmer as postmaster until it closed.

WATSON CREEK a village located nine miles west of Preston and three miles from Wykoff, possibly in Forestville Township. It had a Baptist church, a private school, and a hotel; its post office operated 1865–89.

WAUKOKEE a former hamlet in section 25, Carimona, founded in 1853, derived its name "from an Indian chief, who used to have a fishing and hunting camp at this place." It had a post office, 1854–72.

WEST CHATFIELD a village in Chatfield Township, platted in 1856 by a Mr. Crittenden; it had a sorghum mill.

WHALAN a city in Holt, sections 8, 9, and 16, founded in 1868, is on land previously owned by John Whaalahan, "but usage dropped the redundant a's and an h, and it became Whalan." It was incorporated on February 17, 1876; the post office began in 1869.

WILTON CENTRE a country post office of Harmony Township, 1877–81, with Thomas Thomson postmaster in his general store.

WINDOM see HARMONY.

WYKOFF a city in Fillmore Township, sections 21, 22, 27, and 28, platted in 1871 and incorporated March 8, 1876, commemorates Cyrus G. Wykoff of La Crosse, Wis., who was the surveyor for construction of this railway and was one of the pro-prietors of this townsite. Its post office began in 1858 as Free Soil Prairie, changing to Wykoff in 1871.

YORK settled in 1854, organized May 11, 1858, bears the name of an ancient walled city in England, which was one of the principal seats of Roman dominion there. Thence came the name of the city and state of New York, and numerous villages, cities, and counties in 17 states of the Union are named York, this being the Saxon form derived from Eboracum, the Latin name. The village of York, section 22, had a post office, which began as Canfield in 1857 with Sylvester B. Canfield as first postmaster; it changed to York in 1883 and closed in 1903.

———————————

Rivers and Creeks

A large area of southeastern Minnesota, comprising Fillmore County, also Houston County on the east, Winona and Olmsted Counties on the north, Wabasha and Goodhue Counties, farther north, and Mower County on the west, has no lakes, being strongly contrasted with the abundance of lakes in nearly all other parts of this state. The southeastern lakeless area includes the edge of the great Driftless Area of Wisconsin, which reaches into Houston and Winona Counties. On its other and larger part, in Fillmore County and the other counties named, the formations of glacial and modified drift, spread by the continental ice sheet and by waters from its melting, are relatively ancient and thin, not dominating the surface outlines. The region therefore lacks the more or less uneven contour of alternate swells and depressions, or sometimes more noteworthy ridges, hills, and hollows, that elsewhere are characteristic of the drift, causing it generally to have plentiful lakes.

Root River, more fully noticed in the first chapter, is translated from the Dakota name Hokah, both being used on Joseph N. Nicollet's map in 1843. This river may be said to be formed by the union of its North and Middle Branches in Chatfield Township. A mile and a half below Lanesboro it receives the South Branch. Another large southern affluent, called the South Fork of Root River, drains southeastern Fillmore County and joins the main stream in Houston County.

On the state map published in 1860, the

Middle and South Branches and the South Fork were respectively called Fillmore, Carimona, and Houston Rivers, taking these names from the three villages.

Tributaries of the Root River from the north in this county include Rush Creek, before noted, in Rushford; Pine Creek in the north edge of Arendahl, which is a branch of Rush Creek; and Money and Trout Creeks in Pilot Mound Township.

Houston County has another Money Creek, for which a township is named. There it originated from an incident of the early history, but the reason for its duplication in Fillmore County has not been ascertained, though the two are believed to have some relationship.

Lost Creek, tributary to the Middle Branch, is so named because it flows underground in the creviced limestone beds for two miles, through sections 14 and 13, Jordan.

The North and South Jordan Creeks, before mentioned as giving the township name, and the Brook Kedron, flowing into the Middle Branch in Sumner, are names from the Bible, the latter being a very small stream with a deep valley at the east side of Jerusalem.

Bear, Deer, and Spring Valley Creeks flow into the Middle Branch from the southwest.

Sugar Creek, named for its sugar maples, is tributary to Root River in section 13, Chatfield.

The South Branch receives Watson Creek near the center of Carrolton, commemorating Thomas and James Watson, pioneers of Fountain Township; and from the south it receives Canfield, Willow, and Camp Creeks, the first (which in two parts of its course flows underground) being named for S. G. Canfield of York and the last having been a favorite camping place for immigrants. A small eastern tributary of Camp Creek was formerly called Duxbury Creek for pioneer families there, but on recent maps it is named Partridge Creek for the well-known game birds.

Weisel Creek, flowing into the South Fork of Root River in Preble, was named for David Weisel, who in 1855 built a sawmill and gristmill near its mouth. The mill was carried away, and he and his family were drowned by a flood of this stream, August 6, 1866.

Beaver Creek, before noticed as the source of the name of Beaver Township, was called Slough Creek on the map of 1860.

The head stream of Upper Iowa River, to which Beaver Creek is tributary, flows meanderingly past the south side of Beaver, York, and Bristol, several times crossing the state boundary. Its name, previously considered in the first chapter, like that of the state of Iowa and of the larger Iowa River, farther south, commemorates a Siouan tribe who lived on these rivers, nearly related with the Winnebago.

Eagle Rocks and Chimney Rock

These rocks are craggily eroded and weathered forms of the limestone strata left in the process of very slow channeling of the valley of the South Branch of Root River in section 27, Forestville. The Eagle Rocks are pictured in the *Final Report of the Minnesota Geological Survey* (vol. 1, 1884, p. 296), and on the same page the Chimney Rock is described, "on the side of the bluff of a ravine, . . . having a fancied resemblance to an oven with a low chimney."

Forestville/Mystery Cave State Park

This state park was authorized in 1949 but did not formally become a state park until 1963. The centerpiece of the park is the historic Meighen store, since 1977 administered as a historic site by the Minnesota Historical Society. The park is notable for is diversity of plant life because it embraces both deciduous forest and tallgrass prairie. In 1987 Mystery Cave was added to the state park. The cave, the largest known limestone cave in the state, owes its formation to the karst structure with water percolating through the limestone and eating away the rock. There are 12 miles of passageways through the cave.

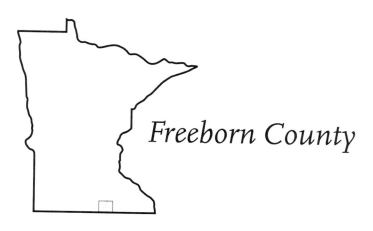

Freeborn County

Established February 20, 1855, this county was named in honor of William Freeborn, member of the council in the territorial legislature for the years 1854 to 1857. He was born in Ohio in 1816; came to St. Paul in 1848 and removed to Red Wing in 1853, where he had large interests, as also at Cannon Falls; emigrated in 1864 to the Rocky Mountains and spent the next winter as a gold miner in Montana; was engaged three years in fruit culture in Oregon; and finally, in 1868, settled in California on a ranch at Santa Margarita in San Luis Obispo County. He was the second mayor of Red Wing, in 1858, but resigned before the end of the year. Although he had traveled much, he wrote in 1899 from his California home that he had never ridden on a railroad train. Thomas M. Newson, in his *Pen Pictures of St. Paul, Minnesota* (1886), wrote of Freeborn as follows: "He was a man of progressive and speculative ideas, energetic, always scheming, and had a happy faculty of getting other parties interested in his enterprises. He was a quietly spoken man, of rugged appearance; self-possessed, and never was afraid to venture." This county was organized March 4, 1857, with Albert Lea as the county seat.

Notes of the origins of geographic names have been gathered from History of Freeborn County *(1882, 548 pp.), including the "Centennial History," by Daniel G. Parker (forming pp. 281–92); the later history of this county, compiled by Franklyn Curtiss-Wedge (1911, 883 pp.); and from Martin Van Buren Kellar of Albert Lea, interviewed in April 1916.*

ADAIR a farmer's post office, 1891–92, in Pickerel Lake Township; also known as Clover Valley; the postmaster was William P. Pickle in his general store.

ALBERT LEA TOWNSHIP first settled in the summer of 1855, organized in 1857, took the name of its village, which was platted in October 1856 and was incorporated as a city March 11, 1878. Its post office began in 1856, and it had a station of the Minneapolis, St. Paul and Sault Ste. Marie Railroad (Soo Line) and the Chicago Great Western Railroad. The name was adopted from the large adjoining lake on the southeast, to which Joseph N. Nicollet gave it in honor of Albert Miller Lea, who in 1835 explored and mapped streams and lakes in this county.

Lea was born in Richland, Grainger County, Tennessee, July 23, 1808; was graduated at West Point in 1831; aided Maj. Stephen H. Long in 1832 in surveys of the Tennessee River; was an assistant on surveys of Lake Michigan in 1833; was in military service on the Missouri and Mississippi Rivers during 1834; and in the summer of 1835 was second lieutenant of a company on the exploring expedition here noticed, in which he was designated as ordnance officer and volunteered his services as topographer and chronicler.

The expedition, under the command of Lieut.

Col. Stephen Watts Kearny, traveled along the northeast side of the Des Moines River from the Mississippi to the mouth of Boone River, thence northeast to the Mississippi at the mouth of Zumbro River (named Embarras River by Lea, because it was encumbered by a raft of driftwood near its mouth), thence southeast to Wabasha's village and the site of Winona, and thence westward to the headwaters of the Cedar and Blue Earth Rivers, and southwestward through the present Winnebago and Kossuth Counties in Iowa, to the Des Moines River. Descending the Des Moines in a canoe from the site of the city of this name to its mouth, Lea mapped it and described it in his journal of the expedition, which was the basis of an unpublished report to the War Department, and of a pamphlet (53 pp., with a map), published the next year in Philadelphia. In this publication, Lea first gave the name Iowa to the district obtained by treaty at the close of the Black Hawk War, in 1832. It was an eastern part of the large area later called Iowa as a territory and state, having reference to the Iowa Indians and the river bearing their name.

An extended autobiographic sketch, written by Albert M. Lea for the Minnesota Historical Society, was published in the *Freeborn County Standard*, March 13, 1879. He resigned from the army in 1836; resided in Tennessee, was a civil engineer, and in 1838 was U.S. commissioner for the survey of the southern boundary of the Territory of Iowa; was professor of mathematics in the East Tennessee University at Knoxville, 1844–51; removed to Texas in 1857; was an engineer of the Confederate service during the Civil War; lived in Galveston, 1865–74, and later in Corsicana, Texas, where he died, January 17, 1891. Two of his brothers were Pryor Lea, a member of Congress, and Luke Lea, who as commissioner of Indian affairs, was associated with Gov. Alexander Ramsey in 1851 in making the treaties of Traverse des Sioux and Mendota.

Further details of this expedition, and notes of the names applied by Lea to lakes and streams in Freeborn County, are given in the later part of this chapter.

ALDEN a city in Alden and Carlston Townships, settled in 1858, was organized April 3, 1866. The railway village was platted in 1869, and the track was completed to this place January 1, 1870; it had station on the Chicago, Milwaukee and St. Paul Railroad. It was incorporated on March 4, 1879, and reincorporated in March 1908; it has had a post office since 1866. This name is borne by villages and townships in seven other states.

ARMSTRONG a village, sections 3 and 4, Pickerel Lake, was established in 1878 and was named for Hon. Thomas Henry Armstrong, who in that year erected a grain elevator there. He was born in Milan, Ohio, February 6, 1829; was graduated at Western Reserve College, 1854; came to Minnesota in 1855, settling in High Forest, Olmsted County; and in 1874 removed to Albert Lea, where he died, December 29, 1891. He was a representative in the legislature, 1864–65, being speaker in 1865; was lieutenant governor, 1866–70; and a state senator, 1877–78. The village had a station of the Chicago, Milwaukee and St. Paul Railroad and the Minneapolis and St. Louis Railroad; its post office operated 1878–1957, and as a rural branch 1957–58.

BANCROFT first settled in July 1855, organized May 11, 1858, had a temporary village of this name, platted in the fall of 1856, in sections 21 and 28, which on March 4, 1857, was an unsuccessful candidate for the county seat. It was incorporated on May 19, 1857, and had a post office, 1857–59, 1863–78, and 1897–1902. The name was chosen in honor of George Bancroft (1800–1891), who was the author of *History of the United States* (ten vols., published 1834–74); U.S. secretary of the navy, 1845–46, and founder of the Naval Academy, Annapolis; minister to Great Britain, 1846–49, and to Berlin, 1868–74.

BATH settled in the spring of 1856, was organized in January 1858 under the name of Porter but was renamed Bath, April 15, 1859, after the name of the county seat of Steuben County, New York, the native town of Frederick W. Calkins, who had settled here in 1857. A country post office was located in section 8, 1877–1904, and it had a station of the Minneapolis and St. Louis Railroad.

BEAR LAKE a post office in Nunda Township, 1858–59 and 1874–77.

BUCKEYE see MANCHESTER.

CARLSTON first settled in August 1855, was organized in January 1858, being then named Stanton in honor of Elias Stanton, a settler on the shore of Freeborn Lake, who had suffered amputation of his feet because of their being frozen, and who died in the spring of 1858. This name was earlier used for another Minnesota township, so that in September 1859 it was changed, the present name being adopted "in respect to the memory of a distinguished Swede of that name, who settled in that town in an early day, and who was drowned in Freeborn lake." He was Theodore L. Carlston (or Carlson), the second settler, drowned in 1858.

CLARKS GROVE a city in Bath Township, sections 34 and 35, was founded in 1890, ten years before the railway was built. Its name had been long borne by a grove a mile east of the present village, in which grove John Mead Clark settled "in the early days." It was incorporated as a village on February 27, 1920, and had a station of the Chicago and Northwestern Railway, sometimes listed as James. Its post office began in 1857 with Clark as postmaster.

CLOVER a post office in Nunda Township, 1895–1909.

CONGER a city in Alden Township, section 24, incorporated as a village on April 27, 1934, was named by railroad officers for Congressman Edwin Hurd Conger of Des Moines, Iowa, who was later ambassador to China, Brazil, and Mexico and died in 1907; the post office began in 1901.

CORNING a village at the corner of Newry and Moscow Townships, with several grocery and general merchandise stores and a blacksmith shop.

CRAYON PARK a station of the Chicago, Milwaukee and St. Paul Railroad in section 6 of Oakland Township.

CURTIS a station of the Chicago, Rock Island and Pacific Railroad in Albert Lea Township.

DEER CREEK a village in London Township, section 33, settled by 1875 with a creamery, a store, a school, and several churches.

EMMONS a city in Nunda Township, sections 32 and 33, on the state line, was incorporated February 27, 1899. Here Henry G. Emmons settled in 1856, and "in 1880 his sons started a store on the present site of the village." He was born in Norway, October 16, 1828; came to the United States in 1850, settling at first in Wisconsin; was postmaster of the State Line post office fifteen years and also of the Emmons post office, which began in 1899; was a representative in the legislature, 1877–78; died in this village, October 2, 1909. The village had a station of the Minneapolis and St. Louis Railroad.

FAIRFIELD a village in Riceland Township, 1857–90, with a grain mill, a sawmill, a store, and four residences.

FREEBORN SPRINGS a post office, 1857–61, in Lyndon Township.

FREEBORN TOWNSHIP was first settled in July 1856 and was organized May 11, 1858. Its village in sections 34 and 35, platted in June 1857, and the lake beside which it lies were named like the county in honor of William Freeborn, whence also the township received this name. The village was incorporated on August 12, 1858, then was in an unincorporated status until reincorporated on March 27, 1949. Its post office was first named Freeborn City, 1857–58, at postmaster Ludwig T. Carlson's home; when Layfayette T. Scott built his hotel in 1858, the post office was moved there, and Scott became postmaster.

FREEMAN first settled in 1854, organized April 2, 1861, was named in honor of John Freeman, a native of Northampton, England, who in 1855 "secured, under the pre-emption law, the whole of section fifteen for himself and three sons." See also KNATVOLD.

FREMONT a post office, 1866–74; location not found.

GENEVA settled in 1855–56, was organized May 11, 1858. Its village in sections 7 and 8, platted in the winter of 1856–57, had been named by Edwin C. Stacy, the first postmaster there and the first probate judge for the county, "in remembrance of Geneva, N.Y.," whence the large adjoining lake and the township received the same name. It was incorporated November 24, 1889; the post office, begun in 1856, was located first in the O. G. Goodnature home, with John Heath and later E. C. Stacy, postmasters.

GLENVILLE a city in sections 5 to 8, Shell Rock Township, was named by officers of the railway company. It was incorporated in 1898. Previous to the building of the railway there in 1877, this had been the site of a smaller village, platted in 1856 when Bartlett, Ellswart and Phillips formed a townsite corporation, bearing the name Shell Rock for the river on which it is situated, thence given also to the township. The post office was first named Shell Rock, 1856–79, when changed to the present name. The village had a station of the Minneapolis and St. Louis Railroad.

GORDONSVILLE a railway village in section 32,

Shell Rock, platted in 1880, received its name from a post office that operated 1862–1965, of which T. J. Gordon and his son, W. H. H. Gordon, were successively postmasters after 1865, residing as farmers in section 28, near the site of this village. The village had an elevator, a creamery, and a number of other businesses, which diminished by the 1930s; the post office was a rural branch 1965–69.

GUILDFORD see OAKLAND.

HARTLAND settled in the spring of 1857, organized May 11, 1858, was named for Hartland in Windsor County, Vt., whence some of its early settlers came. This name was proposed by the wife of O. Sheldon, the first postmaster. The city of Hartland, sections 16, 17, 20, and 21, was platted in 1877 and was incorporated in August 31, 1893; it was originally located one mile south of the present site with a post office, 1857–60; the city moved when the Chicago and Northwestern Railway track was laid, and a new post office was established in 1868.

HAYWARD settled in 1856, organized April 5, 1859, was named in honor of David Hayward, one of its earliest settlers, who came from Postville, Iowa, and returned to that state after living here only two years. The city of Hayward, sections 8 and 9, founded in 1869, was replatted in 1886 and incorporated on June 4, 1924; it had a station on the Chicago, Milwaukee and St. Paul Railroad, and its post office began in 1864.

HOLLANDALE a city in Geneva and Riceland Townships, was developed in 1918 by George H. Payne of Payne Investment Company on 15,000 acres of drained swampland. Beginning in 1924, 400 farm families, many of Dutch descent, quickly settled the area. Its post office began in 1923. Maple Island, a tract of 120 acres covered with trees, two miles east of Hollandale, became a subdivision where many farmers settled; its station of the Chicago, Rock Island and Pacific Railroad was first known as Maple Island.

HOLLANDALE JUNCTION a station of the Chicago, Milwaukee, St. Paul and Pacific Railroad in section 1 of Hayward Township.

ITASCA was a small village or hamlet in section 31, Bancroft, platted in the winter of 1855–56, adjoining a lakelet that also was named Itasca. In 1857 it was an aspirant to be designated as the county seat, but failing in that ambition, it lasted only a few years. The name was derived from that given by Henry R. Schoolcraft to the source of the Mississippi River.

KNATVOLD a village in Freeman Township, sections 27 and 28, began in the early 1890s on the site of the Freeman township hall. It had a store, a creamery, and a post office, 1899–1905, which had briefly been called Freeman from October to December 1899. The village was named for state Senator Thorvald V. Knatvold of Albert Lea.

LANE a station of the Illinois Central and the Cedar Valley Railroads in section 6 of Shell Rock Township.

LERDAL a village in Riceland Township, section 17, with a post office, 1892–1903.

LONDON settled in 1855, organized in 1858, received its name for the city and county of New London, Conn. It was proposed by William N. and James H. Goslee, natives of Hartford County in that state, who settled here respectively in 1856 and 1857. The railway village of London, section 25, was platted in October 1900 on 55 acres of land owned by William Morin. Its post office began in 1877 in the home of postmaster Henry Lang and moved to the general store by 1900; it had a station of the Illinois Central and the Cedar Valley Railroads.

MANCHESTER first settled in June 1856, organized in January 1858, was then named Buckeye, but in May it was renamed Liberty. In October of that year it received the present name, suggested by Mathias Anderson, who came here in 1857 from a township of this name in Illinois. The city in section 15 was founded in 1877–78 and platted in 1882 by Ole Peterson and again in 1898 by H. W. Fish; it was incorporated on October 6, 1947. The village had a station of the Minneapolis and St. Louis Railroad.

MANSFIELD settled in June 1856, was organized in January 1866, being the latest township of this county. Its name, suggested by Capt. George S. Ruble, is borne by a city in Ohio near his former home, and by villages and townships in 14 states of our Union. Originally the name is from a town of Nottinghamshire in England, whence the first Earl of Mansfield (1705–93), a distinguished British jurist and statesman, received his title. The history of this county (1882) refers to him as commemorated by this township name. The village in section 4 was incorporated on June 17,

1858, but is presently unincorporated; it had a creamery, a general store, and a post office, 1872–1908.

MAPLE ISLAND see HOLLANDALE.

MONARCH a village in Geneva Township, three miles east of Geneva, had a post office, 1896–1900, a store, a school, and a creamery; when the creamery closed, the village ceased to exist.

MOSCOW first settled in May 1855, was organized in January 1858. "Some years previous to settlement, the heavy body of timber which covered section seventeen, in Moscow, was set on fire in a dry season, creating such a conflagration as to suggest scenes in Russia under the great Napoleon. From that time it was known as the Moscow timber, and thus the name of the town had its origin" (*History*, 1882, p. 292). The little village of this name, section 22, was platted in June 1857. It had a general store, a hotel, a creamery, a blacksmith, and a school; it also had a station of the Chicago Great Western Railroad and a post office, 1859–1903.

MURTAGH a station on the Chicago, Rock Island and Pacific Railroad in Albert Lea Township, sections 26 and 35.

MYRTLE the railroad village in section 7, London, was founded "in 1900, when the railroad came through" and named for Myrtle Lane, first postmaster, 1887–1900, on the H. N. Lane farm. It was incorporated as a village on May 8, 1937.

NEW DENMARK a locality in Albert Lea Township, sections 8 and 9, which was incorporated into the city of Albert Lea.

NEWRY settled in 1854, organized May 11, 1858, was named on the suggestion of Thomas Fitzsimmons, who was the first township clerk, for a seaport and river in northern Ireland, whence several pioneers of this township came. A post office was located in section 16, 1874–88 and 1895–1904.

NUNDA settled in 1856, organized May 11, 1858, was named by Patrick Fitzsimmons, a native of Ireland, who was one of the first settlers and a prominent citizen, "in honor of towns of the same name in which he had lived in New York and Illinois." This name is "derived from the Indian word *nundao*, meaning 'hilly,' or according to another authority, 'potato ground'" (Henry Gannett, *The Origin of Certain Place Names in the United States*, 1905). See also TWIN LAKES.

OAKLAND settled in 1855, organized April 5, 1857, received its name from the small and scattered oak trees, with occasional groves, that originally occupied fully half of its area, commonly called "oak openings," while the remainder consisted of prairie land and grassy sloughs. The village, section 2, had a store, a creamery, a bank, and a school. Its first post office operated 1857–59 with Thomas Rockford, postmaster; the second post office was at Guildford, 1858–75, transferring in 1875. It had a station of the Chicago, Milwaukee, St. Paul and Pacific Railroad.

OAKVALE a post office, 1859, established earlier in Worth County, Iowa; location not found.

OSLO a post office, 1874–75, in Vernon Township.

PEAVEY a station of the Soo Line in Riceland Township.

PETRAN a village in Hayward Township, sections 10 and 11, which had a station of the Chicago, Milwaukee, St. Paul and Pacific Railroad.

PICKEREL LAKE TOWNSHIP first settled in 1855, organized September 8, 1865, bears the name of the lake crossed by its east boundary, widely known for its abundance of this fish. The lake had been called Bear Lake by the Indians because previous to the coming of white settlers they killed a large bear near it. The present name was given by Austin R. Nichols, through whose mistake in 1854 the former names of Pickerel and Bear Lakes became transposed (*History*, 1882, p. 291).

RICELAND settled in August 1856, organized in January 1858, was at first named Beardsley in honor of Samuel A. Beardsley, one of the first pioneers, who "came by ox team from Illinois, brought considerable stock, and settled on the south side of Rice lake." This large but shallow lake, well filled with wild rice, for which the township was soon renamed, covered some 2,000 acres, but it has been wholly drained away, the lake bed being now farmland. A post office was located in the township, 1858–60.

ST. NICHOLAS was the first village in this county, platted in the summer of 1856 on the south side of Albert Lea Lake in sections 25 and 26 of Albert Lea Township. It had a post office, 1856–59. In March 1857, it aspired to be elected as the county seat, but after the failure of that hope, its buildings were removed and the village site became farmland.

SHELL ROCK TOWNSHIP settled in June 1853,

organized in 1857, received the name of its river, the outlet of Albert Lea Lake, which along its course in Iowa is bordered by rock strata containing fossil shells. The early village of Shell Rock has been noticed in this list as Glenville, its present name.

SIGSBEE a village in the southwest corner of section 26, Riceland Township, which had a post office, 1899–1904, and a store.

SOUTH HOLLANDALE a station of the Chicago, Milwaukee, St. Paul and Pacific Railroad in Riceland Township, section 2.

STATE LINE a post office, 1864–79, of Nunda Township established at the farm home of postmaster Henry George Emmons, who was later a county commissioner and a state legislator.

SUMNER a village in Moscow Township, was platted in 1857 by Rufus Crum, who had a stagecoach station on the site; there was also a store, a school, a cemetery, and a post office, 1857–72; the village was abandoned by 1876.

TRENTON a village in Freeborn Township, section 3, was incorporated on May 23, 1857, until returned to unincorporated status. It had a post office, 1857–1901; the first postmaster was Lester Rogen.

TWIN LAKES a railway village in section 12, Nunda, was partly platted in 1858, being the site of a sawmill and a flouring mill many years previous to the building of the railway in 1877–78. It was incorporated on April 8, 1957. Its post office was named Nunda, 1859–81, then changed to Twin Lakes. The fall of Goose Creek, outflowing from the neighboring Twin Lakes, supplies valuable water power.

WOODLAWN a country post office, 1892–94, 20 miles east of Albert Lea and 5 miles from Oakland, possibly in Oakland Township.

Lakes and Streams,
with Notes of the Expedition in 1835

The pamphlet before mentioned as published by Lieut. Albert M. Lea, titled *Notes on the Wisconsin Territory, particularly with reference to the Iowa District or Black Hawk Purchase* (53 pp., 1836), has a folded map of the country extending from northern Missouri to the foot of Lake Pepin and from the Mississippi to the Missouri River, comprising the present southeast part of Minnesota and near-

ly all of Iowa. In the area of Freeborn County, Lea mapped and named five lakes, each of which is clearly identified on the present more accurate maps.

Fox Lake, doubtless named for a fox seen there, is the largest of these lakes, to which Nicollet's map in 1843 gave its present title, Albert Lea Lake. The outflowing Shell Rock River received this name on Lea's map, which Nicollet copied but called it a creek. Where Lea crossed it on the outward journey of the expedition, "limestone filled with petrifications was abundant," whence he derived the name (*Iowa Historical Record*, vol. 6, p. 548).

Chapeau Lake, meaning in French a hat, so named by Lea for its outline, which reminded him of the old-fashioned three-cornered hat, left unnamed by Nicollet, is now White Lake, commemorating Capt. A. W. White, an early settler who lived beside it till 1861, then removing into the village of Albert Lea.

Fountain Lake, adjoining the north side of the city of Albert Lea, is produced by a dam, so that it does not appear on early maps.

Council Lake of Lea's map, referring to some parley there with "a few straggling Indians," as mentioned in his autobiographic letter to the Minnesota Historical Society, is now Freeborn Lake, outflowing by the Big Cobb River northwesterly to the Blue Earth and Minnesota Rivers. This lake and two others continuing northward are mapped by Nicollet as Ichiyaza Lakes, a Dakota name meaning a row or series.

Trail Lake, named probably for an Indian trail passing by it, mapped too large by Lea, copied by Nicollet, but without a name, is the Upper Twin Lake, outflowing by Lime Creek, which was also named by Lea, now Goose Creek. A very little lakelet of Lea's map, northwest of Trail Lake, represents the Little Oyster Lakes in sections 23 and 26, Pickerel Lake Township, "so called because of their shape."

Lake Boone, named by Lea in honor of Nathan Boone, captain of one of the companies of dragoons in this expedition, is now Bear Lake in Nunda, which was at first called Pickerel Lake in 1853 by the white settlers, as noted in the history of this county (1882, p. 291). Lea mapped it erroneously as the source of Boone River in Iowa, named on his map likewise for Capt. Boone. In this error he was followed by Nicollet, whose map, however, leaves both the lake and river unnamed. Boone (1780–1857) was the youngest of the nine children of the renowned frontiersman Daniel Boone.

"Paradise Prairie," noted by Lea, northward of his Chapeau Lake, was described in the history of the county in 1882 that it enters Bancroft Township "in the southwestern corner and extends northeasterly almost across the entire town, gradually disappearing towards Clark's Grove, in the northeast corner."

In the list of townships, sufficient reference has been made to several lakes, besides those noted by Lea, namely, Geneva Lake, Itasca Lake, Pickerel and Rice Lakes, and the Twin Lakes.

Nicollet's Ichiyaza Lakes, before noticed, doubtless included Lake George, and Spicer and Trenton Lakes, in Freeborn, named for and by early settlers. Another, the little Prairie Lake, also named Penny Lake, is in section 31 of this township.

Le Sueur or Mule Lake, in the east part of Hartland, lies at the head of Le Sueur River. Its second name alludes to the loss of "a fine span of mules belonging to B. J. Boardman," drowned there in 1857.

Lake George, in section 22, Bath, was named in honor of George W. Skinner, Jr., son of a prominent pioneer there.

Newry Lake derived its name from its location, in section 2, Newry Township.

Deer and Turtle Creeks in Newry and Moscow, Goose Lake in section 3, Albert Lea, and Elk Lake, section 21, London, need no explanations.

Spring Lake in the city of Albert Lea, and Fountain Lake at its north side, the latter a mill pond, are named for springs on their shores.

Bancroft Creek is in the township of this name.

Manchester had a notable group of small lakes, namely, Lake Peterson, Silver, Sugar, and Spring Lakes, but the first two have been drained.

Peter Lund Creek in Hayward commemorates a pioneer farmer, an immigrant from Norway, who came to America in 1850, settled here in 1856, and was the first township treasurer.

Steward's Creek in Alden and Mansfield was named in honor of Hiram J. Steward, who was born near Bangor, Maine, September 21, 1831; served in the Civil War, 1862, being severely wounded; came west and in 1869 settled as a farmer in section 12, Mansfield.

Lime Creek is the outlet of Bear Lake and State Line Lake, flowing into Iowa and there tributary to Shell Rock River. It was thought by Lea to be the headstream of Boone River as before noted.

Grass Lake in sections 26 and 35, Freeman, now drained, was named for the grasses and sedges growing in its shallow water.

Woodbury Creek in Oakland and London, flowing into Mower County, received the name of a settler there.

Myre-Big Island State Park

Local efforts to preserve woodlands led to the creation in 1947 of Big Island State Park, with a nucleus of Big Island in Albert Lea Lake. One of those undertaking the campaign was state Senator Helmer C. Myre. In 1990 his work was recognized when the park was renamed Myre-Big Island State Park. Myre served on the Albert Lea police force, was sheriff of Freeborn County, was a state representative, 1939–41, and state senator, 1947–49. He died October 6, 1951. Land on the north side of the lake was added to the park with acquisition in 1976 of a 560-acre parcel from the Interstate Power Company. The chief feature of this addition was an esker, a ridge left by water flowing beneath a melting glacier.

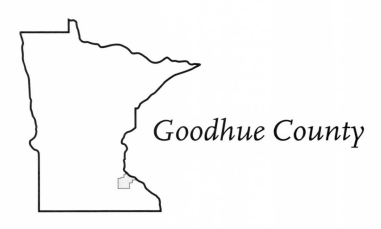

Goodhue County

This county, established March 5, 1853, was named in honor of James Madison Goodhue, who was the first printer and editor in Minnesota, beginning the issue of the *Minnesota Pioneer* on April 28, 1849. He was born in Hebron, N.H., March 31, 1810, and died in St. Paul, August 27, 1852; was graduated at Amherst College in 1833; studied law in New York City and was admitted to the bar about 1840; afterward was a farmer three years in Plainfield, Ill.; practiced law in Galesburg, Ill., and in Platteville and Lancaster, Wis.; became editor of the *Wisconsin Herald*, published in Lancaster; removed to St. Paul in the spring of 1849 and was a most earnest and influential journalist there during the three remaining years of his life.

Goodhue was a man of very forcible character and of high moral principles. As a vigorous writer, he did much to upbuild St. Paul and Minnesota and made strong personal friends and enemies. Because of his scathing editorial against the U.S. marshal Alexander Mitchell and Judge David Cooper, a brother of the latter attacked Mr. Goodhue, January 15, 1851, on the street in front of the building in which the legislature was in session and stabbed him twice, severely wounding him, and being shot in return. From that injury he never fully recovered.

Biographic sketches of Goodhue as founder and editor of the first newspaper of the new Minnesota Territory are in the MHS Collections, by Col. John H. Stevens (6: 492–501) and D. S. B. Johnston (10: 247–53). His successor as editor of the *Pioneer*, Joseph R. Brown, wrote of him in an editorial tribute a year after he died: "James M. Goodhue was a warm and fast friend of Minnesota to the day of his death. He will be remembered with the small band of sturdy men who labored constantly and with iron resolution to establish the pillars of society in our Territory upon a sound moral basis. His press was always found on the side of law, order, temperance, and virtue."

Information of origins and meanings of these names has been gathered from the Geographical and Statistical Sketch . . . of Goodhue County, *by W. H. Mitchell (1869, 191 pp.);* History of Goodhue County *(1878, 664 pp.);* Goodhue County, Past and Present, by an Old Settler, *by Rev. Joseph W. Hancock (1893, 349 pp.); the later history, edited by Franklyn Curtiss-Wedge (1909, 1,074 pp.); and from Dr. William M. Sweney, Albert E. Rhame, city engi-neer, and Charles S. Dana, clerk of the court, interviewed at Red Wing in April 1916.*

ADDINGTON SPUR a station of the Chicago, Milwaukee and St. Paul Railroad, Red Wing Township, section 31.

ALLANDALE a settlement in Vasa Township, just south of Spencer (later Vasa), circa 1860s.

ASHLAND a locality in Wanamingo Township, section 16, circa 1874.

ASPELUND a farming village in Wanamingo Township, sections 16 and 21, founded by veterinarian and first postmaster Dr. Christian Hveem, its post office operating 1872–1905. The name given is the Norwegian designation for the grove of aspen or poplar trees near to the village. It had a station of the Chicago, Milwaukee and St. Paul Railroad.

AURLAND a post office, 1898; location not found.

AYR a farming village in Cherry Grove Township, section 14, was named for the county in Scotland where many of the early settlers had lived. Its first post office, 1863–84, was located in the home of postmaster Israel T. Comstock, discontinuing when the village of Roscoe took over the mail route, and reestablished, 1893–1902, with James Simpson as postmaster.

BAKKO a village in Kenyon Township, section 14, which was never platted but had a milk train stop of the Chicago Great Western Railroad; named for Ole Bakko, who came from Norway to the Kenyon area in 1855.

BARR a small village in Minneola Township, section 21, which had a station of the Chicago, Milwaukee and St. Paul Railroad; it disappeared sometime in the 1920s.

BELLE CREEK TOWNSHIP settled in 1853, organized in 1858, received this French name of its creek, meaning beautiful. The village of Belle Creek, section 8, was platted in 1883 by Prentiss Clark of Minneapolis. Although its post office operated 1860–83, the village did not diminish until after 1910. The Chicago Great Western Railroad had a station by this name in Vasa Township, section 27.

BELLECHESTER a city with Wabasha County, located in Chester and Belvidere Townships, was incorporated as a village on October 5, 1955; its post office operated 1911–17, and as a rural branch, 1930–63; it had a station of the Chicago Great Western Railroad.

BELVIDERE settled in the spring of 1855, organized May 11, 1858, was at first called York, and later Elmira, the present name being adopted December 28, 1858. Illinois has a city of this name, which also is borne by villages and townships in seven other states. See also THOTEN.

BELVIDERE MILLS a post office, 1877–1905, in Belvidere Township, sections 4 and 5. Nelson Beeman Gaylord, farmer and miller, was postmaster for many years in his general store; he was born in Pennsylvania in 1823, came to Goodhue County in 1855, built a gristmill in 1861, and established the post office; he died in 1902. A station of the Chicago, Milwaukee and St. Paul Railroad was located there.

BLACK OAK a settlement of Belle Creek Township, 12 miles from Red Wing, with a number of small businesses and several churches; Orvan G. Rosing was postmaster in the Rosing and Doyle general store, 1877–85.

BOMBAY a village in Wanamingo and Cherry Grove Townships, was named for the city in India. Settlement began when a branch of the Chicago, Milwaukee, St. Paul and Pacific Railroad was built from Faribault to Zumbrota in 1903, the depot being built on John Davidson's farm. Locals wanted to name the village Davidson, but railroad officials selected the name.

BURLEY a community in Featherstone Township, section 7, with a post office, 1897–1900.

BURNSIDE settled in 1854, organized in 1858, was known at first as Union, and in 1859–61 as Milton, but was renamed as now in March 1862 in honor of Ambrose Everett Burnside (1824–81), a distinguished general in the Civil War, 1861–65, governor of Rhode Island, 1866–69, and U.S. senator, 1875–81. The settlement of Burnside in the township, circa 1853–1908, is now part of Prairie Island Reservation. On June 1, 1971, the township was annexed by the city of Red Wing.

BURR OAK SPRINGS a village in Belle Creek Township, which had a stop on the stage coach line between St. Paul and Dubuque, Iowa, and a post office, 1855–57, located in the home of postmaster Henry Doyle.

CANNON FALLS TOWNSHIP settled in 1854, organized in 1858, derived its name from the falls of the Cannon River, as it was named by Zebulon Pike in 1806, by William H. Keating's narrative of Maj. Stephen H. Long's expedition in 1823, and on Joseph N. Nicollet's map, 1843, erroneously changed from the early French name, Riviere aux Canots, which alluded to canoes left near its mouth by parties of Indians on war or hunting expeditions. Cannon Falls city, platted August 27, 1855, was incorporated as a village February 19, 1874, and adopted its city charter on February 13, 1905. The post office was first called Cannon

River Falls 1855–89; it had a station of the Chicago Great Western Railroad.

CANNON JUNCTION a station on the Chicago, Milwaukee and St. Paul Railroad, in sections 21 and 22 of Burnside Township; also known as Hem-Minne-Cha, which means "hill, water, wood."

CANNON VALLEY a post office, 1874–77; location not found.

CASCADE a village in Stanton Township, section 18, was platted but not incorporated; it had a post office, 1882–1901, a mill, a cooper, a chapel, a store, a blacksmith, and several homes.

CENTRAL POINT a township of very small area, settled about 1850, was organized in 1858. Its name refers to a point of land here extending into Lake Pepin, about midway between the head and foot of the lake. The lumber village of Central Point was first settled in 1853 and platted in May 1855; it tried to develop into a city, with two stores, a hotel, a sawmill, a post office, 1855–60, and a station on the Chicago, Milwaukee and St. Paul Railroad. It thrived until about 1857 when Lake City became more attractive to settlers; however, it remained a popular resort area.

CHERRY GROVE settled in 1854, organized in 1858, received its name from a cherry grove in the central part of this township, where a log schoolhouse was built in 1857. The wild red cherry (also called bird cherry) and the wild black cherry are common throughout the greater part of this state.

CLAY PITS see CLAYBANK.

CLAYBANK a post office, 1890–1904, in Goodhue Township, sections 5 and 8, with a station of the Chicago Great Western Railroad; also referred to as Clay Pits.

CRYSTAL SPRINGS a post office, 1858–63; location not found.

DENNISON a city in Warsaw and Northfield Townships with Rice County, was named in honor of Morris P. Dennison, a settler near its site in 1856, on whose land the village was located. The village was settled by 1849, platted in 1884, incorporated as a village on December 3, 1904, and separated from the townships on July 20, 1907. Its post office began in 1885, although there is some confusion as to whether it was named Spring Creek before the post office was established in postmaster Gunnar A. Bonhus's general store. Dennison visited Minnesota in 1849 from Vermont, brought his family in 1856, and filed a land claim,

building a log shanty in the center of the city; he moved to Northfield in 1865 and died in a farm accident in 1879.

EAGLE MILLS see WELCH.

EAST RED WING see RED WING.

EGGLESTON a village in Welch Township, section 1, and Burnside Township, section 6, was named for an early settler and land owner. John E. and Joseph Eggleston settled in the township of Burnside in the spring of 1855, and Harlan P. and Ira E. Eggleston were volunteers in the Civil War from that township, which included Welch until 1864. It had a post office, 1875–1934, and a station on the Chicago, Milwaukee, St. Paul and Pacific Railroad.

EIDSVOLD a farmers post office, 1875–88, in Holden Township, with a general store.

ELMIRA see GOODHUE.

FAIRPOINT a small village euphoniously named, in section 33, Cherry Grove, was platted in 1857; it had a post office, 1857–61 and 1865–1902.

FEATHERSTONE first settled in 1855, organized in 1858, "derived its name from William Featherstone, who with a large family settled there in 1855." A post office was located there 1858–63.

FINNEY a post office, 1882–83; location not found.

FINSETH a station of the Chicago Great Western Railroad in Holden Township, section 29.

FLORENCE settled in 1854, organized in 1858, was named in honor of Florence Graham, oldest child of Judge Christopher C. Graham of Red Wing. She was married January 8, 1872, to David M. Taber, who died April 1, 1880. Mrs. Taber was "known for her interest in all matters which tend toward the betterment of the city and county." Her father (1806–91) served in the Mexican war; came to Red Wing in 1854 as receiver of the U.S. land office and filled that position until 1861; was the municipal judge after 1869. A post office, 1858–67, a store, and a hotel were located in the township between Frontenac and Lake City; the site is now a roadside park.

FOREST MILLS a village in Zumbrota Township, section 29, had a flour mill built in 1867 by H. H. Palmer, store owner in Zumbrota, William S. Wells, and William Bruce Dickey, later a state senator. Two streets were laid out in 1865, with a store, a cooper shop, a sash and door factory, and several other industries; with no railroad facilities the milling operations were abandoned, and the settlement gradually dwindled; a post office operated, 1879–98.

FRONTENAC a railway village and neighboring lakeside village of summer homes in Florence Township, had the early Indian trading post of James Wells before 1850 and was permanently settled in 1854–57. The name commemorates Louis de Buade de Frontenac, who was born in Paris, 1622, and died in Quebec, November 28, 1698. He was the French colonial governor of Canada in 1672–82 and 1689–98. There is no record of his traveling to the Mississippi River. A post office began in 1855 as Westervelt, with Evert V. Westervelt as postmaster then and when the name changed to Frontenac in 1860; it had a station of the Chicago, Milwaukee, St. Paul and Pacific Railroad in section 15.

GOODHUE TOWNSHIP settled in 1854, organized September 13, 1859, was then named Lime, but was renamed as now in January 1860, honoring James M. Goodhue, like the county name. The city in sections 21 and 28 incorporated as a village on April 2, 1897; its post office was noted under several names: Elmira, 1857–58; Goodhue Centre, 1858–79; Goodhue, 1882–84; Goodhue Centre, 1888–89, when returned to its present form. The community developed after the Duluth, Red Wing and Southern Railroad came through in 1889 and built the depot.

HADER a village in Wanamingo Township, section 1, was intended to be the county seat but did not develop as planned; 122 blocks were platted by Otis F. Smith in 1857; however, the streets were never laid out, and only two stores and several houses were built; a post office operated 1857–1903.

HARLISS a village with a station of the Chicago, Milwaukee, St. Paul and Pacific Railroad station; location not found.

HAY CREEK TOWNSHIP settled in the spring of 1854, organized in 1858, received its name from the stream, which had natural hay meadows. The township had a post office, 1874–1902, in section 19, with a station on the Chicago Great Western Railroad in Featherstone Township, section 24.

HOLDEN settled in 1854–55, organized in 1858, has a name that is borne by townships in Maine and Massachusetts and by a city in Missouri. The village, section 9, was formerly called Dunkirk and changed when the first post office operated

March to June 1860 on George Nichol's farm; the second post office began in 1867 in Thomas E. Lajord's general store, closing in 1903.

INDIO a station of the Chicago, Milwaukee, St. Paul and Pacific Railroad in Welch Township.

KENYON settled in 1855, organized in 1858, was named for a pioneer merchant, who in 1856 built the first store there. The city of Kenyon, sections 3, 4, 9, and 10, was incorporated on October 16, 1885, and separated from the township on April 22, 1889. It was platted in 1856 by A. Hilton, Jay A. Day, James M. Le Duc, and a Mr. Howe; Le Duc chose the name to honor Kenyon College in Gambier, Ohio, in honor of his alma mater. It had a station of the Chicago Great Western Railroad, and its post office began in 1856.

LAKE CITY a city with Wabasha County, which see.

LENA a post office, 1879, in Pine Island Township, section 10, with a station of the Chicago Great Western Railroad; named for the wife of hotel keeper John Lee.

LEON settled in the fall of 1854, organized in 1858, bears a foreign name, that of a medieval kingdom, which was later a province of Spain. It is also the name of townships in New York and Wisconsin.

MIAMI a post office, 1858–60, located in Warsaw Township.

MINERAL SPRINGS a station of the Chicago, Milwaukee, St. Paul and Pacific Railroad in Cannon Falls Township, section 2.

MINNEOLA settled in May 1855, organized December 15, 1859, has a name from the Dakota language, meaning "much water." A post office, located six miles east of Aspelund, operated 1863–71.

NANSEN a country post office in Holden Township, section 12, 1898–1905, with Ole H. Pynten as postmaster the entire time in the store he built in 1892 on his farm; Pynten died in 1906. The only other industry was a cheese factory opened in 1904, which ceased in 1954. The post office was named for Arctic explorer Fridtjof Nansen.

NORWAY a village in Wanamingo Township, section 19, and trading center; it had a post office, 1857–1902; the site was never platted, and no traces of the community remain.

OLD FRONTENAC see FRONTENAC.

PINE ISLAND settled in 1854, organized in 1858,

took the name of its village, which was platted in the winter of 1856–57. The city with Olmsted County is located principally in Pine Island Township; it was incorporated as a village on March 6, 1878, and reincorporated on February 28, 1918. It was named in 1855 by Moses Jewell, an early settler, for the solitary large white pine on a small island. The major industry was cheese making, and it had a station of the Chicago Great Western Railroad; its post office began in 1856.

"The island proper is formed by the middle branch of the Zumbro, which circles around the present village, enclosing a tract once thickly studded with tall pine trees. . . . This spot was one of the favorite resorts of the Dakota Indians. They called it Wa-zee-wee-ta, Pine Island, and here in their skin tents they used to pass the cold winter months, sheltered from the winds and storms by the thick branches of lofty pines. The chief of Red Wing's village told the commissioners of the United States, when asked to sign the treaty that would require his people to relinquish their home on the Mississippi River, that he was willing to sign it if he could have his future home at Pine Island" (Hancock, p. 288). "Between the two branches of the Zumbro River, which unite a short distance below, there was quite a forest of pine, which could be seen for a long distance over the prairie, giving it quite the appearance of an Island in the sea" (Mitchell, p. 118).

POPLAR GROVE a post office, 1855–62, in Pine Island Township.

RED WING the location of a mission to the Dakota in 1837 by two Swiss missionaries, Samuel Denton and Daniel Gavin, was first settled for farming and Indian trading in 1850–52; was chosen to be the county seat in 1854; was incorporated as a city March 4, 1857; and received new municipal charters on March 3, 1864, and February 21, 1887. It was platted in 1853, and its post office began in Wabasha County in 1850, known briefly as Wah-coo-ta before transferring to Goodhue County as Red Wing. The village had a station serving several railroad lines.

The village became the site of famous pottery works; the first shop was opened by J. Pohl, a German immigrant potter by trade; the first Red Wing pottery was that of W. M. Philleo, who moved to St. Paul in 1870 after his shop was destroyed by fire. Initial use of clay from the township's extensive clay pits is credited to David Hallum, former associate of Philleo, who opened a shop that developed into the Red Wing Stoneware Company.

A village called East Red Wing was incorporated on March 4, 1857; then the village charter was revoked, and the village was merged in the city of Red Wing on March 19, 1857. The city expanded again on June 1, 1971, by annexing Burnside Township.

Doane Robinson, historian of the Sioux, writes in the *Handbook of American Indians* (Hodge, pt. 2, 1910, p. 365): "RED WING. The name of a succession of chiefs of the former Khemnichan band of Mdewakanton Dakota residing on the west shore of Lake Pepin, Minn., where the city of Red Wing now stands. At least four chiefs in succession bore the appellation, each being distinguished by another name. The elder Red Wing is heard of as early as the time of the Pontiac war, when he visited Mackinaw, and was in alliance with the English in the Revolution. He was succeeded by his son, Walking Buffalo (Tatankamani), who enlisted in the British cause in 1812. The name was maintained during two succeeding generations, but disappeared during the Dakota Conflict of 1862–65. The family was less influential than the Little Crows or the Wabashas of the same tribe."

Col. William Colvill, in a letter to Prof. Newton H. Winchell, wrote (*Geology of Minnesota, Final Report*, vol. 2, 1888, p. 60): "Red Wing's titular name was Wacouta—'the shooter.' This was always the head chief's title,—the same as that of the chief who captured Hennepin. He had the name of Red Wing, Koo-poo-hoo-sha [Khupahu, wing, sha, red], from the swan's wing, dyed scarlet, which he carried."

Pike in 1805–6 called the second of these hereditary chiefs Talangamane, which should be more correctly written Tatanka mani, meaning "Buffalo walking"; and he also gave his titled name in French, Aile Rouge, with its direct English translation, Red Wing.

The Dakota name of this place was Rhemnicha or Khemnicha, applied by Nicollet's map to the present Hay Creek as Remnicha River. It means the Hill-Water-Wood place, formed by three Dakota words, *Rhe*, "a high hill or ridge," *mini*, "water," and *chan*, "wood," referring to the

Barn Bluff and other high river bluffs and to the abundance of water and wood, which made it an ideal camp ground.

REST ISLAND a village in Central Point Township, section 30, located on Lake Pepin, was platted in 1895 by Etta Thompson and had a post office 1892–93.

RICE see WHITE WILLOW.

ROSCOE settled in 1854, organized in 1858, was named by Charles Dana, one of the pioneers, "from the township of Roscoe, Illinois, where he had previously lived." It had a post office, 1857–1905, in section 29.

ROSCOE CENTRE a post office in Roscoe Township, 1863–82, formerly called Sunapee, 1858–63.

RYAN a village in Belle Creek Township, section 14, settled primarily by Irish and developed with a stage coach stop on the route between Red Wing and Kenyon. A post office operated 1882–1903, with Phillip Ryan as postmaster; that site is where St. Colomba's Church stands in Belle Creek village.

SEVASTAPOL a logging settlement located between Red Wing and Wacouta, platted in 1857, flourished until 1864 when better lumbering facilities were developed upstream; many of the area's early lumbermen were said to have fought in the Crimean War near the Russian city for which it is named; no traces of the settlement remain.

SKYBERG a village in Kenyon Township, section 36, was named for Simon O. Skyberg, a Norwegian immigrant, who with Dr. Ole Abelson opened a general store in 1887, Abelson being first postmaster at the store; its post office operated 1879–1951, although the community diminished after the 1920s; it had a station of the Chicago Great Western Railroad in 1885.

SOGN a village in Warsaw Township, section 24, was named for a district of Norway. The post office, 1892–1903, was established in the home of Ole Underdahl with Ola A. Tveitmoe, postmaster. John Underdahl built a store in 1893; a hotel, a blacksmith, and cheese factory also were built.

SPENCER a village in Vasa Township, was platted in 1857 by Phinneus S. Fish; its post office operated, 1856–68, when changed to Vasa.

SPRING CREEK a post office, 1860–1902, in Cherry Grove Township, section 9.

STANTON settled in the fall of 1854, organized in 1858, was named in honor of William Stanton, who with his son of the same name and others, immigrants from New England, came in 1855, settling on Prairie Creek. Rev. J. W. Hancock, who conducted the first religious services of this township at his home in the winter of 1855–56, wrote: "The log house built by William Stanton, Sr., near the road leading to Faribault from the nearest Mississippi towns, was for several years the only place for the entertainment of travelers between Cannon Falls and further west. Mr. Stanton's latch string was always hanging out, and every civil appearing stranger was welcome to such accommodations as he had. He frequently entertained fifty persons the same night." A post office began in 1857 with Stanton as first postmaster; it was located in section 30, with a station on the Chicago Great Western Railroad.

SUNAPEE see ROSCOE CENTRE.

THOTEN a post office, 1878–83, which was briefly called Belvidere; it was located 14 miles from Red Wing on Wells Creek and had a flour mill.

TROY a settlement in Belle Creek Township, also called Troy City, which was platted in 1856 and had one building, a general store.

VASA settled in 1853, organized in 1858, "was named in honor of Gustavus Vasa, king of Sweden, more generally known as Gustavus I, the Christian king, and the founder of the Lutheran Church" (*History*, 1878, p. 428). He was born in Lindholmen, Upland, Sweden, May 12, 1496, and died in Stockholm, September 29, 1560; was king 1523–60. A post office was located in section 15, 1868–1955; formerly called Spencer, 1856–68.

WACOUTA settled in 1850, organized 1858, was named by George W. Bullard, the first settler, who was an Indian trader and in 1853 platted a village around his trading post, which was a rival of Red Wing for designation as the county seat. Hancock wrote as follows of the last chief bearing this name, commemorated by this little township.

"The nephew of Scarlet Wing [Red Wing] was the last reigning chief of this band of Dakotas. His name was Wacouta, the shooter. It was this chief who informed the writer that his uncle, the Scarlet Wing, was buried on a bluff near Wabasha. Wacouta was a man of peace. He was not accustomed to lead in the warpath, although his braves had the privilege of forming war parties and making raids against their enemies whenever they desired.

"Wacouta was very tall, straight, and dignified in his demeanor. He was also a man of good judgment. His authority was not absolute. He rather advised his people than commanded them. He encouraged industry and sobriety; was a friend to the missionaries, and sent his own children to their schools when he was at home himself."

As before mentioned by Colvill in the notice of Red Wing, this name was borne as a title of chieftaincy. With slight difference, it was the name of the head chief of the Issati Sioux about Mille Lacs at the time of the captivity of Hennepin and his companions in 1680. Hennepin wrote of him as "Ouasicoudé, that is, the Pierced-pine, the greatest of all the slati chiefs."

Keating in 1823, as historian of Maj. Long's expedition, gave this name, under another spelling, "Wazekota (Shooter from the pine-top)," for the old Red Wing chief, Walking Buffalo, whom Pike had met 18 years before. It is from two Dakota words, *wazi*, "pine," and *kute*, "to shoot."

The village, section 36, had a station of the Chicago, Milwaukee, St. Paul and Pacific Railroad and various post offices: Wah-coo-ta, which was established in Wabasha County and transferred to Red Wing; Wacoota, 1854–69, and Wacouta, 1874–1904.

WANAMINGO settled in 1854, organized in 1858, is almost wholly occupied by prosperous Norwegian farmers. The origin and meaning of the name remain to be learned. It appears to be of Indian derivation, "the name of a heroine of a novel popular in those days" (*History*, 1910, p. 222). The city in Wanamingo Township, section 25, and Minneola Township, section 30, was platted in 1907 and incorporated as a village on April 23, 1917. Its first building was erected in 1855; it had a station of the Chicago, Milwaukee, St. Paul and Pacific Railroad and has had a post office since 1857.

WANGS a trading center in Warsaw Township, section 22, with a store, a blacksmith, a shoe shop, a creamery built in 1893, and a post office, 1876–1901; little remains of the community.

WARSAW was first settled in June 1855, and was organized in 1858. Indiana has a city of Warsaw, and 12 states of our Union have villages and townships that bear the name of the capital of Poland. It was originally called Klock Township.

WASTEDO a village in Leon Township, sections 21

and 22, was first settled in 1856, the townsite laid out by H. Ferrell. It had a post office, 1857–1903, and a station of the Chicago Great Western Railroad, but the site did not grow, and the plat was vacated, reverting to farms.

WELCH settled in 1857, organized March 23, 1864, was then named Grant in honor of Gen. Ulysses S. Grant, but it was renamed as now in January 1872 to commemorate Abraham Edwards Welch of Red Wing. He was born at Kalamazoo, Mich., August 16, 1839, and died in the army at Nashville, Tenn., February 1, 1864. He volunteered at Lincoln's first call for troops and was first lieutenant in the First Minnesota Regiment; was taken prisoner, paroled, and served as major against the Dakota in 1862. Later he was major in the Fourth Minnesota Regiment and died from the effect of wounds received at Vicksburg. He was the son of William H. Welch, jurist, who was born in Connecticut about 1812, was a graduate of Yale College and later of its law school, came to Minnesota in 1850, and resided at first in St. Anthony and afterward in St. Paul. He was chief justice of the supreme court of Minnesota Territory, 1853–58, removed in 1858 to Red Wing, and died there January 22, 1863.

The village of Welch in section 28 had a flour mill built in 1878; the post office began in 1860–61 as Eagle Mills with Warren Mills, postmaster; when brothers Samuel and Peter Nelson built a store in 1886, the post office was reestablished as Welch.

WESTERVELT See **FRONTENAC**.

WHITE ROCK a village in Vasa Township, section 32, and Belle Creek Township, section 5; it had a post office, 1871–1903, and a station of the Chicago Great Western Railroad.

WHITE WILLOW a village of Zumbrota Township, section 6, was established when the railroad was built between Red Wing and Zumbrota, with a general store, two grain elevators, a blacksmith, and a cheese factory; however, declining railroad transportation caused the cheese factory to close, the post office was removed, and the village dwindled; the post office operated, 1876–1905, transferring to Rice.

ZUMBROTA settled in 1854, organized in 1858, received the name of its village, platted in September 1854, on the Zumbro River, which flows across the southern part of this township. The

Dakota named this river Wazi Oju, meaning Pines Planted, having reference to the grove of great white pines at Pine Island, before noticed; and it bears this name on Nicollet's map, 1843, and the map of Minnesota Territory in 1850. It was called Riviere d'Embarras and River of Embarrassments by Pike, 1805–6, adopting the name given it by the early French traders and voyageurs; Embarrass River by Maj. Long, 1817; and Embarras, the more correct French spelling, by Albert M. Lea's map, 1836. From the reminiscences written by Lea in 1890 of his explorations, we learn that the French name referred to obstruction of the river near its mouth by a natural raft of driftwood. Pronounced quickly and incompletely, with the French form and accent, as heard and written down by the English-speaking immigrants, this name, Rivière des Embarras, was unrecognizably transformed into Zumbro, which is used on the map of Minnesota in 1860. The village and township name adds a syllable, the Dakota suffix *ta*, meaning "at, to, or on," that is, the town on the Zumbro, being thus a compound from the French and Dakota languages.

The city in Zumbrota and Minneola Townships was incorporated as a village on February 14, 1877. Its first store was erected in October 1856 by Thomas P. Kellett, who became the first postmaster in 1857; other businesses included a cheese factory, mills, elevators, and a creamery. The city was the site of the 1857 Zumbrota Covered Bridge, the only existing covered bridge in Minnesota and the first bridge built over the North Branch of the Zumbro River. Flood damage in 1863, 1865, and 1869 required extensive replacement of bridge sections, the latter year's work remaining until 1932 when the bridge was removed to the fairgrounds.

Lakes, Streams, Islands, and Bluffs

The Mississippi River, which has the large Prairie Island at its west side above Red Wing and extending into Dakota County, and the enlargement of the Mississippi named Lake Pepin, adjoining Goodhue and Wabasha Counties, have been considered in the first chapter.

Cannon and Zumbro Rivers are also noticed in that chapter, the former especially in its presumed identification with the fictitious Long River of Lahontan, but the origins and significance of the names of these streams are again mentioned in the foregoing pages for Cannon Falls and Zumbrota Townships.

Other names of streams, etc., whose origins are presented in the list of townships, include Belle Creek, Central Point of Lake Pepin, Hay Creek, and the so-called Pine Island of Zumbro River.

Excepting Lake Pepin, Silver Lake (very small) in Red Wing, and the few small lakes on Prairie Island, this county is destitute of lakes.

Several streams need no explanations for their names, as Pine Creek, tributary to Cannon River from the north in Cannon Falls Township, Prairie Creek in Stanton, Little Cannon River, Spring Creek in Featherstone and Burnside, and the North and South Branches of the Zumbro.

Bullard Creek, in Hay Creek Township and Wacouta, was named in honor of George W. Bullard, early trader, founder of the former village of Wacouta.

Wells Creek commemorates James Wells, often called "Bully" Wells, an early fur trader on Lake Pepin near the site of Frontenac, who was a member of the territorial legislature in 1849 and 1851.

"Rest Island," at the west side of Lake Pepin near the Central Point, was the location of a home for reform of drunkards, founded in 1891 under the earnest work of John G. Woolley of Minneapolis, who in 1888 entered the lecture field as an advocate of national prohibition.

Prairie Island, translated from its early French name, Isle Pelée, visited by Médard Chouart, sieur de Groseilliers and Pierre E. Radisson in 1655–56, as narrated in the MHS Collections (10, pt. 2: 449–594, with maps), has Sturgeon Lake, Buffalo Slough, North Lake, Clear and Goose Lakes, and the Vermillion River or Slough, continuing from this river in Dakota County and being the western boundary of this large island, which forms mainly the northern parts of Burnside and Welch Townships. Buffalo Slough recalls the old times, long before agricultural settlements here, when buffalo sometimes grazed on the extensive prairie of this island.

Sturgeon Lake was named for the shovel-nosed sturgeon, frequent in the Mississippi here and in this lake, a very remarkable and large species of fish, esteemed for food, having a projecting snout, broad and flat, resembling a shovel or a canoe paddle, which was particularly described by Radisson and Father Louis Hennepin, the first writers on the upper Mississippi.

Assiniboine Bluff in Burnside, nearly isolated from the general upland by the erosion of the Mississippi and Cannon valleys, commemorates the former presence of Assiniboine Indians here, of whom Col. William Colvill wrote in the *Final Report of the Geological Survey* of this state (vol. 2, 1888, pp. 57–60).

Barn Bluff, at Red Wing, is translated from its early French name, La Grange, meaning the Barn, which refers to its prominence as a lone, high, and nearly level-crested bluff, quite separated from the side bluffs of the valley, and therefore conspicuously seen at a distance of many miles up the valley and yet more observable from boats passing along Lake Pepin. Maj. Long in 1817 ascended this hill or bluff, called in his journal "the Grange or Barn," of which he wrote: "From the summit of the Grange the view of the surrounding scenery is surpassed, perhaps, by very few, if any, of a similar character that the country and probably the world can afford. The sublime and beautiful are here blended in the most enchanting manner" (MHS Collections 2: 45).

Other bluffs in Red Wing, adjoining the western border of the river valley or forming a part of it, include Sorin's Bluff, named in honor of Rev. Matthew Sorin, who settled here in 1853, was the first treasurer of this county and the second president of the trustees of Hamline University (at that time located in Red Wing), later was a pastor in Missouri and Colorado, and died in 1879; the Twin Bluffs, on opposite sides of a street leading southwestward; and College Hill, the site of the Red Wing Seminary.

Jordan Bluff in Wacouta, and a short stream and ravine called Jordan Creek in Red Wing, were probably named for a pioneer.

Post Bluff, next eastward in Wacouta, commemorates Abner W. and George Post, early settlers there.

Waconia Bluff in Florence, rising on the valley side west of Frontenac, bears a Dakota name meaning a fountain or spring, from a spring at its base.

Near this southeastward is Point No-point, "from whose summit one may see the whole length of the lake. . . . Persons going in boats down the river see this point for six or eight miles, while the boat seems all the time approaching it, yet none of the time getting any nearer till just as they arrive at Frontenac" (Mitchell, 1869, pp. 96–97).

Sand Point, translated from the French name, Pointe au Sable, is a wave-built spit of sand and gravel, a narrow projection of the shoreline jutting half a mile into Lake Pepin, adjoining Frontenac. Wells Creek, here flowing into the lake, was called "Sand Point R." on Nicollet's map in 1843.

Westward from Point No-point, the large and high area of Garrard Bluff in the northern part of Florence, between the railway and the lake, was named in honor of the Garrard brothers, who founded and named Frontenac village. After they had first visited this place in 1854 on a hunting trip, they purchased large tracts of land here, several thousand acres.

Louis H. Garrard settled at Frontenac in 1858 and engaged in farming and development of this estate; was a representative in the legislature in 1859; removed to Lake City in 1870 and was for three years president of the First National Bank there; resided in Cincinnati, Ohio, his native city, after 1880; and died at Lakewood, N.Y., July 1887, aged 58 years.

The older brother, Israel Garrard, was born in Lexington, Ky., October 22, 1825, and died at his home in Frontenac, Minn., September 21, 1901. He was graduated at the Harvard Law School; settled here in 1854 and after the completion of the land purchase, in 1857–58, built the family home, St. Hubert's Lodge, named for the patron saint of huntsmen. At the beginning of the Civil War, he raised a troop of cavalry in Cincinnati; served as colonel of the Seventh Ohio Cavalry and was promoted to brigadier general; returned here in 1865 and was widely known for his liberality.

Beginning in the 1930 there were efforts to set this area aside for a park. Success came in 1957 with the establishment of Frontenac State Park, which includes both the floodplain along the river and the bluffs towering over Lake Pepin. Besides preserving prairie and hardwood forest, the park is a key area in the flyway for migratory birds.

Prairie Island Reservation

The Prairie Island Indian Community is along the Mississippi River north of Red Wing (in the former Burnside Township). Land purchases for the Mdewakanton and Wahpekute bands occurred in 1886, 1889, and 1934, reaching a total of 534 acres, which are tribally owned. Tribal headquarters are at Welch.

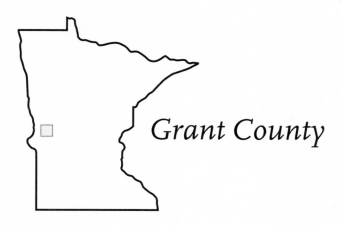

Grant County

This county, established March 6, 1868, and organized in 1874, was named in honor of Ulysses Simpson Grant, whose generalship terminated the Civil War in 1865, with preservation of the Union, after which he was president of the United States, 1869 to 1877. He was born at Point Pleasant, Clermont County, Ohio, April 27, 1822; and died at Mount McGregor, near Saratoga, N.Y., July 23, 1885. Having been graduated at West Point in 1843, he served through the Mexican War of 1846–48; left the army in 1854 and settled in St. Louis; and removed to Galena, Ill., in 1860. He entered the Civil War in June 1861 as a colonel and on April 9, 1865, received the surrender of Robert E. Lee, which ended the war.

On the occasion of the completion of the building of the Northern Pacific Railroad across the continent, Gen. Grant visited Minnesota and was present at the grand celebration held in St. Paul and Minneapolis, September 3, 1883.

Many excellent biographies of Grant have been published. One of his biographers, Louis A. Coolidge in 1917, writes: "His success as President in setting our feet firmly in the paths of peace, and in establishing our credit with the nations of the world, is hardly less significant than his success in war."

The grand courage displayed in his last severe and incurable illness, when during the final months of his life he diligently toiled with the pen in the completion of his memoirs to win a competence for his family and to aid toward payment of creditors after great financial disaster, revealed heroic traits of his character that could never otherwise have found expression.

In 12 states of our Union, counties have been named for him. In New York City his tomb, completed in 1897, has been rightly called "the most imposing memorial structure on the Western Continent."

Information of geographic names in this county has been gathered from the Illustrated Souvenir of Grant County, *by W. H. Goetzinger (1896, 42 pp.);* History of Douglas and Grant Counties, *Constant Larson, editor (1916, 2 vol.; pp. 361–509 in vol. 1 being description and history of this county); and from C. M. Nelson, county auditor, and Hon. Ole O. Canestorp, interviewed during a visit at Elbow Lake, the county seat, in May 1916.*

AASTAD a village in Stony Brook Township, section 2, which was named Aastad Township across county lines in Otter Tail County. The first store was built by Ira Jacobs, who lived in Aastad Township but built on the Stony Brook Township side, later selling it to Knute D. Erickson, who moved the building to his farm in Aastad Township, Otter Tail County, and became first postmaster in 1881; as the Aastad community developed with other stores and businesses, the post office was moved to Grant County in 1894 but returned to Otter Tail County in 1898, closing in 1901.

ASH a post office in Stony Brook Township, 1883–87, with Samuel F. Ash as postmaster on his farm.

ASHBY a city of Pelican Lake Township, sections 2, 3, 10, and 11, platted in 1879, was named for Ashby, England, or possibly in honor of Gunder Ash, a pioneer farmer from Norway, who lived east of the village site and was a friend of James J. Hill. The village was developed on land owned by Simon Larson and was incorporated on March 7, 1884; the post office began operating in 1880.

BARRETT a city of Lien and Elk Lake Townships, platted in May 1887 and incorporated on December 11, 1889, and the adjoining Barrett Lake, commemorate Gen. Theodore Harvey Barrett, who after the Civil War owned and conducted an extensive farm in Grant and Stevens Counties, residing near Moose Island station in Stevens County. He was born in Orangeville, Wyoming County, N.Y., August 27, 1834, and died in this county at Herman, July 20, 1900. He settled in St. Cloud, Minn., 1856, was a captain in the Ninth Minnesota Regiment, 1862–63; was colonel of the 62d U.S. Colored Infantry, 1864–65, and was brevetted brigadier general, March 13, 1865. The post office was established as Fridhem, 1877–87, a Swedish term meaning "home of peace," changing to Barrett in 1887; the village had a station on the Minneapolis, St. Paul and Sault Ste. Marie Railroad (Soo Line).

CANESTORP a village in Stanford Township, section 18, one mile west of Elbow Lake, platted in March 1887, was named for Hon. Ole O. Canestorp, whose birth name was Olof Olofsson, later changed for his farm home in Sweden, Kananstorp. He was born in Sweden, May 21, 1847; came to the United States in 1862 and to Minnesota in 1871, settling at Elbow Lake; was judge of probate of this county, 1878–82, county treasurer, 1882–89, and a state senator, 1891–93 and 1907–9. He died at his home March 24, 1917. The place is also frequently called West Elbow Lake.

CHARLESVILLE a farmers post office, 1904–9, in North Ottawa Township, section 36; it had a station of the Great Northern Railway.

CORK see ERDAHL.

DELAWARE TOWNSHIP organized October 6, 1879, was named by pioneer settlers from that state.

ELBOW LAKE TOWNSHIP organized April 3, 1877, received its name from the adjacent lake in Sanford, shaped like an arm bent at the elbow, to which this name had been given many years previously by early traders and immigrants. Maj. Samuel Woods and Capt. John Pope, in their expedition in the summer of 1849, were the earliest to apply this name, which they each, in their official reports, derived from the shape of the lake.

Elbow Lake village, on a site chosen in 1874 to be the county seat, in Sanford Township, was also named from this lake; it was platted October 28, 1886, and was organized September 2, 1887. The first commercial building was erected in 1884, a boardinghouse and saloon called the Elbow Lake House. The village had a station serving several railroad lines; the first post office operated, 1873–74 and 1876–83, with Henry F. Sanford, postmaster, transferring to Sanford; a second post office began later in the year of 1883.

ELK LAKE TOWNSHIP organized January 4, 1876, was named for its Elk Lake and Lower Elk Lake, tributary to the Chippewa River, where elk were plentiful before agricultural settlers came. The route of Woods and Pope in 1849 passed this Elk Lake, named by the former in his report, writing "Here we saw an elk, . . . the first one that crossed our path." A post office operated in the township, 1877–92, in sections 9 and 16, where a flour mill operated.

ERDAHL organized July 30, 1877, was "named in remembrance of a district in Norway, from which some of the early settlers had come." The same name was borne also by a pioneer Lutheran pastor of this county, Gullik M. Erdahl, who was born in Hardanger, Norway, October 5, 1840, and came to America at the age of seven years with his parents, who settled in Madison, Wis. He was graduated at Luther College, Decorah, Iowa, 1866, and at the Concordia Seminary, St. Louis, 1869; was a missionary and founder of churches in Kansas, Nebraska, and Iowa; was pastor of five congregations in this county, 1875 to 1900, and later of two until his death at his home near Barrett on March 25, 1914. The railway village of Erdahl was platted in October 1887. A country post office operated in section 10, 1883–90, and was called 'Cork, 1890–1901, although the Great Northern Railway station was still Erdahl, the name changing back to Erdahl, 1901–51.

FRIDHEM see BARRETT.

GORTON organized July 21, 1879, received the name given by officials of the railway to a former siding in this township, northwest of Norcross.

HEREFORD a village in section 6, Elbow Lake Township, and section 1, North Ottawa, was platted in September 1887. The history of the county notes the origin of this name as follows: "In 1886, when the railroad was about to establish a station at this point, it was the intention to call the place Culbertson, in honor of the man who owned a tract of land there, but the modest man said that if they wished to compliment him in any way to call the place 'Hereford, after his beautiful herd of white-faced cattle kept on his farm, Hereford Park,' near Newman, Illinois. Accordingly the place was so christened." The breed of cattle came from a county so named in western England. The village had a post office, 1888–1923, formerly at Ireland, and a station of the Great Northern Railway.

HERMAN a city in Logan Township, sections 13 and 24, platted in September 1875, was incorporated February 17, 1881, and again on March 1, 1887, and would doubtless have been chosen as the county seat if its location were near the center of the county. The post office began in 1872 in Norwegian immigrant Sven S. Frogner's general store; the village had a station of the Great Northern Railway. In 1914 it was selected by the State Municipality League on account of its civic merit as the "model town" of Minnesota. Its name was given by the railway officials in honor of Herman Trott, land agent of the St. Paul and Pacific Railroad company. He was born in Hanover, Germany, February 25, 1830, and died in St. Paul, December 29, 1903. He came to this state in 1856 and settled in St. Paul two years later; removed to the state of Washington in 1890 but returned to reside in St. Paul after 1899.

HOFFMAN a railway village in Land Township, platted in April 1887, incorporated June 23, 1891, was named in honor of Robert C. Hoffman of Minneapolis, who during many years was chief engineer of the Soo Line. The village was developed on land purchased by the Minneapolis and Pacific Railroad in 1886 from Andres Lindberg; it had a hotel, several stores, and a grain elevator; its post office began in 1883 as Wanberg, located near Wilson Lake on postmaster Anton Studling (Studien)'s farm; it transferred to the Louis Peterson farm in 1884 and to the village in 1887.

IRELAND a farmers post office, 1881–88, in North Ottawa Township, changing to Hereford in 1888. The area was settled in 1876. R. Ireland was the farm implement dealer, W. H. Ireland owned the hotel, and Rebecca Ireland was the first postmaster.

JACOBS SPUR a station on the Great Northern and Soo Line Railroads in Elbow Lake Township.

LAND TOWNSHIP organized March 6, 1878, was named on the suggestion of Erik Olson, a Norwegian farmer there, "for the town of Land, Wisconsin, whence some of the early settlers had come." In the Norwegian language, it is a general word meaning land or country.

LAWRENCE was organized March 29, 1880. "The first settlers . . . came here in 1870 from St. Lawrence county, New York. It was they who gave the township its name in remembrance of their former home."

LIEN organized July 28, 1874, was named in honor of Ole E. Lien, who was one of its first settlers, coming in 1867 or 1868. He was born in Norway, came to the United States in 1861, settling in Minnesota, and served during the Civil War in the Tenth Minnesota Regiment.

LILLEMON a farmers post office in Lawrence Township, section 2, 1881–1905, formerly located in Aastad Township, Otter Tail County, with Henry J. Lillimon as postmaster.

LOGAN first settled in 1871, organized July 29, 1874, commemorates John Alexander Logan, who was born in Jackson County, Ill., February 9, 1826, and died in Washington, D.C., December 26, 1886. He served in the Mexican War; was a member of Congress from Illinois, 1859–61; was a general in the Civil War, 1861–65; was again a representative in Congress, 1867–71, and a U.S. senator, 1871–77 and 1879–86. In 1884 he was the Republican candidate for vice-president.

MACSVILLE organized September 23, 1878, was named in compliment for Francis McNabb, an early settler and chairman of the first board of supervisors; for John McQuillan, another early settler, who was the first township clerk; also for Coll

McClellan, who in 1875 was chairman of the board of county commissioners.

NORCROSS a city in Gorton Township developed after the Great Northern Railway came, platted in December 1881 and incorporated on February 20, 1904, received its name from Henry Allyn Norton and Judson Newell Cross of Minneapolis, proprietors of the village site. Its post office began in 1881. Norton was born in Byron, Ill., October 17, 1838; died in Minneapolis, February 3, 1906. He served in the army in the Civil War, 1861–65, attaining the rank of major; resided in Chicago until 1882, when he removed to Minneapolis. Cross was born in the state of New York, January 16, 1838; died in Minneapolis, August 31, 1901. He was a student at Oberlin College when the Civil War began; enlisted in the Seventh Ohio Regiment, and during the first year in service was promoted to the rank of captain; in 1864 was made adjutant general of the military district of Indiana. After the war he studied law and in 1875 settled in Minneapolis.

NORTH OTTAWA was organized July 24, 1882. "Thomas H. Toombs from Ottawa, Illinois, gave the township its name." The first township meeting was held at his house, and he was then elected chairman of the supervisors.

ORRIS a country post office, 1898–1905, located 16 miles northwest of Elbow Lake, in Lawrence Township, section 8.

PATCHEN a farmers post office,1897–1907, in Roseville Township, section 26, which had been originally assigned to Keeville in Stevens County. It was located on the Pomme de Terre River; Charles B. Kloos was the postmaster, township clerk, and a real estate developer.

PELICAN LAKE TOWNSHIP organized January 4, 1876, has an extensive lake of this name, which "was noted for the large flocks of pelicans found there in the early days." It was named Lake Ellenora on the earliest state map, in 1860.

PIKOP a post office, 1886–95, formerly at Ramstad, Sanford, and Elbow Lake, located in Sanford Township, sections 22 and 23.

POMME DE TERRE TOWNSHIP organized July 17, 1877, took the name of the large lake at its southeast border, whence also the Pomme de Terre River, flowing from it to the Minnesota River, was named. It is received from the early French voyageurs and traders, meaning literally apple of the

earth, that is, a potato, but it was here applied to the edible ovoid-shaped root of the wild turnip (*Psoralea esculenta*), called Tipsinah by the Dakota. This much esteemed aboriginal food plant, very valuable to these Indians, formerly was common on dry and somewhat gravelly parts of upland prairies throughout southwestern Minnesota. The old village of Pomme de Terre, in section 24, platted in 1874, was the first village in the county, then superseded by railway towns. A post office was located in section 24, 1868–79 and 1880–1902, first established in Stevens County, with a station of the Soo Line.

RAMSTAD a post office, 1883–86, formerly assigned to Sanford and Elbow Lake, and changing to Pikop; its postmaster was Helge H. Ramstad, who also had been postmaster at Sanford.

ROSEVILLE was organized July 24, 1878. "Many names were suggested . . . but the settlers finally decided upon a name which would remind them of the appearance of the virgin prairie when they located there, beautiful with thousands of wild roses" (*History*, 1916, p. 383).

SANFORD organized July 24, 1882, was named by the county commissioners in honor of Henry F. Sanford, who was the first settler in the township, coming here in 1869. He was born in Pleasantville, Pa., June 2, 1845; came to Minnesota and served in Hatch's Battalion of Cavalry against the Dakota, 1863–66; was chairman of the first board of county commissioners, 1873; and was county auditor in 1875–78 and 1887–91. He was killed by an accident in New Mexico in 1914. The post office, 1883, was formerly the first post office in Elbow Lake, changing to Ramstad.

STONY BROOK TOWNSHIP first settled in 1870, organized July 30, 1877, derived its name from the small Stony Brook and Lake in its north part, which are headwaters of Mustinka River.

THORSBORG a post office, 1888–1900, located in Sanford Township, section 13; it had a station of the Great Northern Railway.

WANBORG see **HOFFMAN**.

WENDELL a city in Stony Brook Township, platted in July 1889 and incorporated on March 3, 1904, as a village, received its name from the railway officials when the road was being built, with the location of a depot there in 1887. It was possibly named for Joseph H. Wendell, a judge in Wright County. Its post office began in 1887 with John A.

Beck as first postmaster in his store. It is also the name of a town in Massachusetts and a village in North Carolina.

———————

Lakes and Streams

The foregoing pages have noticed Barrett Lake, Elbow and Elk Lakes, Pelican Lake, the Pomme de Terre River and Lake, and Stony Brook.

Mustinka River has a Dakota name, meaning "a rabbit," the reference being to the common white rabbit, which also is called the "varying hare," because its fur is gray in summer and white in winter. The Dakota dictionaries by Stephen R. Riggs (1852) and John P. Williamson (1902) give it as *Mashtincha*. The larger jack rabbit or hare, also formerly common on the prairies of western Minnesota and on the great plains farther west, was called *mashtintanka*, which means "great rabbit."

Another stream of this county is named Rabbit River, having its sources in Lawrence and flowing west in Wilkin County to Bois des Sioux River.

Two early routes or trails of traders, traveling with trains of Red River carts from the Selkirk and Pembina settlements, in the lower Red River valley, to St. Cloud and St. Paul, passed across the area of Grant County. Both are delineated on the state map of 1860, the more northern passing by Pelican Lake, then called Lake Ellenora, and the central route by Elbow Lake. A more southwestern route led from the Red and Bois des Sioux Rivers to the Minnesota valley and past Swan Lake and Traverse des Sioux to St. Paul.

Woods and Pope in the expedition of 1849, before mentioned, took the middle route, passing Elk Lake, the Little Pomme de Terre Lake (now named Barrett Lake), and onward northwest, having on the left hand, successively, Long, Worm, Elbow, and Lightning Lakes. Three of these last have been named for their shape or outline, the most remarkable being Worm Lake, of very irregular and wormlike form.

Lightning Lake in Stony Brook Township, and Upper Lightning Lake, a few miles farther northwest, in the edge of Otter Tail County, perhaps derived their names from an incident during the expedition of Woods and Pope, when they so named two lakes where they had camped in reference to "a stroke of lightning, which tore in pieces one of the tents, and prostrated nearly all the persons who were in the camp" (Pope, *Report* [1850], pp. 18–19). But the detailed narration of Pope shows that their Lightning Lakes were those now named Grove Lake and McCloud's Lake in Pope County on a more southeastern part of the route, distant about two or three days' journey from these lakes. In a paper by D. S. B. Johnston, who went over this route in 1857, it is stated that the Lightning Lake of Grant County, according to Pierre Bottineau, the famous guide, "took its name from a man in a former expedition being struck by lightning and killed" (MHS Collections 15: 417 [1915]). In the tradition of guides, possibly the experience of the expedition in 1849 had given origin to a misplaced Lightning Lake in 1857, which has been permanently retained.

A large number of other lakes are named mostly in honor of early settlers near them, or for trees, as Cottonwood Lake, birds, as Cormorant Lake, or other animals, as Turtle Lake; or for their size or outlines, as Big, Horseshoe, and Round Lakes. These are noted in the following list, arranged in the numerical order of the townships and ranges.

Patchen, Shauer, and Silver Lakes in Roseville.

Big and Cottonwood Lakes, Burr, Johnson, Olstrud, Neimackl, Barrows, Graham, and Nelson Lakes in Macsville.

Pullman Lake, adjoining Herman, named for Charles Pullman, proprietor of the first hotel there.

Lake Katrina or Sylvan Lake (bordered by a grove), Peterson, Thompson, Torstenson, Ellingson, Olson, and Retzhoff Lakes, Round Lake, Spring and Turtle Lakes, Church Lake (beside a church), and Island Lake in Elk Lake Township.

Cormorant Lake, Eide, Huset, and Jones Lakes in Lien.

Moses Lake or Slough in Delaware.

Island and Round Lakes in Sanford.

Four Mile Lake (so far from the old Pomme de Terre stage station), Field, Horseshoe, and Scott's Lakes in Pomme de Terre Township, of which the second and fourth were named for nearby farmers.

Stony Brook Lake in sections 3 and 10 of Stony Brook Township.

Stony Lake in section 12, Lawrence, and Ash Lake in sections 24 and 25 of this township, the last being named for an early immigrant farmer from England.

Herman and Norcross Beaches of Lake Agassiz

From their excellent development near Herman and at Norcross, the first and uppermost beach and the second beach, which is next lower, of the Glacial Lake Agassiz, received their names as respectively the Herman and Norcross Beaches or Shorelines. Along northern parts of this great ancient lake, which filled the Red River valley, as more fully noticed in the first chapter of this volume, each of these beaches is divided, on account of the northward uplift of the land during the existence of the lake, into two or several beaches, distinct and separate strand lines at small vertical intervals, which there are distinguished as the Upper and Lower Herman Beaches, or the first, second, third, etc., and likewise the Upper and Lower Norcross Beaches. The earliest published use of these names is in the *Eleventh Annual Report of the Geological Survey of Minnesota*, for 1882.

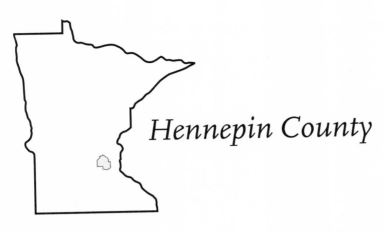

Hennepin County

This county, established March 6, 1852, commemorates Louis Hennepin, the Franciscan missionary, explorer, and author, who was born in Ath, Belgium, about 1640 and died in Holland about 1701. He entered the order of the Recollects of St. Francis, probably in his early youth; spent many years in the service of that order in France, Belgium, Holland, Italy, and Germany; and was present, as a regimental chaplain, at the battle of Senef in 1674. The next year he sailed to Canada, in the same ship with François-Xavier de Montmorency Laval, the bishop of the newly established see of Quebec, and Robert Cavelier, sieur de la Salle, destined to be the greatest French explorer of the New World, arriving at Quebec in September. In 1678 Hennepin joined La Salle's expedition for exploration of Lakes Ontario, Erie, Huron, and Michigan, and the Illinois and Mississippi Rivers.

By direction of La Salle, whom he left near the site of present-day Peoria, Hennepin descended the Illinois River with two companions in a canoe and thence ascended the Mississippi. On their way up the Mississippi they were captured by a band of Dakota, living near Mille Lacs, spent eight months with them, and were rescued by Daniel Greysolon, sieur Du Luth, who enabled Hennepin to reach Green Bay. In the midsummer of 1680, after the early part of their captivity by the Dakota in the region of Mille Lacs, Hennepin and one of his French companions, Anthony Auguelle (also called the Pickard du Gay), were the first white men to see the falls in the Mississippi River, which Hennepin named the Falls of St. Anthony in honor of his patron saint, Anthony of Padua.

He returned to Quebec in 1682 and to Europe soon afterward. In 1683 he published in Paris an account of his explorations, titled *Description de la Louisiane*. A translation of by John Gilmary Shea was published in New York in 1880, with dedication to Archbishop John Ireland and John Fletcher Williams, who were respectively the president and secretary of the Minnesota Historical Society. This volume has an introductory notice of Father Hennepin and an account of his published works (45 pp.), and the main translation is followed by others from La Salle and Du Luth and by a bibliography of Hennepin's works and their many editions and translations.

Extensive quotations from Shea are given in chapter 7 (pp. 205–41) in vol. 1 of *Minnesota in Three Centuries*, published in 1908, which narrates the explorations of Du Luth and Hennepin in the area of this state, with biographic sketches of these great pioneers of New France.

Two hundred years after Hennepin visited and named the falls of the Mississippi at the center of the present city of Minneapolis, a great celebration was held there by the Minnesota Historical Society and the people of the Twin Cities on the grounds of the University of Minnesota, within view of the falls, on Saturday, July 3, 1880. The description of this Hennepin Bi-Centenary celebration, and the addresses of Gov. Cushman K. Davis, Gov. Alexander Ramsey, Gen. William T.

Sherman, and Archbishop Ireland, with a poem by A. P. Miller, are published in the MHS Collections 6: 29–74.

The name of Hennepin, instead of Snelling, which had been proposed by Col. John H. Stevens in the original bill, was adopted for this county on request of Martin McLeod, member of the territorial council.

The origins and meanings of these names have been gathered mostly from the Geographical and Statistical History of the County of Hennepin by W. H. Mitchell and Col. John H. Stevens (1868, 149 pp.); History of Hennepin County and the City of Minneapolis by George E. Warner and Charles M. Foote (1881, 713 pp.); History of Minneapolis, edited by Judge Isaac Atwater, and Hennepin County, edited by Col. John H. Stevens (1895, 2 vols., continuously paged, 1,497 pp.); Compendium of History and Biography of Minneapolis and Hennepin County by Return I. Holcombe and William H. Bingham (1914, 584 pp.); and from Hon. John B. Gilfillan, Dr. Lysander P. Foster, and Maj. Edwin Clark, each of Minneapolis, the second and third being respectively president and secretary of the Hennepin County Territorial Pioneers' Association.

ABEL a village in Maple Grove Township with a flour mill and post office, 1875–79.

ACADEMY a station on the Minnesota Western Railroad, seven miles west of Minneapolis.

ARCOLA a station of the Great Northern Railway in section 15 of Excelsior Township.

ARMSTRONG a station of the Great Northern Railway in Independence Township; see also MAPLE PLAIN.

ATWOOD a station of the Minnesota, Northfield and Southern Railroad; location not found.

BAPTIST ASSEMBLY a post office, 1910–14; location not found.

BEDERWOOD a post office on the north shore of Stubbs Bay, first named Hulda, 1898–99, with Jonathan L. Grave, postmaster; renamed Bederwood, 1899–1901, after the popular strawberry; James W. Robertson was postmaster.

BIBLE COLLEGE a community post office since 1970.

BLOOMFIELD a village in Richfield Township, with a post office, 1886–1902; first postmaster was Alexander Scholz, general store owner and shoemaker.

BLOOMINGTON FERRY according to local history, is the first post office in the county; Joseph Dean requested a post office and received one, two days before Minneapolis received theirs (January 7, 1854); Jonas Staring was postmaster in his home on Staring Lake, and then in a store Horace Goodrich built, for 14 years, until Fred Goodrich became postmaster; however, postal records do not list a post office at Staring Lake. The post office at Bloomington Ferry operated 1865–1902, and Simeon E. Goodrich was appointed first postmaster.

BLOOMINGTON TOWNSHIP first settled in 1843, organized May 11, 1858, was the home of bands of the Dakota, "those of Good Road and Man of the Clouds. They occupied the bluff on the river near the residence of Rev. G. H. Pond." The name was given by settlers from Illinois, who came in 1852. Twelve other states have villages and cities of this name, the two largest being in Illinois and Indiana.

The city of Bloomington was incorporated on April 8, 1953, and is the third largest city in the state; its early post office operated 1853 to 1903, becoming part of the Minneapolis postal system.

BOEVILLE a place name in Minnetrista Township, circa 1930s.

BROOKLYN CENTER is a city created in January 1911 and incorporated as a village February 18, 1911, from part of southeastern Brooklyn Township and eastern Crystal Lake Township. It developed first as a truck garden area, gradually becoming a residential suburb; much of the city was originally the Earle Brown farm, which was deeded to the city on his death in 1969; Brown had been sheriff of Hennepin County and chief of the Minnesota State Patrol.

BROOKLYN PARK a city incorporated on April 14, 1954, was the major part of the original Brooklyn Township, including the early town of Harrisburg.

BROOKLYN TOWNSHIP settled in 1852, organized

May 11, 1858, was named by pioneers from southern Michigan, who came in 1853, for the former township and present railway village of Brooklyn in that state, about 20 miles northwest of Adrian.

Brooklyn was also the name of a post office, 1869–77, formerly named Industriana, 1860–69, at a site platted by the Industrial Mill Company, on which they had built a sawmill about 1858, which did not prove a financial success; after an explosion occurred in the early 1860s, the mill closed, and the site eventually disappeared.

BURSCHVILLE a post office, 1888–1902, located in Corcoran Township, sections 7 and 8, with Julius Bursch, postmaster.

BUSHNELL a community in the western part of Minnetonka Township, named for John B. Bushnell, president of Minneapolis Threshing Machine Company, a major industry of Hopkins; a post office operated 1892–95.

CAHILL see **EDINA**.

CALHOUN BEACH a post office station in 1931.

CAMDEN PLACE a post office, 1888–1900, which was first called Shingle Creek, 1877–88; changed to a branch of Minneapolis.

CHAMPLIN first settled in 1852, organized May 11, 1858, was named from its village, platted in 1853, opposite Anoka and the mouth of the Rum River. The village was first settled in the 1850s by Swiss and Yankees; Joseph B. Holt, Samuel Colburn, and John B. Cook had the site surveyed, platted, and recorded in 1856; it was named for Cook's wife, Ellen E. Champlin, the daughter of Commodore Stephen Champlin, a naval career officer, commander of the *Scorpion*, the gunboat that fired the first shots in the battle of Lake Erie on September 10, 1813, and cousin of Commodore Oliver H. Perry; Cook was a land speculator and partner of Alexander Ramsey in many ventures but did not live here. The city was incorporated on October 14, 1946; its first post office survived only a short time in 1857, a second post office being transferred from Elm Creek in 1858, which had begun there in 1855.

CHANHASSEN a city with Carver County.

CHOWEN a post office, 1882–1902, in section 18 of Minnetonka Township, named for brothers who settled there in 1853, Joseph, George, and William S. Chowen, the last being the postmaster; also known as Chowen's Corner.

CITY OF ATTRACTION see **OSSEO**.

COON RAPIDS a post office, 1897–1901, first located in Hennepin County, which became Coon Rapids, Anoka County.

CORCORAN settled in 1855, organized May 11, 1858, was named in honor of Patrick B. Corcoran, who was the first schoolteacher there, the first merchant, and first postmaster. He was highly commended as a good citizen by Col. Stevens. He was born in Ireland, 1825, came to the United States in 1847, and to this county in 1855, being one of the earliest settlers of this township. The city of Corcoran was incorporated on December 4, 1948; it had a post office, 1863–1903.

CRYSTAL village, as it is now named, incorporated January 11, 1887, would be more suitably termed a small township, under which form of government it was organized April 3, 1860, when Minneapolis and Brooklyn Townships gave up some of their land, being then called Crystal Lake. The northern part was once called Farmersville Township, which in 1858 took two tiers of sections from Brooklyn Township and one from Minneapolis but did not organize, and the boundaries reverted and became part of the new township. The village was the site of a large stockyard in the 1880s; it incorporated as a city in 1960; a post office was located there, 1883–1901. The village has the Twin Lakes and the smaller Crystal Lake, which boasts "a good depth of water and better shores." Besides the title of the township and village, its Crystal Prairie, four miles long and a mile wide, but dotted originally with many small groves, like islands, was also named from the lake.

CRYSTAL BAY a post office first called Markville, 1889–1906, when changed to the present name; Peter M. Mark, a traveling druggist, opened the post office near the Great Northern Railway station in section 10.

CRYSTAL LAKE a post office, 1857–67, in Crystal Township; first settled in 1852, with a flour mill built in 1859 in section 4 of then Brooklyn Township.

DAYTON TOWNSHIP settled in 1851, organized May 11, 1858, was named, like its village, platted in 1855, in honor of Lyman Dayton of St. Paul, one of the original proprietors. He was born in Southington, Conn., August 25, 1810, and died in St. Paul, October 20, 1865. He came to Minnesota in 1849 and invested largely in real estate; was the projector and president of the Lake Superior and Mississippi Railroad (later named St. Paul and Duluth). Dayton is also a city with Wright County; its post office began in 1855.

DEEPHAVEN a city located on Carson's Bay, incorporated as a village in 1900; its post office was first called Northome, 1882–92 (named by Charles S. Gibson of St. Louis, who in 1877 built a house he called "Nort Home"; later he opened the Hotel St. Louis overlooking Bay St. Louis), and was discontinued in 1914. The Hazen J. Burtons moved into a home on Carson's Bay and were asked to name the station of the Minneapolis and St. Louis Railroad located at the foot of their hill; Mrs. Burton suggested Deephaven after the title of a book by her favorite New England author, Sarah Orne Jewett. Hazen J. Burton became the first mayor. The city was the site of the Haralson Brothers tree nursery where the Haralson apple was developed.

DITTER a farmers post office, 1887–1901, in Medina Township, Frank Ditter, postmaster.

DUPONT a post office, 1875–90, Joseph Dupont, postmaster; located six miles from Armstrong in the northwest part of the county, it had a general store and a blacksmith shop.

EDEN PRAIRIE TOWNSHIP settled in 1852, organized in 1858, had a fine natural prairie in its southern portion. "The town was named, in 1853, by a Mrs. Elliot, who gave it the name Eden in expressing her admiration of this beautiful prairie" (*History*, 1881, p. 231). The reference should be for Elizabeth F. Ellet, an author of national reputation, who visited Lake Minnetonka in August 1852, less than three months after it was visited and named by Gov. Ramsey. Other names proposed by her, for bays and a point of Minnetonka, are noted on a later page in this chapter. The city of Eden Prairie was incorporated on October 22, 1962; its first post office operated 1855–1902; the second was transferred from Washburn (1874–1903) in 1903 and operated until 1944.

EDINA a city, originally part of Richfield Township until incorporated as a separate village on December 18, 1888. It was developed out of three different communities: the first, Richfield Mills, lying outside the boundaries of Edina, served as a trading center and the township seat; it had a gristmill and a store. The second a few miles west

on Minnehaha Creek was Waterville Mills with a mill erected in 1856 and sold to Andrew Craik in 1869, a Scottish immigrant from Canada who renamed the enterprise Edina Mills, with a post office, 1881–1902. The third, Cahill Settlement, was established in the 1850s by Irish immigrants and retained a post office named Cahill for the period 1894–1902. The name was derived from the flour mill owned by Andrew and John Craik, who so named the mill in memory of their boyhood home, in or near Edinburgh, Scotland.

ELM CREEK see CHAMPLIN.

ELMWOOD see ST. LOUIS PARK.

EUREKA a post office, 1892–1900 and 1901–43, established for the people at Birch Bluff and Howard's Point, resort areas on Lake Minnetonka; it had a station of the Minneapolis and St. Louis Railroad.

EXCELSIOR organized May 11, 1858, "owes its name and settlement to a colony, under the title of the Excelsior Pioneer Association," which was formed in New York City, November 12, 1852. "They were headed by George M. Bertram and arrived in the summer of 1853." The colony adopted this name in allusion to Henry W. Longfellow's world-famous short poem, "Excelsior," which was written September 28, 1841, and was published a few days later. The city of Excelsior was incorporated as a village on June 14, 1878; the oldest of the Lake Minnetonka communities, it was settled in the early 1850s and platted in 1855; its post office began in 1854. Rev. Charles Galpin, first a minister in Chanhassen, 1853, then moved to Excelsior and was the first postmaster; his brother, Rev. George Galpin, built the town's first hotel, a log cabin, in 1854. The village was the site of many resort hotels with pavilions and yacht marinas and of two amusement parks: the Big Island Amusement Park, 1906–11, was a major attraction for those who came from the Twin Cities; the second, Excelsior Amusement Park, opened in 1925 and was closed and demolished in 1974.

FARMERSVILLE TOWNSHIP see CRYSTAL.

FLETCHER a post office, 1900–1906, located in Hassan Township, and also known as St. Walburg; the site had a hotel and a saloon.

FORT SNELLING the first post office in Minnesota, 1836–1918.

FREEPORT see WAYZATA.

GLEN LAKE a community of one square mile,

mainly private homes, at the crossroad of Excelsior Boulevard and Eden Prairie Road, Minnetonka Township. It had a post office, 1922–63. The original land grant, April 2, 1857, of 160 acres at the south end of Lake Minnetonka was owned by Mary and Robert Glen, later becoming the site of the Hennepin County Home School for Boys and the Glen Lake Sanatorium (state tuberculosis hospital).

GOLDEN VALLEY a western suburb of Minneapolis, euphoniously named for its beautiful valley enclosing a small and narrow lake, was incorporated December 17, 1886, under a village charter, though it was chiefly a farming community. It had been formerly the northwest part of Minneapolis Township. Its post office operated first as Minneapolis Park, 1891–98, discontinuing in 1901; it had a station of the Minneapolis and St. Louis Railroad.

GOODWIN a post office, 1887–89; location not found.

GREENFIELD a city incorporated on March 14, 1958, in Greenwood Township.

GREENWOOD a city formerly part of Excelsior until separated and incorporated on January 10, 1956; primarily a residential community.

GREENWOOD TOWNSHIP settled in 1855, organized May 11, 1858, took the name of a former village, which aspired to be a city, platted by Thomas A. Holmes (founder of many towns) and others in the winter of 1856–57. It was soon superseded by Rockford, on the Wright County side of the Crow River about a mile below the Greenwood city site. "The origin of the name was the charming appearance of the woodlands, as seen by the first settlers, in the early days of summer" (*History*, 1881, p. 311). It had a post office, 1857–75.

GROVELAND see WOODLAND.

HAMEL an unincorporated village in section 12, Medina, founded in 1886, was named for J. O. and William Hamel, merchants there. The post office was called Lenz, 1861–86, when changed to the present; Leonard Lenzen was first postmaster at Lenz, and Joseph O. Hamel was first postmaster at Hamel; it had a station of the Minnesota and Pacific Railroad.

HANOVER a city with Wright County.

HARMONY see RICHFIELD.

HARRIET a suburban post office of Minneapolis, 1895–97.

HARRISBURGH a village of 160 platted acres, located ten miles north of Minneapolis. It had a mill built about 1856, a hotel, several homes, and a store; the mill was torn down a few years later, one house burned, and the rest were removed; a post office operated 1856–66; no trace remains.

HASSAN RAPIDS a post office, 1895–97, located in Hassan Township.

HASSAN TOWNSHIP first settled in 1854, organized April 3, 1860, received its name from the Dakota word *chanhasan*, meaning "the sugar maple tree" (*chan*, tree; *hasan*, from *haza*, the whortleberry or huckleberry, also blueberries; that is, the tree having similarly sweet sap). Carver County has a township named Chanhassen, south of Lake Minnetonka, settled two years earlier and organized in 1858. Not to conflict with that name, the syllable meaning tree was here omitted. A post office operated 1866–1904.

HENCO a post office authorized on September 16, 1921, with Ernest S. Mariette, postmaster, but not established; location not found.

HENNEPIN a short-lived village platted in 1852 on a portion of John H. McKenzie's claim in sections 34 and 35, Eden Prairie, on the Minnesota River, was during several years a shipping point for grain. It was modeled after townsites in the East and was registered in Ramsey County in June 1853 and in Hennepin County, May 17, 1854. It had a store, a gristmill, a sawmill, a blacksmith shop, several homes, and a warehouse by the ferry. It failed to develop because of enterprises elsewhere in the township, and no traces remain.

HIGHLAND PARK a post office, 1855–56; location not found.

HOGBO see LYNDALE.

HOPKINS a city in Minnetonka Township, organized as West Minneapolis on November 27, 1892; the name was changed on July 7, 1928, to honor Harley Hopkins, former adventurer and gold prospector, who settled in the area and became the first postmaster, 1873, in the depot where he was station master. He was born in 1824; came to this county in 1855; engaged in farming on a part of the village site; died in Minneapolis, February 19, 1882. When Hopkins died, his daughter, Florinda, became postmaster at the depot. The city was incorporated December 2, 1947; sometimes referred to as Bushnell.

HULDA see BEDERWOOD.

INDEPENDENCE settled in 1854–55, organized May 11, 1858, bears the name of the largest one of its several lakes. "The lake derived its name from a party of Fourth of July excursionists. Kelsey Hinman, one of the party, named it Lake Independence, in honor of the national holiday" (*History*, 1881, p. 263). The city of Independence was incorporated November 9, 1956.

INDUSTRIANA see BROOKLYN.

ISLAND CITY a settlement on the west shore of Haines Bay, started by William Russell, St. Anthony newspaperman, as an attempt to create the state capitol; the post office was named Tazaska, 1855–56, and Island City, 1856–60.

ISLAND PARK a village incorporated on November 8, 1924, currently unincorporated; its post office was named Phelps Island, 1915–25, changed to Island Park, 1925–27, and became a community post office in 1941.

LAKE SARAH post office, 1895–1906; now an area of Greenfield.

LEIGHTON a village six miles northeast of Wayzata, with a post office, 1857–78, with Nathaniel G. Leighton, first postmaster.

LENZ see HAMEL.

LONG LAKE a Great Northern Railway village in Orono, was named for the adjoining Long Lake, one of our most abundant lake names. Originally part of Medina Township, the village incorporated on February 20, 1906, and again on April 21, separating from the township on April 25; the post office began as Tamarack in 1856 in the home of postmaster Henry Stubbs, changing to the present name in 1869, two years after a station of the St. Paul and Pacific Railroad was built in section 34; Tamarack was named for the vast tamarack swamps in the western part of the county.

LORETTO a Minneapolis, St. Paul and Sault Ste. Marie Railroad (Soo Line) village in section 6, Medina, founded in 1886 and incorporated on March 20, 1940, was named from a Catholic mission for refugees of the Huron Indians near Quebec, Canada, called Lorette, founded and named in 1673, and from the village of Loretto, Ky., where a society of Catholic "Sisters of Loretto at the Foot of the Cross" was founded in 1812. Many schools are conducted by members of this society in the central and southern United States. The original source of the name is Loreto, a small town in Italy, which has a noted shrine of pilgrimage (*Catholic*

Encyclopedia, vol. 9, 1910, pp. 360–61; vol. 13, 1912, pp. 454–56). The city has had a post office since 1887.

LYNDALE an unincorporated village whose post office was named Hogbo, February–June 1892, with Andrew P. Hogland, postmaster; changed to Lyndale and operated until 1904 and 1916–34.

MAPLE GROVE TOWNSHIP first settled in 1851, organized May 11, 1858, was named for the abundance of the hard, or sugar, maple in its forests. The city of Maple Grove incorporated on April 30, 1954, and had a post office, 1866–1901.

MAPLE PLAIN a city in Independence Township, section 25, platted in 1868 when the railway construction was completed to that station of the St. Paul, Minneapolis and Manitoba Railroad, was named, like Maple Grove, for the abundance of the hard, or sugar, maple in its forests. It was incorporated as a village April 19, 1912; its post office began in 1856. Local history states that the post office moved from Armstrong, at which time the postmaster resigned to be depot agent and John Perkins became postmaster; postal records list Irvin Shrewsbury as first postmaster; Armstrong had a depot, a general store, and several houses and is noted on maps as a populated place in Independence Township.

MAPLEWOODS see WOODLAND.

MARKVILLE see CRYSTAL BAY.

MARSHALL TOWNSHIP was organized in 1858 and included all of Dayton and Champlin, but it separated into those two areas that same year.

MEDICINE LAKE a city encircled by Plymouth and located on a peninsula on the south end of Medicine Lake; the village was incorporated April 5, 1944, and had a post office, 1856–64.

MEDINA settled in 1854, organized May 11, 1858, had been previously called Hamburg by the county commissioners, which name was then changed to Medina by a unanimous vote of the 37 settlers present. This name of a city in Arabia, where Mohammed spent his last ten years and died, is borne by villages and townships in eight states of our Union and by counties in Ohio and Texas. The city was incorporated on May 31, 1955.

MINNEAPOLIS founded by Col. John H. Stevens, builder of the first house on the west side of the Mississippi here in 1849–50, organized as a township May 11, 1858, was transformed in 1886 to the village organizations of Golden Valley and

St. Louis Park, excepting the eastern part of the township, which had been comprised in the city area. On the original site of this city, platting of village lots was begun in the spring of 1854 by Stevens, to which other plats were added in 1854–55. The state legislature, in an act approved March 1, 1856, authorized a town government with a council, which was inaugurated July 20, 1858. The city of Minneapolis was incorporated under an act of March 2, 1866, and its first election of officers was held February 19, 1867. It was enlarged, through union of the former cities of Minneapolis and St. Anthony, by a legislative act approved February 28, 1872, and the new city council was organized April 9, 1872. The city's present boundaries were established in 1927; its post office was established in 1854.

The earliest announcement and recommendation of this name was brought by Charles Hoag to the editor of the *St. Anthony Express*, George D. Bowman, on the day of its publication, November 5, 1852. It was then published, without time for editorial comment, which was very favorably given in the next issue on November 12. Soon this new name, compounded from Minnehaha and the Greek *polis*, "city," displaced the various earlier names that had attained more or less temporary acceptance, including All Saints, proposed by James M. Goodhue of the *Minnesota Pioneer*, Hennepin, Lowell, Brooklyn, Albion, and others.

The distinguished parts borne by both Hoag and Bowman in this opportune coinage of the name Minneapolis have been many times related, with gratitude to Hoag for the bright idea and to Bowman for his effective advocacy of it by his newspaper.

But a new claim, for the origination of the name by Bowman during a horseback ride from St. Anthony to Marine Mills on the St. Croix River, was published in the summer of 1915 by a posthumous letter of Benjamin Drake, Sr., a cousin of Bowman, printed on page 1583 in vol. 3 of the late Capt. Henry A. Castle's *History of Minnesota*. The circumstantial evidences of truthfulness there shown for Bowman, as the first to receive the inspiration of uniting "Minnehaha" and "polis" to form this city name, seem quite conclusive.

It is probable, however, that Bowman had mentioned this idea to his friend Mr. Hoag, and that some days or weeks later, when Hoag had en-

tirely forgotten this, it may have come again to his mind and been thought new and original with himself, immediately before his writing the short article by which this name was proposed in November 1852.

So each of these excellent early citizens of Minneapolis may have honestly believed himself the favored first originator of the city's name. They worked together unselfishly and successfully for its adoption, and they seem equally deserving of enduring fame for this service to the young city.

The claims for each are quite fully stated and discussed in the *Minneapolis Journal*, by Hon. John B. Gilfillan, January 7, 1917, and by the present writer a week later on January 14.

MINNEAPOLIS PARK see GOLDEN VALLEY.

MINNEHAHA a post office, 1875–84 and 1888–91; location not found.

MINNEHAHA PARK a post office, 1893–1901, with George Crocker as first postmaster.

MINNETONKA BEACH is a city in Excelsior Township, sections 15, 16, and 22, on a peninsula of Lake Minnetonka, between Crystal and Lafayette Bays, in Orono. It was first settled when John Herrill Holme purchased 100 acres in December 1855; its post office began in 1882; it was platted in 1883 by A. H. Bode of the St. Paul, Minneapolis and Manitoba Railroad and developed as a summer colony and resort area. It was incorporated as the Village of Minnetonka Beach on November 2, 1894; its full name is City of the Village of Minnetonka Beach.

MINNETONKA LAKE PARK see TONKA BAY.

MINNETONKA MILLS see MINNETONKA.

MINNETONKA TOWNSHIP first settled in the spring of 1852, organized May 11, 1858, received the name of the adjoining large lake. The earliest recorded exploration of this lake by white men was in 1822 by two youths, Joseph R. Brown, who became a leading figure in Minnesota history, and William Joseph Snelling, son of the commandant of the fort, accompanied by two soldiers. From their meager and magnified description, William H. Keating, the historian of the United States exploring expedition under Maj. Stephen H. Long in 1823, mentioned this lake, though it was not named nor shown on their map.

Twenty years later, in 1843, Joseph N. Nicollet's map and report of this region, based on preceding maps and filled out by much information from his own explorations and from Indians and white voyageurs whom he questioned, had no intimation of the existence of Minnetonka. It seems to have been entirely forgotten by the officers of the fort with whom Nicollet was intimately acquainted. Because it was in the Dakota country, not ceded for white immigration until the treaties of Traverse des Sioux and Mendota in 1851, ratified by Congress the next year, this fairest one of our myriad lakes remained to be named and published when its first white settlers came.

In the chapter on this township, contributed by Judge Henry G. Hicks to the history of the county in 1895, the exploration of the lower part of this lake by Simon Stevens and Calvin A. Tuttle in April 1852 is well narrated. Two days after their return, the *St. Anthony Express* for April 16 published an article titled "Peninsula Lake," in which it is truly remarked that "almost the entire shore appears to be a succession of bays and peninsulas."

The present more felicitous name was coined about six weeks later by Gov. Ramsey, when, near the end of May, he made a journey to this lake in a company of several prominent citizens from St. Anthony and St. Paul. An article by Goodhue in his newspaper, the *Minnesota Pioneer*, for July 1, says: "The lake was named by Governor Ramsey, Minnetonka, or 'Big Water,' who expressed great admiration of the beauties of the country surrounding."

Minne (also spelled *mini*) is the common Dakota word for water, and *tonka* (also spelled *tanka*) is likewise their common word meaning big or great, but the name thus compounded seems not to have been used by the Dakota till Ramsey coined it for the lake. So far as we have records, indeed, the Dakota appear to have had no term for this large and many-featured body of water.

The city of Minnetonka was first settled at Minnetonka Mills on Minnehaha Creek; it was incorporated on August 28, 1956; a post office operated 1855–1909.

MINNETRISTA settled in 1854, organized in the spring of 1859, was at first named German Home by the county commissioners but was changed to the present name by vote of the settlers at the date of organization. "Several names were proposed and rejected. The name of Minnetrista was finally proposed and accepted, Minne (meaning wa-

ters) and trista (meaning crooked); and from the fact that the town contained so many crooked lakes, this name was considered as the most appropriate" (*History*, 1881, p. 260).

To be more definite, this name seems to have been chosen primarily in allusion to the very irregular and curiously zigzag outline of Whale Tail Lake, which thus not only suggested its own name but also this name for the township. Another lake of curious crookedness, in sections 5 and 6, is called Ox Yoke Lake, from its shape. Minnetrista is partly of Dakota derivation, in its first half, but *trista* is not found in either the Dakota or Ojibwe languages. It is another example of words coined by white men, as if used by Indians. The letter *r*, occurring in *trista*, is not employed by Stephen R. Riggs or Frederic Baraga in their dictionaries of these aboriginal languages, nor are their words meaning "crooked" similar in sound with *trista*, which we may therefore think to be of Yankee invention, to signify twisted or twister.

The city of Minnetrista was incorporated on August 16, 1960; it had a post office, 1860–94.

MORNINGSIDE the first major residential development of Edina by C. I. Fuller, was an 8,500-acre designed community for Minneapolis workers; it seceded from Edina on September 22, 1920, but returned in 1966.

MOUND a city on and near the northwestern shore of Lake Minnetonka, incorporated as a village in 1912, separating from Minnetrista; the post office was first called Mound City when it was begun in 1876, changing to Mound in 1894; it had a station of the Great Northern Railway.

The city is named for its aboriginal mounds. Three groups of these mounds within the area of the village, mapped by Newton H. Winchell, have respectively 4, 18, and 9 mounds; and at the distance of about a mile westward is a remarkable series of 69 mounds, on the north side of Halsted's Bay (*Aborigines of Minnesota*, 1911, pages 224–26, with maps of these mound groups).

Around all the shores of Lake Minnetonka, and on some of its islands, are many mounds, mostly in groups. The aggregate number of these mounds mapped and described by Winchell, in the work cited (pp. 224–42, with 36 maps or plats), is 495, in more than 30 groups, which range in their separate numbers from 2 or 3 up to 98 mounds.

MOUND CITY see MOUND.

NAVARRE a community post office since 1952, is an area of Spring Lake.

NEW HOPE a city separated from Crystal about 1936 and incorporated on July 8, 1953.

NORTHOME see DEEPHAVEN.

NORTHTOWN a post office, 1891–1901; location not found.

OAK GROVE a post office, 1855–56; location not found.

OAK TERRACE a village three miles southwest of Hopkins with a post office, 1921–63, and a former station of the Soo Line.

O'BRIENS a post office, 1887–93; location not found.

ORONO TOWNSHIP was organized in 1889, having previously been the south half of Medina. The name, adopted from the township and village of the same name in Maine, was suggested by citizens who had come to Minnesota from that state. Several years before this township was organized and named, George A. Brackett of Minneapolis purchased for his summer home a point on this part of the lakeshore, before called Starvation Point, which he then renamed as Orono Point. In an address by Hon. Israel Washburn, Jr., at the centennial celebration of Orono, Maine, on March 3, 1874, this name is stated to have been borne by a prominent chief of the Penobscot Indians, who was born in 1688 and died February 5, 1801, aged 113 years. Washburn wrote: "Orono was always inclined to peace and good neighborhood.... What the grand and sonorous name he bore signified, or whence it was derived, I have never heard."

The city of Orono was incorporated on November 23, 1954.

OSSEO a city in Maple Grove Township, platted July 10, 1852, and incorporated February 24, 1875. Among the early settlers was Warren Sampson, who built a store in 1854 and operated the post office, then named Palestine, 1855–56; with Isaac La Bissonniere, Sampson again platted the community in 1856, changing its name to Osseo. A short time later another village, City of Attraction, was laid out to the southeast by A. B. Chaffee, its stores and homes later absorbed by Osseo. Potatoes were a major farm export crop and from that enterprise developed the Osseo Starch Factory owned by the Wilmes brothers. The village had a station of the Great Northern Railway in section 18.

Osseo occupies a part of Bottineau Prairie, where Pierre Bottineau, the noted fur trader and guide, took his land claim in 1852. The village "remained under the township governments ... until the spring of 1875, when it was incorporated by act of Legislature." The source of the name is *The Song of Hiawatha*, by Longfellow, published in 1855, which presents the story of Osseo, "son of the Evening Star," told by Iagoo at the wedding of Hiawatha and Minnehaha. This name, received likewise from Longfellow, is borne also by villages in Michigan and Wisconsin.

OXBORO a village 11 miles south of Minneapolis on the Minnesota and Southern Railroad, with a number of businesses and a post office, 1922–48; also known as Oxboro Heath.

PALESTINE see OSSEO.

PARKER see ROBBINSDALE.

PARKERS LAKE a post office, 1871–94, with James M. Parker, postmaster, located in Plymouth Township.

PERKINSVILLE a post office, 1856–61, in Independence Township, settled when brothers John S. and Needham T. Perkins built houses on the south shore of Lake Independence and platted a portion of their land as a village. Needham Perkins built a sawmill, a general store, and a blacksmith shop and was also postmaster.

PHELPS ISLAND see ISLAND PARK.

PLYMOUTH first settled in October 1853, organized May 11, 1858, took the name of its village previously platted on Parkers Lake in 1856, but the village was only of short duration, in contrast with the township name, which, however, some of the settlers at first wished to change to Medicine Lake. Like all the many Plymouths of the United States, it commemorates the city of Plymouth at the mouth of the River Plym in Devonshire, England, whence the Pilgrims in the *Mayflower* sailed in 1620 to the site of Plymouth, Mass., landing there on a boulder of world renown, called Plymouth Rock.

The city of Plymouth was incorporated on May 18, 1955, and had a post office operating 1865–69, 1879–80, and 1886–1901; it had a station of the Minnesota and Pacific Railroad.

POMEROY a post office, 1892; location not found.

RICHFIELD settled in 1849–52, organized May 11,

1858, was then so named by vote of the people, in preference to Richland, its previous name. Twelve other states have Richfield townships, villages, or cities. The city was incorporated as a village in February 1908 and as a city in 1964. Its first post office was called Harmony, 1856–63, because postmaster James A. Dunsmoor, who came from Maine, had named his home Harmony, and was then called Richfield, 1863–97; the second post office was Richfield Center, 1892–97, continuing as Richfield until 1903. The first flour mill, named Richfield Mills, was built on Minnehaha Creek by Philander Prescott and Willis G. and Eli Pettijohn in 1854; the first store was built near the mills by John S. Mann.

Much of Wold-Chamberlain Field of the St. Paul-Minneapolis International Airport lies within Richfield, an area first developed in 1914 as an automobile racetrack. The airfield's first hangar was built in 1920; the field became the property of Minneapolis in 1928 and was called Minneapolis Municipal Airport; in 1944 the site came under the control of the Minneapolis-St. Paul Metropolitan Airports Commission. The field was named for two Minneapolis airmen killed in France during World War I, Ernest Groves Wold and Cyrus Foss Chamberlain, and retains that name; the terminal building is named theCharles A. Lindbergh Terminal.

RICHFIELD CENTER see RICHFIELD.

RICHFIELD MILLS see EDINA.

ROBBINSDALE a city adjoining Minneapolis on the northwest, was named for Andrew B. Robbins, who purchased lands there in 1887 and platted the village. The city organized as a village in 1893 but was not incorporated until 1938; its post office, begun in 1888 as Parker, changed back and forth with that name several times until 1901, when Robbinsdale became the name, closing in 1938.

ROCKFORD a city with Wright County.

ROGERS the railway village of Hassan, was named by officers of the Great Northern Railway company. It incorporated in 1914. It has had a post office since 1884.

ROSS CREEK a post office, 1860–63; location not found.

ROWLAND a country post office, 1890–1903, located in the general store with Harvey M. Anderson, postmaster; located seven miles from Minneapolis and two miles from Eden Prairie.

RUSSELL a post office, 1882, John Russell, postmaster; location not found.

SAGA HILL a summer colony established in the 1880s on the north shore of the West Arm of Lake Minnetonka.

ST. ANTHONY a city with Ramsey County, incorporated as a city March 3, 1855, and its outlying area that was organized as a township May 11, 1858, received the name of the adjacent falls of the Mississippi, which Hennepin in 1680, as he wrote, "called the Falls of St. Anthony of Padua, in gratitude for the favors done me by the Almighty through the intercession of that great saint, whom we had chosen patron and protector of all our enterprises." St. Anthony was born in Lisbon in 1195, became a Franciscan friar at the age of 23, and spent his last five years in a convent at Padua, Italy, where he died in 1231.

ST. ANTHONY FALLS was platted as a village in 1849 and was included in Ramsey County until March 4, 1856. Another plat, in 1848–49, named St. Anthony City, comprised the site of the University of Minnesota and adjoining area southeastward, which later was popularly called "Cheevertown," in honor of William A. Cheever, a pioneer who settled there in 1847, builder of an observatory tower.

An act of the legislature, "consolidating the cities of St. Anthony and Minneapolis, and incorporating the same into one city by the name of Minneapolis," was approved February 28, 1872. A post office, 1849–73, was first established in St. Croix County, Wis., was transferred to Ramsey County, and then to Hennepin County in 1857, with Ard Godfrey as first postmaster, later merging with Minneapolis.

ST. BONIFACIUS a city in Minnetrista with a post office since 1861, was named from its Catholic church, consecrated to St. Boniface, the Apostle of the Germans. He was born in Devonshire, England, about 680, the son of a West Saxon chieftain; was ordained to the priesthood in 710; went as a missionary to Bavaria in 720 and became archbishop of Mainz; resigned that position as primate of Germany at the age of 74 years, resumed his missionary work, and in the next year suffered "martyrdom at the hands of the pagans of Utrecht." The name *Bonifacius* is Latin, meaning "of good fate or fortune."

ST. LOUIS PARK a city developed by a group of

Minneapolis businessmen through the St. Louis Park Improvement Company, incorporating as a village on October 4, 1886, being named in allusion to the Minneapolis and St. Louis Railroad. Thomas Barlow Walker formed the Minneapolis Land and Investment Company in 1890, purchased all the platted land, encouraging other investors to develop industries, and built the streetcar line to Minneapolis; the development plan did not work, industries discontinued, and the area became mainly residential. Its post office, 1890–1930, was earlier called Elmwood, 1887–90.

SETON a summer resort on Lake Minnetonka, one mile east of Mound, with a post office, 1922–42.

SHINGLE CREEK see CAMDEN PLACE.

SHOREWOOD a city originally part of Excelsior Township and developed as a residential community; incorporated as a village on May 14, 1956.

SOUTH PLYMOUTH see WAYZATA.

SPRING PARK a city located on a peninsula on the west end of Lake Minnetonka, Excelsior Township, incorporated as a village on August 20, 1951. Its post office name was spelled Springpark, 1896–1949, when changed to its present form; it had a station of the Great Northern Railway.

STUBBS BAY a village, first known as Graves or Teas Bay, named for Henry Stubbs who lived on Long Lake, where in his home he was postmaster of Tamarack, 1858–69, before it was removed to Long Lake; it had a station of the Chicago and Northwestern Railway.

TAMARACK see STUBBS BAY, LONG LAKE.

TAZASKA see ISLAND CITY.

TEUTONIA a post office, 1898–1901, of Plymouth Township.

TONKA BAY a city of one square mile developed as a major summer resort area in Excelsior Township, section 27, bears a name abbreviated from Minnetonka. It was incorporated as a village on September 16, 1901, the same area authorized for incorporation in 1879 as Minnetonka Lake Park, but was never developed; it had a post office, 1896–1920, to handle mail formerly distributed through Excelsior.

TUCKEY was probably a postal station of Eden Prairie Township. Henry Tuckey opened a store in the front part of his home on Purgatory Creek in Eden Prairie and acquired the right to operate a post office, which became known as the Tuckey Post Office; no official post office was assigned to this place.

WARWICK a post office, 1891–1901, ten miles north of Minneapolis, with John B. Johnson, postmaster in his general store.

WASHBURN see EDEN PRAIRIE.

WATERVILLE MILLS see EDINA.

WAYZATA a city in Minnetonka and Orono Townships, lying on the north side of Wayzata Bay, was platted in 1854, incorporated on May 5, 1883, and May 1, 1906, when it separated from the townships, and incorporated as a city in 1929. Its early development was as a summer resort area, with a subdivision called Fernwood, a summer residence site that expanded into large estates; it was platted by O. E. Garrison. The post office operated as Wyzata, 1856–61, South Plymouth, 1864, Wayzata, 1866, Freeport, 1867–69, changing back to Wayzata; it had a station of the Great Northern Railway.

This name was formed by slight change from *Waziyata*, a Dakota word meaning "at the pines, the north." *Wazi* is defined as "a pine, pines," and *Waziya*, "the northern god, or god of the north; a fabled giant who lives at the north and blows cold out of his mouth. He draws near in winter and recedes in summer." The suffix *ta*, denotes "at, to, on" (Riggs, *Dictionary of the Dakota Language*, 1852, pp. 192, 239). The name *Wayzata*, originated by white men, refers to the location at the north side of the east end of Lake Minnetonka, not to pine trees, which are found nearest, in very scanty numbers, on the Mississippi bluffs at Dayton and on Bassett's and Minnehaha Creeks in Minneapolis.

WEST ARM a post office, 1858, located on Lake Minnetonka.

WEST MINNEAPOLIS see HOPKINS.

WOODLAND a city located on Wayzata Bay of Lake Minnetonka developed as a residential area; a large part of the community was owned by George Mapes in 1855 and originally named Maplewood, an *s* being added sometime later. Combining Maplewoods and a community called Groveland, the village was incorporated on December 6, 1948, a few months later changing its name to Woodland.

WOODWARD a post office, 1898–1901, with Byron W. Woodward, first postmaster; location not found.

WOOLNOUGH a summer resort on Lake Minnetonka, with a post office, 1905–17, James H. Woolnough, postmaster.

WYZATA see WAYZATA.

ZUMBRA HEIGHTS a summer resort on Lake Minnetonka with a post office, 1889–1902.

Fort Snelling at First Named Fort St. Anthony

The naming of Fort Snelling was preceded by three or four other names. First, when the troops came in August and September 1819 with Col. Henry Leavenworth for construction of the fort, they spent the fall and winter, as also two succeeding winters, in a cantonment or barracks of log houses on the southeastern or Dakota County side of the Minnesota River, about a third of a mile southeast from the site of the fort. St. Peter's Cantonment took the French and English name of the river. It was also called New Hope, noting cheer and trust for the future of this outpost in the wilderness, far from civilized settlements.

At the time of high water of the river in the spring, they were compelled to remove to another camping place, which was selected on the upland prairie about a mile northwest from the fort site. Copious springs of clear and cool water issue on the face of the river bluff below that second campground, which was mostly of tents, named Camp Coldwater.

After three years of alternation in cabin and tent life at New Hope and Camp Coldwater, the troops moved into their barracks within the enclosure of the fort, in the late autumn of 1822. Its cornerstone had been laid September 10, 1820, soon after Col. Josiah Snelling succeeded Leavenworth in the command, and its construction was well completed in 1824, when Gen. Winfield Scott visited it in May or early June on a tour of inspection of western army posts. Up to that time and till the beginning of 1825, it was called Fort St. Anthony, in allusion to the neighboring Falls of St. Anthony.

In the report of the tour of review and inspection, dated at West Point, November 1824, Gen. Scott wrote in part as follows, concerning Fort St. Anthony: "I wish to suggest to the general-in-chief, and through him to the War Department, the propriety of calling this work *Fort Snelling*, as a just compliment to the meritorious officer under whom it has been erected. The present name is foreign to all our associations, and is, besides, geographically incorrect, as the work stands at the junction of the Mississippi and Saint Peter's rivers, eight miles below the great falls of the Mississippi, called after Saint Anthony. Some few years since the Secretary of War directed that the work at the Council Bluffs should be called Fort Atkinson in compliment to the valuable services of General Atkinson on the upper Missouri. The above proposition is made on the same principle."

In accordance with this recommendation, "it was directed in War Department General Orders No. 1, dated January 7, 1825, that the military post on the Mississippi at the mouth of the Saint Peter's, theretofore called Fort Saint Anthony, be thereafter designated and known as Fort Snelling" (Letter of Gen. Henry P. McCain, U.S. Adjutant General, Sept. 24, 1915).

Josiah Snelling was born in Boston, Mass., 1782, and died in Washington, D.C., August 20, 1828. He was commissioned first lieutenant in the Fourth Infantry, U.S. Army, 1808; served in the War of 1812; was promoted to be colonel of the Fifth Infantry, 1819; took command of Fort St. Anthony in 1820 and in the next three years erected its permanent buildings. In 1827 his regiment was removed to St. Louis. (Much history of the officers and their families at Fort St. Anthony, especially for Col. and Mrs. Snelling, is given in a paper contributed by the present writer to the *Magazine of History*, vol. 21, pp. 25–39, July 1915.)

Lakes and Streams

The first chapter has given attention to the origins of the names of the Mississippi, Minnesota, and Crow Rivers, which together form two-thirds of the boundary enclosing this county.

Islands of the Mississippi in the area of Minneapolis, in their descending order, include Boom Island, where log booms formerly retained the lumbermen's logs until they were gradually supplied to the sawmills; Nicollet Island, a residential portion of the city, named, like an avenue, in honor of the French explorer and geographer, Joseph Nicolas Nicollet; Hennepin Island, named also like an avenue and like this county; Cataract Island and Carver's Island, just below the falls, the latter being named for Capt. Jonathan Carver, who visited the falls in 1766; Spirit Island, close below the preceding, formerly a high remnant of the rock strata, held in awe by the Indians; and Meeker Island, an alluvial tract between the Franklin Avenue bridge and the Milwaukee Railway bridge, which was owned by Judge Bradley B. Meeker, for whom also a county is named.

In the preceding list of townships, sufficient mention has been made for Crystal Lake and Lake Independence, Long Lake in Orono, Lake Minnetonka, Whale Tail and Ox Yoke Lakes, the Falls of St. Anthony, and Wayzata Bay.

The earliest detailed map of any part of this state was drafted during the building of the fort, in 1823, titled "A Topographical View of the Site of Fort St. Anthony," as described in the historical paper before cited. Lakes Harriet and Calhoun and the Lake of the Isles, in the series at the west side of Minneapolis, are there mapped and named, with numerous others of the lakes, rivers, and creeks, in the contiguous parts of Hennepin, Ramsey, and Dakota Counties. The region east of the Mississippi River was designated as Michigan and that on the west as Missouri.

Lake Harriet was named for the wife of Col. Leavenworth. Her maiden name was Harriet Lovejoy, her home being in Blenheim, Schoharie County, N.Y. She was born in 1791, was married to Leavenworth in the winter of 1813–14, and died at Barrytown, N.Y., September 7, 1854. She came here with her husband and the first troops, August 24, 1819, and was here about one year. Leavenworth received the brevet rank of brigadier general in 1824 and died at the age of 51, July 21, 1834, in an expedition against the Pawnee and Comanche. Fort Leavenworth in Kansas and a city and county there were named in his honor.

Lake Calhoun commemorates John Caldwell Calhoun (1782–1850), the eminent statesman of South Carolina, who was secretary of war, 1817–25. He was vice-president of the United States, 1825–32; was U.S. senator, 1833–43; and was secretary of state under President Tyler, 1844–45, when he was again elected to the Senate, of which he remained a member until his death. The Dakota name of this lake is given as "Mde Medoza, Lake of the Loons," by Maj. T. M. Newson in his "Indian Legends of Minnesota Lakes" (no. 1, 1881, p. 18).

The Lake of the Isles was named for its islands (now two, but formerly four, as mapped in the Andreas Atlas, 1874); and Cedar Lake, for the red cedar trees of its shores.

Minnehaha Falls received the name of Brown's Falls on the fort map of 1823 in honor of Jacob Brown, major general and commander in chief of the army from 1814 until his death, February 24, 1828; but Minnehaha Creek on that map, quite erroneous in its course, bears no name. A journey up this creek to Lake Minnetonka, which was made, as before mentioned, by Joseph R. Brown and William J. Snelling in May 1822, when they were each only 17 years old, could scarcely have caused the name of that subsequently prominent citizen of Minnesota to be so applied on a map drafted by an army officer.

The name *Minnehaha* is cited by Longfellow's *Song of Hiawatha*, published in 1855, as used by Mary H. Eastman in the introduction of her book, *Dakotah, or Life and Legends of the Sioux around Fort Snelling*, published in 1849. She there wrote: "The scenery about Fort Snelling is rich in beauty. The Falls of St. Anthony are familiar to travelers, and to readers of Indian sketches. Between the fort and these falls are the 'Little Falls,' 40 feet in height, on a stream that empties into the Mississippi. The Indians call them Mine-hah-hah, or 'laughing waters.'"

The common Dakota word for waterfall is *haha*, which they applied to the Falls of St. Anthony, to Minnehaha, and in general to any waterfall or cascade. To join the words *minne*, "water," and *haha*, "a fall," seems to be a suggestion of white men, which thereafter came into use among the Indians.

The late Samuel W. Pond, Jr., in his admirable book, *Two Volunteer Missionaries*, narrating the lives and work of his father and uncle, Samuel W. and Gideon H. Pond, wrote: "The Indian name, 'Little Waterfall,' is given . . . in speaking of the falls now called by white people 'Minnehaha.' The Indians never knew it by the latter name, bestowed upon it by the whites."

Somewhat nearly this name, however, was used in 1835 by Charles J. Latrobe in his book *The Rambler in North America*, telling of his travels in 1832–33, in which he wrote as follows, applying it, with parts of the name transposed, to the larger falls of the Mississippi: "But the Falls of St. Anthony! . . . the Hahamina! 'the Laughing Water,' as the Indian language, rich in the poetry of nature, styles this remote cataract."

Another early book of travel using the same form of the name, under a different spelling, is *A Summer in the Wilderness; embracing a Canoe Voyage up the Mississippi and around Lake Superior*, by Charles Lanman (1847, 208 pp.). He described the present Minnehaha Creek as "a small river, without a name, the parent of a most beautiful waterfall." Of the Falls of St. Anthony he wrote: "Their original name, in the Sioux language, was Owah-Menah, meaning falling water." The same spelling and translation had been given in Henry R. Schoolcraft's *Narrative*, 1820.

Soon this Dakota name took its present form, an improvement devised by white people, probably first published in Mary Eastman's book in 1849, previously quoted. It was more elaborately presented by Rev. John A. Merrick in a paper describing the Falls of St. Anthony, contributed to the *Minnesota Year Book* for 1852, published by William G. Le Duc. Merrick wrote: "By the Dahcota or Sioux Indians they are called Minne-ha-hah or Minne-ra-ra (Laughing water), and also Minne-owah (Falling water), general expressions, applied to all waterfalls; but *par eminence* Minne-ha-hah Tonk-ah (the great laughing water). By the Ojibwe they are termed Kakah-Bikah (the broken rocks)."

The noble American epic of Longfellow, in which he pictured Hiawatha, "skilled in all the crafts of hunters," and

> . . . *the Arrow-maker's daughter,*
> *Minnehaha, Laughing Water,*
> *Handsomest of all the women,*

so well appealed to the imagination of both the United States and Great Britain, indeed of all where English is spoken, that soon after its publication in 1855, this name became known around the world, the most widely honored and loved name in Minnesota history and legends.

The names of other streams and lakes in this county are noted in their order from south to north and from east to west, this being the numerical order of the townships and ranges in the government surveys.

Rice Lake, through which Minnehaha Creek flows, was named for its wild rice, formerly gathered for food by the Indians.

Lake Nokomis was called Lake Amelia by the fort map in 1823, probably for the wife or daughter of Capt. George Gooding, who came with the first troops in 1819. The name was changed to Nokomis by the park commissioners of Minneapolis in 1910 for the grandmother of Hiawatha.

Next to the south and southwest are Mother Lake (drained), Diamond, Pearl, Mud, and Wood Lakes.

Nine Mile Creek received its name from its distance southwest from Fort Snelling.

Long Lake (mostly drained), Grass Lake (on one map named Terrell Lake), and Rice Lake (having wild rice) are on the bottomland of the Minnesota River in Bloomington and Eden Prairie.

On the upland in these townships are another Long Lake (also named Bryant's Lake), Anderson, Bush, Hyland, Neill, Staring, Red Rock, and Moran Lakes, Lake Riley, Mitchell, Round, and Duck Lakes, mostly named for farmers nearby.

Minnetonka Township has Shady Oak Lake in section 26 and Glen Lake in section 34.

In Excelsior are Galpin's Lake, Christmas Lake, and Silver Lake, the first named for Rev. Charles Galpin, the first pastor there, and the second for Charles W. Christmas of Minneapolis, the first county surveyor.

Minnetrista, named for its two remarkably crooked lakes, has also Dutch Lake, adjoining a German settlement; Lake Langdon, which commemorates R. V. Langdon, the first township clerk; and Long Lake in sections 9, 15, and 16.

Minneapolis, in addition to its western series of lakes before noted, has Sandy Lake, northeast of the Mississippi; Powderhorn Lake, named for its original shape, later changed as the center of a park; and Loring Park Lake, named in honor of Charles M. Loring, who was prominent during more than 30 years in the development of the Minneapolis system of parks and public grounds. Glenwood Park, on the west border of this city, includes Glenwood and Brownie Lakes.

Bassett Creek, flowing through the village area of Golden Valley and the city of Minneapolis, was named for Joel Bean Bassett, an early settler and lumberman, who was born in Wolfborough, N.H., March 17, 1817, and died in Los Angeles, Calif., February 1, 1912. He came to Minnesota in

1849, settling in St. Paul, but soon preempted a tract adjoining the Mississippi in Minneapolis, near the mouth of this creek; removed there in 1852 and afterward engaged in lumbering and flour milling; was a member of the territorial council, 1857; was Indian agent for Minnesota 1865–69.

The village area of Golden Valley has Virginia Lake, Sweeney Lake, and Twin Lake.

Again Twin Lakes are found three to four miles farther north in the area of Crystal village, which was named, as before noted, for its Crystal Lake.

Shingle Creek, which crosses Brooklyn Township and the Brooklyn Center village, joining the Mississippi in the north edge of Minneapolis, had near its mouth the first shingle mill in this county, built in 1852. It flows through Palmer Lake, named for a pioneer.

Plymouth has Bass Lake, Pomerleau, Smith, and Turtle Lakes in its northern half. The much larger Medicine Lake, in its southeastern part, was named by the Indians after one of their number was drowned there by the capsizing of his canoe in a sudden storm. This name, in their use, means mysterious and was given to the lake because they could not find his body. Parker's Lake and Gleason and Kraetz Lakes in the southwest part of Plymouth were named for settlers, the first being for six Parker brothers who came from Maine in 1855 and later, opening farms around this lake.

Medina Township has Medina Lake in section 2; Lake Peter in sections 4 and 5; School Lake in the school section 16; Seig and Half Moon Lakes in sections 17 and 18; Hausmann Lake in section 24; Wolsfeld Lake in sections 22 and 27, named for brothers John, Charles, and Nicholas Wolsfeld, who settled at the lake in 1855; and Lake Katrina in sections 19, 20, 29, and 30.

Orono has Lydiard Lake, close east of Long Lake; Classen Lake, a mile and a half west of Long Lake village; and French and Forest Lakes, adjoining the bays and arms of Lake Minnetonka.

Independence has Mud Lake, Haughey and Fox Lakes; and Pioneer Creek, the outlet of Lake Independence, flows southwestward across this township.

Elm Creek flows through Rice Lake, at the center of Maple Grove Township, and Hayden's Lake,

in the southeast corner of Dayton. Midway between these lakes, Rush Creek is tributary to it from the west.

Maple Grove also has Mud Lake in section 2; Weaver Lake in sections 17 to 20; and Fish Lake, Cedar Island, and Eagle Lakes, the last being the largest in the township.

Corcoran has only very small lakes, the largest (which alone is named on maps) being Jubert's Lake in sections 29 and 32.

Lake Sarah, the largest in Greenwood, outflowing to the Crow River by Edgar Creek, was named in 1855 for the wife or sweetheart of a pioneer; and in the same year Lake Rebecca received its name in honor of Mrs. Samuel Allen. Sections 23 and 24 of this township had a series of small lakes, now drained, which were named Hafften, Schendel, Schauer, and Schnappauf Lakes for German farmers.

Besides Hayden's Lake, before mentioned, Dayton has French Lake, named for William, Allen, and Newton French and their sister, Mrs. Templin, Quakers from North Carolina who settled near the lake in 1853 and later moved to Oregon; Grass, Diamond, and Lura Lakes, next northward; Goose Lake at the southeast corner of this township; and Powers Lake in section 34.

Hassan has Lake Harry, Sylvan Lake, and Cowley Lake. The last is also known as Parslow's Lake in honor of Septimus Parslow, who in 1856 was appointed the first postmaster of Hassan and held the office 25 years or more.

Woodland has Marion Lake, named for early land owner Samuel C. Gale's third daughter, Marion, and Woolsey Pond, named for George and Alvira Woolsey who had a home there; also known as Peterson's Pond, Pete's Pond, and Mirror Lake.

Bays, Points, and Islands of Lake Minnetonka

The origin of the name of this lake, and also the story of its early white explorers, have been told for Minnetonka Township. Shortly after its exploration and naming in 1852, it was visited on August 11 of that summer by a prominent author, Elizabeth Fries Ellet of New York City, who gave to Minnesota and Minnetonka nearly 20 pages in her *Summer Rambles in the West*. Besides her notes of the journey to this lake, she named Eden Prairie, which gave its title to a township.

Her name for the first water sheet at the east end of Minnetonka, now named Gray's Lake or Bay, was Lake Browning for the poet Elizabeth Barrett Browning. The next part, wider and larger, which was soon afterward named Wayzata Bay, as before noted, Mrs. Ellet called Lake Bryant for our American poet, from whom she "read aloud a few lines . . . appropriate to the scene."

Between her Lake Bryant and the third large sheet of water, "an extremely narrow . . . headland half a mile in length, running out from the southern shore," since named Breezy Point, was by her named Point Wakon, "the Dakota term for anything spiritual or supernatural." There an oval stone, a waterworn boulder about a foot in diameter, had been found, which the Dakotas had "painted red, and covered with small yellow spots, some of them faded to a brown color," around which stone the Dakota braves were accustomed, after raids against the Ojibwe, to celebrate.

Cedar Point projects into Wayzata Bay from the south, named for its red cedar trees. It was also known as Stetson's Point for the owner in 1892.

Proceeding westward along the south side of the lake, we pass Robinson's Bay, with Sunset Point southwest of it; Carson's Bay at Deephaven; and St. Alban's Bay and Gideon's Bay, respectively east and west of Excelsior. Carson's Bay was formerly named Pig Inlet; the name was changed to honor an early settler, Elijah Carson, brother of the frontiersman Kit Carson.

Gluek's Point and Solberg's Point are passed southwestward, before coming to Excelsior.

A summer village that failed to grow, called St. Albans, was platted in 1856 on the north shore of the bay, which thence took its name.

Gideon's Bay (also called Tonka Bay) commemorates Peter M. Gideon, the horticulturist, who there originated the renowned Wealthy apple, named by him in honor of his wife. He was born in Champaign County, Ohio, February 9, 1820; came to Minnesota in 1853, settling beside this bay, where later he was superintendent of the State Fruit Farm. A small memorial park and a tablet in his honor at Manitou Junction, about a mile west of Excelsior, were dedicated June 16, 1912.

Hull's Narrows, joining the lower and upper parts of Minnetonka, received this name for Rev.

Stephen Hull, who settled on a farm there in February 1853. Originally a short creek, it was widened and deepened as a canal and was opened to steamboat navigation in 1873.

On the south side of the upper lake are Lock's Point, Howard's Point, and a less noteworthy projection of the shore at Zumbra Heights, west of Smithtown Bay.

Hard Scrabble Point on the west, and Cedar Point on the east, divide this upper lake from Cook's and Priest's Bays, at the west end of Minnetonka.

Yet farther west, connected by a strait with Priest's Bay, is Halsted's Bay, named for Frank William Halsted, who was born in Newark, N.J., in 1833, and died here in June 1876. He came to Minnesota in 1855; served in the U.S. Navy during the Civil War; resided in a picturesque house near the shore of this bay, called the Hermitage. His older brother, George Blight Halsted, was born in Elizabethtown, N.J., March 17, 1820, and died here September 6, 1901. He was graduated at Princeton College; studied law; served in the navy, and later in the army, through the Civil War; came to this state in 1876 and afterward resided in the home where his brother had lived.

Phelps Island (originally a peninsula) lies east of Cook's Bay and is indented on its southeast side by Phelps Bay. These names were given in honor of Edmund Joseph Phelps of Minneapolis, who was born near Brecksville, Ohio, January 17, 1845. He came to Minnesota in 1878, settling in Minneapolis; organized, with others, the Minneapolis Loan and Trust Company in 1883, of which he was secretary and treasurer.

Pelican Point and Casco Point are respectively west and east of Spring Park Bay, on the north side of the upper lake.

Carman's Bay, named for a farmer, John Carman, who settled here in September 1853, and Lafayette Bay, named from the Hotel Lafayette, are respectively west and east of the Narrows, on the north side. Lafayette Bay was known as Holmes Bay for many years after John Herrill Holmes, who claimed the first land in 1855 in Minnetonka Beach, sold the land in 1874 to Josiah Huntington, at which time Holmes Point became Huntington Point, and Holmes Bay became Lafayette Bay.

Huntington Point and Starvation or Orono

Point jut into the lower lake from the north, respectively west and east of Smith's Bay.

Branching off from Smith's Bay westward is Crystal Bay, named by Mrs. Templin from its deep, clear appearance, and connected with the latter are Maxwell and Stubbs Bays, the North Arm, and the West Arm and Harrison's Bay.

East of Orono Point is Brown's Bay, and next east are Lookout Point and an upland with fine residences, named Ferndale, which, with the opposite Breezy Point, before noted, are at the entrance of Wayzata Bay.

Haines Bay, in Orono, is named for an early family named Haines.

So we have traversed the entire shoreline, with its multitude of indenting bays and projecting points, of this exceedingly attractive lake, of which I wrote in 1917 that it "may well be called the Kohinoor of Minnesota's ten thousand lakes." For the archaeologist and historian, this lake has great interest in its many groups of aboriginal mounds, before noticed in connection with the village named Mound. For the naturalist, in addition to its beautiful scenery, it has treasures of the native flora and fauna, notably its abundant species of trees and shrubs and its many kinds of fishes and birds. Two points, one near the east end of the lake and another near the west end, are named for their red cedars, and islands in the upper part of the lake received names from their formerly plentiful cranes and more rare nests of the bald eagle.

The islands of Minnetonka include Big Island in the lower lake, which at first was known as Meeker's Island for Judge Bradley B. Meeker of Minneapolis, who visited this lake with Gov. Ramsey and others in 1852; Gale Island, near the southwest shore of Big Island, named for Harlow A. Gale (1832–1901) of Minneapolis, whose summer home was there; and, in the upper lake, Wild Goose Island, Spray Island, Shady, Enchanted, Wawatasso, Eagle, and Crane Islands. The longest of these names may be akin with one in Longfellow's *Song of Hiawatha*: "Wah-wah-taysee, little firefly."

"Picturesque Lake Minnetonka," published in yearly editions by S. E. Ellis (1906, 102 pp.), referred the name of Enchanted Island to its being long ago a favorite place of Dakota medicine dances; and related that Wawatasso was a young Dakota man who rescued the daughter of a white pioneer trapper from drowning. Other Dakota legends about Minnetonka have been written in prose by Thomas M. Newson in 1881 and in poetry by Hanford L. Gordon (*Indian Legends and Other Poems*, 1910, 406 pp.). Like Hiawatha and Minnehaha and like the geographic names in this county that are partly of Dakota derivation, these writings present more white than Indian ways of thought and imagery.

The Fort Snelling Military Reservation in 1839

A map of "Fort Snelling and Vicinity," surveyed and drafted by Lieut. E. K. Smith in October 1837, comprises the near vicinity of the fort, Camp Coldwater, and the post of the American Fur Company on the site of Mendota, having probably been made mainly to show the cabins and fields of settlers permitted to locate on the Military Reservation.

Two years later a more extended survey and map, for the U.S. War Department, by Lieut. James L. Thompson, showed the boundaries established or adopted for the Military Reservation, "done at Fort Snelling, October and November, 1839, by order of Major Plympton."

This map, on the scale of two inches to a mile, is limited to the reservation area, reaching west to the Lake of the Woods (now called Wood Lake), the series of Harriet, Calhoun, and the Lake of the Isles, and northwest to the lower part of Nine Mile Creek (now Bassett's Creek). On the east the reservation was bounded by the middle of the channel of the Mississippi to the island next below the present Meeker Island. From the upper end of that island, the boundary on the north side of the part of the reservation east and north of the Mississippi extended due east 5 miles, to a point near the intersection of St. Peter and Tenth Streets in the city of St. Paul. Next it extended due south 2 miles and 10 chains, crossing the Mississippi just west of the upper end of Harriet Island, to a point near the present corner of Annapolis Street and Manomin Avenue in West St. Paul. Thence the southeastern boundary of the reservation ran 8 miles and 42 chains southwestward, nearly in parallelism with the Mississippi and Minnesota Rivers and about a mile distant from them. Finally the most southern line of this area ran due west 1 mile and 75 chains, to the Minnesota River at the place of beginning, about 6 miles distant from the fort.

Reserve Township of Ramsey County, now included in the city of St. Paul, had its north boundary very near the north line of the reservation, whence the township was named.

The history of the opening for settlement of the greater parts of the reservation in 1852–55, including the southwestern areas of St. Paul and Ramsey County and the area of Minneapolis west of the river, has been related by Dr. William W. Folwell in a paper, "The Sale of Fort Snelling, 1857," in the MHS Collections (15: 393–410 [1915]).

On the reservation map of 1839, "Land's End" is a part of the bluff on the northwest side of the Minnesota River, nearly two miles southwest from the fort, where the bluff is intersected by a tributary ravine; Minnehaha Falls and Creek were called Brown's Falls and Brown's Creek; an "Indian Village" adjoined the southeast shore of Lake Calhoun; and the "Mission," with three cultivated fields, comprising probably 30 acres, was on the northwest side of Lake Harriet.

Fort Snelling State Park

Many people recognized the significance of the area around Fort Snelling and over the years worked to preserve it. Then the situation reached a crisis stage in the 1950s as urban development and highway construction threatened to obliterate the site. The land had become the property of the Veterans Administration in 1946, which in 1960 declared it excess property, thereby making it available for purchase. The bill authorizing the land purchase and establishing Fort Snelling State Park was signed into law on April 20, 1961. The park includes the historic fort as well as Pike Island and the river bottomland below the fort (including land in Dakota and Ramsey Counties), which were developed for recreational use. The Fort Snelling Historic District was declared a National Historic Landmark on December 19, 1960. In 1969 the fort itself was transferred to the Minnesota Historical Society, which manages it as one of its historic sites.

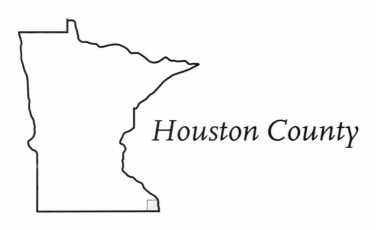

Houston County

Established February 23, 1854, this county was named in honor of Samuel Houston, who was president of Texas before its annexation by the United States and afterward was a senator from that state. He was born near Lexington, Va., March 2, 1793; and died in Huntsville, Tex., July 26, 1863. In his youth he lived several years with the Cherokee Indians near his home in eastern Tennessee; later he served in the Creek War, 1813–14, winning the admiration of Gen. Andrew Jackson by his bravery in a battle, after being severely wounded; studied law and was admitted to practice, 1818–19; was a member of Congress from Tennessee, 1823–27; and was governor of that state, 1827–29.

On account of an uncongenial marriage, he resigned the governorship, retired to life in the Arkansas Territory, whither the Cherokee had been removed, and again lived with them, becoming a trader. In December 1832, he went to Texas under a commission from President Andrew Jackson, looking toward its purchase for the United States. In 1835 he was elected commander-in-chief of the Texans, and in the battle of San Jacinto, April 21, 1836, he defeated the Mexicans and captured their general, Santa Anna, ending the war.

Houston was president of the Texas republic, 1836–38 and 1841–44. Texas was annexed by the United States in 1845, being admitted as a state, and Houston was elected one of its senators, which position he held by reelections for 13 years, until 1859. Later he was governor of Texas, 1859–61, being an opponent of secession.

In the years 1854–56, when antagonism between the North and South on slavery questions gave presages of the Civil War, Houston aspired to nomination as the Democratic candidate for the national presidency; and in October 1854, the general Democratic committee of New Hampshire earnestly recommended him to be "the people's candidate" for the campaign in 1856. His popularity in Minnesota at that time is attested by the name of this county; and he is likewise commemorated by counties in Tennessee and Texas, and by names of cities and villages in Texas, Mississippi, Missouri, and other states.

Several biographies of Sam Houston, as he always styled himself, have been published. Marble statues of him and Stephen F. Austin, sculptured by Elisabet Ney of Texas, and erected as the gift of that state in Statuary Hall of the national capitol, were accepted February 25, 1905, with memorial addresses by members of Congress representing Texas, Tennessee, Missouri, and Arkansas.

Information for the origins of geographic names in this county has been gathered from the History of Houston County *(1882, 526 pp.); and from Charles A. Dorival, judge of probate, interviewed during a visit at Caledonia, the county seat, in April 1916.*

BEE a post office, 1891–1905, of Wilmington Township, section 33, on the Iowa border; first named Bergen, it had a store, a flour mill, a creamery, and a station of the Chicago, Milwaukee and St. Paul Railroad.

BELLVILLE a place name in Spring Grove Township about 1887.

BERGEN see **BEE**.

BLACK HAMMER TOWNSHIP first settled in 1852, organized in April 1859, received this name, meaning Black Bluff, from an exclamation of Knud Olson Bergo, an early Norwegian settler in the adjoining township of Spring Grove, on seeing a prairie bluff here blackened by a fire. It was the name of a bluff at his birthplace in Norway. *Hammer*, as a Norwegian word, has the same spelling and meaning as in English. Doubtless the name was suggested, both in Norway and here, by the shape of the bluff or hill. The village in section 22 had a blacksmith, a post office, 1871–1905, in postmaster Gunder Mattison (Matheson)'s general store in section 15, a school, and a church.

BROWNSVILLE TOWNSHIP first settled in November 1848, organized May 11, 1858, was named for its steamboat landing and village, platted in 1854, by Job and Charles Brown, brothers, who came to Minnesota in 1848 from the state of New York. Biographic notes of both are in the MHS Collections, vol. 14. The city of Brownsville in sections 23 and 26, which is the oldest settlement in the county and was the first county seat, was incorporated as a village on March 2, 1858. When first settled, the community was known as Wild Cat Bluff. By 1870 the village had 50 businesses including a sawmill and a brewery, farming and lumbering being main industries. Its post office was established in Wabasha County and transferred to Houston County in 1852; it had a station of the Chicago, Milwaukee, St. Paul and Pacific Railroad in section 26.

BUTTERFIELD VALLEY in Hokah Township, south of the city of Hokah, was first settled in 1853 by Hiram Butterfield, who came from Illinois.

CALEDONIA settled in 1851, organized May 11, 1858, took the name of its village, which was platted and named in 1854–55 by Samuel McPhail, who had served in the Mexican War and later was colonel of the First Minnesota Mounted Rangers in the Dakota War, 1862–63. This was the ancient Roman name of Scotland north of the firths of Clyde and Forth, and in modern use it is the poetic name of Scotland.

Caledonia village was incorporated by a legislative act, February 25, 1870, and reincorporated on April 8, 1889. It is situated in Caledonia and Mayville Townships and is the county seat. Its post office began in 1855; the railroad was built through in 1879. Extensive clay deposits nearby were utilized in making bricks, creating an early industry. A station of the Chicago, Milwaukee, St. Paul and Pacific Railroad was in section 13.

CROOKED CREEK TOWNSHIP settled in 1852–53, organized May 11, 1858, was named for the creek that flows through it in an exceptionally crooked course, entering a western channel of the Mississippi at Reno. Its valley is the route of the railway from Reno nearly to Caledonia.

DAY VALLEY a village in Mound Prairie Township, section 21, was named for James C. Day, born January 30, 1822, in Fayette County, Pa. He came to Minnesota in 1855, was a member of the State Constitutional Convention in 1857, moved to La Crescent, and died in San Jose, Calif., on February 8, 1911. The village had a post office, 1857–58, known as Dayville.

DEDHAM a post office, 1858–65. Edmund McIntire, railroad contractor, from Dedham, Mass., arrived in 1855 and made a claim in section 33 of Yucatan Township, naming the post office for his hometown, but as Yucatan already had a post office, Dedham closed, the village of Yucatan moving to the Dedham location.

EGBERT a station of the Chicago, Milwaukee and St. Paul Railroad in section 21 of Mayville Township.

EITZEN a city in Winnebago Township, section 32, was incorporated on May 17, 1947. Its name was chosen by Christian Bunge, Jr. for the place of his birth, Eitzen, Germany. He built a log grocery store in 1866 and was postmaster when the post office began in 1868.

FAIRY ROCK a locality in Crooked Creek Township, section 26, about 1874–87.

FREEBURG a village of Crooked Creek Township,

section 30, was named by German settlers for the city of Freiburg in the Black Forest region of Germany. Its post office was first spelled Freeburgh, 1858–94, when changed to the present form, discontinuing in 1947.

GRAND CROSSING a station of the Southern Minnesota Railroad in Hokah Township, section 24.

HACKETTS GROVE a post office, 1856–60, of Brownsville Township, with Emery Hackett, postmaster.

HAMILTON see LA VILLA.

HOKAH TOWNSHIP settled in 1851, organized May 11, 1858, bears the Dakota name of the Root River, which is its English translation. *Hutkan* is the spelling of the word by Stephen R. Riggs and Dr. Thomas S. Williamson in their Dakota dictionaries, 1852 and 1902, but it is spelled *Hokah* on the map by Joseph N. Nicollet, published in 1843, and on the map of Minnesota Territory in 1850. A part of the site of the village, which was platted in March 1855, had been earlier occupied by the village of a Dakota leader named Hokah. This railway village was incorporated March 2, 1871. The city of Hokah reincorporated on April 23, 1923, and separated from the township. It was first settled by Edward Thompson, who built a sawmill in 1852, a flour mill in 1853, and a dam in 1866 across the Root River in anticipation of the Southern Minnesota Railroad coming; the railroad caused the population to increase tenfold. Thompson Creek south of Hokah and Mt. Tom are named for Thompson. Part of the city was called Slab Town for the houses built on slabs from the sawmill. The post office began in 1856.

HOUSTON TOWNSHIP settled in 1852 and organized in 1858, was named, like the county, for Gen. Sam Houston of Texas. The village was incorporated April 7, 1874. It was first settled in June 1852 by William G. McSpadden from La Crosse, Wis., at a site just west of the fork of Root River and its south fork, which he platted in 1856. The first store was built by Ole Knutson, who became first postmaster in 1856. When the Southern Minnesota Railroad laid track in 1866 and Mons Anderson donated the right-of-way and depot site, the town moved west to the present site. The city was reincorporated on October 10, 1889.

HOWES CORNER a post office, 1883–85, located five miles southeast of Houston, in Yucatan Township, section 14.

HULLSVILLE a rural post office, 1879–80, located 30 miles from Caledonia, in the northeast part of the county on a junction of several railroads, with Louis Hull, postmaster, and Lans Hull, railroad agent and telegraph operator; the community had a Catholic church and exported lumber and beer.

JEFFERSON TOWNSHIP organized in 1858, received its name, on the suggestion of Eber D. Eaton of Winnebago Township, for Jefferson County, N.Y., whence he came to Minnesota. Jefferson village, on the west channel of the Mississippi, in sections 26 and 35, was at first called Ross's Landing for John and Samuel Ross, brothers, who came here as the first settlers in 1847. A dispute between the village and the Chicago, Milwaukee and St. Paul Railroad in 1872 led the railroad to build a station farther south in New Albin, Iowa, which then absorbed what little businesses Jefferson had built up.

LA CRESCENT TOWNSHIP settled in 1851, organized May 11, 1858, was named, like its village, platted in June 1856, in allusion to the town of La Crosse, Wis., which had been previously founded on the opposite side of the Mississippi. That French name, meaning the bat used in playing ball and thence applied to the ballgame often played by the Indians, had been given to La Crosse Prairie before the settlement of the town, because the ground was a favorite place for their meeting to play this game. The origin and meaning of the Wisconsin name, however, were disregarded, if known, by the founders of La Crescent, who confused it with La Croix, the Cross. "Recalling the ancient contests of the Crusaders against the Saracens and Turks in their efforts to recapture the Holy Sepulchre, where the Cross and the Crescent were raised aloft in deadly strife, and being mindful of the fate that overtook those who struggled under the banner of La Crosse, they resolved to challenge their rival by raising the standard of La Crescent, and thus fight it out on that line" (*History of Houston County*, 1882, p. 426).

The first building in the city of La Crescent, 1851, was a log cabin trading post built by Peter Cameron and operated by his brother, David Richardson; in 1851 Harvey and William Gillett platted a village naming it Manton, with a post office by that name beginning in 1856, with William Gillett as postmaster; the site was sold to the Kentucky Company, a real estate venture, who renamed it La Crescent. The village had a station of the Chicago, Milwaukee, St. Paul and Pacific Railroad in section 3.

LA VILLA a village in the Root River valley, sections 33, 34, and 35; Enoch Gould, from New Hampshire, came in 1855 establishing a post office named Hamilton, 1856–58, which became La Villa, 1858–67; the area remains farmland with no development of a community.

LIMA a post office, 1862–64; location not found.

LOONEYVILLE a village in Looney valley along the Root River, first settled by John S. Looney, born in Nashville, Tenn.; he lived in Illinois and Wisconsin before coming in 1852, returning to Illinois in 1858. Looney with Elihu Hunt and Daniel Wilson had 40 acres surveyed for a townsite; Corydon Looney opened a store on his father's land in 1855 and moved to the West Coast about 1858, selling the store to Wilson, then postmaster, who moved the post office from his home to the store; the post office operated, 1855–70. James Looney, another son of John, platted 360 acres in sections 27 and 34 in 1857 as St. Lawrence, on the north side of the Root River, in hopes that the railroad would be located there; however, the railroad laid track south of the river, and the town died before it could be developed.

LORETTE see MOUND PRAIRIE.

MANTON see LA CRESCENT.

MAYVILLE settled in 1855 and organized in 1858, was named for Mayville, N.Y., the county seat of Chautauqua County, whence Dr. John E. Pope and others of the early settlers of this township came. A post office was located in the township, 1861–62.

MONEY CREEK TOWNSHIP settled in 1853–54, organized May 11, 1858, and its village, which was platted in the autumn of 1856, received their names from the creek here tributary to the Root River. "Some man having got his pocket-book and contents wet in the creek, and spreading out the bank notes on a bush to dry, a sudden gust of wind blew them into the water again, and some of it never was recovered, so this circumstance suggested the name of the stream, after which the town was named" (*History*, 1882, p. 436). A post office was located in section 12, 1856–1907.

MOUND PRAIRIE TOWNSHIP settled in 1853–54, was organized in April 1860. "The name of the town was suggested by Dr. Chase, an old resident,

in remembrance of a remarkable rounded bluff in section four, surrounded by a wide valley on all sides." The village in section 28 on land owned by William Hunter was platted by Dr. J. G. Sheldon in 1856, who gave it the Castilian name of San Jacinto, and its post office was called that 1856–71. Another post office, called Lorette, was located in the Lorette House (eventually known as Loretta House), a stage coach stop on the territorial road between La Crosse and St. Paul built and operated by postmaster Seth Lore, formerly of New Jersey, who was postmaster, 1856–61. The two post offices of San Jacinto and Lorette were merged as the Mound Prairie post office in the store owned by John A. Eberhard; it had a station of the Chicago, Milwaukee and St. Paul Railroad.

NEW BOSTON a post office that was to be established about November 1855; location not found.

NEWHOUSE a station of the Chicago, Milwaukee and St. Paul Railroad in Spring Grove Township, section 29, with a post office, 1880–1933; named for the family from whom the railroad purchased the land.

NITTIDAL see WILMINGTON.

NORMA a station of the Chicago, Milwaukee and St. Paul Railroad in section 35 of Hokah Township.

OWEN a post office in Yucatan Township, section 9, 1889–1902, located 16 miles from Caledonia.

PERKINS a flag stop of the Chicago, Milwaukee and St. Paul Railroad between Houston and Rushford, Winona County, first known as Money Creek Station, but so as not to confuse it with the village of Money Creek, the name was changed in honor of some railroad men of Money Creek Township.

PINE CREEK a village that lies half in section 2, La Crescent Township, Houston County, and half in section 35, Dresbach Township, Winona County.

PINE VALLEY a locality in Mound Prairie Township, section 2, about 1929.

PORTLAND a post office in Wilmington Township, section 30, also known as Portland Prairie, 1855–61, changed to Wilmington, 1861–93, and reestablished as Portland, 1893–1901. The first settlers came in the early 1850s, among them a large group of Methodists from Rhode Island by way of Lansing, Iowa, and the Everett brothers from New Portland, Maine, in 1851, who named the community.

RENO a railway village and junction in Crooked Creek Township, at first called Caledonia Junction, was renamed by Capt. William H. Harries of Caledonia in honor of Jesse Lee Reno. He was born at Wheeling, W.Va., June 30, 1823; was graduated at West Point in 1846; served in the Mexican War; was a brigadier general and later a major general of United States volunteers in the Civil War; was killed in the battle of South Mountain, Md., September 14, 1862. A post office was located there, 1880–1935, at which time mail was routed through New Albin, Iowa. The village had a station of the Chicago, Milwaukee, St. Paul and Pacific Railroad in section 35.

RICEFORD a village in section 6, Spring Grove Township, platted in 1856, was named in honor of Henry M. Rice of St. Paul, who also is commemorated by the name of Rice County. He visited this place in 1856, following an Indian trail and fording the creek there, which thence is called Riceford Creek. The village developed during the 1850s and 1860s and had a station of the Chicago, Milwaukee, St. Paul and Pacific Railroad, but when the railroad built stations at Newhouse and Mabel in Fillmore County, the village ceased; its post office, first established in Fillmore County, operated 1855–1905.

RIVER JUNCTION a station of the Chicago, Milwaukee and St. Paul Railroad in La Crescent Township, section 3.

SAN JACINTO see MOUND PRAIRIE.

SCHECH'S MILL located in Caledonia Township and on the National Register of Historic Places, is the only complete and active water-powered mill in the state; it was built in 1876 by John Blinn and purchased in 1877 by Michael Schech, head miller of the St. Paul Roller Milling Company.

SHELDON TOWNSHIP settled in June 1853, organized May 11, 1858, took the name of its village, located in the Beaver Creek valley, founded in 1854–57, of which Julius C. Sheldon, who came from Suffield, Conn., was one of the proprietors. Sheldon stayed only long enough to leave his name. The village was incorporated on March 20, 1858, but is presently unincorporated; it had a post office, 1856–1903, a general store, a creamery, a blacksmith shop, and a gristmill.

SPRING GROVE TOWNSHIP settled in 1852 and organized in 1858, received the name of its first post office, which was established in 1855 at the home of James Smith, the earliest settler, beside a spring and a grove. The village in sections 11 and 14 was organized December 31, 1889, and incorporated on January 14, 1890. Smith came from Pennsylvania about 1852, opened the first store in 1853, became the first postmaster, the first justice of the peace, and a member of the county commissioners court. Most of the village was platted on land owned by William J. Flemming, who also opened the first tavern in 1856. A station of the Chicago, Milwaukee, St. Paul and Pacific Railroad was located in section 11.

TOLEDO a village in Hokah Township, section 5, also spelled Teledo, which had a woolen factory and existed about 1870–78.

UNION GROVE a post office, 1865–66, of Union Township.

UNION TOWNSHIP settled in 1853, was organized April 5, 1859. Thirty other states have townships and villages of this name. A post office operated 1857–78, with the township's first settler, Henry Snure, Sr., who had come in 1854, as first postmaster.

WATERTOWN a locality in the Winnebago valley, about 1855, 16 miles south of Brownsville.

WILMINGTON first settled in June 1851, organized May 11, 1858, has a name that is likewise borne in 14 other states by townships, villages, and cities.

WILMINGTON GROVE a village in Wilmington Township, section 15, was founded in the 1860s and first called Nittidal by settlers who came because of its spring water supply. The first business was Crystal Springs Creamery in 1888. A first post office named Wilmington, 1861–93, had been at Portland earlier and changed back to Portland; a second post office became Wilmington in 1893 when the Nittidal post office, 1890–93, changed to Wilmington, discontinuing in 1902; it had a station of the Chicago, Milwaukee and St. Paul Railroad.

WINNEBAGO settled in March 1851, organized May 11, 1858, is drained by Winnebago Creek, which, with the township, received its name from the Winnebago Indians, many of whom, after the cession of their Wisconsin lands in 1832, were removed to northeastern Iowa. Their hunting grounds then extended into this adjoining edge of Minnesota, until they were again removed in 1848 to Long Prairie, in central Minnesota. The township was laid out by Oscar Bloomer and E. D.

Eaton, who came in 1855, and was called Water-town and renamed Winnebago.

The head chief of the Winnebago, Winneshiek, for whom an adjacent county in Iowa is named, lived and hunted in this county. "His principal home was about seven miles west of the village of Houston, on the Root river, Houston county, Minnesota; here he lived, during the winter, in a dirt wigwam" (*History of Winneshiek County, Iowa*, by Edwin C. Bailey, 1913, vol. 1, p. 34).

WINNEBAGO VALLEY a village in section 22 of Winnebago Township, with two mills, a hotel, several stores, and a post office, 1858–1906.

YARINGTON a post office, 1896–98; location not found.

YUCATAN settled probably in 1852 and organized in 1858, was at first called Utica, but to avoid confusion with other places of that name, which are found in 16 states, one being Utica Township in Winona County, it was changed to the present name of somewhat similar sound, which is used nowhere else in the United States. It was taken from the large peninsula of Yucatan, forming the most southeastern part of Mexico, and from the Yucatan channel, between that country and Cuba. The village in section 33 was platted in 1856 by the first settler, Edwin Stevens, who picked the name, built a log home, a mill dam, a sawmill, and five other buildings and by September of that year moved away, first to Iowa and later to Washington Territory. Its post office operated 1856–1905; it had a station of the Chicago, Milwaukee and St. Paul Railroad; see also DEDHAM.

Lakes, Rivers, Creeks, and Bluffs

Houston County lies in a large driftless area, exempted from glaciation and therefore having none of the glacial and modified drift formations by which it is wholly surrounded. This area also includes parts of several other counties of southeastern Minnesota, but its greatest extent is in Wisconsin, with small tracts of northeast Iowa

and northwest Illinois. Its length is about 150 miles from north to south, with a maximum width of about 100 miles. It is characterized by an absence of lakes, excepting on the bottomlands of rivers where they fill portions of deserted watercourses. Such lakes occur in this county along the Mississippi and Root Rivers, one of which, two to three miles southeast of La Crescent, is named Target Lake, from former rifle practice there.

The preceding pages have noted the origins of the names of Crooked Creek, Root River, Money Creek, and Riceford and Winnebago Creeks.

Pine Creek, flowing through La Crescent to the Mississippi, has here and there a few white pines on its bluffs, this region being at the southwestern limit of this tree.

Tributaries of the Root River from the north are Storer, Silver, and Money Creeks; and from the south, in similar westward order, Thompson Creek (formerly also known as Indian Spring Creek), Crystal Creek, and Badger, Beaver, and Riceford Creeks. Thompson Creek was named in honor of Edward Thompson and his brother, Clark W. Thompson, the principal founders of Hokah, for whom biographic notices are given in the MHS Collections, vol. 14.

A prominent bluff of the Root River valley at Hokah is named Mt. Tom.

Wild Cat Creek flows into the Mississippi at Brownsville, and Wild Cat Bluff is a part of the adjacent high bluffs forming the west side of the Mississippi valley. These names, and those of Badger and Beaver Creeks, tell of early times, when the fauna of this region included many fur-bearing animals that have since disappeared or become very scarce.

This stream-dissected area was preserved by the creation of Beaver Creek Valley State Park in 1937. Besides protecting the deep valleys and impressive scenery, the park conserves timber and plant life. In 1978 Schech's Mill was added to the National Register of Historic Places and to the park.

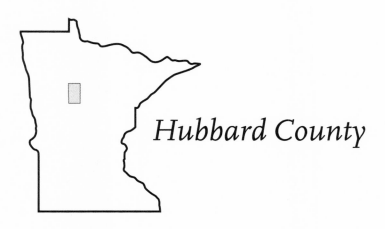

Hubbard County

This county, established February 26, 1883, was named in honor of Lucius Frederick Hubbard, governor of Minnesota from 1882 to 1887. He was born in Troy, N.Y., January 26, 1836; came to Minnesota in 1857, established the *Red Wing Republican* and was its editor till 1861; enlisted in December 1861 as a private in the Fifth Minnesota Regiment; within a year was promoted to be its colonel; and in December 1864 was brevetted brigadier general. In the Spanish-American War, 1898, he again served as brigadier general. In 1866 he engaged in the grain business at Red Wing and after 1870 also in flour milling. From 1877 to 1890 he took a leading part in the construction and management of new railway lines, built to promote the business development of Red Wing and Goodhue County. He was a state senator, 1872–75, and was governor, 1882–87, his second term consisting of three years on account of the change to biennial sessions of the legislature. He removed to St. Paul in 1901 and afterward lived there, except that his home during the last two years was with his son in Minneapolis, where he died February 5, 1913.

In the MHS Collections, vol. 13 ("Lives of the Governors of Minnesota," by Gen. James H. Baker, published in 1908), pages 251–81 give the biography and portrait of Gov. Hubbard, with extracts from his messages.

By an act of the legislature, April 16, 1889, Hubbard was appointed a member of a board of commissioners for preparing and publishing a history titled *Minnesota in the Civil and Indian Wars, 1861–1865*. In this work of two volumes he contributed the "Narrative of the Fifth Regiment" (vol. 1, pp. 243–81), followed by the roster of this regiment (pp. 282–99), published in 1890.

Five other papers by Hubbard, relating to campaigns, expeditions, and battles of the Civil War, are in the MHS Collections 12: 531–638 (1908); and the same volume has also an article by him, titled "Early Days in Goodhue County" (pp. 149–66).

Information for these names and for lakes and streams in this county was gathered from Joseph F. Delaney, who was the county auditor, 1907–15, M. M. Nygaard, register of deeds, and Dr. Pearl D. Winship, a resident since 1887 at Park Rapids, the county seat, interviewed during visits there in October 1909 and September 1916.

AKELEY TOWNSHIP and its railway village were named in honor of Healy Cady Akeley, who built large sawmills here and during many years engaged very extensively in logging and manufacture of lumber. He was born in Stowe, Vt., March 16, 1836, and died in Minneapolis, July 30, 1912. He was admitted to practice law in 1858; served in the Second Michigan Cavalry in the Civil War; settled in Minneapolis in 1887 as a lumber merchant; was president of the Flour City National Bank and of the Akeley Lumber Company. In 1916 these sawmills were closed, having exhausted the available supplies of pine timber.

The city of Akeley was incorporated on December 30, 1916. It was developed on large tracts of timber land that had been surveyed by Thomas Barlow Walker in 1876 and purchased by him and Akeley a short time later; their Red River Lumber Company began in 1893. General settlement began about 1895, with a general store, a brick industry, and hotels; the railroad came in 1899; the post office began in 1895 as Akely in postmaster John A. Plummer's home. Plummer was born in Indiana in 1851, came with his family to Minnesota in 1855 and to Akeley Township in 1894; the name changed to the present spelling in 1927. Dairying replaced the lumber industry by the early 1900s, and the Red River Lumber Company moved its mill to California in 1917.

AMES a post office, 1889–92, at the home of postmaster John Moran, who lived on Moran Lake in section 14 of Straight River Township; Moran was born in the early 1860s in Ohio, came to Minnesota in 1866 and to Park Rapids in 1893, and was county sheriff, 1893–97.

ANN see LAPORTE.

ARAGO TOWNSHIP received its name from Lake Arago on Joseph N. Nicollet's map of 1843, at the place of the present Potato Lake, in the southeast part of this township. The name commemorates Dominique François Arago, an eminent French physicist and astronomer, who was born at Estagel, France, February 26, 1786, and died in Paris, October 2, 1853. A post office was in section 6, 1897–1955.

ARAN see ORAN.

BADOURA TOWNSHIP was named for Mary Badoura Mow, wife of David Mow. They were pioneer settlers on the Hubbard prairie, where she died, after which he removed to southern Minnesota. This was the name of a princess in *Arabian Nights*. The village in section 8 had a post office, 1896–1915, and a station of the Great Northern Railway.

BECIDA a village in Fern Township, sections 23 and 26, with a post office since 1899.

BENEDICT a village in section 35, Lakeport, and Benedict Lake, about two miles distant to the south, were named for a homestead farmer. The village had a station of the Northern Pacific Railroad and has had a post office since 1907.

BURCH a post office authorized on October 19, 1905, Laura E. Schuneman, postmaster, but not established; location not found.

CARNYBELL a post office authorized on September 29, 1904, James E. Pauley, postmaster, but not established; location not found.

CHAMBERLIN a post office, 1898–1916, located in section 28 of White Oak Township.

CLAY TOWNSHIP was named for its generally clayey soil of glacial drift, in contrast with other tracts having more sandy and gravelly soil.

CLOVER TOWNSHIP derived its name from its abundance of white clover, growing along the old logging roads of the lumbermen.

CROW WING LAKE TOWNSHIP was named for its group of nine lakes on and near the Crow Wing River in its course through this township.

DEWEY a post office, 1898–1904, located in Crow Wing Township.

DISTRICT OF STEAMBOAT RIVER TOWNSHIP T. 142N, R. 32W.

DORSET a railway village in sections 10 and 11, Henrietta, was named by officers of the Great Northern Railway company for the place in England, from which a number of the early settlers came. This is the name of a county in southern England, a town in Vermont, and a village in Ohio. The village was platted in 1899 and had two saloons, a general store, a school, a church, and a station of the Great Northern Railway. The post office operated 1898–1964; its first postmaster, Jacob Avenson, was born in Illinois in 1854, came to Minnesota in 1882 and to Henrietta Township in the spring of 1883. Although there were other industries for a time, the community developed into a major fishing resort area along Mantrap chain of lakes.

DOUGLAS LODGE a post office of Lake Alice Township, section 19, which began in 1933 and transferred in 1953 to Lake Itasca in Clearwater County.

EMMAVILLE a post office, 1900–17, located in Clay Township, section 33; it had a station of the Great Northern Railway.

FARDEN TOWNSHIP was named for Ole J. Farden, a Norwegian homesteader there, who removed to West Hope in Saskatchewan.

FARRIS is a railway village of the Great Northern Railway and Minneapolis, St. Paul and Sault Ste. Marie Railroad (Soo Line) in sections 14 and 15, Farden. It was incorporated on June 18, 1898, but is presently unincorporated. It had a post office, 1898–1915, formerly called Graceland 1897–98, Fred A. Silver being postmaster under both names.

FERN TOWNSHIP was named in honor of Richard Fern, who owned a homestead in Lake Emma Township but in 1916 removed to Park Rapids.

FERNHILL a post office of Lake Hattie Township, section 21, 1905–36; it had a station of the Minnesota and International Railway.

FRY a post office authorized on October 3, 1906, C. J. Jencks, postmaster, but not established; location not found.

GRACE LAKE a station on the Great Northern Railway in Farden Township, section 16; its post office was at Cass Lake.

GRACELAND see FARRIS.

GRIMMER see PINEVIEW.

GUTHRIE TOWNSHIP named after its railway village in section 12, commemorates Archibald Guthrie, a contractor for the building of the Minnesota and International Railway. It has had a post office since 1900.

HART LAKE TOWNSHIP was named for its heart-shaped lake in section 17, but the names of the lake and township are misspelled.

HELGA bears the name of a daughter of John Snustad, probably the first white child born in that township.

HENDRICKSON TOWNSHIP commemorates John C. Hendrickson, the former owner of a sawmill there, who removed to Sauk Centre.

HENRIETTA TOWNSHIP was first called Elbow Lake, then Martin for William H. Martin, born in Massachusetts in 1831, and finally for Martin's wife, Henrietta P. Martin, born in Ohio in 1837; their homestead adjoined the southwest end of Elbow Lake. He served during the Civil War in an Ohio regiment, attaining the rank of lieutenant colonel; was a member of the board of county commissioners when this township was organized; and later returned to his former home in Dayton, Ohio, where he died. A post office operated in the township, 1892–94, with Martin as postmaster, and merged with Park Rapids in 1894.

HORTON a station of the Great Northern Railway in section 34, Straight River Township, was named for Edward H. Horton, a cruiser selecting lands for lumbering, who lived many years in Park Rapids but removed to Montana in 1908.

HUBBARD TOWNSHIP notable for its large prairie, was named, like the county, for Gen. Hubbard; it was formerly named Manter. A post office in section 20 began as Manter in 1880 in Cass County with John W. Jarvis, postmaster; he was born in 1846 in Ohio, came to Minnesota in 1880, opened a store in 1882, which housed the post office, moved to Park Rapids in 1894, and served as judge of probate court, 1893–95, and county auditor, 1895–97. The post office was transferred to Hubbard County in 1884, John Jarvis remained as postmaster, and the name was changed to Hubbard, 1884–1965, although called Brighton in 1886; it became a rural branch, 1965–68.

KABEKONA a post office, 1901–5, which merged with Laporte in 1905, located in the Chippewa National Forest; a community named Kabekona Corner exists on the site.

LAKE ALICE TOWNSHIP received its name from a lake that was called Lake Elvira by Capt. Willard Glazier, in memory of his eldest sister, on the maps of his expeditions to Lake Itasca in 1881 and 1891. The lake was renamed by the pioneer settlers to commemorate Alice Glazier, who accompanied her father in the large party of his second expedition, and to whom his book, *Headwaters of the Mississippi* (1893, 527 pp.), was dedicated.

LAKE EMMA TOWNSHIP was named for a beautiful though small lake in the north half of section 23, which is much surpassed in size by several others in this township.

LAKE GEORGE TOWNSHIP has a large lake at its center, which was thus named by Glazier in 1881 for his brother, a member of his first expedition to Lake Itasca, in July of that year. A post office in section 16 began as Yola, in section 5, in 1903, and changed to the present name in 1933.

LAKE HATTIE TOWNSHIP bears the name of its largest lake, derived from Glazier's map in 1881.

LAKEPORT see LAPORTE.

LAKEPORT TOWNSHIP was named, with a change of spelling, for its railway village, Laporte.

LAPORTE meaning, in French, "the door or gate"), a city in Lakeport Township, was incorporated as a village in May 4, 1908, separating from the township on June 22. The first post office, 1899–1901, was established with the arrival of the Northern Pacific Railroad; Nelson Daughters, who had come in 1898 with his wife, Ann, who died shortly thereafter in childbirth, became first postmaster, naming the site Ann in memory of his wife. In 1899, some Indians came to Daughters, requesting whiskey; when he refused, they returned to Walker, charging him with liquor trafficking; while being taken to Walker for trial, he escaped, returned to Ann, and died in a gun battle with the sheriff's posse. When the post office was reestablished in 1900 with justice of the peace J. C. Stuart as postmaster, the name was changed to Lake Port; the mail was being confused with Lake Park, so Mrs. Stuart named it Laporte after the Iowa town where she was married. Most of the village burned on May 11, 1911, but the community immediately began rebuilding; major fires occurred again in 1930, 1931, 1934, and 1936.

LATONA was the name of the post office, 1895–1909, at Horton railway station, which was located on the Wadena County border in Straight River Township, section 33; it merged with Menahga in Wadena County in 1909; Wilton J. Lord, postmaster, named it for Zeus's wife, mother of Apollo and Artemis.

MALTBY a place name in Rockwood Township about 1914.

MANTER see **HUBBARD**.

MANTRAP TOWNSHIP was named for the large Mantrap Lake at its northwest corner, which, by its many bays and peninsulas, entrapped and baffled travelers through this wooded country in their endeavors to pass by it or around it. Crooked and Spider Lakes in this township were also named for their similarly winding and branched outlines. A post office was in section 6, 1912–15.

NARY a railway station of the Northern Pacific Railroad in section 33, Helga Township, was named for Thomas J. Nary of Park Rapids, who during many years was a cruiser selecting timber lands for purchase by lumber manufacturers in Minneapolis. It had a post office, 1899–1924.

NEVIS TOWNSHIP and its railway village were probably named either for Ben Nevis in western Scotland, the highest mountain of Great Britain, or for Nevis, an island of the West Indies. The city, in sections 3 and 10, was incorporated as a village on February 4, 1902, and again on April 9, 1921,

at which time it separated from the township; the post office began in 1899.

NIAWA a post office in Lake George Township, section 28, 1896–1938, which merged with Park Rapids in 1938; the first postmaster, farmer Milo S. Maltby, was born in New York in 1855, came to Minnesota in 1869 and to the county in 1887; it had a station of the Red River Lumber Company logging railroad.

OJIBWAY a post office, 1892–94, which merged with Hackensack, Cass County, in 1894; located on the Crow Wing River, probably in White Oak Township.

ORAN a rural post office, 1903–9, located in Clay Township, section 21; sometimes shown on maps as Aran.

PARK RAPIDS a city in Todd Township, sections 23–26, and the county seat, was named by Frank C. Rice, proprietor of the townsite, who came from Riceville, Iowa, a railway village that he had previously platted. The name was suggested by the parklike groves and prairies there, beside the former rapids of the Fish Hook River, later dammed to supply valuable water power. The village was platted in 1882 by surveyor Joseph Sombs, who was born in Canada in 1834 and came to Minnesota in 1853. The city was incorporated on November 25, 1890; its post office was established in Cass County and transferred to Hubbard County in 1881; the first postmaster was Gilbert F. Rice, a miller born in 1839 in New York, who moved to Park Rapids in 1881, owned a flour mill, and served as judge of probate court, 1883–87.

PINEVIEW a post office in Henrietta Township, 1900–2, first known as Grimmer in 1900, with Albert S. Leland, postmaster and farmer, who was born in Michigan and came to Hubbard Township from North Dakota in 1885. Pineview's postmaster was Sevan (Swan/Sven) Rodin, born in Sweden, and a glassblower in Illinois before moving to Crow Wing Township in 1886; he later lived in Nevis in 1915 and then Dorset.

ROCKWOOD TOWNSHIP was at first named Rockwell, in honor of Charles H. Rockwell, a homesteader there. A lake also bears his name in sections 16 and 17, Henrietta, where likewise he had a farm.

ROSBY a station of the Great Northern and Soo railways in the northeast corner of Helga

Township, section 1, was named for Ole Rosby, a Norwegian farmer. It had a farmers post office, 1900–1909.

SCHOOLCRAFT post office located in section 27 of Rockwood Township, 1905–18, with a station of the Great Northern Railway.

SCHOOLCRAFT TOWNSHIP was named for its river, along which Henry Rowe Schoolcraft and his party canoed in 1832, ascending and portaging to Elk Lake, which he then renamed Lake Itasca. He was born in Albany County, N.Y., March 28, 1793, and died in Washington, D.C., December 10, 1864. He was educated at Middlebury College, Vt., and Union College, Schenectady, N.Y., giving principal attention to chemistry and mineralogy. In 1817–18 he traveled in Missouri and Arkansas; in 1820 was in the expedition of Gen. Lewis Cass to the upper Mississippi River, which turned back at Cass Lake, regarded then as the principal source of the river; in 1822 was appointed the Indian agent for the tribes in the region of the Great Lakes, with headquarters at Sault Ste. Marie and afterward at Mackinaw; and in 1832 led a government expedition to the head of the Mississippi in Lake Itasca. He published, in 1821, 1834, and 1855, narrative reports and maps of the two expeditions up the Mississippi, which supplied many geographic names. During the greater part of his life, Schoolcraft held various official positions connected with Indian affairs; and in 1851–57, under the auspices of the U.S. government, he was the author and compiler of a most elaborate work in six quarto volumes, finely illustrated, titled *Historical and Statistical Information respecting the History, Condition, and Prospects of the Indian Tribes of the United States.*

SHELL CITY a place name in Hubbard Township about 1894.

STRAIGHT RIVER TOWNSHIP was named for the river flowing from Straight Lake in Becker County eastward through the north part of this township. In the usage of the Ojibwe, from whom these are translations, the river took the name of the lake whence it flows.

STREETER a post office, 1889, which merged with Shell City, Wadena County, that same year; farmer John W. Smith, postmaster, was born in Illinois in 1853, came to Minnesota in 1883 and to Park Rapids in 1890, was county treasurer, 1891–95,

and county commissioner, 1900–1; location not found.

THORPE was named for Joseph Thorpe, an early schoolteacher of Hubbard County, who took a homestead claim in this township.

TODD was named, as proposed by Frank C. Rice of Park Rapids, which is situated in this township, for Smith Todd, a homesteader there. He served during the Civil War in the Eighth Maine Regiment, removed about 1910 to Spokane, Wash., and died there in 1915.

WHITE OAK TOWNSHIP was named for this species of oak, having "strong, durable, and beautiful timber," which is frequent or common in southeastern and central Minnesota. Its geographic range continues northwest through this county to the upper Mississippi River and the White Earth Reservation.

YOLA see **LAKE GEORGE**.

Lakes and Streams

The foregoing pages have noted the names of Benedict Lake and railway station, and of Hart Lake, Lakes Alice, Emma, George, and Hattie, Mantrap Lake, and Straight River, for each of which a township is named.

The remarkable series or chain of lakes along the head stream of Crow Wing River, in the southeast part of this county, was mapped by Schoolcraft in 1832. On his return from the expedition to Lake Itasca, his party traveled by canoes from Leech Lake southwest to the head of the Crow Wing and through its lakes, this being a route well known to the Ojibwe and frequently used in their war raids against the Dakota. In the descending order, these eleven lakes on Schoolcraft's map, published in 1834 with his narrative of this expedition, are Kaginogumag, Little Vermilion, Birch Lake, Lac Plè, Ossowa Lake, Lac Vieux Desert, Summit Lake, Long Rice Lake, Allen's and Johnston's Lakes, and Lake Kaichibo Sagitowa. Two of these names were given in honor of Lieut. James Allen and George Johnston, members of the expedition.

On the map of Hubbard County by the Minnesota Geological Survey (in vol. 4, 1899), this series of names is copied, excepting that the first is Longwater Lake, as it was translated by Schoolcraft's narrative.

Lac Plè (or Pelé) was named in allusion to its being partly bordered by a prairie. Lake Ossowa of the map is named Lake Boutwell in the narrative in honor of Rev. William T. Boutwell of this expedition. Lac Vieux Desert is there translated from its French name, as "the Lake of the Old Wintering Ground." Summit Lake was named "from its position," where the river turns southeastward from its previous southwest course. The lowest lake of the series is translated as "the lake which the river passes through at one end."

In the 1916 atlas of Minnesota, these original names were replaced by a numerical list, which came into use by lumbermen and the pioneer settlers. The lowest is called First or Sibley Lake, and the Third and Fourth Lakes are also named respectively Swift and Miller Lakes, these names being for early governors of Minnesota. The other lakes are designated only by their numbers, up to the Eleventh Lake, which, as noted by Schoolcraft, is called Kaginogumag by the Ojibwe, meaning Longwater Lake.

The stream now named Schoolcraft River was called by him the "Plantagenian or South fork of the Mississippi." Lake Plantagenet, through which it flows in the north edge of this county, retains the name that he gave in 1832. These names, for a line of kings of England, who reigned from 1154 to 1399, were derived from the flowering broom (in Latin, *plantagenista*), chosen as a family emblem by Geoffrey, count of Anjou, whose son was Henry II, the first of the Plantagenet kings. Another name sometimes given to this river is Yellow Head, for Schoolcraft's guide, whose Ojibwe name, Oza Windib, has this meaning. It was called River Laplace by Nicollet's map in 1843 for the great French astronomer, who was born in 1749 and died in 1827.

Hennepin Lake and River, La Salle River, and its Lake La Salle, tributary to the Mississippi from the northwest part of this county, bear names given in honor of these early French explorers by Glazier in his first expedition to Lake Itasca in 1881.

Other names received from Glazier's map of his route in that year, passing from Leech Lake west to Itasca, are Garfield Lake, named by Mrs. J. C. Stuart of Laporte in 1899 after the first president for whom she had voted, James Abram

Garfield (1831–81); Lake Sheridan in sections 24 and 25, Lake George Township, for Philip Henry Sheridan (1831–88), the renowned cavalry commander in the Civil War; and Lake Paine, for Barrett Channing Paine, who accompanied Glazier in that expedition.

Steamboat River and Lake were named for their being ascended by steamboats from Leech Lake.

Fish Hook River and Fish Hook Lake are translations from their Ojibwe name, given by Rev. J. A. Gilfillan as Pugidabani.

Belle Taine Lake, formerly Elbow Lake, first named by the white settlers for its sharply bent outlines; it has an Ojibwe name, which means, as translated by Gilfillan, "the lake into which the river pitches and ceases to flow,—dies there." It has no visible outlet, the inflow being discharged south to the Crow Wing River by springs or perhaps westward to the north part of Long Lake in Henrietta and Hubbard Townships.

Kabekona, the name of a lake and river tributary to Leech Lake, is defined by Gilfillan as "the end of all roads," which may be nearly equivalent with Schoolcraft's earlier translation, "the rest in the path."

Many other lakes remain to be noted as follows, in the order of the townships from south to north and of ranges from east to west.

Badoura has Wolf Lake in sections 17 and 18 and Tripp Lake on the south line of section 20, the last being named for Charles Tripp, an early settler.

Crow Wing Lake Township, in addition to the four lower lakes of the Crow Wing River series, has another Wolf Lake; Bladder and Ham Lakes, named for their shape; Palmer Lake in section 29; and Duck Lake in section 31.

Hubbard has Stony Lake in sections 1 and 2 and Little Stony Lake on the east side of section 1, named for ice-formed ridges of boulders and gravel on their shores; Long Lake, extending north from the village six miles; and Upper Twin Lake, partly in section 31, lying on the Wadena County line.

Straight River Township has Lake Moran, nearly three miles long and very narrow, reaching from section 13 to section 27, named for an early settler; and Bass Lake and Hinds Lake in section

24, the last being named for Edward R. Hinds of Hubbard, representative of this county in the legislature in 1903–5, 1909, and 1915–19, who once had a logging camp at this lake.

White Oak Township has Williams Lake in section 13, Hay Lake in section 10, and Loon Lake in section 30.

Nevis has the Fifth to the Eighth Lakes of the Crow Wing series; Elbow Lake, before noted; and Deer Lake, Shallow Lake, and Clausen's Lake, in sections 4, 5, and 6.

Henrietta has Bull Lake, named by the Ojibwe for a bull moose killed there; and Swietzer, Rockwell, and Peysenski Lakes, named for pioneer farmers.

Portage Lake in Todd Township was named for a portage from it westward on an Ojibwe canoe route.

Shingob Lake in sections 25 and 26, Akeley, and the creek flowing thence to Leech Lake, are named, like the adjoining Shingobee Township in Cass County, from the Ojibwe word *jingob*, applied as a general term to several species of evergreen trees, including the balsam fir, spruce, and arbor vitae.

Mantrap Township, with its Mantrap, Crooked, and Spider Lakes, before noticed, has Waboose Lake in section 2, meaning a rabbit in the Ojibwe language; and Dead Lake in section 18, which, though receiving an inlet from Crooked Lake, has no outlet.

Lake Emma Township, besides the small lake of this name, has Bottle Lake, named for the narrow strait, like the neck of a bottle or hourglass, connecting its two broad areas; Stocking Lake, named for its shape; Pickerel Lake, having many fish of this species; Rice Lake, having much wild rice; Blue Lake, named for its depth and color; Big Sand Lake and Little Sand Lake; and Gilmore and Thomas Lakes, the last being named for the owner of a hotel there, frequented for hunting and fishing.

Arago has Potato Lake, named for the wild artichoke, a species of sunflower with tuberous roots, much used as food by the Indians; Eagle Lake, named by timber cruisers for a nest in a large tree near the middle of its east shore; Island Lake; and Sloan Lake in section 32, named for John Sloan, a nearby farmer.

Mud Lake is in sections 19 and 30, Thorpe.

Clay Township has Schoolcraft Lake, crossed by its north line, near the highest sources of Schoolcraft River; Fawn Lake on the west side of section 6; Skunk Lake in sections 29, 30, and 32; and Bad Axe Lake in sections 26 and 35.

Clover Township has Little Mantrap Lake on its west boundary, named for its irregularly branching bays, lying about ten miles west of the larger Mantrap Lake.

Lakeport, with Garfield and Kabekona Lakes, before noted, has also Mirage Lake.

Lake Alice Township, including the eastern edge of the Itasca State Park, which reaches one mile into this county, has Lake Alice in sections 2 and 11, Beauty Lake in section 28, and numerous other little lakes.

Dow's Lake in section 32, Schoolcraft, was named for William Dow, who built a sawmill on the Schoolcraft River near this lake, taking a homestead there, but later removed to Laporte.

Farden has Midge, Grace, Wolf, Mud, and Long Lakes, all lying in the northeast part of this township.

Rockwood, with the large Plantagenet and Hennepin Lakes, before noticed, has Spearhead and Little Spearhead Lakes, probably named for their shape.

Fern Township has Diamond Lake and Lake La Salle.

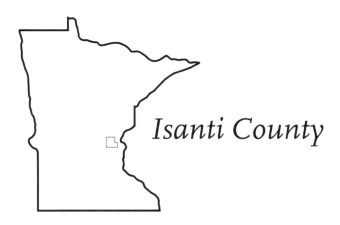

Isanti County

Established February 13, 1857, this county bears the former name, now obsolete, of a large division of the Dakota, or Sioux, anciently Izatys, now Santee, who lived years ago in the region of the Rum River and Mille Lacs, called by Father Louis Hennepin respectively the river and lake of the Isantis. Under different forms of spelling, this name was used by Daniel Greysolon, sieur Du Luth; Hennepin; and Robert Cavalier, sieur de La Salle, the first two seeing these Indians in 1679 and 1680; and the name, spelled Issati, appears on Jean Baptiste Louis Franquelin's map of 1688.

Prof. A. W. Williamson wrote of this word, and of its probable derivation from the Dakota name of Knife Lake in Kanabec County: "Isanti (isanati or isanyati),—isan, knife; ati, dwell on or at; the Dakota name of the part of the nation occupying Minnesota, and comprising the Sissetons as well as those now known as Santees; it is supposed the name was given as this lake was their chief location for a time on their westward journey."

Edward D. Neill's *History of Minnesota* (p. 51) mentions the Isanti division of the Dakota people as follows: "From an early period, there have been three great divisions of this people, which have been subdivided into smaller bands. The first are called the Isanyati, the Issati of Hennepin, after one of the many lakes at the head waters of the river marked, on modern maps, by the unpoetic name of Rum. It is asserted by Dahkotah missionaries now living, that this name was given to the lake because the stone from which they manufactured the knife (isan) was here obtained. The principal band of the Isanti was the M'dewakantonwan. In the journal of Le Sueur, they are spoken of as residing on a lake east of the Mississippi. Tradition says that it was a day's walk from Isan-tamde or Knife lake." The two lakes so referred to are doubtless Mille Lacs (the lake of the Isantis) and Knife Lake, on the Knife River, 15 miles distant southeastward.

Hon. J. V. Brower has shown that the Knife Lake and the Isanti, or Knife, Dakota probably derived their name from the first acquirement of iron or steel knives there by these Indians, in the winter of 1659–60, through their dealings with Groseilliers and Radisson, and with the Hurons and Ottawas of their company (*Memoirs of Explorations in the Basin of the Mississippi*, vol. 6, titled "Minnesota," 1903, pp. 119–23).

Information for this county was received from Hans Engberg, president of the First National Bank of Cambridge, who was the county auditor during the years 1878–88, from Sidney S. Bunker, an early pioneer, and G. G. Goodwin, county attorney, each a resident of Cambridge, the county seat, interviewed during a visit there in August 1916.

ANDREEM a post office, 1898–1904, of Stanchfield Township, section 5.

ATHENS TOWNSHIP bears the name of the most renowned city of ancient Greece, which is now the largest city and capital of that country. An Ohio county and its county seat, townships in Maine, Vermont, and New York, and cities and villages in 14 other states of our Union, are also named Athens. Probably settlers coming from one or more of these states proposed this name. A post office was in section 10, 1883–1903.

BODUM a post office in section 16 of Isanti Township, 1899–1903, with Peter Bodien, first postmaster; it had a store, a creamery, and an icehouse.

BRADFORD was named by Rev. Charles Booth, an Episcopal pastor who took a homestead claim in this township, for his native city of Bradford in Yorkshire, England. The village in section 18 had a post office, 1890–1908.

BRAHAM a city in sections 1 and 2 of Stanchfield Township, administered with Kanabec County, was named by officers of the Great Northern Railway company. It was incorporated as a village March 5, 1901; it had a station of the Great Northern Railway, and the post office began in 1891.

CAMBRIDGE TOWNSHIP was named by settlers from Maine for the township of Cambridge in the central part of that state. The old university city of Cambridge in England, whence we have the names of several cities and villages in the United States, is built on both sides of the little River Cam.

The old city of Cambridge was located a mile and one half south of the present city, platted in 1856 by John Owens, a St. Paul newspaperman, and R. F. Slaughter, a St. Paul real estate developer; Owens retired from the newspaper in 1857 and began farming in North Branch Township. The post office was established in 1856. The new Cambridge was started when Jedediah Kimball of Maine built a boardinghouse in 1859, and most of the townsite had moved there by 1869, the year voters selected Cambridge, rather than Old Isanti, for the county seat; it was incorporated as a village February 26, 1876. A number of businesses began, including a woolen mill, roller mills, and a starch factory, and when the Great Northern Railway came through in 1899, there was increased development.

CARMODY a village in section 32 of Dalbo Township, with a post office, 1899–1908.

CROWN a village in section 9 of Stanford Township, with a post office, 1890–1904.

CUSHMAN a post office, 1894–1901, of Oxford Township.

DALBO TOWNSHIP has a Swedish name, meaning the home of people from the former province of Dalarne, also called Dalecarlia, in central Sweden. A post office was established in 1884 in section 25; some businesses appeared as early as the 1870s, although most development was at the turn of the century, including stores, a feed mill, a creamery, a potato cannery, and a starch factory.

DARMSTADT a post office in Stanford Township, 1880–81, named for the place in Germany from which some of the early settlers had come.

DAY a village in section 7 of Maple Ridge Township, with a post office, 1896–1908.

EAST LAKE FRANCIS SHORES a locality in Bradford Township.

EDGEWOOD a village in Isanti Township that was the site of a District 3 school organized in 1863 and consolidated with Cambridge in 1958.

ELMPARK a post office, 1900–2, of Stanchfield Township; a village now known as Elm Park is located in section 24 of Maple Ridge Township.

GRANDY a village in section 3 of Cambridge Township with a post office established in 1899; it was incorporated as a village on February 13, 1903, but is currently unincorporated.

HEWSON a post office, 1897–1904, in Oxford Township, section 23, named for Stephen Hewson, former bookbinder at the *St. Paul Pioneer Press* newspaper office; it was the site of the courthouse and jail for the Cambridge precinct before Cambridge was named county seat.

ISANTI TOWNSHIP and its railway village were named, like the county, for the Dakota who inhabited this region when the first white explorers and traders came. The old Isanti was first established in sections 29 and 32, with a post office beginning 1865 in the home of Peter Norelius, a store and a hotel built in 1866 by George Nesbitt, and gristmills, a church, and a school. The village was moved in 1899 to the present site to be along the Great Northern Railway; incorporated as a village February 27, 1901.

KARMEL a post office, 1899–1900, first in section 1 of Wyanett Township and moved to section 5 of Springvale Township.

MAPLE RIDGE TOWNSHIP was named for its broad low ridge and the plentiful maples of its original forest. A post office was in section 11, 1869–1904.

MINNESOTA BOYS TOWN a locality in Isanti Township, southeast of Cambridge.

NORTH BRANCH TOWNSHIP is crossed by the North Branch of the Sunrise River. The name Congress Township was first petitioned in 1868 but not selected. See also SPRING LAKE.

OXFORD TOWNSHIP was named by its settlers for Oxford County, Township, and village in Maine. Twenty-five states of our Union have Oxford townships or villages, the earliest having derived the name from the ancient city and university of Oxford in England. It is of Anglo-Saxon origin, meaning the oxen's ford. A post office, 1864–1906, was first in section 13 and later in section 20.

OXLIP a village in section 19 of Bradford Township, with a post office, 1899–1908.

PINE BROOK a village in Springvale Township, section 19, with a post office, 1899–1901.

ST. FRANCIS a village in Stanford Township about 1919.

SPENCER BROOK TOWNSHIP received the name of its brook, which was named for Judge Benjamin Spencer, from Pennsylvania, who came to the area with his family in the late 1850s having been in Minneapolis earlier, and later moved to Sherburne County, where again he served as judge. The village in section 15 had a post office, 1857–1908.

SPRING LAKE a village in section 11 of North Branch Township; its post office was first located in section 26 and called North Branch, 1865–88, and discontinued in 1901.

SPRINGVALE TOWNSHIP has a euphonious name that is also borne by a village in Maine and by townships and villages in seven other states. A post office was in section 2, 1870–1937; the site had a mill, a creamery, and a brickyard.

STANCHFIELD TOWNSHIP the Lower Stanchfield Brook and Lower Stanchfield Lake, and Stanchfield Creek or Upper Brook, with its two Upper Stanchfield Lakes, are named in honor of Daniel Stanchfield, who was the first, in September 1847, to explore the extensive pineries of the Rum River. He was born in Leeds, Maine, June 8, 1820, and died at Fort Logan, Colo., May 23, 1908. He settled at St. Anthony in 1847, engaged in logging on this river and in mercantile business at St. Anthony, was a representative in the territorial legislature in 1853, removed to Iowa in 1861, and returned to Minneapolis in 1889, which was afterward his home. He contributed to the MHS Collections, vol. 9 (1901) a paper titled "History of Pioneer Lumbering on the Upper Mississippi and Its Tributaries, with Biographic Sketches" (pp. 325–62, with his portrait). The village in section 22 had a station of the Great Northern Railway and has had a post office since 1870.

STANFORD TOWNSHIP has the name of a township in New York, villages in Indiana and Illinois, and a small city in Kentucky. A post office was located there 1886–1901.

STANLEY a village in section 1 of Isanti Township, with a post office, 1893–1904.

TARN a post office in Stanford Township, section 2, 1898–1905.

TOLIN a post office in section 7 of Dalbo Township, 1899–1908, with Ole Tolin as postmaster.

WALBO a village in Springvale Township, section 28, founded in 1866 by Swedes from Rattvik; "wal" in Swedish is a type of fish. Its post office, 1892–1903, was located in postmaster Andrew Wicklund's home; there was a sawmill, a blacksmith, a grange store, and a creamery.

WEBER a village in section 31 of North Branch Township, with a post office, 1897–1900.

WEST LAKE FRANCIS SHORES a locality in Bradford Township.

WEST POINT a village in section 1 of Spencer Brook Township.

WYANETT TOWNSHIP was named after a village in northern Illinois, which was platted in 1856. It is noted by Henry Gannett as an Indian word, meaning "beautiful." The village in sections 20 and 21 had a post office, 1890–1900.

Lakes and Streams

The foregoing list has referred to the North Branch of the Sunrise River, Spencer Brook, and the Stanchfield Brooks and Lakes.

Sunrise River is translated from its Ojibwe name, given by Rev. Joseph A. Gilfillan as "Memokage zibi, Keep sunrising river."

Rum River is noticed in the chapter on Mille Lacs County, the name of this river having been suggested by the Dakota name of Mille Lacs.

Oxford has Horse Shoe Lake and Horse Leg Lake, the latter extending into North Branch, each named for its shape; Twin Lakes and Upper and Lower Birch Lakes; and Hoffman, Tamarack, Long, and Typo Lakes.

Athens has Stratton Lake in section 18, named for an early settler.

Marget Lake of section 3 in the east part of Stanford, named for farmers in the area, has been drained. Seelye Creek, flowing south from section 12, Stanford, was named for Moses Seelye, a pioneer settler who came from New Brunswick.

North Branch has Big Pine Lake in sections 4 and 9, named for a large white pine there, near the southern limit of its geographic range.

Isanti Township has Lakes Fanny and Florence, named for wives or children of pioneers.

Bradford has Lakes Elizabeth and Francis, Long Lake, and German Lake, the last being named for German settlers there. The second and third have been also called respectively Lake St. Francis, from the old French name of Rum River, and Lake Henrietta.

In Spencer Brook Township are Tennyson, Baxter, Blue, and Mud Lakes.

Cambridge has Skogman's Lake, named for an early Swedish settler. This township has two Long Lakes, one in sections 4 and 9, and another in sections 12 and 13.

Green Lake in Wyanett is mainly shallow, named for its green scum in summer, and the smaller but deeper Spectacle Lake is named for its shape, like a pair of eyeglasses.

Troolin and Linderman Lakes, in Stanchfield, were named respectively for a blacksmith and a farmer near them; Mud Lake, for its muddy shores; and the Upper and Lower Rice Lakes, for their wild rice.

Lory Lake, in section 5, Maple Ridge, was named for H. A. Lory, the former owner of the east half of that section.

Itasca County

This county, established October 27, 1849, having originally a much greater area than now, derived its name from Itasca Lake, which was named by Henry R. Schoolcraft in his expedition to this source of the Mississippi in 1832. The translation of its previous Ojibwe and French names is Elk Lake. Schoolcraft gave no explanation of the origin and meaning of the name Itasca in his narrative of this expedition published in 1834, but in his later book, on Gen. Lewis Cass's expedition of 1820 and this of 1832, published in 1855, the following statement is made, relating to the meaning of Itasca Lake. "I inquired of Ozawindib the Indian name of this lake; he replied *Omushkos*, which is the Chippewa name of the Elk. Having previously got an inkling of some of their mythological and necromantic notions of the origin and mutations of the country, which permitted the use of a female name for it, I denominated it Itasca."

The existence of this lake, and its French name, Lac la Biche, were known to Schoolcraft by information from Indians and voyageurs before this expedition, and the actual history of his coining this new word, as narrated 50 years afterward by his companion in the expedition, Rev. William T. Boutwell, is told by Hon. J. V. Brower in the MHS Collections (7: 144, 145).

"Schoolcraft and Boutwell were personal associates, voyaging in the same canoe through Superior, and while conversing on their travels along the south shore of the great lake, the name 'Itasca' was selected in the following manner, in advance of its discovery by Schoolcraft's party.

"Mr. Schoolcraft, having uppermost in his mind the source of the river, expecting and determined to reach it, suddenly turned and asked Mr. Boutwell for the Greek and Latin definition of the headwaters or true source of a river. Mr. Boutwell, after much thought, could not rally his memory of Greek sufficiently to designate the phrase, but in Latin selected the strongest and most pointed expressions, 'Veritas,' and 'Caput,'—Truth, Head. This was written on a slip of paper, and Mr. Schoolcraft struck out the first and last three letters, and announced to Mr. Boutwell that 'Itasca shall be the name.'"

The origin of this name had perplexed experts acquainted with the Ojibwe and Dakota languages, as related by Charles H. Baker in the *St. Paul Pioneer*, May 26, 1872. Three weeks later the same newspaper for June 16 published letters received by Alfred J. Hill from Gideon H. Pond, the missionary to the Dakota; Mary H. Eastman, citing a supposed Ojibwe myth or tradition in her "Aboriginal Portfolio"; and Rev. William T. Boutwell, telling how Schoolcraft coined the name by using parts of the two Latin words, Veritas Caput. Twenty years later, Brower's publication of his interview with Boutwell, as here cited, settled this very interesting question beyond any further doubt.

The chapter of Clearwater County contains a review of the explorations of the sources of the Mississippi, which were completed by detailed surveys of the Itasca State Park, lying mainly in that county.

Information of the names in this county was received from Edward J. Luther, deputy county auditor, and John A. Brown, county surveyor, during a visit at Grand Rapids, the county seat, in September 1909; and from Hugh McEwen, deputy auditor, during a second visit there in August 1916.

ACROPOLIS a village in section 34 of Goodland Township on the Wright and Davis logging railroad, many of whose workers were Greek; thus the site was named for their home village; it absorbed Quigg's logging camp nearby; a station of the Great Northern Railway was built in 1918; the village merged into Goodland in the late 1930s.

AFFLECK a post office, 1916–17, located seven miles north of Grand Rapids.

ALDER a village in Marcell Township, also known as Jessie Lake or Jessie Lake Junction, on the Minnesota and Rainy River Railway. A. W. Stickler built a general store in 1910; the only other buildings were accommodations for railroad section workers. The village was platted and owned by a man named Scott from Mankato who never lived there.

ALVWOOD TOWNSHIP is mainly occupied by Swedish settlers, and the first part of its name is probably derived from Sweden. The village in section 8 was first known as Thirteen Mile Corner because of its location on a highway intersection 13 miles from Blackduck to the west and Northome to the north. A post office operated 1904–20 and 1930–74.

ARBO TOWNSHIP was named for an early lumberman, John Arbo, who settled there.

ARCTURUS a station of the Duluth, Missabe and Northern Railway in section 24 of Iron Range Township.

ARDENHURST at first called Island Lake Township, was renamed by its settlers from England. The first part of this name refers to the ancient Ardennes forest, which covered a large area in northern France, Belgium, and western Germany; and *hurst* is an Anglo-Saxon word meaning "a grove or a wooded hill."

ARROW a post office, 1903–6; location not found.

BALL CLUB is the name of a railway village at the south end of Ball Club Lake, which is translated from its Ojibwe name, suggested by the form of the lake. The Indians were fond of playing ball, and their club or bat used in this game was called

La Crosse by the French, being the source of the name given to a city and county in Wisconsin. A post office named Ball Club was established in 1903 in section 2 of T. 144N, R. 26w on the Leech Lake Reservation; it was spelled first as Ballclub until 1950; it became a rural community branch in 1964; it had a station of the Great Northern Railway.

BALSAM TOWNSHIP was named for the Balsam Lake and Creek and for its abundance of the balsam fir, which also is common throughout northeastern Minnesota. The bark of this tree supplies a transparent liquid resin or turpentine, called Canada balsam, used in mounting objects for the microscope and in making varnish.

BASS BROOK TOWNSHIP was named for its brook, having many fish of our well-known bass species. The Ojibwe name of the lake is noted by Rev. Joseph A. Gilfillan as Ushigunikan, "the place of bass," and the outflowing brook, according to the Ojibwe usage, bears the same name. The city of Bass Brook was incorporated in 1992; its post office is named Cohasset.

BASS LAKE a village in section 26 of Wirt Township, was settled as a Czech farming community; its first settler, in 1911, was Vaclav Komarek, whose home was used for a store, the first post office, and the depot of the Minneapolis and Rainy River Railway; the post office operated 1913–43.

BASS LAKE TOWNSHIP was named for its lake.

BEARVILLE TOWNSHIP is named for its principal stream, Bear River, flowing from Bear Lake.

BEAUTYLAKE a post office authorized on May 14, 1900, with Peter A. Olson, postmaster, but not established; location not found.

BEDE a post office, 1903–6; location not found.

BENGAL a station of the Great Northern Railway in section 1 of Goodland Township.

BENNETT a locality in Nashwauk Township associated with the Bennett Mine, with a station of the Great Northern Railway in section 30.

BERGVILLE a village in sections 19 and 20 of Ardenhurst Township; its post office operated 1904–35, with Albert K. Berg, first postmaster.

BIGFORK TOWNSHIP and its railway village are named from their location on the Big Fork River. The city of Bigfork was incorporated as a village on January 17, 1907; settlement began in 1892 when Damase Neveaux built a log cabin on the river and laid claim to a tract of pine timber. It had a station of the Minneapolis and Rainy River Railway, and the post office was established in 1902.

BIRCHGROVE a post office, 1912–13; location not found.

BLACKBERRY TOWNSHIP organized in 1909, was named either for Blackberry Lake and Brook or by railway section foreman Peter Larson for the abundance of blackberry briers in the area. The village in sections 9 and 10 was first settled by Scandinavians; Ora M. Harry, the first merchant, built a log store in 1899 and was the first postmaster, the post office operating 1899–1944; the Duluth and Winnipeg Railroad built its line through in 1889. A plat was recorded by Thomas and Luella Simmons in 1918.

BOVEY a city in Arbo Township developed as a logging site almost 20 years before the townsite company platted 40 acres of forest land in 1904, following the news of iron ore mining operations to open in Itasca County. It was incorporated as a village July 21, 1904, and separated from the township on November 16, 1921. Erick Johnson opened the first store in 1903, became the first postmaster when the post office was established in 1904, and later a bank president.

BOWSTRING TOWNSHIP adjoins the east side of Bowstring Lake, which is a translation of its Ojibwe name, noted as Atchabani or Busatchabani by Gilfillan. This name is also applied by the Ojibwe to the Big Fork, because the Bowstring Lake is its source. The village in section 6 has had a post office since 1902.

BRIDGIE a village and flag station of the Minnesota and International Railway located in Cormorant Township and first settled in 1891; its post office operated 1895–1908, when it transferred to Orth.

BROWN a place name in T. 56N, R. 25W, section 10, about 1874.

BRUCE a site three miles north of Swan River in Goodland Township, section 29, which was created by the A. C. Lumber Company; a station of the Great Northern Railway was built there; the lumber company closed in the early 1920s, and the settlement began disappearing; the name existed until the 1940s, when some local residents began calling it Morrell.

BUSTI a post office authorized on July 19, 1915, with Cara Raberge, postmaster, but not established; location not found.

BUSTICOGAN a township name, is of Ojibwe derivation.

CALUMET a city of Greenway Township, bears the French name (from the Latin *calamus*, a reed) of the ceremonial pipe used by the Indians in making treaties or other solemn engagements. Assent was expressed by smoking the calumet, which, from treaties preventing or terminating wars, was often called the peace pipe. The city began as a logging site in the 1880s, but its chief source of employment was the Hill Annex Mine; 480 acres were platted by the Powers Improvement Company, selling lots beginning in 1908. The Duluth, Missabe and Northern Railway built a line through in 1906; the post office was established in 1908; it was incorporated as a village on May 21, 1909.

CALYX a station with St. Louis County of the Duluth, Missabe and Northern Railway, in Lone Pine Township.

CANISTEO a mine site near Coleraine in Iron Range Township; it had a station of the Great Northern Railway.

CARPENTER TOWNSHIP was named in honor of Seth Carpenter, an aged homesteader, who in 1906 headed the petition for its organization.

CHIEF LIGHTFOOT'S VILLAGE an Ojibwe village, 1880–1900, at Indian Point on Swan Lake.

CLARK a locality in T. 58N, R. 27W, section 14, also known as Clark's Siding, which was developed as a logging operation; it was named for two Clark brothers who held title to most of the land on which Itasca Railroad (later Minneapolis and Rainy River) laid track in 1898 between Bowstring Hill and Smith Lake; the railroad pulled the track and rerouted the line in 1904.

COFFEY a post office, 1911–19, located ten miles northwest of Deer River in T. 145N, R. 26W, with Anna M. Coffey as postmaster.

COHASSET the railway village of Bass Brook Township, received its name from the town of Cohasset on the east coast of Massachusetts. It is an Indian word, meaning, as noted by Henry Gannett, "fishing promontory," "place of pines," or "young pine trees." A post office was established in 1892; the village was incorporated on February 20, 1902; in 1916 the village of Cohasset and Bass Brook Township were separated; in 1957 residents voted again to become one governmental unit; in 1975 the merger was dissolved, with Bass

Brook incorporating as a city in 1992 and Cohasset remaining the post office.

COLERAINE a city in Iron Range and Trout Lake Townships, bears the name of a township in western Massachusetts. It was chosen in honor of Thomas F. Cole, who was prominent in the early development of the iron mines on the Mesabi Range and president of the Oliver Mining Company but later removed to Arizona, becoming president of a copper mining company there. The city was developed in 1904 as an Oliver Mining Company town by John Campbell Greenway, general superintendent; Oliver Mining Company was formed in the 1890s and later became part of U.S. Steel Corporation. The city is located one mile from Bovey and was designed basically as a residential community; the company-controlled administration screened potential residents. It incorporated as a village on April 20, 1909, and separated from the township on October 31, 1921; its post office was established in 1906.

COLLINS a village in Stokes Township, section 17, about 1930–39.

COMPTON a post office, 1891–92, in Bass Brook Township; a townsite was established in August 1891 by George A. Canfield and J. M. Marcum, but lots did not sell well, and gradually the site merged with Cohasset.

CONNORS a locality in Bigfork Township about 1930.

COOLEY a community settled in the early 1900s; Butler Brothers Mining Company operated the Harrison Mine there, 1914–63; the post office was open 1925–54.

CORT a mining village in section 15 of Greenway Township, with a post office, 1908–9, a hotel, a general store, and several saloons.

COUNTY ROAD a village in section 22 of Deer River Township with a station of the Minneapolis and Rainy River Railway.

CUNNINGHAM a post office of Ardenhurst Township, section 3, 1901–13, Edwin O. Cunningham, postmaster; authorized to reestablish on August 25, 1914, with Claud D. Fish, postmaster, but did not do so.

DEER LAKE TOWNSHIP and **DEER RIVER TOWNSHIP** are named for this lake and river, which are translated from the Ojibwe name Wawashkeshiwi, as noted by Gilfillan. See also UNORGANIZED TERRITORY OF DEER LAKE.

DEER RIVER a city in Morse Township, sections 25, 26, 35, and 36, organized as a village on November 23, 1891, incorporated on January 10, 1898, separated from the township on December 5, 1906, and incorporated as a city in 1956. It was first called Itasca City when a trading post was established there by Frank Vance. Its post office began in 1893 and serves other communities of the area: Inger, Talmoon, Jessie Lake, Spring Lake, Max, Wirt, and Ball Club; it had a station of the Duluth and Winnipeg Railroad. The city was developed as a logging community; much of the original village burned in an 1897 forest fire; there are presently many resorts in the area.

DEWEY TOWNSHIP was named in honor of George Dewey, victor in the battle of Manila Bay, May 1, 1898. He was born in Montpelier, Vt., December 26, 1837; was graduated at the U.S. Naval Academy, 1858; served in the Civil War; was promoted as lieutenant commander in 1865, captain in 1884, commodore in 1896, and admiral in 1899.

DICKSON'S SPUR see WARBA.

DORA LAKE a village in a summer resort area of Kinghurst Township, section 1, which had two post offices: the first operated 1913–18; the second had been at Popple, 1905–46, transferred to Dora Lake, and discontinued in 1953.

DUMAS a station of the Great Northern Railway in Morse Township, section 31.

DUNBAR a post office, 1913–33, located in Good Hope Township, section 16.

EFFIE a city seven miles north of Bigfork in Unorganized Territory of Effie, t. 62N, r. 26w, section 27, with a station of the Minneapolis and Rainy River Railway, incorporated June 10, 1940. Its post office began in 1903, with Eva R. Wenaus, postmaster, in the store owned by her husband, O. R. Wenaus; named for Effie Wenaus, daughter of Eva.

ERICKSON a station of the Great Northern Railway in Morse Township, section 33.

EVERGREEN a village in Bigfork Township, section 12, with a country post office, 1908–17; it had a station of the Minneapolis and Rainy River Railway.

FAIRVIEW TOWNSHIP has the euphonious name chosen by its settlers in their petition for organization.

FEELEY TOWNSHIP was named for Thomas J. Feeley of Aitkin, who had logging camps there during several years. He lived in this township from 1899. See also WARBA.

FOX LAKE a station of the Minneapolis and Rainy River Railway in Wirt Township, section 21; also known as Fox Lake Junction.

FRANKLIN TOWNSHIP like the counties of this name in 24 states of the Union, and townships, villages, or cities in 30 states, commemorates Benjamin Franklin, philosopher, statesman, and diplomat, who was born in Boston, January 17, 1706, and died in Philadelphia, April 17, 1790.

GARDNER see GOODLAND.

GOOD HOPE named by the settlers of this township, is also the name of villages in eight other states.

GOODLAND TOWNSHIP has another auspicious name, found likewise in Indiana, Michigan, and Kansas. The village in section 16 began as a logging camp for the Swan River Logging Company and was called Gardner, possibly for a local attorney by that name; it was platted in 1903 by C. H. Phinney Land Company, who renamed the community with a more descriptive term. Its post office began in 1903; it had a station of the Great Northern Railway.

GRAN TOWNSHIP was named for an early settler.

GRAND RAPIDS TOWNSHIP received its name from the location of its village, the county seat, beside rapids of the Mississippi, having a fall of five feet in a third of a mile. The city was incorporated as a village June 11, 1891, and as a city in 1957; established as the county seat on November 8, 1892, following a long fight with La Prairie for the designation. Although logging camps, trading posts, and buildings were on the site earlier, the first permanent building was the Potter Company general store in 1872; Lowe G. Seavey, first postmaster in 1874, built the first hotel; a station of the Duluth and Winnipeg Railroad was built in 1890; one of the major businesses is the Blandin Paper Company and its Blandin Foundation.

GRATTAN TOWNSHIP organized in 1905, was named for the Irish orator and statesman, Henry Grattan (1746–1820); the name was suggested by John W. Skully. A post office, 1920–35, was in section 10, which was formerly at Pinetop, 1901–20, in section 15; also the site of a sawmill and a station of the Minnesota and International Railway.

GREENFIELD BEACH a locality in Spang Township, section 35, circa 1910–40.

GREENROCK a village in Bearville Township, section 24; a post office was authorized on July 15, 1904, with F. A. Venning, postmaster, but was not established.

GREENWAY TOWNSHIP was named for John C. Greenway, who formerly had charge of iron mining at Coleraine for the Oliver Mining Company but removed to be a superintendent of copper mining in Bisbee, Ariz.

GUNN a station of the Great Northern Railway in section 26 of Grand Rapids Township.

HARRIS TOWNSHIP was named for Duncan Harris, who took a homestead claim there, on which he had a fruit farm.

HAUPT see HOUPT.

HAYSLIPS CORNER see TALMOON.

HOLMAN a mining village in Iron Range Township, section 27, with a station of the Great Northern Railway; dissolved as a village in 1917; also had a station of the same name of the Duluth, Missabe and Western Railroad in section 15.

HOUPT a village in section 19 of Nore Township, with a post office, 1903–14, and a station of the Minnesota and International Railway; also known as Haupt.

INGER TOWNSHIP was named for one of its pioneer settlers. A post office was operated in section 17, 1912–54, becoming a rural branch, 1954–55.

IRENE see VANCE.

IRON RANGE TOWNSHIP contains the iron mining railway villages of Coleraine, Bovey, and Holman, which have the most western mines of the Mesabi Range.

JAYNES a station of the Minneapolis and Rainy River Railway in Stokes Township, section 20.

JESSE LAKE see LAKE JESSIE.

JESSIE JUNCTION see ALDER.

JURGENSON a place name in Greenway Township.

KEEWATIN a city of Nashwauk Township, has an Ojibwe name, spelled *giwédin* by Frederic Baraga's *Dictionary*, meaning "north," also "the north wind." It was the name of a former large district of Canada, at the west side of Hudson Bay. This word is spelled *Keewaydin*, as it should be pronounced, in Henry W. Longfellow's *Song of Hiawatha*, with translation as "the Northwest wind, the Home wind." The city was incorporated as a village on November 27, 1906, and separated from the township on October 17, 1921. Logging companies were in the area before 1900, but most were gone by 1910; the first place of business was a tent where whiskey was sold; brothers Max and Harry Shuirman arrived in 1905 and opened Shuirman Brothers' Store; before Max moved away in 1910, he became the first postmaster in 1906 and was instrumental in getting the village incorporated. It had a large Finnish population. The village was platted by members of the Pillsbury, Longyear, and Bennett families; the township company originally selected Apollo as the name, but later Keewatin was substituted. It had a Great Northern Railway station; several mines opened in the area, 1910–30.

KENNY a station of the Minneapolis and Rainy River Railway in Unorganized Territory of Effie, T. 62N, R. 26W.

KESAHGAH a post office in 1857; location not found.

KEVIN a place name in Lone Pine Township.

KINGHURST TOWNSHIP formerly called Popple (a mispronunciation of the poplar tree, very abundant here), was renamed in honor of Cyrus M. King of Deer River, who during many years was a member of the board of county commissioners. See also ARDENHURST.

LA CROIX a post office authorized on June 25, 1907, with Peter Peterson, postmaster, but not established; location not found.

LAKE JESSIE TOWNSHIP has a lake of this name and another called Little Jessie Lake, probably either for the daughter of surveyor Taylor, who was in the area, or for timber cruiser Jessie Harry, who died in Grand Rapids in 1955. A station of the Minneapolis and Rainy River Railway was in section 24; the post office was called Jesse Lake, 1909–54, with Peter Peterson, first postmaster. The Minneapolis and Rainy River Railway was built through in 1905 and discontinued in 1930.

LA PRAIRIE a city of Grand Rapids Township, is near the mouth of Prairie River, which flows through Prairie Lake. It was incorporated as a village December 29, 1890, and developed as a logging community. Its steamboat landing on the Mississippi River was first known as Neal's Landing, named for owner Neal Carr, the name changing to Nealsville, then Saginaw, then La Prairie. It had a Duluth and Winnipeg Railroad station and a post office, 1890–1917. There are many stories about the origin of the name.

LAWRENCE TOWNSHIP T. 57N, R. 24W, previously part of Balsam Township.

LEECH LAKE RESERVATION T. 145N–T. 147N, R. 25W–R. 29W; see Beltrami County.

LEIPOLD a village in section 23 of Sago Township, was named for the John A. Leipold family, who came in 1906; John A. Leipold was postmaster in his home, 1909–25. A branch line of the Great Northern Railway, used primarily for logging, was built in 1906; the tracks were removed in 1935.

LIBERTY TOWNSHIP previously unnamed T. 47N, R. 24W.

LIND a station of the Minneapolis and Rainy River Railway in Marcell Township.

LITTLE BAND LAKE see UNORGANIZED TERRITORY OF LITTLE BAND LAKE.

LONE PINE TOWNSHIP previously unnamed T. 56N, R. 22W.

LONG LAKE TOWNSHIP is similarly named for one of its lakes, this name and also Round Lake being of very frequent occurrence among the almost countless lakes of Minnesota.

MACK see TALMOON.

MARBLE a city in Greenway Township, sections 16–20, was incorporated as a village on April 20, 1909. The first homestead claim was in 1888 by Albert F. Gross of Duluth, which became the Gross-Marble Mining Company property; the village was enlarged in 1908 by the Oliver Mining Company, at which time 20 of its 80 acres were reserved for a public park. The post office began in 1908.

MARCELL JUNCTION a station of the Minneapolis and Rainy River Railway, two miles south of Marcell.

MARCELL TOWNSHIP was named in honor of Andrew Marcell, the first conductor of trains on the Minneapolis and Rainy River Railway, which was originally built for transportation of logs to sawmills. A summer resort community first developed on the shore of Turtle Lake but moved to its present site in section 18, when the Minneapolis and Rainy River Railway built their line; the post office was established there in 1902.

MARTINS a locality in section 30 of Balsam Township.

MAX a post office established in 1906 in Max Township, section 23, which was given a short and easy-to-spell name by the postal department; it had a station of the Great Northern Railway.

MAX TOWNSHIP a previously unnamed township, T. 148N, R. 27W, organized in 1921 and named for its post office.

McCORMICK and **McLEOD TOWNSHIPS** were named for pioneers.

McKINLEY a logging camp, 1905–9, with a sawmill, located in Sago Township.

McVEIGH a station of the Minneapolis and Rainy River Railway in Deer River Township, section 2, named for a pioneer.

MISSISSIPPI JUNCTION a place name in T. 53N, R. 24–25W, possibly the same as the depot of that name in Aitkin County (also known as Mississippi Landing, Jacobson, and Hiawatha); platted in 1922 by the Hill City Railway; a sawmill was on the site.

MOORE a station of the Great Northern Railway in section 36 of Nashwauk Township.

MOOSE PARK TOWNSHIP received this name by the suggestion of C. H. Harper, a pioneer farmer there, who was one of the petitioners for its organization. A post office operated in the township, 1914–20.

MORRELL a station of the Great Northern Railway in Goodland Township (T. 54N, R. 22W), section 29.

MORSE TOWNSHIP T. 145N, R. 25W, formerly part of Oteneagen Township.

NASHWAUK TOWNSHIP has an Algonquin name, from Nashwaak River and village, near Fredericton, New Brunswick. It is probably allied in meaning with Nashua, "land between," the name of a river and a city in New Hampshire. The city of Nashwauk began as a logging community in the 1880s, and the townsite company platted the village on a former lumber campsite; the Great Northern Railway built a depot, and its post office began in 1902; the village was incorporated in 1903.

NASS a post office, 1913–38, transferred from Celina, St. Louis County; located in Carpenter Township (T. 62N, R. 22W) in sections 2, 11, and 14 at various times.

NEAL'S LANDING see LA PRAIRIE.

NEALSVILLE see LA PRAIRIE.

NORE TOWNSHIP was named for Kittil S. and Syver K. Nohre, immigrant settlers from Norway.

NORTH is a railway village of Nore, in the north edge of this county.

NORTHEAST ITASCA see UNORGANIZED TERRITORY OF NORTHEAST ITASCA.

NORWOOD a townsite incorporated on May 19, 1857; location unknown, and no trace found; the town council, which requested incorporation, included O. H. Rice, William George Colville, William Diggins, Henry Storrell, Daniel Case, and E. C. Becker, none of whom was identified in indexes to the Minnesota censuses of 1857 or 1860.

NOWHERE a site in T. 58N, R. 26–27W used for logging; although no community developed, the site, located in the middle of the county, was referred to by name and "might as well have been in the middle of nowhere."

NOYES a station of the Duluth, Missabe and Iron Range Railroad in Lone Pine Township, section 27.

OKOLL a post office authorized on February 9, 1907, with Regis G. Dargle, postmaster, but not established; location not found.

ORCHID a post office in section 20 of Kinghurst Township, 1905–27.

ORTH a post office of Nore Township, section 2, 1908–30, formerly at Bridgie, 1895–1908; it had a station of the Northern Pacific Railroad.

OSLUND a village in section 12 of Max Township, with a post office, 1922–33.

OTENEAGEN was named by William Hulbert, a farmer and lumberman of this township, who came from Michigan. In a different spelling, Ontonagon, it is the name of a river in northern Michigan, tributary to Lake Superior, and of its village and county. Gannett has defined the Michigan name as an Ojibwe word, meaning "fishing place," or, in another account of its origin, adopted because an Indian maiden lost a dish in the stream and exclaimed "nindonogan," which meant "away goes my dish."

PENGILLY a village and post office in section 15 of Greenway Township begun in 1915; established for the station of the Duluth, Missabe and Northern and Great Northern railroads named Swan Lake; a brick company and a general store were early businesses.

PHILBIN a place name in Blackberry Township.

PINECREST a post office, 1912–33, located in

T. 147N, R. 28w, section 18, on the Leech Lake Reservation.

PINES a station on the Minneapolis and Rainy River Railway in section 8 of Marcell Township, T. 59N, R. 26w.

PINETOP see GRATTAN.

PINEWOOD a post office, 1903; location not found.

POKEGAMA TOWNSHIP derived this Ojibwe name from Pokegama Lake, translated by Gilfillan as "the water which juts off from another water," and "the lake with bays branching out." This large lake, having a very irregularly branched shape, nearly adjoins the Mississippi River.

The Pokegama Falls of the Mississippi, named from this lake, about three miles above Grand Rapids, had a descent of 15 feet in a sixth of a mile, but the dam built there in the upper Mississippi reservoir system increases the fall to 21 feet, raising also the level of the lake. Schoolcraft, in his narrative of the expedition with Gov. Cass in 1820, wrote: "The Mississippi at this fall is compressed to eighty feet in width and precipitated over a rugged bed of sand stone, highly inclined towards the northeast. There is no perpendicular pitch, but the river rushes down a rocky channel."

POKEGAMON a village incorporated on May 23, 1857, but location not given and no trace found; supposedly there was also a post office established, August 24, 1857-May 15, 1860, called Pokegamon Falls, but it is not listed in post office lists.

POMROY a station of the Minneapolis and Rainy River Railway in section 3 of Pomroy Township.

POMROY TOWNSHIP T. 150N, R. 26w, previously unnamed.

POPPLE a 1930 map of Itasca County shows two communities by this name, one in Kinghurst Township, section 15, and a second in Deer River Township, which was a station of the Minneapolis and Rainy River Railway; a post office by this name operated 1905-46, before changing to Dora Lake.

RELEASE a post office, 1908-12, in section 3 of Balsam Township.

RENTOLA a logging camp, 1912-15, located in Sago Township and owned by Emil and Abraham Koski; the name means "unencumbered generosity or abundance."

ROSY a village in section 2 of Third River Town-

ship, with a station of the Minneapolis and Rainy River Railway and a post office, 1901-35.

ROUND LAKE TOWNSHIP and railway station are named for the central and smallest one of the three Round Lakes in the north half of this county. The next in size closely adjoins Long Lake, and the largest is at the east side of Good Hope.

Round Lake is also a place name in Stokes Township, section 7, on a 1930 map, with Round Lake Junction, a station on the Minneapolis and Rainy River Railway, in section 10.

SAGINAW see LA PRAIRIE.

SAGO TOWNSHIP was organized September 15, 1903. It received this name after several others had been successively chosen but found inadmissible, being previously used elsewhere in Minnesota. It was suggested by one of the county commissioners because sago pudding was served at their dinner. Another possible origin of the name is as a contraction of Saginaw, Michigan, former home of many of the early loggers and farmers of the Swan Lake region. The township was largely developed by Finnish immigrants.

SAND LAKE TOWNSHIP bears the name of its large lake, through which the Big Fork flows, next below Bowstring Lake.

SAVANNAH a station of the Duluth, Missabe and Northern Railway; location not found.

SIDING NO. 6 see WAWINA.

SIDING NO. 8 see WARBA.

SILVERWOOD a place name northeast of Coleraine in Iron Range Township.

SNOWBALL a village in Lone Pine Township, two miles east of Calumet, about 1910; it had several stores, boardinghouses, and saloons but did not develop, and the merchants moved to Calumet and other places nearby; what was left burned.

SOUTH ITASCA see UNORGANIZED TERRITORY OF SOUTH ITASCA.

SPANG TOWNSHIP was named in honor of Matthew A. Spang, a lumber manufacturer at Grand Rapids, who was the county auditor when this township was organized.

SPLIT HAND TOWNSHIP received the name of its principal lake and creek, translated from the Ojibwe name as "Cut Hand" on Joseph N. Nicollet's map.

SPLITHAND a post office, 1898-99, in Unorganized Territory of South Itasca, T. 53N, R. 24w, section 21.

SPRING LAKE a village in Lake Jessie Township, section 17, with a post office since 1912.

SQUAW LAKE a city in section 20 of Max Township, incorporated December 17, 1940, as a village; its post office began in 1923. It was developed as a trade center and had several CCC camps in the area; also a station on the Great Northern Railway.

STANLEY see WIRT.

STARKS a station of the Minneapolis and Rainy River Railway in Lake Jessie Township.

SUMMIT a station of the Minneapolis and Rainy River Railway in Wirt Township.

SUOMI a village settlement located on small portions of unorganized townships T. 58N, R. 26W, and T. 58N, R. 27W, originally surveyed about 1870, having some homesteaders and logging interests; often referred to by the names Bowstring Hill and Albo. The first of the settlers came in 1916, many from Finland, who named the community for their native country. It had a post office 1921–35.

SWAN LAKE see PENGILLY.

SWAN RIVER a community on the Sago and Wawina Township border, is named for the river near it, which flows from Swan Lake. This is a translation of the Ojibwe name, Wabiziwi, noted by Gilfillan. It was first settled in 1889 but never organized as a village; it had four locations and sites within Sago Township: Old Swan River, 1889–91; Swan River Junction, 1892–99; East Swan River, 1900–40; and West Swan River, 1941-present. Its post office in section 18 of Wawina Township began in 1890; it had stations in Sago Township of the Duluth, Mississippi River and Northern Railroad in section 7 and of the Great Northern Railway in section 12.

TACONITE a city in Iron Range Township, incorporated on April 20, 1909, as a village, was laid out by the Oliver Mining Company, which opened the Holman Mine there. The Diamond Mine was the site of earliest iron mining experimentation in the late 1880s; the first experimental washing plant on the western Mesabi Range was also built there. Its post office began in 1906; it had a station serving several railroad lines in section 22 and Taconite Junction in section 27.

TALMOON a village in Marcell Township, sections 9, 10, and 15; its post office, formerly at Mack, 1912–38, and Hayslips Corners, 1938–39, operated until 1954, changing to a rural branch.

THIRD RIVER TOWNSHIP is crossed by the river of this name, the third in the order from east to west, tributary to the north side of Lake Winnibigoshish. Also the name of a village in the township.

TOGO a post office since 1905 located in Carpenter Township, section 28, was named by Miles A. Nelson, the first postmaster, for Admiral Togo of the Japanese navy, which sank the Russian fleet during the Russo-Japanese War in 1905.

TOLLEF a post office authorized on December 4, 1902, with Emma C. Thomson, postmaster, but not established; location not found.

TROUT LAKE TOWNSHIP is named for its largest lake, translated from *Namegoss* or *Namegosi*, as the Ojibwe word is spelled respectively by Baraga and Gilfillan.

TURTLE JUNCTION a station of the Minneapolis and Rainy River Railway in Marcell Township.

UNORGANIZED TERRITORY OF DEER LAKE T. 54N, R. 26–27W; T. 55N, R. 27W; T. 56N, R. 26–27W; T. 57N, R. 26W; and T. 58N, R. 26–27W.

UNORGANIZED TERRITORY OF EFFIE T. 62N, R. 26W.

UNORGANIZED TERRITORY OF LITTLE BAND LAKE T. 55N, R. 23W.

UNORGANIZED TERRITORY OF NORTHEAST ITASCA T. 58–61N, R. 23W; T. 59–61N, R. 24W; T. 59–62N, R. 25W; and T. 62N, R. 26–27W.

UNORGANIZED TERRITORY OF SOUTH ITASCA T. 53N, R. 24–25W.

VAN CAMPS a station on the Minneapolis and Rainy River Railway in Bigfork Township.

VANCE a post office in Kinghurst Township, 1899–1901, with Frank L. Vance, postmaster; Vance, born in 1854 in Wisconsin, requested a post office named Irene, and it was authorized on May 18, 1905, but not established.

VERNA see WARBA.

WABANA a village in Balsam Township, section 22, with a post office called Wabana, 1904–10, and Wabana Lake, 1916–18; it had a station of the Great Northern Railway.

WABANA TOWNSHIP T. 57N, R. 24W, previously part of Balsam Township.

WARBA a city in Feeley Township, was incorporated as a village in 1911. A logging site named Siding No. 8, also known as Dickson's Spur for a timber man named Dickson, existed 1891–98 and changed its name to Verna. Verna was located side by side with the village of Feeley (also known as Feeley's Spur), named for the sawmill owner Thomas J. Feeley (died in Duluth May 24, 1935), which was platted in 1904. The Feeley post office operated 1901–10, at which time the U.S. Post Office Department thought Feeley was too close to Foley, and a contest to rename the village was held; A. A. Hall won, selecting the Indian word *warbasibi*, which has been variously interpreted as "resting place" or "white swan," the latter being *Wabiziwa* or *Waiba*, converted to Warba; the Great Northern Railway changed the depot name from Verna to Warba, thus both Verna and Feeley became Warba.

WASHBURN a townsite platted in Trout Lake Township on the shore of Trout Lake when it was known that iron ore operations would be developing in the western Mesabi Range; it became part of Coleraine.

WAWINA the most southeastern township of this county, received the name of its earlier railway village, an Ojibwe word meaning "I name him often, . . . mention him frequently," as defined in Baraga's *Dictionary*. The village in section 27, settled primarily by Finnish immigrants, began as a station of the Duluth and Winnipeg Railroad called Siding No. 6; a post office existed for one year, 1912, in the store of postmaster George T. Johnson; a depot was built in 1915.

WELLERS, WELLERS SPUR, or **WELLER'S SPUR** was a Great Northern Railway station and village five miles southeast of Deer River in section 30 of Bass Lake Township.

WHITE FISH LAKE a village in Wirt Township, section 27, with a station of the Minneapolis and Rainy River Railway.

WILDWOOD TOWNSHIP organized 1993.

WINNIBIGOSHISH a post office, 1905–8; location not found.

WINNIBIGOSHISH TOWNSHIP was on the Leech Lake Reservation at the north side of the large lake of this name, which has been fully noticed in the chapter for Cass County. It is now an unorganized territory.

WIRT TOWNSHIP was named by O. E. Walley, its first settler, probably for a township in New York or a county in West Virginia, where the name was given in honor of William Wirt (1772–1834), who was the attorney general of the United States, 1817–29. The village in sections 10 and 15 was established as a logging supply station on the Min-

neapolis and Rainy River Railway; its post office began in 1874 and was changed to a community post office in 1974. Elias O. Walley was the first settler, opening a store and becoming the first postmaster. The first site was on the north side of the Big Fork River with a store, a post office, and a hotel; the present community is across the river on the site of a former logging town, called Stanley by the railroad.

WOLF a station of the Minneapolis and Rainy River Railway in Bigfork Township.

WOODROW a place name on the border of Bigfork and Effie Townships, about 1930.

WYMAN a station of the Duluth and Iron Range Railroad in Nashwauk Township, section 22.

ZEMPLE a city in Morse Township, was incorporated as a village on May 29, 1911, and separated from the township on June 29; named for R. T. Zemple, who owned most of the land and was the first village president.

Lakes and Streams

The preceding pages have given sufficient mention of Ball Club Lake, Balsam Lake and Creek, Bass Brook and Lake, Bear River and Lake, the Big Fork River, Blackberry Lake and Brook, Bowstring Lake, a name that is also given to the Big Fork by the Ojibwe, Deer Lake and River, Lake Jessie and Little Jessie Lake, Prairie River and Lake, Long Lake, Pokegama Lake and Falls, the three Round Lakes, Sand Lake, Split Hand Lake and Creek, Swan River and Lake, Third River, and Trout Lake.

Lake Winnibigoshish lies in the course of the Mississippi on the boundary between Cass and Itasca Counties, so that it has previously received attention.

In addition to the southern Deer Lake and River, which gave their names to townships and a large village, this county has a second lake and river of this name, tributary to the Big Fork.

The following lakes remain to be mentioned, in their order from south to north, and from east to west.

Cowhorn Lake is named for its shape.

Lake Siseebakwet, as spelled on maps but given by Gilfillan as Sinzi-ba-quat, is a name received from the Ojibwe, meaning Sugar Lake, having reference to their making maple sugar.

Rice Lake in Bass Brook Township is named for wild rice.

Southeast of Swan Lake are Hart, Helen, and Beauty Lakes.

Trout Lake Township has Mud Lake, one of our most frequent lake names.

Grand Rapids Township has Horseshoe, Lily, Hale, and Crystal Lakes. The third was named in honor of James T. Hale, a member of the state tax commission, who formerly lived there.

White Oak Point on the Mississippi and a lake of the same name are translated from the Ojibwe name of this point, Nemijimijikan, as noted by Gilfillan.

Northwest and west of Swan Lake are Ox Hide, Snowball, and Panasa Lakes. The last is an Ojibwe name, meaning "a young bird."

Shoal Lake lies between Prairie and Bass Lakes.

Chase Lake, near the west end of Deer Lake, was named for Jonathan Chase, who was born in Sebec, Maine, December 31, 1818, and died at his home in Minneapolis, February 1, 1904. He came to Minnesota in 1854, engaged in lumbering in Mille Lacs County, and later owned an interest in the large sawmills at Gull River, Cass County.

Crooked Lake has very irregularly branched outlines.

Lawrence Lake was named for Hugh Lawrence, a Minneapolis lumberman who had a logging camp there.

Wabano Lake and the Little Wabano Lake are nearly like an Ojibwe word, *waban*, "the east, the morning twilight." *Wabun* is its spelling in *The Song of Hiawatha*, and Waupun as the name of a city in Wisconsin. Longfellow also used another word, *wabeno*, "a magician or juggler," spelled *Wabanow* by Baraga, which is more directly the source of the name of these lakes. Wabeno is a village name in northeastern Wisconsin, defined by Gannett as "men of the dawn" or "eastern men."

Next westward are Blue, Johnson, Moose, and Island Lakes.

Buck Lake was named for a male deer.

Pioneer lumbermen, or their forest cruisers who selected tracts of timber for purchase, are commemorated by Lake Buckman, King, Gunn, Dick, and Smith Lakes.

A further list of lakes, with those last named and westward, comprises another Island Lake, Ruby, Spider, and Little Long Lakes; Wolf Lake, Carriboo Lake (more correctly spelled Caribou), Dead Horse and Grave Lakes, Little Bowstring Lake, and Potato Lake; and Portage Lake, lying between Bowstring and Sand Lakes.

Northward are Eagle, Coon, and Fox Lakes; Turtle and Little Turtle Lakes; Cameron and Sandwick Lakes, the second named for John A. Sandwick, a pioneer farmer; Bustie's Lake and Shine Lake, north of the most eastern bend of the Big Fork; Lakes Bella and Dora; Spring, East, and White Fish Lakes; and Four Towns Lake, of small area, named for its lying in the corner of four townships.

Cut Foot Sioux Lake is translated from its Ojibwe name, referring to a maimed Sioux or Dakota who was killed there in a battle in 1748 (Warren, *History of the Ojibway People*, MHS Collections 5: 184; Winchell, *The Aborigines of Minnesota*, 1911, p. 534). The outlet of this lake is the first stream found flowing into the north side of Lake Winnibigoshish, in the order from east to west. Next are Pigeon River and Third River, the last giving its name to a township.

Downes Creek, flowing into the west part of Round Lake, is the most western stream of the Big Fork basin.

Island Lake in Ardenhurst, the third so named in this county, has Elmwood Island, which is more than a mile long but very narrow, indicating by its mapped outline that it is an esker gravel ridge of the glacial drift.

Maple Ridge

The highest point of Itasca County is a hill four miles west of Grand Rapids in sections 22 and 23, Bass Brook, adjoining the north part of Pokegama Lake, above which it rises about 350 feet. It is commonly called Maple Ridge or Sugar Tree Ridge. Other hills or ridges in this county rarely have even a third of this height, being so low that they have not been named.

State Parks

One of the first state parks in Minnesota was created in Itasca County in 1921 when the legislature authorized Scenic State Park, which was originally to be called Sandwick State Park. Located on Sandwick, Pine, and Coon Lakes, the park is between George Washington Memorial State Forest and the Chippewa National Forest, created in 1908. The combination of the park and forests preserves an area of virgin timber, especially white and red (Norway) pine.

Hill Annex Mine State Park. The land was part of the mining area at the western end of the Mesabi Iron Range. The mine itself operated from 1914 to 1978, producing 63 million tons of ore and ranking sixth in production among Minnesota's mines. When the mine closed, the land was sold to the Iron Range Resources and Rehabilitation Board, who managed the site until the state park was established. The mine pit gradually filled with water once mining ceased and the pumps were turned off. The resulting open-pit lake is a haven for wild birds.

Jackson County

This county, established May 23, 1857, is stated by its best informed old citizens, as also by J. Fletcher Williams, who from 1867 to 1893 was secretary of the Minnesota Historical Society, and by Return I. Holcombe, writing in the *Pioneer Press Almanac for the Year 1896*, to be named "for Hon. Henry Jackson, the first merchant in St. Paul." He was born in Abingdon, Va., February 1, 1811; came to St. Paul in June 1842; was appointed the first justice of the peace, 1843; was the first postmaster, 1846–49; was a member of the first territorial legislature, and a charter member of the Minnesota Historical Society; removed to Mankato in 1853, where he was one of the first settlers; and died there, July 31, 1857. In the summer of 1842 he opened the first store at St. Paul, in a cabin built of tamarack logs on the riverbank near Jackson Street, which was named for him.

The late William P. Murray, who was a member of the legislature in 1857 at the time of formation of Jackson County, dissented from this derivation of the name, asserting that according to his recollection it was their intention to commemorate Andrew Jackson, the seventh president of the United States.

The county seat also has this name, with which its site was christened a few weeks before the legislative act forming the county was passed. So it appears that the name was first adopted by pioneers on the ground, but whether they meant to honor Andrew Jackson, the military hero and statesman, or Henry Jackson, a founder of St. Paul and Mankato, on their route from the east to this area, is not certainly determined.

Counties in 20 other states of the Union are named Jackson, which with only one exception are noted by Henry Gannett as in honor of the president. Twenty-four states have townships, villages, or cities of this name. Pennsylvania, the previous home of some of the pioneers of this county and of Jackson, its county seat, has 17 townships thus named, in so many different counties, surpassing any other state in such expression of admiration of Andrew Jackson.

Information for this county was gathered from An Illustrated History of Jackson County, Minnesota, *by Arthur P. Rose (586 pp., 1910); and from I. W. Mahoney, county abstractor at the office of the register of deeds, and Alexander Fiddes, an early settler, who was the postmaster many years at Jackson, interviewed during a visit there in July 1916.*

ALBA TOWNSHIP organized September 21, 1872, has a Latin name, meaning "white," which is also the name of villages in Pennsylvania, Michigan, Missouri, Texas, and Oregon.

ALPHA a city in Wisconsin Township, sections 11–14, platted in 1895 and incorporated July 3, 1899, bears the name of our letter *A* in the Greek alphabet, which word is formed from the first and second Greek letters. It is also the name of villages in Maryland, Indiana, Illinois, and other states. The post office was established in 1895; it had a station of the Chicago, Milwaukee, St. Paul and Pacific Railroad in section 13.

ARLINGTON a townsite platted in 1885, but no buildings were constructed; location not found.

BELMONT TOWNSHIP was organized January 5, 1867, receiving its name from a settlement of Norwegian immigrants who came here in 1860. One of their leaders, Anders Olson Slaabaken, was also often called Anders Belmont, probably for a locality in Norway. This is also a frequent English name of villages and townships in many other states. The village in section 17 was first called Frog Point before its post office was established; the first operated 1872–74 and then transferred to Brownsburg; the second operated 1877–80 and 1882–86.

BERGEN a village in section 24 of Christiania Township, with a post office, 1889–1900; the postmaster, Sivert O. Harstad, was born in Norway in 1866, came to Minnesota in 1867, and to Jackson County in 1871.

BLUFF a station of the Chicago, St. Paul, Minneapolis and Omaha Railroad in Delafield Township; named for a bluff nearby.

BROWNSBURG a village in Belmont Township, section 28, established in 1875 as a Norwegian settlement and named for brothers Ole A. and Bredey A. Brown, who built flour and feed mills. The post office was transferred from Belmont in 1874; Ole A. Brown became the first postmaster, Bredey following him in 1880; the post office discontinued in 1900.

CHRISTIANIA TOWNSHIP organized March 4, 1871, was named by its settlers for the capital city and chief seaport of Norway. This name was given to the city in honor of Christian IV, king of Denmark and Norway, by whom it was founded in 1624.

DELAFIELD TOWNSHIP finally so named March 4, 1871, was organized October 11, 1870, being then called Pleasant Prairie and afterward Orwell and Bergen, which names were not accepted because they had been earlier given to townships elsewhere in Minnesota. This name is borne by villages in Illinois and Wisconsin.

DESMOIN LAKE a village in Des Moines Township, first settled before 1857; only a few buildings were erected; no trace remains.

DES MOINES TOWNSHIP organized April 2, 1866, was at first called Jackson for the county seat thus named in the eastern part of this township. About six weeks later, on May 16, it was renamed as now by the county commissioners for the river that flows through the township and county. The very interesting origin of this name has been noted in the first chapter.

ELLDORA a post office, 1872–73; location not found.

ELM a farmers post office, 1894–1901, located in Enterprise Township.

ENTERPRISE organized March 4, 1871, was named in accordance with the suggestion of Samuel D. Lockwood and Anders Roe, early settlers of this township.

EWINGTON organized March 28, 1873, was named in honor of Thomas C. Ewing and family, who were its first settlers.

GOLDLEAF a post office, 1888–91, in the northeast part of the county, 25 miles north of Jackson.

HARLIN a post office, 1892–1900, in Belmont Township, sections 1 and 2; the townsite platted in 1888 was named Karlin, but no buildings were constructed.

HERON LAKE a city in sections 19 and 30 of Weimer Township was platted in June 1872 by the Sioux City and St. Paul Railroad and was incorporated as a village on November 17, 1881. Its post office began in 1870, the first postmaster being Daniel F. Cleveland. The post office was called just Heron, 1895–99. The city was the county's second permanent townsite; a large proportion of Austrian and German immigrants settled there.

HERON LAKE TOWNSHIP organized September 7, 1870, was named for the large lake on its west side, which, as noted by Prof. A. W. Williamson, is translated from its Dakota name, Okabena (*hokah*, heron; *be*, nests; *na*, diminutive suffix), meaning "the nesting place of herons." Minnesota has three common species, the great blue heron or crane, from which Crane Island of Lake Minnetonka was named, the green heron, and the black-crowned night heron. The last, found by Dr. Thomas S. Roberts in considerable numbers at Heron Lake, was formerly plentiful or frequent through the greater part of this state.

HUNTER organized February 13, 1872, was named in honor of James Wilson Hunter, a pioneer merchant of Jackson, who at that time was the county auditor. He was born in Scotland, August 16, 1837; came to the United States in 1855 and to Minnesota in 1858; settled at Jackson in 1868, where he died August 13, 1900. He was a representative in the state legislature in 1869.

JACKSON a city in Des Moines Township, sections 23–26, and the county seat, is on the site of the earliest white settlement within the area of this county, founded and named Springfield in the summer of 1856. It consisted of a log store building on the west side of the Des Moines River and a few cabins, quite scattered, on the east side. Several of its settlers were killed, March 26, 1857, by a band of Dakota under the leadership of Inkpaduta, coming from their skirmish with many settlers at Spirit Lake, Iowa. Soon afterward the site of Springfield was renamed Jackson, and on May 23 of that year it was designated to be the county seat by the act establishing this county. But the financial panic of 1857 checked immigration, the Civil War followed, and the village was not platted until the fall of 1866. It was incorporated April 19, 1881. The origin of this name, which was adopted for the county, is discussed at the beginning of this chapter. The post office was established in 1857 as Pisa, Brown County, and changed to Jackson there before being transferred to Jackson County in 1858; it had a station of the Chicago, Milwaukee, St. Paul and Pacific Railroad in Wisconsin Township, section 19.

JACKSON CENTRE a post office in Heron Lake Township, 1879–81; a townsite was planned, and while no major buildings were constructed, there was a general store, a saloon, and a blacksmith shop; it had a station of the Southern Minnesota Railroad.

KARLIN see HARLIN.

KIMBALL TOWNSHIP organized March 23, 1872, was named in honor of Wilbur S. Kimball, the pioneer hardware merchant of Jackson. He was born in Chelsea, Vt., in 1835; came to Minnesota at the age of 21 years, engaging in hardware business at Austin; served in the Fourth Minnesota Regiment during the Civil War; removed to Jackson in 1867 and was a merchant there many years; was later a traveling salesman; and died in Jackson, December 13, 1892.

LA CROSSE TOWNSHIP organized in September 1872, was named for the city of La Crosse, Wis.,

whence many of its settlers came. This name refers to the favorite game of ball often played there by the Indians, the stick or club used to catch and throw the ball being called *la crosse* by the French.

LAKEFIELD a city located at the border of Heron Lake and Hunter Townships, founded in 1879 with the completion of the railway to this point, was named for the adjoining Heron Lake. It was incorporated September 1, 1887, but remained part of Heron Lake Township until April 22, 1889, and reincorporated on May 24, 1909. The village was platted in 1879 by Anders R. Kilen, who was born in Norway in 1846, and came to the United States in 1858 and to Jackson County in 1867. Also in 1879, the Southern Minnesota Railroad built a side track and depot in section 32 of Heron Lake Township on land owned by Kilen. The post office began in 1880; Martin A. Foss, first postmaster, born in Norway, was also a bank director, a farmer, a general merchandise store owner, and the Heron Lake Township treasurer. The major milling industry began in 1892; a well-known establishment was the Winter Hotel, built in 1895 by Grant Winter.

Kilen Woods State Park nearby in Belmont Township is located on part of the land owned by Agil Kilen. The park, at first called Kilen Hills Park, was established by the state legislature in 1945. The park overlooks the Des Moines River valley where the river slices through a hundred feet of glacial drift. The surrounding area slopes gently westward toward the Coteau des Prairies; the park is noted for its timber in the river bottom and the prairie on the uplands.

LOON LAKE a post office, 1882–88, located in Minneota Township.

MIDDLETOWN lying between Petersburg and Minneota, was organized May 10, 1869. "The fact that the township was situated between the two older organized townships suggested the name."

MILOMA a village in section 35 of La Crosse Township, which had a station at the intersection of the Chicago, Milwaukee and St. Paul and Chicago, St. Paul, Minneapolis and Omaha railways; its compound name was formed by putting together the first three letters of each, the roads being known familiarly as the Milwaukee and the Omaha. This crossing was laid August 1, 1879, and for about 25 years it was called Prairie Junction. Its post office began as Prairie Junction, 1881–83 and 1886–1906, at which time it was changed to Miloma; the first postmaster at Prairie Junction was George Maddesin; in 1906 Barbara Readle became postmaster of Miloma. Born in Germany in 1851, Readle came with her family to the United States in 1852, to Alba Township in 1872, and to then Prairie Junction in 1893, first renting a hotel and later purchasing it.

MINNEOTA TOWNSHIP organized October 15, 1866, has a Dakota name, meaning "much water," given partly for its group of several small lakes but mainly for the adjoining large Spirit Lake and Lake Okoboji in northwest Iowa. A village by the same name was located in the township about 1940.

NAMSOS a village in sections 21 and 22 of Kimball Township, with a post office, 1875–1904, and a station of the Chicago, Milwaukee and St. Paul Railroad.

OAK LAKE a post office, 1879–80, in Sioux Valley Township, with Abram McCulla, postmaster, stock raiser, and farmer.

OKABENA a city in sections 7 and 8 of West Heron Lake Township, was founded in September 1879, taking the Dakota name of the lake, which means, as before noted, "the nesting place of herons." It was incorporated as a village and separated from the township on July 30, 1938; its post office operated 1880–84 and reestablished in 1892. In 1897 Henry J. Schumacher purchased the townsite, platted it, and built a hotel; he sold the townsite in 1905 to Ferdinand Milbrath and his son, Edward. The Milbraths purchased the Okebena Clay Works, a brick and tile manufacturing company begun in 1897 and incorporated in 1916 with Edward Milbrath, president.

ORR a post office in section 30 of Hunter Township, 1873–1900.

PETERSBURG organized April 2, 1866, received its name in honor of Rev. Peter Baker, a pioneer Methodist minister, who settled in this township in 1860 and was its first postmaster. The village in section 28 was settled in the 1870s and platted in 1898; its post office operated 1867–1967.

PISA see JACKSON.

PRAIRIE JUNCTION see MILOMA.

ROST TOWNSHIP organized February 3, 1874, was named in honor of Frederick Rost, an early settler who came there in 1869. It was at first erroneous-

ly spelled Rust in the record of the county commissioners and on maps. A branch-line station of the Chicago, Milwaukee and St. Paul Railroad was located in the township.

ROUND LAKE TOWNSHIP organized in October 1869, was named for the beautiful lake in its western part. A post office was in section 30, 1872–84.

SIOUX VALLEY TOWNSHIP organized February 27, 1874, the latest in this county, was named for the Little Sioux River, which flows through it and continues south across northwestern Iowa to the Missouri River. The Little and Big Sioux Rivers, the latter forming the northwest boundary of Iowa, were named for the Dakota or Sioux, who inhabited this region. The name *Sioux* is the terminal part of *Nadouesioux*, a term of hatred, meaning "snakes, enemies," which was applied by the Ojibwe and other Algonquians to this people. The village in section 30 had a post office, 1879–1906.

SOMERSET a post office, 1875–81, in Kimball Township.

SPOFFORD a post office, 1894–1903, in Ewington Township, with farmer and storekeeper John A. Spafford as postmaster. Spafford, born in Ontario, Canada, in 1837, lived in Illinois and other Minnesota places before Jackson County; the post office was on his farm, the post office department misspelling his name, using the older English form.

SPRINGFIELD see JACKSON.

SUMMIT a post office, 1867–72; location not found.

SWASTIKA BEACH a village in section 5 of Christiania Township, on the southwest end of Fish Lake.

TIMBER LAKE see WILDER.

TREBAN a townsite platted in 1887, which had a few buildings, with plans for a brewery; location not found.

VERDAL a post office on the border of Belmont and Christiania Townships, 1883–88; Hans C. Sether, postmaster and farmer, was born in Norway in 1854, came to the United States in 1868, and established a homestead in Belmont Township.

WEIMER organized May 27, 1871, was then named Eden, which was changed to the present name October 20, 1871. "Charles Winzer, the township's first settler, selected the name in honor of his home town in Germany, Saxe-Weimar." It was correctly spelled in the petition for its adoption but was copied erroneously in the county records.

WEST HERON LAKE TOWNSHIP was organized January 7, 1874, "its geographical location suggesting the name."

WILDER a city in sections 6 and 7 of Delafield Township, was located and named in November 1871 in honor of Amherst Holcomb Wilder of St. Paul. He was born in Lewis, N.Y., July 7, 1828, and died in St. Paul, November 11, 1894. He came to Minnesota in 1859 and engaged in mercantile business and also in stage and steamboat transportation. Later he was interested in building numerous railways in Minnesota and adjoining states. By his will, and by the later wills of his widow and daughter, the Amherst H. Wilder Charity was founded, providing an endowment fund, of which the income is used to aid people in need. The building of this village was begun in 1885. It was platted by the Sioux City and St. Paul Railroad, December 7, 1886, and was incorporated March 28, 1899. For a few months, June-November 1871, the railroad station was called Timber Lake, then renamed; its post office was established in 1886. The community development was enhanced by the building in 1895 of the first Breck School as a farm college, the school moving to St. Paul in 1907.

WILLIAMSBURG a townsite platted in 1874, which had a store and postal station; location not found.

WISCONSIN TOWNSHIP organized April 10, 1869, was named in honor of the state from which a majority of its settlers came. This name, given to the state from its large river, is noted by Gannett as "a Sauk Indian word having reference to holes in the banks of a stream, in which birds nest."

Lakes and Streams

The preceding pages have noticed the Des Moines River, Heron Lake, Round Lake, and the Little Sioux River.

Elm Creek, draining the northeastern part of this county, flows east across Martin County to the Blue Earth River.

Independence Lake, on the south line of Christiania, was named by the U.S. surveyors, who came to it on the Fourth of July. Long Lake and Fish Lake are crossed respectively by the east and north boundaries of this township. Lower's Lake in sections 15 and 22 has been drained.

The east part of Wisconsin Township has small creeks flowing into Martin County, which are sources of the East Fork of the Des Moines River.

Minneota has Loon Lake, Pearl, Rush, and Little Spirit Lakes. The last is named in contrast with the much larger Spirit Lake in Iowa, which is translated from its Dakota name, Mini wakan, noted by Joseph N. Nicollet. In its most northern part, Spirit Lake touches the boundary of the state and of this township at the south side of section 36.

Tributary to the West Fork of the Little Sioux River are Skunk and Rush Lakes in Spring Valley, Round Lake in the township bearing its name, and also Illinois Lake, Plum Island Lake, named for the grove of native plum trees on its island, and Iowa or State Line Lake, crossed by the Iowa boundary at the southwest corner of this county.

Des Moines Township has Clear Lake at the middle of its west side, remarkable for the depth and purity of its water.

Heron Lake Township has Lake Flaherty, an early name, but for whom it was given is unknown.

Timber Lake, named for its lone grove in this broad prairie region, adjoins the south side of Wilder village. It has been also called Lake Minneseka, a Dakota name meaning "bad water."

Lake Carroll, formerly mapped in section 4, Delafield, has been drained.

Jack and Okabena Creeks flow into the west side of Heron Lake, the former being probably named from jack rabbits, and the latter bearing the Dakota name for Heron Lake.

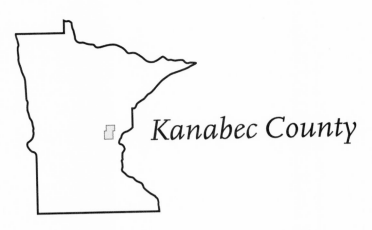

Kanabec County

Established March 13, 1858, and organized in 1882, this county bears a name proposed by William H. C. Folsom of Taylors Falls, who, as a member of the state senate in 1858, introduced the legislative bill for the formation of the county. *Kanabec* is the usual word for a snake in the language of the Ojibwe, given by them to the Snake River flowing through Kanabec and Pine Counties to the St. Croix. It has a heavy accent on the second syllable, with the English long sound of the vowel, being thus pronounced quite unlike the name of the Kennebec River in Maine. The latter name, accented on the first syllable, is of different etymology, meaning "long lake,—a name of Moosehead lake transferred to the river."

This Ojibwe word is variously spelled but has only slight difference of pronunciation. On Joseph N. Nicollet's map it is *Kinebik*; in Edward F. Wilson's manual of this language, *kenabig*; and in Frederic Baraga's *Dictionary*, which is followed by Rev. Joseph A. Gilfillan and Chrysostom Verwyst in their lists of Ojibwe names, it is *ginebig*, but this is pronounced, in French style, nearly like our English form of the word in the county name.

Information of geographic names in this county has been received from Fifty Years in the Northwest, *by W. H. C. Folsom (763 pp., 1888); and from A. V. Sander, county auditor, A. M. Anderson, register of deeds, Olof P. Victorien, judge of probate, and Hon. J. C. Pope, each of Mora, the county seat, interviewed during a visit there in May 1916.*

ANN LAKE TOWNSHIP its lake of this name, and the outflowing Ann River, tributary to the Snake River, commemorate an Ojibwe woman who lived beside the lake (*Kathio*, by J. V. Brower, 1901, p. 114). The township separated from Knife Lake Township and organized July 13, 1904. The village of Ann Lake is in sections 2 and 3.

ARTHUR TOWNSHIP organized in 1883, was named by Charles E. Williams of Mora in honor of Chester Alan Arthur, the twenty-first president of the United States, who was born in Fairfield, Vt., October 5, 1830, and died in New York City, November 18, 1886. He was graduated at Union College in 1848; practiced law in New York City; was inspector general of state troops during the Civil War; was collector of the port of New York, 1871–78; was elected vice-president in 1880, and succeeded James A. Garfield, who died September 19, 1881. His term as president extended to March 4, 1885.

BRAHAM a city with Isanti County, which see.

BRONSON a village in section 15 of Arthur Township, established in 1882 on the side track of the Great Northern Railway as an accommodation site for Isaac Staples's logging business, and abandoned at the end of active logging operations; its post office operated 1882–99.

BRUNSWICK TOWNSHIP organized in 1883, received its name from Brunswick village and township in Maine, at the head of navigation on the

Androscoggin River, whence many pioneer lumbermen came to the pineries of the St. Croix and Snake Rivers. A village of this name, platted in 1856 in section 1 of this township, was the first county seat. The village, in the then Grass Lake Township, now Brunswick Township, section 12, was established as the logging headquarters of Hersey, Staples and Bean; George Staples from Maine named it; in 1856, George and his brother, Isaac Staples, platted the site. George opened the first store and was its first postmaster, the post office operating 1860–1918 and again 1927–1934, the latter period located in Tallman's Mill, built by S. E. Tallman of New York. He also built a dam across the Groundhouse River at Brunswick in 1869, a sawmill in 1870, and a flour mill in 1879; the site was named the county seat on March 13, 1859, remaining so until 1883 when transferred to Mora.

COIN a village in section 35 of Brunswick Township, which earlier had a post office, 1898–1904; it was named during the William Jennings Bryan free silver debate as suggested by Ole E. Olson, the storekeeper and postmaster.

COMFORT TOWNSHIP was named by the first town clerk, Harry Stone, for a popular magazine of that time; it was organized January 6, 1892, and included Whited Township.

FISK see GROUNDHOUSE; OGILVIE.

FORD TOWNSHIP organized in 1916, the latest in this county, was formerly included in Peace Township. It separated from Hillman Township, May 16, 1916, at which time there were only three homesteaders in the township, all in section 32: Henry Weal, who came in 1898, and Charles A. Peterson and Charles Johnson, both of whom came in 1899. The township was named for Henry Ford, of Detroit, Mich., a wealthy manufacturer of automobiles, who conducted a large delegation from this country to Europe in December 1915 to confer with the nations at war and to intercede for restoration of peace.

GRASS LAKE is a village in Brunswick Township; settlement began about 1872 with many Swedish immigrants; its post office operated 1878–1904.

GRASS LAKE TOWNSHIP organized in 1883, formerly had a small lake of this name, now drained, in sections 13 and 24, which was mostly filled with tall marsh grass, the water being very shallow.

GRASSTON a city in section 12 of Grass Lake Township, was incorporated on October 21, 1907, and separated from the township on April 8, 1908; it was established in 1898 on a side track of the Great Northern Railway on June 6, 1899 and platted on June 6, 1899. John A. Swan owned the land and suggested Swanville, but the name was already in use in the state; also suggested was Oxenville, but the railroad selected Grasston, and Swan agreed. The post office began in 1899, with Annie Swan, first postmaster.

GROUNDHOUSE a village in Kanabec Township, which was named for the wooden huts covered by earth of the Hidatsa Indians who once lived in the area. Its post office began in 1889 as Fisk, with Noah Adams, postmaster and sawmill and shingle mill owner, and changed to Groundhouse, 1889–99, Adams continuing as postmaster, at which time the name was changed to Ogilvie. The village was platted by Isaac Staples for Hersey, Staples and Company, on January 17, 1857; the name had a brief rebirth when the original site of Ogilvie was called Groundhouse; see also OGILVIE.

HAY BROOK TOWNSHIP was named for the brook flowing through it, having meadows that supplied hay for winter logging camps. It separated from Hillman Township and organized November 15, 1915.

HEDIN a post office in Knife Lake Township, 1901–6, with Axel Hedin, postmaster.

HILLMAN TOWNSHIP was named in honor of William F. Hillman, a pioneer farmer there. It was organized June 19, 1894, and included several townships later separated out: Hay Brook, Ford, and Kroschel. A post office on the border of sections 20 and 29 was first called Mull when William Currie was appointed postmaster July 17, 1895, at Halfway House on the stage road between Mora and Lawrence in Mille Lacs County, and named for a place in Scotland; when William Hillman was appointed postmaster on October 29, 1895, the name was changed to Hillman, operating several months under both names, and discontinuing in 1906.

KANABEC TOWNSHIP like the county it was named for, bears the Ojibwe name of the Snake River. It separated from Arthur Township and organized on August 28, 1896.

KNIFE LAKE TOWNSHIP received its name from the Knife Lake and River, which are translated from their Dakota and Ojibwe names. The first knives of iron or steel obtained by the Dakota, in the winter of 1659–60, were brought there by Groseilliers and Radisson and the Huron and Ottawa Indians who accompanied them, as noted for Isanti County. The township was organized June 19, 1894, including at that time the townships of Ann Lake, Peace, Pomroy, and Knife Lake.

KROSCHEL TOWNSHIP was named in honor of Herman Kroschel, one of its first settlers. It was organized June 12, 1899.

LEWIS LAKE a village in section 19 of Brunswick Township, with a post office established in 1896 in Isanti County, transferring to Kanabec County in 1899, and discontinuing in 1904.

MILLET RAPIDS site of the Staples family logging headquarters located six miles south of Mora on the Snake River.

MORA a city in Arthur Township, was platted in May 1882, when by popular vote it succeeded Brunswick as the county seat. It was platted by Myron R. Kent, who was first postmaster in 1883; the name was suggested by Israel Israelson, who came in 1871 to the Lewis Lake area, for his home town in Dalarna, Sweden, and so Kent requested that name for the post office. It was incorporated as a village on February 16, 1891. The first permanent resident was Alvin J. Conger, who came to Minnesota in 1859, established a trading post at Spring Brook Hill, two miles southeast of Mora, which he abandoned in 1861, and lived in other Minnesota places until 1882, when he arrived in Mora, later building a hotel.

MUD CREEK see QUAMBA.

MULL see HILLMAN.

OGILVIE a city in Kanabec Township, sections 26 and 35, was incorporated as a village on January 21, 1902. The first land was purchased in 1854 by the Hersey Lumber Company; Noah Adams built a sawmill and store in the late 1880s; the post office was first Fisk and then Groundhouse, before becoming Ogilvie in 1899. Oric Ogilvie Whited purchased the townsite, filing a plat on July 18, 1889, changing the name to Ogilvie, and later that year the Great Northern Railway changed the depot name from Groundhouse to Ogilvie.

PEACE TOWNSHIP was named by vote of its people, this name being suggested in contrast with its village of Warman. It was separated from Knife Lake Township and organized March 2, 1903.

POMROY TOWNSHIP was named, as also Pomroy

Lake, crossed by its west line, in honor of John Pomroy, a pioneer lumberman who had a logging camp beside the lake. It was separated from Kroschel Township and organized March 3, 1903.

QUAMBA a city in Whited Township, platted in 1901 by Oric Ogilvie Whited, and incorporated as a village on July 11, 1952. It was first established in 1882 on the side track of the Great Northern Railway and known as Mud Creek for the creek that the tracks crossed; when the depot was built, the name was changed to Quamba, which according to the railway officials was an Indian word for "mudhole." Its post office operated 1901–3 and 1906–66, at which time it changed to a rural branch.

RARITAN a post office, 1903–4, located in Grass Lake Township, section 9.

RIVERDALE a post office, 1907–10, located in section 34 of Knife Lake Township.

SOUTH FORK TOWNSHIP is crossed by the South Branch or Fork of the Groundhouse River. It was separated from Brunswick Township and organized August 28, 1896.

WARMAN a village in sections 5 and 6, Peace, having granite quarries, was named in honor of S. M. Warman, a quarry owner there, who was killed by the fall of a derrick. Warman opened a granite quarry in 1907, and on July 18 of that year, he and his wife, Sarah J. Warman, platted a village as Warman Creek on the west side of the road (present Highway 65); N. C. Pike of Pike-Horning Granite Company, on July 23, 1907, platted the east side of the road calling it East Mora, a name that did not receive popular acceptance; the site is now part of the Warman community. The post office operated 1907–20.

WHITED TOWNSHIP like Ogilvie village, was named in honor of Oric Ogilvie Whited of Minneapolis. He was born in Fitchville, Ohio, January 20, 1854; was graduated at the State Normal School, Winona, Minn., 1872; taught school several years in Olmsted County, and later was the county superintendent of schools; was admitted to practice law, 1884; settled in Minneapolis in 1890, engaged in real estate business and law practice, and owned numerous tracts of land in this county. He died in Minneapolis, August 6, 1912. The township separated from Comfort Township and organized May 8, 1899; Isaac Staples purchased the first land for logging purposes in 1854; the pine timber was so good in this township that logging companies purchased all of the land.

WOODLAND a village in sections 17–20 of Ford Township.

———————

Lakes and Streams

The foregoing pages have noted the Snake River, Ann Lake and River, Grass Lake, Hay River, Knife Lake and River, Pomroy Lake, and the South Fork of Groundhouse River.

A tradition among the Dakota and Ojibwe, cited by Newton H. Winchell in *The Aborigines of Minnesota* (p. 67), told of Hidatsa Indians, a branch of the great Dakotan stock, anciently living in Minnesota, who were driven westward to the Missouri River by the coming of the Dakota. These Indians lived in wooden huts covered with earth, whence probably came the aboriginal name that we retain in translation as the Groundhouse River, draining the southwest part of this county. It is called Earth Fort River on the map of David D. Owen's *Geological Report*, published in 1852.

Tributaries of the Snake River, in their order from south to north in this county, include, on its east side, Mud Creek, flowing through Mud Lake, Chesley River, also called Little Snake River, and Cowan's River, the second and third being named for pioneer lumbermen; and, on the west side, Rice Creek, named for its wild rice, Groundhouse, Ann, and Knife Rivers, previously noticed, Moccasin River, into which Snowshoe River flows, Hay River, and Bergman's River, near the north line of the county. The last bears the name of a lumberman whose logging camp was on this brook.

The picturesque upper falls and lower falls of the Snake River are respectively about two miles and three miles south of the north boundary of this county.

Among the few lakes that remain to be mentioned, Brunswick has Devil's Lake in section 4; Pennington Lake in section 13, now drained, named for James Pennington, who near it opened the first farm in the county; and Lewis Lake in the southwest corner of this township, named for a pioneer settler beside it.

Arthur Township has Spring Lake in sections 1 and 12; Lake Mora in the village of this name; Kent Lake in sections 16 and 21, commemorating Myron R. Kent, who platted and named this village; and Fish Lake, through which Ann River flows, in sections 33 and 34.

A lake beside Snake River in sections 10 and 15, Peace, is mapped as Full of Fish Lake, a translation from its Ojibwe name.

Kroschel has Bass Lake in section 1; Loon Lake in sections 3 and 4; Long Lake and Bland Lake in sections 4 and 5; Beauty Lake in section 10; Lake Eleven in the section having this number; Pike Lake in section 13; Feathery Lake and Muskrat Lake in section 24; and White Lily Lake in section 27, named for its abundance of the fragrant white water lily.

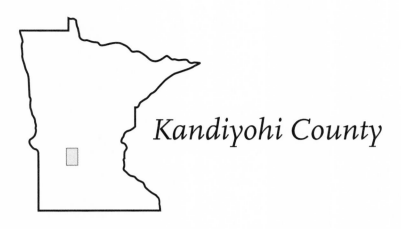

Kandiyohi County

This county, established March 20, 1858, bears the Dakota name of one or several of its lakes, meaning "where the buffalo fish come." Dr. Thomas S. Williamson states that it is from "*kandi*, buffalo fish; *y*, euphonic; *ohi*, arrive in." Our three species of buffalo fish, *Ictiobus cyprinella*, *I. urus*, and *I. bubalus*, at their spawning season in May and June leave the large rivers, in which they live the greater part of the year, and come, sometimes in immense numbers, to the lakes at the head of the small streams. The first named species, when mature, often attains the weight of 30 to 40 pounds; and the second and third are about two-thirds as large.

Victor E. Lawson, the historian of the county, writes: "It is believed that in early times the Indians applied this name to the entire group of lakes which form the sources of the Crow river. Until very recent years buffalo fish and other kindred species came up the rivers and small streams every spring to find spawning places in these waters. . . .

"The name Kandiyohi was first made known to white men by Joseph Nicholas Nicollet, who in 1836–41 explored the region now comprising Minnesota. . . . He did not personally visit this section, but secured his information about the sources of the Crow from Indians. . . . It was not until 1856 that white men acquired any definite

knowledge as to the extent and character of these lakes. In that year four different parties of townsite promoters visited the region now embraced within the boundaries of our county and gave separate names to the different lakes which attracted their attention. The name Kandiyohi was appropriated by one of these companies, and two of the lakes in the southern group were by them named Big and Little Kandiyohi. When a new county was organized the historic Indian name was adopted."

In the accepted pronunciation, which differs somewhat from the Dakota usage, this name accents its first and last syllables, the last having the English long sound of the vowel.

At first the area of this county was divided under legislative acts of March 8 and 20, 1858, in two counties, each comprising 12 congressional townships. The north half was named Monongalia County, and during 12 years Kandiyohi County had only the south half of its present area until in 1870 they were united. The name *Monongalia* was derived from the county so named in Virginia (now in West Virginia), being Latinized from the Delaware Indian word *Monongahela*, "river with the sliding banks," given to the stream that unites with the Allegheny at Pittsburgh, forming the Ohio River.

The origins and meanings of the geographic names in this county have been learned from the Illustrated History and Descriptive and Biographical Review of Kandiyohi County, *by Victor E. Lawson and Martin E. Tew (1905, 446 pp.); and from interviews with Samuel Nelson, county auditor, and Mr. Lawson, editor of the* Willmar Tribune *and principal author of the admirable folio history here cited, during a visit at Willmar, the county seat, in May 1916.*

ADAMSVILLE a village incorporated on March 23, 1857; location not found.

ARCTANDER TOWNSHIP organized April 4, 1879, was named in honor of John W. Arctander, who during ten years, 1876–86, was a resident of this county, being an attorney in Willmar, and thence removed to Minneapolis. He was born in Stockholm, Sweden, October 2, 1849; was graduated at the Royal University of Norway, 1870, and the same year came to the United States; came to Minnesota in 1874 and soon afterward was admitted to practice law. In 1875 he published a handbook of the laws of Minnesota in the Norwegian language.

ASPELIEN a post office, 1893–96, in section 25 of Norway Township, with Andrew H. Espelien, postmaster.

ATWATER a city in sections 1, 2, 11, and 12 of Gennessee Township, founded in 1869, was named in honor of E. D. Atwater, secretary of the land department of the St. Paul and Pacific Railroad. It was incorporated February 17, 1876. Its post office began in 1869 as Gennissee Station, changing in 1870 first to Stockholm and then to Atwater. The area was also known as Summit Lake. Located on the Great Northern Railway, it was a grain storage and milling center.

BLOMKEST a city in Roseland Township, section 14, incorporated as a village April 7, 1952; it was platted in October 1926 and established on the Luce Line (Minnesota Western Railroad) as Kester in honor of C. E. Kester, then mayor of Hutchinson; however, confusion with a town called Kiester in Faribault County resulted in the name Kesterville, 1928–1943; that name, while used, was still not satisfactory, and when its post office began in 1928, it was called Blomkest, a name combining Kester with Blomquist, honoring Ole Blomquist (known as Blom Olof Anderson in his native Sweden), who was one of the early settlers

of the community. The village had a station of the Minneapolis and St. Louis Railroad.

BURBANK TOWNSHIP organized in August 1866, was named in honor of Henry Clay Burbank, a well-known merchant in St. Paul and St. Cloud "held in high esteem by the early settlers for favors extended." He was born in Lewis, N.Y., May 4, 1835, and died in Rochester, Minn., February 23, 1905. At the age of 18 years he came to St. Paul and with his brother, James C. Burbank, engaged in forwarding and commission business and wholesale grocery trade. The firm transported supplies and furs for the Hudson's Bay Company and owned wagon trains and steamboats on the Red River. He was a state senator in 1873. The village in section 19 and 30 was also named for Henry C. Burbank; it was platted in 1866 with a post office, 1867–1904, established when in Monongalia County.

CHARLTON a village established by the Kandiyohi Townsite Company west of Kandiyohi Lake, incorporated on May 23, 1857; location not found.

COLFAX TOWNSHIP organized June 24, 1871, was at first called Lake Prairie, but in September of the same year it was renamed in honor of Schuyler Colfax (1823–85), who in 1869–73 was vice-president of the United States. A post office was located in section 11, 1877–1904.

COLUMBIA a townsite in New London and Green Lake Townships, incorporated as a village on May 19, 1857; the incorporation was dissolved. The town was established in 1858 on the west shore of Green Lake near the present city of Spicer and was the temporary county seat of Monongalia County in 1861.

CROW RIVER a village in section 6 of Burbank Township.

CROYDON a post office, 1875–89, named for the native place in New Hampshire of Mrs. Johnson, whose husband, Charles Johnson, was postmaster; transferred to Raymond in 1889; location not found.

CRESCENT BEACH a resort area in Green Lake Township, section 10, on the south shore of Green Lake.

DAVIS a post office, 1874–76; location not found.

DOVRE TOWNSHIP organized April 6, 1869, received its name from its prominent morainic hills in sections 20 and 21, which the early Norwegian settlers called the Dovre Hills, in remembrance of the Dovrefjeld Mountains and high plateau on the boundary between Norway and Sweden. A post office was located in section 8, 1874–76, with Lars O. Thorpe, postmaster, for whom the community of Thorpe was named.

EAST LAKE LILLIAN TOWNSHIP organized March 6, 1893, had been since 1872 the east half of Lake Lillian, named for the lake crossed by the boundary between these townships.

EDWARDS TOWNSHIP established September 7, 1871, was named in honor of S. S. Edwards, a pioneer settler who was the leader for its organization.

FAHLUN established March 20, 1877, bears "the popular name of the home county in Sweden of a number of the early settlers." The chief city of that district, also named Fahlun or Falun, is sometimes called "the Treasury of Sweden," having mines of copper, silver, and gold. A post office was located in the township, 1879–80 and 1883–85.

FULLERVILLE a townsite in section 25 of Dovre Township, platted in 1857 when part of Monongalia County; it was named for Randall Fuller, promoter of the townsite, which did not develop.

GENNESSEE organized in 1858, was named (with changed spelling) for the Genesee River in New York, whence several of its first pioneers had come in 1857. This name means, according to Henry Gannett, "shining valley" or "beautiful valley," in its native Indian language of New York, but the too liberal spelling here used, yet without change in pronunciation, came from Tennessee.

GENNISSEE STATION see ATWATER.

GEORGEVILLE a village in Burbank Township, section 8, named for Jorgen L. Postmyhr, the first settler about 1874.

GREEN LAKE TOWNSHIP established in January 1868, received its name from the large lake on its north boundary, which was named August 10, 1856, by the first party of settlers. On that day they selected a townsite on the southwestern shore of this lake, now occupied by the village of Spicer, in sections 3 and 4 of this township. "They were enraptured by the beautiful sheet of water, and from its peculiar shade of bottle green christened it Green lake. To their future city they gave the name of Columbia."

A post office called Green Lake was established four times between 1857 and 1906; it was first in Meeker County and then transferred to Monongalia County until 1870; it was then located in New London Township, section 27; the site had a dam built across the Crow River in 1867, several saw- and gristmills, a general store, a church, and a hotel; it had a station of the Great Northern Railway in section 28.

GRUE a post office in section 20 of Green Lake Township, 1886–1906, and a Great Northern Railway loading station, halfway between Willmar and Spicer; no other buildings were erected. It was named for Ole Nelson Grue, state senator, 1898–1901, who was born in Wisconsin in 1857, graduated from St. Olaf College in 1879, became a successful farmer, and died in 1916.

HARRISON TOWNSHIP established April 25, 1858, was named in honor of Joseph D. Harris, who settled here in August 1857 and was the first postmaster and the first town clerk. He was born in Nova Scotia in May 1834 and died May 7, 1878. A post office was in section 8; it was first established and discontinued in Meeker County, 1858–63, was reestablished in Monongalia County in 1866, transferring to Kandiyohi County, 1874–1907. It was laid out as St. Johns in 1856 and reorganized by postmaster Joseph D. Harris and Amos Dodge in 1857, at which time it was renamed.

HAWICK a village in Roseville Township, section 28, originally platted as a townsite on the Willmar-St. Cloud branch of St. Paul, Minneapolis and Manitoba Railroad and named Russell for Russell Spicer, son of the railroad builder; as that name had already been given to another townsite, the name was replaced with Hawick, a Scottish placename, by R. Manvel, a railway superintendent. Its post office was established as Roseville, Burbank Township, Monongalia County in 1867, transferred to Kandiyohi County, 1874–82, and reestablished as Hawick in 1887.

HOLLAND TOWNSHIP was established July 23, 1888. Its settlers "were principally Hollanders, or of Holland descent, but with a sprinkling of Swedes and Germans."

HOLUM a post office, 1891–1905, in section 2 of Norway Lake Township, with Simon E. Holum, postmaster.

HULLS CORNERS a post office, 1874–84, in Harrison Township, with William H. Hull, postmaster.

IRVING TOWNSHIP organized March 27, 1868, took its name from a townsite platted on the east side of Green Lake in 1856 by Eugene M. Wilson of Minneapolis, who later was a congressman, and others. This name was probably selected in honor of the distinguished American author Washington Irving (1783–1859). The village in section 13 was platted in 1856 and organized on March 8, 1858, serving as county seat of Monongalia County; it was incorporated as a village on May 23, 1857; the incorporation was dissolved. Its post office was originally established on the east shore of Green Lake, 1857–62, in what was then Meeker County, reestablished in Monongalia County in 1868, moving to Lake Calhoun, and again to section 13 in 1895. The village had two general stores, a creamery built in 1895, a feed mill, and two blacksmiths.

IVY a post office, 1886–87, of Roseland Township.

JERICHO a village in Arctander Township with a name from the Old Testament, which had two general stores, a church, a creamery, and several shops.

KANDIYOHI TOWNSHIP was established March 1, 1868, then including also the present townships of Fahlun, Whitefield, and Willmar. It was named, like the county, for the Kandiyohi Lakes. The city in section 10, named for the township, was founded when the railway was built in 1869 and was incorporated May 23, 1857, and again on May 6, 1904, separating from the township on May 4, 1905. The first post office, 1867–71, was transferred to Lake Elizabeth; the second post office was known as Kandiyohi Station until 1894. The village had a station of the Great Northern Railway.

An earlier townsite of this name, platted in October 1856, in section 25 of this township and the adjoining section 30 of Gennessee, at the north side of Lakes Kasota and Minnetaga, aspired to become the capital of Minnesota, for which purpose a bill was passed by the legislature in March 1869 but was vetoed by Gov. William R. Marshall. This project was again brought to the attention of the legislature in 1871, and also in 1891 and 1893, but received no favorable action. In 1901 the "capitol lands," which had been acquired there by the state in 1858, were sold for use in farming.

KESTER see **BLOMKEST**.

LAKE ANDREW TOWNSHIP organized March 19, 1872, received the name given to this lake in the summer of 1857 by Andrew Holes, one of the first two settlers, being carved by him "in large, plain letters upon one of the cottonwood trees" of its south shore. A post office was located in the township, 1881–92.

LAKE ELIZABETH TOWNSHIP organized April 16, 1869, bears the name of the lake crossed by its north boundary, given "in honor of the wife of A. C. Smith, the early lawyer and receiver at the United States land office at Forest City." Lakes Ella and Carrie, closely adjoining the north side of this lake, in Gennessee, were named for her daughters. A post office was in section 16, 1871–1906, first established at Kandiyohi, 1867–71; the site had a creamery and a store built in 1891.

LAKE LILLIAN TOWNSHIP was organized January 23, 1872. The lake was named in honor of the wife of artist and author, Edwin Whitefield, who accompanied the first exploring party to the Kandiyohi Lakes in the summer of 1856. The city on the border of Lake Lillian and East Lake Lillian Townships was established as the first village on the Luce Line (Minnesota Western Railroad) in section 18 of East Lake Lillian Township; it was incorporated as a village February 15, 1926, and separated from the township on March 23; its post office operated 1868–1906 and since 1923.

LINTONVILLE see **REGAL**.

LUNDBY a village in Dovre Township, section 18, was named by John Rodman (Rådman), who was born in Värmland in 1823 and died in 1908; the name is a coined word from Mamrelund, his home, and the Swedish *by* meaning "village or farm"; Mamre Township, Rodman Lake, and Mamre are names all associated with Rodman.

MAMRE TOWNSHIP organized April 6, 1870, took the name given in 1866 to the lake in sections 11, 12, and 14 by one of the first three settlers, John Rodman, whose homestead claim was on the southwest arm of this lake. "He gave the name Mamre to his new home locality, from the Biblical reference to the home of Abram in the Promised Land." A post office was in section 14, 1870–74; Rodman, postmaster, suggested the name as a combination of Mamre and honors to Rev. J. P. Lundblad, a pastor who assisted with the Swedish congregation that founded the community; it was also known as Butterfield and Mamre Lund.

NEGORD a post office in section 19 of Arctander Township, 1898–1904, which changed to a rural branch, 1905–9; named for Havor Negord (Negaard), a farmer of the area.

NEW LONDON TOWNSHIP organized August 25, 1866, derived its name from the city in section 10, which was founded in 1865 by building a sawmill and was incorporated April 8, 1889. The name was chosen by Louis Larson "from a similarity he saw with the location of New London, Wis., a prospering village of his old home county." The city was the temporary county seat, 1867–70; the post office began in Monongalia County in 1867; it had a station of the Great Northern Railway.

NORWAY LAKE a village of Lake Andrew Township, which had a post office, 1867–1914, established in Monongalia County and transferred to Kandiyohi County in 1871.

NORWAY LAKE TOWNSHIP organized in August 1866, at first included also the present townships of Arctander, Lake Andrew, Mamre, and Dovre. It was named for the largest lake of its original area, lying mainly in Lake Andrew Township, around which many Norwegian immigrants settled.

PENNOCK a city of St. John's Township, section 3, founded in 1870–71 with the building of this railway, at first bore the township name. In the fall of 1891 it was renamed in honor of George Pennock of Willmar, superintendent of this division of the Great Northern Railway. It was incorporated as a village on March 14, 1903; the post office was called St. John or St. Johns, 1871–92, changing to Pennock at that time; the first postmaster was Erick G. Berglund (1891–1935) at the hardware store he owned with his brother, C. J. Berglund; it had a station of the Great Northern Railway in section 3, first called St. Johns.

PRIAM a village in section 36 of St. Johns Township; it had a creamery, an elevator, a store, a school, a station on the Willmar and Sioux Falls Railway, and a post office operating 1900–1908.

PRINSBURG a city at the center of Holland Township, section 16, platted in 1886, commemorates Martin Prins, member of a land firm in Holland, who came here and in 1884 acquired about 35,000 acres of railroad lands, mostly in this county. He died in 1887. The city was incorporated as a village June 25, 1952; it began when acreage within the 34,000 acres of land in Kandiyohi and Renville Counties, owned by two partners, Prins and Theodore Koch, was offered for sale in 1885, with the promise that as soon as 20 Dutch families had settled, one half of the cost of a church would be contributed by the partners; 40 lots were sold, and

40 acres in the middle of the township were set aside for a village; the post office was established during three periods, 1887–89, 1896–1904, and from 1927, each time located in the general store.

RAYMOND a city in Edwards, section 19, platted in 1887, was named for Raymond Spicer, a son of John M. Spicer of Willmar, who was the founder of Spicer village. It was incorporated as a village on October 20, 1897, and was first known as Raymond Station; two post offices were established, the first operating February-July 1889, with Charles G. Squire as postmaster; the second began in August 1889 when transferred from Croydon, with William H. Harris as first postmaster.

REGAL a city in section 5 of Roseville Township, incorporated as a village April 25, 1940; it was first established as Linton and named after one of the Minneapolis, St. Paul and Sault Ste. Marie Railroad (Soo Line) contractors; however, another town already had that name, so the community became Lintonville; the post office department determined that name not acceptable, so George Weidner, an early settler, suggested three automobile names: Regal, because he owned one; Ford, because a local farmer had one; and Harvard, because it was a solid name; Regal won. It had a station of the Minnesota and Pacific Railroad; the post office was called Lintonville, 1887–1914, changing to Regal in 1915.

RINGVILLE a post office, 1886–1903, located in Burbank Township, section 14, on postmaster Gunder Iverson Ringen's farm, for whom named.

ROSELAND TOWNSHIP was organized March 16, 1889, its name being chosen by Peter Lindquist, the first settler, who came in the spring of 1869. "In Swedish the name is the usual designation for a flower garden." The village in section 18 was the third village created as a result of the Luce Line building through the county; a post office operated 1891–92 and reestablished in 1928–1965.

ROSEVILLE a post office in Burbank Township, 1867–82, established in Monongalia County, becoming part of Kandiyohi County in 1874.

ROSEVILLE TOWNSHIP organized August 25, 1866, was named as suggested by Joseph Cox "on account of the profusion of wild roses growing and in bloom upon the prairie."

ST. JOHNS see PENNOCK.

ST. JOHNS TOWNSHIP first settled in 1868, was established by a special act of the legislature, February 27, 1872, and was organized a month later. It bears a name given to a locality on its north line by an early map of the state, published in 1860, probably noting a proposed site for a Catholic colony, whence the lake in sections 1 and 2 became known as St. Johns Lake.

SAND LAKE a post office in section 11 of Colfax Township, 1868–77, established in Monongalia County, becoming part of Kandiyohi County in 1870.

SCHULTZVILLE a post office, 1890–92, in Harrison Township, with William A. Schultz, postmaster.

SPICER a city of Green Lake and New London Townships, was platted in 1886 on the deserted early townsite of Columbia and was named in honor of John M. Spicer, its founder and owner of the site, who was the president of the company building the railway line. Raymond village was named for his son, as before noted. It incorporated as a village on June 10, 1904; the post office was established in 1886 with Burton B. Swetland as postmaster in William Olson's general store, Olson being the first merchant and operator of a tourist passenger boat on Green Lake; it had a Great Northern Railway station in section 3 of Green Lake Township.

STOCKHOLM see ATWATER.

SUMMIT LAKE see ATWATER.

SUNBURG a city in Norway Lake Township, section 30, incorporated as a village September 8, 1951; the post office was established in 1871 as Sunburgh, changing to the present form in 1894; both versions of the name were suggested by John Sandvigen, a rural mail carrier, the first for a locality in Norway, the second for a strait between two lakes near postmaster Ole Eliason's home, *sund* meaning "strait" in Norwegian.

SVEA a village in section 26 of Whitefield Township; the name was in use by a local Swedish Lutheran congregation founded in 1870, being a feminine form of Sweden, and adopted for the community and post office, which began in 1891, with Nils Nilsson (Nels N. Nelson), first postmaster; he was a Swedish immigrant who came to the area in 1869, becoming a successful farmer and local government member.

THORPE a village in East Lake Lillian Township, section 14, named for Lars Olson Thorpe, a banker

who was born in 1847 in Norway, came to Minnesota in 1865, served as county register of deeds, 1874–81, was state senator, 1895–97 and 1903–9, and died in 1921. The village had a creamery, built in 1896, a station of the Minneapolis and St. Louis Railroad in section 13, and a post office, 1898–1906.

WARNER a post office in section 4 of Colfax Township, 1877–1901, John D. Warner, postmaster.

WEST LAKE a post office, 1871–1905, located in Arctander Township.

WEXFORD a post office in section 17 of Green Lake Township, 1882–87; the name was suggested by John Cody, Sr., for his native Wexford, Ireland.

WHITEFIELD TOWNSHIP was established June 6, 1870. Its name is from a proposed townsite selected by an exploring party in the early autumn of 1856 on the northwest shore of Lake Wagonga, in sections 1 and 11, named in honor of Edwin Whitefield, a landscape artist, who was a member of the party. Lake Lillian, named for his wife, is the source of another township name, as before noted. The village, also named for the artist, was incorporated on May 23, 1857, but the incorporation was vacated.

WILLMAR TOWNSHIP established January 4, 1870, took the name of its village platted in 1869 when the railroad there was built. The townsite was selected and named by George L. Becker, president of the railroad. "Leon Willmar, a native of Belgium, at that time residing in London, was the agent for the European bondholders of the St. Paul and Pacific railroad company, and it was in his honor that the town was named. He afterwards secured several hundred acres of land around the northeastern shores of Foot Lake, and presented the same to his son, Paul Willmar, who a few years before had served as a soldier of fortune under Maximilian, the adventurous invader of Mexico." Expensive buildings were erected in 1871 for the Willmar farm, on section 1 of this township, where during ten years Paul Willmar conducted operations on an extensive scale. In 1881 he sold this large farm and returned to Belgium. Willmar village was incorporated January 16, 1874; and its city charter was adopted November 19, 1901; a later city charter was adopted in 1968. The village had a Great Northern Railway station in section 15, and its post office began in 1869.

Lakes and Streams

The foregoing pages have noted the names of the Kandiyohi Lakes, Green Lake, Lakes Andrew, Elizabeth, and Lillian, Lakes Ella and Carrie, Lake Mamre, Norway Lake, and St. Johns Lake.

Shakopee Creek, flowing west to the lake of this name in Chippewa County, is noticed in the chapter for that county; and Hawk and Chetamba Creeks, having their sources here, are noticed under Renville County.

Many lakes remain to be mentioned, but a considerable number have names that require no explanation. The list follows the numerical order of the townships from south to north, and of the ranges from east to west.

Dog Lake in East Lake Lillian Township and others smaller and without names have been drained and are now farmlands.

Fox Lake, crossed by the south line of Lake Lillian Township, and Grove Lake on its west side, named for the grove on its island, have been drained.

Lake Elizabeth Township has Johnson Lake in sections 10 and 11 and Otter Lake in sections 10 and 15. Lakes Charlotte and Mary, now drained, were in its southwest part.

Fahlun has Lake Fanny and Wagonga Lake, which was formerly called Grass Lake, in translation of this Dakota name. The latter, reaching west into Whitefield, is erroneously spelled Waconda on some maps.

Lake Milton was in sections 7 and 18, Whitefield, and Stevens Lake in section 20, but both are drained.

Edwards has Bad Water Lake, through which Hawk Creek flows at Raymond; Olson Lake in section 26; and Vick Lake, drained, in sections 29 and 30.

Gennessee has Summit Lake in sections 9 and 10, referring to the building of the railroad, which very near the west line of this township crosses its highest land between St. Paul and Breckenridge; Pay Lake, of smaller size, in section 10, where the paymaster in that work had his camp; Lakes Ella and Carrie, before noticed in their relationship with Lake Elizabeth; and Lake Minnetaga, compounded of the Dakota words *minne*, "water," and *taga*, "froth, foam."

In Kandiyohi Township are Lake Kasota, a Dakota name, meaning "a cleared place," and Swan Lake, each lying close to the north side of Little Kandiyohi Lake, with which Lake Kasota is connected by a strait.

Willmar has Foot Lake, adjoining the city, named in honor of the first settler here; Willmar Lake, which adjoins the former Willmar farm, being a northeastern bay of Foot Lake, connected therewith by a narrow passage; and Grass Lake, which was shallow and mostly filled with marsh grass but is now drained.

Solomon R. Foot, commemorated by the lake bearing his name, was born in Dover, Ohio, May 30, 1823; came to Minnesota in 1857 and in June took a homestead claim on the shore of this lake, being the first settler of Willmar Township; removed about six years later to Melrose in Stearns County, where he built a hotel and was the first postmaster; removed to Minot, N.Dak., in 1888; spent his last few years in California, with his children, and died March 15, 1903. Another lake, in Dovre, is also named for him.

The largest lake in Harrison was visited in September 1856 by a party of explorers who came from St. Peter. "The crystal brightness of the lake impressed them, and they named it Diamond lake." Other lakes in this township are Jessie Lake, crossed by the north line of section 6; Rieff and Swenson Lakes, drained, in section 15; Sperry Lake, section 16; Taits Lake, section 19; Thomas Lake, drained, in sections 21 and 22; Schultz Lake, in sections 23 and 26; and Wheeler Lake, in sections 26, 27, and 34.

Green Lake Township has Henderson Lake in section 6; Twin Lakes, sections 7 and 8; Elk Horn Lake, sections 9 and 16, where a pair of very large elk antlers were found in 1857; Eagle Lake, crossed by the west line of this township; and Bur Oak Lake in section 33.

Dovre has Ringo Lake, Florida Slough Lake, and Long or Nevada Lake, each of large size, in its northeast part; Point Lake, King, Skataas, and Swan Lakes at the southeast, the second and third being named for pioneer farmers; and Solomon Lake at the southwest, named, like Foot Lake in Willmar, for Solomon R. Foot, who often visited this lake as a hunter and trapper.

In Mamre Township, besides the lake of this name, are Swan Lake, of clear water, in sections

9 and 10, and Church and Lindgren Lakes, respectively in sections 23 and 26, which are shallow and grassy.

Irving has Calhoun Lake, named for an early settler who raised cattle there; Otter Lake, very small, in section 4, and Shoemaker Lake, crossed by the south line of section 6, both drained; and Long Lake in the north part of section 6, extending into Roseville.

New London has Bear Lake in section 7; Cedar Island Lake in section 17, named for its red cedar trees; Nest Lake in sections 28 and 29, remarkable for the former abundance of nests of double-crested cormorants, commonly called "black jacks," on the trees of its larger island; and George and Woodcock Lakes, respectively in sections 32 and 33, extending south into Green Lake Township. The last was named for Elijah T. Woodcock, the first settler near it. Lake Eight in sections 5 and 8, translated from the name given by Swedish settlers, is a marsh, only covered by water in wet seasons.

Lake Andrew Township, with its lake so named, has also Middle Lake and Norway Lake; Lake Mary, on the west line of section 19; Norstedt Lake, small and shallow, in section 24; and, near the south side of the township, Lake Florida and Crook Lake, the last being named from its crooked outline. "Lake Florida is said to have been first so designated by the early settlers of Norway Lake on account of its location to the south."

Arctander has Swenson Lake in sections 24 and 25. West and Sand Lakes in sections 16 and 17 have been drained.

Burbank has Lake Twenty, in the section so numbered, and Mud Lake, on the south line of this township.

Colfax has Prairie and Stauffer Lakes, shallow, or sometimes dry, in its southeast part; Timber Lake, Skull and Swan Lakes, and Games Lake at the southwest; and Sand, Thompson, and Hystad Lakes in its north half, the last being named for Andrew O. Hystad, an early farmer there.

In Norway Lake Township are Lake Bertha and Even's or Glesne Lake near its center; and Deer Lake, Lake Ole, Lake of Hefta, and Brenner Lake in its north part, with Crook Lake on its north line. Glesne Lake was named for Even O. Glesne, a pioneer farmer beside it, and Lake Bertha for his daughter. "Lake of Hefta was so called in honor of

Mrs. Marie Hefta, . . . who was born on a place of that name in Norway," and Brenner Lake was named for Andreas Hanson "Brenner," the added surname having reference to "his vocation in Norway as manufacturer of tar."

When the first pioneers came, their settlements or small neighborhoods preceding the organization of townships were designated by the adjoining lakes, as the Diamond Lake, Eagle Lake, and Nest Lake settlements. Finally nine townships, among them being Kandiyohi, Mamre, and St. Johns, were thus named for their lakes.

Hills of the Waconia and Dovre Moraines

The north half of this county is crossed by two belts of morainic drift hills, very irregular in contour and attaining heights of 100 to 200 feet above the lowlands and lakes. Names applied to parts of these hilly tracts, and to some of the more conspicuous separate elevations, are Cape Bad Luck and Sugarloaf, in the south edge of Roseville; the Blue Hills, culminating in Mount Tom, about a mile north of Lake Andrew; the hills before noted as giving their name to Dovre Township; and Ostlund's Hill, in section 22, Mamre, named for Lars Ostlund, a farmer at its west side.

Derived from the hills in Dovre, this name is extended to the seventh or Dovre moraine in the series of 12 marginal moraine belts formed successively along the receding border of the continental ice sheet during its final melting in Minnesota.

Eastward in New London, Irving, and the edge of Roseville, the drift hills are referred to a somewhat earlier stage of the glacial retreat, being a part of the sixth or Waconia moraine, named from Waconia in Carver County. At Mount Tom, and thence northwest for about 25 miles, the Waconia and Dovre Moraines are merged in a single belt of drift hills, knolls, and short ridges.

Sibley State Park

Adjoining Lake Andrew with a shore line of one and a half miles, this park, named in honor of Gov. Henry Hastings Sibley, was provided through purchase by the state in July 1919. Initially it was a tract of 356 acres, consisting of high morainic hills, short ridges, and hollows, sprinkled with drift boulders and covered with hardwood timber. Its acquirement as a state park was advocated by

Victor E. Lawson of Willmar, and Peter Broberg of New London; and its supervision and development were first directed by Carlos Avery, state game and fish commissioner. The park includes Mount Tom, which rises 150 feet above the nearby lakes. With various additions, the park grew to almost 3,000 acres.

Kittson County

Forming the northwest corner of this state, Kittson County was established by being thus renamed, March 9, 1878, and by reduction from its area, creating Marshall County, February 25, 1879. Previously it had been a part of Pembina County, one of the nine large counties into which the new Minnesota Territory was originally divided, October 27, 1849. It was named in honor of Norman Wolfred Kittson, one of the leading pioneers of the territory and state. He was born in Sorel, Canada, March 5, 1814; came to the area that afterward was Minnesota in 1834, and during four years was engaged in the sutler's department at Fort Snelling; was later a fur trader on his own account and became manager for the American Fur Company in northern Minnesota; engaged in transportation business, at Fort Snelling, Pembina, and St. Paul; was a member of the territorial legislature, 1851–55, and mayor of St. Paul, 1858; became director of steamboat traffic on the Red River for the Hudson's Bay Company in 1864; and established a line of steamers and barges known as the Red River Transportation Company, whence he was often called "Commodore." He died suddenly, May 10, 1888, on a railway train in his journey of return to Minnesota from the East. The Cathedral of the Archdiocese of St. Paul is built on the site of his home.

With the adoption of the present name of Kittson County, the former Pembina County ceased to exist in Minnesota, but it is still represented by a North Dakota county bearing that name, on the opposite side of the Red River. It was first the name of a river there, was thence applied to an early fur trade post at the junction of this stream with the Red River, was given in 1849 to the great Pembina County, and later to the town that became the county seat of its part in Dakota Territory, near the site of the old trading post. William H. Keating wrote, in his narrative of Maj. Stephen H. Long's expedition in 1823, that it was derived from the Ojibwe word for the fruit of the bush cranberry, "anepeminan, which name has been shortened and corrupted into Pembina." This tall bush (*Viburnum opulus*) is common along the Pembina and Red Rivers, as also through the north half of Minnesota, and its fruit is much used for sauce by the Ojibwe and the white people. Edward D. Neill translated the name as follows (*History of Minnesota*, p. 868): "The Pembina river, called by Thompson 'Summer Berry,' was named after a red berry which the Chippeways call Nepin (summer) Minan (berry), and this by the voyageurs has been abbreviated to Pembina."

Information has been gathered from History of the Red River Valley (2 vols., 1909, the chapter for this county, by Edward Nelson, former register of deeds, being pp. 923–66); and from interviews with Mr. Nelson and Axel Lindegard, a merchant in Hallock, the county seat, during a visit there in August 1909, and Edward A. Johnson, clerk of court, and again with Mr. Lindegard, in a second visit there, September 1916.

ALICE see **NORTHCOTE**.

ARVESON TOWNSHIP organized July 14, 1902, was named in honor of Arve Arveson, a settler in Davis, who was then chairman of the county commissioners.

BEATON a village in section 4 of Deerwood Township, developed as a trading center and was named for one of the former homesteaders. Barney M. Bothum, postmaster, born about 1865, filed a claim in Deerwood Township in 1884, was in the cattle business in 1888, opened a store on his homestead claim in 1891, where he operated the post office, 1892–1907. As lumbering declined and the Minneapolis, St. Paul and Sault Ste. Marie Railroad (Soo Line) laid its track two miles south, trading lessened and most businesses moved north to Halma.

BONISH a post office, 1900–1902, in section 26 of Granville Township, with Matts O. Nordin, postmaster.

BOULDER see **ORLEANS**.

BRIDGEPORT a post office, 1902–12, located in section 22 of Spring Brook Township.

BRONSON see **LAKE BRONSON**.

CANNON TOWNSHIP organized July 11, 1904, was named for Thomas Cannon, a merchant in Northcote, who was one of the county commissioners. It was first named Norman when organized in 1904, and its name was changed a few months later.

CARIBOU TOWNSHIP organized January 8, 1908, had a few reindeer, of geographic limitation in the wooded and partly swampy region of northern Minnesota and Canada, named Rangifer caribou. The second word of the name is of Algonquian origin, meaning "a pawer or scratcher," in allusion to the habit of this animal in winter, pawing in the snow to eat the reindeer moss beneath. The village in section 34 had a post office, 1905–19.

CHATHAN a station of the Great Northern Railway in Skane Township, section 1.

CLOW TOWNSHIP commemorates several brothers of that name, early settlers there, who came from Prince Edward Island, Canada. It was organized in 1883; its first post office was Boulder (also spelled Bolder), housed in the Wisdom farm house, with Laura A. Wisdom, postmaster.

DAVIS TOWNSHIP organized July 24, 1882, was named in honor of Edward N. Davis, a settler in section 30, who was a county commissioner but removed to Georgia. See also **DONALDSON**.

DEER a post office of Deerwood Township, 1898–1910.

DEERWOOD was organized July 23, 1888, receiving this name from its deer and its tracts of woodland.

DONALDSON a city in Davis Township, sections 18–20 and 30, was named for Capt. Hugh W. Donaldson, a veteran of the Civil War, manager of an adjoining farm of several thousand acres, owned by the Kennedy Land Company. It was incorporated as a village on November 21, 1902; its post office was called Davis, 1883–84, when William Couth was postmaster, changing to Donaldson in 1884 at which time Edward Davis became postmaster; Davis, who came in 1879, built the first store, and the post office and township were named for him.

EAST KITTSON see **UNORGANIZED TERRITORY OF EAST KITTSON**.

ENOK a village in section 31 of Jupiter Township, which had a post office, 1896–1907, a store, a creamery, and a blacksmith.

FAIRVIEW see **HUMBOLDT**.

GRAMPION a station on the Soo Line in section 7 of Clow Township; also spelled Grampian.

GRANVILLE TOWNSHIP organized July 27, 1885, took a name that is borne by villages and townships in 12 other states.

HALLOCK TOWNSHIP which includes the county seat, was organized August 2, 1880, and was named in honor of one of the founders of its village, Charles Hallock, the widely known sportsman, journalist, and author. He was born in New York City, March 13, 1834; was graduated at Amherst College, 1854; was during many years editor of *Forest and Stream*, which he founded in 1873; erected a large hotel here in 1890, which was a noted resort of sportsmen until it was burned in 1892; was the author of many magazine articles and books on hunting, fishing, travel in Alaska, Florida, etc.; died in New York on December 2, 1917. Hallock village, platted in 1879–80, was incorporated June 11, 1887; its post office began in 1879.

HALMA a city in Norway Township, incorporated as a village on September 28, 1923. The first merchant was John Edwin Holm, born in Norway in 1872; he came with his family to the United States in 1875, lived in Renville County until 1895, when he moved to a farm near Halma, becoming first postmaster when the post office began as Lafgren in 1902 and continuing when the name changed to Halma in 1904; served as first treasurer of Norway Township and died March 15, 1955, at Hallock. The community developed when the Soo Line came through, many businesses moving there from Beaton.

HAMPDEN TOWNSHIP was the earliest organized in this county, July 28, 1879. It was named on the suggestion of officers of its railway for John Hampden (1594–1643), the celebrated statesman and patriot of England.

HAZELTON TOWNSHIP organized July 23, 1888, was probably named for its plentiful growth of wild hazelnut bushes. Minnesota has two species, each being common through its northern part. A post office was located in section 29, 1892–97 and 1899–1900.

HEMMINGTON a post office, 1903–14, in McKinley Township, section 8, named for John P. Hemming, who petitioned for the post office, Isabel Doupe being first postmaster.

HILL TOWNSHIP organized January 11, 1901, is named in honor of the distinguished railway builder and president, James Jerome Hill, who owned and farmed large tracts in and adjoining this township. He was born near Guelph, Ontario, September 16, 1838, and died at his home in St. Paul, May 29, 1916. He came to Minnesota in 1856 and engaged in steamboat and railway transportation. In 1871 he consolidated the transportation business of Norman W. Kittson in the Red River region with his own; and Donald A. Smith (later Lord Strathcona) managed the company jointly with himself. He was the prime mover in the effort to secure the bonds of the St. Paul and Pacific Railroad, successfully accomplishing this in 1878, with reorganization under the name of the St. Paul, Minneapolis and Manitoba Railroad, of which he was general manager,

1879–82, and president, 1883–90. This railway and its new branches were again changed in name in 1890 to be the Great Northern Railway system, of which Hill continued as president till 1907, becoming then chairman of its board of directors. His biography by Joseph G. Pyle, in two volumes with portraits, was published in 1917. The extensive Hill farm, comprising about 15,000 acres in Hill and St. Vincent Townships, was sold during the summer of 1917, in 127 parts, to make small farms for settlers.

HUMBOLDT a city in sections 23 and 26 of St. Vincent Township, was incorporated as a village on September 29, 1919; its post office was established as Fairview in 1889, changing to Humboldt in 1896, a name selected possibly to honor the many former German stockholders of the Great Northern Railway when it was completed in 1878, or to commemorate Baron Alexander von Humboldt (1769–1859), an eminent German scientist and author, who in 1799 to 1804 traveled in South America and Mexico.

INTERUPOLIS a village, circa 1882–90, which was noted for its saloon business; location not found.

JUPITER TOWNSHIP organized November 10, 1883, was named for the planet Jupiter by Nels Hultgren, an early Norwegian settler there, who had been a sea captain.

KARLSTAD a city in Deerwood Township, sections 18, 19, and 24, was incorporated as a village August 28, 1905, and separated from the township on May 10, 1911. The first settler, Carl August Carlson, was born in Sweden in 1854 and came to the United States in 1881 and to the county in 1883; he sold the townsite to the Soo Line when they built through his farm, which encouraged many businesses to move there from Pelan. Its post office was called Klingville, 1904–5, at which time the name suggested was Clayton, under which it was platted in 1904, but became Karlstad for the city of Karlstad in Sweden.

KENNEDY a city on the border of Skane and Tegner Townships, was platted December 31, 1880, and incorporated as a village on June 15, 1899. It was named in honor of John Stewart Kennedy (1830–1909). From his former home in Scotland he came to America in 1856, settled in New York City, and was an iron merchant, banker, and railway director. He was a generous donor to many public charities and for educational and religious work. The Kennedy Land and Town Company, operating a bonanza farming project, convinced the St. Paul, Minneapolis and Manitoba Railroad, which had planned the site of a station two miles north, to build through the village, expanding the trade opportunities. Its post office began in 1881.

KLINGVILLE see KARLSTAD.

KLONDIKE TOWNSHIP see UNORGANIZED TOWNSHIP OF KLONDIKE.

LAFREN see HALMA.

LAKE BRONSON a city in Percy Township, was platted on February 8, 1905, and became incorporated on March 16. Its post office began as Percy, 1888–1904, was Bronson, 1904–38, changing to Lake Bronson January 2, 1939. The first settlers in the area were the Giles Bronson family, three miles east of the townsite in 1882, the post office of Percy being established on his farm with his wife, Maggie, as postmaster, and named for his home township in Ontario. The post office transferred in 1901 to the Andrew Vik store, Vik becoming postmaster in 1904, when the name was changed to honor the Bronson family. The first building on the site was a hotel erected by Swan Olson.

LANCASTER is a city on the border of Poppleton and Granville Townships; it was incorporated as a village on September 30, 1905; the post office was first called Lanerow 1903, changing to Lancaster in 1904 when the Soo Line came through and named for a railroad official believed to have come from Lancashire County, England. The first business was a hotel built by Bernard Johnson, followed by three grain elevators.

LANEROW see LANCASTER.

LINCOLN a post office, 1883–88; location not found.

MATTSON a village in section 11 of Red River Township, was named for brothers Lars and Hans Mattson from Önnestad, Skåne, Sweden. In 1853 Hans founded the settlement of Vasa in Goodhue County; in 1878 he purchased a large piece of land for a Swedish settlement; his younger brother, Lars, a farmer in Vasa, was among the first Swedish settlers to arrive the next year. Hans Mattson was an emigration agent, colonel in the Civil War, attorney, newspaper publisher, and secretary of state. The village had a post office, 1891–1905.

McKINLEY TOWNSHIP organized July 14, 1902, was named in honor of William McKinley (1843–1901), who was a member of Congress from Ohio, 1877–91; governor of Ohio, 1892–96; and president of the United States, 1897–1901.

NORLAND a village in section 32 of McKinley Township. Harry Norland opened a store in Pete Boyda's house, 1922–25, at which time he built the Norland Store and Cream Station. The post office operated 1928–37 in the Norland store, with his wife, Clara, serving as postmaster. Norland was also township clerk; in 1939 the store burned, and all township records were destroyed.

NORTH RED RIVER TOWNSHIP see RED RIVER TOWNSHIP.

NORTHCOTE the railway village in Hampden Township, section 21, was named in honor of Sir Stafford Henry Northcote (1818–87), an eminent English statesman and financier. He was a commissioner at the treaty of Washington in 1871, which referred the Alabama claims of the United States against England to an international tribunal of arbitration. The village developed as a trading center; the townsite plat was filed on December 21, 1880, by the St. Paul, Minneapolis and Manitoba Railroad, following the building of a depot in July 1879. The post office began as Alice in 1880, changing to Northcote in 1881, and discontinuing in 1974; the first postmaster under both names was Agnes Hawley.

NORWAY TOWNSHIP organized January 9, 1901, was named for the country from which nearly all its settlers came.

NOYES a station of the Great Northern and Soo railways adjoining the international boundary, was named in honor of J. A. Noyes, the U.S. customs collector there. The village was established as a customs port of entry in 1905 in section 25 of St. Vincent Township; it had a station of the St. Paul, Minneapolis and Manitoba Railroad, and its post office began in 1927; it was platted November 15, 1933, but not incorporated.

OAK POINT a village in Caribou Township, section 12, about 1912–38.

ORLEANS a Soo railway village in the east edge of Clow Township, section 24, was named by officers of that railway. Derived from the city of Orleans in France, this name is borne by counties in Vermont and New York and by townships and villages in Massachusetts and seven other states. It was organized in 1904 when the Soo Line was built; its post office began as Boulder, 1897–1904, when changed to Orleans. It had a creamery, an elevator, and a lumberyard.

PARK a post office, 1900–14, located on the Frans Anderson farm in Arveson Township, section 35, where he had the Park Store.

PEATLAND TOWNSHIP see UNORGANIZED TOWNSHIP OF PEATLAND.

PELAN TOWNSHIP organized April 20, 1900, was named for Charles H. Pelan, a pioneer settler there. The village in section 36 was created for pioneers filing homestead claims; it was incorporated as a village on March 3, 1903. The first settler was Norwegian immigrant Hans T. Olson in 1884, who began picking up the mail in 1887 at Hallock to distribute to Pelan residents because there was no authorized post office. A number of businesses developed, including a bank and a roller mill; the townsite began diminishing about 1910, businesses moving away until little remained by the 1930s, and the incorporation dissolved.

PERCY TOWNSHIP organized July 9, 1900, was named for Howard Percy, an early trapper and hunter. See also LAKE BRONSON.

POPPLETON organized April 8, 1893, received its name, by a common mispronunciation, for the plentiful poplar trees and groves in this township. A post office was located in the township, 1899–1905, which had been given the name Poplartown, verbal usage changing it to Poppleton.

RED RIVER TOWNSHIP organized January 5, 1881, having a length of 12 miles from south to north, is named for the river that is its western boundary. It separated on July 30, 1947, into North Red River Township, T. 161N, R. 50W, and South Red River Township, T. 160N, R. 50W.

REINHOLT a country post office, 1901–4, near the Red River, nine miles southwest of Hallock in Red River Township.

RICHARDVILLE TOWNSHIP organized January 8, 1895, was named for George Richards, one of its first settlers, whose homestead claim is the southwest quarter of section 30.

ROBBIN a post office in sections 20 and 29 of Teien Township, 1892–1933, the first postmaster being George C. Teien, brother of Andreas C. Teien for whom the township was named. George came to the United States from Drammen, Norway, in 1865, opened a general store, and named

the post office for the bird with a slight change in spelling.

ST. JOSEPH TOWNSHIP organized January 9, 1901, was named by its settlers, including Catholic immigrants from Poland, for St. Joseph, husband of the Virgin Mary. The north part sends its drainage west to the Joe River, a small stream so named by the early fur traders and voyageurs.

ST. VINCENT TOWNSHIP organized March 19, 1880, is opposite Pembina, N.Dak. Its name had been earlier given, before 1860, to a post of fur traders here, in honor of the renowned St. Vincent de Paul, founder of missions and hospitals in Paris, who died September 27, 1660, at the age of 80 years. The city in sections 2 and 11, located on the site of an XY Fur Company trading post, was incorporated as a village on May 23, 1857, and again on March 8, 1881; it had a station of the Great Northern Railway in section 2, and at St. Vincent Junction in section 6; its post office began in 1878.

SCONE a country post office in Red River Township, 1900–1904.

SIGGESTAD a farmers post office, 1902–17, 12 miles northeast of Hallock in Hill Township; Ole Peterson, its postmaster, was a jeweler and watch repairer.

SKANE TOWNSHIP organized May 10, 1887, was named for the old province of Scania, the most southern part of Sweden.

SOUTH RED RIVER TOWNSHIP see RED RIVER TOWNSHIP.

SPRING BROOK TOWNSHIP organized January 2, 1884, received the name of a brook flowing through its southern part.

SULTAN a station of the Soo Line in sections 31 and 32 of St. Vincent Township.

SVEA TOWNSHIP organized February 15, 1884, bears a name given in poetry to Sweden, the native country of many of its settlers.

TEGNER organized July 24, 1882, was named in honor of Esaias Tegner (1782–1846), a famous Swedish poet. In 1811 he was awarded the prize of the Academy of Sweden for a long poem titled "Svea," and in 1825 he published his most celebrated work, *Frithjof's Saga*, based on the old Norse saga of this name.

TEIEN organized April 5, 1882, was named for Andreas C. Teien, an early Norwegian homesteader in section 4. A post office was in sections 15 and 16, 1886–1903.

THOMPSON organized July 24, 1882, was named for William, Robert, and George Thompson, brothers, who took homestead claims in this township as pioneer farmers. The organizers met in the home of Robert Thompson and named the township Garfield, changing it in 1883 to honor the three Thompson brothers. Robert Thompson came from Ireland in 1861, being the second settler in the county; he died in Fort Dodge, Iowa, in 1922, where he had moved in 1890.

TWIN RIVERS a post office, 1878–79; location not found.

UNORGANIZED TERRITORY OF EAST KITTSON T. 161–162N, R. 45W.

UNORGANIZED TOWNSHIP OF KLONDIKE T. 161N, R. 45W.

UNORGANIZED TOWNSHIP OF PEATLAND T. 162N, R. 45W.

VISBY a post office in Richardville Township, 1899–1906, located in the general store of Anderson and Gabrielson; when the post office discontinued, the store was moved to Orleans.

Lakes and Streams

This county, lying wholly within the great area of the Glacial Lake Agassiz, has now only very few and very small lakes. These are the Twin Lakes in Arveson, Scull Lake in section 22, St. Joseph, and Lake Stella (a star), adjoining the village of St. Vincent. The last was called "Lac du Nord Ouest" on the map of Minnesota in 1860, meaning, in its use by the French voyageurs, "Lake of the Northwest" corner of this North Star State.

Spring Brook, giving its name to a township, is one of the sources of Tamarack River (a translation of the Ojibwe name), which, after flowing through large swamps, joins the Red River in South Red River Township.

The South Branch of Two Rivers receives the Middle Branch at Hallock, and it unites with the North Branch about two miles above the mouth of the united stream. The Ojibwe name, given by Rev. Joseph A. Gilfillan, "is Ga-nijoshino zibi, or the river that lies two together as in a bed; no doubt, from its two branches running parallel."

Joe River, before noted, deriving its headwaters from St. Joseph Township, and flowing through Richardville, Clow, and the northeast part of St. Vincent, reaches the Red River about three miles north of the international boundary. In Clow the channel is lost for several miles in a wide swamp.

Lake Bronson State Park

Following the extended drought of the 1930s, state authorities authorized a dam on the South Fork Two Rivers in order to create a reservoir to supply water to the county seat of Hallock. Subsequently and in part to address the lack of lakes as recreational areas in the northwest corner of the state, the legislature in 1937 established Two Rivers State Park, renamed Lake Bronson State Park in 1945. Park facilities were added as a WPA project. The dam itself is located in a notch in the McCauleyville ridge that was formed as the ice in Glacial Lake Agassiz melted and the lake retreated northward.

Koochiching County

This county, established December 19, 1906, bears the Cree name applied by the Ojibwe to Rainy Lake and also to the Rainy River and to its great falls and rapids at International Falls. It is translated by Rev. J. A. Gilfillan as Neighbor Lake and River or, under another interpretation, a lake and river somewhere. He remarked that this word is of difficult or uncertain meaning and that, although in common Ojibwe use, it does not strictly belong to that language.

Jacques de Noyon, a French Canadian voyageur, who was probably the first white man to traverse any part of the northern boundary of Minnesota, about the year 1688 found this name used in the Cree language for the Rainy River. As narrated by an official report of the Intendant Begon, written at Quebec, November 12, 1716, published in the Margry Papers (vol. 6, pp. 495–98), de Noyon, about 28 years previous to that date, had set out from Lake Superior by the canoe route of the Kaministikwia River, under the guidance of a party of Assiniboine Indians, in the hope of coming to the Sea of the West. He passed through Rainy Lake, called the Lake of the Crees, and wintered on its outflowing river, the Takamaniouen, "otherwise called Ouchichiq by the Crees," evidently the Koochiching or Rainy River and Falls, from which this county is named.

Another early narrative of travel, 1740–42, by a French and Ojibwe mixed blood named Joseph la France, containing a description of the Rainy Lake and River, is given in a book published by Arthur Dobbs in London in 1744, titled *An Account of the Countries Adjoining to Hudson's Bay*. La France passed through Rainy Lake in the later part of April and early May 1740 and stayed ten days at the Koochiching Falls on the Rainy River near the outlet of this lake. For the purpose of fishing, the Moose band of Ojibwe had "two great Villages, one on the North Side, and the other on the South Side of the Fall," being respectively on or near the sites of Fort Frances and International Falls. The narrative tells the origin of the French name, Lac de la Pluie (Lake of the Rain), which in English is Rainy Lake, that it "is so called from a perpendicular Water-fall, by which the Water falls into a River South-west of it, which raises a Mist-like Rain." This refers to the outflowing Rainy River in its formerly mist-covered falls, since 1908 dammed and supplying waterpower in the city of International Falls for the largest paper-making mills in the world.

The original meanings of Ouchichiq (for Koochiching), the Cree name of Rainy River 200 years ago, and Takamaniouen, variously spelled, an equally ancient Indian name of the Rainy River and Lake, are uncertain, but it may be true that one or both gave in translation the French and English names, which refer to the mists of the falls, resembling rain.

Takamaniouen, as written by Begon in 1716, placed in another spelling on the map drawn by Auchagah (Ochagach) for Pierre Gaultier de Varennes, sieur de la Vérendrye in 1728, was received from the Assiniboines. It is thought by Horace V. Winchell and U. S. Grant (*Geology of Minnesota*, vol. 4, p. 192) that this name was translated to Lac de la Pluie.

Information for this county was gathered from Louis A. Ogaard, county surveyor, during a visit at International Falls, the county seat, in September 1909; and from L. H. Slocum, county auditor, during a second visit there in August 1916.

All townships of the county were dissolved in 1950; thus, in the entries below township numbers are given with the names of townships established before 1950.

Between 1900 and 1936–37, about 150 lumber camps were in the county, many with names that appear on maps, but these are not included here unless later development created a more established settlement.

BALDUS TOWNSHIP (T. 159N, R. 29W), was named for August Baldus, who was influential in obtaining the post office of the same name, 1912–26, with James McCallister (or McAlister), postmaster.

BANNOCK TOWNSHIP (T. 157–158N, R. 26W) received this Gaelic name from Scotland by vote of its bachelor settlers, for their bannock bread, "in shape flat and roundish, . . . baked on an iron plate or griddle." A post office was located in section 27, 1907–25.

BEAR RIVER TOWNSHIP (T. 67N, R. 26W) is crossed by a little river of this name, flowing north to the Big Fork.

BEAVER TOWNSHIP (T. 67–68N, R. 23W) had formerly many beaver dams on its Beaver Brook, a tributary of the Little Fork.

BERGMAN a station of the Minnesota, Dakota and Western Railway in T. 65N, R. 25W (Dentaybow).

BESCEMAR a post office, 1914–26, located in T. 155N, R. 25W (Grand Falls), with a station of the Minnesota and International Railway.

BIG FALLS TOWNSHIP (T. 154N, R. 25W) includes the village of this name, which was incorporated on May 10, 1904. One of the first settlements in the county, the trade center for loggers and homesteaders began about 1896 and was platted in 1901 by E. J. Swedback of Bemidji. Its post office was established in Itasca County as Ripple in 1901, and with the arrival in 1906 of the Minnesota and International Railway, its name changed to the present in honor of the swift and beautiful rapids of the Big Fork River. The community vied with International Falls to become the county seat.

BIRCHDALE a village in section 3 of T. 159N, R. 27W (Sault), was named for the many groves of white birch found there in early days, as suggested by Mae Whitney Buell. It was settled primarily by Scandinavians beginning in 1899; it had a station of the Duluth, Winnipeg and Pacific Railroad; its post office was first established in Itasca County in 1906 in the home of postmaster Herbert T. Whitcomb.

BOIS FORT a post office, 1922–26 and 1930–32, located in T. 65N, R. 23W of the Bois Forte Reservation.

BORDER a post office, 1912–53, located on the Rainy River in T. 160N, R. 28W (Murphy), section 8, with a station of the Canadian National Railroad.

BRAMBLE a logging village in section 28 of T. 63N, R. 22W (Summerville), named for the prickly bramble bush abundant in the area. The post office, 1928–36, was located in the home of Edward Johnson, his daughter Lillian serving as postmaster; the Elmdale School was built on his homestead.

BRIDGIE TOWNSHIP (T. 151N, R. 29W) was named for a girl, Bridgie Moore, the first white child born there. It had a station of the Minnesota and International Railway, where C. W. Fields had a stopping place and provided postal service.

BUDD a post office, 1912; location not found.

CALDWELL BROOK a village in T. 152N, R. 25W (Wicker Township), was named for an early logger who had camps along the brook in the early 1880s. The first homestead claims were filed in 1902; most settlers left their homesteads in 1936 when the resettlement program was started.

CALDWELL TOWNSHIP and the Caldwell Brook, flowing to the Big Fork, were named for an early pioneer.

CAMP FIVE a station of the Minnesota, Dakota and Western Railway in т. 66 N, R. 25w (Dentaybow).

CEDARDALE a station on the Minnesota, Dakota and Western Railway in т. 64 N, R. 26w.

CENTRAL a village located on the Rainy River, 14 miles from Baudette in т. 160 N, R. 29w (Williams), sections 2 and 3. The village had a post office, 1909–28, the first postmaster being Joseph A. Nolin (also spelled Nolan) (1855–1926), who had come from Canada and opened a general store with his wife, Marguerite (1869–1944).

CINGMARS TOWNSHIP (т. 67–68 N, R. 24w) was named for E. F. Cingmars, a French settler there, who removed to the West.

CRAIGSVILLE a village in section 36 of т. 63 N, R. 26w, was named for a logging foreman in the area named Craig; it was platted in 1924 by James Reid. The site had such extensive logging around it that during logging season up to 5,000 loggers might be found in the local taverns. Its post office, 1915–52, was established in Itasca County and transferred to Koochiching County in 1918; it had a station of the Minneapolis and Rainy River Railway.

CROSS RIVER TOWNSHIP (т. 67 N, R. 25w) was named for this small stream, flowing northeastward through it to the Little Fork.

DEHART a station of the Minnesota, Dakota and Western Railway in section 32 of т. 68 N, R. 25w (Jameson).

DENTAYBOW TOWNSHIP (т. 65 N, R. 25w) uniquely honors three of its homestead farmers, named Densmore, Taylor, and Bowman, each represented by a syllable in the name. A post office was located in section 22 of the township (т. 66 N, R. 25w), 1908–33, the first postmaster being Alice Bowman; it had a station of the Minnesota, Dakota and Western Railway.

DINNER CREEK TOWNSHIP (т. 153–154 N, R. 26w) is crossed by a creek so named, where timber cruisers and estimators had a meeting place for dinner, tributary northwestward to the Sturgeon River.

ELEANOR a station on the Minnesota, Dakota and Western Railway in т. 63 N, R. 26w.

ENGELWOOD TOWNSHIP (т. 151 N, R. 28w) received its name in compliment to its numerous settlers named Engelking, who came from the vicinity of Fort Ridgely, Nicollet County.

ERICSBURG a village in section 7 of т. 69 N, R. 23–25w (Rat Root), was founded by a real estate agent named Erik Franson, for whom the village is named; Franson built a sawmill at the site and in 1907 purchased the first settler Lou Boulin's 1897 homestead and platted the village. Franson was born in Sweden in 1872, came to the United States in the 1890s, spent a few years in Canada before settling in International Falls in 1905, where he died in 1914. The post office was established in 1907 with Gust Franson, brother of Erik, as postmaster; it had a station of the Duluth, Virginia and Rainy Lake Railroad.

EVERGREEN TOWNSHIP (т. 152 N, R. 27w) has a general forest of the evergreen trees, including black and white spruce, balsam fir, arbor vitae or white cedar, and three species of pines.

FAIRLAND a settlement in section 31 of т. 158 N, R. 27w, was begun about 1902 when the first settlers arrived; it was known until 1912 as Feldman for an early settler. Ole K. Scheie, another early settler, operated a store on Fred Smith's place three miles east, where he was postmaster of the post office called Fairland, which was named for his home place in Norway, called Fjaarland; when Scheie opened a general store with Ole Sandsmark at Sandsmark's home, the post office was moved and operated there until 1936.

FALLS JUNCTION a residential community east of International Falls, in т. 70 N, R. 23–24w (Koochiching), section 36; it had a station serving the Duluth, Winnipeg and Pacific and the Minnesota, Dakota and Western railways.

FELDMAN a township organized in 1916, is named for one of its first settlers.

FOREST GROVE TOWNSHIP (т. 152 N, R. 28w) received this descriptive name by the vote of its people. The village in sections 15, 16, 21, and 22 of the township is in the Pine Island State Forest.

FORSYTH a post office, 1904–22, of т. 69 N, R. 23–25w (Rat Root), section 7, was named for the first postmaster, Elizabeth Forsyth White (d. 1930); her husband, Francis White, requested the post office and was listed as the official postmaster; their log house near the Little Fork River bridge on Highway 71 is on the National Register of Historic Places.

FRONTIER a village in т. 159–160 N, R. 28w (Murphy), section 20, which had a post office, 1904–44, first established in Itasca County.

GALVIN JUNCTION a station on the Minnesota,

Dakota and Western Railway in T. 70N, R. 23–24W (Koochiching), sections 20 and 21.

GATES CORNER a place name in Pine Island State Forest.

GEMMELL a townsite located on the homestead of Peter McHugh in T. 152N, R. 27W (Evergreen), sections 20 and 21; it was first called Clear Lake, then Stoner, with a post office begun in Itasca County in 1904; it was then changed to Gemmell in 1905, when the Northern Pacific Railroad came, in honor of W. H. Gemmell of Brainerd, general manager of the Minnesota and International Railway. The post office discontinued in 1974.

GOWDY TOWNSHIP (T. 156N, R. 25–26W) commemorates its several pioneers of this name, who took homestead claims on and near the Big Fork. A community called Gowdy was located in the township circa 1902–37.

GRAND FALLS TOWNSHIP (T. 155N, R. 25W) is crossed meanderingly by the Big Fork. Its Grand Falls, in the southeast edge of this township, with descent of 29 feet over ledges of gneiss and mica schist, gave also the name Big Falls to the adjoining railway village and township on the south. The village of Grand Falls was located in section 36 of the township; it had a station of the Minnesota and International Railway and a post office, 1906–11, first established in Itasca County, and then known as Granfalls.

HANNAFORD a village in section 31, T. 69N, R. 26–27W (Reedy); it was platted in 1894 when part of Itasca County and had a post office, 1895–96; the community was promoted but not developed, although there were several small flourishes of industry, including a mill, which closed in 1910.

HANSON see MANITOU.

HAPPYLAND a flag stop of the Northern Pacific Railroad in T. 68N, R. 26W (Meadow Brook), section 24. There are several versions of its name's origin, one being that in 1907 when railroad construction gangs, with mosquitoes and a muskeg bog to contend with, reached the high pine area five miles south of Littlefork, the mosquitoes let up, and the walking was good, so a grateful crew named it "a happy land." The first homesteaders came in 1904; it had a station on the Minnesota and International Railway and a post office, 1908–5, Charles S. Romens listed as the official postmaster.

HARRIGAN TOWNSHIP was named for an early settler.

HAY CREEK a village in T. 159N, R. 29W, developed when the area opened for homesteading in 1911; all the families were gone by 1938, and the area became a game refuge.

HENRY TOWNSHIP (T. 66N, R. 26W) was named for a prominent pioneer in the township.

HOLLER see SOUTH INTERNATIONAL FALLS.

INDUS TOWNSHIP (T. 159N, R. 25W) received this name of a great river in western India by the suggestion of Rev. M. F. Smootz, a homesteader beside the Rainy River, who had been a missionary in that country. The village in section 4 of the township had a post office, 1902–74, first established in Itasca County.

INTERNATIONAL BOUNDARY a station of the Duluth, Virginia and Rainy Lake Railway in section 34 of T. 71N, R. 24W.

INTERNATIONAL FALLS the county seat, founded as Koochiching village in the township of this name, was platted in April 1895 by teacher and preacher L. A. Ogaard for the Koochiching Company and named Koochiching; it was incorporated as a village on August 10, 1901, consumed by fire on June 15, 1902, and when rebuilt changed its name to International Falls; it was incorporated as a city in 1909. Its name notes its location on the international boundary at the Koochiching Falls of Rainy River. The descent of the river there, in broken rapids on irregularly jutting ledges of granitoid gneiss, was 23 feet, mainly within a distance of about 300 feet, but a dam close above the falls, completed in 1908, increased their head to 26 feet, raising the river to the level of Rainy Lake and permitting the lake steamboats to come to this city. Before the stream was thus used for its waterpower, operating the great paper mills of International Falls, the plentiful mists and spray of the falls, which nearly always formed a rainbow in the sunshine, well accounted for the aboriginal origin of the names of Rainy Lake and River.

A post office was established as Koochiching in 1894 while part of Itasca County; it had a station of the Canadian Northern Railway and the Northern Pacific Railroad; the first resident was Alexander Baker of Scotland (1827–99), a miner and homesteader; the first postmaster was Ernest J. Holler (1877–1915), who published a newspaper in Big Falls and served as a deputy sheriff;

he was the son of John Acey Holler (see RANIER; SOUTH INTERNATIONAL FALLS).

Fort Frances, the village on the Canadian side of Rainy River opposite to this city, was built around a former fur trade post, which was so named in honor of Frances Ramsey Simpson (d. 1853), wife of Sir George Simpson (1792–1860). He was governor for the Hudson's Bay Company in Canada nearly 40 years, from 1821 until his death, September 7, 1860, at his home in Lachine, near Montreal.

ISLAND VIEW a resort and residential village in sections 31–33 of T. 70–71N, R. 22W (Ray), at the mouth of the Black Bay on Rainy Lake; it was established as a village on October 30, 1939, but not incorporated.

JAMESON a village east of International Falls in T. 70N, R. 24W.

JAMESON TOWNSHIP (T. 68N, R. 25W) was named in honor of Charles S. Jameson, a homesteader on the site of the village of Littlefork in this township. He came from Northfield, Minn., founded the first newspaper of Koochiching (now International Falls), and was editor of the *Little Fork Times*.

KLINE TOWNSHIP (T. 154N, R. 29W) was named for a pioneer settler.

KOOCHICHING see INTERNATIONAL FALLS.

KOOCHICHING TOWNSHIP (T. 70N, R. 23–25W), like the county, took this name from the falls of Rainy River.

LAUREL a village located on the Rainy River in T. 70N, R. 26W (Reedy), section 32, which had a post office, 1903–35, first established in Itasca County, and a station on the Minnesota, Dakota and Western Railway.

LINDFORD TOWNSHIP (T. 157N, R. 25W) was named in honor of Andrew L. Lindvall, a Swedish farmer beside the Big Fork in section 13, who also owned a store and was the first Lindford postmaster. A post office was located in sections 13 and 24 of the township, 1905–31. Lindvall, who was born Nordanbro Anders Larsson in Sweden in 1850, came to the United States in 1878, and to Lindford in 1903, submitted many names for the settlement; the name selected included part of his name and that of Henry Ford, the automobile industrialist; Lindvall opened a store in his home in 1905 and built a sawmill in 1907; he died in International Falls in 1919.

LITTLEFORK a farming and logging city in T. 68N,

R. 25W (Jameson), sections 9 and 10, is named for its location on the Little Fork of the Rainy River. The first settlers came to the Littlefork Valley in 1884; the first building was erected by William Slingerland as a "stopping place," where he became the first postmaster in 1902, when the post office was established; the city was incorporated August 20, 1904.

LOMAN a residential community located in T. 158N, R. 25W (Watrous), section 11, was named for the George and Mary Loman family, homesteaders who came from Canada in 1889 and opened the first post office in their home in 1901, with Jennie R. Mourhess, postmaster; it had a station on the Minnesota, Dakota and Western Railway.

LUNDGREN a village in T. 155N, R. 27W (Sturgeon River), section 28, also known as Sturgeon River. When Augustin and Matilda Lundgren, with their six children, arrived at the site, there had been only one previous settler. A post office operated 1908–19 with Augustin Lundgren as postmaster; no business community developed.

LUOMA a station on the Duluth, Winnipeg and Pacific Railway in T. 70N, R. 23W (Koochiching).

MANITOU TOWNSHIP (T. 159N, R. 26W) received its Ojibwe name, meaning a spirit, from the Manitou Rapids of Rainy River, which forms the north boundary of this township. The river falls about three feet in these rapids, a short pitch over solid rock on the bottom and in both banks. The village in section 4 had a station of the Dakota, Western and Pacific Railroad and a post office, first established as Hanson in 1903, with Andrew M. Hanson as postmaster, and changed to Manitou, 1904–71, Hanson also being its first postmaster under that name.

MARGIE a station of the Northern Pacific Railroad in T. 153N, R. 26W (Dinner Creek), section 2, with a post office established in 1903 and named for the daughter of postmaster Westley Horton, the post office being located in their store. It was located at a site on high land between two swamps; there were several stores and a sawmill.

McCLELLAN a post office, 1915–36, in T. 155N, R. 29W (White Birch), with a station of the Minnesota and International Railway.

McDONALD a station of the Minnesota, Dakota and Western Railway in T. 67N, R. 25W (Cross River), section 32.

MEADOW BROOK TOWNSHIP (T. 68N, R. 26W) has a small stream of this name, tributary to the Bear River.

MEDING TOWNSHIP (T. 67–68N, R. 22W) was named for Paul Meding, an early German farmer here.

MIZPAH the name of a city in sections 19, 20, 29, and 30 of T. 151N, R. 28W (Engelwood), is the Hebrew word for a watchtower. It is used as a parting salutation, meaning "The Lord watch between me and thee, when we are absent one from another" (Genesis 31:49). It was incorporated as a village on January 2, 1905, and separated from the township on June 3, 1915. The first settlers were the Potter brothers, Will, Walter, and Sam, in January 1900, Walter becoming the first postmaster when the post office was established in 1901 and Will building a sawmill in 1904 .

MURPHY TOWNSHIP (T. 159–160N, R. 28W) was named in honor of an Irish pioneer, whose homestead farm here nearly adjoined the Rainy River.

NAKODA a station of the Minnesota and International Railway in T. 70N, R. 24W (Koochiching), section 29.

NETT LAKE a village with St. Louis County, located in T. 65N, R. 22W.

NETT LAKE TOWNSHIP and **NETT RIVER TOWNSHIP** (T. 66N, R. 23–24W) border on the Bois Forte, or Nett Lake, Reservation, which is more fully noticed, with the origin of these names, at the end of this chapter.

NORDEN TOWNSHIP and its earlier Norden post office were named for Norwegian settlers. The post office was in section 30 of T. 154N, R. 29W (Kline), 1908–34, which also had a station on the Minnesota and International Railway.

NORTHLAND a station on the Duluth, Winnipeg and Pacific Railway in T. 69N, R. 23W (Rat Root), sections 17 and 22.

NORTHOME a city in T. 151N, R. 28W (Englewood), sections 19, 20, 29, and 30, was incorporated as a village on September 16, 1903; it was first settled by Claude Fish and C. W. Fields on the homestead of A. M. Brohiem, Fields having had a business earlier at Bridgie and Orth in Itasca County; the site was called New Bridgie; when the post office was established in 1902, it was named Phena; when the Northern Pacific Railroad came in August 1903, the post office department requested a name change, and the community became Northome.

PELLAND a village in T. 70N, R. 25W (Koochiching), section 29, was established when brothers Frank and Joe Pelland and their families came from Quebec in 1894 to an area near the junction of the Rainy and Little Fork Rivers, the community being named for them. Emma Pelland (Mrs. Joseph Pelland) was the first postmaster when the post office was established in 1902, the post office discontinuing in 1918; it had a station of the Minnesota, Dakota and Western Railway.

PHENA see **NORTHOME**.

PINE TOP TOWNSHIP (T. 151N, R. 27W) was named for an exceptionally tall white pine, which had at its top a peculiar cluster of small branches. A village was located in sections 9, 10, 15, and 16.

PLUM CREEK TOWNSHIP (T. 151N, R. 25W) has a little stream so named for its wild plum trees.

RAINY LAKE CITY was a gold mining station, during a few years, at the east side of the strait between Rainy Lake and Black Bay (also called Rat Root Lake). A stamp mill was built there in 1894 for crushing the ore mined on the southwest end of Dryweed Island, less than a mile distant, but the work failed to repay its expenses. A village was incorporated April 3, 1894, and its post office, 1894–1900, was established and discontinued while part of Itasca County. At its peak there were four or five stores and a number of other businesses, following the "gold fever" boom when five mines operated within a five-mile radius of the community; by 1906 only one resident remained, and most of the buildings had been dismantled.

RANIER a city in T. 71N, R. 24W (Koochiching), northeast of International Falls, was incorporated on March 24, 1908, and separated from the township on March 31, 1919. The first permanent resident was John Acey Holler in 1898, U.S. customs officer at Koochiching, where he moved in 1906, selling his homestead to Cook and O'Brien Company, which surveyed the townsite. The Duluth, Rainy Lake and Winnipeg Railway came in 1907 along with a building boom; the post office began in 1908. The city was named by officers of the railroad.

RAPID RIVER TOWNSHIP (T. 157–158N, R. 29W) contains the sources of the East Fork of the river so named, flowing thence north to the Rapid and Rainy Rivers.

RAT ROOT TOWNSHIP (T. 69N, R. 23–25W) is crossed by the circuitous course of the river so named, tributary to Rat Root Lake, which also is very commonly called Black Bay, connected with Rainy Lake by a strait. The name of the river and lake, adopted for the township, is a translation of the Ojibwe name, referring to roots eaten by muskrats. All the streams in this district become somewhat darkly stained by the peaty swamps through which they sluggishly flow, so that they give the same dark color to the water of the Rat Root Lake, whence came its other name, Black Bay.

The muskrat is an abundant fur-bearing animal of the northern United States and Canada, a small brother or cousin of the beaver, which it almost equals in its industry and skill for house building. Its favorite food, stored for winter use in the houses of mud and rushes built in shallow lakes, consists of the roots of the common yellow water lilies, which gave the name of Rat Root. Another place named for the muskrat is Rat Portage, now Kenora, at the mouth of the Lake of the Woods.

RAUCH a village located in T. 63N, R. 22W, sections 9 and 10, on the Bois Forte Reservation; it was named for its first settler, John Rauch, born in Simac, Austria, in 1864; he came to the United States in 1886, first working in the mines at Soudan and Nashwauk before filing a homestead at this site in 1906, moving to it in 1908, and opening a general store in his log building home along with a post office in 1909; the post office discontinued in 1953.

RAY TOWNSHIP (T. 70–71N, R. 22W) was named for Edwin Ray Lewis of Grand Rapids, who was a land surveyor and timber cruiser, often traversing this region. A village in section 6 developed about 1893 with the gold mining boom; its post office was established in 1907, and it had a station of the Duluth, Winnipeg, and Pacific Railway.

REEDY TOWNSHIP (T. 70–71N, R. 26W) commemorates David Reedy, its first settler, an immigrant from Ireland, who took a land claim at the west side of the mouth of the Big Fork.

RIDGE a station of the Northern Pacific Railroad in section 2 of T. 152N, R. 27W (Evergreen).

RIPPLE see BIG FALLS.

ROCKTON a station of the Minnesota, Dakota and Western Railway in T. 64N, R. 26W.

SAULT TOWNSHIP (T. 159–160N, R. 27W) received its name, the French word for "a leap or jump," from the Long Sault Rapids of Rainy River, which is its north boundary. The rapids are about a mile long, falling about seven feet.

SCARLETT and **STEFFES TOWNSHIPS** were named in honor of pioneers.

SEYMOUR a station on the Minnesota, Dakota and Western Railway in T. 68N, R. 25W (Jameson), section 17.

SHELLAND a post office, 1914–17, located in T. 63N, R. 22W; it had a station on the Duluth, Winnipeg and Pacific Railway.

SILVERDALE a village in sections 35 and 36 of T. 64N, R. 22W, was named for Johan Johansson Silverdahl, who was born in Sweden in 1858 and came to Minnesota in 1897, filing a homestead claim of 160 acres at the site in 1903; his home was the location of the post office, 1909–18, with Silverdahl serving as postmaster. The first school was built on his land; Silverdahl's family came in 1922, and he died in 1939.

SOUTH INTERNATIONAL FALLS incorporated as a village August 8, 1912, and as a city on August 9, 1921; it has the longest of any Minnesota name and is larger in acreage than International Falls. It was referred to as Holler's Addition for many years; its post office was named Holler 1927–48, when changed to the present; Holler was named for John Acey Holler, customs agent at Koochiching and state legislator, born in Cleveland, Ohio, in 1843, and died in International Falls September 15, 1917; his son, George, was the first mayor. The village had a station of the Northern Pacific Railroad.

STALS a post office, 1921–35, with Peter Stal, first postmaster, located in T. 155N, R. 26–27W (Sturgeon River).

STONER see GEMMELL.

STURGEON RIVER TOWNSHIP (T. 155N, R. 26–27W) is traversed in its south part by this river, flowing east to the Big Fork. The name, probably translated from the Ojibwe, refers to the ascent of the lake or rock sturgeon to this stream.

SUMMERVILLE TOWNSHIP (T. 63N, R. 23W) was named by vote of its people for Margaret Sommers, a widow and the only woman residing in the original township in 1905. There are villages or townships of this name in Pennsylvania, North and South Carolina, Georgia, and other states of the Union, and also in Nova Scotia and Ontario.

TURNER a station of the Minnesota, Dakota and Western Railway in T. 63N, R. 26w.

WARREN TOWNSHIP (T. 151N, R. 29w), organized in 1916, has a name that is borne by counties in 14 states, and by townships, villages, and cities in 24 states, a large majority being in commemoration of Joseph Warren, who fell in the battle of Bunker Hill.

WATROUS TOWNSHIP (T. 158N, R. 25w) was named for Charles B. Watrous from Pennsylvania, who was a farmer and owned a large sawmill on the Rainy River near the east line of this township.

WAUKANHA a post office, 1922–35, in T. 67N, R. 26w (Bear River), sections 30 and 31; it had a station of the Northern Pacific Railroad.

WAYLAND a village in T. 158N, R. 29w (Rapid River) first settled about 1907 by Canadians; its post office operated 1911–35; with little prospect of the railroad coming to the area to aid in their farming efforts and with their properties logged off, most settlers left by the mid-1930s.

WHITE BIRCH TOWNSHIP (T. 155N, R. 29w) has an abundance of the paper, or canoe, birch, used to make birch-bark canoes.

WICKER TOWNSHIP (T. 152N, R. 25–26w) was named for Harry Wicker, a homesteader in its sections 10 and 11, on the Big Fork.

WILDWOOD TOWNSHIP (T. 151N, R. 26w) received this name in the petition of its people for organization. A logging village in sections 15, 16, 21, and 22 had a post office, 1911–35, variously located in the homes of the postmasters.

WILLIAMS TOWNSHIP (T. 160N, R. 29w) was named in honor of James Williams, well known for operating a portable sawmill, whose homestead farm on the Rainy River was in sections 6 and 7, at the northwest corner of this township and of the county.

WISNER a station of the Northern Pacific Railroad and the Minnesota and International Railway in T. 67N, R. 26w (Bear River), section 10.

ZORA a village in T. 151N, R. 25w (Plum Creek), created by Albert Joseph Porter, postmaster from Maine, who filed a claim in 1901 to log the land;

Porter died in 1938; the post office operated 1907–10.

――――――

Lakes and Streams

Foregoing pages have sufficiently noted the names of the Rainy Lake and River, the Koochiching or International Falls, the Big and Little Forks of Rainy River, Bear River, Beaver Brook, Caldwell Brook, Cross River, Dinner Creek, the Grand Falls of the Big Fork, the Manitou and Long Sault Rapids of Rainy River, Meadow Brook, Plum Creek, the East Fork of Rapid River, the Rat Root River and Lake (this lake, united to Rainy Lake by a strait, being also named Black Bay), and the Sturgeon River.

Names of islands, bays, and points of the part of Rainy Lake belonging to this county, in their order from east to west, are Dryweed Island before mentioned for its gold mining, Sha Sha Point and Black Bay, Grindstone Island, Grassy Island and Grassy Narrows separating it from the south shore, Red Sucker Island, Jackfish Island and Bay, Stop Island, Kingston Island, and Sand Bay and Pither's Point at the mouth of the lake.

The Big Fork is known by the Ojibwe as Bowstring River, from its source in the large Bowstring Lake, which is translated from the name Atchabani or Busatchabani, given by them to the lake and its outflowing stream, before noticed in the chapter for Itasca County.

The Little Fork bears a peculiarly descriptive Ojibwe name, recorded by Gilfillan as Ningtawonani zibi, the river separating canoe routes, which name is also applied, with a slight change, to the Nett River. In the thought of these Indians, expressed by the name, canoe voyageurs ascending the Little Fork may go forward to its source or may turn aside and go up Nett River, having thus the choice of separate routes.

The Ojibwe name of Nett Lake was written Asubikone by Gilfillan, meaning "taken or entangled in the net." Its origin, as told by the Bois Forte Ojibwe, is presented in the notice of their reservation.

Only a few other names of streams and lakes in this county remain to be listed.

South of Nett Lake, Prairie Creek and Willow Creek flow into the Little Fork from the east; Reilly Creek is a small eastern tributary of the Big Fork, about ten miles south of Big Falls; Black River, named for its peat-stained water, joins Rainy River about three miles west of the Big Fork; Tamarack River flows from Gemmell northwestward to the north part of Red Lake; and the headstream of Battle River (formerly mapped here as Armstrong Creek), tributary to the south part of that lake, crosses Bridgie Township, in the southwest corner of this county.

Among the few and little lakes, limited to the south edge of the county above the highest shoreline of Lake Agassiz, are Bartlett Lake, at Northome, and Battle Lake, through which the Battle River flows.

Bois Forte Reservation

This Ojibwe reservation, also called Nett Lake Reservation, comprising the whole or parts of nine surveyed townships and enclosing Nett Lake, lies in Koochiching and St. Louis Counties. In addition, the band has reservation land near Lake Vermilion in St. Louis County and on Deer Creek in the northern part of Itasca County. They call themselves Sugwaundugah wininewug, meaning "Men of the thick fir woods," but the early French traders named them Bois Fortes, "Hard Wood Indians."

In the treaty at Washington, April 7, 1866, providing this reservation, the name given to Nett Lake by the Ojibwe was spelled As-sab-a-co-na. Albert B. Reagan, who was the U.S. agent here in 1909–14, writes the traditional origin of this name, received as a myth of the Bois Forte medicine men. The Ojibwe, coming first by the route of Vermilion and Pelican Lakes, are said to have found on the little island of Nett Lake many strange beasts, "half sea lion and half fish," who fled westward by swimming and wading though the shallow and mostly rice-filled lake. "On coming to the island the canoemen paddled around it, and by the track of the muddied water pursued the beasts across the lake and up a creek till they found where the earth had swallowed them, as if they had been caught in a net." The myth is thought to refer to the flight and escape of a party of their enemies, the Dakota, whom the Ojibwe by many raids and battles drove away from the wooded north part of Minnesota.

The northeast side of this island, which is named Picture Island by the white people, but Drum Island by the Ojibwe, has a smoothly glaciated rock surface, as described by Reagan, "covered with crudely made pictographs of human beings, dance scenes, and outlines of the animal gods worshipped by the men making the pictures. . . . The drawings seem to be similar to those at Pipestone, Minnesota, which are known to be Siouan. Furthermore, the Ojibways say that their people did not make the rock pictures."

Coutchiching Rock Formation

Reports on the geology of the parts of Canada and Minnesota surrounding Rainy Lake, published in 1889–1901, give the name Coutchiching to a large series of Archaean micaschists, outcropping in this county on Rainy Lake, around Black Bay, and southward on the Little and Big Forks and at and near Nett Lake (*Geology of Minnesota, Final Report*, vol. 4, 1899, ch. 8, pp. 166–211, with maps and sections; vol. 6, 1901, pl. 65). This name is a variant form of the Cree and Ojibwe name of Rainy Lake and River, which is applied to this county and a township, the pronunciation in the two forms being alike.

Franz Jevne State Park

State planners were intending to add land along the Rainy River to the park system when they had the good fortune to receive a gift from the family of Franz Jevne. Jevne had been a lawyer in International Falls and Minneapolis and was described by his son as a true pioneer of northern Minnesota. The park was created as a state wayside in 1967 and upgraded to state park status in 1969. The park is northeast of Birchdale and includes the Sault Rapids and some of the most scenic land along the Rainy River. The remainder of the park is largely peatland, which was once entirely covered by Glacial Lake Agassiz.

Lac qui Parle County

This county was established March 6, 1871. Nine years earlier a county bearing this name but of entirely different area, situated north of the Minnesota River, had been authorized by a legislative act, February 20, 1862, but it was not ratified by the people. This French name, meaning "the Lake that Talks," is translated from the Dakota name, Mde Iyedan (*mde*, lake; *iye*, speaks; *dan*, a diminutive suffix), applied to the adjacent lake, which is an expansion of the Minnesota River. The lake, nearly 10 miles long with a maximum width of 1 mile and a maximum depth of 12 feet, owes its existence to the deposition of alluvium from the Lac qui Parle River, which enters the Minnesota valley near the foot of the lake. Its name most probably was suggested to the Dakota by echoes thrown back from its bordering bluffs. Prof. Andrew W. Williamson wrote: "It is very uncertain how it received the name; one tradition says from an echo on its shores, but it is doubtful if any such existed; another tradition is that when the Dakotas first came to the lake voices were heard, but they found no speakers; some think the word has changed its form." The Qu' Appelle River in Saskatchewan, also a French translation of its Indian name, having nearly the same significance, "the River that Calls," is similarly enclosed by somewhat high bluffs, likely to reply to a loud speaker by echoes.

Rev. Moses N. Adams, who during our territorial period resided as a missionary at Lac qui Parle, told of a very remarkable creaking, groaning, and whistling of the ice on the lake in winter and spring, due to fluctuations of the water level allowing the ice to rise and fall, grating upon the abundant boulders of the shores. At the same time these strange sounds are echoed and reverberate from the enclosing bluffs. To these "voices" he ascribed the Dakota and French name.

In the history of the county (1916, p. 99), a different explanation is offered, "that at times when the wind was from the right quarter the breaking of waves against the stones on the shore gave off a distinct musical note, or sound, which accounted for the giving of the name to the lake by the early voyageurs."

Information of the origins and meanings of these names has been gathered from History of the Minnesota Valley *(1882, 1,016 pp.), in which pages 937–55 relate to this county;* History of Chippewa and Lac qui Parle Counties *(1916, two vols., 605 and 821 pp.), edited by Lycurgus R. Moyer and Hon. Ole G. Dale; and from interviews with these editors and Hon. J. F. Rosenwald of Madison, the county seat, during a visit there in July 1916.*

AARHUS a country post office, 1898–1902, of Garfield Township.

AGASSIZ TOWNSHIP settled in 1870, organized April 12, 1887, was named for the Glacial Lake

Agassiz, in the basin of the Red River and of Lake Winnipeg, which outflowed by the Glacial River Warren along the Minnesota valley at the north side of this township. Jean Louis Rudolphe Agassiz, in whose honor that ancient lake received its name, was born in Motier, Switzerland, May 28, 1807, and died in Cambridge, Mass., December 14, 1873. His observations of the Swiss glaciers and his principal writings concerning them and the glacial origin of the drift were during the years 1836 to 1846. In the autumn of 1846 Agassiz came to the United States, and the remainder of his life was mostly spent here in zoological researches and in teaching in Harvard College, where he founded the Museum of Comparative Zoology.

ARENA a Latin word meaning "sand," is the name of a township settled in 1878 and organized January 3, 1880. Its earliest pioneers came from southern Wisconsin, where this name was earlier given to a township and village on the Wisconsin River in Iowa County.

AUGUSTA TOWNSHIP organized February 5, 1880, was named for Augusta in Eau Claire County, Wis., the former home of its first settlers, a party of 11 families, who came in April 1879.

BAXTER TOWNSHIP settled in the summer of 1870 and organized September 30, 1871, was named in honor of Hiram A. Baxter, at whose home the township meeting for organization was held.

BELLINGHAM a city in Perry Township, sections 3, 4, 9, and 10, incorporated as a village on May 5, 1890, and platted by the owners, William R. and Mary P. Thomas and Robert and Phebe (Morse) Bellingham (d. 1889). The county newspaper first suggested the name Perry after its township name, but Phebe (Morse) Bellingham named it for her father-in-law, Charles Thomas Saker Bellingham (b. 1823, England; d. 1905, Bellingham), the patriarch of the large Bellingham family (seven sons, one daughter), who lived in the area. The Great Northern Railway came in 1887, and the depot was built in 1888. Banker Hans M. Hagestead was the first postmaster when the post office opened in 1887, and he later was township manager and brought the newspaper to the village in 1891.

BLENHEIM a post office, 1880–81; location not found.

BOAT CREEK a post office, 1880–85, in the farmhouse of James B. Smith, postmaster; located in Augusta Township, 25 miles west of Lac qui Parle.

BOYD a city in Ten Mile Lake Township, sections 15, 16, and 22, platted in 1884 and incorporated on February 10, 1893, was named by officers of the Minneapolis and St. Louis Railroad. The post office began in 1884.

CAMP RELEASE TOWNSHIP first settled in 1868, organized April 5, 1871, has the site of Camp Release, marked by a monument, where the captives taken by the Dakota in the war of 1862 were surrendered on September 26 to Gen. Henry H. Sibley. A post office was located in the township, 1873–80.

CERRO GORDO TOWNSHIP settled in the spring of 1868, organized April 7, 1871, received this Spanish name, meaning "Big Mountain," in accordance with the suggestion of Col. Samuel McPhail, who participated in the battle of Cerro Gordo in the Mexican War, April 18, 1847. A post office was located in section 3, 1877–85 and 1887–1904.

DAWSON a railway city near the center of Riverside Township, platted in 1884, incorporated as a village on November 12, 1884, and as a city in 1911, was named in honor of William Dawson, a banker of St. Paul, who was one of the proprietors of its site. He was born in County Cavan, Ireland, October 1, 1825; came to America in 1846; settled in St. Paul in 1861, was its mayor, 1878–81, and died there February 19, 1901. The original site of the city was in section 21 on the Minneapolis and St. Louis Railroad, purchased and platted by the Dawson Townsite Company in 1884 and filed in 1892. The post office began in 1884 with Charles J. Coghlan, postmaster and newspaper publisher.

FLENSBORG a post office begun as a special supply post office called Norman, 1880–83, and changed to Flensborg, 1883–84, located 16 miles west of Lac qui Parle, originally misspelled Fleusborg.

FREELAND was settled in 1877 and organized in March 1880. The petitioners at first requested that the name Freedom be given to the new township in compliment to J. P. Free, one of its pioneers, but this was changed, because another township of the state was earlier so named. A post office was located in the township, 1891–1904, with farmer and school board member John Palmgren as postmaster (b. Sweden; d. 1893).

GARFIELD TOWNSHIP settled in 1873, organized January 24, 1881, was named in honor of James Abram Garfield, president of the United States. He was born at Orange, Ohio, November 19, 1831; was an instructor and later president of Hiram College, Ohio, 1856–61; served in the Civil War and was promoted to major general in 1863; was a member of Congress from Ohio, 1863–80; was elected president in 1880 and was inaugurated March 4, 1881; was shot at Washington by Charles J. Guiteau, July 2, and died at Elberon, N.J., September 19, 1881.

HAMLIN TOWNSHIP settled in April 1874 and organized September 10, 1879, commemorates its first settler, John R. Hamlin, who died in 1876.

HANTHO TOWNSHIP organized November 4, 1878, was also named for its first settler, Halvor H. Hantho, an immigrant from Norway, who took a homestead in section 15 in 1872. Later in the same year his brothers, Nels and Ole, located on section 13. A post office was in section 29, 1899–1903.

HAYDENVILLE a village in section 20, Arena, with a station of the Minneapolis and St. Louis Railroad, platted October 10, 1910, was named in honor of Herbert L. Hayden, owner of the site. He was born in Onondaga County, N.Y., March 23, 1850, and died in Madison, Minn., November 20, 1911. He came to Minnesota in 1875; settled at Lac qui Parle in 1878; was admitted to practice law, 1881; removed to Madison in 1884, was secretary and treasurer of the townsite company and engaged in banking and farming; was county attorney, 1891–92 and 1895–96.

LAC QUI PARLE TOWNSHIP first settled by homesteaders in 1868, organized January 12, 1873, took its name, like the county, from the lake on its northern boundary. Its village is located in section 27, on the site of a former Indian village; it was surveyed in May 1871 by L. R. Moyer and registered on September 14, 1872; it was the county seat until May 1889 when the county offices were permanently located in Madison. The village had a station of the Chicago, Milwaukee and St. Paul Railroad, and its post office operated 1870–1907. Two earlier townsites had been platted in the township: the first in section 30 in the fall of 1869 on the homestead of William Mills and called Williamsburg had a store, which moved to Lac qui Parle; the second in section 20 platted in December 1869 had a store but no formal name and also moved to Lac qui Parle.

LAKE SHORE TOWNSHIP settled in 1874, organized March 11, 1879, received this name because it borders on Marsh Lake, four miles long, through which the Minnesota River flows, a body of shallow water, or more generally in the summer a grassy marsh.

LOKEN a post office, 1880–85, 18 miles from Lac qui Parle; location not found.

LONSET a post office, 1895–1901, in Cerro Gordo Township, with Christian E. Kittleson, postmaster; he was born in Norway and came to the eastern part of the county in 1893, later being in the mercantile business in Lac qui Parle.

LOUISBURG a city in section 33 of Lake Shore Township, was platted on September 12, 1887, by Ole Thompson and William R. Thomas and incorporated as a village on November 2, 1905; it is said that Ole Thompson, who owned the land of the townsite, named it for his father, Louis Thompson, who had settled in section 34 in 1876. When the post office opened in 1888, the first postmaster was Thomas R. Thompson, son of Ole; it had a station of the Great Northern Railway.

MADISON TOWNSHIP first settled in 1877, organized in October 1879, was named on the suggestion of Claus P. Moe, "in memory of his former home at Madison, Wisconsin." The city of Madison is located in sections 20, 21, 28, and 29; the townsite company organized by H. A. Larson, general store owner, purchased the land from John Anderson in 1884 and platted the townsite; the post office began as True in 1883, changing its name to Madison in 1884; it had a station of the Minneapolis and St. Louis Railroad. The city was incorporated in 1886, became the county seat in 1889, and adopted its city charter March 12, 1902.

MANFRED TOWNSHIP settled in 1876, was organized March 11, 1879, being then named Custer in honor of Gen. George A. Custer (1839–76). The name was changed to Manfred in 1884 for the principal character in a wild and weird dramatic poem by Lord Byron, having its scenes in the Alps of Switzerland.

MARIETTA a city of August Township, sections 21, 27, and 28, platted in 1884 and incorporated on January 12, 1900, was named by officers of the Minneapolis and St. Louis Railroad. This name is borne by cities in Ohio and Georgia and by villages in 11 other states. Pioneers from Marietta, Ohio, had settled here. The post office began in 1884.

MARTINVILLE a farmers post office, 1898–1905, 18 miles southeast of Madison in Freeland Township, in section 27 or 28.

MAXWELL TOWNSHIP settled in 1871 and organized in 1878, was named in honor of Joseph Henry Maxwell, one of its earliest pioneers. He was born in West Virginia, March 5, 1840; served in a West Virginia regiment during the Civil War; came to Minnesota in 1871, taking a homestead claim in this township; died in Minneapolis, January 27, 1916. A post office was located in the township, 1882–84.

MEHURIN TOWNSHIP organized October 14, 1879, was named in honor of its first homesteader, Lucretia S. Mehurin, and her father, Amasa Mehurin, who each came to this township in 1877. He was born in Rutland County, Vt., June 28, 1808; lived in Iowa 21 years, 1833–54, and later in Freeborn County, Minn.; came to Lac qui Parle County in 1873, being the first settler in Garfield. The village of Mehurin was located in sections 15, 16, 21, and 22; it had a post office, 1901–3, with Anders A. Henningsgaard as postmaster; he was born in Norway in 1853, came to the United States in 1893, and to Minnesota in 1899.

MILLROY a post office, 1878–79, which was transferred to Odessa, Big Stone County; location not found.

NASSAU a city of Walter Township, was platted in December 1893 and incorporated as a village in 1897. This name, received from Germany, is borne by counties of New York and Florida. The village had a station of the Great Northern Railway and has had a post office since 1888.

NORMAN see FLENSBORG.

PERRY TOWNSHIP was settled in 1878 and organized in 1880. Its name is borne by counties of 10 states of the Union and by townships and villages or cities in 19 states, mostly in honor of Oliver Hazard Perry (1785–1819), victor in the celebrated battle of Lake Erie, September 10, 1813. Some of the first settlers here had come from a township of this name in Dane County, Wis.

PROVIDENCE TOWNSHIP settled in 1877, organized October 31, 1878, received its name from the large city and capital of Rhode Island, founded by Roger Williams in 1636. Villages and townships in 12 other states also bear this name. The village in sections 23 and 24 had a post office, 1879–96 and 1898–1907.

RIVERSIDE settled in 1868 and organized September 21, 1872, took its name from the Lac qui Parle River, which traverses this township, being formed here by the union of its West and East Branches.

ROSEN a village in section 3 of Walter Township; it had a post office, 1897–1907 and 1952–55, which changed to a rural branch, 1956–68.

SVERDRUP a post office, 1881–82; location not found.

TEN MILE LAKE TOWNSHIP first settled in 1876, organized November 4, 1878, was named for its former lake, now drained, which was ten miles distant from the Lac qui Parle mission and trading post. The lake outflowed by Three Mile Creek, so named because it joins the Lac qui Parle River about three miles south of the mission site.

TRUE see MADISON.

VAALER a Norwegian settlement of Riverside Township, which had a Norwegian Lutheran church, a school, and a post office, 1878–84, with farmer John Olsen as postmaster; exporting wheat was the main industry.

WALTER TOWNSHIP settled in 1878 and organized October 18, 1884, was named in honor of Henry Walter, who was its first settler, served as a county commissioner, and after living here about 30 years removed to the state of Washington and died there.

WILLIAMSBURG see LAC QUI PARLE.

YELLOW BANK TOWNSHIP organized January 28, 1878, received the name of the Yellow Bank River, referring to the yellowish glacial drift seen in its newly eroded bluffs. This stream, having its sources on the high Coteau des Prairies, was called by William H. Keating the Spirit Mountain Creek, translated from its Dakota name, in the narrative and map of Maj. Stephen H. Long's expedition in 1823. It is Yellow Earth River on the map of Minnesota published in 1860.

Lakes and Streams

Keating mapped the Lac qui Parle River as Beaver Creek, adopting this name from the fur traders. His narrative adds that the Dakota called it Watapan intapa, "the river at the head," because they considered Lac qui Parle as the head of the Minnesota River, probably referring rather to the limit of favorable canoe travel during the usually low stage of water in the summer. Its name on Joseph N. Nicollet's map, published in 1843, is Intpah River, and this is repeated on maps of Minnesota in 1850 and 1860.

Canby, or Lazarus, Creek, which flows past Canby in Yellow Medicine County, crosses several sections in Freeland and Providence, thence being tributary southeastward to the East Branch of the Lac qui Parle River; and Cobb, or Florida, Creek, from sources in Florida Township, Yellow Medicine County, flows north to the West Branch.

Salt Lake, also called Rosabel Lake, is crossed by the state boundary at the west side of sections 5 and 8, Mehurin.

Emily Creek, in Hantho Township, flows to Lac qui Parle.

Yellow Bank River has South and North Forks.

Whetstone River flows from South Dakota through the northmost corner of this county, being tributary to the Minnesota at Ortonville. It is a translation of the Dakota name, given as Izuzah River by Nicollet.

Antelope Hills and Moraines

Through the west border of this county runs a narrow belt of low morainic hills, knolls, and irregular short ridges. In Freeland the most prominent of these glacial drift accumulations are named the Antelope Hills. Northward in Mehurin and Augusta the belt is called Stony Ridge, one of its knolls or hillocks at the north side of the West Branch of Lac qui Parle River being styled Mount Wickham. Farther north it is known as Yellow Bank Hills, cut through by the river of that name.

It is a part of the Antelope, or Third, Moraine of the continental ice sheet, in the series of 12 mapped in Minnesota. At its west side in this county a wider tract of lowlands is known as the Antelope Valley, named, like this moraine, for their once frequent antelope herds.

The only American species of these graceful deerlike animals is *Antilocapra americana*, the pronghorn antelope, proverbially timid and fleet in escape from pursuers. Prof. Clarence L. Herrick wrote of their geographic range as follows in his *Mammals of Minnesota*, published in 1892. "The habitat is limited to the temperate parts of North America west of the Mississippi river. Formerly their range included all of the territory between the tropics and about fifty-four north latitude and from the Mississippi to the coast, except in the wooded and mountainous portions. At the present time they are restricted to the less accessible and arid regions between the Missouri river and the Mountains and southward. Southwestern Minnesota once furnished them congenial pasturage, but they have long since retired beyond the Missouri."

Lac qui Parle State Park

As the land along the Minnesota River was developed for farms, local residents began to pressure government authorities for flood-control measures. In the 1930s a series of dams was built on the river, creating reservoirs at Lac qui Parle Lake and Marsh Lake. In 1941 an area on the south side of the lake became Lac qui Parle State Park. The park is adjoins the Lac qui Parle Wildlife Management Area, which is a haven for thousands of migrating waterfowl.

Lake County

This county, established March 1, 1856, received its name from its being bounded on the southeast by Lake Superior, which the Ojibwe call "Kitchigumi, meaning great water," as spelled by Rev. Joseph A. Gilfillan, or "Gitche Gumee, the Big-Sea-Water," of Longfellow in *The Song of Hiawatha*. Its very early French name, Lac Superieur, used by Father Jacques Marquette, Father Louis Hennepin, and Jean Baptiste Louis Franquelin, denotes its situation as the highest in the series of five great lakes tributary to the St. Lawrence River, which are named collectively the Laurentian lakes. This largest body of fresh water in the world by surface area has a mean level 602 feet above the sea and a maximum depth of 1,026 feet.

Information of origins and meanings of the geographic names was gathered from John P. Paulson, county auditor, and A. E. Holliday, assistant superintendent of the Duluth and Iron Range Railroad, each being interviewed during a visit at Two Harbors, the county seat, in August 1916.

ALGER a railroad station and junction in section 23 of Two Harbors Township, was named for Hon. Russell A. Alger, senior member of a lumbering firm in Saginaw, Mich., formerly owning much pine timber in this county and large sawmills in Duluth. He was born in Medina County, Ohio, February 27, 1836; served in the Union army during the Civil War and was brevetted major general in 1865; was governor of Michigan, 1885–87; was secretary of war, 1897–99, and U.S. senator from Michigan, 1902–7; and died in Washington, D.C., January 24, 1907.

AVERY a post office, 1899–1902; location not found.

BAPTISM a village in t. 56n, r. 7w, on the Baptism River.

BEAVER a station of the Duluth and Northern Minnesota Railroad in Silver Creek Township (t. 55n, r. 9w), section 18.

BEAVER BAY TOWNSHIP the first organized in this county, before 1885, received its name from Beaver Bay village, platted by Thomas Clark, on the west side of the small bay bearing this name, where the Beaver River flows into Lake Superior. The Ojibwe name of this bay is noted by Gilfillan and Chrysostom Verwyst alike, "Ga-gijikensikag, the place of little cedars." The city in section 12 was platted on June 24, 1856, the day that 25 immigrants arrived to settle, and became the first permanent settlement in the county; its post office began in 1856, the year the Wieland brothers started their sawmill operation. The county government was organized in 1866, naming this community the county seat until it was moved to Two Harbors in 1886. Fishing developed in the 1890s, the last load of logs was shipped out in 1910, and mining development became the main industry. The city was incorporated August 13, 1953. The township split in 1981, creating Stony River Township, which see.

BRITTON a railroad station of the Duluth and Iron

Range Railroad in Two Harbors Township (T. 54N, R. 11W), section 4, was named for a superintendent of logging in its vicinity.

BRULE RIVER a post office, 1870–73; location not found.

BUCHANAN a platted townsite in T. 52N, R. 11W of 1856 on the west side of the Knife River; site of an early U.S. land office and named for President James Buchanan.

BURLINGTON see TWO HARBORS.

BUTTERFLY LAKE a settlement in section 16 of Two Harbors Township (T. 61N, R. 9W), on Butterfly Lake.

CASTLE DANGER a lakeshore village in section 33 of Silver Creek Township, was settled in 1890 by three Norwegian fishermen, although the land was owned by lumber companies. The origin of its name has several stories, among them that it was for the cliffs along the shore resembling a castle or for a boat named *Castle* that ran aground here.

CLARK/CLARK'S CROSSING see SILVER CREEK.

CRAMER TOWNSHIP organized July 14, 1913, and its railway village, were named in honor of J. N. Cramer, a homesteader and later a merchant in the village, who removed to Pennsylvania. The township (T. 57–62N, R. 6W) dissolved in 1950 and became the Unorganized Territory of East Lake. The village in section 9 had a post office, which was first named Silver, 1908–11, then Cramer, 1911–17; it had a station of the Duluth and Northern Minnesota Railroad.

CRYSTAL BAY TOWNSHIP organized April 26, 1904, received this name from a very little bay of Lake Superior, having such crystalline rocks as were formerly worked at two localities farther southwest on the lakeshore in this county to supply emery, a variety of corundum, used for grinding and polishing.

The village of Crystal Bay in T. 56N, R. 7W (Beaver Bay) was developed by Minnesota Mining and Manufacturing Company when it purchased acreage in 1902 for mining corundum to use in producing sandpaper, selling the property in 1916; 40 acres were eventually incorporated into what is now Tettegouche State Park, and 40 acres developed as Illgen City.

CYR a station of the Duluth and Northern Minnesota Railroad in section 2 of T. 55N, R. 8W (Beaver Bay).

DARBY/DARBY JUNCTION a station of the Duluth, Missabe and Iron Range Railroad in section 8 of T. 56N, R. 10W (Silver Lake).

DELLACROSS a post office, 1918, 16 miles northeast of Two Harbors.

DRUMMOND a village in T. 54N, R. 11W (Two Harbors), section 17, with a post office, 1901–18, and a station of the Duluth, Missabe and Iron Range Railroad; it was named for the owner of nearby logging camps.

EAST BEAVER BAY a settlement near Beaver Bay, on Lake Superior.

EAST LAKE, UNORGANIZED TERRITORY OF see CRAMER TOWNSHIP.

EMETTA see WALES.

ENCAMPMENT ISLAND a fishing station in T. 54N, R. 11W, incorporated as a village on May 23, 1857; no trace remains.

FALL LAKE TOWNSHIP organized April 4, 1899, comprising the northern quarter of this county (T. 63–66N, R. 6–11W), received its name from Fall Lake, in the southwest part of the township. The Ojibwe apply the name Kawasachong to this lake, meaning mist or foam lake, referring to the mist and spray rising from rapids and falls of the Kawishiwi River, which descends about 70 feet in a short distance between Garden Lake and Fall Lake. This aboriginal name of the falls and lake, noted by Prof. N. H. Winchell (*Geology of Minnesota*, vol. 4, p. 408), is in origin and meaning like the French and English names of Rainy Lake and River, and in form it is somewhat like Koochiching, their Cree and Ojibwe name. The village of Fall Lake is in section 19 of T. 63N, R. 11W.

FINLAND a village in section 20 of Crystal Bay Township (T. 57N, R. 7W), was developed primarily by Finnish immigrants, who began coming to the area about 1895, although the place name was not noted until about 1911. The Alger-Smith logging railroad extended through the community in 1907; its post office began in 1915; it was the site of a CCC camp, 1933–38, and an Air Force station, 1950–80. The Duluth and Northern Minnesota Railroad station was in section 17.

FOREST CENTER a post office, 1950–65, located in Boundary Waters Canoe Area Wilderness; it had a station of the Duluth, Missabe and Iron Range Railroad.

GAKADINA see MARCY.

GOOSEBERRY a station of the Duluth and Northern Minnesota Railroad in section 9 of T. 54N, R. 10W (Silver Creek).

GREENWOOD a station of the Duluth, Missabe and Iron Range Railroad in section 21 of T. 57N, R. 10W (Silver Creek).

GUSTAFSON HILL a land elevation, 1,339 feet, about halfway between Two Harbors and Silver Bay and about five miles inland from Lake Superior, was named for Johannes Olof Gustafson, a Swedish laborer, carpenter, and road construction worker, born in 1856; Gustafson homesteaded in 1899 on the site but logged the area instead of farming, selling the property in 1908; he died on September 12, 1911, in Two Harbors; the site later reverted to the state.

HAWLETT a station of the Duluth and Iron Range Railroad in section 26 of T. 54N, R. 11W (Waldo).

HIGGINS a station of the Duluth and Northern Minnesota Railroad in section 20 of Two Harbors Township (T. 53N, R. 11W), was named for a former owner of an adjacent tract of pine timber.

HIGHLAND a Duluth and Iron Range Railroad station, is near the highest land crossed between Lake Superior and the Cloquet River.

ILGEN/ILLGEN CITY a village in section 11 of T. 56N, R. 7W (Beaver Bay Township) named for the Rudolph Ilgen family, who settled the area in 1924 after coming from Des Moines, Iowa, purchased 40 acres from the Minnesota Mining and Manufacturing Company, and put up a sawmill, a store, a hotel, and cabins.

ISABELLA the "highest" community in the state, being located in section 4 of T. 59N, R. 8W (Stony River Township) on the Laurentian Divide 200 feet above sea level; an isolated community begun about 1906, its post office opened in 1912, becoming a rural branch in 1965.

JAY SEE LANDING a locality in section 4 of T. 58N, R. 9W (Waldo), in the Finland State Forest; also seen as J C Landing and Jaysee, incorrectly; named for the J. C. Campbell Lumber Company, which had logging operations at the site.

JOHNSON a station of the Duluth and Northern Minnesota Railroad in section 17 of T. 57N, R. 6W (Cramer).

JORDAN a place name, possibly near Jordan Lake in T. 64N, R. 8W (Fall Lake) in the Superior National Forest.

KENT site of a CCC camp in Crystal Bay Township.

KNIFE RIVER a railroad village in T. 52N, R. 11W (Two Harbors), section 31, platted in 1899 following the building of the Alger-Smith Lumber Company's railroad in 1898; it is at the mouth of the river of this name, which is translated from Mokomani zibi of the Ojibwe. It had a number of businesses with fishing a prime industry; its post office began as Mellie in 1899, changing to Knife River in 1903; it was incorporated October 2, 1909.

LARSMONT a village in T. 52N, R. 11W (Two Harbors), section 16, was once the site of major logging operations in the 1880s and 1890s. The name dates to 1914 and was coined by Gust Mattson, a native of Larsmo, Finland, and one of the earliest settlers of the place, from Larsmo and *nt* from the English words *mount* and *mountain*; the majority of settlers were from Larsmo, although Norwegians and Swedes also came to the area. Fishing, farming, and railroading were main occupations; it had a station of the Duluth and Iron Range Railroad. Its post office began in 1915, changing to a rural branch in 1966. Much of the area was destroyed in a forest fire in 1926.

LAUREN a station of the Duluth and Iron Range Railroad in T. 54N, R. 11W (Waldo), section 2.

LAX LAKE a village in section 11 of T. 56N, R. 8W (Beaver Bay Township), with a post office, 1913–15, was named for the Johannas Waxlax family, Swedish immigrants who came in 1896 and acquired the first homestead; Johannas was killed in a train accident in 1910. The community developed about 1907 when the Alger-Smith Lumber Company's Duluth and Northern Minnesota Railroad reached the area; after the logging was done, the community became largely residential and later a resort area.

LENNOX a station of the Duluth and Northern Minnesota Railroad in section 9 of T. 55N, R. 9W (Silver Creek).

LITTLE MARAIS a village in section 20 of Cramer Township (T. 57N, R. 6W), was named by the early French voyageurs for its little marsh, in contrast with the larger marsh of Grand Marais in Cook County. Scandinavian fishermen first settled the area in the late 1880s, and the community developed following establishment of the post office in Benjamin Fenstad's home in 1905; he came in 1890 with his family (seven sons and two daughters); his home was later rebuilt into a hotel, and the first school began in his home; he died in 1932 and his wife, Serine, in 1945. The Fenstad sons had a fish company, took over the hotel, built cabins, a filling station, and a store, and established the telephone company. The post office became a rural branch in 1964.

LONDON a village in section 35 of T. 55N, R. 10W (Silver Creek) with a station of the Duluth and Northern Minnesota Railroad.

MALMOTA/MARMATA a village in T. 53N, R. 10W, on the Kinewabic River, 38 miles north of Duluth; incorporated on August 2, 1858; no trace remains.

MANITOU JUNCTION a locality in section 30 of T. 59N, R. 7W (Crystal Bay).

MAPLE a place name; location not found.

MARCH see MARCY.

MARCY a village in section 34 of T. 55N, R. 11W (Two Harbors), which had a station of the Duluth and Iron Range Railroad and a post office named Marcy, 1899–1940; also known as Gakadina and March.

MARMATA see MALMOTA.

McNAIR a station on the Duluth and Iron Range Railroad in section 24 of T. 56N, R. 11W (Waldo).

MELLEN a post office, 1907; location not found.

MELLIE see KNIFE RIVER.

MURPHY CITY a village located between Hoyt Lakes and Taconite Harbor, developed in 1954 by Arthur L. Porter as a residential area for employees of the Erie Mining Company and completed in 1957.

NIGGER HILL a village in section 24 of T. 60N, R. 6W (Cramer) with a station of the Duluth and Northern Minnesota Railroad, was named for the engine, called nigger, used for hoisting materials.

NORSHOR JUNCTION a station of the Duluth and Iron Range Railroad; location not found.

NORTH BRANCH a station of the Duluth and Northern Minnesota Railroad in section 8 of T. 55N, R. 9W (Silver Creek).

PALISADE a post office, 1892–96; location not found.

PIGEON RIVER a post office, 1867–77, in T. 56N, R. 7W (Beaver Bay), Finland State Forest.

PORK BAY a village in T. 58N, R. 6W (Cramer).

PRAIRIE PORTAGE a village in section 2 of T. 64N, R. 9W (Fall Lake), near the site of a portage of that name in section 1.

RAPER a post office, was authorized on January 27, 1897, with Charles S. Reeves to be postmaster, and again on December 18, 1897, with

Pascal J. Rosso to be postmaster, but neither was established; location not found.

SAWBILL LANDING a village with a post office, 1954–63, and rural branch, 1963–65, and a station of the Duluth, Missabe and Iron Range Railroad; location not found.

SCOTT JUNCTION a station of the Duluth and Iron Range Railroad in T. 57N, R. 10W (Silver Creek), section 21.

SECTION THIRTY a village in T. 63N, R. 11W (Fall Lake), was developed as a residential community for miners of the Merritt Mining Company at the Section 30 Mine, with boardinghouses, private homes, dormitories, and company houses, a general store, and a school. Its post office began as Sellwood, 1906–8, reestablished as Section Thirty, 1910–33; it had a station on the Duluth, Missabe and Northern Railway.

SELLWOOD see SECTION THIRTY.

SILVER see CRAMER.

SILVER BAY a city in T. 56N, R. 7W (Beaver Bay Township), was incorporated as a village on October 19, 1956; its post office began in 1954 in the home of the postmaster, Faith Erickson. Fishermen were at the site in the early 1900s, but officially the city developed when Reserve Mining Company built its plant in 1951 and platted the townsite in 1952. There are several accounts of the name's origin, the most common being that the captain of the *America* needed a name for the shipping point at the site about 1903 and suggested the name for the bay, the city taking its name from the bay.

SILVER CREEK TOWNSHIP organized May 3, 1905, received the name of a creek flowing into Lake Superior four miles northeast of Two Harbors, translated from the Ojibwe name. The village in section 34 (T. 54N, R. 10W) was begun about 1890 by Henry Clark at what was known first as Clark or Clark's Crossing in section 10, which had a station of the Duluth and Northern Minnesota Railroad in section 21.

SILVER RAPIDS a village in section 32 of T. 63N, R. 11W (Fall Lake), one mile north of White Iron.

SPLITROCK a small settlement and logging campsite at the mouth of Split Rock River and the terminus of the Split Rock and Northern Railway, was begun in 1899 with a wharf for removal of timber by the Split Rock Lumber Company, owner and controller of the harbor, the railroad, the coal dock, and the store, which held the post office during its operation, 1900–5; almost all traces of the site were gone by 1906.

STANLEY a station of the Duluth and Northern Minnesota Railroad in section 7 of T. 52N, R. 11W (Two Harbors).

STEWART a station of the Duluth and Northern Minnesota Railroad in section 11 of T. 53N, R. 11W (Waldo).

STONY RIVER TOWNSHIP T. 59N, R. 8W, organized in 1981; formerly part of Beaver Bay Township.

TOIMI a village in section 20 of T. 57N, R. 11W (Two Harbors).

TWO HARBORS TOWNSHIP organized February 20, 1894, was named after the lake port of the Duluth and Iron Range Railroad, bearing the same name. It formerly included T. 52–62N, R. 11W and T. 60–62N, R. 9–10W; it divided in 1950, T. 57–62N, R. 11W, and T. 60–62N, R. 9–10W becoming part of Unorganized Territory of West Lake; the rest remained as the Unorganized Territory of Two Harbors, which also absorbed part of Waldo Township, T. 53–57N, R. 11W.

The city of Two Harbors is the county seat and a major shipping point for iron ore on Lake Superior; it lies on two little bays, natural harbors, named Agate and Burlington Bays, the ore docks being on the western Agate Bay. Beach sand and gravel here contain frequent pebbles of banded chalcedony called agate. The city was platted in 1885 as Agate Bay, although its post office was known as Two Harbors when established in 1883; it was incorporated as a village March 9, 1888, and as a city February 26, 1907. The townsite of Burlington at Burlington Bay was platted in 1856, first incorporated on May 23, 1857, and later incorporated with Agate Bay as Two Harbors; Burlington had a post office, 1856–62. The first shipment of ore arrived from the Soudan Mine on July 31, 1884. It is the site of the *Edna G.*, a tugboat owned by the Duluth, Missabe and Iron Range Railroad, built in 1896 and named for Edna Greatsinger, daughter of Jacob Greatsinger, president of the railroad; the tug was placed on the National Register of Historic Places in 1975 as the only steam-powered tug operating on a Great Lake. Segog, named for developer Ray F. Segog, is one of several additions to the city.

UNORGANIZED TERRITORY OF EAST LAKE see CRAMER.

UNORGANIZED TERRITORY OF TWO HARBORS see TWO HARBORS.

UNORGANIZED TERRITORY OF WEST LAKE see TWO HARBORS, WALDO.

WALDO TOWNSHIP (T. 53–59N, R. 9–11W), organized August 3, 1909, took its name from an earlier Duluth and Iron Range Railroad station. This is also the name of a county in Maine, and of villages and townships in nine other states. A station of the Duluth, Missabe and Northern Railroad was in section 23. In 1950 it split, T. 53–57N, R. 11W being transferred to the Unorganized Territory of Two Harbors and T. 58–59N, R. 9–10W to the Unorganized Territory of West Lake.

WALES a village in section 21 of T. 55N, R. 11W (Two Harbors), which had a station of the Duluth, Missabe and Iron Range Railroad, and a post office named Emetta, 1919–23, changing to Wales, 1923–65.

WANLESS a station of the Duluth and Northern Minnesota Railroad in section 35 of T. 60N, R. 6W (Cramer).

WATERVILLE a village in T. 54N, R. 9W at the mouth of the Split Rock River, noted on an 1858 map.

WELCH a station of the Duluth, Missabe and Iron Range Railroad in section 3 of T. 55N, R. 11W (Two Harbors).

WEST LAKE, UNORGANIZED TERRITORY OF see TWO HARBORS, WALDO.

WHITE IRON a locality in section 31 of T. 63N, R. 11W (Fall Lake), which had a resort on the north end of White Iron Lake.

WHYTE a station on the Duluth and Iron Range Railroad in section 1 of T. 57N, R. 10W (Silver Creek).

YORK a station of the Duluth, Missabe and Iron Range Railroad in section 35 of T. 54N, R. 11W (Waldo).

Lakes and Streams

Much aid for the following pages has been received from the descriptions and maps of the Minnesota Geological Survey, which in the fourth volume of its *Final Report* has a long chapter on Lake County and three other chapters on its parts of the Vermilion and Mesabi Iron Ranges.

The coast of Lake Superior in this county has the following islands, points, bays, and tributary streams bearing names, in their order from southwest to northeast: Knife Island and Granite Point, near the mouth of Knife River; Agate and Burlington Bays, before mentioned, at Two Harbors; Burlington Point, at the east side of the latter bay, which received its name from a townsite platted on its shore in 1856; Flood Bay, named for a man who took a land claim there in the same year; Stewart River, where likewise in 1856 John Stewart and others took claims; Silver Creek, which gave its name to a township; Encampment River and an island of this name, about a mile and a half farther east, named in Joseph G. Norwood's geological report, as assistant with David D. Owen, published in 1852; Gooseberry River, a name given on the map of Maj. Stephen H. Long's expedition in 1823, noted by Gilfillan as a translation of the Ojibwe name (and identified by others as an anglicization of Groseilliers, for the explorer Médard Chouart, sieur des Groseilliers, whose name appears a river on a 1760 French map of the area); Split Rock River and Point, named from the rock gorge of the stream near its mouth (a name that appears on a lake survey map as early as 1825); Two Harbor Bay (not to be confounded with the bays at the city of Two Harbors); Beaver River and Bay, whence the village and township of Beaver Bay are named; the Great Palisades, turretlike rock cliffs, rising vertically 200 to 300 feet at the lakeshore; Baptism River, named Baptist River on Long's map; Cathedral Bay, bordered by rock towers and pinnacles; Crystal Bay, source of the name of a township; an unnamed bay and point at Little Marais; Manitou River, retaining its Ojibwe name, which means a spirit; and Pork Bay, in notable contrast with the grandeur and awe of some of the preceding names.

Lakes tributary to Lake Superior include Stewart Lake and Twin Lakes, sources of Stewart River; Highland Lake, west of Highland station; Thomas, Christensen, Amberger, Clark, Kane, and Spruce Lakes, mostly named for cruisers selecting tracts of timber or for lumbermen in charge of logging camps; Bear Lake, three miles northwest of Beaver Bay; Lax Lake (formerly called Schaff's Lake), for which a railroad station is named, as before noted; Nicado, Micmac, and Nipissiquit Lakes, having aboriginal names; Moose, Nine Mile, and Echo Lakes, outflowing south to Manitou River; Long Lake, Shoepack,

Crooked, Artlip, and East Lakes; and, farther north, Harriet Lake, Wilson Lake and Little Wilson Lake, Windy Lake, Elbow, Lost, and Frear Lakes, the last three being crossed by the east line of the county.

Many of the lakes and waterways in the northern part of the county are included in the Boundary Waters Canoe Area Wilderness, for which see Cook County. On the north, the basin of Rainy Lake comprises about three-fifths of Lake County. Its chief streams, sending their waters to the series of lakes on the international boundary, are Isabella River, Stony and Birch Rivers, and Kawishiwi River. The last is an Ojibwe name, meaning, as defined by Gilfillan, "the river full of beavers' houses, or, according to some, muskrats' houses also."

The abundant lakes of this northern district include Bellissima, or Island, Lake, Parent and Syenite Lakes, Lake Isabella, Gull, Bald Eagle, and Gabbro Lakes, the last being named from the rock formation of its shores; Copeland's Lake, Clearwater, Pickerel, and Friday Lakes; Greenwood Lake, named for George C. Greenwood, who was a hardware merchant in Duluth, often called West Greenwood Lake, in distinction from a lake of this name in Cook County; Sand, Slate, Birch, White Iron, Farm, and Garden Lakes, the last two noting that the Ojibwe had cultivated ground adjoining them; Fall Lake, called Kawasachong Lake by the Ojibwe, noticed on a preceding page for the township named from it; Boulder Lake, Lake Polly, Lake Alice, and Wilder Lake; Fraser and Thomas Lakes, named for John Fraser and Maurice Thomas, who selected timber lands and engaged in lumbering near these lakes; Gabimichigama and Agamok Lakes, each extending into Cook County; Ogishke Muncie Lake, somewhat changed from its Ojibwe name, meaning "a kingfisher," spelled *ogishkimanissi* by Frederic Baraga's *Dictionary*; Cacaquabic, or Kekequabic, Lake, translated by Gilfillan as "Hawk-iron lake"; Marble Lake, Cherry, Currant, Doughnut, Spoon, Pickle, and Plum Lakes; Lake Vira and Ima Lake, the latter named in honor of the eldest daughter of Prof. N. H. Winchell, the state geologist; Illusion Lake, Jordan, Alworth, Disappointment, and Round Lakes; Ensign Lake, named in honor of Josiah D. Ensign of Duluth, judge in this district, 1889–1920; Snowbank Lake, a translation of its

Ojibwe name, which means, as Gilfillan defined it, "snow blown up in heaps lying about here and there"; Newfound Lake, Moose, Jasper, Northwestern, and Crab Lakes; Manomin Lake, meaning "wild rice"; Wood or Wind Lake, Pine, Sucker, Oak Point, and Saturday Lakes; Triangle and Urn Lakes, whose names were suggested by their outlines; Newton Lake, named by Dr. Alexander Winchell in honor of his brother, Newton H. Winchell; and, near the northwest corner of the county, Horse Lake and Jackfish Lake.

Snowbank Lake has Boot and Birch Islands, the first being named for its shape; and a small lake between Ensign and Snowbank Lakes is for a like reason named Boot Lake.

During the examination of this region for the Minnesota Geological Survey, much care was taken to secure correctly the Ojibwe names of the streams and lakes. Their translations were commonly used in that survey, as also by the earlier explorers and fur traders, government surveyors, and lumbermen. But nearly all the lakes of relatively small size lacked aboriginal names, and in many instances remained unnamed. The need for definite description and location of geologic observations led frequently to arbitrary adoption of names, where none before existing could be ascertained. For example, Dr. Alexander Winchell in 1886 gave to six little lakes on the canoe route between Kekequabic and Ogishke Muncie Lakes, occurring within that distance of less than two miles, the names of the first six letters of the Greek alphabet, the series being Alpha, Beta, Gamma, Delta, Epsilon, and Zeta Lakes. When farmers and other permanent settlers come, new names will doubtless replace some that have been thus used or proposed without local or historical significance.

The lakes on the north side of this county were surveyed and mapped, with full details of their shores and islands, by David Thompson in 1822–23, for determination of the course of the international boundary, following a canoe route that had been long used by the fur traders. An excellent description of this route, from Grand Portage to the Lake of the Woods, was published in 1801 by Sir Alexander Mackenzie in his *General History of the Fur Trade from Canada to the Northwest.*

Cypress, or Otter Track, Lake is the most east-ern in this series bordering Lake County. Its first name, used by Thompson, refers to its plentiful cypress trees, now commonly called arbor vitae or white cedar. Otter Track is for the Ojibwe name, noted by Gilfillan, "Nigig-bimi-kawed sagaiigun, the lake where the otter make tracks, from four tracks of an otter on the rocks by the side of the lake, as if he had jumped four times there." More probably, however, the name alludes to peculiar slides where otters took amusement by sliding into the water from a bank of snow or rock or mud, as described in Clarence L. Herrick's *Mammals of Minnesota* (pp. 129–35).

Next westward is Knife Lake, having several branches or arms, translated from Mokomani sagaiigun of the Ojibwe. Prof. N. H. Winchell in 1880 wrote of their reason for this name, derived from an adjoining rock formation, "a blue-black, fine-grained siliceous rock, approaching flint in hardness and compactness, with conchoidal fracture and sharp edges; sometimes it is nearly black. It is this sharp-edged rock that gave name to Knife lake. It is only local, or in beds, or sometimes in ridges."

The outlet of Knife Lake flows through three little lakes, which Dr. Alexander Winchell named in 1886, from east to west, Potato, Seed, and Melon Lakes. Next are Carp Lake (also called Pseudo-Messer Lake) and Birch, or Sucker, Lake, named for their fish and trees, succeeded westward by the large and much branched Basswood Lake, on the northern limit of the geographic range of this tree, which was generally common throughout Minnesota and was abundant in the Big Woods.

For the last of these lakes Mackenzie used the French name of the basswood, Lac Bois Blanc (white wood), adding, "but I think improperly so called, as the natives name it the Lake Pascau Minac, or Dry Berries." This Ojibwe name was spelled *Bassimenan* by Prof. N. H. Winchell, and *Bassemenani* by Gilfillan, whose translation of it is "Dried blueberry lake." Although the first syllable may have suggested the English name Basswood, which is a translation from that given by the early French voyageurs, the Ojibwe had no reference to the tree but only to their gathering and drying berries here for winter use.

Adjoining the northwest part of Lake County, the river flowing from Basswood Lake along the boundary enters Crooked Lake, translated from its old French name, with reference to its very irregularly crooking and branching outlines.

Hunter Island

Joseph N. Nicollet's map, published in 1843, shows a more northern route of canoe travel from Saganaga Lake west to Lac la Croix, which follows the stream and series of lakes outflowing from Saganaga, whereas the international boundary crosses a water divide between Saganaga and Cypress, or Otter Track, Lake, thence passing westward along a continuous stream and its lakes. The tract between that northern route of water flow and the southern or boundary route, bordering the north side of Lake County, is named Hunter's Island by Nicollet's map and Hunter Island by later maps. It is estimated by Dr. U. S. Grant to have an area of about 800 square miles (MHS Collections 8: 1–10 [1898]).

Greenwood Mountain and Other Hills

This county is traversed from southwest to northeast by the continuations of the Vermilion and Mesabi Iron Ranges, belts of rock formations more fully noticed in the chapter for St. Louis County, where they contain vast deposits of iron ores. These belts are not marked by ridges or hills along large parts of their course, and they nowhere attain heights worthy to be called mountains.

The general highland rises about 1,000 feet above Lake Superior, or 1,600 feet above the sea, within eight or ten miles north from the lakeshore. Onward this average height, much diversified by valleys, low ridges, and hills, reaches nearly to the international boundary, on which Otter Track and Crooked Lakes are respectively 1,387 feet and 1,245 feet above the sea. Names have been given to only a few of the highest hills. Though these vary in their altitude to about 500 feet above the adjoining lowlands and lakes, they are unduly dignified by being called mountains and peaks.

Greenwood Mountain is only 145 feet above the lake of this name at its north side.

Disappointment Hill, a mile east of the lake so named, has a height of 350 feet above it.

Mallmann's Peak, named for John Mallmann, employed by the Minnesota Geological Survey,

situated close north of the east end of Kekequabic Lake, rises steeply to the height of 230 feet.

About two miles southeast from the last are the Twin Peaks, and nearly two miles farther east is Mount Northrop, named in honor of Cyrus Northrop, president of the University of Minnesota, 1884–1911, attaining altitudes about 2,000 feet above the sea, or 500 feet above Kekequabic Lake.

Superior National Forest

A great part of the north half of Lake County is included in this National Forest, which also comprises considerable areas in Cook and St. Louis Counties. The date of its establishment in 1909 and the steps taken by an act of Congress and by a special recommendation from Minnesota, leading to the designation of these lands as a public reservation for forestry uses, have been noted in the chapter for Cook County.

Glacial Lake Elftman

When the continental ice sheet of the glacial period was finally melting away from this area, its northwardly receding border held temporarily an ice-dammed lake in the basin of Kawishiwi River, with outflow southward and westward. This ancient lake, first described by Arthur H. Elftman, an assistant of the Minnesota Geological Survey, was named in his honor by Prof. N. H. Winchell in the *Bulletin of the Geological Society of America* (vol. 12, 1901, p. 125). "It had an area of about 100 square miles at the time of its greatest extent and an elevation of about 1,700 feet above the sea."

State Parks

The land for Gooseberry Falls State Park, the first park to be established on the North Shore, was acquired in 1933 by the state as part of the expansion of Highway 61 and because of its exceptionally high scenic value and recreational potential, which the highway would make accessible. The Civilian Conservation Corps began building trails, campgrounds, and structures in 1934; the park was formally incorporated into the system in 1937. It features the waterfalls along the lower Gooseberry River, which drops more than a hundred feet over bedrock formed by lava flows.

George H. Crosby, a mining magnate who was active in the development of the Mesabi and Cuyuna Iron Ranges, donated the land on the Manitou River to the state to be used for George H. Crosby–Manitou State Park. Established in 1955, it was formally opened in 1971. It has been designed primarily for use by backpackers.

When Split Rock Lighthouse State Park was established in 1967, its lands surrounded one of the most photographed lighthouses in the United States. The lighthouse, built after a November gale sank six ships within twelve miles of the river, operated from 1909 to 1969; two years later the federal government gave the property to the state as a historic site. The Minnesota Historical Society has operated the lighthouse since 1976.

Tettegouche State Park was created in 1979 when, with the help of the Nature Conservancy, the state purchased the former lands of the Tettegouche Club, a hunting club begun by Duluth businessmen in 1910 and owned privately after 1921. That property was combined with the undeveloped Baptism River State Park, established in 1945. The park's name is said to mean "retreat." The seven-square-mile area contains Mount Baldy, the highest point in the state at 1,620 feet; Lakes Micmac, Tettegouche, Nipissiquit, and Nicado; and Lindstrom and Nicado Creeks. With rugged mountains and magnificent views, it has been called the "crown jewel" of the state park system.

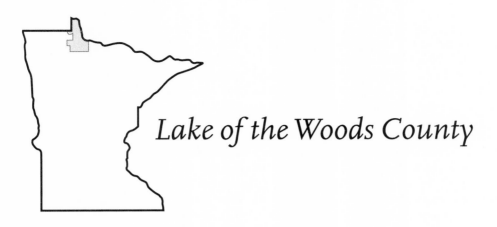

Lake of the Woods County

Lake of the Woods County separated from Beltrami County in 1922. All post offices established before 1922 were therefore created while part of Beltrami County. All townships dissolved in 1960, but old names are noted as locations here; former unnamed townships were given letters of the alphabet, A to H, and Angle was divided into ten townships, noted in the entry for Northwest Angle. Scattered parcels of land within the county are part of Red Lake Reservation, for which see Beltrami County.

AMERICAN POINT see **PENASSE ISLAND.**

ANGLE INLET a post office in T. 168N, R. 34W (Angle 2) since 1936, located on the west bank of the Pine River; the site grew at a location where travelers left the steamboats from Fort Frances to board stagecoaches for their overland journey to Winnipeg.

ANGLE TOWNSHIP received this name from its being bounded on the north by the inlet (about 10 miles long) of the Lake of the Woods leading to its Northwest Angle, or "most northwestern point," as it was described by the treaty of 1783 and by later treaties defining the boundary between the United States and Canada. The area thus named Angle comprises about 120 square miles, bounded by the lake on the south, east, and north. Excepting Alaska, it is the most northern tract of the United States, lying between 10 and 26 miles north of the 49th parallel.

ARNESEN (also **ARNESSEN**), a fishing village on the shore of the Lake of the Woods, in Lakewood Township, section 5, formerly known as Rocky Point, was founded by Bernard A. Arnesen, who settled there in 1897. The village had a post office, 1903–23, with Arnesen as postmaster; it had a station on the Canadian National Railroad.

BANKTON a post office, 1915–32, of Meadowland Township, sections 27, 28, and 30, with a station on the Canadian National Railroad.

BAUDETTE a city and the county seat, located in Spooner and Baudette Townships (T. 161N, R. 31W), was incorporated as a village in 1907; it merged with Spooner in 1954. The city began as a steamboat landing and lumber town with a sawmill, following the railroad coming through in 1901; it was named for Joseph Baudette, a trapper who had been in the area since the early 1880s. The first family was the Cathcarts in 1893, Thomas Cathcart having worked in the area in 1891. The post office began in 1900 as Port Hyland, with Daniel Hyland as postmaster, changing to Baudette in 1901; it had a station of the Minnesota and Manitoba Railroad (Canadian National).

BEAVER DAM TOWNSHIP (T. 159N, R. 36W).

BIRCH BEACH a village in Prosper Township on the Lake of the Woods lake front.

BLAISE a post office of 1920, established and discontinued while part of Beltrami County; location not found.

BOONE TOWNSHIP (T. 159N, R. 31W).

CARP a village in section 17 of Swift Water Township, was named by a lumber camp cook who saw suckers running up the Rapid River and mistakenly called them carp. The village developed when the railroad came through; its post office operated 1912–33.

CEDAR SPUR a post office, 1909–17, established and discontinued while part of Beltrami County, located in section 21 of McDougald Township; it had a station of the Northern Pacific Railroad.

CHILGREN TOWNSHIP (T. 162N, R. 34W) was named for Albert Chilgren, of Swedish descent, who was a farmer and lawyer there.

CLEMENTSON a small village on Rainy River at the mouth of Rapid River in section 12 of Gudrid Township, was named for Helec Clementson, owner of a sawmill there, formerly a county commissioner, who came in May 1896. A post office was established in 1901, with Ole Clementson as postmaster, changing to a rural branch in 1964.

CLOVER POINT a post office in Lakewood Township, first named Concord, 1914–15, with Agnes McGuire, postmaster; then named Dutchie, 1915–22, with McGuire continuing as postmaster; and finally named Clover Point in 1922, with Edward W. Collins, postmaster.

CLOVERDALE TOWNSHIP (T. 159N, R. 34W).

CONCORD see CLOVER POINT.

DRIFTWOOD POINT a locality in T. 166N, R. 33W (Angle 9).

DUTCHIE see CLOVER POINT.

EAST GRACETON see GRACETON.

ENGLERVILLE a village located one mile south of Baudette on the river, which grew around the Engler Mill and existed about 1909–19.

EUGENE TOWNSHIP (T. 160N, R. 34W) was named probably for Eugene V. Debs, of Indiana, candidate of the Socialist Party for president of the United States in 1904, 1908, and 1912.

FAUNCE a village in section 18 of Cloverdale Township, which had a post office, 1917–38.

FORT SAINT CHARLES a fort built in 1732 by Pierre Gaultier de Varennes, sieur de la Vérendrye, as an exploration center and abandoned in 1793; the Minnesota Fourth Degree Knights of Columbus have reconstructed the site.

GRACETON a village in section 23 of McDougald Township, which has had a post office since 1905, changing to a rural branch in 1973; it had a station

on the Canadian National Railroad, with another station called East Graceton in section 25.

GUDRID TOWNSHIP (T. 160N, R. 30W) has a Norwegian feminine name, probably for the wife of an immigrant homesteader.

HACKETT a village in section 36 of Wheeler Township, near the Rainy River, with a post office, 1905–23, John L. Hackett, postmaster; it had a station on the Canadian National Railroad.

HIWOOD TOWNSHIP (T. 160N, R. 36W) had a post office, 1919–36, located in section 32.

INTERNATIONAL BOUNDARY a station of the Canadian National Railroad; location not found.

JACOBS a place name on a 1980 map, located in Zippel Township.

KEIL TOWNSHIP (T. 157N, R. 31W) was probably named for a German settler.

KNUTSON a post office in Keil Township, 1908–09, with Con Knutson, postmaster.

LAKEWOOD TOWNSHIP (T. 163N, R. 34W) was named for its timber and for its situation on the south shore of the Lake of the Woods.

LE CLAIRE a small village notable as the first truly American settlement in the county, was the site of the first post office, 1898–1902, and customs house in the county; it grew around two fisheries at Oak Point, at the east end of Curry's Island at Four Mile Bay; see also PENASSE ISLAND.

LONG POINT a village in sections 35 and 36 of Lakewood Township, on Long Point peninsula; the first settlers were the Asmus family in 1890.

LOVEDALE a post office, 1919–35, of Pioneer Township, section 15, with Sophia A. Love, postmaster.

LUDE a post office, 1904–34, with Alexander Lude as postmaster, located in Prosper Township, section 8.

McDOUGALD TOWNSHIP (T. 161N, R. 33W) was named for John McDougald, a member of the first board of county commissioners, later engaged in real estate business at Black Duck.

MEADOWLAND TOWNSHIP (T. 158N, R. 33W) was named for its grasslands along streams, open areas used for hay making in this generally wooded region.

MORRIS POINT a peninsula located in section 17 of Wheeler Township, which has a small community.

MYHRE TOWNSHIP (T. 161N, R. 34W) was named for L. O. Myhre, of Norwegian descent, a former member of the board of county commissioners, who resided near Bemidji.

NORRIS TOWNSHIP (T. 159N, R. 35W).

NORTHWEST ANGLE was named for its triangular shape and from its position north of the 49th parallel; Angle is 75,000 acres and divided into ten townships: Angle 1: T.168N, R.35W; Angle 2: T.168N, R.34W; Angle 3: T.168N, R.33W; Angle 4: T.167N, R.35W; Angle 5: T.167N, R.34W; Angle 6: T.167N, R.33W; Angle 7: T.166N, R.35W; Angle 8: T.166N, R.34W; Angle 9: T.166N, R.33W; Angle 10: T.166N, R.32W. See also PENASSE ISLAND.

NOYES TOWNSHIP (T. 160N, R. 35W).

OAK ISLAND a village in T. 167N, R. 33W (Angle 6), section 2; the post office was established in 1920, first at Oak Island Trading Post, three-eighths mile west of its present location on the northwest end of Oak Island at the Bay store.

OAK POINT a peninsula in section 7 of Wheeler Township, which has a small community.

OAKS CORNER a place name of Angle Township.

PARK TOWNSHIP (T. 159N, R. 33W).

PENASSE ISLAND a locality in T. 168N, R. 33W (Angle 3) named for Tom Penasse, a local Indian; the post office, established in 1920 on the east bank of the Poplar River, operated until 1969, when it became a rural branch. The community was first located on the east bank of the Poplar River until it was moved in 1929 from the mainland to the island of American Point, where a post office to be named American Point had been authorized on October 23, 1926, with George Arnold to be postmaster, but was not established; it officially became Penasse Island in 1975. See also NORTHWEST ANGLE; LE CLAIRE.

PILGRIM HALL a place name on a 1980 map in T. 158N, R. 34W (Township F).

PIONEER TOWNSHIP (T. 157N, R. 32W) received this name in compliment to its pioneer settlers.

PITT a village in section 35 of Wabanica Township, named for the large gravel pit located nearby; its post office began in 1903; everything but the Minnesota and Manitoba Railroad depot was destroyed in a 1910 fire, and only a few buildings were reconstructed.

PORT HYLAND see BAUDETTE.

POTAMO TOWNSHIP (T. 160N, R. 33W) has the name of a town on the east coast of the island of Corfu, Greece.

PROSPER TOWNSHIP (T. 163N, R. 33W) received this name of good promise in accordance with the petition of its settlers.

RAKO a post office in sections 16 and 21 of Keil Township, 1919–36.

RAPID RIVER TOWNSHIP (T. 159N, R. 30W) was named for the stream crossing it, a tributary of the Rainy River. It was mapped and described by William H. Keating of Maj. Stephen H. Long's expedition in 1823 as the River of Rapids, "so called from the fine rapids which it presents immediately above its mouth."

ROOSEVELT a city with Roseau County.

RULIEN TOWNSHIP (T. 159N, R. 32W) was named for William Rulien, who was engaged in real estate business in Baudette.

SPOONER TOWNSHIP (T. 160N, R. 31W) and its village, on the Rainy River, located across the Baudette River from Baudette, were named for Judge Marshall A. Spooner of Bemidji, who helped obtain the incorporation papers; Spooner was born in Indiana in 1858, came to Minnesota in 1882 and to Bemidji in 1901, served as judge of the 15th district, 1903–8, and died in 1927. The village was incorporated on August 22, 1905, reincorporated on January 17, 1907, and separated from the township, merging with Baudette in 1954. The village was settled in 1905 as a lumber community and station of the Great Northern Railway; its lumber mill, built in 1905, was the industry center until it was destroyed by a fire in 1921. The post office operated 1907–54.

SUGAR POINT a post office, 1911–12, located in T. 167N, R. 33W (Angle 6), sections 17 and 20.

SWIFT WATER TOWNSHIP (T. 158N, R31W) received its name, like Rapid River Township before noted, from the Rapid River flowing through these townships.

VICTORY TOWNSHIP (T. 158N, R. 32W).

WABANICA TOWNSHIP (T. 161N, R. 32W) received its name from *waban*, the Ojibwe word for the east and also for the twilight or dawn of the morning. It had a post office, 1906–14.

WALHALLA TOWNSHIP (T. 160N, R. 32W) is named from Norse mythology, for the hall of Odin, also spelled Valhalla, into which were received the souls of warriors slain in battle.

WHEELER TOWNSHIP (T. 162N, R. 32W), at the west side of the mouth of Rainy River, was named for Alonzo Wheeler, a pioneer farmer there.

WHEELERS POINT a peninsula in section 19 of

Wheeler Township, which has a small community.

WILLIAMS a city in section 18 of McDougald Township and gateway to Zippel Bay State Park, located on the south shore of Lake of the Woods, was incorporated as a village April 1, 1922; it developed with the Minnesota and Manitoba Railroad as a shipping center for timber products and was originally just called "The Siding"; it was named for William Mason and George Williams, who had followed the track roadbed in 1901 to stake claims at the site; its post office began in 1903 with William H. Dure, postmaster.

ZIPPEL TOWNSHIP (T. 162N, R. 33W) was named for William M. Zippel, of German descent, who through many years was a fisherman on the Lake of the Woods, living in this township at the mouth of the creek that was earlier named for him. The aboriginal name of this stream, which continued in use in translated form for several years, was Sand Creek. Zippel first settled at Rat Portage in 1884 and removed three years afterward to the mouth of this creek, where the fishing village bearing his name existed for several years. A post office was in section 11, 1901–34, with Zippel serving as first postmaster. Zippel Bay State Park, created in 1959 to provide public access to Lake of the Woods, was made up of lands in the vicinity of the village that were mostly tax-forfeited.

Townships formerly unnamed noted on the 1992 plat map with letters: Township A: T. 157N, R. 30W; Township B: T. 157N, R. 33W; Township C: T. 157N, R. 34W; Township D: T. 157N, R. 35W; Township E: T. 158N, R. 30W; Township F: T. 158N, R. 34W; Township G: T. 158N, R. 35W; Township H: T. 165N, R. 32W.

Lakes and Streams

The names of the Lake of the Woods and Rainy River have been considered in the first chapter of this work.

David Thompson's map of the international boundary survey from Lake Superior to the Lake of the Woods in 1826 shows the mouths of Rapid River, Riviere Baudette, and Winter Road River flowing into the Rainy River from this county. The first was named, as before noted, for its picturesque rapids or falls, descending about 20 feet, close above its mouth, and the second is thought to be a French personal surname.

The third of these streams received its name, as noted by Nathan Butler of Minneapolis, who during many years was engaged in surveying and land examinations in northern Minnesota, for "a winter road, or dog sled trail, leaving the Rainy River at the mouth of the Winter Road River and running about S. 20° W. fifty miles, to the middle of the north shore of the north Red Lake. The whole distance is one continuous swamp, tamarack and open, except where the streams have cut down into the ground from six to twelve feet below the surface, thus draining the land on either side for forty or fifty rods" (*Geology of Minnesota*, vol. 4, 1899, p. 160).

Winter Road Lake, in Eugene Township, is translated, like this outflowing river, from their Ojibwe name.

Peppermint Creek, tributary to the Winter Road River, is named for its native species of mint, including most notably the wild bergamot (*Monarda fistulosa*).

Points and Islands, Lake of the Woods

The Rainy River enters the Lake of the Woods by flowing through Four Mile Bay, so named for its length from east to west. This bay is separated from the main lake by Oak Point, also four miles long, which is a narrow sandbar bearing many bur oaks, a species that is common or abundant throughout Minnesota excepting far northeastward.

On the Canadian side, opposite Oak Point, a similar wave-built sandbar, or barrier beach, named Sable Island, skirts the original lakeshore for about six miles northeastward. Its French name, if anglicized, would be Sand Island. The geologic origin or formation of Oak Point and Sable Island is the same as that of Minnesota Point and Wisconsin Point, which enclose the harbors of Duluth and Superior.

The sand dunes of this island and of Oak Point caused this large southwest part of the Lake of the Woods to be formerly often called Sand Hill Lake.

From the mouth of Rainy River, at the east end of Oak Point, the international boundary runs nearly due north across the main southern area of the lake, passing close west of Big Island, which belongs to Canada. As it approaches the

Northwest Angle inlet (also called "Angle river"), which has been noted on a preceding page in its relation to Angle Township, the boundary sets off to this state, on its west and south side, Oak, Flag, and Brush Islands, in this order from southeast to northwest, besides several islands of smaller size.

Eight miles south of Oak Island is Garden Island (or Cornfield Island), also belonging to Minnesota, named from its former cultivation by the Ojibwe. John Tanner, the white captive who lived the greater part of his life among the Ottawa and Ojibwe, had his home for some time on this island, as told in his *Narrative*, published in 1830. The state added the island to the state park system as Garden Island State Recreation Area in 2000.

In coasting along the south shore westward from the mouth of Rainy River, Long Point and Rocky Point are passed at the north side of Lakewood Township.

Cormorant Rock, about a mile north from Rocky Point, is a small island of bare rock, named from its being the nesting place of multitudes of the double-crested cormorant, the same species for which lakes and a township in Becker County are named, as also a river and a township in Beltrami County.

Next to the west, Muskeg Bay, mostly adjoining Roseau County, is the most southwestern part of the lake, lying between Rocky Point on the east and Buffalo Point, in the edge of Manitoba, on the north. The bay received this Ojibwe name from tracts of swamp on its shore, and the Buffalo Point was named for its being on or near the northeastern limit of the former geographic range of the buffalo.

The site of Fort St. Charles, which was established by Pierre Gaultier de Varennes, sieur de la Vérendrye, in 1732 and named by him in honor of the governor of Canada, Charles de Beauharnois, was discovered in 1908 on the Minnesota shore of the Northwest Angle inlet nearly three miles distant from the bend of the boundary at American Point, the north end of a small island, where it turns from its north course to run westward up the inlet. From this fort the eldest son of La Vérendrye and a Jesuit missionary named Father Aulneau, with 19 French voyageurs, started in canoes June 5, 1736, to go to Mackinac for supplies. Early the next morning, at their first camping place, they were surprised and killed by a war party of the Prairie Sioux. This encounter, from which not one of the Frenchmen escaped, was on a small island of rock, since called Massacre Island, in the Canadian part of the Lake of the Woods, about 20 miles distant from the fort by the canoe route (Rev. Francis J. Schaefer, in *Acta et Dicta*, published by the St. Paul Catholic Historical Society, vol. 2, pp. 114–33, July 1909, with two maps between pages 240 and 241 in the same volume).

Le Sueur County

Established March 5, 1853, this county commemorates a Canadian French trader and explorer, Pierre Charles Le Sueur, before mentioned in the chapter for Blue Earth County as mining what he supposed was copper ore there in 1701, whence the name of the Blue Earth River and of that county were derived. He was born in 1657 of parents who had emigrated to Canada from the ancient province of Artois in northern France. At the age of 26 years, in 1683, he came to the Mississippi by way of the Wisconsin River. The remaining years of the century, excepting expeditions for the sale of furs in Montreal and absence on voyages to France, he spent principally in the country of the Dakota. He was at Fort St. Antoine, on the eastern shore of Lake Pepin, with Nicolas Perrot at the time of his proclamation in 1689, which he signed as a witness. At some time within a few years preceding or following that date, he made a canoe trip far up the Mississippi, this being the first recorded exploration of its course through the central part of Minnesota.

Within the first few years after Le Sueur came to the area of this state, he had acquired acquaintance with the language of the Dakota and had almost certainly traveled with them along the Minnesota River. From his first Christian name, Pierre, as Edward D. Neill and Justin Winsor think, came the French name St. Pierre, in English the St. Peter, by which this river was known to the white people through more than a century and a half, until its aboriginal Dakota name was adopted for the new Minnesota Territory.

A letter of Antoine de la Mothe, sieur de Cadillac, written in 1712, cited in the Margry Papers, states that after the appointment of Pierre Le Moyne, sieur d'Iberville, a cousin of Le Sueur's wife, to be the first governor of Louisiana, Le Sueur had his family remove there and that his wife and children were then living in Louisiana, where he had died. Another account indicates that he died during the return voyage from France, after his visit there in 1702, carrying the green or blue earth, supposed to be an ore of copper, which he mined on the Blue Earth River.

Information for these names was gathered from History of the Minnesota Valley (1882, 1,016 pp.), having pages 477–532 for this county, and History of Nicollet and Le Sueur Counties (1916, two vols., 544 and 538 pp.), edited by Hon. William G. Gresham; and from Edward Solberg, register of deeds, who has made many land surveys throughout the county,

Frank Moudry, former register of deeds, and Patrick G. Galagan, former judge of probate, each being interviewed during a visit at Le Sueur Center, the county seat, in July 1916.

ANAWAUK a post office, 1858–87, located ten miles southeast of Le Center, with a sawmill, a planing mill, a church, a school, a hotel, and a general store.

BABCOCK'S LANDING the claim of Joseph Babcok in Kasota Township (T. 110N, R. 26W), adjoined Kasota on the north at the mouth of the Shanaska Creek, opposite the present St. Peter; it had a sawmill.

BEVERDAM a post office, 1896–1904, located in Cordova Township, section 33.

BLUE GRASS GROVE a post office, 1864–67; location not found.

CAROLINE a village in section 5 of Kasota Township, had a station of the Chicago, St. Paul, Minneapolis and Omaha Railroad in section 17, a church, a school, and a post office, 1878–93, with Conrad Smith, a lime manufacturer, as postmaster.

CHEHALIS a post office, 1887–1902, located in section 30 of Kilkenny Township, and a station of the Minneapolis and St. Louis Railroad.

CLEVELAND TOWNSHIP organized in 1858, was named for the city of Cleveland, Ohio, several of the first settlers here, in 1855–56, having come from that state. The city, in sections 15, 16, 21, and 22, founded and thus named in 1857, was the county seat during one year, 1875–76, being succeeded by Le Sueur Center. It was organized on June 24, 1858, and incorporated as a village on March 9, 1904; its post office was first called Grandville, 1856–57, then changed to Cleveland. It had a station of the Chicago, St. Paul, Minneapolis and Omaha Railroad. In Ohio this name refers to Gen. Moses Cleaveland (1754–1806), agent of the Connecticut company that colonized the Western Reserve, under whose direction the site of the city named in his honor was surveyed in 1796.

CORDOVA TOWNSHIP settled in 1856 and organized in 1858, bears the name of an ancient city of Spain, renowned for its Moorish antiquities, which in the Middle Ages was "the most splendid seat of the arts, sciences, and literature in the world." The village, in section 14, located on Lake Gorman and the Cannon River, was platted September 28, 1867, and incorporated on February 27, 1878, but not separated from the township. It had a post office, 1857–1907, called Simons for a few months in 1857.

DERRYNANE TOWNSHIP organized in 1858, was settled partly by immigrants from Ireland. Its name was derived from Derrynane Abbey beside the little bay of this name on the southwest coast of Ireland. It is also borne by a village in the province of Ontario, Canada. A post office was located in the township, July-November 1861, with Andrew Hower as postmaster.

DOYLE a village in section 34 of Montgomery Township, was probably named to honor Dennis Doyle, a pioneer settler of Kilkenny in the same township; it had a post office, 1880–1935, and a station of the Minneapolis and St. Louis Railroad.

DRESSELVILLE a village located in section 10 of Sharon Township, had a post office, 1865–1900, and was named for its first postmaster, Philip Dressel, an immigrant from Germany, who was also the county auditor. The village was settled about 1855; businesses included a sawmill and a broom handle factory.

EAST HENDERSON a village in section 7 of Tyrone Township, located on the east side of the Minnesota River, opposite the city of Henderson in Sibley County, was organized in 1855, platted December 22, 1877, incorporated as a village on March 2, 1883, and separated from the township on March 20, 1908, incorporation dissolved. The village had a ferry, 1856–77, a general store, and a grain elevator, which closed in 1960.

EAST ST. PETER a village in sections 21 and 22 of Kasota Township, on the east side of the Minnesota River, opposite St. Peter in Nicollet County, was platted October 1, 1856; it had a station of the Chicago, St. Paul, Minneapolis and Omaha Railroad.

ELYSIAN TOWNSHIP organized in 1858, received this name from its village, which had been platted September 20, 1856, and was incorporated in January 1884. It was adopted from the Greek names Elysium and the Elysian Fields, "the dwelling place of the happy souls after death, placed by Homer on the western margin of the earth, by Hesiod and Pindar in the Isles of the Blessed in the Western Ocean."

The city of Elysian, with Waseca County, the Le Sueur County section being in section 35 of Elysian Township, adjoins the northeast end of Lake Elysian, called Okaman Lake on Joseph N. Nicollet's map in 1843, which is crossed by the county line and lies almost wholly in Waseca County. The city was incorporated on March 2, 1883, and separated from the township on March 20, 1908; it had a post office called Elysium, 1856–58, which was transferred to Okaman, Waseca County, and in 1859 was transferred back.

FOREST PRAIRIE a post office, 1857–58; location not found.

GERMAN LAKE a post office, 1859–60; location not found; however, the lake of this name is in Elysian and Cordova Townships.

GORMAN a post office, 1857–59, in Cordova Township.

GRANDVILLE see CLEVELAND.

GREENLAND a village in section 32 of Elysian Township, which had a post office, 1883–1914, and a station on the Chicago Great Western Railroad.

HEIDELBERG a city in sections 19 and 20 of Lanesburg Township, was platted December 4, 1878, and was named by its German settlers for the city of Heidelberg in Germany, widely known for its great university, which was founded in 1386. It was incorporated as a village on June 26, 1894, and had a post office, 1872–1903.

HENDERSON a station of the Chicago, St. Paul, Minneapolis and Omaha Railroad in section 6 of Tyrone Township.

HILLSDALE a post office, 1858–60; location not found.

JEFFERSON LAKE a post office, 1866–72, located on Lake Jefferson.

KASOTA TOWNSHIP settled in 1851, organized May 11, 1858, took the Dakota name of its village, in sections 29, 32, and 33, which was platted March 23, 1855, and was incorporated on April 28, 1890. It means, as noted by Prof. A. W. Williamson, "clear, or cleared off; the name sometimes applied by the Dakotas to the naked ridge or prairie plateau south of the village." This Kasota terrace of the valley drift, three miles long from north to south and averaging a half mile wide, is about 150 feet above the river and 75 feet lower than the general upland.

The post office was established in Blue Earth County in 1854 and transferred to Le Sueur County in 1857. One of the first settlers was Joseph W. Babcock, who built a sawmill in 1852 on Shanaska Creek and began quarrying limestone that same year, building a ferry on the Minnesota River in 1854; Babcock became the first postmaster when the post office was established in 1854 in the store owned by C. Schaefer; it had a station on the Chicago and North Western Railway.

KILKENNY TOWNSHIP settled in 1856, was named by its Irish people for a city and county of southeastern Ireland. The city, in sections 22 and 27, was platted in 1877 and was incorporated June 3, 1883. Among its first settlers was Dennis Doyle (1818–1902), born in Kilkenny County, Ireland, who came to the United States in 1851, settled one mile west of the present city site, in section 21, and opened a store in his home in 1857, where he taught in the first school and became the first postmaster, serving 1857 to 1888; he was the first township clerk and served as a state legislator. Doyle was the first to marry in the community; Catherine Raway, born in France in 1839, was his wife. The Minneapolis and St. Louis Railroad station was named Washburn until Doyle requested the change to coincide with the post office name.

LAKE DORA a post office, 1871–72, eight miles southeast of Lexington.

LAKE JEFFERSON a post office, 1885–88; location not found but probably on the lake of that name.

LAKE WASHINGTON a post office, 1862–1902, located in Kasota Township, section 8, with a station on the Chicago and North Western Railway.

LANESBURG TOWNSHIP was named in honor of its first settler, Charles L. Lane, who came in 1854 and opened a farm in section 33.

LANESBURGH see MONTGOMERY.

LE CENTER a city in sections 28 and 29 of Lexington Township, was platted on December 2, 1876, as Le Sueur Center and established as the county seat; its post office was established as Union Centre in 1864 on the farm of postmaster John Chapman, in section 32, and discontinued when the new post office of Le Sueur Centre was created in 1877 one mile north; it was incorporated as a village February 21, 1890. The name was variously spelled Lesueur Center, 1893–1928, and Le Sueur Center, 1928–31; although the name was changed on December 5, 1930, to Center, it changed again on January 23, 1931, to the present form. It had a station on the Chicago, St. Paul, Minneapolis and Omaha Railroad.

LE SUEUR TOWNSHIP and city were founded in 1852, with the village plats bearing this name, which in the next year was given to the new county. Two rival villages, each with a post office, one called Le Sueur and the other Le Sueur City, were incorporated respectively on June 10 and 17, 1858. Nine years later, by an act of the state legislature,

March 9, 1867, they were united in a borough town, Le Sueur, which was incorporated as a city March 16, 1891. It was the first county seat until 1875, being then succeeded by Cleveland for one year, and by Le Center since 1876. Its major industry is canning, which began in 1903 with the Minnesota Valley Canning Company, furnishing seed and supervising the growing and harvesting of crops from 200 acres; its first production was 11,750 cases of Evergreen Cream Corn; 25 years later crops were raised on 20,000 acres. The Jolly Green Giant first appeared in 1928, created in the image of Paul Bunyan and representing the biggest peas grown in the world and located in a green valley; the figure became so well known that the company changed its name to Green Giant Company in 1950. The home of Dr. William Worral Mayo was built there in 1859; it was added to the National Register of Historic Places in 1969.

A stream here tributary to the Minnesota River is called Le Sueur Creek or River, and its northern branch is known as Little Le Sueur Creek or "Forest and Prairie Creek." The last name refers to its course through an originally wholly wooded area, but near its mouth coming to the north end of the extensive Le Sueur prairie, five miles long and two to four miles wide, which is a terrace of valley drift similar to the much smaller Kasota prairie terrace, previously noted.

LE SUEUR CENTRE see **LE CENTER**.

LEXINGTON TOWNSHIP settled in 1855 and organized in 1858, was named after its village in sections 3, 9, and 10, which was platted by pioneers from New England in 1857; it had a station on the Minneapolis and St. Louis Railroad and a post office, 1856–1907. This name is borne by a village of Massachusetts, where the battle of Lexington was fought, beginning the Revolutionary War, April 19, 1775, by cities in Kentucky and Missouri, and villages and townships in 19 other states.

LINDER BAY a village in section 17 of Washington Township, on the southeast shore of Lake Washington, about 1928.

LLOYD a post office located in section 33 of Sharon Township, 1894–1903.

MARYSBURG a hamlet in the south edge of Washington Township, in section 15, platted January 24, 1859, was named by its first settler, John L. Meagher, an immigrant from Ireland, who was

its postmaster during many years and was also the probate judge for this county. It had a post office, 1858–1903, spelled Marysburgh until 1894.

MAYLARDVILLE a post office, 1858–63, with John Maylard as postmaster; location not found.

MONTGOMERY TOWNSHIP was settled in 1856 and organized in 1859. Its city, in sections 3, 4, 9, and 10, incorporated in 1902, was platted as a village September 5, 1877, by John and Jane Martin, who purchased the townsite in 1877, when the Minneapolis and St. Louis Railroad was built there, its site being "in the midst of a dense forest of very heavy timber." It had a post office established as Lanesburgh 1857–66, on a farm in section 33 of Lanesburg Township, with Charles L. Lane, postmaster; it then moved to Montgomery Township, the name changing to Montgomery, and operated on farms until opened in the village general store in 1877. The area was settled by Czech, German, and Irish families; it is the largest Czech-populated area in the state.

Fifteen states of the Union have counties of this name, and it is borne also by a similar number of villages and townships, commemorating Gen. Richard Montgomery, who in the American Revolution commanded an expedition invading Canada, in which he was killed December 31, 1775, while leading an attack on Quebec.

MORRISTOWN see **RICE COUNTY**.

NEW PRAGUE incorporated as a village in March 1877, and as a city in April 1891, is crossed along its main street by the line of Le Sueur and Scott Counties. It was named for the ancient city of Prague, the capital of Bohemia, from which many immigrants came here. The community was first settled in 1854; the Minneapolis and St. Louis Railroad came in 1877; its post office was named Oral, 1857–72, when the community was part of Scott County only, changed to Praha, 1872–79, and Prague, 1879–84, at which time the name was permanently changed to the present one.

OKAMAN at the east side of the northern end of Lake Elysian, was an early village, platted March 30, 1857, lying partly in Waseca County. Its site was vacated in 1867 and reverted to farm uses. The name Okaman, supplied by the Dakota, was given to this lake by Nicollet, derived, according to Williamson, from *hokah*, "heron, man, nests." It thus had the same meaning as the Okabena Creek and Lakes in Jackson and Nobles Counties.

ORAL see NEW PRAGUE.

OTTAWA TOWNSHIP was settled in 1853 and organized in 1858. Its village, in sections 27 and 34, platted April 4, 1855, was then named Minnewashta, from Dakota words meaning "water" and "good," in allusion to its excellent springs. On June 20, 1856, it was surveyed anew and renamed Ottawa, for a tribe of the great Algonquian family, nearly related to the Ojibwe. Their name, originally meaning traders, is given to the Ottawa River and the capital of Canada, to cities in Illinois and Kansas, a village in Ohio, and a township in Wisconsin. The post office was established in Dakota County in 1856 and transferred to Le Sueur County in 1857; it had a station of the Chicago, St. Paul, Minneapolis and Omaha Railroad; the settlement existed about 1853–1907.

PETTIS a station of the Chicago, Milwaukee and St. Paul Railroad in section 35 of Kasota Township.

PRAGUE/PRAHA see NEW PRAGUE.

ROGERS a station of the Minneapolis and St. Louis Railroad in Waterville Township.

RUDOLPH a village in Tyrone Township, with boardinghouses, an elevator, and a post office, 1868–79, in postmaster Edward Winkelman's general store.

ST. HENRY a village in section 25 of Sharon Township, named for the Catholic church built by its first settlers; the post office operated 1870–77 and 1880–1902.

ST. HUBERTUS a post office, 1865–81, located in section 24 of Montgomery Township.

ST. THOMAS a community in sections 18 and 19 of Derrynane Township, which had a post office, 1872–1902, and a station on the Chicago, St. Paul, Minneapolis and Omaha Railroad.

SHARON TOWNSHIP was settled in 1854 and organized in 1858. Its name, derived from the fertile plain of Sharon in Palestine, is borne also by villages and townships in 19 other states of the Union. A post office was located in section 17, 1871–80 and 1883–99; it was first called Young Town, before being renamed by its Welsh settlers.

SIMONS see CORDOVA.

TYRONE TOWNSHIP settled in 1855–56 and organized in 1859, was named, on the suggestion of Irish immigrants, for a county in northern Ireland. New York and Pennsylvania have townships of this name. The township originally contained

37 sections, not the usual 36, and was known in 1858 as Hillsdale, changing to the present name when organized.

UNION CENTRE see LE CENTER.

UNION HILL a locality in section 1 of Derrynane Township.

WARSAW see RICE COUNTY.

WASHBURN see KILKENNY.

WASHINGTON first settled in 1858 and in the same year designated as a township, has two large lakes, which the government surveyors had named in honor of Washington and Jefferson, presidents of the United States.

WATERVILLE TOWNSHIP settled in 1855 and organized in 1858, received this name from its village in sections 21, 22, and 26–28, which was incorporated as a village on February 28, 1878, and as a city in 1898. It is also the name of a city in Maine and of villages and townships in ten other states. The choice of the name had reference chiefly to the adjoining Lakes Tetonka and Sakatah (Dakota names, used by Nicollet), through which the Cannon River flows, and to White Water Creek, here tributary to Lake Sakatah. The city developed when the first settlers arrived in 1855 from New England; the post office began in 1856, and the first general store and hotel were built in 1857; it was platted by E. L. Wright for the Minneapolis and St. Louis Railroad in 1877. Set in a tourist area, the city is the site of a fish hatchery and Sakatah State Park, for which see Rice County.

WEST TROY a post office, 1858–60; location not found.

YOUNG TOWN see SHARON.

Lakes and Streams

Lakes Elysian, Washington, Jefferson, Tetonka, and Sakatah, Le Sueur Creek or River, the Little Le Sueur Creek, and White Water Creek are noted in the preceding list of townships.

Other lakes and creeks of this county are as follows, in the order of the townships and ranges, from south to north and from east to west.

Horseshoe Lake is crossed by the east line of Waterville, and Goose Lake is in its section 2.

Elysian has Lake Francis, Rays Lake (named for George E. Ray, a pioneer farmer there), and Lake Tustin (partly drained), at the north side of the village; Rice Lake in section 3, named for its wild rice; German Lake, mostly in sections 4 and 5, bordered by farms of German settlers; Sasse Lake in section 10, named for early German homesteaders, William and Frederick Sasse; Silver Lake in section 20; Steele Lake, on the north line of section 22; Fish Lake in sections 23 and 24; and Round Lake in sections 29 and 30.

Kasota is crossed by Shanaska Creek (also Shahaska and Chankaska, a Dakota name, used by Nicollet, meaning "forest-enclosed"), the outlet of Lake Washington; Spring Creek, about three miles farther north; and Cherry Creek at the north end of this township, flowing into the Minnesota River near Ottawa village. Lake Williams or Plaza, and Long Lake, each very small, are in the southern part of Kasota, and the larger Lake Emily near its center. Another Lake Emily is mapped in section 31, Cleveland, only two miles southeast from the last.

Kilkenny has Sunfish, Saber, and Diamond Lakes, in its south half, which is crossed by Little Cannon Creek or River; and its north half has Lakes Dora, Mabel (drained), and Volney, the last being named for Volney J. Brockway, a pioneer farmer in section 31, Montgomery, at its north side.

Cordova Township has Lake Gorman, named in honor of Willis Arnold Gorman (1816–76), who was governor of Minnesota Territory, 1853–57, and served in the Civil War as colonel of the First Minnesota Regiment in 1861, and later as a brigadier general; Sleepy Eye Lake, in section 15, named for the Dakota leader who is also commemorated by a lake and village of Brown County; Goose Lake in section 28; and Bossuot Lake in sections 29 and 32.

Scotch Lake in Cleveland received its name for pioneers from Scotland; Lake Henry, Decker Lake (also called Silver Lake), and Savidge and Goldsmith Lakes were likewise named for settlers; and this township also has a little Rice Lake in sections 7 and 8, Dog Lake in sections 32 and 33, and no fewer than three Mud Lakes, in sections 24, 25, and 33.

Montgomery has another Rice Lake, named for the wild rice (but also called Hunt Lake), in section 1; another Mud Lake in section 27; Kuzel Lake in section 16; Borer Lake in section 19, commemorating Felix A. Borer, formerly county auditor; and Green Leaf Lake, named from the foliage of the surrounding woods, in sections 19, 20, 29, and 30.

Beside Hockridge Lake, in the northeast corner of Lexington, a farm claim was taken by Granville Hockridge in October 1860, and a second claim was taken by his brother in 1863; Clear Lake and Lake Mary adjoin Lexington village; and farther south in this township are Tyler Lake, named for William L. Tyler, who settled there in 1858, and Mud Lake in sections 24 and 25.

Sharon has a large Rice Lake, shallow in wet seasons and filled with wild rice, but only a marsh in the summer, this being the fourth Rice Lake noted in Le Sueur County.

In the northwest part of Lanesburg are Graham Lake and yet another Mud Lake, the sixth so named on one map of this county; and in its southern part, outflowing east and north into Scott County by Sand Creek, are Eggert Lake, Lake Pepin, named for some reason after the large Lake Pepin of the Mississippi River, and Lake Sanborn, the last being in honor of Edwin Sanborn, who took a homestead here in April 1857.

In Derrynane are Sheas Lake, named for Timothy Shea, an early settler whose farm adjoined it, and School Lake in the school section 36.

Elysian Moraine

Le Sueur County is crossed at and near its southern border by a belt of low morainic drift hills, ridges, and small knolls, much strewn with boulders, occupying a width of three to four miles, reaching from Waterville and Elysian northwesterly by Lake Jefferson and the two Lakes Emily to the wide Minnesota valley at St. Peter and Traverse des Sioux. In Nicollet County this belt continues but is less clearly developed, passing westward by the north side of Swan Lake. It is named the Elysian Moraine by the chapters on these counties in the *Final Report of the Minnesota Geological Survey*, being the fifth in a series of 12 marginal moraines partly mapped in their courses through this state.

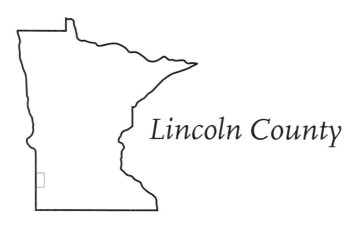

Lincoln County

This county, established March 6, 1873, was named in honor of Abraham Lincoln, president of the United States during the Civil War, who was born February 12, 1809, near Hodgenville, Ky., and died in Washington, April 15, 1865. In his youth and early manhood he was a farm laborer, a salesman, a merchant, and a surveyor. He served in the Black Hawk War, 1832; was a member of the Illinois legislature, 1834–42; began practice of law at Springfield, Ill., in 1837; was a member of Congress, 1847–49; was Republican candidate for U.S. senator in 1858, and held a series of debates throughout Illinois with the Democratic candidate, Stephen A. Douglas, on questions of national legislation against slavery; was president from 1861 until his death, and was assassinated five days after the surrender of Robert E. Lee, which had ended the war.

Born of humble but worthy parents in their small log cabin on the lonely frontier, Lincoln became the foremost statesman of our American republic, its preserver in the direful war of secession, emancipator of the millions of slaves, and his life was crowned by martyrdom for the sacred cause of justice, liberty, and law.

The patriotic legislature of Minnesota in the year 1861 desired to honor Lincoln by giving his name to a county established from the north-eastern part of the present Renville County, with addition of the two most southern townships now in Meeker County, but this act failed of the requisite ratification by the people of the counties thus changed. Next, by an act approved March 9, 1866, the name of Rock County was changed to Lincoln. This law, however, was ineffectual, being ignored by the people of Rock County. Therefore a third unsuccessful attempt was made, by an act of February 12, 1870, on the anniversary of Lincoln's birthday, to establish a county named Lincoln, taking it, as in 1861, from eastern Renville County, but not with the same boundaries as before. It again failed of adoption by the people. Finally, in 1873, Lincoln County was made from the former western part of Lyon County, the legislative act was ratified by the popular vote in November, and the new county was proclaimed by Gov. Horace Austin, December 5, 1873. Counties have been named for President Lincoln in 15 other states.

Among the many biographies of Lincoln, one of the most complete is by John G. Nicolay and John Hay, in ten volumes, published in 1890. *Lincoln Bibliography, a List of Books and Pamphlets relating to Abraham Lincoln*, by Judge Daniel Fish, of Minneapolis, 380 pages, was published in 1906.

Information was received from Leroy P. Sisson, register of deeds, and George Graff, clerk of the court, during a visit at Ivanhoe, the county seat, in July 1916.

ACORN PLANTING an Indian village dating from before 1858, located in section 18 of Lake Benton Township, also known as Indian Planting.

ALTA VISTA TOWNSHIP meaning "high view," was named by Col. Samuel McPhail, whose home as a farmer during several years was in the southeast quarter of its section 12; the township was called McPhail County during the 1860s. A post office was located in section 12, 1876–81. This area is 300 to 600 feet above the Minnesota River, about 30 miles distant to the northeast, in which direction it has a very extensive view.

ARCO a city in section 31 and 32 of Lake Stay Township, was platted in 1900 as Arcola and first incorporated under that name in June 30, 1903, being named by the Chicago and North Western Railway officials for the ancient city of Arcola in Italy; the name was later shortened to avoid confusion with a railway station named Arcola in Washington County, and the city was reincorporated July 28, 1903. Its post office began in 1900 in the general store of postmaster Christian Larsen; it had a station of the Minnesota and South Dakota Railway.

ASH LAKE TOWNSHIP received the name of its lake in section 17, which was bordered by a grove of white ash trees, a species that is frequent or common throughout Minnesota, excepting far northward.

DANEBOD a district in Hope, Marshfield, and Diamond Lake Townships, became the second largest settlement of Danes in the state, developing when a colony of Danes, led by Rev. Hans Jorgen Pedersen (1851–1905), came in the early 1880s, built a college, and established a land agreement with the Winona and St. Peter Railroad for 35,000 acres where, for three years, the land was to be sold only to Danes. The first 70 settlers arrived on June 27, 1885, at Lake Benton and traveled to Tyler and the area called Danebod; by sundown 3,000 acres had been sold, and the community was established. The name refers to the name given to Queen Thyra in tenth-century Denmark, meaning "one who mends or saves the Danes."

DIAMOND LAKE TOWNSHIP was named from its lake of diamond shape in sections 23 and 24, adjoining the north side of Lake Benton.

DRAMMEN TOWNSHIP was named by its Norwegian settlers for the seaport, river, and fjord in Norway, bearing this name, about 25 miles southwest of Christiania.

HANSONVILLE the most northwestern township and the last organized in this county, was named in honor of one of its earliest settlers, John Hanson, who was a representative in the state legislature in 1887 and for some years the historian of the Lincoln County Old Settlers Association.

HENDRICKS TOWNSHIP and railway village received their name from Lake Hendricks, crossed by the state boundary at the west side of this township. The lake has this name on the map of Minnesota published by J. S. Sewall and C. W. Iddings in 1860, which shows the boundary line and its relation to Lakes Hendricks, Shaokatan, and Benton. Such delineation was derived from a survey after the passage in 1857–58 of the acts of Congress defining the western limits of Minnesota for its admission as a state. The name Hendricks was given to the lake during that survey, in honor of Thomas Andrews Hendricks, commissioner of the General Land Office from 1855 to 1859, who was born near Zanesville, Ohio, September 7, 1819, and died in Indianapolis, Ind., November 25, 1885. He was a member of Congress from Indiana, 1851–55; U.S. senator, 1863–69; governor of Indiana, 1873–77; and was vice-president of the United States in 1885.

The city of Hendricks in sections 17 to 19 was incorporated as a village on October 27, 1900, and again on February 17, 1908; the post office began in 1884. The city developed as a trade center for a large area of southwestern Minnesota and eastern South Dakota. It had a station of the Winona and St. Peter and Minnesota and South Dakota railroads.

HOPE TOWNSHIP was named by vote of its settlers. Fourteen other states have villages and townships of this auspicious name.

IDLEWILD a post office in section 18, Ash Lake Township, which was first called Morse, 1878–82, then Shaokatan, 1882–88, and finally Idlewild, 1888–1902, in Sylvester Stanley Mack's general store; Mack was born in Connecticut in 1847, came to Minnesota in 1878, operated the general store, and later moved to Long Prairie.

INDIAN GROVE an Indian village predating its first recording in 1855; located in Hope Township, it was the site of the first township government.

INDIAN PLANTING see ACORN PLANTING.

IVANHOE a city in Royal Township, section 34, was named by officers of the Chicago and North Western Railway for the hero of the novel thus titled, written by Sir Walter Scott. It was platted by the Western Town Lot Company in 1889 on land owned by Mike Pukrop; many of the streets were also named for characters in the novel. The post office was first called Wilno, 1883–1901, at which time it was changed to Ivanhoe. It was incorporated as a village on January 22, 1901, and as a city in 1968. It succeeded Lake Benton as the county seat in 1902, officially since August 5, 1904.

LAKE BENTON TOWNSHIP the first organized in the area of Lincoln County, and its village, which was the county seat for 20 years, 1882–1902, succeeding Marshfield, bear the name given to the lake on Joseph N. Nicollet's map, published in 1843. In his journey to the Pipestone Quarry and to this lake in the summer of 1838, Nicollet was accompanied by John C. Frémont, then a young man, who afterward was known as "the Path Finder," for his explorations of the Rocky Mountains, and who in 1856 was the presidential candidate of the newly organized Republican Party. Lake Benton was named by Frémont and Nicollet for Sen. Benton, whose daughter Jessie was married to Frémont in 1841; and a lake in North Dakota was named Lake Jessie in honor of her on this map. Thomas Hart Benton was born near Hillsborough, N.C., March 14, 1782, and died in Washington, D.C., April 10, 1858. He was U.S. senator from Missouri during 30 years, 1821–51.

The city of Lake Benton was platted on August 29, 1879, for the Chicago and North Western Railway by Marvin Hughitt, later president of that railroad, on land owned by A. W. Morse and John Snyder; it was incorporated as a village October 24, 1881. The post office was established in Lyon County in 1873 and transferred to Lincoln County in 1877.

The depth and area of Lake Benton vary much with fluctuations of average moisture or dryness during successive years. At its high stage the water surrounds an island in the east part, called Bird Island.

LAKE STAY TOWNSHIP has a lake, adjoining Arco village, named in honor of Frank Stay, who was wounded there in 1865, near the end of his service of three years in campaigns against the Dakota after the war in 1862. He was born in Canada, June 10, 1837; came to Minnesota in 1854; was farming on the site of Hanley Falls, Yellow Medicine County, at the time of conflict, in August 1862, and only escaped after great exposure and suffering. After 1868 he lived on his homestead farm in the township of Camp Release, Lac qui Parle County, where he was the first settler. A post office was located in section 14, 1879–1900.

LIMESTONE TOWNSHIP occupied in its greater part by the knolly and hilly glacial drift of the Gary Moraine, which is more fully noticed near the end of this chapter, received its name in allusion to the plentiful limestone boulders, with many others of granite and gneiss.

MAHKAHSAHPAH see RUSSELLVILLE.

MARBLE TOWNSHIP likewise mainly belonging to the Gary Moraine, was similarly named for its light yellowish magnesian limestone boulders, some of which resemble marble in hardness, durability, and adaptation to be polished for building or ornamental uses.

MARSHFIELD TOWNSHIP received the name of its village, previously platted in 1873 in the northeast quarter of section 30, which was the first county seat until 1882, being then succeeded by Lake Benton. It was named in honor of Charles Marsh and Ira Field, pioneer settlers. The former, who came here in 1871, was the owner of its site and was appointed the first auditor of the county in January 1874. The village had a post office, 1872–81, established in Lyon County and transferred to Lincoln County in 1877, at which time it was located in postmaster Marshall Phillips's store, the first store built in the county. The community had several stores and hotels, but when the railroad built a distance west, the townsite was abandoned, and most buildings moved to Tyler or Lake Benton.

MORSE a post office, 1878–82, on the Charles M. Morse farm in section 19, Ash Lake Township, where he had built a store in 1878; it was transferred to Shaokatan, 1882–88. After the railroad built south of the site, the community did not develop, and most buildings were moved to section 18 in Ash Lake Township, where the Shaokatan post office had moved, the name becoming Idlewild.

MOUNTAIN PASS a village in Hendricks Township, incorporated on May 23, 1857; no trace remains.

NEW GROVE a post office in section 8 of Shaokatan Township,1884–1901. William F. Dorn, the postmaster, was born in 1850 in Germany, came to the county in 1883, and also served as township supervisor and school director; he died November 27, 1937.

PRAIRIE FARM a postal station in Hendricks Township.

ROYAL TOWNSHIP was organized as York, but because that name was already in Fillmore County, the name was changed to Royal in honor of LeRoy Royal who was active in organizing the township.

RUSSELLVILLE a post office called Mahkahsahpah 1867–69, and Russellville from July to November 1869, with Edward U. Russell as postmaster under both names; location not found.

SHAOKATAN TOWNSHIP has the Dakota name of its lake, found on an early map of this state, before mentioned for Lake Hendricks, published January 1, 1860. Its origin and meaning remain to be learned. A post office was in section 14, 1882–88, on postmaster Samuel D. Pumpelly's farm; he was born in Kentucky and came to Minnesota in 1876; after serving as postmaster for seven years, he became county auditor at Lake Benton, later moving to Oregon, where he died. The post office had earlier been at Morse and later moved to Idlewild.

TOWNVILLE a post office, 1885–88; location not found.

TYLER a city platted September 8, 1879, in sections 3 and 4 of Hope Township, was named in honor of C. B. Tyler, who was born in Montrose, Pa., September 2, 1835; came to Minnesota in 1857; was register of the U.S. land office in New Ulm after 1873; owned and edited the *New Ulm Herald*, 1875–78; removed to Tracy in 1880 and later to Marshall, where he engaged in banking. The city was incorporated as a village on July 23, 1887; its post office began in 1879; it had a station of the Chicago and North Western Railway.

VERDI TOWNSHIP was named for the renowned Italian operatic composer Giuseppe Verdi (1813–1901). This name means "verdant or verdure," descriptive of the greenness of the township, which in all its extent is during the spring and summer a far-reaching green prairie. The village in section 35 had a post office beginning in 1879, first located in John C. Enke's general store; Enke died in Lake Benton on January 25, 1935. It had a station of the Chicago and Dakota Railway and a number of businesses, including a creamery and a hotel.

WILNO a village in section 23 of Royal Township, was primarily settled by Poles and was platted on February 10, 1883, with most streets named for Polish cities or heroes. The village was named for the second city, Vilnius, or Wilnius, of old Poland, now the capital of Lithuania. Two post offices were established; the first, 1883–1901, was transferred to Ivanhoe; the second operated 1902–4. The Church of St. John Cantius was built as a wooden church about 1882, was replaced in 1902 with a brick building, and was known as the "Cathedral in the Cornfield," in reference to its location in this center of Polish-American farming.

Lakes and Streams

The preceding pages have noticed Ash and Diamond Lakes; three lakes of special geological interest, named Benton, Shaokatan, and Hendricks, which will be again noticed at the end of this chapter; and Lake Stay, which in dry seasons is represented by two lakelets.

Other lakes bearing names to be listed are Swan Lake, a mile south of Tyler; Cottonwood Lake, which has been drained, north of Tyler; Lake Nova, or Dead Coon, Lake, in the northeast corner of Marshfield; Blackman and Rush Lakes, in sections 9 and 16 of Diamond Lake Township; Perch Lake in section 17, Royal, and Eagle Lake in sections 25 and 36, and the Twin Lakes, in sections 28 and 29, Hansonville.

The streams of this county are named only as branches of the Redwood, Yellow Medicine, and Lac qui Parle Rivers.

Altamont and Gary Moraines

The description and map of Lincoln County in the *Final Report of the Minnesota Geological Survey* (vol. 1, 1894, chap. 20, pp. 589–612) direct attention to its two well-developed belts of marginal drift hills and short low ridges and knolls, abundantly sprinkled with boulders. The western or outer moraine, lying on the crest of the great highland called the Coteau des Prairies, extends north-northwestward through the southwestern part of the county, past the western ends of Lakes Benton, Shaokatan, and Hendricks, and thence it continues in South Dakota, to cross the Chicago and North Western Railway at Altamont, a dozen miles west of the interstate boundary. Parallel with this and about 15 miles distant to the northeast, the similar but broader second moraine passes across the northeast part of this county, where its profusion of limestone boulders gave the names of Limestone and Marble Townships. It crosses the same railway at and west of Gary, in the east edge of South Dakota.

From these localities, described by the Minnesota reports, these first and second marginal moraines of the continental ice sheet, in a successive series of 12 traced partly in this state, were named in 1883 by Prof. T. C. Chamberlin as the Altamont and Gary Moraines. Next northeastward, being also parallel with these, is the Antelope, or Third, Moraine, also named by him in 1883, noted in the chapter for Lac qui Parle County.

The Hole in the Mountain

The outer or Altamont Moraine belt, and the thick sheet of till that descends thence westward, are cut in the west part of Lake Benton Township by a deep channel or valley, which is called, translating the Dakota name, the "Hole in the Mountain." The railroad between Lake Benton and Verdi village goes south-southwest four miles through this gap, bounded on each side by picturesque bluffs. Its depth, wholly in the glacial drift, is from 150 to 200 feet below the knolly surface of the moraine, and its highest point is about 10 feet above Lake Benton, which has its outlet eastward into the Redwood River. This valley, from an eighth to a fourth of a mile wide, was evidently excavated by a river that flowed from northeast to southwest across this great ridge, which is the highest land in southwestern Minnesota, being

1,000 feet above the Minnesota River on the northeast, 350 feet above the Big Sioux River on the west, and about 1,960 feet above the sea.

At three other places, 11, 14, and 18 miles northwest from Lake Benton, similar channels have been eroded through the massive ridge of this moraine and through the smooth sheet of drift that slopes downward from its west side. The first of these channels begins at the southwest end of Lake Shaokatan and extends about 2 miles southwest in the same course with this lake, through the knolly belt of the moraine, beyond which its course for the next 3 miles is northwest along its west side, crossing the state line. Lake Shaokatan outflows northeastward to the Yellow Medicine River, but the highest part of the valley that extends from it westerly is only slightly elevated above the lake.

The most northwestern of these remarkable channels or valleys, lying in Brookings County, S.Dak., and extending southward from the southwest end of Lake Hendricks, was called by the Dakota "the Brother of the Hole in the Mountain," because of its close likeness to the pass southwest from Lake Benton.

While the ice sheet covered the basin of the Minnesota River and deeply overspread all the country northward, rising high above the Coteau des Prairies, streams outflowed from its melting border in the courses of these channels, at the same time with the accumulation of the Altamont moraine. Much glacial drift was borne away by the streams from the lower part of the ice in which it had been held, producing hollows when that drift was deposited, in which lie the Lakes Benton, Shaokatan, and Hendricks, respectively about 10, 15, and 20 feet in depth. The general surface of the drift is about 10 feet above these lakes, showing that the drift enclosed in the basal part of the ice sheet adjoining the outermost moraine, measured by the action of the glacial rivers and the resulting hollows of the three lakes, was equal to a thickness of 20 to 30 feet.

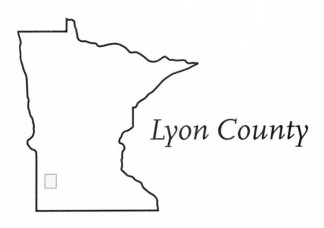

Lyon County

This county, established by two legislative acts, March 6, 1868, and March 2, 1869, was named in honor of Gen. Nathaniel Lyon, who was born in Ashford, Conn., July 14, 1818, and was killed in the battle of Wilson's Creek, Mo., August 10, 1861. He was graduated at the U.S. Military Academy in 1841; served in Florida during the later part of the Seminole War, 1841–42, and also served in the Mexican War, 1846–47; was promoted captain in 1851 and was on frontier duty during the years 1853–61 in Kansas, Dakota, Minnesota, and Nebraska. At the beginning of the Civil War he took a prominent part in the contest against secession in Missouri, rendered efficient aid to the national government as commander of the U.S. arsenal in St. Louis, and was appointed general of the Department of Missouri in June 1861.

A series of his letters in 1860, in which he advocated the election of Lincoln as president, titled *The Last Political Writings of Gen. Nathaniel Lyon*, was published in 1861, soon after his death (275 pp., including a memoir of his life and military services). His biography was more fully written by Dr. Ashbel Woodward (360 pp., 1862), and his devotion to the Union, for which he gave his life, is the theme of a volume by James Peckham, *Gen. Nathaniel Lyon and Missouri in 1861, a Monograph of the Great Rebellion* (447 pp., 1866). He is also commemorated by the names of counties in Iowa, Kansas, and Nevada.

Information of the origins of names was gathered from History of the Minnesota Valley *(1882, 1,016 pp.), having pages 848–82 for this county,* History and Description of Lyon County, *by C. F. Case (1884, 98 pp.), and* An Illustrated History of Lyon County, *by Arthur P. Rose (1912, 616 pp.); and from interviews with Mr. Rose, author of the later work, and Richard R. Bumford, former register of deeds, visited at Marshall, the county seat, in September 1916.*

AMIRET TOWNSHIP settled in 1868 and organized March 17, 1874, was at first called Madison, which was changed in 1879 to the present name, taken from its railway village. The name was chosen in honor of Amiretta Sykes, wife of M. L. Sykes, vice president of the Chicago and North Western Railway company. The first townsite in the area of Lyon County had been platted in 1857 about three miles southwest from the site of this village and was named Saratoga, which name was given in 1874 to the railway village then platted in section 19. When the railway was being built, in 1872, a post office had been established there and named Coburg in honor of William Coburn, the pioneer merchant and first postmaster. In 1879 the name Amiret was chosen, superseding both these names and the former township name of Madison.

BALATON a city in sections 22 and 23 of Rock Lake Township, platted in July 1879 and incorporated on December 12, 1892, was named for the large and picturesque Lake Balaton in western Hungary. Other versions of the name's origin include that it was named for a Chicago and North Western Railway stockholder named Balaton, that the name is a corruption of Belltown for David Bell, store owner and first merchant, and that indecision about choosing a name required a "ballot-on" situation. The city had a station of the Chicago and North Western Railway, and the post office began in 1879 with hotel owner Ralph E. Town as postmaster.

BLAEN AVON a post office located in section 34 of Custer Township, 1873–76.

BRENNER a post office, 1876–1903, located in section 4, Vallers Township, with Ole O. Brenner as postmaster.

BURCHARD a railway station in section 11, Shelburne, received this name in 1886 in honor of H. M. Burchard, a Chicago and North Western land agent at Marshall. It had a post office, 1886–1910 and 1920–45. The Winona and St. Peter Railroad station was also known as Redwood Station and Shelburne.

CAMDEN a post office, 1874–1900, in Lynd Township; a small community with a store and a school developed around the Camden gristmill, which had been built in 1868; it was located near the present-day Camden State Park, established in 1935 in Lyons and Lynd Townships; no traces of the settlement remain. The park, originally known as Camden Woods, overlooks the Redwood River valley on the eastern side of the Coteau des Prairies. It contains the Altamont Moraine, the second highest and most eastern of the Coteau moraines.

CERESCO a post office located on the Redwood River in Stanley Township, established in 1869 in McPhail County, transferred to Lyon County in 1872, and discontinued in 1882.

CLIFTON TOWNSHIP settled in 1872 and organized October 7, 1876, bears a name proposed by Christopher Dillman, which is also borne by villages and townships in 21 other states.

COBURG a post office, 1873–77, located in Amiret Township, with William Coburn as postmaster, which was transferred to Amiret.

COON CREEK TOWNSHIP organized August 4, 1883, has a creek so named from Dead Coon Lake near its source, in Lincoln County, to which that name was given by the early government surveyors because they found a dead raccoon there.

COTTONWOOD a city in Lucas Township, section 9, platted in July 1888, received its name from the adjacent lake, which has cottonwood trees on its shore. The city was first settled about 1871 on a townsite of 372 acres and was incorporated as a village January 12, 1892. The mail was first received at Vineland, Yellow Medicine County, 1873–88, where Ole S. Reishus was postmaster on his homestead; when Reishus moved to the Cottonwood site in 1888, the post office also moved and changed its name; his wife, Igebor O. Reishus, became postmaster; it had a Great Northern Railway station.

COTTONWOOD LAKE a post office, 1888, in Lucas Township with Ole S. Dahl, postmaster; Dahl became postmaster of Cottonwood following Ole and Igebor Reishus.

CUSTER TOWNSHIP settled in 1868 and organized October 14, 1876, was named in honor of George Armstrong Custer, who was born in Ohio, December 5, 1839; was graduated at the U.S. Military Academy in 1861; served through the Civil War; was brevetted a major general in 1866; commanded an exploring expedition to the Black Hills in 1874; and was killed with all his attacking troops by the Indians in Montana, June 25, 1876.

DUDLEY a village in section 17, Clifton, platted December 20, 1901, was named for Dudley village and township in Massachusetts. It had a post office, 1903–8, and a station on the Chicago and North Western Railway in section 18.

EIDSVOLD TOWNSHIP first settled in June 1871 and organized September 20, 1873, was named by vote of its Norwegian settlers for a parish in Norway, noted as the meeting place of the National Assembly in 1814.

FAIRVIEW settled in June 1870, organized April 1, 1873, was described by Case in 1884, "as its name implies, a beautiful prairie township, which, especially in early summer, spreads out a landscape of loveliness nowhere else equalled but on the green, rolling prairies, and under the clear atmosphere of Minnesota."

FLORENCE a city in section 20, Shelburne, platted October 9, 1888, and incorporated as a village on February 16, 1920, was named for Florence Sherman, daughter of its founder. It had a Great Northern Railway station, and the post office was established in 1889.

GARVIN a city in section 27, Custer, was developed

by the Chicago and North Western Railway in 1879, although a depot was not built until 1886. It was platted April 30, 1886. It was first identified as Siding No. 7, and then called Terry (1886), and afterward Kent (1887) for Chicago missionary Father Kent, which was changed to the present name in July 1891 in honor of H. C. Garvin, traveling freight agent of the railway. Area residents often referred to the community as Seefield, the post office name, 1887–91, for a resident who built the first building, a grain elevator, near the station.

GHENT a city in section 15 of Grandview, platted in June 1878 by the Winona and St. Peter Railroad and incorporated May 15, 1899, at first bore the name of the township but was renamed in September 1881 for the ancient city of Ghent in Belgium, in compliment to Belgian colonists coming in 1880–81, who were led by Bishop John Ireland to settle in this part of the county. The post office was established as Grandview in 1874; however, in 1882 a residents' petition requesting the name be changed to Ghent was granted, the railroad changing the name of the station as well.

GRANDVIEW see GHENT.

GRANDVIEW TOWNSHIP first settled in August 1871 and organized two years later, was named, like Alta Vista in Lincoln County, for the extensive outlook northeastward from the Coteau des Prairies.

GREEN VALLEY a Great Northern Railway village in section 10, Fairview Township, platted in May 1888, refers to the vast green prairie there traversed by the Redwood River. A post office began in 1889 and changed to a rural branch in 1964.

HECKMAN a station of the Chicago and North Western Railway, five miles southeast of Marshall in Lake Marshall Township, was named for a dining-car superintendent. A post office was in section 25, 1901–14, located at the east end of the lake.

HILDRETHSBURGH a post office, 1874–80, located in postmaster Charles Hildreths's home, section 14 of Lyons Township, although Henry Mupler was postmaster; the post office moved to the home of Mrs. Libby Willard in section 17 and changed its name to Leo, 1880–92.

ISLAND LAKE TOWNSHIP first settled about 1868 and organized in March 1879, was named for its lake in section 34, having a small wooded island. A post office was located in section 34 of the township, 1874–1901; the small community had a church and a cheese factory.

LAKE MARSHALL TOWNSHIP settled in 1869 and organized March 8, 1872, received the name of its lake, given in honor of Gov. William Rainey Marshall, for whom also a county is named.

LEO see HILDRETHSBURGH.

LONESOME see TAUNTON.

LUCAS was settled in 1871. "The town was set off for organization in July 1873, as Canton, which was changed to Lisbon, and again to Moe, and lastly to Lucas. The first town meeting was held August 5, 1873" (*History of the Minnesota Valley*, p. 865). This name is borne by counties in Ohio and Iowa, a township in Wisconsin, and villages in these and other states.

LYND TOWNSHIP settled in 1867, organized January 9, 1873, was named in honor of James W. Lynd, who had a fur trading station in section 5, Lyons, during 1855–57, and afterward removed one or two miles down the Redwood River to the northeast quarter of section 33 in this township. He was born in Baltimore, Md., November 25, 1830, and was killed in the Indian attack at the Lower Sioux Agency, August 18, 1862. He came to Minnesota about 1853 and lived among the Dakota to learn their language, habits, and characteristics, on which he intended to publish a book. The manuscript for it was completed but was mostly destroyed in the Dakota War. He was a state senator in 1861.

The city of Lynd began with the development of three communities, all called Lynd: (1) Upper Lynd in section 33 was named for trading post owner James W. Lynd and was the county seat when the county was established in 1870; (2) Lower Lynd was laid out in June 1870 in section 27 with a hotel, a store, and a church; businesses transferred from Upper Lynd to Lower Lynd by common consent and the county seat moved to Lower Lynd in 1872; when the Winona and St. Peter Railroad built north of Lynd in 1872 and the town of Marshall developed, the county seat was moved to Marshall in January 1874; this site became Old Lynd; (3) the (New) Lynd site was platted in November 1888 at the siding established by the Great Northern Railway in section 27, creating the present community, which incorporated as a village January 4, 1954; the post office was established in 1872.

LYONS TOWNSHIP first settled in January 1868, organized April 1, 1873, received its name from that of the county, with an added letter, which gives to it the English form of the name of the ancient and large city of Lyon in France.

MARSHALL the county seat, sections 4, 5, and 9 in Lake Marshall Township, platted in August 1872, incorporated as a village March 18, 1876, and as a city February 20, 1901, was named for Gov. Marshall, like Lake Marshall Township, in which it is situated. The first settlers began arriving in the early 1870s in an area chosen and platted by the Winona and St. Peter Railroad (which later became part of the Chicago and North Western Railway) as a site for a future village to be named Redwood Crossing; one of the first settlers was Charles H. Whitney, first postmaster when the post office opened in 1870 as Lake Marshall, who requested shortening the name to Marshall in 1872.

MINNEOTA a city in Eidsvold Township, sections 25, 26, 35, and 36, which was incorporated on January 21, 1881. It was first known locally as Pumpa, so designated by early Norwegian settlers because of the railroad water pump, and then called Upper Yellow Medicine Crossing for its location. It was platted as Nordland village by the Winona and St. Peter Railroad in August 1876; when the post office was established in 1878, it was given the name Nordland, with railroad section boss Harvey D. Frink, postmaster, at his homestead store on railroad land, located on the left side of the tracks west of Yellow Medicine Creek; when the railroad built its depot on the right side of the tracks and other buildings went up nearby, the post office moved to new postmaster Nils Winther Luth Jaeger's store, and the name changed to Minneota, as suggested by Thomas D. Seals, another storekeeper. Jaeger was born in Norway in 1841, came to Minnesota in 1868 and to Lyon County in 1874, and was prominent in business for many years. The name Minneota is a Dakota name, meaning "much water." Prof. A. W. Williamson wrote of its origin, that it is "said to be so named by an early settler on account of an abundance of water flowing into his well."

MINNESOTA a locality on the border of Lincoln County, in Island Lake Township.

MONROE TOWNSHIP first settled in 1871, organized January 5, 1874, was named by Louis and Ole Rialson, pioneers who came from Monroe, the county seat of Green County in southern Wisconsin. Seventeen states of the Union have counties of this name, and a larger number have townships and villages or cities, including eight townships in Pennsylvania, all being named in honor of James Monroe (1758–1831), who was the fifth president of the United States, 1817–25.

NORDLAND see MINNEOTA.

NORDLAND TOWNSHIP settled in 1870, organized May 9, 1873, has the name of a northern district of Norway, crossed by the Arctic Circle. Nearly all its settlers came from that country.

PUMPA see MINNEOTA.

REDWOOD STATION see BURCHARD.

RIPON see TAUNTON.

ROCK LAKE TOWNSHIP organized October 26, 1876, took its name from the lake in its northwest corner, which refers to the abundance of boulders around the shore, pushed up in some places by the lake ice to form a rock wall. A post office was located in the township, 1873–83, after being located in Lyon Township, 1873–74.

RUSSELL a city in section 19, Lyons, founded in May 1888, platted on January 19, 1889, and incorporated September 2, 1898, was named for Russell Spicer, son of a promoter of the building of this branch railway. The post office, begun in 1889, was first located in Ephraim Skyhawk's store, his family for some time having been the only residents; the store and an elevator and section house for the Willmar and Sioux Falls Railroad were built in 1888.

SARATOGA a district in 1874 that included four townships: Sodus, Amiret, Custer, and Monroe; a community developed in section 19 of Amiret Township by this name until it was changed to Amiret.

SEEFIELD see GARVIN.

SHAM LAKE a post office, 1873–78, located in section 2 of Lucas Township, with a station of the Great Northern Railway.

SHELBURNE see BURCHARD.

SHELBURNE TOWNSHIP settled in 1871, organized September 6, 1879, has a name that is borne also by townships and villages in New Hampshire, Vermont, and Massachusetts, and by a county and its county seat in Nova Scotia.

SHETEK see TRACY.

SODUS TOWNSHIP first settled in the spring of

1871, organized October 27, 1876, was named for Sodus Township and village in Wayne County, N.Y., adjoining Sodus Bay of Lake Ontario. This name is of Indian origin, but its meaning is uncertain.

STANLEY TOWNSHIP settled in 1867, was organized in March 1877. A city in Wisconsin, villages and post offices in a dozen other states, and a county in South Dakota bear this name.

SUMMIT see TRACY.

SVERDRUP a post office, 1883–88; location not found.

TAUNTON a city in section 17, Eidsvold, platted in April 1886 and incorporated March 27, 1900, was named by C. C. Wheeler, an officer of Winona and St. Peter Railroad, for the city of Taunton in Massachusetts. It was first called Lonesome in August 1886 when the post office was established, indicative of its position on the prairie, changed three months later to Ripon after a community in Wisconsin, and changed again in 1888 to Taunton.

TRACY a city in Monroe Township, platted in 1875, incorporated as a village February 5, 1881, and as a city August 3, 1893, was named in honor of John F. Tracy, a former president of the Chicago and Northwestern Railway. Its post office was called Summit, 1874–75, and transferred to Lyon County from Redwood County; it was next called Shetek, 1875–77, and then became Tracy. While it was Summit, Levi Montgomery was the postmaster on his homestead, the name relating to this being the highest point on the railroad between Chicago and Lake Campeska, S.Dak.; when Montgomery left his claim during the grasshopper scourge, the post office was moved to the new village, called variously Shetek, Shetek Station, or Shetek Bend, with postmaster Horatio N. Joy in his store, the first building in the community; it had a station of the Winona and St. Peter Railroad in section 23.

UPPER YELLOW MEDICINE CROSSING see MINNEOTA.

VALLERS TOWNSHIP organized October 7, 1876, was named by Ole O. Brenna, a pioneer settler from Norway. "His desire was to name it Valla, a Norwegian word, meaning valley, but because of incorrect spelling in the petition or illegibility the county commissioners made the name read Vallers" (*History of Lyon County*, by Rose, p. 57).

WESTERHEIM TOWNSHIP first settled in June 1871

and organized May 9, 1876, received this Norwegian name, meaning "western home," by vote of its people, mostly immigrants from Norway.

Lakes and Streams

Coon Creek, Cottonwood Lake, Island Lake, Lake Marshall, and Rock Lake, giving their names to townships, a city, and a village, have been duly noticed in the foregoing list.

Meadow Creek is a name given to the stream flowing from Lake Marshall to the Cottonwood River.

Three Mile Creek is a northern tributary of the Redwood River, with which it is nearly parallel and three to five miles distant along most of its course.

Monroe has Lake Sigel and the shallow or sometimes dry Twin Lakes, the former being named in honor of Gen. Franz Sigel (1824–1902), distinguished for his service in the Civil War.

The Lake of the Hills, often dry, is in sections 20 and 21, Custer. Long Lake, on the south line of this township, and Lake Yankton, adjoining Balaton, outflow southeastward to Lake Shetek and the Des Moines River.

Black Rush Lake, drained, was in Lyons; Marguerite or Wood Lake is in Coon Creek Township; and Goose Lake lies about a mile west of Island Lake.

Swan Lake is on the east side of section 12, Stanley.

School Grove Lake was in the school section 36 of Lucas; Lady Slipper and Lady Shoe Lakes were in the south half of this township, having species of the Minnesota state flower, commonly known by these names, also called moccasin flower; and Sham Lake was in section 3. These former lakes, however, have been drained. Only Cottonwood Lake, beside the village named from it, and Lone Tree Lake, in sections 5 and 6, remain in Lucas Township.

Between the lakes of Stanley and Lucas, in the northeast corner of this county, and the numerous lakes before mentioned, in its higher southwest part, a wide tract extending from southeast to northwest through its center is destitute of lakes, excepting Lake Marshall, named for a governor of this state and giving his name to the county seat.

Mahnomen County

This county, established December 27, 1906, was previously the east part of Norman County. It comprises half the area of the White Earth Reservation, which also extends south into Becker County and east into Clearwater County, the name of the reservation as noted in the chapter for Becker County, being derived from White Earth Lake. The south line of Mahnomen County crosses the north end of this lake, and its outlet, the White Earth River, flows through the south half of this county to the Wild Rice River.

Mahnomen is one of the various spellings of the Ojibwe word for the wild rice. From this excellent native grain we receive the English name, through translation, of the Wild Rice Lakes in Clearwater County and of the Wild Rice River, which has its source in these lakes and flows across Mahnomen and Norman Counties to the Red River. The same word has been more commonly written "manomin," as in Frederic Baraga's *A Dictionary of the Ojibway Language*, and in this spelling it was the name of a former very small county in this state, between Anoka and St. Anthony (the east part of Minneapolis), existing from 1857 to 1869. With other orthographic variations, it gave the names of the Menominee Indians, Menominee River, County, and city in Michigan, and Menomonee River as well as the towns of Menomonee Falls and Menomonie in Wisconsin.

The county seat of Mahnomen County has the same name, which was given to this railway village before the county was established. Its spelling here adopted is similar to Mahnomonee, written by Henry W. Longfellow in *The Song of Hiawatha*.

In the Dakota language, according to its dictionary by Rev. Stephen R. Riggs, wild rice is called *psin*. From that word probably came the earliest published name, Du Siens for the Wild Rice Lake and River, given by the narration of Joseph la France in 1744, as noted in the chapter for Clearwater County. He described the plant as "a kind of wild Oat, of the Nature of Rice." It was commonly known by the early French traders and voyageurs as *folle avoine*, meaning "fool oat or false oat," and thence their name for the Menominee, living in the north part of Wisconsin and Michigan, was Folles Avoines, and that region of many lakes and streams, having abundance of wild rice, was named the Folle Avoine country. Dr. Douglas Houghton, writing in 1832 as a member of Henry R. Schoolcraft's expedition to Lake Itasca, defined this term to comprise "that section of country lying between the highlands southwest from Lake Superior and the Mississippi river."

A very interesting monograph, titled "The Wild Rice Gatherers of the Upper Lakes," was contributed by Prof. Albert E. Jenks in the *Nineteenth Annual Report of the Bureau of American Ethnology*, for 1897–98, published in 1900 (forming its pp. 1,013–137, illustrated with 13 plates). Derived mainly from that elaborate work, a summary notice of the wild rice and its use by the Ojibwe was given by Prof. N. H. Winchell, in part as follows. "The plant is an annual, springing from seed every year, growing in lakes and slow-flowing streams which have a mud-alluvial bottom. The grain is from about a half an inch to nearly an inch in length, cylindrical, dark slate color when ripe, and is embraced in glumes, or husks, arranged in an appressed panicle at the top of the long stem. . . . Its leaves are broad (for a grass) and numerous. Its botanical name is *Zizania aquatica*. The fruit is ripe in September. While it is perpetual when once established in favorable situations, it becomes necessary to sow it artificially when it is destructively gathered. . . . In August the green, standing, rice stalks are tied into bunches by the women. This is for protecting the grain from injury and loss by water-fowl as well as by winds, and also to facilitate the subsequent harvesting. The twine used is the pliable inner bark of the bass-wood. . . . Much rice is gathered, however, without previous tying. When it is ripe it is gathered in canoes which are pushed through the rice-field, one woman acting as canoeman and the other as harvester. The stalks, whether tied in bundles or not, are bent over the gunwale and beaten with a stick so as to dislodge the grain. As the fruit is easily loosened, whether by the wind or by birds, as well as by handling, it is necessary to gather it just before maturity, and subsequently subject it to a process of drying and ripening" (*The Aborigines of Minnesota*, 1911, pp. 592–94).

About 10,000 bushels of wild rice were formerly harvested yearly by the Ojibwe in northern Minnesota, being an average of a bushel or more for each of the population. In later years, the amount of wild rice used is much diminished. But it has considerable salable value, especially when marketed to white people.

Rev. Joseph A. Gilfillan, in his paper on "The Ojibways in Minnesota" (MHS Collections 9: 55–128 [1901]), presented a vivid description of the gathering of wild rice, as seen at a large rice lake in the north part of this reservation.

Information of the origins and meanings of names in this county was received from Alfred Aamoth, auditor, and Arthur J. Andersen, treasurer, during a visit at Mahnomen, the county seat, in September 1909; and from John W. Carl, auditor, and Martin M. Bowman, clerk of the court, in a second visit there in September 1916.

BEAULIEU TOWNSHIP and village were named for Henry and John Beaulieu, who served in the Civil War and afterward owned farms here. The village in section 31 was first established with the trading post of John H. Beaulieu in 1868; the post office began in 1891 with Lizzie Beaulieu, postmaster, changing to a rural route in 1960 and discontinuing in 1968. John Beaulieu was during many years the village postmaster. Records of the Beaulieu family and allied families, prominent in the history of the Ojibwe in this state, descendants of a French fur trader, Bazille Beaulieu, and his Ojibwe wife, Queen of the Skies, are given by Winchell in *The Aborigines of Minnesota*, page 722. During the 1890s a government boarding school for Indian children was built, closing in 1912.

BEJOU TOWNSHIP and its railway village received this name, changed in pronunciation and spelling, from the French words *Bon jour* ("Good day") of the former fur traders and voyageurs. It is the common Ojibwe salutation on meeting friends or even strangers, used like the familiar English and American greeting, "How do you do?" The city in sections 22, 23, 26, and 27, incorporated as a village on January 13, 1921, was created by the Minneapolis, St. Paul and Sault Ste. Marie Railroad (Soo Line) in 1904 as a railroad village; its post office began in 1906.

BEMENT a post office, 1905–6, which was located 25 miles north of Detroit Lakes and named for a pioneer family, two of whom were Thomas Bement, who built a hotel here in 1904, and William (Bill) Bement, who built the first livery barn and later ran a butcher shop; the post office name was changed to Waubun.

CHIEF TOWNSHIP was named in honor of Maysha-ke-ge-shig (also spelled Me-sha-ki-gi-zhig), a leader of the Ojibwe on the White Earth Reservation, described by Winchell as "a man revered for many noble qualities and for his distinguished presence." He died "nearly 100 years old," August 29, 1919, at the Old Folks Home in Beaulieu; he had lived as a farmer on this reservation since 1868.

CLOVER TOWNSHIP T. 145N, R. 39W.

DUANE a post office in section 32 of Heier Township, 1904–24, named for Rev. Duane Porter, pastor of the Methodist church.

GREGORY was named for Joseph Gregory, an early farmer, who was one of the first taking an allotment of land in this township.

HEIER TOWNSHIP commemorates Frank Heier, who was teacher of an Ojibwe school in this township and later was superintendent of the government school at Pine Point, Becker County, near the southeast corner of the White Earth Reservation.

ISLAND LAKE TOWNSHIP has a large lake of this name, containing an island of many acres.

LAGARDE TOWNSHIP was named for Moses Lagarde, who served in the Civil War, received a farm allotment here, and was owner of a hotel in Beaulieu village.

LAKE GROVE TOWNSHIP is mostly a broadly undulating and rolling prairie but has several small lakes bordered with groves. A post office was located there, 1914–16.

LITTLE ELBOW LAKE TOWNSHIP also known as Little Elbow Township (T. 143N, R. 39W), dissolved in 1950, becoming part of the Unorganized Territory of Southeast Mahnomen.

MAH KONCE a village in sections 3 and 4 of Twin Lakes Township, which had a post office, 1924–30.

MAHNOMEN a city in Pembina Township, sections 2 and 11, and the county seat, is north of the Wild Rice River, whence came this Ojibwe name, later given to the county; it was incorporated as a village on March 21, 1905. One of the government buildings of the Pembina Mission (Wild Rice Church) was the site of the first post office in February 1904, named Perrault with Lawrence W. Pettijohn, postmaster; the post office name was changed to Mahnomen in December 1904 and moved to the Olson Hardware Store with Sigurd Bernard Olson, postmaster; Olson was born in Gaylord in 1877 and died at Mahnomen in 1962.

MARSH CREEK TOWNSHIP bears the name of the creek flowing across it.

NAY-TAH-WAUSH a village located in Twin Lakes Township, section 28, was first known by the name Twin Lakes; the name changed in 1906 to Nay-tah-wash, which means "smooth sailing." The site had several sawmills, stores, and government offices; its post office began in 1907 with Star Bad Boy, postmaster.

OAKLAND TOWNSHIP T. 143N, R. 40W.

PEMBINA TOWNSHIP like Pembina River and County in North Dakota, is named from the bush cranberry, excellent for making sauce and pies, called by the Ojibwe *nepin ninan*, "summer berry." The Ojibwe words were transformed into this name by the French voyageurs and traders.

PERRAULT see **MAHNOMEN**.

POPPLE GROVE TOWNSHIP has mainly a prairie surface, interspersed with occasional groves of the common small poplar, often mispronounced as in this name.

ROSEDALE TOWNSHIP consisting partly of prairie and partly of woodland, was named for its plentiful wild roses.

SNIDER LAKE was possibly an early name for Little Elbow Township. It has a lake of this name, beside which Frank Schneider, a German married to an Ojibwe, formerly lived as a farmer but later removed to Waubun village.

SOUTHEAST MAHNOMEN Unorganized Territory of, includes former Little Elbow Lake Township (T. 143N, R. 39W) and Twin Lakes Township (T. 144N, R. 39W).

TWIN LAKES TOWNSHIP (T. 144N, R. 39W) is named for its two lakes, separated by a narrow strip of land with a road. It dissolved as a township in 1950, becoming part of Unorganized Territory of Southeast Mahnomen.

UNORGANIZED TERRITORY OF SOUTHEAST MAHNOMEN see **LITTLE ELBOW LAKE TOWNSHIP, TWIN LAKES TOWNSHIP**

WAUBUN a city in section 24 of Popple Grove Township, has an Ojibwe name, meaning "the east," "the morning," and "the twilight of dawn." It is spelled *waban* in Baraga's *Dictionary*, and *wabun* by Longfellow in *The Song of Hiawatha*, with definition as the east wind. Another spelling of this name is borne by Waupun, a city in eastern Wisconsin. The city was incorporated as a village on December 18, 1907. When the Soo Line built through the county in 1903–4, the general manager, Pennington, and his chief engineer, Thomas Green, named the stations as they moved the line north; all towns on the reservation had to have

Indian names. The post office for this community was established in 1905 as Bement, changing to Waubun in 1906.

———————

Lakes and Streams

The foregoing pages have sufficiently noticed the White Earth and Wild Rice Rivers, Island Lake, Marsh Creek, Snider Lake, and the Twin Lakes.

The origins of the names of White Earth and Tulaby Lakes, crossed by the south line of this county, are given in the chapter for Becker County.

Numerous other lakes are to be here listed, in the order of townships from south to north and of ranges from east to west.

Big Bass Lake was named for its fish, and Little Elbow Lake for its bent form.

Simon Lake, crossed by the middle part of the east boundary of the county, commemorates Simon Roy, who had a cattle farm there and died many years ago, leaving several sons living on the White Earth Reservation.

Lake Erie is in section 7, Lagarde. Why it received this name is unknown.

Rosedale has Gardner, Sandy, and Fish Lakes. The first was named for Charles Gardner, who was a log driver on the Snake and Pine Rivers and later was a successful farmer at this lake.

Lone Lake is two miles north of Simon Lake, and Washington Lake lies four miles northwest of Lone Lake, being just north of Wild Rice River.

Aspinwall, Vanoss, and Warren Lakes in Chief Township were named respectively for Henry Aspinwall, a farmer beside the lake of his name, Francis Vanoss, of Canadian French and Ojibwe descent, who in his old age took a land allotment, and Budd Warren, a nephew of William W. Warren, the historian of the Ojibwe. This township also has Chief Lake named, like the township, for an Ojibwe chief.

Sugar Bush Lake in section 7, Island Lake Township, received its name from its maple trees used for sugar-making.

Gregory Township has Lake Beaulieu and Church Lake. The first was named for Alexander H. Beaulieu, who long ago was allotted land there, which he farmed until 1916, then removing to Fosston. Church Lake was named for Charles Church, an American farmer there, having an Ojibwe wife.

Tamarack Lake in section 29, Bejou, is partly bordered by tamarack woods. Sand Hill River, flowing through the northwest part of this township, is named from the dunes or windblown sand hills of its delta in Polk County, which was deposited at the highest stage of the Glacial Lake Agassiz.

White Earth Reservation

Because Mahnomen County is included within this reservation, special attention should be here directed to the concise notice of its name and date before given for Becker County, in which are the Reservation Agency at White Earth and the lake whence the name is taken. It is the largest of the several Ojibwe reservations in this state, having an area of 1,300 square miles, of which only a small part is still Indian owned. It contains many lakes, mostly of small size.

The White Earth Reservation was established by a treaty at Washington, March 19, 1867. In the summer of the next year many Ojibwe of the Mississippi and Gull Lake bands, led respectively by Wa-bon-a-quot (White Cloud) and Na-bun-ash-kong, removed there. June 14, 1868, was the day of arrival of the pioneers in the removal, and its anniversary is celebrated at White Earth each year. Twelve townships in Becker County, the entire 16 townships of Mahnomen County, and the next 4 of Range 38 in Clearwater County are included in the reservation area.

Marshall County

This county, established February 25, 1879, was named in honor of William Rainey Marshall, governor of Minnesota. He was born near Columbia, Mo., October 17, 1825, but his boyhood was spent in Quincy, Ill., to which place his parents removed in 1830. At the age of 15 years, in company with his older brother Joseph, he went to the lead mines of Galena, where he worked several years and learned land surveying.

In 1847 he came to St. Croix Falls, Wis., and in 1849 to Minnesota, settling at St. Anthony Falls and opening a general hardware business, with his brother Joseph. For Franklin Steele and others, he surveyed the St. Anthony Falls townsite, his plat being dated October 9, 1849. Two years later he removed to St. Paul, which thenceforward was his home, and became its pioneer hardware merchant. In 1855 he founded a banking business, which failed in the financial panic of 1857, and subsequently he engaged in farming and stock-raising and brought to Minnesota its earliest high-bred cattle.

Marshall was commissioned in August 1862 as lieutenant colonel of the Seventh Minnesota Regiment; aided in the fight against the Dakota during the war in 1862 and in the expedition of 1863 in Dakota Territory; and afterward served through the Civil War in the South, being promoted colonel of his regiment in November 1863 and brevetted brigadier general March 13, 1865. He was governor of Minnesota during two terms, 1866–70, being "one of the best chief magistrates the state has ever bad." In 1876–82 he served as the state railroad commissioner.

In 1893 he was elected secretary of the Minnesota Historical Society, of which he had been president in 1868, but he resigned in 1894 on account of ill health and went in hope of recovery to Pasadena, Calif., where he died January 8, 1896. An obituary sketch by Rev. Edward C. Mitchell was published in the eighth volume of the MHS Collections (1898, pp. 506–10, with a portrait), and the thirteenth volume of this series, "Lives of the Governors of Minnesota," by Gen. James H. Baker, published in 1908, has a more extended biography (pp. 145–65, with a portrait), including extracts from his addresses and messages as governor.

———

Information of the origins of names was received from History of the Red River Valley *(2 vols., 1909), having pages 831–59 for this county; from August G. Lundgren, county auditor, and Peter Holan, deputy auditor, John P. Mattson, editor of the* Warren Sheaf, *and Hon. Andrew Grindeland, district judge, each being interviewed during a visit at Warren, the county seat, in August 1909; and again from Mr. Lundgren, also from Alfred C. Swandby, clerk of the court, R. C. Mathwig, Albert P. McIntyre, and Charles L. Stevens, editor of the* Warren Register, *during a second visit there in September 1916.*

AGDER TOWNSHIP organized in 1902, has the name of a district in southern Norway, southwest of Christiania. A post office, formerly called Thorwick, 1896–1909, was located in the township, 1909–10, with Marie Thorwick as first postmaster.

ALMA organized in 1882, was named for Alma Dahlgren, the first child born in this township, daughter of Peter O. Dahlgren, who during several years was the county treasurer. A settlement called Alma was in section 13.

ALVARADO a city in Vega Township, has the name of a seaport and river in Mexico, about 40 miles southeast of Vera Cruz. It is also the name of a small city in Texas and of villages in Indiana and California. It was first settled in 1879 and incorporated as a village on October 16, 1907; its post office began as Snake in 1888, named for its location on the Snake River, with Ole Sand, postmaster, in his store. When the Minneapolis, St. Paul and Sault Ste. Marie Railroad (Soo Line) came in 1903, its construction crew established the station name as Alvarado, so Sand with his brother moved the store and the post office in 1905, changing the post office name, and Sand's son, Martin H. Sand, became the new postmaster.

ANITA a station of the Soo Line in section 24 of New Solum Township; a request for a post office was authorized on June 5, 1905, with John Meyers to be postmaster, but it was not established.

ANSTAD a post office in section 10 of Moylan Township, 1906–18.

ANTWINE a post office, 1903–4, on the Red River, 23 miles northwest of Warren.

APPLE a post office, 1899–1913, in section 31 of Wright Township.

ARGYLE a city in sections 10 and 15 in Middle River Township, bears the name of a county in western Scotland, which is borne also by a township in Maine and by villages in nine other states. This name was proposed by Hon. Solomon G. Comstock for Argyle, Maine, where he was born in 1842 and for whom a township of this county is named. The city was incorporated as a village December 12, 1883. Settlers were on the site in the early 1870s, which was first called Frenchtown and then Louisa; its post office was established in 1878 as Middle River, changing to Argyle in 1882. The city developed on a Great Northern Railway

site and had a flour mill, a general store, a hotel, and a number of other businesses.

ASPELIN a village in Big Grass Township, section 30, about 1915–30.

AUGSBURG TOWNSHIP organized in 1884, was named by its Lutheran people for the ancient city of Augsburg in Bavaria, Germany. The chief Lutheran creed, called the Augsburg Confession, was submitted to the Diet of Augsburg in 1530; and a treaty was made there between the Lutheran and Catholic states of Germany, September 25, 1555, which secured the triumph of the Reformation by granting authority for the separate states to prescribe the form of worship within their limits. A country post office was located in the township 20 miles north of Warren, 1901–6.

BALTIC a post office located on the John A. Johnson farm in section 24 of New Folden Township, 1905–8.

BEND a post office, 1894–1905, in section 9 of Wanger Township.

BIG WOODS TOWNSHIP organized in 1882, has a wide border of timber along the Red River. The village in section 28 had a post office, 1886–1909, first postmaster being Hans B. Imsdahl, who also served as register of deeds for the county for many years; the post office operated at the general store; the community also had an elevator and a sawmill in its early years.

BLOOMER TOWNSHIP also organized in 1882, received its name from the village of Bloomer in Chippewa County, Wis., whence some of its settlers came. A post office called Bloomer was in section 6 of Vega Township, 1903–5.

BLOOMWOOD a post office, 1903–7, in section 18 of Bloomer Township.

BOXVILLE TOWNSHIP organized in 1884, was named for William N. Box, an early homesteader there, who removed to Northfield, Minn., and later to the Pacific Coast.

BREESE see **MIDDLE RIVER**.

CEDAR TOWNSHIP organized in 1892, has groves of the arbor vitae, more often called white cedar.

COMO TOWNSHIP organized in 1900, received its name from Lake Como in St. Paul, as probably proposed by George F. Whitcomb, a landowner here who lived in that city. Seven states of the Union have villages of this name, derived from the Italian city and province and their mountain-bordered lake so named at the south side of the Alps. A post office called Como existed, 1902–3; location not found.

COMSTOCK TOWNSHIP organized in 1881, was named in honor of Solomon G. Comstock, an attorney for the Great Northern Railway company, who named the village of Argyle. He was born in Argyle, Maine, May 9, 1842; came to Minnesota in 1869, settling in Moorhead; was admitted to practice law in 1871; was a representative in the state legislature, 1876–77 and 1879–81; a state senator, 1883–87; and a representative in Congress, 1889–91.

DECOY a post office, 1904–7, in Thief Lake Township.

DONNELLY TOWNSHIP organized in 1895, commemorates Ignatius Donnelly, who was born in Philadelphia, November 3, 1831, and died in Minneapolis, January 1, 1901. He was admitted to practice law in his native city; came to Minnesota in 1857; was lieutenant-governor, 1860–63, and a representative in Congress, 1863–69; later served several terms in the state legislature and was a national leader in the Farmers' Alliance movement and in the Populist Party; author of many published speeches and addresses and of numerous books. He lived many years at Nininger, a few miles west of Hastings, and was often called "the Sage of Nininger."

EAGLE POINT organized in 1890, was named from an eagle's nest near the center of this township at a point of the woods that reached eastward from the Red River.

EAST PARK organized in 1899, is the second township east of Nelson Park, previously organized, whence this name was suggested.

EAST VALLEY TOWNSHIP organized in 1896, crossed by the Thief River, had settlers from the earlier West Valley Township on the Middle River.

ECKVOLL TOWNSHIP organized in 1901, received this Norwegian name, meaning "Oak Vale," in allusion to its abundant oak groves. It was proposed by Nels K. Nelson, previously a resident of Warren, being taken from a former Eckvoll post office in section 15 of Oak Park Township, 1892–1907.

EDD a post office, was authorized on June 15, 1903, with Edward K. Johnson to be postmaster, but not established; location not found.

ELDEN a post office in Oak Park Township, 1905,

formerly called Valborg, 1901–5, Nils Elden being postmaster under both names.

ELLERTH a village in Marsh Grove Township; the post office was named for Ellerth Sagnes, wife of Edward Sagnes, postmaster, and was established in his home in section 18 in 1898, moved in 1902 to the Korstad store in section 6 with Anders Korstad, postmaster; it closed in 1913.

ELMBO a post office, 1902–8, 20 miles northeast of Warren.

ENGLUND a village first located in Augsburg Township and later moved to section 30 of Nelson Park Township after Mamie Stromgren put up a building and started a store; it was named for its first postmaster, Andrew J. Englund; the post office operated 1889–1908. Most of the first settlers to the area came from Jämtland and Ångermanland, Sweden.

ESPELIE TOWNSHIP organized in 1903, is likewise named from Norwegian words meaning "Poplar Slope," for its many groves of poplars. The village in section 21, had a post office, 1901–35, with Robert S. Espelee, postmaster.

EXCEL TOWNSHIP organized in 1884, was named from the village and township of Excelsior in Hennepin County, being shortened to avoid exact repetition of that name, which was taken from the well-known poem titled "Excelsior," written by Henry W. Longfellow in 1841. A post office in section 29, 1889–1905, was formerly named Labree, 1883–89, with Adolph Labree as postmaster.

FARLEY see **WARREN**.

FIR a post office, 1883–1905, in section 10 of Nelson Park Township, in the country store owned by Knute Hodne, who also owned the store in Koland.

FLAKNE a post office located in the general store in section 8 of Mud Lake, 1912–16.

FLORIAN a village in section 8 of Wright Township, which was first settled by Polish immigrants and named for Father Florian Matuszewske, who received the franchise to operate a post office, 1903–8, with Andrew Iglinski, postmaster, in his store. It was originally named Stanislawo for Stanislog Gryglaszewski, but the name was found too difficult to pronounce.

FODVANG a village in section 13 of Marsh Grove Township, which had a post office, 1887–1913.

FOLDAHL organized in 1883, is named for a

locality in Norway, the country from which most of the settlers in this township came. The village in section 8 had a post office, 1883–1913. Old Mill State Park, begun in the 1930s as Middle River State Park and formally established in this township in 1951, features a restored gristmill built about 1896 by John Larson.

FORK TOWNSHIP organized in 1896, was so named because the Red River receives the Snake River at its west side. Boatmen ascending the Red River may here take either one of two routes, like prongs or tines of a fork. A post office was located in section 29, 1894–1926.

FRAM a post office in section 15 of Rollis Township, 1903–10.

FRENCHTOWN see ARGYLE.

GATZKE a village in section 10 of Rollis Township; the first settlers were Louise and Ole Stordahl in 1897; the post office began in 1901 on Carl E. Johnson's farm about a mile east and north of the present site and was given his wife's maiden name. A creamery was built at the present site in 1907, and other businesses followed, so those who had built near the post office moved their buildings, including the general store.

GERMANTOWN a post office in section 35 of Grand Plain Township, 1897–1928.

GOLDEN VALLEY a post office in sections 15 and 22 of Mud Lake Township, 1912–26. An experimental peat farm was operated near here, 1918–23, by the state of Minnesota on land leased from Selmer Dahl and Mrs. Carl Dahl.

GOTLAND a post office, 1900–5, in section 12 of Vega Township, named by postmaster, farmer, and storekeeper Gotfred Stromgren for his home area in Sweden.

GRAND PLAIN TOWNSHIP organized in 1898, is in the nearly level and plainlike east part of the county.

GRANVILLE see OSLO.

GRATZEK a post office, 1888–90, in section 9 of Wright Township with John Gratzek, postmaster.

GRYGLA a city in section 26 of Valley Township, was incorporated as a village on February 7, 1917. It was first settled by Arne Fladeland, who opened his store there in 1898; when a post office was requested that same year, a number of names were proposed. The city, founded in 1902, was named for Frank Grygla, better known as the "Father of the Polish National Alliance," of which he was

president for ten years; his father was a count in one of the ancient and noble families of Poland.

HALVOR a post office in section 29 of Oak Park Township, 1901–5.

HELLEM a post office, 1886–1908, first located in section 9 of New Solum Township on the Rasmus Nelson farmstead and later moved to other farms in section 17 and section 16.

HOLT TOWNSHIP organized in 1890, and its city in sections 32 and 33 were named, with a slight change in spelling, in honor of a pioneer Norwegian settler, Halvor Holte, who came to the area in 1886. This is an ancient Anglo-Saxon and Scandinavian word meaning "a grove" or "a wooded hill." The village was incorporated on March 16, 1915, and separated from the township on February 18, 1916. Its post office operated 1886–1969; the Sandridge post office, 1901–8, merged with Holt in 1908.

HOMOLKA a post office, 1901–25, in section 6 of Thief Lake Township, was first located in Poplar Grove Township, Roseau County, until 1918, at John Homolka's sawmill.

HUMBOLDT see NEWFOLDEN.

HUNTLEY TOWNSHIP organized in 1902, having been a noted hunting ground for moose, was at first Huntsville, which was changed because an earlier township in Polk County had received that name.

IDUN a post office, 1902–4, in East Park Township.

INGALLS a post office, 1888–1912, in section 21 of Spruce Valley Township, with William H. Ingalls, postmaster and notary; settlement in the area began in 1886.

JACOBUS a post office, 1884–86; location not found.

JANE a post office, 1912–22, in section 33 of Thief Lake Township.

JEVNE a post office in section 35 of East Park Township, 1902–24, with Knute O. Jevne, postmaster.

JONSTAD a post office, 1902–14, located in section 31 of Moose River Township.

JUVIK a farmers post office, 1897–1907, 14 miles northeast of Warren, in section 10 of Comstock Township.

KLEP a post office, 1902–9, in section 29 of New Folden Township on the farm of Samuel Tunheim, postmaster, who named the post office for his home in Norway. Tunheim (1863–1918) was a pioneer evangelist, teacher, and editor who held many township offices.

KOLAND a post office, 1902–9, in section 8 of East Park Township; John Koland was postmaster in the store owned by Knute Hodne, who also owned the country store in Fir.

LABREE see EXCEL.

LINCOLN TOWNSHIP organized in 1892, was named in honor of the martyr president of the United States in the Civil War.

LINER a post office, 1899–1910, in the store on postmaster Ole H. Langlie's farm, in section 19, Valley Township, on the south side of the Mud River.

LINSELL the most northeastern township of this county and one of the latest organized, in 1908, was named by its Swedish people for the town of Linsell in central Sweden.

LLEWELLYN a post office, 1901–9, in section 3 of New Solum Township in general store of postmaster Per P. Hagen.

LOUISA see ARGYLE.

LOVEID a post office, 1901–5, in section 12 of New Maine Township.

LUNA a station on the Great Northern Railway in section 11 of Warrenton Township.

LUND see STRANDQUIST.

MAGNUS a post office, was authorized on May 5, 1902, with Hans Hallin to be postmaster, but was not established; location not found.

MANOR a post office in section 10 of Excel Township, 1901–8.

MARSH GROVE TOWNSHIP organized in 1884, formerly had numerous marshes and poplar groves, now mostly changed to well-cultivated farms. A village was in section 6 about 1928.

MAVIE a village in Grand Plain Township about 1918.

McCREA TOWNSHIP organized in 1882, was named for Hon. Andrew McCrea, farmer and lumberman, who had land interests in this county and whose sons were residents of Warren during many years, thence removing to the West. He was born in New Brunswick in 1831, came to St. Paul in 1854, afterward lived in Colorado and other states but in 1870 settled in Perham, Minn.; he was a representative in the legislature in 1877 and a state senator in 1879.

MIDDLE RIVER a city in section 11, Spruce Valley Township, on the Middle River, was incorporated as a village on July 23, 1904. The post office, in section 7 of Cedar Township, was named Breese, 1890–1904, and transferred to Middle River in 1904. The Great Northern Railway station was first named Breese and also changed in 1904 to Middle River.

MIDDLE RIVER TOWNSHIP the earliest organized in this county, October 14, 1879, is on the stream so named, which flows through the central and western part of this county, being tributary to the Snake River near its mouth.

MOE a post office was authorized on February 13, 1893, with Tosten O. Moe to be postmaster, but was not established; location not found.

MOOSE RIVER TOWNSHIP organized in 1904, took the name of its river, flowing into Thief Lake.

MOYLAN TOWNSHIP organized in 1902, was named for Patrick Moylan, an Irish settler, who removed to Oregon or Washington.

MUD LAKE TOWNSHIP organized in 1914, includes the east half of the area of Mud Lake tributary to Thief River.

NAIL a post office was authorized on December 23, 1904, with Forrest Holton to be postmaster, but was not established; location not found.

NASET a post office in East Park Township, 1905–7.

NELSON PARK TOWNSHIP organized in 1884, was named for James Nelson, a Yankee hunter and trapper, who was its earliest homesteader, and for several other settlers named Nelson, immigrants from Sweden and Norway.

NEW FOLDEN TOWNSHIP organized in 1884, and its railway village received their name from a seaport in northern Norway, on the south branch of the Folden fjord.

NEW MAINE TOWNSHIP organized in 1900, was named in compliment to settlers from the state of Maine. An alternate version is that it was named for the historic battleship *Maine*, destroyed in Havana harbor in 1898 shortly before the settling of the township.

NEW SOLUM TOWNSHIP organized in 1884, is named for a district in Norway.

NEWFOLDEN a city in New Folden Township, was incorporated as a village on February 8, 1916; it was first settled in 1882 but not developed until the Soo Line came in 1904. The city was originally named Baltic by the Soo Line for the numerous

Baltic elevators along the line; however, residents requested the name be the same as their post office, and the name Baltic was given to another community in the township in 1884 and changed to Newfolden in 1896; another site of this name, located two miles south, had developed in 1886 with several stores and disappeared almost overnight when the railroad platted the "new" Newfolden in 1904. The post office began as Humboldt and operated 1884–96 in section 14 of New Solum Township, first located on postmaster Ole Olson Lie's farm in New Folden Township; the name was changed to Newfolden in 1896, and the post office moved to Oyve B. Bakke's store, at which time he became postmaster.

OAK PARK TOWNSHIP organized in 1883, has many oaks in its woods bordering the Red River. The name of a discontinued post office of this township, Eckvoll, meaning "Oak Vale," was transferred, as before noted, to a township in the east part of this county.

OPDAHL a post office, 1900–14, in section 20 of New Maine Township.

OSLO a city in sections 31 and 32 of Oak Park, bears the name of a large medieval city that occupied the site of Christiania, Norway. The old city was mostly burned in 1547 and again in 1624, and the new city was founded and named at the later date by Christian IV, king of Denmark and Norway. The city was incorporated on November 21, 1905, as Oslo; the name changed to Soo City in 1907 and back to Oslo in 1908; it was reincorporated on December 11, 1912, at which time it separated from the township. The post office began as Granville, Polk County, in 1881 and transferred to Oslo in 1905, associated with postmaster Andrew Hilden, who was born in Norway in 1853, moved to the United States in 1869 and to Granville, Polk County, in 1896, buying the one existing store and taking over the post office in 1897; he moved the store to the present Oslo in 1905 along with the post office; Hilden moved to Baudette in 1910, where he died in 1922.

PARKER TOWNSHIP organized in 1884, was named for George L. Parker, a pioneer settler there, who after several years moved away.

PIEHOTTA a post office, was authorized on February 13, 1901, with Jacob Piehotta to be postmaster, but was not established; location not found.

RADIUM is a small village of the Soo railway in section 19 of Comstock Township, named for the very wonderful metallic element radium, discovered in 1902. It has had a post office since 1905.

RANDEN a post office, 1905–27, in section 19 of Linsell Township, with Hans E. Randen, postmaster; a store and a church were also at the location.

RINGBO a village in section 7 of Holt Township, was named for a small Norwegian town near Gudbransdhal from which many of the area settlers came; *ring* meaning "circle" and *bo* meaning "place where people live" together mean "community." There was a post office, 1891–1907.

ROCKSTAD a post office in northeast New Folden Township, 1899–1907, located on the Ole Folden homestead with Jens P. Folden, postmaster.

ROLLIS organized in 1899, was named for Otto Rollis, formerly of Warren, who became a storekeeper and first postmaster in this township but later removed to Colorado. The post office was in section 21, 1898–1923.

ROSEWOOD a village in section 3 of New Solum Township; the first post office, located in Enoch and Tina Nelson's farmstead general store, was called Strip, 1900–12, in reference to a land correctional area shown on a geographic survey; when the Soo Line came through in 1905, local residents requested the name be changed to Rosewood for the roses growing on a ridge nearby; however, the post office did not change its name until 1912; the post office closed in 1954.

SANDRIDGE a post office, was named by the Great Northern Railway in 1904 to describe the area; when the Agassiz National Wildlife Refuge was created in 1937, many dairy and grain farmers had to leave their properties, and the economy of the village diminished. The post office merged with Holt in 1908.

SINNOTT TOWNSHIP organized in 1883, was named for Pierce Joseph Sinnott, who was born in Ireland in 1846, moved to United States in 1878 and to this township in 1878, and died in 1922, and for his brother, James P. Sinnott, who was born in Ireland in 1844 and came in 1882 to the area where his brother had already homesteaded; he died in 1920.

SKOG a village in section 10 of Eagle Point Township, first settled by Swedish immigrants about

1881; its post office, 1902–14, was named for its first postmaster, Peter P. Granskog.

SKRAMSTAD a post office, 1904–6, located in Como Township with Gunder D. Skramstad as postmaster.

SNAKE see ALVARADO.

SOO CITY see OSLO.

SORUM a post office, 1901–8, in section 19, East Valley Township, located on the east side of Thief River on the H. M. Olson farm.

SPRUCE VALLEY TOWNSHIP organized in 1888, is named for its spruce trees along the Middle River, which are common or abundant throughout northeastern Minnesota but here reach their southwestern limit.

STANISLAWO see FLORIAN.

STEINER a Great Northern Railway station in section 28 of Excel Township.

STEPHEN a city in sections 5 and 6 in Tamarac Township and north of Tamarac River, was named in honor of George Stephen, a prominent financial associate of James J. Hill in the building of the Great Northern Railway system. He was born at Dufftown, in Banffshire, Scotland, June 5, 1829; came to Canada in 1850, settling in Montreal, and engaged in dry goods business and manufacturing cloth; was president of the Bank of Montreal, 1876–81, and president of the Canadian Pacific Railway company, 1881–87; was knighted by Queen Victoria in 1886; was a founder in 1887, with Sir Donald Smith, of the Royal Victoria Hospital, Montreal; removed to England in 1888 and resided in London. In 1891 he received the title of Baron Mount Stephen, referring to a peak of the Rocky Mountains named for him during the construction of the Canadian Pacific Railway. The city was incorporated as a village December 18, 1883; the original settlement, known as Tamarack, was in 1878 in a sheltered location south of the Tamarac River where the first building was the Great Northern Railway section house; the post office was established in 1879 on the John Hughes farm in section 8 and moved to the new site when developed in 1883.

STONE a post office located in section 13 of New Solum Township, 1900–9, in the general store on the farm of postmaster Ole Hall.

STRANDQUIST a city in section 22, Lincoln Township, was named in honor of John Erik Strand-quist, a merchant there, who was born in Sweden in 1870 and settled in this county in 1892; it was incorporated as a village on July 31, 1923. A Mr. Lund operated a post office west of town called Lund, 1897–1905, although Charles M. Carlson was listed as postmaster; Strandquist, born in Sweden in 1870, came to the United States in 1892, had a farm in the Strandquist area on which he opened a general store and where in 1899 he established the Strandquist post office; when the railroad came in 1904, Strandquist moved his business into the village, then called Lund, so that the village had two post offices until the Lund post office closed in 1905; Strandquist died in 1919.

STRIP see ROSEWOOD.

TAMARAC TOWNSHIP organized in 1879, received its name from the Tamarac River, here crossed by the Great Northern Railway.

TAMARACK see STEPHEN.

THIEF LAKE TOWNSHIP organized in 1896, is named for its large lake, the source of the Thief River. The origin of these names, related by William W. Warren in the *History of the Ojibway People*, is given in the chapter for Pennington County, which has its county seat at Thief River Falls.

THORWICK see AGDER.

VALBORG see ELDEN.

VALLEY TOWNSHIP organized in 1900, is crossed by Mud River or Creek, tributary to Mud Lake by a valley scarcely below the general level.

VEGA TOWNSHIP organized in 1883, bears the name of the ship in which Baron Nordenskjöld, the Swedish explorer, in 1878–79 traversed the Arctic Ocean along the north coast of Russia and Siberia, passed through the Bering Strait to the Pacific, and returned around Asia and through the Suez Canal. A post office was located on postmaster Andrew P. Norland's farm in section 30, 1898–1907.

VELDT TOWNSHIP organized in 1902, was at first called Roosevelt for Theodore Roosevelt, the president of the United States. Because that name had been earlier given to another township of Minnesota, it was changed to this Dutch word, used in South Africa, meaning "a prairie or a thinly wooded tract."

VIKING TOWNSHIP organized in 1884, was named by Rev. Hans P. Hansen, a Norwegian Lutheran pastor in Warren. This Scandinavian word, often translated as "a sea king," more correctly denoted any member of the early medieval pirate crews of Northmen who during several centuries ravaged the coasts of western and southern Europe. The city in section 26 was incorporated as a village April 12, 1921; the post office was established in 1890. The community developed with the railroad; there were three elevators and a number of small businesses.

WANGER TOWNSHIP organized in 1882, was named for a German hunter and trapper who lived there before the coming of agricultural settlers.

WARE a post office, 1896–1908, in Como Township.

WARREN a city in Boxville and Warrenton Townships and the county seat, platted in 1879–80, incorporated as a village in 1883 and as a city April 3, 1891, was named in honor of Charles H. Warren, general passenger agent of the St. Paul, Minneapolis and Manitoba Railroad, which in 1890 was renamed the Great Northern Railway. The community developed with the Great Northern, Northern Pacific, and Soo Line railroads. The railway was built to the site of Warren in the summer of 1878, and in November of that year trains ran through to Winnipeg. The post office was established as Farley in 1878 and changed to Warren in 1880.

WARRENTON TOWNSHIP organized in 1879, has a name of the same origin as the city of Warren, which is at its southeast corner.

WEST VALLEY TOWNSHIP organized in 1884, is named from the Middle River, which here is enclosed by low bluffs. A post office was in section 28, 1884–1913.

WHITEFORD TOWNSHIP organized in 1910, has a name that is borne also by small villages in Maryland and Michigan. A post office was located in the township, 1904–7.

WRIGHT TOWNSHIP organized in 1884, probably received this name in honor of one of its first settlers.

Streams and Lakes

Middle River was named by the fur traders, whose trains of Red River carts crossed it on the old Pembina trail about halfway between Pembina and their crossing of the Red Lake River.

Snake River is translated from its Ojibwe name, written by Rev. Joseph A. Gilfillan as Ginebigo zibi.

Tamarac River is also noted by him as a similar translation, from Ga-mushkigwatigoka zibi. Tamarack is elsewhere the common spelling for the tree and geographic names derived from it.

In the place of these three streams, only one is found on the map of Maj. Stephen H. Long's expedition in 1823, named Swamp Creek, where the present Tamarac ditch in Donnelly and Eagle Point Townships carries to the Red River the drainage of a large swamp area, in which Tamarac River was formerly lost, thence emerging northward and joining the Red River in the southwest part of Kittson County. Swamp Creek, translated from the Ojibwe name of Tamarac River, was copied on Joseph N. Nicollet's map in 1843 and on the map of Minnesota Territory in 1850, but the state map of 1860 has the present Tamarac, Middle, and Snake Rivers, although their courses are erroneously drawn.

Preceding pages have noticed Moose River, Thief Lake and River, and Mud River and Lake, whence three townships are named.

Green Stump Lake and Elm Lake, each shallow and drained for use as farmlands, were respectively about one mile and three miles southwest of Mud Lake, which was before noted.

Whiteford has two little lakes, about midway between Thief and Mud Lakes, of which the eastern one is named Olson Lake.

Marshall County is wholly in the area of the Glacial Lake Agassiz.

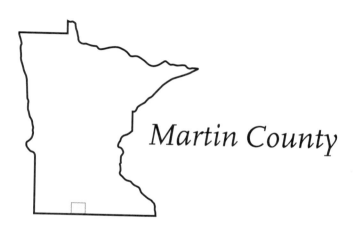

Martin County

This county was established May 23, 1857, being named, according to the concurrent testimony of its best informed early citizens, in honor of Henry Martin of Wallingford, Conn., who then was a resident of Mankato, having land interests there and probably expecting to live permanently in Minnesota. He was born in Meriden, Conn., February 14, 1829; went to California in 1849 and engaged in auction business in San Francisco until 1851; returned to Connecticut and was state bank commissioner, 1854–56; came to Minnesota in 1856 and selected and purchased, for eastern associates and himself, about 2,000 acres of lands in Mower, Fillmore, and other counties, including the area, then in Brown County, which in 1857 was set apart as Martin County; resided temporarily in Mankato and visited the chains of lakes in this county for hunting and fishing, one of which, Martin Lake in the northwest corner of Rutland Township, was named for him. Beside this lake he built a house and partly planned to settle there. Within about one year be returned to Wallingford, Conn., where his family had continuously resided, and that town was ever afterward his home. He engaged in manufacturing there, was deputy sheriff of New Haven County, 1884–87, and after 1895 was assistant town clerk. (These biographic notes are in a letter and personal sketch received from him in 1905.) He died in Wallingford, July 18, 1908, in the home to which he brought his bride in 1853.

Members of the territorial legislature, who passed the act establishing Martin County, may have been partly influenced in favor of this name by remembering that Morgan Lewis Martin, of Green Bay, Wis., as delegate to Congress from Wisconsin Territory, on December 23, 1846, introduced the bill for the organization of the Territory of Minnesota. He was born in Martinsburg, Lewis County, N.Y., March 21, 1805; was graduated at Hamilton College, 1824; came to Green Bay in 1827 and during his long life resided there, being, as a lawyer and judge, prominently identified with the history of his state. He died December 10, 1887. An autobiographic narrative by him, with notes by R. G. Thwaites, was published in the Wisconsin Historical Society Collections (vol. 11, 1888, pp. 380–415); and his portrait is given in vol. 9 of that series, facing page 397.

The honor of the county name, ascribed to Henry Martin by William H. Budd (*History of Martin County*, p. 114), was again so stated, with historical details given by George S. Fowler, in an article published by the *Martin County Sentinel*, July 15, 1904. Two weeks later, a second article on this subject, by A. N. Fancher, presented the rival claim that the honor belongs in an equal or larger degree to Morgan L. Martin.

Information of geographic names has been gathered from History of Martin County, *by William H. Budd, published in 1897 (124 pp.); from George S. Fowler and Christian N. Peterson, interviewed during a visit at Fairmont, the county seat, in October 1910; and from R. M. Tyler, clerk of the probate court, Hon. Albert L. Ward, state senator, Hon. Frank A. Day, and Miss Minnie Bird, librarian, during a second visit at Fairmont in July 1916.*

AMBER a post office, located on the lake of the same name in section 30 of Fairmont Township, operated 1867–74. The lake was also known as Bardwell Lake after former residents who lived there before moving away in 1879.

ANDREW JOHNSON a post office, 1865–72, in section 22 of Tenhassen Township, three miles from the old Tenhassen post office on the east side of the creek, is named for the president of the United States.

BELMONT a post office, 1864–68; location not found.

BENONI a post office, 1873–74, in Tenhassen Township.

BUCEPHALIA see FOX LAKE.

CADWELL a post office, 1899–1901, located in section 11, Galena Township.

CARDONA see IMOGENE.

CEDAR TOWNSHIP established January 2, 1872, was named for Cedar Lake, at its east side, which has red cedar trees on its shores.

CEDARVILLE a village and trade center on the north shore of Cedar Lake in section 24 of Cedar Township, was platted in 1892 by R. L. Patrick and consisted of four blocks; it had two stores, a hotel, a blacksmith, and a gristmill; its post office operated 1868–1903.

CENTER CHAIN a post office, 1882–1905, and trade center in section 33 of Silver Lake Township, which had a store, a creamery, and a church; the post office was originally called Chain Lake Center, 1858–82, but was shortened to Center Chain by request of the postmaster.

CENTER CREEK TOWNSHIP bears the name of the creek flowing through it from the Central Chain of lakes. A post office called Center Creek began as Colfax 1861–65, in section 24, Winnebago City Township, Faribault County, at the home of postmaster S. B. Hazen; then in 1863 it was moved to R. N. Feiro's farm one half mile east, and again in 1865 to postmaster James Olden's farm in section 29 of Center Creek Township; the name was changed to Centre Creek and discontinued in 1879.

CEYLON a city in sections 23–26 in Lake Belt Township, has the former name of a large island adjoining India. It is also the name of villages in Pennsylvania and Ohio. It was incorporated as a village October 22, 1900; it developed when the Minnesota and International Railway came through in 1898, the railroad choosing the townsite and naming it Tenhassen; however, that name was already in use, so a group of men sitting in Tom Sahr's general store suggested Ceylon for the boxes of Ceylon tea in the store. The post office began in 1899.

CHAIN LAKE CENTRE see CENTER CHAIN.

COLFAX see CENTER CREEK.

DE SOTA a site in Lake Fremont Township, was platted in 1899 as a station of the Minneapolis and St. Louis Railroad and named for the explorer, Hernando de Soto; residents protested the Spanish name, the Spanish-American War having just ended. Accessibility was so limited that a request was made to move the site two miles south, creating the community of Dunnell, the De Sota site being totally vacated within three months and reverting to farmland.

DUNNELL a city in sections 10, 11, 14, and 15 of Lake Fremont Township, was named in honor of Mark H. Dunnell, congressman, who was born in Buxton, Maine, July 2, 1823, and died in Owatonna, Minn., August 9, 1904. He was graduated at Waterville College in 1849 and was admitted to practice law in 1856; was appointed U.S. consul to Vera Cruz in 1861; came to Minnesota in 1865, settling at Winona, and later removed to Owatonna; was a representative in the legislature in 1867; state superintendent of public instruction, 1868–71; and a member of Congress, 1871–83, and again in 1889–91. The city was organized in 1899 and incorporated as a village on October 23, 1901; it had a station on the Minneapolis and St. Louis Railroad, and the post office began in 1873.

EARL a post office, 1891–96, at the home of postmaster Wallace B. Mayo in section 17 of Jay Township; there was no significance attached to the name when Mayo consulted the post office guide and picked a name not already in use.

EAST CHAIN TOWNSHIP was named for the East Chain of lakes, described in the later part of this chapter. The village in section 7 was first settled about 1859 and developed as a trading place from the early 1860s when a Mr. Chatfield built the first store near the site of the post office called East Chain Lakes (1862–1906), later shortened to East Chain.

ELM CREEK TOWNSHIP established in March 1867, is crossed by the creek of this name, which flows through the north half of the county, for the many elms in the woods along its course.

FAIRMONT a city in Fairmont Township and the county seat, platted as a village in 1860 by W. S. Campbell, from which the township took this name, was incorporated February 28, 1878, and adopted its city charter in 1902. It was at first called Fair Mount, referring to its situation beside and above the Central Chain of lakes, having a fine outlook across the lakes and the adjoining county. The first post office of the county was established here in 1858; several railroads came through in the late 1870s and aided in developing the townsite as a trading center.

FORT BRITT a fort established during the Dakota War of 1862 at the home of George Britt in section 32 of Silver.

FOX LAKE TOWNSHIP established January 2, 1872, is named for the long and narrow lake at its south side, which also gave this name to the railway village at its east end, in section 34, platted in 1899. The post office began as Walnut Grove in 1867, became Bucephalia in 1873, then Fox Lake later that year, and again Walnut Grove, 1874–76, and was discontinued and reinstated as Fox Lake in 1901, becoming a rural branch, 1955–1965; it had a station of the Iowa, Minnesota and Northwestern Railroad.

FRASER TOWNSHIP was named in honor of Abraham N. Fraser, who took one of its first homestead claims, on Elm Creek.

GALENA TOWNSHIP was named by settlers from the city of Galena in Illinois, which received this name from mines of galena, a lead ore.

GRANADA a city in sections 20, 29, 30, and 31 of Center Creek Township, bears the name of a renowned medieval Moorish city and kingdom in Spain. It was founded in 1888 and incorporated as a village on May 11, 1895; it was originally called Handy with a post office of that name, 1888–91,

Albert H. Reynolds, postmaster, named in honor of Abner S. and Sally M. Handy, who had settled in section 31 of the township in 1859; it was platted in 1890 by Ed Anderson, and the name changed in 1891, with Reynolds continuing as postmaster under the new name; it had a station of the Minneapolis, St. Paul and Sault Ste. Marie Railroad (Soo Line).

HANDY see GRANADA.

HAYES a post office, 1877–79, in Westford Township on the section 2 farm of postmaster James Brownlee; named for President Rutherford B. Hayes.

HAZELMERE a village in Fairmont Township, section 17, about 1913–16.

HILLSBOROUGH see ROSE LAKE.

HORICON a post office first located in Rutland Township, section 5, in 1867 but moved to the Murphy farm in Westford Township in 1887, discontinuing in 1900; it may have been named by settlers from Horicon, Wis.

IMOGENE a railway village in section 5 of Pleasant Prairie Township, platted in 1900, has the name of the daughter of Cymbeline in one of Shakespeare's plays. It was first platted in 1899 under the name Cardona, but residents did not like the Spanish name, and when a post office was requested, 1901–13, the name was changed; the Chicago and North Western Railway depot was the center of town, and a few businesses were present, but the townsite was never incorporated.

JAY TOWNSHIP established January 2, 1872, has the name of a county in Indiana and of villages and townships in Maine, Vermont, and New York, commemorating John Jay (1745–1829), who was an eminent statesman of the American Revolution, first chief justice of the U.S. Supreme Court, 1789–95, and governor of New York, 1795–1801.

JERICO a site in the Nashville Township area that existed about 1856, when the area was still part of Brown County.

KIRTLAND TOWNSHIP former name of Rutland Township.

LAKE BELT TOWNSHIP established in March 1867, was named for its series of three lakes, to be again noticed in the later part of this chapter. An alternate version is that it was named for Lake Belle (later changed to Clear Lake), but an error in recording created the name as it is. Lake Belt was also a post office, 1873–1900, in the township, later merging with Ceylon.

LAKE FREMONT TOWNSHIP established January 2, 1872, formerly had a small lake, now drained, in the west part of section 34, which was named in honor of John C. Frémont (1813–90), assistant with Joseph N. Nicollet in his expedition through this region in 1838. He was later called "the Pathfinder," from explorations of the Rocky Mountains and the Pacific slope in 1842–45, and was the Republican candidate for the presidency of the United States in 1856.

LAKE PUZAH a post office of Rutland Township, 1858–60, established when part of Brown County; it may have been in same area as a later post office named Horicon.

LILY CREEK see **WELCOME**.

LONE CEDAR a post office, 1867–79, in sections 7 and 18, Fairmont Township, was named by postmaster Kilburn J. Archer for the single cedar on his farm, the only cedar tree in section 18; Archer also had a halfway house tavern in a sod building on his land, which ceased to exist when the railroad was built through Sherburn and the post office was transferred there.

LONE WILLOW a post office, 1871–72, in section 20 of Rolling Green Township.

MANYASKA TOWNSHIP bears a Dakota name, given to lakes of this vicinity on Nicollet's map, probably meaning "white bank or bluff," but to be then more correctly spelled *mayaska*. It has been otherwise translated as "white iron" or silver, from *maza*, "iron," *ska*, "white." This name is also borne by a lake in section 19, a railway station, and a village in section 25. The village was established as a shipping point for stock and grain with a station of the Chicago and North Western Railway in 1899; the post office operated 1900–8.

MAY see **NORTHSTAR**.

METHVEN a post office, 1873, in Elm Creek Township.

MONROE a post office, 1875–1903, in section 19 of Waverly Township, with John Hollister, first postmaster and first chairman of the Galena Township board of supervisors.

MONTEREY see **TRIMONT**.

MULE FARM/MULE TOWN a farm located in sections 13, 14, and 23 of northeast Jay Township, representing a thousand acres and developed in the 1870s by a Wisconsin syndicate (Cargill, Bassett, and Hunting) using mule and horsepower and up to 40 workers; the farm failed through mismanagement, and in 1888 a fire destroyed the buildings. The same company platted the community of Sherburn, which was located in section 7 next to Mule Farm.

NASHVILLE was named in honor of A. M. Nash, a pioneer farmer, at whose home this township was organized, May 3, 1864.

NASHVILLE CENTRE a village in section 9 of Nashville Township, was established about 1864; the post office began in 1867, with Alonson M. Nash, postmaster, and the village developed in sections 3 and 10 after the post office moved to a general store there; the post office discontinued in 1904.

NORTHROP a city in section 9, Rutland, platted in 1899, was named in honor of Cyrus Northrop, who was born in Ridgefield, Conn., September 30, 1834; was professor of rhetoric and English literature at Yale University, 1863–84; and was president of the University of Minnesota, 1884–1911. The city was incorporated as a village on July 6, 1933; the post office operated 1900–72, when it became a branch of Fairmont; it had a station of the Chicago, St. Paul, Minneapolis and Omaha Railroad.

NORTHSTAR a post office in section 4, Fraser Township, 1875–95, was named for the Minnesota sobriquet "North Star State." It was spelled North Star, 1895–98, discontinued that year but reestablished as Northstar, 1898–1904, when the May post office, 1867–98, was transferred there; the May post office was in section 8 at the home of postmaster Hugh P. Simpson, who picked the name simply because there was no other post office by that name in Minnesota.

ORMSBY a city in Galena and Long Lake Townships with Watonwan County, was incorporated as a village on September 5, 1902; the main street is on the county line, dividing the community between the two counties. It was named for E. S. Ormsby, formerly of Emmetsburg, Iowa, who owned the bank.

PIXLEY a post office, 1881–1902, and stage stop, was first located in section 34 of Pleasant Prairie Township on George F. Pixley's 160-acre farm, which he purchased in 1874; Pixley also built the country store on his farm in 1881, where the post office remained until 1894.

PLEASANT PRAIRIE TOWNSHIP organized March 7,

1865, has a euphoniously descriptive name, chosen by its settlers. A post office, 1867–84 and 1886–1902, was first located in section 23 and then in section 11.

PRAIRIE CREEK a post office, 1868–71; location not found.

ROLLING GREEN TOWNSHIP bears a name chosen for its undulating and rolling contour of the green and far-viewing prairie.

ROSE LAKE a post office first called Hillsborough, 1864–65, with Charles W. Hill, postmaster, and then Rose Lake until discontinued in 1882; location not found; a lake of this name is in Fairmont Township.

RUTLAND TOWNSHIP was named on the suggestion of one of its early settlers, Amasa Bowen, register of deeds, for the city and county of Rutland in Vermont. It was formerly called Kirtland Township. A post office was located in section 12, 1867–88.

SHERBURN a city in section 7 of Manyaska Township, incorporated as a village on March 8, 1879, was named in honor of the wife of an officer of the Chicago, Milwaukee and St. Paul Railroad, living in McGregor, Iowa, or possibly in honor of Sherburne S. Merrill, a Southern Minnesota Railroad official. It was platted by the Cargill, Bassett, and Hunting syndicate of Wisconsin about 1878, as was Mule Farm. A post office called Lone Cedar, 1867–79, was located about one mile south of the present Sherburn, where it transferred to in 1879.

SILVER LAKE TOWNSHIP was first established as Nevada Township in 1860, but as that name was already given to another township in the state, the name was changed in 1863. It has the South and North Silver Lakes in the Central Chain.

SPERRY a post office in section 29 of Nashville Township, began as Waverly, 1862–87, moving to the home of Oliver H. Sperry in 1887 and changing its name, discontinuing in 1900. Sperry was born in New York in 1809 and came to the county in 1864.

TENHASSEN TOWNSHIP established March 7, 1865, received this Dakota name, changed in form, from the "Tchan Hassan lakes," mapped in this vicinity by Nicollet. More correctly spelled, it is the name of Chanhassen Township in Carver County, meaning the "sugar maple," from *chan*, "tree," and *hassen*, related to *haza*, "huckleberry or blueberry," thus denoting "the tree of sweet juice." A

post office was located in section 20 and 21, 1862–1900, with a sawmill, a general store, and a stage station.

TRIMONT a city in Galena and Fox Lake Townships, is the result of the merger between Triumph and Monterey. The village of Triumph, platted in 1899 and named by John Stein, in compliment for the Triumph Creamery company, had a station of Minnesota and International Railway in section 32 of Galena Township; the post office began in 1880, and the village was incorporated on August 15, 1901. Monterey had a station of the Minneapolis and St. Louis Railroad in section 31 of Galena Township; the post office began in 1899, and the village was incorporated on October 14, 1902. As these two railroad communities grew, the few miles between them diminished, and they merged into one city on January 1, 1959.

TRIUMPH see TRIMONT.

TRUMAN a city in sections 4, 9, and 10 in Westford, platted in 1899, was named for Truman Clark, a son of J. T. Clark, who was then the second vice-president of the Chicago, St. Paul, Minneapolis and Omaha Railroad. Also several families named True lived near this village. It was incorporated as a village on March 31, 1900, having developed when the Watonwan Valley Railroad came in 1899. Most settlers lived on Elm Creek near the west ford, and as there were no bridges, the stream had to be crossed where fording was possible, thus the name of its post office, Westford, which began in section 36 in 1871 and changed to Truman in 1899. It had a station of the Chicago, St. Paul, Minneapolis and Omaha Railroad.

WALNUT GROVE see FOX LAKE.

WAVERLY see SPERRY.

WAVERLY TOWNSHIP was named by a pioneer settler, who was from the large village of Waverly in Tioga County, N.Y.

WELCOME a city at the intersection of Manyaska, Fox Lake, and Rolling Green Townships, eight miles west of Fairmont, was named in honor of Alfred M. Welcome, whose farm lay at its southwest side. It was incorporated as a village on May 7, 1890, and separated from the townships on April 24, 1907. It was established in 1880 by the Southern Minnesota Extension Company on land owned by S. L. Campbell at a point called Campbell's Switch; the post office was established in

July of 1881 as Lily Creek, but as that name was already in existence, the name was changed in September to Welcome.

WESTFORD see TRUMAN.

WESTFORD TOWNSHIP has a name that is borne also by villages and townships in Vermont, Massachusetts, Connecticut, New York, Pennsylvania, and Wisconsin.

WILBERT a village in section 15 and 22 of Tenhassen Township, named for the first postmaster, Wilbert L. Robinson, who died in 1901; the community had a general store where the post office operated 1898–1907.

Chains of Lakes

Three remarkable series of lakes in this county, named the East, Central, and West Chains, are of great interest in glacial geology because they give evidence of a prolonged warm or temperate interglacial stage or epoch, preceded and followed by long stages of severe cold, when the continental ice sheet covered this area and extended far to the south.

The East Chain extends in a somewhat irregular northerly course for 12 miles from the Iowa line, with outflow northeastward by South Creek. This chain comprises eight lakes, varying from a half mile to two miles in length, with a half to two-thirds as great widths. The lakes are bordered by rolling areas of till, to which their shores ascend 30 to 40 feet, mostly by quite steep slopes. Between the lakes are, in some cases, marshes as wide as the narrower parts of the lakes, but some of the adjoining lakes are connected by contracted channels, such as may have been cut by the outflowing stream. Thus the series does not occupy depressions in any well-marked continuous valley.

About 20 lakes form the Central Chain, which extends 22 miles in an almost perfectly straight course from south to north, lying 3 to 6 miles west of the East Chain. Its outlets are South, Center, Elm, and Perch Creeks, all flowing eastward. The shores and the country on both sides consist of till, which rises to a moderately undulating expanse 30 to 40 or 50 feet above the lakes. Though forming a very distinct, straight series, these lakes do not occupy a well-defined valley, for its width varies from one mile or more to less than an eighth of a mile, and it is interrupted in three places by water divides, their lowest points being 10 to 15 feet above the adjoining lakes.

The West Chain is less distinctly connected than the East and Central Chains, from which it also differs in having the longer axes of some of its lakes transverse to the course of the chain, and in having the shorter series of lakes joined with it as branches. Tuttle Lake at the south end of the chain lies on the state line, about 4 miles west of Iowa Lake, the south end of the Central Chain. Thence the West Chain reaches 20 miles northwesterly, then 9 miles northerly, and then northwest and west for 8 miles to Mountain Lake in Cottonwood County, its whole extent being 37 miles. Its successive portions from south to north are tributary to the East Fork of the Des Moines River, to Center and Elm Creeks, and to the South Fork of Watonwan River. This West Chain comprises about 25 lakes, extending through a region of undulating till, the direct deposit of the ice sheet, with no noteworthy areas nor unusually thick included layers of water-deposited gravel and sand, as is true of all this county.

A series of three lakes in Lake Belt Township lies somewhat west of the direct course of the West Chain and may be regarded as a branch of it, and 3 miles east of this lake belt, another series of seven lakes, very plainly a branch of the West Chain, diverges from it and reaches almost due north 12 miles from Tuttle and Alton Lakes. To these, as a continuation of the same branch, ought perhaps to be added four other lakes, which are situated 4 to 9 miles farther north.

The explanation of these series of lakes that appears most probable is that they mark interglacial avenues of southward drainage and occupy portions of valleys that were excavated in the till after ice had long covered this region and had deposited most of the drift sheet but before the later glacial stage or epoch again enveloped this area beneath a lobe of the continental glacier, partially refilling these valleys and leaving along their courses the present chains of lakes.

In the order from north to south, the East Chain includes Lone Tree Lake, named for a tall cottonwood tree beside it, which was a landmark for travelers; Lake Imogene, whence the neighboring railway village was named; Rose Lake, having many roses along its shores; Sager Lake, named for a pioneer settler; and Clear Lake and East Chain Lake. This chain also has two lakes of small size.

In the same order, the Central Chain has Perch Lake, outflowing northward by Perch Creek; Murphy Lake, named for John Murphy, an early Irish homesteader; Martin Lake, named for Henry Martin, as before noted; High Lake, Lake Charlotte, Twin Lakes, Canright Lake, and Buffalo Lake in Rutland, the last being named for its buffalo fish; Lake George, named for George Tanner, a settler there in the north edge of the present city of Fairmont; Lake Sisseton, bearing the name of a tribal division of the Sioux, this region being noted on Nicollet's map as the "Sissiton Country"; Budd Lake, named in honor of William H. Budd, historian of the county, who took a land claim here in July 1856; Hall Lake, commemorating E. Banks Hall, who also came in the summer of 1856; Amber Lake, Mud Lake, and Bardwell and Wilmert Lakes; North and South Silver Lakes, the former also called Summit Lake; and Iowa Lake, crossed by the Iowa line.

The West Chain comprises in this county, besides several small lakes, Fish, Buffalo, and North Lakes, the second named for the buffalo fish; Cedar Lake, which gave the name of a township; Big Twin Lakes, the smaller one of which has been drained; Seymour and McGowan Lakes, the latter now dry, named respectively for W. S. Seymour and Daniel McGowan, pioneers; Fox Lake, naming a township; Temperance Lake, Munger Lake, now drained, named for Perry Munger, an early farmer, and Manyaska and Prairie Lakes, the latter drained, in Manyaska Township; Smith Lake, formerly called Goose Lake, and Holmes Lake, each drained, on the north line of Lake Belt; and Alton or Inlet Lake and Tuttle Lake in Tenhassen. The last, crossed by the state line, is named in honor of Calvin Tuttle, one of the earliest settlers in Martin County, who came in March 1856. This lake was called Okamanpidan Lake on Nicollet's map, a Dakota name referring to its nests of herons.

A western branch of the West Chain, before noted, giving the name of Lake Belt Township, consists of Susan, Fish, and Clear Lakes.

Between the Central and West Chains, a longer but less continuous branch of the latter includes, with several small lakes and several drained, Long and Round Lakes in Waverly; Patten or Patton Lake in section 25, Galena, named for Lieut. Patton, whose platoon of troops built a sod fort there in May 1863 (previously called Chanyaska Lake for its trees), and Creek Lake on Elm Creek, crossed by the south line of section 36; Eagle and Swan Lakes in Fraser; Pierce and Mud Lakes in Rolling Green; and a second Mud Lake or Rice Lake, Babcock or Bright Lake, and Clayton Lake in Tenhassen.

Other Lakes and Streams

Only a few lakes and fewer streams remain to be noted in addition to the chains of lakes and the streams outflowing from them.

Burnt Out Lake, adjoining a burned peat bed, in sections 21 and 28, East Chain, was formerly called Calkins Lake, for pioneer farmers of this name at its east side. Ash Lake, shown by early maps in sections 26 and 27 of this township, has been drained.

Timber Lake or Marsh, mostly in section 2, Rolling Green, is named for its grove.

The head stream of the East Fork of the Des Moines, flowing across Jay and Lake Belt Townships and through Alton Lake to Tuttle Lake, has given to the former of these lakes a second name, Inlet Lake.

Lily Creek, having water lilies, is the outlet of Fox Lake flowing east into Swan and Eagle Lakes.

Clam Lake is in sections 15 and 16, Fox Lake Township.

Badger Lake, a shallow lake in sections 17 to 20, Galena, was named for its badgers, formerly frequent here, but more common in Wisconsin, "the Badger State."

Duck Lake, once noted for its wild ducks, in sections 2 and 11, Elm Creek Township, and Watkins Lake, in sections 8, 9, and 16, have been drained.

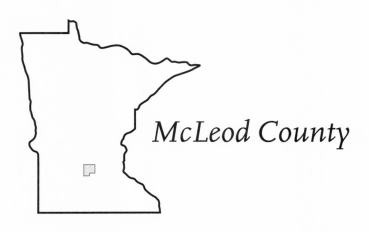

McLeod County

Established March 1, 1856, this county was named in honor of Martin McLeod, a pioneer fur trader of Minnesota, who was born in Montreal, August 30, 1813, of Scottish parentage, and there received a good education. In 1836 he came to the Northwest, voyaging in an open boat on Lake Superior from its mouth to La Pointe, Wis., and thence walking more than 600 miles to the Pembina settlement on the Red River, where he arrived in December. The next March, having set out with two companions, young British officers, and Pierre Bottineau as guide, he came to the trading post of Joseph R. Brown at Lake Traverse, arriving March 21, after a journey of 19 days and a most perilous experience of hunger and cold due to successive blizzards, by one of which the two officers perished. Coming forward to Fort Snelling in April 1837, he was afterward during many years engaged as a fur trader for Chouteau and Company, under the direction of Gen. Henry H. Sibley, being in charge of trading posts successively on the St. Croix River, at Traverse des Sioux, Big Stone Lake, Lac qui Parle, and Yellow Medicine.

McLeod was a member of the council in the territorial legislature, 1849–53, being president of the council in 1853. With Col. John H. Stevens and others, he was one of the founders of Glencoe in 1855. He died November 20, 1860, on his farm, to which he had removed his family in 1849, at Oak Grove in Bloomington, Hennepin County. He was a charter member of the Minnesota Historical Society and was one of its two vice-presidents elected at the time of its organization, November 15, 1849. (The name is pronounced as if spelled McLoud, with English sound of the diphthong.)

Information of the origins of geographic names has been received from an address by R. H. McClelland at the fiftieth anniversary of the founding of Hutchinson, October 4, 1905; History of McLeod County (1917, 862 pp.), edited by Franklyn Curtiss-Wedge and Return I. Holcombe; and interviews with Capt. Axel H. Reed, Henry L. Simons, and Henry Wadsworth, each of Glencoe, the county seat, during a visit there in July 1916.

ACOMA TOWNSHIP was named by Dr. Vincent P. Kennedy for the Indian pueblo village of Acoma in western New Mexico, about 50 miles west of Albuquerque. A post office was located in section 31, 1892–1905.

BEAR LAKE a village in section 11 of Hutchinson Township, with a post office, 1899–1903; the first township school was built in section 14 in 1869.

BEAVER DAM a post office, 1860–62; location not found.

BERGEN TOWNSHIP was named by its Norwegian settlers for the large city and seaport of Bergen in southwestern Norway. A post office was located in section 2, 1867–83 and 1887–88.

BISCAY a city in Hassan Valley Township, section 25, received its name from the large Bay of Biscay adjoining Spain and France. It was incorporated as a village in 1949; the post office operated 1888–1954, changing to a rural branch, 1954–1965; it had a station on the Chicago, Milwaukee, St. Paul and Pacific Railroad.

BROWNTON a city in sections 29 and 32 in Sumter, platted October 15, 1877, incorporated February 20, 1886, was named by Capt. Alonzo L. Brown, whose farm included this townsite, in honor of his brother, Charles, who died in 1862 in the Civil War, both men serving with Company B of the Fourth Minnesota Regiment. Alonzo Brown was born in Auburn, N.Y., November 8, 1838, and died at his home in Brownton, October 11, 1904. He came to Minnesota in 1857, settling here; served in the Civil War and became captain; was author of the *History of the Fourth Regiment, Minnesota* (1892, 594 pp.). The first settlers came about 1856, and the community was shown on territorial maps as Grimshaw's Settlement for Robert E. Grimshaw, one of the 1856 settlers; the post office began in 1878 with Alonzo L. Brown, postmaster; it had a station of the Chicago, Milwaukee, St. Paul and Pacific Railroad.

BRUSH PRAIRIE a post office in section 14, Bergen Township, 1867–83.

CEDAR a post office, 1859–63, in section 6 of Lynn Township; the village was incorporated on May 19, 1857, as Cedar City, but no trace remains.

COLLINS see STEWART.

COLLINS TOWNSHIP was named in honor of one of its early settlers. This name is borne by a township in New York and by villages in ten other states.

EAST HUTCHINSON a post office, 1867–73, of Hutchinson Township.

FERNANDO a village in sections 28 and 29 of Round Grove Township, which formerly had a station of the Chicago, Milwaukee and St. Paul Railroad, a church, and a creamery where the post office was located, 1899–1903, with Ferdinand W. Fenske as postmaster and buttermaker.

FREMONT a post office, 1856–61, established in Hennepin County and transferred to McLeod County in 1859; location not found.

GLENCOE TOWNSHIP received the name of its village founded on June 11, 1855. It was chosen by Martin McLeod, for whom this county was named and who was a member of the townsite company, in commemoration of the historic valley called Glencoe in Scotland where the MacDonalds were massacred in February 1692. The city in sections 13, 14, and 33 was incorporated in 1873 and adopted its charter as a city March 4, 1909. From the beginning of the county, it has been continuously the county seat; it has had a post office since 1856. The city boomed when the Hastings and Dakota Railway came in 1872, followed by the Chicago, Milwaukee, St. Paul and Pacific Railroad, changing from a small settlement to a trade center. John Harrington Stevens is considered the founder.

GLENDALE a post office, 1858–63 and 1868–71, located in Hutchinson Township.

GRIMSHAW'S SETTLEMENT see BROWNTON.

HALE TOWNSHIP was named either for an early settler or for John P. Hale of New Hampshire, a distinguished American statesman and the Free Soil candidate for president in 1852. It is said that the Hutchinsons and other antislavery men of the county induced the county board to name the township for the eminent New England Free Soiler (*History* of this county, p. 264). John Parker Hale was born in Rochester, N.H., March 31, 1806, and died in Dover, N.H., November 19, 1873. He was a member of Congress from New Hampshire, 1843–45; U.S. senator, 1847–53 and 1855–65; and was minister to Spain in 1865–69. A post office was located in section 13, 1872–78 and 1880–81.

HASSAN VALLEY TOWNSHIP the last organized in this county, is crossed by the Hassan River, as it was named on maps of Minnesota in 1860 and 1869, but on later maps called the South Fork of Crow River. This Dakota word, *hassan*, is derived from *haza* or *hah-zah*, the "huckleberry or blueberry." With another Dakota word, *chan*, "tree," it supplied the name of the sugar maple, *chanhasan*, the tree of sweet juice, whence came the name of Chanhassen Township in Carver County and Hassan Township in Hennepin County.

HEATWOLE a village in section 25 of Lynn Township, named for Joel P. Heatwole; he was born in Indiana in 1856 and came to Minnesota in 1882, first publishing newspapers at Glencoe and Duluth before publishing the Northfield newspaper in 1884; he served as U.S. Representative, 1895–1903, and died at Northfield in 1910. The post office operated 1899–1903.

HELEN TOWNSHIP was named in honor of Helen Armstrong, its first white woman resident, whose husband, J. R. Armstrong, was sheriff of the county. A post office was in section 33, 1873–75.

HUTCHINSON TOWNSHIP took the name of its village founded November 19, 1855, by the brothers Asa, Judson, and John Hutchinson, with others. These brothers were members of the famous family of many singers, born in Milford, N.H., who gave concerts of popular and patriotic songs throughout the United States after 1841 until the close of the Civil War. Asa Burnham Hutchinson, youngest of the brothers founding Hutchinson, where he afterward lived, was born March 14, 1823, and died at his home there November 25, 1884. Adoniram Judson Joseph Hutchinson, commemorated by the name of Judson Lake, now drained, about a mile north of this city, was born March 14, 1817, and died in Lynn, Mass., January 10, 1859. John Wallace Hutchinson, born January 4, 1821, resided many years in Lynn, Mass., and was author of the *Story of the Hutchinsons* (2 vols., 495 and 416 pp.), published in 1896.

Hutchinson, in Hutchinson and Hassan Valley Townships, was incorporated as a village February 9, 1881, and as a city in 1904; the post office began in 1856. The station in section 6 of Hassan Valley Township served several rail lines. The city has the second oldest park system in the United States.

KARNS CITY a townsite laid out by Gen. S. D. Karns in July 1856 and incorporated on May 23, 1857, on the south shore of Lake Marion in Sumter Township in hope that the railroad would be built through it; the community did not develop, and no trace remains.

KEYSTONE a post office, 1867–70; location not found.

KOMENSKY a village in Hutchinson Township, section 34, which had a general store, a station of the Luce Line and other rail lines, and a school until 1959.

KONISKA a village platted in 1856 in Rich Valley Township, section 20, on the South Fork of Crow River, for utilization of its waterpower. It was laid out in 1856 and first called McLeod, with a post office named Koniska, 1860–63 and 1866–82; little remains of the townsite.

LAKE ADDIE a post office in section 7, Sumter Township, 1868–79.

LAKE TODD a post office, 1870–71, which became

Bonniwells Mills, then Lamson, Meeker County; location not found.

LESTER PRAIRIE a city in section 2 in Bergen, platted in 1886 and incorporated on September 13, 1888, was named in honor of John N. Lester and his wife, Maria Lester, whose homestead farm included a part of its site. The city was incorporated again on March 19, 1912, when it separated from the township. Its first store opened in 1887, and the post office opened in 1888 at George Chamber's lumberyard with Lena McConahy as postmaster; it had a Great Northern Railway station.

LYNN TOWNSHIP was named probably by recommendation of the Hutchinson brothers for the city of Lynn in Massachusetts.

McLEOD see **KONISKA**.

PENN TOWNSHIP settled largely by Germans from Pennsylvania, was named for William Penn, the founder of that state.

PLATO a city in sections 11 and 14, Helen Township, bears the name of a renowned Greek philosopher (d. 347 B.C.), who was a disciple of Socrates and the teacher of Aristotle. This is also the name of small villages in New York, Illinois, Kentucky, and Missouri. The city was incorporated as a village January 1, 1889; its post office, established in 1858, was located on the north end of Kennison Lake, and when the Chicago, Milwaukee, St. Paul and Pacific Railroad came through the township, the village moved to be near it.

RICH VALLEY was named on the suggestion of A. B. White, an early settler at its village of Koniska, for the fertility of its soil and for the South Fork of Crow River flowing through this township.

ROUND GROVE TOWNSHIP was named for the large grove in the northwest quarter of its section 6, adjoining the east side of Round Grove Lake, less than a mile southwest from Stewart village. A village in section 2 was laid out by Dr. D. A. Stewart of Winona, with a post office, 1872–79.

ST. GEORGE is a village on the South Fork of Crow River in the east edge of Rich Valley in sections 13 and 24. It was first settled about 1850 on five acres of land, with a dam on the Crow River providing power for a gristmill and sawmill; it had a post office, 1870–81.

SCHAEFER'S PRAIRIE the largest and one of the last virgin prairies left in Minnesota, is located on 160 acres in section 34, Sumter Township; it was originally owned by Fred and Frederica (Peik)

Schaefer; after their deaths, their daughter, Lulu Schaefer Leonard, sold the land to The Nature Conservancy, which turned over management to the University of Minnesota.

SHERMAN a village in section 28 of Winsted Township, with a station serving several lines including the Minnesota and Western Railroad.

SILVER LAKE a city in sections 33 and 34 of Hale Township platted in 1881 and incorporated on December 23, 1889, is situated at the north side of Silver Lake. It was settled primarily by Czechs and Poles. Its post office was established as Fremont in Hennepin County in 1856 and transferred to McLeod County in 1859, continuing until 1861; a farm post office was established in 1867 as Silver Lake, and the site was called Fremont until the general store was built in 1881, at which time the townsite was laid out as Silver Lake; the farm post office moved a number of times; it had a station of the Minneapolis and St. Louis Railroad.

SOUTH SILVER LAKE a village in section 4 of Rich Valley Township, with a station on the Great Northern Railway.

STEWART a city on the Chicago, Milwaukee and St. Paul Railroad in section 31, Collins, platted in 1878 and incorporated on May 15, 1888, was named in honor of its founder, Dr. Darwin Adelbert Stewart, a Winona physician. He was born in 1842 in New Hampshire, came to this area in 1878, the same year as the railroad, and helped in its organization. The post office was first called Collins, 1871–79, then changed to Stewart; the Chicago, Milwaukee and St. Paul Railroad had a station called Collins in section 17 and one named Stewart in section 31. The city was separated from the township on March 18, 1913.

STOEVERVILLE a station in Round Grove Township on the Hastings and Dakota Railway; about 1871, Capt. Cushman K. Davis of St. Paul and Col. Stoever of the railroad laid out a townsite, but it was not developed.

SUMTER TOWNSHIP was named for Fort Sumter, built on a small artificial island three miles southeast of Charleston, S.C., as a defense of its harbor. The bombardment of this fort by the Confederates, April 12 and 13, 1861, with its evacuation by Maj. Robert Anderson on April 14, began the Civil War. A village in section 10 had a post office, 1869–75; following the arrival of the Chicago, Milwaukee and St. Paul Railroad, a townsite developed on 20 acres of land originally owned by Jeremiah Nobles; a post office again operated 1880–1937. During the 1940s most of the business section of the village was purchased for a mink ranch, which closed in 1976.

VOLLMAR a post office, 1881–83; location not found.

WINSTED TOWNSHIP its village, and the adjoining Winsted Lake, received their name from Winsted in Connecticut, one of the county seats of Litchfield County, the native place of Eli F. Lewis, founder of this village. The lake was originally named by him Lake Eleanor, in honor of his wife.

The city of Winsted in sections 2 and 11 was incorporated August 27, 1887; the first settlers came in the early 1850s, most of German ancestry; Lewis began to develop the site in 1857, platting the townsite on January 2, 1867; Lewis was born in Winsted, Conn., in 1820 and came to Minnesota in 1846, eventually moving to Ketchum, Idaho, in 1883, where he died in 1885. The post office operated 1858–61, was reestablished as Winsted Lake in 1866, and changed back to Winsted in 1886.

Lakes and Streams

Crow River, belonging to several counties, has been considered in the first chapter. McLeod County lies mostly in the basin of its South Fork, which in early years of the county was called Hassan River, as before noted. That name, received from the Dakota and meaning sugar maple, is applied to a township, Hassan Valley; and the next township on this stream, also named from it, is Rich Valley. Its chief tributary, flowing across the south half of the county, is Buffalo Creek, named for abundant buffalo bones found throughout the area when it was first settled and brought under cultivation.

Silver Creek in Bergen Township is a smaller southern tributary of the South Fork, and from the north it receives Crane, Otter, and Bear Creeks, the last being the outlet of Bear Lake, Lake Harrington, and Silver Lake.

High Island Creek, crossing the two most southern townships, flows eastward through Sibley County to the Minnesota River, passing High Island Lake, whence came its name, as noted for that county.

The list of townships and villages contains due notice of Judson Lake, near Hutchinson, Round Grove Lake, Silver Lake, and Winsted Lake.

It is noteworthy that the long and narrow Otter Lake, intersected by the course of the South Fork or Hassan River, Lake Marion in the northeast edge of Collins, Lake Addie at Brownton, and Bakers Lake, crossed by High Island Creek in Penn Township, form together an almost straight series, extending 17 miles from north to south, more than half of which is water. This series of lakes may be of similar origin with the three very remarkable series or chains of lakes in Martin County, described and named in its chapter.

Lakes Addie and Marion were named before 1860 by Charles Hoag for his two daughters. He lived there during a few years, though previously and also afterward his home was in Minneapolis, where in 1852 he bore a principal part in naming that city.

Bakers Lake was named in honor of Augustus C. Baker, who settled there as a farmer in 1865. He was born in Freedom, Ohio, December 19, 1838, came to Minnesota and served during the last year of the Civil War in the Fourth Minnesota Regiment, engaged in mercantile business in Brownton after 1878, and in recent years was its postmaster.

Kings Lake, in sections 10 and 15, Penn, and Wards Lake, crossed by the south line of Round Grove Township, were named for early settlers.

Helen Township formerly had Kennison Lake in sections 1 and 12 and Bear and Brian Lakes in section 32, but they have been drained.

Glencoe has Rice and Swan Lakes in sections 7 and 8, and Brewster and Thoeny Lakes in its southwest part. Mathias Thoeny, for whom the last is named, was born in Switzerland, September 28, 1837; served through the Civil War in the Second Minnesota Regiment, rising to the rank of captain; was a merchant in Glencoe, 1865–70, auditor of this county in 1873–83, and afterward was cashier of the First National Bank of Glencoe during 30 years.

Sumter, with Lake Addie before noted, has Lake Mary in section 17, Clear Lake in section 13, and Nobles Lake adjoining Sumter village. The last was named for three brothers, Alexander, Daniel, and Jeremiah Nobles, whose homesteads were on or near this lake.

In Collins, with Lake Marion, are Eagle Lake and Lake Whitney, the last being named for a pioneer farmer.

Lake Barber, similarly named, is in sections 26 and 27, Lynn, but Lake Allen, in its sections 22 and 23, and another shallow lake in section 34 have been drained.

Winsted has South Lake, lying a half mile south of Winsted Lake; Roach and Higgins Lakes, both drained, in the east edge of this township; Grass Lake in sections 3 and 10; Coon Lake, crossed by the north line of section 5; and Cloustier Lake in section 31. Crane and Otter Creeks, in the south half of Winsted, flow southeastward to the South Fork of Crow River.

With Silver Lake, beside the village of this name in Hale Township, are Mud Lake, on the east, and Swan Lake, about a mile distant northwestward. Another Mud Lake, in sections 23, 24, and 26, Hale, has been drained, as also the former Bullhead Lake in section 21, named for its small species of catfish, called the bullhead or horned pout.

Hutchinson Township has Lake Byron in section 2, and a group of a dozen other lakes in its northern half, including Bear and Little Bear Lakes, Emily and Echo Lakes, Lakes Harrington, Hook, and Todd, and Loughnan's Lake.

Lewis Harrington, honored by one of these lakes, was born in Greene, Ohio, November 22, 1830; was surveyor of the townsite of Hutchinson, 1855–56, and its first postmaster; was captain of a company defending this place against the Dakota in 1862; was a representative in the state legislature, 1866–68; and died by an accidental fall, August 14, 1884, while engaged on government surveys in the state of Washington.

Lake Hook was named for Isaac Hook, who came in the spring of 1856 and lived beside this lake many years as a recluse.

Lake Todd commemorates Daniel S. Todd, a pioneer farmer.

Walker's Lake, two miles northeast from the city of Hutchinson, and Judson Lake, before noticed, have been drained for use of their beds as farming land.

In the north half of Acoma are Cedar and Belle Lakes, crossed by the north line of the township and county, and Stahl Lake in sections 10 and 11, named for Charles Stahl, a German farmer, who settled there in June 1857. Ferrel Lake, formerly in sections 16 and 17, is drained.

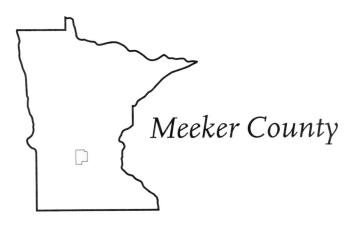

Meeker County

Established February 23, 1856, this county was named in honor of Bradley B. Meeker of Minneapolis, who was an associate justice of the Minnesota supreme court from 1849 to 1853. He was born in Fairfield, Conn., March 13, 1813; studied at Yale College; practiced law in Richmond, Ky., 1838 to 1845, and later in Flemingsburg, Ky.; was appointed judge in the new territory of Minnesota in 1849 and presided at the first term of court on the site of Minneapolis, which was held in the old government gristmill on the west side of the river below the falls, August 20, 1849. Judge Meeker was a charter member of the Minnesota Historical Society, 1849, and was one of the first board of regents of the University of Minnesota, elected by the territorial legislature in 1851. After leaving the bench, he engaged in real estate business and was a member of the constitutional convention, 1857. He purchased a large tract of land on the Mississippi below St. Anthony, including Meeker Island and extending eastward, and he foresaw and often spoke of the coming great prosperity of Minneapolis. He died very suddenly in Milwaukee, where he had halted on a journey to the East, February 20, 1873.

Information of the origin and meaning of names has been gathered from A Random Historical Sketch of Meeker County, *by A. C. Smith (1877, 161 pp.);* Album of History and Biography of Meeker County *(1888, 610 pp.); and from Norris Y. Taylor, who during many years was county surveyor, J. W. Wright, who was county superintendent of schools, 1879–87, and a state senator, 1907–9, and William H. Greenleaf, for whom a village and township are named, each being interviewed during a visit at Litchfield, the county seat, in May 1916.*

ACTON organized in April 1858, was named for the village of Acton in Ontario, Canada, whence the Ritchie family came to settle in this township in 1857. The village in sections 26, 35, and 36 was incorporated on February 8, 1858, but the incorporation was dissolved; it had a post office, 1857–63 and 1899–1904.

ARVILLA a station of the Great Northern Railway in Dassel Township.

BECKVILLE a locality in Greenleaf Township whose first Swedish settlers came in the late 1850s, followed in 1869 by a Swedish Lutheran congregation of about 30 under the leadership of Rev. Peter Beckman, the site taking the name Beckville in his honor.

BONNIWELL, BONNIWELLS MILLS see LAMSON.

BRIGHTWOOD a locality on the south shore of Lake Ripley near Litchfield in section 23 of Litchfield Township, about 1913–16; also known as Brightwood Beach.

CASEY a post office, 1897–1904, in section 11 of Ellsworth Township.

CEDAR MILLS TOWNSHIP organized January 25, 1870, received the name of its village founded in 1860, which was named from the large Cedar Lake, about two miles distant to the east. This lake has many red cedars on its shores and islands, as noted by its name on Joseph N. Nicollet's map, Rantesha Wita or Red Cedar Island Lake. The city in sections 12–14 was incorporated as a village in 1950; the site was originally owned by the City Investment Company and was platted in December 1922. The post office, begun in 1870 in Renville County, was transferred to Meeker County in 1872, discontinued in 1904, reestablished in 1927, and changed to a rural branch in 1955; its station served several railroad lines including the Minneapolis and St. Louis Railroad.

COLLINWOOD organized May 8, 1866, bears the name (changed in spelling) of Collingwood, a port on the southern part of Georgian Bay in Ontario. This township was at first called New Virginia but was renamed as now in 1868, taking the name of the village platted in its northeast corner by Canadian settlers in 1866, beside Lake Collinwood, which is crossed by its east line. A post office was in section 1, 1869–78.

CORVUSO a village in section 17 of Cedar Mills Township; the name is corrupted Latin for "gathering of the crows," as given by an early resident for the number of crows present. The village was originally owned and platted by the Penn Investment Company in 1923. It had a creamery, a general store, a post office, 1898–1905 and 1923–53, and a station of the Minneapolis and St. Louis Railroad in section 20.

COSMOS TOWNSHIP organized January 25, 1870, has a name proposed by Daniel Hoyt, one of its first settlers, who came in 1867, was a surveyor, and was elected the first township clerk. It is an ancient Greek word meaning "order, harmony," and thence the universe as an orderly and harmonious system. The city in sections 15, 16, 21, and 22 was incorporated as a village on September 21, 1926, and as a city in 1969; a post office was established in Renville County in 1870 and transferred to Meeker County in 1872, closing in 1906 and reestablishing in 1924; it had a station serving several rail lines including the Minnesota and Western Railroad.

CROW RIVER a village in section 33, Union Grove Township; the post office was first called Lake Lydia, 1867–68, discontinuing in 1909.

DANIELSON settled in 1857, organized March 12, 1872, was named for Daniel Danielson, its first township clerk and assessor, and for Nels Danielson, an immigrant from Norway, who took a land claim here in 1861 and died in 1870.

DARWIN TOWNSHIP organized April 5, 1858, was then called Rice City, which was changed in 1869 to the name of its railway village, platted in October of that year. It was chosen in honor of E. Darwin Litchfield of London, England, a principal stockholder and promoter of the St. Paul and Pacific (now the Great Northern) Railroad, for whom also, as well as for his wife and his brothers, the village and township of Litchfield were named. The village in sections 22–27 was first organized by a party of surveyors from Dubuque, Iowa, who made claims on paper; the townsite was platted as Stella City and then named Rice City for Hon. Edmund Rice of St. Paul; it was incorporated as a village on June 16, 1919; the post office, established as Rice City, operated 1862–63 and again in 1868, the name changing to Darwin in 1869.

DASSEL TOWNSHIP first settled in 1856, was organized in the fall of 1866 under the name of Swan Lake, from the Big Swan Lake in its northeast part, but it was renamed in 1871 for its railway village in sections 27 and 34, platted in 1869, which was incorporated February 28, 1878. The village and township thus commemorate Bernard Dassel, who in 1869 was secretary of the St. Paul and Pacific Railroad company. The site was platted in 1869 by Parker Simons, civil engineer for the St. Paul and Pacific Railroad; Simons liked the area and built the first frame building on the site; the early townsite had a general store, a sawmill, a hotel, and a number of small businesses; the post office was called Dassel Station, 1869–70, before changing to the present form.

DICKSON a post office, 1888; location not found.

EAST KINGSTON a village in section 14 of Kingston Township, a few miles northeast of the city of Kingston, first settled in 1860 and platted on January 24, 1871.

EDEN VALLEY a railway village in the north edge of Manannah, platted in 1886, was euphoniously named by officers of the St. Paul, Minneapolis and Sault Ste. Marie Railroad (Soo Line). The city with Stearns County began as Pappelbusch (often spelled Popple Bush) in Manannah Township in 1877, a German name meaning "stand of popple trees," on a site two and one-half miles east of the present Eden Valley; it was incorporated as a village on April 25, 1894. August Loegering came to the site about 1880, bought a farm on the border of Stearns and Meeker Counties, opened a general store and a post office called Logering, 1884–93, the post office department misspelling his name. Loegering was born in 1857 in Waconia, later moved to Long Prairie, where he died in 1938. When the Minneapolis and Pacific Railroad built through sections 2 and 3 of the present city, all businesses moved there; the post office, begun as Eden Lake in Stearns County in 1872, was transferred to Eden Valley in 1887.

ELLSWORTH TOWNSHIP first settled in June 1856, organized September 1, 1868, was named at the suggestion of Jesse V. Branham, Jr., in honor of Ephraim Elmer Ellsworth, colonel of a Zouave regiment from New York City, who soon after the beginning of the Civil War was killed in Alexandria, Va., May 24, 1861.

FOREST CITY TOWNSHIP on the west border of the Big Woods, organized April 5, 1858, received the name of its village, platted in the summer of 1857, which was the county seat until the autumn of 1869, being then succeeded by Litchfield. The village was originally intended to be in Harvey Township but was platted in Forest City, section 17, after a post office was established there in 1856 on Walter C. Bacon's farm, the first post office in the county; the post office discontinued in 1907. The village was incorporated on May 19, 1857, but later unincorporated.

FOREST PRAIRIE TOWNSHIP consisting mainly of woodland but having a small prairie nearly a mile long in its northwest corner, was organized in the summer of 1867. Its name was chosen "because there was not a bit of prairie in the town." A farmers post office operated, 1879–81.

GREENLEAF TOWNSHIP settled in 1856 and organized August 27, 1859, was named, like the village on its east border, in section 30, Ellsworth, platted in 1859, in honor of William Henry Greenleaf, one of the founders of the village. He was born in Nunda, N.Y., December 7, 1834; came to Minne-

sota in 1858, settling here; was county treasurer, 1860–62; county surveyor, 1864–70; and a representative in the legislature, 1871–73. He removed to Litchfield in 1872; for several years after 1878 he was receiver of the U.S. land office in Benson; he died in 1917. The village was once the county seat and land office site; it had a post office, 1860–1906.

GROVE CITY a city in section 3 and adjoining Swede Grove Township, was platted in the summer of 1870 and was incorporated February 14, 1878. It was first settled in 1869 as Swede Grove in Swede Grove Township with a post office of that name; in 1870 the St. Paul and Pacific Railroad established a station named Grove City two miles east and one mile south, platting the site on August 26, 1870; the post office moved in 1879 and the name changed to Grove City

HARVEY TOWNSHIP settled in the spring of 1856, organized in 1867, was named for James Harvey, who took a homestead claim here in 1860.

HOPE LAKE a village in Acton Township about 1937.

JENNIE a village in section 20 of Collinwood Township, which formerly had a post office, 1898–1903.

KANDIYOHI a post office, 1857–58; location not found.

KINGSTON settled in 1856 and organized April 5, 1858, took the name of its village, proposed by George A. Nourse, a lawyer of St. Anthony. Twenty-five other states, and also the Canadian provinces of Ontario and New Brunswick, have villages or cities and townships of this name. The city in section 22 was platted in 1871 and incorporated as a village on September 13, 1961; the post office began in 1857, changed to a rural branch, 1907–10, and reestablished as a community post office in 1954.

KORONIS a post office, 1868–74; location not found, but probably associated with a townsite of this name in Paynesville Township, Stearns County.

LAKE HAROLD a post office, 1862–86, in section 28 of Acton Township.

LAKE LYDIA see CROW RIVER.

LAMSON a village in section 25, 26, and 35, Collinwood Township, whose post office had a number of earlier names: established as Lake Todd in

McLeod County in 1870, changed to Bonniwells Mills, 1871–95, with George Boniwell, postmaster, at his mill site in section 27; called Bonniwell, 1895–97; and Lamson until 1903 when discontinued.

LITCHFIELD TOWNSHIP organized April 5, 1858, was at first named Ripley for the lake in the township and then Ness in honor of Ole Halvorson Ness, one of its original party of Norwegian settlers, who came in July 1856. It continued to bear that name until its village was platted in 1869 on the St. Paul and Pacific Railroad, then being built. By petition of its citizens, the township received the village name, Litchfield, in honor of a family who prominently aided in the construction and financing of the railway, including three brothers, Egbert S., Edwin C., and E. Darwin Litchfield. They were the contractors by whom the line from St. Paul to St. Cloud and Watab was built in 1862 to 1864, and later they aided to provide the means for building this more southern line through Meeker County to Breckenridge (*Life of James J. Hill*, by J. G. Pyle, 1917, 2 vols.). Partly in appreciation of the honor of the name given to the village and township, generous donations to the Episcopal church here were received from Mrs. E. Darwin Litchfield in London. Another of this family, William B. Litchfield, was in 1869 the general manager of this railroad, and his son, Electus D. Litchfield, was the architect, in 1915–17, of the new building of the St. Paul Public Library and the Hill Reference Library. Litchfield village was established and platted in 1869 when the Great Northern Railway came through and succeeded Forest City as the county seat in the fall of 1869; the townsite was owned by George B. Waller and was incorporated February 29, 1872; the post office began in 1869 with John A. C. Waller, postmaster.

LOGERING see EDEN VALLEY.

MANANNAH TOWNSHIP organized October 13, 1857, took the name of its early village, which was surveyed and platted in 1857 in section 30 by a Mr. Halcott. It had a mill until 1862, a store, and a hotel, but nothing remains of this site. The present village of this name in sections 30 and 31 was platted in 1871 and is primarily residential; it was incorporated as a village on May 19, 1857, but is presently unincorporated; a post office operated 1857–1907.

NESS a post office, 1860–65, in Litchfield Township, then named Ness Township.

NEW HOPE a post office, 1882–88; location not found.

NORTH KINGSTON a village in the north part of Kingston Township, about 1937, its post office being Kimball in Stearns County.

ODON a post office, 1857–58; location not found.

OSTMARK a farming community on the border of Kingston and Forest City Townships; the settlement began in 1886 when the first Swedish immigrants came; by 1893 they had developed a Swedish Lutheran congregation named after Östmark parish, Värmland, from where most of its members had come.

PAPPELBUSCH see EDEN VALLEY.

RICE CITY see DARWIN.

ROSENDALE a residential community in section 8 of Danielson Township, which earlier had a post office, 1871–1906.

ST. ANDREW a post office of 1857; location not found.

SOMERVILLE a village in Cosmos Township, incorporated on July 20, 1858, but no trace remains.

STAR LAKE a village in Green Leaf Township.

STELLA CITY a village in Darwin Township, about 1856, located on the road leading from Henderson to the Red River.

STROUT a village in section 17 of Greenleaf Township, named for Capt. Richard Strout, leader of an army company during the Dakota War in the Acton area; it had a post office, 1896–1904.

SWEDE GROVE see GROVE CITY.

SWEDE GROVE TOWNSHIP organized March 15, 1868, bears the name of a post office established there in 1864, referring to its many Swedish settlers and the frequent tracts of woodland.

SWIFT LAKE a post office, 1868–75; location not found; however, a lake of this name is in section 33 of Manannah Township and may be related.

SYLVAN HILL a post office, 1868–73; location not found.

UNION GROVE TOWNSHIP settled in 1856 and organized April 18, 1866, received its name from the grove where a union church had been built, this name for the settlement being proposed by Lyman Allen, one of its pioneer farmers, who came from Massachusetts in 1856 and returned there in 1860.

WASHINGTON MILLS a village in section 29 of Dassel Township, then Swan Lake Township, about 1874.

WATKINS a city in section 2 in Forest Prairie Township, was named by officers of the Minneapolis and Pacific Railroad for an official of the railroad. It was incorporated as a village on May 2, 1893, and separated from the township on March 23, 1917; the post office began in 1887. It developed when the Minneapolis and Pacific Railroad came in 1886, the site being on a farm then owned by Danville D. Spaulding.

WESTON a village in Harvey Township, incorporated on March 7, 1857; no trace remains.

Lakes and Streams

The foregoing pages have noticed Cedar Lake, crossed by the south line of Ellsworth, which gave a part of the name of Cedar Mills Township; Collinwood Lake, adjoining the township of this name; and Big Swan Lake, whence Dassel Township was originally named.

Crow River, having its North, Middle, and South Forks in Meeker County, is considered in the first chapter, treating of rivers and lakes that belong partly to several counties.

In the order of the townships from south to north, and of the ranges from east to west, this county has the following many lakes and creeks.

The north line of Cedar Mills crosses Harding, Coombs, and Atkinson Lakes, named for pioneers, extending also into Greenleaf, the first being in honor of Rev. W. C. Harding, who later was a Presbyterian pastor in Litchfield. Vincent Coombs and John Atkinson were farmers beside the lakes bearing their names. Hoff Lake is in section 1, and Pipe Lake, named for its shape, was in sections 16 and 21 but has been drained. Mud Lake, also drained, was crossed by the west line of this township.

Cosmos has Thompson Lake, named for an early homesteader, and the greater part of the dry bed of Mud Lake.

Collinwood has Butternut Lake, named for its trees, in section 3; Washington Lake, on the northwest, named for the first president of the United States, extending into Dassel, Darwin, and Ellsworth; Pigeon or Todd Lake and Spencer Lake, both drained; Maple, Long, and Wolf Lakes, and Lakes Byron and Jennie. Silver Creek flows into Collinwood Lake from this township.

Belle Lake and Cedar Lake, named for its red cedars, as before noted, are crossed by the south line of Ellsworth, continuing into McLeod County. Fallon Lake, mostly drained, a small Long Lake in section 23, Lake Erie, Sioux Lake, and Greenleaf and Willie Lakes are in the south half of the township, the last two being named for William H. Greenleaf, like the next township, and for U. S. Willie (or Wiley), a young lawyer, a member of the legislature in 1859, who lived a year or two at Forest City and died there. In the north half are Birch, Hurley, Benton, and Manuella Lakes; and Stella Lake is on the north line, reaching into Darwin.

In Greenleaf, besides the three lakes on its south side, lying partly in Cedar Mills Township, are Goose and Mud Lakes, the second being drained, Lake Minnie Belle, Evenson Lake, Hoosier Lake, and Star Lake, the last, extending into Litchfield, being named for its arms like rays of a star.

Danielson has King Lake, beside which Hon. William S. King of Minneapolis had a large stock farm, raising Durham cattle, later called March Lake for a subsequent owner of this farm, with King Creek outflowing to the South Fork of Crow River; and Bell Lake and Creek, similarly named for another farmer.

In Dassel Township are Spring and Little Spring Lakes, Long Lake, Sellards Lake, named for Thomas Sellards, a settler from Kentucky, Big Swan Lake, before noted, Lake Arvilla, and Maynard Lake, with Washington Creek, outflowing from Washington Lake to the North Fork.

Darwin Township has Lake Darwin, Stevens and Casey Lakes, Rush Lake, Mud Lake (drained), and Round Lake, the last being crossed by the west line of sections 30 and 31.

Adjoining Litchfield village is Lake Ripley, which commemorates Dr. Frederick N. Ripley, frozen to death there in the winter of 1855–56. The township has also Stone Lake in section 3, and Lake Harold in sections 19 and 30, with five or six other small lakes mapped and named, which are merely marshes or dry lake beds, excepting in the spring or in very rainy summers.

Acton has a large Long Lake, most frequent of our geographic names; Hoop Lake (mapped wrongly as Lake Hope), named because its water, like a hoop, surrounds a central island; and fully a dozen marshes that sometimes become shallow lakes, including Kelly, Butter, and Lund Lakes.

Lake Francis, outflowing by Eagle Creek to the North Fork, and Lake Betty, on the Clearwater River, are in Kingston.

Powers, Dunn, Richardson, Plum, Rice, and Mud Lakes are in Forest City Township, besides the Mill Pond, formed by a dam on the North Fork of Crow River. Michael Powers, Timothy Dunn, and William Richardson were pioneer farmers living near the lakes named for them.

Harvey has Schultz Lake, Lake Mary, Half Moon Lake, named for its shape, and Tower Lake. The first was named for three brothers, German farmers, and the last for an early homesteader who was killed by the Dakota in 1862. Jewett and Battle Creeks here flow to the North Fork of Crow River, the second being translated from its Indian name.

In Swede Grove Township are Helga Lake or Marsh, Peterson Lake, and Wilcox, Miller, and Mud Lakes, the last two being shallow and mainly drained. Peterson Lake was named for Hans Peterson, a settler, father of the late Hon. Peter E. Hanson of Litchfield, who was a state senator, 1895–97, and secretary of this state, 1901–7.

Clear Lake, named for its deep and clear water, situated in the center of Forest Prairie Township, is the chief source of Clearwater River, which flows thence eastward to the Mississippi. This is a translation from the Ojibwe, who named the river for the lake at its source, their name of each being Kawakomik, as spelled on Nicollet's map, Ga-wakomitigweia in the lists of Rev. Joseph A. Gilfillan and Chrysostom Verwyst. It was a frequent Ojibwe name, being retained in Wisconsin by the equivalent French name of the Eau Claire lakes, river, city, and county.

Manannah has Swift's Lake in section 33, and Pigeon Lake, crossed by its west line. Stag Creek runs south in this township to the North Fork. Horseshoe Lake, formerly in section 23, nearly adjoining the north side of Tyrone Prairie, has been drained.

Union Grove Township comprises a part of Pigeon Lake, on its east side; Lake Emma and Mud Lake, mostly in section 10; and a part of the large Lake Koronis on the north, which lies mainly in Paynesville, Stearns County.

Mille Lacs County

The ten southern townships of this county, Dailey, Mudgett, Page, Hayland, Milaca, Borgholm, Milo, Bogus Brook, Greenbush, and Princeton, were known as Monroe County until Mille Lacs County was established in 1860. The county was named for the large lake, called Mille Lacs, meaning a thousand lakes, which is crossed by the north boundary of the county. It was named Lac Buade by Father Louis Hennepin in 1680, for the family name of Count Frontenac. By the Dakota it was called Mde Wakan, that is, Wonderful Lake or Spirit Lake. Pierre Charles Le Sueur's journal, written in 1700 and 1701 and transcribed by Bernard de la Harpe, states that the large part of the Dakota who lived there received from this lake their distinctive tribal name, spelled, by La Harpe, Mendeouacantons. The same name, with better spelling, was given by William H. Keating in 1823, and the lake, on the map accompanying his *Narrative*, is named Spirit Lake, but this group of the Dakota, the Mdewakanton, had before that time been driven from the Mille Lacs region by the Ojibwe and then lived along the Mississippi.

Wakan Island, noted on a later page for the present village of Wahkon, was the source of the name Mde Wakan, given to the lake and to this great subtribe of the Siouan people, and was also accountable, by a punning translation, for the Rum River, the outlet of this lake.

The Ojibwe name of the lake, as given by Joseph N. Nicollet, is Minsi-sagaigon, which is also applied to the adjoining country, "from *minsi*, all sorts, or everywhere, etc., *sagaigon*, lake." He adds that the first is an obsolete word, "pronounced *misi* or *mizi*." Rev. Joseph A. Gilfillan gave the meaning of the Ojibwe name as "Everywhere lake or Great lake." This name, spelled Mississacaigan, appeared on Guillaume de l'Isle's map in 1703. It is evidently of the same etymology as Mississippi (great river).

The French voyageurs and traders, as Nicollet states, following their usual practice of translating the Indian name, called the country, having "all sorts of lakes," the Mille Lacs (Thousand Lakes) region; whence this name came to be applied more particularly to this largest lake of the region. It was used by Zebulon Pike, in application to the lake, being well known at the time of his expedition in 1805; and Jonathan Carver learned much earlier, in 1766, of the name, but supposed it to refer to "a great number of small lakes, none of which are more than ten miles in circumference, that are called the Thousand Lakes." Dr. Elliott Coues discussed this name somewhat lengthily in his edition of Pike (vol. 1, pp. 311–14).

Mille Lacs has an area of about 200 square miles, slightly exceeding Leech and Winnibigoshish Lakes but much surpassed by Red Lake. It is shallow near the shore, and there it is often made muddy by the waves of storms, but its large central part is always clear water, varying mainly from 20 to 50 feet in depth, with a maximum depth of 84 feet.

Information of geographic names has been received from History of the Upper Mississippi Valley, *1881, having pages 663–80 for Mille Lacs County;* Memoirs of Explorations in the Basin of the Mississippi, *by Hon. J. V. Brower, vol. 3, Mille Lac, 1900, pages 140, and vol. 4, Kathio, 1901, pages 136, each having maps and many other illustrations; and from Hon. Robert C. Dunn, Judge Charles Keith, and Joseph C. Borden, deputy county treasurer, each being interviewed during a visit at Princeton, the county seat, in October 1916.*

BAYVIEW a locality in South Harbor Township, the site of the lakeside village and resort called Izatys. This name was given by Daniel Greysolon, sieur Du Luth, in the report of his service to France, writing of his first visit to the Dakota at Mille Lacs: "On the 2d of July, 1679, I had the honor to plant his Majesty's arms in the great village of the Nadouecioux, called Izatys, where never had a Frenchman been." It is a variation of Issati or Isanti, also Santee, noting this division of the Sioux, or Dakota.

BOCK a city in section 15 of Borgholm Township, was named by officers of the Great Northern Railway company. It was incorporated as a village on January 30, 1923; its Great Northern Railway siding was first called Tosca by the railroad and renamed for the first businessmen, the Bock brothers of New Ulm, who built a sawmill, which they sold in 1890 to Charles W. Burnhelm, for whom the Burnhelm Siding nearby was named. The post office operated 1892–1910 and since 1915; Burnhelm was the first postmaster.

BOGUS BROOK TOWNSHIP bears the name of its large eastern tributary of the Rum River, derived from the early Maine lumbermen, but the reason for the adoption of this name, meaning spurious and originally referring to counterfeit money, is unknown.

BORGHOLM TOWNSHIP has the name of a seaport of Sweden, on the island of Oeland, whence some of its settlers came.

BRICKTON a village in Princeton Township, section 17, about two miles north of Princeton had a station of the Great Northern Railway, a post office, 1901–28, and several brickyards. Its large brick industry ceased in 1920 in part because the clay resources gave out and the transportation costs became too high.

BRIDGMAN see FORESTON.

BURNHELM SIDING see BOCK.

COVE a post office in section 21 of South Harbor Township, 1893–1916, briefly called Southshore from May 1904 to July 1905.

DAILEY TOWNSHIP was named in honor of Asa R. Dailey, an early settler there, who removed to Montana.

EAST SIDE TOWNSHIP adjoins the east shore of Mille Lacs. It contains Father Hennepin State Park, established in 1941.

EDITH a farmers post office, 1895–1901, 50 miles north of Princeton.

ERIKSONVILLE see ONAMIA.

ESTES BROOK a village on the border of Greenbush and Milo Township, was named, as was its brook, for Israel H. Estes, an early settler in Milo Township, who had a logging camp, a sawmill, and a boardinghouse. There was one main street; those living on the north side of the street were in Milo Township with the post office in section 31, and those on the south side of the street were in Greenbush Township with the railroad station in section 6. A supply depot of the Great Northern Railway became a general store, and the post office, 1874–1905, was located there.

FITZPATRICK a station of the Great Northern Railway; location not found.

FORESTON a city in section 33 of Milo Township about three miles west of Milaca, is partly surrounded by a hardwood forest. It was incorporated as a village on May 9, 1889. The lumber industry created the community on the west branch of the Rum River, naming it Bridgman, and established a post office, 1882–89, with Coleman Bridgeman as postmaster; the name was changed to Foreston in 1889.

FREER a post office, 1899–1911, in section 1 of Greenbush Township.

GREENBUSH TOWNSHIP settled in 1856, organized in 1869, was named for the township of Greenbush adjoining the east side of Penobscot River in Maine. Many of the settlers in this county, both for its pine lumbering and for farming, came from that "Pine Tree State," being therefore commonly called "Mainites."

HAYLAND TOWNSHIP was named for the natural meadows on its several brooks, supplying hay for oxen and horses of winter logging camps.

ISLE HARBOR TOWNSHIP and **ISLE** a city and port

of Mille Lacs, are named for their excellent harbor, partly enclosed and sheltered in storms by Malone Island, also called Great or Big Island. The townsite was established in 1906 and incorporated as a village on November 1, 1913; it first opened up for homesteading in 1891, and the first business was a general store and hotel built in 1894 by Charley Malone, who became first postmaster in 1896 and first mayor in 1913. Malone acquired the title to the large island off the southeast shore of Mille Lacs, which he named Ethel for his eldest daughter; when the post office was established he requested the name Ethel's Island, but the department felt the name was too long and they shortened it to Isle.

IZATYS see **BAYVIEW**.

JOHNSDALE a village in section 17 of Bradbury Township, which had a post office, 1918–1934.

KATHIO TOWNSHIP adjoining the southwest shore of Mille Lacs and including its outlet, Rum River, here flowing through three small lakes, bears an erroneously transcribed form of the foregoing name, Izatys, published by John R. Brodhead in 1855 (*Documents Relating to the Colonial History of New York*, vol. 9, p. 795). In the original manuscript of Du Luth's report, before cited, Brodhead copied *Iz* of *Izatys* as "K," and *ys* as "hio," giving to that name a quite new form, Kathio, which error was followed by Edward D. Neill, Newton H. Winchell, Alfred J. Hill, Brower, Coues, and others. It has been so much used, indeed, that it will be always retained as a synonym of Izatys or Isanti (MHS Collections, vol. 10, pt. 2, 1905, p. 531). Mille Lacs-Kathio State Park, established in this township in 1957, contains rich archaeological resources that reflect 9,000 years of human habitation, including the site of the great Dakota village of Izatys.

LAWRENCE see **WAHKON**.

LONG SIDING an unincorporated railway village about four miles north of Princeton in section 7 of Princeton Township, was named for Edgar C. Long, a lumberman and landowner. It had a Great Northern Railway station, a creamery built in 1904, a dance hall in 1907, and a number of other businesses; the post office operated 1903–54 and as a rural branch until 1959.

MILACA a city in sections 25 and 26 of Milaca Township and the county seat since 1920, at first called Oak City, and the township of that name, organized after the village was platted, have a shortened and changed name derived from Mille Lacs. The village was platted in 1892 and incorporated on February 20, 1897; it was first developed by lumber companies, hence the early name of Oak City. Its post office was established in March 1883 as Oak City and changed that November to Milaca.

MILO TOWNSHIP settled in 1856 and organized in 1869, received its name from a township and its manufacturing village in the central part of Maine, on the Sebec River.

MUDGETT TOWNSHIP organized in 1916, was named in honor of Isaiah S. Mudgett, who was born in Penobscot County, Maine, June 7, 1839, came to Minnesota in 1858, settled at Princeton in 1865, and was during several years the county auditor.

OAK CITY see **MILACA**.

ONAMIA TOWNSHIP bears the name given on the government survey plats by Oscar E. Garrison, surveyor, to the third and largest of the three lakes through which the Rum River flows next below the mouth of Mille Lacs. A city on the border of South Harbor and Onamia Townships on the south side of Onamia Lake also has this name. It was received from the Ojibwe, but its meaning is uncertain, unless it be like *Onamani*, noted in Frederic Baraga's *Dictionary*, whence Vermilion Lake in St. Louis County is a translation. The city was platted on November 12, 1901, and incorporated as a village on August 4, 1908; it had a station of the Great Northern Railway, and its post office began in 1901, incorporating the post office of Ericksonville, which had been established in 1898 in section 6 of Onamia Township on postmaster Lars Erickson's farm, for whom it was named.

OPSTEAD is the name of a post office, 1889–1933, and a hamlet of Swedish settlers in sections 2 and 3 of East Side Township.

PAGE TOWNSHIP was named in honor of Charles H. and Edwin S. Page, lumbermen there, who came from Maine. The village in section 14 had a post office, 1894–1921, with Charles Page as first postmaster, and a station of the Great Northern Railway.

PEASE a city in section 13, Milo, was incorporated as a village on August 6, 1923. In 1882 Benjamin Soule, a Maine lumberman, who had a sawmill at

Princeton, built a second sawmill and a hotel two miles northeast of the present Pease called Soule's Crossing and located on the east branch of the Rum River; in 1886 when the railroad completed the tracks from Princeton to Milaca, Soule built another sawmill near the tracks, which was then called Soule Siding; following the Hinckley fire in 1894 that destroyed the sawmills, the first Dutch arrived at Soule Siding, settling on land around the Siding, and requested a post office, at which time the name was changed to Pease, either by the railroad for James J. Hill's friend Granville S. Pease of Anoka, or as a misspelling of Peace, the name requested by the residents.

POTTS TOWN see WAHKON.

PRINCETON a city with Sherburne County and the county seat of Mille Lacs County until 1920 when Milaca was named, received its first permanent settlers in 1854 and was named in honor of John S. Prince of St. Paul, who with others platted this village in the fall or winter of 1855, the plat being recorded April 19, 1856. He was born in Cincinnati, Ohio, May 7, 1821; came to St. Paul in 1854 as agent of the Chouteau Fur Company; afterward engaged in insurance, real estate, and banking; was a member of the constitutional convention of Minnesota, 1857; mayor of St. Paul, 1860–62 and 1865–66; was president of the Savings Bank of St. Paul for many years; and died in that city September 4, 1895. Princeton Township was organized in 1857, and the village separated from the township and was incorporated March 3, 1877. Major industries were brickmaking and a potato starch factory; the village had a station of the Great Northern Railway in section 33, and its post office began in 1861.

SNOW a post office, was authorized on October 15, 1891, with Arthur L. Snow to be postmaster, but not established; location not found.

SOULE SIDING, SOULE'S CROSSING see PEASE.

SOUTH HARBOR TOWNSHIP was named for its good harbor on the south side of Mille Lacs.

SOUTHSHORE see COVE.

VINELAND a village and port of Mille Lacs near its outlet, in Kathio, was named for the early Norse settlement on the northeast coast of North America in the year 1000, visited by numerous later voyages, which was called in the Icelandic language Vinland, meaning Wineland, from grapes found there. Its post office was called Vineland

from 1891 to 1921 and Wigwam Bay from 1921 to 1929, at which time it was discontinued.

WAHKON a city in section 17 of Isle Harbor Township, was incorporated as a village on November 6, 1912; it was established in 1885 as Potts Town, changed to Lawrence in 1891 when the post office was established, and changed again in 1910 to Wahkon. This name is the Dakota name of Mille Lacs, spelled *wakan* in the Dakota dictionary by Rev. Stephen R. Riggs, defined as "spiritual, sacred, consecrated, wonderful, incomprehensible." The Dakota applied this name especially to a very remarkable but small island far out in the lake, about seven miles northwest from Wahkon, consisting of rock, granitic boulders piled by the ice of the lake to a height of nearly 20 feet, a noted resort of gulls and pelicans, called on maps Spirit Island or Pelican Island. Only 1 or 2 feet below the lake level, and visible under the water for 100 feet or more to the north and east, is a ledge of the bedrock described by David I. Bushnell in Brower's memoir of Mille Lac (p. 121, with a picture, on p. 118, of the heaped rock masses forming the island). Wonderful as the island is, it was the origin of the Dakota name of the lake, of this village, and, by a punning perversion noted on a later page, the name of the Rum River.

WIGWAM BAY see VINELAND.

WOODWARD BROOK a village in sections 21 and 28 of Bogus Brook Township.

Bays, Points, and Islands of Mille Lacs

From the map and descriptive notes of this lake by Hon. J. V. Brower, in his memoirs titled "Mille Lac" and "Kathio," the following names are copied for its south half in Mille Lacs County, with their derivations or significance, and with notes of more recent names.

Hunter Point, earlier called Halfway Point, is on the north edge of Mille Lacs County, near the middle of the east shore.

Accault Bay is next south, named for one of the two Frenchmen who were at Mille Lacs with Hennepin in 1680.

Big Point and Cedar Point are the northwest and southeast limits of Radisson Bay, named for Pierre E. Radisson, the earliest writer of travels in the area of Minnesota, who came with Médard

Chouart, sieur de Groseilliers to Prairie Island in 1655 and to the region of Kanabec County, not far southeast of Mille Lacs, in the midwinter of 1659–60.

Next in order southward are Cedar Bay and Island, Ojibway Point, North and South Courage Bays, now renamed Twin Bays, with Courage Point between them, Boulder Point, now named Hawk Bill Point, Big Island, and Gim-i-nis-sing Bay. The Courage Bays and Point were named for an Ojibwe, "A-ya-shintang, He-is-encouraged," and the bay last named, now called Isle Harbor, bears on Brower's map the Ojibwe name that is translated for Big Island. This island is now named Malone Island, for Charley Malone, a resident of Isle village.

West of Isle Harbor are Be-dud, Na-gwa-na-be, and Wadena Points, named for Ojibwe of Mille Lacs, the second a spiritual leader, and the third a leader who was severely wounded in their last battle against the Dakota, near Shakopee, May 27, 1858.

Wahkon Bay, adjoining the village of this name, was mapped by Brower as Sa-ga-wa-mick Bay, meaning a long shoal or sand bar, which in this bay extends from its shore to Mulybys Island, named for a lumberman of the Snake River and Stillwater. Other islands farther north in this bay, named by Brower as Sumac and Pelican Islands, are on a later map called Half Moon Island, for its shape, and Wilson Island, for its owner, Guy G. Wilson of Mora. Northeast from the last is Pine or Spider Island. Between Wahkon Bay and Cove Bay or South Harbor, called South End Bay by Brower are Coming-in-sight Point, translated from its Ojibwe name, Carnelian Beach, named from its carnelian pebbles, Maple Point, and Mo-zo-ma-na (or Mazomannie) Point, named for a former Mille Lacs leader, signer of treaties in 1863 and 1889.

Portage Bay or Cove Bay, next westward, was the usual starting place for canoe journeys down the Rum River, making first a portage about a mile long from the south side of Mille Lacs to the east end of Lake Onamia.

Anderson Point, next west of Portage Bay, is named for a Swedish settler, owner of a summer hotel. Thence to Sah-ging Point and Outlet Bay, a nearly straight shore reaches four miles, named Rogers Shore by Brower for Oren S. Rogers, drowned near there June 27, 1896.

Sah-ging, the Ojibwe word meaning an outlet, was applied by Brower to the point southeast of Outlet Bay, but later maps rename these as Libby's Point and Vineland Bay. Hay Island and the small Robbins Bay adjoin Vineland village, and at the north limit of Vineland Bay is Cormorant Point, with Robbins Island, named by Brower for David H. Robbins, which is now called Rainbow Island.

Shore View Bay and Sa-gutch-u Point, next northward, as they were mapped by Brower, the latter being named for an Ojibwe living there, are called on a recent map Sha-bosh-kung Bay and Point, commemorating a former leader of Mille Lacs, who signed treaties in 1863, 1867, and 1889. This name, spelled in several ways, is translated "Who passes under" (*Aborigines of Minnesota*, pp. 726–27).

Wigwam Bay, west of the last named point, is succeeded northward by Reel Point, Fenley Shore, named for William E. Fenley, and Aitkin and Crow Wing Points, which adjoin the corner of the counties so named.

Hennepin Island, also named Prisoner's Island, alluding to the captivity of Hennepin, who probably, however, never came to this island, lying nearly five miles north of Wahkon village, is a small and low reef of boulders, called Deception Crest by Brower. The only other island far from the shore is the Wakan or Spirit Island, before noted as the source of the old Dakota name for Mille Lacs, Mde Wakan, and the differently spelled village name, Wahkon. By proclamation of the president of the United States in 1915, Spirit Island is a bird refuge or reservation, for protection of water-loving birds that have resting places and nests there.

A very interesting and reliably historic locality, identified and named by Brower, is Aquipaguetin Island, a tract of hard ground about a half mile long and a quarter of a mile wide, in the northeast part of section 25, Kathio, enclosed by Rum River on the east, the western part of Third or Onamia Lake on the south, and a swamp on the west and north.

In a Dakota village there, Aquipaguetin, the band leader, lived, who adopted Hennepin as his son and befriended him during his enforced stay in the vicinity of Mille Lacs from May to September in 1680, excepting their midsummer absence on a great hunting expedition far down the Mississippi.

Brower mapped 22 ancient village sites, scattered around the entire circuit of Mille Lacs, which were probably all occupied for some time by the Dakota. They are most frequent about the southwestern third of the lake, from Wahkon to Aquipaguetin Island, Vineland, and the west side of Wigwam Bay, 13 sites of the former villages being found in that distance of about 20 miles. "The great village," called Izatys by Du Luth, misread "Kathio" by Brodhead, is thought to have been near the present Vineland.

Other Lakes and Streams

The name of Rum River, which Carver in 1766 and Pike in 1805 found in use by English-speaking fur traders, was indirectly derived from the Dakota. Their name of Mille Lacs, Mde Wakan, translated Spirit Lake, was given to its river but was changed by the white men to the most common spirituous liquor brought into the Northwest, rum, which brought misery and ruin, as Du Luth observed of brandy, to many of the Indians. The map of Maj. Stephen H. Long's expedition in 1823 has these names, Spirit Lake and Rum River. Nicollet's map, published in 1843, has "Iskode Wabo or Rum R.," this name given by the Ojibwe but derived by them from the white men's perversion of the ancient Dakota name Wakan, being in more exact translation "Spirit Water." More frequently, as noted by Gilfillan, the Ojibwe name for Rum River was taken from their name for the lake and meant simply the Great Lake River.

Three lakes on the course of the Rum River in its first eight miles from the mouth of the Mille Lacs were called Rice Lakes by Daniel Stanchfield in the autumn of 1847, for their abundance of wild rice then being harvested by the Ojibwe. On a map of Minnesota published in 1850 they are Roberts' Lakes. In the government survey, by Oscar E. Garrison, they were named Ogechie, Nessawae, and Onamia Lakes. The first was from the Ojibwe word for an intestinal worm, referring to its long, narrow, and curved shape, but its more common name used by the Ojibwe, as noted by Gilfillan, is " Netumigumag, meaning First lake." In the Ojibwe dictionary the second name is spelled Nassawaii, meaning "in the middle," but on later maps this is called Shakopee Lake. The third name, Onamia, meaning Vermilion Lake, given to a township and village, probably referred, like the larger Vermilion Lake and Red Lake in northern Minnesota, to the vermilion and red hues of the western sky and of the lake at sunset, as seen from the eastern shore. According to Gilfillan, however, the Ojibwe commonly call this "Eshquegumag, the Last lake."

Whitefish Lake is a half mile west of Wigwam Bay, to which it outflows.

Chase Brook, named for Jonathan Chase of Minneapolis, who had a logging camp there, flows into Mille Lacs from East Side Township. He was born in Sebec, Maine, December 31, 1818; came to Minnesota in the spring of 1854 and engaged in lumbering on Rum River; later owned an interest in the large sawmills at Gull River in Cass County; died in Minneapolis, February 1, 1904.

Tributaries to Rum River from the east include, in their order from north to south, Black Brook, darkly colored by peat swamps; Whitney, Mike Drew, O'Neill, and Vondel Brooks, named for early lumbermen; and Bogus Brook, before noticed for its naming a township.

From the west, Rum River receives Bradbury Brook, having North and South Forks; Hanson Brook, named for Gilbert S. Hanson, a lumberman from Maine; Burnt Land, Whiskey, and Tibbetts Brooks, the last being named for two brothers, lumbermen, who lived in Princeton; Chase Brook, named for Nehemiah Chase (a brother of Jonathan, before mentioned), killed by an accident when breaking a log jam on the Rum River at the mouth of this brook.

The West Branch of Rum River receives Stony Brook, Estes Brook, named for Jonathan Estes of St. Anthony, and Prairie Brook.

Battle Brook, in Greenbush, named from a fight there between employees of Sumner W. Farnham, a Minneapolis lumberman, flows through Rice Lake, named for its wild rice, and thence is tributary southward to the St. Francis and Elk Rivers in Sherburne County.

Mud Lake is crossed by the north line of section 1, Princeton; Fogg Lake is at the southeast corner of section 17, named for Frederick A. Fogg, an early homesteader, who removed to Sauk Rapids; and Silver Lake is a mile east of Princeton village.

Branches of the Ground House River and of Ann and Knife Rivers, drain eastern parts of this county, being tributary to Snake River.

Mille Lacs Indian Reservation

This reservation is located in Mille Lacs, Aitkin, and Pine Counties. The original reservation, established in an 1855 treaty, included four townships at the south end of Mille Lacs Lake with their islands. Most of the original land has passed from Indian ownership; a large tract was ceded in 1864, reserving to the band one section granted to Sha-bosh-kung, for whom a bay and point on the west side of Mille Lacs are named. Through the late 1800s and early 1900s, members of the band strenuously and successfully resisted the persistent efforts of the U.S. government to remove them to White Earth Reservation, preferring to remain on their ancestral lands in an area of remarkable beauty and rich natural resources.

Morrison County

This county, established February 25, 1856, was named in honor of William and Allan Morrison. The older of these brothers, William, was born in Montreal, March 7, 1785, and died on Morrison's Island, near Sorel, Canada, August 7, 1866. He entered the service of the XY Fur Company in 1802, coming to Grand Portage, Leech Lake, and the headwaters of Crow Wing River. From 1805 to 1816 he was engaged there for a new company formed by the coalition of the XY and North West Companies. Later, through ten years, he was in the service of the American Fur Company, under John Jacob Astor, and established a series of trading posts on or near the northern boundary of Minnesota from Grand Portage west to Lake of the Woods. In 1826 he retired, and afterward lived in Canada. During his journeys as a fur trader he explored a large region of northern Minnesota. In 1804 he visited Lake Itasca, then called Lac La Biche or Elk Lake, thus long preceding Henry R. Schoolcraft in the discovery of the source of the

Mississippi, as is related by Hon. J. V. Brower in vol. 7 of the MHS Collections, with publication of the full text of a letter on this subject, which William Morrison wrote to his brother Allan, January 9, 1856. This letter was forwarded to Gov. Alexander Ramsey, then president of the Minnesota Historical Society, a few days before the act was passed establishing this county.

Allan Morrison, who is also commemorated by this name, was born at Terrebonne, near Montreal, June 3, 1803, and died at White Earth, Minn., November 21, 1877. He came to Fond du Lac and northern Minnesota in the fur trade, associated with his brother William, in 1820; had charge of trading posts at Sandy Lake, Leech Lake, Red Lake, and Mille Lacs; was the first trader at Crow Wing, continuing there many years; and finally removed in 1874 to the White Earth Reservation. He was a representative in the first territorial legislature.

Information has been gathered from History of the Upper Mississippi Valley *(1881, having pp. 586–636 for this county);* The History of Morrison County *by Nathan Richardson, a series of weekly articles in the* Little Falls Transcript *during 1876, collected in a scrapbook in the public library of Little Falls;* History of Morrison and Todd Counties *by Clara K. Fuller (1915, 2 vols., 708 pp.); and from Ed-*

ward F. Shaw, judge of probate, interviewed during a visit at Little Falls, the county seat, in May 1916.

AGRAM TOWNSHIP received this name by request of its settlers, in July 1886, for the city of Agram, which was the German spelling of Zagreb, at that time in Austria-Hungary and the capital of Croatia and Slavonia.

AUSLAND a post office, 1899–1914, located in Rail Prairie Township, section 12.

BELLE PRAIRIE TOWNSHIP first settled in 1849, organized April 6, 1858, adopted this name, meaning "beautiful prairie," from the French fur traders and voyageurs, for its tract of grassland five miles long and averaging about a mile in width, nearly adjoining the Mississippi River. The village in section 13 had a station of the Chicago, St. Paul, Minneapolis and Omaha Railroad, and a post office, 1852–1904, first established while in Benton County; the name has also been spelled as Bell Prairie and Belleprairie.

BELLEVUE TOWNSHIP settled in 1852, organized in the spring of 1858, has another French name, meaning "beautiful view," in reference to the outlook from its prairie beside the Mississippi, which reaches south into Benton County.

BLANCH RAPIDS a village about four miles north of Royalton, circa 1937.

BLANCHARD a village in section 32 of Swan River Township, near the Blanchard Rapids Dam, which was built in 1924, seven miles south of Little Falls on the Mississippi River.

BOWLUS a city in sections 11–14 of Two Rivers Township, platted in July 1907, was named by officers of the Minneapolis, St. Paul and Sault Ste. Marie Railroad (Soo Line). It was incorporated as a village on September 8, 1908, and separated from the township on February 27, 1919. The Soo Line came in 1907, the same year the post office opened, and the townsite was platted by Tri-State Land Company on land originally owned by Henry Armstrong, Sr., whose son developed the post office of Stella.

BRIGGS a post office, 1886, with Emegene Briggs as postmaster; location not found.

BUCKMAN TOWNSHIP organized in 1874, was named in honor of Clarence B. Buckman, one of its first settlers. He was born in Bucks County, Pa., April 1, 1850; came to Minnesota in 1872, settling here as a farmer and lumberman; removed to Little Falls in 1880; was a representative in the legislature, 1881, and a state senator in 1889 and 1899–1901; was a member of Congress in 1903–7; and died in a sanitarium at Battle Creek, Mich., March 1, 1917. The city in sections 4, 5, 8, and 9 was incorporated as a village on May 4, 1903, and separated from the township on March 22, 1920; the

post office began in section 20 on the farm of Edward S. Arnold, postmaster, moved several times, discontinued in 1910, but reestablished in 1921.

BUH TOWNSHIP organized in July 1895, was named in honor of Joseph Francis Buh, a Catholic priest, who was born in Austria, March 17, 1833; came to the United States in 1864; was a missionary in Minnesota during 18 years, until 1882; and later through more than 20 years was a pastor at various places in this state.

CAMP RIPLEY MILITARY RESERVATION controls sections 5–8, 17–19, and 30–32 of Clough Township, which was originally part of Green Prairie Township. Old Fort Ripley was established in 1849 in section 8 of Green Prairie Township, with a government ferry in section 16; the old Fort Ripley grounds and powder magazine rubble are on the reservation. It had a station of the Northern Pacific Railroad in section 36 of Ripley Township; the U.S. military training camp is located in section 36. See also **FORT RIPLEY**.

CENTER VALLEY a post office, 1910–12, and station of the Soo Line, in section 8 of Hillman Township.

CHAMBERS a post office, 1903–4, with Jay R. Chambers, postmaster; location not found.

CLOUGH TOWNSHIP organized in October 1890, was named in honor of David Marston Clough, who engaged extensively in lumbering here, with sawmills and manufacturing in Minneapolis. He was born in Lyme, N.H., December 27, 1846; came to Minnesota in 1857 with his father's family, who settled at Spencer Brook, Isanti County; removed to Minneapolis in 1866; was a state senator, 1886–90; lieutenant-governor, 1893–95, and governor of Minnesota, 1895–99; removed in 1899 to Everett, Wash., and there also engaged in a large lumber business; he died in Everett on August 27, 1924.

CULDRUM see **SWANVILLE**.

CULDRUM TOWNSHIP organized June 2, 1870, was named by John Workman, who had previously lived at Little Falls and settled here soon after the Civil War, this being the name of his birthplace in Ireland.

CURTIS SIDING a Northern Pacific Railroad siding in section 9, Cushing Township; William Long is said to have built a sawmill and planing mill here before 1890.

CUSHING TOWNSHIP organized October 30, 1891, and its village in sections 21 and 22, platted in December 1907, probably were named for an eminent jurist, congressman, and diplomatist, Caleb Cushing (1800–1879) of Massachusetts, who in 1847 was financially associated with Franklin Steele and others in founding St. Anthony and beginning the great lumber industries of the upper Mississippi. The village had a station of the Northern Pacific Railroad and has had a post office since 1890.

DARLING TOWNSHIP established January 7, 1891, at first called Randall, which continues as the name of its railway village, in section 7, was renamed in October 1907 for William L. Darling of St. Paul. He was born in Oxford, Mass., March 24, 1856, was graduated at Worcester Polytechnic Institute, 1877, settled in St. Paul, engaged in railway engineering, and from 1905 was chief engineer of the Northern Pacific Railroad. This is also the name of a village in section 35; it had a post office, 1903–11, and during the 1930s the Northern Pacific Railroad used Darling as a switching spur and boxcar cleaning station.

DIXVILLE a country post office, 1895–1907, in Buckman Township, 17 miles southeast of Little Falls and 9 miles east of Royalton.

DULCE a post office, 1903–11, in Mt. Morris Township; a sawmill was on the site.

ELMDALE a city in sections 2, 3, 10, and 11 of Elmdale Township, was settled in the 1870s and incorporated as a village on April 23, 1947. The founder, Knud Hans Gunderson, was the first postmaster and storekeeper; Gunderson was born in Denmark in 1841, came to the United States in 1867 and to Elmdale in 1871, building his store in 1878; the Danish settlement was surveyed by Jens Hansen in 1866. The post office operated 1878–1907.

ELMDALE TOWNSHIP settled in 1865, organized April 11, 1881, was named for the abundant elms in its woods, and its western part has many low morainic hills and dales.

FAWNDALE a country post office in section 18 of Swan River Township, 1897–1911, located on the Swan River, 12 miles southwest of Little Falls; postmaster Lars Larson was a carpenter.

FLENSBURG a city in Culdrum, platted in March 1890 by Olaf and Dagmar Searle, was named for a seaport and fjord of Schleswig, at that time a province of Prussia, adjoining Denmark. The post office began in 1892; the city was incorporated as a village on June 17, 1911, and separated from the township on March 19, 1918. After the Little Falls and Dakota Railroad was completed in 1882, there was a sidetrack to a mill, called Flen's Landing or Flynn's Siding, with a depot and named for J. C. Flynn of Little Falls, a teacher in the Little Falls schools in the late 1870s; later he was an inspector for the Northern Pacific Railroad and a representative in the state legislature.

FORT RIPLEY was a military post of the United States until July 1878. It was at first named Fort Gaines, in honor of Edmund Pendleton Gaines (1777–1849), who served in the War of 1812 as a colonel and later as a brigadier general. Eleazar Wheelock Ripley, for whom this fort was renamed November 4, 1850, was born in Hanover, N.H., April 15, 1782; served in the War of 1812, being promoted to the rank of brigadier general, and was brevetted major general; was a member of Congress from Louisiana, 1835–39; and died in Louisiana, March 2, 1839. See also CAMP RIPLEY MILITARY RESERVATION.

FRANKFORD a place name noted in 1856; location not found.

FREEDHEM a village in sections 1, 2, and 11 of Belle Prairie Township; the first Swedes in the area came in 1897, with many more following, emigrating mainly from Östergötland and Småland; they named the community Fridhem, a common Swedish place name meaning "home of peace," which was anglicized to Freedhem when the post office operated, 1902–10.

GENOLA is a city in sections 17 and 18 in Pierz Township, platted in August 1908 and at first called New Pierz; on April 15, 1915, it was incorporated as Grainville but changed immediately to Genola, the name of a village in Piedmont, Italy; it separated from the township on May 3, 1921. The village developed when the Soo Line came in 1907; the post office began in 1912 as New Pierz, changed to Genola in 1915, and became a rural branch in 1951.

GILBERT a post office in section 11 of Ripley Township, 1891–1905.

GOSHEN a post office, 1897; location not found.

GRACEVILLE a village in section 36 of Belle Prairie Township, about 1916.

GRAHAM/GRAHAMS SPUR a village in section 33

of Little Falls Township, with a station of the Northern Pacific Railroad in section 4 of Bellevue Township.

GRANITE TOWNSHIP organized in July 1902, has in its section 21 many outcrops of a granitic rock, coarse gray gneiss, adjoining the Skunk River for a half mile or more, where a village named Granite City was founded by Tallmadge Elwell in 1858. It had a sawmill, hotel, and other buildings, which were deserted in 1861–62, on account of the Civil War and the Dakota War, the site being permanently abandoned. It had a post office, 1858–63.

GRAVELVILLE a former village on the Platte River in sections 35 and 36 of Belle Prairie Township, was founded in 1876 by D. O. Goulet and Charles Gravel, who, with their older brother Narcisse, built a sawmill and gristmill there and also engaged in mercantile business; the post office operated 1879–1905.

GREEN PRAIRIE TOWNSHIP organized in the spring of 1868, was named in honor of its first settler, Charles H. Green, a native of Glens Falls, N.Y., who came here in 1855, enlisted in the Third Minnesota Regiment in 1861 and was killed in the battle of Murfreesboro, July 13, 1862. The prairie in this township, bordering the Mississippi, was about three miles long and nearly a mile wide. A post office operated in section 5, 1867–1903.

GREGORY a station and small village of the Northern Pacific Railroad in section 28 of Little Falls Township in the north edge of Bellevue, is named for John Gregory Smith of Vermont, president of the Northern Pacific Railroad company in 1866–72, more fully noticed in the chapter for Crow Wing County, where the city of Brainerd was named in honor of his wife.

HARDING a city in Pulaski Township, sections 8 and 17–20, was incorporated as a village on March 15, 1938; it developed around the Holy Family Church in the early 1920s; the post office operated 1923–53 and as a rural branch 1966–75.

HILLMAN a city in sections 21 and 28 in Leigh Township, platted in July 1908, was incorporated as a village November 7, 1938. The Soo Line built through in 1906. Primarily settled by German immigrants, the village was founded by Osmer Leigh. Its post office began in 1913 with Ethel A. Leigh as postmaster.

HILLMAN TOWNSHIP organized July 7, 1902, and the brook much earlier so named, with its south-ern tributary, Little Hillman Brook, commemorate a pioneer of the county.

HUFF a post office in section 24 of Parker Township, 1881–1904; first called Lafond; see ST. STANISLAUS.

LAKIN TOWNSHIP organized July 6, 1903, was named for Fred H. Lakin, a settler from Maine, who during many years was one of the county commissioners, living in Royalton. Before 1885 the township was known as Oakwood Township and then Morrill Township.

LASTRUP is a city in Buh and Granite Townships comprised of two earlier settlements; it was incorporated as a combined village on March 1, 1916, and separated from the township on January 27, 1923: East Lastrup was platted in 1892 in Granite Township and had a creamery and saloon among its businesses; West Lastrup was settled in Buh Township, had a blacksmith, and was the site of its first post office, called Lastrup, 1898–1907, and reestablished in 1923.

LEDOUX see SOBIESKI.

LEIGH TOWNSHIP organized February 15, 1908, was named in honor of Joseph P. Leigh, a pioneer farmer there, who came from Maine.

LINCOLN a village in section 30, Scandia Valley Township, platted in September 1893 by Elizabeth Bauman, having numerous summer homes beside Fish Trap Lake, was named for the martyr president of the United States in the Civil War. The townsite had a lumber mill, a railroad station, several stores, and a post office, 1890–1954; by the 1960s it had developed as a resort area. The north extension was platted in 1899 as the McKinley Addition (for the president) by William B. and Sarah Hash, who owned Edgemoor on Hash Hill, an early store and resort.

LITTLE FALLS the county seat, first settled in 1848 and platted in 1855, was incorporated as a village February 25, 1879, and as a city in July 1890. James Fergus is considered the founder of the village, living there until he moved to Fergus Falls and began that city. The post office opened in 1852 while part of Benton County. The city area mainly belonged to Little Falls Township, which was organized May 11, 1858, but it extends also into the adjoining Belle Prairie Township, and its part west of the Mississippi is in Pike Creek Township. Lt. Zebulon Pike in 1805–6 called the rapids or falls of the river here "Painted Rock or Little Falls," the first of these names being translated from the French traders. Mill Island, a slate outcrop a quarter of a mile long, divides the river into east and west channels, and the original descent of the rapids at this island and southward was 11 feet in three-fourths of a mile. About the year 1890 a dam was built, which raised the river 9 feet above the former head of the rapids, giving thus a total fall of 20 feet and holding the river as a mill pond for about 3 miles to the middle of the Little Elk Rapids, which previously had a descent of 7 feet in one mile.

During an exceptionally high flood stage of the Mississippi in June 1858, the steamboat *North Star* from Minneapolis passed over the Sauk Rapids and the Little Falls and made a pleasure trip to the Grand Rapids in Itasca County (MHS Collections, vol. 9, p. 48).

The discovery in 1878 by Frances E. Babbitt, a schoolteacher at Little Falls, of artificially flaked quartz fragments in the Mississippi valley drift gave evidence of the presence of human habitation there during the closing part of the Ice Age. "Kakabikansing," the Ojibwe name of Little Falls, meaning "the place of the little squarely cut-off rock," is the title of a memoir on this subject by Hon. J. V. Brower, published in 1902 (126 pp., with maps and many illustrations from photographs).

LITTLE FALLS WEST a village incorporated in March 1856, now part of the city of Little Falls.

LITTLE ROCK a village in section 32 of Buckman Township, also known as Little Rock Lake.

LITTLE TEXAS a post office, 1878–80 and 1884, located in the southwest part of the county, nine miles from Little Falls; John Hamlin, postmaster, was a blacksmith and general store owner.

MANDERSON a post office in section 14 of Elmdale Township, 1891–97; named for a local family; no traces of a community remain.

MORRILL TOWNSHIP settled in 1874, organized April 11, 1881, was at first called Oakwood but after a few years was renamed in honor of Ashby C. Morrill, a member of the board of county commissioners. He was born in Canterbury, N.H., January 9, 1830; was graduated in the law school of Harvard College; came to Minnesota in 1857, settling in Minneapolis; engaged after 1868 in milling and lumbering and had a farm in Buckman Township; resided after 1884 at Little Falls,

where he erected the Little Elk mills; and died in Minneapolis, May 5, 1904. The village in sections 28, 29, 32, and 33 began as a single store erected about 1910, although an earlier settlement of the name had a post office, 1891–1907.

MOTLEY TOWNSHIP organized in the spring of 1879, took the name of its railway village, founded in 1874, which was named by officers of the Northern Pacific Railroad company. The city, with Todd County, was organized in 1885, incorporated as a village on May 1, 1905, and separated from the township on April 1, 1918; it was originally platted in section 18 of Motley Township by the Lake Superior and Puget Sound Company in 1870 but not recorded until 1879; the post office was established in Todd County in 1873 and transferred to Morrison County in 1874; it had a station of the Northern Pacific Railroad.

MOUNT MORRIS TOWNSHIP organized March 17, 1897, was named by Dunkard settlers who came from Pennsylvania and Ohio. This name is borne also by townships and villages in New York, Pennsylvania, Illinois, Michigan, and Wisconsin.

NEW PIERZ see **GENOLA**.

NORTH PRAIRIE a small village in section 20 of Two Rivers Township, platted in the summer of 1885, is in the oldest Polish settlement of this county, founded by its pioneer immigrants in 1868–70. The village had a post office, 1867–1904, established in Stearns County and transferred to Morrison County in 1873.

PARKER TOWNSHIP organized in the spring of 1880, was named in honor of George F. Parker, its first settler. He was born in Bridgewater, Mass., December 26, 1846, served during the Civil War in Massachusetts regiments, and came here as a homesteader, April 17, 1879.

PIERZ TOWNSHIP organized March 9, 1869, was named in honor of Francis Xavier Pierz (or Pirec), a Catholic missionary. He was born in Godic, Carniola, Austria, November 20, 1785; was ordained a priest in 1813; came to the United States in 1835; was a missionary to the Ottawa Indians in Michigan and from 1852 to 1873 labored mainly among the Ojibwe in northern Minnesota; was a leader in forming the Benedictine community of St. John's, Collegeville, and in bringing German colonists to Stearns and Morrison Counties; returned to Austria in 1873 and died in Laibach, Carniola, January 22, 1880. The city in section 8 of Pierz was platted in 1891, was incorporated as a village on August 17, 1894, and separated from the township on October 21, 1916. The post office, began in 1870 in the home of postmaster Frank Konen, located in section 28 of Buh Township, was called Rich Prairie, 1876–92, and was moved into the village in 1878; the village had a station of the Soo Line.

PIKE CREEK TOWNSHIP organized in 1880, with its creek of this name, commemorates Zebulon Montgomery Pike, explorer of the upper Mississippi, whose stockade camp in the winter of 1805–6 was on its west bank in Swan River Township, about a quarter of a mile south from the mouth of Swan River. He was born in Lamington, N.J., January 5, 1779; entered the U.S. Army in 1799 and became a captain in 1806; conducted an expedition to the headwaters of the Mississippi in 1805–6, being overtaken by an early snow and cold on October 16, so that his party then made their winter encampment, as noted, at the west side of Pike Rapids; advanced thence afoot in the midwinter, with a few of his men, to Sandy, Leech, and Cass Lakes; discovered Pike's Peak of the Rocky Mountains in the next year on an expedition to the headwaters of the Arkansas and Red Rivers; was promoted in the War of 1812 to the rank of brigadier general and was killed April 27, 1813, while commanding an attack at York (now Toronto), Canada. In 1807 and 1810 he published accounts of his explorations in Minnesota and in the Southwest. His journals and reports of these expeditions were more fully published in 1895, edited and annotated by Dr. Elliott Coues, in three volumes. A paper in the *Somerset County (N.J.) Historical Quarterly*, October 1919 (vol. 8, pp. 241–51), shows that Pike's birthplace was at Lamington in that county.

A paper town called Pike Creek was located in Pike Creek Township, circa 1891.

PIKE RAPIDS a post office in Swan River Township, 1868–78.

PLATTE TOWNSHIP organized January 24, 1899, was named for the Platte River, which crosses it. This stream has its main source in a large Platte Lake on the north line of the county, and it flows through a smaller Platte or Rice Lake in the east part of Little Falls Township. Its name, given by the early French fur traders, meaning "dull, flat, shallow," is borne also by a remarkably shallow

river, though long, in Nebraska and Colorado. The village in section 24, on the Platte River, had a post office, 1902–7, and a station of the Sauk Rapids-Brainerd branch of the St. Paul and Pacific Railroad.

PULASKI TOWNSHIP organized in January 1899, was named in honor of the Polish general Casimir Pulaski, who greatly aided Washington in the Revolutionary War. He was born in Poland, March 4, 1748; entered the American service in 1777; formed a corps called Pulaski's Legion in 1778; defended Charleston in 1779; was mortally wounded near Savannah, Ga., October 9, 1779, and died two days later.

RAIL PRAIRIE TOWNSHIP organized January 27, 1890, was named in honor of Case Rail, a pioneer farmer in section 18, beside the Mississippi, whose homestead was mostly a prairie. The village in sections 17 and 18 of Rail Prairie Township had a post office, 1888–1910, which was originally spelled as Rails Prairie. Rail built a store in section 17, where he was the postmaster; the *s* of the name was lost over time.

RAMEY a village in section 34 of Morrill Township about a mile and a half from Morrill; it once had a sawmill, a creamery, a number of businesses, and a post office, 1899–1923.

RANDALL a city in section 7 in Darling Township, platted in March 1890, incorporated on August 14, 1900, and separated from the township on April 11, 1907, was named in honor of John H. Randall of St. Paul. He was born in Roxbury, Mass., in 1831; came to Minnesota in 1856; engaged in official service for the St. Paul and Pacific Railroad company and from 1887 to 1907 for the Northern Pacific Railroad company; and died in St. Paul, March 11, 1916. The post office opened in 1889; it was considered the railroad terminus for the township of Darling at one time and had a station of the Northern Pacific Railroad. Darling Township was originally named Randall in 1891, after the village, and received its present name in 1907, as before noted.

RICH PRAIRIE see PIERZ.

RICHARDSON TOWNSHIP organized January 7, 1903, was named in honor of Nathan Richardson, who was the author of a newspaper history of this county in 1876. He was born in Clyde, N.Y., February 24, 1829; came to Minnesota in 1854 and in the next year settled at Little Falls; was during many years register of deeds for the county and later was judge of probate; was postmaster of Little Falls for about ten years; was a representative in the legislature in 1867, 1872, and 1878; and died at his home in Little Falls, January 9, 1908.

RIPLEY TOWNSHIP received its name from Fort Ripley, built in 1849–50 on the west bank of the Mississippi, opposite the mouth of the Nokasippi River.

ROSING TOWNSHIP organized July 7, 1902, was named in honor of Leonard August Rosing, who in that year was the Democratic candidate for governor of Minnesota. He was born in Malmo, Sweden, August 29, 1861; came to the United States in 1869 with his parents, who settled in Goodhue County, Minn.; resided in Cannon Falls after 1881, being a merchant there; was private secretary of Gov. John Lind, 1899–1901; was a member of the State Board of Control, 1905–9; and died in St. Paul, April 14, 1909.

ROYALTON a city in sections 26, 35, and 36 of Bellevue Township, platted in 1878 and incorporated as a village on March 3, 1887, was named by settlers from the township and village of Royalton in Vermont. The village was begun by Rudolphus D. Kinney, a Vermont missionary, as a post office and mission, 1854–57, which was transferred to Langola in Benton County when Kinney moved east and the site was abandoned; when the Northern Pacific Railroad built a station in section 35 in 1877, settlement began anew, and a post office, again established in 1878, was named Royalton, as previously chosen by Kinney.

RUCKER a post office, 1905–17, in Granite Township, located five miles northwest of Hillman, with Carrie Rucker, postmaster.

ST. STANISLAUS a post office in Pike Creek Township, section 29, seven miles west of Little Falls, was called Lafond from June 1883 to April 1887, with Moses Lafond as postmaster, and was then called St. Stanislaus from April to September 1887, with Joseph Harris as postmaster.

SCANDIA VALLEY TOWNSHIP organized in October 1893, was named by its Scandinavian settlers. In ancient times the name Scandia designated what was supposed to be a large island north of the Baltic Sea, before exploration made it known as the south part of the peninsula of Sweden and Norway.

SOBIESKI a city in sections 3–9 of Swan River Township, was incorporated as a village on December 2, 1915, and separated from the township on June 10, 1920. It was developed on the site of earlier communities; the first was a post office in section 4, 1875–1904, called Ledoux for Frank X. Ledoux, who owned a store and was first postmaster; the community was then called Swan River, although that post office, 1854–79, was established in Benton County, the name continuing until 1918 when changed to Sobieski for Prince Sobieski, hero of Poland; Swan River was also known as Green's Ferry and Aitkinsville, the latter because William A. Aitkin, the fur trader for whom Aitkin County was named, is buried there.

STELLA a post office located a half mile west of Bowlus in Two Rivers Township at postmaster Henry Armstrong, Jr.'s, homestead and stage stop, 1895–98; Armstrong's father owned the land on which Bowlus was developed.

STRAND a post office, 1903–7, in Scandia Valley Township, five miles east of Lincoln.

STROMAN a village in section 5 of Elmdale Township, with a post office, 1889–95 and 1897–1902, begun by August Stroman (or Strommen), postmaster, who also owned the general store and a sawmill in section 18.

SULLIVAN a country post office, 1904–17, located in Richardson Township; postmaster Mason Cadwell was a livestock breeder.

SWAN RIVER see SOBIESKI.

SWAN RIVER TOWNSHIP organized in December 1874, bears the name of the stream flowing through its northern part to the Mississippi. Its source is Swan Lake in Todd County, the name of both the lake and river being received by translation from their Ojibwe name, spelled Wabisi by Frederic Baraga and Wabizi by Rev. Joseph A. Gilfillan. When the first settlers came, Minnesota had two species of swans, the whistling swan and the trumpeter swan.

SWANVILLE TOWNSHIP organized October 12, 1892, likewise crossed by the Swan River, took the name of its railway village, platted by John Williams, Jr., and Henry Albert and Matilda Rhoda in section 7 in November 1882 and incorporated May 24, 1893; the name was selected by Williams. The major industry was lumber, and the village had a station of the Northern Pacific Railroad. Its post office in section 32 was first called Culdrum, 1867–83.

SWEDBACK'S SETTLEMENT see UPSALA.

TOPEKA a switching spur of the Northern Pacific Railroad to accommodate grain cars, with a store and elevator, located in section 25 of Ripley Township from the early 1890s to 1930s.

TWO RIVERS TOWNSHIP first settled in 1855 and organized in September 1865, received the name of its streams tributary to the Mississippi, a translation from the Ojibwe, as noted by Gilfillan. The larger one of the Two Rivers is formed by the South and North Two Rivers, which unite about three miles above its mouth, the former being the outlet of Two River Lake in Stearns County. Little Two River flows into the Mississippi a third of a mile north from the mouth of the larger stream. A post office was located in the township, 1857–58 and 1867–84.

UPSALA a city in Elmdale Township, was named from the ancient city of Uppsala in Sweden, renowned for its university founded in 1477. It was incorporated as a village on January 2, 1917, and was first called Swedback's Settlement for the site where Charles Swedback built his store; as more settlers from Sweden arrived, the name was changed. Its post office began in 1883, was discontinued in 1911, and was reestablished in 1917.

VAWTER a small village of the Soo Line in section 6 of Bellevue, was platted in the summer of 1908. It had a post office, 1922–40.

ZERF a post office, 1897–1902, in section 8 of Hillman Township, 19 miles east of Little Falls; there were a number of businesses, including several mills, a church, and a school.

Lakes and Streams

The preceding pages have noticed the Hillman and Little Hillman Brooks, Pike Creek, Platte Lake and River, Swan Lake and River, and the Two Rivers.

Near the northwest corner of the county, Scandia Valley Township has a fine group of lakes, beautiful for their hilly and wooded shores, numerous points, bays, and islands, and abounding in fish and waterfowl. Lake Alexander, the largest of this group, named before 1860 for Capt. (and later Maj.) Thomas L. Alexander, stationed at Fort Ripley, has Crow, Potato, and High Islands. It outflows to Fish Trap Lake and thence by Fish Trap Brook to the Long Prairie and Crow Wing Rivers.

Shamano Lake, about two miles farther north, has this spelling on the map of Minnesota in 1860, derived, according to Gilfillan, "from an old Indian named Shamanons, who lived there long ago," but on the most recent maps it is spelled Shamineau, a French form of this Ojibwe name.

Smaller lakes in Scandia Valley are Stanchfield Lake, named for a lumberman, on the south line of sections 1 and 2; Duck Lake in sections 9 and 10; Round Lake in section 13; McDonald Lake, section 17; Lena Lake, section 18; and Ham Lake, named for its shape, adjoining the northeast shore of Fish Trap Lake.

Mud Lake is in section 36, Rosing.

Tamarack and Alott Lakes are respectively in sections 11 and 34, Rail Prairie. The latter, erroneously printed Mott Lake on one map, was named with a slight change in spelling for F. Aiott, a pioneer farmer there.

Clough Township has Round Lake in section 27, and Goose and Clough Lakes in sections 26 and 35.

Lake Madaline is in sections 5 and 8, Cushing.

Fish Lake is on the east line of Darling Township.

In the northwest part of Elmdale are Long, Pine, and Cedar Lakes.

Little Elk River, translated from its Ojibwe name, is tributary to the Mississippi from the west, giving name to Little Elk Rapids of the great river, between two and three miles north of Little Falls. Hay Creek, named from its meadows that supplied hay for winter logging teams, flows into the North Fork of Little Elk River; and the South Fork receives Tidd, Shingle, and Sturgis Brooks.

Another Hay Creek flows to the Mississippi from the south part of Swan River Township.

Below the Little Elk River and Rapids, the Mississippi has Big Island, a mile north of Mill Island at Little Falls; Newton and Hobart Islands, about a mile north of Pike Rapids; and between three and five miles south of Swan River are Cash's, Muncy's, and Blanchard's Rapids.

On its east side the Mississippi receives Fletcher Creek from Ripley and Belle Prairie.

At the head of Platte River are Platte Lake, before noted, and Sullivan Lake, the latter crossed by the east line of Pulaski. Skunk River, the large eastern tributary of the Platte, was called Little Platte River on the map of Minnesota in 1860.

Joseph N. Nicollet mapped the Platte as "Pekushino river"; it was named "Flat river" on the map of Minnesota Territory in 1850; and Joseph G. Norwood's map in David D. Owen's geological report, published in 1852, first presented its French name, Platte River.

Four small lakes are tributary to the lower part of this river, namely, Fish Lake in sections 13 and 14, Agram; Pelkey Lake, bearing the name of pioneer farmers beside it, in sections 34 and 35, Belle Prairie; Rice Lake, formerly mapped as Platte Lake, having much wild rice, through which the river flows in Little Falls Township; and Skunk Lake, closely adjoining this Rice Lake and also very near the mouth of Skunk River.

Little Rock Creek flows into Benton County.

Mount Morris and Lakin Townships are drained to the Rum River by its West Branch and Tibbetts Brook.

Prairies and Hills

Four townships of this county, Belle Prairie, Bellevue, Green Prairie, and Rail Prairie, are named for small natural prairies on the valley drift bordering the Mississippi. A larger area, called Rich Prairie, consisting mainly of similar valley drift, adjoins the Platte and Skunk Rivers in Buh, Pierz, Agram, and the southeast part of Little Falls Township. With the exception of these and some other such limited grasslands, Morrison County originally was well wooded, and amidst its principally hardwood forests it had numerous extensive tracts of valuable white pine timber.

Considerable parts of this county are occupied by belts of low morainic drift hills, but only two hills are named on maps. One is widely known as "Hole-in-the-Day's bluff," because the second hereditary Ojibwe chief of this name was buried on its top. He was born in 1828 and died at Crow Wing, June 27, 1868, being assassinated by three members of the Pillager band. This hill is on the south edge of Belle Prairie, about a mile and a half northeast of Little Falls. It rises 40 feet above the average height of neighboring hillocks in the same belt, being about 150 feet above the Mississippi, but even this slight elevation commands a wide prospect of the adjoining valley plain.

The second morainic hill distinguished by a name is in the eastern section 26 of Belle Prairie, known as Tanner's Hill, which has a height of only about 100 feet above the country around it.

Pike's Wintering Place

The site of log houses and a stockade built by Pike and his soldiers as their winter quarters in 1805–6 on the west bank of the Mississippi at Pike Rapids, before noticed for Pike Creek Township, is marked by a bronze memorial tablet upon a cairn of stones, given by the Daughters of the American Revolution and unveiled September 27, 1919, with an address by Mrs. James T. Morris of Minneapolis, state regent.

The Mississippi at its stage of low water falls three feet by its rapids in the distance between about a quarter and an eighth of a mile north of this site. Its bed, strewn with boulders, has many low outcrops of staurolite-bearing mica schist.

Charles A. Lindbergh State Park

Charles A. Lindbergh State Park, containing the boyhood home of the great aviator, was established in 1931. Soon after Lindbergh's historic transatlantic flight, souvenir hunters invaded and vandalized the building, and the family donated the property to the state. The Minnesota Historical Society operates the home as a historic site. The park is named for Charles A. Lindbergh, Sr., a progressive Republican Congressman who represented central Minnesota from 1907 to 1917 and lost the governor's race in 1918.

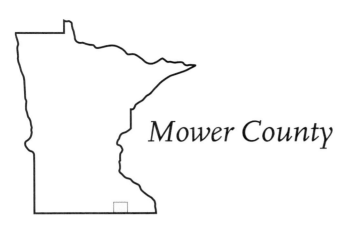

Mower County

Established February 20, 1855, this county was named in honor of John E. Mower, who was born in Bangor, Maine, September 15, 1815, and died in Arcola, Minn., June 11, 1879. He came to St. Croix Falls, Wis., in 1842; removed to Stillwater, Minn., in 1844; and settled at Arcola, near Stillwater, in 1847, where he afterward resided, being chiefly engaged in lumbering. He was a member of the council of the territorial legislature, 1854–55, and a representative in the state legislature, 1874–75.

His brother, Martin Mower, born in Stark, Maine, in 1819, came to Stillwater in 1843; had large business interests of building, manufacturing, and lumbering in Stillwater and Arcola; selected the latter place as his home in 1846 and died there in July 1890.

The family name here has been pronounced with the long sound of *o*, as for one mowing grass, not like a mow of hay in a barn, but the county title, by common usage, is spoken in the latter way.

Information of the origin and meaning of names has been gathered from History of Mower County *(1884, 610 pp.); the later history of this county, edited by Franklyn Curtiss-Wedge (1911, 1,006 pp.); and from Henry Weber, Jr., judge of probate, Eugene Wood, register of deeds, and Flora Crane Conner, librarian, each interviewed during a visit at Austin, the county seat, in April 1916.*

ADAMS TOWNSHIP was organized in May 1858. Its city of the same name in section 11 was platted by Selah Chamberlain on January 30, 1868, and was incorporated as a village February 17, 1887. This name is borne by counties in nine states of the Union and by villages and townships in 14 states, mostly in honor of John Adams, the second president of the United States, 1797–1801, and his son, John Quincy Adams, the sixth president, 1825–29. The first postal service was provided in 1859 from the farm home of John Ingens; the post office was established in 1861 with

Harold M. F. Ingens, postmaster; it had a station of the Chicago, Milwaukee, St. Paul and Pacific Railroad.

ANDYVILLE a village in Lansing Township.

AUSTIN the county seat, platted in the spring of 1856, incorporated as a village on March 6, 1868, and as a city on February 28, 1871, and February 28, 1876, and also Austin Township, organized in 1858, were named for Austin R. Nichols, their first settler. He was born in Lawrence County, N.Y., June 13, 1814; came to Minnesota in 1851 and took a land claim in 1853 on the site of this city; built a sawmill here in 1854 but sold this claim later in the same year; was a pioneer farmer subsequently at several other places in this state; removed to Minneapolis in 1865 and to the northwest shore of Mille Lacs in 1879, where Nichols post office, named in his honor, was established at his home, at the west edge of Aitkin County. He died there, almost a century old, April 5, 1914.

The post office began in 1855; the city had a

station of the Chicago, Milwaukee, St. Paul and Pacific Railroad. The most well known of the many businesses in the city is George A. Hormel and Company, begun by Hormel on borrowed money in 1891; its national advertising, begun in 1910, made its products household names; Hormel, born in Ohio, died in 1946 in California at age 85.

AUSTIN ACRES a suburb of Austin, located in section 8 of Austin Township.

BELLEVUE a station of the Chicago Great Western Railroad in section 16 of Lodi Township.

BENNINGTON TOWNSHIP at first named Andover by the county commissioners in 1858, was organized in the autumn of 1860, then receiving its present name from Bennington, Vt., renowned for a battle of the Revolutionary War, August 16, 1777, in which the British were defeated by the Americans. A post office was located in the township, 1888–92.

BROWNSDALE a city in sections 9 and 10 of Red Rock Township, was platted in the summer of 1856 by Andrew D. and Hosmer A. Brown and was incorporated on February 16, 1876. Andrew D. Brown was born in North Stonington, Conn., in 1818; came to Minnesota in 1856, settling here, and engaged in lumber business and milling; died in Minneapolis in May 1911. Hosmer A. Brown was born in North Stonington, Conn., September 30, 1830; came to this state in 1855, settling on the site of Brownsdale as a farmer and carpenter; was a representative in the legislature in 1870 and 1877.

The village was one of three communities wanting to be the county seat, and in anticipation of success, its name was changed to Mower City; when the vote of June 1, 1857, named Austin as county seat, the name was changed back to Brownsdale. The post office operated 1857–58, and then the name became Mower City, 1858–71, changing back to Brownsdale in 1871; the village had a station of the Chicago, Milwaukee, St. Paul and Pacific Railroad.

CANTON a post office, 1862–68, in Windom Township at a time when the township was named Canton.

CEDAR CITY a farm community in Lyle Township, which had a stone and timber dam built by Caleb Stock and John Phelps, who with T. N. Stone built a sawmill and gristmill and platted part of their claim in 1856. Caleb Stock was postmaster

January-September 1857, at which time the post office was transferred to Mineral Springs. The dam and mills were washed away during flooding in 1858 and not rebuilt.

CLAYTON TOWNSHIP originally named Providence in 1858, was organized June 20, 1873, being then renamed in honor of William Z. Clayton, owner of a large tract of land in this township. He was born in Freeman, Maine, in 1837; came to Minnesota about 1857; served in the First Minnesota Battery of Light Artillery, 1861–65, becoming its captain; later resided in Winona County, and during several summers in this township, being a farmer and dealer in real estate; removed to Bangor, Maine.

COLFAX a post office, 1868–70; location not found.

CORNING a village in section 32 of Udolpho Township and in section 6 of Lansing Township, was settled about 1884. Its post office, 1894–1906, was established in Freeborn County and transferred to Mower County in 1902. Little of the community remained by 1906.

DEXTER TOWNSHIP organized June 6, 1870, was named for Dexter Parritt, who came from Ohio with his father, Mahlon Parritt, in 1857, these being the first settlers. The city of Dexter in sections 13, 14, 23, and 24 was platted in 1874 and was incorporated February 28, 1878; it had a station of the Chicago, Milwaukee, St. Paul and Pacific Railroad, and the post office was established in 1874.

ELKHORN see HAMILTON.

ELKTON a city in Marshall and Dexter Townships, was platted January 25, 1887, and incorporated as a village on February 6, 1906. It had a station of the Chicago Great Western Railroad in section 1 of Marshall Township, and its post office began in 1887.

ESBA a post office, 1867–77, in Windom Township, three miles north of Rose Creek.

FRANKFORD TOWNSHIP was organized May 11, 1858, taking the name of its village in section 13, which had been settled in 1854 and platted in 1856. The village was named the county seat until a vote was taken and Austin was chosen. It had three stores, a hotel, a number of businesses, a school, a church, and a post office, 1855–1900; when the Southern Minnesota Railroad came in 1870, many towns were developed along the route, but Frankford was not one of them, and eventually the land returned to farm use.

GAINESVILLE see GRAND MEADOW.

GERMANIA a farming village six miles south of Adams in Adams Township, which had a post office, 1878–81 and 1890–91.

GRAND MEADOW TOWNSHIP named by the county commissioners in 1858, in allusion to its being an extensive prairie, was organized April 20, 1862. Its city of this name in Grand Meadow and Frankford Townships, on the Chicago, Milwaukee and St. Paul Railroad, was platted in 1870, when this railway line was built through the county. It was incorporated as a village on February 24, 1876, and again on April 13, 1906; its post office began in 1858 as Gainesville and changed to Grand Meadow in 1859, with Cyrus G. Langworthy as postmaster under both names.

HAMILTON a former village on the east line of Racine, lying mainly in Fillmore County, was platted in 1855, as noted for that county. The village was in section 1 of Frankford Township, section 36 of Racine Township, and into Sumner Township, Fillmore County; it was earlier called Elkhorn while it was only in Fillmore County. A post office was located there, 1855–63.

JOHNSBURG a village in section 33 of Adams Township, whose first settlers came in 1855, many from the German community of Johnsburg in McHenry County, Illinois; the early village centered around the Catholic church and school; its post office operated 1891 to 1900.

LANSING TOWNSHIP organized May 11, 1858, received this name from the capital of Michigan in compliment to Alanson B. Vaughan, a pioneer settler, on account of its similarity in sound with his first name. Lansing village in section 10, of which he was the first proprietor, was also platted in 1858; it was incorporated as a village on February 17, 1881; incorporation was dissolved on February 24, 1885. It had a station of the Chicago, Milwaukee, St. Paul and Pacific Railroad, a flour mill, a hotel, and a general store where the post office began in 1857.

Vaughan was born in Clinton County, N.Y., June 6, 1806; removed to Rock County, Wis., in 1843; came to Minnesota in 1854 and settled in this township, with his five sons, in 1855; was the first merchant and first postmaster in the adjoining village of Austin; was a member of the state

constitutional convention in 1857 and the first judge of probate in this county; died October 3, 1876.

LE ROY TOWNSHIP was organized May 11, 1858. The city in sections 33 and 34, bearing the same name, was platted in 1867, when this Iowa and Minnesota division of the Chicago, Milwaukee and St. Paul Railroad was being built. It was originally platted on April 24, 1857, in section 28 of the township by Lewis Mathews, Daniel Caswell, Martin L. Shook, and Adoniran J. Palmer near the site of the first settler, Henry Edmonds, who had built a mill in April 1855. When the railroad came in August 1867, two miles south, the depot was called Le Roy Station, and eventually businesses began in that area, and the "old town" of Le Roy diminished; the post office began in 1856, with Daniel Caswell as postmaster. The village was incorporated on February 26, 1876. The land around the millpond in the "old town" was donated to the village as a park; in 1962 it became Lake Louise State Park. The pond was named for Louise Hambrecht, a member of the family that built the mill.

LODI TOWNSHIP organized in February 1874, had received this name from the county commissioners in 1858. A village was in section 15 about 1913. The name is borne by villages and townships in New York, New Jersey, Wisconsin, and several other states, being derived from a medieval city of Lombardy in Italy, made famous by a victory won at the bridge of Lodi by Napoleon against the Austrians, May 10, 1796.

LYLE TOWNSHIP organized in 1858, was named in honor of Robert Lyle, a native of Ohio, who settled here in November 1856, was judge of probate for the county, and in 1868 removed to Missouri. Lyle, a city in section 36, platted in 1870, was incorporated March 9, 1875. The post office was established in 1862 with Nathaniel P. Williams, postmaster; then was called Minnereka, 1870–71, with William Shellback as postmaster; and returned to Lyle in 1871, with Thorwald Irgens, postmaster; also known as Lyle Center. It had a station serving several lines, including the Chicago Great Western Railroad.

MADISON a village in section 21 of Udolpho Township, began on September 3, 1857, when Warren A. Brown opened a general store, the site of the post office, 1857–75. The village had a hotel, a livery stable, a sawmill, and a station of Chicago, Milwaukee, St. Paul and Pacific Railroad, but the community did not grow, and by 1903 the townsite had reverted to farmland.

MANILA a post office, 1899–1907, located in Red Rock Township with Louis F. King as postmaster in his general store.

MAPLEVIEW a city in Lansing Township, was incorporated as a village on June 6, 1946, when the community had about 100 families; its name originated from a row of hard maple trees on the west side of town.

MARSHALL TOWNSHIP which had been called York by the county commissioners in 1858, was organized June 6, 1870, being named in honor of William Rainey Marshall, who was governor of this state from 1866 to 1870.

MAYVILLE a village in sections 31 and 32 of Waltham Township, with a station of the Chicago Great Western Railroad and a post office, 1895–1912.

MINERAL SPRINGS a post office, 1857–70, which was earlier at Cedar City; location not found.

MINNEREKA see LYLE.

MOWER CITY see BROWNSDALE.

NEVADA TOWNSHIP first settled in 1854, was organized in May 1858, receiving this name from the Sierra Nevada, meaning Snowy Range, which forms the eastern border of the great valley of California. Nevada Territory was organized three years later, in 1861, and was admitted to the Union as a state in 1864. A post office operated in section 21, 1858–78.

PLEASANT VALLEY TOWNSHIP organized May 11, 1858, was named by Sylvester Hills, its pioneer settler, who came here in 1854 from the village and township of Pleasant Valley in Dutchess County, N.Y. A post office was located in the township, 1858–59.

PRAIRIE a post office, 1863–71; location not found.

RACINE TOWNSHIP organized May 11, 1858, bears the French name, meaning "root," of the Hokah or Root River, which receives tributaries from this township. The city of Racine in section 26 was platted October 3, 1890, and incorporated as a village on June 30, 1959. It had a station of the Chicago Great Western Railroad, and its post office was established in 1879.

RAMSEY a railway junction and small village three miles north of Austin, in Lansing Township, section 23, was named in honor of Gov. Alexander Ramsey, for whom a biographic sketch is presented in the chapter of Ramsey County. The village had a post office, 1874–75, and a station of Chicago, Milwaukee, St. Paul and Pacific Railroad.

RED ROCK TOWNSHIP organized in 1858, was named by its first settler, John L. Johnson, who came from Rock County, Wis., in October 1855. His first home here was in Red Rock grove in section 4, this name being suggested by a large red rock in the grove, the only one of the kind to be found for miles around.

RENOVA a little village of the Chicago Great Western Railroad in section 9, Dexter, was platted March 30, 1900. It had a post office, 1890–1934.

ROOT RIVER a post office, 1860–83, located in section 16 of Pleasant Valley Township.

ROSE CREEK a city in section 26, Windom, developed when the Chicago, Milwaukee and St. Paul Railroad came in 1867; it was incorporated February 17, 1899; the post office began in 1865. It is situated beside the creek of this name, which is the largest eastern tributary of Cedar River in this county.

SARGEANT TOWNSHIP organized September 16, 1873, was named in honor of Harry N. Sargeant, one of its pioneer farmers. He was born in the Province of Quebec, June 19, 1817; came to Wisconsin in 1858 and to this county in 1865, settling in section 11 of this township; was elected the first township clerk; died January 25, 1884. Sargeant, a city in sections 18 and 19, was platted September 7, 1894, incorporated as a village on August 25, 1900, and reincorporated on March 10, 1921. It had a station on the Chicago Great Western Railroad; the post office was established in 1881.

SUTTON a village in section 26 of Dexter Township, had a general store, a creamery, a blacksmith, a station of the Chicago Great Western Railroad, and a post office, 1886–1907.

TAOPI a city in sections 9 and 16 in Lodi Township, platted in 1875, was named in honor of Taopi (Wounded Man), a leader of the farmer band of the Dakota, who died in March 1869. He was one of the first converts to Christianity at the Redwood mission on the Minnesota River and at the time of the Dakota War of 1862 was friendly to the whites and aided in the rescue of many. He is commemorated in a book, *Taopi and His Friends, or the Indians' Wrongs and Rights*, by Rev. S. D.

Hinman, Bishop Whipple, and others (125 pp., with his portrait, published in 1869). The village was incorporated on March 6, 1878, and reincorporated on April 25, 1907. It was the site of the largest steam flouring mill in the southern part of the state and had a station serving several rail lines, including the Chicago Great Western Railroad; the post office began in 1875.

TROY CITY a townsite on the Red Cedar River eight miles south of Austin, platted in sections 4 and 8 of Lyle Township by John Tift on March 24, 1857; Tift built a sawmill, and the site also had a hotel, but the community did not develop.

UDOLPHO TOWNSHIP organized in 1858, was named by one of its pioneers, Col. Henry C. Rogers, from his having read *The Mysteries of Udolpho* by Mrs. Ann Ward Radcliffe of England, published in 1794. This is a highly fanciful and weird romance of Italy in the seventeenth century, representing Udolpho as a medieval castle in the Apennines. A post office was located in section 11, 1873–85.

VARCO a village in section 26 of Austin Township, four miles south of Austin, was platted November 17, 1875, on the farm of Thomas Varco, in whose honor it was named. He was born in England, came to Minnesota in 1856, settling here, and died February 12, 1893. The village had a station of the Chicago Great Western Railroad, and the post office operated 1875–82.

WALTHAM TOWNSHIP organized June 4, 1866, had been named April 16, 1858, at a meeting of the county commissioners, one of whom, Charles F. Hardy of Red Rock, was a native of Waltham in Massachusetts. The city of Waltham, in sections 9, 10, and 16, was platted September 8, 1885, and incorporated as a village on February 21, 1898. It was originally platted in 1865 one mile west of the present site by A. J. Burbank for land speculators; Burbank erected a three-story hotel on the town-site, and a post office opened, 1867–74. When the Chicago Great Western Railroad came in 1885, the railroad platted the new site, and the original townsite land was sold off for farming. A new post office was established in 1886.

WINDOM TOWNSHIP organized May 11, 1858, at first called Brooklyn and later Canton, was renamed in May 1862 in honor of William Windom of Winona, who then was a member of Congress. His name is borne also by the county seat of Cottonwood County, for which a biographic notice of him is presented.

Rivers and Creeks

Mower County, with a large adjoining tract of southeastern Minnesota, differs from nearly all other parts of this state by the absence of lakes.

The North and South Branches of the Root River, and Bear and Deer Creeks, headstreams of its Middle Branch, drain the northeast part of the county, the French name of this river, Racine, being given to its most northeastern township.

Upper Iowa River flows eastward from Lodi, receives the Little Iowa River in Le Roy, and crosses the state line at the southeast corner of this county.

Cedar River, called Red Cedar River on Joseph N. Nicollet's map in 1843, flows through the west part of this county. Its tributaries here received from the east, in the order from north to south, are Wolf Creek, Dobbins Creek, Rose Creek, before noted as giving its name to a railway village, and Otter Creek. Little Cedar River, another of its eastern tributaries, which joins the Cedar River much farther south in Iowa, has its sources in Marshall, Clayton, and Adams Townships. From the west, Cedar River in this county receives Turtle, Orchard, and Woodbury Creeks.

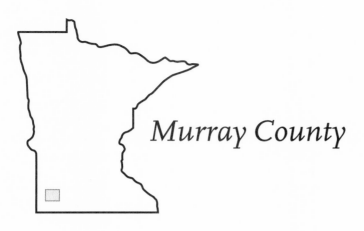

Murray County

This county, established May 23, 1857, and organized June 17, 1872, was named in honor of William Pitt Murray, who was born in Hamilton, Ohio, June 21, 1825, and died in St. Paul, June 20, 1910. He studied at Miami University, Oxford, Ohio; was graduated in law at the State University of Indiana, 1849, and came to Minnesota the same year, settling in St. Paul; was a member of the territorial legislature in 1852–53 and in 1857, and of the council, 1854–55, being its president in 1855; was a member of the state constitutional convention, 1857; a representative in the state legislature in 1863 and 1868; and a state senator, 1866–67 and 1875–76. He was a member of the St. Paul City Council, 1861–68 and 1870–79, being 6 years its president; and for 13 years was the city attorney, 1876–89. He contributed a paper, "Recollections of Early Territorial Days and Legislation," in the MHS Collections (12:103–30 [1908], with his portrait); and was a member of the board of editors of *Minnesota in Three Centuries* (4 vols.), published in 1908. During more than 60 years he was an eminently useful and greatly beloved citizen of the capital of this state.

Information of geographic names in Murray County was received from Alfred Terry of Slayton, during many years a dealer in real estate here, E. V. O'Brien, county auditor, W. J. McAllister, judge of probate, and Robert Hyslop, clerk of the court, each being interviewed during a visit at Slayton, the county seat, in July 1916; and from Neil Currie, interviewed several times in St. Paul in 1918.

AVOCA a city in sections 27, 28, 33, and 34 of Lime Lake Township, was named in 1879 by Archbishop John Ireland, who founded near it a Catholic colony of immigrant farmers. The name is taken from a river in County Wicklow, Ireland, about 40 miles south of Dublin, noted for the picturesque beauty of its valley, called Sweet Vale of Avoca in a poem by Thomas Moore. From the fame given by the poet's praise, this name also has been chosen for villages in 13 other states of the Union.

The townsite was laid out in 1878 by a Mr. Reed of Minneapolis and Benjamin W. Woolstencroft and replatted on October 31, 1879, by the Northwest Town Lot Company. The city was incorporated as a village on November 22, 1881, and reincorporated on April 13, 1913. The post office began in 1872 as Lime Lake and was located in postmaster Peter Erickson's log cabin, changing to Avoca in 1878; the village had a station of the Chicago, St. Paul, Minneapolis and Omaha Railroad.

BELFAST TOWNSHIP organized July 19 and September 3, 1878, bears the name of a large seaport city in northern Ireland, whence the city of Belfast in Maine, on Penobscot Bay, was named, as also villages of eight other states and townships in New York and Pennsylvania.

BEN FRANKLIN see DOVRAY.

BONDIN see FULDA.

BONDIN TOWNSHIP organized November 2, 1874, received the name of a post office previously established at the home of William M. Davis, a pioneer farmer in the northwest quarter of its section 24. See also FULDA.

CAMERON TOWNSHIP organized September 10, 1878, and first named Stanley, has a name that is borne also by villages or cities or townships in 14 other states. It was selected here in compliment for Charles Cameron Cole, an early settler. The village of the same name was established by a colony of Scots numbering 35 persons in 1883; a post office, 1878–80, was established with Edix Connor as postmaster; his daughter, Mabel, was the first child born in the community; the community did not develop, and most of the settlers returned to Scotland.

CHANARAMBIE TOWNSHIP organized July 25, 1879, and first named Lime Stone, is drained by the headstreams of Hidden Wood Creek, or Tchan Narambe Creek, as it is named on Joseph N. Nicollet's map, published in 1843. This Dakota name referred to trees or a grove in its valley concealed from any distant view, called Lost Timber by the early settlers.

CHANDLER a city in Leeds and Moulton Townships, was named in honor of John Alonzo Chandler, who was in official service of the Chicago, Milwaukee and St. Paul Railroad company more than 40 years, beginning this service in 1856. He was born in West Randolph, Vt., January 18, 1831; was captain in the Nineteenth Wisconsin Regiment, 1861–62, and a state senator in Wisconsin, 1864–65; came to Minnesota in 1870, settling in St. Paul, where he died March 31, 1902.

The village was platted on June 7, 1886, and the settlement began with grain elevators, a creamery, a depot of the Southern Minnesota Railroad, and a post office, opened in 1886 in first postmaster Samuel P. Rockey's general store. The city was incorporated as a village on October 6, 1900, and separated from the township on April 1, 1926.

CONWELL CITY was a paper city to be located in Mason Township and incorporated on May 23, 1857. According to the 1857 census, there were 91 people residing at the townsite, which was planned by William Pitt Murray and named for his wife's family name, and an 1859 newspaper referred to the site as the county seat; however, no trace of a community was found; also referred to as Council City, Connwell City, Cornwall City, Cornwell City, Canwell City, Coldwell, and Caldwell.

CRESWELL a post office in section 34, Belfast Township, 1874, transferred to Nobles County.

CURRENT LAKE a village in section 24, Ellsborough Township, began with a store built in 1902 by Aaslog Gravley, although its postal service began earlier, first at Charley Bergstom's homestead in section 22, then in 1877 at Hans H. Molin's farm, and then at Andrew Borg's home, 1886–1900.

CURRIE a city in sections 16, 17, and 20 of Murray Township, was founded in 1872, when Neil Currie and his father, Archibald Currie, built a flour mill there, using waterpower of the Des Moines River about a mile below the mouth of Lake Shetek. Archibald Currie was born in Argyllshire, Scotland, November 13, 1816; came with his parents to America when five years old and to Minnesota in 1862; was a merchant in Winona County until 1874; then removed to Currie, where he engaged in merchandising and milling; was treasurer of this county, 1879–83; died July 15, 1904. This village, which was the first county seat, from 1872 to 1889, being succeeded by Slayton, was named in honor of him and of Neil Currie, who was born in Canada, December 15, 1842. He built the first store here in 1872 and aided in organizing the Murray County Bank in 1874; was postmaster of Currie, 1872–90, and clerk of the court, 1874–87; resided here as a merchant until 1905, when he removed to St. Paul.

The village was platted in July of 1873, and the village post office was established as Lake Shetek, 1870–74, before becoming Currie; the village was incorporated on September 1, 1900; it had a station of the Chicago, St. Paul, Minneapolis and Omaha Railroad in section 16.

DES MOINES RIVER TOWNSHIP organized May 31, 1878, is crossed by the river of this name, which has its sources in the west edge of this county.

DOVRAY TOWNSHIP organized March 18 and April 22, 1879, was named for Dovre, a village in Norway and for the Dovrefjeld, a high mountainous plateau of that country, this name being given by Nels S. Taarud, the county treasurer. Ten years earlier, in 1869, a township of Kandiyohi County received the name Dovre, having the same derivation, for which reason the spelling was changed here, while retaining nearly the original pronunciation. In the 1874 Andreas atlas the township was called Skandia.

Dovray, a city in section 20, was platted in 1904 and incorporated as a village on January 2, 1924. Old Dovray began in 1895 when a cooperative creamery was built in section 16, one mile north and one mile east of the present site; when the Chicago, St. Paul, Minneapolis and Omaha Railroad came in 1899, the townsite was moved to section 20 and platted on June 12, 1904. The post office began as Ben Franklin, in section 14 of Holly Township, 1872–95, and was transferred here in 1895.

EAST DES MOINES a post office, 1879–80, located in Des Moines Township; the first postmaster was Benjamin G. Weld, one of four brothers who were pioneer settlers of the township.

ELLSBOROUGH TOWNSHIP organized March 21, 1874, was named for Elfsborg, Sweden, a community where many of the early Swedish emigrant settlers had lived.

FAIRVIEW a post office, 1873–75, in Shetek Township, section 18.

FENTON TOWNSHIP the latest organized in this county, March 19, 1886, was named in honor of P. H. Fenton, a pioneer farmer, who removed to the state of Washington.

FULDA a city in sections 25 and 26 in Bondin, was named for an ancient city in central Germany on the river Fulda, noted for its early medieval abbey founded in 744, and its beautiful cathedral, built in 1704–12. The village was platted on July 19, 1879, by Benjamin W. Woolstencroft and incorporated as a village in November 21, 1881. The townsite at Seven Mile Lake first had a post office called Bondin in section 24, 1874–79, the name changing at that time to Fulda; the village had a station serving the Southern Minnesota Railroad and the Chicago, Milwaukee, St. Paul and Pacific Railroad.

GROSWAL a place name in Belfast Township in 1887.

HADLEY a city in section 11 of Leeds, has a name that is borne by villages and townships in Massachusetts, New York, Pennsylvania, and other states. It was incorporated as a village on September 1, 1903; it was originally known as Summit Lake when platted on October 31, 1879; the name changed to Hadley when its post office was established in 1880. A number of businesses, including a creamery, a general store, and an elevator, developed at its early settlement, and it had a station of the Chicago, St. Paul, Minneapolis and Omaha Railroad.

HOLLY the name of one of the oldest townships of this county, organized June 17, 1872, was chosen in honor of John Z. Holly, one of its early pioneers, who after a few years returned to Illinois.

IBSEN a post office, 1890–92; location not found.

IONA TOWNSHIP organized March 17, 1880, was named after its city in sections 8 and 9, platted in 1878 by Rev. Martin McDonnell, who here founded a Catholic industrial school for orphans. This is the name of a small island on the west coast of Scotland, celebrated for its ancient abbey, founded by St. Columba in the sixth century, and for a ruined cathedral, which was founded in the thirteenth century. The city of Iona was incorporated as a village on January 22, 1896; the post office began in 1880 with McDonnell as postmaster; it had a station of the Chicago, Milwaukee, St. Paul and Pacific Railroad.

IRON LAKE a post office, 1879–80; location not found; however, a lake of this name is in sections 14 and 15 of Skandia Township and may be related to the post office site.

KELLEY a post office, 1897–1902, in section 29 of Holly Township.

LAKE SARAH TOWNSHIP organized March 11, 1873, was named for its largest lake, doubtless commemorating, like the companion Lake Maria, the wife or daughter of one of the government land surveyors or of a pioneer settler, but surnames for these honorees remain to be learned.

LAKE SHETEK see CURRIE.

LAKE WILSON a city in sections 12 and 13 of Chanarambie, platted in 1883 and incorporated as a village on July 12, 1900, was named by Jonathan E. Wilson, formerly of Chicago, Ill., who also named the nearby lake for himself. He owned at one time 17,000 acres of land in this vicinity (W. H. Stennett, *Place Names of the Chicago and Northwestern and the Chicago, St. Paul, Minneapolis and Omaha Railways*, 1908, p. 180). The village had a station of the Chicago, St. Paul, Minneapolis and Omaha Railroad, and the post office opened in 1883.

LEEDS TOWNSHIP organized March 11, 1873, received its name from Leeds Township and village in Columbia County, Wis. It is near Lowville in that county, whence the Low brothers came to Murray County. A post office was located in the township, 1879–80.

LIME CREEK a village in section 20, Belfast, was named for this creek by Nicolaus Costello, who with Anton Hager founded the village in 1888. The village was platted on December 27, 1898, on land then owned by Anton and Josefa Hager. The post office operated 1889–1971; the village had a station on the Chicago, St. Paul, Minneapolis and Omaha Railroad.

LIME LAKE see AVOCA.

LIME LAKE TOWNSHIP organized September 24, 1873, was named for this lake, which has plentiful boulders of limestone, pushed up by its ice into ridges along parts of its shore.

LIME STONE a post office, 1879–81, located on postmaster William N. Luce's farm two miles west of Lake Wilson in Chanarambie Township at a time when the township was still called Lime Stone.

LOUISA a post office, 1883–84; location not found, but mail thereafter went to Ben Franklin, then Dovray.

LOWVILLE TOWNSHIP organized September 2, 1873, was named for John H. and Bartlett M. Low, brothers, who came here from New York and Wisconsin. Each of these states has a township named Lowville in honor of their family. John H. Low came first in the winter of 1865–66 for trapping in the vicinity of the Bear Lakes. In 1866 the brothers took land claims in and adjoining the Great Oasis of timber, as the extensive grove beside these lakes was named on Nicollet's map, in allusion to the surrounding region of treeless prairie. John H. Low was the county auditor, 1881–84, continued as a farmer on his homestead 48 years, and removed to Slayton in 1914. Bartlett Marshall Low was born in Poughkeepsie, N.Y., in 1839; served in the Forty-second Wisconsin Regiment during the Civil War; came to Minnesota in 1865 and settled here a year later; was a representative in the legislature, 1887–89. (The family and township names here have an exceptional pronunciation, like how, now.) A post office was in section 8, 1874–1900, with Stephen Manchester as postmaster.

MASON TOWNSHIP organized July 20, 1872, was at first called Okcheeda (or Oksida, as in the 1874 Andreas atlas), but in 1879 was renamed in honor of Milo D. Mason, one of its pioneer settlers, who was a mail carrier between Currie and Pipestone. A post office was in section 11, 1890–1900.

MOULTON TOWNSHIP organized October 28 and November 18, 1879, was named in honor of Justin P. Moulton of Worthington. He was born in Gilbertsville, N.Y., July 4, 1828; came to Minnesota in 1855; kept a hotel in Saratoga, Winona County, and later engaged in mercantile business in Rochester; was a representative in the legislature, 1862–63; was receiver of the U.S. land office in Worthington, 1875–81.

MURRAY CENTRE a post office, 1872–81, in section 34 of Oksida Township, later named Mason Township.

MURRAY TOWNSHIP organized July 20, 1872, was named, like this county, for William Pitt Murray of St. Paul.

OWANKA a Dakota word, meaning a camping place, is the name of grounds platted for summer homes in Shetek Township on and near the northeastern shore of Lake Shetek. A part in the southwest quarter of section 29 had been earlier named Tepeeota, meaning a place of Dakota tents or tepees. About a mile southward, in the center and southwest part of section 32, the high shore is called "Ball's bluff," for Ezra Ball, a pioneer settler there, on whose land a party of state cavalrymen camped as rangers through this region after the Dakota War in 1862. A village in section 30 had a post office, 1900–1902.

PRAIRIE LODGE a post office, 1874–78; location not found.

SCOVELL a post office in section 27 of Cameron Township, 1880–91, with James W. Parshall, postmaster, at the home of H. Schovell, for whom named.

SHETEK TOWNSHIP at first called Lake Shetek, organized July 20, 1872, was named for its large lake, of which the broadest expanse is in the southwest part of this township and which also reaches south into Mason and Murray. Nicollet wrote of his visit here in the summer of 1838: "I pitched my tents, during three days, about the group of Shetek or Pelican Lakes, that occupy a portion of the space forming the Coteau des Prairies. This name belongs to the language of the Chippewas and has been given to them by the voyageurs. The Dakota call this group of lakes the *Rabechy*, meaning the place where the pelicans nestle [have nests]" (*Report*, 1843, p. 13). Shetek is thus noted as an Ojibwe word, meaning a pelican, but it differs somewhat from its original form. It is spelled Shada in Henry W. Longfellow's *Song of Hiawatha*, Shede (each vowel being pronounced like long *a*) by Rev. Joseph A. Gilfillan, and jede (nearly the same as each of the preceding in pronunciation) by Chrysostom Verwyst.

Six years after Nicollet was here, Lieut. James Allen, with a company of dragoons, explored the Des Moines valley in August and September 1844, from its junction with the Mississippi to Lake Shetek, which, not having Nicollet's report and map, he called "the Lake of the Oaks, . . . the highest source of the Des Moines that is worth noticing as such."

Lake Shetek State Park, located primarily in this township, was established in 1929. Its origins relate to the Dakota War of 1862; legislative acts in 1905 and 1921 provided for the reinterment of the bodies of twelve white people killed in the conflict and the building of a memorial.

SHETIC a post office, August to December 1862; location not found.

SILLERUD a Swedish Lutheran congregation located in Skandia Township settled by emigrants from Värmland and Skåne; the name was suggested by G. F. and August Gren, natives of Sillerud, Värmland; the church was built in 1878 on the northeast shore of Currant Lake and listed on maps as Sillerud Church.

SKANDIA TOWNSHIP first settled in 1870 and organized January 7, 1873, bears the ancient name of southern Sweden, whence a longer form of the same name, Scandinavia, is used to designate the great peninsula of Sweden and Norway, or, in a wider sense, to include also Denmark and Iceland. The township was called Leeds in the 1874 Andreas atlas.

SLAYTON TOWNSHIP organized July 20, 1872, was then called Center (or Centre, as in the 1874 Andreas atlas) for its central position in the county; but in 1882, a year after Slayton railway village was platted, the township was thus renamed in honor of Charles W. Slayton, its founder and chief proprietor. He was a real estate dealer, lived in this village about two years, 1881–82, removed afterward to New Mexico, but returned to Minnesota and lived in St. Paul several years. The county seat was removed from Currie to Slayton by a vote of the county, June 11, 1889. The city in section 15 was incorporated on February 26, 1883, and reincorporated on September 30, 1918; it had a station on the Chicago, St. Paul, Minneapolis and Omaha Railroad, and the post office was established in 1881.

Charles Wesley Slayton was born at West Potsdam, N.Y., August 24, 1835; came to Wisconsin with his parents in 1855; was a farmer and after 1868 a manufacturer of furniture in Berlin, Wis., and a traveling salesman; removed to Minnesota in 1878, settling in St. Paul as a land agent of the St. Paul and Sioux City Railroad company; platted Slayton village in 1881; went to England early in 1882 and returned in April with 67 colonists, most of whom settled in or near this village; was a partner after 1882 in gold and silver mining in New Mexico, but thereby in failure of his associates he lost his entire property; removed in 1892 to Phoenix, Ariz., there engaging again in real estate business and in mining (*History of the Slayton Family*, 1898, pp. 123–24, with his portrait). On account of failing health, he went in hope of recovery to Little Rock, Ark., and died there, June 5, 1906.

THRALL a post office, June to December 1878; location not found.

WIROCK a village in section 24 of Iona Township, was platted on April 15, 1907, and established by Herran Weirauch and named for him, the spelling changed to make pronunciation easier. Weirauch was the first settler and the first postmaster, the post office operating 1907–34.

Lakes and Streams

The foregoing pages have noticed the Des Moines River, Chanarambie Creek, Lakes Sarah and Maria, Lake Wilson, Lime Lake and Creek, and Lake Shetek.

Okshida Creek, as named on Nicollet's map, called also Oksida or Beaver Creek on later maps, being the headstream of Des Moines River, gave its name in the early years to Okcheeda Township, from 1872 to 1879, since called Mason. This is evidently the same Dakota word that in Nobles County is applied to Lake Ocheeda and Ocheyedan Creek or River, south of Worthington. Its meaning is indicated by Nicollet on his map, which, in the belt of morainic drift hills that is intersected by this lake and its outflowing stream, has Ocheyedan Hillock or Mourning Ground. In the Dakota *Dictionary* by Stephen R. Riggs, 1852, *acheya* and *akicheya* are verbs meaning "to mourn, as for a dead relative," these words being allied closely with the names cited in Nobles County and with Okshida, variously spelled, in Murray County. Here the name commemorates the mourning for two boys killed by a war party of enemies.

The southeast part of Moulton is drained by Champepadan Creek, flowing southward into Nobles and Rock Counties. Its Dakota name, given by Nicollet, with translation, as Tchan Pepedan River, or Thorny Wood River, was derived from its thorn bushes and small trees.

Currant Lake, on the west line of Skandia, and Plum Creek in Holly Township, each flowing northeast to the Cottonwood River, received these names from their wild currants and wild plum trees.

Skandia also has Iron Lake and Lake Oscar.

Hawk or Rush Lake crossed by the south line of Skandia, was the most northeastern of the group of Bear Lakes, four in number, lying mainly in Lowville, the others being Crooked and Bear Lakes and Tibbetts or Great Oasis Lake. All are now represented by dry lake beds, having become valuable farming lands. The fourth, also drained, was called Great Oasis Lake, from this name applied by Nicollet to the adjoining grove, which had an area of more than 300 acres, before noted for Lowville Township.

Lake Wilson, just east of the railway village so named, was earlier called Sand Lake.

Summit Lake adjoins Hadley village, whence the railway descends both to the east and west.

Lake Elsie, now drained and in cultivation, in the east part of Slayton village, was named for a daughter of Arthur Simpson, a settler beside it, who came from England, was the first owner of the Park Hotel, and removed to southern California.

Lake Cora Belle, in Iona, and Lake Iva Delle (spelled Ivedalle on some maps), in Ellsborough, were named by the U.S. surveyors in honor of daughters of the proprietor of the principal hotel in Worthington.

The North and South Badger Lakes, in the northeast corner of Iona, are named for badgers formerly found here.

In the southeast part of Mason are Lake Beauty, so called by Henry Edwards, a settler near it, and Mud and Clear Lakes, which are described by their names.

Another Clear Lake, now dry, was crossed by the west line of section 6, Shetek; and James Lake, named for James P. Corbin and James W. Matthews, early settlers beside it, is in the east half of section 4, outflowing eastward to Plum Creek.

The Inlet is a long and narrow northwestern arm or branch of Lake Shetek, receiving a tributary creek from Long Lake, which is crossed by the north line of this county.

Several small lakes adjoining the northeast end of Lake Shetek, are Bloody Lake, for victims of the Dakota War of 1862, Fox Lake, Isabella or Round Lake, and Lake Fremont. The last commemorates John C. Frémont (1813–90), who was here with Nicollet in 1838, renowned later as an explorer and as the Republican candidate in 1856 for the presidency of the United States.

Smith Lake, named for Henry Watson Smith, a pioneer farmer at its west side, is near the southeast shore of Lake Shetek, in sections 6 and 7, Murray. He settled here before the Dakota War, left his claim at that time, and never returned.

In Dovray are Skow Lake in section 1, Long Lake on the west side of sections 3 and 10, Rush Lake in section 15, Lake Buffalo in section 18, Duck Lake a half mile southeast of Dovray village, and Star Lake at the middle of the south line of this township.

Lake Louisa (earlier mapped as Lake Eliza) is in sections 11 and 12, Des Moines River.

Seven Mile Lake, south of Fulda, was named for its distance on an old trail from the Graham Lakes in Nobles County.

Center Lake, also called Central Lake, is at the center of Belfast. Talcott Lake, on the east line of its sections 24 and 25, was named by Nicollet in honor of Andrew Talcott (1797–1883), as noted in the chapter of Cottonwood County.

Buffalo Ridge

The highest land in this county, extending about two miles along the crest of the Coteau des Prairies in the central part of Chanarambie, is called Buffalo Ridge, in translation of its Dakota name. It rises 100 to 200 feet above the lowest adjoining valleys. On its highest knoll the Dakota had delineated various animals by "a series of boulder outlines, mostly formed of small stones. The best preserved of these figures apparently represents a buffalo. . . . It heads to the northeast, and its greatest length is nearly 12 feet" (T. H. Lewis, in the *American Anthropologist*, July 1890, quoted in *The Aborigines of Minnesota*, 1911, pages 106–8, with a diagram of the buffalo outline).

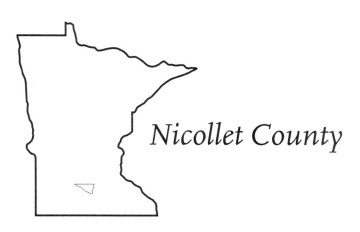

Nicollet County

Established March 5, 1853, this county was named in honor of Joseph Nicolas Nicollet, geographer and explorer, whose admirable map and report of the region that now comprises Minnesota and the eastern parts of North and South Dakota were published in 1843 soon after his death. His name is also commemorated by an island of the Mississippi at Minneapolis and by a principal avenue of that city. (In pronunciation the name is anglicized, with accent on the first syllable and sounding the final letter.)

Nicollet was born July 24, 1786, at Cluses, in Savoy; completed his studies in Paris, where in 1817 he was appointed an officer of the astronomical observatory; in 1819 he became a citizen of France, and in 1825, or earlier, he received the Cross of the Legion of Honor. He was financially ruined by results of the Revolution of 1830 and came to the United States in 1832 to travel in unsettled parts of the South and West. Under the direction of the U.S. War Department and Bureau of Topographical Engineers, he made a canoe journey in 1836 from Fort Snelling up the Mississippi to Itasca Lake and in 1838 a trip up the Minnesota River and past Lake Shetek to the red pipestone quarry. He died in Washington, D.C., September 11, 1843.

In the U.S. government reports and maps of his work, his name appears varyingly as I. N. or J. N. Nicollet, and it is given as Jean N. by Gen. Henry H. Sibley, Dr. Edward D. Neill, Prof. N. H. Winchell, and other writers of Minnesota history. Research by Horace V. Winchell, however, in 1893, published in the *American Geologist* (vol. 13, pp. 126–28, for February 1894), show that his name was Joseph Nicolas Nicollet. A biographic sketch of him, with a portrait, was given by N. H. Winchell in the *American Geologist* (vol. 8, pp. 343–52, December 1891), and additional details were given by H. V. Winchell in the article before cited.

The error of this name, during half a century so generally mistaken, may have come from its being confounded with that of the much earlier French explorer Jean Nicolet (also spelled Nicollet), who came to Canada in 1618 and who was a most energetic and honored agent of the proprietors of Canada for the promotion of the fur trade. In 1634 this Nicolet visited Sault Ste. Marie and thence came to Green Bay in eastern Wisconsin, being the first white man known to explore any part of that state. He died on the last day of October 1642, being drowned by shipwreck on the St. Lawrence River near Quebec.

Information of geographic names has been gathered from History of the Minnesota Valley, 1882, having pp. 637–97 on this county; History of Nicollet and Le Sueur Counties, edited by Hon. William G. Gresham, 2 vols., pages 544 and 538, 1916; and from Judge Gresham, the editor here cited; Z. S. Gault, cashier of the Nicollet County Bank, Henry Moll, judge of probate, and Mary Briggs Aiton, widow of Rev. John F. Aiton, each being interviewed during a visit at St. Peter, the county seat, in July 1916.

BELGRADE TOWNSHIP first settled in 1854 and organized in 1858, was named from a township and village in Kennebec County, Maine, and from the ancient city of Belgrade on the River Danube.

BERNADOTTE TOWNSHIP settled in 1859, organized January 23, 1869, received this name at the suggestion of John Miller, one of its pioneer settlers, in honor of Charles XV (1826–72), king of Sweden and Norway. He was the son of Oscar I and was the grandson of a French general, Jean Baptiste Jules Bernadotte (1764–1844), who was elected crown prince of Sweden in 1810 and became the king in 1818, with the title Charles XIV. The village in section 3 had a post office, 1871–1904. A township and village in Illinois also bear this name.

BRIGHTON a post office, 1879–1902, in Bernadotte Township, section 33; the site had three blacksmith shops and a creamery.

BRIGHTON TOWNSHIP settled in 1855, but the latest township organized in this county, October 16, 1877, had several families who came from Brighton Township in Kenosha County, Wis.

CLARKESVILLE a post office, May–October 1872; location not found.

COURTLAND TOWNSHIP organized in 1858, was then called Hilo, from its post office established in 1856, which received that name from a bay and town in Hawaii. It was renamed in 1865 for Cortland County and its county seat in New York, whence some of its settlers came. A city in sections 5–8, having the same name, designated as a railway station in 1872, was platted February 14, 1882, and incorporated as a village on December 3, 1892. The post office was first established in the home of William Duprey as Hilo, 1856–64, and was reestablished in 1866 as Courtland, although the spelling was Cortland until 1874. By 1882, the village had become a trade center with

a number of businesses, a hotel, a creamery, an elevator, and a depot of the Winona and St. Peter Railroad.

DAKOTA CITY a townsite in section 34 of Nicollet Township, across the river from Judson in Blue Earth County, laid out in 1856 with a sawmill, a store, and two houses; a post office was established as Hebron at the site, 1857–85.

EUREKA see NICOLLET.

FLANDREAU a post office, 1894–97; location not found.

FORT RIDGELY a fort and townsite in section 6 of Ridgely Township; the post office, 1854–1903, was called Ridgely. The fort was built 1853–54 and was used as a U.S. military post until the spring of 1867. The fort was named in 1854 by Jefferson Davis, then secretary of war, in honor of three army officers from Maryland who died in the Mexican War, Lieut. Henderson Ridgely, Capt. Randolph Ridgely, and Capt. Thomas P. Ridgely. Dakota Indians attacked the fort twice during the Dakota War of 1862; the restored commissary and reconstructed foundations of its buildings are now enclosed in Fort Ridgely State Park, which was established in 1911.

GRANBY TOWNSHIP settled in May 1855, organized May 11, 1858, has the name of townships and villages in Vermont, Massachusetts, Connecticut, New York, and the Province of Quebec. A post office was located in section 7, 1862–81.

HEBRON see DAKOTA CITY.

HILO see COURTLAND.

KASOTA a place name in Oshawa Township, south of St. Peter, which appears as early as 1874 in the Andreas atlas; it was probably across the Minnesota River from Kasota in Le Sueur County.

KERNS a village in section 31 of Belgrade Township, was named for early settlers John and William Kern. The first settler was LeRue P. Parsons in 1853, who owned the land, was a blacksmith by trade, and built the school east of his home in 1861. The post office operated 1898–1902; there was a creamery and a number of other businesses.

KLOSSNER a railway village in section 3 of Lafayette, platted in October 1897, was named for Jacob Klossner, proprietor of its site. He was born in Switzerland, December 23, 1846; came with his parents to the United States when three years old, and to Minnesota in 1856; served against the

Dakota, with the First Minnesota Mounted Rangers, 1862–63; owned a farm in New Ulm; was a representative in the legislature in 1878. The village developed when the Minneapolis and St. Louis Railroad came in 1895; its post office began in 1896.

LAFAYETTE TOWNSHIP settled in 1853 and organized May 11, 1858, was named, like townships and villages or cities of 20 other states of the Union, with counties of six states, in honor of the Marquis de Lafayette (1757–1834) of France, who came to America and greatly aided Washington in the Revolutionary War and later was an eminent French statesman and general. The city of this name, in sections 1, 2, and 11, was platted on August 22, 1896, and incorporated as a village May 11, 1900. John Bush and his family came in 1854 and kept a "stopping place" for travelers, where the first post office was located in 1858, discontinuing in 1870. The village became a trading center when the Minneapolis and St. Louis Railroad was built through in October 1895, and the post office was reestablished in 1897.

LAKE PRAIRIE SETTLEMENT see SCANDIA GROVE.

LAKE PRAIRIE TOWNSHIP settled in the summer of 1853, organized in 1858, was mainly an extensive prairie with numerous small lakes, some of which have been drained.

LANGE a post office in section 9 of Belgrade Township, 1900–1902.

LITTLE ROCK TRADING POST was located in section 22 of Ridgely Township and established by Joseph La Framboise for the American Fur Company, 1834–56.

MIDDLE LAKE a post office, 1862–69 and 1871–73; location not found; however, a lake of this name is at the intersection of Oshawa, Traverse, and Granby Townships, which may relate to the post office site.

MORELAND a place name in section 19 of Lake Prairie Township, which the 1874 Andreas atlas notes as a post office, although it is not listed in post office directories.

NEW SWEDEN TOWNSHIP organized January 25, 1864, has many Swedish settlers, but its earliest settlement, in 1855–57, was by immigrants from Norway, taking homesteads near a grove in its north part, which therefore was named Norwegian Grove. A village in section 22 had a post office, 1884–1905.

NICOLLET TOWNSHIP named after the county, was first settled in the spring of 1854 and was organized May 11, 1858. An early village of this name, in section 17, was platted in 1857 but lasted only three years; "old" Nicollet was originally laid out in 1856 with a hotel, a sawmill, blacksmith shop, several buildings, and a stagecoach stop; the first post office, 1856–58, called Eureka, was a community in section 33 of 500 acres with a sawmill and moved to "old" Nicollet in 1857; the name was changed to Nicollet until April 1877; another post office was established as Nicollet Station in 1873 and combined with the first post office in 1878. The present city in sections 3 and 4 was incorporated November 17, 1881, and separated from the township on April 17, 1889; when the Winona and St. Peter Railroad was completed in 1870, the village (first called Nicollet Station) was laid out in section 3 along the tracks.

NORSELAND a village in section 19 of Lake Prairie Township, was first organized in 1854 when a small Methodist congregation came. In 1858 a Norwegian Lutheran church was formed, and a community developed with stores, a creamery, and a post office, 1864–1905.

NORTH MANKATO in Belgrade Township, is a city on the Minnesota River, opposite to the city of Mankato, Blue Earth County. It was originally platted in 1857 with two ferry landings connecting to Mankato; a bridge between the communities was built in 1898. It was incorporated as a village and separated from the township on December 19, 1898.

NORTH STAR a village in section 33 of Oshawa West Township.

NORWEGIAN GROVE a village in New Sweden Township established in 1855 by a group of Norwegian immigrants who came to a grove in the northern part of the township.

OSHAWA TOWNSHIP first settled in 1852, organized May 11, 1858, received its name from the Canada town of Oshawa on the northwest shore of Lake Ontario, noted by Henry Gannett as an Indian word meaning "ferry him over," or "across the river." A community called Oshawa in section 29 had a post office, 1858–60 and 1862–1909, and a railroad station.

PLANO a post office, 1888–96; location not found.

REDSTONE a village site platted in 1856 in sections 34 and 35 in the west part of the present

Courtland Township was named for adjacent out-crops of red quartzite beside the Minnesota River. The site was on land owned by Marshall B. Stone, the first postmaster; the post office operated 1857–62 and 1867–71. A few years later this site was mostly vacated by removal of its settlers to New Ulm, Brown County.

RIDGELY see FORT RIDGELY.

RIDGELY TOWNSHIP organized September 26, 1871, was named for Fort Ridgely in its section 6. During 13 years before its organization, from 1858 to 1871, this township was a part of West Newton, which was named from the steamboat that brought the first troops and supplies to build Fort Ridgely, as noted for that township.

ROCK BEND, ROCKY POINT see ST. PETER.

ST. GEORGE a village in section 26 of West Newton Township with a post office, 1894–1904.

ST. PETER the county seat, located in Traverse and Oshawa Townships, first settled in the fall of 1853 by Capt. William B. Dodd, platted in June 1854, was incorporated as a borough March 2, 1865, and as a city January 7, 1873. It was named for the St. Pierre or St. Peter River, as the Minnesota River was called by the early French and English explorers and fur traders, probably in honor of Pierre Charles Le Sueur, whose surname is borne by the adjoining county on the east side of this river. In early years it was also known as Rock Bend and Rocky Point. The city had a station of the Chicago and North Western Railway, and the post office was established in 1856. The city is the site of Gustavus Adolphus College, which was first founded in Red Wing in 1862, moved to East Union, Carver County, in 1863, at which time it was called St. Ansgar's Academy, and moved to St. Peter in 1876 and was renamed. The Minnesota Hospital for Insane was established here in 1866.

SCANDIA GROVE a settlement about 13 miles northwest of St. Peter and one of the oldest Swedish settlements in Minnesota, although the first settlers were Norwegians who arrived about 1855. The community developed, however, in 1858 with the arrival of a small Swedish Lutheran congregation from Skåne who settled in the west portion of Lake Prairie Township, eventually extending into most of New Sweden Township.

SOLEM a post office, 1895–98; location not found.

STRAUS see TRAVERSE.

SWAN CITY a townsite in section 5 of Nicollet Township, was settled in 1856, with a post office, 1857–65.

SWAN LAKE a site in section 29 of Nicollet Township, formerly the site of the village of Sleepy Eye, a Dakota leader.

TIMBER LAKE a post office, 1867–69; location not found.

TRAVERSE DES SIOUX a village in Traverse Township, which developed with the lumber trade; it had a post office, 1853–73.

TRAVERSE TOWNSHIP organized May 11, 1858, took the name of its village, platted in 1852, commonly called Traverse des Sioux "Crossing of the Sioux," because the Minnesota River was crossed here on a much-used trail from St. Paul and Fort Snelling to the upper Minnesota valley and the Red River valley. In 1823 this place was named "the Crescent" by Maj. Stephen H. Long's expedition, referring to a bend of the river, but before 1838, when Nicollet was here, it had received this French name, Traverse des Sioux. The *Dakota Dictionary*, published in 1852, notes its Dakota name as Oiyu-wege, meaning "the place of crossing, a ford." The village in section 12 had a post office called Straus in 1886, which changed to Traverse in 1896 and discontinued in 1915; it had a station of the Winona and St. Peter Railroad.

UNION CITY a place name of the 1850s; location not found.

WAHEOKA a place name of the 1850s; location not found.

WEST NEWTON TOWNSHIP settled in the spring of 1856 and organized May 11, 1858, originally included Fort Ridgely and the present Ridgely Township. It was named partly in compliment to James Newton, one of its first settlers, who was born in Kentucky in 1829, took a homestead claim here in 1856, and served in the Second Minnesota Regiment in the Civil War. A further and principal reason for the choice of this township name was the steamboat named *West Newton*, under command of Capt. D. S. Harris, which made the trip from Fort Snelling to the site of Fort Ridgely in the last four days of April 1853, bringing two companies of the Sixth Regiment, with lumber and supplies for building the fort. "This was the first steamer that had ascended the Minnesota river any distance above the mouth of the Blue Earth," as Maj. Benjamin H. Randall wrote in a paper on the history of Fort Ridgely, especially narrating its defense against the Dakota, August 18–22, 1862, published in the *Winona Republican*, 1892.

The steamboat, *West Newton*, 150 feet long and of 300 tons burden, was built for Capt. Harris in 1852 for the Mississippi River traffic between Galena and St. Paul. It was the earliest boat arriving at St. Paul in the spring of 1853, on April 11, and during that season it made 27 trips to and from St. Paul until in September it was sunk near Alma, Wis. (George B. Merrick, *Old Times on the Upper Mississippi*, 1909, p. 293).

The township had a post office, 1862–1910, and the area also had a sawmill, a gristmill, Henry Diepolder's hotel built in 1853, and a number of businesses. Alexander Harkin's store, listed on the National Register of Historic Places, was built there in 1867; Harkin, an emigrant from Scotland, served as justice of the peace, coroner, and postmaster, among other positions.

Lakes and Streams

The Dakota name Mini Sotah, borne with changed spelling by the river that borders this county and by the state, is also applied on Nicollet's map to the lake crossed by the county line on the north side of West Newton, translated as Clear Lake. The outlet of Clear Lake is Eight Mile Creek, crossed eight miles from Fort Ridgely on the road to Traverse des Sioux.

Little Rock Creek or River, also called Mud Creek, joins the Minnesota River near the east line of Ridgely. About three miles northwest from its mouth is an outcrop of gneiss and granite in the Minnesota valley, adjoining the site of a former Indian trading post, called Little Rock in translation of the French name, Petite Roche, given to it by the early traders and voyageurs.

Fort Creek, flowing past the east side of the site of Fort Ridgely, is the most western tributary of the Minnesota River in this county.

Nicollet Creek, flowing south through Nicollet Township to the Minnesota, is the outlet of the large Swan Lake, which Nicollet mapped as Marrah Tanka (for *maga*, goose, *tanka*, great), the Dakota name of the swan. William H. Keating, in the *Narrative* of Long's expedition in 1823, wrote of this lake, "The Indian name is Manha tanka

otamenda, which signifies the lake of the many large birds." Two species, the trumpeter swan and the whistling swan, were formerly found in Minnesota. The first nests here, but the second, which yet is rarely seen in this state, has its breeding grounds far north of our region.

Eastward from Swan Lake are Middle Lake, Little Lake, Horseshoe Lake, named for its shape, Timber Lake, having trees and groves on its shores and on its large island, Fox Lake, and Rogers Lake, the last, in section 3, Traverse, being named for a pioneer farmer.

Oakleaf Lake, formerly called Cowan's Lake, in section 25, Oshawa, received its present name in honor of H. J. Eckloff, a Swedish farmer, whose name has this meaning.

Goose Lake, named for its wild geese, on the line between Traverse and Oshawa, has been drained.

Site of the Dakota Treaty, 1851

Near the ford of the Minnesota River, called the Traverse des Sioux, whence Traverse village and township were named, a treaty with the Dakota had been made in 1841 by Gov. James D. Doty of Wisconsin, which, however, failed of ratification in the U.S. Senate. Ten years later, on July 23, 1851, a treaty with the Wahpeton and Sisseton Dakota of the Minnesota valley was concluded here by Gov. Alexander Ramsey and Col. Luke Lea, whereby these Indians ceded to the United States, for white settlement, the greater part of their lands in southern Minnesota. A year later this treaty, with changes afterward accepted by the Dakota, received ratification by the Senate, and it was proclaimed by President Millard Fillmore on February 24, 1853 (see the account of these treaties, by Thomas Hughes, MHS Collections 10: 101–29 [1905]).

The site of the Treaty of Traverse des Sioux in 1851 was appropriately marked June 17, 1914, by a brass tablet on a granite boulder, unveiled by Mary B. Aiton. This historic memorial was presented to the state from the Capt. Richard Somers Chapter of the Daughters of the American Revolution, St. Peter, by Mrs. H. L. Stark, regent (*St. Peter Herald*, June 19, 1914). The Treaty Site History Center operated by the Nicollet County Historical Society interprets the site.

Nobles County

Established May 23, 1857, and organized October 27, 1870, this county was named for William H. Nobles, who was a member of the Minnesota territorial legislature in 1854 and 1856. In the autumn of the latter year he began the construction of a wagon road for the U.S. government, crossing southwestern Minnesota and this county, to extend from Fort Ridgely to the South Pass in the Rocky Mountains. This work was continued in 1857 but was not completed.

Nobles was born in New York State in 1816; was a machinist by trade and came to St. Croix Falls, Wis., in 1841, to assist in building the first mill there but soon removed to Hudson, Wis.; in 1843 he began his residence in Minnesota, at Stillwater; and in 1848 came to St. Paul, where he commenced wagon making and blacksmithing, building for Henry H. Sibley the first wagon made here. In 1849 he went to California and lived there, in Shasta County, until May 1852, when he led a party of citizens to inspect a pass that he had discovered, crossing the Sierra Nevada, since bearing his name. Returning to Minnesota, he earnestly advocated the building of an immigrant road (and ultimately a railroad) from St. Paul, by way of the South Pass and Nobles Pass, to San Francisco. He served as lieutenant colonel in the Seventy-ninth New York Regiment during a part of the Civil War and afterward held several government positions. A few years of ill health ensued, and he died in St. Paul, December 28, 1876, having returned a few days previous from seeking in vain for recovery.

The U.S. steamship *Nobles*, named in honor of this county's Liberty Loan record in World War I, was launched August 23, 1919.

Information of geographic names has been received from An Illustrated History of Nobles County *by Arthur P. Rose (1908, 637 pp.); and from Dr. George O. Moore, president of the State Bank of Worthington, and Julius A. Town, attorney, who came here as pioneer settlers in 1872, interviewed at Worthington, the county seat, in July 1916.*

ADRIAN a city on the border of Olney and West Side Townships, the main street being the boundary of the two townships, platted in May 1876, and incorporated November 17, 1881, was named in honor of Adrian Iselin, who was the mother of Adrian C. Iselin, one of the directors of the St. Paul and Sioux City Railroad. In the vicinity of Adrian a Catholic colony of immigrant farmers was founded by Archbishop John Ireland in 1879. The city developed when the St. Paul and Sioux City Railroad came in 1876 and was aided by the Catholic colonization project. The post office began as Hibbards in 1872 in section 20 of West Side Township, with William F. Hibbard as postmaster, changing to Adrian in 1876 and located at that time in George H. Carr's general store, the first merchant in the community; the city had a station of the Chicago, St. Paul, Minneapolis and Omaha Railroad.

AIRLIE see KINBRAE.

BIGELOW TOWNSHIP organized May 20, 1872, and its railway village, platted in the same year, were named in honor of Charles Henry Bigelow, who was born in Easton, N.Y., June 4, 1835, and died in St. Paul, Minn., July 31, 1911. He settled in St. Paul in 1864, engaged in lumber business and insurance, and was president of the St. Paul Fire and Marine Insurance Company, 1876–1911. The city, the third established in the county, in section 31, was incorporated as a village on February 17, 1900, and separated from the township on July 25, 1908. Its first building was the Chicago, St. Paul, Minneapolis and Omaha Railroad depot in 1872, the same year the post office was established.

BLOOM TOWNSHIP organized in April 1879, was named in honor of Peter Bloom and his family, including three sons, who were its first settlers, locating on section 22 in 1874. A country post office was located in the township, 1892–99.

BREWSTER a city in sections 23–26 of Hersey Township, platted April 22, 1872, was called Hersey until August 1880, being then renamed either for the village and township of Brewster in Barnstable County, Mass., or, according to Elias F. Drake, then president of the St. Paul and Sioux City Railroad, was named for a director of the Chicago, St. Paul, Minneapolis and Omaha Railroad. The city was incorporated as a village on December 19, 1898; the post office began as Hersey in section 25, 1872–86, then changed to Brewster, although the Chicago, St. Paul, Minneapolis and Omaha Railroad station was already known as Brewster by 1880. Peter Geyerman became postmaster in 1886 at his general store, The Big Store.

CRESWELL see KINBRAE.

DE FOREST see KINBRAE.

DEWALD TOWNSHIP organized September 20, 1872, was named in honor of Amos and Hiram Dewald, pioneer settlers, who came in April 1872. A post office was in section 20, 1872–76; John B. Churchill, postmaster, came in 1872 and built a store in 1873, which became a stopping place known as the ten-mile house.

DUNDEE a city in section 1 of Graham Lakes Township, platted in 1879 and incorporated February 15, 1898, has the name of a city in Scotland, which is also borne by villages in 12 other states. When the site was selected in 1879, it was named Warren in honor of Joseph Warren, who died in the battle of Bunker Hill; however, when the post office was established in September of that year, the name chosen was Dundee.

ELK TOWNSHIP established September 16, 1872, took the name given by early trappers to the creek that has its sources here, flowing eastward. A lone elk was seen in this township ten days before the petition for its organization was granted by the county commissioners. A post office was located in the township, 1878–80.

ELLSWORTH a city in sections 28, 29, 32, and 33 of Grand Prairie Township, platted in September 1884 and incorporated January 21, 1887, was named in honor of Eugene Ellsworth of Cedar Falls, Iowa. The village and its post office began in 1884, the latter in postmaster B. Frank Garmer's general store; it had a station of the Chicago, St. Paul, Minneapolis and Omaha Railroad in section 29.

ELWYN a post office, 1899–1900; location not found.

GRAHAM LAKES TOWNSHIP organized April 21, 1871, received this name from its East and West Graham Lakes, mapped as Lake Graham by Joseph N. Nicollet. James Duncan Graham and Andrew Talcott, for whom Nicollet named Lake Talcott in the southwest corner of Cottonwood County, were commissioners in 1840–43, with James Renwick, for the survey of the northeastern part of the international boundary between the United States and Canada. Graham was born in Virginia, April 4, 1799, and died in Boston, Mass., December 28, 1865. He was graduated at the U.S. Military Academy in 1817, served in the corps of topographical engineers after 1829, and was brevetted lieutenant colonel for his valuable work on the northeastern boundary survey. A post office was in section 24, 1868–79.

GRAND PRAIRIE TOWNSHIP organized October 30, 1873, is in a very extensive prairie region, which has mostly an undulating or rolling surface, but the greater part of this township is nearly level. A post office was in section 10, 1875–85, in Austin Ayers's home, which was also used as a halfway house and stopping point for travelers and farmers between Sibley and Pipestone. Ayers was born in New York and lived in Wisconsin and Minnesota for a number of years before moving to South Dakota in 1883.

GRETCHTOWN a place name before 1867; location not found.

HERSEY see BREWSTER.

HERSEY TOWNSHIP organized June 11, 1872, took the early name of its railway village, which was changed to Brewster in 1880, as before noted. The township name commemorates Samuel Freeman Hersey of Bangor, Maine, who was a director of the St. Paul and Sioux City Railroad. He was born in Sumner, Maine, April 12, 1812; engaged in lumber business and banking in Maine, Minnesota, and Wisconsin and established large sawmills in Stillwater, Minn.; was a member of Congress from Maine, 1873–75; and died in Bangor, February 3, 1875.

HIBBARDS see ADRIAN.

INDIAN LAKE see ROUND LAKE.

INDIAN LAKE TOWNSHIP established April 22, 1871, bears the name of its lake in sections 27 and 34, where the first white settlers, coming in 1869, found the camp of a considerable band of Dakota, who remained in this vicinity during several years.

JACK CREEK a country post office, 1878–80, located ten miles from Worthington in Graham Lakes Township.

KINBRAE a city in section 11 in Graham Lakes Township, founded in 1879 by the Dundee Land Company of Scotland, was at first called Airlie for the Earl of Airlie, who was president of the land company; when the townsite was platted, it was changed to De Forest but received the present Scottish name in August 1883. It was incorporated February 17, 1896. The petition for a post office was as Airlie, 1879–82, was changed to De Forest, 1882–83, and then Kinbrae in 1883 on request of the Chicago, Milwaukee and St. Paul Railroad; the post office discontinued in 1971. An earlier post office named Creswell was established in 1873 in section 34 of Belfast Township, Murray County, and was transferred to Graham Lakes Township in 1876, combining with Airlie in 1879.

LAKEVIEW a village in section 15 of Graham Lakes Township, shown in the 1874 Andreas atlas.

LARKIN TOWNSHIP the latest organized in this county, March 27, 1883, was named in honor of John Larkin of New York City, a prominent worker in the Catholic colonization association that brought many settlers to southwestern Minnesota.

LEOTA TOWNSHIP was organized April 5, 1879. "The name was suggested by W. G. Barnard, one of the township's earliest settlers. It is the only township, village or physical feature in Nobles county named in honor of an Indian. Leota was an Indian maiden who figured in a story of Indian adventure" (history of this county by Rose, p. 102). The village in sections 5 and 8 grew out of a place of the same name in Orange County, Iowa, when a large number of Dutch immigrants moved from there to this site in the 1890s. The post office operated in 1879 with Horace N. Holbrook as postmaster, was reestablished in 1894 with James TenCate as postmaster in the store he owned with John and Nick DeBoer, discontinued in 1918, and was reestablished a third time in 1931. The townsite was surveyed by M. S. Smith for TenCate in 1902.

LISMORE TOWNSHIP organized August 9, 1880, to which many Irish Catholic settlers came during that year, was named after a village of County Waterford in Ireland, noted for a fine baronial castle. The city of Lismore in sections 1 and 12 was platted in the summer of 1900 and was incorporated May 31, 1902. The first business was the St. Croix Lumber Company, the first building was a saloon owned by James Beacom, and the second building was a general store owned by Ollis B. Bratager, first postmaster in 1900; the village had a station of the Cedar Rapids, Iowa Falls and Northwestern Railroad.

LITTLE ROCK TOWNSHIP organized September 20, 1872, is crossed by the Little Rock River, which here receives its West Branch. Thence it flows southwestward through Lyon County in Iowa to the Rock River, which is named, like Rock County of Minnesota, from the Mound, a precipitous hill of red quartzite near Luverne in that county. A post office was located in section 22, 1875–1903.

LORAIN TOWNSHIP was organized September 20, 1872, being then named Fairview, from its beautiful panoramic outlook over this great prairie region but was renamed June 15, 1874, "after the town of Loraine, Adams county, Ill., the superfluous 'e' being dropped." This name in Ohio and Illinois came from the ancient large district of Lorraine in France and Germany.

MILLER see RUSHMORE.

OKABENA see WORTHINGTON.

OLNEY TOWNSHIP established July 10, 1873, was at first called Hebbard in honor of William F. Hebbard, an early settler. On June 15, 1874, it received the present name after the county seat of Richland County, Ill., which was named for Nathan Olney of Lawrenceville in that state.

ORG a village in section 4 of Bigelow Township, about four miles southwest of Worthington, was originally named Iselin for Adrian C. Iselin, who owned much of the land in this vicinity; it was then called Sioux Falls Junction, but received this name, of unknown derivation, in 1890, the change being ordered by W. A. Scott, then general manager of the Chicago and North Western Railway. Platted in 1899, the village developed a number of businesses, although it did not become incorporated; the post office operated 1895–1917; it had a station of the Chicago, St. Paul, Minneapolis and Omaha Railroad.

PFINGSTON a village in section 17 of Seward Township with a post office, 1894–1900.

RANSOM TOWNSHIP organized September 20, 1872, was at first named Grant, for Ulysses S. Grant, Civil War general and U.S. president, but was changed because he had been thus honored earlier by another Minnesota township. July 10, 1873, the present name was given by the county commissioners in honor of Ransom F. Humiston, the founder of Worthington. He was born in Great Barrington, Mass., July 3, 1822; was educated at Western Reserve College, Ohio, and was principal of a classical school that he established in Cleveland, Ohio; organized the National Colony Company in 1871 and brought many settlers to Worthington and other parts of this county; returned to live in the East and died in April 1889. The village in sections 21 and 22 had a post office, 1895–1903.

READING the village in section 24 of Summit Lake Township, platted in June 1900, was named in honor of a pioneer farmer, Henry H. Read, the original owner of a part of the village site. It began when the Cedar Rapids, Iowa Falls and Northwestern Railroad built a depot; the post office opened in 1900 with Albert N. Cheney as postmaster in his general store.

ROUND LAKE a city in sections 13, 14, 23, and 24 of Indian Lake Township, founded in 1882, was named for the adjoining Round Lake in Jackson County, on request of O. H. Roche, who owned a ranch of nearly 2,000 acres surrounding that lake. An alternative version of the naming is that when the Round Lake post office in Round Lake Township, Jackson County, was discontinued in July 1884, residents of Indian Lake requested the name of the village be changed to Round Lake, the post office following in January of 1885. The village was developed by the railroad and was platted in December 1882 and again in 1889 because no sites were sold under the original platting except for two railroad buildings; it was incorporated on October 14, 1892. The post office was established as Indian Lake in 1883, with Edgar Adelbert Tripp as postmaster.

RUSHMORE a city in section 19 of Dewald Township, platted in July 1878, on the Sioux Falls branch of the Chicago, St. Paul, Minneapolis and Omaha Railroad, bears the name of its pioneer merchant, S. M. Rushmore. It was incorporated March 27, 1900. The city was first called Miller Station when the Worthington and Sioux Falls Railroad was completed in 1876 in honor of former Gov. Stephen Miller; when the post office was established in 1878, the name was changed to Rushmore.

ST. KILIAN a village in section 27 of Willmont Township, which developed around the St. Kilian Catholic Church, built in 1887. The village was platted in 1891; the post office operated 1892–1907, with general store owner John Mock as postmaster.

SAXON a country post office, 1899–1902, located in section 31 of Indian Lake Township.

SEWARD TOWNSHIP organized October 30, 1872, commemorates William Henry Seward, the noted statesman, who was born in Florida, N.Y., May 16, 1801, and died in Auburn, N.Y., October 10, 1872. He was governor of New York, 1839–42, and a U.S. senator, 1849–61; was secretary of state, 1861–69, and concluded the purchase of Alaska from Russia in 1867. A post office was located in the township, 1874–80.

SUMMIT LAKE TOWNSHIP organized June 5, 1873, was first called Wilson, later Akin, and received its present name July 27, 1874, from its former lake in section 11, whence the general surface descends in very gentle slopes both eastward and westward.

SWEDEN a village in Indian Lake Township named for its large concentration of immigrants from Sweden.

TRENT a station of the Chicago, St. Paul, Minneapolis and Omaha Railroad located in Worthington Township.

WARREN see DUNDEE.

WEST SIDE TOWNSHIP organized February 24, 1877, is at the west side of the county. It had a post office, called Westside 1874–86, in section 18.

WILFRED a farmers post office in Summit Lake Township, 1892–95.

WILLMONT TOWNSHIP was organized December 12, 1878. "One faction wanted the township named Willumet, the other Lamont. When the commissioners, on November 22, provided for the organization, they named the township Willmont, a combination of parts of the names suggested by the two factions" (history by Rose, p. 100). Thomas H. Brown the Burlington, Cedar Rapids and Northern Railway right-of-way man, is said to have selected the name for the township.

WILMONT a city in Larkin and Willmont Townships, platted on January 22, 1900, omitting one letter of the township name, was incorporated June 4, 1900. Its post office began in 1900 with lumberyard owner Charles William Becker, postmaster; it had a station of the Cedar Rapids, Iowa Falls and Northwestern Railroad.

WORTHINGTON a city in sections 23–26 of Worthington Township and the county seat, platted in the summer of 1871, was incorporated as a village March 8, 1873, and as a city in 1912. Its site had been called Okabena during the grading of the railway in 1871 for the two adjoining lakes, meaning the nesting place of herons, a Dakota name from *hokah,* "heron," *be,* "nests," and *na,* a diminutive suffix, as noted by Prof. A. W. Williamson. Its railroad station was named Okabena, as was the post office for the first year of operation, 1872, with Herbert W. Kimball as first postmaster. In the autumn of 1871 that name was changed to Worthington in honor of the mother of Mary Dorman Miller, wife of Dr. A. P. Miller, who was intimately associated with Ransom F. Humiston in forming the National Colony Company and founding Worthington, before noticed because Ransom Township was named for him. Mrs. Miller in 1888 wrote of the origin of this name: "My mother's maiden name was Worthington.

Her father was Robert Worthington, of Chillicothe, Ohio, who was the brother of Thomas Worthington, governor of Ohio; and the now beautiful, prosperous town of Worthington, Minn., was named for the Chillicothe family." Worthington Township was organized May 20, 1872.

Dr. A. P. Miller, whose wife and her family were thus honored, came from Ohio to Minnesota in 1871; was editor and owner of the *Worthington Advance,* 1872–87; removed to California and in 1908 was in the newspaper business at Los Angeles. He is author of an excellent poem read at the Hennepin Bi-Centenary celebration in Minneapolis, 1880 (MHS Collections 6: 55–61).

Lakes and Streams

The foregoing pages have noticed Elk Creek, from which Elk Township is named, the Graham Lakes, Indian Lake, Little Rock River, and Summit Lake, all of which likewise give their names to townships. The railway village of Round Lake is for a lake and township of Jackson County.

Another Elk Creek, formed by small streams from Lismore and West Side Townships, flows southwest into Rock County to the Rock River.

Okabena Creek, flowing east from Worthington to Heron Lake in Jackson County, is the outlet of the West Okabena Lake, whence the site of Worthington was at first named Okabena, as before noted. From this name, given to Heron Lake on Nicollet's map in 1843, the present name of that lake was translated, while the Dakota name, referring to these lakes and the creek as "the nesting place of herons," was retained for the creek and for two lakes at Worthington, of which the east one has been drained.

Jack Creek, in the northeast part of this county, probably named for its jack rabbits, also flows into Heron Lake.

Lake Ocheda (or Ocheda Lake), its outflowing Ocheyedan Creek, and Okshida Creek in Murray County, are names received by Nicollet from the Dakota, having reference to their mourning for the dead, as before noted in the chapter on Murray County.

Kanaranzi Creek, which gathers its headstreams from the central part of Nobles County, running southwest to the Rock River and giving its name to a township in Rock County, was mapped by Nicollet as "Karanzi R., or R. where the Kansas were killed," referring to Kansas or Kaw Indians who had ventured thus far into the Dakota country.

Champepadan Creek, crossing the northwest corner of this county, is likewise a Dakota name given by Nicollet, somewhat transformed in spelling, which his map translates as "Thorny Wood river," from its having thorn bushes and trees.

Eagle Lake, formerly in sections 4 and 9, Graham Lakes Township, has been drained. Clear Lake or Kinbrae Lake adjoins Kinbrae village in this township, and State Line Lake or Iowa Lake is at the southeast corner of this county.

Norman County

This county, established February 17, 1881, had been thought by R. I. Holcombe and others to be named, like Kittson County three years before, in honor of Norman W. Kittson, who accomplished much for the extension of commerce and immigration to the Red River valley. The actual choice of this name, however, as better known by residents of the county and by surviving members of the convention held at Ada for securing its establishment by the state legislature, was for commemoration of the great number of Norwegian (Norseman or Norman) immigrants who had settled there. Norse delegates were a majority in the convention, and the name was selected on account of patriotic love and memories of their former homes across the sea. Similarly a township organized in March 1874, in Yellow Medicine County, had been named Norman; and another township there in the same year received the name Normania. "In Norway a native is referred to as a Norsk or Norman."

By the federal census of 1910, in a total population of 13,446 in Norman County, 2,957 were born in Norway, and both parents of 4,651 others among those born in America were Norwegian. No other county of Minnesota had so large a proportion of Norwegian people in that year.

Information of the origins and meanings of names has been gathered from History of the Red River Valley, *2 vols., 1909, having pages 967–72 for Norman County; and from David E. Fulton, county auditor, historian for the Norman County Old Settlers' Association, and Conrad K. Semling, clerk of the court, interviewed during visits at Ada, the county seat, in September 1909 and again in September 1916. Additional notes were also received in 1916 from Alexander Holden of Ada and Anund K. Strand of Lake Ida Township, pioneers who came respectively in 1872 and 1880.*

AABYE see **PERLEY.**

ADA a city in sections 8, 9, 16, and 17 of McDonaldsville Township and the county seat, founded in 1874 and incorporated as a village February 9, 1881, was named in honor of a daughter of William H. Fisher of St. Paul, then attorney and superintendent of the St. Paul and Pacific Railroad, under whose superintendency this line of the Red River valley was constructed. A biographic notice of him is given in the chapter of Polk County, where his name is borne by Fisher Township and village. Ada Nelson Fisher died at the age of six years, in 1880, but this prosperous and beautiful village and the county perpetuate her name and memory. The post office began as MacDonaldsville in 1874, the postmaster being Finnian McDonald on his farm, until it was moved to the village in 1876 and the name changed; the village had a Great Northern Railway station.

ANTHONY TOWNSHIP organized in 1879, was

named for Anthony Scheie, one of its first settlers, who came here in 1872. His father, Andreas A. Scheie, the first pastor in this county, was born in Vigedal, Norway, February 17, 1818; came to the United States in 1840; was ordained to the ministry in 1855; was pastor in Fillmore County, Minn., 1857–76, and afterward in Ada; and died in 1885. A village was in section 29 and had a post office, 1901–7.

BEAR PARK TOWNSHIP organized in 1881, received this name in accordance with the request of its settlers in the petition for organization.

BETCHER a village in section 7 of Green Meadow Township, was begun about 1900 by Arthur H. Betcher, general store owner and postmaster during the post office years of operation, 1902–7.

BIJOU a post office, was authorized on February 28, 1905, with B. B. Brosvick to be postmaster, but not established; location not found.

BORUP a city in section 16 in Winchester Township, was named in honor of Charles William Wulff Borup, who was born in Copenhagen, Denmark, December 20, 1806, and died in St. Paul, July 6, 1859. He came to the United States in 1828 and to St. Paul in 1848, where in 1854 he established the banking house of Borup and Oakes, the first in Minnesota. His sons, Gustav J. and Theodore Borup, were also prominent businessmen in St. Paul. The city was first settled two miles south of the present location, in section 28, with a Great Northern Railway station and grain warehouse; it was moved in 1892 to its present site, platted in 1899, and incorporated as a village February 15, 1951; the post office was established in 1906.

COLDNER see GOLDNER.

COLENSO a post office in section 28 of Shelly Township, 1880–97, first established in Polk County, transferring to postmaster Peter Olson Holte's farm, which had a general store and blacksmith shop on the site.

FAITH a village in section 14 of Fossum Township, which had a post office, 1883–1911.

FLAMING is a Northern Pacific Railroad village in section 16 of Sundahl; it had a post office, 1902–19.

FLOM TOWNSHIP at first called Springfield, organized in 1881, was named for Erik Flom, a native of Norway, who came here as a pioneer farmer in 1871. The village in section 28 began

about 1880 with a small grocery store owned by N. E. Nelson, followed shortly by a large store built by Melvin Kleven, Hans Skansgaard, and Henry Vehle, the last being the first postmaster when the post office was established in 1895.

FOLKEDAHL a village on the Wild Rice River in Lake Ida Township, with a sawmill and post office, 1884–96, with Theodore A. Folkedahl as postmaster.

FOSSUM TOWNSHIP settled in 1872 and organized in 1881, was named for a village in southern Norway. The village in section 31 had a post office, 1882–1911, first located in Anton Johnson's general store, the first building on the site.

GALLITZIN a village in Hendrum Township incorporated on May 23, 1857; no trace remains.

GARY a city in sections 16 and 21 of Strand Township, founded in 1883, received this name in compliment to Garrett L. Thorpe, its first merchant, who came here from Manchester, Iowa, became an extensive landowner in this county, and settled at Ada. The village was incorporated on February 21, 1901; a number of businesses, including a creamery, developed in 1886 with the Northern Pacific Railroad's coming; the post office was established in 1887.

GOLDNER a post office in section 16 of Mary Township, 1887–1903, with Ole K. Hamre, postmaster; Hamre was born in Norway in 1865, came to Minnesota in 1875 and to the county in 1881, and died in Gary in 1942; sometimes shown on maps as Coldner.

GOOD HOPE TOWNSHIP was the latest organized, in 1892, its auspicious name being chosen by vote of its people.

GREEN MEADOW TOWNSHIP organized in 1880, bears a name that was likewise chosen by its people, having reference to the summer verdure of its prairie surface.

HADLER a village in section 16 of Pleasant View Township, was named for Jacob Hadler, an early settler there, who in 1909–15 was a member of the board of county commissioners. The village had a post office, 1903–8 and a station of the Great Northern Railway.

HALSTAD TOWNSHIP organized in 1879, and its city in sections 19 and 30, were named for Ole Halstad, a pioneer farmer, who came from Norway. During many years he was the postmaster of Marsh River post office in this township, now discontinued. The city was platted in 1883 and incorporated as a village on February 13, 1893; a post office was established in 1884, with Erik K. Brandt, postmaster, and it had a station of the Great Northern Railway.

HEGNE TOWNSHIP organized in 1881, was named for Andrew E. Hegne, one of its first settlers, coming from the district of Stavanger, Norway, who removed to Evansville, Minn., and was a hardware merchant there.

HEIBERG a railway village in Wild Rice Township, was named in honor of Jorgen F. Heiberg, owner of its flour mill. A post office called Heiberg was located in section 16 of Wild Rice Township, at the general store owned by Karl Stenseth on the former site of Twin Valley; Stenseth came from Norway in 1882, became postmaster in 1888, serving until 1916 when the post office merged with Twin Valley; the railroad siding called Heiberg was located about two miles north of the post office site in section 9.

HENDRUM TOWNSHIP organized in 1880, and its city in section 30, founded in 1881, are named from a district or group of farms in Norway, whence some of the early settlers of this township came. The village was platted in 1883 and incorporated on August 26, 1901. Johanas Hagen (1820–1902) was postmaster on his farm, two miles north of the present site, when the post office was established in 1878; Hagen helped organize the township and village. An alternative version of the origin of the village's name is that it was for his wife, Olava Hindrum Hagen (1831–97). It had a station of the Great Northern Railway.

HOME LAKE TOWNSHIP organized in 1881, has two lakelets in section 13, to which this name was given as a compliment for John Homelvig, the former clerk of this township.

KALMER a country post office, 1891–1900, located in section 9 of Shelly Township.

LAKE IDA TOWNSHIP organized in 1879, bears the name of a small lake at in its sections 7 and 8, given in honor of Ida Paulson, daughter of an early homesteader in Anthony Township.

LEE TOWNSHIP at first called Norman, organized in 1882, was named for Ole Lee, a pioneer settler, who came from Kongsberg, Norway.

LOCKHART TOWNSHIP organized in 1882, was named for its very large Lockhart farm, which

bore the name of the owner, a resident in Pennsylvania. Lockhart railway village, in the north edge of section 29, superseded the former Rolette station of the Great Northern Railway, the village, and the post office in section 17. A post office has been located in section 29 since 1883.

MacDONALDSVILLE see ADA.

MARSH RIVER a post office, 1879–1903, in section 11 of Halstad Township, with Alex Running as first postmaster, followed by Ole Halstad on his farm, until he moved into the village of Halstad in 1884; other postmasters carried on the work at their homes, moving the office several times.

MARY TOWNSHIP organized about the year 1880, was named in honor of the wife of Jacob Thomas, an early settler there.

McDONALDSVILLE TOWNSHIP the first organized in the area of this county, in 1874, was named in honor of one of its pioneer farmers, Finnian McDonald, a native of Scotland, who came to Minnesota from Glengarry, Ontario, settling here beside the Wild Rice River.

NAVARRE a post office, 1900–1905, in Spring Creek Township, which opened after Peter Sheets, Jr., built a store and petitioned for a post office; Sheets, born in Ohio in 1872, moved to Illinois and Iowa before coming to Minnesota in 1899; his sister, Carrie, was the mail carrier and his wife, Hattie Starks Sheets, the postmaster.

PERLEY a city in section 30 of Lee Township, was named in honor of George Edmund Perley of Moorhead. He was born in Lempster, N.H., August 19, 1853; was graduated at Dartmouth College, 1878; was admitted to practice law in 1883 and came to Minnesota the next year, settling in Moorhead; was a representative in the legislature in 1903–5. The city began as a Great Northern Railway village in 1883 and was incorporated as a village on September 27, 1906. The post office was first named Aabye, 1884–85, located four miles southwest on the river in the trading post of Andrew T. Aabye, postmaster, who moved his store into the village and continued as postmaster when the name changed to Perley.

PLEASANT VIEW TOWNSHIP organized in 1880, received this euphonious name by suggestion of James Preston, one of its pioneers, who later removed to Duluth.

POLEITE a station of the Great Northern Railway in section 17 of Lockhart Township.

POLK CITY   a village in Hendrum Township, 20 miles from Ada, established for steamboat traffic on the Red River. The post office operated 1877–82, being first established in Polk County and transferred to Norman County in 1881. The site had a gristmill and blacksmith, with Austin J. Austin serving as postmaster and justice of the peace in his general store.

QUAL   a post office in section 25 of Fossum Township, 1901–3, with Edward Qual, postmaster.

RANUM   a village in section 16 of Bear Park Township, which had a post office, 1900–1905.

RINDAHL   a village in section 4 of Bear Park Township.

ROCKEY   a post office, 1887–89, in Rockwell Township, with John S. Wenburg, postmaster in his general store.

ROCKWELL TOWNSHIP   at first called Wheatland, organized in 1882, was named by settlers who came from Rockwell in Cerro Gordo County, Iowa.

ROLETTE   a former Great Northern Railway village in section 17 of Lockhart Township, was superseded by Lockhart village. Its name commemorated Joe Rolette, who was born at Prairie du Chien, Wis., October 23, 1820, and died at Pembina, Dakota Territory, May 16, 1871. He was employed by the American Fur Company at their trading post at Pembina in 1840; established a cart route from the Red River to St. Paul, extending the fur trade of that city into a large region in competition with the Hudson's Bay Company; was a representative in the territorial legislature of Minnesota, 1853–55, and a member of the territorial council, 1856–57. During the latter year occurred his notorious exploit of carrying away the bill to remove the seat of government to St. Peter, and thus he saved the capital for St. Paul.

Rolette was also the name of a post office in section 17 of Lockhart Township, established three times: August-October 1880 in Polk County, June-November 1881, and February-October 1901, at which time it was merged with Lockhart.

SHELLY TOWNSHIP   organized in 1879, was named for John Shely, with a variant form of his name, a trapper, who was the first homestead farmer of this township, was later a wheat buyer at Ada, and thence removed to Duluth as an assistant grain inspector for the state. Shely was born in Vermont in 1847, came to Minnesota in 1854, and died in 1898 in Crookston. The city in section 18 was plat-

ted in 1896 and incorporated as a village on July 11, 1902; it had a Great Northern Railway station, and the post office began in 1896.

SPRING CREEK TOWNSHIP   organized in 1880, was named for the creek flowing through it, a tributary of the Marsh River.

STRAND TOWNSHIP   organized in 1880, was so named by the Norwegian settlers because its poplar groves bordering the beaches of the Glacial Lake Agassiz, seen at a long distance from the vast prairie of the Red River valley, resembled an ocean strand or shore. The village in sections 13 and 24 had a post office, 1882–99, located in the general store of postmaster Tron Rishoff, who came to the United States from Norway in 1869 and to the county in 1880; a small village grew up around the store.

SUNDAHL   organized in 1880, received its name from a village and a river in Norway. The village in section 13 had a post office, 1882–1905.

SYRE   a village in section 27 of Home Lake Township, was begun in the early 1900s and named for Swen Syre, who homesteaded in section 28; the site had a post office, 1891–1936, a general store, an elevator, a creamery, a lumberyard, and station of the Northern Pacific Railroad.

TWIN VALLEY   a city in sections 27 and 28 in Wild Rice Township, was named from its situation between the Wild Rice River and a tributary creek. In 1874, S. P. Olson selected a site in section 16 on which to build a flour mill; the site attracted farmers, and a village was established by 1880; when the Northern Pacific Railroad came in 1886, the businesses of Twin Valley moved to its present site, and the old townsite became Heiberg. The village was incorporated on August 27, 1894, and a post office was established in 1878.

ULLMAN   a post office, 1897–1903, located eight miles from Ada and six miles from Twin Valley, probably in Lake Ida Township, with farmer and thresher Ole S. Dalby as postmaster.

WAUKON TOWNSHIP   organized in 1880, has a Dakota name, meaning "spiritual, sacred, wonderful." It probably refers to the grandeur of the view westward over the broad Red River valley, this township being crossed by the highest shoreline of Lake Agassiz. A village in section 16 had a post office, 1895–1905.

WHEATVILLE   was a Great Northern Railway

station and a post office, 1895–1910, located in section 4, Winchester Township.

WILD RICE a post office, 1874–92, located in section 6 of Flom Township in the home of Andrew J. Hanson; Hanson was born in Norway, came to the United States in 1869, and farmed in Fossum Township before moving to Flom Township and building a general store.

WILD RICE TOWNSHIP organized in 1881, is crossed by the Wild Rice River, translated from its Ojibwe name, Manomin or Mahnomen.

WINCHESTER TOWNSHIP organized in 1854, was named by settlers from Winchester in Van Buren County, Iowa. This name is borne by townships and villages or cities of 21 states of the Union.

Lakes and Streams

The Red River has been considered in the first chapter, and the Wild Rice River is most fully noticed for Mahnomen County, which bears the aboriginal name of that river and of the lakes at its source.

Marsh River, which diverges from the Wild Rice River about two miles southeast of Ada, flowing thence northwest to the Red River, is a sluggish and marshlike stream in dry seasons but carries a great part of the Wild Rice waters during flood stages.

Spring Creek, for which a township is named, receives a tributary, South Spring Creek, from Green Meadow Township.

Two tributaries of the Wild Rice River in this county are named on maps, these being its South Branch, a considerable stream, and the little Marsh Creek in Fossum.

With Lake Ida and Home Lake, in the townships so named, only two other lakes are mapped with names, these being Long Lake, close east of Ada, and Love Lake, a former rivercourse in the northwest corner of Lee. Lake Ida and Long Lake have been drained.

Several other lakelets are found in the most eastern townships, above the highest beach of Lake Agassiz, but for these no names were learned, excepting Stene Lake on the farm of Mons L. Stene, in section 35, Fossum, but it has been drained.

Frenchman's Bluff

The first settlers of Flom, coming in 1871, found three old log cabins, long deserted, in a grove adjoining a prominent and irregularly outlined hill of morainic drift near the center of the area of that township. Thinking the cabins to have been built by early fur traders, they named the hill Frenchman's Bluff. It rises 150 feet or more above the upper shoreline of the former Lake Agassiz, about three miles distant at the northwest, and affords a wide view on all sides.

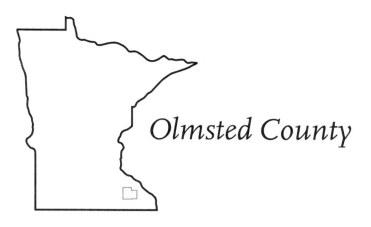

Olmsted County

This county, established February 20, 1855, was named in honor of David Olmsted, first mayor of St. Paul, in 1854, who in 1855 removed to Winona, in the county of that name, adjoining Olmsted County. He was born in Fairfax, Vt., May 5, 1822; came to the Northwest, first to the Wisconsin lead mining region, in 1838; was a pioneer settler of Monona, Iowa, in 1840; engaged in trading with the Indians at Fort Atkinson, Iowa, in 1844; was a member of the convention that framed the state constitution of Iowa, in 1846; came in 1848 to Long Prairie, Minn., when the Winnebago Indians were transferred there, and established a trading post, which he continued several years. He was a charter member of the Minnesota Historical Society and a member of the council of the first territorial legislature, 1849 and 1850, being its first president. In 1853, having removed to St. Paul, he became proprietor and editor of the *Minnesota Democrat*, which under his management

began its issue as a daily newspaper in May 1854. After his removal to Winona, ill health compelled him, in 1857, to give up business, and he then returned to his old home in Vermont, where he died February 2, 1861.

Another prominent citizen of this name but of another family, with slightly different spelling, for whom, however, some have supposed this county to be named, was S. Baldwin Olmstead, a farmer and contractor of Belle Prairie and Fort Ripley, who was a member of the territorial council in 1854 and 1855, when this county was created, having been president of the council in the former year. He was born in Otsego County, N.Y., in 1810; came to the Northwest in early manhood and resided in Iowa and Minnesota; was engaged with government contracts about Fort Ripley for a time; removed to Texas at the close of the Civil War and settled on a farm in Burnett County, where he died, January 27, 1878.

Information of geographic names has been gathered from the Geographical and Statistical History of the County of Olmsted *by W. H. Mitchell (1867, 121 pp.); "History of Olmsted County," pp. 617–1,148, in the* History of Winona and Olmsted Counties *(1883);* History of Olmsted County *by Hon. Joseph A. Leonard and others (1910, 674 pp.); and from Hon. Charles C. Willson and Timothy H. Bliss, each of Rochester, the county seat, interviewed during a visit there in April 1916.*

BEAR GROVE see BYRON.

BLACK OAK GROVE a post office, 1861–64; location not found.

BYRON a city in sections 29 and 32 in Kalmar Township, platted in 1864, incorporated on February 12, 1873, and separated from the township in 1912, was named at the suggestion of G. W. Van Dusen, an early grain buyer, for his former home, Port Byron, N.Y. (W. H. Stennett, *Origin of the Place Names of the Chicago and Northwestern*

Railway, 1908, p. 50). The post office was first named Bear Grove, 1857–68, for the numerous bears found in the vicinity; the village had a station of the Chicago and North Western Railway.

CARROLLVILLE a post office, 1872–1902, on the border of High Forest and Pleasant Grove Townships; Thomas J. Carroll was the first postmaster.

CASCADE a post office in section 33 of Oronoco Township, 1867–79.

CASCADE TOWNSHIP organized in 1859, was named for the beautiful Cascade Creek, which flows through the south edge of this township, joining the Zumbro River in the city of Rochester.

CEDAR BEACH a village in section 14 of Oronoco Township.

CHATFIELD a city in Elmira Township, section 31, with Chatfield Township in Fillmore County, was incorporated as a village on March 6, 1857, and in 1871 and as a city in 1891; it had a station of the Chicago and North Western Railway.

CHATFIELD JUNCTION a station of the Chicago and North Western Railway located in section 15 of Eyota Township.

CHESTER a village in section 11 of Marion Township, six miles east of Rochester, has a name that is also borne by townships and villages or cities in 25 other states. The post office, established in 1868, became a rural branch in 1957; the station of the Chicago and North Western Railway was the first east of Rochester, taking part of that name as its own.

CORRA a post office, 1880–1904, in Viola Township, which had been formerly at Viola; it had a station of the Chicago and North Western Railway.

CUMMINGSVILLE a former village on the North Branch of the Root River, in section 28 of Orion Township, was platted by Francis H. Cummings, who settled here in 1855, building a sawmill.

CURTIS a stagecoach stop, 1854, between Rochester and Pickets.

DANESVILLE a village in sections 6 and 7 of Kalmar Township.

DOTY a station of the Chicago and North Western Railway in section 34 of Viola, was named by G. W. Van Dusen of Rochester, on whose farm the station was located, for former Governor James Duane Doty of Wisconsin (1799–1865); also known as Dotyville.

DOUGLAS formerly spelled Douglass, a railway village in section 1 of Kalmar Township, eight miles northwest of Rochester, was named for Harrison Douglass, owner of its site. He was born in Macedon, N.Y., March 21, 1825; came to Minnesota in 1855, settling here as the first blacksmith in the county; built a grain elevator at this village in 1878; died in Fargo, N.D., March 7, 1902. The village had a post office, 1878–1963, which operated as a rural branch, 1963–1974, and it had a station serving the Chicago and Great Western and the Chicago and North Western Railways.

DOVER CENTRE see DOVER.

DOVER TOWNSHIP originally named Whitewater in 1858 for its river flowing east into Winona County, was organized in May 1859, being then renamed for Dover in New Hampshire, whence some of its settlers came. The city of this name in sections 21 and 22, platted in the spring of 1869, was at first called Dover Center, from its location at the center of this township; it was incorporated as a village on December 22, 1908, and separated from the township on February 26, 1909; the post office, established in 1858, was known for a time as Dover Centre.

DURANGO see NEW HAVEN.

ELMIRA TOWNSHIP organized May 11, 1858, was named by settlers from the vicinity of Elmira, N.Y.

EYOTA TOWNSHIP organized in 1858, was at first named Springfield, which was changed in 1859 to this Dakota word, spelled *iyotan* by Rev. Stephen R. Riggs in the Dakota *Dictionary*, meaning "greatest, most." The city of Eyota in sections 11 and 14, platted in November 1864, was incorporated February 16, 1875. The post office was established as Greenfield in 1857 and changed to Eyota in 1864; it had a station of the Chicago Great Western and the Winona and St. Peter Railroads.

FAIRFIELD a post office, 1857–64; location not found.

FARM HILL a post office, 1863–89, located in section 7 of Farmington Township.

FARMINGTON organized in 1858, is an excellent farming township, whence it received this name, borne also by a railway village in Dakota County and by townships and villages or cities in 25 other states of the Union. Five counties in Wisconsin have each a Farmington Township.

FINLEY see MARION.

GENOA a little village in section 34, New Haven, first settled in 1856 and platted in 1865, bears the name of an ancient seaport in northern Italy, the birthplace of Columbus. Nine other states of the Union have villages of this name. The village had a post office, 1872–1905.

GOLDEN HILL a locality in Rochester Township.

GRANT a post office, 1864–65, which was formerly Waterloo, 1856–64; location not found.

GREENFIELD see EYOTA.

GROESBECK a village and post office, 1883–90, located in sections 4 and 5 of Pleasant Grove Township, was named for an early settler named John H. Groesbeck, who was born in 1833 in New York, came to the township in 1860, built an inn and stage stop in 1869, developed grain and livery businesses, and died in 1903. When the post office was transferred to the newly platted Simpson a short distance away, the community reverted to farmland.

HANSON a post office, 1875–1900, in section 11 of Rock Dell Township, with Thomas Hanson, first postmaster.

HAVERHILL a post office, 1866–67, in Marion Township, section 11, with a station on the Chicago and North Western Railway.

HAVERHILL TOWNSHIP organized in 1858, originally called Zumbro for the principal river of this county, was renamed Sherman in 1865 and Haverhill in 1866, this name being suggested by settlers who had come from Haverhill in Massachusetts.

HIGH FOREST TOWNSHIP organized in 1858, took the name of its village in section 5, platted in 1855, on high land partly surrounded by forest along the North Branch of the Root River. The village was incorporated on February 28, 1869; the incorporation was repealed, and the village was made part of the township again on April 10, 1919. The post office, established in Mower County, was called Pleasant Valley 1855–56; its name was changed to High Forest in 1856, and it was transferred to Olmsted County in 1858, discontinuing in 1902.

HORTON a station of the Chicago Great Western Railroad and a post office, 1892–1905, in section 34 of Eyota, was named for Charles Horton, a lumber merchant of Winona. He was born in Niles, N.Y., March 31, 1836; came to Minnesota in 1858, settling in Winona; founded the Empire Lumber Company in 1858 and was its president; died in Winona, May 15, 1913.

JUDGE a village in section 14 of High Forest Township, which had a post office, 1897–1902, and a station of the Chicago Great Western Railroad, which was located on the farm of Edward Judge, a native of Ireland, who came here as a pioneer settler in 1854 and died in September 1904. In October 1940, the last building in the village, the store and home of the Matthew Judge family, for whom the town was named when established in 1891, was destroyed by fire.

KALMAR TOWNSHIP organized in May 1858, bears the name of a seaport in southern Sweden, noted for a treaty made there July 20, 1397, uniting the kingdoms of Sweden, Norway, and Denmark. A post office called Kalmar, 1856–59, was probably located in the township.

KEPNER'S CORNERS a village in Quincy Township, three miles south of Kingsley Corner, about 1885.

KINGSLEY CORNER a village in sections 11 and 14 of Quincy Township.

LAIRD a railway station of the Chicago Great Western Railroad in section 26, Eyota, was named in honor of William Harris Laird of Winona, who was born in Union County, Pa., February 24, 1833, and died in Baltimore, Md., February 5, 1910. He came to Minnesota in 1855, settling in Winona; was active in the firm of Laird, Norton and Co., formed in 1856, engaged extensively in lumbering and lumber manufacturing. He was the donor of the public library building in Winona and president of the trustees of Carleton College. A post office was also located in section 26, 1891–1905, with George W. Plank as postmaster.

LANDALE a post office, 1880–81; location not found.

LITTLE VALLEY a post office, 1863–1902, in section 16 of Quincy Township.

MARION TOWNSHIP organized in 1858, received the name of its village, in section 35, founded in 1855–56. The post office operated 1857–1905. The village was called Finley about 1854 and contended with Rochester for the county seat. Seventeen states of the Union have counties of this name, and it is borne also by townships and villages or cities of 25 states, in honor of Francis Marion (1732–95) of South Carolina, a distinguished general in the Revolutionary War.

NEW HAVEN TOWNSHIP organized in May 1858,

was named for the city of New Haven in Connecticut. A post office, 1857–70, first named Durango 1856–57, was located in section 23; no trace remains.

OAKWOOD a post office, 1879–81; location not found.

OLMSTED a post office in section 36 of Kalmar Township, 1874–81, and a station of the Winona and St. Peter Railroad.

ORION MILLS a place name in Orion Township, section 18, on the 1878 atlas of the county.

ORION TOWNSHIP organized in 1858, received this name of a constellation from a township and village in Richland County, Wis.

ORONOCO TOWNSHIP organized in 1858, was named for its village in section 17, founded in 1854, which Dr. Hector Galloway, one of its first settlers, named for the large Orinoco River (differently spelled) in South America, in allusion to the valuable waterpower of the Middle Branch of the Zumbro River at this village. The village was incorporated on March 6, 1968; the post office was established in 1854, with Robert K. Whitely, an early settler from St. Louis, Mo., as postmaster; the station for Oronoco on the Chicago and North Western Railway was located west of the city in section 22 of New Haven Township.

OTHELLO a post office, 1864–79 and 1881–1902, located in section 31 of New Haven Township and section 6 of Milton Township, Dodge County.

PINE ISLAND a city with Goodhue County.

PLAINVIEW JUNCTION a railroad station in section 15 of Eyota Township on the Chicago and North Western Railway.

PLANKS a railroad station in Eyota Township, section 34, on the Chicago and North Western Railway, perhaps named for George W. Plank, postmaster of nearby Laird, or for John A. Plans, who ran a country tavern there; also known as Planks Crossing and Planks Junction.

PLEASANT GROVE TOWNSHIP organized May 11, 1858, and its village platted in 1854 in section 28 and incorporated on March 7, 1878, derived their name "from a beautiful grove of oaks, where the little village is located." The village developed around a lumber mill, flour mill, a creamery, and a brick kiln; the post office, 1854–1905, was established in Fillmore County and transferred to Olmsted in 1855; the founder of the community and its first postmaster, Philo S. Curtis, was also

a hotel owner, a sheriff, and a philanthropist; he died in 1859 in Dakota Territory.

PLEASANT VALLEY SEE HIGH FOREST.

POTSDAM a village in section 11 of Farmington, founded about the year 1860, was named by its German settlers for the German city of Potsdam, noted for its royal palace and beautiful parks, 16 miles southwest of Berlin. The village had a post office, 1873–1905.

PREDMORE a station in section 36 of Marion, established in 1891, was named for J. W. Predmore, who came in 1854 as one of the pioneer settlers of this township. The village had a station of the Chicago Great Western Railroad and a post office, 1892–1905.

QUINCY TOWNSHIP organized May 11, 1858, bears the name of cities in Massachusetts and Illinois and of villages and townships in 14 other states. A post office was located in section 26, 1858–1902.

RINGE a village in section 33 of Farmington Township; the post office operated 1898–1902.

ROCHESTER the county seat, often called "the Queen City," was platted on July 25, 1854, and was incorporated as a city August 5, 1858. It was named for Rochester, N.Y., by George Head, a pioneer settler, often referred to as the father of Rochester, who had lived there and afterward in Wisconsin before coming to this place in July 1855. The rapids of the Zumbro River here reminded him of the Genesee River in New York and its great water power at Rochester, having a vertical fall of 95 feet (Leonard, *History of Olmsted County*, p. 185). Head's wife, Henrietta, was the first white woman in the community. Head was born in England in 1822 and died in Bermuda in 1883; his body was returned in 1884 and buried in Rochester. The city's station served a number of rail lines, including the Winona and St. Peter; the post office was established in 1855. The city is the home of the world-famous Mayo Clinic.

ROCK DELL TOWNSHIP organized May 11, 1858, has narrow gorges or dells, with ragged cliffs of limestone, eroded by little streams flowing northward to the South Branch of the Zumbro River. The village in section 17 had a post office, 1858–1905.

SALEM TOWNSHIP organized in 1858, was named by Cyrus Holt, a pioneer who came here in 1855 and was appointed postmaster of an office established in the winter of that year. The post office, 1856–74, in section 15, and later the township, received this name from Salem, the county seat of Marion County, Ill. A station of the Chicago, St. Paul, Minneapolis and Omaha Railroad was located in the township; also known as Salem Corners.

SIMPSON a railway village and junction in section 5 of Pleasant Grove Township, platted in 1890, was named in honor of Thomas Simpson of Winona, Minn., secretary of the Winona and Southwestern Railway company. He was born in Yorkshire, England, May 31, 1836; came to the United States with his parents while quite young; studied surveying and in 1853 took the government contract for running the meridian and parallel lines in the southeast part of Minnesota Territory; settled in Winona in 1856; was admitted to the bar in 1858; practiced law, engaged in many important business enterprises, and during many years was president of the State Normal School board; died in Winona, April 26, 1905. The post office began as Groesbeck in 1883 with Joshua S. Whitney as postmaster and was transferred to Simpson in 1890, Whitney continuing as postmaster; it operated as a rural branch from 1956 to 1964; Whitney, from Maine, was also a music teacher, a farmer, and owner of a livery, a hardware store, and a hotel.

SIX OAKS a post office, 1868–1902, located in section 5 of Quincy Township.

SPRINGFIELD a post office, 1855–59; location not found.

STEWARTVILLE in section 34 of High Forest Township, was founded by Charles Stewart, born in New York in 1816, who came from there in the spring of 1857 and built a mill here in 1858. When the railroad passing this place was constructed in 1891, additions to the village were platted by Stewart and others. The village was incorporated on November 21, 1893, reincorporated on April 14, 1919, and separated from the township. Stewart was the first postmaster when the post office was established in 1858; he served in the legislature, 1868 and 1870, and died in Stewartville in 1886. The village had a station of the Chicago Great Western Railroad.

VIOLA CENTRE see VIOLA.

VIOLA TOWNSHIP at first named Washington, organized in May 1858, was renamed at the suggestion of Irwin N. Wetmore, for the village of Viola in Wisconsin, about 40 miles southeast of La Crosse. The railway village in section 21, bearing the same name, was platted in September 1878. It had a station of the Chicago and North Western Railway and two post offices; the first operated 1862–68 and 1875–80 before transferring to Corra, and the second, called Viola Centre, 1878–80, changed to Viola until 1963, when it became a rural branch. The Viola Gopher Count began in 1874 when the abundance of gophers was a problem and over the years has become an annual celebration.

WATERLOO see GRANT.

YANKEE RIDGE a post office, 1863–67; location not found.

ZUMBRO a post office, 1856–67; location not found.

ZUMBROTA JUNCTION a railroad station of the Chicago Great Western Railroad located west of Rochester in section 34 of Cascade Township.

Lakes and Streams

Olmsted County is drained by the Zumbro, Whitewater, and Root Rivers, flowing to the Mississippi.

The origin and meaning of the first of these names are fully noticed in the chapter of Goodhue County, where a village and township on this river are named Zumbrota. Its earlier Dakota name, Wazi Oju, applied to the river by Joseph N. Nicollet, referring to its large grove of white pines at the village of Pine Island, is also duly explained for that village and township in Goodhue County.

Large affluents of the Zumbro in Olmsted County are its Middle Branch, formed at Oronoco village by union of the North and South Middle Branches, Cascade Creek, whence a township is named, the South Branch, Silver Creek, Bear Creek, to which Badger run is a tributary, and Willow Creek.

Bear Creek has its farthest source in a spring on the farm in Eyota that was taken as a homestead claim in 1853 by Benjamin Bear, a pioneer from Pennsylvania, the first settler in that township, for whom the creek received this name.

Whitewater River, having in this county its North, Middle, and South Branches, is translated from its Dakota name, Minneiska, borne by a township and village in Wabasha County at the mouth of this stream.

Root River, to which its North Branch flows through the south edge of Olmsted County, is also a translation of the Dakota name Hutkan, spelled Hokah on Nicollet's map, which gave the name Hokah of the village and township adjoining the mouth of Root River in Houston County.

Partridge Creek is a small tributary to this branch of the Root River from the south in Pleasant Grove Township.

The only lakes in this county are two picturesque mill ponds formed by dams, Shady Lake at the village of Oronoco, and Lake Alice or Florence at Stewartville. The second "was named Lake Alice by Charles N. Stewart, in compliment to his wife" (as noted in the *History of Olmsted County* by Leonard, 1910, p. 270), but by 1916 was called Lake Florence. Lake Zumbro, Oronoco, also is formed by a dam on the river of that name.

Hills

The bedrocks, sculptured by rains and streams before the Ice Age and only thinly overspread by the glacial drift, present beautiful valleys and ravines, most noteworthy in Rock Dell Township, and in some places form hills or small and low plateaus. College Hill is such a plateau, about 75 feet high, in the west part of the city of Rochester; Sugarloaf Mound, more conspicuously seen, rises south of the railroad two miles east of this city; and Lone Mound is in section 11, Farmington.

Otter Tail County

This county, established March 18, 1858, and organized September 12, 1868, received its name from the Otter Tail Lake and River. The lake, from which the river was named, derived its peculiar Ojibwe designation, thus translated, from a long and narrow sandbar, having an outline suggestive of the tail of an otter, formed very long ago and now covered with large woods, which extends curvingly southeast and south between the last mile of the inflowing Otter Tail (or Red River) and the lake, at its eastern end, in section 10 of Otter Tail Township. At its northwestern base the bar is connected with the main shore by a gradually widening higher tract between the river and lake, to which, with the prolonged bar, the Indians very fittingly, in view of their geographic outlines, gave this name. Its Ojibwe form is given by the late Rev. J. A. Gilfillan as Nigigwanowe, that is, Otter Tail, both for the lake and for the outflowing river to its junction with the Bois des Sioux River. The otter was formerly frequent or common in and near the rivers and lakes of all parts of this state. It subsists on fish, capturing them by rapid and expert swimming.

The late Hon. J. V. Brower, who visited the locality three times, in 1863, 1882, and 1899, on the last occasion giving it a careful examination as a part of his archaeologic survey of the region, stated that the height of the bar varies from 10 to 25 feet above the lake; that its length slightly exceeds a mile, while its width, somewhat uniform, is only about 50 to 75 feet; and that it appears to have been amassed by wave and ice action of the lake. It was probably built by the waves during storms, nearly to its present extent and form, within the first few centuries after the lake began its existence, which was at the time of uncovering this region from the receding ice sheet at the close of the glacial period.

Otter Tail City, which about the years 1850 to 1860 was an important trading post on the route from the then flourishing town of Crow Wing to Pembina and the Selkirk settlements, stood on the main shore at the northeastern end of Otter Tail Lake, adjoining the mouth of the river and the end of the Otter Tail bar. The U.S. land office for this district was located there during several years and was thence removed to Alexandria in 1862. But all the buildings of the "city" were long since removed or destroyed, and only the cellar holes remain.

The Otter Tail River was known to the Ojibwe at the time of David D. Owen's geological exploration, in 1848, as the Otter Tail from this lake to its junction with the Red Lake River at Grand Forks. Present usage retains the name Otter Tail for the river above the lake of this name (though other names, derived from successive lakes, are used there by the Ojibwe), as well as along its portion continuing below this lake to the axis of the Red River valley at Breckenridge and Wahpeton, where it receives the Bois des Sioux River and turns from a westward to a northward course.

Information of the origins and meanings of geographic names has been supplied by the History of Otter Tail County, *edited by John W. Mason (1916, 2 vols., pp. 694, 1009); from William Lincoln, county auditor, and P. A. Anderson, register of deeds, interviewed during visits at Fergus Falls, the county seat, in September 1909, and again in September 1916; and from Hon. E. E. Corliss, formerly of Fergus Falls, custodian of the state capitol, 1910–17.*

AASTAD TOWNSHIP organized March 14, 1871, was named for Gilbert Aastad, one of its early settlers, a native of Norway. A post office was located in section 34, 1880–81, before changing to Lillemon in Grant County; one block was platted at the site and one store built.

ALMORA is a Minneapolis, St. Paul and Sault Ste. Marie Railroad (Soo Line) village in section 17 of Elmo Township. The post office operated 1903–54; the Depression, a bank robbery in 1924, and fires that destroyed many of the buildings, including an elevator, a cheese factory, and the depot, left the site with only a few buildings and homes.

ALTONA see VERGAS.

AMBOY see TOPELIUS.

AMES a station of the Northern Pacific Railroad on the border of section 6 of Orwell Township and section 32 of Oscar Township.

AMOR organized April 5, 1879, has a Latin name, meaning love, adopted in the Norwegian language of the settlers of this township as the name of Cupid, the god of love in the ancient Roman mythology. A village in section 17 had a post office, 1878–1906.

ARTHUR a post office, 1897–1906, in section 12 of Maplewood Township.

AURDAL TOWNSHIP organized January 24, 1870, was named for a village in Norway, 80 miles northwest of Christiania. A post office operated, 1871–82 and 1899–1901.

AXEL a post office, 1897–1906, in section 34 of Clitherall Township, with Axel Person (or Pierson) as postmaster.

BALMORAL a lakeside village of summer homes in section 31, Otter Tail Township, received its name from Balmoral Castle in Scotland, which was a favorite summer residence of Queen Victoria. The post office in section 31 operated during three periods between 1870 and 1905; the site had several mills including a gristmill begun by

postmaster James G. Craigie in 1868, a hotel, a cheese factory, and a school, and was often noted on maps as Balmoral Mills; the site later became a golf course.

BANGOR see SCAMBLER.

BARKEY a village in Star Lake Township.

BASSWOOD a village in section 35 of Dead Lake Township, which had a post office in 1901.

BATEMAN a post office, November 1858-January 1859, with Matthew Wright as postmaster, who was also postmaster at Waseata; location not found.

BATTLE LAKE a city located in Everts and Clitherall Townships, platted October 31, 1881, and incorporated as a village on May 2, 1891, adjoins the western end of the large West Battle Lake, which lies mainly in Everts and Girard Townships. Near this lake and the East Battle Lake, in the southeast part of Girard, a desperate battle was fought, about the year 1795, by a war party of 50 Ojibwe, coming from Leech Lake, against a much greater number of Dakota. A graphic narration of the battle, in which more than 30 of the Ojibwe were killed, is given in William W. Warren's *History of the Ojibway People* (MHS Collections 5: 336–43 [1885]). The post office operated 1871–74 and since 1881; a station of the Northern Pacific Railroad was in section 4 of Clitherall Township.

BEAVER DAM a post office, 1878–82, located 12 miles northeast of Fergus Falls and 25 miles southwest of Perham, probably in Maine Township; the settlement exported timber, fencing, and cordwood.

BENTON'S CROSSING see TOPELIUS.

BERKEY a post office in section 8 of Maine Township, 1903–5.

BESSIE a post office, 1895–1906, located in section 34 of Lida Township.

BLOWERS TOWNSHIP organized April 9, 1884, was named "in honor of A. S. Blowers, one of the prominent citizens of the early history of the county, and a member of the board of commissioners for many years." A post office was in section 9, 1899–1905, located in the home of postmaster August Aho; the site was never platted.

BLUFFTON TOWNSHIP organized July 17, 1878, and the city in sections 28, 29, 32, and 33, platted in March 1880, incorporated as a village on February 26, 1903, and separated from the township on March 19, 1909, received this name in allusion to the high banks or bluffs of the Leaf River along its course in the south edge of this township. North Bluff Creek is tributary here to the Leaf River from the north, and South Bluff Creek from the south. The village began with a creamery, a sawmill, a gristmill, and a station of the Northern Pacific Railroad; the post office was established in 1878.

BOARDMAN a village platted in 1880 in section 7 of Newton Township with four blocks, although no buildings were erected at the time; later, when New York Mills was laid out one-half mile away, the site was eventually absorbed into that city.

BONITA a site in the southwest tip of what was later Western Township, is shown on J. S. Sewall's 1857 map but was not developed.

BRENT a station of the Great Northern Railway in section 13 of Carlisle Township.

BUSE was organized October 3, 1870. "Ernest Buse, in whose honor the township was named, was one of the earliest settlers and became one of the most influential men of the county." He was born in 1836; came to Minnesota in 1857, when his parents settled at Red Wing; served in the Third Minnesota Regiment, 1864–65; was the first homesteader on the site of Fergus Falls, 1869; removed to Vancouver, B.C.; returned to Minnesota and resided at Red Lake Falls; died during a visit to Lodi, Calif., February 1, 1914.

BUTLER TOWNSHIP organized August 15, 1883, was named in honor of Stephen Butler of Fergus Falls, who during many years was the county treasurer. A village was in section 15, and the post office operated, 1897–1954, and as a rural branch, 1954–57. The first postmaster was Amasa J. Pierce at his home; Pierce was born in Indiana in 1848, came to Minnesota in 1876 and to this county in 1879, served as justice of the peace and chairman of the township board for many years, moved to Boot Lake in 1922, where he died in 1939. The site was not a municipality and was governed by the township board; it had a township hall, a store, and a cheese factory. The community was developed by a group of about 200 Dutch, who came direct from Holland in 1910.

CANDOR see VERGAS.

CANDOR TOWNSHIP organized January 8, 1880, has a name that is also borne by a township and village in New York and by villages in Pennsylvania and North Carolina.

CARLISLE TOWNSHIP organized February 24, 1881, received the name of its village in section 2 on the Great Northern Railway, which was platted in December 1879. The post office began in 1880 and has been a rural branch since 1960. A city in England, a county in Kentucky, and villages and townships in 11 other states bear this name.

CENTER GROVE a village located at the corner of sections 27, 28, 33, and 34 of Norwegian Grove, with a post office, 1898–1905.

CLEAR VIEW a village in sections 1 and 2, Scambler Township.

CLITHERALL a village in section 6 of Nidaros Township, settled in 1865, platted in October 1881, and incorporated October 6, 1898, was named like the lake for George B. Clitherall. The village had a station on the Northern Pacific Railroad, and the post office began in 1868.

CLITHERALL TOWNSHIP the first organized in this county, October 24, 1868, received its name from Clitherall Lake, lying in Clitherall and Nidaros Townships and adjoining the village of Clitherall. "The lake took its name from Major George B. Clitherall, who was register of the United States land office at Otter Tail City from 1858 to 1861" (*History of Otter Tail County*, 1916, p. 169). He was born at Fort Johnson, N.C., June 13, 1814, and died in Mobile, Ala., October 21, 1890. He is well remembered by the Minnesota Historical Society for his donation to its museum, a carved mahogany armchair that was owned by George Washington in his home at Mount Vernon.

COMPTON TOWNSHIP organized July 31, 1875, commemorates James Compton, an early pioneer of this county. He was born near Meadville, Pa., January 14, 1840; served during the Civil War in Pennsylvania and Illinois regiments, attaining the rank of captain; came to Minnesota in 1872, settling at Fergus Falls; assisted in organizing the First National Bank there and was its cashier until 1891; was a state senator, 1883–89; was commandant of the Minnesota Soldiers' Home in Minneapolis after 1900; and died in Minneapolis, January 14, 1908.

CORLISS TOWNSHIP organized January 3, 1884, was named in honor of Eben Eaton Corliss of Fergus Falls, who was born in Fayston, Vt., September 1, 1841, and died in St. Paul, July 21, 1917. He came to Minnesota in 1856 when his parents settled in Winona County; served during the Civil

War in the Second Minnesota Regiment; was admitted to practice law in 1870 and in the same year settled near Battle Lake, building the first frame house in Otter Tail County; removed to Fergus Falls in 1874; was the first county attorney, 1871–75, and again held this office in 1879–85; was a representative in the legislature in 1872; was a member of the State Capitol Commission, 1893–1908; and after 1910 was custodian of the capitol.

DALTON a Great Northern Railway village in sections 11 and 12 of Tumuli Township, platted in 1882 and incorporated May 2, 1905, was named in compliment for Ole C. Dahl, proprietor of its site. The post office began in 1880 as Tumuli, changing to Dalton in 1882.

DANE PRAIRIE TOWNSHIP organized May 10, 1870, received this name by choice of its people, nearly all being natives of Denmark. It had much timber beside its many lakes, with small intervening prairies.

DANIA a post office, 1876–79, located in Tordenskjold Township, an area first settled in 1868; it had a Lutheran church, a school, and a general store; the community exported wheat.

DAVIES a village in section 14 of Homestead Township; the post office operated 1886–1905, with first postmaster Andrew J. Davies at his home; the site had a general store and a blacksmith.

DAYTON probably named for Lyman Dayton of St. Paul, was a village in Buse Township founded before 1860 with the building of a sawmill on the Otter Tail River, about four miles southwest from the site of Fergus Falls, and its post office was named Waseata, but this settlement was permanently abandoned in August 1862 on account of the Dakota War. The village, also known as Dayton Hollow, was first settled by Joseph Whitford in 1857 and then by the Matthew Wright family, their home being a regular stopping place and the location of the post office of Waseata, 1858–63 and 1870–74, with Wright as postmaster; see also BATEMAN.

DEAD LAKE TOWNSHIP the last organized in this county, April 10, 1897, took the name of its large lake, which extends west into the townships of Star Lake and Maine. It is translated from the Ojibwe name, referring to a grave, given by Gilfillan as Tchibegumigo, "House of the Dead, . . . from the custom of the Indians to build the re-

semblance of a little house over a grave." Dead River, named from the lake, is its outlet. About the year 1843, beside the eastern part of this lake, some 30 or 40 Ojibwe, comprising only old men, women, and children, were killed by a war party of Dakota, whence the lake and river were named (*History of Becker County*, by Wilcox, 1907, pp. 212–14).

DEER CREEK TOWNSHIP organized July 1, 1873, and the city in sections 26 and 27, platted in May 1882, and incorporated December 28, 1899, are named for the creek flowing north through the east part of this township to the Leaf River. The post office began in 1879; the early site had a brick factory, a creamery, an elevator, a flour mill, a blacksmith, and a station of the Northern Pacific Railroad.

DENT a city in section 34 on the Soo Line in Edna Township, platted August 19, 1903, and incorporated September 8, 1904, was named for the variety of corn called Northwestern Dent Corn that was used so abundantly by farmers of the area. The post office was established in 1900.

DOPELIUS see TOPELIUS.

DORA TOWNSHIP organized August 9, 1879, was probably named in honor of the wife or daughter of a pioneer homesteader, but her surname is not known. A post office, 1880–1906, was first located in postmaster Gottlieb Baer's store in section 15.

DREXEL a post office, 1903–4, in section 17 of Aurdal Township, with Carl Drechsel, postmaster.

DUNN TOWNSHIP organized March 16, 1880, was named in honor of George W. Dunn, at whose home the first election was held. A post office called Dunn was authorized on December 19, 1903, with Roy E. Dunn to be postmaster, but not established; location not found but probably in Dunn Township.

DUNVILLA a village and summer resort in section 20 of Dunn Township, nine miles north of Pelican Rapids. The post office began in 1916 as Lake Lizzie with hotel owner Roy Emery Dunn as postmaster, changed to Dunvilla in 1930, with Anna L. Dunn, postmaster, and discontinued in 1949.

EAGLE LAKE TOWNSHIP organized September 5, 1870, has the name of its largest and deepest lake.

EASTERN organized July 29, 1875, is the most southeastern township of this county. Its name was chosen with reference to Western, the township forming the southwest corner of the county, which had been organized in January 1873.

ECHOTA a village in Everts Township, incorporated on June 11, 1858, was platted by Benjamin Densmore in May 1857 for the Echota and Marion Land Company but failed to develop beyond the stage of incorporation; no trace remains.

EDNA TOWNSHIP organized March 21, 1882, was named probably for one of its pioneer women.

EDWARDS a village in section 5 of Friberg Township; the post office was spelled Edward, 1890–99, and Edwards, 1899–1906; Edward M. Nelson was the first postmaster.

EFFINGTON organized March 21, 1872, received its name on the suggestion of Matthew Evans, an early settler, who had found it in a novel (*History of Otter Tail County*, 1916, pp. 216–18). A post office was in section 26, 1884–1906.

ELIZABETH TOWNSHIP organized September 5, 1870, was named in honor of the wife of Rudolph Niggler, a pioneer merchant and first postmaster, at whose store the first township meeting was held. The city in sections 31 and 32, bearing this name, platted in 1872, was incorporated November 21, 1884. The post office was first called Elizabethtown, 1871–82; it had a station of the Northern Pacific Railroad.

ELMO TOWNSHIP organized March 16, 1880, has a name that is borne also by villages in Wisconsin, Missouri, and other states, and by a lake near Stillwater in this state, with the railway village of Lake Elmo beside it. A post office located five miles north of Parkers Prairie operated 1872–75 and 1884–85.

ELMWOOD a townsite platted in 1911 in sections 34 and 35 of Candor Township.

ERHARD a city in section 28 of Erhards Grove Township, was platted in July 1882 and incorporated as a village on October 13, 1949. The post office was established as Erhards Grove, 1871–72 and 1874–76, and was first located in section 17 of Erhards Grove Township, with Alexander Erhard as postmaster, and reestablished as Erhard in 1880; it had a station of the Great Northern Railway.

ERHARDS GROVE a township organized September 24, 1870, was named for Alexander E. Erhard, a signer of the petition for organization, at whose house the first election was held.

ESSEX a post office, 1886–94, in section 26 of Eastern Township.

EVERTS TOWNSHIP organized July 22, 1879, was named in honor of Rezin Everts and his son, Edmund A. Everts, pioneers of this township. A biographic sketch of the latter, contributed by E. E. Corliss in the *History of Otter Tail County*, notes that he was born in Carroll County, Ill., November 12, 1840; came to Minnesota in 1855 with his parents, who settled in Winona County; served in the Second Minnesota Regiment during the Civil War; settled as a homestead farmer in section 27 of this township in the spring of 1871; removed to Battle Lake village in 1881 and was a merchant there until his death, March 9, 1915.

FAIR HILLS a village in section 4 of Dunn Township.

FAUST a country post office, 1901–2, in Rush Lake Township.

FERGUS FALLS platted in August 1870, on a site that had been selected and named in 1857, was incorporated as a village February 29, 1872, and as a city March 3, 1881. Within the city limits, along a course of about three miles, the Otter Tail River descends nearly 70 feet, having originally comprised here a nearly continuous series of rapids, flowing over boulders of the glacial drift. The county seat was first located in 1868 at Otter Tail City and was removed to Fergus Falls in the later part of 1872. The township of this name, which included the north half of the present city area, was organized June 29, 1870.

The first permanent settler was Ernest Buse, who came in 1865 and became the first mayor; George Burdick Wright of Minneapolis, who came in 1867 and built a dam in 1870 and a sawmill and flour mill in 1871, was instrumental in the development of the community. The site was platted in August 1870 by George Wright. The post office began in 1870, with H. N. Hannigson (Henreich Hanigsen) as first postmaster.

James Fergus, for whom the township and city were named, was born in Lanarkshire, Scotland, October 8, 1813. "At the age of nineteen he came to America with the idea of improving his fortune. He located in Canada at first, where he spent three years and learned the trade of millwright.... In 1854 he removed to Little Falls, Minnesota, and, in company with C. A. Tuttle, built a dam across the Mississippi and platted a village. Here he remained for two or three years. During the townsite speculation fever, in the winter of

1856 and 1857, Joseph Whitford, a blacksmith and steamboat engineer, a natural frontiersman, possessed of uncommon courage, energy and prudence, proposed to go out and take up a townsite at what was known as Graham's Point, on the Red [Otter Tail] river. Mr. Fergus furnished the necessary outfit for this expedition. Procuring a dog train and a half-breed guide, Whitford went to Graham's Point and staked out a town. On their way back, at Red river, an Indian family told them of a better place for a town twenty miles distant. Leaving his half-breed to recruit, Whitford took an Indian as a guide and went to the place designated and staked off what is now Fergus Falls, the name being given by the exploring party in honor of the man who had furnished the outfit for the expedition. Mr. Fergus himself never visited the place.

"In 1862 Mr. Fergus drove his own team from Little Falls, Minnesota, to Bannock, Montana territory. He became quite prominent in territorial affairs and was influential in the organization of the new county of Madison in that territory, and held many positions of trust and responsibility. He served two terms in the Montana legislature, and was a member of the constitutional convention of 1887" (*History of Otter Tail County*, 1916, pp. 479, 480). Fergus County in Montana was named in his honor. He died near Lewistown in that county, June 25, 1902.

FOLDEN TOWNSHIP organized February 24, 1881, bears the name of a seaport on the Folden fjord in Norway, about 70 miles north of the Arctic Circle.

FRENCH is a village in section 34 of Carlisle Township, six miles west of Fergus Falls, which had a Northern Pacific Railroad station and a post office, 1884–1906; sometimes called French Stub.

FRIBERG TOWNSHIP organized January 6, 1874, was at first called Florence and later Woodland but was renamed June 1, 1874, for the city of Germany, spelled Freiberg, in Saxony. A post office was located on postmaster John Seeba's land in section 34, 1881–91.

GIRARD TOWNSHIP organized March 21, 1882, has a name that is borne by townships and villages or cities in Pennsylvania, Ohio, Illinois, Kansas, and other states, in honor of Stephen Girard (1750–1831) of Philadelphia, a wealthy merchant and philanthropist, founder of Girard College.

GORMAN TOWNSHIP organized September 4, 1873, was named in honor of John O. Gorman, at whose home the first township election was held.

GRAND a post office, January-September 1883; location not found.

GRESHAM a post office, 1883–1905, first located on the land of Charles B. Green, postmaster, in section 14 of Candor Township.

HEINOLA a village in section 6 of Deer Creek Township, was begun in 1873 and named for Matt Heinola, who had a grocery store in his home about 1908. The principal business was the creamery, which opened in 1908 and closed in 1946.

HENNING TOWNSHIP organized July 17, 1878, was at first called East Battle Lake, which was changed August 1, 1884, to the present name, borne also by villages in Illinois and Tennessee. The city of Henning, incorporated September 24, 1887, had several years earlier received this name in honor of John O. Henning, of Hudson, Wis., who during many years was a druggist there and died April 15, 1897. The post office was established in 1881; it had a station of the Northern Pacific and Soo Line railroads.

HEPSY a post office, 1883–85; location not found.

HILLVIEW a village in section 17 of Paddock Township, also known as Red Eye. The post office began as Paddock in 1883 in section 32, changed to Hillview in 1907, and closed in 1914; the site had one block platted, several stores, and a sawmill.

HOBART TOWNSHIP organized July 10, 1871, and its village in sections 1 and 2 on the Northern Pacific Railroad, platted in the spring of 1873, have a name that is borne also by villages and post offices in New York, Indiana, and several other states. The post office was first called New Rose Lake 1871–72, then Hobart, 1872–75, with Nicholas Hendry as postmaster under both names; it had a station of the Northern Pacific Railroad, which was moved in 1874 to the new community at Frazee's Mills, later called New York Mills.

HOFF a post office, 1883–96, located in section 17 of Eagle Lake Township; one block was platted, and a gristmill was built nearby. On November 25, 1890, the post office authorized a name change to Pansey, but the change did not occur.

HOMESTEAD TOWNSHIP organized July 26, 1880, as Runyan, later received this name in allusion to the many homestead farms received by its settlers from the U.S. government.

HOOT LAKE a station of the Northern Pacific Railroad in Buse Township.

INGLEWOOD a village in section 6 of Girard Township, about 1902–21.

INMAN TOWNSHIP organized March 18, 1878, was named in honor of Thomas Inman, a pioneer homesteader from Indiana, noted as a deer hunter, at whose house the first township election was held. A post office, with Inman as postmaster, was located in section 22, 1879–84. Inman was a Baptist minister and served as a captain in the Fourth Minnesota Regiment during the Civil War.

JOHNSON STATION see LUCE.

JOY a post office, 1873–1905, in section 28 of Eastern Township, was established in Douglas County and transferred to Otter Tail County in 1892. The post office was in Francis M. Prettyman's general store and later consolidated with Parkers Prairie.

JOYCE a post office, 1899–1902, located on Otter Tail Lake, 25 miles northeast of Fergus Falls.

KITCHENER a Great Northern Railroad station in section 8 of Oscar Township.

LAKE LIZZIE see DUNVILLA.

LAKE SYBIL a post office, 1880–92, located in section 32 of Hobart Township.

LEAF CITY a village in Leaf Lake Township, six miles east of Otter Tail City, about 1857.

LEAF LAKE TOWNSHIP organized July 22, 1879, was named for its West and East Leaf Lakes, further noticed also for the next township.

LEAF MOUNTAIN TOWNSHIP organized January 7, 1874, was at first called Dovre Fjeld, for the mountainous plateau of that name in Norway. It was renamed March 18, 1874, for its Leaf Hills or "mountains," a belt of conspicuous morainic drift hills, more fully noticed at the end of this chapter. Their aboriginal name, given by Gilfillan as Gaskibugwudjiwe, translated as "Rustling Leaf mountain," was applied alike by the Ojibwe to these drift hills, the two Leaf Lakes, and their outflowing Leaf River, the lakes and river being named from the hills. A post office was in section 16, 1878–1904.

LEAF SIDE a summer resort in section 25 of Leaf Lake Township, platted in 1906 by O. H. Molden for A. D. and Mary E. Peck.

LIDA TOWNSHIP organized March 19, 1879, bears the name of its largest lake, which probably commemorates the wife or daughter of a pioneer settler or of the government surveyor of the sections in this township. On the early state maps published in 1860–70, Lake Lida is incorrectly outlined and named Lake Anna, but it is rightly mapped, with the present name, in the first atlas of Minnesota, 1874. A post office, 1882–1906, was first located in postmaster Henry Moore's store in section 14.

LOOMIS a townsite, was laid out 1871 by the Northern Pacific Railroad at the rapids of Pelican River in honor of Col. John S. Loomis, Northern Pacific land commissioner; Lord Gordon was the proprietor and planned to establish a Scottish colony on 26 sections of land, but it was not developed.

LUCE a village on the Northern Pacific Railroad in section 30 of Gorman Township, was first known as Johnson before being platted in May 1884 for John and Caroline Dinehart, owners of the townsite; it was incorporated June 13, 1905; the incorporation was dissolved by town agreement during the late 1920s. The Northern Pacific Railroad station was also known as Johnson Station. A post office operated 1883–1948.

LYMAN a village in section 8 of Oak Valley Township, began about 1900 with a creamery, a blacksmith, and a post office, 1901–5, in postmaster Arthur Lyman Dickinson's general store.

MAINE TOWNSHIP organized September 5, 1871, was named at the request of R. F. Adley, one of its first settlers, a native of the state of Maine, at whose home the first election of this township was held. The village's first post office in 1875 was in section 23; a later post office, 1877–1909, was in section 14; the site had one block platted by 1882.

MAPLEWOOD a village in section 35 of Sverdrup Township, about 1894.

MAPLEWOOD TOWNSHIP organized July 26, 1880, was then called St. Agnes but was renamed May 2, 1882. The sugar maple is a common or abundant tree throughout nearly all of the forested region of this state.

MARION a townsite in Everts Township, at the southwest end of Otter Tail Lake, was platted in May 1857 by Benjamin Densmore for the Echota and Marion Land Company and incorporated on June 11, 1858, but it failed to develop, and no trace was found.

MILL PARK a milling village in section 31 of Aurdal Township, which had a post office, 1885–1901.

MILLTOWN a village in section 4 of Everts Township, was incorporated on May 23, 1857, but no trace remains.

MONITOR FALLS a post office, 1884–85, located in section 35 of Maine Township, with one store and one block platted.

MYHRE a post office, February-November 1883, with Torston Myhre as postmaster; location not found.

NEW ROSE LAKE see **HOBART**.

NEW YORK MILLS a city in section 8 of Newton Township, was platted on October 12, 1883, and incorporated on May 27, 1884. One of first settlers, Randolph L. Frazee, owned most of townsite land and had a sawmill, which he sold to the New York Mills Company in 1873, moving to the village in Becker County named for him, although later returning to Pelican Rapids. The community expanded with the sawmills built by Dr. Van Aerman, commissioner of pensions in Washington, D.C., and his partners; their company was organized in Olean, N.Y., in 1872 and was called New York Mills for Aerman's home state, a name adopted by the community; the company dissolved in 1882. The Northern Pacific Railroad came in 1871, and the post office was established in 1874. Although Yankees were the first to settle in the city, it was the Finnish immigrants who stayed and developed the community.

NEWTON TOWNSHIP organized March 22, 1877, was at first called New York Mills, which remains as the name of its principal village. The township name was changed July 26, 1883, the present name being adopted for its having the same first syllable as before.

NIDAROS TOWNSHIP organized September 5, 1871, bears an ancient name for the city of Trondhjem in Norway, derived from Nidrosia, its medieval Latin name, which has reference to its situation at the mouth of the River Nid.

NIRVANA a village in section 3 of Nidaros Township and section 34 of Girard Township, on the north shore of Stuart Lake, about 1933.

NORWEGIAN GROVE TOWNSHIP organized January 7, 1873, was settled entirely by people from Norway. The village in sections 9 and 10 had a post office, 1878–1906.

OAK VALLEY TOWNSHIP organized January 2, 1877, is drained northward to the Leaf River by two small streams, named Oak and South Bluff Creeks.

ORWELL TOWNSHIP organized July 27, 1886, had been previously known as West Buse but was then called Liberty, which was changed November 3, 1880, to the present name. This is borne also by townships and villages in Vermont, New York, Pennsylvania, and Ohio. It was adopted here in compliment to Charles D. Wright, who was born in Orwell, Vt., November 8, 1850; came to Minnesota in 1869 and was employed seven years in the office of the U.S. surveyor general in St. Paul; settled in Fergus Falls in 1877; was mayor in 1885 and 1888 and president of the First National Bank, 1882–1912.

OSCAR TOWNSHIP organized July 1, 1873, was named in honor of Oscar II, who was born in Stockholm, January 21, 1829, and was the king of Sweden and Norway from 1872 until his death, December 8, 1907. A post office was in section 32, 1889–1905.

OTTER TAIL CITY the early station on a route of fur traders from St. Paul and Crow Wing to the Red River valley, noted at the beginning of this chapter, was in the area of Otter Tail Township, being for several years the place of the U.S. land office, and later it was the first county seat. The village began about 1870 as a trading post owned by Donald McDonald on the east shore of Otter Tail Lake; it developed with a sawmill, a flour mill, five hotels, 28 saloons, and a number of other businesses, but when the railroad did not come through by 1885, the site became a ghost town.

OTTER TAIL TOWNSHIP organized September 5, 1870, was named like this county, for its largest lake.

OTTERTAIL a city and resort community in Otter Tail Township, developed when the Soo Line came through one mile east of the old Otter Tail City; it was first platted on September 3, 1903, by the Minnesota Loan and Trust Company and was incorporated as a village on May 5, 1904. The post office began in 1858 and was variously misspelled as Otter Tail City or Otter Tail; it had a Northern Pacific Railroad station in section 20.

OTTO TOWNSHIP organized March 22, 1883, was named thus by the county commissioners, who disregarded the request of the petitioners that it be called Lake View. Whether the commissioners intended to honor a pioneer, or derived it from the county name, was not recorded. Eight other states have Otto townships and post offices.

PADDOCK see HILLVIEW.

PADDOCK TOWNSHIP organized March 21, 1882, was named for L. A. Paddock, at whose sawmill the first election was held.

PARKDALE a small village of the Great Northern Railway in section 3, Tumuli, was platted in 1876 as Hazel Dell, which was changed to the present name by an act of the state legislature, February 7, 1878. Its post office operated during three periods from 1877 to 1893 at a site in section 4, with a mill, a store, and a school. A Great Northern Railway station of this name was several miles north in section 19 of Dane Prairie Township.

PARKERS PRAIRIE TOWNSHIP organized January 4, 1870, being then called Jasper, was renamed March 1, 1873, for an early settler on its principal tract of prairie. Its railway village of the same name, platted in the summer of 1880, was incorporated November 17, 1903. The city in section 22 developed around the Soo Line depot built in 1904 located one-half mile north of the original site; its post office was established in 1870.

PARKTON a railway station of the Northern Pacific Railroad in section 5, Inman.

PEARE PRAIRIE a post office, 1879–80, located 40 miles east of Fergus Falls; the 1879–80 business gazetteer spelled it Pease Prairie.

PELICAN LAKE a post office, 1873–1905, located in section 2 of Scambler Township.

PELICAN RAPIDS a city in sections 21, 22, 27, and 28 of Pelican Township, was platted in 1872 where the river descends with rapids over drift boulders and incorporated December 10, 1883. The Ojibwe gave to Lake Lida their name of the pelican, spelled Shada by Henry W. Longfellow's *Song of Hiawatha*, and they applied the same name to the Pelican River from this lake and Lake Lizzie to its junction with the Otter Tail River. W. G. Tuttle, considered its founder, came from New York in 1870 and built a sawmill; O. A. Edward Blyberg, first postmaster from 1872, when it was established, until 1886, first merchant, and first builder of a frame house, was born in Norway in 1850, came to the United States in 1865 and to this community in 1871; he also opened the first drugstore with Frank E. Blodgett; he died in 1921. The vil-

lage had a Great Northern Railway station in section 27.

PELICAN TOWNSHIP organized September 5, 1870, took its name from the Pelican River flowing through it.

PERHAM TOWNSHIP organized March 19, 1872, was then called Marion Lake Township, for the lake adjoining its southwest corner, but March 1, 1877, it was renamed, to be like its village, by an act of the legislature. Josiah Perham, commemorated in this name, was the first president of the Northern Pacific Railroad company, in 1864–65. He was born in Wilton, Maine, in 1803 and died in Boston, Mass., in 1868. Very interesting biographic notes, with narration of his enthusiastic efforts for construction of this transcontinental railway line, are given in Eugene V. Smalley's *History of the Northern Pacific Railroad* (1883, pp. 97–132). Perham, a city in sections 14 and 15, on this railroad, platted March 6, 1873, was incorporated February 14, 1881. Its original townsite was laid out in June 1872 by the Lake Superior and Puget Sound Land Company; the post office began in 1872, with Henry Kemper as postmaster.

PHELPS a village in section 35 of Maine Township, began with a power dam and mill built by William E. Thomas on land he purchased from Mathew Sharp. The mill, located ten miles downstream from Otter Tail Lake on Otter Tail River, opened in 1889 as the Maine Roller Mills. Thomas, born in Wisconsin in 1856, came to this county in 1878, married Liona Phelps (1860–1906), the daughter of Osee and Margaret Phelps, early settlers in Maine Township, served as postmaster during its years of operation, 1891–1909, and died in California in 1941.

PINE LAKE TOWNSHIP organized January 5, 1883, was named for its large Pine Lake, through which the Otter Tail River flows, originally bordered by valuable white pine timber. The three pine species of this state, each common or frequent through northeastern Minnesota, reach the southwestern limit of their geographic range in the east part of this county.

RAMSDELL a post office, 1880–81, located in Oak Valley Township. George Ramsdell settled in section 8 in 1878, built a store in 1880, which housed the post office, with teacher Rufus A. Darling as postmaster, who later became county auditor.

RED EYE see HILLVIEW.

REDINGTON a post office, 1899–1906, located in section 8 of Dead Lake Township; a school one-half mile east also served the community.

RICHDALE the village in section 33 of Pine Lake Township, was platted in September 1899 as a farmers' trading village and was called Richland but was changed to the present name because that name was already used in the state. This village and the next were named in honor of Watson Wellman Rich, civil engineer, who was born in Dayton, N.Y., March 9, 1841, and died in Shanghai, China, January 12, 1903. He served in the Fourth Minnesota Regiment in the Civil War, attaining the rank of captain; engaged in engineering work for several railroad lines in Minnesota and after 1897 was chief consulting engineer of the Imperial Chinese Railway Administration. The village had a Northern Pacific Railroad station, a general store, a cream station, and a potato warehouse; its post office operated 1900–1916.

RICHVILLE in section 17 of Rush Lake Township, platted in the fall of 1903, was incorporated October 25, 1904. Under Richdale, preceding, the origin of this name has been noted. The city developed following the arrival of the Soo Line in 1901; businesses included an elevator, a creamery, and a pickle company; the post office began in 1904 in postmaster Charley A. Friberg's general store.

ROBERTS a village in section 2 of Western Township; it had a post office, 1897–1906.

ROTHSAY a city with Wilkin County.

RUMSEY a post office, 1890–1906, was first in section 16 of Friberg Township, with Hiram P. Rumsey as postmaster, and later in sections 20 and 29.

RUNYAN TOWNSHIP see HOMESTEAD TOWNSHIP.

RUSH LAKE TOWNSHIP organized January 3, 1871, bears the name of its large lake, which is translated from the name given to it by the Ojibwe, used also by them for the Roseau Lake and River. Rush Lake gives its name, in the usage of the Ojibwe, to the part of the Otter Tail River flowing from it to Otter Tail Lake. A post office was located in section 22, 1870–78, with John Doll the first postmaster, succeeded by Henry Kemper, who moved the post office to Perham.

SAGAWNOMA a switching station of the Soo Line, in Otter Tail Township, about 1872.

ST. JOSEPH a village in section 33 of Perham Township.

ST. LAWRENCE a post office, 1886–1906, in section 4 of Rush Lake Township.

ST. OLAF TOWNSHIP organized March 20, 1869, was at first called Oxford but was renamed May 10, 1870, in honor of St. Olaf, born in 995, an early king of Norway, in 1015–30, who consolidated the kingdom and aided the establishment of Christianity but was killed in a battle with his rebellious subjects, July 29, 1030. He is the patron saint of Norway and is regarded by its people as the great champion of national independence. A post office was in section 2, spelled St. Oloff, 1870–94, and St. Olaf, 1894–1904.

SCAMBLER TOWNSHIP organized August 8, 1871, was named for Robert Scambler, a homesteader, at whose house the first township election was held. A post office was in section 15, 1873–79, was changed to Bangor, 1879–89, and was reestablished as Scambler, 1889–91, in section 34.

SOUTHWICK a locality on the 1882 county atlas in section 32 of Sverdrup Township, its post office being Turtle Lake.

SPIRIT LAKE a post office, 1879–1906, in section 4 of Dora Township, was first located in postmaster Ellis L. Thomas's store on his homestead.

SPRING CREEK a site of flour and saw mills, 1875–85, in section 2 of Scambler Township.

SQUIRE a village in section 28 of Aastad Township, with a post office, 1894–1905.

STAR LAKE TOWNSHIP organized January 18, 1880, has a large and remarkably branched Star Lake in its northern part, "which in shape bears a striking resemblance to a star fish." A post office in section 34 opened during three periods between 1880 and 1906; although never platted, it was a stopping place for stagecoaches and travelers between Fergus Falls and Perham.

STOD a post office, 1888–1906, in section 10 of Trondhjem Township.

SUNNYSIDE a locality on the border of Nidaros and Girard Townships.

SVERDRUP TOWNSHIP organized March 18, 1878, was at first called Norman. Because that name had been previously given to another Minnesota township, it was renamed July 17, 1878, in honor of George Sverdrup, president of Augsburg Seminary, Minneapolis. He was born in Balestrand,

Norway, December 16, 1848; was graduated in theology at the University of Norway, 1871; became a professor of Augsburg Seminary in 1874 and its president in 1876; died in Minneapolis, May 3, 1907.

SVERRE a post office in section 11 of Elizabeth Township, 1900–1906.

TANGLEWOOD a locality in section 4 of Everts Township.

TEN MILE LAKE a post office, 1871–72, located in Tumuli Township.

THRONDHEIM a post office, 1878–79, in Trondhjem Township.

TOPELIUS a farmers' trading village in section 25 of Newton, platted in the summer of 1901, was named for Zachris Topelius, although it was erroneously spelled Dopelius for many years, possibly first by the railroad, and later by its post office, 1901–16; other maps use the correct form. Topelius (1818–98) was a distinguished Swedish editor, educator, historian, poet, and novelist of Helsingfors, Finland. The village was first known as Benton's Crossing and then as Amboy (1899).

TORDENSKJOLD TOWNSHIP organized September 8, 1869, as Blooming Grove, was renamed May 10, 1870, in honor of Peder Tordenskjold, a renowned Norwegian admiral in the Danish service. He was born in Trondhjem, Norway, October 28, 1691, and was killed in a duel at Hanover, Germany, November 20, 1720. His original surname was Wessel, and the name of this township, meaning "Thunder Shield," was conferred on him by the king of Denmark as a title of nobility. A post office, sometimes found spelled Tordenskiold, was located in section 30, 1870–1904.

TOWN SITE a country post office first called Woodside, 1878–79, in Woodside Township, was changed to Town Site, 1879–82, with Knud K. Tvete as postmaster under both names; it was located 18 miles from Fergus Falls and 11 miles from Dalton, its nearest railroad point, possibly in Aastad Township.

TRONDHJEM TOWNSHIP organized July 7, 1873, bears the name, meaning "Throne Home," of an ancient city in Norway on the south side of the great Trondhjem fjord, noted for its cathedral, an early burial place for the kings of Norway and in later times the place of their coronation.

TUMULI see DALTON.

TUMULI TOWNSHIP organized September 8, 1869, was then called Union but on May 10, 1870, received this Latin name, meaning "mounds, as of burial," having reference probably to the morainic drift hills in the east part of this township.

TURTLE LAKE see UNDERWOOD.

UNDERWOOD a city in section 32 of Sverdrup, platted in the fall of 1881 and incorporated November 22, 1912, was named in honor of Adoniram Judson Underwood, who was born in Clymer, N.Y., May 26, 1832, and died in Fergus Falls, December 21, 1885. He came to Minnesota in 1854; served in the First Minnesota and other regiments in the Civil War; was a representative in the legislature, 1871–72; settled at Fergus Falls in 1873, and was the founder and editor of the *Journal*, 1873–85. The post office was first called Turtle Lake, 1871–72 and 1876–84, at which time it was changed to Underwood; it had a station of the Northern Pacific Railroad.

URBANK a city in section 30 of Effington Township, was incorporated as a village August 16, 1947; it had a post office, 1903–6.

VERGAS a city in sections 24 and 25 of Candor Township, was platted under the name of Altona in the fall of 1903 and was so incorporated February 23, 1905. Its present name is for one of four in the "V" series used to designate Soo Line sleeping cars that traveled between Minneapolis and Winnipeg, the others being Viking, Venlo, and Venus. The post office began as Candor in 1904, the railroad station was Vergas, and the townsite was Altona, all names changing to Vergas in 1903. A major tourist attraction is the Vergas Loon, a 20-foot-tall replica overlooking Loon Lake, dedicated in 1963 to the memory of the community's third postmaster Edward (Ewald G.) Krueger, who served from 1933 until his death in 1962, a major advocate of a community park opened in 1958.

VIDA a post office in section 4 of Amor Township, 1899–1904.

VINING a city in sections 1, 11, and 12 of Nidaros, platted in the fall of 1882 and incorporated April 26, 1908, has a name, given by officers of the Northern Pacific Railroad company, which is borne also by villages in Georgia, Iowa, and Kansas. The village had a Northern Pacific Railroad station, and the post office began in 1882.

WADENA a city with Wadena County, Otter Tail County's part being in section 1 of Compton Township; the Northern Pacific Railroad station of Wadena Junction is also in section 1.

WALL LAKE a village in section 34 of Aurdal Township, is near the north end of the lake so named for a low and flat-topped gravel ridge, like a wall, on its west side, through which the lake has cut its outlet, leaving a distinct old shoreline at its formerly higher level. The village had a post office, 1870–73 and 1886–1906, and a Northern Pacific Railroad station.

WASEATA see DAYTON.

WEGGELAND a post office, 1897–1909, in section 35 of Friberg Township.

WESTERN organized January 7, 1873, received its name as the most southwestern township in the county. Eastern Township was named similarly, in July 1875, at its southeast corner. The village in section 14 had a post office, 1872–1906, first established in Wilkin County and transferred to Otter Tail County in 1874.

WIMER LAKE a resort village in section 3 of Hobart Township on Wimer Lake, was platted September 11, 1907, by O. G. Molden for landowner Solomon F. Anderson.

WOODLAND a post office, 1888–1910, in section 3 of Corliss Township, which transferred to Becker County.

WOODSIDE see TOWN SITE.

WOODSIDE TOWNSHIP organized January 2, 1877, was then Wrightstown, for several pioneer settlers named Wright, which remains as the name of a hamlet in section 2. The present name of the township was adopted March 22, 1877, referring to its original woodlands and its situation at the east side of the county.

WORDEN a post office, 1892–1906, located in section 22 of Maplewood Township, with Harrison Worden as postmaster.

WRIGHTSTOWN a village in section 2 of Woodside Township, which was never platted but had a store, a church, a town hall, and several homes. The first settler was Edmund Wright, a Baptist minister and surveyor, who came with his family in 1873; John H. Aldrich, born in New York in 1830, came with his family in 1874, built a store in the front room of his house, where he opened the post office in 1875. See also WOODSIDE TOWNSHIP.

Lakes and Streams

The preceding pages have considered the names of Otter Tail Lake and River, the West and East Battle Lakes, the North and South Bluff Creeks, Clitherall Lake, Dead Lake and River, Deer Creek, Eagle Lake, the West and East Leaf Lakes and Leaf River, Lake Lida, Oak Creek, Pelican River, and Pine, Rush, Star, and Wall Lakes.

Pomme de Terre River, receiving its headwaters in the south part of this county, has been previously noted, with derivation of its name, in the chapter for Grant County, which has a township named from it.

Wing River, flowing from southeastern Otter Tail County northward to join the Leaf River in Wadena County, gives its name to a township there, so that it is to be better noticed for that county.

Similarly the Red Eye River, crossing the northeast corner of Otter Tail County, passes a township that bears this name in Wadena County and is to be again mentioned there, with the origin of the name from species of fish in this stream.

Toad River, the outlet of Toad Lake in a township of that name in Becker County, each translated from their Ojibwe name, flows into the north end of Pine Lake.

Only a few other streams remain for notation, as Willow Creek, tributary from Henning to the East Leaf Lake; Belle River, flowing from Eastern Township into Douglas County and there giving the name of Belle River Township; Pelican Creek, which flows from St. Olaf southwest through Pelican Lake Township of Grant County to the Pomme de Terre River; and the headstream of Mustinka River, running south across Aastad into Grant County. The last name is from a Dakota word, *mashtincha*, meaning "a rabbit."

"According to Rev. J. B. Hingeley, there are 1,029 lakes, by actual count, in Otter Tail County, not including sloughs and ponds" (*Geology of Minnesota*, vol. 2, 1888, p. 535). To give a systematic enumeration of such as are named on maps, excepting those on the courses of the Otter Tail and Pelican Rivers, they may well be arranged in the order of the townships from south to north, and of ranges from east to west.

The Otter Tail River, earlier called the Red River as stated at the beginning of this chapter, runs through Rice Lake in Hobart, Mud Lake and Little Pine Lake in the southeast corner of Gorman, Big Pine Lake in the township named for it, Rush and Otter Tail Lakes, Deer Lake in the northwest corner of Everts, East Lost Lake in the northeast corner of Sverdrup, West Lost Lake in Maine Township, and three smaller expansions of the river, called Red River Lake, in sections 25 and 27 to 29, Friberg.

On the Pelican River in this county are Pelican Lake, as it is named by the white people, called by the Ojibwe, in Gilfillan's translation, "the lake with the smooth-shorn prairie coming down to it on one side"; Lake Lizzie, probably commemorating a pioneer woman, possibly the Elizabeth who is honored by the name of a township on this river, but here lacking knowledge of her surname; and Prairie Lake, in Pelican Township, lying in the eastern edge of the great prairie region.

Eastern Township has Lake Annalaide, Long Lake, Lake Mary, Rice Lake, named for its wild rice, and North and South Maple Lakes.

Parkers Prairie Township has Horsehead Lake, Cora Lake and Lake Augusta, Rainy Lake, Lake Adley, and Clarino, Resser, Nelson, and Fish Lakes.

In Effington are Mud Lake, Meyer, Arken, Block, and Stemmer Lakes.

In Leaf Mountain Township are Lake Jessie, Lake George, Toms Lake, Johnson, Samson, and Spitzer Lakes.

In Eagle Lake Township, besides the lake of that name are Middle and Torgerson Lakes; Lake Jolly Ann is crossed by its west line.

St. Olaf Township has Long Lake, Lakes Johannes, Johnson, Lacy, and Sewell, Vinge Lake, and Sonmer Lake.

In Tumuli the Pomme de Terre River runs through Rose and Ten Mile Lakes, the second being the largest of this township, which also has Clear Lake, Hansel Lake, and Mineral and Alkali Lakes. The last two are sometimes reduced to mostly dry lake beds, with alkaline crystals resulting from evaporation. Ten Mile Lake tells, by its name, the distance on an old Indian trail from the lake to the crossing of the Otter Tail River.

Aastad has Mud Lake in sections 23 and 24.

Western Township has Upper Lightning Lake, more than three miles long, lying about four to seven miles northwest from Lightning Lake of the Mustinka River in Grant County. The chapter of that county has comments on the origin of these names.

Elmo Township has Wing River Lake.

In Nidaros are Stuart, Bredeson, Siverson, Johnson, and Belmont Lakes; Bullhead Lake, having the small species of catfish known by this name, also called the horned pout; and the northeast end of Clitherall Lake.

In Clitherall Township, besides the large lake of this name and the southwest edge of West Battle Lake, are Crane Lake and Lake Lundeberg.

Tordenskjold has German and Dane Lakes, named from the nationality of their first settlers, and Fiske, Tamarack, Long, Volen, Black, Stalker, and Sugar Lakes.

In Dane Prairie Township, with Wall Lake, before noted for the railway station so named, are Stang Lake, Rosvold and Larson Lakes, Indian Lake, Bronseth, Fossen, Lye, and Swan Lakes.

Buse Township has One Mile Lake, at the southeast edge of Fergus Falls, Pebble, Horseshoe, and Iverson Lakes. In the southeast part of the city area of Fergus Falls, originally belonging to this township, are Lake Charles and Grotto Lake.

Orwell has Rush Lake in section 12, and Orwell Lake, which is a wide part of the Otter Tail River.

Henning has East Battle Lake, which lies partly in that township.

Girard, with the East and West Battle Lakes, has Beauty Shore Lake, Mason, Tamarack, and Hanson Lakes, and Lakes Emma and Ethel.

In the eastern edge of Everts, the outlet of West Battle Lake flows through the Molly Stark Lake, Annie Battle Lake, and Lake Blanche, the first being named for the wife of John Stark, a noted general of the Revolutionary War, who won the victory of Bennington, August 16, 1777. In the west part of this township are Elbow Lake, the two Silver Lakes, and Round and Deer Lakes.

Sverdrup has the South and North Turtle Lakes, Bass Lake, Lake Onstad, Norway Lake, Crooked and Horseshoe Lakes, East Lost Lake, Lake John, Anna and Little Anna Lakes, and Pleasant Lake.

Aurdal has Loon, Mud, and Nelson Lakes, Little Lake, and Spring and Fish Lakes.

Fergus Falls Township has Lake Alice in the city area, Opperman and Hoot Lakes, nearly adjoining the city, and Wedell Lake in section 6.

Carlisle has Johnson and Fjestad Lakes and Oscar Lake, crossed by its north line and extending into Oscar Township, and also Skogen Marsh.

Leaf Lake Township, in addition to the East and West Leaf Lakes, whence it is named, has Grass Lake in section 19, and Portage Lake, to which the traders and canoemen made a portage from the West Leaf Lake on their route to the Red River valley.

Otter Tail Township, with the west part of Portage Lake and the northeastern half of Otter Tail Lake, has Lake Buchanan, named by Maj. Clitherall in honor of Pres. James Buchanan (1791–1868), two Long Lakes, respectively northwest and southeast of the old Otter Tail City, Donalds Lake, Gourd Lake, named for its curved outline, with a strait connecting its larger and smaller parts, and Pickerel and Round Lakes.

Amor has Walker Lake, through which Dead River flows, close above its mouth, Mud Lake, and the eastern one of the Twin Lakes.

Maine Township has the western Twin Lake, Pickerel and Peterson Lakes, Leon Lake, and the West Lost Lake, the last being on the course of the Otter Tail River.

Elizabeth Township has Long Lake, Reed and Zimmerman Lakes, Lakes Jewett and Mason and Devils Lake.

Oscar Township has Oscar Lake, which commemorates King Oscar II, like this township. Its southern part, lying in Carlisle, has an island of 29 acres.

Otto Township has the east half of the large Rush Lake, which gave its name to a township.

In Rush Lake Township, besides the west half of the lake so named, are Round and Head Lakes, the greater eastern part of Marion Lake, and Rice and Boedigheimer Lakes, the last two being on the outlet of Marion Lake.

In Dead Lake Township are the eastern part of that large lake and the west part of Marion Lake.

Star Lake Township, with the great and triply branched Star Lake, includes a major part of the western body of Dead Lake and much of Mud

Lake, both being crossed by the south line of the township.

Maplewood Township has Beers Lake, Twin and Crystal Lakes, and Lake 21, named from its section.

Erhards Grove Township has Sandberg and Grandrud Lake and Lake Knobel.

Pine Lake Township has the Big Pine Lake.

Perham has the southern parts of Little Pine Lake and Mud Lake, also the southeast part of Devils Lake, each of which reaches north into Gorman.

In Edna Township are the Big and Little McDonald Lakes, Pickerel, Rice, Wolf, Paul, Ceynowa, Moenkedick, Grunard, Wendt, and Mink Lakes, with a part of Lake Sybil in the north edge of sections 5 and 6.

Dora Township has the western continuation of Lake Sybil, the south half of Loon Lake, which reaches north into Candor, and Spirit Lake, these being in its northern half, and the two long Silent Lakes on its southern border.

Lida Township has the large Lakes Lida and Lizzie, before noted.

In Pelican Township is Prairie Lake, the lowest through which the Pelican River flows.

Norwegian Grove Township has Grove Lake at its northeast corner, reaching northeastward into Scambler and Pelican, and having a grove on its large island, which is mostly in section 1 of this township; also Lakes Alfred, Olaf, Jacob, and Annie.

Paddock, the most northeastern township, has Mud Lake, one of our most abundant names, likely to be given to any lake with mainly muddy shores.

Butler has Bear and Edna Lakes, each crossed by its west line.

Corliss, with parts of the two lakes last noted and also parts of Big and Little Pine Lakes, has also Indian Lake in its sections 8 and 9.

Gorman, in addition to the three lakes on its south side, reaching into Perham, as already mentioned, has a small Dead Lake in section 1, and Silver Lake in sections 6 and 7.

In Hobart are Gray and Keyes Lakes, Rice Lake on the Otter Tail River, Graham, Wimer, and Fairy Lakes, Five and Six Lakes, named from their being in sections 5 and 6, Scalp Lake, and Rose, Jim, and Long Lakes.

Candor Township has Sauer Lake, crossed by its north line, Cooks and Schram Lakes, Hand Lake and T Lake, named from their outlines, and Leek, Lawrence, Hook, and Otter Lakes.

Dunn Township, with the northwest part of Lake Lizzie, Pelican Lake, and Little Pelican Lake, which are on the Pelican River, has also Lake Emma, Elbow Lake, and Franklin Lake.

Scambler, with the west part of Pelican Lake, has Tamarack and Sand Lakes, Lake Harrison, Ranklev, Pete, and Grove Lakes. The last has been earlier mentioned for its reaching southwest into Norwegian Grove Township.

In general, only the rivers and a few large lakes retain names used by the Indians, or translations from them. Nearly all the other names, of townships, villages, and lakes, numbering hundreds in this very large county, were selected or invented by the incoming white agricultural settlers.

Hills of the Marginal Moraines

In the series of 12 marginal moraines of the continental ice sheet mapped for parts of their courses across Minnesota, the eighth and ninth are very prominently developed in this county, being thence named respectively the Fergus Falls and Leaf Hills Moraines. These belts of drift hills extend in a semicircle from Fergus Falls southeast to the south line of the county and thence east and northeast to East Leaf Lake, a distance of 50 miles. Through five townships, Tordenskjold, St. Olaf, Eagle Lake, Leaf Mountain, and Effington, the two moraines are merged together and form a range 5 to 3 miles wide, composed of very irregular, roughly outlined hills, 100 to 300 feet high, commonly called the Leaf Mountains. This is a translation from the Ojibwe, as was noted for Leaf Mountain Township, and they also applied their name of the hills to the Leaf Lakes and River. The common designation as "mountains" has currency because they are the only hills in this part of Minnesota that are conspicuously seen at any great distance. In the highest portions they rise 200 to 350 feet above the adjoining country, which is itself deeply covered with drift (*Geology of Minnesota, Final Report*, vol. 2, 1888, pp. 544–51).

From the crests of the Leaf Hills, extensive views are obtained northward over the greater part of this county and southward across Douglas and Grant Counties, but the separate hills, of which there are many supplying such wide and grand views, have not received names on maps.

Indian Hill, in section 9, Oscar, near the middle of the west side of this county, has a fine outlook eastward upon that part of the Fergus Falls Moraine, and at the west it overlooks the plain of Wilkin County, which was the bed of the Glacial Lake Agassiz, stretching with a slight descent 20 miles to the Red River.

State Parks

Maplewood State Park was established on the south end of Lake Lida in 1963 in response to the need for recreational opportunities in a large region of the state. This a large area of hilly, lake-dotted land, which contained some working farms, rural schools, and churches, was judged more suited to recreation than to farming.

Glendalough State Park consists of land that was a summer retreat and private game farm from 1903 to 1990, when the Cowles Media Company donated it to the Nature Conservancy, which deeded it to the state in 1992. The park contains Molly Stark and Annie Battle Lakes; the latter is designated as a "heritage fishery" on which no motors or electronic equipment are allowed.

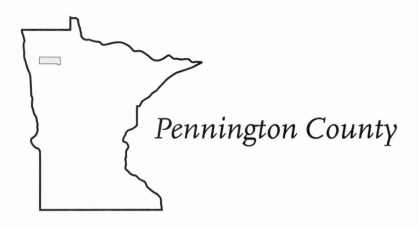

Pennington County

This county, established November 23, 1910, was named in honor of Edmund Pennington of Minneapolis. He was born in La Salle, Ill., September 16, 1848; began his life work in railroad service in 1869; was since 1888 successively superintendent, general manager, and vice-president of the Minneapolis, St. Paul and Sault Ste. Marie Railroad (Soo Line), and from 1909 was its president. From 1858 to 1896 this area was included in Polk County, and from 1896 to 1910 it was a part of Red Lake County.

Information of geographic names in Pennington County was received from Edward L. Healy, real estate dealer, of Red Lake Falls, interviewed during a visit there in August 1909; and from Harry E. Ives, clerk of the court, Lars Backe, former mayor, and Joseph Johnson, each of Thief River Falls, the county seat, interviewed there in September 1916.

All post offices created before 1910 were established in Red Lake County.

AANSTAD a village in Goodridge Township, about 1915.

ANTON a village in section 10 of Smiley Township, circa 1911, noted as a post office although not listed in the post office directory; it had a school and a cemetery.

BLACK RIVER TOWNSHIP slopes mostly southwestward, sending its drainage to the stream of this name, given on Joseph N. Nicollet's map in 1843, which alludes to its dark water, stained by the peaty soil of some parts of its course.

BRAY TOWNSHIP was named in honor of Damase Simon Bray, one of its pioneer farmers. He was born at Cedars, near Montreal, Canada, March 17, 1828; came to Minnesota in 1880, settling on a homestead in this township, as it was later organized; removed to Red Lake Falls, 1886; and died there, September 24, 1908. The village of Bray was in section 25 about 1914–30.

BRUNKEBERG a post office, 1905–11, located in section 36 of Cloverleaf Township.

CLOVER LEAF TOWNSHIP was named for its white clover, growing abundantly in many places beside roads and on pastured lands.

DAKOTA JUNCTION a station of the Soo Line in section 16 of North Township.

DEER PARK TOWNSHIP was a favorite hunting ground for deer.

ERIE a village in section 13 of Highlanding Township and section 18 of Star Township. Erie post office, 1905–38, first located in section 24 in Highlanding Township, was named by Alexander F. Lattimore, who came from near Erie, Pa. He was owner and editor of the *Eleven Towns*, a newspaper especially representing a group of 11 townships in the eastern part of this county, formerly in the Red Lake Reservation but opened to white settlers June 20, 1906. Lattimore served as first postmaster; the post office was moved in 1915 to section 13 with Edward Singer, postmaster, until it was discontinued.

GOODRIDGE TOWNSHIP and its city, in section 21, are named for a broad but very low ridge, only a few feet above the adjoining areas at each side, which reaches from the village about four miles southeastward. The city was incorporated as a village on August 19, 1915; it developed when the Minnesota and Northwestern Railway came in 1914 and was platted that year by Northern Townsite Company. Jay Payne was the first mayor; Payne and his wife, Jennie Noble Payne, came to Cloverleaf Township in 1905, purchasing a stone and lumber claim, then moved to Goodridge in 1915; Jennie Payne was born in New York in 1875, came to Minnesota in 1890, and was postmaster for 19 years beginning when the post office was established in 1915.

HAZEL is a village in sections 1 and 2, River Falls; it had a station of the Soo Line; the post office operated 1904–54. Two species of hazel, much sought by children and squirrels for their excellent nuts, are generally common in this county and throughout northern Minnesota.

HICKORY TOWNSHIP the most southeastern in the county, is at or near the northwestern limit of the swamp hickory, or bitternut. This species furnished nearly all the hoop-poles for flour barrels cut in the southern and central parts of the state. According to the 1976 county history, Christine Olson submitted the name because she thought she had hickory trees in her yard; however, there were no hickory trees in the entire township; her husband, Julius Olson, was postmaster of Rudell.

HIGHLANDING TOWNSHIP and its village High Landing, at the corner of sections 10, 21, 28, and 29, on the north bank of the Red Lake River, are named from the relatively high ground there adjoining the stream, which made this a favorable place for the landing of steamboats on their passage between Thief River Falls and Red Lake. The village had a creamery, several stores, a church, and a school; the post office operated 1905–14, with Thomas Jacobson as postmaster. Jacobson was born in Wisconsin in 1869, came to the township in 1904, homesteading in section 29; he was a farmer, a cattle breeder, township clerk, and justice of the peace.

HILDA a post office, 1905–15, in section 6 of Hickory Township, in the general store of Olaf Hanson and named for his wife, Hilda Clemenson Hanson. The post office was a stopping place for riverboats to and from Thief River Falls; Hanson operated a steamboat and owned the only sawmill in the township, located on the north side of the Red Lake River.

HOMME a post office, 1913–15, in section 27 of Hickory Township; postmaster Halvor G. Homme was born in Norway in 1849, farmed in Echo, Yellow Medicine County, before moving to this township in 1912; he returned to Echo in 1916, where he died in 1929.

KOKESH see NEPTUNE.

KRATKA TOWNSHIP and village beside Red Lake River, were named in honor of Frank H. Kratka, an early merchant of this county. He was born at Sugar Island, Wis., May 21, 1850; settled in 1884 at the site of Thief River Falls, then called Rockstad as a trading post for the Ojibwe of the adjacent Red Lake Reservation; learned their language and was an interpreter; was the first postmaster of Thief River Falls, in 1887–88, when the village was platted and named; was its president in 1891 and 1893, the first mayor after its incorporation as a city, 1896–97, and again in 1902–3; likewise for a second time was the postmaster, 1907–14; removed to Pasadena, Calif., where he died January 27, 1915. The Ojibwe called him Ogema, meaning a chief, but in 1896 he opposed an endeavor to rename this city as Ogema Falls.

A post office was first located in section 22, 1904–28, in Carl Jensen's general store; when Stephen Singer purchased the store in 1907, he moved it and the post office to section 15, where it remained until it closed.

KUEHNEL a post office, 1905–13, was first located in section 20 of Highlanding Township with Miss Auguste Kuehnel as postmaster; in 1907 Peter Wold was named postmaster and moved the office to section 19.

LIEGAARD a post office, 1913–14, in section 4 of Hickory Township, with Lars Lee, postmaster.

MALONE a post office in section 12 of Mayfield Township, 1907–15; it was also known as Austad while Grunde Austad was postmaster, 1907–12.

MAVIE a village in sections 20 and 21 of Cloverleaf Township, was platted originally in 1914 on

11 acres in section 21 by Northwestern Townsite Company; it had an elevator, stores, a bank, a hotel, a livery, and a depot of the Soo Line. The post office, 1907–44, was first located on Charles P. Quist's farm in section 25 of Silverton Township and named for his daughter's nickname; the post office moved to section 31 of Cloverton Township in 1910 and moved again in 1914 to section 21 when the site was platted.

MAYFIELD TOWNSHIP was named in honor of A. C. Mayfield, who was one of its early homesteaders, coming from Wisconsin.

NEPTUNE a post office, 1909–32, was located in Hickory Township; it was first in section 2 and then moved to section 12 in 1910. First postmaster Archibald D. Brown was born in New Brunswick, moved to Virginia, Minn., where he was a carpenter and later police chief, and came to Hickory Township in 1904, where he homesteaded and built the schoolhouse; he applied for the post office under the name Kokosh, which was used for only a few months; Brown died in 1921.

NORDEN TOWNSHIP at the north side successively of Polk, Red Lake, and Pennington Counties, received this name, meaning northern, from the languages of its Norwegian and Swedish settlers.

NORTH TOWNSHIP next east of Norden, is named similarly for its location and for its including the most northern part of the Red Lake River, at the city of Thief River Falls.

NUMEDAL TOWNSHIP bears the name of a river in Norway and of the series of farms and pasture lands along its valley.

POLK CENTER TOWNSHIP the most southwestern in this county, was named for its situation near the center of the original area of Polk County.

RADNY a village in section 11 of Deer Park Township; the post office operated 1905–10 in section 10 while still part of Red Lake County, with John L. Radniecki, for whom it was named, as postmaster. Radniecki was born in Poland in 1883, came to the United States in 1886 and to Minnesota in 1903; he was the first storekeeper, postmaster, and president of the telephone company; he died in 1970.

REINER TOWNSHIP was named in compliment for Reinhart Johnsrud, who later was the township treasurer. A post office was in section 27,

1905–30, with Reinhart Johnsrud as postmaster.

RHODA a post office, 1905–30, in section 17 of Deer Park Township, which was also known as Singer when general store owner Edward Singer was named first postmaster.

RIVER FALLS TOWNSHIP has rapids of the Red Lake River, flowing over glacial drift boulders, at St. Hilaire village, and in other parts of its course through this township.

ROCKSBURY TOWNSHIP was named in honor of Martin Rockstad, one of its first settlers, whose homestead farm in section 4 nearly adjoined Thief River Falls.

ROCKSTAD more exactly bearing Martin Rockstad's name, was the earliest post office in Rocksbury Township, established in 1881 with Rockstad as postmaster at a trading station in or near the south edge of the present city area, as before mentioned in the notice for Kratka Township. Rockstad came from Wisconsin in 1880 and died in 1946 at age 99. The post office operated until 1891.

RUDELL a post office, 1905–22, was located in section 19 of Hickory Township, with Julius Olson as postmaster the entire time at his country store; Olson submitted the name Dellerud, for his home in Sweden; when the name was not accepted by the post office department, he reversed the syllables.

ST. HILAIRE a city in section 6 of River Falls Township, on the west side of the Red Lake River in the northwest corner of River Falls, was platted in 1882 and incorporated as a village on July 4, 1883. It had a station of the Great Northern Railway; the former railway branch from Crookston to St. Hilaire began its regular train service on July 4, 1883. There are three versions of the city's naming: first, a Frenchman named St. Hilaire lived in a shack near the river, selling items like gunpowder and tobacco, and when an item was needed, residents would "go to St. Hilaire" for it, and the name stuck; second, in 1882, a Frenchman named Arthur Yvernault bought land on which the townsite was then platted and named it for his hometown in France; third, and most likely, it was named by Hon. Frank Ives for the French statesman and author Jules Barthélemy-Saint-Hilaire, who was born in Paris, August 19, 1805, and died November 24, 1895. Ives was the postmaster when the post office began in 1882 while still part of Polk County.

SANDERS TOWNSHIP was named in compliment for Sander Engebretson, a native of Hallingdal, Norway, who was one of its pioneer farmers.

SILVERTON TOWNSHIP received this euphonious name by vote of its people. It is near the eastern limit of the silverberry, a shrub having whitish leaves and bearing edible berries of the same silvery color, common along the Red River valley and thence far westward. A village with a station of the Soo Line was in section 21 about 1914–38.

SMILEY TOWNSHIP was named in honor of William C. Smiley, who in 1904 was the county surveyor of Red Lake County and afterwards practiced law in St. Paul.

STAR TOWNSHIP for which the name Zenith had been proposed by Joseph Johnson, received its name by vote of its people, who thought Zenith difficult to pronounce. It has reference to the polar, or north, star, in the French language "L'Etoile du Nord" of the state seal, whence Minnesota is popularly called "the North Star State."

SUNBEAM a post office in section 29 in Highlanding Township, 1905–19, was named by William G. Hunt, publisher of its local newspaper, which has the same name; Hunt was postmaster during all the post office's years of operation.

THIEF RIVER FALLS a city in North and Rocksbury Township and the county seat, was platted as a village in 1887 and was incorporated as a city September 15, 1896. A post office named Thief River operated February-May 1884 while still part of Polk County and was then reestablished in 1891 when the Rockstad post office moved here. The city was a former terminus for the Great Northern and Soo Line railroads. The Red Lake River within the city area originally flowed in rapids over boulders. Above the present dam, which has a head of 15 feet, supplying valuable water power, this river is navigable by steamboats to Red Lake. On the northeast side of the city it receives Thief River, which is translated from the Ojibwe name, noted by Rev. Joseph A. Gilfillan as "Kimod akiwi zibi, the Stolen Land river or Thieving Land river." The map of Maj. Stephen H. Long's expedition, in 1823, and Nicollet's map, published in 1843, give the present name.

William W. Warren's *History of the Ojibway People* (MHS Collections 5) explains the origin of this name and notes its true translation, as it was at first used. "For a number of years, on the headwaters of Thief river . . . a camp of ten Dakota lodges succeeded in holding the country by evading or escaping the search of the Ojibwe war parties. Here, loath to leave their rich hunting grounds, they lived from year to year in continual dread of an attack from their conquering foes. They built a high embankment of earth, for defense, around their lodges, and took every means in their power to escape the notice of the Ojibwe—even discarding the use of the gun on account of its loud report, and using the primitive bow and arrows, in killing such game as they needed. They were, however, at last discovered by their enemies. The Crees and Assiniboines, during a short peace which they made with the Dakotas, learned of their existence and locality, and, informing the Ojibwe, a war party was raised, who went in search of them. They were discovered encamped within their earthen enclosure, and after a brave but unavailing defense with their bows and arrows, the ten lodges, with their inmates, were entirely destroyed." From the Dakota earthwork, constructed for concealment and defense, the Ojibwe gave to the stream its early name, meaning "Secret Earth river," as translated by Warren, in allusion to the hiding and protecting earth embankment. Through erroneous pronunciation of the name, however, with a misunderstanding of its intended significance, the French and English fur traders, and afterward also the Ojibwe, changed it to "Stealing Earth river," and thence to Thief River. The same name is applied by the Ojibwe to Thief Lake, the head of this stream, the lake and nearly all the course of the river being in Marshall County.

TORGERSON a post office in section 29, Reiner, 1909–15, was named for Mikkel Torgerson, a homestead farmer, who was the first clerk of this township.

TWEET a post office, 1887–1906, located in section 29 of Norden Township, was named for Jacob Tweet, who came from Norway in 1888, settling on a farm seven miles west of Thief River Falls. Justus L. Johnson was postmaster 1887–89, at which time Ole J. Tweet, son of Jacob, was appointed postmaster, operating the office in his home, which had a general store and a creamery station. A log school across the road was established for Norwegian-speaking children of the area.

WYANDOTTE TOWNSHIP bears the aboriginal name of a confederation of four Iroquoian tribes, called Hurons by the French, who lived in the part of Canada southeast of Lake Huron and the Georgian Bay. It is also the name of counties in Ohio, Michigan, and Kansas. In the year 1655, Huron and Ottawa exiles, driven from their homes by raids of the Iroquois, accompanied Médard Chouart, sieur de Groseilliers, and Pierre E. Radisson to Prairie Island of the Mississippi on the southeast boundary of the present state of Minnesota. It had a post office, 1895–1905, in section 23.

Rivers

Black River and Thief River have been noted in the preceding pages for the township and city named for them.

Red Lake and the streams to which its name is given, Red Lake River, crossing this county, and the Red River on the west boundary of the state, are considered in the first chapter, which treats of lakes and rivers that belong partly to several counties, and they are again somewhat fully noticed in the chapter of Red Lake County.

The glacial and modified drift in Pennington County, and the relatively thin lacustrine and alluvial beds that in some parts of this area cover the drift, were spread very evenly on the bed of the Glacial Lake Agassiz, so that the surface has no hollows holding lakes.

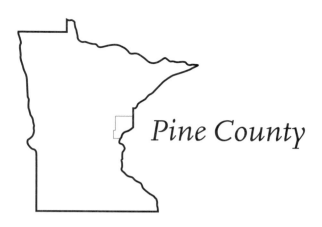

Pine County

Established March 1, 1856, and organized in 1872, this county was named with reference to the extensive pineries of white and red (Norway) pine in various parts of this district, since much worked and practically all cut off by lumbermen. Perhaps also this name was adopted partly for the Pine Lakes and River, here tributary from the west to the Kettle River. Pine City, the county seat, received its name from that of the county and also from the adjacent Ojibwe village, Chengwatana.

Minnesota has three pine species, each limited to its northeastern part. The white pine is commercially the most valuable for its excellent lumber; the red pine, more commonly but wrongly called the Norway pine, is plentiful in many large tracts, preferring a more sandy soil, and is nearly as much esteemed for its lumber as the foregoing; and the jack pine, of smaller size, grows on areas of yet more sandy and gravelly soil, being least valued for lumber and commonly utilized only as fuel.

Information of names in Pine County has been gathered from Fifty Years in the Northwest *by William H. C. Folsom, 1888, having pp. 260–85 for this county; and from W. H. Hamlin, county auditor, and Robert Wilcox, judge of probate, interviewed during a visit at Pine City, the county seat, in May 1916.*

ALHAMBRA see CHENGWATANA.

ARLONE TOWNSHIP organized May 15, 1911, was named in honor of Lois Arlone Hamlin, daughter of the county auditor.

ARNA TOWNSHIP organized March 7, 1910, has a name proposed by W. H. Hamlin, county auditor, not known in use elsewhere, either as a personal or place name.

ASKOV a city in sections 19, 20, 29, and 30 of Partridge Township, was incorporated as a village on April 25, 1918, and separated from the township on April 8, 1921. It was founded by the Danish Peoples Society in 1906; the name is of ancient origin meaning "ash wood" and is the name of Denmark's largest folk high school. Most of the village was destroyed in the 1894 Hinckley fire. It had a Great Northern Railway station, and its post office began as Partridge, 1889–1909, before changing to Askov.

BANNING is a settlement in section 34, Finlayson, having sandstone quarries beside the Kettle River. It was named in honor of William L. Banning, who was born in Wilmington, Del., January 1814; settled in St. Paul, Minn., 1855, and engaged in banking; served in the Third Minnesota Regiment in the Civil War; afterward was a contractor in railroad construction; died in St. Paul, November 26, 1893. The settlement was first called Quarry Village when the spur line from Miller Station (Groningen) was built in 1891–92 by the St. Paul and Duluth Railroad, the contractor being Banning. It was platted by quarryman and first postmaster Martin Ring, who renamed it for

Banning. The village was almost gone by 1912, along with its post office, 1896–1912.

BARRY TOWNSHIP organized January 8, 1902, was named in honor of Edward Barry, a heroic engineer of the Great Northern Railway train that rescued nearly 500 people of Hinckley and its vicinity from death in a great forest fire, September 1, 1894, carrying them to West Superior, when the villages of Hinckley and Sandstone were burned (*Memorials of the Minnesota Forest Fires* by Rev. William Wilkinson, 1895, pp. 127–87). The township was originally organized on September 30, 1901, as Arthur in honor of President Chester A. Arthur but was changed as a township of that name already existed in the state.

BELDEN a lumbering and pulpwood village in section 1 of Belden Township, 16 miles north of Markville, was established on the Minneapolis, St. Paul and Sault Ste. Marie Railroad (Soo Line) in 1912 and incorporated as a village on September 14, 1921. It had a store, several businesses, and a post office, 1913–43; the village was disincorporated and auctioned off in November 1943, most buildings being removed from the site.

BELDEN TOWNSHIP organized July 11, 1921, was named for Grace Belden, who worked in the Tri-State Land Office in Minneapolis; the township became part of New Dosey in 1949.

BELKNAP see GRONINGEN.

BERGMAN see TUXEDO.

BEROUN a village in section 34 of Mission Creek Township, six miles north of Pine City, was named by Joseph Chalupsky for a location in his native Czechoslovakia and translated to mean "an official or other important person." Chalupsky came to the township in 1896 with four sons and five daughters, built the first general store in 1899 and a sawmill, and platted the townsite, which also had a cheese factory, a pickle factory, a brewery, a creamery, and a Northern Pacific Railroad station; the post office began in 1895. See also BROWNS HILL.

BIG SPRING a village in section 15 of Hinckley Township, about 1874.

BIRCH CREEK TOWNSHIP organized July 13, 1896, the most northwestern in this county, was named for the creek that flows through it, tributary to the Kettle River. The township was first called Swede Park, but the name was changed at the first election on August 1, 1896.

BLOMSKOG a locality in Windemere Township established in 1897 by a Swedish Lutheran congregation, who named it for a parish of that name in Värmland.

BREMEN TOWNSHIP organized January 2, 1906, was named by its German settlers for the city of Bremen in Germany.

BROOK PARK TOWNSHIP organized April 18, 1894, and the city in sections 15 and 22 have a euphonious name suggested by Dr. C. A. Kelsey, who envisioned a parklike setting along Pokegama Creek. The city was incorporated as a village on October 1, 1919, and separated from the township on March 3, 1920. The village began about 1874 with a lumber camp on the site called Pokegama and had a station of the Great Northern Railway. After the Hinckley fire of 1894 destroyed all the buildings, the village was rebuilt with a number of stores and businesses and named Brook Park after the township, although the post office form of the name was Brookpark from 1894 to 1950, at which time the present name was adopted.

BROWNS HILL a village in sections 3 and 4 of Pokegama Township and sections 33 and 34 of Mission Creek Township, which may have been an early site of Beroun.

BRUNO TOWNSHIP organized May 11, 1903, and the city in section 19 were named in honor of an early hotel owner there. The township was formerly named Mansfield, but the name was changed as another township in the state already had that name. The city was incorporated as a village on August 29, 1903; the original townsite in section 19 was owned and platted by Fitzhugh Burns. The Eastern Railway Company of Minnesota station was known as Mansfield Station in 1887; the post office began in 1896. Because many of the early settlers were from Czechoslovakia, the city may also have been named for Brno, a village in the Czech Republic.

CENTRAL STATION see HINCKLEY.

CHENGWATANA TOWNSHIP organized March 2, 1874, bears an Ojibwe name, stated by Folsom to be formed by the words meaning "pine" and "city," which are spelled *jingwak* and *odena* in Frederic Baraga's *A Dictionary of the Ojibway Language*. It was the name of "an Indian village which from time immemorial had been located near the mouth of Cross Lake. This locality had long been a rallying point for Indians and traders."

The village of Chengwatana in section 26 was originally platted in 1856 as Alhambra by Judd, Walker and Company and Daniel G. Robertson, but the plans and name were not well accepted; it was named as the first county seat when the county was established in 1856 until established at Pine City in 1870. The village was garrisoned as a frontier military post, 1862–63. The post office began as Snake River Dam in Chisago County (March-May 1856), transferred to Pine County as Alhambra, 1856–57, and as Chengwatana, 1857–73.

CLINT a post office, 1900–1902, in section 29 of Royalton Township at an area developed by Swedish immigrants and named with the Swedish word *klint*, meaning "hill," for its location on a hill; the site had a store, a sawmill, and a cemetery.

CLOVER TOWNSHIP organized April 25, 1905, was named for its profuse growth of the cultivated red clover in fields and of the native white clover in pastures and beside roads, both giving evidence of a rich clayey soil.

CLOVERDALE a village in section 22 of Arlone Township, which began as Turpville, named for the turpentine industry operated in 1903–4 by the Capilovich brothers and renamed about 1921 for both the wild and cultivated clover in the area.

CLOVERTON a village in section 35 of Dosey Township, five miles north of Markville, organized about 1917 and named for the vast growth of wild clover in the area and for the Iowa corporation Red Clover Land Company, which owned half of the township in 1916; the Soo Line came through in 1911, and a post office operated 1912–72.

CROSBY organized July 13, 1908, was named in honor of Ira Crosby, a pioneer farmer in this township.

CROSSROADS an Ojibwe village in section 2 of Ogema Township.

DANEWOOD a settlement by a group of Danish immigrants in southwest Royalton Township, existing in the late 1890s.

DANFORTH was named for N. H. Danforth of Sandstone, a landowner in this township, who removed to the state of Washington. The township was established as Crooked Creek March 15, 1904, was changed to Dexter on May 24, 1904, and changed to Danforth on July 11, 1904.

DELL GROVE TOWNSHIP organized October 11, 1895, was named for the valley of Grindstone Lake and the North Branch of Grindstone River and for its groves of pines, which were burned by the forest fires in September 1894.

DENHAM a city in section 24 of Birch Creek Township, established in 1908 and incorporated as a village on February 28, 1939, was named for an employee of the Soo Line. The post office began in 1909, becoming a community post office in 1974.

DOSEY TOWNSHIP organized June 7, 1909, was named in honor of Julius Dosey, a former lumberman there, who in 1916 was the mayor of Pine City. The township became part of New Dosey in 1949.

DUQUETTE a village in section 24 of Kerrick Township, was built on an early Indian village site; the first settlers were French Canadians, among them Frank Duquette, who built a sawmill and store. The village was named Kerrick until the Great Northern Railway depot was moved three miles south, keeping that name, and for a period Duquette was called Old Kerrick, the new site being called New Kerrick; the names were corrected when the Duquette post office was established in 1905.

DUXBURY a village in Wilma Township, originally platted in section 15 two miles east of the present townsite in sections 8, 9, 16, and 17. The early site was picked in anticipation of the railroad, which did not come. The village was named for Frank R. Duxbury, a large landholder, who came to the township before 1910 from southeastern Minnesota. The post office operated 1915–26.

EAGLEHEAD a post office, 1911–17, located in section 7 of Wilma Township.

ELLSON a village in sections 4 and 9 of Bremen Township, was established about 1895 as a lumber community; it had a sawmill and halfway house and store owned by Edwin C. Ellson, Sr., who was also the postmaster; the post office operated 1904–25.

FINLAYSON TOWNSHIP organized October 22, 1895, and the city in Finlayson and Pine Lake Townships were named in honor of David Finlayson, the former proprietor of a sawmill in this village. The city was incorporated as a village on August 24, 1905; it had a station of the Northern Pacific Railroad, a sawmill, a pickle factory, and two potato warehouses among its early businesses; the post office was established in 1887.

FLEMING TOWNSHIP organized May 7, 1907, was named for William Fleming; he was born in Ireland in 1835, came to Canada and then to the United States, settling in Emerald Township, Washington County, in 1858; he owned and sold more than 3,000 acres in various areas of the state; he died in 1908.

FORTUNA a village in section 15 of Sandstone Township, was incorporated on May 19, 1857; it was platted at the junction of the Government Road and the Kettle River in 1857 by W. A. Porter and had 200 residents by 1887, but little evidence remains of the site; it was mostly absorbed into the city of Sandstone.

FRIESLAND a village in sections 25 and 36 of Dell Grove Township, five miles north of Hinckley, was named for a province of The Netherlands; it had a station of the Great Northern and Northern Pacific railroads and a post office, 1896–1917.

GLASSPOOL a post office, July-November 1905; location not found.

GREELEY a village in sections 27 and 34 of Royalton Township, was named for Elam Greeley, a lumberman, who settled in section 15 in 1849; born in New Hampshire in 1818, Greeley had a logging business in Stillwater and owned the Chengwatana toll dam at the outlet of Cross Lake; he died in 1883. The post office operated first under the spelling Greely, 1886–88, with William Ambrose as postmaster, and as Greeley, 1899–1902, with John O. Lindgren as postmaster in his general store.

GRONINGEN a village in section 1 of Dell Grove Township and section 6 of Sandstone West Township, bears the name of the most northeastern province of The Netherlands, adjoining the east side of Friesland. It began with two general stores, a potato warehouse, and several small businesses; it had a Northern Pacific Railroad station, first called Miller Station, and a post office called Belknap, 1877–81, and Groningen, 1896–1913 and 1917–54.

HARLIS a village in section 1 of Nickerson Township, had a depot of the Soo Line, a school, and a post office, 1914–32.

HENRIETTE a city in section 17 of Pokegama Township, formerly called Cornell, was named for a local sawmill of that name; the village developed around the depot of the Eastern Railway Company of Minnesota, which came in 1898. It was platted in 1901, the same year the post office was established, and incorporated as a village on March 13, 1920.

HINCKLEY TOWNSHIP organized March 2, 1874, and its city in Barry and Hinckley Townships, incorporated in 1885, were named in honor of Isaac Hinckley, who was born in Hingham, Mass., in 1815, and died in Philadelphia, Pa., March 28, 1885. During 16 years, from 1865 to 1881, he was president of the Philadelphia, Wilmington and Baltimore Railroad company. He was a stockholder for building the St. Paul and Duluth Railroad, later part of the Northern Pacific company. The township originally included Barry, Arlone, Clover, and Ogema Townships. The city, first known as Central Station, separated from the township in 1907 and reincorporated on November 27, 1907; its post office began in 1870. The city was destroyed by the forest fire of 1894, along with much of the county; a museum, located in the rebuilt Great Northern and Northern Pacific depot and dedicated in 1976, tells the story of the fire.

INDIAN VILLAGE a place name in Wilma Township on a 1930 map of county.

KEENE TOWNSHIP organized April 29, 1920, is said to be named for an employee of the Soo Line but is more likely named for either local resident Frank Keene or an Ojibwe family of that name living in Ogema Township. The township was set off from Dosey Township, was dissolved May 25, 1938, and was reorganized as part of New Dosey in 1949.

KERRICK TOWNSHIP organized October 22, 1895, and its city in section 35 have a name that is borne also by a village in central Illinois. It was chosen in honor of Cassius M. Kerrick, who was born at Greensburg, Ind., in 1847; came to Minnesota, settling in Minneapolis, as master mechanic for the Great Northern Railway; later was a contractor, erecting many railway bridges; removed to Pasadena, Calif., in 1913, and died there March 12, 1918. The city was incorporated as a village on October 22, 1946; the post office was established in 1891, with Frank Duquette as first postmaster, for whom the village of Duquette, previously named Kerrick, in section 24 of the township is named. The city had a station of the Great Northern Railway.

KETTLE RIVER TOWNSHIP organized March 2,

1874, received the name of the river flowing through it, a translation from the Ojibwe name, noted by Rev. Joseph A. Gilfillan, "Akiko zibi; Akik, kettle, zibi, river, and o, connective." This name was given to the river in allusion to the waterworn rocks, copper-bearing trap rock and conglomerate, of its rapids along a distance of five miles next above its junction with the St. Croix River. Through the central part of the county, from the south line of this township to the mouth of Grindstone River, the Kettle River flows 15 miles in a valley or gorge about a quarter to two-thirds of a mile wide, eroded in horizontally bedded sandstone, which forms bluffs on each side 75 to 100 feet high, their upper half being usually vertical cliffs.

The village of Kettle River, in sections 27 and 28, had a post office, which began as Kettle River Station, 1870–81, was called Kettle River, 1881–92, and transferred to Rutledge; the village had a station on a branch of the Great Northern Railway.

KINGSDALE a village in section 1 of Dosey Township, five miles north of Cloverton, was organized about 1912 on land owned by C. R. Grace, who had come in 1911 and built a hotel and general store; it had a station of the Soo Line and a post office, 1913–61.

LAKE LENA a village in section 28 of Ogema Township, had a post office, 1913–21, with Lena L. Thayer as postmaster.

MANSFIELD a station of the Great Northern Railway in section 19 of Bruno Township.

MARKVILLE a village in section 26 of Arna Township, was named for Mark Andrews, who platted the site soon after the Soo Line tracks were laid in 1912; the unincorporated village had an early sawmill about 1890 and a number of businesses. The post office began in 1912, with E. J. Steinbring opening the first store; his wife, Edith Steinbring, was postmaster 1912–31.

MIDWAY a village platted in 1855 in section 34 of Mission Creek, north of present Beroun, by Frank B. and Julia L. Lewis, but not developed.

MILBURN a village in eastern Pine City Township, section 32, was named for a local disaster; a lumber mill built in 1892–93 was destroyed by fire in 1894, and only the foundations can still be seen. The first settler was J. P. Floodquist from Sweden, who came in 1885. The site had two churches, a cemetery, and a school.

MILLE LACS a post office, 1856–59; location not found but possibly in Ogema Township.

MILLER STATION see GRONINGEN.

MISSION CREEK TOWNSHIP organized March 17, 1880, and its village in section 10 bear the name of the creek flowing through the east part of this township. It joins the Snake River east of Lake Pokegama and received its name from a mission to the Ojibwe founded beside that lake in 1836, which was broken up by the attack of a large war party of the Dakota, May 24, 1841. Before the Hinckley fire of 1894, the village had a station of the Northern Pacific Railroad, a hotel, a sawmill, a general store, a blacksmith, and 26 houses, all of which were destroyed in the fire except one house and the cemetery; only the latter remains of the original village; the post office operated 1876–1908.

MORTIMER a post office authorized on February 19, 1889, with Thomas Creeper to be postmaster; appointment records indicate that the post office may have operated until April, but it is likely that it was never established; location not found.

MUNCH TOWNSHIP was organized October 2, 1905, as Cedar Lake and separated from Chengwatana Township; the name was changed to Munch on January 2, 1906, in honor of three brothers, natives of Prussia, who were lumbermen in this county. Adolph Munch born in 1829, came to the United States in 1850 and to Minnesota in 1854; resided at Taylors Falls, Chisago County, and at Pine City; removed to St. Paul in 1871 and died there November 26, 1901. Emil Munch, born in 1831, came to this country in 1849 and settled at Taylors Falls in 1852; was a representative in the legislature, 1860–61; was captain of the First Minnesota Battery, 1861–65; was state treasurer, 1868–72; owned a flouring mill at Afton, Washington County, after 1875; died August 30, 1887. Paul Munch, born in 1833, came to the United States in 1854, settling at Taylors Falls; served in the First Minnesota Light Artillery in the Civil War, attaining the rank of first lieutenant; removed to Chengwatana, where he died July 26, 1901.

NESHODANA a townsite platted in 1856 in sections 35 and 36 of Arna Township and sections 1 and 2 of Ogema; no settlement developed.

NEW DOSEY TOWNSHIP consolidated Dosey, Keene, and Belden Townships in 1949.

NICKERSON TOWNSHIP organized September 10, 1907, and its village in section 4 were named in honor of John Quincy Adams Nickerson of Elk River, Sherburne County, who promoted the building of this line of the Great Northern Railway. He was born in New Salem, Maine, March 30, 1825; came to St. Anthony, Minn., in 1849, and four years later settled at Elk River, buying land on which a part of that village was afterward built; conducted a hotel and also engaged in lumbering; was postmaster of Elk River and treasurer of Sherburne County. The village developed around a sawmill in section 9 and shifted to section 4 when the Great Northern Railway and highway were built; it had a post office, 1895–1954, with Ernest A. Nickerson, first postmaster.

NORMAN TOWNSHIP organized March 15, 1906, was named by its Swedish and Norwegian settlers to commemorate their Scandinavian origin as Northmen, being thus like the names of Norman County and Norman Township in Yellow Medicine County.

OGEMA TOWNSHIP organized August 16, 1915, has an Ojibwe name, meaning "a chief."

OUTFLOW an Ojibwe village in section 18 of Ogema Township.

PARK TOWNSHIP was set off from Bruno Township and organized September 25, 1922.

PARTRIDGE TOWNSHIP organized January 8, 1901, may have been named in honor of one of its first settlers, although local residents believe it was named for the game bird indigenous to the area or, more likely, for a ridge that runs southwest to northeast dividing or "parting" the township. The village in sections 19, 20, 29, and 30 was totally destroyed in the 1894 forest fire; it had a post office, 1889–1909, which was transferred to Askov.

PINE CITY TOWNSHIP organized March 2, 1874, and the city, the county seat, platted in 1869, incorporated February 14, 1881, and reincorporated and separated from the township on June 30, 1908, were named from the county. It is also especially significant that the name of the nearly adjacent Ojibwe village, Chengwatana, was derived, as before noted, from the two words for "pine" and "city." Probably this aboriginal village, as well as the pine forests, shared in the naming of the village and township of Pine City and also in the earlier selection of the county name. Hiram Brackett, born in Maine in 1817, came to Pine City in 1868 and built the hotel, where his wife, Louise D. Brackett, was first postmaster when the post office was established in 1870; Brackett died in 1883. The city had a station of the Northern Pacific Railroad in section 33.

The township was separated into **PINE CITY WEST**: T. 38N, R. 21W, sections 1–12, and T. 39N, R. 21W, sections 25–27 and 32–36; and **PINE CITY EAST**: T. 38N, R. 20W, sections 1–12, and T. 39N, R. 20W, sections 28–34.

PINE LAKE TOWNSHIP organized October 22, 1895, has the Big Pine Lake and the Upper and Lower Pine Lakes, which outflow northeastward by the Pine River, all these names, as likewise of the county and of its ancient Ojibwe village, being derived from the majestic pine woods.

POKEGAMA TOWNSHIP organized January 7, 1895, bears the Ojibwe name of its creek and lake, meaning "the water which juts off from another water," applied to this lake because its south end is very near the Snake River. It is also the name of a large lake beside the Mississippi in Itasca County and likewise was given by the Ojibwe to the little lake now called Elk Lake, closely adjoining Lake Itasca. A townsite in section 35 had a tuberculosis sanatorium, 1905–43, and a post office, 1912–43; an earlier place by this name was renamed Brook Park.

QUARRY VILLAGE see **BANNING**.

ROCK CREEK TOWNSHIP settled in 1872, organized March 2, 1874, and its city in section 22, bear the name of the creek that here flows south into the northeast corner of Chisago County, tributary to the St. Croix River. The city was incorporated as a village on November 4, 1970; it was established soon after the Lake Superior and Mississippi Railroad built through the area in 1870 and was a lumbering and sawmill center, having five mills in the area. The post office began in 1874; its name was Rockcreek, 1894–1950.

ROCK CREEK WEST TOWNSHIP is T. 38N, R. 21W, sections 13–36, and T. 38N, R. 20W, sections 13–34.

ROYALTON organized March 17, 1880, the most southwestern township of Pine County, was named in honor of Royal C. Gray, who in 1854 settled on section 15, at the south side of the Snake River, on a farm that had been opened in 1849 by Elam Greeley, a pioneer lumberman.

RUTLEDGE a city in sections 28, 33, and 34 of Kettle River Township, was incorporated as a village on February 17, 1893. It was first called Kettle River when the post office opened in 1881, changing to Rutledge in 1892. Located on the Kettle River, it had a sawmill by 1870 and a station of the Northern Pacific Railroad.

ST. JOHNS LANDING a townsite in section 32 of Ogema Township, platted in October 1857, began as an Indian village and is now a recreational campsite.

SANDSTONE TOWNSHIP organized October 22, 1895, and its city platted in June 1887, were named for their extensive quarries of St. Croix sandstone in the bluffs of the Kettle River, which were first worked in August 1885. The city was incorporated as a village on September 28, 1887, and reincorporated and separated from the township on April 14, 1920. Quarries owned by William Henry Grant, Sr., a St. Paul attorney, were operated by his son, W. H. Grant, Jr., who was also the first postmaster when the post office was established in 1887. The village was destroyed during the Hinckley fire of 1894, the townsite abandoned, and a new village built on land donated by W. H. Grant, Sr.

SILVERTON a townsite in section 27 of Park Township.

SPRINGDALE a townsite in sections 23 and 24 of Arlone Township two miles east of Cloverdale, which was not developed; no post office was established.

STURGEON LAKE TOWNSHIP organized October 5, 1897, and its city in sections 11–14 were named for the large lake in Windemere Township, two miles east of this city. The city was platted on August 14, 1889, by the St. Paul and Duluth Railroad, owner of the land, and incorporated as a village on August 2, 1889; the post office operated 1881–82 and was reestablished in 1888.

TURPVILLE see CLOVERDALE.

TUXEDO a summer resort in section 26 of Pokegama Township on Pokegama Lake, six miles northwest of Pine City; the post office was called Bergman, 1898-April 1905, with postmaster August Bergman, changed to Tuxedo, and discontinued in October 1905.

VILLSTAD a locality in section 4 of Partridge Township, was established in 1898 by Swedish immigrants, first as a cemetery, and named after Villstad parish in Småland, the birthplace of some of the leading settlers; a church was built in 1900, and the congregation organized in 1909.

WAREHAM a village in section 21 of Sandstone Township, with a station of the Great Northern Railway.

WEST ROCK a village in section 19 of Rock Creek Township, was settled by Swedish immigrants in the 1870s; it had a church, a school, a store, and a creamery.

WHALENS a paper town in section 21 of Keene Township; not developed.

WILLOW RIVER a city in sections 2, 10, and 11 of Kettle River Township, is at its crossing of this stream, the largest eastern tributary of the Kettle River. The city is located on the site of an early Indian village; a sawmill and lumbering were the main industries, and it had a station of the Northern Pacific Railroad. The city was incorporated as a village on November 7, 1891, and the post office was established in 1889.

WILMA TOWNSHIP organized October 22, 1907, was named in honor of a daughter of Wilma Abbott, a former resident of this township, who removed to Caledonia, Minn.

WINDEMERE TOWNSHIP organized January 3, 1882, received its name, with change in spelling, from Lake Windermere, the largest lake in England. The name was suggested by an early homesteader, William Pitt, who was born and raised on the shores of the English lake.

Lakes and Streams

The foregoing list has noticed Birch Creek, Kettle River, Mission Creek, the Pine Lakes and River, Pokegama Creek and Lake, Rock Creek, Sturgeon Lake, and Willow River, from which seven townships and four villages in this county received their names.

The St. Croix and Snake Rivers are considered in the first chapter, treating of large rivers and lakes that are partly included in several counties; and the Snake River, translated from Kanabec, its Ojibwe name, is also noticed in the chapter of Kanabec County.

Cross Lake, so named from its being crossed by the Snake River, is a translation of its Ojibwe name, Bemidji. The same aboriginal name is borne by a lake and city on the upper Mississippi, in Beltrami County. In each case, the name alludes to the river flowing across the lake.

Grindstone River, formed by union of its South and North Branches, and Grindstone Lake, outflowing by the North Branch, are named from the finely gritty sandstone outcrop at the north side of this river adjoining Hinckley village, which was used for sharpening iron and steel tools by the Ojibwe and early fur traders. Quarrying to supply stone for bridge masonry and other building uses was begun there in 1878, and seven years later more extensive quarries were opened in the similar rock beds at the village of Sandstone.

Other lakes and streams in this county, mostly needing no explanations of the derivations and meanings of their names, include Rock Lake, one of the sources of Rock Creek, and Devils Lake, of small area, respectively about two miles and one mile south of Pine City, each bordered by low morainic drift hills, abundantly strewn with boulders; Hay Creek, in the west part of Royalton, flowing north to the Snake River; Cedar Lake, in Munch Township; Deer and Skunk Creeks, tributary to the Kettle River from the west in Barry and Sandstone Townships; Elbow and Bass Lakes, crossed by the north line of Dell Grove Township; Indian and Fish Lakes, in the east edge of Pine Lake Township; Little Pine River, flowing through the Upper and Lower Pine Lakes; Moose River, a large eastern branch of Kettle River, coming from several lakes in Carlton County that are named from moose found in this region; Island and Grass Lakes, in the north edge of Windemere; Oak Lake in Kerrick, near the head of Willow River; Net Lake and River, flowing northeastward into Carlton County; Bear Creek, Sand River, its East Fork, and Hay Creek, also flowing to Sand River from the east, Crooked Creek, with its West and East Forks, Tamarack River, with its West Fork, and Spruce River, these numerous streams, in their order from west to east, being tributary to the St. Croix between the Kettle River and the east line of the county and state; and Rock Lake and Lake Lena in Ogema.

The Kettle River at its Upper Falls or Dalles, east of Banning, flows in rapids about a half mile through a narrow gorge formed by ragged cliffs of sandstone, 50 to 100 feet high. Its Lower Falls, on each side of an island a half mile southeast of Sandstone village, descend about 8 feet within a distance of an eighth of a mile. In the three miles between these falls the river flows with a gentle current.

Opposite the mouth of this river, and for three miles above and one mile below, the St. Croix River is turned in two channels by three long islands, which together are called the "Big island" or the St. Croix Islands. The eastern large channel is the state boundary, and the western is commonly called Kettle River Slough. In both the river has a strong current, with numerous rapids, so that this extent of four miles on the St. Croix is named Kettle River Rapids.

Between four and five miles farther south, the St. Croix has its Horse-race Rapids, a half mile long, over a smooth rock bed, not broken by boulders.

State Parks

St. Croix State Park began in the 1930s as the St. Croix Recreational Demonstration Area, a Depression-era project. Lands in the "cutover," the area heavily logged by lumber companies and subsequently used as farmland, were purchased by the federal government, which planned to show that submarginal agricultural lands could be used for the benefit of the public. Workers from the Civilian Conservation Corps built the campgrounds, trails, and structures of the park. Most of their efforts remain in use today, with many of the buildings and structures listed on the National Register of Historic Places. The area was transferred to the state in 1943.

Banning State Park, which preserves the remains of the above-mentioned village and provides challenging whitewater experiences for canoeists and kayakers on the Kettle River, was established in 1963.

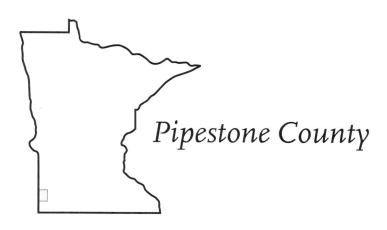

Pipestone County

This county, established May 23, 1857, was organized 22 years later by a legislative act approved January 27, 1879. Its name was at first applied, however, by an error of the original act in 1857 to the area that is now Rock County, while that name was given to the present county of Pipestone. These counties therefore exchanged names by an act of the legislature, February 20, 1862. The transposition was needful, as Pipestone County now includes the celebrated quarry of red pipestone, to which its name refers, and Rock County now has the prominent rock mound near Luverne, which similarly was the source of its name.

Jonathan Carver, wintering in 1766–67 with the Dakota on the Minnesota River, near the site of New Ulm, learned of the highland farther west, since named Coteau des Prairies, as "a mountain, from which the Indians get a sort of red stone, out of which they hew the bowls of their pipes."

George Catlin, the painter of Indian portraits, wrote the earliest printed description of this quarry, which he visited in the summer of 1836. Two years later it was visited by Joseph N. Nicollet, as noted in the report with his map of the upper Mississippi region. These descriptions are reprinted in the *Final Report of the Geological Survey of Minnesota* (vol. 1, 1884, pp. 62–70). The great veneration of many tribes of Indians for the stone here quarried and the legend of its first use to make the peace pipe, or calumet, are known to all readers of Henry W. Longfellow's *Song of Hiawatha*, published in 1855, which derived its account of the pipestone from Catlin and Nicollet. The red pipestone, also called catlinite, occurs as a layer about 18 inches thick, enclosed in strata of red quartzite. It has been quarried by the Indians along an extent of nearly a mile from north to south, their earliest quarrying having been done hundreds of years ago.

Information of the origin and meaning of names has been gathered from An Illustrated History of the Counties of Rock and Pipestone *by Arthur P. Rose, 1911, having pp. 241–421 and 657–802 for this county; and from Charles H. Bennett, Warrington B. Brown, and L. G. Jones, the county treasurer, each of Pipestone, interviewed during a visit there in July 1916.*

AETNA TOWNSHIP the latest organized, July 19, 1880, was named in honor of Aetna Johnson, a

stepdaughter of Christ Gilbertson, an immigrant from Norway, who settled in this township in 1878.

AIRLIE a village six miles west of Pipestone in Sweet Township, section 6, was founded in 1879 by Dundee Land and Improvement Company of Scotland, being named in honor of the earl of Airlie, who was its president. The post office was known as Clausen, 1881–82, and Airlie, 1882–1934. The village had three elevators, a lumberyard, and a Chicago, Milwaukee and St. Paul depot.

ALTONA/ALTOONA see CRESSON.

ALTONA TOWNSHIP organized February 28, 1880, received its name by vote of its settlers, for the city of Altoona in Pennsylvania, but an error in spelling changed it to the name of a city in Germany, adjoining Hamburg. Altona is also the name of a village and township in New York and of villages in Michigan, Indiana, Illinois, and Missouri.

BURKE TOWNSHIP organized April 26, 1879, was at first called Erin but was renamed a few weeks later in honor of Rev. Thomas N. Burke of Ireland, who in 1871 had visited America on a lecturing tour in defense of the political rights of that country.

CAZENOVIA a village in section 21 of Troy, founded in 1884, was named for a town and lake in Madison County, N.Y., whence many farmers of this vicinity had come. The village had a post office, 1885–1938, and a station of the Chicago, Rock Island and Pacific Railway.

CLAUSEN see AIRLIE.

CONVERSE a post office, 1879–80, with Frederick A. Converse as postmaster; location not found.

CRESSON a village in section 36 of Altona Township, was originally surveyed in September 1885 as Altoona with a plat of 14 blocks. The first business was a grain warehouse built by Ezra Rice in 1885; Alex McNaughton built a general store in his farm home in February 1894, and the post office of Altoona was established, closing in 1896. By 1910, the village was known as Cresson after the station of the Chicago, Rock Island and Pacific Railroad; maps variously show the site as Altoona, Altona, and Cresson.

EATON see ETON.

EDEN TOWNSHIP organized September 27, 1879, was named by a popular vote, on the recommendation of Richard O'Connell, after much discussion of other proposed names. "The beautiful stretch of country comprising the township suggested the Garden of Eden to the pioneers."

EDGERTON a city in sections 21, 22, 27, and 28 of Osborne Township, incorporated October 13, 1887, was named in honor of Gen. Alonzo J. Edgerton, who was born in Rome, N.Y., June 7, 1827, and died in Sioux Falls, S.D., August 9, 1896. He was graduated at Wesleyan University

in 1850; came to Mantorville, Minn., in 1855 and was there admitted to practice law; served as captain of the Tenth Minnesota Regiment, 1862–64, and in 1865 was brevetted brigadier general; removed to Kasson in 1878; was a state senator in 1859 and again in 1877–78; and was a U.S. senator by appointment from March to December 1881.

The village was first settled by Alonzo D. Kingsbury in 1876, who sold his land and interest in the village when it was platted in 1886. The post office was called Osborne, September-December 1879, with Kingsbury as postmaster, who continued when the name changed to Edgerton following the arrival of the Southern Minnesota Railroad.

ELMER TOWNSHIP organized August 28, 1879, has a name that is also borne by villages in New Jersey, Pennsylvania, Michigan, and Missouri.

ETON a station of the Chicago, St. Paul, Minneapolis and Omaha Railroad in section 11 of Gray Township, established in 1895 as Gray Siding, was renamed in November 1906 for the town of Eton in England, having a celebrated school where the Close brothers, local grain elevator owners, were educated.

FOUNTAIN PRAIRIE organized June 2, 1879, was named by Charles Heath, one of its early settlers, for his former home township in Columbia County, Wis.

GILLARD a post office, 1883–86, with Handy J. Gillard, postmaster; location not found.

GRANGE TOWNSHIP organized April 26, 1879, received this name in compliment to the Patrons of Husbandry, an agricultural order whose lodges are called granges, from French words, *grange*, "a barn," and *grangier*, "a farmer." This order was founded in 1867 by Oliver H. Kelley (1826–1913), who from 1849 was a Minnesota farmer in Sherburne County.

GRAY SIDING see ETON.

GRAY TOWNSHIP organized June 28, 1879, was named in honor of Andrew O. Gray, its first permanent settler.

HATFIELD a city in Burke and Gray Townships, founded in 1880, has a name that is borne by a township and village in Massachusetts and by villages of Pennsylvania, Wisconsin, and other states. A local story of its naming says that in 1879 one of the men on a railroad grading crew had his hat blown off by the wind a number of times, and after retrieving it from the field, he suggested the name "hat field." The city was incorporated as a village on September 9, 1919; it had a station of the Southern Minnesota Railroad, and the post office began in 1880.

HEATH a farmers post office, 1880–96, ten miles north of Pipestone, with Caleb Heath as postmaster.

HICKOX PRAIRIE see WOODSTOCK.

HOLLAND a city in Rock and Grange Townships, nine miles northeast of Pipestone, founded in 1888, was incorporated May 15, 1898, being named for "a large colony of Hollanders in that vicinity." The village was first platted as a 13-block townsite in May 1888 following the arrival of the Willmar and Sioux Falls Railroad. The post office was established in 1889, with first postmaster Janus Huibregtse in his general store; his wife, Clara, proposed the name in honor of their homeland.

IHLEN a city in sections 9, 10, and 16 , Eden, was named in honor of Carl Ihlen, on whose land it was originally platted in section 9 in July 1888. The site was selected as a freight division point in 1916 for the Great Northern Railway. The post office began in 1889 with Ihlen as postmaster.

JASPER a city with Rock County, in the south edge of Eden, incorporated May 13, 1889, was named for its quarries of red quartzite, commonly called jasper, an excellent building and paving stone. Twelve blocks were platted on April 19, 1888, by Pipestone County surveyor Alfred S. Tee on part of the Joseph Warren Drew homestead. The main industry was the quarries nearby. The village had a station of the Great Northern Railway; the post office was established in 1888, with newspaper publisher Selah S. King, postmaster.

JOHNSTON a quarry village located one mile north of Pipestone, was founded in 1890. By 1900 most quarrying had ceased; the last stones were removed in 1933; little remains of the village.

LUCTOR a post office, 1902–5, in Fountain Prairie Township, section 33.

McVEY a country post office, 1882–96, with James McVey as postmaster, located 15 miles north of Pipestone and 7 miles from Lake Benton, Lincoln County, probably in Fountain Prairie Township.

NORTH SIOUX FALLS a quarry village located in

section 27, Eden Township, was founded in 1890. The post office, 1891–93, was located in Archie True's general store. The railroad came in 1892, and a hotel and several other buildings were built, but the quarrying diminished by 1905.

OSBORNE see EDGERTON.

OSBORNE TOWNSHIP organized March 31, 1879, was named on the suggestion of William J. Dodd, an early settler, in honor of his cousin, J. C. Osborne, of Newark, N.J.

PINNEY a railroad station of the Great Northern located in section 32 of Grange Township, which was also known as Pinny and Penny; it had an elevator built by the New London Milling Company of Willmar in 1905, which burned down in 1914.

PIPESTONE the county seat, at first named Pipestone City, platted in October 1876, was incorporated as a village February 10, 1881, and as a city July 23, 1901. Its area was mostly in section 12 of Sweet Township, adjoining the south border of the quarry, before noted at the beginning of this chapter, which is mostly comprised in section 1.

RIDGE a post office, 1878–83, in Elmer Township, eight miles from Pipestone.

ROCK a post office, 1879–81, ten miles east of Pipestone in Burke Township; the site had a gristmill, and postmaster William M. Ware was a farmer and a blacksmith.

ROCK TOWNSHIP organized June 2, 1879, has several small streams, sources of the Rock River flowing southward past "the Mound" of red quartzite in Rock County, whence the river and that county received their name, given also to this township for its location at the head of the river.

RUTHTON a city in sections 10 and 11 of Aetna Township, platted in June 1888 and incorporated November 2, 1897, was established by the Willmar and Sioux Falls Railroad and named in honor of the wife of W. H. Sherman, one of the townsite proprietors. Its post office began in 1888.

SWEET TOWNSHIP organized February 20, 1879, was named in honor of Daniel E. Sweet, the first settler of this county. He was born in Pennsylvania, April 10, 1838; came to Wisconsin with his parents and in 1860 removed to Iowa; served in the Eleventh Iowa Regiment during the Civil War; took a land claim on the site of Pipestone in 1874; platted Pipestone City, in company with Charles H. Bennett, in 1876, was its first postmaster, and later was the county surveyor and probate judge; removed to Louisiana in 1886, where he had charge of a steamboat line and engaged in other business enterprises; died at Siloam Springs, Ark., October 2, 1902.

TROSKY a city located in Elmer Township, platted in September 1884, was incorporated June 10, 1893. The significance of this name, not found elsewhere in the United States, is unknown. The village had a station of the Chicago, Rock Island and Pacific Railroad, and the post office was established in 1884. The site developed further after 1890 when L. P. Kenyon of Rock Rapids purchased the townsite and promoted it.

TROY TOWNSHIP organized December 3, 1879, received its name from Troy, N.Y., by vote of the settlers after many other names had been proposed and rejected. Daniel B. Whigam, at whose home in section 10 the township meeting was held, finally suggested this name from its being stamped on his kitchen stove as its place of manufacture. "The stove instrumental in supplying the name of the township had a history of its own. It was the first stove sold by the first dealer in Pipestone county, and came from the store of William Wheeler, of Pipestone" (Rose, *History* of this county, p. 277).

WOODSTOCK a city in sections 2, 3, 10, and 11 of Burke, platted in September 1879 and incorporated July 11, 1892, "was named after Woodstock, the county seat of McHenry County, Illinois, which was named after Woodstock, Vermont, and that after a town in England." The city is located on a site earlier called Hickox Prairie for first landowners, Granger and Kasson Hickox; the post office began as Hickox in 1878 with Granger Hickox as postmaster, who continued after the name was changed to Woodstock in 1879; it had a station of the Chicago, St. Paul, Minneapolis and Omaha Railroad.

━━━━━━

Streams and Lakes

The Rock River has been noticed in the first chapter and again for the township in this county named from it.

Redwood River, having sources in Aetna, the most northeastern township of this county, is fully noticed in the chapter for Redwood County.

Flandreau Creek, in Fountain Prairie and Altona Townships, flowing southwest to the Big Sioux River in South Dakota, and the village of this name near its mouth, commemorate Charles Eugene Flandrau (but with a change in spelling), who was born in New York City, July 15, 1828, and died in St. Paul, Minn., September 9, 1903. He was admitted to practice law in 1851; came to Minnesota in 1853, settling in St. Paul; was a member of the state constitutional convention, 1857; was associate justice of the supreme court of Minnesota, 1857–64; author of *The History of Minnesota and Tales of the Frontier* (1900, 408 pp.), and many papers in the Minnesota Historical Society Collections. During the Dakota War, in August 1862, Judge Flandrau commanded the volunteer forces in their defense of New Ulm against the attacks of the Dakota and on account of his important services received from Gov. Alexander Ramsey the commission of colonel.

Pipestone Creek, named from its flowing past the red pipestone quarry, had a series of four little lakes on its course, Pipestone, Crooked, Duck, and Whitehead Lakes, the first being in the east part of the quarry monument and the others within about a mile west from the quarry. These lakes have been drained.

At the quartzite bluff between Pipestone Lake and the quarry, this stream "passes over the ledge from the upper prairie to the lower with a perpendicular fall of about 18 feet," as noted by Prof. N. H. Winchell (*Geology of Minn., Final Report*, vol. 1, 1884, p. 539). His later map of the pipestone quarry names this cascade as Winnewissa Falls (*Aborigines of Minn.*, 1911, plate at p. 564), from the Dakota verb *winawizi*, "to be jealous or envious." The name had been used much earlier in an excellent poem by Adelaide George Bennett of Pipestone, titled "The Peace-Pipe Quarry," first read at a celebration there July 4, 1878, which was reprinted as pp. 77–85 in *Indian Legends of Minnesota*, compiled by Cordenio A. Severance and published in 1893. In the reprint Mrs. Bennett inserted new lines with this name, "Falls of Winnewissa."

Close west of the falls are Leaping Rock, a little columnar cliff left by erosion in front of the verge of the bluff and within leaping distance from it, and Inscription Rock, bearing the name of J. N. Nicollet and initials of five members of his exploring party, inscribed when they visited the pipestone quarry in July 1838.

Nearly on the south line of the national monument, about a half mile south from the falls and the present quarry pits, an exceptionally huge granite boulder, the largest known in Minnesota, lying on the quartzite, has fallen in six pieces under the action of frost, separating it along the natural seams or joints. "The largest three pieces, each about twenty feet long and twelve feet high, are the Three Maidens, so called . . . from the tradition that after the destruction of all the tribes in war, the present Indians sprang from three maidens who fled to these rocks for refuge" (*Geology of Minn.*, vol. 1, p. 546).

Split Rock Creek, named from its flowing through gorges eroded in the quartzite at Jasper and on lower parts of its course, in Rose Dell Township of Rock County and in South Dakota, receives its headstreams from Sweet and Eden Townships in the southwest corner of Pipestone County. In 1937 the WPA built a dam of quartzite on the creek in Eden Township to create a lake in the Split Rock Creek Recreational Reserve, later renamed Split Rock Creek State Park.

In Osborne, the most southeastern township, the West Fork of Rock River flows to it from Elmer, and nearly opposite to that stream it receives Chanarambie Creek, bearing a Dakota name that means "hidden wood," as noted for Murray County, which has a township of this name.

The Altamont Moraine, the outermost marginal belt of knolly and ridged glacial drift, forms the crest of the Coteau des Prairies in the northeast part of this county, extending across Rock and Aetna Townships, with the sources of the Des Moines and Redwood Rivers on its slope declining eastward and the highest springs of Rock River on its western slope.

Pipestone National Monument

This tract, one mile north of Pipestone, was originally an Indian reservation, one mile square, which was set apart for the Yankton Sioux in accordance with a treaty made in Washington, April 19, 1858. The reservation was provided solely for quarrying by the Indian tribes, and no trespassing there by white men was permitted. The federal government bought the reservation in 1928. Following many years of work to create a national monument, sponsors introduced the first legislative acts in 1934, but it was not until 1937 that the national monument was established. Of the one-mile-square tract, 116 acres is level prairie land that has never been cultivated. Another 167 acres was added to the site in 1956.

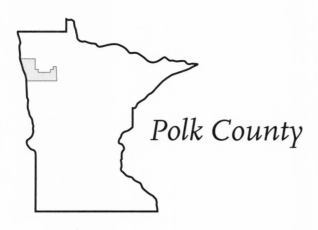

Polk County

Established July 20, 1858, and organized in 1872–73, this county was named in honor of James Knox Polk, the eleventh president of the United States. He was born in Mecklenburg County, N.C., November 2, 1795, and died in Nashville, Tenn., June 15, 1849. His home was in Tennessee after he was 11 years old. He was admitted to practice law in 1820; was a member of Congress, 1825–39, and served as speaker the last four years; was governor of Tennessee, 1839–41; and as Democratic candidate for president was elected in 1844. On March 3, 1849, the next to the last day of his presidential term, he approved the act of Congress that organized Minnesota Territory.

Return I. Holcombe, in the history of this county, wrote of Polk as follows: "He advocated the war against Mexico and was an efficient President during that contest. But he was opposed to wars in general, and it was largely his great influence during his administration which prevented war with Great Britain in 1846 over the Oregon question—a war of which many unwise Americans were decidedly in favor—and when he was in Congress he and some other Congressmen prevented a war with Spain. He was a man of pure and high character and personally popular. This county need be well satisfied with its name."

Information of names has been gathered from History of the Red River Valley *(1909, 2 vols., continuously paged), having a chapter for this county, pp. 860–86, by Judge William Watts and Arthur A. Miller;* Compendium of the History and Biography of Polk County *by Return I. Holcombe and William H. Bingham (1916, 487 pp.); interviews with Judge Watts and Arthur A. Miller of Crookston, the county seat, during a visit there in August 1909; from Henry J. Welte, county auditor, Amund L. Hovland, judge of probate, Hans L. Waage, clerk of court, Elias Steenerson, David H. Turner, and Judge Watts, during a second visit at Crookston in September 1916; and from A. F. Cronquist and Thomas Vollen of Erskine, interviewed there in September 1916 for the southeast part of this county.*

ALDAL a post office in Garfield Township, 1881–87, located in the store built by Edward H. Cornelius, first postmaster, was named for Jacob Aldal, who was born in Norway in 1847 and came to the United States in 1871 and to the area in 1879; the site had a sawmill, a church, and a school.

ANDOVER TOWNSHIP organized in 1877, has a name that is also borne by townships and villages in Maine, New Hampshire, Massachusetts, and ten other states.

ANGLIM a village in section 19 of Crookston Township, with a station serving the Northern Pacific Railroad.

ANGUS TOWNSHIP organized in 1879, and its village in section 9, were named in honor of Richard Bladworth Angus, a banker of Montreal, who financially aided the construction of this line of the Great Northern Railway. He was born in Bathgate, Scotland, May 28, 1831, and came to Canada in 1857; was successively a director, general manager, and president in 1910–14 of the Bank of Montreal; was a principal promoter for building the Canadian Pacific Railway, which was completed in 1885. The village had a post office established in 1879, with Duncan McLennan, first postmaster; it had a station of the Great Northern Railway and four grain elevators nearby.

BADGER TOWNSHIP has a lake of this name, adjoining Erskine village, and its outlet, Badger Creek, flows northwest through this township. The lake and creek were named for the burrowing animal, frequent in Minnesota, which gave to Wisconsin its sobriquet as the "Badger State."

BEHAIM a post office, 1884–86, with Johannes E. Beim, postmaster, located 37 miles southeast of Crookston and 27 miles from Beltrami, possibly in Hubbard Township.

BELGIUM TOWNSHIP organized in 1880, had immigrants from Belgium as its first settlers.

BELTRAMI a city in sections 16 and 21 of Reis Township, was named in honor of Giacomo Costantino Beltrami (1779–1855), an Italian exile, who traveled to the Red River and the upper Mississippi in 1823, as narrated in the chapter on Beltrami County. The city was first settled about 1870 and was incorporated as a village on September 11, 1901. The first post office, 1878–1900, was named Edna for Edna Webb, wife of Isaac W. Webb; he was postmaster 1878–83, and she was postmaster 1883–84. The site was located about three miles south of the Great Northern Railway depot built in 1885 and one and a half miles south of the present Beltrami; in 1900 the post office was moved near the railroad station site.

BENOIT a village in section 22 of Kertsonville Township, which had a station of the Great Northern Railway in section 23, the tracks running across Frederick Benoit's land in section 26; Benoit was postmaster of the Lawton post office, 1899–1903, in section 23, one mile from the railroad station.

BIRKHOLZ a post office, 1900–1908, located in section 33 of Higdem Township in the store on postmaster Marie Rose Northrup's farm.

BOCKERSVILLE see KEY WEST.

BRANDSVOLD TOWNSHIP was named in honor of one of its pioneer settlers, an immigrant from Norway.

BRANDT TOWNSHIP has a name that is borne by villages in Pennsylvania, Ohio, and South Dakota.

BRIAN CITY a trade center store built in 1898 by Edward Groven on his homestead in Winger Township, which was later sold and moved into Winger.

BRISLET TOWNSHIP organized in 1880, was probably named for one of its early settlers.

BUFFINGTON a village in section 5, Fanny Township, and section 32 of Euclid Township, had a post office, 1887–93, with George Buffington as postmaster, and a station of the Northern Pacific Railroad.

BULLAN a post office, May-October 1890, with Jesse P. Bullan, postmaster; location not found.

BURWELL a village in section 12 of Fairfax Township, had a Great Northern Railway station and a post office, 1899–1907.

BYGLAND TOWNSHIP organized in 1877, was named for a village in southern Norway, whence several of its pioneer settlers came. The village in section 16 was established when Sveinung K. Flaat built the Bygland Store in 1897. Flaat was born in Norway in 1871, came to the United States in 1889, and died in 1953. The post office operated 1897–1906, with Flaat as postmaster 1897–1903.

CARMEN a village in section 1 of Andover Township, with a post office, 1880–91, was established about 1878; it had several businesses and a hotel; Knud Knudson was postmaster in his general store.

CARTHAGE a station of the Northern Pacific Railroad in section 33 of Sullivan Township; Carthage Junction was in section 34.

CHESTER TOWNSHIP has a name that is borne also by townships and villages or cities in 25 other states, by counties in Pennsylvania, South Carolina, and Tennessee, and by a city and county in England.

CHOWELL a locality in section 6 of Nesbit Township.

CISCO a post office in section 11 of Badger Township, 1904-7.

CLIMAX a city in sections 29 and 30 of Vineland,

is named with an ancient Greek word meaning "a ladder or a stairway," hence the highest point attained in an oration or in any series of endeavors, chosen here from its use in an advertisement of "Climax Tobacco." The city was incorporated as a village on August 18, 1897; it was first located one and a half miles southwest of the present site on the Steenerson farm, with a general store, a post office, a flour mill, a bank, a harness shop, and a doctor/veterinarian; when the St. Paul, Minneapolis and Manitoba Railroad came in 1896, the village moved to the present site, adding a depot, three elevators, a roller mill, a lumberyard, and a stockyard. The post office operated first as Meos, 1881–88, then as Climax, 1888–91, and was reestablished in 1894.

COLONY a post office, 1904–5; location not found.

COLUMBIA see LENGBY.

COLUMBIA TOWNSHIP has a name borne by counties in eight states, townships and villages or cities in 27 states, and the largest river of our Pacific Coast, in honor of Christopher Columbus, the explorer of America.

In 1896 several propositions for the establishment of new counties from the eastern part of Polk County were submitted to the vote of the people, resulting in the formation of Red Lake County. One of the petitions had sought to form a county named Columbia, and this was again attempted in 1902, for the southeast part of the present Polk County, which then received a large vote in its favor. Columbia County was proclaimed by the governor in December 1902 as established, but the proceedings in the popular vote, when three different names, Nelson, Columbia, and Star, had been submitted and adopted to be applied to the new county, were declared invalid and of no effect by a decision of the state supreme court, April 16, 1903.

CROOKSTON the county seat, first settled in 1872, incorporated as a city February 14, 1879, was named in honor of Col. William Crooks of St. Paul, who was the chief engineer in locating the first railroad here, then known as the St. Paul and Pacific Railroad, which was constructed in 1872 from Glyndon through Crookston to the Snake River at the site of Warren in Marshall County. He was born in New York City, June 20, 1832; was graduated from the department of civil engineering at West Point Military Academy;

settled in St. Paul in 1857 as engineer for this railroad; served as colonel of the Sixth Minnesota Regiment in the Civil War; was a representative in the state legislature, 1875–77, and a state senator, 1881; died in Portland, Ore., December 17, 1907. The first locomotive used in Minnesota, in 1862, was named William Crooks in his honor.

His father, Ramsay Crooks, who was born in Greenock, Scotland, January 2, 1787, and died in New York City, June 6, 1859, was probably also intentionally honored by the adoption of this name. As a member, and subsequently president, of the American Fur Company, he was well known throughout the Northwest. During many years he was identified with the fur trade in Minnesota and had great influence with the Indians.

The city began as Hawley in 1872 (September-November); Edward M. Walsh was postmaster and continued when the name changed to Crookston; it was platted in September 1875. Crookston Township was organized March 28, 1876. The city area was taken partly from this township and also from Lowell, Andover, and Fairfax.

CROOKSTON JUNCTION a station of the Great Northern Railway in section 1 of Andover Township, west of Crookston.

CUMMINGS a station of the Northern Pacific Railroad in section 14 of Huntsville Township, the tracks crossing land owned by James Cumming.

DAVIDSON a village in section 29, Nesbit Township, had a post office, 1900–1910, and a station of the Northern Pacific Railroad.

DAVISON a place name on a 1902 county map noted as a post office and station of the Northern Pacific Railroad, section 14, Keystone.

DEETT a post office, 1884–85, 38 miles northwest of Crookston and 20 miles northwest of East Grand Forks; location not found.

DOMESTIC a post office, 1883–84, with William Martin as postmaster; location not found.

DOVER see OVETIA.

DUGDALE a village in section 26, Tilden Township; the station serving the Great Northern and Northern Pacific railroads was first called Albert; the post office operated in 1884 and 1889–1927.

EAST GRAND FORKS a city in Grand Forks and Rhinehart Townships, incorporated as a city March 7, 1887, is on the east side of the Red River, opposite the city of Grand Forks, N.D., where the confluence of the large Red Lake River with the upper part of the Red River presents two navigable courses or forks for ascending boats. The city began after the Civil War as a trading center and stopping-off place for Red River cart teamsters going between St. Paul and Winnipeg; the St. Paul, Minneapolis and Manitoba Railroad came in 1880. The city was first known as Nashville when the post office opened in 1874, for William C. Nash, fur trader and government mail carrier between Abercrombie and Pembina; the name changed to East Grand Forks in 1883. Nash was born in Pennsylvania and came to the area in 1863, securing the mail contract in 1864, and was postmaster of Tillia, 1872–73. Regular flooding of the rivers has caused difficulties for the community. After a devastating flood in 1997, the U.S. Army Corps of Engineers built levees along the Red River to protect the cities of Grand Forks and East Grand Forks; the land between the levees was designated as the Greenway, to be developed as a recreational area. In 2000, the Minnesota legislature established the Red River State Recreation Area on the state-managed portion of Greenway lands.

EBERT a post office, 1882–83, four and a half miles from Crookston, with saw- and gristmills; location not found.

EDEN TOWNSHIP was named, like a township of Pipestone County and Eden Prairie Township in Hennepin County, for the Garden of Eden, to express the happiness of the settlers in their new homes.

EDNA see BELTRAMI.

ELDRED a village in section 35 of Roome Township, was founded by John Elg, for whom it is named; when the village was platted in 1897, the form of the name was Eldridge, a name already in the state, so Eldred was selected. When the Great Northern Railway came, Elg donated the land for the right-of-way; he owned a confectionery, was postmaster for three years, and died in 1928. The post office, 1897–1968, changed to a rural branch in 1968; first postmaster and merchant was Theodore M. Boyer, later a township treasurer; the first building was the Northwestern Elevator in 1897.

ERSKINE a city in section 4 of Knute Township, founded in 1889, was named in honor of George Q. Erskine, who platted the original townsite; he was born in New Hampshire, December 1, 1828, and died at Crookston, January 15, 1908. He came from Racine, Wis., to this county about 1885 and was president of the First National Bank of Crookston. The city was incorporated as a village on March 8, 1897, and reincorporated and separated from the township on April 24, 1917. The early village had a flour mill, three elevators, a hotel, a general store, and a station of the Great Northern and Soo Line railroads; the post office was established in 1889.

ESPETVEH a post office, 1897–1910, James H. Espetveh, postmaster, in section 8, Chester Township.

ESTHER TOWNSHIP was named in honor of the daughter of Grover Cleveland, president of the United States.

EUCLID TOWNSHIP organized in 1879, and its village in section 23, were named by Springer Harbaugh, manager of the large Lockhart farm in Norman County, for the beautiful Euclid Avenue in Cleveland, Ohio, where he had formerly lived. The village was first settled about 1872, platted as six blocks in 1880 by the Keystone Farm Association, the land owned by Harbaugh and Charles Lockhart, who built a hotel there in 1881; the post office was established in 1879. There were two stations at the site: Euclid for the Great Northern Railway and South Euclid for the Northern Pacific Railroad.

FAIRFAX TOWNSHIP organized in 1879, bears the name of a county in Virginia and of townships and villages in Vermont, Ohio, Indiana, Iowa, and several other states.

FANNY TOWNSHIP organized in 1880, commemorates the wife or daughter of a pioneer, but her surname is unknown.

FARLEY TOWNSHIP organized in 1878, was named in honor of Jesse P. Farley, who was born in Tennessee in 1813 and died in Dubuque, Iowa, May 9, 1894. He was a merchant in Dubuque and established a steamboat line to St. Paul; came to Minnesota in 1873 as receiver of the St. Paul and Pacific Railroad; resided in St. Paul several years, engaging in railroad enterprises.

FERTILE a city in sections 20 and 21 of Garfield, was named for Fertile village of Worth County in northern Iowa, whence some of its first settlers came. The city was incorporated as a village on May 22, 1888; it was first settled in 1879 and was platted on May 25, 1887, by James B. and

Caroline F. Holms of Minneapolis, owners of the property, as 19 blocks with the Duluth, Crookston and Northern Railroad tracks through the middle and a public park in the southwest corner. John S. LaDue had a grocery store in LaDue Grove, three miles west of Fertile, where he was first postmaster when the post office began in 1881; he moved it to the townsite in 1887.

FISHER TOWNSHIP organized in 1876, and its city in sections 21 and 22 of the same name, received it from the earlier railway terminal village of Fisher's Landing, founded here in the fall of 1875 on the Red Lake River at its head of practicable steamboat navigation. It was first called Shirt-tail Bend because a shirt had once been tied to a pole to warn steamboats of the bend in the river and was renamed Fisher's Landing when the post office began in 1874, changing to the present name, Fisher, in 1882; it was incorporated as a village on February 9, 1881. During a few years, until the railway lines to Winnipeg and Grand Forks were completed, respectively in 1878 and 1879, Fisher's Landing surpassed Crookston in population and business. It closely adjoined the site of the present village, by which it was superseded, so that the old Landing village area "has changed to an unpretentious cow pasture." These names were adopted in honor of William H. Fisher, who was born in Hunterdon County, N.J., December 24, 1844; engaged in railroad business after 1864; settled in St. Paul in 1873 as attorney for the receiver of the St. Paul and Pacific Railroad, and as its assistant manager and superintendent; later was president and manager of the St. Paul and Duluth Railroad company, 1883–99; was vice-president and general manager of the Duluth and Winnipeg Railroad company, 1888–93.

FOSSTON a city in sections 3 and 4 of Rosebud Township, was named in honor of Louis Foss, its earliest merchant, who removed to Tacoma, Wash. Foss opened the post office in 1883 at his general store in the southwest part of the township. The present townsite was organized by W. J. Hilligoss, who selected and purchased the townsite in 1884, had it surveyed, platted a four-block area, and built a hotel; Hilligoss died in 1941. When the townsite was named for him, Foss moved his store and the post office there. The village was incorporated on August 22, 1895. It had a Great Northern Railway depot.

FREEMAN a Northern Pacific Railroad village in section 11 of Fisher Township.

GARDEN TOWNSHIP organized in 1881, was named by its people for its beauty and fertility, like Eden before noted. A village named Garden was located in the township about 1937.

GARFIELD TOWNSHIP organized in 1880, commemorates President James Abram Garfield, who was born at Orange, Ohio, November 19, 1831, and died at Elberon, N.J., September 19, 1881. He was an instructor and later president of Hiram College, Ohio, 1856–61; served in the Civil War and was promoted to major general in 1863; was a member of Congress, 1863–80; was president of the United States in 1881.

GENTILLY TOWNSHIP organized in 1879, received its name from a village on the St. Lawrence River in the Province of Quebec, which was named for the town of Gentilly in France, a southern suburb of Paris. The village of Gentilly was a French Catholic community that began as a rest stop for the stage line, with a saloon, eating, and sleeping accommodations; Joseph Beaudette settled a claim there in 1876 and named it for his native village in Quebec. It had a post office, 1880–1963, which changed to a rural branch, 1963–77, with Phillipe Beaupre, as first postmaster.

GIRARD a village in section 15 of Andover Township, with a Great Northern Railway station.

GODFREY see MAPLE BAY.

GODFREY TOWNSHIP organized in 1881, was named in honor of Warren N. Godfrey, an early settler at the southwest end of Maple Lake in this township, who removed to the state of Washington.

GOSSEN a post office in section 5 of Winger Township, was first located in 1889 at the farm home of Knute H. Rollag; it was passed around to several farms before locating in the Gossen Store in 1893, remaining there until it closed in 1905; the townsite also had a wool-carding factory.

GRAND FORKS TOWNSHIP organized in 1882, has a translated name, like the adjoining city of East Grand Forks and the city in North Dakota on the opposite side of the Red River, from the Ojibwe name of the junction of the Red River and the Red Lake River, noted by Rev. Joseph A. Gilfillan as "Kitchi-madawang, the big forks, that is, where the rivers are so large in either fork that you don't know which to go into."

GRAND VIEW a village in section 26 of Woodside Township, about 1930.

GRANVILLE see Oslo, Marshall County; maps sometimes show this place name in Higdem Township, Polk County.

GREENVIEW a village in section 19 of Russia Township, had a station on the Great Northern Railway.

GREGG a post office, 1898–1907, in section 31 of Winger Township; in 1898 Charles Odden homesteaded in section 31 and established the Gregg Store on his farm, which was operated by the Christenson Brothers; Martin G. Christenson was postmaster.

GRIEBROK a village in sections 1 and 2, Chester Township, with a general store and a post office, 1901–18.

GROVE PARK TOWNSHIP organized in 1880, has groves bordering the northeast part of Maple Lake, with Lakeside Park on the shore of this lake in the adjoining edge of Woodside Township.

GULLY TOWNSHIP and its city in sections 34 and 35 are named for a gully or ravine there crossed by the railway, adjoining the highest beach ridge of Glacial Lake Agassiz. The city was incorporated as a village on July 16, 1924; the early townsite had a Soo Line station, a roller mill, a hotel, and a lumberyard; the post office was established in 1896.

HAMMOND TOWNSHIP organized in 1880, was named in honor of one of its early settlers.

HANDY a farmers post office, 1898–1901, 13 miles north of Fosston, with Eric C. Jacobson, postmaster.

HANSVILLE a post office, 1884–97, with Hans Jacob Hanson, postmaster, about 50 miles southeast of Crookston and 35 miles east of Edna.

HAROLD a station of the Northern Pacific Railroad in section 25 of Fairfax Township.

HAWLEY see CROOKSTON.

HELGELAND TOWNSHIP was so named by its Norwegian people for the district of Helgeland in the north part of Norway.

HIGDEM TOWNSHIP organized in 1879, was named in honor of Arne O. Higdem, a pioneer farmer there, who was a member of the board of county commissioners. A post office was located in the township, May-November 1880, with Olaf Sandin, postmaster.

HILL RIVER TOWNSHIP has a stream that was so named for morainic hills adjoining its course near the north line of this township. It has also been called the South Fork of Clearwater River.

HIXON a village in Lowell Township, developed around two railroad sidings in sections 9 and 21.

HOLMES see MELVIN.

HUBBARD TOWNSHIP settled in 1871 and organized in 1882, was named in honor of Lucius Frederick Hubbard, governor of Minnesota in 1882–87, for whom a biographic notice is presented in the chapter of Hubbard County.

HUNT a Great Northern Railway station in section 8 of Huntsville Township.

HUNTSVILLE the first township organized in the county, March 17, 1874, was named in honor of Bena Hunt, one of its first settlers, who came here from Winona in 1871.

JOHNSON TOWNSHIP organized in 1898, was named in honor of John O. Johnson, a Norwegian homesteader in Columbia, who then was one of the county commissioners.

KANKEL a station of the Great Northern and Northern Pacific railroads, in section 6 of Onstad Township.

KERTSONVILLE TOWNSHIP organized in 1881, was named for one of its pioneer settlers.

KEY WEST a village in Keystone and Nesbit Townships; the post office was called Bockersville, 1892–96, with blacksmith Andrew Dieffenbaugh as postmaster, changed to Keywest in 1896, with Redvald P. Skarstad as postmaster in his store, discontinuing in 1910. The Northern Pacific Railroad station was sometimes called the Keystone Station for its location on the townships' border.

KEYSTONE TOWNSHIP organized in 1881, had the very large Keystone farm, owned by capitalists in Pittsburgh, Pa. This farm was named for Pennsylvania the "Keystone State," which was located at the center in the series of the 13 original states, like the keystone of an arch.

KING see MCINTOSH.

KING TOWNSHIP was named in honor of Ephraim King, an early settler, who was the first postmaster there.

KITTSON a station of the Great Northern Railway in section 31 of Fairfax Township, seven miles south of Crookston, was named for Norman W. Kittson, of whom a biographic sketch has been given in the chapter for Kittson County.

KNUTE TOWNSHIP was named for Knute Nelson, a Norwegian farmer near Fertile, who was a member of the board of county commissioners. He had the same name as Governor Nelson, who was also a U.S. senator.

KOHLER a Northern Pacific Railroad station in section 32 of Belgium Township.

LAFONTAINE a farming community and post office, 1881–83, in Lake Pleasant Township; farmer Joseph Marchildon was postmaster.

LAKESIDE PARK is a village of summer homes in section 4 of Woodside, on the northwest shore of Maple Lake.

LAWTON see BENOIT.

LEESTON a post office, 1898–1910, in section 8 of Godfrey Township, with Teman K. Temanson, postmaster; an elevator was located on T. G. Lee's property; the Northern Pacific Railroad station of Lees was in section 20.

LENGBY a city in sections 28 and 33 of Columbia Township, was incorporated as a village on March 9, 1904; it was first settled about 1883 when Swedish settlers arrived. The post office was established in 1890 as Columbia in section 21, with Carl Hasselton as postmaster. In 1898 when the Great Northern Railway came and the first buildings were erected, the post office was changed to Lengby, a distortion of Lindby, as it was supposed to be named to honor a local settler named Lindahl with the addition of the Swedish *by*, meaning "village."

LESSOR TOWNSHIP received its name, changed in spelling from Lessard, in honor of a French Canadian pioneer farmer.

LIBERTY TOWNSHIP organized in 1880, was named by its people in the petition for township organization.

LINDSAY a post office, 1884–1912, in section 5, Hill River Township.

LOWELL TOWNSHIP organized in 1877, was named for the city of Lowell in Massachusetts, whence some of its settlers came.

MALLORY a village in section 26 of Huntsville, was named in honor of Charles P. Mallory, a lumber merchant in Fisher. He was born in the Province of Quebec, March 7, 1844; came to Minnesota in 1871, settling in Minneapolis; and removed to Fisher in 1878. The village had a post office, 1880–1916, and a station of the Great Northern Railway.

MAPLE BAY a village in section 14 of Godfrey Township, located on Maple Lake, was platted in 1882

and diminished in size by the early 1920s. The post office began as Godfrey in 1881, with Warren Godfrey, postmaster, changed to Maple Bay in 1882, with Fred H. Date, postmaster; the form of the name was Maplebay from 1895 until the post office closed in 1941.

MAPLE LAKE a village four miles southwest of Mentor, about 1937.

McDONALD a Great Northern Railway station in section 29 of Nesbit Township.

McINTOSH a city in sections 9, 10, and 16 of King Township, was named for Angus J. McIntosh, the owner of a part of the village site. He built a store and lodging house one and a half miles east of the present townsite, where he was postmaster when the post office began in 1884; he purchased land in the new townsite and lived there for a number of years before moving to Detroit Lakes, where he died in 1923. The city was incorporated as a village in April 1891 and reincorporated and separated from the township on July 11, 1911. The city includes the area formerly called King, which was principally a post office, 1883–89, in section 10 in the store of Ephraim King, three miles northeast of McIntosh, which consolidated with McIntosh in 1889. It had a Great Northern Railway station.

MELVIN a village in section 21 of Onstad Township, served as a trade center; it had a Northern Pacific Railroad station called Holmes in section 22; the post office operated 1890–1943, with Cyrus H. Holmes, first postmaster.

MENTOR a city in sections 22, 26, and 27 of Grove Park Township, was named for the village of Mentor in northeastern Ohio, where President Garfield purchased a farm, which was his country home during his last three years. The village was established in 1882, platted on September 21, 1892, and incorporated as a village on January 11, 1902. It had a Great Northern Railway station; the post office was established in 1882, George H. Tripp, postmaster.

MEOS see CLIMAX.

MERRILL SIDING a Northern Pacific Railroad siding in section 3 of Fisher Township on land owned by A. C. Merrill.

MOSLEY a post office, 1883–84; location not found.

MOVOLD a post office, January-April 1884, with Thron Movold, postmaster; location not found.

NASHVILLE see EAST GRAND FORKS.

NEBY a village in sections 25 and 36 of Tynsid Township, with a post office, 1881–1903.

NESBIT TOWNSHIP organized in 1880, was named in honor of James and Robert Nesbit, brothers, born in Lanark County, Canada, who settled here in 1875. A Great Northern Railway station was in section 19.

NIELSVILLE a city in sections 19, 20, 29, and 30 of Hubbard, incorporated as a village on May 7, 1920, was named for Nels C. Paulsrud, who first settled in the area in 1872 about one and a half miles northwest of the present site. Paulsrud came from Norway in 1869, his name originally being Nils Olson; he provided mail service at his home, which was called Old Nielsville after the post office of Nielsville began at the present location in 1883. The village had a station of the Great Northern Railway.

NOBLE a post office in section 28, Helgeland Township, 1901–23.

NOEL a post office, 1890–91, Eli H. Noel, postmaster; location not found.

NORTHLAND TOWNSHIP was named for Norway, the native land of many of its settlers. A post office was in section 18, 1892–1908, in the store owned by postmaster John Votvedt (Vaatveit), a Norwegian immigrant who came about 1888.

NOYES JUNCTION a village in section 19 of Crookston Township with a Great Northern Railway station.

OLGA a village in section 29, Eden Township, which had a post office, 1889–1914.

OMERA a Northern Pacific Railroad station in section 14 of Keystone Township.

ONSTAD TOWNSHIP organized in 1882, was named in honor of Ole P. Onstad, one of its pioneer farmers, an immigrant from Norway.

OSVETA a post office, 1881–83, located in Tabor Township, one mile south of the present community of Tabor; the postmaster was John Mikulicky, who later moved to Thief River Falls.

OVETIA a post office, 1886–96, in Tabor Township, which was earlier called Dover, 1884–86; Herman Helgeson was postmaster under both names.

PARNELL TOWNSHIP was named by settlers from Ireland in honor of Charles Stewart Parnell, the Irish statesman. He was born in Avondale, Ireland, in 1846; was a member of parliament, 1875–91; visited the United States in the interest of the Irish agitation for home rule in 1879–80; and died in Brighton, England, October 6, 1891.

QUEEN TOWNSHIP is the second east of King Township, which suggested this name. A post office was in section 2, 1899–1910.

REDLAND a station of the Great Northern Railway in section 1, Andover Township.

REIS TOWNSHIP organized in 1880, was named in honor of George Reis, an early settler, who came here from Pennsylvania and after a residence of several years removed to Michigan.

RHINEHART TOWNSHIP was named in honor of Capt. A. C. Rhinehart of East Grand Forks, who was a member of the board of county commissioners.

RINDAL/RINDAHL a post office, 1882–1905, established in Norman County and transferred to section 33 of Garden Township, Polk County, in 1901.

ROAN a village in section 19 of Brislet Township, with a station of the Great Northern Railway; some maps show this site as Roon.

ROCKWOOD a locality in sections 3 and 4 of Nesbit Township.

ROHOLT a post office, 1881–83, established as a supply post office for the western part of the county, 26 miles north of Ada, Norman County.

ROMSDAHL a post office, 1885–86; location not found.

ROOME TOWNSHIP organized in 1879, was named for one of its pioneer farmers.

ROON see ROAN.

ROSEBUD TOWNSHIP was named either by John Flesch, first settler in the Thirteen Towns district, who suggested the name to the county auditor for the abundance of wild roses on his claim, or for Rose Eikens, daughter of Herman Eikens, the first white child born in the settlement.

ROSS a station of the Great Northern Railway in section 19 of Lowell Township.

ROUXVILLE a post office, 1883–84, Esdras Roux, postmaster; location not found.

RUSSIA TOWNSHIP organized in 1882, and its railway village, bear the name of the largest country of Europe and of a township and village in New York. It had a post office, 1894–1907, named Russia located in section 18, with Felix Raulenbuehler, postmaster.

SANDSVILLE TOWNSHIP organized in 1882, was named in honor of Casper and Martin Sand, brothers, natives of Norway, who came here as homesteaders in 1880, opening a large stock farm.

SCANDIA TOWNSHIP bears the ancient name of the southern part of the peninsula of Sweden and Norway, whence those countries, and also Denmark and Iceland, are together named Scandinavia.

SCOTTSVILLE a post office, 1884–85, Thomas Scott, postmaster; location not found.

SHERACK a village in section 36 of Tabor Township and section 2 of Keystone Township, had a Northern Pacific Railroad station in section 3 of Keystone Township, and a post office, 1901–5.

SHIRLEY a village in section 25 of Fanny Township, seven miles north of Crookston, had a station of the Great Northern Railway, next to which was a 14-block platted townsite called Wakeman, which did not develop.

SLETTEN TOWNSHIP was named in honor of Paul C. Sletten, who was receiver of the U.S. land office in Crookston. A post office was in section 21, 1884–91 and 1896–1904.

SOLIE a post office, 1884–86, 37 miles northeast of Crookston and 16 miles northwest of St. Hilaire, Pennington County.

SOUTH EUCLID see EUCLID.

SPRAGUE a Great Northern Railway station in section 5 of Fisher Township.

SULLIVAN TOWNSHIP organized in 1880, was named in honor of Timothy Sullivan, municipal judge in East Grand Forks. A station of the Northern Pacific Railroad was in section 32.

TABOR TOWNSHIP settled by Bohemians, was named for a city of Bohemia about 50 miles south of Prague. Joe Bren built the first store in 1886 in the village in section 8; the post office operated 1889–1944, with Frank J. Cernousek as first postmaster; he was also a justice of the peace and legal adviser.

THEODORE a post office, 1903–17, in section 35 of Queen Township.

THIRTEEN TOWNS the area or district of the county encompassing the original thirteen townships opened for settlement in 1883: Badger, Brandsvold, Chester, Columbia, Eden, Fosston, Hill River, King, Knute, Lessor, Queen, Rosebud, and Sletten; a newspaper of this name, established in 1884, was published in Fosston.

TILDEN/TILDEN JUNCTION a village in section 21 of Tilden Township, had four blocks platted by 1902. A Great Northern Railway station was in section 22 and a Northern Pacific Railroad station in section 27; the post office, 1883–94, was called Tilden.

TILDEN TOWNSHIP organized in 1882, was named in honor of Samuel J. Tilden, who was born in New Lebanon, N.Y., February 9, 1814, and died at Greystone, near Yonkers, N.Y., August 4, 1886. He was governor of New York in 1875–76 and was the Democratic candidate for president of the United States in 1876.

TILL a post office, 1884–91, 35 miles southeast of Crookston, with Hogen B. Hogenson, postmaster and justice of the peace.

TILLIA a post office, 1872–73, with William C. Nash, postmaster; location not found.

TRAIL a city in section 30 of Gully Township, was named for its location where a former trail between the Red River valley and the Red Lake Agency was crossed by the railway. The city was incorporated as a village on April 17, 1950; it had a station of the Minneapolis, St. Paul and Sault Ste. Marie Railroad (Soo Line), and the post office was established in 1910.

TYNSID TOWNSHIP settled in 1871, and organized in 1879, was named for Tönset, a railway village in Norway, about 100 miles south of Trondheim. It was thus incorrectly written in the petition for the township organization.

VALLEY a post office, 1884–1905, located in section 19 of Garden Township, three and a half miles east of Fertile, its general store serving as a trading center.

VANNET a station of the Northern Pacific Railroad in section 3 of Nesbit Township.

VICTOR a post office, 1899–1901; location not found.

VINELAND TOWNSHIP organized in 1876, was named in compliment to Leif Steenerson, its first settler, who took a homestead claim here in May 1871. The name refers to the voyage of Leif Ericsson from Greenland, about the year 1000, when he explored a country to which he gave the name Vinland or Wineland, for its grape vines, having sailed probably to the coast of Maine and Massachusetts.

WAKEMAN see SHIRLEY.

WALKER SIDING/WALKERTON a Northern Pacific Railroad station in section 32 of Keystone Township, on the north side of the tracks.

WANKE a post office, 1896–1931, in section 28, Johnson Township, with Edward J. Wanke as first postmaster; the site had a store and a hotel.

WIG a post office, 1889–1900 and 1902–3, in section 33 of Bygland Township.

WILDS a station of the Great Northern Railway; location not found.

WILLEWATER a post office, 1884–89, in section 14 of Knute Township, located in Anders W. Anderson's store on the shore of Willewater Lake.

WINGER TOWNSHIP was named by Norwegian settlers for a group of farms in the valley district called Gudbrandsdal in central Norway. The city of Winger in section 22 was platted by the Soo Line in 1905 and was incorporated as a village on January 5, 1921; it began with a general store built by Ingebret Messelt in 1885, where he also was first postmaster when the post office was established in 1886. The major part of the village site in 1889 was on Gullek Overland's land, which he sold in 1904 to the Minnesota Land and Trust Company, moving to Fertile, where he died in 1909.

WINTHROP a post office, 1861–63; location not found.

WOODSIDE TOWNSHIP organized in 1882, lies mainly on the wooded southeastern side of Maple Lake, which is bordered westward by the vast prairie area of the Red River valley. A post office was in section 22, 1882–1905.

Lakes and Streams

The Red River and the Red Lake River are noticed in the first chapter, and they are more fully considered in the chapter on Red Lake County.

An older channel of the Red Lake River, branching from it in Fisher, extending about 25 miles northwestward and joining the Red River near the north line of Esther, was named the Grand Marais, meaning "great marsh," by the early French fur traders and voyageurs. Like Marsh River, which similarly extends from the Wild Rice River at Ada northwest to the Red River in Norman County, it has during most of the year only a small and nearly stagnant stream, which is changed into a great river with the snow melting of spring and at times of heavy rains.

The Snake River, translated from Kanabec, its Ojibwe name, crosses the north line of this county for a few miles in Sandsville, and by several creeks receives the drainage of its northeastern townships, from Belgium and Euclid northward.

Lost River, in Gully and Chester, flowing west to the Clearwater River in Red Lake County, was lost in a large swamp along a part of its lower course.

Hill River, from which a township received its name, was translated from Peqwudina zibi of the Ojibwe, as written by Gilfillan.

Poplar River, having its sources in Columbia and joining the Clearwater River near the northwest corner of Poplar River Township in Red Lake County, is a translation of the Ojibwe name, Asadi zibi.

Badger Lake and Creek, giving their name to a township of Polk County, have been before noticed.

Burnham and Anderson Creeks are southern tributaries of the Red Lake River in Fisher.

Sand Hill River, flowing westward through the south edge of this county from unnamed lakes near its sources in Rosebud Township, is another translation from the Ojibwe, given more fully by Gilfillan as "Ga-papiqwutawangawi zibi, or the river of sand hills, scattered here and there in places." The short English name is used on the map of Maj. Stephen H. Long's expedition in 1823. Plentiful dunes of windblown sand, forming hillocks 25 to 75 or 100 feet high, to which this name refers, occur within two miles west of Fertile and thence for a distance of five miles southward, lying on the sand delta deposited here at the highest level of the ancient Lake Agassiz.

Maple Lake, before noticed for its villages of Lakeside Park and Maple Bay, has many sugar maple trees in the forest at its southeast side.

Cable Lake is about a mile west of Lakeside Park.

Union Lake, in Woodside and Knute Townships, was named for its comprising three wide parts united by straits.

Crystal Lake, in Woodside, has exceptionally transparent water.

Lake Sarah, in the southwest part of Knute

Township, adjoins the east end of Union Lake. In the north part of this township are Lake Cameron beside Erskine village, named for Daniel Cameron, an early homesteader on the site of this village, and Oak Lake, named for its oak groves.

Lake Arthur, in Garfield Township, was named in honor of Chester Alan Arthur (1830–86), who succeeded Garfield as president of the United States, 1881–85.

Cross Lake, named from its outline, on the headstream of Hill River in the central part of Queen Township, had a very long Ojibwe name, translated by Gilfillan as "the lake with pines on one side of the water."

Turtle Lake, a mile west of Cross Lake, is translated from the Ojibwe, their name, noted by Gilfillan, being "Mekinako sagaiigun, or Turtle lake, from its form, which, seen from a canoe in the middle, closely resembles a turtle."

Perch Lake adjoins the west side of Cross Lake, and Connection Lake forms the greater part of a canoe route between Cross and Turtle Lakes.

White Fish Lake, on the south line of Queen Township, a mile south of Turtle Lake, is one of the sources of the Poplar River, which also receives the outflow of six smaller lakes in the west part of Columbia.

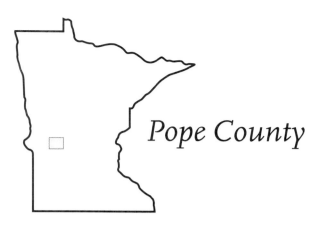

Pope County

This county, established February 20, 1862, and organized September 4, 1866, was named in honor of Gen. John Pope, who was born in Louisville, Ky., March 16, 1822, and died in Sandusky, Ohio, September 23, 1892. He was graduated at West Point in 1842 and served as a lieutenant in the Mexican War. In the summer of 1849 he was a member of an exploring expedition under the command of Maj. Samuel Woods, which went from Fort Snelling up the Mississippi and Sauk Rivers and past White Bear Lake (later named Lake Minnewaska), in the present Pope County, to the Red River, and thence northward by a route at a considerable distance west of the river to Pembina. On the return, in order to make a thorough examination of the Red River (later Otter Tail River), Pope and a small number of the party embarked in canoes and ascended this river to Otter Tail Lake, made the portage to Leaf Lakes, and thence descended the Leaf, Crow Wing, and Mis-

sissippi Rivers. He wrote in his report: "On the 27th of September we arrived at Fort Snelling, and completed a voyage of nearly one thousand miles, never before made by any one with a like object."

At the time of this expedition, Pope was a captain. He was afterward, in 1853 to 1859, commander of the expedition making surveys for a Pacific railroad near the 32d parallel. In the Civil War he was a most energetic defender of the Union, and early in 1862 was commissioned major general. September 6, 1862, shortly after the outbreak of the Dakota War in Minnesota, General Pope was appointed commander of the Department of the Northwest, with headquarters at St. Paul, and he continued in charge of this department until January 1865. To his efficient direction and cooperation was due, in a large degree, the success of Gens. Henry H. Sibley and Alfred Sully in their campaigns of 1863 and 1864 against the Dakota.

Information of the origins and meanings of names was received from the Illustrated Album of Biography of Pope and Stevens Counties, *1888, having pp. 145–364 for Pope County; and from Ole Irgens, county auditor, Casper T. Wollan, a pioneer merchant, and his brother, M. A. Wollan, president of the Pope County State Bank, each of Glenwood, the county seat, interviewed during a visit there in May 1916.*

ANDERSON a post office, 1868–83, in the wheat-growing area of Barsness Township, with Ole N. Barsness, postmaster.

BANGOR TOWNSHIP bears the name of a city in Maine and of villages and townships in New York, Pennsylvania, Michigan, Wisconsin, and several other states.

BARSNESS TOWNSHIP was named in honor of three brothers, Nels N., Erik N., and Ole N.

Barsness, born in Norway respectively in 1835, 1842, and 1844, who settled in this township in 1865–66. The village in sections 10 and 11 had a post office, 1897–1906, and a Minneapolis, St. Paul and Sault Ste. Marie Railroad (Soo Line) station in section 15.

BELCHER see WESTPORT.

BEN WADE see LOWRY.

BEN WADE TOWNSHIP was named in honor of Benjamin Franklin Wade, who was born near Springfield, Mass., October 27, 1800, and died in Jefferson, Ohio, March 2, 1878. He removed to Ohio with his parents, about 1820; began law practice in 1827; was a district judge, 1847–51; and was a U.S. senator, 1851–69. He was an anti-slavery leader and supported the Homestead Act of 1862.

BLUE MOUNDS TOWNSHIP is crossed by a belt of low morainic drift hills, to which this name was given by settlers from Blue Mounds, a village in Dane County, Wis. The hills thus named in each of these states appear bluish when seen from a distance. A post office operated in the township, 1874–84.

BROOTEN a city with Stearns County.

CAMP DAKOTA a place name shown on a 1910 county map in section 24, Glenwood Township, on the east shore of Lake Minnewaska.

CHIPPEWA FALLS see TERRACE.

CHIPPEWA FALLS TOWNSHIP was named for its falls in Terrace village, descending 16 feet, on the East Branch of the Chippewa River, supplying water power for a flour mill. This village and its post office at first were called Chippewa Falls but were renamed by request of the settlers to prevent their mail from going to the city of Chippewa Falls in Wisconsin.

CYRUS a city in sections 19, 20, 29, and 30 of New Prairie Township, was incorporated as a village on March 16, 1899, and platted in 1881 by O. H. Dahl and Charles Olson on their 1866 homestead, who set aside part of the land for a village. It was first called Scandiaville but changed in 1882 when the post office, requested by first postmaster M. Frank Cronquist, who built a store in 1881, was established as Cyrus, a name suggested by Olson.

EGGEN a post office, 1897–1901, in Hoff Township, with Ole Eggen, postmaster.

ERICKSON a post office, 1884–98, in Lake Johanna Township, with Peter Erickson, postmaster.

FARWELL a city in section 16 of Ben Wade Township, was platted in April 1887, and incorporated as a village on June 12, 1905; its name is possibly a form of the Norwegian word *farväl* meaning "farewell." The city was established in 1886 when the Soo Line arrived; Ole Irgens was postmaster when the post office opened in 1887 in a small building before he built a store with Jacob Jacobson in 1890, serving until 1900.

FLINT a station of the Soo Line in section 26 of Reno Township.

FOWLDS see SEDAN.

FRON a post office, 1883–87, located six miles north of Starbuck and associated with a congregation organized in 1888 at Starbuck.

GILCHRIST TOWNSHIP was named for the first syllables of the surnames of Ole Gilbertson and Gunder Christopherson, early settlers. Gilbertson's cousin was Olaus Olson Grove, the first settler in the county (1859) and in Barsness Township (1861); another of the township's first families was that of Knut Simon, for whom Simon Lake in this township was named. A post office was in section 17, 1868–1905.

GLENWOOD TOWNSHIP on the southeast side of Lake Minnewaska, was named for the great glen or valley occupied by this lake and for the woods around its shores, contrasted with the prairies that form the far greater part of this county. The city of Glenwood, the county seat at the northeast end of the lake, in Glenwood and Minnewaska Townships, was first settled in 1856 and was first platted in part on September 26, 1866, by Kirk J. Kinney and Alfred W. Lathrop on land owned by Kinney, who named it for his home in New York; it was incorporated as a village on February 23, 1881, and as a city in 1912. The first building was the Kinney and Lathrop store, where Lathrop served as first postmaster when the post office was established in 1867; the Little Falls branch of the Northern Pacific Railroad came in 1882 and the Soo Line in 1886.

GROVE CITY a village, was incorporated on June 24, 1858; no location and no trace found.

GROVE LAKE TOWNSHIP has Grove Lake and McCloud Lake near its south side, which are more fully noticed in the later part of this chapter. The village of Grove Lake is in section 24, one mile east of the lake for which it is named; it was incorporated as a village on June 24, 1858, but the incorporation was dissolved; it had a post office, 1872–1907.

HOFF TOWNSHIP was named for the village of Hof in Norway, about 50 miles north of Christiania. A Great Northern Railway station was in section 19; it was also known as Hynes.

HOREB a post office, 1874–83 and 1898–1901, in Blue Mounds Township.

HOVERUD a farmers post office, 1884–93, located 18 miles southwest of Glenwood and eight miles from Hancock, Stevens County, name of township unknown; the community was settled in 1872.

HYNES see HOFF.

LAKE AMELIA a post office, 1876–83, located on the Little Chippewa River in Glenwood Township; Frank A. West was the first postmaster.

LAKE JOHANNA TOWNSHIP bears the name given to its large lake on the map of Minnesota in 1860, probably in honor of the wife or daughter of an early settler, but her surname is unknown. A post office was located in the township, 1868–1903, with John Johnson as first postmaster.

LANGHEI TOWNSHIP has a Norwegian name, meaning "a long highland." Its northeastern part gradually rises to an elevation about 300 feet above Lake Minnewaska, being the highest land in the south half of the county, with a very extensive prospect on all sides. A post office was in section 12, 1871–1904.

LEVEN TOWNSHIP was named for a loch, or lake, in eastern Scotland the Leven River outflowing from it, and the seaport at its mouth, on the north side of the Firth of Forth.

LONG BEACH a city on the northwest side of Lake Minnewaska in Minnewaska Township, was incorporated as a village on May 18, 1938.

LOWRY a city in section 24 of Ben Wade Township, platted in March 1887 and incorporated as a village on May 5, 1896, was named in honor of Thomas Lowry, who was born in Logan County, Ill., February 27, 1843, and died in Minneapolis, February 4, 1909. He was admitted to the bar in 1867 and in the same year came to Minnesota, settling in Minneapolis, where he practiced law and dealt in real estate; was president and principal stockowner of the company operating the street railways of Minneapolis and St. Paul, called the Twin City Rapid Transit Company. The post office began as Ben Wade in 1884, with John L.

Johnson, postmaster; when the Soo Line came in 1887, the name was changed to Lowry, and John E. Benson, who had a store in the township for many years, moved it to Lowry, becoming the first postmaster.

MINNEWASKA TOWNSHIP adjoining the northern shore of the largest lake in this county, bears the name given to the lake by the white settlers made from two Dakota words, *mini* or *minne*, "water," and *washta* or *waska*, "good." Prof. N. H. Winchell wrote of the lake and its successive names, as follows: "This lake, according to statements of citizens of Glenwood, was originally designated by an Indian name, meaning *Dish Lake*, because of its being in a low basin. After that, when the chief, White Bear, was buried in a high hill on the north shore, it was called *White Bear Lake*. After a time it was changed to *Lake Whipple*, from Bishop Whipple, of Faribault, and by act of the state legislature in 1883 it was again changed to *Minnewaska*, or Good-water. It is said to be 85 feet deep in its deepest part and averages about 40 feet, and there is no known evidence of its having ever stood at a higher level" (*Geological Survey of Minnesota, Thirteenth Annual Report*, for 1884, p. 14).

Joseph N. Nicollet's map, published in 1843, has no delineation nor name for this lake, which, with its grandly picturesque basin and enclosing bluffs, is the most noteworthy topographic feature of the county. Woods and Pope, in their exploration in 1849, first mapped it as White Bear Lake. The name Lake Whipple, in honor of Henry Benjamin Whipple (1822–1901), the revered and beloved Episcopal bishop of Minnesota, was applied to it during several years, when it was confidently expected that an Episcopal school would be founded at Glenwood.

NEW PRAIRIE a village trade center and station of the Northern Pacific Railroad in section 30 of White Bear Lake Township, with a post office, 1872–83 and 1920–46.

NEW PRAIRIE TOWNSHIP was named by its settlers, as their new home in the great prairie area of western Minnesota.

NORA TOWNSHIP is reputed to have been named for Norway, the native country of many of its people. A post office was in section 21, 1876–1903.

OTTO a post office, 1867–89, located in section 30 of Westport Township, was named for the youngest son of the first postmaster, Norman

Shook, who operated the post office in his home and was the first settler in the area; he was later judge of probate.

RENO TOWNSHIP received the name of its large lake, commemorating Jesse Lee Reno, major general of U.S. volunteers, who was born in Wheeling, W.Va., June 20, 1823, and was killed in the battle of South Mountain, Md., September 14, 1862. He was graduated at West Point in 1846, served in both the Mexican and Civil Wars, and made a survey in 1853 for a military road from Mendota, Minn., to the mouth of the Big Sioux River. A post office was in section 18, 1868–76.

ROLLING FORKS TOWNSHIP was named for its contour as an undulating and rolling prairie, crossed by the East Branch, or Fork, of the Chippewa River, which here receives a considerable tributary from the north. A post office was located in the township near the county border, 1870–76 and 1879–83.

SEDAN a city in Grove Lake and Bangor Townships, is named for a city of France, famous for the battle fought on September 1, 1870, between the Germans and the French, which resulted in the surrender of the French army, leading directly to the establishment of France as a republic. The city was incorporated as a village on November 19, 1897; it was surveyed in 1887 as Thorson but was changed soon after to Fowlds for Jim Fowlds, one of the first settlers; a post office operated under that name, 1887–92, with Charles A. Warner, postmaster, at which time it was changed to Sedan, with John H. Warner, new postmaster, in the Warner general store. The Minneapolis and Pacific Railroad came in 1887.

STARBUCK platted in the spring of 1882 and incorporated as a village on June 6, 1883, is a city in sections 23–26 of White Bear Lake Township. There are four versions of the city's naming: (1) for the oxen Star and Buck, owned by Andrew Hagenson, who hauled the materials for an early bridge and on whose homestead lay the railroad right-of-way; (2) for Sidney Starbuck, a director of the Little Falls and Dakota Railroad; (3) for W. H. Starbuck, a New York capitalist with interests in railroad construction; or (4) for an early settler whose last name was Sagbaken. The post office began in 1869 in section 12 as White Bear Centre, with Nels B. Wollan, one of eight brothers who came from Norway, as postmaster in his general

store three miles north and one-half mile east of the present townsite; he moved the store to Starbuck in 1882 when the name changed, continuing as postmaster.

STAY-A-WHILE PARK a subdivision or populated place south of Glenwood in section 18 of Glenwood Township, is shown on the 1910 county map.

STOCKHOLM a village in section 18 of Gilchrist Township, was designated the county seat in 1862 and officially organized as the county seat in September 1866; at the 1867 fall election, the county seat was moved to Glenwood, and this site was abandoned.

TERRACE is a village formerly called Chippewa Falls, in section 33 of the township of that name, platted in June 1871. The village is built on a terrace plain of the valley drift bordering both sides of the Chippewa River. The post office was first named Chippewa Falls, 1871–81. William Moses and the two Wheeler brothers, John and George, came to Owatonna from Canada in 1868, where they built a gristmill; they moved to Pope County in 1870 and built a mill in 1871 and a store, where John Wheeler was first postmaster; the post office discontinued in 1974.

THORSON see SEDAN.

VILLARD a city in Westport and Leven Townships, platted in August 1882, was named in honor of Henry Villard, who was born in Bavaria, April 11, 1835, and died at Dobbs Ferry, N.Y., November 12, 1900. He came to the United States in 1853, engaged in journalism and in the management of railroads, and was president of the Northern Pacific Railroad company in 1881–83, when the construction of its transcontinental line was completed. E. V. Smalley, in his history of this railroad, devoted two chapters (pp. 245–76) to the very remarkable career of Villard, up to the time of its publication in 1883. The city was incorporated as a village on October 4, 1883, and separated from the township on March 18, 1908; it had a station of the Northern Pacific Railroad in section 24 of Leven Township, and the post office was established in 1882.

WALDEN TOWNSHIP has the name of a township and village in Vermont and of villages in New York, Georgia, and Colorado. Henry D. Thoreau lived alone in 1845–47 beside Walden Pond, near Concord, Mass., as narrated in his book, *Walden,* *or Life in the Woods*, published in 1854. A post office was in section 14, 1897–1901.

WESTFIELD a post office in section 33 of Grove Lake Township, 1868–76.

WESTPORT TOWNSHIP and its city in sections 14 and 23, which was incorporated as a village on March 13, 1926, have a name that is borne by townships and villages in Maine, Massachusetts, Connecticut, New York, Wisconsin, and ten other states. The city was first platted in 1866 by D. M. Durkey on the northeast bank of Lake Westport, where he built a log two-story way station for travelers on the Red River trail; the city was replatted in October 1882; growth of the village was encouraged when the Little Falls and Dakota Railroad came through. The post office began as Belcher 1883–88, changing its name in 1888, and serving as a rural branch, 1966–1970.

WHITE BEAR CENTRE see STARBUCK.

WHITE BEAR LAKE TOWNSHIP includes the western end of this lake, which has been known by several names, before mentioned for Minnewaska Township. The grave of the Ojibwe leader White Bear is an elongated mound on a knoll in the south edge of section 3, Minnewaska, about 90 feet above the lake, as described by Prof. N. H. Winchell (*Aborigines of Minnesota*, 1911, p. 298).

"Waube-Mokwa (the White Bear), who was a chief among the Ojibways and dwelt by these waters," is represented to have lived here more than two centuries ago by "*The Tribe of Pezhekee, a Legend of Minnesota*" (1901, 232 pp.), written by Alice Otillia Thorson of Glenwood. It is known in history, however, that the warfare of the Ojibwe against the Dakota, acquiring the region of northern Minnesota by conquest, took place much later.

WINTHROP is referred to as the oldest site in county, but no location is noted.

Lakes and Streams

Excepting its eastern border, this county is drained by the Chippewa River, which is fully noticed for the origin of its name in the chapter on Chippewa County. Its tributaries in Pope County are the Little Chippewa River, Outlet Creek, which flows from Lake Minnewaska and through Lake Emily, and the East Branch, from which Chippewa Falls and Rolling Forks Townships are named, flowing into Swift County.

Signalness Creek, tributary to Outlet Creek from the north side of the Blue Mounds, and a small lake crossed by the south line of section 14 in Blue Mounds Township, were named in honor of Olaus Signalness, a pioneer farmer in the northwest quarter of that section. He was born in Norway, November 12, 1851; came to the United States in 1864, with his parents, who settled in Wisconsin; and in 1869 they removed to this county, being the first settlers in this township. The lake is also known as Mountain Lake. Its entire watershed is within the boundaries of Glacial Lakes State Park, established in 1963 to preserve the rich prairie flora.

Mud Creek flows from Lake Johanna Township southwestward to the East Branch.

Grove Lake, having a grove beside it, which gives its name to a township, and McCloud Lake, closely adjoining its west end, are at the head of the North Fork of Crow River, flowing east into Stearns County. These lakes were on the route of Woods and Pope, in the expedition to the Red River in 1849, and their party camped here during a week, from June 27 to July 3, but they were then named Lightning Lakes, referring to a severe thunderstorm, with "a stroke of lightning, which tore in pieces one of the tents, and prostrated nearly all the persons who were in the camp." The name of the Lightning Lakes, however, although clearly shown by Pope's journal to belong to the Grove and McCloud Lakes, has been transferred to two other lakes much farther west on their course, in Grant County and southwestern Otter Tail County.

Westport Lake, in the township of this name, is the source of Ashley Creek, which flows into Stearns County and is a tributary of the Sauk River.

The other lakes of Pope County, including many named for pioneer settlers, are noted as follows, in the order of the townships from south to north, and of the ranges from east to west.

Lake Johanna Township has the large lake of this name.

Gilchrist Township has Lakes Gilchrist, Linka, Nilson, and Johnson, Scandinavian Lake and Goose and Simon Lakes. Lake Linka was named in honor of the wife of Rev. Peter S. Reque, a Lutheran pastor.

Rolling Folks Township has Lakes Hanson,

Helge, Anderson, and Rasmusson. The first named, which is the largest, was formerly called Woodpecker Lake.

Langhei has Lake Benson and Swan Lake.

Hoff, the most southwestern township, and Bangor, the most eastern of the townships numbered 124, have no lakes.

Chippewa Falls Township has Round Lake and Lakes Swenoda and Anderson. The second is a composite name, for its adjoining Swedish, Norwegian, and Danish settlers; and Swenoda Township, 25 miles distant to the southwest, in Swift County, was named in the same way.

Barsness has Lakes Stenerson, Gilbertson, Ben, Mary, Celia, Nelson, and Edwards.

Lake Emily, on Outlet Creek in Blue Mounds and Walden Townships, quite surely commemorates the wife or daughter of a pioneer, but her surname, as for other feminine names of lakes in this county, remains to be ascertained for a more definite historical record.

Grove Lake Township, beginning the tier numbered 125, has Lake Lincoln and Mud Lake, with Grove and McCloud Lakes, which earlier had been named Lightning Lakes, as before noted.

Lake Alice is mainly in section 12, Glenwood, and Camp Lake is crossed by the west line of its sections 30 and 31.

Minnewaska Township, with its large and beautiful lake of this name, has also Pelican Lake.

White Bear Lake Township has Lake Malmedard, crossed by its north line, named for Christian Malmedard, a pioneer Norwegian farmer there.

On the west line of New Prairie Township are Lakes Charlotte and Cyrus, the latter being southwest of Cyrus village.

In Westport, the most northeastern township, Westport Lake, as before mentioned, is connected southward by a strait with the wider Swan Lake.

Leven has a series of four lakes, the most southern being Lake Amelia, the source of the East Branch of the Chippewa River; Lake Villard, next northward, adjoining the village of this name; and Lakes Leven and Ellen. Rice Lake, west of Lake Villard, is named for its wild rice.

In Reno Township, with its lake so named, are Lakes Ann and John, and Mud Lake, crossed by its north boundary.

Ben Wade Township has Lake Jorgenson.

Nora, the most northwestern township, has Pike Lake, named by Woods and Pope in 1849 for many pike fish caught there.

Hills

The Blue Mounds, before mentioned for the township named for them, are overtopped by the great highland of Langhei, also before noted in the list of townships. The very massive Langhei Hill and the deep basin and high bluffs of Lake Minnewaska are undoubtedly due to the contour of the bedrocks, though no outcrop of them is seen because of their concealment under the glacial drift.

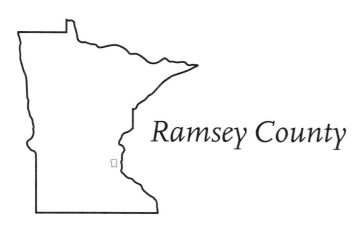

Ramsey County

Established October 27, 1849, this county was named in honor of Alexander Ramsey, the first governor of Minnesota Territory. He was born near Harrisburg, Pa., September 8, 1815; studied at Lafayette College; was admitted to the practice of law in 1839; was a Whig member of Congress from Pennsylvania, 1843–47; was appointed by Pres. Zachary Taylor, April 2, 1849, as governor of this territory; arrived in St. Paul, May 27; and commenced his official duties here June 1, 1849. He continued in this office to May 15, 1853. In 1851 Gov. Ramsey negotiated important treaties with the Dakota at Traverse des Sioux and Mendota and in 1863 with the Ojibwe where the Pembina trail crossed the Red Lake River, by these treaties opening to settlement the greater part of southern and western Minnesota. He was the second mayor of St. Paul in 1855. After the admission of Minnesota as a state, he was elected its second governor and held this office from January 2, 1860, to July 10, 1863, during the very trying times of the Civil War and the Dakota War. Being in Washing-

ton on business for the state when the news of the fall of Fort Sumter was received, he at once tendered to Pres. Abraham Lincoln a regiment of 1,000 men from Minnesota, this being the first offer of armed support to the government. Ramsey was U.S. senator, 1863–75, and secretary of war in the cabinet of Pres. Rutherford B. Hayes, 1879–81. He was president of the Minnesota Historical Society, 1849–63, and from 1891 until his death in St. Paul, April 22, 1903. The Minnesota legislature provided that his statue be placed in the Statuary Hall of the national capitol.

When this county was established in 1849, as one of the nine counties into which the new territory was originally divided, it reached north to Mille Lacs and to the upper Mississippi in the present Aitkin County. In 1857, with the formation of Anoka, Isanti, Mille Lacs, and Aitkin Counties, Ramsey retained only a small part of its former area and became the smallest county of Minnesota. Its county seat, St. Paul, has been continuously the capital of the territory and state.

Information of the origins of names has been gathered in A History of the City of Saint Paul and of the County of Ramsey *by J. Fletcher Williams, published in 1876 as vol. 4 of the Minnesota Historical Society Collections (475 pp.);* History of Ramsey County and the City of St. Paul *(1881, 650 pp.);* Fifty Years in the Northwest *by William H. C. Folsom (1888), having pp. 532–90 for this county; and*

History of St. Paul, *edited by Gen. C. C. Andrews (1890), 603 pp., with biographical sketches, 217 pp., by R. I. Holcombe.*

ARDEN HILLS a city, formerly part of Mounds View Township, was incorporated on February 14, 1951.
BALD EAGLE a village on the southern shore of Bald Eagle Lake, in sections 11 and 12 of White

Bear Township. The lake was so named because "a small island near the center was the home of several bald eagles at the time of the government surveys." The village had an industrial park and a depot built by the St. Paul and Duluth Railroad.

BELLAIRE a village in White Bear Township.

BELLVILLE a village incorporated on May 23, 1857, location not found.

BLAINE a city with Anoka County.

BROOKLYND a place name across the Mississippi River from the St. Paul levee, about 1859.

BROPHY SETTLEMENT a site six miles northeast of St. Paul and four miles from St. Anthony, was settled in the fall of 1850 by Michael Brophy, a soldier in the Mexican War, and his wife; the 160 acres, with Lake Johanna in the center, attracted a number of other settlers, 1850–55.

CARDIGAN JUNCTION a village in section 25 of Mounds View Township, halfway between Owasso and Vadnais Lakes, in what is now Shoreview; a Minneapolis, St. Paul and Sault Ste. Marie Railroad (Soo Line) station was in section 36 in 1880, and a post office operated as Cardigan, 1894–1912.

CASTLE see **NORTH ST. PAUL.**

CENTERVILLE a post office, 1856–59; location not found.

CLAYMOUNT a Northern Pacific Railroad station in section 32 of New Canada Township.

CUENCA a Soo Line station in section 1 of Rose Township, on the east shore of Lake Owasso.

FALCON HEIGHTS a city, formerly part of Rose Township, incorporated as a village on April 1, 1949.

FORDSON a station of the Chicago, Milwaukee, St. Paul and Pacific Railroad, five miles west of St. Paul's Union Depot.

FRENCHMAN'S BAR a locality in the bend of the Mississippi River, below the mouth of the Minnesota River, about 1867.

GEM LAKE a city, next to White Bear Lake, incorporated as a village on July 1, 1959.

GLADSTONE a village and junction of the Northern Pacific Railroad and the Soo Line, in New Canada, was named in honor of William Ewart Gladstone (1809–98), the eminent British statesman, for whom villages are also named in New Jersey, Illinois, Michigan, and other states. A post office named Gladstone in section 15 of New Canada Township, 1888–1923, was later known as Gloster or Glouster from about 1928 to 1941.

GLENWOOD a village in White Bear Township, about 1930.

HAMLINE a post office, 1880–91, at a site now within St. Paul city limits, near Hamline University and the state fairgrounds; it was also known as Johanna Crossing before 1873, then College Centre, then College Place.

HARVESTER WORKS a post office, 1876–79; location not found.

HAZEL PARK a neighborhood within east St. Paul city limits, which had a railway station of the Chicago, St. Paul, Minneapolis and Omaha Railroad nearly four miles northeast from the Union Depot in St. Paul; it "was so named because it was located in the midst of a dense hazel shrubbery" (Stennett, *Place Names of the Chicago and Northwestern Railways*, 1908, p. 178).

HIGHWOOD a railway station of the Chicago, Burlington and Quincy Railroad and a post office, 1901–7, in the southeast part of the area of St. Paul, having the same name with villages in Connecticut, New Jersey, and Illinois.

HOFFMANS CORNER a locality between St. Paul and White Bear Lake at U.S. Highway 61 and County Road E.

HOWARDS LAKE a post office, 1855–61, with John P. Howard, postmaster; location not found.

IRONDALE a townsite, was begun in 1891 when the Harris Brothers established an ironworks, the name probably in reference to that enterprise; located at the northern end of Long Lake, the site had 25 company houses, a general store, a hotel, a number of saloons, and a post office, 1892–93; most of the company homes were moved to sites in New Brighton, two miles south, and Mounds View Township.

LAKE SHORE PARK a station in section 23 of White Bear Township of the Union Pacific Railroad and an interurban rail line.

LAKEWOOD a village in White Bear Township, which became part of White Bear city.

LAUDERDALE a city incorporated as a village on January 21, 1949, once in Hennepin County and formerly part of Rose Township, was named for William Henry Lauderdale; he was born in 1830 in New York, arrived in Hennepin County in 1854, owned land in the area later known as Prospect Hills, was a veterinarian, had a dairy and real estate business, and died in the early 1900s.

LITTLE CANADA a city in section 32 of New Canada Township with a post office, located in section 13, 1852–76; the first settler was French Canadian farmer, voyageur, and trader Benjamin Gervais, who came in 1844. Abraham Lambert, born in 1790 in Lauzon, Canada, came to the area in 1845, was postmaster, 1852–54, and died in 1875.

MACALESTER a post office, 1886–89, in section 3 of Reserve Township, near Macalester College, within St. Paul city limits.

MAPLEWOOD a city and suburb of St. Paul with 12 miles of common boundary with that city, which was formerly was New Canada Township, exclusive of North St. Paul; it was incorporated as a village on February 28, 1957.

McLEAN TOWNSHIP organized in April 1858, was named in honor of Nathaniel McLean, who in 1853 settled on its sections 3 and 4, east of Dayton's Bluff adjoining the Mississippi. He was born in Morris County, N.J., May 16, 1787; came to St. Paul in 1849; was the Indian agent at Fort Snelling, 1849–53; and died in St. Paul, April 11, 1871. This former township was annexed to the city of St. Paul in 1887.

MERRIAM PARK a large residential district in the western part of St. Paul, was named for Hon. John L. Merriam (1825–95) and his son, Gov. William R. Merriam, who with others were the original proprietors of this addition to the city.

MOUNDS VIEW TOWNSHIP organized May 11, 1858, has a tract of hills of morainic drift extending from south to north about three miles through its central part, affording a fine panoramic view from their northern and highest points, which are about 200 feet above the surrounding country. When the township was organized, it included the present Shoreview, Arden Hills, New Brighton, Mounds View, and parts of North Oaks and St. Anthony; the township changed when New Brighton incorporated in 1891, Arden Hills in 1951, and Spring Lake Park in 1956. The city of Mounds View was incorporated as a village on April 24, 1958; its post office operated 1858–59 and again 1887–89, before being transferred to New Brighton, St. Paul providing that service since 1950.

MOUNTVILLE a village in section 3 of McLean Township, about 1867–74.

NEW BRIGHTON a city formerly part of Mounds View Township, incorporated as a village on November 20, 1890, having stockyards and meat-packing business, was named for Brighton, Mass., which formerly was an important cattle market with abattoirs, now a suburban district of Boston. The post office was at Mounds View earlier and then here from 1889, with William L. Marston, postmaster; the post office consolidated with St. Paul in 1950. The city was the site of the first owner-occupied townhouse complex in the state, Windsor Green, begun in 1964.

NEW CANADA TOWNSHIP also at first called Little Canada, organized May 11, 1858, was named in compliment for its French Canadian settlers. A post office was located in the township, 1884–1903, with Antoine Lanoux as postmaster.

NORTH OAKS a city incorporated on July 18, 1956, was formerly part of White Bear and Mounds View Townships.

NORTH ST. PAUL a city in section 1 of New Canada, adjoining Silver Lake, incorporated as a village on January 17, 1888, was at first named Castle in honor of Capt. Henry Anson Castle (1841–1916) of St. Paul, by whom it was founded in 1887, the next year after the Wisconsin Central Railroad was built there. The post office began as Castle in 1885, changed to North St. Paul in 1887, and discontinued in 1936, the service then provided through St. Paul.

OAKLAND a station of the Chicago, Burlington and Quincy Railroad in section 11 of McLean Township.

OTTER LAKE a post office, 1856–60; location not found.

OWASSO a station of the Northern Pacific Railroad, seven miles north of St. Paul.

PIG'S EYE a locality on the Mississippi river opposite Kaposia, circa 1849–70, with one street two miles long; also known as Weldsville, Wellsville, and LeClaire's Settlement. The name is also given to a lake, an island, a sandbar, and a lighthouse. All were named for Pierre (Pig's Eye) Parrant.

PLEASANT LAKE SETTLEMENT a locality of 1851, about ten miles north of St. Paul.

RESERVE TOWNSHIP organized May 11, 1858, had been until 1853 a part of the Fort Snelling military reserve. The north line of this reservation east of the river, surveyed in 1839, as noted in the chapter of Hennepin County, coincided nearly with the north line of this township and with the present Iglehart Avenue of St. Paul. In 1887, with the enlargement of St. Paul to the present area, this township became a suburban part of the city.

RIVERVIEW formerly called West St. Paul or simply the West Side, being the part of the city on the western (but here really the southern) side of the Mississippi, received this name February 15, 1918, by action of the city council. Its high river bluffs, in part known as Cherokee Heights, give very extensive and grand views of this valley. The petition for the change to the name Riverview bore 3,434 signatures, while 50 opposing it preferred that the new name should be South Side.

ROSE TOWNSHIP organized May 11, 1858, was named in honor of Isaac Rose, who settled here in the summer of 1843, purchasing 170 acres of land, which included the site of Macalester College. He was born in New Jersey in 1802; was a land agent, selecting farms for immigrants; died at Ottawa, Minn., in February 1871.

ROSEVILLE a city in Rose Township, was incorporated as a village on April 19, 1948, and separated from the township. One of its first settlers was Isaac Rose, who was the postmaster, 1857–61, its years of operation, and for whom the township and village were named. The townsite changed over the years from a rural community to a suburb of St. Paul.

ST. ANTHONY a city with Hennepin County.

ST. ANTHONY PARK the most northwestern part of St. Paul, includes a residential area of nearly two square miles, adjoining the St. Paul campus of the University of Minnesota, with the state fairgrounds, which are in Rose Township. The name was applied to additions of the city area, in allusion to the former city of St. Anthony, now the east part of Minneapolis, bordering the west side of St. Anthony Park. Both refer to St. Anthony Falls of the Mississippi, named by Father Louis Hennepin in 1680 after his patron saint. A post office called St. Anthony Park was in section 29 of Rose Township, 1886–91, and a station of the Great Northern Railway.

ST. FRANCIS a townsite incorporated on May 23, 1857, on White Bear Lake, but no trace found.

ST. JOHNS a locality in section 5 and 6 of New Canada Township in 1874.

ST. PAUL the county seat and the capital of Minnesota, first settled by Pierre Parrant in 1838, received its name from a little Catholic chapel built in 1841 under the direction of Father Lucian Galtier, who in the preceding year had come to Mendota, near Fort Snelling. The history of the building and naming of the chapel, with the adoption of the name for the village and city, was written in part as follows by Galtier in 1864, at the request of Bishop Thomas L. Grace.

"In 1841, in the month of October, logs were prepared and a church erected, so poor that it would well remind one of the stable at Bethlehem. It was destined, however, to be the nucleus of a great city. On the 1st day of November, in the same year, I blessed the new *basilica*, and dedicated it to 'Saint Paul, the apostle of nations.' I expressed a wish, at the same time, that the settlement would be known by the same name, and my desire was obtained. I had, previously to this time, fixed my residence at Saint Peter's [Mendota], and as the name of PAUL is generally connected with that of PETER, and the gentiles being well represented in the new place in the persons of the Indians, I called it Saint Paul. The name 'Saint Paul,' applied to a town or city, seemed appropriate. The monosyllable is short, sounds well, and is understood by all denominations of Christians. . . . Thenceforth the place was known as 'Saint Paul Landing,' and, later on, as 'Saint Paul'" (*History of the City of Saint Paul* by Williams, 1876, pp. 111–12).

Lucian Galtier was born in France in 1811 and died at Prairie du Chien, Wis., February 21, 1866. He studied theology in his native land; came to the United States in 1838 with a band of missionaries; was ordained a priest at Dubuque, Iowa, in 1840, and the same year settled at Mendota. In 1844 he removed to Keokuk, Iowa, and four years later returned to France. Afterward he again came to America and resided at Prairie du Chien until his death.

The post office was established in St. Croix County, Wisconsin Territory, on April 7, 1846; Jacob Wales Bass, born in Vermont in 1815, came to St. Paul in 1847 and was considered the first postmaster, although he served from 1849–53 at his hotel, the St. Paul House; he died in St. Paul in 1889.

St. Paul was organized as a village or town November 1, 1849, and was incorporated as a city March 4, 1854, then having an area of 2,560 acres, or 4 square miles. It received a new city charter March 6, 1868, when its area was 5.45 square miles, to which about 7 square miles were added February 29, 1872, and again 3 square miles March 6, 1873. West St. Paul, now Riverside, which had belonged to Dakota County, was annexed November 16, 1874, by proclamation of the popular vote ratifying the legislative act of March 5, 1874, whereby the total area of the city was increased to 20 square miles. Further large annexations, March 4, 1885, and February 8, 1887, adding the former McLean and Reserve Townships, extended St. Paul to its present area, 55.44 square miles, which is very nearly the same as the area of Minneapolis.

Prof. A. W. Williamson, in his list of geographic names in this state received from the Dakota, wrote: "Imnizha ska, — *imnizha*, ledge; *ska*, white; the Dakota name of St. Paul, given on account of the white sandstone cropping out in the bluffs." In the simplest words, this Dakota name means "White Rock."

As a familiar sobriquet, St. Paul is often called "the Saintly City"; Minneapolis similarly is "the Mill City" or "the Flour City"; and the two are very widely known as "the Twin Cities."

A few districts of St. Paul have been noted in the preceding list, namely Merriam Park, Riverview, and St. Anthony Park; and the railway stations of Hazel Park and Highwood, likewise before noted, also are in St. Paul. This city has numerous other residential or partially mercantile and manufacturing districts, which may properly be briefly mentioned here. Several districts designated as parks, however, are wholly or partly occupied by residences, this being the case with each of the districts called parks in the following list.

Dayton's Bluff, at the east side of the Mississippi in the southeast part of St. Paul, has a large residence district on the plateau extending backward from its top. The name commemorates Lyman Dayton, a former landowner there for whom a village and township in Hennepin County were named. On the edge of the southern and highest part of the bluff, in Mounds Park, is a series of seven large aboriginal mounds, 4 to 18 feet high, from which a magnificent prospect is obtained, overlooking the river and the central part of the city. Dayton was born in Southington, Conn., August 25, 1810, and died in St. Paul, October 20, 1865. He came to Minnesota in 1849, settling in this city, and invested largely in real estate; was the projector and president of the Lake Superior and Mississippi Railroad.

Arlington Hills and Phalen Park are northeastern districts, the second being named from Phalen Lake and Creek for Edward Phelan (whose name was variously spelled), one of his successive land claims, in the earliest years of St. Paul, having been on this creek.

Como Park, the largest public park of the city, with adjoining residences, encloses Lake Como, named by Henry McKenty in 1856 for the widely famed Lake Como adjoining the south side of the Alps in Italy. He was born in Pennsylvania in 1821, settled in St. Paul at the age of 30 years, dealt largely in city lots and farmlands, and died in this city August 10, 1869.

Lexington Park is a western central district, named from Lexington, Mass., where the first battle of the Revolutionary War was fought, April 19, 1775.

Farther northwest and southwest, respectively, are the districts of Hamline and Macalester Park, having the Methodist Hamline University and the Presbyterian Macalester College, named in honor of Bishop Leonidas Lent Hamline (1797–1865) of Ohio, and Charles Macalester (1798–1873) of Philadelphia, a generous donor to this college.

In and near Groveland Park, a district at the west side of the city, bordering on the Mississippi, are three large Catholic institutions, St. Paul Seminary, University of St. Thomas, and College of St. Catherine.

St. Anthony Hill, often called simply the Hill District, comprises a large residential area on a broad plateau that was crossed by the earliest road leading from the central part of St. Paul to the Falls of St. Anthony and the city of this name, which in 1872 was united with Minneapolis.

At Seven Corners, southwest from the business center of St. Paul, streets radiate in seven directions, with buildings on the intervening corners of the city blocks.

ST. PAUL PARK a city with Washington County.

SHOREVIEW a city, separated from Mounds View Township when it was incorporated as a village on

April 24, 1957. The first settler was Socrates A. Thompson in 1850. Named for its many lakes, the site began as a rural farming community and developed into a suburban trade and residential center.

SPRING LAKE PARK a city with Anoka County.

SUBURBAN HILLS a locality in section 4 of McLean Township about 1867.

VADNAIS HEIGHTS a city formerly in White Bear Township, was incorporated on July 24, 1957, as a village; it was named for Lake Vadnais, which was named for Jean Vadnais, a French Canadian who settled on its southeast shore in 1846 just north of the first settler of record, Paul (Paulette) Bibeau, in 1845.

WEST ST. PAUL which had been incorporated as a city in Dakota County, March 22, 1858, returned to township government in 1862 but was annexed to Ramsey County in 1874, becoming a ward of the city of St. Paul, and was renamed Riverview in 1918, as before noted.

WHITE BEAR BEACH a resort village on the north shore of White Bear Lake in section 12 of White Bear Township; it had a station of the Northern Pacific Railroad.

WHITE BEAR LAKE a city in White Bear Township, incorporated as a village on February 18, 1881, developed around a resort trade. Its first hotel was built in 1853 by Villeroy B. Barnum and sold in 1856 to John M. Lamb, first postmaster in 1857 and sergeant-at-arms in the territorial legislature; the depot was built in 1868 when the Lake Superior and Mississippi Railroad came; its first store was built in 1870 by Daniel Getty (died 1903).

WHITE BEAR TOWNSHIP organized May 11, 1858, and its village, which was incorporated in 1881, received the name of the large White Bear Lake, "from an old Indian legend, in which they suppose it to be possessed with the spirit of a white bear, which was about to spring on the wife of one of their young braves, but was shot by him, and its spirit had haunted the island and lake since and had mysteriously disposed of several of their braves. The island, which they named Spirit island, is located near its northwestern shore and has about fifty-four acres of land, covered with quite a heavy growth of timber" (history of this county, 1881, p. 281). It is now commonly called Manitou Island, its original Ojibwe name.

William H. C. Folsom, in his *Fifty Years in the Northwest* (1888, on its p. 545), wrote of the Dakota name as follows: "The Indians called this a grizzly, polar, or white bear, and named an adjacent locality [now a village on the northeastern shore, in Washington County] 'Mah-to-me-di,' or 'M'de, i. e., Mahto, gray polar bear, and M'de, lake. It is not probable, however, that a polar bear ever reached this spot, and a visit from a grizzly is nearly as improbable. Indian legends are very frequently made to order by those who succeed them as owners of the soil."

WILSON a station of the Soo Line in section 31 of Mounds View Township.

Lakes and Streams

Pike Island, on the Dakota County side of the Mississippi at the mouth of the Minnesota River, adjoining the former Reserve Township (now the most southwestern part of St. Paul), was named in honor of Zebulon Montgomery Pike, who in 1805 there purchased from the Dakota for the United States a large tract as a military reserve, on which Fort Snelling (at first called Fort St. Anthony) was built in 1820–24.

Beside the center of St. Paul, at the foot of the bluff of Riverview, are Harriet and Raspberry (later Navy) Islands of the Mississippi. Harriet Island, containing 28 acres, donated to this city by Dr. Justus Ohage, May 26, 1900, is used as a public playground. It was named very long ago in honor of Harriet E. Bishop, who was born in Vergennes, Vt., January 1, 1817, and died in St. Paul, August 8, 1883. She came to St. Paul in 1847 to open the first permanent school in this city. Through her influence a Sunday school also was soon organized, and in the next year a public building was erected to accommodate the school and preaching services. She was the author of *Floral Home, or First Years of Minnesota* (1857) and other books.

The little Cozy Lake, in Como Park, adjoins Lake Como.

Rice Creek, the outlet of White Bear and Bald Eagle Lakes, flows through shallow lakes in Centerville Township, Anoka County, thence passing into Mounds View, and reaching the Mississippi in Fridley, Anoka County, a few miles north of Minneapolis. Hon. Henry M. Rice of St. Paul, was an early landowner and summer resident near the lower course of this creek, in Fridley Township, the stream being named in his honor, as noted in the chapter for that county.

Shadow Falls Creek, a very little stream, is named for its cascade in springtime or after any heavy rains, on its descent to the great river, north of the St. Paul Seminary. Finn's Glen, having a similar brooklet, is about a mile farther south, named for William Finn, the first permanent settler in Reserve Township.

Trout Brook, flowed through St. Paul, was tributary to Phalen Creek just before their united waters reached the Mississippi, and was the outlet of McCarron Lake in Rose Township. John E. McCarron, a farmer who lived beside this lake, was born in 1839, came there in 1849, served in the Fourth Minnesota Regiment in the Civil War, and died in St. Paul, March 27, 1897.

Phalen Creek and Lake have been previously noted for the northeastern district and public park of St. Paul adjoining this lake, which was the original source of the city water supply. Northward a series of lakes has been added to that first source, partly by artificial channels, including Spoon Lake named for its outline, Gervais, Fitzhugh (or Kohlman), Vadnais, Pleasant, and Charley Lakes, Long and Deep Lakes, and Wilkinson and Otter Lakes, reaching to the north line of the county.

Gervais Lake commemorates Benjamin Gervais, a pioneer French Canadian farmer, who was born at Riviere du Loup, Canada, July 15, 1786, and died here in January 1876. He settled on the Red River in the Selkirk Colony in 1812; came to Fort Snelling in 1827; and when settlers were ordered to leave the military reservation, in 1838, he opened a farm in the central part of the present area of St. Paul. In 1844 he removed to this lake, being the first settler in the area of New Canada.

Vadnais Lake was named "for John Vadnais, who made a claim on its banks as early as 1846"; and Wilkinson Lake, for "Ross Wilkinson, who first took up a claim on its shores."

Pig's Eye Lake and Marsh, on the alluvial bottomland of the Mississippi about two miles southeast from Dayton's Bluff and the Indian Mounds, were named in allusion to Pierre Parrant, a whiskey dealer, before mentioned as the first settler in St. Paul, who about the year 1842 removed to the vicinity of that lake. He had a defective eye,

whence he received this nickname, applied also to the village of St. Paul at its beginning, until displaced by the present name in 1841. Pig's Eye Lake had been previously called Grand Marais, meaning the Great Marsh, by the early French fur traders and voyageurs (*History of Saint Paul*, by Williams, 1876, pp. 64–88).

Battle Creek, named for the battle of Kaposia in 1842, between the Ojibwe and Dakota, flows into Pig's Eye Lake from the high land east of the river valley. Another great ravine there, having numerous tall white pines, is named Pine Cooley, from the French word *coulée*, meaning "a ravine or run" (*History* by Williams, pp. 122–25).

Kaposia, the Dakota village of the successive hereditary chiefs named Little Crow, early located on the east bank of the Mississippi near the Grand Marais, where Pike saw it in 1805 and Maj. Stephen H. Long in 1817, was several times changed in place, being even removed to the vicinity of the mouth of Phalen Creek or near the site of the Union Depot in St. Paul, as known by the narratives of Gen. Lewis Cass and Henry R. Schoolcraft at this village in 1820, Long and William H. Keating in 1823, and Charles J. Latrobe in 1833. Again in 1835 it was near the Grand Marais, as noted by George W. Featherstonhaugh. After the treaty at Washington in 1837, by which the Dakota ceded their lands east of the Mississippi here, the Kaposia band had their village at its west side, occupying a part of South Park, a suburb of South St. Paul in Dakota County, which was its site at the time of the battle. The approach of the Ojibwe for the attack, and the course of their retreat, were by way of these ravines of Battle Creek and Pine Cooley.

The name Kaposia, changed from Kapozha in the Dakota language, means "light or swift of foot in running," as defined by Prof. A. W. Williamson in his list of Dakota geographic names. Little Crow's band had received this name, which thence was applied to their village, "in honor of their skill in the favorite game of lacrosse."

The following lakes remain to be noticed in this county.

Beaver Lake is about two miles east from the south end of Lake Phalen.

New Canada has Silver Lake, adjoining North St. Paul, and Savage Lake in sections 6 and 7, the latter being so named because "the Indians frequented its shores in large numbers."

White Bear Township, with its numerous lakes before noted, has also Birch, Black, Poplar, Sucker, and Gilfillan Lakes, the last being named in honor of Charles D. Gilfillan of St. Paul.

The north line of Rose Township crosses Lake Owasso, formerly called Big Bass Lake, and Lake Josephine. The first of these names is nearly like "the bluebird, the Owaissa," in Henry W. Longfellow's *Song of Hiawatha*. For the companion lakes Josephine and Johanna, the latter lying in Mounds View Township, Judge Edmund W. Bazille stated that the surname McKenty may be added, these names being in honor respectively of the daughter and wife of Henry McKenty, by whom Lake Como was named.

Other lakes in Mounds View are Turtle, Snail (also Maryland), Round, Island, Valentine, Long, and Silver Lakes. Marsden Lake has been drained.

Hills and Caves

The Mounds View Hills, in the township named for them, are the highest points in the county.

The Arlington Hills, in a district of St. Paul platted with that name, are merely an undulating and somewhat prominently rolling tract of morainic drift. St. Anthony Hill, another district in this city, is an extensive plateau about 225 to 240 feet above the Mississippi. Dayton's Bluff and Cherokee Heights, respectively east and west or south of this river in St. Paul, are parts of the prolonged series of river bluffs that bound the valley on each side, rising from its bottomlands to the general level of the adjoining country.

Carvers' Cave, in the lower part of Dayton's Bluff, was named for Capt. Jonathan Carver, who there on May 1, 1767, received a deed written by himself and signed by two Dakota chiefs, granting to him and his heirs a large tract of land in the present states of Minnesota and Wisconsin. This cave was well known to the Dakota, whose name for it, as noted by Carver, was "Wakon-teebe, that is, the Dwelling of the Great Spirit."

A biographic sketch of Carver is given in the chapter for the county bearing his name. All the vast inheritance that had been claimed for his heirs and others, under the Dakota deed, was denied and annulled in 1821–25 by the U.S. Congress. Long afterward Carver Lake, which is in the edge of Washington County, five miles southeast from Carver's Cave and the Mound Park, was named for one of his descendants who settled as a farmer beside it.

Fountain Cave, about four miles farther up the Mississippi, at the base of its bluff in the southwest part of St. Paul, was discovered in 1811. Major Long explored and described it in 1817, giving to it this name because a brook runs through the cavern and issues, like a fountain, at its mouth. Cass and Schoolcraft examined it in 1820 but erroneously called it Carver's Cave.

Glacial Lake Hamline

A map and description of a glacial lake, lying mostly within the area of St. Paul, are presented by the present writer in the *Bulletin of the Geological Society of America* (vol. 8, 1897, pp. 183–96). Its deposits form nearly level sand and gravel plains and plateaus, 260 to 225 feet above the river, extending from near the St. Paul campus of the University of Minnesota eastward to the northwest end of Lake Como, thence southward past Hamline University, with a narrow connection southeast to another wide expanse in the Hill District or plateau crossed by Summit Avenue. The length of the Glacial Lake Hamline was thus about six miles, with maximum widths exceeding one mile.

Red Lake County

Established December 24, 1896, this county received its name from the Red Lake River, which flows through it, giving also its name to Red Lake Falls, the county seat. The river derives its name, in turn, from Red Lake, these both being translations of their Ojibwe names.

Why these Indians originally so designated the lake was uncertain until it was ascertained by the late Rev. Joseph A. Gilfillan. It had been affirmed, with poetic license, by Giacomo C. Beltrami, who traveled here in 1823, publishing in 1824 and 1828, that the aboriginal names of Red Lake and its outflowing river, the latter translated by him Bloody River, refer to the "blood of the slain," in the wars between the Ojibwe and Dakota. Gilfillan, who was a missionary to the Ojibwe of northwestern Minnesota from 1873 to 1898, wrote in 1885 that the Ojibwe name of this lake, written by him "Misquagumiwi sagaigun, Red-water lake," perhaps alludes to "reddish fine gravel or sand along the shore in places, which in storms gets wrought into the water near the edges," or to the reddish color of streams flowing into the lake from bogs on its north side, probably reddened by bog iron ore. He later wrote, however, in a letter of February 1899, that these are erroneous conjectures of some of the Ojibwe and that he had obtained more reliable information, so that he could then confidently state the origin of this name as follows: "Red lake is so called from the color of the lake [reflecting the redness of sunset] on a calm summer evening, when unruffled by wind and in a glassy state, at which times it is of a distinctly wine color. . . . It is not called Red lake from any battle fought on its shores."

Red Lake and Red River appear with these names, in French, on the map by La Vérendrye (1737) and on Philippe Buache's map (1754), and the lake is so named on the somewhat later maps of Thomas Jefferys and Jonathan Carver. From information obtained during his travels in Minnesota in 1766 and 1767, Carver mapped Red Lake and the Red Lake River giving them exactly their present names. Their earliest delineation, however, from personal examination, was by David Thompson (in 1813–14), who in April 1798 reached Red Lake, coming by way of the Red Lake and Clearwater Rivers, and thence going onward to Turtle and Cass Lakes.

It tells us something of the appreciation of natural beauty and grandeur by the Indians that they took from the hues of sunset the name of the largest lake in Minnesota, whence we now have, by derivation, the names of two large rivers, of a county, and of its county seat.

*Information of names was received from Edward L.
Healy, real estate dealer, Z. A. Chartier, deputy county auditor, Ovid Emard, county treasurer, and Frank
Jeffers, register of deeds, each of Red Lake Falls, interviewed during visits there, the first in August 1909,
and the others in September 1916. The effort to form
Red Lake County from Polk County in 1896 was followed by a fight to name Red Lake Falls as the county seat rather than Thief River Falls, which forced another fight to create Pennington County in 1910, with
Thief River Falls as its county seat.*

*Post offices operating before 1896 were established
in Polk County and may also have discontinued
there.*

ANTON a post office, 1904–10, located in Peter O.
Berg's general store, 27 miles northeast of Red
Lake Falls.

BADGER a post office, 1885–89, in section 7 of
Terrebonne Township; the first postmaster was
Onzieme Ducharme.

BEAUDRY a post office, 1882–94, in Lake Pleasant
Township, with John T. Beaudry, postmaster; the
area was settled in 1882.

BRAY a post office, 1889–1904, in section 23 of
Browns Creek Township.

BROOKS a city in section 14 in Poplar River Township, was incorporated as a village on April 7,
1955. The post office was established in 1883, with
Daniel Little, postmaster. The city was platted in
1904 as a farm community with a number of
small stores and a station of the Minneapolis,
St. Paul and Sault Ste. Marie Railroad (Soo Line)
in section 15.

BROWNS CREEK TOWNSHIP has a stream so
named, tributary to the Black River, probably
commemorating a pioneer settler or an early
hunter and trapper. The township was part of
Black River Township before it was separated
from Polk County.

BUCKTOWN a village in Lambert Township, two
and a half miles southeast of Lambert post office.

DELORME a village in sections 33 and 34 of Lake
Pleasant Township, was named for Ambrose Delorme, a homestead farmer. The village was established as a station of the Northern Pacific Railroad and located on land owned by Charles
Perrault; the station was later called Perrault, although the community remained Delorme.

DOROTHY a village in section 5 of Louisville, was
named by J. F. Matthews of Red Lake Falls for
St. Dorothy's Catholic Church, which was built
here in 1880 for the French Canadian families
in the area. This feminine name, derived from
the ancient Greek language, means "the gift of
God." The village had a station of the Northern
Pacific Railroad and a post office, 1898–1908 and
1920–45.

EMARD a post office, 1883–93, in section 17 of
Emardville Township.

EMARDVILLE TOWNSHIP received its name in hon-
or of Pierre Emard, who was born in Longueuil
on the St. Lawrence River in Canada, opposite
Montreal, in 1835 and came to Minnesota in 1878,
settling as a homesteader in section 24, Red Lake
Falls.

EQUALITY TOWNSHIP was named by its people in
the petition for its organization. A village name
Equality was located in the township about 1937.

GARNES TOWNSHIP bears the name of one of the
earliest settlers, E. K. Garnes, an immigrant from
Norway. The name of the township and the village in section 14 is a phonetic spelling of E. K.
Gjernes, first postmaster, who built a store in section 10 in 1896; Gjernes later moved to Oklee; the
post office operated 1896–1910.

GERVAIS TOWNSHIP was named in honor of Isaiah Gervais, who was born at Fort Garry (now
Winnipeg), Manitoba, December 10, 1831, came
to Minnesota and lived in St. Paul, settled as a
homestead farmer in section 26, Red Lake Falls,
in 1876, and died there, November 2, 1888.

GRIT a post office, 1898–1913, located in postmaster Edward E. Havik's store in section 19,
Equality Township; the name was supposedly
chosen because it required considerable "grit" to
undertake hauling goods on the 20 miles of bad
roads from Lambert.

HILLTOP a station of the Northern Pacific Railroad in section 13 of Louisville Township.

HUOT a village on the Red Lake River in section
28, Louisville. The village and township were
each named for Louis Huot, an early French
Canadian homesteader there, who came to the
area in 1876. It had a post office, 1881–1936, with
Huot the first postmaster.

IVES a station of the Great Northern Railway in
section 5, Louisville Township.

LAKE PLEASANT TOWNSHIP was named for the
former lake and marsh in its section 18, now

drained. A village called Lake Pleasant was located in the township about 1937.

LAMBERT TOWNSHIP was named for Francois Lambert, who was born at St. Ursule, Province of Quebec, March 10, 1847. He came to Minnesota in 1881, settling as a farmer on section 10 in this township, of which he was the treasurer during many years. A post office was in section 15, 1883–1912, and was transferred to Oklee in 1912. Many of the buildings on the site were moved to Oklee between 1910 and 1917.

LILLO a post office in section 3 of Equality Township, 1899–1919, with Magnus Johnson as postmaster; Johnson changed his name to Lillo, and Mrs. Lillo operated the general store.

LOST a post office in section 34, Emardville Township, 1896–1911.

LOUISVILLE TOWNSHIP like its village of Huot, before noted, commemorates Louis Huot, a pioneer farmer.

MARCOUX / MARCOUX CORNER a locality at the intersection of Highways 2 and 32 in Lake Pleasant Township, with a café and service station, which were begun in 1927 by Edward Marcoux, who moved to California in 1936.

OKLEE a city in sections 1 and 12 of Lambert, incorporated as a village on February 6, 1914, bears the name of Ole K. Lee, a Scandinavian settler, on whose farm the village was built. The Soo Line came in 1909, and the townsite was platted by Tri-State Land Company, who purchased the land from Lee that year.

PERRAULT a Northern Pacific station near the center of Lake Pleasant Township, was named for Charles Perrault, a homestead farmer, who died in 1915. See also DELORME.

PLUMMER a city in sections 4, 8, 9, and 10 of Emardville, incorporated as a village on February 14, 1905, received its name in honor of Charles A. Plummer, who about the year 1881 built a sawmill and gristmill on the Clearwater River near the site of this village. He removed to Iowa. The city was platted in 1904 when the Soo Line came; when the post office was established in 1903, the name Scotland was requested after the Hotel Scotland, but because there was already a village by that name, Plummer was chosen; the hotel changed its name to Hotel Plummer shortly after. Hubert H. Finrow, later a mayor of the village, was first postmaster at a site west of the present village; the village moved to the present site in 1904.

POPLAR RIVER TOWNSHIP is crossed by this stream, tributary to the Clearwater River. Its name, which is translated from the Ojibwe, appears as Aspen Brook on Thompson's map from his travel here in 1798. Two species of poplar, or aspen, are common throughout most of this state, one of them being especially plentiful northward.

RED LAKE FALLS the county seat, near the center of a township bearing this name, was incorporated as a village February 28, 1881, and as a city in 1898. The name has reference to rapids and falls within the city area, supplying valuable waterpower, on both the Red Lake and Clearwater Rivers. These are translations of their Ojibwe names, received from the lakes whence they flow. The post office was established in 1878 with Ernest Buse as first postmaster. He was born in Germany in 1837, came to the United States in 1852 and to Minnesota in 1854, being first settler and founder of Fergus Falls; he moved to Red Lake Falls in 1877; he died in California in 1914 and is buried in Fergus Falls. The city had stations serving the Great Northern Railway and the Northern Pacific Railroad.

RIVER TOWNSHIP part of River Falls Township until separated from Polk County, is named for the Red Lake River flowing through it.

ROLAND a village in section 33 of Deer Park Township, Pennington County, is located on the north shore of Clearwater River; the land was first owned by A. A. Rolandson; when the county lines changed, it became located in Equality Township. Its post office operated 1910–17, and it had a station of the Soo Line.

TERREBONNE TOWNSHIP has a French name, meaning "good land," received from the county and town of this name in the Province of Quebec. The village in section 25 had a post office, 1881–1915.

WYLIE TOWNSHIP and its village in section 25 were named in honor of William Wylie, an early farmer there. He was born in England in 1850, married Mary Jane Barnes in Ontario in 1874, moved to Crookston in 1880, and then to section 25 of the township in 1883; he was a schoolteacher but needed more income to support his family so he went to Colorado in 1892 to work in the mines and died there in an accident in 1901. It had a post office, 1883–1937, with Mary Jane Wylie the first postmaster, and a station of the Great Northern Railway. The village was part of Bray Township in Pennington County before the county lines changed.

Streams and Lakes

Lost River, Hill River, Poplar River, and Badger Creek, southern tributaries of Clearwater River in this county, have their headwaters in the southeast part of Polk County, so that the origins and meaning of their names have been given in the chapter for that county. The second of these streams was mapped by Thompson in 1798 as "Wild Rice rivulet," for several small lakes of its upper course, having much wild rice.

Black River, flowing from the north through Wylie and Louisville to the Red Lake River at Huot, is named from the dark color of its water received from peaty swamps. Its largest tributary is Browns Creek, for which a township is named.

This county, like others lying within the area of the Glacial Lake Agassiz, has a smoothed surface of its drift sheet, with no hollows holding lakes. Formerly it had a single lake, which gave the name of Lake Pleasant Township, but that was rather a marsh, becoming occasionally a shallow lake, which has been drained, its bed being now good farming land.

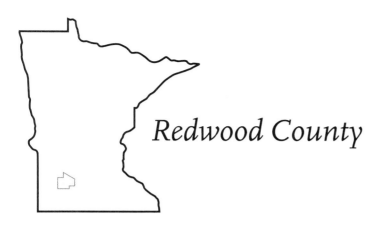

Redwood County

Established February 6, 1862, this county was named for the Redwood River, whence also comes the name of the county seat, Redwood Falls, situated on a series of cascades and rapids of the river. Prof. A. W. Williamson wrote of this name: "Chanshayapi;—*chan,* wood; *sha,* red; *ayapi,* are on; Redwood river; so called by the Dakotas on account of the abundance of a straight slender bush with red bark, which they scraped off and smoked, usually mixed with tobacco. This name is spelled by Nicollet Tchanshayapi." William H. Keating and George W. Featherstonhaugh each gave both the Dakota and English names of this river; and the latter traveler expressly defined their meaning, as follows: "This red wood is a particular sort of willow, with an under bark of a reddish colour, which the Indians dry and smoke. When mixed with tobacco it makes what they call *Kinnee Kinnik,* and is much less offensive than common tobacco."

The inner bark of two *Cornus* species, *C. sericea,* the silky cornell, and *C. stolonifera,* the red-osier dogwood, were used by the Indians, both the Dakota and the Ojibwe, to mix with their tobacco for smoking. The Algonquian word *kinnikinnick* for such addition to the tobacco included also the leaves of the bearberry and leaves of sumac, gathered when they turn red in the autumn, which were similarly used.

Cornus sericea is frequent throughout Minnesota, excepting far northward, and *C. stolonifera* abounds through the north half of this state and is common southward to Winona, Mower, and Blue Earth Counties, but its southward geographic range scarcely reaches into Iowa. Dr. C. C. Parry stated that the bark of the former species, wherever it is found, is preferred for use as *kinnikinnick* and that the bark of the latter is commonly substituted for it by the Indians about Lake Superior.

It has been supposed also that the Dakota name of the Redwood River alludes to the red cedar trees on its bluffs at Redwood Falls or to trees there marked by spots of red paint for guidance of a war party at some time during the ancient warfare between the Ojibwe and the Dakota for ownership of this region, as told in a Dakota legend to early white settlers (history of this county, 1916, pp. 613–14). Either of these alternative suggestions has seemed to many of the settlers more probable than the testimony for the *kinnikinnick,* which was received from an earlier and more intimate knowledge of the Dakota people and their language. *Chan,* as a Dakota word, may mean "a tree or any woody shrub," being a more general word than *wood* in our language, which in its most common use is applied only to trees.

But two or even all three of these reasons for the naming of the river may be included together as each contributing to its origin, namely, the *kinnikinnick,* the red cedars, and also painted trees. In support of the third as a part of the origin, we should quote from Giacomo C. Beltrami who was here in 1823, accompanying Maj. Stephen H. Long's expedition, for he wrote that the Redwood

River was "so called from a tree which the savages paint red every year and for which they have a peculiar veneration" (Beltrami, *A Pilgrimage in America*, vol. 2, p. 316).

———

Information of the origins and meanings of names has been gathered from History of the Minnesota Valley *(1882), having pages 762–98 for this county;* The History of Redwood County, *compiled by Franklyn Curtiss-Wedge, reviewed by Julius A. Schmahl (1916, 2 vols., 1,016 pp.); and William H. Gold, Hiram M. Hitchcock, Major M. E. Powell, and Hon. Orlando B. Turrell, each of Redwood Falls, the county seat, interviewed during a visit there in July 1916.*

ASHFORD a post office, 1886–1904, which began on postmaster Robert H. McKittrick's farm in section 20, Underwood Township, and moved to section 30 in 1888.

BELVIEW a city in section 8 of Kintire, platted in 1889 and incorporated January 3, 1893, has a name derived from French words, meaning "a beautiful view." It was first called Rolling Prairie and Jones Siding, but when the post office was established in 1887, the name changed. The first postmaster was Charles Jones, son of Hibbard F. Jones, who platted the site in 1889. It had a station of the Chicago and North Western Railway.

BOX ELDER a post office begun in 1880 in section 24 of Underwood Township, with Eben Martin as postmaster on his farm, and moved in 1883 to section 20 of Vesta Township, discontinuing in 1884.

BROOKVILLE TOWNSHIP settled in 1869 and organized April 19, 1873, has a name that is borne also by villages in Pennsylvania, Ohio, Indiana, Illinois, Wisconsin, and six other states.

CERESCO a post office in section 20 of Underwood Township, 1872–76, which was transferred to Lyon County.

CHARLESTOWN organized May 25, 1872, was named in honor of Charles Porter, who was the first settler in this township, coming in 1864. It had a post office, 1874–77; Anthony A. Praxel was first postmaster; it was also called Cottonwood Crossing.

CLEMENTS a city in section 33 of Three Lakes Township, platted in 1902 and incorporated as a village on June 29, 1903, was named in honor of Peter O. Clements, a nearby farmer. He was born in Sweden, April 17, 1847; came to the United States, settling first in Washington County, Minn.; and removed in 1877 to section 32 in this township; he died in 1940. The site was first settled about a mile north of the present site as a trade center with a dairy and a post office established in 1900, with Lewis J. Rongstad as postmaster in the Rongstad-Thorston store. The Western Town Lot Company purchased the present site from Henry Petrie and platted six blocks in 1902; the post office was moved, and a number of businesses developed.

COTTONWOOD CROSSING see CHARLESTOWN.

DELHI TOWNSHIP first settled in 1865, organized February 19, 1876, was named by Alfred M. Cook, builder and owner of a flour mill at Redwood Falls, who came from Delhi, a village in Ohio, near Cincinnati. Six other states have villages of this name, derived from the large city of Delhi in India. The city in sections 7, 8, 17, and 18, bearing the same name, was platted in 1884 and was incorporated as a village November 13, 1902. The post office, begun in 1884 in section 17, had Rodman R. Hurlbut as postmaster and depot agent at the station serving the Minneapolis and St. Louis and the Wisconsin, Minnesota and Pacific Railroads.

ENDERLY a post office in section 15, Sherman Township, which began as the Lower Sioux Agency post office, 1868–84, and was transferred to Enderly in 1884, discontinuing in 1889.

GALES TOWNSHIP organized July 18, 1876, received its name in honor of its first settlers, A. L. and Solon S. Gale, who came in May 1872.

GILFILLAN a village in section 36 of Paxton, was named in honor of Charles Duncan Gilfillan, owner of a large farm there, comprising about 8,000 acres, who was born in New Hartford, N.Y., July 4, 1831, and died in St. Paul, December 18, 1902. He came to this state in 1851 and settled in St. Paul in 1854; was for three terms a representative in the legislature and a state senator in 1878–85. During his later years he engaged largely in farming in this county and was president of the Minnesota Valley Historical Society, interested in the erection of monuments and tablets commemorating events of the Dakota War in 1862. Several railroads went through the village, the station having been established to provide shipping facilities for the vast Gilfillan estate, along with an elevator and storage buildings.

GRANITE ROCK TOWNSHIP first settled in 1871–72 and organized in 1890, has small outcrops of the granitic bedrock in sections 6 and 12. Excepting these outcrops and the similar but far more extensive rock exposures along the Minnesota valley and in the adjacent gorge of the Redwood River at and below its falls, all the surface of the county is a moderately undulating sheet of glacial drift, which deeply covers the bedrocks.

GRUNDEN a post office, 1898–1903, section 14, Gales Township, with Andrew M. Grunden, postmaster, formerly a postmaster at Logan.

HILL TRACK a station of the Minneapolis and St. Louis Railroad in Delhi Township.

HOLLAND see MORGAN.

HONNER TOWNSHIP earlier called Baldwin, first settled in 1864 and organized January 24, 1880, was named for J. S. G. Honner, who was one of the first settlers of Redwood Falls and later took a claim on the Minnesota River in this township. He was born in New York in 1831; came to Minnesota in 1856 and to this county in 1864; was the first register of deeds for the county and was a representative in the legislature in 1865 and 1870 and a state senator in 1872.

JOHNSONVILLE TOWNSHIP settled in 1872, organized January 9, 1879, "was named for the Johnsons living in it." Four members of the first board of township officers had this surname.

KINTIRE TOWNSHIP first settled in the summer of 1872 and organized May 25, 1880, received its name from the large peninsula of Kintyre, 40 miles long, on the southwestern coast of Scotland.

LAMBERTON TOWNSHIP settled in July 1864, organized April 1, 1874, and its railway village, founded in 1873 and incorporated March 3, 1879, commemorate Henry Wilson Lamberton, who was born in Carlisle, Pa., March 6, 1831, and died in Winona, Minn., December 31, 1905. He settled there in 1856, became president of the Winona Deposit Bank in 1868, was elected president of the Winona and South Western Railway in 1894, and was one of the state capitol commissioners from the organization of that board until his death.

The city of Lamberton in section 23 was incorporated as a village on March 1, 1879, and separated from the township on April 16, 1891. The post office was established in Yellow Medicine County and transferred to Redwood County in 1873, with Charles R. Kneeland as postmaster in his general store. The site was laid out by Capt. T. G. Carter in 1875; it had a station of the Chicago and North Western Railway and the Winona and St. Peter Railroad.

LEILA a post office requested but not established, with John Dittbrenner to be postmaster; location not found.

LOGAN a post office, 1887–1903, first located in section 14 of Gales Township, with Elisha E. Slover as postmaster on his farm; it was later in sections 7 and 10 of Johnsonville Township.

LOWER SIOUX a village in Paxton and Sherman Townships, six miles east of Redwood Falls; the post office operated 1868–84, when it was transferred to Enderly.

LOWER SIOUX AGENCY established in 1853–54, on the southern bluff of the Minnesota River in the present northwest quarter of section 8, Sherman, had several government buildings and became a considerable village before its abandonment on account of the Dakota War in 1862.

LUCAN a city in sections 21 and 22 of Granite Rock, platted in January 1902, and incorporated as a village November 19, 1902, was named for a village in Ireland, seven miles west of Dublin. Another version of its name origin is that one of the railroad surveyors was named Lou Kartak, and when another surveyor was asked if he could think of a name for the townsite, he replied, "No, but maybe Lou can." The post office began as Rock in 1890, with Robert Schanberger, postmaster, on his farm in section 14; it then moved to section 6 of Vail Township, then back to Granite Rock Township in section 20, moving to several more sites until Jens Larson took over in 1903, changing it to Lucan in 1908. The village had a station of the Chicago and North Western Railway; it was also known as State Line.

MILROY a city in sections 16 and 17 of Westline, next west of Lucan, platted in March 1902 and incorporated on November 18 of the same year, "was named for Major General Robert H. Milroy, a gallant Union soldier during the early days of the war of the rebellion" (Stennett, *Place Names of the Chicago and Northwestern Railways*, 1908, p. 102). He was born near Salem, Ind., June 11, 1816; was graduated at Norwich University, Vt., 1843; served in the Mexican War and in the Civil War; was superintendent and agent for Indian affairs in Washington Territory, 1872–85; and died in Olympia, Wash., March 29, 1890.

The post office opened in 1902, with Jerry A. Looney as postmaster; when platted by the Western Town Lot Company, the townsite covered a large tract of land in sections 16–20; lots were sold on auction on April 9, 1902; a petition presented on February 7, 1905, reduced the townsite size to 160 acres in sections 16 and 17. A well-known business, the Milroy Eating House, built in 1898 in Vesta, was moved to a site near the Chicago and North Western Railway tracks in 1902.

MORGAN TOWNSHIP organized in May 1880, and its city in sections 15, 16, 21, and 22, platted August 14, 1878, incorporated as a village February 11, 1889, and separated from the township on April 16, 1891, were named in honor of Lewis Henry Morgan, the eminent soldier, explorer, and author, who has been called "the Father of American anthropology." He was born near Aurora, N.Y., November 21, 1818, and died in Rochester, N.Y., December 17, 1881. Among the numerous books of his authorship is a history of the American beaver and its works, for which in 1861 he traveled through Minnesota to the Red River settlements in Manitoba and in 1862 for this research he ascended the Missouri River to the Rocky Mountains.

The city was called Brookville for a number of years before its first platting as nine blocks in sections 15 and 16. Thomas G. Holland, section boss for the Chicago and North Western Railway, had a boxcar home on the site where, with his assistant, Mel Tolman, he opened the first post office, 1878–80. The post office became Holland, 1881–86; in 1886 the name changed back to Morgan.

MORTON village, lying mainly in Renville County, includes also a suburb on the south side of the Minnesota River in the extreme eastern corner of Honner. A station of the Minneapolis and St. Louis Railroad in section 36 of Honner was associated with the village.

NEW AVON TOWNSHIP first settled in March 1870, organized September 5, 1872, was named in compliment to Joshua S. and Jonathan P. Towle, early settlers there, who had come from Avon Township in Maine. A post office, 1876–88, was first located on Joshua Towle's farm, five miles northeast of Wabasso; the second post office, 1898–1906, was in section 6.

NORTH HERO TOWNSHIP settled in 1871 and organized September 27, 1873, "was named by Byron Knight, after his old home, the island of North Hero in Lake Champlain, Vermont. This island was named in honor of Ethan Allen, of Revolutionary fame" (*History of Redwood County*, 1916, p. 360). The township was named Barton Township in the 1874 Andreas atlas.

NORTH REDWOOD a city in sections 29 and 30 of Honner, was platted in the autumn of 1884, incorporated August 15, 1903, and separated from the township on April 9, 1915; the post office was established in 1885. The Minneapolis and St. Louis Railroad depot, called Redwood, was where Richard W. Sears, depot agent in 1886, began selling watches as a side venture; he moved to Chicago in 1887, and with Alvah R. Roebuck as partner, he developed the Sears, Roebuck and Company mail order business; Sears died in 1916. The original depot building was moved to the Redwood County fairgrounds to be used as a museum but was destroyed by fire in August 1961 before the museum opened.

OKAWA see **SEAFORTH**.

ORIOLE a post office, 1884–93, in section 30, Sheridan Township, with Harriet M. McCormick, first postmaster.

PAXTON TOWNSHIP organized September 13, 1879, was named in honor of James Wilson Paxton, a lawyer of Redwood Falls, who became owner of a large tract of land in this township but removed to Tacoma, Wash. He was born in Pennsylvania, December 21, 1827, and died January 6, 1892 (*The Paxton Family*, 1903, p. 399). The township was earlier called Blackwood and was part of Honner. A post office was in section 26, 1879–82; the site was surveyed in 1878; it had a station of the Chicago and North Western Railway.

PLUM CREEK a village north of Walnut Grove,

which had a gristmill in 1898 built by Julius Dahms. Laura Ingalls Wilder wrote a series of children's books about frontier life, one of which, *On the Banks of Plum Creek*, centered around the area of Plum Creek and Walnut Grove.

PRAIRIE LEA a post office, 1875–77, in section 18 of Sundown Township, near the Redwood Falls-to-Springfield stage route.

REDWOOD CENTER a townsite incorporated on May 23, 1857; location not found.

REDWOOD FALLS a city in Redwood Falls and Honner Townships and the county seat, first settled by Col. Samuel McPhail, J. S. G. Honner, and others in the spring and summer of 1864, was platted October 1865 and incorporated as a village March 9, 1876, and as a city April 1, 1891. The name is taken from the falls of the Redwood River, which descends about 140 feet by vertical falls and by rapids in its last three miles. The greater part of this descent takes place in a picturesque gorge close below the city area, within a distance of less than a half mile. The township of this name, having the city in its northeast corner, was organized January 22, 1880. The city is located in an area first opened to white settlers in 1851; the U.S. government built a sawmill at the falls of the Redwood River in 1855 and later a gristmill. McPhail platted the town in 1854 and built the first house; the post office began in 1864. The village had a station serving several rail lines, including the Chicago and North Western. The former county poor farm is the site of the Redwood County Museum and houses the Minnesota Inventors Hall of Fame.

REVERE a city in sections 23–26 of North Hero, platted in May 1886, and incorporated as a village February 21, 1900, was named in honor of Paul Revere, a patriot in the American Revolution, renowned for his ride from Boston to Lexington, April 18–19, 1775, to arouse the Minutemen, as told by Henry W. Longfellow in "The Midnight Ride of Paul Revere." He was born in Boston, January 1, 1735, and died there May 10, 1818. The city was first platted as two blocks in 1886 by John E. Blunt for the Chicago and North Western Railway land company; Lewis J. Rongstad built a general store, where he opened the post office in 1893.

RIVERSIDE a river village in section 20 of Honner Township, which had a boat landing built in 1853 but did not develop until about 1874, when

E. B. Daniels, his son Horace, and Peter A. Schiek opened a general store at the ferry crossing; Schiek was postmaster during the two years of the post office operation, 1875–76; Daniels had the site surveyed but never filed the plat. Most buildings had been moved to North Redwood by 1882.

ROCK see LUCAN.

ROCK VALLEY a post office, 1870–71, with Ole A. Hare, postmaster; location not found.

ROWENA a village in section 27 of New Avon, on the Chicago and North Western Railway bears the name of the ward of Cedric in Sir Walter Scott's *Ivanhoe*. She is the rival of Rebecca and marries Ivanhoe. The village was platted in March 1902, but it was not incorporated.

SANBORN a city in sections 25, 26, 35, and 36 of Charleston, incorporated as a village on November 11, 1891, was named in honor of Sherburn Sanborn, who during many years was an officer of this railway company. The village was platted in June 1881 by John Yaeger on both sides of the Winona and St. Peter Railroad tracks, which crossed his farmland; he filed the plat on October 10 as Sanborn for the Chicago and North Western superintendent. Thomas Poole served as first postmaster, beginning in May 1880.

SEAFORTH a city in sections 29–32 of Sheridan, platted in October 1899 and incorporated as a village on February 13, 1901, received its name from Loch Seaforth, an arm of the sea in the Hebrides, which partially divides Lewis from Harris. The post office began in 1899, with W. J. Carlton Pratt, postmaster; the site was first called Okawa, the name meaning "pike" in Ojibwe, a name chosen by Harry I. Orwig, chief engineer for the Chicago and North Western Railway's land company, who platted it in 1894.

SHERIDAN TOWNSHIP organized January 22, 1870, first named Holton, was named for Philip Henry Sheridan (1831–88), a famous Union general in the Civil War.

SHERMAN TOWNSHIP organized October 4, 1869, was named for William Tecumseh Sherman (1820–91), a heroic general of the Civil War, renowned for his march through Georgia, "from Atlanta to the sea," November 15 to December 21, 1864.

SPRINGDALE TOWNSHIP at first called Summit, having the highest land of this county, at its southwest corner, was first settled in June 1867 and was organized November 21, 1873, being named for its numerous springs and brooks or creeks, flowing in dales and ravines.

STEAMBOAT LANDING a site near the mouth of the Redwood River, which in the 1860s was used by Redwood Falls businessmen as a freight shipping point.

SUMMIT a village in section 30 of Springdale Township, noted as a post office in the 1874 Andreas atlas.

SUNDOWN TOWNSHIP settled in 1871 and organize in 1873, has an almost unique name meaning the sunset. It is also the name of a village in Ulster County, N.Y. A post office was first established in 1878 in section 24 on postmaster William H. Hawk's farm and was moved in 1877 to the farm of Lord M. Rowe in section 26 until it was discontinued in 1879; it was reestablished in section 18, 1896–1906.

SWEDES FOREST TOWNSHIP first settled in September 1865 and organized September 21, 1872, was named in compliment to its many immigrant settlers from Sweden. It is mostly prairie but has a continuous forest along the bluff fronting the Minnesota River valley. The township was formerly part of Kintire and Delhi. A post office was in sections 26 and 35, 1868–77, with Peter Swenson, postmaster.

THREE LAKES TOWNSHIP settled in 1868, organized April 4, 1876, derived this name from the former group of three lakes in its northern part, now drained. A post office was in section 8, 1875–77, with Abel Leighton, postmaster.

UNDERWOOD TOWNSHIP settled in August 1869, organized May 2, 1876, has a name that is borne also by a village in Otter Tail County and by villages in Iowa and North Dakota.

VAIL TOWNSHIP earlier called Center, first settled in 1869 and organized September 16, 1879, was named in compliment of Fred Vail Hotchkiss, who was chairman of the board of county commissioners. A post office was in section 8, 1899–1900, with John Longbottem as postmaster; Longbottem, also first clerk of the township, was born in Canada in 1850, came to Minnesota in 1869, and was among the first settlers.

VESTA TOWNSHIP settled in 1868, organized May 29, 1880, was named on the suggestion of Fred Vail Hotchkiss for his sister, Vesta Vail Hotchkiss. The city, in sections 15 and 16, was platted in 1899

and was incorporated February 9, 1900. The post office began in 1899, with Timothy L. Crowley as first postmaster; the Chicago and North Western Railway had a station after 1898.

WABASSO a city in sections 23 and 26 of Vail Township platted in September 1899, was incorporated May 1, 1900. Its name is from Longfellow's *Song of Hiawatha*, for the Ojibwe word *wabos* (pronounced wahbose), meaning "a rabbit." The site was developed by the Chicago and North Western Railway in 1898 and platted by the Western Town Lot Company as four full blocks and two partial blocks, lots selling at auction on November 1, 1899. The post office was established in 1900, with hardware store owner John H. Rahskoph as postmaster.

WALNUT GROVE a city in North Hero and Springdale Townships, platted in April 1874, incorporated March 3, 1879, and separated from the townships on March 30, 1891, was named for a grove of about 100 acres, including many black walnut trees, on Plum Creek in the southeast corner of Springdale, from one to two miles southwest of this village. It is at the northern limit of the geographic range of this tree. The first postmaster, Lafayette Bedal, a native of Canada, built a shanty near the Chicago and North Western Railway right-of-way called Walnut Station in 1872 in what became North Hero Township, across the line from Springdale Township; Bedal's brother, Elias, transferred his grain-buying business from Eyota to the new settlement and filed the plat on September 10, 1874, naming it Walnut Grove. With Gustave Sunwall, Lafayette Bedal built a store, and when the village was incorporated in 1879, Bedal was the first president of its council; Charles Ingalls, father of Laura Ingalls Wilder, was elected the first justice. The post office was first called Walnut Station, 1873–81, and then became Walnut Grove.

WANDA a city in section 19 of Willow Lake Township, platted in September 1899, incorporated as a village on April 12, 1901, and separated from the township on March 20, 1906, is named from "the Ojibway Indian word *wanenda*, and means 'to forget' or 'forgetfulness'" (Stennett, *Place Names of the Chicago and Northwestern Railways*, p. 135). The post office began in 1900.

WATERBURY TOWNSHIP settled in the spring of 1872 and organized April 9, 1878, was named for the township and large village of Waterbury in Vermont.

WAYBURNE a railway station of the Chicago and North Western Railway in section 4 of Brookville, was platted in 1902 on land owned by Hans Madsen; the name is fanciful and has no historical significance.

WELDON a post office in Sheridan Township, 1869–74, with Thomas Barr, postmaster, and again 1879–80, with William W. Obert, postmaster.

WEST LINE a post office in section 26, Westline Township, 1878–80, with Lizzie H. Weymouth, postmaster; it was reestablished in 1887 as Westline, in section 26, with John N. Jones, postmaster, moving to several other sections before closing in 1902.

WESTLINE TOWNSHIP settled in 1872 and organized October 14, 1878, was named for its situation on the west side of the county.

WILLOW LAKE TOWNSHIP first settled in 1871, organized September 27, 1873, was named for its lake adjoining Wanda village.

Streams and Lakes

Tributaries of the Minnesota River in this county include Big Spring Creek in Swedes Forest; Rice Creek in Delhi; the Redwood River, noticed in the first pages of this chapter; Crow Creek, five miles farther east; and Wabasha Creek in Sherman. Beside Crow Creek were the villages of Little Crow and Big Eagle, after their removal from the Mississippi, until the time of the Dakota War in 1862; and the villages of two other Dakota leaders, Wabasha and Wacouta, adjoined Wabasha Creek. The Lower Sioux Agency was nearly midway between these creeks.

The Redwood River receives Ramsey Creek from the south edge of Delhi, flowing from Ramsey Lake (now drained), each named in honor of Gov. Alexander Ramsey, and Clear Creek, from Granite Rock Township, joins this river at Seaforth.

The Cottonwood River, crossing the southern part of this county, has been well noted in the chapter of Cottonwood County. It may be here added that a very large and lone cottonwood tree beside this stream, about seven miles northwest of Lamberton village, was reputed to be a chief

reason for its name; but the Dakota had used the name Waraju, as spelled by Joseph N. Nicollet, which the white traders and explorers translated, for probably more than a century before the growth of that tree began.

Sleepy Eye Creek, flowing from this county east to join the Cottonwood River in Brown County a few miles south of the city of Sleepy Eye, has been noticed under that county.

On its north side the Cottonwood River receives no tributary in Redwood County. On the south it receives three creeks from Gales Township; Plum Creek, from Springvale and North Hero, named for its wild plums; and farther east, flowing from Cottonwood County, Pell Creek, Dutch Charley Creek, to which Highwater Creek is a tributary, and Dry Creek, so named from its being often dried up during summer droughts.

The preceding pages have noticed the former Ramsey Lake in Delhi; the Three Lakes, now drained, which were formerly in the township named for them; and Willow Lake, also giving its name to a township.

Only a few other lakes remain to be listed, as Hackberry Lake in Brookville, now drained, which was named for its hackberry trees; Snyder Lake in section 33, Morgan, now dry; Rush Lake, also now dry, two miles southeast of Willow Lake; Nettiewynnt Lake (formerly Hall Lake), now drained, in Gales Township, bearing the fanciful name of a large farm that adjoined it and extended more than two miles south, containing about 3,000 acres; Horseshoe Lake, of curved shape, now drained, in Westline; Goose and Swan Lakes in the northwest part of Underwood; and Tiger Lake on the Minnesota bottomland in Honner, named probably for a puma or "mountain lion." This animal, also often called a panther, was described by Capt. Jonathan Carver as "the Tyger of America."

Ramsey State Park

Adjoining the city of Redwood Falls, a mainly wooded tract of about a hundred acres was acquired by the state of Minnesota in 1911 as a public park. It includes a half mile of the picturesque gorge of the Redwood River below its falls, with the tributary gorge of Ramsey Creek, which in this park has a waterfall descending nearly 50 feet. The Redwood River flows one and a half miles in its gorge before it opens into the broad bottomland of the Minnesota valley, being quite unique in its grand and beautiful scenery. The state park is named in honor of Gov. Alexander Ramsey, who was prominent in making treaties in 1851 with the Dakota, by which they ceded the great prairie region of southwestern Minnesota for white settlers and agricultural development. Soon after the establishment of the Lower Sioux Agency, about eight miles east of Redwood Falls, it was visited by Gov. Ramsey, for whom then Ramsey Creek and Lake were named. In 1957 the state turned the park over to the city of Redwood Falls for a city park.

Lower Sioux Reservation

Following the signing of the Treaties of Mendota and Traverse des Sioux in 1851, the Dakota moved to reservations along the Minnesota River. Their lands were reduced by half in 1858. After the Dakota War of 1862, they lost all lands in the state. Beginning with congressional action in 1887 and 1893, the federal government bought land in the vicinity of Lower Sioux Agency for Dakota living in Minnesota in 1886. The Lower Sioux Reservation was established in 1888 and consists of 1,743 acres along the Minnesota River in Redwood County.

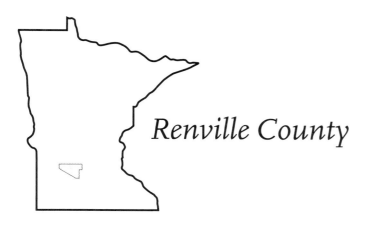

Renville County

This county, established February 20, 1855, and organized March 1 and November 8, 1866, was named for Joseph Renville, a "bois brule, " whose father was French and mother Indian, of whom Dr. E. D. Neill gave an appreciative sketch in the first volume of the MHS Collections. Renville was born at or near the Kaposia village of the Dakota, on the Mississippi a few miles below St. Paul, about the year 1779. After a few years at school in Canada, he became a voyageur for an English company in the fur trade of the Northwest. In the War of 1812 he received the appointment and rank of a captain in the British army and led a company of Dakota warriors against the U.S. frontier. He was employed by Maj. Stephen H. Long as the interpreter of his expedition to the Red River and Lake Winnipeg in 1823; and William H. Keating, the historian of the expedition, derived from him a large amount of information relating to the Dakota people. Afterward, having become an agent of the American Fur Company, Renville erected a trading house at Lac qui Parle and resided there until his death, which was in March 1846.

He was a friend of Rev. Thomas S. Williamson, who came as a missionary to the Dakota of the Minnesota valley in 1835. "Renville warmly welcomed him," wrote Dr. Neill, "and rendered invaluable assistance in the establishment of the missions. Upon the arrival of the missionaries at Lac qui Parle, he provided them with a temporary home. He acted as interpreter, he assisted in translating the Scriptures, and removed many of the prejudices of the Indians against the white man's religion."

Information of names has been gathered in History of the Minnesota Valley *(1882), having pages 798–848 for this county;* The History of Renville County, *compiled by Franklyn Curtiss-Wedge (1916, 2 vols., 1,376 pp.); and from Charles N. Matson, judge of probate, and Hon. Darwin S. Hall, each of Olivia, the county seat, interviewed during a visit there in July 1916.*

BANDON TOWNSHIP first settled in April 1869 and organized January 4, 1871, was named by its Irish settlers for a town in southern Ireland, on the River Bandon, about 20 miles southwest of Cork. A post office in section 6 was begun in 1881 with Andreas Hohle, postmaster; Hohle was born in Norway in 1869, came with his parents to the United States that year and to the township in 1871, became a teacher, and died in 1899; post office closed in 1900.

BEAVER FALLS TOWNSHIP organized April 2, 1867, and its village in section 22, platted July 25, 1866, and incorporated January 21, 1890, received their name from Beaver Creek, which is a translation of the Dakota name Chapah River, noted on

Joseph N. Nicollet's map in 1843. This village was the first county seat, until a very long contest, begun in 1885, was finally decided in October 1900 by removal of the county offices to Olivia. An act to invalidate the incorporation was approved on April 14, 1891. The village was platted on land owned by David Carrothers and Sam McPhail, the latter residing in Redwood Falls; a post office operated 1867–1904.

BECHYN a village in sections 28 and 29 of Henryville Township, which had a post office, 1888–1904.

BIRCH COOLEY see MORTON.

BIRCH COOLEY TOWNSHIP organized April 2, 1867, and its former village, platted in June 1865 but burned in 1871, were named for their small stream. "Coulée is a French word meaning the bed of the stream, even if dry, when deep and having inclined sides. The original name of the stream in the coulée was La Croix Creek, but the vicinity was known from the early days as Birch coulée, and this was finally corrupted to Birch Cooley, now the official name of the township" (history of this county, 1916, p. 1,290). This name was translated from Tampa Creek of the Dakota, as it was mapped by Nicollet, referring to its many trees of the paper or canoe birch, which in this vicinity reaches the southwest limit of its geographic range.

BIRD ISLAND TOWNSHIP settled in the spring of 1872, was organized October 21, 1876, and its city in sections 13, 14, 23, and 24 of the same name, platted in July 1878, was incorporated March 4, 1881, and was reincorporated on June 1, 1908, and separated from the township. The name was derived from a grove of large trees, including many of the hackberry, in section 15, about a mile west of the village and on the south side of the railway, surrounded by sloughs, like an island, whereby it was protected from prairie fires. This grove, named Bird Island for its plentiful wild birds, was a favorite camping place of Indians and trappers, and it supplied timber for the early settlers. The village developed when the Hastings and Dakota Railway came in 1878; the post office began in 1878.

BOON LAKE a post office, 1882–1902, was located first in section 24 of Brookfield Township and then in section 30 of Boon Lake Township.

BOON LAKE TOWNSHIP organized September 6, 1870, bears the name of its largest lake, probably given in honor of a pioneer settler.

BROOKFIELD a townsite in section 1 of Brookfield Township and section 6 of Boon Lake Township, which had a post office established in 1897, a general store, a blacksmith, a creamery, and a feed mill; the post office merged with Buffalo Lake in 1914.

BROOKFIELD TOWNSHIP settled in 1871 and organized April 7, 1874, has a name that is borne also by a city in Missouri and by villages and townships in 12 other states.

BUFFALO LAKE a city in section 30 of Preston Lake Township, platted in 1881 and incorporated as a village on November 6, 1891, was a half mile south of a picturesque little lake whence it received this name. John C. Riebe came in 1880 and purchased land that was a former fort site; he had the village platted on his land and became the first postmaster when the post office opened in 1882; he was also first village council president and was instrumental in establishing Olivia rather than Beaver Falls as the county seat. The townsite developed with the Hastings and Dakota Railway's arrival, although passengers departed at Monson's Crossing a half mile west until the depot was built in 1882.

CAIRO TOWNSHIP settled in 1859 and after the Dakota War again settled in 1864, was organized April 7, 1868. It was at first called Mud Lake Township, for its lake on Mud Creek (Little Rock Creek), but received its present name July 8, 1869. This name, derived from the capital of Egypt, is borne also by a city of Illinois and by villages and townships in ten other states.

CAMP TOWNSHIP was organized April 2, 1867. A post office was in section 23; it was first called Renville during two periods, 1862–63 and 1873–80, and then Camp, 1880–1904.

CHURCHILL a village in section 34 of Brookfield Township.

CREAM CITY a creamery site in section 14 of Osceola Township with three platted blocks.

CROOKS TOWNSHIP the latest organized in this county, was named in honor of H. S. Crooks, who settled here as a homestead farmer in 1870. It was organized as Aurora Township in November 1884 and changed to Crooks in 1885.

DANUBE is a city in sections 5 and 6 of Troy Township, founded in 1899. This name, received from the large river in Europe, is borne also by a township and village in New York. The city was called Miles when it was incorporated on November 5, 1902, and was changed to Danube in 1903 and separated from the township on April 19, 1917. The city developed as a local trade center for farmers with the arrival of the Hastings and Dakota Railway; the post office began in 1898 as Miles changing to Danube in 1903.

EDDSVILLE a farmers post office, 1877–1905, in section 18 of Palmyra Township, with Edwin H. Oleson as first postmaster at his home in section 28.

EMMET TOWNSHIP first settled in June 1869 and organized September 21, 1870, was named in honor of Robert Emmet (1778–1803), the Irish patriot.

ERICSON TOWNSHIP settled in 1871 and organized January 27, 1874, was named in honor of Eric Ericson, a prominent pioneer of this county, who served as county auditor and during many years was the county superintendent of schools. A country post office was in the township, 1877–79, with Fred H. Wolstad, postmaster.

FAIRFAX a city in sections 5–8 of Cairo, platted August 22, 1882, and incorporated January 5, 1888, was named by Eben Ryder, president of the Minneapolis and St. Louis Railroad company, for his native county in Virginia. The city began as a settlement one-half mile east on land owned by Edmond O'Hara and moved to its present site when the Chicago and North Western Railway came in 1882. The post office also was established that year; the first merchant and postmaster was Luke T. Grady. The site was originally on an island with a deep slough around it, requiring a great deal of drainage.

FINN TOWN a village in Camp Township, south of Franklin, where only ruins remain; formerly the village had a hotel and inn and a landing for steamboats loading grain.

FLORA TOWNSHIP first settled in the spring of 1859 and again in 1865, was organized April 2, 1867, receiving the name of "the first horse brought here" by Francis Shoemaker.

FLORITA a post office in Flora Township, 1886–1905, first in section 26 and then in section 22.

FRANKLIN is a city in sections 1, 2, 11, and 12 of Birch Cooley Township, platted in 1882 and in-

corporated as a village on April 24, 1888. Holder Jacobus was postmaster, 1869–82; the village had a station of the Minneapolis and St. Louis Railroad. Eighteen townships in so many counties of Pennsylvania, and also townships and villages or cities in 29 other states, bear this name, with counties in 24 states, mostly in honor of Benjamin Franklin (1706–90).

GORDON a post office, 1875–79, 20 miles from Beaver Falls; Charles B. Gordon was the first postmaster.

HAWK CREEK TOWNSHIP organized April 2, 1867, received the name of its creek, translated from its Dakota name, Chetambe, noted on Nicollet's map. When organized, the township included the present townships of Sacred Heart, Ericson, Hawk Creek, and Wang and land to the west in Chippewa County. A locality called Hawk Creek was noted in the 1874 Andreas atlas as a post office in section 8, although it is not on official post office lists.

HECTOR TOWNSHIP settled in 1873 and organized June 30, 1874, was at first called Milford but was renamed a month later for the township and village of Hector in Schuyler County, N.Y. whence many of its settlers had come. The city in sections 20, 21, 28, and 29 of this township, bearing the same name, was platted in September 1878, when the Hastings and Dakota Railway did a ten-block survey on land they owned, and was incorporated February 23, 1881. The post office was first located in 1875 in section 2 about four miles northeast of the village site, with John Baker as postmaster. It had a station serving the Minneapolis, St. Paul and Sault Ste. Marie Railroad (Soo Line) and the Hastings and Dakota Railway.

HENRYVILLE TOWNSHIP settled in May 1866 and organized March 16, 1871, was named in honor of Peter Henry, one of its pioneer farmers. A post office was in section 10, 1879–92, with Henry Schoregge, first postmaster.

HERZHORN a post office, located in Flora Township, 1868–79.

JEANNETTVILLE a village in section 28 of Hawk Creek Township; the post office was established in 1869 as Hawk Creek in Chippewa County, with Isaac S. Earl as postmaster, and became Jeannettville in 1871; it was discontinued in 1881.

KINGMAN TOWNSHIP settled in May 1877, organized September 3, 1878, was named by S. T.

Salter, the first township clerk, in honor of W. H. Kingman, his former fellow townsman in Winn, Maine, who removed to Wisconsin and purchased much land in this township but did not settle here.

LAKESIDE a village in section 27 of Boon Lake Township, was so named for its location near Allie Lake. A post office began operating in section 33 in 1871, with Ira S. Sheppard as postmaster; the post office was discontinued in 1902.

MARTINSBURG TOWNSHIP settled in 1873, organized September 3, 1878, was named for Martin Grummons whose father, W. F. Grummons, of this township, was then a member of the board of county commissioners.

MELVILLE TOWNSHIP was settled in 1872 and organized January 1, 1878. A station called Melville of the Chicago, Milwaukee, St. Paul and Pacific Railroad was located in the township, three miles east of Bird Island.

MILES see DANUBE.

MORTON a city in sections 30 and 31 of Birch Cooley Township, adjoining the Minnesota River, platted in 1882 and incorporated as a village on August 1, 1887, was named by officers of the Minneapolis and St. Louis Railroad company. The city developed with the granite quarries across the tracks from the townsite; it served several rail lines, including the Minneapolis and St. Louis Railroad. The Birch Cooley post office was established in 1867, and when the second postmaster, W. G. Bartley, who ran a mill in section 22, moved into Morton in 1882, he brought the post office with him; the name changed to Morton in 1894.

NEW LISBON a post office, 1872–1901, located briefly in section 6 of Wang Township in the home of Christopher Hutchins.

NORFOLK TOWNSHIP settled in the fall of 1868 and organized July 26, 1869, was at first called Houlton but on January 4, 1871, was renamed Marschner, which in 1874 was changed to Norfolk. This name, derived from a county in England, is borne also by counties in Massachusetts and Virginia and by townships and villages or cities in these states and in Connecticut, New York, and Nebraska. A post office was located in section 29, 1879–80 and 1882–1902, with James Brown, postmaster.

OLIVIA the county seat, a city in Troy and Bird Island Townships, was first platted in September 1878 in section 7 of Bird Island Township and for some time called Station in Section 7, until named Olivia. It may have been named by Albert Bowman Rogers, an eminent civil engineer, who located this railway. "The first station agent to be placed at Ortonville, Minn., was a woman. Her name was Olive. She was a particular friend of Chief Engineer Rogers, and it was for her he named Olivia" (history of this county, p. 1359). Or the city may have been named for Margaret Olivia Sage, wife of Russell Sage, an official of the Chicago, Milwaukee and St. Paul Railroad. The city was incorporated March 4, 1881, and reincorporated and separated from the townships on September 28, 1906. After much contention extending through 15 years for removal of the county seat from Beaver Falls to Olivia, this was finally provided by a vote of the county, October 25, 1900. Isaac Lincoln was named first postmaster in 1879; it had a station serving several lines, including the Soo Line.

OSCEOLA TOWNSHIP settled in 1875 and organized September 30, 1879, was named by L. L. Tennis, then a county commissioner, for the village of Osceola in Wisconsin. Counties in Florida, Michigan, and Iowa and townships and villages or cities in 15 states of the Union are named in commemoration of a Seminole leader, Osceola, who was born in Georgia in 1804 and died at Fort Moultrie, S.C., January 30, 1838. A post office was in section 18, 1893–1905.

PALMYRA TOWNSHIP organized January 2, 1872, was named by settlers who came from Palmyra in southeastern Wisconsin. Sixteen other states also have villages and townships named from the ancient Palmyra, "city of palms," which was in an oasis of the Syrian desert. A post office was in section 22, 1873–80, located in T. A. Risdall's house with Edwin H. Oleson as postmaster.

PLAINFIELD a place name in section 30 of Hector Township, which is not the same as Plumfield but is often confused with that post office.

PLUMFIELD a post office, 1875–78, with John B. Perkins, postmaster, on his farm in section 30, Hector Township, about one and a half miles southwest of Hector.

PRESTON LAKE TOWNSHIP settled in 1866 and organized September 7, 1869, was named for its largest lake probably commemorating a pioneer settler or a hunter and trapper.

REISHUS see SACRED HEART.

RENVILLE a city in sections 5 and 8 of Emmet Township, platted in September 1878, and incorporated February 19, 1881, was named in honor of Joseph Renville, like this county. A post office with this name was established first in section 23 of Camp Township, operating 1862–63 and again 1873–80, before changing its name to Camp; a second post office was established at the present site as Renville Station, 1878–86, in reference to its Hastings and Dakota Railway station; it became Renville in 1886.

SACRED HEART TOWNSHIP organized April 6, 1869, was settled mostly by Lutherans, so that the adoption of a name apparently Roman Catholic in origin seems surprising. It was derived, however, from the name given by the Dakota to an early trader, Charles Patterson, who about 1783 established a trading post at the rapids of the Minnesota River in the present section 29, Flora, later called Patterson's Rapids. He wore a bearskin hat, whence, "the bear being a sacred animal to the Indians, they called him the 'Sacred Hat' man, which gradually became Sacred Heart" (*History of the Minnesota Valley*, p. 817). The name so applied to the trader was afterward used by the Dakota for the site of his trading post and thence it was given, in this accepted translation, to the adjacent township.

Another explanation for the origin of this name has been told by Louis G. Brisbois, a French pioneer of Hawk Creek Township. "He declared that in the early days the mouth of the Sacred Heart Creek formed in the shape of a heart, and that a French missionary priest, inspired by this, had given the name of Sacred Heart to a mission of French half-breeds and Indians that he had established here, and that the locality gradually took the name of this early mission, still retaining it long after the mission had passed into oblivion" (history of this county, p. 1,332).

Sacred Heart, a city in section 7, was platted in October 1878, was incorporated on May 16, 1883, was separated from the township on March 20, 1906, and was reincorporated on June 6, 1908. Settlement began in the early 1860s with many settlers from Norway. Post offices were established at three different times: the first, 1867–71, was transferred to Vicksburg; the second operated 1875–77; and the third was established as Minnesota Crossing, 1868–77, with German P. Greene, postmaster, township clerk, and first

teacher in the township. Greene came to the township in 1865, naming the site, then in section 8, Minnesota Crossing for the ford in the river below his log house; the house was the center of township activity until 1876; the post office then became Reishus, 1877–78, with Olaf S. Reishus, postmaster, who continued when the name changed to Sacred Heart; it had a station of the Hastings and Dakota Railway and Soo Line.

SWANSEA a farmers post office, 1867–85, in Preston Lake Township.

TROY TOWNSHIP settled in 1871–72, organized March 21, 1876, has the name of an ancient city in Asia Minor, renowned as the scene of the Trojan War, the theme of the *Iliad* of Homer. It is also the name of a large city in New York and of townships and villages or small cities in 25 other states.

VICKSBURG a river town in section 30, Flora, was first settled in 1871; its post office, located in section 19 of Sacred Heart Township, operated 1871–1901. Its name was from Vicksburg, Miss., which was besieged in the Civil War and surrendered July 4, 1863.

WADSWORTH a post office in Emmett Township, 1875–79, and a station on the Hastings and Dakota Railway.

WANG TOWNSHIP settled in 1867 and organized July 28, 1875, was named for a district or group of farms in Norway.

WELLINGTON TOWNSHIP settled in 1868 and organized June 4, 1873, commemorates the Duke of Wellington (1769–1852), victor over Napoleon at Waterloo in 1815. A city of Kansas and villages and townships in ten other states bear this name. A post office was located in the township, 1880–1904, on postmaster, justice, and town clerk William Schoenfelder's land.

WINFIELD TOWNSHIP settled in 1872, organized December 27, 1878, was named in honor of Gen. Winfield Scott (1786–1866), chief commander in the Mexican War. Winfield is the name also of a city in Kansas and of villages and townships in 16 other states. A post office, 1885–1902, was first on Ulrick Julson's farm in section 14 and then on Nels Swanson's farm in section 11.

Streams and Lakes

The Minnesota River flows in strong rapids over a bed of glacial drift boulders adjoining section

29, Flora, named Patterson's Rapids for a fur trader, as was noted under Sacred Heart Township. The descent here is about five feet within a third of a mile.

On the southwest border of this county the Minnesota River receives Hawk Creek and Sacred Heart Creek in the townships bearing these names, the first being a translation from its Dakota name, Chetamba, which is now given to a creek flowing into it from Ericson and Wang; Middle Creek in Flora; Beaver Creek, with West and East Forks, translated from the Dakota, as noted for Beaver Falls Township; Birch Cooley or Creek, also from the Dakota and before noticed for the township named from it; and Three Mile Creek in Camp, so named for its distance northwest from Fort Ridgely. Farther east, in Cairo, are Fort Creek and Mud or Little Rock Creek, flowing into Nicollet County and there tributary to the Minnesota River respectively near Fort Ridgely and near the site of a former trading post called Little Rock, adjoining an extensive rock outcrop in the Minnesota valley.

Buffalo Creek flows eastward into McLeod County, from Brookfield and Preston Lake Townships.

Besides Boon, Buffalo, and Preston Lakes, whence two townships and a village are named, these townships have Hodgson, Phare, and Allie (or Alley) Lakes, named for early settlers.

In section 23, Brookfield, Boot Lake, named from its outline, has been drained, and a lake formerly in the central part of Wellington has also been drained.

Mud Lake is on Mud or Little Rock Creek in Cairo.

Fox Lake, formerly about four miles long, crossed by the county line at the north side of Kingman, and another lake on the north line of Ericson, have been drained. Thus, too, the former Pelican Lake, adjoining the southeast side of Bird Island village, and Long or Lizard Lake in Winfield have disappeared.

Monuments of the Dakota War of 1862

Through the work of the Minnesota Valley Historical Society, under the direction of its president, Hon. Charles D. Gilfillan, many localities in Renville and Redwood Counties of great historical interest in events of the Dakota War in August 1862 and 1862–63 were carefully identified and marked in 1895–1902 by granite monuments and tablets. A report of this work, including many illustrations and much history and biography, written by Return I. Holcombe, was published in 1902 (79 pp.).

Two of these monuments are erected beside the railway southeast of Morton, one being in memory of the soldiers killed in the battle of Birch Couley, September 2, 1862, and the other in memory of several Dakota who were friendly to the white people, doing all they could to rescue them.

In Redwood County, this society erected numerous tablets in the vicinity of the Lower Sioux Agency and also similarly marked the site of Camp Pope, about a mile northwest from the present city of Redwood Falls, named, like Pope County, in honor of Gen. John Pope. There Gen. Sibley and his troops were encamped from April 19 to June 16, 1863, in preparation for his expedition against the Dakota in the present area of North Dakota.

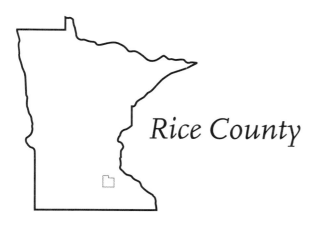

Rice County

Established March 5, 1853, this county was named in honor of Henry Mower Rice, one of the two first U.S. senators of Minnesota, 1858 to 1863. He was born in Waitsfield, Vt., November 29, 1816; came west to Detroit in 1835 and four years later to Fort Snelling; was during many years an agent of the Chouteau Fur Company; aided in the negotiation of several Indian treaties by which lands were ceded for white immigration in Minnesota; and was the delegate from this territory in Congress, 1853 to 1857. Excepting when absent in Washington, he resided in St. Paul from 1849 onward and was a most generous benefactor of this city. To Rice County he presented a valuable political and historical library. He was a charter member of the Minnesota Historical Society and was its president, 1864 to 1866. He died in San Antonio, Tex., while spending the winter months there, January 15, 1894. His portrait and a sketch of his life and public services, written by Gov. William R. Marshall, are published in the MHS Collections (9: 654–58 [1901]).

In accordance with the state enactment, a statue of Senator Rice is one of the two selected to represent Minnesota in the Statuary Hall of the U.S. Capitol in Washington, as unveiled February 8, 1916.

Information of the origin and significance of names has been gathered from History of Rice County *(1882, 603 pp.);* History of Rice and Steele Counties, *compiled by Franklyn Curtiss-Wedge (1910, 2 vols.), in which pages 1–628, in vol. 1, are the history of this county; and from Frank M. Kaisersatt, county auditor, and Martin M. Shields, judge of probate, interviewed at Faribault, the county seat, during a visit there in April 1916.*

All the townships of this county were organized May 11, 1858, on the date of admission of Minnesota as a state.

AUGHEIM a post office, 1880–81, with Edward Keirnan, postmaster; location not found.

BERG a post office, 1889–1901, in Webster Township, on land originally owned by a settler named Berg, who opened a general store on his farm; the site had Martin Elyward's saloon in the area of Berg nicknamed Little Chicago.

BRIDGEWATER TOWNSHIP first settled in 1853, has a name that is borne by a seaport city in southern England and by townships and villages in Maine, New Hampshire, Vermont, Massachusetts, and ten other states. The township had a post office in section 32, 1890–91, and a station of the Dan Patch Electric Line.

CANNON CITY TOWNSHIP settled in October 1854, was named like its village, platted in the fall of 1855, but not recorded until 1857, and never incorporated, for the Cannon River, flowing across the west part of the township. Ambitiously called a city, this village had the honor of being the first place of meeting of the county commissioners, in

1855, but within that year Faribault was selected as the county seat. The post office operated 1855–80, and then Dean post office was located in a general store in the center of the platted community, next to the public square, 1880–1901. The village and its vicinity were the scene of a widely read novel by Edward Eggleston, *The Mystery of Metropolisville*, published in 1873.

CEDARTOWN a post office, 1860–63, with Richard Leahy, postmaster; location not found.

CHESTER a post office, 1859–61, with Edwin S. Drake, postmaster; location not found.

CLARK'S CROSSING a station of the Dan Patch Electric Line, in section 27, Bridgewater Township, located on George Clark's land.

COMUS a community in section 29 of Bridgewater Township, formerly a station of the Chicago, Milwaukee and St. Paul Railroad.

DEAN a post office at Cannon City after 1880, named in honor of J. W. Dean, an early merchant there; the post office was discontinued in 1901.

DENNISON is a city with Goodhue County, on the east line of Northfield, lying mostly in Goodhue County. The village railroad station was called Spring Creek by the Chicago Great Western Railroad for more than 20 years until the community requested that the name be changed to Dennison for the previous owner of its site, Morris P. Dennison, a farmer, who removed to the city of Northfield.

DIAMOND a post office, 1863–65, with Patrick Smith, postmaster; location not found.

DODGE see EKLUND.

DUNDAS a city in Bridgewater, platted in 1857 and chartered in 1879, bears the name of a large town in Ontario and of villages in Ohio, Illinois, and Wisconsin, commemorating Henry Dundas (1742–1811), an eminent British statesman. This village was named by its founders, Edward T. and John M. Archibald, who came from Dundas in Ontario, built a flour mill here and made the best flour in the state (MHS Collections 10: 41 [pt. 1, 1905]; 14: 19 [1912]). The post office was established in 1859.

EAST PRAIRIEVILLE see PRAIRIEVILLE.

EAST RICHLAND a post office, 1872–75, located in section 34 of Richland Township.

EKLUND a townsite in Walcott Township; its post office began as Dodge City in Steele County, became Dodge, 1894–97, was then transferred to Rice County, and was discontinued in 1905.

ERIN a station of the Chicago, Milwaukee and St. Paul Railroad in Bridgewater Township.

ERIN TOWNSHIP settled in the spring of 1855, received this ancient and now poetic name of Ireland at the time of its organization, in 1858, by vote of its people, many of whom were Irish immigrants.

FARIBAULT a city in Cannon City Township and the county seat, platted in February 1855, organized as a township of small area May 11, 1858, and incorporated as a city February 29, 1872, was named in honor of Alexander Faribault, the eldest son of Jean Baptiste Faribault, who is commemorated by the county of this name. Alexander was born at Prairie du Chien, Wis., June 22, 1806, and died in this city that he had founded, November 28, 1882. He came to the Cannon River as a trader among the Indians in 1826, and during the next eight years he established trading posts on the sites of Waterville in Le Sueur County and Morristown in this county and also at a large Dakota village on the northwest shore of Cannon Lake. In 1834–35 he persuaded these Dakota to remove their village to the site of Faribault. Faribault served as first postmaster when the post office was established in 1853 and built the first frame house, which is on the National Register of Historic Places. A sawmill was built in 1854 and a gristmill in 1855. The city became the county seat in 1855. Shattuck, a military-style school for boys, was established in 1866, St. Mary's School for Girls in Bishop Henry B. Whipple's home in 1866, Seabury Divinity School in 1858, the institution for deaf, dumb, and blind in 1863, and the institution for the feebleminded in 1879.

FOREST TOWNSHIP first settled in 1854, was named probably for the originally wooded condition of nearly all its area. Townships and villages in ten other states and counties in Pennsylvania and Wisconsin bear this name.

FOUNTAIN GROVE see NORTHFIELD.

FOWLERSVILLE a post office, 1858–79, located in section 20 of Erin Township, with Bartholomew Foley, first postmaster.

GILBERT a post office, 1880–81, six miles east of Faribault, in Wheeling Township.

HAVEN a post office, 1861–67.

HAZELWOOD a community in section 10 of Webster Township; its post office, 1857–1905, was first located in section 12 in postmaster John J. McCabe's general store.

HILDEBRAND a station of the Chicago Great Western Railroad in Wheeling Township on the Goodhue County border.

KASPER a siding of the Chicago and North Western Railway in section 16, Walcott Township.

LAKE CITY a townsite platted in section 3 of Warsaw Township on the east shore of Cannon Lake, was considered to be a resort community at the turn of the century; although the site had a hotel, a school, and several buildings, it never developed.

LESTER a post office, 1872–1901, in section 8 of Forest Township.

LITTLE CHICAGO see BERG.

LITTLE PRAIRIE a station of the Dan Patch Electric Line in section 29 of Bridgewater Township.

LONSDALE is a city in section 26 of Wheatland, founded in 1903 by the Chicago, Milwaukee and St. Paul Railroad, having the same name as villages in Rhode Island and Arkansas. Its post office was established in 1902, the year of village incorporation; it was known first as Willoughby for James Wilby, who had settled on a claim in that section in 1857.

MILLERSBURG a village in section 15 of Forest Township, was platted in 1857 by George W. Miller. The first settler was James Fitzimmons in 1855, who sold his 160 acres in 1856 to Miller; Miller platted the acreage, built a mill and a hotel, and became first postmaster. The post office was begun in 1858 and discontinued in 1901.

MOLAND a post office, 1882–1905, located in section 36, Richland Township, with Peter Lund, first postmaster.

MORRISTOWN a city platted in the autumn of 1855 and incorporated as a village in 1874, and its township, organized May 11, 1858, received this name in honor of Jonathan Morris, who was born in Pennsylvania, January 9, 1804, and died here November 27, 1856. After being for 25 years a minister of the denomination called Christians or Disciples in Indiana and Ohio, he came to Minnesota in 1853 and settled here in 1855. The post office was established in 1856, with Walter Morris, son of Jonathan, as postmaster.

NERSTRAND a city in Wheeling Township, settled in 1855, platted in 1885 by Osmund Osmundson, and incorporated January 30, 1897, bears the name of an earlier post office, which was named by Osmundson for his former home in Norway. Osmundson was born in Norway in 1826, came to the United States in 1850 and to Nerstrand in 1856, served as a county commissioner and in the legislature, 1872–73, and died in 1914. The post office began in 1877, with Augen H. Brokke as postmaster in his store.

NORTHFIELD a city with Dakota County, in Bridgewater and Northfield Townships platted in October 1855, incorporated as a village in 1871 and as a city February 26, 1875, and the adjoining township of this name, organized in 1858, commemorate John W. North, principal founder of the village, who was born in Onondaga County, N.Y., in February 1815, and died in Oleandar, Calif., February 2, 1890. He was educated at Wesleyan University, Middletown, Conn.; was admitted to practice law in 1845; came to Minnesota in 1849 and settled here in 1855; was a member of the territorial legislature in 1851 and presided over the Republican wing of the convention in 1857 that framed the state constitution; was influential in founding the University of Minnesota and was treasurer of its board of regents, 1851–60. In 1861 he removed to Nevada, being appointed by Pres. Abraham Lincoln surveyor general of that territory. He presided over the convention that formed the state constitution of Nevada in 1864 and was one of the judges of its supreme court. Later he organized the company that established the fruit-growing settlement of Riverside near Los Angeles, Calif., and was U.S. judge for that state.

Another citizen of Northfield, who has been thought to be included in the honor of this name, was Ira Stratton Field, born in Orange, Mass., January 25, 1813, who came to Minnesota early in 1856, settling in Northfield as a blacksmith and farmer, and died here June 2, 1892. For 20 years before his coming here, he had lived in Jamaica, Vt., and had been elected twice to the Vermont legislature. He was an earnest advocate for temperance and for abolition of slavery. His removal to Northfield with his family soon after the village was platted and received its name, and the tradition that the name was intended to honor each of these prominent early settlers, may be explained by acquaintance between North and Field before the latter came west. An obituary sketch of Field in the *Northfield Independent*, June 9, 1892, states that "early in 1856 . . . he was gladly welcomed by Mr. North and the other few here at that time."

Northfield's post office was established as Fountain Grove in 1855 and changed to Northfield in 1856. The city was the scene of the bank robbery by the James-Younger gang in 1876. It is the site of Carleton College, known as Northfield College when established in 1866 by the Congregational Church; its name was changed in 1877 to honor William Carleton of Charlestown, Mass., who gave the college a gift of $50,000. Also located there is St. Olaf College, established in 1874 through the support of the Evangelical Lutheran Church.

OAK HARBOR a place name in Warsaw Township, circa 1930.

PRAIRIEVILLE a community in Cannon City Township, was platted in 1855 but not incorporated; its post office was called East Prairieville and operated 1857–79. Alexander Anderson was the first postmaster.

RICHLAND TOWNSHIP settled in 1854, has a name borne by counties in Wisconsin and five other states and by villages and townships in 20 states. A post office was in section 22, 1878–1901.

RUSKIN a community in Richland Township.

SCOTTS MILLS a station of the Dan Patch Electric Line in section 8 of Cannon City Township.

SHEFFIELD MILL a place name in Warsaw Township, circa 1930.

SHIELDSVILLE TOWNSHIP settled in 1855, was named in honor of Gen. James Shields, who induced many Irish colonists to take homestead farms in this township and in Erin. He was born in Atmore, Tyrone County, Ireland, December 12, 1810; came to the United States in 1826; studied law and in 1832 began practice in Kaskaskia, Ill.; was a member of the legislature in that state, 1836–39, state auditor in 1840–43, and a judge in its supreme court, 1843–45; served in the Mexican War, attaining the brevet rank of major general; was U.S. senator from Illinois, 1849–55; settled in Faribault, Minn., 1855, being attorney for the townsite company; was one of the senators elected to Congress when this state was organized and served in 1858–59; removed to California in 1860; served in the Civil War, 1861–63; resided on a farm in Carrollton, Mo., after 1866, devoting much time to lecturing, and was again a U.S. senator in 1879, from Missouri; died in Ottumwa, Iowa, June 1, 1879. At the unveiling of his statue in the Minnesota capitol, October 20, 1914, an address was given by Archbishop John Ireland, which, with the portrait of Shields and a biographic paper by Capt. Henry A. Castle, was published in the MHS Collections (15: 711–40 [1915]). His statue is also placed in the Statuary Hall at Washington as one of the two representing Illinois. The village of Shieldsville, in the northeast corner of this township, was platted June 12, 1856; it had a post office, 1856–1905.

SPRING CREEK see **DENNISON**.

TAFF a post office, 1871–72, with Nels Husebo as postmaster; location not found.

TENOD a post office, 1899–1900, in section 32 of Northfield Township.

TENROD a station on the Chicago, Milwaukee and St. Paul Railroad in Bridgewater Township.

TOWER CITY a station of the Dan Patch Electric Line, in section 17, Cannon City Township.

TREBON a place name in Shieldsville Township, circa 1930.

TRONDJEM a community of Webster Township, which flourished in the late 1860s to early 1900s; it had a post office, 1889–1905, three stores, a creamery, and a blacksmith.

UNION LAKES a townsite in section 6 of Bridgewater Township, was named for Union Lake in Forest and Webster Townships. The first settlers were German immigrants Friederich Albers and his family, who came to the United States in 1853. Its post office, 1856–87, was first located in Henry M. Humphrey's home in section 35 until 1873.

URLAND a post office, 1878–79, with Nils N. Kvernoden, postmaster; location not found.

VESELI a village in Wheatland, platted in 1880 in sections 10 and 15 and incorporated in 1889, was named for a city in southern Bohemia, whence its early settlers came. The post office was called Wesely, 1879–1908, at which time the name was changed to its present form, a word that means "hilarity, happiness, contentment, cheerfulness"; in the center of the village is the Czech Catholic church, school, and cemetery.

WALCOTT TOWNSHIP first settled in February 1854, "was named in honor of Samuel Walcott, from Massachusetts, who was a very able, energetic and talented man, but after a time his mind became distraught, and he found an abiding place in an insane retreat in his native state" (history of this county, 1910, p. 147). A siding of the Minneapolis, St. Paul and Sault Ste. Marie Railroad (Soo Line) was in section 18 of the township, with a post office, 1856–66 and 1890–1901.

WARSAW TOWNSHIP settled in 1854 and organized in 1858, was at first called Sargent but was renamed in 1864, then taking the name of its first post office, which had been established in 1856. This name was given "in honor of a town in New York, from whence a number of the early settlers had come" (history of this county, 1882, pp. 507, 513). A post office has operated in section 18 of the township since 1858; the site was platted in 1857 on the three farms of J. Freeman Weatherhead, Christian Hershey, and A. Lamb, on both sides of the Cannon River, but was not incorporated.

WEBSTER TOWNSHIP first settled in the spring of 1855, commemorates Ferris Webster, one of its most prominent pioneers. He was born in Franklin, N.Y., February 2, 1802; came to Minnesota in 1856, settling here as a farmer; he had a store in section 35; he died August 24, 1880. A post office was established in the township in 1879, first in section 8 in the home of Ferdinand Butzke and later in the store in section 10 on Magnus Olson's land, along with a creamery.

WELLS TOWNSHIP settled in 1853, was named for James Wells, more commonly called "Bully Wells," a fur trader and farmer. He was born in New Jersey in 1804; served 15 years in the U.S. Army, having come to Minnesota with Col. Henry Leavenworth in 1819; was a trader at Little Rapids, near the site of Chaska, and in 1836 established a trading post on the site of Okaman in Waseca County; removed in 1837 to the head of Lake Pepin, being a trader there 16 years; came to this township in 1853 and founded a trading post on section 34, beside Wells Lake on the Cannon River but gradually gave his attention mainly to farming; was murdered mysteriously in 1863.

WESELY see VESELI.

WHEATLAND TOWNSHIP settled in 1855–56, has a name that is borne also by townships and villages in New York, Pennsylvania, Indiana, Wisconsin, Iowa, and six other states. A community named Wheatland had a post office, which operated

1857–1907, with Peter O'Brien as first postmaster in his store in section 19, serving until 1859, followed by Patrick Cody in his section 32 home until 1876. Cody was born in Ireland in 1808, came to the county in 1855, and died in 1880. The village was laid out in section 33 next to Cody's land.

WHEELING TOWNSHIP first settled in June 1854, bears the name of a city in West Virginia and villages in Indiana, Illinois, and Missouri. A post office was in section 27, 1865–86.

WILLOUGHBY see LONSDALE.

Lakes and Streams

The name of the Cannon River and Lake has been noticed in the first chapter, and it is also considered for Cannon Falls, Goodhue County. Straight River, lying in Steele County, is noted in its chapter.

Cannon River has its source in Shields Lake, crossed by the north line of Shieldsville, named like that township for Gen. James Shields. It flows through Rice Lake, named for its wild rice, and Hunt Lake is tributary to it, before passing westward into Le Sueur County. Returning into Rice County, from Waterville, it flows through the Lower or Morristown Lake, Cannon Lake, and Wells Lake, the last named, like its township, for the fur trader, James Wells.

From the north and west, the Cannon River receives Devil Creek, which brings the outflow of Cedar and Mud Lakes; three creeks, unnamed on maps, flowing from Dudley, French, and Roberds Lakes; Wolf Creek, deriving outflow from Mazaska, Fox, and Circle Lakes; and Heath Creek, flowing from Knowles Lake and through Union Lake.

In the preceding list, we may additionally note that Cedar Lake has red cedars on its shores; Roberds Lake was named for William Roberds, a native of North Carolina, who settled beside it and built a sawmill; *Mazaska*, meaning "white iron," is the Dakota word for silver; Circle Lake encircles a large island, containing 97 acres; and in Union Lake the two headstreams of Heath Creek are united.

Small tributaries of Cannon River from the south and east are outlets of Sprague Lake in Morristown; Mackenzies Creek flows through Warsaw to Cannon Lake; and Prairie Creek, flowing northeastward from Cannon City through Northfield

Township, passes across an eastern prairie area, contrasted with the mainly wooded country west of the Cannon River.

Straight River in this county receives Mud Creek from the west, and Rush and Falls Creeks from the east.

Crystal Lake, named for the clearness of its water, adjoins Dean village in Cannon City.

The northeast part of Morristown has three little lakes, namely, Pats Lake and Boneset and Mormon Lakes. The second is named for its abundance of boneset, also called thoroughwort, and the third was used by a Mormon missionary as a place for baptism of converts.

Hatch Lake, in sections 16 and 17, Wheatland, was named in honor of Zenas Y. Hatch, a pioneer homesteader, who was prominent in township affairs. Other lakes in Wheatland are Rezac Lake or Metogga Lake, in section 20, first named for Frank Rezac, a farmer near it, who served in the Union army; Cody Lake, named in honor of Patrick Cody, a nearby farmer; and Phelps Lake, formerly called Cedar Lake, extending across the township line into Erin. Their outflow goes west and north by Sand Creek, tributary to the Minnesota River near Carver.

State Parks

The county's two state parks preserve parts of the Big Woods, the deciduous forest that covered much of southeastern Minnesota before white settlers cleared it for farmland and lumber. The first was Nerstrand State Park, established in 1945, just west of the town of Nerstrand, and renamed Nerstrand Big Woods State Park in 1990. Sakatah Lake State Park, created in 1963, includes Upper and Lower Sakatah Lakes, reaching into Le Sueur County. At the time the park was established, a railroad bisected it; when the line was abandoned in 1976, the road was converted to become the Sakatah Singing Hills Trail.

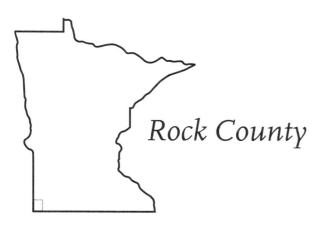

Rock County

This county was established May 23, 1857, and was organized by a legislative act March 5, 1870. Its name and also that of the Rock River refer to the prominent rock outcrop (called "The Rock" on Joseph N. Nicollet's map in 1843) of reddish gray quartzite, forming a plateau of gradual ascent from the west and north, but terminated precipitously on the east and south, which occupies an area of three or four square miles, situated about three miles north of Luverne, on the west side of the Rock River, above which it has a height of about 175 feet. In this generally prairie region, "the Mound," as this plateau is now called, commands an extensive prospect. The name is translated from the Dakota "Inyan Reakah or River of the Rock," as it was mapped by Nicollet.

By the original legislative act of 1857, the names of Rock and Pipestone Counties were respectively transposed from their intended and appropriate areas, which error was corrected by the legislature in 1862.

Information of names has been gathered from History of Rock County, *pages 5–8 in a plat book of this county, published in 1886;* An Illustrated History of the Counties of Rock and Pipestone *by Arthur P. Rose, 1911, having pp. 31–239 on this county, with pp. 423–655 for its biographical history; and from Joseph H. Adams, county register of deeds, Charles O. Hawes, and Caroline M. Watson, each of Luverne, the county seat, interviewed during a visit there in July 1916.*

ASH CREEK a community in section 23 of Clinton, platted in August 1883, is near the mouth of the creek so named for its ash trees. The owner of this townsite, Col. Alfred Grey, an English capitalist and an extensive landowner in this section of Minnesota and Iowa, "was fully honored in the names bestowed upon the streets running east and west, which were Colonel, Grey, and Alfred" (history of this county, 1911, p. 209). A post office was located there, 1871–1939, the first site being in section 14, with Lina B. Kniss as postmaster, on property owned by her husband, George W. Kniss. Col. Grey sold all of his property, 894 acres, to Ezra Rice and James Gray in 1891.

ASH GROVE a place name on a county map; location not found.

BATTLE PLAIN TOWNSHIP organized July 16, 1877, was at first called Riverside but was renamed March 19, 1878, for "the Indian battlefield located within its boundaries."

BEAVER CREEK TOWNSHIP organized September 16, 1872, received this name from its creek, on the suggestion of James Comar, a homesteader on section 14. Rose, in the history of the county (p. 234), gives an interesting account of the former great abundance of the beaver, as follows: "Beaver and other fur-bearing animals were taken along the streams for many years after the county was settled. During the early seventies quite a number of beaver were trapped by the settlers along Beaver Creek in the township of the same name. A pioneer settler of the precinct tells me that at the mouths of the many deep holes, which are a feature of the stream, these cunning animals would cut down the willows and build formidable dams within a few days if unmolested. The local press in the fall of 1876 reported Rock River lined with implements of destruction for the taking of the valuable pelts. Beaver were taken along this stream up into the eighties."

The city of Beaver Creek, incorporated October 2, 1884, was established with the arrival of the Worthington and Sioux Falls Railroad; Charles Williams donated 80 acres of his land in section 28 to the railroad for platting in October 1877, and the post office was established in his home, three-fourths of a mile east of the village.

BRUCE a railway station in Martin Township, platted in May 1888, was named in honor of one of the chief officials of the Illinois Central Railroad company. Its post office operated 1888–1936.

CARNEGIE a townsite, was platted in section 6 of Rose Dell Township in competition with Jasper, which had been platted across the county line in Eden Township, Pipestone County; Jasper attracted more business, and the Carnegie site diminished.

CLINTON see KONGSBERG.

CLINTON TOWNSHIP organized February 18, 1871, was named by vote of its people, for the village of Clinton in Oneida County, N.Y. the seat of Hamilton College.

DENVER TOWNSHIP the latest organized in this county, July 24, 1878, was at first called Dover until January 6, 1880. It was renamed with this slight change in spelling, after the capital of Colorado, "Queen City of the Plains," because another township of Minnesota had been earlier named Dover. A post office was on postmaster Horace Goodale's farm in section 10, 1885–87.

GRANT TOWNSHIP was settled earlier, but when organized in 1871 it included Clinton, Kanaranzi, and Martin, and the name changed to Clinton.

HANDY a post office, 1874–85, in southeast Kanaranzi Township.

HARDWICK a city in Denver, platted as four blocks in 1891, and incorporated October 10, 1898, was named in honor of J. L. Hardwick, the master builder of the Burlington, Cedar Rapids and Northern Railway. The community developed with the establishment of a Burlington station in 1886 on the Otter Otterson farm; a second rail line came in 1900 with a branch line from Worthington. John Otterson built the first building and opened the post office in 1891.

HILLS a city in Martin Township, section 28, platted in November 1889 and incorporated November 15, 1904, was at first called Anderson, in honor of Goodman Anderson, a resident there, but was renamed March 1, 1890, for Frederick C. Hills, who then was president of the Sioux City and Northern Railway. The city was located at the intersection of the Illinois Central and the Sioux City and Northern railroads. The post office was established in 1890, when postmaster Jacob N. Jacobson and his partner moved their store from Bruce, Jacobson having served as a postmaster there. Southwest of the village is the historic Old Iron Post erected in 1870, which marks the point of meeting for Minnesota, South Dakota, and Iowa.

JASPER a city in section 3 of Rose Dell and reaching into Pipestone County, platted April 19, 1888, and incorporated May 9, 1889, was named for its excellent quarries of "jasper," more correctly to be termed red quartzite. See also Jasper in the chapter of Pipestone County.

KANARANZI TOWNSHIP organized January 15, 1873, bears the name of its creek, which is spelled Karanzi on Nicollet's map, a Dakota word, translated as meaning "where the Kansas were killed." The community of this name in section 3 was platted in August 1885; its post office was established in 1886, with Glenn T. Bandy as postmaster on his farm.

KENNETH a city in sections 1 and 2 of Vienna, platted in July 30, 1900, and incorporated as a village on July 20, 1921, was named for a son of Jay A. Kennicott, owner of "a section farm half a mile south of the new town." The city developed when the Chicago, Rock Island and Pacific Railroad came through in 1899; its post office began in 1900, with James L. Hogan, postmaster, in his general store.

KONGSBERG a post office of Clinton Township, began as Clinton, 1876–77, and changed to Kongsberg, 1877–84; Nils Clemetson was postmaster under both names.

LUVERNE a city in Luverne Township and the

county seat, first settled in 1867–68, platted as a village in 1870, was incorporated by a legislative act February 14, 1877, and by vote of its people November 12, 1878. Nearly 26 years later, on September 7, 1904, it was organized as a city. This name was adopted for the post office begun in the winter of 1868, being in honor of Eva Luverne Hawes, the eldest daughter of the first settler here, Philo Hawes; Hawes's step-brother, Edward McKenzie, was postmaster. She was born at Cannon Falls in Goodhue County, November 14, 1857; accompanied her parents to the Rock River home in 1868; was married to P. F. Kelley, September 5, 1876; and died in Luverne, June 9, 1881. In the early years the name was spelled as two words, Lu Verne, "but the style was gradually replaced by the present form." The personal name was found in a novel or romance, then probably a new book or published in a magazine, which was read by Philo Hawes's cousin Lucy Cotter, of Red Wing, at whose request the baby Luverne was so named.

As her father and mother are also honored by the name of the village and city, this notice may desirably add that he was born in Danby, N.Y., December 18, 1830, and died at Luverne, August 10, 1908. He came to Minnesota in 1853; served as second lieutenant in the Eleventh Minnesota Regiment in the Civil War; was a mail carrier in 1867 between Blue Earth, Minn., and Yankton, Dakota Territory; settled on the site of Luverne in March 1868; was chairman of the board of county commissioners, 1871–73; was postmaster of Luverne, 1871–74 and 1888–93; and engaged in real estate and insurance business.

Luverne Township, named from its earlier village, was organized February 16, 1871; initially it included Luverne, Mound, and the west half of Magnolia Township.

MAGNOLIA TOWNSHIP organized November 27, 1872, was named for the township and village of Magnolia in Rock County, Wis., on suggestion of Philo Hawes, who had lived there. The city of this name, platted in October 1891, was incorporated September 4, 1894. When first established as a station in 1877, it was called Drake for Hon. Elias F. Drake of St. Paul, president of the Minnesota Valley Railroad, who owned a large farm here, but on May 2, 1886, the name was officially changed to that of the township. A post office was established in 1886 in section 14, following the

transfer of the post office called Westside in Nobles County, with Ira E. Crosby, first merchant, as postmaster.

MANLEY a community in the south edge of Beaver Creek Township, platted in October 1889, was named in honor of W. P. Manley, cashier of the Security National Bank in Sioux City, Iowa, one of the leading stockholders of the Sioux City and Northern Railway. Its post office operated 1890–1914, the first postmaster being Mary E. McCallen.

MARTIN TOWNSHIP organized March 12, 1873, was named for John Martin, its first settler, who located on section 13 in 1869 and built the first house in this township. A post office was located on postmaster John O. Tyler's farm, 1876–80.

MEADOW a post office, 1877–95, first located on first postmaster Knud K. Steen's homestead, section 14, Rose Dell Township.

MOUND TOWNSHIP established April 21, 1877, contains the large plateau of rock, called "the Mound" by the white settlers, whence the Rock River and this county are named, as before noted. An earlier township, named Gregory, at first including all the north half of the county, had been organized May 2, 1873, at the home of Horace G. Gregory in section 35 of the present Mound Township, but the six surveyed townships originally forming Gregory were later separately organized under other names. The quarries of the Mound supplied to Luverne the stone used in building the courthouse, high school, and numerous other buildings. The Mound and the tallgrass prairie around it are now protected within Blue Mounds State Park, developed in the 1930s and formally established in 1961.

PLEASANT VALLEY a post office, 1879–80, with Charles A. Reynolds, postmaster; location not found.

ROSE DELL TOWNSHIP organized August 17, 1877, bears a name proposed by W. T. Vickerman, for "a rocky gorge, filled in the summer months with beautiful wild roses." This gorge is about 200 feet wide and 40 feet deep, on section 25, "a few rods west of Mr. Vickerman's pioneer home" (history of the county, 1911, p. 67).

SPRING WATER a post office, 1876–79, in Rose Dell Township, with Marion Brock, postmaster.

SPRINGWATER TOWNSHIP organized May 5, 1874, was then called Albion but was renamed as now on June 15 in that year. "Mike Mead had immigrated to the township from Springwater, New York, and when he discovered a large spring on section 32 it doubtless suggested to him the appropriateness of Springwater for the township, which through his eloquence he persuaded the majority of the citizens to accept" (history of the county, p. 65).

STEEN a city in Clinton, platted in the summer of 1888 and incorporated as a village on February 5, 1942, was named in honor of John P. Steen and his brother, Ole P. Steen, immigrants from Norway, who were respectively homesteaders of its site and an adjoining quarter section and gave land for the townsite. The community was settled primarily by German immigrants; it was called Virginia for a number of years, a name given to its Illinois Central Railroad station. Its post office was established as Steen in 1888, with Christian Clemmetson as first postmaster in his furniture store.

VIENNA TOWNSHIP organized February 10, 1874, was named by D. A. Hart, at whose home the first township meeting was held. This name, received from the large capital city of Austria, is borne by villages and townships in Maine, New York, Ohio, Wisconsin, and 13 other states of the Union.

WARNER a station of the Chicago, St. Paul, Minneapolis and Omaha Railroad in section 7 of Magnolia Township.

Rivers and Creeks

This is one of the very few counties in Minnesota having no lakes. It lies south and west of the remarkable marginal moraines referable to the later part of the Ice Age, and therefore it has a relatively smooth drift sheet destitute of low hills or swells, with hollows and lakes, which are characteristic of the drift generally in this state.

The Rock River, Ash Creek, Beaver Creek, and Kanaranzi Creek have been already noticed.

Elk Creek, flowing through Magnolia, testifies of former pasturage of elk there.

Champepadan Creek in Vienna, flowing from Nobles County, has a Dakota name, translated "Thorny Wood" on Nicollet's map.

Mud Creek flows south from Martin into Iowa, and Brush or Blood Run and Four Mile Creeks flow southwestward into South Dakota.

Beaver Creek receives Little Beaver and Springwater Creeks as tributaries.

In Rose Dell Township are Split Rock and Pipestone Creeks, which have been noted in the chapter of Pipestone County.

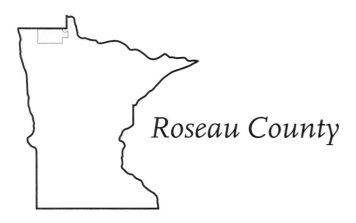

Roseau County

This county was established December 31, 1894, and received an addition from Beltrami County, February 10, 1896. It is named from the Roseau Lake and River, of which the former appears, with this name, on the La Vérendrye map (1737). The river is shown on David Thompson's map (1814), with the name Reed River, translated from this French name, which is in turn a translation of the Ojibwe name. Rev. Joseph A. Gilfillan wrote it, "Ga-shash-agunushkokawi-sibi or the-place-of-rushes-river, or briefly, Rush river." It is more accurately called Reed-grass River on Maj. Stephen H. Long's map (1823) and on Gen. John Pope's map (1849). The very coarse grass, or reed, referred to is *Phragmites communis*, which is common or frequent in the shallow edges of lakes throughout the prairie region of Minnesota and Manitoba. During a canoe trip around all the shore of Red Lake in September 1885, this species was observed in great abundance at many places, growing 8 to 12 feet in height.

Information of the origins and meanings of geographic names has been received from Syver G. Bertilrud, county auditor, interviewed at Roseau, the county seat, during a visit there in September 1909; and from him a second time, also from D. H. Benson, dealer in real estate, and J. W. Durham, janitor of the high school, each of Roseau, interviewed there in September 1916.

All townships organized before December 31, 1894, were organized in Kittson County.

ALGOMA TOWNSHIP (T. 163N, R. 37W) bears a name of Indian derivation, "formed by Schoolcraft from *Algonquin* and *goma* meaning 'Algonquin waters.'" It designates a large district in Canada, bordering Lakes Huron and Superior. The township was organized April 8, 1902, was dissolved September 20, 1937, and became part of Lake Township in 1960.

AMERICA TOWNSHIP (T. 161N, R. 37W), organized July 13, 1903, and dissolved December 20, 1937, was named by its settlers, mostly born in the more eastern states and thence called Americans, in distinction from the foreign immigrants who settled many townships of this county. A post office, 1903–21, was first located on postmaster Harry E. Sanders's land in section 12 of America Township, and by 1913 on land next to his in section 7 of Clear River Township at Frank Stacy's general store.

BADGER a city on the east edge of Skagen, incorporated as a village in 1906 and as a city in 1968, took its name from Badger Creek, flowing northwestward, tributary to the Roseau River. Its post office was established in 1889.

BARNETT TOWNSHIP (T. 160N, R. 42W) was named in honor of Myron E. Barnett, one of its American homesteaders; it was organized November 2, 1901, changed briefly to Wittak, and changed back to Barnett.

BARTO TOWNSHIP (T. 161N, R. 43W), organized July 8, 1895, was named for a Bohemian settler there; among the first settlers was Nike Barto, first township chairman.

BEAVER TOWNSHIP (T. 160N, R. 38W), organized August 13, 1912, was named for its former colonies of beavers, living on the headstreams of the North Fork of Roseau River. That river was dammed in the early 1970s to create the artificial lake that is the centerpiece of Hayes Lake State Park, which was formally opened in 1973. They are named for A. F. Hayes, an early settler and an advocate of the creation of the lake.

BENWOOD a post office, 1904–25, in section 3 of Poplar Grove Township, was first settled in 1903. Andrew Lang owned the first general store on John Modahl's land, site of the first post office, with Anna Fitzgerald as postmaster.

BLOOMING VALLEY (T. 163N, R. 44W), organized April 3, 1908, is the most northwestern township of the county, named for its prairie and woodland flowers in the slight depression of the Roseau valley.

BOOBAR a post office, 1898–1901, in section 12, Stokes Township.

CASPERSON post office, 1903–17, first in section 18 and later in section 21 of Golden Valley Township, was named for brothers who took homestead claims near it.

CEDARBEND TOWNSHIP (T. 162N, R. 37W), organized July 22, 1902, has a bend of the West Branch of Warroad River, bordered by many trees of white cedar, also known as the American arbor vitae. A post office, 1899–1934, was begun in section 29 with Mary C. Stoltz as postmaster.

CLEAR RIVER TOWNSHIP (T. 161N, R. 36W) received this name in allusion to the clearness of the West Branch of Warroad River in its southwestern part, contrasted with the frequently dark color of streams in this region, stained by seepage from peaty ground. The township was organized July 13, 1903, and dissolved February 19, 1941; it was first called Sutton, then River, and then Clear River. A post office was in section 33, 1909–31, in a store on postmaster Serene B. York's farm.

CONRAD a post office in America Township, 1913–34, with Mary Anderson, wife of Conrad Anderson, postmaster; the post office was moved in 1919 to section 29, where Richard Goldner was postmaster until it was discontinued.

DAWD a post office in section 20 of Stafford Township, 1910–13.

DEER TOWNSHIP (T. 159N, R. 43W) was named for its many deer, being a favorite hunting ground. It was organized as Tordenskjold and was changed to Deer on December 17, 1900.

DEWEY TOWNSHIP (T. 160N, R. 44W) commemorates Adm. George Dewey, hero in the Spanish-American War, 1898, who was born in Montpelier, Vt., December 26, 1837, and died in Washington, D.C., January 16, 1917. He was graduated at the U.S. Naval Academy, 1858; served in the Civil War; was promoted to be a captain in 1884, commodore in 1896, and admiral in 1899. Soon after the outbreak of the war with Spain, he destroyed the Spanish fleet off Cavite in the Bay of Manila, May 1, 1898, and on August 13 his fleet aided the troops under Gen. Wesley Merritt in the capture of Manila. The township was organized as Two Rivers on March 4, 1899, and changed to Dewey in July 1899.

DIETER TOWNSHIP (T. 163N, R. 41W), organized July 15, 1890, was named in honor of a German settler, Martin Van Buren Dieter, who later removed to Montana.

DOCK a country post office, 1901–5, located 30 miles southwest of Roseau, with Ole K. Dock, postmaster; location not found.

DUXBY a post office in section 26 of Pohlitz, 1897–1938, with Charles Peterson, first postmaster, was named from two Norwegian words, *dux* meaning "ducks," and *by* meaning "*town*," for the many ducks on the river there.

EDDY post office, on the Roseau River in section 1 of Grimstad Township, 1897–1911, was named in honor of Frank Marion Eddy of Sauk Centre. He was born in Pleasant Grove, Minn., April 1, 1856; taught school a few years and was land examiner for the Northern Pacific Railroad company; was clerk of the district court of Pope County, 1884–94; representative in Congress, 1895–1903; and later was editor of the *Sauk Centre Herald*. Joseph E. Budd was postmaster, in his general store.

ELKWOOD TOWNSHIP (T. 159N, R. 37W), dissolved November 15, 1937, had elk formerly on its small prairie tracts, but most of its area is woodland.

ENSTROM TOWNSHIP (T. 162N, R. 38W), organized August 16, 1915, and first named Woodland, received its name in honor of Louis Enstrom, a homestead farmer and lawyer in Malung, who was a member of the board of county commissioners. He was born in Sweden in 1873 and settled here in 1889.

FALUN TOWNSHIP (T. 161N, R. 38W), organized January 10, 1907, bears the name of an important mining town in central Sweden, famous for its mines of copper, silver, and gold, whence it is sometimes called "the Treasury of Sweden." A post office, 1901–16, was first located in section 9 and then in section 16.

FOX a community in section 23 of Ross, was named for foxes, as the next village and creek westward are named for badgers. The site was platted in 1891 by Nels White, who became mayor, but the townsite was not incorporated. Its post office operated 1891–99 and 1903–37, first on Tellef S. Nomeland's farm and then in a store built in section 27; in 1909 it was moved one mile east.

GARLAND a post office, 1902–27, located in section 14, Neresen Township, first at Hans Christianson's homestead and then at Bernt Dallum's.

GOLDEN VALLEY TOWNSHIP (T. 159N, R. 39W), organized March 10, 1906, crossed by the South Fork of Roseau River, was thus auspiciously named by vote of its settlers.

GOOS a post office, 1899–1912, in Malung Township, with Dora Goos, postmaster, on the Claus Goos farm.

GORDON a post office, 1905–8, located 20 miles southwest of Roseau, with Olaf N. Gordon as postmaster; location not found.

GREENBUSH a city in section 10 of Hereim, was named for the first evergreen trees seen near the "ridge road," as one comes eastward from the Red River valley. These are spruce trees, about two miles northeast of the village. An early trail, later a wagon road, and latest the Great Northern Railway, here began a curving course along a gravel beach ridge of Glacial Lake Agassiz, following this beach for about 20 miles, or nearly to the site of Roseau. Early settlers were Polish, Bohemian, and Scandinavian immigrants; the city was called West Greenbush or New Greenbush for many years because the first site, now called Old Greenbush, was located on a ridge two miles northeast in section 10. The post office was established in 1892, first on the Hedges farm in section 36 of Barto Township, with Fedelia Hedges, post-

master; in 1899 it was moved to Olaf Hildahl's general store in section 31 of Skagen Township and in 1904 was moved again to the present townsite when Hildahl moved his store there.

GRIMSTAD TOWNSHIP (T. 160N, R. 40W) was named for John Grimstad, a Norwegian homesteader there, who removed to North Dakota.

HAUG a community in section 27, Soler Township; its post office, 1897–1931, was named for postmaster Theodore E. Haug, a homestead farmer from Norway, and was first located in section 35 on land owned by him; the post office was moved in 1905 to Lorentz and Regina Hegstad's store, where it remained until it was discontinued.

HERB a post office, 1901–15, located on postmaster Peter Johanson's (Johnson) land, in section 30, Deer Township.

HEREIM TOWNSHIP (T. 160N, R. 43W), organized May 31, 1900, was named for a Norwegian farmer, Ole Hereim.

HOMOLKA a post office in section 34 of Poplar Grove Township, was named for Anton Homolka, a Polish settler; it was established on January 19, 1901, with John Kovars, postmaster, and was discontinued on February 28, 1925.

HUSS TOWNSHIP (T. 159N, R. 42W), organized May 20, 1905, bears the name of the great Bohemian religious reformer and martyr John Huss (1369–1415). He followed John Wycliffe of England, "the Morning Star of the Reformation." A post office was located in section 7 of Huss Township on postmaster Lewis Christopherson's farm, 1903–17.

JADIS the township (T. 162–163N, R. 40W) in which Roseau is situated, organized July 15, 1890, was named in honor of Edward W. Jadis, agent for the Sprague Lumber Company of Winnipeg. He was born in England and received a liberal education there; came from eastern Canada to Minnesota before 1875 and was a lumberman on Mud and Pine Creeks, floating the logs down the Roseau and Red Rivers to Winnipeg; removed to Hallock, was auditor of Kittson County, 1887–92, and died November 1, 1892. A post office, 1888–95, was located a half mile north of Roseau in Horace W. Sutton's store; the site became part of Roseau.

JUNEBERRY a post office, 1905–23, in section 7 of Juneberry Township, is named for a small tree, variously called Juneberry, service berry, or shad bush, which is common or frequent throughout Minnesota. Juneberry Township (T. 162N, R. 44W) was named for the post office.

KLECTZEN post office, 1909–18, was located in section 19 of Neresen Township in postmaster Semon Klectzen's store; Klectzen was well known in the area as a peddler going from home to home selling his goods.

LAKE TOWNSHIP was organized May 3, 1960, and includes T. 163–164N, R. 36W (Warroad); T. 163–164N, R. 37W (Algoma); it is the largest township in the county and surrounds the city of Warroad.

LAONA TOWNSHIP (T. 162N, R. 35W), organized April 4, 1902, was at first called Roosevelt like its railway village, but was renamed because another Minnesota township, in Beltrami County, had earlier received that name.

LEO a community in Barto Township, section 19, was named in honor of Leo XIII (1810–1903), who was the pope 25 years, from 1878 until his death. Its first post office, begun in 1897, was located one mile east of the present townsite, with Peter Y. Johnson as postmaster until 1908; the post office was then moved to A. P. Kukowski's general store and was discontinued in 1915.

LIND the most southwestern township (T. 159N, R. 44W), organized January 3, 1900, is in honor of John Lind, the fourteenth governor of this state. He was born in Kanna, Sweden, March 25, 1854, and came to the United States in 1867 with his parents, who settled in Goodhue County, Minn. He attended the University of Minnesota in 1875; was admitted to the bar in New Ulm in 1877 and practiced there, excepting terms of absence in official duties, until 1901; represented his district in Congress, 1887–93; was governor of Minnesota, 1899–1901; removed to Minneapolis in 1901 and was again a member of Congress, 1903–5; president of the board of regents of the University of Minnesota, 1908–13; was envoy of Pres. Woodrow Wilson in Mexico, 1913–14.

LOLITA post office, 1894–1902, was located in section 9 of Moose Township, with Andrew O. Gordon, postmaster and township treasurer until 1900. Gordon was born in 1863 in Dodge County, came to section 9 in 1890, and died in 1917; he had one of the few threshing rigs in the county.

LONGWORTH a community, formerly a railway station, in Algoma, six miles north of Warroad, is named in honor of Nicholas Longworth of Cincinnati, Ohio, where he was born November 5, 1869. He was graduated at Harvard University, 1891, and in its law school, 1893; was married to Alice Lee Roosevelt, daughter of Pres. Theodore Roosevelt, in 1906; was a member of Congress, 1903–13 and 1916–31.

MacKENZIE a post office, 1903–5, with Andrew M. Pearson, postmaster, real estate agent, and justice of the peace in his general store; the site was first settled about 1892 on Bear Creek, ten miles southeast of Roseau Township; location not found.

MALUNG TOWNSHIP (T. 161N, R. 39W), organized January 17, 1894, and village have the name of a town in Dalecarlia, in west-central Sweden. The community in section 17 was first settled in 1889 by settlers from Dalecarlia; the oldest of these was Hed Lars Larsson, born in Ytter-Malung in 1841, where he later was a teacher; he suggested the name for the settlement. Its post office operated, 1895–1954.

MANDUS railway station, formerly called Lucan, was named for Mandus Erickson, a Swedish farmer and owner of the land on which it was located. The post office, 1911–13, in section 14 of Spruce Township, with postmaster Nils A. Erickson, was named for the railroad station. Mandus Erickson was born in Vilhelmina, Västerbotten, Sweden, and came to the United States in 1892.

MANDVILLE a post office, April-September 1905, with Oliver Mandville, postmaster; location not found.

MICKINOCK TOWNSHIP (T. 160N, R. 39W), organized May 28, 1900, commemorates a leader of the Ojibwe, whose home was near Ross post office, west of Roseau Lake. He was described as "one of the best Indians that ever lived, intelligent, sociable, and honest."

MOODY post office in Ross Township, 1896–1910, was named for Charles A. Moody, first Roseau County auditor and known as "the father of Warroad." The first postmaster was Albert O. Skagen on his section 7 farm. Moody was born in 1863 in Illinois, came to the county in 1893, served on many boards, was mayor of Warroad in 1910, and died in Minneapolis in 1922.

MOOSE TOWNSHIP (T. 162N, R. 42W), organized February 14, 1892, was named for its frequent moose. This is one of our few English words received, with slight change, from the Algonquian languages.

MORANVILLE TOWNSHIP (T. 162N, R. 36W), organized December 8, 1892, received its name in compliment for Patrick W. Moran, its first settler.

NERESEN TOWNSHIP (T. 160N, R. 41W), organized May 28, 1900, was named in honor of Knut Neresen, one of its Norwegian homesteaders.

NORACRES a post office in section 33 of Blooming Valley Township, 1923–38, with Axel T. Norland as postmaster.

NORLAND TOWNSHIP (T. 163–164N, R. 38W) was organized April 30, 1913; when first settled, it was called Vesterbotten, after Västerbotten, Sweden, from where most of the settlers had come, but as this proved too difficult for Americans to pronounce, it was changed to Norland, a generic term for the Norrland region of Sweden.

OAK POINT a post office, 1910–42, established in Kittson County and transferred to Roseau County in 1910 and located in the northwest corner of Blooming Valley Township; Emma Poirier was first postmaster.

OAKS TOWNSHIP (T. 161N, R. 35W), organized March 10, 1906, and dissolved January 8, 1937, was named for Charles Oaks, an American homesteader near the center of this township, who was a stage driver between Stephen and Roseau but removed to the Peace River valley in Alberta.

PALMVILLE TOWNSHIP (T. 159N, R. 40W), organized July 11, 1905, was named in compliment for Louis Palm, a Swedish homesteader there.

PELAN a post office, was located in Kittson County, 1888–1912, and in Dewey Township, 1913–38; the site was first settled in 1880, and the post office opened with Frederic W. ("Billy") Clay as postmaster, who disappeared with a mail sack in 1889; Hans T. Olson, farmer and blacksmith one mile north of first site, became postmaster. The village of Pelan was incorporated in 1903 and ceased in 1909; the post office moved across the river to Roseau County, with John and Clara Pedersen providing service, 1913–17.

PENCER a community in section 12 of Mickinock; its post office, also named Pencer, 1899–1981, was intended to honor John C. Spencer, a traveling salesman from St. Paul, but the proposed name was thus changed by the U.S. postal department. He took a homestead claim near Wannaska, about six miles distant to the southwest.

PENTUREN a post office, 1908–37, was established in section 19 of Elkwood Township, with Ben Penturen as postmaster for the first year; it moved to various locations in sections 29, 32, and 36.

PEQUIS a post office established in section 26 of Enstrom Township, with Gena Heicie, postmaster.

PINECREEK a community in section 3 of Dieter Township; it had a post office, 1896–1975; Gulbrand Haugen was the first postmaster.

POHLITZ TOWNSHIP (T. 163–164N, R. 42W), organized January 17, 1895, was named for the place in Germany where William Schmidt, first settler in the area, was born.

POLONIA TOWNSHIP (T. 161N, R. 44W), organized March 8, 1899, was settled mostly by immigrants from Poland.

POPLAR GROVE TOWNSHIP (T. 159N, R. 41W), organized July 21, 1904, was named by vote of its people, this being chosen from the ten or more names proposed.

REINE TOWNSHIP (T. 159N, R. 38W), organized January 8, 1918, was named for a pioneer family; they had two general stores, one in section 31, and one in section 13, which was moved to Elkwood Township in 1912.

RIVER a post office, 1907–46, in section 30 of Beaver Township; the first postmaster was Frank Trach in the store he built on his Riverside Farm land, located on a branch of the Roseau River; in 1911 the post office was moved to Axel Tornquist's store, where it remained until it was discontinued.

ROOSEVELT a city in section 36 of Laona, adjoining the east boundary of the county, its governing associated with Lake of the Woods County, was named in honor of Theodore Roosevelt, the eminent author and statesman. He was born in New York City, October 27, 1858; served as a colonel in the Spanish-American War, 1898; was governor of New York, 1899–1900; president of the United States, 1901–9; was later an editor of *The Outlook*; died at his home, Oyster Bay, N.Y., January 6, 1919. The post office was established in 1901, and the Canadian National Railroad built through the city in 1904.

ROSEAU the county seat, a city in sections 13 and 24 of Jadis, was named like this county for the

Roseau Lake and River. The city was platted in 1892 and incorporated in 1895, the same year the post office was established. The city became a port of entry to Canada in 1930 on the Richardson farm, made official in 1937, and became a commercial entry port in 1989.

ROSS a community in section 27 of Dieter Township, which had a post office established in 1890; it was first located a half mile west of the present site on Ole Johnson's farm and then moved to a farm east of the site.

ROSS TOWNSHIP (T. 162N, R. 41w) was organized on January 10, 1891, while part of Kittson County and reorganized January 1, 1895, after Roseau County was established. Its name is borne by a county in Ohio and by villages in Ohio, Indiana, Iowa, and other states.

SALOL a community in section 9 of Enstrom, was named by Louis P. Dahlquist, formerly a druggist clerk, who was county superintendent of schools and later the county treasurer. Salol is a white crystalline powder, used as a remedy for rheumatism and neuralgia. The community developed with the timber industry, and a post office was established in 1907; it became a near ghost town but revived as a residential area when Marvin Windows and Polaris Industries, both in Warroad, increased employment opportunities.

SANWICK a post office in section 3 of Dewey, 1899–1914, was named for Aven Sanwick, a Norwegian settler. Halver N. Johnson was postmaster, 1899–1908, and then Albert Teske until it discontinued in 1914.

SKAGEN TOWNSHIP (T. 161N, R. 42w), organized March 14, 1899, is in honor of Albert O. Skagen of Ross, who was chairman of the board of county commissioners. This is the name of a seaport and cape at the north extremity of Denmark.

SKIME a community in section 31 of Reine Township; the first store was built in 1910 by Alfred Skime and sold to Alfred Loken, who opened the post office there, 1910–60, and as a rural branch, 1960–64.

SOLER TOWNSHIP (T. 162N, R. 43w), organized January 7, 1896, is named for the district of Solör in Norway.

SPRUCE TOWNSHIP (T. 162N, R. 39w), organized April 8, 1893, had formerly much spruce timber. Our larger species, called black spruce, attaining a height of 70 feet and diameter of 1 to 2 feet, is much used for papermaking, but the white spruce, of somewhat more northern range, is a smaller tree, here growing to the height of about 20 feet, with a diameter of 6 to 8 inches. Both are common in northern Minnesota, extending westward to the Roseau River.

SPRUCE VALLEY TOWNSHIP (T. 163–164N, R. 39w) was organized January 6, 1920, and dissolved April 5, 1932; when organized, it had 36 people and a school.

STAFFORD TOWNSHIP (T. 161N, R. 40w), organized March 8, 1892, was named for William Stafford, a settler who came from Michigan.

STOKES TOWNSHIP (T. 161N, R. 41w), organized March 16, 1896, was named for George Stokes, who lived in Badger village, adjoining the west line of this township.

STRATHCONA a city in section 35 of Deer Township, commemorates Donald Alexander Smith, later Lord Strathcona, who was born in Forres, Scotland, August 6, 1820, and died in London, January 21, 1914. He came to Canada in 1838 in the service of the Hudson's Bay Company; was stationed during 13 years at trading posts on the Labrador coast and later in the Canadian Northwest; was promoted to be resident governor for that company; was one of the principal financial promoters for construction of the transcontinental Canadian Pacific Railway and was a friend of James J. Hill, under whose leadership the Great Northern Railway was built; was during many years a member of the Dominion House of Commons; after 1896 was High Commissioner for Canada in London and in 1897 was raised to the peerage as Baron Strathcona and Mount Royal; was a very generous donor from his great wealth to many institutions of education and charity.

The compound title of his peerage referred to Glencoe, his summer home in the county of Argyle, Scotland, and to Mount Royal in Montreal, his former home in Canada. "Glencoe, the glen or valley of Conan, has its equivalent in Strathcona" (*The Life of Lord Strathcona*, by Beckles Willson, 1915, vol. 2, p. 265).

Hans Lerum, postmaster, 1905–41, and his partner, Charlie Gunheim, built the first store in the city in 1904.

SWAMP a post office, April-July 1905, John Nelson, postmaster; location not found.

SWIFT a community of Moranville Township, had

a station of the Canadian National Railroad, first called Muirhead Siding for pioneer settler Harry Muirhead; when Muirhead and several others, including first postmaster Carl Carlquist, watched the train speed through the area, they remarked on how "swift" it traveled, thus arriving at the name. Carlquist opened the post office in 1905 in his general store; several sawmills were located nearby because of the extensive lumbering done in the area.

TORFIN a community in section 12 of Palmville; its post office, 1907–14, was named in honor of Iver Torfin, postmaster, a Norwegian pioneer and a farmer in that township. Torfin was born in 1863 in Iowa; came to the county in 1887; served as first clerk of court for Roseau County, 1895–1905; moved to Wannaska, where he was, among other positions, fire warden, 1911–18; and died in 1918. His wife, Petra, a former midwife, owned and operated the Torfin Hotel and Restaurant in Wannaska, 1915–25, and died in 1945.

WANNASKA a community in section 24 of Grimstad, on a camping ground of the chief Mickinock, is said to bear an early Ojibwe name of the Roseau River. Probably it referred rather to a deep place of the river, being derived from *woanashkobia*, defined by Frederic Baraga as "a reservoir or basin of water." Its post office began in 1896 at the home of postmaster John C. Spencer, the site also of the first school.

WARROAD a township (T. 163–164N, R. 36W) on the southwest side of the Lake of the Woods, and its city on the Warroad River near its mouth, incorporated November 9, 1901, are named from this river, which was in a neutral tract between the warring Ojibwe and Dakota. Jonathan Carver's map from his travel to the Minnesota River in 1766–67 explains this term as follows: "All Countries not Possessed by any one Nation, where War Parties are often passing, is called by them the Road of War." Warroad's first post office, begun in 1897, was located at Jacob N. Laughlan's trading post on the shore of Lake of the Woods; the depot of the Canadian National Railroad, built in

1900, is on the National Register of Historic Places. The city is a port of entry to Canada with customs and immigration offices; major industries are the Polaris Industries and Marvin Windows; the Marvin family, pioneers to the area, built the public library and a heritage center in 1991. See also LAKE TOWNSHIP.

WINNER a community of Elkwood Township, which had a post office, 1913–37; Georgine Moen was first postmaster.

Lakes and Streams

The name of the Lake of the Woods is fully considered in the first chapter, treating of our large rivers and lakes, and Roseau Lake and River are noticed at the beginning of this chapter.

Marvin Lake, near the international boundary, in Algoma (Lake), and Mud Lake, quite small, in sections 10 and 11, T. 160N, R. 37W, complete the meager list of lakes in this county, which lies within the area of Glacial Lake Agassiz, having therefore a smoothed surface with few hollows for lakes or sloughs.

Mud and Pine Creeks, flowing from the edge of Manitoba, join the Roseau River and Lake and were formerly routes of driving pine logs to Winnipeg.

In Laona is Willow Creek, tributary to the Lake of the Woods, and in Moranville the Warroad River is formed by union of its East and West Branches, having also between them a small affluent called Bulldog Run River.

Roseau River, formed by its North and South Forks, which unite in Malung, receives also Sucker Creek, Hay Creek, flowing into the North Fork, and Cow Creek, these being tributaries above Roseau Lake; and farther west it receives Badger Creek, which runs in a drainage ditch along most of its course.

On the southwest, the headstream of the South Branch of Two Rivers flows past Greenbush, and thence it crosses Kittson County to the Red River.

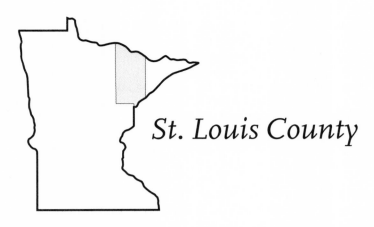

St. Louis County

This county, established by legislative acts of March 3, 1855, and March 1, 1856, is named from the St. Louis River, the largest entering Lake Superior, which flows through this county. The river was probably so named by Pierre Gaultier de Varennes, sieur de la Vérendrye (1685–1749), who was a very active explorer, in the years 1731 and onward, of the vast country from Pigeon River and Rainy Lake to the Saskatchewan and Missouri Rivers, establishing trading posts and missions. The king of France in 1749, shortly before the death of La Vérendrye, conferred on him the cross of St. Louis as a recognition of the importance of his discoveries, and thence the name of the St. Louis River appears to have come. On Jean Baptiste Louis Franquelin's map (1688) and Philippe Buache's map (1754), it is called the Riviére du Fond du Lac, and the map by Gilles Robert de Vaugondy (1755) and Jonathan Carver's map (1778) are the earliest to give the present name. St. Louis County has the distinction of being the largest county in this state, having an area of 6,611.75 square miles.

Saint Louis was born at Poissy, France, near Paris, April 25, 1215, and died near Tunis, Africa, August 25, 1270. From 1226 he was King Louis IX of France, his mother Blanche being regent during his minority. He undertook a crusade to the Holy Land in 1248, from which, after a terrible war, he returned to France in 1254. His second crusade was undertaken in 1267, for which he finally sailed from France on July 1, 1270, but in this expedition he died by an illness less than two months later. He is commemorated by the name of the city of St. Louis, but Louisiana was named for Louis XIV, who was king of France from 1643 to 1715.

Information about names has been gathered from History of the Upper Mississippi Valley *(1881), having pp. 681–99 for this county;* History of Duluth, and of St. Louis County, to the Year 1870 *by Hon. John R. Carey, in the MHS Collections 9: 241–78 (1901);* History of Duluth and St. Louis County, *edited by Dwight E. Woodbridge and John S. Pardee (1910, 2 vols.), pp. 1–412, 413–899; and from J. O. Walker, deputy county auditor, George H. Vivian, county treasurer, Edward K. Coe, county engineer of roads, J. W. Marvin, of the land department, Duluth, Missabe and Northern Railway, Hon.*

Josiah D. Ensign, district judge, Hon. William E. Culkin, Jerome E. Cooley, Leonidas Merritt, and John G. Williams, each of Duluth, the county seat, and James Bardon, of Superior, Wis., and J. D. Lamont, of the Cole-McDonald Exploration Company, Virginia, all being interviewed during visits in Duluth, Superior, and Virginia in August 1916.

ADMIRAL a station in sections 20 and 21, Clinton Township.

ADOLPH a village in section 30 of Herman, 12 miles west of Duluth, has a personal name derived from the old German language, meaning "noble wolf," that is, "noble hero." It had a station of the Duluth, Missabe and Iron Range Railroad. The post office began in 1899, with Per Adolph Bjorlin, first postmaster, giving it his middle name; Bjorlin, born in Sweden in 1872, was postmaster about 15 years in his store; he then moved to Duluth, opened a furniture store, and died in 1925.

AERIE LAKE a Duluth, Missabe and Iron Range Railroad station in Alborn Township.

AGNEW JUNCTION a station of the Duluth, Missabe and Iron Range Railroad; location not found. A post office was authorized for Agnew on May 7, 1898, with Henry T. Agnew to be postmaster, but did not become established.

AGNEW LOG a station of the Duluth, Missabe and Iron Range Railroad; location not found.

AGNEW MINE a station of the Great Northern Railway in section 11 of Stuntz Township (T. 57N, R. 21W) and its spur station located in section 2 of Balkan Township (T. 58N, R. 20W).

ALANGO TOWNSHIP (T. 61N, R. 19W) received its name, probably from Finland, by choice of its settlers.

ALBANY a station of the Duluth, Missabe and Iron Range Railroad and the Great Northern Railway for the Albany Mine, located in section 32, Balkan Township (T. 58N, R. 20W).

ALBORN TOWNSHIP (T. 52N, R.18W) was named by its settlers, the Norwegians being probably more numerous than those of any other nationality. The village had a post office, which began in 1900 in section 23 and was later moved to section 18. Its station of the Duluth, Missabe and Northern Railway in section 24 was at first named Albert for Albert S. Chase, brother of Kelsey D. Chase, who was president of the Duluth, Missabe and Northern Railway company in 1890–93.

ALDEN JUNCTION a place name in section 34, Normanna Township (T. 53N, R. 13W), on a 1911 county map.

ALDEN LAKE is the name of a village in Normana Township, sections 19 and 20, on the Cloquet River, beside a lake of the same name through which the river flows.

ALDEN TOWNSHIP T. 53–54N, R. 12W.

ALICE a Great Northern Railway station in Stuntz Township, now within Hibbing city limits, was named for a daughter of a proprietor of its site; al-

so a spur station of the Great Northern Railway for the Alice Mine in section 6 of Fayal Township.

ALLEN JUNCTION a village in T. 58N, R. 14W, section 15, was named for William Prescott Allen of Cloquet; the village was also known as Okwanim; it was established as a Duluth, Missabe and Northern Railway station and had a post office, 1899–1958, known as Allen, first located in section 3.

ALLEN TOWNSHIP (T. 61N, R. 14W) was named in honor of William Prescott Allen, lumberman, who was born in Thomaston, Maine, September 1, 1843, and died in Portland, Maine, in August 1908. He served in the First Iowa Cavalry and later in the 65th U.S. Infantry, attaining the rank of captain; settled in Minnesota at the close of the war; after 1881 resided at Cloquet and was general manager and vice-president of the C. N. Nelson Lumber Company; was a member of the state senate, 1891–95. The township became part of Unorganized Territory of Birch Lake.

ALPENA MINE a station of the Duluth, Missabe and Iron Range Railroad in section 5 of Missabe Mountain Township.

ALVIN/ALVINA see GHEEN.

ALWORTH MINE a Great Northern Railway station; location not found.

ANATOL a post office, 1921–43, in Grand Lake Township (T. 52N, R. 16W), section 10, with a station of the Duluth, Winnipeg and Pacific Railway.

ANDERSON a station of the Duluth, Winnipeg and Pacific Railway, circa 1937–38; location not found.

ANGORA TOWNSHIP (T. 61N, R. 18W) and the village in section 9 bear the name of a town in Turkey, celebrated for its long-haired goats, whose wool is largely exported. The village began as a station of the Duluth, Winnipeg and Pacific Railway; its post office was established in 1903.

ANNIE a post office, 1902–9, in section 20, Midway Township.

ARBUTUS in T. 67N, R. 21W, section 9, was the most northwestern station of the Duluth, Winnipeg and Pacific Railway in this county, named for the fragrant spring flower, *Epigaea repens*, often called trailing arbutus, commonly known in New England as the mayflower. This locality is near the western limit of its geographic range.

ARGO a Duluth, Missabe and Northern Railway station in T. 60N, R. 12W, sections 17 and 20.

ARGO TOWNSHIP (T. 59–61N, R. 12–13W), was divided in 1970; T. 59N, R. 13W, and T. 60N, R. 12–13W became part of the city of Babbitt, and T. 59N, R. 12W became part of the Unorganized Territory of Birch Lake.

ARLBERG a village in section 10 of Culver Township with a station of the Great Northern Railway.

ARMSTRONG LAKE a station of the Duluth and Iron Range Railroad; location not found, but a lake of this name is in Eagles Nest Township, sections 13, 14, and 23.

ARNOLD a village in sections 22 and 27, Rice Lake Township had a post office, 1898–1907.

ARONA a Great Northern Railway station in section 8 of Clinton Township.

ARROWHEAD TOWNSHIP formerly unnamed T. 50–51N, R. 19W.

ARTHUR is a station of the Duluth, Missabe and Iron Range Railroad about three miles east of French River, in sections 2 and 3, Duluth Township (T. 51N, R. 12W).

ASH LAKE is a village in section 9 of T. 66N, R. 20W and a station of the Duluth, Winnipeg and Pacific Railway, adjoining a small lake of this name, about eight miles north of Cusson and Pelican Lake. The village had a post office, March-August 1908.

ASHAWA see COOK.

ATHENS a Duluth, Missabe and Northern Railway station in section 32 of Kugler Township, was named for the capital city of Greece.

ATKINS MINE a station of the Great Northern Railway; location not found.

AULT TOWNSHIP (T. 55N, R. 12–13W) bears the name of a village on the coast of France near the mouth of Somme River, also of a village in Colorado.

AURORA founded in 1898 and incorporated on November 25, 1903, is a city in sections 9 and 10 of White Township (T. 58N, R. 15W). The post office was established in 1903 and had a Duluth and Iron Range Railroad station. This Latin name, meaning "the morning," is borne by cities in Illinois, Indiana, Missouri, and Nebraska, a township of this state in Steele County, and villages and townships in 13 other states.

BABBITT a city in Babbitt Township (T. 60N, R. 12W), section 18, was incorporated as a village on September 12, 1956; it was named for Judge Kurnal R. Babbitt of New York City; the post office began in 1920. See also ARGO TOWNSHIP.

BADEN a village in section 11 of Alborn Township, had a station of the Great Northern and Duluth, Missabe and Northern Railways.

BAILEY a station of the Duluth, Winnipeg and Pacific Railway in section 1, Ellsburg Township (T. 55N, R. 17W).

BAKER a post office, 1892–93; location not found.

BALKAN TOWNSHIP (T. 58–59N, R. 20W) was named for the Balkan Mountains of southeast Europe.

BALSAM a station of the LTV railroad; location not found.

BANGOR a place name of 1916 in section 6, White Township (T. 58N, R. 15W), associated with the Bangor Mine.

BARCLAY JUNCTION a station of the Great Northern Railway in section 28, Balkan Township (T. 58N, R. 20W).

BARTLETT is a village in section 11, Grand Lake Township (T. 51N, R. 16W), which began as a Duluth, Winnipeg and Pacific Railway station, three miles south of the Cloquet River.

BASSETT TOWNSHIP (T. 57–58N, R. 12–13W) was named for William Bassett, a cruiser, who selected tracts valuable for their pine timber. See also ARGO TOWNSHIP.

BATES a post office, 1904–7, in section 18 of Lavell Township (T. 55N, R. 19W).

BEACHMAN a station of the Duluth, Missabe and Iron Range Railroad; location not found.

BEAR RIVER a village in sections 7 and 18, Morcom Township, which had a post office, 1903–54.

BEATTY TOWNSHIP (T. 63–64N, R. 18W) honors five brothers, pioneers there in lumbering and farming.

BELGRADE a village in T. 58N, R. 16W, associated with the Belgrade Mine.

BELLVILLE a village site in T. 50N, R. 13W, sections 7 and 18, was approved to incorporate on May 19, 1857, but did not develop; named for a speculator named Bell.

BENGAL a village in T. 55N, R. 21W, section 6, had a post office, 1904–21, and a station of the Great Northern Railway.

BERGER SPUR a station of the Duluth, Winnipeg and Pacific Railway, noted on a 1965 county map as Berger in section 5, T. 66N, R. 20W.

BERWIND JUNCTION a station of the Northern Pacific Railroad in Duluth Township.

BIG LAKE a station of the Cypress Mining Railroad; location not found.

BILLINGS MINE SPUR a Great Northern Railway station in section 23 of Stuntz Township (T. 58N, R. 20W).

BINISBI a station of the Duluth, Missabe and Iron Range Railroad; location not found.

BIRCH a village in section 35 of Payne Township with a station of the Duluth, Missabe and Northern Railway was named in honor of Charles J. Birch of Proctor, trainmaster of this railway.

BIWABIK TOWNSHIP (T. 58N, R. 16W) and its city in sections 1–4, 9–11, on the Mesabi Iron Range, have an Ojibwe name, meaning "iron." The city was incorporated as a village on November 10, 1892, and reincorporated and separated from the township on April 8, 1909; its post office began in 1893.

BLISS a station of the Duluth, Winnipeg and Pacific Railway in section 36, T. 63N, R. 19W (unorganized township of Gheen).

BOEING MINE SPUR a station of the Great Northern Railway in section 6, Stuntz Township (T. 57N, R. 20W).

BOULDER a Duluth and Iron Range Railroad station in Babbitt Township (T. 60N, R. 13W).

BRACE JUNCTION a Great Northern Railway station; location not found.

BRADFORD a Duluth, Missabe and Iron Range Railroad station, was associated with the mine station of the Great Northern Railway, located in section 29, Stuntz township (T. 58N, R. 20W).

BREDA a village in section 29, Fairbanks Township (T. 56N, R. 12W), with a station of the Duluth, Missabe and Iron Range Railroad, four miles southeast of Fairbanks, was named for one of its Norwegian settlers; also known as Wissacode.

BREITUNG TOWNSHIP (T. 62N, R. 15W) was named in honor of Edward Breitung, of Negaunee, Mich., who opened the Minnesota Mine, the first worked on the Vermilion Iron Range. He was born in Schalkau, Germany, November 10, 1831; was educated at the College of Meiningen, Germany; was mayor of Negaunee, 1879–82; was a member of Congress in 1883–85. Breitung Township split in 1990, and the east half became Eagles Nest Township.

BREVATOR TOWNSHIP (T. 50N, R. 17W), had a village in section 18, with a station of the Great Northern Railway. It was first settled about 1903 by Ludwig Alzant; it had a post office, 1913–16; also known as Brevator Junction.

BREWER a Duluth, Missabe and Iron Range Railroad station in section 32 of Midway Township.

BRIMSON a village in section 4 of Ault Township (T. 55N, R. 12W), had a station of the Duluth, Missabe and Northern Railway, near its crossing of the Cloquet River, was named in honor of W. H. Brimson, who was superintendent of this railroad in 1888–89. Its post office began in 1897.

BRITT is a village in section 32, Sandy Township, with a station of the Duluth, Winnipeg and Pacific Railway, eight miles north of Virginia. Its post office was known as Brittmount 1919–50, at which time it changed to the present name, which was the railway station name.

BRITTMOUNT see BRITT.

BROOKLYN is a village in section 7 of Stuntz Township (T. 57N, R. 20W), with Duluth, Missabe and Iron Range Railroad stations in sections 7 and 18; it became part of Hibbing in 1910.

BROOKSTON is a city in sections 27 and 34 of Culver Township; it was platted about 1905 and incorporated as a village on April 13, 1907; the post office began in 1899. The city was destroyed by a forest fire in 1918 and rebuilt. It was formerly known as Stoney Brook Junction, the Duluth, Missabe and Iron Range Railroad station located in section 28.

BROWN a Duluth, Winnipeg and Pacific Railway station; location not found.

BROWNS a Duluth, Missabe and Iron Range Railroad station; location not found.

BRUCE MINE a Great Northern Railway station in section 27 of Balkan Township (T. 58N, R. 20W).

BRUNT MINE was a siding and spur station of the Great Northern Railway in section 10 of Nichols Township (T. 58N, R. 18W).

BUBOLITZ a place name in Field Township on a 1911 county map.

BUCHANAN a townsite platted in October 1856, "named after James Buchanan, then candidate for the presidency of the United States, . . . was located on the shore of Lake Superior southwestward from the mouth of Knife River. Like many other paper towns on the north shore, it never amounted to anything" (Carey, p. 272). The town was created as a location from which to explore for copper and was incorporated as a village on July 30, 1858. Its post office existed 1858–62, with William G. Cowell, postmaster and proprietor of the site, which he had surveyed in October 1856; it had the U.S. land office from 1857 until May 1859, when the office was removed to Portland, later a part of Duluth. The site was destroyed by fire.

BUHL a city in sections 20 and 21 of Great Scott Township (T. 58N, R. 19W), on the Mesabi Range, incorporated on February 25, 1901, was named in honor of Frank H. Buhl, of Sharon, Pa., president of the Sharon Ore Company, which corporation opened the first mines in this locality in the spring of 1900 (history of the county, 1910, p. 727). The post office began in 1900.

BUNKER a village in section 31 of Stuntz Township (T. 56N, R. 20W), with a Duluth, Missabe and Iron Range Railroad station noted as Darrow in 1916.

BURNETT a village in section 17 of Industrial Township, with a post office, 1896–1907, 1913, 1920, and since 1922. The Duluth, Missabe and Northern Railway station with the same name was named for a roadmaster of this railway.

BURNTSIDE/BURNTSIDE LAKE a village and resort community in section 36, Morse Township (T. 63N, R. 13W), had a post office, 1923–25, and a Duluth, Missabe and Iron Range Railroad station.

BURT MINE a Duluth, Missabe and Iron Range Railroad station in section 31, Stuntz Township (T. 58N, R. 20W).

BURTON a Duluth, Missabe and Iron Range Railroad station; location not found.

BUTLER BROTHERS two spur line stations of the Great Northern Railway; locations not found.

BUYCK TOWNSHIP formerly T. 65N, R. 17W, was named for one of its pioneers, Charles Buyck, who became treasurer of this township but later removed to Canada. It later became part of Portage Township. The village, at the intersection of sections 9, 10, 15, and 16, had a post office, 1913–63, which became a rural branch from Orr in 1963.

CAIN a Duluth, Missabe and Iron Range Railroad station; location not found.

CALYX a station with Itasca County of the Duluth, Missabe and Iron Range Railroad in section 5, T. 55N, R. 21W.

CAMERON a station of the Duluth, Winnipeg and Pacific Railway; location not found.

CANOSIA TOWNSHIP (T. 51N, R. 15W) was named for a lake crossed by its west line, now more commonly called Pike Lake. This widely used Algonquian word for the pike fish, spelled *kinoje* in Frederic Baraga's *A Dictionary of the Ojibway Language*, is the same with Kenoza, the name of a lake in Haverhill, Mass., theme of a short poem by John Greenleaf Whittier, who translated it "Lake of the pickerel." It is spelled Kenosha as a city and county of Wisconsin. A post office was located in section 31, 1889 and 1891–1919.

CANYON a village in section 34, Northland Township, which has had a post office since 1905.

CARDIFF a station of the Great Northern Railway in Nichols Township (T. 58N, R. 18W), section 16.

CAROLAN a place name in section 34, Duluth Township (T. 52N, R. 12W), shown on a 1911 county map.

CARSON LAKE is a village in section 25, Solway Township, with a post office, 1910–53. The Great Northern Railway and Duluth, Missabe and Iron Range Railroad station was called Carson.

CARSON LAKE mine spur station of the Duluth, Missabe and Iron Range Railroad in section 10 of Stuntz Township (T. 57N, R. 21W).

CASCADE JUNCTION a station of the Duluth and Northeastern; location not found.

CASCO a Great Northern Railway station in section 12 of Lavell Township (T. 55N, R. 19W).

CATLIN see POUPORE.

CEDAR VALLEY TOWNSHIP (T. 53–54N, R. 21W) is named for its abundant growth of the arbor vitae, more frequently called white cedar, bordering the Floodwood River.

CEDRIC a post office, 1912–15; location not found.

CELINA a village in T. 62N, R. 21W at the intersection of sections 7, 8, 17, and 18, which had two early post offices; the first, 1908–13, was transferred to Nass, Itasca County; the second operated 1914–35; Theodore Hall was postmaster for both.

CENTRAL LAKES was a station of the Duluth, Winnipeg and Pacific Railway, about six miles south of the St. Louis River, and a post office, 1914–23, in section 34 of T. 56N, R. 17W.

CHANDLER PIONEER MINE a station of the Duluth, Missabe and Iron Range Railroad in section 28, Morse Township (T. 63N, R. 12W).

CHATTACO MINE a Great Northern Railway station; location not found; the mine office was in Chisholm.

CHATWICK a place name of 1916 in section 20 of Clinton Township (T. 57N, R. 18W).

CHERRY TOWNSHIP T. 57N, R. 19W, had a village of the same name in section 24, which had a post office, 1914–18.

CHESTER was a Duluth, Missabe and Iron Range Railroad station and a mine spur station of the Great Northern Railway located in section 27, Stuntz Township (T. 58N, R. 20W).

CHISHOLM a city in Balkan Township (T. 58N, R. 20W), which was incorporated July 23, 1901, was burned September 5, 1908, but was soon rebuilt; the post office was established in 1901. Its great mine, first worked in 1889, and the village are named in honor of Archibald Mark Chisholm, a principal explorer of the Mesabi Range. He was born in Alexandria, Ontario, April 25, 1864; came to Minnesota and in 1888–94 was paymaster of the Chandler and Ely Mines on the Vermilion Range; removed in 1894 to Hibbing, where he was a bank cashier, dealing also in real estate and mining properties; was discover and partner of several very productive Mesabi mines, including this one bearing his name; had large interests of copper mining in Arizona and New Mexico; removed in 1900 to Duluth. A junction of the Duluth, Missabe and Iron Range Railroad was in section 28 of Balkan Township associated with the Chisholm Mine.

CHRYSLER see CRYSLER.

CLARK NO. 4 was a station of the Duluth, Missabe and Iron Range Railroad in section 28 of Stuntz Township (T. 58N, R. 20W).

CLEMENT a place name in section 20 of French Township in the 1916 plat book but not shown on a 1930 map.

CLIFTON in section 24 of Lakewood Township, was the first village site platted in this county, in 1858 by John S. Watrous, "on the north shore of Lake Superior about nine or ten miles from Duluth. The plat of the townsite showed two long parallel piers or breakwaters extending for hundreds of feet into the lake, indicating a commodious harbor; but it was all on paper; the name was the only existence that Clifton ever had" (Carey, p. 253). It had a post office, March-September 1879. A Duluth, Missabe and Iron Range Railroad station of this name was on the old village site.

CLINTON TOWNSHIP (T. 57N, R. 18W) was named in honor of Clinton Markell, who was one of the proprietors of Portland, removed from Superior to Duluth in 1869, was mayor of Duluth in 1871–72 and aided much in making this city a market for shipment of grain.

CLOQUET RIVER a station of the Duluth, Missabe and Iron Range Railroad, in section 15 of Fredenberg Township.

CLOVER VALLEY was a post office, 1914–15, in Duluth Township (T. 52N, R. 12W), and a Northern Pacific Railroad station, also known as Stanley.

CLUB HOUSE a Northern Pacific Railroad station; location not found.

CLYDE IRON WORKS a Duluth, Missabe and Iron Range Railroad station; location not found.

COLBY is a village in section 6 of Hoyt Lakes Township (T. 58N, R. 14W), which had a Duluth, Missabe and Iron Range Railroad station.

COLE a Duluth, Missabe and Iron Range Railroad station; location not found.

COLERAINE a village in section 25 of Alborn Township and a station of the Duluth, Missabe and Iron Range Railroad.

COLISEUM a Duluth, Missabe and Iron Range Railroad station; location not found.

COLLINGWOOD a Duluth, Missabe and Iron Range Railroad station; location not found.

COLUMBIA JUNCTION see CULVER.

COLUMBIA MINE SPUR a mine spur station of the Great Northern Railway in section 8, Missabe Mountain Township.

COLVIN TOWNSHIP (T. 56N, R. 15W) was named for Frank S. Colvin, a lumber dealer in Biwabik.

COMMODORE a Great Northern Railway station in section 8, Missabe Mountain.

COMO OIL a Duluth, Winnipeg and Pacific Railway station; location not found.

CONDON a Duluth, Missabe and Iron Range Railroad station; location not found.

CONGO a Great Northern Railway station and post office, 1912–14, in section 27 of Arrowhead Township (T. 51N, R. 19W).

COOK a city in section 18, Owens Township, platted in 1903, was named in honor of Wirth H. Cook, a lumber dealer of Duluth, chief promoter of the construction of Duluth, Winnipeg and Pacific Railway, who became its president. The city was incorporated as a village on May 13, 1926; it had a station of the Duluth, Missabe and Iron Range Railroad and the Duluth, Winnipeg and Pacific Railway. The post office was formerly at Ashawa, 1903–8, a Duluth, Rainy Lake and Winnipeg Railway station in section 19 of Field Township, moving to Cook in 1908.

COONS a Duluth, Missabe and Iron Range Railroad station in Solway Township.

CORBIN a post office, 1906–9, in T. 56N, R. 16W.

CORSICA a Duluth, Missabe and Iron Range Railroad station in section 18, Biwabik Township.

COSTIN a village in section 4 of Nichols Township (T. 58N, R. 18W), near the large village of Mountain Iron, was platted about 1912 by John Costin, Jr., of Virginia, who was born in Hancock, Mich., and came here in 1893.

COTTON TOWNSHIP (T. 54N, R. 16–17W) was named in honor of Joseph Bell Cotton, a lawyer of Duluth. He was born in Albion, Ind., January 6, 1865; was graduated at the Michigan Agricultural and Mechanical College, Lansing, 1886; was admitted to the bar and two years later settled in Duluth; was a representative in the legislature in 1893. The village in section 15 has had a post office since 1905.

CRANE LAKE a village in section 24 of T. 67N, R. 17W; its post office was established in 1922.

CRETE MINE a Hibbing company mine, which had a Great Northern Railway station; location not found.

CRONIN a Duluth, Missabe and Iron Range Railroad station; location not found.

CROSBY a post office, 1885–86; location not found.

CROXTON MINE a Buhl mine, which had a station of the Great Northern Railway in section 13, Stuntz Township (T. 58N, R. 20W).

CRUSHER JUNCTION a Duluth, Missabe and Iron Range Railroad station; location not found.

CRYSLER a Duluth, Winnipeg and Pacific Railway station in section 14 of Grand Lake Township (T. 52N, R. 16W).

CULVER TOWNSHIP (T. 51N, R. 18W) and its village in section 12 commemorate Joshua B. Culver, one of the founders of Duluth. He was born in Delaware County, N.Y., September 12, 1829; came to Minnesota in 1848 and engaged in the Indian

trade on the upper Mississippi until 1855, when he removed to Superior, Wis.; but two years later he settled at Duluth as a proprietor of its site. He was in that year appointed the first postmaster and was also the first clerk of the district court; was register of the U.S. land office in 1860 and till May 1861. Soon after the Civil War began, he removed to Michigan, helped to organize the Thirteenth Michigan Regiment, went with it as adjutant, and succeeded to its command as colonel. He served with this regiment through the war, being in its later part brigade commander. In 1868 he returned to Duluth and in 1869 was appointed the first county superintendent of schools; was elected the first mayor of Duluth, in 1870; and "continued as one of its most honored and leading citizens until his death on July 17th, 1883" (Carey, p. 257). The village has had a post office since 1894; the Duluth, Missabe and Iron Range Railroad station was first known as Columbia and Columbia Junction.

CUMBERLAND an authorization for a post office under this name was approved on November 9, 1905, with G. Mattson to be postmaster, but was not established; location not found.

CUSSON is a village in section 24 of Leiding Township (T. 65N, R. 20W) near Pelican Lake, which had a station of the Duluth, Winnipeg and Pacific Railway and was named by officers of this railway. It had a post office, 1909–29.

DALE MINE a Great Northern spur station of the Kelly Lake Mine in section 3, Stuntz Township (T. 57N, R. 21W).

DARROW see BUNKER.

DAVIS a station of the Duluth, Missabe and Iron Range Railroad in section 4 of Fayal Township; also spelled Daves.

DEACON MINE a Duluth, Missabe and Iron Range Railroad station in section 12 of Great Scott Township (T. 58N, R. 19W).

DEAN MINE a Great Northern Railway spur station of the Buhl Mine located in section 15 of Great Scott Township (T. 58N, R. 19W).

DEERFIELD a post office, 1913–16, in T. 66N, R. 21W.

DE FOREST a settlement with a station of the Duluth, Winnipeg and Pacific Railway in section 35 and 36 of Nichols Township (T. 58N, R. 18W).

DEWEY BEACH a place name in French Township, section 13, in 1916.

DEWEY LAKE a station of the Great Northern Railway in section 23 of French Township, circa 1930, bears the name of its adjacent lake, perhaps given in honor of Adm. George Dewey, who was previously noticed for Dewey Township in Roseau County. The station was called Powers on some maps.

DIBBELL a station of the Duluth, Missabe and Iron Range Railroad in section 3 of T. 55N, R. 18W.

DICK JUNCTION a Duluth, Missabe and Northern Railway station, circa 1937; no location found.

DIERCKS a Duluth, Winnipeg and Pacific Railway station, about 1937; no location found.

DINHAM LAKE a station of the Duluth, Winnipeg and Pacific Railway, in section 29, Ellsburg Township (T. 55N, R. 16W), is beside a lake of this name.

DIVIDE a Duluth, Missabe and Iron Range Railroad station in sections 24 and 25 of T. 60N, R. 13W.

DOLAN a station of the Duluth, Missabe and Iron Range Railroad; location not found.

DONNER MINE the Chisholm company had a Great Northern Railway station; location not found.

DORMER JUNCTION a Great Northern Railway station; location not found.

DRACO a Great Northern Railway station in section 22 of Brevator Township.

DULNOR a settlement in section 28, Fairbanks Township (T. 56N, R. 13W).

DULUTH the county seat, first settled in 1850–51, platted and named in 1856, was incorporated as a town May 19, 1857, as a city March 5, 1870, and received a new city charter March 2, 1887. "In 1868, Duluth, Portland, and Rice's Point, until then three separate organizations, were consolidated, and all assumed the name of Duluth." Later the city area was extended on the west to include Oneota and Fond du Lac and eastward to Endion, Lakeside, and Lakewood. The city has had a post office since 1857, and its union depot served several rail lines including the Duluth, Missabe and Iron Range Railroad, Great Northern Railway, and Minneapolis, St. Paul and Sault Ste. Marie Railroad (Soo Line).

The choice of the name of this city is narrated by Hon. John R. Carey, as follows: "In February, 1856, . . . Rev. Joseph G. Wilson, of Logansport, Ind., then sojourning at Superior as a home missionary, under the home mission board of the New School Presbyterian Church, was appealed to, to suggest a name for the future city. Mr. Wilson, who that winter lived with the writer and his family, informed me that he was promised two lots by the proprietors in the new town, in case he would suggest an appropriate name which they would accept. He asked for any old books in my possession, which might mention the name of some early missionary or noted explorer in the Lake Superior country, but I had then but a few books and not of the kind required. Mr. Wilson set about his task to earn the reward of the deed of the two lots in the great city. He visited the homes of citizens that he expected might be possessed of a library, and in his search found among some old books belonging to George E. Nettleton, an old English translation of the writings of the French Jesuits, relating to themselves and the early explorers and fur traders of the Northwest. In this he ran across the name of Du Luth, along with others of those early traders and missionaries who visited the head of the lake in the remote past. With other names, that of Du Luth was presented by Mr. Wilson to the proprietors at their meeting one evening in the home of George E. Nettleton, and after discussion of the relative merits of the several names submitted, the name Du Luth was selected" (MHS Collections 9: 254). On the first plat of Duluth, surveyed by Richard Relf and recorded May 26, 1856, the name appeared in its present form.

Daniel Greysolon, sieur Du Luth, was born at St. Germain Laval near Roanne, France, and died at his home in Montreal, February 25, 1710. His surname was otherwise variously spelled, as Du Lhut, Du Lhud, and Du Lud. It seems most suitable to adopt the spelling here first given, which, written as a single word, is borne in his honor by this great city, built on or near the site of his convocation of many Indian tribes in the early autumn of 1679.

With seven Frenchmen, Du Luth made the canoe journey to Lake Superior in 1678 for the purpose of exploring the country farther west, occupied by the Dakota and Assiniboine, among whom he spent the next two years, endeavoring to bring them into alliance with the French for fur trading. In the summer of the second year, 1680, Du Luth met Father Louis Hennepin and his two French companions and secured their liberation from captivity with the Dakota of Mille Lacs.

The sobriquet of Duluth, "the Zenith City of the Unsalted Seas," was originated by Dr. Thomas Foster (1818–1903), who established the first newspaper in Duluth in 1869. It was an expression in an enthusiastic speech by Foster at a celebration of July 4, 1868, by Duluth and Superior people in a park on Minnesota Point. It has been sometimes erroneously attributed to a very famous speech in Congress, January 27, 1871, by James Proctor Knott (1830–1911), who was a member from Kentucky, ridiculing Duluth in connection with the bill for a land grant to the St. Croix and Lake Superior Railroad company.

"Twin Ports" is a name frequently used for these adjoining great cities of Duluth and Superior, as the term "Twin Cities" is applied to Minneapolis and St. Paul.

DULUTH TOWNSHIP (T. 51–52N, R. 12W) adjoins the east boundary of the county, including the former sites of Buchanan and Clifton.

DUMBLANE a settlement, which had a Great Northern Railway station, located in section 22, Kelsey Township.

DUNKA JUNCTION/DUNKA RIVER railroad stations in sections 9 and 10 of T. 60N, R. 12W, on the Dunka River about one mile south of Birch Lake.

DUNNING a post office, was authorized under this name on December 7, 1904, with F. H. Gillmor to be postmaster, but not established; location not found.

DUNWOODY CONNECTION/JUNCTION a settlement, which had a Duluth, Missabe and Iron Range Railroad station in section 24 of Balkan Township (T. 58N, R. 20W), with a mine spur of the Great Northern Railway in section 3, Stuntz Township (T. 58N, R. 20W).

DUPONT SPUR a Great Northern Railway station; location not found.

EAGLES NEST TOWNSHIP was created in 1990 from the eastern half of Breitung Township and included all but the western tier of six sections of T. 62N, R. 14W. Eagles Nest, a settlement, had a Duluth, Missabe and Iron Range Railroad station in section 22.

EAST JUNCTION was the name of three Great Northern Railway stations located in section 18 of Clinton Township.

EAST MORRIS a Duluth, Missabe and Northern Railway station; location not found.

EAST VIRGINIA a station of the Duluth, Missabe and Northern Railway, about 1937, in Missabe Mountain Township.

ELBA a place name of 1916 in section 13, Missabe Mountain Township.

ELCOR a community in section 13, Missabe Mountain Township, with a post office, 1920–56, and a railroad station of the Duluth, Missabe and Iron Range Railroad spelled Elcore.

ELDES CORNER a settlement in section 20 of Midway Township.

ELIZABETH MINE a Great Northern Railway station in section 22 of Balkan Township (T. 58N, R. 20W).

ELLIS a Great Northern Railway station in section 18 of Nichols Township (T. 58N, R. 18W).

ELLSBURG see MELRUDE.

ELLSBURG TOWNSHIP (T. 55N, R. 16–17W) was named by its Swedish settlers for a place in Sweden.

ELLSMERE see MELRUDE.

ELMER a community in section 5 of Meadowlands Township, with a post office, 1906–73, which had a station of the Duluth, Missabe and Iron Range Railroad and Great Northern Railway.

ELMER TOWNSHIP T. 53N, R. 20W.

ELSDON was a railroad station of the Duluth, Winnipeg and Pacific Railway next north of Cusson; location not found.

ELWOOD a Duluth, Missabe and Iron Range Railroad station in Hermantown Township.

ELY a city on the Vermilion Range, in sections 27, 28, 33, and 34 of Morse Township, platted as a village in 1887, incorporated as a city March 3, 1891, was named in honor of Arthur Ely of Cleveland, Ohio, one of the financial promoters of the construction of the Duluth and Iron Range Railroad, which was opened to traffic here in July 1888. He also was prominent in the development of the iron mines at Tower.

Another citizen distinguished in the history of the county, for whom this city has been thought to be named, was Rev. Edmund Franklin Ely, who was born in Wilbraham, Mass., August 3, 1809, and died in Santa Rosa, Calif., August 29, 1882. He came to Minnesota in 1832 as a missionary to the Ojibwe, under appointment by the American

Board for Foreign Missions, and located at Sandy Lake. In 1834 his mission school was removed to Fond du Lac, where he labored until May 1839, then removing to Pokegama. In 1854 he came as a homesteader to the site of Superior, Wis., and in the next year he settled at Oneota, now a part of Duluth. He platted the Oneota town site, built a steam sawmill and docks, and was the postmaster six years but removed in 1862 to St. Paul.

The post office was established as Florence in 1887 and was changed to Ely in 1888; it had a Duluth, Missabe and Iron Range Railroad station.

EMBARRASS TOWNSHIP (T. 60N, R. 15W) and its railway station received this name from the Embarrass River, referring to the driftwood formerly on some parts of this stream, which was a difficulty and hindrance to canoes. The community in section 24 has had a post office since 1896; the Duluth, Missabe and Iron Range Railroad had stations at the mine of this name in section 5 of White Township (T. 58N, R. 15W).

EMCO a Duluth, Missabe and Iron Range Railroad station in section 17, Hoyt Lakes (Mesaba) Township (T. 59N, R. 14W).

EMMERT a Duluth, Missabe and Iron Range Railroad station in section 4 and a Great Northern Railway station in section 5 of Stuntz Township (T. 57N, R. 20W); the latter also had stops at the Emmert Siding and Yard.

ENDION the name of a village site platted in 1856 in section 23 of Duluth Township and incorporated on May 19, 1857, now a part of Duluth, is an Ojibwe word, meaning "my, your, or his home." The site was surveyed by proprietors Charles Martin, M. P. Niel, and others.

ERIE MINING COMPANY a station of the Cypress Railway; location not found.

EUCLID MINE a Great Northern Railway station in section 21 of Balkan Township (T. 58N, R. 20W).

EVELETH a city on the Mesabi Range, in section 32 of Missabe Mountain Township, founded in 1894 but mostly removed about one mile in 1900, and incorporated in 1913, was given this name for Erwin Eveleth, former postmaster and mayor of Corunna, Michigan, who died in 1922. The post office was established in 1895.

EXMOOR a Great Northern Railway station in section 22 of Balkan Township (T. 58N, R. 20W).

FABER see TABER.

FAIRBANKS TOWNSHIP (T. 56N, R. 12–13W) and its community in section 1 (T. 56N, R. 12W), formerly called Bassett Lake, eight miles south of the St. Louis River, were named in honor of Charles Warren Fairbanks of Indiana. He was born in Union County, Ohio, May 11, 1852; was graduated at the Ohio Wesleyan University, 1872; was admitted to practice law, 1874, and settled in Indianapolis; was U.S. senator, 1897–1905; and vice-president of the United States, 1905–9; died at his home in Indianapolis, June 4, 1918. The community had a post office, 1905–53, with a Duluth, Missabe and Iron Range Railroad station, also known as Bassett.

FAIRLANE a Duluth, Missabe and Iron Range Railroad station; location not found.

FAIRLANE TACONITE a Duluth, Winnipeg and Pacific Railway station; location not found.

FALLS OF ST. LOUIS was a post office, 1856–59; location not found.

FAY MINE a Great Northern Railway spur station for the Virginia-based company, located in section 6, Missabe Mountain Township.

FAYAL TOWNSHIP (T. 57N, R. 17W) and the great Fayal Mine were named for the most western island in the central group of the Azores, which has an excellent harbor. A Duluth, Missabe and Iron Range Railroad station called Fayal was in section 6.

FENS a Duluth, Missabe and Iron Range Railroad station in McDavitt Township (T. 55N, R. 18W), section 10.

FERMOY was a station and junction of the Great Northern Railway, four miles north of Kelsey, in section 28, McDavitt Township (T. 55N, R. 18W).

FERMOY Unorganized Territory of, T. 55N, R. 18W.

FERN TOWNSHIP (T. 60N, R. 20W) received its name by vote of its people, who represent several nationalities; it became part of Unorganized Territory of Sand Lake.

FERNDALE a Great Northern Railway station; location not found.

FIELD TOWNSHIP (T. 62N, R. 19W) was named for a newspaper editor, one of the organizers of the township, who later removed to Canada.

FINE LAKES TOWNSHIP (T. 50N, R. 20W) was named by its Scandinavian people for its numerous little lakes.

FLANDERS a Great Northern Railway station in section 23, Balkan Township (T. 58N, R. 20W).

FLINT CREEK a Duluth, Winnipeg and Pacific Railway station; location not found.

FLINT GRAVEL PIT a Great Northern Railway station; location not found.

FLOODWOOD TOWNSHIP (T. 51N, R. 20W) and the city in sections 5–8, at the mouth of Floodwood River, received their name from the stream, which formerly was obstructed by natural rafts of driftwood. It was called Embarras River by Joseph N. Nicollet's map in 1843, which designated the present river of that name as Second Embarras River. Both these streams, like the Zumbro River in southeastern Minnesota, derived their old French name, Embarras, from their driftwood hindering canoe travel. The city was incorporated as a village on May 10, 1899; the post office began in 1890; it had a Great Northern Railway station.

FLORENCE SEE ELY.

FLORENTON a village in section 10, Wuori Township, with a post office, 1908–65.

FOND DU LAC bearing a French name that signifies "Farther end of the lake," or, as we should commonly say, "Head of the lake," was a trading post of the North West Company in 1792, being then on the south or Wisconsin shore of the St. Louis River where it comes to the still water level of Lake Superior, 12 miles distant in a straight line from the Minnesota Point. Later the post of this name occupied by the American Fur Company was on the opposite or Minnesota side of the river on a part of the village site that was platted in 1856. The site is now a suburban area of Duluth, which had a post office, 1857–1938, and Northern Pacific and Chicago, Milwaukee and St. Paul railroad stations.

FORBES is a village of McDavitt Township (T. 56N, R. 18W), section 3, with a post office since 1905; a Duluth, Missabe and Iron Range Railroad station of this name was in section 34 of Clinton Township.

FORSMAN a village and a former Duluth, Winnipeg and Pacific Railway station, in T. 60N, R. 18W, between Virginia and Vermilion Lake, named for a Finnish-Swedish settler named Victor Forsman, who lived in the area around 1920; also nearby is Forsman Creek, a small stream that runs into the Rice River.

FOUR CORNERS a settlement in section 32 of Canosia Township.

FRANKLIN a city in sections 4, 5, 8, and 9 of Missabe Mountain, was incorporated as a village on March 10, 1915; it had a Duluth, Missabe and Iron Range Railroad station.

FRANTZ MINE a Great Northern Railway spur station for the Buhl company in section 21 of Great Scott Township (T. 58N, R. 19W).

FRASER a village in section 23, Balkan Township (T. 58N, R. 20W), was incorporated as a village on October 6, 1913, but later unincorporated; it had a station of the Duluth, Missabe and Iron Range Railroad and Great Northern Railway.

FREDENBERG TOWNSHIP (T. 52N, R.15W) was named in honor of Jacob Fredenberg, one of its German pioneer settlers. A community by this name in the township had a post office, 1908–9.

FREDERICK a station of the Duluth, Missabe and Iron Range Railroad in section 18 of Stuntz Township (T. 56N, R. 20W).

FRENCH LICK a place name in section 18, Duluth Township, on a map of 1916 but not found in 1930; it may be the same as French River.

FRENCH RIVER is a community located on the shore of Lake Superior, in sections 17 and 18 of Duluth Township, with a station of the Duluth and Iron Range Railroad, at its crossing of this river. A post office of this name was established and discontinued in Superior County, Wis., 1856–58, before Minnesota's statehood.

FRENCH TOWNSHIP (T. 59–60N, R. 21W) was named for William A. French, an early homesteader, who became an officer of this township. A Duluth, Winnipeg and Pacific Railway station named French was located in the township. See also UNORGANIZED TERRITORY OF MCCORMACK LAKE.

FULTON a Duluth, Missabe and Iron Range Railroad station; location not found.

GAKADINA a Duluth, Missabe and Iron Range Railroad station; location not found.

GALLAGHER JUNCTION a place name in section 27, Normanna Township (T. 53N, R. 13W), circa 1911.

GAPPAS a site in T. 69N, R. 21W, section 27.

GARY a village in section 3 of T. 48N, R. 15W, which had a Duluth, Missabe and Iron Range Railroad station.

GENOA a place in T. 58N, R. 17W, sections 33 and 34.

GHEEN is a village in section 5 of Leiding Township (T. 63N, R. 19W). About 1890, mixed-blood Ojibwe brothers William and Stephen Gheen homesteaded a tract east of Gheen at Elbow Lake, developing a government farm and trading post, where Stephen was Indian agent for ten years. It had a post office, 1906–16, with William as postmaster, for whom the community was named. The post office name was changed to Alvina 1916–18, and changed back to Gheen in 1919; it had a Duluth, Winnipeg and Pacific Railway station.

GHEEN CORNER a village south of Gheen in section 7 of T. 63N, R. 19W and sections 1 and 12 of T. 63N, R. 20W.

GILBERT a city in section 23, Missabe Mountain Township, platted in August 1907 and incorporated as a village on April 10, 1908, may have been named in honor of E. A. Gilbert, a prominent businessman of Duluth, or may have been named for Giles Gilbert (died May 4, 1908), who owned mining and timber land at the townsites of Calumet and Marble. The post office began in 1907; it had a Duluth, Missabe and Iron Range Railroad station.

GLEN MINE a Duluth, Missabe and Iron Range Railroad spur station in section 29, Balkan Township (T. 58N, R. 20W).

GLENDALE is a village in section 13, Leiding Township (T. 64N, R. 20W) and section 18 of Leiding (T. 64N, R. 19W), with a former Duluth, Winnipeg and Pacific Railway station.

GNESEN TOWNSHIP (T. 52–53N, R. 14W) was named by Polish settlers for a city in the province of Posen, Prussia, reputed to be the oldest of Polish cities, where until 1320 the kings of Poland were crowned and which was returned to Poland in 1919 and the spelling changed to Gniezno.

GNESER a post office, was authorized under this name on January 17, 1905, with George Trader to be postmaster, but not established; location not found.

GODFREY a Duluth, Missabe and Iron Range Railroad station in section 33, Balkan Township (T. 58N, R. 20W).

GOWAN a community in section 34, Floodwood Township, with a post office, 1905–71; the Great Northern Railway station in section 27 was named Mirbat.

GRACE MINE a Great Northern Railway station for the Emmert-based company in section 33 of Balkan Township (T. 58N, R. 20W).

GRAFF a Duluth, Missabe and Iron Range Railroad station in section 25, Stuntz Township (T. 56N, R. 21W).

GRAND LAKE a village in section 26 of Industrial Township, had a station of the Duluth, Missabe and Iron Range Railroad. It had a post office named Stonehouse, 1904–6, which moved to Saginaw in 1910.

GRAND LAKE TOWNSHIP (T. 51–52N, R. 16W) received its name from a lake, which is large or grand in comparison with smaller neighboring lakes.

GRANITE a Duluth and Iron Range Railroad station in section 19 of T. 60N, R. 12W.

GRANT a village at the former Grant Mine site in section 20 of Great Scott Township (T. 58N, R. 19W).

GRATWICK a station of the Duluth, Missabe and Iron Range Railroad and Great Northern Railway in section 20, Clinton Township.

GREANEY a village at the intersection of sections 3, 4, 9, and 10 of T. 63N, R. 21W, ten miles west of Gheen, was named for Patrick Greaney, a merchant there and first postmaster; the post office operated, 1909–54.

GREAT SCOTT TOWNSHIP (T. 58–59N, R. 19W) was named by the board of county commissioners, this being a common expletive of one of the board members.

GREENWOOD TOWNSHIP T. 62–63N, R. 16W.

GUNDERSON a Duluth, Winnipeg and Pacific Railway station; location not found.

GUTHRIE a Duluth, Winnipeg and Pacific Railway station; location not found.

HALDEN TOWNSHIP (T. 51N, R. 21W) is named in honor of Odin Halden of Duluth. He was born in Norway, May 6, 1862; came to the United States in 1881 and settled at Duluth in 1882; was a grocer, 1883–90; was deputy auditor of this county, 1890–94, and then the county auditor.

HALEY a village in section 23 of Leiding Township (T. 63N, R. 19W), with a former Duluth, Winnipeg and Pacific Railway station.

HAMNAH a post office, was authorized under this name on March 23, 1903, with John T. Joyce to be postmaster, but not established; location not found.

HANNA a station of the Great Northern Railway; site not found.

HARDING a post office, 1896–1902, on Crane Lake in section 23 of T. 67N, R. 17W.

HAROLD MINE a South Hibbing company, which had a Great Northern Railway station in section 11, Stuntz Township (T. 57N, R. 21W).

HARRELL a post office, 1908–18, in section 28 of Prairie Lake Township, with James Harrell, first postmaster.

HARRIGAN a Duluth, Winnipeg and Pacific Railway station; location not found.

HARRIS LAKE/HARRIS JUNCTION was a station of the Duluth and Northeastern Railroad in section 27 of T. 55N, R. 14W, about eight miles southwest of Fairbanks, adjoining a small lake of this name.

HARRY a place name near Angora, circa 1937.

HARTLEY a village that began as a spur station of the Great Northern Railway in section 23 of Balkan Township (T. 58N, R. 20W); it was related to the Hartley Mine, which also had a station in the same section.

HAY LAKE Unorganized Territory of, T. 59N, R. 16W.

HECTOR a Duluth, Missabe and Iron Range Railroad station in section 1, Biwabik Township.

HEIKKILA LAKE Unorganized Territory of, T. 56–57N, R. 16W, T. 56N, R. 17W.

HELMER a Duluth, Missabe and Iron Range Railroad station, junction, and mine spur in section 14 of Great Scott Township (T. 58N, R. 19W).

HEMLOCK a post office, 1911–12, in section 9 of Alborn Township, which on later maps (1930) was shown as Turney.

HERMAN TOWNSHIP (T. 50N, R. 15W) was named by German settlers in honor of the early German hero, who was born in the year 17 B.C. and died in A.D. 21, renowned for his defeating the Roman troops in Germany. The township was absorbed by the city of Hermantown.

HERMANTOWN a city in sections 9, 10, 15, and 16 of Herman Township, was incorporated as a city on December 13, 1975.

HIBBING a large mining city of the Mesabi Range in Stuntz Township, was named in honor of Frank Hibbing, its founder. He was born in Germany in 1857; came to the United States with his parents when a boy; engaged in lumbering in Duluth and also acquired large interests in the Mesabi iron mines; discovered the Hibbing ore beds in the autumn of 1892; died in Duluth, July 30, 1897. The post office began in 1893; the city had stations of the Duluth, Missabe and Iron Range Railroad and Great Northern Railway.

HIBBING HEIGHTS was a village platted in 1908, which became part of Alice in 1910 and then was annexed by Hibbing.

HIGGINS a place name in section 4 of T. 58N, R. 18W, about 1965.

HILL SPUR a Duluth, Winnipeg and Pacific Railway station; location not found.

HINSDALE is a village in section 17 of Mesaba Township, with a post office of this name, 1887–88, and a Duluth, Missabe and Iron Range Railroad station located in section 8.

HOBSON a settlement in section 34 of French Township, about 1921–37, on the lake of the same name.

HOLTER a post office, 1908–11, located in section 11 of Mesaba Township, and a Duluth, Missabe and Iron Range Railroad station.

HOODOO POINT a village in Morse Township (T. 63N, R. 12W), in sections 19, 20, 30, and 31, on the peninsula of the same name; it had a station of the Duluth, Missabe and Iron Range Railroad.

HOPPER a village in Nichols Township (T. 58N, R. 13W), section 13, with a post office, 1914–18 and 1920–53, which transferred to the community of West Virginia.

HORNBY a station of the Duluth, Missabe and Iron Range Railroad in sections 7 and 18 of Fairbanks Township (T. 56N, R. 12W), two miles south of Fairbanks, named for Henry Cook Hornby.

HORNBY JUNCTION a station of the Duluth and Northeastern Railroad in section 7 of Ault Township (T. 55N, R. 13W), is named for Henry Cook Hornby of Cloquet. He was born in Gilbert, Iowa, April 29, 1866; came to Minnesota in 1884 and from 1888 was in the employment of the Cloquet Lumber Company, being assistant manager, 1897–1904, and afterward manager and president.

HOWARDS a Duluth, Missabe and Iron Range Railroad station; location not found.

HOYT LAKES a city in Hoyt Lakes Township (T. 58N, R. 14W), was incorporated as a village on November 17, 1955; the community was developed by Pickands Mather and Company and named in 1952 for Elton Hoyt II, head of the firm; the post office established in 1955.

HOYT LAKES TOWNSHIP T. 58–59N, R. 14W, includes former Mesaba Township.

HUGHES a post office, 1910–17, in T. 63N, R. 21W, with Clarence A. Hughes, postmaster.

HULL JUNCTION a village in section 31 of Lavell Township (T. 55N, R. 20W), formerly a station of the Duluth, Missabe and Iron Range Railroad.

HULL RUST MINE had a Great Northern Railway station in section 1, a station for the Duluth, Missabe and Iron Range Railroad and Great Northern Railway in section 2 of Stuntz (T. 57N, R. 21W), and a yard station of the Duluth, Missabe and Northern Railway in section 12 of T. 57N, R. 14W.

HUNTERS PARK is an area of Duluth.

HURLEY a place name in section 20 of Duluth Township (T. 52N, R. 12W), circa 1911.

HUTTER a Duluth, Missabe and Iron Range Railroad station in the west part of Biwabik Township (T. 58N, R. 16W), was named for H. A. Hutter of Duluth, an ore dock agent.

IDINGTON is a village in section 28 of Angora Township, which had a Duluth, Winnipeg and Pacific Railway station in section 27.

INDEPENDENCE is a village in section 26 of New Independence Township, which had a post office, 1890–1916.

INDUSTRIAL TOWNSHIP (T. 51N, R. 17W) received this name by choice of its settlers. It is also the name of a village in West Virginia.

IRON a city in sections 14, 15, and 22 of Clinton Township, was incorporated as a village in 1893; the post office was called Iron Junction, 1893–95, and then shortened to Iron; it had a Duluth, Missabe and Iron Range Railroad station.

IRON JUNCTION see IRON.

IRONTON is a western district of the city of Duluth, located in Midway Township. It had a manufacturing plant of the United States Steel Corporation.

IROQUOIS a station of the Duluth, Missabe and Iron Range Railroad and Great Northern Railway for the Iroquois Mine, located in section 10, Mountain Iron Township (T. 58N, R. 18W).

ISLAND is a settlement in section 16 of T. 52N, R. 21W, which had a post office, 1908–13, and a Great Northern Railway station; it was named for its having a tract of dry farming land surrounded by a very extensive swamp region.

ISLAND LAKE JUNCTION a Duluth and Northeastern Railroad station in section 32 of Gnesen Township (T. 53N, R. 14W).

JENNINGS MINE a Great Northern Railway station in section 14 of Great Scott Township (T. 58N, R. 19W).

JERICHO a place name in T. 60N, R. 13W, about 1930–37.

JONES is a railway station of the Duluth, Missabe and Iron Range Railroad in sections 19 and 20 of Biwabik Township, named in honor of John T. Jones, one of the discoverers of the iron mines of Biwabik and Virginia; also known as Jones Junction.

JUDSON MINE a Great Northern Railway station in section 20 of Great Scott Township (T. 58N, R. 19W), maintained by the Buhl company.

KABETOGAMA a settlement in Kabetogama Lake Township, with a post office, 1931–59.

KABETOGAMA LAKE TOWNSHIP (T. 69N, R. 21W).

KALMAN a Duluth, Missabe and Iron Range Railroad station; location not found.

KEENAN is a village in section 34 of Clinton Township, with a Duluth, Missabe and Iron Range Railroad station, named for C. J. Keenan, a station agent.

KELLY was a Duluth, Winnipeg and Pacific Railway station in section 31 of T. 64N, R. 19W.

KELLY LAKE a village in sections 15 and 21 of Stuntz (Hibbing) Township (T. 57N, R. 21W), is beside a little lake so named. The village has had a post office since 1907.

KELSEY TOWNSHIP (T. 54N, R. 18W) and its village in section 22 were named in honor of Kelsey D. Chase of Faribault. He was born in Little Valley, N.Y., December 1, 1841; came to Minnesota in 1860; served in the Second Minnesota Regiment during the Civil War; engaged in mercantile business, real estate, and railway and mining development, residing successively in Rochester, Owatonna, Duluth, Crookston, and Faribault; was president of the Duluth, Missabe and Northern Railway Co., 1890–93; president of the Chase State Bank in Faribault. The village was located near an early Indian village; the post office began in 1897; it had a Duluth, Missabe and Iron Range Railroad station in section 15.

KENNY MINE a Great Northern Railway station in section 14, Great Scott Township (T. 58N, R. 19W).

KERR a village in section 3 of Stuntz Township (T. 57N, R. 21W), with a former Duluth, Missabe and Iron Range Railroad station.

KETTLE FALLS a settlement with a post office, 1912–13; location not found.

KEVIN PATRICK MINE a Great Northern Railway station; location not found.

KINMOUNT a post office, 1909–12, in section 24 of т. 67 n, r. 21w, had a station of the Duluth, Winnipeg and Pacific Railway, five miles northwest of Ash Lake.

KINNEY a city in section 15, Great Scott Township (т. 58 n, r. 19w), incorporated as a village on November 11, 1910, was named in honor of O. D. Kinney, a discoverer of the iron mines of Virginia and a founder of that city. The post office began in 1907.

KINROSS a station of the Great Northern Railway in section 17, Nichols Township (т. 58 n, r. 18w).

KIRK a village in section 18, Clinton Township, formerly a Duluth, Missabe and Iron Range Railroad station.

KITZVILLE a settlement in section 5 of Stuntz Township (т. 57 n, r. 20w), with a post office, 1913–16.

KNOX DEPOT an LTV railroad station; location not found.

KUGLER TOWNSHIP (т. 61 n, r. 15w) was named in honor of Fred Kugler, a former member of the board of county commissioners.

LAKE / LAKE JUNCTION a Duluth, Missabe and Iron Range Railroad and Duluth, Winnipeg and Pacific Railway station in section 32 of Sandy Township.

LAKENAN LOGGING SPUR a Duluth, Missabe and Iron Range Railroad station; location not found.

LAKESIDE is an area of Duluth, with a Duluth, Missabe and Iron Range Railroad station; an act to incorporate as a city was approved on April 2, 1891, and provided for future annexation to the city of Duluth; the post office was called Lakeview 1889–1902, a name also applied to the railroad station for that period.

LAKEVIEW see LAKESIDE.

LAKEWOOD a village in sections 26 and 34 of Lakewood Township, had a post office, 1901–35, and a Duluth, Missabe and Iron Range Railroad station in section 35.

LAMBERTON MINE SPUR a Great Northern Railway station in section 9, Stuntz Township (т. 57 n, r. 21w).

LANSWORTH a Duluth, Winnipeg and Pacific Railway station, circa 1937; location not found.

LARGO a settlement and a former Duluth, Missabe and Iron Range Railroad station called Largo Junction, located in т. 58 n, r. 18w, one mile west of Eveleth.

LAURA MINE a Great Northern Railway station in section 31, Balkan Township (т. 58 n, r. 20w), maintained by the South Hibbing company.

LAVELL TOWNSHIP (т. 55–56 n, r. 19w, т. 55 n, r. 20w) is named in honor of a French homesteader, who developed a good farm.

LAVINIA a townsite in section 25 of Stuntz Township (т. 58 n, r. 21w), platted in 1909 by Day Development Company.

LAWRENCE LAKE a Duluth, Missabe and Iron Range Railroad station; location not found.

LEANDER a village in sections 32 and 33 of Owens Township, developed as an agricultural district following the arrival of two Swedish settlers in 1894; in 1902 a station for the Duluth, Missabe and Iron Range Railroad and Duluth, Winnipeg and Pacific Railway was built and named for Peter Leander, on whose farm it was located.

LEETONIA a village in Stuntz Township (т. 57 n, r. 21w), was associated with the mine of the same name; its Great Northern Railway spur station was in section 10.

LEFFINGWELL a post office, 1902–4, with Charles E. Leffingwell as postmaster; location not found.

LEIDING TOWNSHIP (т. 63–65 n, r. 19w, т. 64–65 n, r. 20w) was named for one of its families of Scandinavian settlers. A post office was probably located in the township, January-June 1908.

LEIGHTON a Great Northern Railway station in section 9 of Stuntz Township (т. 56 n, r. 21w).

LENONT a Duluth, Missabe and Northern Railway station, circa 1937, in Balkan township (т. 58 n, r. 20w).

LEONARD MINE SPUR a Great Northern Railway station in section 28, Balkan Township (т. 58 n, r. 20w).

LEONETH a post office, 1922–60, in section 1 of Clinton Township.

LEONIDA a city in section 36, Mountain Iron Township (т. 58 n, r. 18w), and section 1 of Clinton Township, was incorporated in 1917 as a village; it had a Duluth, Missabe and Iron Range Railroad station.

LEOPOLD a Great Northern Railway station; location not found.

LESTER PARK a section of Duluth, located on the shore of Lake Superior near the Lester River; it had a station so named on the Duluth and Iron Range Railroad at its crossing of the river.

LEWIS a Duluth, Rainy River and Winnipeg Railway station in T. 65N, R. 20W.

LINCOLN MINE SPUR a Duluth, Missabe and Iron Range Railroad station in section 4, Missabe Mountain Township.

LIND see STURGEON RIVER.

LINDEN see MEADOWBROOK.

LINDEN GROVE TOWNSHIP (T. 62N, R. 20W) is named for its timber of basswood, our American linden tree. The village of the same name is located at the corner of sections 10, 11, 14, and 15.

LITTLE SWAN a community in Stuntz Township (T. 56N, R. 20W), sections 26 and 35, with a post office, 1914–32, later became part of the city of Hibbing.

LONDON a section of Duluth, also known as New London.

LONGTIN a post office, June-July 1915, with Wilfred Longtin as postmaster; location not found.

LONGYEAR MINE and **SPUR** a Great Northern Railway and Duluth, Missabe and Iron Range Railroad station in section 5 of Stuntz Township (T. 57N, R. 20W).

LUCKNOW is a village in section 15 of Great Scott Township (T. 58N, R. 19W), which had a Great Northern Railway station in section 22 for freighting iron ore. It is named after a city of India, where the British garrison made a heroic defense against the Sepoy mutineers in 1857.

LYNWOOD formerly called Stuart, was a railway station in section 29 of Stuntz Township (T. 56N, R. 21W), 12 miles southwest of Hibbing.

LYTLE a station of the Duluth, Rainy Lake and Winnipeg Railway in sections 29 and 30 of T. 67N, R. 20W, with a siding station of the Duluth, Winnipeg and Pacific Railway.

MACE MINE NO. 2 a Great Northern Railway station in section 32, Stuntz Township (T. 57N, R. 21W).

MACON a station of the Duluth, Missabe and Iron Range Railroad in section 5 of Clinton Township.

MADEIRA MINE a Great Northern Railway station in section 36, Stuntz Township (T. 58N, R. 21W).

MAHONING a village associated with the mine of the same name in section 2, Stuntz Township (T. 57N, R. 21W); it had a Great Northern Railway mine spur station.

MAKINEN a village in T. 56N, R. 16W, at the intersection of sections 3, 4, 9, and 10; the post office began in 1922, with John Makinen as first postmaster.

MALDEN a station of the Great Northern Railway in section 33, Clinton Township.

MANEY a village in section 15 of Alborn Township, formerly a station of the Duluth, Missabe and Northern Railway, was named for E. J. Maney of Duluth, general superintendent of the Shenango Furnace Company.

MARBLE a Duluth, Missabe and Iron Range Railroad station; location not found; a townsite platted before 1908 at the Oliver Iron Mining Company's development of the Hill open pit mine.

MARFIELD see MOUNTAIN IRON.

MARGARET MINE SPUR the Buhl company's Great Northern Railway station in section 16, Great Scott Township (T. 58N, R. 19W).

MARISKA a Duluth, Missabe and Iron Range Railroad station in section 9 of Missabe Mountain Township.

MARKHAM a community in section 27, Colvin Township, with a post office, 1908–22, near a lake of this name; it was named for a pioneer.

MARTINS a station serving the Duluth and Northeastern Railroad and Great Northern Railway in section 33 of Grand Lake Township (T. 52N, R. 16W), associated with the Martin Brothers Spur station of the Duluth, Winnipeg and Pacific Railway.

MASABA see MESABA.

MATAWAN a Duluth, Missabe and Iron Range Railroad station; location not found.

McCOMBER a community in Breitung (Eagles Nest) Township (T. 62N, R. 14W), section 18, with a post office, 1916–25.

McCORMACK LAKE Unorganized Territory of, T. 59N, R. 21W; formerly part of French Township.

McCORMACK LAKE TOWNSHIP T. 60N, R. 21W, formerly French Township.

McDAVITT TOWNSHIP (T. 55–56N, R. 18W) was named for J. A. McDavitt of Duluth, who was a pioneer lumberman here.

McDONALD a station of the Duluth, Winnipeg and Pacific Railway in T. 65N, R. 20W.

McKINLEY a city in sections 17 and 18 of Biwabik Township, first settled in 1890 and incorporated in the autumn of 1892, is named from the mine developed by the McKinley brothers, John, William, and Duncan. The city has had a post office since 1892; a Duluth, Missabe and Iron Range Railroad station was in section 17.

MEADOWBROOK a village in section 31, Willow Valley Township, was named for the Farrington family farm; the first post office was named Linden, 1908–9, with George Lindsey as postmaster; the second post office was called Meadow Brook, 1908–54.

MEADOWLANDS TOWNSHIP (T. 53N, R. 19W) has a tract of natural mowing and farming land, called meadows, adjoining the White Face River and giving the name of the railway village and the township, but much of its area consists of extensive swamps, called muskeg. The city in section 15 was incorporated as a village on October 15, 1924; the post office began in 1906; it had a Duluth, Missabe and Iron Range Railroad station.

MELRUDE a village in Ellsburg Township (T. 55N, R. 16W), with a Duluth, Winnipeg and Pacific Railway station in section 18; the name is an anglicized form of Mellerud, a town in Dalsland, Sweden. A Duluth, Winnipeg and Pacific Railway station named Ellsburg was established here about 1910, and a post office opened in 1913 under that name; in 1918 the station name was changed to Ellsmere, but the post office remained Ellsburg; in 1927, because of confusion with the two names and other places in the state with similar names, both the post office and the station were renamed Melrude.

MERRITT a mining townsite one mile east of Biwabik was named in honor of Alfred and Leonidas Merritt of Duluth, widely known for the discovery and development of the iron ore of the Mesabi Range and for promoting the construction of the Duluth, Missabe and Northern Railway and of the great ore docks in Duluth. Leonidas Merritt, the older of these brothers, commonly called Lon, was born in New York State in 1845; served in Brackett's Battalion, Minnesota Cavalry, in the Civil War; was a representative in the legislature in 1893; and is shown as one of the statues at the base of that of Gov. John Albert Johnson in front of the state capitol, being the prospector carrying a pack on his back. A post office named Merritt was in sections 1 and 2 of Biwabik Township, 1892–93.

MESABA HEIGHTS a Duluth, Missabe and Iron Range Railroad station; location not found.

MESABA TOWNSHIP (T. 59N, R. 14W) and mining railway village in section 28 were named from the Mesabi Iron Range. The diverse spellings of this Ojibwe name, and its significance as the Giant's Range, are considered later in this chapter. The township became part of the city of Hoyt Lakes. The village was incorporated on July 7, 1891, but later unincorporated; the post office operated 1889–92, changed to Masaba, 1892–99, and was renamed Mesaba, 1900–1943; it had a Duluth, Missabe and Iron Range Railroad station.

MIDDLETON a site on Minnesota Point (Duluth) owned by Robert Reed and T. A. Markland and surveyed on August 1, 1856.

MIDWAY a Great Northern Railway station in section 10, Great Scott Township (T. 58N, R. 19W).

MIDWAY TOWNSHIP (T. 49N, R. 15W) is named from Midway Creek, halfway between Fond du Lac and the head of the falls and rapids on the St. Louis River. The village in section 8 had a post office, 1889–1911.

MILFORD a steam sawmill site located one mile above Oneota, in 1857, built by Henry C. Ford, who had a claim of 80 acres at this point; Ford returned to Philadelphia in 1860; the mill disintegrated and was destroyed by fire in 1868; the area was later platted as the fourth division of West Duluth.

MILLER a station of the Duluth, Winnipeg and Pacific Railway, about 1937; location not found.

MINNESOTA DRAW an Northern Pacific Railroad station in section 3, T. 49N, R. 14W.

MINNTAC a Duluth, Missabe and Iron Range Railroad station; location not found.

MINORCA JUNCTION a Duluth, Winnipeg and Pacific Railway station, probably related to the mine of the same name; location not found.

MIRBAT see GOWAN.

MISSABE JUNCTION a village in section 4, T. 49N, R. 14W, formerly a railroad station of the Duluth, Missabe and Iron Range and Soo Line railroads.

MISSABE MOUNTAIN MINE a Duluth, Missabe and Iron Range Railroad station in section 9, Missabe Mountain Township.

MISSABE MOUNTAIN TOWNSHIP (T. 58N, R. 17W) has a high portion of the Mesabi Range, with the large mining cities of Virginia and Eveleth and the village of Gilbert. It was absorbed by the cities of Virginia, Eveleth, and Gilbert.

MITCHELL a village in section 5 of Stuntz Township (T. 57N, R. 20W), formerly a station of the Duluth, Missabe and Iron Range Railroad and Great Northern Railway, was named in honor of Pentecost Mitchell, vice-president of the Oliver Mining Company.

MOLDE a post office, 1902–14, in section 3 of Duluth Township (T. 52N, R. 12W).

MONROE a Duluth, Missabe and Iron Range Railroad station in section 28, Balkan Township (T. 58N, R. 20W), also called Monroe Junction, and the Great Northern Railway mine spur-to-shaft station located in section 34.

MONTEZUMA a site at the mouth of the Sucker River, 17 miles from Duluth, which was surveyed in May 1856 by Vose Palmer and owned by Frederic Ottoman.

MOOSWA MINE a Buhl-based company, had a Great Northern Railway station; location not found.

MORCOM TOWNSHIP (T. 61N, R. 21W) was named in honor of Elisha Morcom of Tower, a Cornishman, one of the promoters of mining development on the Vermilion Range, being the first superintendent of the Soudan Mine, who was chairman of the board of county commissioners when the new courthouse was built.

MORGAN PARK an area of Duluth, which had a station of the Duluth, Missabe and Iron Range and Northern Pacific Railroads.

MORRELL a station in section 3 of T. 55N, R. 18W, on the Duluth, Missabe and Northern Railway.

MORRIS MINE the Great Northern Railway had a station in section 8 of Missabe Mountain Township (T. 58N, R. 17W) and a yard station in section 32 of Balkan Township (T. 58N, R. 20W).

MORSE TOWNSHIP (T. 62–63N, R. 12–13W), in which the city of Ely is situated, was named in honor of the late J. C. Morse of Chicago, who was one of the members of the Minnesota Iron Company.

MORTON MINE AND SPUR a Great Northern Railway station in section 11 of Stuntz Township (T. 57N, R. 21W).

MOUNT IRON see **MOUNTAIN IRON**.

MOUNTAIN IRON a city in Nichols Township (T. 58N, R. 18W), first settled in the spring of 1892, was incorporated as a village on November 28, 1892, separated from the township on May 16, 1908, and reincorporated on June 20, 1913. Its name is from the Mountain Iron Mine, the earliest to ship ore from the Mesabi Range, in August 1892. The post office began as Marfield in 1892, with Roscoe Merritt as postmaster, changed to Mount Iron in 1894, and to Mountain Iron in 1913; it had a Duluth, Missabe and Iron Range Railroad station in section 3.

MUELLER a Duluth, Missabe and Iron Range Railroad station; location not found.

MUNGER a village in sections 22 and 23 of Solway Township, was named in honor of Roger S. Munger of Duluth. He was born in North Madison, Conn., February 25, 1830; came to Minnesota in 1857 and was partner with his brother, Russell C. Munger, in the pioneer music store of St. Paul; removed to Duluth in 1869, engaging in lumber business; in 1872 organized a firm, Munger, Markell and Co., who built grain elevators and made this city a great grain-buying and shipping market; and was president of the Imperial Mill Company, organized in 1888, and of the Duluth Iron and Steel Company, organized in 1898. The village had a post office, 1903–31, and a station of the Duluth, Missabe and Iron Range Railroad and Duluth, Winnipeg and Pacific Railway.

MURPHY a station of the Duluth, Winnipeg and Pacific Railway in T. 54N, R. 15W, section 26; also known as Murphy's Spur.

MURRAY a village in section 30 of Breitung Township (T. 62N, R. 14W), formerly a Duluth, Missabe and Iron Range Railroad station, was named for a foreman or superintendent of the Tower Lumber Company.

MUSKEG an LTV station; location not found.

MYERS MINE SPUR a Duluth, Missabe and Iron Range Railroad station in section 22 of Balkan Township (T. 58N, R. 20W).

NAGONAB a station of the Great Northern Railway in section 34 of Brevator Township, bears the name of an Ojibwe leader of the Fond du Lac band, who was born in 1795 and died at Fond du Lac in June 1894. He was influential in persuading the Ojibwe and Dakota to sign a treaty at Prairie du Chien in 1825, acknowledging the sovereignty of the United States; was a signer of a treaty at La Pointe, Wis., in 1854, in which the Ojibwe ceded large tracts of land in northern Minnesota and Wisconsin, including the Vermilion and Mesabi Iron Ranges; and in 1889, at the age of 94 years, he with his son signed further agreements for cessions of lands and rights in the Fond du Lac and Red Lake Reservations. His name, spelled in five or six ways, with accent on the second syllable, is translated as "Sitting ahead" (*Aborigines of Minnesota*, 1911, pp. 719, 720, 722).

NASSAU MINE a station of the Duluth, Missabe and Iron Range Railroad and Great Northern Railway in section 5, Stuntz Township (T. 57N, R. 20W).

NEA a post office, 1898–1909, in section 20 of Normanna Township (T. 52N, R. 13W).

NELSON a village in section 5 of Stuntz Township (T. 57N, R. 20W), circa 1921–38.

NE-NE-MIK-KATO a place name in section 6 of Breitung (T. 62N, R. 15W), 1916–21.

NESS TOWNSHIP T. 52N, R. 19W, formerly unnamed.

NETT LAKE a village with Koochiching County, located in sections 18 and 19 of T. 65N, R. 21W, part of the Bois Forte Reservation; the first post office, 1909–28, was moved from St. Louis County to Koochiching County shortly after it was established; a second post office was begun in 1940, becoming a rural branch in 1956.

NEVADA a Duluth, Missabe and Iron Range Railroad station; location not found.

NEW DULUTH a village southwest of Duluth city limits, in sections 10 and 11 of T. 48N, R. 15W, had a post office, 1891–1914, and a Northern Pacific Railroad station in section 10.

NEW INDEPENDENCE TOWNSHIP (T. 52N, R. 17W) was named by choice of its settlers, who came mostly from Norway when that country and Sweden had the same sovereign.

NICHOLS TOWNSHIP (T. 58–59N, R. 18W) was named in honor of James A. Nichols, a foreman or captain of ore prospectors, who discovered for the Merritt brothers the first large bed of iron ore found on the Mesabi Range. It became the city of Mountain Iron.

NIKILA a station of the Duluth, Winnipeg and Pacific Railway, about 1937; location not found.

NILES MINE a station of the Duluth, Missabe and Iron Range Railroad in section 27 of Balkan Township (T. 58N, R. 20W).

NOLANS MILL a Duluth, Missabe and Iron Range Railroad station; location not found.

NOMI JUNCTION a Duluth, Missabe and Iron Range Railroad station; location not found.

NOPEMING the site of a tuberculosis treatment center in Midway Township, section 29; it had a post office, 1913–66, and a station of the Duluth, Winnipeg and Pacific Railway and Duluth, Missabe and Iron Range Railroad.

NORMAN is the post office name for the railway village of Skibo, five miles southeast of Allen Junction, chosen in honor of Peter Norman, foreman of a railway section.

NORMANNA TOWNSHIP (T. 52–53N, R. 13W) was named in compliment for immigrants from Norway.

NORTH CYPRESS MINE a Great Northern Railway station; location not found.

NORTH EDDYS MINE a Great Northern Railway station in section 11, Stuntz Township (T. 57N, R. 21W).

NORTH JUNCTION a station of the Duluth, Winnipeg and Pacific Railway in T. 58–59N, R. 17–18W, about 1937; also known as North Loop Junction.

NORTH MITCHELL a Great Northern Railway station in T. 57N, R. 20W.

NORTH SPRUCE a place name in section 13, Clinton Township; probably a railroad station.

NORTH STAR TOWNSHIP (T. 53N, R. 13W) was formerly part of Normanna Township.

NORTH UNO MINE SPUR a Great Northern Railway station in section 2, Stuntz Township (T. 57N, R. 21W).

NORTHEAST ST. LOUIS, UNORGANIZED TERRITORY OF see UNORGANIZED TERRITORY OF NORTHEAST ST. LOUIS.

NORTHLAND a post office in section 12 of T. 57N, R. 21W, in 1910–22; it became a station of Hibbing.

NORTHLAND TIE COMPANY SPUR a Great Northern Railway station; location not found.

NORTHLAND TOWNSHIP (T. 53N, R. 17W) had many Norwegian settlers.

NORTHWEST ST. LOUIS, UNORGANIZED TERRITORY OF see UNORGANIZED TERRITORY OF NORTHWEST ST. LOUIS.

NORWAY a Duluth and Iron Range Railroad station in sections 10 and 14 of Embarrass Township.

NOVA a Great Northern Railway station in section 19 of Mountain Iron Township (T. 58N, R. 18W).

NYSTROM a Duluth, Winnipeg and Pacific Railway station, about 1937; location not found.

OIT a station of the Duluth, Winnipeg and Pacific Railway in Leiding Township (T. 64N, R. 20W).

OKWANIM see ALLEN.

OLANDER a post office, 1905–7, established in Itasca County and transferred to St. Louis County in 1906; location not found.

OLCOTT a Great Northern Railway station in section 19 of Mountain Iron Township (T. 58N, R. 18W).

OLD ALBANY a Duluth, Missabe and Iron Range Railroad station; location not found.

OLD MESABA see MESABA.

OLIVER a Duluth, Missabe and Iron Range Railroad station for the Oliver Mine in Biwabik Township.

OMEGA/ONEGA a village in section 24 of Stuntz Township (T. 56N, R. 20W), later part of the city of Hibbing; it had a Great Northern Railway station; it is found on maps under both spellings.

ONEOTA a village on the northwest shore of St. Louis Bay, in section 12 of Midway Township, platted in 1856, incorporated as a village on May 23, 1857, and annexed to Duluth in 1889, received its name from a book published by Henry R. Schoolcraft in 1845 titled *Oneota, or Characteristics of the Red Race of America*. In the preface he wrote: "The term Oneota is the name of one of these aboriginal tribes (the Oneidas). It signifies, in the Mohawk dialect, the people who are sprung from a rock." His larger work, *History, Condition, and Prospects of the Indian Tribes* (6 vols., 1851–57), has an article of pt. 1 (pp. 176–80) on "An Aboriginal Palladium, as exhibited in the Oneida stone," with a large colored picture of it. This stone, named Oneota, visited by Schoolcraft in the summer of 1845, was found to be a boulder of syenite on the top of one of the highest hills in the country of the Oneida Indians in western New York. The village had a post office, 1856–93, and a Northern Pacific Railroad station.

ONKKA a station of the Duluth, Winnipeg and Pacific Railway, about 1937; location not found.

ONONDAGA MINE a Duluth, Missabe and Iron Range Railroad and Great Northern Railway station in section 4, Missabe Mountain.

ORR a city in Leiding Township, was incorporated as a village on June 7, 1935. The former Duluth, Winnipeg and Pacific Railway station, located in section 12 of T. 64N, R. 20W, was the nearest railway station for the Bois Forte Reservation. The post office was established in 1907; William Orr was the postmaster and owner of a general store.

ORWELL MINE a Great Northern Railway station in section 21 of Balkan Township (T. 56N, R. 24W).

OSBORNE a Duluth, Missabe and Iron Range Railroad station; location not found.

OWENS/OWENS SPUR a station of the Duluth, Winnipeg and Pacific in Owens Township.

OWENS TOWNSHIP (T. 62N, R. 18W) was named in honor of three brothers, John L., Samuel H., and Thomas Owens. The first, who owned a farm near Cook village in this township, was formerly a lumberman and owner of a sawmill at Tower, was one of the first to ship ore from the Vermilion Range, and lived at Lakeside, an eastern suburb of Duluth. The second came to Tower in 1883, was engineer at its first sawmill, and in 1902 became yardmaster in Eveleth for the Fayal Mine. Thomas Owens, of Two Harbors, became superintendent of the Duluth and Iron Range Railroad in 1892.

PADGETT a station on the Duluth, Winnipeg and Pacific Railway, about 1937; location not found.

PALMERS a village in section 3 of Duluth Township (T. 51N, R. 12W), with a post office, 1913–25, and Duluth, Missabe and Iron Range Railroad station.

PALO a village at the intersection of sections 16, 17, 20, and 21 of White Township (T. 57N, R. 15W), with a post office, 1907–33; its name is likely of Finnish derivation.

PANAMA a Duluth, Missabe and Iron Range Railroad station in section 31 of Stuntz Township (T. 57N, R. 20W).

PARA a Great Northern Railway station in section 33, McDavitt Township (T. 56N, R. 18W).

PARK POINT a village encompassing all that part of Minnesota Point lying south of and below the Duluth ship canal; it was incorporated as a village on March 7, 1881, by special law and annexed later by Duluth.

PARKVILLE a settlement in sections 2, 11, and 12 of Nichols Township (T. 58N, R. 18W), with a station of the Great Northern Railway and a post office since 1923.

PAUPORES see POUPORE.

PAUPORI a Great Northern Railway village eight miles west of Brookston, is diversely spelled, Poupore (in three syllables) being the post office name. The postmaster, Phil Poupore, and the railway agent, W. S. Poupore, were sons of an Ojibwe farmer who lived there. See also POUPORE.

PAYNE a village in sections 10 and 11 of Payne Township (T. 53N, R. 18W), with a post office, 1904–11 and 1915–72, and a former Duluth, Missabe and Iron Range Railroad station in section 10, was named in honor of a former secretary of this railway company.

PAYNE TOWNSHIP (T. 53N, R. 18W) became part of Meadowlands Township.

PEARY is a station of the Duluth, Winnipeg and Pacific Railway, in section 6, T. 56N, R. 17W, at its crossing of the St. Louis River, named in honor of Robert Edwin Peary, the noted Arctic explorer. He was born at Cresson, Pa., May 6, 1856; traversed the inland ice of northwestern Greenland in 1891; traced the northern limit of the Greenland archipelago in 1900; and on April 6, 1909, he reached the North Pole.

PELICAN a Duluth, Winnipeg and Pacific Railway hoist and spur station in section 6 of Leiding Township (T. 64N, R. 19W).

PENOBSCOT MINE a spur station of the Great Northern Railway in section 1, Stuntz Township (T. 57N, R. 21W).

PEQUAYAN TOWNSHIP (T. 54N, R. 12W) was created from the north part of Alden Township. Pequaywan Lake was a community post office, 1970–74, located in section 8.

PERUS/PEUS a Duluth, Missabe and Iron Range Railroad station; location not found.

PETERSON a station of the Duluth, Winnipeg and Pacific Railway, about 1937; location not found.

PETREL a village in section 10 of Fairbanks Township (T. 56N, R. 12W); the post office, 1909–20, was spelled Petrell, with Alga Petrell as postmaster.

PETTIT a Duluth, Missabe and Iron Range Railroad station in section 25 of Missabe Mountain Township (T. 58N, R. 17W).

PEYLA is a village in section 10 of Vermilion Lake Township, with a post office, 1907–24, of which Peter Peyla was the first postmaster.

PHILBIN MINE SPUR a Great Northern Railway station in section 29, Stuntz Township (T. 57N, R. 20W).

PIERCE a village in section 28 of Balkan Township (T. 58N, R. 20W), about 1921.

PIKE TOWNSHIP (T. 60N, R. 16W) has Pike River flowing through it, tributary to Vermilion Lake. This stream, called Vermilion River on the map of David Owen's geological survey, published in 1852, is named from the fish. A post office was in section 29, 1903–15, with a station on the Duluth, Missabe and Northern Railway.

PILLSBURY a Great Northern Railway junction

and a Duluth, Missabe and Iron Range Railroad station for the mine in section 29 of Balkan Township (T. 58N, R. 20W).

PILOT MINE SPUR a Great Northern Railway station in section 2, Mountain Iron Township (T. 58N, R. 18W).

PINE LAKE ROAD a Cypress railroad station; location not found.

PINEVILLE a settlement in section 6, White Township (T. 58N, R. 15W), with a post office, 1909–20.

PIONEER and **CHANDLER MINE** a Great Northern Railway station in section 27, Morse Township (T. 63N, R. 12W).

PLANKINGTON a Duluth, Missabe and Iron Range Railroad station; location not found.

POLAND a post office, 1895–1900, in section 8, Rice Lake Township.

PONA CREEK SPUR a Duluth, Missabe and Iron Range Railroad station; location not found.

PORTAGE TOWNSHIP (T. 65N, R. 17–18W, T. 66N, R. 17–19W). See also **BUYCK TOWNSHIP**.

PORTLAND a townsite settled in 1855 on the north shore of Lake Superior, adjoined the original plat of Duluth. It was platted in 1856 by owners Aaron B. Robbins, James D. Ray, C. Marshall, and J. J. Post, incorporated as a village on May 19, 1857, and consolidated with Duluth on March 30, 1861.

POT SHOT LAKE, UNORGANIZED TERRITORY OF see **UNORGANIZED TERRITORY OF POT SHOT LAKE**.

POTLATCH a Duluth, Winnipeg and Pacific Railway station; location not found.

POUPORE a post office in sections 28 and 29 of Arrowhead Township (T. 51N, R. 19W), which was called Paupores, 1902–4, Catlin, 1904–6, and Poupore, 1908–32, with Valentine W. Rock as postmaster under all three names; a Great Northern Railway station was in section 29.

POWERS a post office, 1900–9, with Albert H. Powers, postmaster, in section 23 of T. 58N, R. 21W, established for the convenience of the Power and Simpson Logging Company; it may be the same as Dewey Lake; it is found in section 7 on a 1911 map; it became part of the city of Hibbing.

PRAIRIE LAKE TOWNSHIP (T. 50N, R. 21W) is named from the Prairie Lake and River, flowing through it, tributary to Sandy Lake in Aitkin County. Hush-kodensiwi, meaning "little prairie," is the Ojibwe name, noted by Rev. Joseph A. Gilfillan, for the lake and river.

PRINDEL a station of the Duluth, Missabe and Iron Range Railroad and Duluth, Winnipeg and Pacific Railway; location not found.

PROCTOR a city in sections 3, 10, and 15 of Midway Township, incorporated as a village on November 6, 1894, commemorates James Proctor Knott of Kentucky, before mentioned for his humorous speech in Congress in 1871, ridiculing Duluth, but really aiding the young city much by its advertisement. He was born near Lebanon, Ky., August 29, 1830; was a representative in Congress, 1867–71 and 1877–83; governor of Kentucky, 1883–87; professor of civics and law in Center College, Danville, Ky., 1892–1901; and died at Lebanon, Ky., June 18, 1911. The village's post office was established as Proctorknott from 1894 to 1904, changing to Proctor, 1904–43, and then becoming a branch of the Duluth postal service.

PROCTORKNOTT see **PROCTOR**.

PROSIT a village in section 10, Alborn Township, with a post office, 1916–66, and a Duluth, Missabe and Iron Range Railroad station.

PUTNAM a station of the Duluth, Winnipeg and Pacific Railway in section 7, Wuori Township.

RAINY JUNCTION a village south of Virginia in Missabe Mountain Township, with a Duluth, Missabe and Iron Range Railroad station in section 19.

RAMSHAW a village in Grand Lake Township (T. 52N, R. 16W), had a station of the Duluth, Missabe and Iron Range Railroad and Duluth, Winnipeg and Pacific Railway; the name is also noted on a 1965 map in section 13 of Clinton Township.

RATHBUN SPUR NO. 8 a Duluth, Missabe and Iron Range Railroad station; location not found.

REDORE a village in Stuntz Township (T. 57N, R. 20W), section 5, which had a post office, 1917–67, and a Great Northern Railway station.

RENO is a village in section 14 of Bassett Township (T. 57N, R. 13W), formerly a railroad station of the Duluth, Missabe and Iron Range Railroad.

RICE LAKE TOWNSHIP (T. 51N, R. 14W) is named for the Wild Rice Lake, crossed by its west line. The Ojibwe name of this lake means, according to Gilfillan, "the place of wild rice amidst the hills."

RICE RIVER a station of the Duluth, Winnipeg and Pacific Railway, in section 18, Sandy Township.

RICE'S POINT a district of Duluth on Minnesota Point, between the harbor and St. Louis Bay, was named in honor of its pioneer landowner, Orrin Wheeler Rice of Superior, Wis., who was a younger brother of Henry M. and Edmund Rice, prominent citizens of St. Paul. He was born in Waitsfield, Vt., October 6, 1829, and died in Minneapolis, March 9, 1859. He filed a land claim for this point in 1854 and was a member of the first town council of Duluth in 1857. The first election in St. Louis County was held at his house on this point in September 1855.

RIDGE a village in section 6 of Argo Township (T. 59N, R. 13W), with a former station of the Duluth, Missabe and Iron Range Railroad.

RILEY a station of the Duluth, Missabe and Iron Range Railroad and Great Northern Railway in section 1 of Stuntz Township (T. 56N, R. 21W).

RIVERS a station of the Duluth, Missabe and Iron Range Railroad in section 8, Kugler Township, was named from its location near the crossing of the West Two Rivers. The eastern one of these rivers flows through Tower.

RIVERSIDE a village seven miles southwest of Union, probably in Clinton Township, formerly a Northern Pacific Railroad station, which may be the same as Riverside Junction station.

ROBERTS MINE SPUR a Great Northern Railway station in section 8, Biwabik Township.

ROBINSON a village in section 7 of Morse Township (T. 62N, R. 13W), formerly a Duluth, Missabe and Iron Range Railroad station, was named for a lumberman whose logging camp was beside a small lake there. The Robinson Lake Iron Company in section 18, who platted the townsite in 1910, requested a post office and built a hotel.

ROLLINS a village in sections 10 and 15 of Ault Township (T. 55N, R. 12W), formerly a Duluth, Missabe and Northern Railway station, was likewise named for a lumberman.

ROSS a place name in section 32 of Normanna Township (T. 53N, R. 13W) shown on a 1911 map.

ROSSOM a station of the Duluth, Winnipeg and Pacific Railway, about 1937; location not found.

ROTHMAN a village in Bear Island State Forest, located in section 14 of T. 61N, R. 13W.

RUBY JUNCTION a village in section 7 of Stuntz Township (T. 57N, R. 20W), northeast of Hibbing, formerly a station of the Duluth, Missabe and Iron Range Railroad and Great Northern Railway.

RUSH LAKE a railway station for logging on the Duluth and Northeastern Railroad, in section 24 of T. 54N, R. 15W, is beside a lake of this name.

RUST a Duluth, Missabe and Iron Range Railroad station in section 12 of Stuntz Township (T. 57N, R. 21W), probably related to the Hull Rust Mine.

SAARI a station of the Duluth, Winnipeg and Pacific Railway, also listed as Saari Bros. Spur, Saari Spur, and Sarri; location not found.

SAGINAW is a village in section 36 of Industrial Township, with a post office established in 1906, named probably by lumbermen from the city and county of Saginaw in Michigan. It formerly had a station of the Duluth and Northeastern and Duluth, Missabe and Iron Range Railroads.

ST. CLAIR a village east of Chisholm, formerly a station of the Duluth, Missabe and Iron Range Railroad and Great Northern Railway.

ST. LOUIS JUNCTION a Duluth and Northeastern Railroad station in section 28 of Bassett Township (T. 58N, R. 13W).

ST. LOUIS RIVER a village in sections 21 and 22 of Bassett Township (T. 58N, R. 13W), with a Duluth, Missabe and Iron Range Railroad station.

ST. LOUIS TOWNSHIP (T. 58N, R. 12W), named like this county for the St. Louis River, crossed in its south part by the Duluth and Iron Range Railroad, became part of Bassett Township.

SALO CORNER a place name, also known as Salo's Corner, circa 1941, but no location found.

SAND LAKE, UNORGANIZED TERRITORY OF see UNORGANIZED TERRITORY OF SAND LAKE.

SANDY TOWNSHIP (T. 60N, R. 17W) is named for Sandy Lake and an adjacent Sand Lake, each tributary by the Pike River to Vermilion Lake. Sandy, its post office, 1911–27, was in section 23.

SAVOR and SIBLEY MINE SPUR a Duluth, Missabe and Iron Range Railroad station in section 27 of Morse Township (T. 63N, R. 12W).

SAX a village in sections 26 and 27, McDavitt Township (T. 55N, R. 18W), with a post office, 1916–30, and a former railroad station. A 1916 map shows it as Wallace, and the 1930 map spells it Saxe; the Duluth, Missabe and Iron Range Railroad has it Sax, and the Great Northern Railway as Saxe. The railroad station was named for Solomon Saxe of Eveleth, who was a landowner there.

SAXE a second place name in section 17 of Clinton Township in 1916.

SCOTT a village in Great Scott Township (T. 58N, R. 19W), section 36, which had a Duluth, Missabe and Iron Range Railroad station and siding.

SCRANTON a village associated with the mine site, which had a Great Northern Railway station in section 13 of Stuntz Township (T. 57N, R. 21W).

SELLERS MINE a Duluth, Missabe and Iron Range Railroad station in section 6 of Stuntz Township (T. 57N, R. 20W).

SEMER a post office, 1916–20, ten miles northeast of Tower.

SEVEN BEAVERS LAKE a Cypress railroad station in Bassett Township (T. 58N, R. 12W).

SEVILLE a Great Northern Railway station in section 10, Great Scott Township (T. 58N, R. 19W).

SHAGAWA a post office, 1887–88; location not found, but probably near the lake of the same name in Morse Township (T. 63N, R. 12W).

SHAN see SHAW.

SHARON a Great Northern Railway and Duluth, Missabe and Iron Range Railroad station in sections 16 and 17, Great Scott Township (T. 58N, R. 19W), along with the Great Northern Railway mine station in section 17.

SHATTUCK a Duluth, Missabe and Iron Range Railroad station; location not found.

SHAW a village, developed around its Duluth, Winnipeg and Pacific Railway station in section 34 of Cotton Township (T. 54N, R. 16W); the post office was called Shan, 1919–50, and Shaw, 1950–59, with Mathilda Roberg as postmaster under both names. The village was first settled by Gust Sundvick in 1907. The post office supposedly was named Shan, as selected by the postal department, because there already was a Shaw in Missouri and Mississippi; however, the station and village were known as Shaw.

SHELDON/SHELTON a Duluth, Missabe and Iron Range Railroad station in section 25 of Nichols Township (T. 58N, R. 18W); the Duluth, Winnipeg and Pacific Railway station at the same site was called Shelton Junction.

SHENANGO a mining railway station of the Duluth, Missabe and Iron Range Railroad in section 22 of Balkan Township (T. 58N, R. 20W), was named for the Shenango Furnace Company of Pennsylvania; also known as Shenango Junction.

SHERIDAN-KERR MINE Duluth, Missabe and Iron Range Railroad stations in sections 3, 34, and 35, Stuntz Township (T. 58N, R. 21W). See also KERR.

SHERMAN CORNER a village in section 8 of Angora Township.

SHERWOOD a village in section 3 of Cherry Township, formerly a Duluth, Missabe and Iron Range Railroad station.

SHIELS a station of the Duluth and Northeastern Railroad in section 34 of T. 55N, R. 14W.

SHIRAS MINE a Great Northern Railway station in section 16, Great Scott Township (T. 58N, R. 19W).

SHORT LINE PARK a post office, 1889–90, in section 32 of Midway Township and the site of a station of the Great Northern Railway, Northern Pacific Railroad, and Chicago, Milwaukee and St. Paul Railroad.

SIDE LAKE a village in section 21 of French Township (T. 60N, R. 21W), with a post office established in 1927.

SILICA a village at the intersection of sections 4, 5, 8, and 9 of T. 55N, R. 21W, at a former station of the Duluth, Missabe and Iron Range Railroad.

SILLIMANS a Great Northern Railway station; location not found.

SIMAR a village in section 15, Solway Township, with a station of the Duluth, Winnipeg and Pacific Railway in section 14.

SIMPSON a Duluth, Missabe and Iron Range Railroad station; location not found.

SIMS a Great Northern Railway station in section 16, Stuntz Township (T. 56N, R. 21W).

SKIBO a village in sections 21 and 28, Bassett Township (T. 58N, R. 13W), formerly a station of the Duluth, Missabe and Iron Range Railroad, was named for Skibo Castle, the summer home of Andrew Carnegie, on the north shore of Dornoch Firth in the northern part of Scotland. The village had two post offices: the first operated 1902–13; the second was at Norman, 1897–1918, with Peter Norman as postmaster, was transferred to Skibo in 1918, and was discontinued in 1919.

SLIVER MINE a Great Northern Railway station in section 5, Missabe Mountain Township.

SMITHVILLE a suburban area of West Duluth (T. 49N, R. 15W), sections 26 and 27, which had a post office, 1888–1918. Part of its platted area is Lenroot's Addition, named for Lars Lenroot (Lönnrot), who immigrated from Sweden in 1854, lived for a time in Duluth, moved to Vermilion Lake in 1860, working as a farmer and blacksmith, and then moved to Superior, Wis.; his son, Irvine Luther Lenroot, born in 1869, become a well-known U.S. senator from Wisconsin. The Northern Pacific Railroad station was in section 27 of Midway Township.

SNOWBALL a platted townsite six miles west of Nashwauk; not developed.

SNOWDEN a village associated with the former Duluth, Missabe and Iron Range Railroad station called Snowden Junction; location not found.

SNYDER a post office, January–November 1908, in sections 5 and 6, T. 62N, R. 21W, with Lorin K. Snyder as postmaster.

SOLWAY TOWNSHIP (T. 50N, R. 16W) was named for the Solway Firth, an arm or inlet of the Irish Sea, between Scotland and England.

SOUDAN a village in section 28, Breitung Township (T. 62N, R. 15W), near Tower, and its mine, which was the first in this state to ship iron ore, in 1884, were so named by D. H. Bacon, general manager of this mine, because the severe winter cold here is very strongly contrasted with the tropical heat of the Soudan (or Sudan) region in Africa. The village had a post office, established as Tower Mines in 1887 and changed to Soudan in 1888; associated with Tower Junction.

SOUTH AGNEW MINE SPUR a Great Northern Railway station in section 11, Stuntz Township (T. 57N, R. 21W).

SOUTH CYPRUS MINE SPUR a Great Northern Railway station in section 3, Stuntz Township (T. 57N, R. 21W).

SOUTH JUNCTION and **SOUTH LOOP** stations of the Duluth, Winnipeg and Pacific Railway; no locations found.

SOUTH UNO MINE SPUR a Great Northern Railway station in section 10, Stuntz Township (T. 57N, R. 21W).

SPARTA a settlement in section 34, Missabe Mountain Township, incorporated in 1897, may have been named for ancient Greece, like Athens station near Tower, but probably was named by pioneers coming from Sparta in Wisconsin. It had a Duluth, Missabe and Northern Railway station and a post office, which was first named Weimer in 1896, changed to Sparta in 1897, and discontinued in 1919.

SPATTEN a post office, 1903–5, in section 19, Herman Township.

SPAULDING is a village in sections 23 and 26 of Morse Township (T. 63N, R. 12W), at the east end of Long Lake; the Duluth, Winnipeg and Pacific Railway station was located in section 23.

SPINA a village in section 14 of Great Scott Township (T. 58N, R. 19W), was developed when W. J.

Power secured controlling interest in the Kinney Mine in 1909; it was located at the Kinney Mine and had a Great Northern Railway station.

SPIRIT LAKE a village in section 35 of T. 49N, R. 15W, with a Northern Pacific Railroad station in section 26.

SPRAY a Duluth, Missabe and Iron Range Railroad station; location not found.

SPRIC a station of the Duluth, Missabe and Northern Railway, circa 1937; location not found.

SPRING a Duluth, Missabe and Iron Range Railroad station in section 11 of Mesaba Township, associated with the mine of the same name.

SPRUCE a village in section 13, Clinton Township, was the site of a former railroad station of the Duluth, Missabe and Iron Range Railroad; also known as Spruce Junction.

STANBURY a Great Northern Railway station; location not found.

STEELTON a village in section 3, T. 48N, R. 15W, formerly a station of the Duluth, Missabe and Iron Range Railroad.

STEVENSON is a village in section 7, Stuntz Township (T. 57N, R. 21W), associated with the mine of the same name; the Great Northern Railway had a station in section 7, and a spur station in section 15; the post office operated 1902–50.

STONEHOUSE see GRAND LAKE.

STONEY BROOK JUNCTION see BROOKSTON.

STONEY BROOK TOWNSHIP (T. 50N, R. 18W).

STROUD a Duluth and Northeastern Railroad station six miles southwest of Rush Lake in section 8 of T. 53N, R. 15W.

STUART a place name of 1916 in section 26 of Stuntz Township (T. 56N, R. 21W), which may be the same as Lynwood.

STUNTZ TOWNSHIP (T. 56–57N, R. 20W, T. 55–58N, R. 21W), which includes Hibbing, was named in honor of George R. Stuntz of Duluth. He was born in Albion, Erie County, Pa., December 11, 1820; came to the site of Duluth in 1852; was a land surveyor and civil engineer and made extensive surveys in northern Wisconsin and northeastern Minnesota, including the iron ore lands along the Mesabi Range; died in Duluth, October 23, 1902. The township became part of the city of Hibbing.

STURGEON PARK a place name in the 1916 plat book in section 21 of French Township (T. 60N, R. 21W) but not shown on the 1930 map.

STURGEON RIVER a post office in section 30, Linden Grove Township, was first named Lind, 1910–14, with Austin Lind as postmaster; it was changed to Sturgeon River, located in section 34 of T. 62N, R. 21W, and was discontinued in 1916.

STURGEON TOWNSHIP (T. 61N, R. 20W) was named from the Sturgeon River, which flows through it northwestward, being tributary to the Little Fork of Rainy River. The rock sturgeon of northern Minnesota attains a length of six feet and a weight of 100 pounds. "On portions of the Lake of the Woods sturgeon fishing is the chief occupation, thousands of large fish being taken annually" (Ulysses Orange Cox, *A Preliminary Report on the Fishes of Minnesota*, 1897, p. 13). The village of Stroud is in sections 10, 11, 14, and 15 of the township.

SUMMIT stations of the Duluth, Missabe and Iron Range Railroad in section 7, and of the Great Northern Railway in section 8, White Township (T. 58N, R. 15W).

SUN HILL a place name in Allen Township, circa 1911.

SUNDBY a post office, 1902–15, in section 3, Solway Township, with a station of the Great Northern Railway.

SUSQUEHANNA MINE a Duluth, Missabe and Iron Range Railroad station in section 6 of Stuntz Township (T. 57N, R. 20W), and a Great Northern Railway spur station in section 7.

SWAN RIVER LOGGING a Great Northern Railway station; location not found.

SWEENEY MINE the Kelly-based company had a Great Northern Railway spur line with a station in section 3 of Stuntz Township (T. 57N, R. 21W).

SYRACUSE MINE a Great Northern Railway station in section 33, Balkan Township (T. 58N, R. 20W).

TABER a Duluth, Winnipeg and Pacific Railway station in sections 1 and 12 of T. 60N, R. 18W, six miles southeast of Angora; also known as Faber.

TAFT a village in section 14 of Grand Lake Township (T. 52N, R. 16W), formerly a station of the Duluth, Winnipeg and Pacific Railway and the Duluth and Northeastern Railroad, was named in honor of William H. Taft. He was born in Cincinnati, Ohio, September 15, 1857; was graduated at Yale University, 1878; was U.S. circuit judge, 1892–1900; was president of the U.S. Philippine Commission, 1900–1901; first civil governor of the Philippine Islands, 1901–4; U.S. secretary of war, 1904–8; and president of the United States, 1909–13. A second place of this name is found in section 9, Portage Township (T. 66N, R. 17w), about 1916.

TENER a Duluth, Missabe and Iron Range Railroad station; location not found.

THEEN a Duluth, Winnipeg and Pacific Railway station in section 5 of Leiding Township (T. 63N, R. 19w).

THOMAS a Duluth, Missabe and Iron Range Railroad station; location not found.

THORNE MINE the Buhl company had a Great Northern Railway spur line with a station in section 10 of Great Scott Township (T. 58N, R. 19w).

THUNDERBIRD a Duluth, Missabe and Iron Range Railroad station; location not found.

TIOGA a Duluth, Missabe and Iron Range Railroad station in section 28 of Balkan Township (T. 58N, R. 20w).

TOIMI a post office, 1910–35, in section 36 of Bassett Township (T. 57N, R. 12w), and located 1915–20 in Lake County.

TOIVOLA TOWNSHIP (T. 54N, R. 19–20w) bears a Finnish name, equivalent to "Hopeville" or "Land of Promise," given by Thomas Arkkola, a pioneer immigrant from Finland. The village in sections 7 and 18 (T. 54N, R. 20w) had a post office, 1913–74, continuing as a community post office since 1974. Toijala is a village in the southwest part of that country.

TORNVILLE a place name in sections 3 and 4 of Morse Township (T. 62N, R. 13w), circa 1965.

TOURNEY (OR TURNEY) see HEMLOCK.

TOWER a city in section 32 of Breitung Township (T. 62N, R. 15w), first platted as a townsite in 1882, with a post office from 1883, reached by the Duluth and Iron Range Railroad in 1884, and incorporated as a city March 13, 1889, was named in honor of Charlemagne Tower, Sr., of Philadelphia, Pa. He was born in Paris, N.Y., April 18, 1809; was graduated at Harvard College, 1830; studied law and was admitted to the bar in 1836; practiced law in Pennsylvania 25 years; was captain in the Sixth Pennsylvania Regiment in the Civil War; was connected with the Minnesota Iron Company and the Duluth and Iron Range Railroad company, and was thus instrumental in opening in 1884 the great iron industry of Minnesota.

The name also honors Charlemagne Tower,

Jr., who was born in Philadelphia, April 17, 1848; was graduated at Harvard University, 1872; was admitted to the bar in 1878; resided in Duluth, 1882–87, where he was president of the Duluth and Iron Range Railroad company and managing director of the Minnesota Iron Company; was U.S. ambassador to Austria-Hungary, 1897–99, to Russia, 1899–1902, and to Germany, 1902–8.

TOWER JUNCTION a village in section 33, Breitung Township (T. 62N, R. 15w), formerly a Duluth, Missabe and Iron Range Railroad station.

TOWER MINES see SOUDAN.

TRIMBLE a station of the Duluth and Iron Range Railroad in section 12, Mesaba Township.

TROY a place name in section 7 of Fayal Township, about 1921–37.

TRUNK ROAD a Duluth, Winnipeg and Pacific Railway station; location not found.

TUDOR a Great Northern Railway station in section 15, Payne Township.

TURNEY (OR TOURNEY) see HEMLOCK.

TWIG a community in section 27 of Grand Lake Township (T. 51N, R. 16w), was formerly a Duluth, Winnipeg and Pacific Railway station known as Twig Station; the post office operated 1901–16 and since 1947.

UNION a Duluth, Missabe and Iron Range Railroad station in section 9 of Missabe Mountain Township.

UNORGANIZED TERRITORY OF BIRCH LAKE see ALLEN TOWNSHIP.

UNORGANIZED TERRITORY OF FERMOY T. 55N, R. 18w.

UNORGANIZED TERRITORY OF HAY LAKE T. 59N, R. 16w.

UNORGANIZED TERRITORY OF HEIKKILA LAKE T. 56–57N, R. 16w; T. 56N, R. 17w.

UNORGANIZED TERRITORY OF JANETTE LAKE T. 55N, R. 21w.

UNORGANIZED TERRITORY OF LAKE VERMILION T. 61–64N, R. 17w.

UNORGANIZED TERRITORY OF MCCORMACK LAKE T. 59N, R. 21w.

UNORGANIZED TERRITORY OF NETT LAKE T. 64–65N, R. 21w (western half).

UNORGANIZED TERRITORY OF NORTHEAST ST. LOUIS T. 64–66N, R. 12w; T. 64–67N, R. 13w; T. 63–67N, R. 14w; T. 63–67N, R. 15w; T. 62–67N, R. 16w; T. 61–64N, R. 17w.

UNORGANIZED TERRITORY OF NORTHWEST ST.

LOUIS T. 67–69N, R. 17W; T. 67–69N, R. 18W; T. 67–70N, R. 19W; T. 66–71N, R. 20W; T. 64–71N, R. 21W.

UNORGANIZED TERRITORY OF POT SHOT LAKE T. 52N, R. 21W.

UNORGANIZED TERRITORY OF SAND LAKE T. 60N, R. 18–20W.

UNORGANIZED TERRITORY OF WHITEFACE RESERVOIR T. 54N, R. 13W; T. 54–58N, R. 14W; T. 53–55N, R. 15W; T. 53N, R. 16W.

UTICA a Great Northern Railway station for the Utica Mine yard, section 2, Stuntz Township (T. 57N, R. 21W).

VAN BUREN TOWNSHIP (T. 52N, R. 20W) was named in honor of Martin Van Buren, who was born at Kinderhook, N.Y., December 5, 1782, and died there, July 21, 1862. He was U.S. senator from New York, 1821–28; governor of New York, 1828–29; secretary of state under Pres. Andrew Jackson, 1829–31; vice-president of the United States, 1833–37; and president, 1837–41.

VERMILION DAM a post office, 1920–27, on the Vermilion River where it runs into Vermilion Lake; location not found.

VERMILION GROVE was a proposed village site for summer homes on the south side of Frazer Bay (formerly called Birch Bay) of Vermilion Lake; location not found.

VERMILLION LAKE a post office, 1867–71, and a Duluth, Missabe and Iron Range Railroad station; location not found.

VERMILION LAKE TOWNSHIP (T. 61N, R. 16W), adjoining the most southern arm of this lake, thence derived its name, a translation of Onamuni, the Ojibwe name of the lake. George H. Vivian, the county treasurer, who formerly lived in Tower, stated that the aboriginal name refers to the red and golden reflection from the sky to the smooth lake surface near sunset, being thus of the same significance as the Ojibwe name of Red Lake.

VINCE a station of the Duluth, Winnipeg and Pacific Railway; location not found.

VIRGINIA a city in Missabe Mountain Township, having a courthouse as the seat of the judicial district for the north part of the county, was founded in September 1892 and was incorporated as a city in 1894, after having been almost entirely destroyed by a fire in June 1893. It was again almost wholly burned in the summer of 1900 from a forest fire. The site of the city was originally heavily wooded. This name was proposed by David T. Adams, an explorer who was looking for mining lands; he suggested the name for the virgin country around him and for the home state of a fellow town and mine promoter, A. E. Humphreys. The post office was established in 1893; the station serving the Duluth, Missabe and Iron Range Railroad, Duluth, Winnipeg and Pacific Railway, and Great Northern Railway was in section 7.

VIRGINIA AND RAINY LAKE SPUR a Duluth, Winnipeg and Pacific Railway station; location not found.

VIRMOUNT a Duluth, Winnipeg and Pacific Railway station; location not found.

WAASA TOWNSHIP (T. 60N, R. 14W) was named for the province of Vasa (or Waasa) in western Finland.

WABEGAN a Duluth, Missabe and Iron Range Railroad station; location not found.

WABIGON MINE the Buhl company had a Great Northern Railway spur line with a station in section 17, Great Scott Township (T. 58N, R. 19W).

WACOOTA a village in section 10 of Nichols Township (T. 58N, R. 19W), associated with the Wacoota Mine.

WACOTAH MINE the Virginia-based company had a Great Northern Railway station in section 2, Nichols Township (T. 58N, R. 18W).

WADE a Duluth, Missabe and Iron Range Railroad station in Great Scott Township (T. 58N, R. 19W).

WAGONER a post office in sections 5 and 6 in Alango Township, 1912–18.

WAHLSTEN a village in section 29 of Kugler Township, which had a Duluth, Missabe and Iron Range Railroad station, named for August Wahlsten, a Swedish lumberman and homesteader in this township.

WAKEMUP a village in section 21, Beatty Township (T. 63N, R. 18W) named for an Ojibwe community nearby.

WALLACE a railway station four miles north of Kelsey, was named for a lumberman there, who later lived in Duluth. See also SAX.

WALSH a station of the Duluth, Missabe and Iron Range Railroad in section 4 of Kugler Township; a second place with this name was in section 6 of T. 56N, R. 17W.

WANLESS a Duluth, Missabe and Iron Range Railroad station and a Great Northern Railway station in section 16, Great Scott Township (T. 58N, R. 19W).

WARREN MINE SPUR a Great Northern Railway station in section 10, Stuntz Township (T. 57N, R. 21W).

WEBB LINE JUNCTION a Great Northern Railway station for the Webb Mine, located in section 6 of Stuntz Township (T. 57N, R. 20W).

WEBSTER a Duluth, Missabe and Iron Range Railroad station; location not found.

WEGGUM MINE a Hibbing mine with a Great Northern Railway station in section 6, Stuntz Township (T. 57N, R. 20W).

WEIMER see SPARTA.

WENTWORTH a Duluth, Winnipeg and Pacific Railway station; location not found.

WEST DULUTH a village in sections 4, 5, and 6 of Oneota Township, which had depots in section 7 and 17 serving the Duluth, Winnipeg and Pacific Railway, Northern Pacific Railroad, and Soo Line, and under the name West Duluth Junction in section 13; a post office operated 1889–1900; the village was annexed to Duluth on January 1, 1894.

WEST VIRGINIA a village in sections 12 and 13 of Nichols Township (T. 58N, R. 18W); the post office was transferred from Hopper and operated 1953–60; it had a Duluth, Winnipeg and Pacific Railway station.

WHEELING MINE a Virginia company mine with a Great Northern Railway station in section 1, Nichols Township (T. 58N, R. 18W).

WHITE TOWNSHIP (T. 57–59N, R. 15W) was named in honor of a mining captain on the Mesabi Range in the employ of the Kimberly Mining Company.

WHITEFACE a village in section 3 of Cotton Township (T. 54N, R. 16W) on the Whiteface River, formerly a Duluth, Winnipeg and Pacific Railway station; the Duluth, Missabe and Iron Range Railroad called the station White Face River.

WHITEFACE RESERVOIR, UNORGANIZED TERRITORY OF see UNORGANIZED TERRITORY OF WHITEFACE RESERVOIR.

WHITESIDE a junction and spur station of the Duluth, Missabe and Iron Range Railroad, in section 15, Great Scott Township (T. 58N, R. 19W).

WICK a place name in section 15, McDavitt Township (T. 56N, R. 18W), in 1911.

WILLOW VALLEY TOWNSHIP (T. 63N, R. 20W) needs no explanation of its name.

WILLS MINE SPUR a Duluth, Missabe and Iron

Range Railroad station in section 18, Biwabik Township.

WILPEN a village in sections 2 and 11 of Stuntz Township (T. 57N, R. 20W), had a Duluth, Missabe and Iron Range Railroad station and Wilpen Junction station of the Duluth, Missabe and Iron Range Railroad and Great Northern Railway. The post office operated 1910–42.

WINPON see WINTON.

WINSTON-DEAR STRIPPING a Great Northern Railway station in section 18, Stuntz Township (T. 57N, R. 20W).

WINTON a city in section 24 of Morse Township (T. 63N, R. 12W), incorporated as a village on July 23, 1901, reincorporated on April 6, 1906, and separated from the township on April 23, 1906; the post office began in 1895; it had a Duluth, Missabe and Iron Range Railroad station, also shown as Winpon. The village was named in honor of William C. Winton, a member of the Knox Lumber Company of Duluth, which did much logging around Ely and Winton. He was superintendent for building the first sawmill at Winton in 1898.

WISSACODE see BREDA.

WOLF a village in section 3 of Clinton Township, was developed at the site of a former station of the Duluth, Missabe and Iron Range Railroad.

WOODBRIDGE a Duluth, Missabe and Iron Range Railroad station in section 16, Great Scott Township (T. 58N, R. 19W).

WOODHULL a Duluth, Winnipeg and Pacific Railway station; location not found.

WOODHURST a post office, 1918–2; location not found.

WOODLAND a suburban area of Duluth.

WUORI TOWNSHIP (T. 49N, R. 17W) has a Finnish name, meaning "a mountain." The southwest part of this township has an exceptionally high and massive hill of the Mesabi Range, culminating in sections 25, 28, and 29, with its top about 2,150 feet above the sea, being the highest land in this county, 700 feet above the mining city of Virginia, three miles distant to the southwest.

WYMAN a village in section 3 of T. 58N, R. 14W, was named in honor of an old sea captain, George Wyman, who lived at Two Harbors.

YATES a Great Northern Railway station in section 11 of Great Scott Township (T. 58N, R. 19W).

ZENITH a dredge company spur and furnace

station of the Northern Pacific Railroad; location not found.

ZIM a community in section 27 of McDavitt Township (T. 56N, R. 18W), with a post office since 1899 and a former Duluth, Missabe and Iron Range Railroad station. The village is near the former site of the logging camp of a lumberman named Zimmerman.

––––––––––

Lakes and Streams

The foregoing pages contain notes of the St. Louis River, Alden Lake, Ash Lake, Canosia or Pike Lake, the Central Lakes, Dewey and Dinham Lakes, Dunka River, Embarrass River, the Fine Lakes, Floodwood River, French River, Grand Lake, Harris and Kelly Lakes, Midway Creek, Pike River, Prairie Lake and River, Wild Rice Lake, the West and East Two Rivers of Tower, Robinson Lake, Rush Lake, Sandy and Sand Lakes, Sturgeon River, and the large Vermilion Lake.

Vicinity of Duluth

Knife River, having its sources in Duluth Township, is the most eastern flowing into Lake Superior from this county. Its name is noted by Gilfillan as translated from Mokomani zibi of the Ojibwe.

Sucker River, next westward, is likewise a translation from the Ojibwe name, Namebini zibi.

French River, "R. des Français" of Owen's geological report in 1852, is called Angwassago zibi in the Ojibwe language, meaning Floodwood River, the aboriginal name being thus of the same significance with two tributaries of the St. Louis River.

Talmadge River, the next considerable stream westward, was named for Josiah Talmadge, a north shore pioneer at Clifton in 1856.

Lester River, named in honor of a pioneer, is called Busabika zibi by the Ojibwe, meaning "Rocky Canyon River, or the river that comes through a worn hollow place in the rock," as translated by Gilfillan. Its aboriginal name comes from its picturesque gorge in Lester Park. Amity Creek is tributary to it from the west.

Farther west, within the city limits of Duluth, are Tischers Creek, Chester Creek, Miller, Keene, and Kingsbury Creeks, Knowltons Creek, Stewart Creek, Sargents Creek, and Mission Creek. The last, flowing into St. Louis River at Fond du Lac, was named from the early mission there for the Ojibwe.

Miller Creek was named for Robert P. Miller, who enlisted from Duluth in the Fourth Minnesota Regiment in December 1861 and was promoted as first lieutenant in the Fiftieth U.S. Colored Infantry in 1863.

Kingsbury Creek was named in honor of William Wallace Kingsbury, who was born in Towanda, Pa., June 4, 1828, and died April 17, 1892. He settled in Endion (later a part of Duluth); was a member of the territorial legislature, 1855–56, and of the constitutional convention, 1857; was delegate to Congress from Minnesota Territory, 1857–58; later returned east.

On the Lake Superior shore are Knife Island, very small, and Granite Point, each about a quarter of a mile south from the mouth of Knife River; Stony Point and Sucker Bay, adjoining the mouth of Sucker River; Crystal Bay, a mile northeast from Lester River; and Minnesota Point, a very prolonged and somewhat broad sandbar beach reaching from the north shore near the center of Duluth about seven miles southeastward, which, with the similar but shorter Wisconsin Point, encloses the Duluth and Superior harbor, also known as the Bay of Superior. Through the base of this long point a ship canal was cut in 1871, which, with its lighthouse and the long piers built out into the lake, gives a protected and deep entrance to the harbor.

West of the main harbor are two shorter and wider sandbar points, namely, Rice's Point, before noted on the Minnesota side, and Connor's Point of Superior, Wis., which divide the harbor or Bay of Superior, from St. Louis Bay. Proceeding thence up the St. Louis River, one passes Grassy Point, the large Clough Island, Spirit Lake and its Spirit Island, Mud Lake, and Bear Island, before coming to Fond du Lac, Nekuk Island, and the foot of the long series of rapids and falls of the St. Louis River, which were passed in the former canoeing travel by a portage of seven miles to the head of these falls near Cloquet.

Along a distance of about six miles, from Thompson and Carlton nearly to Fond du Lac, the river flows in a rock-enclosed gorge, called the Dalles of the St. Louis, with frequent reaches of towering cliffs. It makes a descent of 400 feet, utilized by a canal and penstocks to supply water power for Duluth and to generate for the Twin Ports electric power, light, and heat. In the chapter of Chisago County, which has the Dalles of the St. Croix River, the derivation and significance of this French name have been previously noted.

Bays, Points, and Islands of Vermilion Lake

For Vermilion Lake Township the aboriginal origin and meaning of this name have been stated, being the same as for Red Lake.

In the *Fifteenth Annual Report* of the geological survey of Minnesota, for 1886, Prof. Newton H. Winchell presented a large map of Vermilion Lake, with the names of its many bays, points, and islands, noting for most of these features both the Ojibwe name and its translation. It will be sufficient here to note the translated names and to designate other names that are applied only by the white people, either on that map or in later maps and atlases.

Beginning at the east end of the lake and taking the names in their order from east to west, we have Armstrong River flowing into Bear Bay and Armstrong Bay, the river and bay being named for a white pioneer, who prospected for the Minnesota Iron Company; the large Bear Island, later named Ely Island in honor of Arthur Ely, like the city of this name; the very little Ant Island and Kid Island, respectively at the northwest side and west end of Ely Island; Stuntz Island, named, like a township, in honor of George R. Stuntz, at the entrance of Pelican Rock Bay, which has Stuntz Bay as its indented southern part; Beef Bay, and its western part called Jones Bay, names from white men, with Basswood and Birch Islands, the former called by the white men Whiskey Island; Hoo doo Point, projecting into the east part of Beef Bay, and Sucker Point, with the little Fish Island, the last two names being from the Ojibwe, at the north side of its entrance; Mission Bay, also called Sucker Bay, next west of Beef Bay, and Beef Lake, about two miles farther west, these being named from an Indian mission school and from provision used by mining and timber prospectors; Birch Point, three miles long and narrow, and Black Duck Point, the latter a wide peninsula of very irregular outline; Black Duck Bay and Tree Island; and Birch Bay, later called Frazer Bay.

The foregoing names belong to the southern side of the eastern and relatively broad two-thirds of Vermilion Lake. On the northern side of that part, in the same order from east to west, are the very little Newfoundland Island; Cedar Island, called Key Island by white people in allusion to its outline; Brush Bay and River; Spring and Rice Lakes, the latter connected by a very narrow strait, a mile long, with the main lake; Pine Island, six miles long, of very irregular form, having a Narrows north of its east end, a little portage crossing an isthmus of this island, and Porcupine Bay and Island north of its western part; Bear Trap Creek, a mile west of the Narrows; Trout River, Short Portage, at its rapids, and the large Trout Lake, with Pine Island in its northern part; Silver Island, at the northeast side of Birch or Frazer Bay; and Menan Island, the most eastern in a series of five islands on the north side of Birch Bay.

Advancing northward and westward beyond Birch or Frazer Bay, one passes Avis Island, nearly two miles long, named for a daughter of Prof. N. H. Winchell; Birch River or Narrows and Oak Island, coming to Outlet Bay and the rapids in the Vermilion River at the mouth of this lake; Bear Narrows, leading into the West Bay; Farm Island, named from its cultivation by the Ojibwe, at the center of this bay; Long Bay, its northeast arm; Partridge Bay on the north, connected by a long strait, called the Partridge River, with the West Bay; and Big Island, Little Farm Island, Little Sucker River, and Sturgeon Portage, at the west end of the lake.

The map of Maj. Stephen H. Long's expedition, in 1823, gives the name of Vermilion Lake as if it were on or very near the international boundary; Nicollet mapped it somewhat correctly; and the map of Owen's survey, published in 1852, shows both the lake and the inflowing Pike River, which it calls Vermilion River, a name later restricted to the outflowing stream.

On a later map of Vermilion Lake by Prof. N. H. Winchell, in the *Final Report* of the geological survey (vol. 4, 1899), the same nomenclature is presented as in 1886, excepting omission of minor details and insertion of Wakemup's village on the southwest shore of West Bay.

A very large drafted map of the county, used in the office of the county auditor, agrees with the atlas of the state published in 1916 by designating the several broad parts of Vermilion Lake, in order from east to west, as Armstrong Bay, east of Ely Island; Pike Bay, close west of Tower, formerly called Beef Bay, into which the Pike River flows; Big Bay, the main broad body of the lake; Daisy Bay, next northwest of the very long and narrow Birch Point; Frazer Bay, called Birch Bay by the Ojibwe; Niles Bay, also known as Outlet Bay; and Wakemup Bay, formerly called West Bay. Armstrong, as before noted, was a mining prospector; Frazer Bay commemorates the late John Frazer of Duluth, who was a timber explorer or cruiser; and Wakemup was the anglicized name of an Ojibwe leader, Way-ko-mah-wub, a signer of the treaty in 1889, whose village was at the southwest side of that western bay.

Other changes from Winchell's map in 1886 are found in the atlas of 1916, including Lost Lake, instead of Beef Lake, two miles west of Mission Bay; Hillsdale Island, instead of Avis Island; Norwegian Bay, for the Long Bay of the Ojibwe, branching off northeast from Wakemup Bay; and Black Bay, for Partridge Lake and River, the long northern arm of Wakemup Bay. Here immigrants from Norway and the dark, peat-stained water have given the newer names last noted.

Railway advertising pamphlets claim 365 islands in Vermilion Lake, counting many formed by rock ledges, very small in area.

The International Boundary

Lakes and streams, flowing westward to Rainy Lake, were traversed by the former canoe route on the boundary of St. Louis County in the following order from east to west as described by Sir Alexander Mackenzie in his "General History of the Fur Trade from Canada to the Northwest" (forming a part of his *Voyages from Montreal . . . in the Years 1789 and 1793*).

Crooked Lake, adjoining also the northwest corner of Lake County, is translated from its old French name, Croche, meaning "crooked, bent," given by the early voyageurs and traders in allusion to its exceedingly irregular outlines. Next was the Portage de Rideau, meaning Curtain Portage, 400 paces long, named "from the appearance of the water, falling over a rock of upwards of thirty feet." About three miles farther, after crossing the similarly very irregular Iron Lake, the canoemen passed over the Flacon Portage, meaning a flagon

or decanter, hence translated as Bottle Portage, "which is very difficult, is 400 paces long, and leads to the Lake of La Croix [the Cross], so named from its shape."

Thence the route on Lac la Croix, for nearly 30 miles, was first northward, next a long distance westward, and at last southward, to the Portage la Croix, 600 paces long. Beyond are the Loon Lake and River, the latter also called Little Vermilion River, reaching about four miles to the Little Vermilion Lake, narrow and riverlike, "which runs six or seven miles north-northwest, and by a narrow strait communicates with Lake Namaycan [also spelled Namekan or Nemeukan, an Ojibwe word, meaning Sturgeon], which takes its name from a particular place at the foot of a fall, where the natives spear sturgeon."

Sand Point Lake, as named on later maps, and Lake Namekan, connected by a winding and riverlike strait, having a descent of only a few inches, were described by Mackenzie as a single lake, spelled by him Namaycan. Thence the descent to Rainy Lake is nine feet, at the Chaudiere Falls and Portage, which is the French name given to the fall, meaning "a great boiling kettle." The preferred canoe route, however, passed westward a few miles on Lake Namekan and thence crossed the Nouvelle or New Portage as a more expeditious route to Rainy Lake.

Early maps by Long, Nicollet, Owen, and Alfred T. Andreas, from 1823 to 1874, note Namekan or Sturgeon Lake as reaching far west toward the Black Bay, near the west end of Rainy Lake, but on later maps the western half of this irregular and partly constricted body of water bears another Ojibwe name, Kabetogama Lake, meaning, as defined by Gilfillan, "the lake that lies parallel or double, namely with Rainy lake." David Thompson, in 1826, mapped this western part as "Lac Travere" (probably meant for Travers) and the east part as "Lake Nemeukan." The French name, "Travere" or Travers, which may be translated as "abreast or alongside," referred doubtless to the aboriginal name, Kabetogama.

Within the half of Rainy Lake that borders St. Louis County, it is nearly divided in two by the "Grande Detroit," as named on Thompson's boundary map in 1825–26, meaning the Great Strait. The part of the lake east of this strait was mapped by Thompson with the aboriginal name

"Wapesskartagar or Rainy lake," which is not found in Baraga's *Dictionary*. The larger part west of the strait is designated by his map as "Koocheche sakahagan or Rainy lake," for which a full consideration has been presented in the chapter of Koochiching County.

Returning to the northeast corner of this county, we need to note that it borders on the western part of Hunter Island, a large tract of Canada, as before explained in the chapter for Lake County.

Adjoining the Flacon or Bottle Portage, a very large island on the Canadian side of the southeast part of Lac la Croix is called Shortiss Island by the 1916 atlas, but it was named Irving Island on the map of St. Louis County in the *Final Report* of the Minnesota geological survey. Next northwestward this lake has Coleman Island, about four miles long and irregularly branched, on the Minnesota side of the boundary.

For this large and very diversified lake, named La Croix by the French, "from its shape," the map by Thompson, in 1826, gives also an Ojibwe name, Nequawkaun, spelled Nequowquon on recent maps, which seems to be the same word as Negwakwan, defined by Baraga as "a piece of wood put in the incision of a maple tree" (apparently the spout to collect sap for sugar-making). Throughout northern Minnesota the Ojibwe, according to Thomas Clark, commonly made much maple sugar at the time of sap-running each spring, averaging north of Lake Superior from 100 to 500 pounds for each lodge. A different name used by the Ojibwe people for this lake is given by Gilfillan, "Sheshibagumag sagaiigun, the lake where they go every which way to get through."

Loon Lake is translated from its Ojibwe name.

Gilfillan noted their name of the river north of Hunter Island, "Ga-wasidjiwuni zibi, or River shining with foam of rapids." This stream, the outlet of Lake Saganaga, lies in Canada; and the international boundary, following the canoe route, crosses a water divide between Saganaga and the Otter Track or Cypress Lake. Thereby Hunter Island, an area of about 800 square miles, is set off to Canada, although it lies south of the continuous watercourse from North and Saganaga Lakes to Rainy Lake.

Again the boundary, if it followed the natural water flow, instead of the established route of canoe travel, would lead from Lake la Croix by its outlet, Namekan River, more directly westward into Namekan Lake, instead of taking the circuitous course, easier for canoes, through Loon, Little Vermilion, and Sand Point Lakes, thus giving to Canada a tract of about 125 square miles south of the natural and uninterrupted watercourse. These and other features of our northern boundary are more fully noted in two papers by Dr. U. S. Grant and Prof. Alexander N. Winchell in the MHS Collections (8: 1–10 and 185–212, with a map at p. 40 [1898]).

Another very interesting historical paper, with references to early surveys by Thompson and his admirable detailed maps, published in 1898, is also included in the Collections (15: 379–92 [1915]), titled "Northern Minnesota Boundary Surveys in 1822 to 1826, under the Treaty of Ghent," by Hon. William E. Culkin of Duluth.

Bays, Points, and Islands of Rainy Lake

From a geological map of Rainy Lake by Horace V. Winchell and Dr. U. S. Grant (*Final Report*, Geol. of Minnesota, vol. 4, 1899, p. 192), the following names are noted.

Near Kettle Falls, between Namekan and Rainy Lakes, the latter lake has Tierney Point, Hale Bay, and a large Oak Point Island, these being on the Canadian side of the boundary.

Westward, along the Minnesota shore, are Lobstick Point, Rabbit Island, and Sand Narrows; a nameless coast for the next seven miles; then Big Island, the Pine Islands, Saginaw Bay, and Point Observe; Brule Narrows, which Thompson called "Grande Detroit," the newer French name Brule being given in allusion to adjacent burned woodlands; Cranberry Bay and Dryweed Island, which has its east extremity at the northwest corner of St. Louis County and reaches west three miles, beside the Itasca County shore.

In both Namekan and Kabetogama Lakes this map shows many islands, from the smallest size to a mile or more in length, including Big Pine Island in Kabetogama.

Other Parts of this County

There remain many other lakes and streams, to be additionally cataloged. The further names are arranged in the order of the townships from south to north, and of the ranges from east to west.

White Pine Creek flows from Canosia or Pike Lake, through Mud Lake, to the St. Louis River about a mile above Nagonab.

Lake Antoinette is in section 28, Rice Lake Township.

Caribou Lake, named for reindeer formerly frequent here, adjoins the west side of Canosia Township.

Close south of Grand Lake is the smaller Second Grand Lake, and the stream flowing thence west and north to the Cloquet River is named Grand Lake River.

Sunset Lake is in section 15, Industrial.

Cloquet River received this French surname on Nicollet's map in 1843, but 20 years earlier it was called Rapid River on the map of Long's expedition.

Artichoke River, joining the St. Louis River in Culver, is named from its wild artichokes, a sunflower species having tuberous roots, much used as food by the Indians, which is common or frequent throughout this state.

East Savanna River, having its mouth near Floodwood village, was a part of the canoe route from Lake Superior and the St. Louis River to the West Savanna River, Sandy Lake, and the upper Mississippi. The word *savanna*, more frequently used in Georgia and Florida, is of American Indian origin, meaning "a treeless area," and it is here applied to tracts of partly marshy grassland, over which the portage between the East and West Savanna Rivers was made.

Gnesen Township has Eagle Lake, named for nesting eagles, and Dalka, Jacobs, and Schultz Lakes, named for pioneer farmers.

Fredenberg has Cooks, Gibson, and Orchards Lakes, each named for a pioneer; and Beaver River, the outlet of Wild Rice Lake.

In New Independence Township are Artichoke or Benson Lake and Schelin Lake; and in Alborn are Crooked and Olson Lakes.

Ness has Spider Lake, probably named for its small tributary creeks, reminding one of the legs of a spider.

White Face River, joining the St. Louis in the east edge of Van Buren, was first mapped and named by Owen in 1852, the name being translated from the Ojibwe.

North Star has Alden, Barrs and Lieung Lakes, named for lumbermen and trappers.

The next township westward has Island Lake, on the Cloquet River, and Boulder and Thompson Lakes, the last being named for an early lumberman.

T. 53N, R. 15W, has Otter Lake and Boulder Creek, flowing southward to Cloquet River.

T. 53N, R. 16W, is crossed by Ushkabwahka River, and Leora Lake is in its northwest corner. The Ojibwe name of the river is translated by Gilfillan as "the place of the wild artichokes," being thus of the same meaning as another stream before noted, tributary to the St. Louis River.

Northland Township has Nichols Lake.

Pequaywan has a lake of the same name, an Ojibwe word of undetermined meaning.

Cotton has Witchel Lake, Bug Creek is there tributary to the White Face River, and Kaufit and Williams Lakes.

Sand Creek is a western tributary of the St. Louis River in Toivola.

Floodwood Lake, source of the river of this name, which was earlier noted, is in the west edge of this county in Cedar Valley.

Ault has Brown, White, and Stone Lakes.

T. 55N, R. 14W, has Sullivan Lake in sections 23 and 24.

T. 55N, R. 15W, has Comstock and Wasuk Lakes, the second being of small area in sections 17 and 18.

Ellsburg has Dinham Lake, which it gave also to the adjacent railway station.

The next township westward has Young Lake, and these townships are crossed by the Pale Face River, tributary to the White Face.

East Swan River, and its tributary, West Swan River, are translated from the Ojibwe name.

Faribanks has Wolf and Harris Lakes on its southern border, the latter giving its name to a railway station.

Linnwood Lake is in T. 56N, R. 14W.

Colvin has Markham Lake.

Next are Mud Hen Lake and Creek, and Long Lake, which outflows westward by the Water Hen River.

T. 56N, R. 17W, has in its southern half Elliott, Fig, Anchor, Murphy, and Stone Lakes. The singularly branched form of Anchor Lake suggested its name.

McDavitt has in its section 18 the St. Louis River that receives from the north two small tributaries, named the East and West Two Rivers.

Bassett has Bassett and Cadotte Lakes in its southwest corner, Pine Lake and Long Lake, which also has been called Jack Pine Lake, and Seven Beaver Lake, the principal head of the St. Louis River, named by the Ojibwe for beavers trapped or shot there; Big Lake, named Dead Fish Lake on Nicollet's map, but on some maps called Devil Fish Lake; also Swamp and Stone Lakes.

T. 57N, R. 16W, has Bass Lake in its sections 1 and 2.

Fayal Township, next west, has Ely Lake, which was formerly called Cedar Island Lake, St. Mary Lake, and Forbes Lake.

Clinton has Elbow Lake, named from its shape; and the next township has McQuade Lake.

Hibbing and its vicinity have Carson and Kelly Lakes, Lake Alice, and Carey Lake.

Partridge River, flowing through the lake of this name or Colby Lake, is a northern affluent of the St. Louis River; and Sunfish (Whitewater) Lake lies southwest of Partridge Lake.

Embarrass River, previously noticed, flows through a series of four long lakes, where it intersects the Mesabi Range, named Wine (Wynne), Embarrass, Cedar Island, and Esquagama Lakes, the first and second being translated from their Ojibwe names. The first, which is the most northern, is named Sabin Lake on several maps, but the people of the Mesabi mining range universally know it by the translation of its aboriginal name, given by Gilfillan as "Showiminabo, or Wine Lake, literally Grape-liquid Lake." The name of the second of these lakes, as of the river, comes through the French language of the former fur traders and voyageurs, referring to driftwood that obstructed parts of the river; and the fourth name, Esquagama, means "Last water or Last lake."

White and Leaf Lakes are on the west edge of Biwabik Township.

In the city of Virginia are Silver and Virginia Lakes.

Nichols (Mountain Iron) Township has Manganika and Mashkenode Lakes, Ojibwe names that need further inquiry for their meanings; and the first is also called on some maps Three Mile Lake.

Longyear Lake, at Chisholm, was named in honor of brothers superintending mines there.

T. 58N, R. 21W, has Rock, Day, and Moran Lakes.

T. 59N, R. 15W, has Little Mesaba Lake.

T. 59N, R. 20W, has Long Lake; and in French Township are Dewey, Island, Hobson, and Gansey Lakes.

In T. 60N, R. 13W, Iron Lake has been also called Thevot Lake.

Big Rice Lake is in Sandy Township, outflowing by Rice River to the South Branch of the Little Fork of Rainy River.

Sturgeon Lake, on the west line of the county, is the head of Sturgeon River, tributary to the Little Fork; and adjoining it on the east is Side Lake, named from its position.

In the townships numbered 61 are Birch Lake, Bear Island Lake, which is called Stuntz Lake on the map of this county by the Minnesota geological survey, Bear Head Lake, and Putnam Lake; the East and West Two Rivers, tributary to Vermilion Lake; and, in the west edge of the county, Bear River, flowing to Sturgeon River.

T. 62N, R. 12W, has White Iron Lake and One Pine Lake.

Eagle Nest Township has the Eagle Nest Lakes; Sand or Armstrong Lake, flowing west to Armstrong Bay of Vermilion Lake, before noted; and Mud Lake and Creek.

T. 63N, R. 12W, has Long (Shagawa) Lake, adjoining Ely.

Burntside Lake and River are translated from their Ojibwe name, referring to burned tracts of forest. The scenery of this lake, having more than 60 islands, was highly praised by Prof. Alexander Winchell.

T. 63N, R. 15W, has Pine and Crab Lakes, the last being named from the four arms or claws stretching out from its north side.

Trout Lake, of large area, has been noticed in connection with Vermilion Lake.

Next westward is Wolf Lake.

In T. 63N, R. 18W, Black Lake and Creek are tributary to Black Bay of Vermilion Lake, each being named from the peat-stained water.

Willow River and Beaver Creek flow westward to the Little Fork.

Elbow and Susan Lakes outflow by Elbow River, through Rice Lake, to the Pelican River at Glendale.

Pelican Lake and River are translated from

their Ojibwe name, given as Shetek on Owen's map in 1852, which also is the name of a large lake in Murray County.

т. 65N, R. 15W, has in its east part the Indian Sioux River, also called Loon River, which flows north to Loon Lake on the international boundary; and in its west part are Lakes Crellin and Jeanette.

Finstad Lake is in section 30, т. 65N, R. 16W; Olive Lake in sections 27 and 28, т. 65N, R. 17W; Kjostad and Myrtle Lakes are in т. 65N, R. 18W; Moose Lake, in sections 28 and 33, т. 65N, R. 19W; and Nett Lake, into which Lost River flows, is crossed by the west line of т. 65N, R. 21W, which is the county boundary.

The townships numbered 66 to 71, extending to the Canadian line, have many lakes, of which those along the boundary have been already noticed. Others bearing names on maps include Shell Lake, east of Loon River; Herriman and Echo Lakes, east of the Vermilion River; Crane Lake, through which that river flows near its mouth; Marion Lake in sections 16 and 17, т. 67N, R. 18W; Elephant and Black Duck Lakes in т. 66N, R. 19W; Ash Lake, at the railway station of that name, with Ash River running thence north to Kabetogama Lake; Long Lake and Moose Lake and River, tributary to Namekan Lake; Johnson and Little Johnson Lakes, flowing by the small Namekan River to the lake so named, before considered; and a little Net Lake in sections 4 and 9, т. 68N, R. 18W.

Hills, Mountains, and the Iron Ranges

The highest elevations in this county, popularly designated as "mountains," would be classed merely as hills in any really mountainous region. Furthermore, it must be noted that the so-called iron ranges are belts of land along which very great beds of iron ore have been found, comprising hills and ridges in parts of their course but in other large parts having no considerable height above the adjoining country on each side.

With topographic exaggeration, Schoolcraft in 1820 and again with Lieut. James Allen in 1832 called the belt of highland north and west of the west end of Lake Superior, adjoining the sites of Duluth and Fond du Lac, the Cabotian Mountains. This name was derived from Cabotia, applied by Joseph Bouchette, a French author, "to all

that part of North America lying north of the Great Lakes," in honor of John and Sebastian Cabot, father and son, who were the earliest making voyages of discovery to the mainland of this continent, in 1497 and 1498. The Dalles of the St. Louis River, before noted, are in the westward extension of this range, as mapped by Allen, but his delineation of its continuation farther west has no warrant in the land contour. Eastward from this river, the Cabotian Range may be regarded as continuous along all the northwest shore of Lake Superior in this state, since practically the same highland adjoins all the lake coast to the Sawtooth Mountains and Mt. Josephine in Cook County. Within the western limits of Duluth, about a mile west of Morgan Park, one of the hills of the range is called Bardon's Peak in honor of James Bardon, of Superior, Wis.

Grandmother Hill is in section 8, т. 57N, R. 13W.

Bald Mountain, merely a hill, is in section 23, т. 64N, R. 19W.

The Vermilion Iron Range, named from Vermilion Lake on its north side, has Sunset Peak in section 15, т. 63N, R. 12W, about two miles west of Winton; Chester Peak, three miles east of Tower, named in honor of Prof. A. H. Chester but often by error called Jasper Peak; and the North and South Ridges, respectively near Soudan and Tower.

Albert Huntington Chester, commemorated by Chester Peak, was born at Saratoga Springs, N.Y., November 22, 1843; was graduated at the Columbia School of Mines, 1868; was professor of chemistry, mineralogy, and metallurgy in Hamilton College, 1870–91, and later in Rutgers College; and died in 1903. For the Minnesota Iron Company in 1875, he made explorations of both the Mesabi and Vermilion Ranges, but his observations remained unpublished until 1884, when they were presented in the *Eleventh Annual Report of the Minnesota Geological Survey* for 1882 (pp. 154–67).

To work the Vermilion iron mines, the construction of the Duluth and Iron Range Railroad was completed to Tower in 1884 and to Ely in 1888. The first trainload of ore was taken from Tower to Two Harbors, the Lake Superior port of this railroad, in August 1884.

On the very productive central part of the

Mesabi Iron Range, the Mountain Iron mine was the first discovered, November 16, 1890, "by a crew of workmen under Capt. J. A. Nichols," for whom Nichols Township, including this mine, was named, as before noted. "In August 1891, the next large deposit was discovered by John McCaskill, Capt. Nichols, and Wilbur Merritt; this has since developed into the Biwabik group of mines. In 1892 two railroads were built to the range, and in 1893 the shipments amounted to 620,000 gross tons" (Horace V. Winchell, "Historical Sketch of the Discovery of Mineral Deposits in the Lake Superior Region," *Twenty-third Annual Report*, Minn. Geol. Survey, for 1894, pp. 116–55). More full description and history of this range are presented in "The Mesabi Iron-bearing District of Minnesota" by Charles K. Leith, this work being Monograph 43, U.S. Geol. Survey, 1903 (pp. 316, with maps and many other plates).

Nicollet mapped this highland range as "Missabay Heights," the earliest published form of the name, but Dr. Joseph G. Norwood, who explored the St. Louis, Embarrass, and Vermilion Rivers in 1848 for Owen's geological survey, wrote it "Missabé Wachu, or 'Big Man Hills,' which form a portion of the dividing highlands between the waters of Hudson's Bay and Lake Superior." Gilfillan noted the Ojibwe name as "Missabe wudjiu or Giant mountain," in which spelling the final *e* is to be pronounced with the English sound of long *a*, as if having the accent given by Norwood, being thus equivalent to Nicollet's spelling. Chrysostom Verwyst, in his later list of Ojibwe geographic names, uses the same orthography, and both these lists copy the spelling of Baraga's *Dictionary*, published in 1880, which defines this word as "Giant; also, a very big stout man." Gilfillan added the following note in his list: "Missabe is a giant of immense size and a cannibal. This is his mountain, consequently the highest, biggest mountain."

But the spelling used by Norwood, Baraga, Gilfillan, and Verwyst, having a final *e* sounded as in French and other European languages, is apt to be mispronounced by American and English readers, who would in analogy with the usage of our language pronounce Messabe in two syllables, with *a* as in fate or babe. Although the Duluth, Missabe and Northern Railway compa-

ny adopted that form, as also the township of Missabe Mountain, while another township makes it Mesaba, the Minnesota and U.S. geological surveys use the preferable form of Mesabi, which readers will surely pronounce in three syllables. Yet they must by analogy give to the last syllable the short sound of *i*, as in Mississippi, whereas Nicollet's spelling is strictly in accordance with the Ojibwe pronunciation, requiring the final syllable to be sounded as *bay*. More satisfactory would be Missabi, if we should not fully follow the spelling by Nicollet, for then the name would show its meaning, great, like Mississippi, Great River.

Henry H. Eames, state geologist of Minnesota in 1865–66, wrote this name as Missabi Wasju; and Col. Charles Whittlesey, in his report on the "Mineral Regions of Minnesota" published in 1866, set the example of spelling it as "the Mesabi Range."

Several references along this range to mountainous heights attained in portions of its extent, including Mesaba (that is, Giant), Wuori, and Missabe Mountain Townships and the village of Mountain Iron, would seem to imply greater altitudes than from 200 to 300 feet above the average of the adjoining region, up to the exceptional 700 feet in Wuori above Virginia city. Such ridges and hills, however, are noteworthy only in comparison with the relatively slight elevations found generally throughout this state.

Marginal Moraines and Glacial Lakes

In the series of 12 successive marginal moraines formed along the borders of the continental ice sheet at pauses that slackened or interrupted its final melting, the latest two are well exhibited on or near the iron ore ranges. Thence they are named the Mesabi or Eleventh and the Vermilion or Twelfth Moraines.

Contemporaneous with the wavering retreat of the ice border, the basins of the Red and Rainy Rivers and of Lake Superior were filled by great ice-dammed lakes, called glacial lakes. Prof. N. H. Winchell, the state geologist, reviewed the evidences of these glacial lakes, enumerating 26 for this state, in a paper read before the Geological Society of America and published in its bulletin (vol. 12, 1901, pp. 109–28, with a map).

Within the basin of Lake Superior and lying

partly in the area of St. Louis County, the list includes Lake Upham, first described and named in 1901 (*Final Report*, Geology of Minnesota, vol. 6, pl. 66), which had an estimated extent of about 1,000 square miles in the St. Louis basin, outflowing past Sandy Lake to the Mississippi; and Lakes St. Louis, Nemadji, and Duluth, flowing to the St. Croix River, the first two by way of Carlton County and the Kettle River, and the last by the Brule River in Wisconsin to the Upper St. Croix Lake and River. Lakes St. Louis and Nemadji received their names from the present rivers, of which the latter, emptying into Lake Superior in the city of Superior, was called Nemadji by the Ojibwe, meaning Left Hand, because in entering Superior Bay, west of the Wisconsin and Minnesota Points, which enclose the harbor, that stream was on the left hand, the St. Louis River being on the right.

The basin of Lake Winnipeg held a much larger glacial lake, named Lake Agassiz in 1879, described most fully in the U.S. Geological Survey Monograph 25 (1896, 658 pp., with many maps and other plates). In the *Twenty-second Annual Report* of the Minnesota survey, for 1893, this ancient lake was mapped as reaching eastward, during its highest stage on the international boundary, to the west part of Hunter Island. By the recent fieldwork and map of Frank Leverett and Frederick W. Sardeson for the Minnesota and U.S. geological surveys, published in 1917, the highest shore of Lake Agassiz is traced eastward in the Little Fork valley nearly to the middle of the south side of Vermilion Lake. Other observations by Prof. N. H. Winchell imply that this glacial lake stood about 10 or 15 feet above the level of Vermilion Lake (*Final Report*, Geology of Minn., vol. 4, 1899, p. 523). Hence we know that it must have extended east along the boundary to Knife and Otter Track Lakes, on the southeast side of Hunter Island, if the ice sheet there was melted away before Lake Agassiz receded from its highest stage.

Between its mouth, at Lakes Traverse and Big Stone, and Vermilion Lake, in a distance of 240 miles, the old lake level at its highest or Herman stage shows now an ascent from 1,050 to 1,370 feet above the sea, or an average gradient of one foot and a third per mile. In other words, since the time of the Herman level of the glacial lake, this area in northern Minnesota has been differentially uplifted or tilted, giving now to the highest and earliest lake beach an ascent of 320 feet in 240 miles from southwest to northeast.

Indian Reservations

By a treaty at La Pointe, Wis., September 30, 1854, the Ojibwe ceded to the United States a great tract in northeastern Minnesota, including Cook and Lake Counties and the greater part of St. Louis County, reaching west to the St. Louis, East Swan, and Vermilion Rivers. Less than a year later, in a treaty at the city of Washington, February 22, 1855, they ceded lands farther west and southwest, from the St. Louis and East Swan Rivers to the Red River, Otter Tail Lake, and Crow Wing River; and in another treaty at Washington, April 7, 1866, the Ojibwe lands of northwestern St. Louis County and eastern Koochiching County were ceded, excepting the Bois Forte Reservation, including and surrounding Nett Lake. This reservation, more fully noticed under Koochiching County, reaches three miles into the west edge of St. Louis County, with an extent of 12 miles from north to south.

The Fond du Lac Reservation, in St. Louis and Carlton Counties, was provided under the treaty of La Pointe in 1854, comprising a tract on the southwest side of the St. Louis River, reaching from Cloquet, Nagonab, and Brevator, west nearly to the middle of Range 19.

Latest provided, by an executive order of the president, December 20, 1881, the Vermilion Lake Reservation, which is part of the Bois Forte Reservation, comprises only about two square miles, being an irregular tract between Pike Bay and Mission or Sucker Bay, between two and four miles west of Tower.

Parks and Forests

Voyageurs National Park, named for the canoemen of the fur trade, contains about 55 miles of the old fur-trade route between the Great Lakes and the continent's interior. Established in 1975, it is the only national park without a road.

In the chapters for Cook and Lake Counties, the large area of the Superior National Forest has been previously considered, with the date, February 13, 1909, when its earliest part was reserved by the U.S. government for forestry uses. From western Cook County this public forest area crosses north-central Lake County, and it continues halfway across northeastern St. Louis County, to Echo Lake and nearly to the Vermilion River.

This county also contains large parts of the Boundary Waters Canoe Area Wilderness, for which see Cook County.

Residents of the Mesabi Iron Range had been picnicking and camping on the land in French Township that became McCarthy Beach State Park for years before 1943, when its owner, John A. McCarthy, died and the property was sold to a lumberman. Local people called for the purchase of the land and the establishment of a state park, which was accomplished in 1945.

Bear Head Lake State Park, T. 61N, R. 14W, established in 1961, provides recreational opportunities in a landscape much like the Boundary Waters Canoe Area Wilderness, not far to the north.

Soudan Underground Mine State Park, originally known as Tower Soudan State Park, was established in 1965 after United States Steel donated the mine, its equipment, and surrounding forested lakeshore land to the state for this purpose. Visitors descend a half a mile into the earth to tour the mine's workings and learn about underground mining on the Vermilion Iron Range.

Scott County

Established March 5, 1853, this county was named in honor of Gen. Winfield Scott, who was commander in chief of the U.S. Army from 1841 to 1861. He was born near Petersburg, Va., June 13, 1786, and died at West Point, N.Y., May 29, 1866; entered the army as a captain in 1808; served with distinction in the War of 1812 and was made a brigadier general and brevet major general in 1814; was chief commander in the Mexican War, 1847; and was an unsuccessful Whig candidate for president in 1852. General Scott visited Fort St. Anthony in the spring of 1824 for inspection of its construction, then completed, and on his recommendation its name was changed to Fort Snelling by a general order of the war department, January 7, 1825.

Information of names was gathered in History of the Minnesota Valley *(1882), having pp. 290–351 for Scott County; and from Nicholas Meyer, judge of probate since 1880, and William F. Duffy, clerk of the court, interviewed at Shakopee, the county seat, during a visit there in July 1916.*

ALBRIGHT see BLAKELEY.

AVA see HELENA.

BADEN/BADDEN see MUDBADEN.

BARDEN a settlement in section 12, Eagle Creek Township, was first named Sibley for Henry H. Sibley and had a Sibley station of the Sioux City and St. Paul Railroad under that name; it was then named Long Lake for a nearby lake; it received its present name in 1885 in honor of J. W. Barden, "who was largely interested in grain elevators and other business enterprises here and hereabouts" (Stennett, *Place Names of the Chicago and Northwestern Railways*, 1908, p. 167).

BEAVER a site on the Minnesota River noted in an 1857 law that granted ferry rights to James B. Sly and Aaron R. Russell of that place.

BELLE FONTAINE a post office, 1857–65; location not found.

BELLE PLAINE TOWNSHIP first settled in 1852–53, and its village founded in 1854, were named by Hon. Andrew G. Chatfield, an associate justice of the supreme court of Minnesota Territory, who settled here in 1854. It is a French name, meaning "beautiful plain." The city of Belle Plaine, in Belle Plaine and St. Lawrence Townships, was incorporated as a borough on March 5, 1868; it has had a post office since 1854, the first postmaster being Edward P. Berry on his section 7 farm of Belle Plaine Township.

BENEDICT see ST. BENEDICT.

BLAKELEY settled in 1853 and established as a township by a legislative act, March 9, 1874, received the name of its railway village, founded in 1867 by Elias F. Drake and I. N. Dean, by whom it was named in honor of Capt. Russell Blakeley, who was born in North Adams, Mass., April 19, 1815, and died in St. Paul, February 4, 1901. His connection with steamboating from Galena to St. Paul began in 1847, and he continued in it, as clerk and afterward as captain and traffic manager, during many years. Later he engaged in staging and expressing in Minnesota and Dakota and had large interests in banking, insurance, and railway companies. He settled in St. Paul in 1862. He was president of the Minnesota Historical Society in 1871 and vice-president from 1876 until his death and contributed to its Collections the "History of the Discovery of the Mississippi River and the Advent of Commerce in Minnesota" (8: 303–418 [1898], with his portrait and 11 plates of early steamboats). A biographic sketch of him is in these Collections (9: 665–70 [1901]).

The village in section 8 was shown on Joseph S. Sewall's 1857 map as Albright and was incorporated as a village under that name on May 19, 1857; it had a post office, 1868–1966, and developed with a creamery, a brickyard, a sawmill, and a station of the Chicago, St. Paul, Minneapolis and Omaha Railroad.

BRENTWOOD a village site platted in September 1860, was united with Jordan when that place was incorporated as a village in 1872. A station named Brentwood of the St. Paul and Sioux City Railroad was located in west section 12 of St. Lawrence Township.

CEDAR LAKE a village in section 22 of Credit Lake Township; the post office operated 1857–1903.

CEDAR LAKE TOWNSHIP settled in 1855 and organized April 11, 1858, was named from the lake crossed by its west line, having red cedar trees on its shores.

CREDIT RIVER TOWNSHIP settled in 1854 and organized in 1858, bears the name of the stream flowing through it, called Credit or Erakah River on Joseph N. Nicollet's map in 1843. Twenty years earlier it was named Elk Creek on the map of Maj. Stephen H. Long's expedition. The village in section 19 had a creamery, a blacksmith, a station of the Chicago, Milwaukee and St. Paul Railroad, and a post office, 1884–1903.

DOOLEYVILLE a post office, 1861–65 and 1868–70; location not found.

EAGLE CREEK TOWNSHIP first settled by Rev. Samuel W. Pond in the fall of 1847, was organized in 1858, receiving the name of a creek, which has its source in Pike Lake, in section 23, and flows northeastward to the Minnesota River. A village named Eagle Creek was incorporated on May 19,

1857; no trace remains, but it was probably in Eagle Creek Township.

EIDSWOLD a village in section 25 of New Market Township, with a post office, 1896–1902.

ELKO a city in section 27 of New Market, has a name that is also borne by villages in Virginia, South Carolina, and Georgia and by a county and its county seat in Nevada. It was incorporated as a village on October 25, 1949; the post office began in 1907; it had a station of the Chicago, Milwaukee and St. Paul Railroad.

GLENDALE TOWNSHIP first settled in the spring of 1852, has a name borne by villages in Massachusetts, Ohio, Wisconsin, and 14 other states. See also SAVAGE.

GRAINWOOD a village in section 35 of Eagle Creek Township, which had a hotel and a post office for a brief period, July-September 1905; also noted on maps as Grainwood Park and associated with the resort area of Prior Lake; it had a station of the Chicago, Milwaukee and St. Paul Railroad.

GREENWOOD is the name of a railway station, with a village mainly consisting of summer homes, between Prior and Long Lakes, in the south edge of Eagle Creek Township.

HAMILTON STATION see SAVAGE.

HELENA TOWNSHIP first settled in 1854, organized May 12, 1858, and the railway station on its north line, bear the name of an earlier village platted in 1856 on section 11 by John C. Smith. It is the name also of the capital of Montana, a city in Arkansas, and villages in eight other states. A post office in the township was first known as Ava 1857–58, with Calendar W. Peutherer as postmaster there and later in Lydia; the name changed to Helena in 1858 and discontinued in 1904.

HILLTOP a station of the Minneapolis and St. Louis Railroad in Sand Creek Township.

JACKSON a township of small area, adjoining the city of Shakopee, was first settled in the spring of 1851 and was organized May 11, 1858. It was called Shakopee Township until the incorporation of the city, when the remaining part of the township was renamed Jackson by a legislative act, January 17, 1871. Like many counties, townships, villages, and cities throughout the United States, it was probably named in honor of Pres. Andrew Jackson (1767–1845).

JOEL a village in Blakeley Township, had a post office, 1899–1903, located in August C. Schmidt's general store, which also served as a saloon, a telephone exchange, and a dance hall; a creamery was built in 1897 by the Milton Dairy of St. Paul; the creamery and the store discontinued in 1917.

JORDAN a city in sections 18, 19, 20, and 30 of Sand Creek Township, platted by Thomas A. and William Holmes in 1854, established in 1856 with the opening of the Sand Creek post office, incorporated as a village February 26, 1872, and as a city March 11, 1891, was named by William Holmes for "the River Jordan in Palestine. The name was given at the end of a somewhat angry and prolonged discussion amongst the citizens as to what the name should be" (Stennett, *Place Names of the Chicago and Northwestern Railways*, p. 180). Sawmill owner William Holmes was postmaster; he was born in 1853 in Ohio, died in 1873, and was the brother of Thomas Holmes of Shakopee. The post office name changed to Jordan in 1872; it had a station of the Minneapolis and St. Louis Railroad.

KEATINGS CROSSING a station of the Chicago, Milwaukee and St. Paul Railroad, was located in sections 8 and 17 of Credit River Township.

LASHEEN a way-station post office established as New Dublin, 1856–71, and Lasheen, 1871–81, located ten miles southeast of Shakopee.

LAWRENCE a village in section 16 of St. Lawrence Township, was incorporated as a village on July 27, 1858, but later unincorporated. The post office, established as St. Lawrence, 1857–79, was named to honor John Lawrence, an early settler; in 1901 the name was shortened to Lawrence; it had a station of the Chicago, St. Paul, Minneapolis and Omaha Railroad.

LIBERTY a post office, 1872–81, in section 34 of Spring Lake Township, near Lake Cynthia.

LISHEEN a place name shown as a post office in section 8 of Credit River Township in the 1874 Andreas atlas.

LOUISVILLE TOWNSHIP named like its former village for the large city of Louisville in Kentucky, the previous home of H. H. Spencer, who settled here in 1853, was originally a part of Shakopee, from which it was set off April 13, 1858. The village of Louisville, platted in 1854, grew well during four or five years, until it had 30 houses or more, but within a few years later its buildings were mostly removed to Carver or were torn down, and the site became farming land. A post office, called Yank-

ton for a period, August 1857-February 1858, was located in Louisville Township, 1855–61.

LYDIA a village in section 29 of Spring Lake Township, had a post office, 1861–1903, begun in the home of Calendar W. Peutherer, who had earlier been Ava's postmaster.

MAPLE GLEN see SPRING LAKE.

MARYSTOWN a village in sections 35 and 36 of Louisville Township, had a post office, 1866–69 and 1873–1903, and a station of the Chicago, St. Paul, Minneapolis and Omaha Railroad.

MERRIAM a proposed village of the St. Paul and Sioux City Railroad, platted in 1866 but abandoned in 1871, and the present station of Merriam Junction in Louisville, established in 1875, were named by Gen. Judson W. Bishop, chief engineer of this railroad, in honor of John L. Merriam, who was born in Essex, N.Y., February 6, 1825, and died in St. Paul, January 12, 1895. He came to Minnesota in 1860, settling in St. Paul, where he engaged with J. C. Burbank and Capt. Russell Blakeley in the staging and expressing business. He helped to organize the First National Bank and the Merchants' National Bank of St. Paul and was president of the latter. In 1870–71 he was a representative in the legislature, being speaker of the house.

A village called Merriam was in section 28 of Louisville Township and had a post office, 1872–73 and 1879–1905; it was also shown on maps as Sioux City Junction; it had a station of the Minneapolis and St. Louis Railroad.

MOUNT PLEASANT a post office, 1856–57, in section 1 of Spring Lake Township.

MUDBADEN a site in section 8 of Sand Creek Township, one mile north of Jordan, was noted for its sulfur springs and spas. A post office operated 1922–51; it had a station of the Chicago, St. Paul, Minneapolis and Omaha Railroad.

MURPHY'S LANDING a ferry landing site, is presently a settlement reconstruction of the 1840–80 period under the guidance of the Scott County Historical Society, known as the Minnesota Valley Restoration Project. The site has a fur trader's cabin, 1850 and 1880 farms, an Indian village, a pond and gristmill, an 1880 townsite, and an interpretive center.

NEW DUBLIN see LASHEEN.

NEW MARKET TOWNSHIP settled in the spring of 1856, was at first named Jackson, when it was organized in May 1858, but it was renamed at the election held October 12, 1858. The name is thought to have been adopted from the town of New Market near Cambridge in England, famous for its horse races. Thirteen other states have villages of this name. The city in sections 20, 21, and 28 was incorporated as a village on August 28, 1895; the post office began in 1867.

NEW PRAGUE founded in 1856, incorporated as a village March 1, 1877, and as a city April 4, 1891, was named for the ancient city of Prague, the capital of Bohemia (Czech Republic), whence many of its first colony of settlers came. This city lies, in about equal parts, in Scott and Le Sueur Counties; the main street, running east and west, is on the county line. See also entry in the chapter of Le Sueur County.

NORTH HENDERSON a townsite platted in the 1850s in Blakeley Township.

PLUM CREEK a post office, 1873–87, in section 25 of Cedar Lake Township, at Robert Gardner's farm.

PORT CARGILL a settlement at Savage on the Minnesota River, with a station of the Minneapolis, Northfield and Southern Railroad.

PRIOR LAKE a city in sections 1 and 2 of Spring Lake Township, near the lake so named, was platted in 1875, taking the name of a post office that had been established in 1872. It was incorporated as a village on February 11, 1891, and reincorporated on June 1, 1921. The area was first settled in the 1850s and developed in 1871 with the Chicago, Milwaukee and St. Paul Railroad routing through the area. The lake, post office, and village, thus successively named, are in honor of Charles H. Prior of Minneapolis, who in 1871–86 was superintendent of the Minnesota divisions of the Chicago, Milwaukee and St. Paul Railroad and from 1886 was a dealer in real estate. He was born in Norwich, Conn., August 1, 1832; he studied at Oberlin College and Ohio State University.

RAVEN STREAM a post office, 1864–1903, in section 36 of Belle Plaine Township and named for the stream in section 3 of Helena Township, was first located on the farm of Leonard Rech; the rural services combined with Union Hill in 1940.

ST. BENEDICT a community in sections 17 and 20 of Helena Township with a post office, 1873–80; it was later named Benedict, 1896–1903.

ST. LAWRENCE TOWNSHIP first settled in 1854, was organized May 11, 1858. Its village, platted in the fall of 1858, was all vacated for farming uses before 1882. New York has a county and a village of this name, which also is borne by villages and townships in five other states, derived from the river and gulf of St. Lawrence. The name was first applied by Jacques Cartier to a bay at the north side of the gulf, August 10, 1536, this being the festal day of St. Lawrence, who suffered martyrdom on August 10, 258. See also LAWRENCE.

ST. PATRICK a village in sections 17 and 18 of Cedar Lake, with a station of the Minneapolis and St. Louis Railroad; the post office operated 1874–1903, with Patrick O'Flynn as first postmaster in his general store.

SAND CREEK TOWNSHIP was first named Douglass at its organization, May 11, 1858, but in September it was changed to St. Mary and in December to Jordan. The present name was adopted at the annual town meeting, April 5, 1859, being taken from the stream that flows through this township and supplies water power at Jordan. It was mapped by Nicollet as "Batture aux fieves," meaning "shallow, with fevers." Next on the map of Minnesota dated January 1, 1860, it is called Fever River and also has a Dakota name, Chankiyata River, of undetermined meaning, while a settlement near the site of Jordan is named Sand Creek. Numerous outcrops of soft white sandstone occur there, whence the stream and township were named. See also JORDAN.

SANTOR a station of the Chicago, St. Paul, Minneapolis and Omaha Railroad in Sand Creek Township.

SAVAGE a city in the northeast corner of Glendale, incorporated as a village on November 7, 1892, and separated from the township on March 5, 1920, after being called Hamilton during many years, was renamed in honor of Marion Willis Savage, who here owned a horse-training farm, with a covered track for practice in racing. He was born near Akron, Ohio, March 26, 1859; removed to Minneapolis in 1886 and engaged in manufacture of stock foods; purchased the world's champion racing horse Dan Patch for $60,000 in 1902; constructed the Dan Patch Electric Line railway from Minneapolis to Savage, Northfield, and Faribault; died in Minneapolis, July 12, 1916, on the next day after his famous horse died. The Dan Patch line soon afterward became insolvent, but in July 1918 it was purchased by a reorganized company, being renamed theMinneapolis, North-field and Southern Railroad.

The city was first named Hamilton by William Byrne, an Irishman who had immigrated to Hamilton, Canada, in 1840 before coming to Minnesota in 1855. The post office was called Hamilton Station, 1866–94, was changed to Glendale, and then to Savage in 1905. During World War II, a military intelligence school was established there, called Camp Savage.

SHAH-K'PAY see SHAKOPEE.

SHAKOPEE a city in Jackson and Eagle Creek Townships, the county seat, was founded by Thomas A. Holmes in 1851 as a trading post, to which he gave this name of the leader of a Dakota band living here. The village, platted in 1854, was incorporated as a city May 23, 1857, but surrendered its charter in 1861, returning to township government. It was incorporated as a village on March 1, 1866. It again received a city charter March 3, 1870, and the former township of Shakopee, excepting the city area, was renamed Jackson, as before noted, January 17, 1871. Holmes, born in Pennsylvania in 1804, is considered the "father" of Shakopee; he served in the 1849 territorial legislature and was influential in the community; he moved to Cullman, Ala., in 1878, where he died in 1888. The post office began in 1853 and was spelled Shah-k'pay until changed to the present spelling in 1857; Holmes was the first postmaster. The village had a station of the Chicago, Milwaukee and St. Paul and Chicago, St. Paul, Minneapolis and Omaha Railroads.

The Dakota name of their village here was Tintonwan, signifying "the village on the prairie," and Rev. Samuel W. Pond, who settled as their missionary in the adjacent edge of Eagle Creek Township in 1847, translated the native name as Prairieville.

Shakopee (or Shakpay, as it was commonly pronounced), meaning Six, was the hereditary name, like Wabasha, of successive leaders, in lineal descent from father to son. The first of whom we have definite knowledge is the Shakopee who was killed when running the gauntlet at Fort Snelling in June 1827, as related by Charlotte O. Van Cleve (*Three Score Years and Ten*, 1888, pp. 74–79). The second, who is commemorated by the name of this city, characterized by Samuel W. Pond, Jr., as "a man of marked ability in council and one of the ablest and most effective orators in the whole Dakota Nation," died in 1860. His son, who had been called Shakpedan (Little Six), born on the site of the city in 1811, became at his father's death the leader of the band, numbering at that time about 400. He was hanged at Fort Snelling, November 11, 1865, for his actions in the Dakota War of 1862.

SIOUX CITY JUNCTION see MERRIAM.

SPRING LAKE TOWNSHIP first settled in 1853, organized May 11, 1858, was named from "Spring lake, a large and beautiful body of water, situated in the northern part of the town, which in turn derives its name from a large spring tributary to it" (*History of the Minnesota Valley*, p. 341). A village named Spring Lake was in sections 3 and 4, with a post office called Maple Glen 1861–95, and Mapleglen, 1895–1903.

SUEL a post office, 1874–87, located in Credit River Township, about four miles from Prior Lake, with blacksmith Peter Barbeau as first postmaster; the site was settled in 1857 and had a sawmill and a hotel.

UNION HILL a post office in section 25 of Belle Plaine Township, which was established in 1876 in Le Sueur County, transferred to Scott County in 1883 and discontinued in 1903.

YANKTON see LOUISVILLE.

Lakes and Streams

At the Little Rapids, in the north part of the southeast quarter of section 31, Louisville, the Minnesota River has a descent of two feet, very nearly, at its stage of low water, flowing across an outcrop of the Jordan sandstone. About a quarter of a mile up the river, which turns at a right angle between these points, there is another rapid, in the east part of the same quarter section, which at the lowest stage of water has a fall of one foot.

In the foregoing pages attention has been directed to the names of Cedar Lake, Credit River, Eagle Creek and Pike Lake, Prior Lake, Sand Creek, and Spring Lake.

Other lakes and streams to be noticed are arranged in the order of the townships from south to north and of the ranges from east to west.

New Market has Rice Lake, crossed by its east line, named from its wild rice.

Cedar Lake Township is crossed from southeast to northwest by Porter Creek, named for George Porter, a pioneer farmer there, which flows through Bradshaw and Mud Lakes. This township also has Ready's or Lennon Lake, in sections 11 and 12; O'Connor's Lake or Cedar Lake, in section 22; McMahon or Carl's Lake, St. Catherine Lake, and Cynthia Lake, on its north line; and Hickeys and Cedar Lakes at its west side.

Helena has Pleasant Lake and Raven Stream, a tributary of Sand Creek.

Belle Plaine had a Rice Lake, now drained, in the western section 25, and Brewery Creek joins the Minnesota River close east of the village.

From Blakeley the Minnesota River receives Robert Creek, named in honor of Capt. Louis Robert of St. Paul, who established a trading post on this creek in 1852; and Big and Little Possum Creeks, flowing through the village, but it seems doubtful that the geographic range of the opossum, common in the southern states, reaches into Minnesota. Clarks Lake, near the center of this township, has an outlet that flows southward into Le Sueur County and joins the Minnesota River at East Henderson. Though unnamed on later maps, this stream was called Abert River on Nicollet's map in 1843 in honor of Col. John James Abert, of the U.S. topographical engineer corps, under whose commission Nicollet conducted his surveys in the Northwest.

Credit River Township has Murphy Lake in sections 3 and 4, and Cleary Lake in section 7, the last being named for John, Peter, and Patrick Cleary, who settled here in 1855.

Spring Lake Township has Kane and Markley Lakes, crossed by its east line; Crystal and Rice Lakes in section 10 and 11; Fish Lake in sections 27 and 28; Spring, Prior, and Little Prior Lakes; and Campbell Lake in sections 5 and 6.

In Sand Creek Township are Geis and Sutton Lakes.

Glendale has Hanrahan Lake, named for a farmer, Edward Hanrahan, whose home was near its western end.

Eagle Creek Township has Prior and Spring Lakes. These two, connected by a strait, have been sometimes called Credit Lake, from the Credit River to which they have probably an underground flow. This township also has O'Dowd, Pike, Dean, Rice, Fisher, and Blue Lakes. O'Dowd Lake was named for three brothers, farmers near it; Dean Lake commemorates Matthew Dean, a settler who came there in 1855; and the last three lakes are on the bottomland of the Minnesota River.

Thole (or Haam) and Gifford (or Schneider) Lakes are in Louisville.

Strunk Lake, beside the Minnesota River in Jackson, was named in honor of H. H. Strunk, a nearby farmer, who afterward was a druggist in Shakopee.

Spirit Hill and Shakopee Prairie

The eastern part of a high terrace of the Minnesota valley drift, adjoining the Sand Creek at Jordan, was named Spirit Hill by the Dakota, who frequently held councils and dances there.

Another remnant of this valley drift is the plateau called the "Sand prairie," which lies a mile north of Spirit Hill.

Through Jackson and Eagle Creek Townships a similar but longer and wider valley drift terrace, 140 to 125 feet above the Minnesota River and nearly 100 feet below the crest and general expanse of the adjoining upland, has a width from a half mile to one and a half miles, with a length of about ten miles. All of this county was originally wooded, excepting much of the bottomland of the Minnesota valley and large parts of its terraces, such as those of Belle Plaine and near Jordan and this south of Shakopee, which last has therefore received the name of "Shakopee prairie."

Shakopee Mdewakanton Reservation

The Dakota in the Minnesota River valley negotiated treaties in 1837 and 1851 for sale of their land. Following the Dakota War of 1862, the people lost their reservation land in the upper Minnesota River valley. Beginning in 1887 the federal government bought land in the Prior Lake area for the returning Mdewakanton Dakota. The reservation consists of 1,500 acres northwest of Prior Lake.

State Park

As early as the 1930s the state recognized the value of having a state park in the Minnesota River valley. The Minnesota Valley State Recreation Area, established in 1969, fulfills that purpose. The park covers parts of Carver, Dakota, Hennepin, Le Sueur, Scott, and Sibley Counties, with administrative offices in Jordan. The park preserves the remains of the pioneer settlement of St. Lawrence, as well as the wildlife of the river valley wetlands.

Sherburne County

This county, established February 25, 1856, was named in honor of Moses Sherburne, who was an associate justice of the supreme court of Minnesota Territory from 1853 to 1857. He was born in Mount Vernon, Kennebec County, Maine, January 25, 1808; came to St. Paul in April 1853 and resided there 14 years, engaging in law practice after 1857; was one of the two compilers of the statutes of Minnesota, published in 1859; removed to Orono in Sherburne County, 1867, and died there, March 29, 1868.

An interesting biographic sketch of Judge Sherburne, with his portrait, was contributed by Rev. Simeon Mills Hayes in the MHS Collections (10: 863–66, pt. 2 [1905]). This paper includes special notice of his life and public services in Maine before coming to Minnesota. His professional and personal character is portrayed as follows: "Sher-burne was a successful lawyer from the beginning of his practice. His absolute integrity, imposing presence, accurate learning, and oratorical endowments drew clients from neighboring counties, and brought him almost immediately into prominence. Although never an office-seeker, his popularity and the general respect felt for his ability made him a recipient of public offices during the greater portion of his professional life. . . . When the Territory of Minnesota applied for admission to the Union as a state, Judge Sherburne took a prominent part in the deliberations which resulted in the adoption of the State Constitution, and his remarks during the Constitutional Convention are among the valuable original sources to which the future historian of Minnesota will apply for an insight into the problems and motives of the Fathers of the North Star State."

Information of the origin and meaning of geographic names has been gathered from History of the Upper Mississippi Valley *(1881), having pp. 294–339 for Sherburne County;* Fifty Years in the Northwest *by W. H. C. Folsom, noting this county in pp. 453–59; and from Charles S. Wheaton, attorney at Elk River since 1872, and Hiram H. Mansur, photographer, each being interviewed during a visit at Elk River, the county seat, in October 1916.*

BAILEY a village in section 25 of Big Lake Township, five miles west of Elk River, formerly having a station of the Great Northern Railway and Northern Pacific Railroad in section 26, was named in honor of Orlando Bailey, a pioneer farmer there. He was born in Chautauqua County, N.Y., in 1820; came to Minnesota in 1852, settling in this township; kept a stage station and hotel nine years; was the first sheriff of this county; and died in 1897; his son, Albert Bailey, was a probate judge. The village was also known as Baileys, Bailey Siding, and Bailey's Siding.

BALDWIN TOWNSHIP first settled in 1854 and organized September 13, 1858, received this name in honor of Francis Eugene Baldwin of Clear Lake Township. He was born in Wayne County, Pa., March 7, 1825; was graduated at Illinois College in 1846; was admitted to practice law in 1847; came to Minnesota in 1855 and resided in Minneapolis and at Clear Lake in this county; was the county attorney two years and owned a farm; was a state senator, 1859–60.

BECKER TOWNSHIP settled in 1855, organized in 1871, and its city in sections 31 and 32, founded in 1867, were named in honor of George Loomis Becker of St. Paul, for whom a biographic sketch has been presented in the chapter of Becker County. The township was divided into **BECKER NORTH TOWNSHIP**: T. 34N, R. 29W, sections 1, 2, 11–14, 23–26, and **BECKER SOUTH TOWNSHIP**: T. 33N, R. 28W. The city was platted on December 5, 1870, and incorporated as a village on November 22, 1904; the post office began as Pleasant Valley in 1866, changing to Becker in 1870; it had a station of the Great Northern Railway and Northern Pacific Railroad.

BENTON see CLEAR LAKE.

BIG LAKE TOWNSHIP settled in 1848, organized in 1858, and its city in sections 19, 20, and 30, at first called Humboldt, are named from the lake adjoining the village, a favorite place for picnics. Humboldt was the county seat until 1867, being succeeded by Elk River, and its name was changed to that of the township when the railroad was built in 1867. The village was incorporated on December 29, 1898; the post office began as Elk Prairie in 1854 while still part of Benton County, changing to Big Lake in 1855.

BLUE HILL TOWNSHIP settled in 1857 or earlier, organized March 20, 1877, had previously been a part of Baldwin. It has a lone hill of glacial drift in the northwest quarter of section 28, called the Blue Mound from its appearance when seen at a far distance, which rises about 75 feet above the surrounding flat plain of sand and gravel. The post office named Blue Hill was probably in the township, 1896–1902.

BRANTFORD a post office, 1857–71; location not found.

BRIGGS LAKE a village in section 22 of Palmer Township, with a post office, 1874–85; Caroline M. Briggs was first postmaster.

CABLE a village in section 21 of Haven Township across the Northern Pacific Railroad tracks from Haven, with a post office, 1884–92; Violetta Cable was first postmaster.

CLEAR LAKE TOWNSHIP settled in 1850, organized in 1858, and its city in sections 7 and 18, founded in 1867, were named for a lake in sections 10 and 11, two miles west of the village. The township was divided into **CLEAR LAKE EAST TOWNSHIP**: T. 34N, R. 29W, sections 3–10, 15–22, and 27–34; and **CLEAR LAKE WEST TOWNSHIP**: T. 34N, R. 30W.

The city of Clear Lake was incorporated as a village on March 13, 1900; it was platted in 1879 and again on March 24, 1882, on 40 acres owned by Alanson C. Potter, who was the depot agent, 1866–84, and died in 1908. The post office was established while still part of Benton County in 1853, the name changing to Benton, 1855–56, and back to Clear Lake. It had a Great Northern Railway and Northern Pacific Railroad station.

DAIRY a store and post office, 1900–1904, in section 22 of Santiago Township.

EAST MONTICELLO a post office, 1858–60; location not found, but probably in Becker Township, across the Mississippi River from Monticello in Wright County.

EAST ST. CLOUD a village in section 6, Haven Township, platted in 1853, which had a granite quarry noted on an 1874 map and a sawmill about 1890; it had a station of the Great Northern Railway and Northern Pacific Railroad.

ELK PRAIRIE see BIG LAKE.

ELK RIVER TOWNSHIP settled in 1848 by Pierre Bottineau, who established a trading post near the site of the village, received its first farming settlement in 1850. Its village of Orono, to be again noticed, was platted in 1855, and the village of Elk River, platted in 1865, was incorporated in 1881, the two villages being united under the latter name.

The township was divided into **ELK RIVER NORTH TOWNSHIP**: T. 33N, R. 26W; and **ELK RIVER SOUTH TOWNSHIP**: T. 32N, R. 26W. The city of Elk River in sections 33 and 34 of Elk River North Township was incorporated as a village on February 19, 1881, and reincorporated on February 6, 1911. The first post office, 1851–67, was established while in Benton County and transferred to Orono; the second post office was at Elk River Station, 1866–76, and became Elk River. The business district developed on the north side of the Great Northern Railway and Northern Pacific

Railroad tracks. The county seat was first established at Humboldt, now Big Lake village, as before noted, but its offices were removed in 1867 to Elk River village, then known, in distinction from Orono, as "the Lower Town."

The river, whence this township and village are named, was called the St. Francis River by Jonathan Carver, Zebulon Pike, Maj. Stephen H. Long, and Henry R. Schoolcraft, taking the name given to the present Rum River by Father Louis Hennepin. Joseph N. Nicollet's map, in 1843, applied the name St. Francis as it is now used, for the chief northern tributary of Elk River. Giacomo C. Beltrami and Nicollet used an Ojibwe name for Elk River, translated as Double River, or by Lieut. James Allen as Parallel River, alluding to its course nearly parallel with the Mississippi. On account of the herds of elk found there by Pike and later explorers and fur traders, the present name was given to this river and to Elk Lake, through which it flows, on the first map of Minnesota Territory in 1850.

FITZPATRICK a Great Northern railway station, in sections 4 and 9 of Elk River Township, six miles north of Elk River.

HAVEN TOWNSHIP first settled in 1846, organized in 1872, had previously been a part of Briggs (now Palmer) Township. Its name is in honor of John Ormsbee Haven, who was born in Addison County, Vt., October 3, 1824, and died at his home in Big Lake Township, September 1, 1906. He was graduated at Middlebury College, 1852; came to Minnesota in 1854; settled on a farm at Big Lake in 1866; was register of deeds, county auditor, county superintendent of schools, and clerk of the district court. In 1872–73 he was a representative in the legislature. A post office was in section 21, 1877–80, of the township, across the Great Northern Railway tracks from Cable.

HILDERS QUARRY SPUR a station of the Great Northern Railway in section 6 of Haven Township.

HOULTON a Great Northern Railway station in section 33 of Elk River Township, about three miles north of Elk River, was named for William Henry Houlton, who was born in Houlton, Maine, March 29, 1840, and died at his home in Elk River Township, August 1915. He came to Monticello, Minn., in 1856; served in the Eighth Minnesota Regiment, 1862–65; entered partner-

ship with his brother Horatio at Elk River in 1866 and engaged in mercantile business, manufacture of lumber and flour, banking, and farming; was a state senator in 1878 and 1883–85; was superintendent of the Minnesota State Reformatory, 1896–1900. A Great Northern Railway spur line was in section 16. The station and spur line were also known as Houlton Siding and Houlton's Mill Spur.

INDIAN MEDICAL SPRINGS a Northern Pacific Railroad station in Big Lake Township, about 1937, four miles west of Elk River.

LAKE FREMONT a village on the Great Northern Railway in Livonia, incorporated in 1912, Zimmerman by the railway company and as a post office, in honor of Moses Zimmerman, who was owner of the farm on which the village was located. The adjoining lake received its name in 1856, when John Charles Frémont (1813–90) was the Republican candidate for president of the United States. He was the assistant of Nicollet, 1838–43, in the surveys and mapping of the upper Mississippi region including Minnesota. See also ZIMMERMAN.

LIVONIA TOWNSHIP settled in 1856 and organized in 1866, is said to bear the Christian name of the wife of Livonia Spencer, who settled in this township in 1864 and was the probate judge of the county for two terms. This is the name of a province in Russia, adjoining the Gulf of Riga. A post office was in section 26, 1867–83 and 1890–1903.

ORLANDO a post office, 1857–82; location not found; named for Orlando Bailey, first postmaster, for whom the community of Bailey was also named.

ORONO a village located in Elk River Township, sections 32 and 33, which in 1881 became a part of the village of Elk River, as before noted, was platted in May 1855 by Ard Godfrey of Minneapolis, who named it for his native town in Maine. Godfrey was given the right to build and maintain a bridge across the Elk River at Orono in 1857. The post office, 1867–78, was transferred from Elk River.

Much interesting biographic information of Orono, the Penobscot chief, for whom the Maine town and village are named, was given in an address of Hon. Israel Washburn, Jr., at the centennial celebration of that town, March 3, 1874. Orono was born in 1688 and died at Oldtown,

Maine, February 5, 1801, aged 113 years. His life is also sketched somewhat fully in the *Handbook of American Indians*, edited by F. W. Hodge (pt. 2, 1910, p. 155).

ORROCK TOWNSHIP settled in 1856 and organized in 1875, after being previously a part of Big Lake, was named in honor of Robert Orrock, its earliest settler. He was born in Scotland, July 15, 1805, came to America in 1831, settled here in 1856 as a farmer and died at his home, January 4, 1885. The village in section 7 had a post office, 1877–1906, a sawmill, and a station of the Northern Pacific Railroad.

PALMER TOWNSHIP settled in 1855, "was organized in 1858, with the name of Briggs, in honor of Joshua Briggs, who resided on the west bank of the lake bearing his name. . . . A few years afterwards, the name was changed to Clinton Lake, and subsequently to Palmer, in honor of Robinson Palmer, the father of Mrs. Joshua Briggs" (*History of the Upper Mississippi Valley*, p. 336).

Benjamin Robinson Palmer, physician, was born in South Berwick, Maine, March 15, 1815; came to Minnesota in 1856, settling in St. Cloud; was assistant surgeon in the U.S. Army, 1862–66, being stationed at Sauk Centre and Fort Ripley, Minn.; lived afterward at Sauk Centre, had an extensive medical practice, and died there May 6, 1882.

PLEASANT VALLEY see BECKER.

PRINCETON a city with Mille Lacs County, which see.

REFORMATORY a station of the Northern Pacific Railroad and Great Northern Railway in section 7 of Haven Township, related to the state reformatory.

ST. CLOUD the county seat of Stearns County, extends also as an incorporated city across the Mississippi to include wards 5 and 6 in Benton County and ward 7 in the northwest corner of Sherburne County. The Minnesota State Reformatory, established in 1889, is in the part of St. Cloud lying in this county. Its ground, 1,057 acres, includes a large granite quarry. See the chapter of Stearns County.

SALIDA a station of the Great Northern Railway at the intersection of sections 9, 10, 15, and 16 of Becker South Township.

SANTIAGO TOWNSHIP settled in 1856, organized in 1868, and its village in section 10, platted in April 1857, have the Spanish name for St. James, borne by the capital of the republic of Chile, as also by a city and province in Cuba. The post office operated at three periods, 1858–60, 1869–1914, and since 1927; the site had a Great Northern Railway station.

ZIMMERMAN a city in sections 9 and 16 of Livonia, was named for a farmer there. It was incorporated as a village in 1910; the post office began in 1890, with Henry Zimmerman as first postmaster; Lake Fremont village in section 5 of Livonia Township, with a post office, 1865–1902, became part of Zimmerman.

―――――――

Lakes and Streams

In the foregoing pages, attention has been given to Big Lake, Clear Lake, the Elk River and Lake, St. Francis River, Lake Fremont, and Briggs Lake, the last being named in honor of Joshua Briggs, a former English sea captain who settled there.

The other lakes and streams bearing names on maps of this county include Twin Lake, on the east line of Elk River, outflowing by Trott Brook, named for Joseph Trott, its earliest settler, who came in 1854; Tibbetts Brook, the outlet of Lake Fremont, named for four brothers from Maine, Joshua, Nathaniel, Ben, and Jim, who were lumbermen and farmers; Battle Brook, named from a fight of two white men, as noted in the chapter for Mille Lacs County, flowing through a second Elk Lake; Rice Lake, on the St. Francis River, filled with wild rice, called St. Francis Lake on old maps; Catlin and Sandy Lakes, in the south part of Baldwin; Stone Lake in sections 25 and 36, Livonia, and a Lake of the Woods (drained) in its section 30; Lakes Ann and Josephine, Big Mud Lake, and Eagle Lake in Orrock; Birch, Mud, and Thompson Lakes in Big Lake Township; Lake Julia and Rush Lake, joined by straits with Briggs Lake; Rice or Strong Creek, in Palmer, flowing through a lake having much wild rice; Pickerel and Long Lakes, crossed by the south line of Haven; and Biggerstaff Creek in Haven, named for a pioneer farmer, Samuel Biggerstaff.

Rapids and Islands of the Mississippi

From the "Historico-Geographical Chart of the Upper Mississippi River," accompanying Dr. Elliott Coues's edition of Pike's *Expeditions*, published in 1895, the following names are listed, in the descending course of the river on the border of Sherburne County, from St. Cloud to the mouth of Crow River at Dayton.

The Thousand Islands, within two miles south of St. Cloud, so named, with great exaggeration, in allusion to the Thousand Islands of the St. Lawrence River along many miles next below the mouth of Lake Ontario, were called Beaver Islands by Pike in 1805, and an "archipelago" by Beltrami in 1823.

Next southward are Mosquito Rapids and Grand Island, which is more than a mile long.

Boynton's Island and Smiler's Rapids adjoin the south side of Clear Lake Township.

Bear Island, Cedar Rapids, Cedar Island, and Lane's Island are at the south side of Becker.

Boom Island, Battle Rapids, Brown's Island, Spring Rapids, and Baker's and Dimick's Islands adjoin Big Lake Township. The Boom Island has reference to booms for storing logs. Battle Rapids, adjoining section 32, received this name in commemoration of the battles of Elk River, between the Ojibwe and the Dakota, narrated by William W. Warren in his *History of the Ojibway People*

(MHS Collections 5: 235–41 [1885]). These battles are referred by Newton H. Winchell to the years 1772 and 1773 (*Aborigines of Minnesota*, 1911, p. 539). "From the circumstances of two battles having been fought in such quick succession on the point of land between the Elk and Mississippi rivers, this spot has been named by the Ojibways, Me-gaud-e-win-ing, or 'Battle Ground'" (Warren, p. 240).

Next are Davis, Wilson, Jameson, and Nickerson Islands, extending to the vicinity of the mouth of the Elk River; and near the southeast corner of Elk River Township and of this county are Dayton Island and Dayton Rapids, named, like the adjoining village and township in Hennepin County, for Lyman Dayton of St. Paul.

Craig Prairie

A large opening in the woods in the west part of Orrock, having an area of about two square miles, is named Craig Prairie, in honor of Hugh E. Craig, its pioneer farmer. Other and more extended open tracts, originally prairies but unnamed, or partly brushland, adjoined the Mississippi through this county and are now mainly occupied by farms.

Sibley County

Established March 5, 1853, this county was named in honor of Gen. Henry Hastings Sibley, pioneer, governor, and military defender of Minnesota. He was born in Detroit, Mich., February 20, 1811; went to Mackinaw, entering the service of the American Fur Company, in 1829; came to what is now Minnesota in 1834, as general agent in the Northwest for that company, with headquarters at Mendota (then called St. Peter's), where he lived 28 years; removed to St. Paul in 1862 and resided there through the remainder of his life. He was delegate in Congress, representing Minnesota Territory, 1849–53; was first governor of the state, 1858–60; and during the Dakota War of 1862 led the army against the Indians and in the next year commanded an expedition against these Indians in Dakota Territory. He was during more than 20 years a regent of the University of Minnesota; was a charter member of the Minnesota Historical Society and was its president in 1867 and from 1876 until his death, at his home in St. Paul, February 18, 1891.

In 1835–36 Sibley built at Mendota the oldest surviving stone dwelling house in Minnesota, in which he and his family lived until their removal to St. Paul. The house is managed by the Sibley House Association.

His biography (596 pp.) by Nathaniel West, D. D., was published in 1889; an excellent memoir of him, by J. Fletcher Williams, is in the MHS Collections (6: 257–310); and a shorter biography, by Gen. James H. Baker, is in his "Lives of the Governors of Minnesota" (MHS Collections 13: 75–105).

Among the Dakota, with whom Sibley had a very intimate and wide acquaintance, he was called "Wah-ze-o-man-ee, Walker in the Pines, a name that had a potent influence among them far and near, as long as the Dakota race dwelt in the state" (Williams, p. 167).

Information of names has been gathered from History of the Minnesota Valley (1882), having pp. 410–77 for Sibley County; and from Florenz Seeman, register of deeds, and Julius Henke, a pioneer who came here in 1860, during a visit at Gaylord, the county seat, in July 1916.

ALFSBORG TOWNSHIP organized January 26, 1869, received this name of a district in Sweden by vote of its Scandinavian settlers. A post office was located in the section 10 home of Swen Anderson, 1881–82.

ANNA a post office, 1873–83, located in section 23 of Faxon Township.

ARLINGTON TOWNSHIP settled in 1855, organized May 11, 1858, and its city in sections 9 and 10, platted in 1856 and somewhat changed in location when the railway was built in 1881, have a name that is borne also by a village in Virginia and by villages and townships in 25 other states. The village was incorporated on March 8, 1860, June 19, 1883, April 3, 1912, and as a city in 1948; it had a station of the Chicago and North Western Railway; the post office began in 1857.

ASSUMPTION a place name in section 13 of Washington Lake Township, on the border of Carver County.

BIG HILL see FAXON.

BISMARCK TOWNSHIP settled in 1867, organized July 24, 1874, was named by its German settlers in honor of the great Prussian statesman "the creator of German unity." He was born at Schönhausen, Prussia, April 1, 1815, and died at Friedrichsruh, July 30, 1898. A post office was located in the township, 1879–91, with James H. Houston, postmaster; the first township meeting was held at Houston's home, and he was elected treasurer.

BRACK a country post office in Grafton Township, 1899–1903, with August Ahlbrecht as postmaster.

CORNISH TOWNSHIP settled in 1868, organized January 25, 1871, received this name on the recommendation of J. B. Wakefield, who settled here in 1869, "in memory of his native town in New Hampshire." A post office was in section 22, 1869–82.

DEERFIELD a village in sections 34 and 35 of Kelso Township, was incorporated as a village on May 19, 1857; it appears in Henderson Township on J. S. Sewall's 1857 map; no trace of the site remains, but it is possibly the same as Rush River.

DOHENY'S LANDING see JESSENLAND.

DRYDEN TOWNSHIP settled in 1854 and organized May 11, 1858, was at first called Williamstown but was renamed by request of Hamilton Beatty and others, he being chairman of the first township board of supervisors. This name, in honor of the celebrated English poet and dramatist John Dryden (1631–1700), is borne also by villages and townships in Maine, New York, Virginia, Michigan, and Arkansas. A post office was located in postmaster John B. Dorr's home on the south shore of Lake Titlow, 1858–61; it ceased during the Civil War and was reestablished in 1864 in section 4 of Dryden Township with Patrick Mohan, postmaster, at his cabin until the post office was merged with Gaylord in 1886.

EAGLE CITY see WINTHROP.

FAXON TOWNSHIP first settled in May 1852, organized May 11, 1858, and its former village in sec-

tions 4 and 5, platted in April 1857, were named for a member of its townsite company. The village was known as Walker's Landing in 1852 until platted in 1857. A post office was established as Big Hill in 1857, changing to Faxon in 1859 and discontinuing in 1901; Hartwell Walker was the first postmaster under both names. A ferry service was begun in 1872 by Mike Sheely and William Murphy across the river to a site in Scott County, which was known as Murphy's Landing; the village was a major wheat shipping center in 1866.

GAYLORD a city in sections 29 and 32 of Dryden, platted in 1883 on 40 acres owned by William and Mina Maas, was named by officials of the Minneapolis and St. Louis Railroad company. Gaylord succeeded Henderson in 1915 as the county seat. Edward W. Gaylord, of Minneapolis, was master of transportation for this railway, 1874–77, and its superintendent, 1878–80. The city was incorporated as a village on June 13, 1883, and as a city on September 19, 1947. The first building was the general store owned by Henry A. Boettcher, postmaster and justice of the peace. The city had a station of the Chicago and North Western Railway; the post office was established in 1881.

GIBBON a city in section 2 in Severance, incorporated as a village on October 28, 1887, and reincorporated on July 3, 1912, was named by officials of the Minneapolis and St. Louis Railroad company for Gen. John Gibbon (1827–96), who was temporarily stationed at Fort Snelling in 1878 and was its commandant during parts of 1880–82 and was commander-in-chief of the Loyal Legion when he died. An alternate version of the naming is that it is for the English historian Edward Gibbon. The first settler, August Peterson, came to the United States in 1867 from Sweden and established a tree claim in 1878, which became known as Peterson's Grove or Settler's Grove; Peterson donated 40 acres for the townsite, and when the lots were sold in 1882, one was reserved for Peterson, who died in 1910; the second lot was for the first person who would build a saloon, who was Wenzel Friedl. The village had a station of the Chicago and North Western Railway; the post office was established in 1883.

GRAFTON TOWNSHIP settled in 1870 and organized in September 1873, has a name that is borne by a county and a town in New Hampshire and by villages and townships in 17 other states. A post office was located in the township, 1875–79.

GREEN ISLE TOWNSHIP settled in 1857, and organized May 11, 1858, received its name, referring to Ireland "the Emerald Isle," by suggestion of Christopher Dolan, an Irish immigrant. The city of this name, in the adjacent section 18 of Washington, was platted in August 1881 and incorporated as a village on December 8, 1883. It had a station of the Minneapolis and St. Louis Railroad and has had a post office since 1866. Lake Erin, next eastward from this village, testifies similarly to the loyal spirit of its settlers from Ireland.

HARTFORD a village in Kelso Township, section 8, noted on Sewall's 1857 map, was located eight miles west of Henderson and earlier called Freemont; it was incorporated on May 19, 1857, but the site was never developed.

HENDERSON TOWNSHIP and its city, founded in 1852 and platted in 1855 by Joseph R. Brown, who is commemorated by Brown County, were named by him in honor of his father's only sister, Margaret Brown Henderson, and for her son Andrew Henderson. During several years this village was Brown's home, and he founded and edited its first newspaper, the *Henderson Democrat*, 1857–61. He was first president of the village council, 1856–57, and was followed as president by his son-in-law, Charles Blair, 1857–58, who was also the first postmaster when the post office was established in 1853. The village was the county seat until 1915, when the county offices were removed to Gaylord. It was incorporated as a town on February 21, 1855; as a borough, January 23, 1866; and as a city, March 23, 1891.

HIGH ISLAND see NEW AUBURN.

JESSENLAND TOWNSHIP settled in 1853, organized May 11, 1858, is "supposed to have received its name from the fact that Jesse Cameron was the first to arrive; it was for some time known as 'Jesse's Land'" (*History of the Minnesota Valley*, p. 428). The village in section 13 had a post office, Jessen Land, 1857–62, located in the section 14 home of postmaster John H. Miller; also at this site was Doheny's Landing, owned by Thomas Doheny, who had come in 1852.

JOHNSTOWN a post office, 1858–59, in Faxon Township, section 20, with John J. Ahern as postmaster.

KELSO TOWNSHIP settled in 1855–56 and organized in 1858, bears a name that was originally given by A. P. Walker, a surveyor, in 1854 or 1855, which "is of Scotch derivation," being the name of a town on the Tweed River in southern Scotland. Two post offices in the township were named Kelso; the first, 1857–65, was a stagecoach stop only, located in the section 20 home of postmaster John Q. A. Grant until it was transferred to Sibley; the second, established in 1866, was located in William T. Barnes's home in section 22 until it was moved in 1875 to section 26 and the home of Henry and Pauline Osterman, she being the postmaster until 1886; the post office was moved again, to section 20, before merging with Rush River post office in 1891.

LEON a post office, 1857–58; location not found.

MOLTKE TOWNSHIP settled in 1875 and the latest organized in this county, August 21, 1878, was named by its German pioneers in honor of the famous Prussian general, Count Helmuth von Moltke (1800–1891). A post office was located in the township, 1879–87, with John P. Blake, postmaster and justice of the peace; the township hall was located there.

MOUNTVILLE a post office, 1872–1902, located in section 12 of Transit Township at the hotel and store managed by Mrs. Louis Uber, where her husband was postmaster.

NEW AUBURN TOWNSHIP settled in 1855, organized May 11, 1858, and its city in sections 17 and 20, platted in 1856, were named by settlers from Auburn, N.Y. The city was incorporated as a village on May 23, 1857, and again on May 24, 1895; the post office began as High Island January-June 1857, and then changed to New Auburn.

NEW ROME a village in section 5, Kelso Township, with a post office, 1876–1902, which had previously been at Prairie Mound, and was named by Capt. John Groetsch, postmaster at his hotel.

PETERSON'S GROVE see GIBBON.

PRAIRIE MOUND a post office, 1856–59, in section 1 of Kelso Township, and then reestablished at New Rome. The site was considered the summer resort area for Henderson.

RUSH RIVER a village in section 34 of Kelso Township, with a post office, 1868–79 and 1891–1903, which then merged with Le Sueur; Sewall's 1857 map shows Deerfield at this site.

SETTLER'S GROVE see GIBBON.

SEVERANCE TOWNSHIP settled in 1867–68 and

organized in 1870, was at first called Clear Lake, for the lake crossed by its south line, but because that name had been earlier given to another Minnesota township, it was renamed in honor of Martin Juan Severance of Mankato. He was born at Shelburne Falls, Mass., December 24, 1826, and died in Mankato, Minn., July 11, 1907. He was admitted to practice law in 1853; came to this state in 1856, locating at Henderson; served in the Tenth Minnesota Regiment, 1862–65, attaining the rank of captain; afterward lived in Le Sueur till 1870, then removing to Mankato; was a representative in the legislature in 1862; judge of the sixth judicial district, 1881–1900. A post office was probably located in the township, May–August 1881.

SIBLEY TOWNSHIP settled in 1856 and organized July 9, 1864, was named like the county, in honor of General Sibley. A post office, transferred from Kelso, was located in section 22, 1865–86.

TRANSIT TOWNSHIP settled in 1858, organized in 1866, has a unique name, as if from the transit instrument used for railway surveys. A post office was in section 8, 1869–1903, located first in Lemont S. Crandell's home and moved in 1881 to William F. Babcock's home.

WASHINGTON LAKE TOWNSHIP settled in 1854–55, organized May 11, 1858, bears the name of a large lake at its center, which "was so called from the fact that two of the first settlers on its borders were from Washington, D.C." (*History of the Minnesota Valley*, p. 435).

WINTHROP a city in section 6 of Alfsborg Township and section 31 of Transit Township, incorporated as a village before 1891 and as a city in 1910, was named by officers of the Minneapolis and St. Louis Railroad. The post office was known as Eagle City, 1858–82, and was first located in Michael Cummings's halfway house and tavern, a stagecoach stop that accommodated travelers on the Old Fort Ridgely Road; the post office was moved in 1868 to Charles A. Swanson's in section 6 of Alfsborg Township, and moved again in 1870 to section 29 of Transit Township and Ole Olson's home until 1881. Eagle City was incorporated on May 19, 1857; when Winthrop requested a post office in 1882, Elford Andrew Campbell, then postmaster of Eagle City, moved that post office to Winthrop; Campbell owned a number of buildings, was agent for the land company, and oper-

ated a law firm. The townsite was platted on land owned by Erick and Brita Olson, who had homesteaded the land in 1869 and platted the site in 1881. The village had a station serving several rail lines including the Minneapolis and St. Louis Railroad.

Lakes and Streams

The Minnesota River, forming the east border of Sibley County, and Clear Lake in Severance, crossed by the south boundary, had the same Dakota name, printed "Mini sotah" on Joseph N. Nicollet's map (*Mini*, "water," *sotah*, "whitishly clouded").

High Island Lake, the largest in the county, has a small but high island of glacial drift in its northern part, rising 20 or 30 feet above the lake. The same name is given likewise to the outflowing High Island Creek, being partly a translation of the Dakota name, recorded by Nicollet as Witakantu, meaning Plum Island (*Wita*, "island," *kantu*, "plum trees").

Nicollet also noted the Dakota name Wanyecha Oju River, and its translation, Rush River, which, with its North and South Branches, drains the southern part of the county.

Bevens Creek, the outlet of Washington Lake in the township of that name, flows northeastward into Carver County.

Buffalo Creek, lying mainly in McLeod County, traverses also the north edge of New Auburn.

Round Grove Lake, giving its name to a township of McLeod County, lies partly in the northeast corner of Grafton.

Other lakes having names on maps include Rice Lake in section 34, Sibley, named for Andrew Rice, a homesteader who settled at its east end and made proof of his claim in 1860; Sand Lake and Cummings or Mud Lake (drained), on the west line of Alfsborg, lying respectively in the course of the South and North Branches of Rush River, the latter being named for A. Cummings, a pioneer who built a hotel there for travelers on the old road from Henderson to Fort Ridgely; Cottonwood (drained) and Swan Lakes, respectively in the west parts of Cornish and Severance; Alkali Lake (drained), having somewhat bitter water, in Moltke; Ward Lake, on the north line of Bismarck; Buck Lake (drained) in the north part of

Grafton, named in honor of Adam Buck of Henderson; Indian Lake in section 21, Transit; Titlow, Mud, Beatty, and Kirby Lakes in Dryden; Silver Lake in Jessenland; Kerry Lake in sections 20 and 21, Faxon; Lake Erin, or Mud Lake, in Washington; Lake Severance in Green Isle, named, like a township, in honor of Judge Severance, who in June 1858, made proof for a homestead in section 17, beside this lake; and Hahn and Schilling Lakes in New Auburn.

Adam Buck was born in Germany, October 12, 1830; came to the United States and in 1852 settled as a farmer in this county; removed to Henderson in 1862 and opened a drugstore; served in the Dakota War of 1862 and in the Civil War as a captain in the Eleventh Minnesota Regiment, 1864–65; was county surveyor, 1868–79; was a representative in the legislature in 1862, 1868, and 1872 and a state senator in 1867; died at his home in Henderson, about 1895.

Robert Beatty was born in the north of Ireland in 1803, came with his parents to Pennsylvania, and removed, with his several sons, in 1857 to Dryden in this county. His son Samuel B. Beatty, born in Pennsylvania in 1841, settled in Dryden in 1857; served in the Tenth Minnesota Regiment, 1863–65; was a representative in the legislature in 1877.

Joseph Patterson Kirby was born in Ireland, August 6, 1838; came to the United States when very young, with his parents; settled as a homestead farmer in New Auburn, 1856; served in the Third Minnesota Regiment, 1861–65, attaining the rank of first lieutenant; lived in Le Sueur, 1865–74; removed to Henderson in 1874 and was judge of probate for Sibley County, 1875–94.

Hahn Lake was named for William Hahn, who was born in Prussia in 1849; came to America at the age of five years, with his parents; and settled in New Auburn in 1879, beside this lake.

Schilling Lake commemorates John Schilling, whose homestead was the southwest quarter of section 5 in this township.

Stearns County

This county, established February 20, 1855, was named for Hon. Charles Thomas Stearns, member of the council of the territorial legislature, 1854 and 1855. The name, however, was decided by a mistake, told in the *History of the Upper Mississippi Valley* as follows: "The bill, as originally introduced, bore the name of Stevens county, in honor of Governor Stevens, then prominently connected with the survey of the Northern Pacific railroad and passed both branches of the Legislature in that shape; but in the enrollment of the bill the change occurred from Stevens to Stearns, and when discovered, it was concluded best to let the matter stand, as the name was still in the line of honorable mention, and Mr. Stearns well entitled to public recognition in this way."

Stearns was born in Pittsfield, Mass., January 9, 1807; came from Illinois to Minnesota in 1849 and first settled in St. Anthony; thence removed in 1855 to St. Cloud, the county seat of Stearns County, where he was proprietor of a hotel during 14 years; and about the year 1870, having sold his hotel to be one of the buildings of the State Normal School, he removed to Mobile, Ala. Later he resided in New Orleans, La., and died there May 22, 1898. He was the last survivor of the founders of the Masonic Grand Lodge of Minnesota.

Information of the origins and meanings of names has been gathered from History of the Upper Mississippi Valley *(1881), which has pp. 369–483 for this county;* History of Stearns County *by William Bell Mitchell (1915, 1,536 pp., in 2 vols., continuously paged); from the author of this county history, also from Hon. Charles A. Gilman and John Coates, each of St. Cloud, the county seat, interviewed during a visit there in May 1916; and from Edwin Clark of Minneapolis, formerly of Melrose for 25 years, 1867–92.*

ALBANY TOWNSHIP settled in 1863, organized in 1868, and its city, incorporated in January 20, 1890, and reincorporated in 1958, have a name that is borne by the capital of New York and by townships, villages, and cities in 17 other states. The first settlers in the city were the Obermiller and Schwinghammer families in section 22 in 1862; Isador Obermiller, married to Maria Schwinghammer, was the first postmaster in 1870 in Halfway House, their home, which also served as a hotel. The site was first called the Schwinghammer Settlement and then Two River Mission Settlement of Two Rivers; when the Great Northern Railway came in 1871 and built a depot a half mile away, it was renamed Albany and platted in 1872; the first building at the new site was Carl Herberger's general store.

ARBAN a post office, 1895–1905, in section 27 of Holding Township; it was also known as Young's Settlement.

ARCADIA a post office, 1855–56; location not found.

ASHLEY the most northwestern township, settled

in 1865 and organized in 1870, received its name from Ashley Creek, flowing through this township, which was named in 1856 by Edwin Whitefield, an eastern artist traveling to Stearns, Todd, and Kandiyohi Counties, in honor of his friend, Ossian Doolittle Ashley of Boston and New York City. Ossian Doolittle Ashley was born in Townshend, Vt., April 9, 1821; was a member of the Boston Stock Exchange, 1846–57, being its president in 1856–57; removed to New York City in 1857 and was a member of its Stock Exchange; was elected president of the Wabash Railroad in 1887.

AVON TOWNSHIP settled in 1856 and organized in 1866, and its city, founded in 1873 and incorporated on January 26, 1900, bear the name of three rivers in England and two in Wales and of villages and townships in Maine, Massachusetts, Wisconsin, and 12 other states of the Union. The city had a station of the Great Northern Railway in section 27; the post office was established in 1873.

BAXTER'S SPUR a station of the Great Northern Railway in section 24 of St. Joseph Township.

BEAVER LAKE a lakeshore community established about 1865 on the border of St. Augusta and Fair Haven Townships.

BELGRADE a city in sections 18 and 19 of Crow River Township, has the name of the capital of Serbia, of a township and its village in Maine, and of villages in Missouri, Nebraska, and Montana. It was platted in 1887 by the Pacific Land Company and incorporated as a village on March 19, 1888; the post office began as Crow Lake in 1871, changing to Belgrade in 1886. When the railroad came in 1886, there already were a number of businesses; it had a station of the Minneapolis and Pacific Railroad.

BIG FISH LAKE a lakeshore village, established about 1938 in Collegeville Township.

BIG LAKE a lakeshore village in Munson Township, was founded about 1950.

BIG WATAB LAKE a lakeshore village in Collegeville Township, established about 1945.

BIRCH KNOLL a village in St. Joseph Township, established about 1970.

BISCHOF'S CORNER a village in Eden Lake Township.

BROCKWAY TOWNSHIP settled in 1855 and organized in 1858, was then called Winnebago but was renamed as now in 1860 after a post office established in September 1857, honoring a lumberman and farmer there. The post office, first located in section 24, was established during three different periods between 1867 and 1905.

BROOTEN a city in North Fork Township, with Pope County, founded with the building of the Minneapolis, St. Paul and Sault Ste. Marie Railroad (Soo Line) in 1886, was named for one of its Scandinavian farmers. The village was incorporated on February 16, 1892. The townsite was on land owned by Reier O. Liabraaten, and the site was given a form of his name; that family was known as the Brootens from then on. The early site in section 31 had a station of the Soo Line, Embrick E. Knudson was postmaster when the post office was established in 1886; Knudson was earlier postmaster at North Fork.

CLEARWATER a village lying for its greater part in the township of this name in Wright County, reaching also into Lynden in Stearns County, received its name from the river there tributary to the Mississippi, called on Joseph N. Nicollet's map "Kawakomik or Clear Water R."

CLINTON see ST. JOSEPH.

COLCHESTER a post office, 1903–4, and station of the Great Northern Railway; location not found.

COLD SPRING a village in Wakefield, was platted in the fall of 1856 and incorporated as a village on June 26, 1889. The post office was established in 1857 as Cold Spring City and changed to the present name in 1889; a station of the Great Northern Railway was in section 22. "The vicinity abounds in natural mineral springs, and the two companies that have made the water famous over a wide territory do a business amounting to some $20,000 a year" (*History of Stearns County*, p. 1,333).

COLD SPRING CITY see COLD SPRING.

COLLEGEVILLE TOWNSHIP settled in 1858, organized in January 1880, is named for St. John's College, which was chartered by the legislature March 6, 1857. The college was opened in the fall of that year, being at first in St. Cloud, but in 1867 it was removed to its present site, in section 1, Collegeville. "In 1880 the name of the Monastery, St. Louis on the Lake, was changed to correspond with the name of the college, . . . as St. John's Abbey" (*History of the Upper Mississippi Valley*, p. 373). By an act of the legislature, February 27, 1883, the legal name of the college was changed to St. John's University. The village of Collegeville, one mile and a half distant, is in section 32, St. Wendell. It has had a post office since 1879 and had a station of the Great Northern Railway.

COLLEGEVILLE ESTATES a village established about 1975 in Collegeville Township.

COONVILLE a village in Brockway Township founded about 1950.

CROW LAKE see BELGRADE.

CROW LAKE TOWNSHIP settled in 1861, organized in 1868, and **CROW RIVER TOWNSHIP**, settled in 1860 and organized in 1877, are named respectively for Crow Lake, in the former township, and the North Branch of Crow River, which flows across the township bearing that name. The stream, belonging partly to several counties, is fully noticed in the first chapter and again in the chapter of Crow Wing County.

DEEP LAKE a lakeshore village in Eden Lake Township, founded about 1970.

EDEN LAKE TOWNSHIP settled in 1856, organized February 16, 1867, received this name by choice of its people, expressing their very high admiration. The lake of this name lies mostly in sections 25 and 26 and outflows northward to the Sauk River. The village of Eden Lake had a post office, 1872–87, which was changed to Eden Valley and transferred to Meeker County; the present community was redeveloped about 1960.

EDEN VALLEY a city with Meeker County, which see.

ELROSA a city in section 9 of Lake George Township, was incorporated as a village on March 1, 1938; it was settled about 1907, and the post office was established in 1913; it had a station of the Soo Line.

FAIR HAVEN TOWNSHIP organized April 5, 1859, and its village, platted in May 1856, received their name from an exclamation of Thomas C. Partridge, "This is a fair haven!" when in the spring of 1856 he came there in an exploring tramp from Clearwater (*History of Stearns County*, p. 1,267). The incorporation as a village was approved on March 16, 1858, but it later unincorporated. The post office of Fair Haven was established in Wright County before transferring to Stearns County; it operated 1857–1961 and was changed to a community post office until 1976, when it was discontinued.

FARMING TOWNSHIP settled in 1858 and orga-

nized March 11, 1873, has a rare name, adopted in allusion to the occupation of all its people. A village in section 32 had a post office, 1883–1904.

FORNER ADDITION a village founded about 1972 in St. Wendel Township.

FREEPORT a city in sections 2 and 3 of Oak Township, incorporated on August 19, 1892, was named by settlers who came from the city of Freeport in Illinois. Its early 1860s settlement of ten families had a general store and a Great Northern Railway station known as Oak Dale and then Oak Station. The post office began as Oak Station in 1875, with Frank Benolken, postmaster, who requested the change to Freeport in 1881; Benolken, born in 1846, came from Johnsburg, Ill., near Freeport, Ill.; worked as a salesman for St. Paul Harvester; became a farmer in the township; served as a state legislator, 1899–1901; and died in 1906.

GAMRADT'S CORNER a village, was established about 1975 in Ashley Township.

GATES see ST. ANTHONY.

GEORGEVILLE a village in section 26 of Crow River Township, had a post office, 1868–1953, which was established in Monongalia County and was transferred to Kandiyohi County in 1871 and to Stearns County in 1888; it had a station of the Minneapolis and Pacific Railroad.

GETTY TOWNSHIP was organized in 1865. "John J. Getty, in honor of whom the town is named, was undoubtedly the first permanent settler. He came on the 6th of July, 1857, and settled on section nineteen, in what has since been known as Getty's Grove" (*History of the Upper Mississippi Valley*, p. 416). He was born in Onondaga County, N.Y., September 15, 1821. A post office was in section 19, 1871–79, located on Getty's property, with F. M. Bipell as postmaster.

GOODNER LAKE a lakeshore village in Maine Prairie Township, was established about 1945.

GRAND LAKE a lakeshore village in Rockville Township, was founded about 1906.

GREENWALD a city in Grove Township, was established in 1907 and incorporated on June 10, 1915. *Wald* is a German word, meaning "a grove." The townsite had a Soo Line station in section 29, and the post office began in 1910.

GROVE TOWNSHIP settled in the fall of 1858, was organized in 1867. It had previously been a part of Oak Grove Township, organized in 1860, which included this surveyed township and another next east. When they took separate organizations, in 1867, they adopted respectively the names Grove and Oak.

HILLVILLE a village founded about 1940 in Avon Township.

HOLDING TOWNSHIP organized in 1870, was named in honor of its first permanent settler, who made a homestead claim in May 1868. Six years later he platted the village of Holding's Ford, giving it this name from its fording place of the South Stream of the Two Rivers. Randolph Holding was born in McHenry County, Ill., July 27, 1844; came to Minnesota in 1861, settling at Clearwater; served in the Eighth Minnesota Regiment, 1862–65; engaged in freighting from St. Cloud to the Red River, 1866–68; settled in this township, 1868; was the township clerk, 1870–81; and a representative in the legislature, 1872.

HOLDINGFORD a city in section 17 of Holding Township; the village incorporated on October 23, 1896, merging two sites: the Soo Line railroad station of Holdingford and the village named Wardeville for Dr. A. G. Warde, a Minneapolis physician, who had purchased the land and platted the townsite. The post office was established in 1872 as Holding's Ford and was changed to Holdingford in 1894.

HURLEY a site south of St. Cloud that may be associated with the Great Northern Railway station at Hurley's Brickyard.

ISABEL a country post office, 1903–5, in Millwood Township at postmaster Moritz J. Hoeschen's general store.

ISLAND LAKE a lakeshore village established about 1972 in Collegeville Township.

JACOBS PRAIRIE a village in sections 1 and 12 of Wakefield Township, founded about 1861 but never incorporated.

KALISCH a post office, 1861–55; location not found.

KANDOTTA a post office, 1859–65, with Edwin Whitefield, author and artist, as first postmaster; location not found.

KENNEBEC a post office, 1857–68; location not found.

KIMBALL a city in Maine Prairie Township; its first post office, Kimball Prairie, operated 1867–70 and was reestablished as Kimball in 1887; it had a station of the Minneapolis and Pacific Railroad.

KIMBALL PRAIRIE a Soo Line village in Maine Prairie Township, founded in 1886, incorporated in February 1892, was named in honor of Frye Kimball, an early farmer there.

KING'S LAKE a settlement founded about 1973 in Millwood Township.

KORONIS a place name in section 8, Paynesville Township, next to the Paynesville station on an 1896 map, and southeast of that site on a 1930 map.

KRAIN TOWNSHIP settled in 1868, and organized in 1872, bears the name of a province of southern Austria, also called Carniola. This was the native province of Rev. Francis Xavier Pirec (or Pierz), who was a leader in founding St. John's College and in bringing German colonists to Stearns County and other adjoining counties, for whom Pierz Township in Morrison County was named.

KRAMER LAKE a lakeshore village in St. Joseph Township, established about 1960.

LAKE GEORGE TOWNSHIP settled in 1856 and organized in 1877, has a lake so named in honor of George Kraemer, one of its pioneer settlers. It was called Lake Henry by the expedition of Samuel Woods and John Pope in 1849. A post office was in section 21, 1892–1905, near the Soo Line.

LAKE HENRY TOWNSHIP settled in 1855 and organized in 1869, took the name of a lake in sections 10 and 15. This lake name, as noted for the last preceding township, was received from the expedition of Woods and Pope, whose route passed the north ends of Lakes David and Henry, named by their journals and maps, identifiable respectively as Lakes Henry and George of later maps. The city in section 14 was incorporated as a village on October 6, 1913; it had a post office, 1883–1905.

LAKESIDE PARK a resort village on Pleasant Lake in section 20 of Rockville Township, noted on maps of 1896 and 1930.

LEEDSTON SEE ST. MARTIN.

LE SAUK TOWNSHIP settled in 1854, organized in 1860, received this French name, meaning "the Sauk," from the same derivation as Sauk Rapids, the Sauk River, Sauk Centre, and Lake Osakis, before explained in the chapter for Benton County.

LONG HILL a post office, 1868–73; location not found.

LONG LAKE a village established about 1970 in Millwood Township.

LONG-CROOKED LAKES a lakeshore village in Lynden Township, established about 1968.

LUXEMBURG is a village in section 19 of St.

Augusta, named by its Luxembourg settlers for the grand duchy and its capital city in western Europe. The post office was known as West St. Augusta, 1863–65, and as Luxemburgh until 1894, when the *h* was omitted from the name, and was discontinued in 1905.

LUXEMBURG TOWNSHIP settled in 1861 and organized in 1866, was named by its German settlers for the province and city in western Germany.

LYMAN a post office, 1889–90, in an area settled about 1866, 12 miles from Sauk Centre and 55 miles from St. Cloud.

LYNDEN TOWNSHIP settled in 1853, organized January 15, 1859, was then named Lyndon, like townships in Vermont and Wisconsin, and like townships and villages in five other states, honoring Josiah Lyndon (1704–78), governor of Rhode Island in 1768–69, a patriot for the American Revolution. From near its earliest record, however, the name has been spelled Lynden, in analogy with the linden tree.

MAINE GROVE a post office, 1879–80, located in the southeast part of the county, 15 miles from St. Cloud.

MAINE PRAIRIE TOWNSHIP organized in 1858, was named by its many pioneers from Maine, who came as its first settlers in 1856. One of its villages or hamlets, named Maine Prairie or Maine Prairie Corners, founded in 1865–66, is on the site of a stockade and fort constructed in 1862 as a refuge from the Dakota War. The name of this township was proposed by Aaron Scribner, who came from Aroostook County, Maine, and who later removed to Otter Tail County and there proposed the name of Maine Township. He died in Washington State in March 1916. A post office was in sections 23 and 24, 1863–1905.

MARTY a village in Maine Prairie Township, established about 1889, which had a post office, 1901–4, a general store owned by postmaster Louis Weiber, and a creamery.

MEIRE GROVE is a city founded about 1858 in sections 17 and 20 of Grove Township; it was incorporated as a village on December 24, 1896; the post office, 1873–1905, was also noted as Meire's Grove and Meiregrove.

MELROSE TOWNSHIP settled in 1857 and organized in 1866, was either named by first settlers Warren and Napoleon Adley and Robert Wheel-er, all from Scotland, for the city of Melrose in Scotland, having ruins of an ancient abbey, near the home of Sir Walter Scott, or by Warren Adley, in honor of Melissa (or Melvina) and Rose, who were his daughters or were other near kindred or friends. The city of Melrose in Millwood and Grove Townships, platted in December 1871 by Edwin and William H. Clark, brothers, was the terminus of the railroad from November 18, 1872, until 1878, was first incorporated in 1881 and in 1896 as a city and received a city charter in 1898. Edwin Clark, considered the "father of Melrose" came in 1871, built a general store and mill, and encouraged development of the community. The post office began in 1859; it had a station of the Great Northern Railway.

MERKLING a post office, 1883–84; location not found.

MILLWOOD TOWNSHIP settled in 1866 and organized in 1871, has a name that is borne also by villages in Massachusetts, New York, Pennsylvania, and seven other states.

MOELLER ADDITION a village in St. Augusta Township, was established about 1970.

MUNSON TOWNSHIP settled in 1856, organized in 1859, has the name of villages in Ohio and Pennsylvania.

MURPHY'S SETTLEMENT a village in Collegeville Township, was founded about 1975.

NAUSDAL a post office, 1885–93, located 17 miles south of Melrose and 45 miles southwest of St. Cloud, probably in Lake Henry Township, with John J. Turtum, postmaster, steamship agent, and constable.

NEENAH a post office, 1856–66; location not found.

NEW MUNICH a city in section 18 of Oak Township, was founded about 1856 and incorporated on January 28, 1896; its post office was established in 1859 as Oak and changed to New Munich in 1863; it had a station of the Soo Line. "It received its name from a Bavarian hunter, who came from Munich, Bavaria, and stayed with the first settlers for several years" (*History of Stearns County*, p. 1,298).

NEW PAYNESVILLE platted as a village on the Soo Line, was organized in 1890, being situated about a mile east of the previous village of Paynesville. In the fall of 1904 it received the old townsite by annexation, and in 1905 its name was changed to Paynesville by popular vote. A post office was begun in 1891. See also PAYNESVILLE.

NORTH FORK TOWNSHIP settled in 1864 and organized in 1867, is crossed by the North Fork of Crow River. A post office was in section 23, 1868–88, with Embrick Knudson as first postmaster; the last postmaster was Dr. Preto Tyrol, for whom the Tyrol post office was named; Knudson was also the first postmaster at Brooten in 1886.

OAK see NEW MUNICH.

OAK TOWNSHIP settled about 1856, organized in 1860, was then called Oak Grove. Its present name dates from 1867, when Grove Township, formerly a part of Oak Grove, was separately organized, as before noted.

OAK DALE/OAK STATION see FREEPORT.

O'BRIEN a Great Northern Railway station in section 17 of St. Cloud Township, related to a quarry of that name in the area.

OPOLE a village in section 8, Brockway Township, with a post office, 1890–1905.

PADUA a village in Raymond Township at the intersection of sections 22, 23, 26, and 27, with a post office, 1900–1905.

PAYNESVILLE TOWNSHIP organized September 20, 1867, had previously been included in Verdale. Edwin E. Payne was its first settler, coming in 1857 and making a homestead claim, on which in the same year he platted and named the first village site. This city, incorporated as a village on July 2, 1887, was annexed to New Paynesville in 1904, and the resultant village in March 1905 dropped "New" from its name. The post office began in 1857 with Edwin Payne as postmaster; it had a station of the Minneapolis and Pacific Railroad in section 18 and of the Great Northern Railway in section 8.

PEARL LAKE a hamlet adjoining the lake of this name in the north part of Maine Prairie, founded by the building of a church in 1889–90, received a post office in 1901, named Marty, which has been discontinued.

PHILLIPI ADDITION a village, was founded about 1973 in St. Joseph Township.

PICARDY a Great Northern Railway station; location not found.

PINE EDGE a village begun about 1948 in Brockway Township, north of the city of St. Cloud.

PINE LAKE a village founded about 1970 in Albany Township.

PLEASANT LAKE a city in Rockville Township, was settled about 1890 and incorporated as a village on July 11, 1938.

PORTSIDE a village founded about 1965 in Brockway Township.

PRAIRIE LAKE a post office, 1879–80; location not found.

RAYMOND TOWNSHIP settled in 1860 but deserted from 1862 to 1866, was organized in 1867, being named in honor of Liberty B. Raymond, one of its early settlers. A post office operated in the township, 1870–78, with Raymond as postmaster. The area was settled by 13 families in 1865, and by 1878 had two churches and four schools; the site was eventually abandoned.

REBISCHKE ADDITION a village in St. Joseph Township, west of St. Cloud.

RICE LAKE a village on the border of Paynesville and Eden Lake Township, was founded about 1900.

RICHMOND a city on the Sauk River, in section 24 of Munson, bears the surname of one of its earliest settlers; and it also partly commemorates Reuben Richardson, by whom this village was platted in 1856. The city was incorporated as a village on January 18, 1890; the post office began as Torah in 1856 and was changed to Richmond in 1909.

ROCKVILLE TOWNSHIP settled in 1855, organized June 25, 1860, and its city, platted in 1856, received their name from the outcrops of granite adjoining the Sauk River and Mill Creek. The city was incorporated as a village on July 14, 1903; the post office was established in 1857; it had a station of the Great Northern Railway in section 9.

ROLLING ACRES a village in Lynden Township, was founded about 1970.

ROSCOE a city in section 25 of Zion Township, formerly called Zion, was incorporated as a village on March 10, 1911. The post office was established as Zion, 1865–1914, changing that year to Roscoe; it had a station of the Great Northern Railway.

ROTHSCOPP a village approved for incorporation on May 23, 1857; location not found, and no trace remains.

ST. ANNA a village on Pelican Lake in section 5 of Avon Township, was incorporated as a village on

October 14, 1915, but later unincorporated; it had a post office, 1884–1905.

ST. ANTHONY a city of Krain Township, was settled about 1880 and incorporated as a village on May 31, 1911; it had a rural post office known as Gates, 1886–89, changed to St. Anthony and discontinued in 1905.

ST. AUGUSTA TOWNSHIP settled in 1854 and organized in 1859, was originally called Berlin and later Neenah, but in 1863 adopted the present name, which had been given by Father Pierz in 1856 to the first church here. The village of St. Augusta in section 7 was first platted in 1854 by Augusta Wilson, who also platted a section of St. Cloud, and was named for his daughter, Augusta, who had died shortly before. The village was approved for incorporation on May 19, 1857, but was not incorporated. It incorporated in 2000 under the name Ventura, for Minnesota Governor Jesse Ventura, but changed by popular vote to St. Augusta in November 2000. It had a post office, 1857–1903, and a station of the Great Northern Railway.

ST. CLOUD the county seat, first settled in October 1851, was platted in the fall of 1854 by John L. Wilson, "familiarly called the 'Father of St. Cloud.'" The history of the county says: "The choosing of St. Cloud as the name for his new town was due to the fact that while reading the life of Napoleon I, Mr. Wilson had observed that the Empress Josephine spent much of her time at the magnificent palace at St. Cloud, a few miles out of Paris, a circumstance which appealed so strongly to his fancy that he adopted it."

St. Cloud, or Clodvald or Chlodvald, was the youngest son of Clodomir, the king of Orleans, who was the son of Clovis. *The History of France* by Guizot (8 vols.) tells in its first volume how the two brothers of Clodvald were murdered by their uncles, king Childebert of Paris and king Clotaire of Soissons, in A.D. 524. The murdered brothers were ten and seven years old, and they were greatly mourned by their grandmother, Queen Clotilde. Of the younger brother, St. Cloud, Guizot wrote: "The third, named Clodvald (who died about the year 560, after having founded, near Paris, a monastery called after him St. Cloud), could not be caught, and was saved by some gallant men. He, disdaining a terrestrial kingdom, dedicated himself to the Lord, was shorn by his own hand,

and became a churchman; he devoted himself wholly to good works, and died a priest. And the two kings divided equally between them the kingdom of Clodomir."

The city with Benton and Sherburne Counties is the only city in the state that is located in three counties; three communities, all developed at the same time, were merged into one: (1) Middle Town, platted in 1854 by John L. Wilson, is the central business district and was primarily settled by German Catholics; (2) Lower Town was developed on land purchased by George Fuller Brott for his St. Cloud Township Company; his partners included Charles T. Stearns, for whom the county is named, and Joseph Wilson, brother of John, the Middle Town developer, who was later involved in development of East St. Cloud; and (3) Upper Town was platted by Sylvanus P. Lowry as Acadia and later replatted as Lowry's Addition to St. Cloud. While John Wilson's area did not develop as fast as the other two, he was the only one who remained in the area; he served in both the territorial and state legislatures, held numerous positions, and founded the community of St. Augusta. The post office began in 1855; it had a station of the Great Northern Railway. The city was incorporated as a town March 1, 1856, and as a city March 6, 1868.

Alluding to the granite quarries in the wards east of the river, St. Cloud is called "the Granite City," and in 1916 the street department automobile, used for street sprinkling, bore the popular slogan, conspicuously painted in large letters, "Busy, gritty, Granite City."

ST. DOMINGO a village approved for incorporation on May 23, 1857; location not found.

ST. FRANCIS a village founded about 1914 in Krain Township.

ST. JACOB a post office, 1866–67; location not found.

ST. JOSEPH TOWNSHIP settled in 1854, organized in 1858, and its city, founded in 1855 and incorporated January 18, 1890, bear the name of its church. The first settler, German immigrant Peter Loso, came in 1854, made a claim on sections 9 and 10, on which the village was platted, owned a store, a mill, and a hotel, and died in 1877. The post office was established as Clinton in 1856, with John Linnemann as postmaster; when the name was changed to St. Joseph in 1870, Loso was postmaster; it had a station of the Great Northern Railway in section 10.

ST. MARTIN TOWNSHIP settled in 1857 and organized in 1863, and its city, founded in 1866 and incorporated as a village on January 7, 1890, are named in honor of St. Martin, bishop of Tours, who was born about the year 316, for whom November 11 is celebrated as Martinmas. The community had a post office, established as Leedston in 1868; its name was changed in 1891, and it was discontinued in 1905 and reestablished in 1928.

ST. NICHOLAS a village in section 15 of Luxemburg Township, with a post office, 1877–1905.

ST. ROSA a city in Millwood Township, was founded about 1904 and incorporated as a village on August 9, 1939.

ST. STEPHEN is a city in Brockway, founded about 1858 and incorporated May 18, 1914, including the former townsite named Brockway, which was platted in 1857. The city has had a community post office since 1957.

ST. WENDEL TOWNSHIP settled in 1854 or earlier, was organized under the name of Hancock in the spring of 1868 but was renamed as now in the summer of the same year. The village in section 5 was founded about 1867; the post office was called Spring Brook 1873–74, and was changed to St. Wendall (a spelling error by the post office), 1874–1905.

SALZAR ADDITION a village founded about 1975 in Wakefield Township.

SAND/SAND'S ADDITION a place name in Albany Township.

SARTELL a city with Benton County, on the Mississippi in Le Sauk, at the mouth of the Watab River, opposite the great paper mill of the Watab Pulp and Paper Company, is named in honor of Joseph B. Sartell, the first settler of Le Sauk, who came in 1854, built a sawmill in 1857, and continued to reside here, with seven sons, until his death, January 27, 1913. He was born at East Pepperell, Mass., January 15, 1826. The paper mill and dam of the Mississippi were built in 1905–7, and the bridge over the Mississippi in 1914. This village, including the mill and railway station in Benton County and the workers' homes mainly in Stearns County, was incorporated on October 19, 1907. The city was first known as the "third rapids" by French fur traders, Elk River being the "first rapids," and Sauk Rapids being the "second rapids"; the Sartell family donated land and money to establish the village; a Sartell was on each city council roster until 1973, the last being Ripley B. Sartell, mayor for 31 years. The post office began in 1906.

SAUK CENTRE TOWNSHIP settled in 1856 and organized in 1858, received this name in allusion to its central location on the Sauk River, between the Sauk Rapids of the Mississippi and Lake Osakis, which likewise was named for its former occupation by a small band of Sauk Indians, as related in the chapter of Benton County. The city of this township, platted in 1863, was incorporated February 12, 1876, and received a city charter March 5, 1889. Alexander Moore obtained the townsite in 1855 in his mother's name, platted the site and suggested the name, and built a dam across the Sauk River and a mill. The post office was established in 1857 in postmaster Warren Adley's home, using the spelling Sauk Center until 1936, when the city won its fight to have the name spelled as Moore suggested. The city had a station of the Great Northern Railway in section 9 and of the Northern Pacific Railroad in section 10. The city is the birthplace of Sinclair Lewis and is thought to be the subject of his book *Main Street*, although he denied its being the sole source of the book's subject matter.

SCHOOL SECTION LAKE a lakeshore village in Maine Prairie Township, established about 1975.

SCHREIFEL'S SETTLEMENT a village established in 1974 in St. Joseph Township.

SCHWINGHAMMERS SETTLEMENT a village, which changed its name to Albany, which see. It is also shown on a 1976 map as a hamlet founded in 1975 south of St. Cloud in St. Cloud Township.

SENTERVILLE a village whose incorporation was approved on March 3, 1858; location not found.

SPAULDING a village with Todd County, which see.

SPRING BROOK see ST. WENDEL.

SPRING HILL TOWNSHIP settled in 1857, organized July 10, 1871, was named from its springs and low morainic hills. The city in section 28 was incorporated as a village on July 8, 1900; the post office operated 1867–1907.

STAPLE'S RIVER VIEW KNOLL a village in St. Joseph Township since 1973.

STARLITE ACRES a village in St. Augusta Township, established about 1975.

STILES a Northern Pacific station in Ashley, five miles west of Sauk Centre, commemorates A. M. Stiles, a pioneer farmer. He was born in Steuben County, N.Y., April 10, 1838; came to Minnesota in 1862, settling first in Rochester; was a miner in Idaho, 1864–66; removed in 1866 to the farm in section 11, Ashley, which was afterward his home; was chairman of the first board of township supervisors, 1870, and was town clerk 1871–80; was a representative in the legislature, 1879.

THIERSE a post office, 1871–74; location not found.

THIESEN'S SETTLEMENT a village, was established about 1975 in St. Joseph Township.

TORAH see RICHMOND.

TWO RIVERS see ALBANY.

TYROL a post office, 1883–1900, in section 36 of Raymond Township, named for Dr. Preto Tyrol of North Fork.

UNITY a post office, 1896–1901, in Getty Township.

VERDALE was a large township or district, organized in 1858, originally including St. Martin, Spring Hill, Lake Henry, Zion, and Paynesville. All its surveyed townships, when separately organized, took the other names here noted.

WAITE PARK a city in section 17 of St. Cloud, containing the Great Northern Railway shops, which were built in 1890–91, was incorporated as a village March 20, 1893, being named in honor of Henry Chester Waite of St. Cloud. He was born in Rensselaerville, N.Y., June 30, 1830; was graduated at Union College, Schenectady, in 1851 and was admitted to practice law in 1853; came to Minnesota in 1855, settling in St. Cloud as its first lawyer; later engaged in banking, flour milling, and as a merchant; was register of the U.S. land office, 1865–69; was a member of the state constitutional convention, 1857, a representative in the legislature, 1863, and a state senator in 1870–71 and 1883–85; died on his farm near the city of St. Cloud, November 15, 1912. He owned flouring mills at Cold Spring and in Clearwater. The post office operated 1897–1972.

WAKEFIELD TOWNSHIP settled in 1855, and organized May 27, 1858, was at first called Springfield

but was renamed as now in 1870, in honor of Samuel Wakefield, chairman of its first board of supervisors in 1858.

WARDEVILLE see HOLDINGFORD.

WEST ST. AUGUSTA see LUXEMBURG.

WOODSTOCK a post office, 1858–59, with David Wood, postmaster; location not found.

YANKEE SETTLEMENT a townsite located in southeast St. Joseph Township, in section 27, was begun by Jacob C. Staples in October 1854, who came from Maine with his six sons.

YARMOUTH a post office, 1859–60, which was approved for incorporation as a village on June 10, 1858; location not found.

YOUNG'S SETTLEMENT see ARBAN.

ZION TOWNSHIP settled in 1860 by German Lutherans, organized in 1867, is named from the hill or plateau of Mount Zion, the highest part of the city of Jerusalem, praised in the 48th Psalm for the beauty of its situation. The railway village of this township, formerly called Zion, is renamed Roscoe, which see.

Lakes and Streams

The rapids and islands of the Mississippi at St. Cloud and southeastward are noted in the chapter for Sherburne County.

In the foregoing pages, attention has been given to the names of Ashley Creek, Clearwater River, Crow Lake and River, with the North Fork of this river, Eden Lake, the South Stream of Two Rivers, Lakes George and Henry, Pearl Lake, and the Sauk River.

The Watab River, joining the Mississippi at Sartell, received this name from jack pines growing near its mouth. The long and slender roots of this pine, as also of the tamarack, were called *watab* by the Ojibwe and were used for sewing birch-bark canoes. In the treaty of 1825 at Prairie du Chien, this river was designated as a part of the boundary agreed upon to be a dividing line between the country of the Ojibwe and that of the Dakota. The entire course of this boundary was noted by Prof. N. H. Winchell in *The Aborigines of Minnesota* (p. 617).

Other tributaries of the Mississippi in this county, smaller than the Sauk, Watab, and Clearwater Rivers, include the southern one of the Two

Rivers, which was crossed by "Holding's ford"; Spunk Brook, translated from the Ojibwe name "Sagatagon or Spunk R." on Nicollet's map in 1843, meaning exceptionally dry and shredded wood or punk, used as tinder for making a fire; St. Augusta Creek, in the township of this name, also called Johnson's Creek, in honor of L. P. Johnson, a pioneer who came here in 1854 and was the first chairman of the township supervisors, in 1859; and Plum Creek, in Lynden, named for its wild plum trees.

Sauk River receives from its north side Adley and Getchell Creeks, named for prominent pioneers; and from its south side Silver and Ashley Creeks, in Ashley Township, Stony Creek in Spring Hill, another stream, which is the outlet of Eden Lake and of the Rice Lakes, and Mill Creek at the village of Rockville.

Warren Adley was born in Maine in 1822, came to Minnesota in 1856, served in the Fourth Minnesota Regiment in the Civil War, kept a hotel first at Melrose and later at Osakis, was a representative in the legislature in 1873.

Nathaniel Getchell was born in Wesley, Maine, November 9, 1828; came to Minnesota in 1852 and three years later was one of the founders of Brockway Township in this county; served in the Minnesota Mounted Rangers, 1862–63.

From the township of Crow Lake flow Skunk River or Creek, the outlet of Skunk or Tamarack Lake, and the Middle Fork, or Branch, of Crow River, having its source in Crow Lake.

Lakes that are named on the maps, in addition to such as have already been noticed, are Lakes Maria, Caroline, and Augusta and Clearwater, Grass, and Center Lakes, a series through which the Clearwater River flows on the southern boundary of Fair Haven and Lynden; another Lake Maria, Crooked and Long Lakes, and Warner Lake, on Plum Creek; Beaver and Block Lakes, in the southwest corner of St. Augusta; Lake Laura and Otter Lake, in Fair Haven; Goodners and Days Lakes, Island Lake, Carnelian and Willow Lakes, and School Section Lake, named from its situation in the school section 36, all being in Maine Prairie; Grand and Pleasant Lakes, in Rockville; Cedar Island Lake, Great Northern, Kray, Park, and Knaus Lakes, on the course of the Sauk River in Wakefield; Mud, Eden, Browns, and Long Lakes, in a se-

ries running from south to north through the east part of Eden Lake Township; the large Rice Lake and a small Pirz Lake, in the west part of that township; Big Lake, Schroeder, Becker, and Horseshoe Lakes, in Munson, the last being on the Sauk River; Lake Koronis in Paynesville, extending south into Meeker County; Fish Lake in Crow Lake Township; Sand Lake (drained) in the southeast corner of Raymond; Black Oak and Elrings Lakes, in Grove Township; a little Lake George in the city of St. Cloud; Kraemer Lake in St. Joseph; Sagatagan and Stump Lakes, adjoining St. John's University, and Big Fish Lake, Long and Sand Lakes, Pitts, and Kreigle Lakes, and Big Watab and Little Watab Lakes, all in Collegeville, the last two being on the South Fork of the Watab River; another Watab (or Rossier) Lake, on the middle course of this river in St. Wendel, and yet another and smaller Watab Lake, also called Bakers Lake, on a northern tributary of this river, in sections 8 and 17, Le Sauk; Shepard Lake (drained) in Brockway; Achman and Kepper Lakes, Lake Anna and Linneman and Minnie Lakes, and the Big, Middle, and Lower Spunk Lakes, in the south half of Avon; Pelican and Pine Lakes in northwestern Avon; the large Two Rivers Lake in Holding; Clear and Mud Lakes, Big and Little Rice Lakes, Lake Henry, another Mud Lake, and Sand Lake, in Farming; North Lake at the north side of Albany village; Vos Lake and Lake St. Anna, in Krain; Gravel Lake in section 1, St. Martin; Sand and Getchell Lakes, Lake Maria, Frevels and Uhlenkolts Lakes, in Oak Township; Kings Lake, Long Lake, Swamp, Cedar, and Wolf Lakes, in the south half of Millwood, and Lake Mary and Big Birch Lakes, crossed by its north line; Lake Sylvia and Little Birch Lake, in the northeast part of Melrose, the former being named for the wife of Alfred Townsend; and McCormic, Cedar, and Sauk Lakes, the last being on the Sauk River, in Sauk Centre Township.

Hills and Prairies

Among many morainic hills from 50 feet, or less, to about 100 feet in height, or rarely 150 to 200 feet high, occurring in numerous long tracts or belts in this county, maps name only Cheney Hill in section 1, Melrose.

Winnebago Prairie, also known as Brockway Prairie, adjoins the Mississippi for about four or five miles in Le Sauk and Brockway; and the North Prairie similarly borders the river in the northeast part of Brockway, continuing into Morrison County.

Besides these relatively small prairie areas of the valley drift in the generally wooded part of this county, it has a large area of prairie west of Richmond and southwest of the Sauk River, continuous with the great prairie region of southern and western Minnesota.

Steele County

Established February 20, 1855, this county was named in honor of Franklin Steele, a prominent pioneer of Minneapolis. He was born in Chester County, Pa., May 12, 1813; came to Fort Snelling as sutler of that frontier post in 1838; became owner of valuable lands at the Falls of St. Anthony; and was active in improvements of the waterpower and in the building up of St. Anthony and Minneapolis. He was a charter member of the Minnesota Historical Society and at the time of his death was chairman of its department of American history. In 1851 he was elected by the legislature as a member of the first board of regents of the University of Minnesota; and during all his later life he was identified with the promotion of many public interests but never held political office. He died in Minneapolis, September 10, 1880.

Biographic notes, with portraits, of Franklin Steele and his associates in founding the lumber industries on the upper Mississippi, with the sawmills of Minneapolis, are given in the MHS Collections 9: 325–62 (1901).

Information of names has been gathered from History of Steele and Waseca Counties *(1887, 756 pp.);* History of Rice and Steele Counties *by Franklyn Curtiss-Wedge (1910), having pp. 629–1,026 for this county; and Hon. Charles S. Crandall, Jesse Healey, Willard E. Martin, and W. E. Kenyon, judge of probate, these being interviewed at Owatonna, the county seat, during visits there in April and October 1916.*

ADAMSVILLE see **BERLIN**.

ANDERSON is a Chicago and North Western Railway station in section 22 of Havana, seven miles east of Owatonna. It was named either for Thomas M. Anderson, a well-known farmer of the township on whose land the railroad station and post office of Lysne were located, or for William Anderson, a local farmer and landowner. Its village or hamlet is called Lysne (pronounced in two syllables).

AURORA CENTRE see **AURORA**.

AURORA TOWNSHIP first settled in 1856, organized February 17, 1857, was named by Hon. Amos Coggswell for the city of Aurora in Illinois. He was born in Boscawen, N.H., September 29, 1825; settled in 1856 on a homestead claim in this township; removed to Owatonna and was a lawyer there; was speaker of the legislature in 1859 and a state senator in 1872–75; died in Owatonna, November 15, 1892. The name Aurora, from the Latin language, means "the morning," or especially "the redness of the dawning light." The village of Aurora had two post offices: the first, 1856–57, was transferred to Oak Glen; the second, in section 17, operated 1857–66 as Aurora Centre and then as Aurora, 1868–94. The community was important in the early days of the railroad, but after it was destroyed by fire, it was replaced by Bixby.

BERLIN TOWNSHIP organized February 17, 1857, was named from the city of Berlin in Wisconsin.

Twenty-three other states of the Union have townships and villages or cities likewise named after the capital of Germany. A post office was in section 22, 1856–1904; it was called Adamsville for the first year, with Hiram Pitcher as first postmaster under both names. The community included a boathouse and summer resort on Beaver Lake and a station of the Minneapolis and St. Louis Railroad.

BIXBY a village in section 34 of Aurora, founded about 1890, was named in honor of John Bixby, who was born in Moretown, Vt., January 28, 1814, and died in Aurora, January 15, 1890. He came to Minnesota in 1856, settling on a homestead claim a mile west of the site of this village. His eldest son, Jacob S. Bixby, on whose farm the new railway station was located, was the first postmaster when the post office opened in 1889. The name Oak Glen, to be later noticed, was proposed for the post office but was changed to Bixby by Hon. Mark H. Dunnell of Owatonna, member in Congress for this district. After Aurora burned, Jacob Bixby convinced the Chicago, Milwaukee and St. Paul Railroad authorities to select his land as a more advantageous location for a new station.

BLOOMING PRAIRIE TOWNSHIP settled in 1856, was organized in 1867, being then called Oak Glen, as further noted in this list. The township was renamed as now in January 1873, taking the name of its railway village, which was platted in 1868. It is euphonious, referring to the abundant flowers of this prairie region, and it has the merit of uniqueness, no other village or post office in the world having adopted this name. The city of Blooming Prairie was incorporated as a village on March 3, 1874; Charles W. Gardner was a merchant and the first postmaster when the post office opened in 1868; the community had a Soo Line depot.

CLINTON FALLS TOWNSHIP settled in 1854, organized May 11, 1858, and its village in section 20, platted in 1855, are named from the falls of the Straight River, having ten feet head at its dam here. Nine other states have counties named Clinton, and 30 states have townships and villages or cities of this name, mostly commemorating George and De Witt Clinton, who were governors of New York, the latter being also the projector of the Erie Canal. The post office, operated 1857–1933, was called Tudor, February-May 1857, with Tudor

T. Beall as postmaster; the name was changed when Timothy A. Bemis became postmaster; it had a station of the Chicago, Rock Island and Pacific Railroad.

COOLEYSVILLE see ELLENDALE.

DEERFIELD TOWNSHIP first settled in May 1855, and organized in the spring of 1858, has a name that is also borne by townships and villages in New Hampshire, Massachusetts, New York, Ohio, Wisconsin, and nine other states. The village in section 16 had a post office, 1857–1906, and a station of the Chicago, Rock Island and Pacific Railroad.

DODGE CITY a post office, located in Merton Township, ten miles northwest of Owatonna, was begun in 1856 and transferred to Dodge, Rice County, in 1894; the community was started by a person named Colburn, who opened a store in the northeast corner of the township in 1856 but sold out soon afterward.

EAST MERIDEN a post office, 1867–88, in section 35 of Meriden Township.

ELLENDALE a city in sections 24–26 of Berlin, was platted in the autumn of 1900 and was incorporated August 16, 1901, its site having been selected by the railway officials, C. J. Ives being president. "The name was given in memory of Mrs. C. J. (Ellen) Ives, who died a few years previous to this time. She was the laboring man's friend. She seemed to know every section man and every brakeman on the road; and her many acts of tender, thoughtful kindness endeared her to the hundreds of employees. Her maiden name was Ellen Dale, so this beautiful, prosperous village will perpetuate the memory of that good woman" (*History of Rice and Steele Counties*, p. 944). The post office began in 1858 as Cooleysville in section 30 of Summit Township, with William Cooley as postmaster, and was then moved to section 25 of Berlin Township; the name was changed in 1901.

ELMIRA a townsite of 80 blocks, was platted in 1857 in section 18 of Somerset Township but never developed.

ELWOOD a village in section 24 of Clinton Falls Township, was platted in 1854 by W. Wilbur Fisk, first postmaster; the post office operated 1856–71.

HAVANA TOWNSHIP settled in 1855, was organized February 27, 1857, being then called Lafayette. In September 1858, the name was changed to Freeman, and in the next month to Dover. Thus it continued till 1869, when it was renamed Havana, on request of Elijah Easton, for Havana, the county seat of Mason County, Ill. As a Spanish word, meaning "a haven, a harbor," it became the name of the chief city and capital of Cuba. The village of Havana, at the corner of sections 17–20, was founded and so named in 1867, with the completion of the Winona and St. Peter Railroad. Its post office, 1869–79, was spelled Havanna and was discontinued in 1911; it had a Chicago and North Western Railway station. It contains Rice Lake State Park, established in 1963.

HOBSON a post office, 1898–1905, in section 24 of Merton Township.

HOPE is a village in sections 19 and 30 of Somerset Township, with a post office since 1916, a creamery built in 1891, and a station of the Chicago, Rock Island and Pacific Railroad.

JUNO a post office, 1857–62; location not found.

LEMOND TOWNSHIP settled in 1856 and organized in April 1858, bears probably a personal surname, but it is nowhere else used as a geographic name, excepting a railway station in Queensland, Australia.

LENOX a post office, 1857–59; location not found.

LITOMYSL a village at the corner of sections 25, 26, 35, and 36 of Somerset Township, received its name from the old town of Litomysl situated in western Bohemia, many of the first settlers being either from there or villages adjacent to it.

LYSNE is a Scandinavian name, in two syllables, of a railway village in Havana, before noted as Anderson, which is its official railway name. A post office called Lysne was in section 22, 1897–1912.

MEDFORD TOWNSHIP first settled in 1853, was organized August 29, 1855, and its city was platted in 1856. The first township meeting was held at the house of William K. Colling, an Englishman who had come here in 1854 and taken a homestead claim, but who after several years' residence returned finally to England. "At a meeting of the settlers to consult upon a name wherewith to christen the town, Mr. Colling said that he had a son who was born on board the ship Medford, and was named Medford, in honor of the ship, and proposed that the town should be named Medford in honor of the boy, which proposition was unanimously adopted" (*History of Steele and Waseca Counties*, p. 303). The city was incorporated as a village on May 22, 1936; the post office was

established in 1855 in Rice County and was transferred to Steele County in 1857 as the first post office in the county; the first postmaster, Smith Johnson, Sr., originally owned the land on which he had the townsite platted, having come to Minnesota in 1853 and died at age 65 in 1857.

MELVILLE a place name in Lemond Township, circa 1887.

MERIDEN TOWNSHIP settled in 1855 and organized in 1857–58, was named by F. J. Stephens, one of its founders, from the city of Meriden in Connecticut, which is famed for its manufacture of silverware and thence is sometimes called the "Silver City." The village of Meriden in section 17 was established as a Chicago and North Western Railway station in 1867; the post office opened in 1856.

MERTON TOWNSHIP settled in 1855, was at first called Union Prairie but was organized in 1857–58 as Orion and was renamed Merton in 1862, probably for the township and village of Merton in Wisconsin. A village in section 17 had a post office, 1862–1903. This is the name of a village in Surrey, England, which in the Middle Ages had a famous Augustinian abbey.

MOLAND a village in section 1 of Merton Township.

OAK GLEN was a stagecoach station at the lakes of this name in section 2 of the present township of Blooming Prairie, where a village site named Oak Glen was platted in 1857 in section 35. Thence the township took this name when it was organized in 1867, but it was renamed Blooming Prairie, as before noted, in 1873. The village site was platted with 111 blocks around a town square, which did not develop and was replaced by Blooming Prairie; it had a post office, 1857–71, which had been transferred from Aurora.

OMRO a post office, 1898–1902, located in section 11 of Summit Township.

OWATONNA the county seat, earliest settled in 1854 and platted in September 1855, was incorporated as a town August 9, 1858, and as a city February 23, 1865. Its post office was established in 1855. The townsite is on land originally owned by A. B. Cornell, W. F. Pettit, and John Abbott, with 120 acres platted into 21 blocks and a public square; it had a station of the Chicago and North Western Railway. The township was organized, with its present area, February 27, 1857. This was the Dakota name of the Straight River, which is its translation. The river was mapped, but not named, on the map of Minnesota Territory in 1855; on the early state maps, in 1860 and 1869, it is called Owatonna River, but in 1870 it is named Straight River.

PRATT a village in section 6 of Aurora, was named in honor of William A. Pratt, a nearby farmer. Its post office operated, 1879–1955, and as a rural branch until 1956; it had a station of the Chicago, Milwaukee and St. Paul Railroad.

RICE LAKE a village in section 1 of Havana Township.

RIVER POINT a village in section 29 of Somerset Township, had a post office, first called Lemond, 1856–57, called Somerset, 1857–59, and then changed to River Point, discontinuing in 1903.

SACO is a village in section 7 of Somerset Township, with a station of the Chicago and North Western Railway in section 6, named from the Saco River and city in Maine.

SOMERSET TOWNSHIP first settled in 1855 and organized in 1857–58, received the name of its first post office, which was established in 1857, with Dr. Thomas Kenyon as postmaster, who came in the spring of 1856. The name of the settlement and post office is said to have come from the overturning of his tent by a high wind, when dinner was ready in it. The somersault of the tent, with change of spelling, became the township name. It is a common geographic name, thus spelled Somerset, for a county in England, counties in Maine, New Jersey, Pennsylvania, and Maryland, and villages and townships in 15 states of the Union. See also RIVER POINT.

STEELE CENTER a village in sections 15 and 16 of Somerset Township; the post office operated 1848–1902.

SUMMIT TOWNSHIP settled in the summer of 1856, organized May 10, 1858, has near its south line the summit or water divide between the sources of the Straight River and Geneva Lake in Freeborn County, which outflows southward to the Cedar River.

SWAVESEY a post office, 1856–64, which transferred to Blooming Grove, Waseca County; location not found.

TUDOR see CLINTON FALLS.

Lakes and Streams

Straight River, translated from its Dakota name, Owatonna, as before noted, has been said to be so named "in derision, as it is about the crookedest river in the state" (Stennett, *Place Names of the Chicago and Northwestern Railways*, 1908, p. 11), but while the stream meanders, the general course of its valley is remarkably straight, from south to north.

Its tributaries from the east are the outlet of the three Oak Glen Lakes and of Rickert Lake, in Blooming Prairie; Turtle Creek, four miles south of Owatonna; Maple Creek, flowing from Rice Lake, named for its wild rice, crossed by the east line of Havana; and Rush Creek, flowing northwest into Rice County.

From the west this river receives the outlet of Lonergan, Beaver, and Mud (or Fosilen) Lakes in Berlin, and Crane Creek, which flows through Bradley Lake, on the line between Meriden and Deerfield.

Only three other lakes bearing names in this county remain to be noted, these being Wilker or Willert Lake or Slough, now drained, in section 6, Lemond, and Pelican and Swan Lakes in Deerfield. The last two, with the adjacent Crane Creek, tell of large wild birds that formerly were frequent here.

Stevens County

Established February 20, 1862, this county was named in honor of Isaac Ingalls Stevens, who in 1853 commanded the expedition making the northern surveys for a Pacific railroad. The expedition started from St. Paul and traveled to the present sites of Sauk Rapids and St. Cloud, and by White Bear (now Minnewaska) and Elbow Lakes, to the Bois des Sioux River, thus passing near the northeast corner of this county. Stevens was born in Andover, Mass., March 28, 1818; was graduated at West Point in 1839; served in the Mexican War; was governor of Washington Territory, 1853–57; was a delegate to Congress, 1857–61; and was a gallant leader for the Union in the Civil War, entering it as colonel of the 79th Regiment of New York Volunteers, known as the Highlanders; attained the rank of major general, July 4, 1862; and lost his life in the battle of Chantilly, in Virginia, on the first day of September in the same year. An earlier attempt to give his name to a county of Minnesota, in 1855, was frustrated by a clerical error in the enrollment of the legislative act, which changed it to Stearns County.

Information for the origins and meanings of names has been received from a pamphlet, "Stevens County, Minnesota, Its Villages, History . . . ," (22 pp.), published in 1879 by the Board of Trade of Morris; Illustrated Album of Biography of Pope and Stevens Counties (1888), having pp. 367–530 for this county; and from Edwin J. Jones, a life member of the Minnesota Historical Society, who has resided in Morris since 1878, and A. L. Stenger, judge of probate, each being interviewed at Morris, the county seat, during a visit there in May 1916.

ALBERTA a city in sections 3 and 4 of Scott Township, incorporated as a village on May 6, 1912, formerly called Wheeler, was renamed in honor of the wife of E. B. Lindsey, a farmer there. The post office was also first known as Wheeler, 1883–84, then as Clearfield, 1884–87, and as Alberta from 1896; it had a station of the Great Northern Railway.

BAKER TOWNSHIP has a common personal surname, which is also borne by counties in Georgia and Florida, a county and city in Oregon, and villages in eight other states. The township was organized on November 15, 1882, as Emmett and was renamed Baker in January 1883 for Miclos and Chatrine Baker, who farmed in the township from about 1880.

BELFAST a special supply post office, 1879–80, 16 miles from Morris.

CHO-KI-O / CHOKAGO see CHOKIO.

CHOKIO (accented on the second syllable, like Ohio) is a city in sections 3 and 10 of Baker. This name is a Dakota word, meaning "the middle." The city was incorporated as a village on August 11, 1898. The post office was called Chokago

1878–79, and Cho-ki-o, 1879–81, and was reestablished as Chokio in 1891; the early site had a creamery, a cheese factory, and a station of the Great Northern Railway.

CLEARFIELD see ALBERTA.

DARNEN TOWNSHIP first settled at a stage station in section 12 by Henry Gager in 1866 and organized January 3, 1878, had many immigrants from Ireland, who probably proposed this name, which is a form of the Irish place name Darien, the name first given and changed in 1879; it was also called Derrynane. The site of Gager's station, at the crossing of the Pomme de Terre River on a state road from Glenwood to Browns Valley, was later occupied by the Riverside mill, owned by Hon. H. W. Stone and Company.

DONNELLY TOWNSHIP and its city in section 24, platted on December 8, 1871, incorporated as a village in June 1900, and at first called Douglas, are named in honor of Ignatius Donnelly, the distinguished politician and author, who owned a farm in section 31, Rendsville, about a mile east of this village. He is also honored by the name of a township in Marshall County, for which a biographic sketch has been presented. The city's railroad station, Douglas, was in section 25, a name used until 1877. John Gavin Donnelly, brother of Ignatius Donnelly, was depot agent when the railroad came in 1872, and when the post office was established in 1876, he became postmaster at the depot (he died in 1889); it is shown as Douglas on an 1874 map in section 25, with the Great Northern Railway station.

DOUGLAS see DONNELLY.

ELDORADO TOWNSHIP organized July 22, 1880, has a Spanish name, meaning literally "the gilded," which is borne by a county in California, a city in Kansas, and villages in ten other states.

EVERGLADE TOWNSHIP organized on August 2, 1880, as Potsdam and later changed to the present name, bears a unique name, received from the Everglades in southern Florida, a large marshy region that has much area of water from 1 to 10 feet deep, enclosing "thousands of little islands, covered with dense thickets of palmetto, cypress, oaks, vines, and shrubs, and in part inhabited by remnants of the Seminole tribe of Indians."

FRAMNAS TOWNSHIP was organized January 11, 1873, as Scandia; its name was changed on June 7, 1873, because many of the settlers were from a cape off the coast of Norway that had the name spelled Framnes.

GAGER'S STATION see POTOSI, and ST. LAWRENCE HOMESTEAD COLONY.

HAIG a village in Morris Township, about 1937, located four miles northwest of Morris, receiving mail from Donnelly.

HANCOCK a city on the border of Hodges and Moore Townships, founded in 1871 when this railway line was completed to Morris, received its name in honor of Joseph Woods Hancock, who was born in Orford, N.H., April 4, 1816, and died in Minneapolis, October 24, 1907. He came to Red Wing in 1849 as a missionary teacher among the Indians; organized a Presbyterian church there in 1855 and was its pastor until 1861; was superintendent of schools for Goodhue County, 1864–81; author of *Goodhue County . . . Past and Present, by an Old Settler* (349 pp.), published in 1893. He continued to reside in Red Wing until about a week before his death. The city was platted in 1872 and incorporated as a village on February 9, 1881; the original site was in section 3 of Moore Township. The post office was established in 1871; it had a station of the Great Northern Railway.

HODGES TOWNSHIP was named in honor of Leonard Bacon Hodges, tree planter for the St. Paul, Minneapolis and Manitoba Railroad, who set out trees in many villages along this railway, including the hundred evergreen trees, or more, of the courthouse square in Morris. He was born in West Bloomfield, N.Y., July 15, 1823, and died in St. Paul, April 14, 1883. He came to Minnesota in 1854, opened a farm in Olmsted County, and founded the town of Oronoco; was a state senator in 1871; removed to St. Paul in 1872; and afterward was much engaged in forestry. The township was organized on March 18, 1878, as Honolulu, but was changed to the present name on March 6, 1879.

HORTON TOWNSHIP organized February 20, 1879, was named in honor of William T. Horton, its earliest settler, who was a farmer in section 14. He was born in Ulster County, N.Y., in 1825; came to Minnesota and engaged in farming in Fillmore and Mower Counties; served in the Eleventh Minnesota Regiment, 1863–64; removed to this township in 1878 and here gave attention largely to stock raising.

KEEVILLE a post office, 1889–97, in section 12 of Rendsville Township, with Samuel Bradley Smith as postmaster until the office was changed to Patchen and moved to Grant County; the name's origin is unknown, but there was supposedly a postal clerk named Kee who lived in Morris for a time.

LARSON a post office, 1891–99, in Swan Lake Township, with Peter G. Larson, postmaster.

MEDINA a post office, 1887–1902, 17 miles from Morris and 10 miles from Chokio; Richard Northcott was postmaster in his general store.

MOORE TOWNSHIP organized on September 9, 1872, as Hancock, and changed to the present name on June 7, 1873, was named for a family of its pioneer settlers.

MOOSE ISLAND a business site in section 4 of Donnelly, was named for the former Moose Island Lake, noted in the list of lakes, five to eight miles distant southward, which is mostly drained. The site began with a Great Northern Railway section house, a lumberyard, a coal and wood yard, a grain warehouse, and elevators. The post office operated 1891–96 and 1905–8 to handle mail for the Barrett Ranch, owned by Gen. Theodore H. Barrett, who had served with the Ninth Minnesota during the Civil War; he was the largest landholder in the township.

MORRIS a city in Morris and Darnen Townships and the county seat, platted in 1869, incorporated as a village February 21, 1878, and as a city in 1902, was named in honor of Charles A. F. Morris, who was born in Ireland in 1827 and died in Excelsior, Minn., June 2, 1903. He came to the United States in 1849 and to St. Paul in 1854; was connected with the engineering departments of several railroads, among them being the Manitoba and the Northern Pacific; removed to Oregon but a few years later returned to Minnesota and resided in Excelsior. The city became the county seat on February 3, 1872. It began as a tent town following the arrival of the Great Northern Railway and Northern Pacific Railroad; the first building was postmaster Henry B. Wolff's general store, where the post office was established in 1871, moving from John B. Folsom's farm at Pape de Terre (1870–71). The city is the site of the University of Minnesota at Morris. Morris Township was organized on January 11, 1873.

NASH a post office, 1876–89, in section 12 of Morris Township, located on Erick E. Solseth's farm.

PAPE DE TERRE see MORRIS.

PEPPERTON TOWNSHIP organized March 11, 1879, was named for Charles A. Pepper, its first settler, who in the fall of 1875 took a soldier's homestead claim in section 34. He was born in Burlington, Iowa, June 1, 1845; served in the Seventh Iowa Cavalry, 1863–66; came to Minnesota in 1871, first settling in Washington County; removed to his homestead in this township in 1875 and to Morris in 1883, where he was a dealer in farm machinery and also in grain; was later a resident of St. Paul.

POTOSI a post office, 1870, was located at the first trading post in the county, Gager's Station, on Wintermute Lake in section 12 of Morris Township. Henry Gager came from Sauk Centre, where he had a store and saloon, and moved from Potosi in 1871 to Bismarck, N.Dak., selling the trading post to Charles Wintermute. The name Potosi means "great riches."

RENDSVILLE TOWNSHIP was organized March 25, 1878; Archibald Young, first clerk of the township, 1878–93, brought a group of settlers here from the East in 1870, later moving to Canada; the township was named for his wife, Lorenda (Rends) Young, whose nickname was "Rends."

SAHLINARK a post office, May-November 1878, with Adolph Tranton as postmaster May to July on Charles A. Sahlmark's farm in Swan Lake Township (originally named Sahlmark Township); Sahlmark was postmaster until the office was discontinued; the post office erred in reading the application, misspelling the name.

SAHLMARK TOWNSHIP see SWAN LAKE TOWNSHIP.

ST. LAWRENCE HOMESTEAD COLONY was formed in 1871 by persons from St. Lawrence County, N.Y.; many settled in section 10, Morris Township, near Gager's Station, their area becoming known as Yankee Ridge Road.

SCANDIA the first permanent settlement and the first post office in the county, 1867–71, settled in 1866 by Scandinavian families; the settlement was not incorporated, and it became part of Scandia Township, renamed Framnes Township.

SCOTT TOWNSHIP organized June 19, 1877, had settlers from southern Minnesota and may thence have received this name from Scott County.

STEVENS TOWNSHIP organized March 16, 1880, was named like this county.

SWAN LAKE TOWNSHIP organized on July 24, 1876, as Sahlmark Township, was renamed for its fine lake in sections 26 and 35. Charles Sahlmark, for whom the township was first named, was elected clerk of the township, serving 1876–78; the township was renamed after the Sahlmark family moved away.

SYNNES TOWNSHIP organized on January 7, 1880, was named for P. Synnes, who settled in section 32. A post office was located in the township, 15 miles southwest of Morris, 1892–1900, with music teacher Ole E. Loftus as postmaster.

WHEELER see ALBERTA.

Streams and Lakes

Pomme de Terre River, flowing across this county, has been noticed in the first chapter and also in the chapter for Grant County, where this river flows through the upper Pomme de Terre Lake and gives its name to a township.

The Chippewa River, flowing through the east edge of Swan Lake Township, was a route of travel for Chippewa, or Ojibwe, war parties in coming from their wooded northern country to the prairie region of the Dakota in the Minnesota valley.

Mud or Muddy Creek is a western tributary of the Pomme de Terre River, and Twelvemile Creek, flowing from Echo or Fish Lake through Eldorado, joins the West Branch of Mustinka River in Traverse County.

The following lakes are found in Stevens County, bearing names on maps, in the order of townships from south to north and of ranges from east to west.

Page Lake in Hodges was named for the late William H. Page, who owned a farm beside it.

Scott Township has Frog or Gorder and Little Frog Lakes, Lake Hattie, and Clear Lake.

Baker Township has Clark (drained) and Gravel Lakes, the first being named for a pioneer farmer who lived near Chokio.

Framnas has Long Lake, formerly called Morse Lake, crossed by its south line; Lake Cyrus in sections 25 and 36; Olson or Charlotte, Hanse, and Hanson Lakes, Lake Moore, and Scandia Lake, forming a very noteworthy group in the east part of this township; and Foss Lake in sections 8 and 17.

Crystal Lake lies in the southwest part of the city of Morris; Gould's Lake (drained) was a mile farther west, in sections 4 and 5, Darnen, named for John L. Gould, an adjoining farmer; and Maughan Lake named similarly for George W. Maughan, was two miles north of Morris, mostly in section 22, but it also has been drained.

Wintermute Lake in sections 1 and 12, Morris, the largest lake of this township, was a favorite resort of the Dakota for fishing and hunting. It was named in honor of Charles Wintermute, one of the earliest settlers of the county, who came in 1871, purchased the Gager stage station, before mentioned, and also took a homestead and bought other land. He was born in Chemung County, N.Y., March 14, 1834; came to Minnesota in 1861; served against the Dakota in the conflict, 1862–63; was a trader at Fort Wadsworth, S.Dak., 1865–71; was a farmer beside this lake, 1871–85, when he removed to Morris; and later continued in farming, with interests in mercantile business and in the lumber trade. In 1875–77 he was chairman of the board of county commissioners.

Moose Island Lake, branched like the horns of a moose, lying in Pepperton and Donnelly, remains only in part, as a large marsh; and Fish Lake, formerly also called Echo Lake, is mostly in sections 6 and 7 of this township.

Swan Lake Township, with the lake so named, has two Pomme de Terre Lakes, on the course of that river.

Harstad Lake, or Slough in the southwest part of Rendsville, commemorates Lars E. Harstad, an early settler there.

Cottonwood Lake, crossed by the north line of section 1, Donnelly, lies for its greater part in Grant County.

Swift County

Established February 18, 1870, this county was named in honor of Henry Adoniram Swift, governor of Minnesota in 1863. He was born in Ravenna, Ohio, March 23, 1823; was graduated at Western Reserve College; was admitted to the practice of law in 1845; came to Minnesota in 1853, first settling in St. Paul but removing in 1856 to St. Peter; and was a member of the state senate, 1862 to 1865. For the latter half of the year 1863, having been elected lieutenant-governor in place of Hon. Ignatius Donnelly, who resigned in consequence of his election as a representative in Congress, Swift succeeded to the governorship when Gov. Alexander Ramsey resigned to take his seat in the U.S. Senate. In 1865, Governor Swift was appointed register of the U.S. land office in St. Peter and held this office until his death, February 25, 1869.

A memoir of Governor Swift by John Fletcher Williams, secretary of the Minnesota Historical Society, is in its vol. 3, pp. 91–98, published in 1870. Gen. James H. Baker in the "Lives of the Governors of Minnesota" (MHS Collections 13 [1908]) presented his biography in pp. 109–27, with his portrait. In the closing pages of this sketch, General Baker wrote: "The memory of Governor Swift will ever be held in the highest regard by the people of this state. The integrity of his character, his fidelity to public duty, his exemplary and spotless life as a citizen, and his devotion to family ties, made him a model worthy of the regard and admiration of the youth of Minnesota."

Information of geographic names has been gathered in History of the Minnesota Valley *(1882), having pp. 955–72 for Swift County; and from J. N. Edwards, judge of probate, H. C. Odney, register of deeds, and the late Ernest R. Aldrich, each of Benson, the county seat, the two former being interviewed during a visit there in May 1916 and the last at later visits by him in St. Paul.*

APPLETON TOWNSHIP organized on March 30, 1870, was at first called Phelps in honor of its first settler, Addison Phelps, who came in the autumn of 1868. Appleton city, named for the city of Appleton in eastern Wisconsin, was founded in 1871–72; the railway was built there in 1879; and the village was incorporated February 19, 1881. The post office was first known as Clarksfield, 1872–73, and was originally platted on an Indian camp site; it had a station of the Great Northern Railway in section 14 and of the Minneapolis, St. Paul and Sault Ste. Marie Railroad (Soo Line) in section 15. The township was renamed Appleton on request of Mr. Phelps, who was one of the county commissioners, September 4, 1872. In Wisconsin this name commemorates Samuel Appleton, one of the founders of Lawrence University, located there.

BENSON a city in sections 5–8 of Torning Township and named the county seat on February 18, 1870, was platted for the railway company by

Charles A. F. Morris, for whom Morris in Stevens County was named, in the spring of 1870; it was incorporated as a village February 14, 1877, and as a city in 1908. The post office was established in 1870; it had a station in section 6 of the Great Northern Railway.

BENSON TOWNSHIP first settled in 1867, was organized in April 1871. The name was adopted in honor of Ben. H. Benson, who was born in Norway in 1846, came to the United States in 1861, and settled in this township in 1869, engaging in mercantile business. After 1875 he owned a farm in Hantho, Lac qui Parle County (*History of the Minnesota Valley*, p. 950). Later he removed to Duluth.

Others have regarded this name as chosen in honor of Jared Benson of Anoka, who at that time and during many years was a prominent citizen and a political leader. He was born in Mendon, Mass., November 8, 1821; came to Minnesota in 1856, settling at Anoka, and engaged in farming and cattle raising; was a member and speaker of the House of Representatives in the state legislature in 1861–62 and 1864 and was again a representative in 1879 and 1889; and died in St. Paul, May 18, 1894.

CAMP LAKE TOWNSHIP first settled in 1866, was named from its lake, which was the site of the camp of government surveyors for this and adjoining townships.

CARLSON a post office, 1890–1904, in section 31 of Kerkhoven Township, with Andrew Peter Carlson, postmaster; it had a station of the Great Northern Railway. Carlson was born in Sweden in 1833, came to the United States in 1863, served in the Sixth Minnesota Regiment during the end of the Civil War, and then settled in section 31 of the township with a farm and a general store on the site where the post office was located; Carlson died in 1910.

CASHEL TOWNSHIP settled in 1873 and organized March 23, 1878, received its name from the ancient city of Cashel in Tipperary County, southern Ireland. A farmers post office was located in section 7, 12 miles southeast of Benson and 8 miles from De Graff, 1895–1905.

CLARKSFIELD see APPLETON.

CLONTARF TOWNSHIP which received its first settler in June 1876, was organized January 16, 1877. "The town was named by Bishop Ireland.

The inhabitants are mostly Irish, a colony having settled here in 1878" (*History of the Minnesota Valley*, p. 969). This name is from the town and watering place in a suburb of Dublin, Ireland. The site was chosen in 1876 by the Catholic Colonization Bureau to develop as its second colony in Minnesota. The city of Clontarf was platted in 1876, incorporated as a village on November 17, 1881, reincorporated on April 21, 1904, and separated from the township on April 7, 1916. The Great Northern Railway came in 1870. The post office began in 1876, with postmaster Dominick F. McDermott, who came from Ireland in 1834 and to Minnesota in 1856.

DANVERS a city in sections 13 and 24 of Marysland, bears the name of a township and village in Massachusetts and of a village in Illinois. The city was incorporated as a village on January 19, 1900, and separated from the township on April 9, 1906. It had a station of the Great Northern Railway, and its post office was established in 1892.

DE GRAFF a city in section 29 of Kildare, founded and platted in 1875, was incorporated February 10, 1881, being named in honor of Andrew De Graff of St. Paul. He was born near Amsterdam, N.Y., October 21, 1811; came to Minnesota in 1857 and built many railroads in this state, including the Great Northern line through this county; he died in St. Paul, November 7, 1894. The post office was established in 1875; it had a station of the Great Northern Railway.

DRY WOOD a place name about 1937; location not found.

DUBLIN TOWNSHIP organized February 14, 1878, having chiefly Irish settlers, is named for the capital and largest city of Ireland.

EDISON TOWNSHIP settled in 1872 and organized March 23, 1878, was originally called New Posen for a Polish city and province of Prussia but was renamed in honor of Thomas Alva Edison, the great inventor. He was born in Milan, Ohio, February 11, 1847; was a newsboy and afterward a telegraph operator; removed to New York City, 1871, to Menlo Park, N.J., 1876, and later to West Orange, N.J. Among his inventions are the duplex telegraph, the phonograph, and the incandescent electric lamp.

FAIRFIELD a village in section 5 of Moyer Township, which had a post office, 1873–1907, and a creamery.

FAIRFIELD TOWNSHIP settled in 1867, organized April 16, 1872, has a name borne by counties in Connecticut, Ohio, and South Carolina and by townships and villages or cities in 29 states of the Union.

HAYES TOWNSHIP settled in 1868 and organized in 1877, was named in honor of Rutherford Birchard Hayes, nineteenth president of the United States. He was born in Delaware, Ohio, October 4, 1822; served in the Union army during the Civil War and was brevetted major general of volunteers in 1865; was a member of Congress, 1865–67; governor of Ohio, 1868–72 and 1876–77; was president, 1877–81; died at Fremont, Ohio, January 17, 1893.

HEGBERT a farmers post office, 1884–1906, in section 28 of Hegbert Township, 24 miles from Benson and 10 miles from Appleton.

HERBERT TOWNSHIP was first settled by Ole Hegstad in 1869 and was organized in a meeting at his house, April 8, 1876.

HOLLOWAY a city in Moyer and Edison Townships, was named by officers of the Great Northern Railway in honor of a pioneer farmer. The village was first called Norton. It was incorporated as a village on February 14, 1903, and the post office was established in 1889; it had a station of the Great Northern Railway in section 35 of Moyer Township.

KERKHOVEN TOWNSHIP first settled in 1865, and the city of this name in section 21 of Pillsbury Township, platted in 1870 and incorporated on March 3, 1881, as Pillsbury, received this Scottish name on February 17, 1883, in honor of Johannes Kerkhoven, who with his brother, Theodores, was given the contract to build rail lines west from St. Paul to Willmar to Kerkhoven; their company was the Kerkhoven Brokerage Company of Amsterdam, Holland. The post office was established in 1871 in Chippewa County, with Matts Rasmussen, postmaster, and was transferred to Swift County, with J. B. Jacobson as postmaster; it had a station of the Great Northern Railway. Monson Lake State Park, established in 1937 in the southeast corner of the township, originated as a memorial to two white families killed in the Dakota Conflict of 1862.

KILDARE TOWNSHIP settled in 1868 and organized April 20, 1875, was named for a county and a town in Ireland.

LOUISBURG a village, was named for Lewis Thompson, who had a store and processed mail; the site was platted in 1887, but its location was not found, and no trace remains.

LYONSDALE a post office, April-November 1879, with John D. Lyons, postmaster; location not found.

MARYLAND a post office, 1884–88; location not found but probably in Marysland Township.

MARYSLAND TOWNSHIP organized March 11, 1879, was settled and named by Catholic immigrants from Ireland.

MOYER TOWNSHIP was first settled in June 1869 by William Moyer, in whose honor it received this name at its organization, January 25, 1879.

MURDOCK a city in Dublin, was platted and named by Samuel Sabin Murdock in 1878, was incorporated on January 28, 1881, and was reincorporated on December 31, 1898. Murdock, former manager of St. Paul Harvester Works, owned 3,000 acres in the area; he was born in Vermont in 1830, was Minnesota railway commissioner in 1894, and retired to Phoenix, Ariz., where he died in 1900. The post office was established in 1878, with general store owner, George Botham, postmaster; it had a station of the Great Northern Railway in section 11.

NORTON see HOLLOWAY.

PHELPS TOWNSHIP see APPLETON TOWNSHIP.

PILLSBURY TOWNSHIP settled in 1869, organized January 29, 1876, was named in honor of John Sargent Pillsbury, who was born in Sutton, N.H., July 29, 1827, and died in Minneapolis, October 18, 1901. He came to Minnesota in 1855, settling in St. Anthony, now the east part of Minneapolis, engaged in the hardware business until 1875, and afterward in lumbering and flour milling; was a state senator, 1864–68 and 1871–75; and governor, 1876–82. He was greatly interested in upbuilding the state university; one of its chief buildings was donated by him and is named in his honor; and he was a member of the board of regents from 1863 until his death, being president of the board after 1891. His biography and portrait are in "Lives of the Governors of Minnesota" by General Baker (MHS Collections 13: 225–50 [1908]).

RIDGEVILLE a post office, 1878–81, in Tara Township, 12 miles from Benson.

ST. AGNES a post office, 1880–82, 28 miles from Benson and 14 miles from Appleton.

SHIBLE TOWNSHIP organized July 8, 1876, was named for Albert Shible, its earliest settler, who came here in August 1869 but removed in 1870.

SIX MILE GROVE TOWNSHIP settled in April 1866 and organized November 1, 1877, is named for its grove, six miles distant from Benson.

SWENODA TOWNSHIP first settled in the spring of 1869, organized April 7, 1873, has a composite name, in compliment to its Swedish, Norwegian, and Danish settlers. The same name is borne by a lake about 25 miles distant northeastward, in Pope County. A post office was located in the township, ten miles southwest of Benson on the Chippewa River, 1877–1901.

SWIFT see SWIFT FALLS.

SWIFT FALLS a village in section 3 of Camp Lake Township, was named for the falls of the East Branch of the Chippewa River. The post office operated 1873–1910.

TARA TOWNSHIP settled in the spring of 1877, organized December 21, 1878, is named for a hill in County Meath, Ireland, about 20 miles northwest of Dublin. "It was in antiquity a chief seat of the Irish monarchs, and is regarded with patriotic veneration by the Irish people." The township was first named Ridgeville because of the hills; the name was changed on January 29, 1879.

TORNING TOWNSHIP organized April 5, 1879, bearing the name of a village in central Denmark, had previously been the south part of Benson Township. It has the city of Benson in its northwest corner.

WEST BANK TOWNSHIP settled in 1868 and organized March 11, 1879, lies at the west side of the Chippewa River.

Streams and Lakes

The Minnesota River, forming a part of the south boundary of Appleton, and the Chippewa and Pomme de Terre Rivers, which cross this county, are considered in the first chapter; and the second and third are also noticed in chapters for Chippewa, Grant, and Stevens Counties.

Mud Creek is tributary to the East Branch of the Chippewa River; Shakopee Creek flowing through Shakopee Lake in Chippewa County, joins the Chippewa River in Swenoda; and it also receives Cottonwood Creek, from West Bank Township.

This county has relatively few lakes. Lake Monson and Lake Frank are crossed by the line between Hayes and Kerkhoven. The former, with a slight change in spelling, was named for Andrew Manson, a pioneer farmer from Norway.

Lake Hollerberg in Kildare was likewise named for a pioneer farmer.

Shible Township has Hart Lake in section 20 and Lake Shible, but Pelican Lake is now dry. The first was named for Isaac Hart, an early settler; and the second for Albert Shible, like the township.

Camp Lake has been before noticed, for the township so named.

In Benson Township are Lakes Hassel, Moore, Frovold, and Johnson. The first is a Norwegian name meaning "the hazel," and the third is in honor of Knut P. Frovold, one of the earliest settlers, who was county auditor and removed to Benson.

Hegbert has Lakes Oliver and Henry in its southern part, and Lake Griffin at the northwest, which is more commonly called Dry Wood Lake, with outflow in rainy seasons by Dry Wood Creek to the Pomme de Terre River. The names Oliver and Griffin are derived from the plat of the government survey of this township. In its southwestern edge Artichoke Creek, flowing only in wet years, runs northwesterly to Artichoke Lake, in the township of this name in Big Stone County. The name refers to a species of wild sunflower having tuberous roots, much used by both the Dakota and Ojibwe for food.

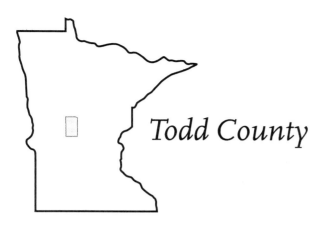

Todd County

This county, established February 20, 1855, and organized January 1, 1867, was named for John Blair Smith Todd, commander of Fort Ripley (at first called Fort Gaines), 1849–54, which was in the part taken from Todd County in 1856 to form a part of Morrison County. Todd was born in Lexington, Ky., April 4, 1814; was graduated at the U.S. Military Academy, West Point, 1837; served in the second Seminole War and the Mexican War; resigned from the army in 1856; was an Indian trader at Fort Randall, Dakota Territory, until 1861; was a brigadier general in the Civil War; was a delegate in Congress for Dakota Territory, 1861 and 1863–65, and governor of that territory, 1869–71. He died in Yankton, Dakota Territory, January 5, 1872.

Information on names has been received from History of Morrison and Todd Counties *by Clara K. Fuller (2 vols., 1915), having pp. 211–307 on the history of this county; from E. M. Berg, county auditor, Otis B. De Laurier, Hon. William E. Lee, John H. Sheets, and Mrs. John D. Jones, each of Long Prairie, the county seat, interviewed during a visit there in May 1916; and from Wilfred J. Whitefield, the oldest resident of Sauk Centre, Stearns County, also interviewed at his home in May 1916.*

ALBURY a place name in Kandota Township, circa 1916.

BARTLETT TOWNSHIP organized March 22, 1883, was named for a family of pioneer homesteaders.

BATAVIA a former townsite, also known as Batavia Station, was at the confluence of Turtle Creek and Long Prairie River in section 12 of Ward Township. Charles A. Jones was the postmaster during the entire period the post office operated, 1890–1904.

BEAR HEAD a post office, 1878–79, in sections 16 and 21 of Bruce Township, was named for the bear killed in 1849 by a government road crew near the Indian agency at Long Prairie. C. D. Batchelor was the postmaster. The site did not develop.

BERTHA TOWNSHIP organized January 4, 1878, and city platted in August 1891 and incorporated on July 16, 1897, commemorate Bertha Ristau, the first white woman settler there and wife of John C. Ristau, postmaster, who established the post office in 1880 in his log cabin store. The city developed following the arrival of the railroad, and three blocks were platted on August 25, 1891, by Francis M. and Louisa Riggs.

BIRCH LAKE see WARD SPRINGS.

BIRCHDALE TOWNSHIP organized March 24, 1869, was named from its Birch Lakes, to be more fully noticed on a later page, and its morainic hills and dales. A post office was located in the township, 1872–74.

BROWERVILLE a city in sections 5, 7, and 8 of Hartford, platted in 1882 by Jacob Vradenberg Brower when the Sauk Centre branch of the Great Northern Railway was built, commemorates

Abraham D. Brower, one of the first settlers of this county, who came in 1860, settled in Round Prairie Township, and was chairman of the first board of county commissioners, in 1867; his fourth son, Jacob Vradenberg Brower (1844–1905) was the first auditor of this county, 1867; a younger son, Walter C. Brower, was editor of the *Stearns County Tribune*, Sauk Centre. These sons were proprietors of the townsite. The biography of Hon. Jacob V. Brower is presented by Josiah B. Chaney in the MHS Collections (12: 769–74 [1908]) and by Prof. N. H. Winchell in *The Aborigines of Minnesota* (1911), pp. x–xiv, with his portrait and autograph.

The city was incorporated as a village on March 10, 1884. James Hart, born in England in 1841, came to the United States in 1855 and to the county in 1872, where he built a mill on Turtle Creek, the area known as Hart's Mill, with a post office called Batavia, 1890–94. Hart then purchased a store, where he opened the Browerville post office in 1894, which was transferred from Hartford; it had a station of the Great Northern Railway.

BRUCE TOWNSHIP was named by George Balmer, a Scottish pioneer farmer there, who was a county commissioner, in honor of Robert Bruce (1274–1329), a famous king and national hero of Scotland.

BURLEENE TOWNSHIP organized in 1888, has a unique name; it is a phonetic spelling of Berlin, a name suggested by several early German settlers at the organization meeting; but their accents were heavy, and the clerk misspelled the name.

BURLINGTON see LITTLE SAUK.

BURNHAMVILLE TOWNSHIP organized September 8, 1870, and its railway village, platted in February 1883, are named in honor of David Burnham, who was a blacksmith for the Winnebago Indians at Long Prairie and settled as a homestead farmer here soon after the Civil War. See also PILLSBURY.

BURTRUM a city in sections 16 and 27 of Burnhamville Township, was incorporated as a village on March 20, 1894; it was platted in April 1884 under the name Hansen and developed when the Northern Pacific Railroad came through; the post office was established in 1888.

CATES STATION see MORAN.

CLARISSA a city in section 27 of Eagle Valley Township, was incorporated as a village on April 22, 1897. Lewis Bischoffsheim, a land speculator, owned the land but never came to the area; his agent, George G. Howe, platted the townsite on July 21, 1879, and gave it a form of Clarisse Bischoffsheim's name. Howe was born in 1825 in New York, came to Minnesota in 1855 and to Todd County in 1878, and moved to Washington Territory in 1890, where he died in 1897. The post office was established in 1880; the Great Northern Railway had a spur station in section 36 and stopped at the Clarissa gravel pit in section 26.

CLOTHO a village in section 35 of Burleene Township, was named for a Greek mythological goddess. The post office was established three times between 1879 and 1908.

COGEL a Northern Pacific Railroad station and post office, 1885, in section 33 of Burnhamville Township.

DAYLIGHT a post office, 1876–78, located in Little Sauk Township, seven miles from Long Prairie.

DOWER LAKE a post office, 1882–90, in section 4 of Staples Township, was platted on November 26, 1884, by A. M. Darling, as a logging site, with a Northern Pacific Railroad station. By 1890, the trees were gone, the sawmill moved, and the townsite ceased; many buildings were moved to Presto, which became Staples.

DRYWOOD a post office, 1899–1906, of Burleene Township, was located in the general store of John Hoosline, a native of Indiana who first settled at Oak Hill before moving to this site. The post office was named for the many acres of dead trees still standing following a forest fire in 1893; the only other building was a school.

EAGLE BEND a city in sections 11–14 of Wykeham Township, received this name from its location at a notable bend of Eagle Creek. The original townsite was purchased in 1883 by Benjamin F. Abbott, a former railroad executive, who became a merchant and helped develop the community. It was incorporated as a village on January 21, 1890. The post office, established in 1882, was first located in postmaster Charles G. O'Dell's general store; it had a station of the Great Northern Railway.

EAGLE VALLEY TOWNSHIP organized March 17, 1880, is crossed by Eagle Creek, which was named for the bald or white-headed eagle, "the bird of freedom," emblem of the United States, found throughout Minnesota.

EGLY a post office, 1880–84, located between Wadena and Long Prairie; location not found.

FAWN LAKE TOWNSHIP organized July 28, 1881, bears the name early given to a lake in the east part of its section 30.

FAY a country post office, 1891–1900, in Moran Township.

GERMANIA TOWNSHIP organized March 17, 1880, was named by its German settlers, this name being proposed by Paul Steinbach, from the ship *Germania* in which he came to America.

GORDON TOWNSHIP organized in January 1869, was named in honor of J. M. Gordon, a pioneer farmer, who was a member of the first board of county commissioners.

GREY EAGLE TOWNSHIP organized September 15, 1873, and its city in sections 7 and 8, platted in September 1882 and incorporated as a village on April 27, 1898, were named from an eagle shot here in 1868 by A. M. Crowell, who many years afterward removed to Bemidji and was its municipal judge. Among the first settlers were the Huffman brothers from Pennsylvania: James, who was the first postmaster when the post office opened in 1877, and Joseph M., hotel owner and justice of the peace. The city had a station of the Northern Pacific Railroad.

GUTCHES GROVE a village in sections 33 and 34 of Reynolds Township.

HARTFORD a village in section 33 of Ward Township; the first settler in the township, John Bassett, arrived in 1865, built a log cabin and the first school in the county, served as county commissioner and a justice of the peace, and opened the post office, 1870–94, which then was transferred to Browerville; a second post office, 1900–1901, had Joseph Sutton as postmaster.

HARTFORD TOWNSHIP organized March 12, 1867, has a name that is borne by a city and county in Connecticut and by townships and villages or cities in Maine, Vermont, New York, Wisconsin, and 12 other states.

HAYDEN a Northern Pacific Railroad station in section 9 of Villard Township.

HEWITT a city in sections 15, 16, 21, and 22 of Stowe Prairie Township, platted in April 1891 on land donated by Henry Hewitt and incorporated as a village on February 20, 1899, was named in honor of Hewitt, a nearby farmer. The post office was established in 1880 as Powell in the farmhouse of George Hildreth and was moved to Hewitt in 1891, where Hildreth continued as postmaster; it had a station of the Great Northern Railway.

IONA TOWNSHIP at first called Odessa, organized January 6, 1881, has the name of a historic island of the Hebrides, which also is borne by a railway village in Murray County.

KANDOTA TOWNSHIP organized in April 1870, took the name of a proposed townsite platted here in 1856, on the shore of Fairy Lake, by Edwin Whitefield, an artist from Massachusetts. This name, derived by him from the Dakota language, is said to mean "Here we rest." The townsite, the first platted in the county, was incorporated as a village on February 27, 1878, and had a station of the Great Northern Railway but did not develop as planned.

LEE'S SIDING a Great Northern Railway station in section 5 of Long Prairie Township, is named for William E. Lee, who was born in Alton, Ill., January 8, 1852; came to Minnesota with his parents in 1856; organized the Bank of Long Prairie in 1882, was its cashier, and in 1896 was elected its president; was a representative in the legislature, 1885–87 and 1893, being speaker of the house in 1893; was a member of the state board of control, 1901–3; was Republican candidate for governor in 1914. He died in 1920.

LESLIE TOWNSHIP organized in September 1876, and its railway village, platted in May 1898, were named in honor of John B. Leslie, a pioneer settler from Kentucky. A farmers post office, 1894–1903, was located in section 33.

LINCOLN a village of Morrison County, which extends into section 25 of Fawn Lake Township.

LITTLE ELK TOWNSHIP is crossed in its northeast part by the headstream of the South Fork of the Little Elk River, flowing east into Morrison County.

LITTLE SAUK TOWNSHIP organized in the spring of 1870, and its village in section 26, on the Sauk River, refer to a band of five Sauk Indians formerly living at Lake Osakis, as previously noted for the cities of Sauk Rapids and Sauk Centre. The village was first called Burlington, although the post office, begun in 1872, and the Great Northern Railway station were called Little Sauk.

LONG PRAIRIE TOWNSHIP organized March 12, 1867, had been occupied 1848–55 by the agency of a reservation for the Winnebago Indians. Long Prairie, the county seat, was platted in May 1867 and was incorporated as a village on December 22, 1883. The name is received from the Long Prairie River, flowing through this county to the Crow Wing River; the stream was named for a long and relatively narrow prairie, from a half mile to one mile wide, bordering its east side for about 20 miles, from Lake Charlotte and Long Prairie village northward to the west line of Fawn Lake Township. When the post office was established in 1850, David Olmsted was the postmaster until he moved to St. Paul in 1853; he was influential in Todd County and the state, and Olmsted County is named for him.

MIRAN BROOK see MORAN.

MORAN TOWNSHIP organized March 27, 1877, is crossed by Moran Brook, here joining the Long Prairie River, named for an early lumberman. The post office began as Miran Brook, 1874–76, and combined with Cates Station, 1874–80, with James H. Cates, postmaster; it was transferred to the village of Moran and located in postmaster and justice of the peace William J. Graves's hotel; the post office was discontinued in 1890 and was reestablished as Moranbrook, 1899–1914, with John Warzeha, postmaster.

MORANBROOK see MORAN.

NEBO a post office, 1880–93, in Stowe Prairie Township, just north of Hewitt; the area was settled in 1873; also known as Mount Nebo.

OAK HILL a hamlet in Leslie Township, is named for its plentiful oak trees and morainic drift hills. A post office with the same name was in sections 16 and 17 of Leslie Township, with a station of the Great Northern Railway.

OSAKIS a city lying mainly in Douglas County but also extending into section 30 of Gordon Township, on the south shore of Osakis Lake, received its name, like the lake and its outflowing Sauk River, from a small band of Sauk Indians, before noted for Little Sauk Township. The post office, 1859–63, was transferred to Douglas County in 1864.

PEORIA a post office, 1883–86; location not found.

PHILBROOK a village on the border of Villard and Fawn Lake Townships, platted November 10, 1889, was named by officers of the Northern Pacific Railroad. The area was first settled in 1859; its post office began as Riverside in 1889 and was changed to Philbrook in 1890; Benjamin F. Hartshorn was postmaster under both names; the post office served as a rural branch, 1956–64, and was then discontinued; a station of the Northern Pacific Railroad was in section 33 of Villard Township.

PILLSBURY a village in section 2 of Burnhamville Township and on the Swan River in section 35 of Bruce Township, was first called Burnhamville, the site of David Burnham's mill. A post office of that name was located at the mill, 1860–77, and was changed to Pillsbury, 1877–1908. The community adopted the name Pillsbury to honor Gov. John S. Pillsbury and his actions regarding the grasshopper scourge of 1877.

POWELL see HEWITT.

PRESTO see STAPLES.

REYNOLDS TOWNSHIP has a name that is borne by a county in Missouri and by villages in Pennsylvania, Indiana, Illinois, and seven other states. Reynolds is also a place name in the township, six miles west of Long Prairie.

RIVERSIDE see PHILBROOK.

ROUND PRAIRIE TOWNSHIP having one of the earliest settlements in this county, was named for the Round Prairie, so called, about five miles long from north to south and two miles wide, in the western third of this township and the east edge of Little Sauk. The village of this name in section 18 was platted in October 1903; it had a post office, 1868–1963, which served as a rural branch until 1969, and a station of the Great Northern Railway.

SPAULDING a village of Stearns County, which extends into section 29 of Birchdale Township, the site of a former Northern Pacific Railroad station.

STAPLES TOWNSHIP organized January 5, 1882, and the city of this name on the Northern Pacific Railroad, founded in 1885, platted as a village called Staples Mill in June 1889, and incorporated as a city on September 5, 1906, commemorate the Stillwater lumber family named Staples, who had logging and manufacturing interests here. Two prominent pioneer lumbermen of this family, coming to Stillwater in 1853–54 from Topsham,

Maine, were Samuel Staples (1805–87) and Isaac Staples (1816–98). The city is governmentally associated with Wadena County. It was established in 1889, when it was incorporated as the 325-acre village of Presto in sections 1 and 12; the post office was named Presto, March-April 1890, with William A. Miller, postmaster; it was then changed to Staples, with Kate P. Staples as postmaster, although the name was not officially changed until 1895; it had a station of the Northern Pacific Railroad in section 12.

STOWE PRAIRIE the most northwestern township, organized March 27, 1877, was named for three brothers, Amos, Isaac, and James Stowe, who were early settlers on and near a prairie area in the north part of this township, continuing also northward into Wadena County.

TURTLE CREEK TOWNSHIP organized in July 1890, has Turtle Creek flowing through its west edge and Turtle Lake at its northwest corner.

UPSHUR a post office, 1880–82, on the Long Prairie River, seven miles from Long Prairie city, with farmer Levi Whitesell as postmaster.

VILLARD TOWNSHIP organized July 28, 1882, was named in honor of Henry Villard (1835–1900), president of the Northern Pacific Railroad company in 1881–83, when its transcontinental line was completed. This name is also borne by a village in Pope County, for which a biographic notice has been presented.

WARD SPRINGS a village in section 23 of Birchdale Township, platted by J. W. and Martha J. Ward, was previously called Birch Lake City, from its location beside Little Birch Lake. The post office was called Birch Lake, 1882–1909; it became a rural branch in 1959 and was discontinued in 1965; it had a station of the Northern Pacific Railroad.

WARD TOWNSHIP organized in July 1877, was named for a township in Randolph County, Ind. by settlers who had come from there. A post office was in the township, 1882–87.

WEST UNION TOWNSHIP was organized March 12, 1867; its city, platted in June 1881, was incorporated in 1900; the townsite was platted on land first owned by Joel Myers; the post office operated 1860–61 and since 1872; it had a station of the Great Northern Railway in section 21.

WHEELER a post office, 1858–59; location not found.

WHITEVILLE was the name commonly given to an early settlement in 1865–66, about five miles west of Long Prairie, for three sisters, wives of L. S. Hoadley, Albert Madison, and Horace Pierce, "whose maiden name was White" (*History of Morrison and Todd Counties*, p. 225).

WYKEHAM TOWNSHIP originally called Eden, organized January 10, 1880, has a unique name, received from England. A country post office was located in the township, 20 miles northeast of Long Prairie, 1880–83, with livestock dealer Joseph Claring as postmaster; a reestablished post office was authorized on March 14, 1901, with Martin O. Hulberg to be postmaster but was never established.

Streams and Lakes

Crow Wing River has been fully noticed in the chapter of Crow Wing County. Long Prairie River is a translation of its Ojibwe name, given by Rev. Joseph A. Gilfillan as "Ga-shagoshkodeia zibi, Long-narrow-Prairie river." These streams were described by Henry R. Schoolcraft as "the war road between the Chippewas and Sioux," the country through which they flow being found by him in 1832 quite uninhabited. No dwelling place, "even a temporary wigwam," was observed in his canoe journey from the head of the Crow Wing along all its course to the Mississippi (*Summary Narrative*, 1855, p. 267).

Gilfillan wrote of Ojibwe names in this county, with their translations, as follows:

"Osakis lake is Osagi sagaiigun, the Sauk's lake."

"Sauk lake" (in Kandota and extending south to Sauk Centre) "is Kitchi-osagi sagaiigun, the great lake of the Sauks."

"Birch Bark Fort lake" (called Big Birch Lake on maps), "Ga wigwassensikag sagaiigun, the-place-of-little-birches lake."

"Sauk river, Osagi zibi, the river of the Sauks."

Wing River flows northeastward through Bertha and Stowe Prairie, being tributary to the Leaf River in Wadena County.

Bear Creek, Little Partridge Creek, and Egly Creek are tributary to Partridge River in Bartlett, which runs northeast to Crow Wing River.

From its north and west side, Long Prairie River receives Dismal Creek, Freemans Creek, Eagle Creek, to which Harris Creek is tributary, Moran

Brook, and Stony Brook; and from the east this river receives Turtle Creek and Fish Trap Creek.

In the southeastern borders of the county are Prairie Brook, flowing into Little Birch Lake; Swan River, having Molly Creek tributary to it from the south, and Little Swan Creek from the north; and headstreams of both the South and North Forks of Little Elk River.

The south boundary of Todd County crosses Crooked or Mary Lake, Big and Little Birch Lakes (formerly called respectively Birch Bark Fort Lake and Middle Birch Bark Lake), and the large and long Sauk Lake, through which the river of this name flows.

Grey Eagle Township, besides the Crooked or Mary and Big Birch Lakes, on its south line, has also Goose, Mound, Buckhorn, Bass, Twin, and Trace Lakes, the last being named for Ferdinand Trace, a homesteader beside it. Twin Lake has two wide parts, united by a strait.

Birchdale has Long Lake, mostly in section 19.

Fairy Lake, in Kandota, was thus fancifully named by Edwin Whitefield, mentioned in connection with this township.

William Lake is at the east side of section 12 and 13, West Union; and in section 1 the Sauk River flows through Guernsey Lake.

In Burnhamville are Buck and Moose Lakes, Lady Lake, named for its plentiful flowers of the lady's slipper, Big Swan Lake, Looney or Long Lake, Bass, Mons, and Little Swan Lakes.

In Round Prairie Township are Felix, Hansman, and Center Lakes, and Lakes Latimer and Lashier. The largest is named for Alfred Eugene Latimer of South Carolina, who, being a lieutenant in the U.S. Army, was in service at Fort Ripley. In the winter of 1859–60 he was detailed, with his company, to be stationed at Long Prairie, as is noted by Charlotte Van Cleve (*Three Score Years and Ten*, p. 158).

Little Sauk Township has Cedar Lake, in section 35, reaching south into Kandota. The northwest part of Little Sauk has Mud Lake and Maple Lake. The last, extending west into Gordon, is also often called Henry Lake, for Lewis Henry, a pioneer farmer beside it.

Gordon has Slawson and Stallcopp Lakes (drained), named for William Slawson and Levi E. Stallcopp, early settlers there, and Faille Lake, adjoining the east edge of Osakis village.

Bruce has Little Rice Lake and Beauty Lake.

In Long Prairie Township are Lake Charlotte and Meyer Lake, the former being named in honor of Charlotte O. Van Cleve, who, with her husband, Gen. Horatio P. Van Cleve, and their family, lived at Long Prairie, 1856–61. Charlotte Ouisconsin Clark Van Cleve was born at Prairie du Chien, Wis., July 1, 1819, and died in Minneapolis, April 1, 1907. Her parents, Lieut. and Mrs. Clark, accompanied the troops who came to the present state of Minnesota to establish the first military post, afterward named Fort Snelling. Their destination was reached when she was a few weeks old, and her childhood was passed there and at other army posts. She was married, March 22, 1836, to Lieutenant (afterward General) Van Cleve. After resignation of his commission, they lived a few years in other states but in 1856 returned to Minnesota, settling at Long Prairie, and five years later removed to Minneapolis, where Mrs. Van Cleve afterward resided, greatly honored and beloved. She wrote an autobiography, *Three Score Years and Ten* (176 pp.), published in 1888. Two chapters in this book narrate remembrances of her life at Long Prairie.

Two miles west of Lake Charlotte is McCarrahan Lake, in Reynolds, named for William McCarrahan, a Scotch-Irish farmer.

Leslie has Little Osakis Lake, through which the Sauk River flows. On the long northeastern arm of Lake Osakis, which projects into this township, are Long, Gutches (or Caughren and Lindbergh), Coon, Buck, and Babbett or Battle Points.

Little Elk Township has Mill Lake, Coal Lake, named from the frequent fragments of lignite coal in its glacial drift, and Long and Round Lakes.

Burleene has Lake Gray, Lowe's Lake, and Lake Eli (all drained). The second was named for Lewis Lowe, a farmer there, who removed to Long Prairie; and the third for Isaac N. Eli, who lived in Reynolds, several miles southeast from that lake.

In Turtle Creek Township are Big Lake, Pine Island or Pine, and Thunder Lakes; Mud Lake, on the course of Turtle Creek; Rice and Little Rice Lakes, having wild rice; Star, Cranberry, and Long Lakes, the last reaching north into Fawn Lake Township; and Peat and Turtle Lakes in section 6.

Horseshoe Lake, named from its curved outline, is in sections 27 and 34, Ward, near the Long Prairie River.

Pendergast Lake is in sections 7 and 8, Wykeham.

Bertha had Deer Lake (drained), on the east edge of section 5.

In Fawn Lake Township, with the lake so named, are also a second Pine Island Lake, Little Fish Trap Lake and Little Fish Trap Creek (or Brook), and Mud Lake.

Villard had Nelson Lake (drained), in section 36, and Hayden Lake and Brook (or Creek) flowing north to the Crow Wing River.

In Staples Township are Rice Lake, named from the wild rice, in sections 25 and 36, and Dower Lake, about two miles west of the city, named in honor of a prominent pioneer settler, Sampson Dower, who came from England.

Hills and Prairies

Although Todd County is traversed by several belts or series of morainic drift hills, mostly from 50 to 100 feet high, only two localities of these hills have received names on maps. The Dromedary Hills, rising with rounded outlines like a camel's hump, are in the northwest part of section 28, Little Elk; and Mount Nebo, in sections 4 and 9, Stowe Prairie, is named for the peak east of the north end of the Dead Sea, whence Moses viewed the Promised Land.

With the Long and Round Prairies and Stowe Prairie, which gave their names to townships, Pleasant Prairie is also to be noticed, a mile in diameter, in the south edge of Round Prairie Township, at the east side of Prairie Brook.

The northeast boundary of the great prairie region of southwestern Minnesota crosses the southwest corner of this county and includes sections 31 and 32 and parts of adjoining sections in Gordon, nearly all of West Union, and the south edge of Kandota. From the higher parts of West Union, an extensive view of limitless prairie is seen toward the south and southwest.

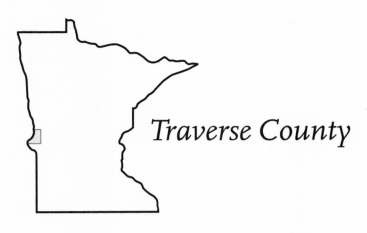

Traverse County

This county, established February 20, 1862, organized March 8, 1881, received its name from Lake Traverse (Lac Travers in French), a translation of the Dakota name. William H. Keating wrote of its significance: "The lake has received its present appellation from the circumstance that it is in a direction nearly transverse to that of the Big Stone and Lac qui Parle lakes, these being directly to the northwest, while Lake Travers points to the northeast." Prof. A. W. Williamson gave its Dakota name and meaning: "Mdehdakinyan, lake lying crosswise."

By the way of Lakes Traverse and Big Stone, whence two counties are named, and by the Minnesota River valley, whence this state is named, the River Warren outflowed from the Glacial Lake Agassiz, which in the closing part of the Ice Age filled the basin of the Red River and Lake Winnipeg. The Ojibwe have given quite another name to Lake Traverse, referring to this deeply channeled ancient watercourse of the continental divide, noted by Rev. Joseph A. Gilfillan as follows: "Lake Travers is Ga-edawaii-mamiwung sagaii-gun, the lake with a breast or pap (like a woman's) on either end; one on the northern, and one on the southern (flowing into Big Stone lake in high water); so flowing either way."

In exceptionally high flood stages of the upper Minnesota River, flowing into this channel of the Glacial River Warren at the village of Browns Valley, a part of its water goes northward into Lake Traverse, so that canoes or boats can then have a continuous water passage from Big Stone Lake to Lake Traverse; but probably no flood conditions in recent time have permitted any southward outflow from Lake Traverse.

At the east side of the southwest end of Lake Traverse, Maj. Stephen H. Long and his party in 1823 were entertained by Wanotan, leader of the Yankton, for whom, with changed spelling, Wahnahta County of Minnesota Territory in 1849 was named, including the present Traverse County.

Information of the origin and meaning of names has been gathered in History of Traverse County, Brown's Valley and its Environs *by J. O. Barrett (1881, 32 pp.); History of the Minnesota Valley (1882), having pp. 986–90 for this county; and from E. J. Fortune, judge of probate, Patrick H. Leonard, sheriff, George G. Allanson, postmaster, James H. Flood, and Ole Odenborg, all of Wheaton, the county seat, interviewed during a visit there in September 1916.*

ARTHUR TOWNSHIP organized in 1881, originally called Hoff in honor of Abel Hoff, its first settler, was renamed on the suggestion of James H. Flood for Arthur village, Ontario, about 70 miles west of Toronto.

BARKER a farmers post office, 1888–96, first called Parnell from 1886–88, located 12 miles from Wheaton; location not found.

BOISBERG a village site platted on May 17, 1901, in section 3 of West Monson, is named from the

Bois des Sioux River, to be noticed on a later page, and from the large granite boulder (berg) on the opposite or South Dakota side of this river in the village of White Rock, whence that village derived its name. The village was never incorporated, and no businesses developed.

BROWNS VALLEY in sections 32 and 33 of Folsom Township, a city founded in 1866–67 by Joseph R. Brown, platted in 1878, was the first village in the county and the first county seat, being succeeded by Wheaton in 1886. The settlement and post office, established in 1867, were at first called Lake Traverse but were renamed Browns Valley after the death of the founder in 1870. Biographic notes of him are presented in the chapter on Brown County, which also was named in his honor. His son, Samuel J. Brown, who during 50 years was a resident of this village, was its first postmaster, 1867–78. A vivid sketch of Joseph Renshaw Brown was given in the pamphlet history of this county by J. O. Barrett in 1881. The city was incorporated as a village on February 23, 1881; it had a station of the Great Northern Railway.

CHARLESVILLE a townsite platted on March 5, 1904, in section 36 of Tintah Township, which had a Great Northern Railway station.

CLIFTON TOWNSHIP the latest organized in this county, was named for a township in Monroe County, Wis., about 40 miles east of La Crosse, as proposed by Bartlett Ashbough, a former settler here, who removed to Saskatchewan.

COLLIS a village in section 11 of Tara, comes from the Latin word *collis*, "a hill," this name being proposed by a priest, with reference to the hill Tara in Ireland, whence the township was named. The village was platted on July 15, 1881, with a Chicago, Milwaukee and St. Paul Railroad station; the post office operated 1885–1954.

CROKE TOWNSHIP organized in 1881, was named, on the suggestion of P. D. O'Phelan, a homestead farmer in Tara, who was a member of the board of county commissioners, in honor of Thomas William Croke, who was born in County Cork, Ireland, May 24, 1824, and died at Thurles, Ireland, July 22, 1902. He was a Catholic bishop in Australia, 1870–74, and afterward was archbishop of Cashel in Ireland, taking an active interest in political affairs and in support of the home rule movement. In 1876 the Catholic Colonization Bureau was organized, with Bishop John Ireland as president and Dillon O'Brien as secretary, each

of St. Paul, through whose efforts many Irish colonists were brought to this county and to Swift, Murray, and other counties in southwestern Minnesota.

DAKOMIN a village in sections 11, 14, and 15 of Windsor Township on a spur line of the Great Northern Railway; it had a barge service on Lake Traverse to haul grain; it had a post office, 1916–17. The village was never platted or incorporated, and when the boat line discontinued in 1917, the town ceased.

DOLLYMONT TOWNSHIP organized in 1881, bears the name of a seaside suburb of Dublin, Ireland, about four miles northeast from the center of that city. It was chosen also partly or mainly in honor of Anthony Doll, who was a pioneer settler here.

DUMONT a city in sections 14, 22, and 23 of Croke, was named by officers of the Chicago, Milwaukee and St. Paul Railroad company, perhaps for a local French hunter who supplied food to the railroad men. The same name is borne by villages in New Jersey, Iowa, and Colorado. The city was incorporated as a village on May 3, 1898; it began in 1884 when the Fargo and Southern Railroad came and was platted on April 1, 1885; the post office was established in 1886.

EVANSVILLE JUNCTION a Great Northern Railway station in section 10 of Tintah Township.

FELIX a post office in sections 32 and 33 of Clifton Township, was established first as Maydwell, 1880–83, changed to Felix in 1883, and discontinued in 1884.

FERNSLEIGH BEACH a station of the Great Northern Railway in sections 16 and 21 of Folsom Township.

FOLSOM TOWNSHIP organized September 2, 1880, was named in honor of Maj. George P. Folsom, who came from New Hampshire and was one of the first merchants of Browns Valley. In the north part of this township, adjoining the shore of Lake Traverse in sections 2 and 10, a trading post was established about the year 1815 by Robert Dickson, "a red-haired Scotchman," whom the British government had appointed "superintendent of the western tribes." In 1823, the expedition of Long and Keating found the Columbia Fur Company occupying this post (or another location near it), under the superintendence of "Mr. Moore," probably Hazen Mooers (1789–1858). He was also trading here in 1835 when Joseph R.

Brown first came to this post; a few years later, in 1838–39, Mooers and Brown were associated at Grey Cloud Island, below St. Paul, in trading and farming.

INVER a post office, 1880; location not found.

LAKE TRAVERSE see BROWNS VALLEY.

LAKE VALLEY see WHEATON.

LAKE VALLEY TOWNSHIP organized in 1881, is named for the northern part of Lake Traverse bordering its west side. This part of the lake, northward from its marshy tract at the mouth of Mustinka River, is called Buffalo Lake on the map of Long's expedition, and Joseph N. Nicollet's map called it Intpah Lake, a Dakota name meaning "the end." It has an extent of eight or ten miles from south to north, being at the ordinary stage of low water an area of marsh one to two miles wide, in which are several spaces of open water a mile or two in length. The lake later became a reservoir and was named Mud Lake. The township was divided into **LAKE VALLEY EAST TOWNSHIP**, T. 127N, R. 46W; and **LAKE VALLEY WEST TOWNSHIP**, T. 127N, R. 47W.

LAKE VIEW see MAUDADA.

LEONARDSVILLE TOWNSHIP organized in 1881, commemorates Patrick Leonard who came from Philadelphia, Pa., settled in Hastings, Minn., in 1855, removed to this township as a homestead farmer in May 1878, and died here in 1900.

LEONARDVILLE a post office, 1879–80, in Leonardsville Township, with Patrick Leonard, postmaster.

MAUDADA a village in section 6 of Walls Township, platted on July 12, 1888, by A. C. Earsley and Charles F. Washburn of Herman, was designated in the first county election, November 8, 1881, to be the county seat, but business of the new county had been earlier transacted at Browns Valley, from which its offices were not removed until in 1886 they were transferred to Wheaton. The name Maudada was in honor of Maud and Ada, daughters of Earsley and Washburn. This proposed village, though manifesting much vigor in its first year, had only a brief existence. The post office was called Lake View, 1878–79, Round Mound, 1879–82, and Maudada, 1882–84.

MAYDWELL see FELIX.

MONSON TOWNSHIP organized in 1881, was named for Peter Monson, a Swedish pioneer homesteader. A post office was located in the township, 1885–86. The township was divided into **EAST MONSON TOWNSHIP**, T. 128N, R. 46W; and **WEST MONSON TOWNSHIP**, T. 128N, R. 47W.

PARNELL see BARKER.

PARNELL TOWNSHIP also organized in 1881, was named, like Croke and Tara, by P. D. O'Phelan, one of the county commissioners, in honor of Charles Stewart Parnell (1846–91), the prominent Irish statesman, who visited the United States in 1879–80.

PIONEER a post office, 1879–80; location not found.

PLEASANT HILL a country post office, 1878–81, on the stage road from Herman in Grant County to the Sisseton Agency in South Dakota; farmer Abel M. Huff was postmaster.

REDPATH TOWNSHIP organized in 1881, was named by its Swedish settlers for a trail or path of the Dakota there.

ROUND MOUND see MAUDADA.

TARA TOWNSHIP organized in 1881, received this name on recommendation of one of its pioneer settlers, P. D. O'Phelan, a county commissioner, for the renowned hill of Tara in Ireland. This extensive hill, adjoining the village of Tara, has a height of about 500 feet. Here was the "ancient seat of sovereignty in Ireland from a remote period to the middle of the sixth century."

TAYLOR TOWNSHIP organized in 1881, was named for one of its pioneer homesteaders.

TERRITTIN a post office, 1879–80; location not found.

TINTAH TOWNSHIP organized in 1881, received its name from the Dakota, this being their common word meaning "a prairie." The city in sections 3 and 10 was incorporated as a village on May 2, 1889, and separated from the township on April 27, 1906. The Great Northern Railway built a station in section 3 in 1872. The village was organized in 1881 and platted on March 1, 1887. Charles Smith became postmaster when the post office opened in 1880.

Hennepin wrote of the Dakota as "the Nation of the prairies, who are called Tintonha," a name derived from *tintah*. Later it has been written Tintonwans, Titonwans, or Tetons, comprising many Siouan bands ranging over southern and western Minnesota and onward to the vast country of plains west of the Missouri.

Shorelines of the Glacial Lake Agassiz extending past the railway village of Tintah are therefrom named the Tintah Beaches, being traced, like other shorelines higher and lower, along great distances on each side of the Red River valley.

TRAVERSE a post office, July-October, 1883; location not found.

WALLS TOWNSHIP organized in 1881, was named for three Scottish brothers, William, Robert, and George Walls, who came from New Brunswick, taking homestead claims in this township.

WHEATON which succeeded Browns Valley in 1886 as the county seat, is a city in sections 17–20 of Lake Valley Township, named in honor of Daniel Thompson Wheaton of Morris, a surveyor for the Fargo and Southern Railroad. He advised that this new village be named Swedenburg in compliment to the Swedish owners of its site, Swan C. and Ole Odenborg, but they preferred to give it this name of the surveyor. He was born in Barre, Vt., January 21, 1845; was graduated at Dartmouth College, 1869; came to Minnesota in 1871 and settled at Morris in 1876; was county surveyor of Stevens County, 1877–1910. The city was incorporated as a village on May 25, 1887; it was first platted on September 1, 1884. The post office began in 1879 as Lake Valley, changing to Wheaton in 1884. It had a station of the Chicago, Milwaukee and St. Paul Railroad.

WINDSOR TOWNSHIP first settled in September 1871 and organized in 1881, was named by one of its pioneer farmers, William J. Smith, who came here from Hastings, Minn. This name is borne by an ancient borough on the River Thames in England, a seaport town of Nova Scotia, a city in Ontario, and townships and villages or cities in 19 other states of the Union.

Lakes and Streams

Lake Traverse, whence the county is named, has been noticed at the beginning of this chapter. Its northern part, called Mud Lake, is more definitely described, with comments on its nomenclature, under Lake Valley Township.

The most southern island of Lake Traverse, about halfway across the lake opposite to the former trading post, which has been noticed for Folsom Township, is called Snake (or Jensen) Island,

"covering about 20 acres, once the village home of the Indians."

Battle Point, in section 29, Windsor, commemorates a battle between the Ojibwe and the Dakota, about the year 1830, narrated by Barrett (history of this county, 1881, p. 8).

Two other islands, nearer to the South Dakota shore, lie about one to two miles north of Battle Point, the more southern being Plum Island and the other North Island. The former translates a Dakota name, Kanta Wita, which is placed farther north on Nicollet's map, in the extreme northern end of this lake. The islands are also called Carlson and Jackson Islands.

Bois des Sioux River, outflowing from Lake Traverse to the Red River, has an early French name, meaning "Woods of the Sioux," with reference to the woods or narrow groves by which it is bordered along its lowest five miles, next to Breckenridge and Wahpeton. On the map of Long's expedition, in 1823, it is called Sioux River; and in the *Narrative* by Keating, as also in the description of the country by Long, it is mentioned as the Sioux River or Swan River. The name Bois des Sioux was used by Keating to note only its fringe of timber. On Nicollet's map, 1843, it is named Sioux Wood River.

Keating's *Narrative* spells the name of the Mustinka River, tributary to Lake Traverse, with a more correct rendering of its Dakota pronunciation, Mushtincha, meaning "Rabbit." The main stream receives in this county South and West Branches or Forks, and the latter has an affluent named Twelvemile Creek.

Hills

Pelican Hill, two miles northeast of Browns Valley, is a knoll on the crest of the bluff of Lake Traverse, about 25 feet higher than the adjoining portions of the bluff. Similar knolls or hillocks on or near the lake bluff close south of the Mustinka River were mapped by Nicollet with Dakota names, Plan Kara and Manstitsa Kara. One of these is now called Round Mound, from which, as noted by Barrett, very impressive views are obtained, especially when the effects of mirage bring Herman and the Tokua Lakes into sight.

Wabasha County

This county, established October 27, 1849, commemorates a line of Dakota leaders, whose history is told by Hon. Charles C. Willson in the MHS Collections (vol. 12: 503–12 [1908]). Wapashaw (variously spelled) was the name, in three successive generations, of the hereditary leaders having greatest influence among the Mississippi bands of the Dakota. Thomas L. McKenney and James Hall, in the first volume of their *History of the Indian Tribes of North America* (1836), gave a portrait of the second man bearing this name, who wore a covering over his left eye. The third Wapashaw's band occupied the country below Lake Pepin, his principal village being on the Rollingstone Creek, near the site of Minnesota City. A beautiful prairie in the Mississippi valley three to five miles southeast of this village, commonly called Wapashaw's Prairie 60 to 80 years ago, became the site of the city of Winona.

The town (now a city) of Wabasha, which was named in 1843 for the last of these three leaders, is situated at a distance of 30 miles up the Mississippi from his village. It was at first called Cratte's Landing, for the earliest white man to build his home there, in 1838.

From this town the county containing it, which was later established, received its name. The more remote origin of the name, which means "red leaf," and thence "red hat or cap," and "red battle-standard," as applied to the first man named Wapashaw, was on the occasion of his return, as tradition relates, from a visit to Quebec, at some time after the cession of Canada to Great Britain in 1763. He had received from the English governor presents of a soldier's uniform, with its red cap, and an English flag, which, being displayed triumphantly on his arrival among his own people, led to their hailing him as Wapashaw (*History of Winona County*, 1883, p. 31).

This name is widely different, as to its origin and meaning, from the Wabash River, which is said to signify in its original Algonquian, "a cloud blown forward by an equinoctial wind." In pronunciation, Wabasha should have the vowel of its accented first syllable (formerly spelled *Waa* and *Wah*) sounded like the familiar word *ah*; and its final *a*, like *awe*. There is, however, a tendency or a prevalence of usage departing from the aboriginal pronunciation for each of the four names of Wabasha, Wadena, Waseca, and Watonwan, by giving to the first *a* its broad sound as in *awe* or *fall*.

Information of names has been collected from the Geographical and Statistical Sketch of the Past and Present of Wabasha County *by W. H. Mitchell and U. Curtis (1870, 164 pp.);* History of Winona and Wabasha Counties *(1884), having pp. 561–1,314 for this county; and from Joseph Buisson, Jr., and David Cratte, sons of founders of Wabasha, the county seat, interviewed during a visit there in April 1916.*

BEAR VALLEY a village in section 24 of Chester, is in a valley tributary to the Zumbro River. "Through this valley a bear was pursued by the early settlers." The village had a post office, 1857–1902; the grange association established in 1870 was one of the earliest in the state; the grange hall was built in 1874.

BELLECHESTER a city in sections 4 and 5 of Chester, which extends into Goodhue County, founded in 1877, prefixes to the township name the French word meaning "beautiful." The city was incorporated as a village on October 5, 1955; the post office operated 1879–1903; a Chicago Great Western Railroad station was located in the Goodhue County part of the city.

BREMEN a village in section 36 of Zumbro, first settled in sections 30 and 31 of Oakwood Township, was also known as Bremen Corner, and earlier as Pell. The village was established in 1864 by Danish immigrant John Behrens (Berns), who built a store and a hotel; his brother, Claus, was postmaster; the post office operated 1872–88.

BRIGHT a siding of the Chicago, Milwaukee and St. Paul Railroad in section 9 of Mazeppa Township, for the use of A. H. Bright's mill, which was built two and a half miles south of Mazeppa on the Zumbro River.

CAMP LACUPOLIS a place name on Lake Pepin in section 22 of Pepin Township.

CENTERVILLE see PLAINVIEW.

CHESTER TOWNSHIP organized May 11, 1858, has a name borne also by a city and county of England, counties in Pennsylvania, South Carolina, and Tennessee, and townships and villages or cities in 26 states of the Union.

CONCEPTION a village in section 11 of Highland Township, which earlier had a post office, 1894–1902; the village was named for the Catholic church, the Church of the Immaculate Conception, which was built in 1866 in section 10.

COOK'S VALLEY a post office, 1858–93, in section 30 of Greenfield Township, was located in a valley named for Aaron and Levi Cook, who were among the first settlers of the township.

DUMFRIES a community in section 10 of Glasgow Township, received its name from a town and county of Scotland, the town being the former home and now the burial place of Robert Burns. The community had a post office, 1894–1912, an elevator, a general store, and a station of the Chicago, Milwaukee and St. Paul Railroad.

ELGIN TOWNSHIP first settled in April 1855, organized May 11, 1858, likewise bears the name of an ancient town and its county in Scotland. It is also the name of a city in Illinois and of villages in ten other states. The city of Elgin in sections 27 and 28, first known as West Greenwood, was founded in November 1878, when the railway branch from Eyota to this place and Plainview was completed, and incorporated as a village on January 4, 1895. The first settlers were George and Curtis Bryant, Henry Atherton, and George Farrar, all having come from Vermont in 1855; George Bryant was the first postmaster when the post office was established in 1857.

FOREST MOUND a post office, 1858–74, located in Elgin Township, at various times in sections 9 and 16, was named for a prominent hill of considerable height and area in section 8.

FUNK a station of the Chicago, Milwaukee and St. Paul Railroad; location not found.

GILLFORD TOWNSHIP organized May 11, 1858, was named for Mr. and Mrs. Gill from Illinois. He came here and took a homestead claim in the summer of 1855, returned to Illinois, and soon died there. "His widow, in order to carry out her husband's wishes, removed to the claim he had selected, and entered upon the toils and privations of a frontier life. In honor of her energy and perseverance, and in memory of her husband, the town was called Gillford." This uniquely spelled name has the same pronunciation as Guilford, which is the name of townships and villages in Maine, Vermont, New York, and nine other states.

GLASGOW TOWNSHIP settled in 1855 and organized in 1858, "was named in honor of the city of Glasgow, Scotland, there being several Scotchmen in the township, and the first settler was a Scotchman." A post office was in section 18, 1863–79.

GOPHER PRAIRIE a post office, 1860–72; location not found.

GREENFIELD TOWNSHIP settled in 1854, organized May 11, 1858, has a name borne by townships and villages or cities in 14 other states.

GREENVILLE a village in sections 10 and 11 of Plainview Township, established in 1855 by Ezra Eddy, later a banker in Plainview, Artemas T. Sharpe from Ohio, William Boatman, and Thomas Todd; 320 acres were platted in 1856 as the first townsite in the township. Two post offices were established: the first, 1856–57, was located in a store built by Mr. Richards of Reads Landing and Rodman Burchard, the latter being postmaster, transferring to Plainview; the second post office operated 1858–65, with Sharpe as postmaster in the same store. The townsite diminished as Centerville, later named Plainview, developed and was abandoned by 1858.

GREENWOOD PRAIRIE an area of tableland in Plainview Township, also known as the Plateau of Plenty, was settled beginning in 1855 when some 40 families moved there, mainly Norwegian immigrants.

HAMMOND a city in sections 27 and 28 of Zumbro, was named for Joseph Hammond, the farmer on whose land it was platted. He was born in New Hampshire, March 28, 1816, and came to Minnesota, settling here in 1856. The city was incorporated as a village in 1900; the post office was first known as Hammondsford, 1878–81, was changed to Hammond in 1881, and became a community post office in 1965.

HIGHLAND TOWNSHIP organized May 13, 1858, was at first called Smithfield, but soon "the more euphonious title of Highland was substituted, which also truthfully implies the fact of its elevated surface."

HYDE PARK a post office, 1857–80, located in section 33 of Gillford Township.

HYDE PARK TOWNSHIP organized in 1858, was at first called Troy and later Zumbro, but received its present name in 1862, in accord with the suggestion of an Englishman, "so that the township is named after one of the most famous places in London" (*History of Winona and Wabasha Counties*, p. 788). The choice of this name was decided mainly in compliment for John E. Hyde of Mazeppa. He was born in Portland, Maine, in 1819; came to Platteville, Wis., in 1849 and to this state in 1855, settling in Mazeppa, where he was a merchant for ten years; served in the 156th

Illinois Regiment, 1865, receiving a sunstroke, after which he never regained good health; but his mercantile business was continued by his wife until 1872. He was the first postmaster of Mazeppa, 1856, and was one of its most useful citizens.

INDEPENDENCE a post office, 1856–62, located in postmaster Seth L. McCarty's home in Plainview Township, west of Woodland.

JACKSONVILLE a post office, 1859–67, in section 11 of Gillford Township.

JARRETT a village in section 23 of Hyde Park, is near a former crossing of Zumbro River, called Jarrett's Ford, for the nearest original settler. The village had a post office, 1879–1919, and a station of the Chicago, Milwaukee and St. Paul Railroad; it was also known as Jarretts and Jarretts Ford.

KEEGAN a post office, 1879–1917, in section 3 of Oakwood Township, was named for an Irish settler there. It had a station of the Chicago, Milwaukee and St. Paul Railroad.

KELLOGG a city in sections 22 and 27 of Greenfield Township, founded in 1870, incorporated February 14, 1877, was named by officers of the Chicago, Milwaukee and St. Paul Railroad company, "in honor of a Milwaukee gentleman who furnished the depot signs," L. H. Kellogg, who died in 1873 (*History of Winona and Wabasha Counties*, p. 885). The post office was called Pawselin, 1862–72, and then changed to Kellogg.

KINGS COOLEY see MAPLE SPRINGS.

LAKE TOWNSHIP beside Lake Pepin, was first settled in 1853–54; the village of Lake City was platted in 1856; and on May 13, 1858, this township was "named Lake City by a vote of the people." The city was incorporated February 26, 1872, and the remaining part of the township "one year thereafter received by legislative enactment the curtailed name of 'Lake,' as it now is" (*History of Winona and Wabasha Counties*, p. 796). The city, governed with Goodhue County, was incorporated as a village in 1909; the post office was established in 1856 in Harvey F. Williamson's general store; the village had a station of the Chicago, Milwaukee and St. Paul Railroad.

LAKE VIEW had a station of the Chicago, Milwaukee and St. Paul Railroad; location not found.

LAKEOPOLIS is noted as a post office on C. M. Foote's map of 1887 in section 21, Pepin Township.

LAKEY a post office in section 27 of West Albany Township, 1881–1903, and a station of the Chicago, Milwaukee and St. Paul Railroad.

LINCOLN a post office, 1861–78, in sections 17 and 18 of Gillford Township.

LYON a post office, 1862–80, in section 17 of Highland Township, located in Alfred W. Lathrop's general store, which was near a gristmill on West Indian Creek.

MAPLE SPRINGS a village on Lake Pepin in sections 17 and 20 of Pepin Township, originally called Kings Cooley, with a railway station of the Chicago, Milwaukee and St. Paul Railroad. Kings Cooley was named for the coulee, or ravine, on the farm of a settler named King.

MAZEPPA TOWNSHIP settled in 1855, organized May 11, 1858, and its village platted in 1856 by Joseph Ford and his son Orville and incorporated in 1877, are named for Ivan Mazeppa (1644–1709), a Cossack chief, commemorated in a poem by Byron. The post office was established in 1856; it had a station of the Chicago, Milwaukee and St. Paul Railroad.

McCRACKEN a railway station in section 20 of Glasgow, is named in honor of William McCracken from Scotland, the first settler in that township. He was born August 15, 1815, came to New Brunswick in 1841, and to Minnesota in 1855, settling here.

MIDLAND JUNCTION a village in section 15 of Greenfield Township, with a station of the Chicago, Milwaukee and St. Paul Railroad.

MILLVILLE a city in section 18 of Oakwood Township, was incorporated as a village in June 1899. It was founded by Charles R. Read, for whom Reads Landing was named, on a site selected for its good gristmill possibility, although none was built. When the post office was established in 1867, Read was the first postmaster in his home. It had a station of the Chicago, Milwaukee and St. Paul Railroad.

MINNEISKA TOWNSHIP settled in 1851, organized April 5, 1859, and its city with Winona County, located in sections 33–35, platted in 1854, are named from the Whitewater River, which is a translation of its Dakota name (*Minne* or *Mini*, "water"; *ska*, "white"). The city was incorporated on March 4, 1857, reincorporated on April 7, 1921, and separated from the township on May 9, 1921. The post office operated January–April 1856, when it was changed to Mount Vernon in Winona County, returning to Minneiska in September.

MOUNT PLEASANT TOWNSHIP first settled in June 1854, was organized May 11, 1858. "The appropriate name was suggested by the magnificent view presented to an observer from the tops of some of the elevations in the south central part, and from the summit of Lone Mound the sight is truly grand" (*History of Winona and Wabasha Counties*, p. 752). A post office was in section 28, 1859–68.

NELSONS LANDING see WABASHA.

OAK CENTER is a village in section 5 of Gillford, named "on account of the abundance of oak trees in that vicinity." The village had a post office, 1875–1907.

OAKWOOD TOWNSHIP similarly named as the preceding, was settled in 1855 and organized in 1859. It was at first called Pell in honor of John H. Pell, an early settler, who was a state senator in 1861 and later was captain of Company I in the First Minnesota Regiment, 1861–63; was renamed Sherman in 1868; but because another Minnesota township had earlier received that name, it was finally changed to Oakwood in 1872.

OLD ABE a post office in section 20 of Plainview Township, 1864–68.

PAUSELIM the origin and meaning of which are unknown, was an early village in Greenfield, platted in 1863, which was superseded by Kellogg.

PAWSELIN see KELLOGG.

PELL see BREMEN.

PEPIN TOWNSHIP organized May 11, 1858, is named from Lake Pepin, receiving thus an ancient and honored French name, as noticed in the first chapter.

PLAINVIEW TOWNSHIP settled in 1854 and organized May 11, 1858, took the name of its city, platted in the summer of 1857 and incorporated as a village on March 9, 1875, and reincorporated on June 10, 1908. The village was at first called Centerville but was changed when the post office was applied for in 1857 because another place in this state had been earlier so named. "In view of location, it being the watershed of the Zumbro and Whitewater Rivers, and in plain view of a large tract of surrounding country, the name was changed to Plainview" (Mitchell and Curtis, 1870, p. 140). Villages in Illinois, Nebraska, and four other states also bear this name. The township contains Carley State Park, established in 1949 and named for James A. Carley a state senator, 1915–29 and 1935–51, who donated much of the land.

PLEASANT PRAIRIE a post office, 1857–64; location not found.

READS LANDING a village in section 24 of Pepin, adjoining the city of Wabasha, is on the site occupied as a Dakota trading post by Augustine Rocque from about 1810 to 1825 or 1830; and later by Charles R. Read, who came here in 1847. Read was born about 1820 in England; came to the United States when ten years old; served in the American army in the Canadian rebellion, 1837–38; was captured by the British and sentenced to be hanged; was pardoned and returned to the United States; in 1847 took charge of this trading post; died at Millville in this county, October 9, 1900. The village of Reads Landing was platted in 1856 as Pepin, but that name was never used; it was incorporated March 5, 1868, and during 10 to 15 years later had flourishing commercial and transportation business, but afterward was superseded by Wabasha. The post office, spelled Reeds Landing, began in 1850, with Charles R. Read as postmaster; the name was changed to Reeds in 1894, to Reads in 1916, and to the present form in 1950; it had a station of the Chicago, Milwaukee and St. Paul Railroad.

SMITHFIELD a hamlet in Highland, retains the original name of that township. A post office was in section 26 of Highland Township, 1858–1903; it was requested by Thomas Israel Smith, who had built a store in 1857, but the store burned down before a post office was granted; James Felton became first postmaster, although the name was selected to honor Smith.

SOUTH TROY a village in Zumbro Township, section 36, which had a post office, 1858–1903.

TEPEEOTA an early village in Greenfield, was founded in 1856 on an island of the Mississippi, a former camping ground of Wapashaw's band, but its hopes came to naught by the financial panic of 1857. On a March night in 1859, its deserted steam sawmill, three-story hotel, and stores, mostly then empty, were burned by incendiarism. This Dakota name means "many houses" (Mitchell and Curtis, 1870, pp. 93–96). A post office was in sections 12 and 13 of Greenfield, 1857–62.

THEILMAN a village in section 36 of West Albany and in section 31 of Glasgow Township, was named for Henry Theilman, on whose land this village was platted. The village was formerly a station of the Chicago, Milwaukee and St. Paul Railroad; the post office began as Thielmanton, 1878–95, was then Thielman, 1895–1904, when the name was changed to its present form.

TRACY a station of the Chicago, Milwaukee and St. Paul Railroad; location not found.

WABASHA the county seat, founded and named in 1843, as related at the beginning of this chapter, was platted in 1854 and was incorporated as a city March 20, 1858. The city is in Pepin and Greenfield Townships. Augustin Rocque built a trading post here in 1833, and Father Ravoux built a Catholic church in 1845; the post office began as Nelsons Landing in 1848 in Chippewa County, Wisconsin Territory; was transferred to Wabasha County in 1850, with Alexis P. Bailly as postmaster, and the name was changed to Wabashaw; it had a station of the Chicago, Milwaukee and St. Paul Railroad.

WATOPA TOWNSHIP settled in 1855 and organized May 11, 1858, has a Dakota name, being a verb, "to paddle a canoe." A post office named Wautopa was located in the township, 1858–60, and was reestablished as Watopa, 1867–71.

WEAVER a village in sections 29 and 30 of Minneiska, platted in 1871, was named in honor of William Weaver, a pioneer settler, who came from the state of New York in 1857 and was one of the proprietors of this village site. Weaver was the first postmaster; the post office operated 1871–1971; it had a station of the Chicago, Milwaukee and St. Paul Railroad.

WEST ALBANY TOWNSHIP first settled in June 1855, organized May 3, 1858, took this name from its village in section 29, which was platted in the spring of 1857 by settlers from Albany, N.Y. The village had a post office, 1857–81.

WEST NEWTON a village in section 9 of Minneiska Township, first settled in 1851 and platted in 1853, was named for the steamboat *West Newton*, which sank in the Mississippi River at the site. The village retreated as the river wore down the banks, and by 1857 the original site was under water; it later became a summer home and cottage community. The village had a post office, 1856–59.

WOODLAND a post office, 1860–75, in section 25, Plainview Township, at the home of postmaster George W. Sylvester.

ZUMBRO TOWNSHIP settled in 1855, was originally a part of Mazeppa and Troy Townships, which were organized in 1858, and had for each the area of a township of the government survey. The inconvenience of crossing the Zumbro River, flowing through these townships, led to the organization of Zumbro, March 19, 1861, comprising the area east and south of the river; and the north part of Troy was renamed Hyde Park.

ZUMBRO FALLS is a city at the falls of the Zumbro River in section 31 of Gillford. It was incorporated as a village on February 8, 1898; the post office has been established and reestablished three times since 1856. The townsite was platted by Uriah S. Whaley, who later served as one of the postmasters in his cabin. The Chicago, Milwaukee and St. Paul Railroad built a narrow gauge railroad in 1877, changing later to standard track.

Rivers and Creeks

Zumbro River is derived, by changes of pronunciation and greater change of spelling, from the early French name, Rivière des Embarras, meaning River of Difficulties or Encumbrances, that is, a stream on which canoeing was hindered by driftwood. On Joseph N. Nicollet's map, 1843, this stream is named Wazi Oju, "Place of Pines," referring to its grove of large white pines at Pine Island in Goodhue County. The North and South Branches of the Zumbro unite at the east side of Mazeppa.

From the north the Zumbro receives West Albany Creek and Skillman or Trout Brook; and from the south its tributaries are Long, Middle, and West Indian Creeks. Skillman Brook, later called Trout Brook, was named from its mill in section 19, Chester, built by brothers of this name. Francis M. Skillman was born at Riverhead, Long Island, N.Y., November 23, 1812; came to Minnesota in 1856, settling on a farm in this county; was a representative in the legislature in 1859–60. Evander Skillman, born in German, N.Y., May 12, 1838, came to this county in 1856; served as first lieutenant in the Third Minnesota Regiment in the Civil War; engaged in mercantile business in Mazeppa, and in 1873 with his brother built this mill.

Whitewater River, before noticed for Minneiska Township, flows through the southern edge of this county.

Lake Pepin, whence Lake City and Lake and Pepin Townships are named, receives Gilbert and King Creeks.

The Zumbro River in its southward course, after coming to the Mississippi bottomland, receives Snake Creek and Indian Creek.

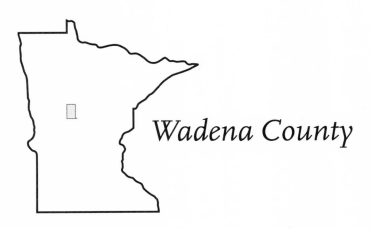

Wadena County

Established June 11, 1858, and organized February 21, 1873, this county took its name from the Wadena trading post of the old trail from Crow Wing to Otter Tail City and Pembina, situated on the west bluff of the Crow Wing River at its crossing in the present township of Thomastown. The former ferry and trading post were between the mouths of the Leaf and Partridge Rivers. Hon. J. V. Brower, who visited the place in 1863 and again examined it in May 1899, stated that in its most populous period, about the years 1855 to 1860, more than a hundred people lived at this trading post, but that in 1899, like Crow Wing and the original Otter Tail City, its buildings had disappeared, and only their cellar holes remained to mark the spot, the trail or road having been long previously abandoned. Soon after the building of the Northern Pacific Railroad, the county seat was located on this railroad, in 1872, 15 miles west of the original Wadena trading post, from which its name was transferred.

This name, an archaic Ojibwe word, signifies "a little round hill," according to Rev. J. A. Gilfillan. It probably had reference, as Brower thought, to the rounded outlines of the Crow Wing bluffs at the old Wadena ferry. It is also a somewhat frequent personal name among the Ojibwe. One of this name, the eldest son of Bad Boy, the last Gull Lake leader, was living in 1899, an old man, on the White Earth Reservation. Prof. N. H. Winchell defined his name as "Sloping Hill," with notation that he signed treaties in 1857 and 1889 (*Aborigines of Minnesota*, 1911, p. 729). Asher Murray, of Wadena, has a portrait of him. The name accents the middle syllable and sounds each *a* as in *father*.

Information of origins and meaning of geographic names was received from Eugene Boss, county auditor since 1903, and Asher Murray, each of Wadena, the county seat, interviewed during a visit there in May 1916. Mr. Murray came to Minnesota in 1880 and has since resided in Wadena, being the county judge of probate in 1889–1902.

ALDRICH TOWNSHIP received the name of the city in section 35, given by officers of the Northern Pacific Railroad company in honor of Cyrus Aldrich, who was born in Smithfield, R.I., June 18, 1808, and died in Minneapolis, October 5, 1871. He came to this state in 1855, settling in Minneapolis, and engaged in real estate business; was a representative in Congress, 1859–63; a member of the state legislature, 1865; and postmaster of Minneapolis, 1867–71. The city was incorporated as a village on March 4, 1938; the post office was established in 1877, with Michael W. Kelly as postmaster; it had a station of the Northern Pacific Railroad.

BLUE GRASS a village on the border of North Germany Township, sections 31 and 32, and Wing River Township, sections 5 and 6.

BLUEBERRY TOWNSHIP has Blueberry River and Lake, which are translated from their Ojibwe name. The low blueberry, supplying abundant berries much prized as food by both Indians and white people, is common in northern Minnesota, extending somewhat farther south and west than our species of pine, spruce, and fir.

BULLARD TOWNSHIP was named in honor of Clarence Eugene Bullard, who was born at Fort Madison, Iowa, in 1843; served in the Sixth Wisconsin Regiment in the Civil War, attaining the rank of first lieutenant; came to Minnesota in 1864; settled in Verndale in 1878; was clerk of the district court of this county, 1881–86; removed to Wadena and during many years was the county attorney; died at his home in Wadena in April 1916. A post office was in section 27, 1896–1907.

CENTRAL a post office, 1897–1904, in section 1 of Aldrich Township, with James F. Oliver, postmaster; Oliver, born in 1847 in Wisconsin, served with the Forty-third Wisconsin Regiment during the Civil War. The site had a station of the Northern Pacific Railroad. It was also known as the "Boyd settlement" for the several Boyd families in the area.

COOK'S CORNER a place five miles north of Verndale in section 21 of Wing River, which is the site of the township hall on Robert Cook's land.

FARNHAM a post office, 1888–89, in section 15 of Bullard Township, on Farnham Lake.

HARTSHORN a post office in sections 11 and 12 of Thomastown Township, 1888–1903, which had earlier been established in Cass County and was transferred to Wadena; it may have been named for Benjamin F. Hartshorn, an attorney in Verndale and a legislator, 1895–97.

HOPATCONG a post office, 1887–1903, in section 30 of Rockwood Township, with Walter Aron Forbes, postmaster, formerly of Vermont.

HUNTERSVILLE TOWNSHIP was named for its being a "hunters' paradise." A settlement in sections 8 and 17 had a post office, 1903–19, and a station of the Northern Pacific Railroad.

KINDRED see SHELL CITY.

LEAF RIVER TOWNSHIP crossed by the river of this name, and its village in section 22 are a translation from the Ojibwe name of the Leaf Hills or "mountains" and the Leaf Lakes and River, before noted in the chapter of Otter Tail County. It is written by Gilfillan as "Gaskibugwudjiwe, Rustling Leaf mountain," the same name being also applied to the lakes and river. The village began as a railroad station for the Great Northern Railway; it had a post office, 1880–82 and 1902–8, as Leaf-river.

LOTTA a post office, 1898–1904, in Rockwood Township.

LUKENS a post office, 1888–1904, in section 30 of Wing River Township; Theophilus Gilbert Lukens (1829–1906) purchased 80 acres on the Hubbard Wheat Trail, built a halfway house, served as postmaster the entire time the post office operated, and provided blacksmith services.

LYONS TOWNSHIP was named in honor of Harrison Lyons of Verndale, who for many years was a member of the board of county commissioners.

MEADOW TOWNSHIP was named for its relatively small tracts of prairie, natural grassland, enclosed in the general woodland.

MENAHGA a city in sections 21, 22, 27, and 28 of Blueberry Township, platted in 1891, very appropriately bears the Ojibwe name of the blueberry, spelled Meenahga by Henry W. Longfellow in *The Song of Hiawatha*. The city was incorporated on August 20, 1892, following a petition entered by Charles Lane, known as Uncle Charlie, and considered the founder of the city, but the name was chosen by Col. William Crooks of the Great Northern Railway. While the first settlers, 1875–80, were Yankees, the largest number of later settlers were Finnish immigrants. The Great Northern Railway came in 1891, the same year the post office was established. A major industry was the American Wire Grass Company, which made rugs and mats from the tough wire grass grown nearby.

METZ was a post office, 1896–1907, in section 13 of North Germany Township, now discontinued, bearing the name of the chief city of Lorraine, which on October 27, 1870, after a siege of two months, was surrendered by the French to the Germans. Amund K. Berg was postmaster at his home, which was also a hostel and grocery store.

NIMROD a city in section 32 of Orton, is named for the grandson of Ham, called, in Genesis, "a mighty hunter before the Lord," who is reputed to have directed the construction of the Tower of Babel. The city was incorporated as a village on August 20, 1924, and as a city on December 4, 1946; the post office operated 1887–1916 and was reestablished as a rural branch in 1938. The city became a halfway stop for wheat haulers between Shell City and Verndale on what was called the Wheat Trail; in 1885 Paluski Williams took over the halfway house of Jake Graba, developing it into a hotel, where his wife, Mary L. Williams, was the first postmaster until 1903. The village had a station of the Great Northern Railway.

NORTH GERMANY TOWNSHIP was named by its many German settlers.

OLEAN a village townsite incorporated on March 9, 1858; location not found.

ORION TOWNSHIP was named in honor of one of its pioneer farmers.

OSSIPEE a post office, January-April 1890; location not found.

OYE a post office, was located in section 22 of Lyons Township, 1902–8, in a store on postmaster John Olson's land.

OYLEN a village in section 24 of Lyons Township, which had a post office, 1906–8, in the store on Gina P. Dahlvang's land, with Henry J. Trana, postmaster; it had a station of the Northern Pacific Railroad.

PASSAIC a post office, 1888 and 1891, located in the Red Eye Township home of postmaster Thomas Olson.

RED EYE TOWNSHIP is traversed by the Redeye River, named, in translation from the Ojibwe for its red-eye fish, a species that is also called "blue-spotted sunfish" or "green sunfish" (Cox, *Fishes of Minnesota*, 1897, p. 67), but a later manual (*American Food and Game Fishes*, by Jordan and Evermann, 1902) places this name, red-eye, as a synonym for the rock bass. The two species are nearly allied, and the latter is stated by Cox to be "a very common and valuable food fish in all the lakes and streams of the state" (p. 56).

ROCKWOOD TOWNSHIP is thought to have been named from its glacial drift boulders and hardwood timber. A spur station of the Great Northern Railway was in section 34.

SEBEKA a city in Red Eye and Rockwood Townships, beside the Redeye River, founded in 1891, was named, like Menahga, by Col. William Crooks, chief engineer of the Manitoba (now Great Northern) Railway. Like Menahga, this is a name of Ojibwe derivation, from *sibi* or *zibi*, "a river," meaning "the village or town beside the river." The city was incorporated as a village on April 30,

1898; the post office was established in 1891 in postmaster John Anderson's store. Logging was the first major industry; the city was developed when the Great Northern Railway came in 1892, mostly by Finnish immigrants.

SHELL CITY a village, was established in section 2 of Shell River Township. The post office began in 1879 as Kindred, was changed to Shell City in 1882, and was discontinued in 1901. William E. Kindred came in May 1879 from Verndale, cleared ten acres for a homestead, petitioned for the post office, and encouraged other families to come that year. The townsite was purchased from Kindred by Francis M. Yoder and Sewall Chandler, who platted it in 1881, changing the name to Shell City. Yoder built a sawmill, and his son, James M., became the postmaster.

SHELL RIVER TOWNSHIP gets its name from the mussel or clam shells of this river and of Shell Lake at its source in Becker County. The Ojibwe, according to Gilfillan, call the lake by a different name, meaning "the lake lying near the mountain," that is, near a portage crossing the water divide between the Crow Wing and Otter Tail Rivers. Thence they also give that name to the Shell River.

STAPLES a city with Todd County, which see.

TAYLOR'S LANDING a post office, 1884–86, with William Taylor as postmaster; location not found.

THOMASTOWN the most southeastern township of this county, was named in honor of Thomas Scott, a pioneer homesteader, who was a lumberman and farmer, but he removed about the year 1875 to the state of Washington.

VERNDALE a city in the west part of Aldrich, was named in honor of Helen Vernette "Vernie" Smith, a granddaughter of Lucas W. Smith, one of its pioneers. He was born in Caledonia County, Vt., September 15, 1816; settled on a homestead claim near the site of this village, which he named; built the first house here and engaged in mercantile business. The city, developed as a wheat trading center for the county, was incorporated as a village on May 24, 1883, and separated from the township on March 11, 1919. The site was first settled in 1876 and was platted in 1877 in section 30 by Lucas W. Smith, with an addition in 1879 in section 19; Smith was the first postmaster when the post office was established in 1878 and built the first store and dwelling. The community had a station of the Northern Pacific Railroad.

WADENA TOWNSHIP and its city with Otter Tail County, in sections 5–8 of the township, the county seat, first settled in the fall of 1871, incorporated February 14, 1881, and separated from the township on March 11, 1921, are named, like this county, from the old trading post. The post office was established in 1873; it had a station serving the Great Northern Railway and Northern Pacific Railroad.

WING RIVER TOWNSHIP has the stream of this name, flowing from Otter Tail and Todd Counties to join the Leaf River. Its name probably was translated from the Ojibwe, like the Crow Wing River. A post office was located in the township, 1880–83, on the Leaf River, with postmaster Alidon W. Amidon, known as Albert; he was born in 1847 in New York, was the first settler of Empire Township in Dakota Township before moving to Verndale about 1878, and died in Columbia Heights in 1926.

———————

Streams and Lakes

On the map of Maj. Stephen H. Long's expedition in 1823, the Crow Wing River is named "R. de Corbeau," meaning River of the Raven, the Leaf River is called its "West Fork," and the other streams of this county are unnamed, being indeed mostly without delineation. Joseph N. Nicollet's map, published in 1843, names the Crow Wing, Leaf, Redeye, and Shell Rivers; and the Partridge River bears its equivalent French name, "Riv. aux Perdrix." The early state map of 1860 adds Union Creek and Wing and Partridge Rivers.

Blueberry River and Lake, and Leaf, Redeye, Shell, and Wing Rivers, from which townships are named, have been noticed in the preceding pages, and the French and English names of Partridge River are translations of its Ojibwe name. The ori-

gin of the name of Union Creek is not known.

The Twin Lakes, on the course of the Shell River, are crossed by the north line of this county.

Kettle Creek is a tributary of Blueberry River.

Stocking Lake, named from its shape, outflows by Stocking Creek to the Shell River.

Spirit Lake, without outlet, adjoins Menahga.

Jim Cook Lake was named for an early farmer, who cut logs there.

Finn Lake, in Shell Lake, has several adjacent settlers from Finland.

In Meadow Township, Yaeger Lake was named for an early German or Swiss homesteader beside it; Mud Lake lies close west, and Rice Lake close south, the latter being named for its wild rice.

Cat River, flowing to the Crow Wing, was named for wildcats encountered by the pioneer settlers. This species, also called the lynx, was formerly frequent throughout Minnesota.

This county has two Hay Creeks, one a tributary of Redeye River, the other of Leaf River, each being named for their small tracts of natural hay meadows.

Lovejoy Lake, in section 16, Thomastown, was named for Charles O. Lovejoy, a homesteader beside it; Hayden Creek, also named for a pioneer, flows through the southeast corner of this township; and Simon Lake is in its section 12.

From its east side, the Crow Wing River receives Big and Little Swamp Creeks, Beaver Creek, and Farnham Brook or Creek, the last being named in honor of Sumner W. Farnham, a Minneapolis lumberman. He was born in Calais, Maine, April 2, 1820; came to Minnesota in 1848 and engaged in logging and lumber manufacturing; opened the first bank at St. Anthony Falls in 1854; was a member of the territorial legislature in 1852 and 1856; died in Minneapolis, April 2, 1900. A lake crossed by the east line of Bullard, about a mile east from the mouth of Farnham Brook, is also named for him; and Sand Lake is in section 1 of this township.

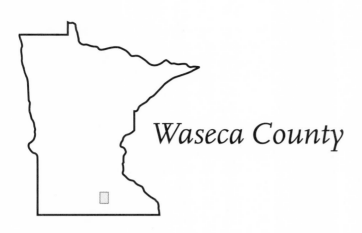

Waseca County

This county was established February 27, 1857. Its name is a Dakota word, which has been explained by Prof. A. W. Williamson as follows: "Waseca (wasecha),—rich, especially in provisions. I was informed in 1855 by a gentleman who was a stranger to me, who professed to be one of the first settlers, that this name was given in response to inquiries as to the Indian word for fertile, and adopted as a name. In Dakota writing and books the word *waseca* is spelled as we spell the name, and is a word likely to be given in answer to such a question. The soil is also very fertile." The name was first applied to the earliest farming settlement in 1855, near the present city of this name.

The county seat, originally located in Wilton, which became an important village, was removed to Waseca in 1870, soon after the building of the Winona and St. Peter Railroad.

The dictionary of the Dakota language, by Rev. S. R. Riggs, published in 1852, shows that this word was pronounced as if written *washecha*. It has the same accent and vowel sounds as Wadena.

Information of names has been derived from History of Steele and Waseca Counties *(1887), having pp. 413–733 for this county;* History of Waseca County *by James E. Child (1905, 848 pp.); from Edward A. Everett and John F. Murphy, each of Waseca, the county seat, who came here respectively in 1867 and 1857, interviewed during a visit at Waseca in October 1915; and from later letters of Mr. Everett, giving testimony from D. J. Dodge, the county clerk of the court, Edward Hayden, of Alton, and Mrs. A. C. Cleland.*

ALMA CITY a village in Alton and Freedom, platted in 1865 for Sam Larabee, who built a hotel, was named in honor of Alma Hills, daughter of Elijah Hills, one of the first settlers in Alton. Alma is also the name of a city in Wisconsin and of townships and villages or cities in 18 other states. The post office began as Peddler's Grove in 1864, was changed to Alma City, 1870–1957, and served as a rural branch until 1963. Peddler's Grove in section 3 of Freedom Township had a station of the Minnesota Stage Company on the route between Owatonna and Mankato, and when two traveling peddlers, Ed Steele and Steve Robinson, settled there, the name was given to the grove of bur oaks at the site.

ALTON TOWNSHIP organized April 27, 1866, was named for the city of Alton, Ill., by James Hayden and William Stewart, pioneers.

BLOOMING GROVE TOWNSHIP was organized April 5, 1858. The origin of the name is told by Mrs. A. C. Cleland, whose father, E. R. Connor, was one of the committee for selecting the township name. "A meeting was held at the residence of a Mr. Isaacs, . . . one mile north of Rice lake. This section of the township is a series of hills, like large and small islands surrounded by meadows and sloughs, which give the appearance of groves rather than a solid forest; and on all edges of these groves grew great plum thickets, and at the time the name was suggested by Mr. Isaacs the plums were in bloom, which gave them their idea of calling the township Blooming Grove." Townships and villages in New York, Pennsylvania, Indiana, and Texas bear this name. A post office, which was formerly Swavesey, Steele County, was located in section 4 of the township, 1864–79; the site was first called Blivens for J. M. Blivens, the first township settler in section 32.

BYRON TOWNSHIP organized November 1, 1858, was named for Byron F. Clark, then a resident of Wilton. He was a money lender, accepting 6 percent monthly interest, even from this county, during the financial depression after the panic of 1857 (*History of Waseca County*, pp. 95–96).

BYRONVILLE a village five miles from New Richland, about 1937.

CLEAR LAKE CITY a village in section 18 of Woodville Township, platted in August 1867, was started as a rival to Waseca but within a few years became part of that city.

COBB RIVER a post office, 1864–73; location not found.

CREAM a postal station in Freedom Township, 1898, located near Alma City.

ELKS PARK a place name in section 4, Woodville Township, about 1937, on the north shore of Clear Lake.

ELYSIAN a city with Le Sueur County, in section 2 of Janesville Township, was platted in 1856, incorporated as a village in 1883, and developed as a resort area.

EMPIRE a townsite in Iosco Township, existed 1856–57, but was not developed when Wilton became the county seat; see also JANESVILLE.

FREEDOM TOWNSHIP organized in March 1864, was named by Fletcher D. Seaman, one of its homestead farmers, who settled there in the spring of that year. Ten other states have townships and villages so named. A post office was in the township, 1879–92.

IDE'S SETTLEMENT a village in Blooming Grove Township on land owned by Mel P. Ide, which did not develop.

IOSCO TOWNSHIP organized April 5, 1858, has a rare name, borne elsewhere only by a county and village in Michigan. It is from Algonquian derivation, coined by Henry R. Schoolcraft in his book, *The Myth of Hiawatha and other Oral Leg-*

ends . . . of the North American Indians, published in 1856. Henry Gannett defined the word as meaning "water of light," or "shining water." A post office, established while part of Steele County, was located in sections 12 and 13 of the township, 1856–60.

JANESVILLE TOWNSHIP organized May 17, 1858, received the earlier name of its village. Old Janesville, the original village, on the west side of Lake Elysian, was called Empire, but an addition was platted in 1856 by J. W. Hosmer, who "named it Jane for Mrs. Jane Sprague, and then, by general consent of the villagers, the 'Jane' was enlarged by adding to it 'ville,' and Janesville resulted and was accepted as the name of the whole village" (Stennett, *Place Names of the Chicago and Northwestern Railways*, 1908, p. 87). During the winter of 1869–70 nearly all the buildings of the previous townsite were removed to the new railway village site, called East Janesville, platted in August 1869, for the Winona and St. Peter Railroad company. On May 10, 1870, the new village was incorporated as Janesville (*History of Steele and Waseca Counties*, pp. 616, 617, 622); the village was reincorporated on April 10, 1877. Old Janesville was also known as Ike Terill Trading Post when located in section 28. The post office was established in 1858. Among the first settlers was the Woolson family; son Albert Henry Woolson, who joined the army during the Civil War, was the last surviving member of the Union Army in the United States (born 1847 in New York and came to Minnesota in 1862, died in Duluth in 1956).

MAINE a post office, 1868–71; location not found.

MAPLEWOOD PARK a station on a spur line of the Winona and St. Peter Railroad, in section 9 of Woodville Township.

MATAWAN a village in section 31 of Byron, bears the name of a village and township in New Jersey. The village had a station of the Chicago, Milwaukee and St. Paul Railroad and a post office, 1907–72.

MAXSON GROVE a post office, 1857–62; location not found.

MELVILLE a post office, 1874–77, in Otisco Township.

NEW RICHLAND TOWNSHIP first settled by a colony from Wisconsin in June 1856, organized November 2, 1858, and its city in sections 17 and 20, platted in August 1877, received this name from the township and county of Richland in Wisconsin. The city was incorporated as a village on February 15, 1878, and reincorporated on March 25, 1920. It was first settled by Norwegian immigrants about 1857–58, the Minneapolis and St. Louis Railroad came in 1873, and the village was platted in 1877 by Henry T. Wells in section 17. John Larsen built a store, where he opened the post office in 1870.

OAKEL a post office, 1878–99; location not found.

OKAMAN a former village on the northeast shore of Lake Elysian, in section 1, Janesville, platted in May 1857, extended also north into the edge of Le Sueur County. This Dakota name has nearly the same meaning as Okabena in Jackson and Nobles Counties, each being from *hokah*, "a heron," having reference to these localities as nesting places of herons. A post office with the same name, transferred from Elysium, Le Sueur County, was in section 1 of Janesville, 1858–75.

OTISCO TOWNSHIP settled in 1856 and organized April 5, 1858, had a village so named that was platted in July 1857, but its railway village dates only from the building of the Minneapolis and St. Louis Railroad in 1877. The post office operated 1857–63 and since 1870. This is the name of a lake and a township in Onondaga County, New York, and of villages in Indiana and Michigan.

PALMER an early railway station in section 13 of Iosco, was platted as a village in September 1915. A village of this name in section 19 of Blooming Grove Township had a post office, 1895–1901.

PEDDLER'S GROVE see **ALMA CITY**.

PLAINVIEW the site of a creamery, 1898, in Iosco Township.

RED TAVERN a place name in 1874 in section 19 of Vivian Township.

ROSE SIDING a railroad siding, circa 1930, in Janesville Township.

ROSS is a station of the Chicago and North Western Railway, two miles east of Janesville, "named for Ross Redfield, who lived nearby."

ST. MARY TOWNSHIP organized April 5, 1858, was named from its Catholic church, which was organized in 1856. The village in section 33 had post offices, 1856–68 and 1872–73, as St. Marys; the village received the name in 1856 from the original owner, Patrick McCarthy; it was platted in 1857 and developed until the Civil War, when most of the men enlisted, at which time it ceased.

SILVER LAKE a post office, 1857–62; location not found but probably in Wilton Township, where Silver Lake is located.

SMITHS MILL a village in section 30 of Janesville, "was named for Peter Smith, the earliest settler here, who owned a mill here before the railroad reached the place" (Stennett, p. 125). Smith was the first postmaster; the post office, 1876–1963, became a rural branch until 1967 and was variously spelled Smith's Mill, Smith Mill, and Smithmill. The townsite had a depot of the Chicago and North Western Railway.

SWANESEY a village in Blooming Grove Township, about 1856.

UNION CITY a village in St. Mary Township, incorporated on March 4, 1857; no trace remains.

VISTA a village in Otisco Township, was first settled in 1856 by the Norwegian Brattland Colony, who had come to the United States in 1846; however, it was the Swedish immigrants arriving in 1856 who named the site for a district in Sweden, Vista härad, Jönköpings län, where many were from, and established the Swedish Evangelical Lutheran Church as the center of the community. A post office operated 1874–78, with Lars Peterson, postmaster.

VIVIAN a post office, 1858–1905, in Freedom Township, which moved several times to the homes of the various postmasters.

VIVIAN TOWNSHIP settled in the summer of 1856, organized April 5, 1858, has a name borne by villages in West Virginia and Louisiana.

WALDORF a city in section 3 of Vivian Township and section 34 of Freedom Township, was incorporated as a village on November 22, 1920; the post office was established in 1908; it had a station of the Chicago, Milwaukee and St. Paul Railroad.

WASECA the county seat, in Woodville Township, platted in July 1867 on the line of the Winona and St. Peter Railroad, was incorporated as a village on March 2, 1868, and as a city on February 23, 1881. It succeeded Wilton as the county seat in 1870. The post office began as Woodville in 1864 and was changed to Waseca in 1867.

WATERLYNN was a village in Otisco Township on the Le Sueur River; in 1856 Mr. Waters and Mr. Chamberlain bought the 1855 claims of George and William Robbins, built a store, and tried to develop a village, with no success.

WILTON TOWNSHIP first settled in August 1854, and organized May 11, 1858, took the name of its village, platted in the autumn of 1855, which was the county seat from the date of the county organization in 1857 until 1870, when the county offices were removed to Waseca. A post office operated 1856–81; fire destroyed much of the village. Wilton is the name of a town in Wiltshire, England, famous for its manufacture of carpets, and of townships and villages in Maine, New Hampshire, Connecticut, New York, Wisconsin, and seven other states.

WOODVILLE see WASECA.

WOODVILLE TOWNSHIP organized April 5, 1858, was named in honor of Eri G. and Loren Mark Wood, brothers, who were pioneer settlers here in 1856. Eri Wood was born in Franklin County, N.Y., March 17, 1832, and died at his home in this township, February 10, 1903. The first township meeting, May 11, 1858, was held at his house.

Lakes and Streams

The map of Minnesota Territory in 1855 has the Le Sueur and Cobb Rivers, the latter being named by the government surveyors, and the former in honor of Pierre Charles Le Sueur, of whom biographic notice is given in the chapter for Le Sueur County.

Boot Creek is a western tributary of the Le Sueur River, and it receives the Little Le Sueur River and McDougal Creek from the east. The last is named for Robert McDougal, who was born in Scotland, March 26, 1821; came to Canada in boyhood with his parents and to Minnesota in 1855, taking a homestead claim in section 6, Otisco, beside this creek and the Le Sueur River; traveled in 1858–60 to the gold mines of the Saskatchewan River and to the Pacific Coast; returned to Minnesota in 1861 but soon went back to Canada; came again to this state in 1866 and was a farmer in Otisco until his death, January 15, 1887.

Little Cobb River and Bull Run Creek, the outlet of Silver Lake, flow west into Blue Earth County.

Iosco Creek, to which Silver Creek is tributary, flows into Lake Elysian; and Crane Creek has its source in Rice Lake, named for its wild rice.

Other lakes of this county include Trenton Lake, crossed by the south line of Byron; Thompson Lake in section 13, New Richland, which on later maps was named Norwegian Lake, but is usually called St. Olaf Lake; Wheeler Lake (drained) in section 5, Vivian, named for John A. Wheeler, who took a claim on section 4 in 1858, served in the Tenth Minnesota Regiment, 1862–65, afterward was first lieutenant in the 66th U.S. Colored Infantry, and died about 1876; Lake Canfield (drained), in the northeast corner of Otisco, named in honor of Job A. Canfield, who was born in Ohio, settled here in 1856, was county judge of probate, 1857–60 and 1870–77, served in the Tenth Minnesota Regiment, 1862–65, and died January 28, 1884; Mott Lake in sections 23 and 26, Freedom; Goose and Watkins Lakes in the northeast part of Woodville, the latter named for Henry Watkins, who came here in 1856 and took a claim on the banks of the lake but about 15 years later removed to Iowa; Clear Lake, remarkable for the clearness of its water, northeast of Waseca; Gaiter Lake, named for its shape, a quarter of a mile south of Clear Lake, and Loon Lake, adjoining the northwest side of this city; Buffalo Lake in Alton; Hayes, Remund, Everson, and Knutsen Lakes, in Blooming Grove Township; Toners, Reeds, and Lily Lakes, the last having many white water lilies, in the northwest part of Iosco; Helena Lake (drained) in section 31, Iosco, and section 36, Janesville; and Rice Lake, having wild rice, Willis, Lilly, and Fish Lakes, in the northwest part of Janesville.

Lake Elysian, extending nearly across Janesville Township, is the largest and most beautiful in this county, extending also north into Le Sueur County, where a township and village bear this name.

Samuel Remund, for whom a lake in Blooming Grove was named, was born in Canton Berne, Switzerland, January 26, 1833; came to the United States in 1855 and in 1856 settled on section 9 in this township; died February 8, 1903.

Gullick Knutsen, commemorated by another lake, was born in Roldat, Norway, May 25, 1840; came to the United States in 1851 with his parents, who settled in Dane County, Wis., and removed to Blooming Grove in June 1856; he served against the Dakota in 1862–63, in Company B, First Minnesota Mounted Rangers; was township treasurer and later township clerk; died at his home, August 11, 1901.

Richard Toner, a blacksmith, for whom Toners Lake was named, settled in Iosco in 1856 and was burned to death in a fire that destroyed his house, August 27, 1878.

Reeds Lake was named for John Reed, a veteran of the War of 1812, who settled in Iosco in 1856.

Willis Lake was named for Abner Willis, who was born in Connecticut, August 15, 1816, and was a farmer in section 8, Janesville.

Lilly Lake, a mile west of Willis Lake, commemorates Terrence Lilly, a cooper, who was born in 1808 at Enniskillen, Ireland, came to the United States in 1849 and to this state in 1857, settling in St. Mary Township, and died May 15, 1891.

Washington County

Established October 27, 1849, this county was named for George Washington, "first in war, first in peace, and first in the hearts of his countrymen." He was born in Westmoreland County, Va., February 22, 1732; was commander-in-chief during the Revolutionary War, 1775–83; was the first president of the United States, 1789–97; and died at his home, Mount Vernon, Va., December 14, 1799. Thirty-two counties in as many states bear his name. This is one of the nine original counties into which Minnesota Territory was divided in 1849. Five others of these counties yet remain, namely, Benton, Dakota, Itasca, Ramsey, and Wabasha, each, like Washington County, being much reduced from its original area.

Information of names has been gathered from History of Washington County and the St. Croix Valley *(1881, 636 pp.);* Fifty Years in the Northwest *by William H. C. Folsom (1888), having pages 355–431 for this county;* History of the St. Croix Valley, *edited by Augustus B. Easton (1909, 2 vols., paged continuously, 1,290 pp.); and from Nicholas A. Nelson, county auditor, and Alpheus E. Doe, judge of probate, each of Stillwater, the county seat, interviewed during a visit there in October 1916.*

AFTON TOWNSHIP first settled in 1837, organized in May 1858, has a city in section 22, on the shore of Lake St. Croix, platted in May 1855 and incorporated as a city in 1971, named by C. S. Getchell, "from Burns' poem, 'Afton Water,' which gives a fine description of the 'neighboring hills, and the clear winding rills'" (*History of Washington County and the St. Croix Valley*, p. 402). The post office began as Milton Mills in 1854, named for the first flour mill in the county and the first privately owned mill north of Prairie du Chien, built in 1853 by Lemuel Bolles, the first postmaster; the name was changed to Afton in 1857; it had a station of the Chicago, Milwaukee, St. Paul and Pacific Railroad.

ARCOLA a former village of sawmills in sections 30 and 31 of May Township, on the St. Croix about four miles south of Marine Mills, was founded in 1846–47. The village developed with the lumbering industry; two mills were built, in 1846 and 1856; the village was platted but never incorporated; it had a station of the Minneapolis, St. Paul and Sault Ste. Marie Railroad (Soo Line). Its name is borne by an ancient town of Italy and by villages in Pennsylvania, Indiana, Illinois, Georgia, and seven other states.

ATKINSON a post office, 1861–62, in Cottage Grove Township, with John Atkinson, postmaster.

BANGOR a village of the 1880s near Bayport.

BASS LAKE a place name, circa 1874, in section 13 of Oakdale Township.

BASSWOOD GROVE a village in section 15 of Denmark Township.

BAYPORT a city in Baytown Township, formerly South Stillwater, was incorporated in 1957. The townsite was settled in 1842 but not developed until 1852, when it was platted as a village called Baytown by mill owner Socrates Nelson and others; it was resurveyed in 1872 by a railroad, which had purchased the land, and renamed it South Stillwater, building a spur line from Stillwater. The post office began in 1873 in the office of the St. Croix Lumber Company, with one of the owners, William Graves, as postmaster, and became Bayport in 1922; it had a station of the Chicago, Milwaukee, St. Paul and Pacific Railroad.

BAYTOWN a small township on the south side of Stillwater, organized in May 1858, was named by Socrates Nelson for the adjoining bay of Lake St. Croix, divided from the main lake by Mulvey's Point. See also BAYPORT.

BIRCHWOOD a city in section 30 of Grant Township, was incorporated on September 10, 1921. It began as a group of summer homes on the south shore of White Bear Lake, its first growth due in part to the building of Wildwood Amusement Park in 1899; the streetcar line into St. Paul and White Bear Lake was a vital link. When all villages in the state became cities in 1974, the community voted to rename the city Birchwood Village to retain the small community feeling of the past, although for legal purposes, it is still known as Birchwood.

CAMPGROUND a post office, 1889–90, in Newport Township, was first settled in 1843 and was known as Red Rock Park.

CARNELIAN JUNCTION a settlement in May Township.

CENTERVILLE see HUGO.

COMBS see OAKBURY.

COPAS a village of the Soo Line, adjoins the former site of Vasa. It has a unique name, not known elsewhere. A post office with the same name was located in section 30 of New Scandia Township, 1906–27, and was transferred to Scandia. The site was named later in honor of John Copas when the Soo Line depot was built. Copas was born in Italy in 1825, came to the United States in 1852 and to Marine Township in 1854, served in the Fourth Minnesota Regiment during the Civil War, had a log cabin store with John Columbus in Vasa in 1854, and died in 1911.

COTTAGE GROVE TOWNSHIP was settled in 1844 and organized in May 1858; its city in section 12, bearing the same name, in allusion to the mingled tracts of groves and prairies, was platted in April 1871 by J. P. Furber, with J. W. Furber, surveyor, four miles from the Chicago, Milwaukee and St. Paul Railroad station of the same name, on 40 acres; the city was incorporated on July 21, 1965. The post office began in 1849, with Joseph W. Forbes, postmaster. The farm community of East Cottage Grove and the railroad village of Langdon were transformed from rural community to "bedroom" suburb by 1958 with the Panorama City addition in 1955, the (Orrin) Thompson Grove additions in 1958 and 1959, and Thompson Grove Estates additions in 1960–70. The city absorbed the township, which then ceased to exist.

DAHKOTAH see STILLWATER.

DELLWOOD a city in Grant Township of euphonious name, having many summer homes beside White Bear Lake, was platted in September 1882 and incorporated as a village in 1919.

DENMARK TOWNSHIP the most southern of this county, was first settled in 1839, and was organized October 20, 1858. A post office was in section 14, 1878 and 1890–1901, with William H. Clother as postmaster in his general store. Maine and New York have townships and villages of this name, which also is borne by villages or hamlets in 13 other states.

DOLPHIN a post office, 1858–60, in Woodbury Township, with John Tanner, postmaster; Tanner came to what was then Red Rock Township in 1850.

DULUTH JUNCTION a village in section 32 of Grant Township, was a former station of the Northern Pacific Railroad.

EAST COTTAGE GROVE see COTTAGE GROVE.

ELEVATOR BAY a station of the Chicago, Milwaukee and St. Paul Railroad in section 14 of Denmark Township.

FOREST LAKE TOWNSHIP organized March 11, 1874, took the name of its city at the west end of a large lake so named from the heavy timber skirting its shores. The city was incorporated in 1896 as a village; it was laid out in 1868 by the St. Paul and Duluth Railroad as a fuel stop on the shore of the lake. A post office was established in 1869, with Michael Marsh as postmaster in his hotel; he was born in Germany in 1828, came to Minnesota in 1855, first to Hastings and then to Forest Lake, later moving to St. Paul.

GRANT see MAHTOMEDI.

GRANT TOWNSHIP organized in May 1858, was then named Greenfield by Socrates Nelson for his former home in Massachusetts, but because that name had been previously given to another Minnesota township, it was renamed in 1864 in honor of Gen. Ulysses S. Grant, whose biography is presented in the chapter of Grant County. The city of Grant incorporated in 1996, and the township ceased to exist.

GREY CLOUD a post office, 1857–63, in Newport Township, section 24.

GREY CLOUD ISLAND TOWNSHIP created from the former Newport Township.

HASTINGS a city with Dakota County, which see.

HUGO a city in section 20 of Oneka Township, was formerly called Centerville for the adjacent township and village of Anoka County but was renamed in honor of Trevanion William Hugo of Duluth. He was born in Cornwall, England, July 29, 1848, came to America in 1852 with his parents who settled in Kingston, Ontario; was a marine engineer on the Great Lakes, 1869–81; settled in Duluth, 1882, and became chief engineer of the Consolidated Elevator Company, the largest such company in the United States; was mayor of Duluth, 1900–1904. It had a station of the St. Paul and Duluth Railroad; the post office began in 1882. The townsite of Hugo was platted on April 26, 1906, and when incorporated in 1972, the Township of Oneka consolidated with the village.

IDLEWYLDE a place name in May Township, circa 1930.

KAPOSIA see NEWPORT.

LAKE ELMO a city in sections 13 and 14 of Oakdale, was named for the adjoining lake, which was formerly called Bass Lake but was renamed Lake Elmo in 1879 by Alpheus B. Stickney of St. Paul, "from the novel, 'St. Elmo'" (Stennett, *Place Names of the Chicago and Northwestern Railways*, 1908, p. 180). The city was incorporated as a village on December 21, 1925; 100 acres was platted in 1874 by the Chicago and North Western Railway as Bass Lake and renamed later. The post office, first called Lohmanville, was established in 1866 in a halfway house, with Peter Stoltz as postmaster, and reestablished at Bass Lake with the same name.

LAKE ST. CROIX a post office, 1840–50, established in Crawford County, Wisconsin Territory, July-December 1840, reestablished in St. Croix County, December 1841-January 1850, at which time it was transferred to Point Douglas, the first post office in the county in Minnesota Territory. See also POINT DOUGLAS.

LAKE ST. CROIX BEACH a city in Baytown Township, was platted and incorporated on December 31, 1951.

LAKELAND SHORES a city located next to Lakeland in section 36 of Lakeland Township and section 2 of Afton Township, was platted and incorporated as a village on November 16, 1949.

LAKELAND TOWNSHIP settled in 1839 and organized October 20, 1858, received the name of its city in section 35 of Lakeland Township and section 2 of Afton Township, platted in 1849 beside Lake St. Croix and incorporated as a village on September 27, 1951. The center of the business district in 1857 was on a ravine (coulee) called "Shanghai Cooley," so named for the large Shanghai chickens raised by Freeman C. Tyler, first postmaster when the post office began in 1854; Tyler, born in New York in 1821, came to the area in 1853 and operated the Shanghai Mill. The village had a station of the Chicago, Milwaukee, St. Paul and Pacific Railroad.

LAKEVIEW is a village site platted in sections 20 and 29, Grant Township, on White Bear Lake in the 1880s.

LAKEWOOD PARK a place name in Grant Township, circa 1930.

LANDFALL a city in section 31 of Oakdale Township, was incorporated as a village on April 6, 1959; it was established in 1956 as a private trailer park; in 1991 it was purchased by the Washington County Housing and Redevelopment Authority, which has aided the development beyond the manufactured home concept, with a school, community center, and city hall.

LANGDON a village in section 21 of Cottage Grove Township, platted in 1871 by J. T. Dodge, chief engineer for the Chicago, Milwaukee and St. Paul Railroad, was named in honor of Robert Bruce Langdon, who was born in New Haven, Vt., November 24, 1826, and died in Minneapolis, July 24, 1895. He came to St. Paul in 1858 and removed to Minneapolis in 1866; was prominently engaged in the construction of railroads in Minnesota and other northwestern states and in

Manitoba and westward, besides the construction of canals, bridges, and many city blocks and flour mills in Minneapolis and elsewhere. He was a state senator, 1873–78 and 1881–85. The post office operated 1871–1933, with depot agent Aaron G. Gillette as first postmaster; see also COTTAGE GROVE.

LINCOLN TOWNSHIP formerly the western third of Grant, was organized December 7, 1918, having been established by the board of county commissioners November 19. It included the villages of Dellwood, Mahtomedi, and Wildwood, with the east half of White Bear Lake. It received its name from Camp Lincoln, a group of summer homes about a mile north of Wildwood Park, named for President Lincoln by Samuel Bloomer, Civil War veteran and founder of Camp Lincoln about 1900. Over the years, parts were annexed by Mahtomedi, and on January 12, 1972, the township merged fully with the city and ceased to exist.

LOHMANVILLE see LAKE ELMO.

MAHTOMEDI a city in section 20 of Grant Township, on the northeast shore of White Bear Lake, was platted in July 1883, by the Mahtomedi Assembly of the Chautauqua Association. This is "the Dakota name of White Bear lake" (from *mato*, the "white or polar bear," or *matohota*, the "grizzly bear," with *mde*, "a lake"). It was incorporated as a village August 14, 1931; its post office operated in 1884 and 1888–89, became Grant 1889–1904, was again named Mahtomedi in 1904, and was discontinued in 1954; it had a station of the Northern Pacific Railroad.

MAPLE ISLAND a village in section 16 of May Township, was created by the Soo Line in 1886. Isaac Staples, Stillwater businessman, was the owner of a 3,000-acre farm known as Maple Island Farm, located on Mud Lake, which had an island with maple trees; thus the name, which was used for the post office, 1885–1900.

MARINE MILLS see MARINE ON ST. CROIX.

MARINE ON ST. CROIX a city in May Township, was incorporated in 1959. The village of Marine was platted in 1853, incorporated on March 4, 1875, and reincorporated on October 7, 1912, the name changing to Marine on St. Croix in 1917 but not officially approved by the U.S. Board on Geographic Names until April 1968. The post office, established in 1838 in St. Croix County, Wisconsin Territory, was called Marine Mills, 1848–1917,

and was first located in the mill company store, with Orange Walker the postmaster for 25 years.

MARINE TOWNSHIP which was organized October 20, 1858, comprised from 1860 to 1893 the present townships of May and New Scandia. It received this name from the Marine Lumber Company, coming from Marine, a village in Madison County, Ill., which in 1838–89 began lumber manufacturing here. The Illinois village was "so named because settled by several sea captains from the east" (Gannett, *The Origin of Certain Place Names in the United States*, 1908, p. 199).

MAY TOWNSHIP organized in 1893, having previously been the south part of Marine, was named in honor of Morgan May, a farmer here and owner of much land, who was a native of England.

MIDDLETOWN a village of the 1880s; location not found.

MIDVALE a railway village in the west edge of Oakdale, was formerly called Castle, in honor of Capt. Henry A. Castle (1841–1916) of St. Paul, author of a *History of St. Paul* (1912) and *History of Minnesota* (1915), each in three volumes. A station of Chicago, St. Paul, Minneapolis and Omaha Railroad in section 19 of Oakdale Township was also called Midvale.

MILTON MILLS see AFTON.

NEW SCANDIA TOWNSHIP organized in January 1893, was formerly the north part of Marine. The first Swedish settlement in Minnesota was made in this township in October 1850, whence this name was chosen, in allusion to the ancient name of the Scandinavian peninsula. It contains William O'Brien State Park, named for the lumber baron whose daughter donated the initial parcel of land for the park. Established in 1947, it was the first state park accessible to the Twin Cities metropolitan area.

NEWPORT TOWNSHIP organized in May 1858, received the name of its city which was so named by Mrs. James H. Hugunin. This is also the name of cities in Rhode Island and Kentucky and of villages and townships in 30 other states. The first settlement was in 1841 near the Dakota village of Kaposia (1839–43). Newport was also the name of a post office in St. Croix County, Wisconsin Territory, February 1843, with William R. Brown, postmaster; when John A. Ford built a trading post in the village, the post office was relocated in 1844;

the name was changed to Red Rock in 1849 and to Newport in 1857. The village was platted as Red Rock on December 19, 1849, was renamed Newport on May 4, 1857, replatted in 1861, and incorporated in 1889 as a village; it had a station of the Chicago, Milwaukee, St. Paul and Pacific Railroad. See GREY CLOUD ISLAND TOWNSHIP.

NORTH STILLWATER a place name in Stillwater Township, section 17, circa 1900–1930.

OAK PARK was a village site, platted in May 1857 by John Parker as a residential community, in the present section 3 of Baytown.

OAK PARK HEIGHTS a city in sections 3 and 4 of Baytown Township and 34 of Stillwater Township, was platted in 1938 and incorporated as a village on April 6, 1959; it had a station of the Chicago, St. Paul, Minneapolis and Omaha Railroad.

OAKBURY a village in Woodbury Township, section 4, had a post office first called Combs, 1886–1900, changed to Oakbury in 1900, and discontinued in 1901.

OAKDALE TOWNSHIP settled in 1848 and organized in May and November 1858, "originally was covered with white, black, and bur oak timber" (Folsom, *Fifty Years*, p. 386). The city of Oakdale was incorporated March 12, 1968, as a village. The township was absorbed by the cities of Lake Elmo and Oakdale.

OAKWOOD a post office, 1887–88, 24 miles from Stillwater, with two sawmills, a barrel factory, and a general store; William A. Donalds was postmaster.

ONEKA TOWNSHIP see HUGO.

OTISVILLE a village two miles north of Marine, at the Soo Line crossing, New Scandia Township, had a post office, 1886–1914; Charles Ekdahl was postmaster; see also VASA.

PINE SPRINGS a city on the border of Grant and Oakdale Townships, was incorporated as a village on June 24, 1959.

POINT DOUGLAS a former village in section 8 of Denmark Township, near the point so named, at the west side of the mouth of Lake St. Croix, was platted August 18, 1849, commemorating Stephen A. Douglas (1813–61). The post office, the first in the county, was transferred from Lake St. Croix, Wisconsin Territory, to Minnesota Territory in 1850 and was discontinued in 1903; Levi Hurtsell was the first postmaster. The site served

as a trade center and had a mill, warehouses, and a lime kiln in 1856; it also had a station of the Chicago, Milwaukee, St. Paul and Pacific Railroad. See also LAKE ST. CROIX.

RED ROCK a railway village one mile north of Newport, was near the site of a mission for the Dakota in 1837–42. The name is from an ovally rounded boulder of granite, about five feet long, which originally lay on the neighboring bank of the Mississippi, but it was removed to the west side of the railroad at the station. This rock was held in great veneration by the Dakota, who often visited it till 1862, and less frequently afterward, bringing offerings and renewing its vermilion paint. Folsom wrote of it in 1888: "It is painted in stripes, twelve in number, two inches wide and from two to six inches apart. The north end has a rudely drawn picture of the sun, and a rude face with fifteen rays." See also NEWPORT.

RED ROCK TOWNSHIP established in 1858, was renamed Woodbury Township in 1861, with a portion transferred to Newport Township.

ST. CROIX JUNCTION a place name in Afton Township, circa 1930.

ST. MARY'S POINT a city in section 14 of Afton Township, was platted in 1951, and incorporated as a village October 30, 1971; it was originally platted as St. Mary's in 1857; the early site had a sawmill operating 1857–58.

ST. PAUL PARK once part of Newport Township, was platted in 1887 on 1,300 acres of farmland owned by William Fowler; it was incorporated as a village in 1909. The village had six hotels, the largest of which was The Parker House, named for one of the city's founders, Charles Parker, whose name is also represented by the Park part of the city name. Its post office was established in 1888; it had a station of the Chicago, Burlington and Quincy Railroad.

SCANDIA a village in section 14 of New Scandia Township, to which the first Swedish settler to the state came in 1850. Two post offices were located here: the first, established on John M. Jonassen's (Johnson) land, operated 1878–1907; the second and present post office was transferred from Copas in 1927.

SHADYSIDE a place name in Oneka Township, circa 1930.

SHANGHAI COOLEY see LAKELAND.

SIEGEL a village in section 9 of Baytown Township.

SOUTH AFTON a village one mile south of Afton, had a general store, an elevator, a warehouse, and a rope ferry across the river, built in 1879 by J. P. Furber.

SOUTH STILLWATER see BAYPORT.

STILLWATER the county seat, was founded in 1843, and on October 26 of that year its name, "proposed by John McKusick, was adopted. This name was suggested by the stillness of the water in the lake, the anomaly of building a mill beside still water, and by fond recollections of Stillwater, Maine" (*History of Washington County and the St. Croix Valley*, p. 500). The city was incorporated on the same date as St. Paul, March 4, 1854, and the township was organized in May 1858. The earliest settlement here was by Joseph R. Brown, 1838–41, platting a townsite that he named Dahkotah on the north part of the present city area. The city was the county seat of St. Croix County, Wisconsin Territory, and continued as the county seat when the name was changed to Still Water, the post office name when it was established in 1846, with Elam Greeley as the first postmaster; the post office was transferred to Minnesota Territory in 1849, and Stillwater became the county seat of Washington County, the oldest county seat in the present state boundaries. Section 4 of Baytown Township was platted as an addition to Stillwater in 1856.

STILLWATER JUNCTION a station of the Chicago, St. Paul, Minneapolis and Omaha Railroad in section 9 of Baytown Township.

VALLEY CREEK a village in section 9 of Afton Township; the first settler and first postmaster, Erastus Bolles, was born in New York in 1821, came to Afton in 1856 and to this site in 1857, built a house, was a blacksmith, and manufactured agricultural tools until 1875. The post office operated 1873–1901.

VASA TOWNSHIP organized or at least named in 1858, was united with Marine on September 7, 1860. Its former village was located in section 30 of Scandia Township. Francis Register, a clerk with the Marine Lumber Co., wanted to create a new community to attract the trade and business away from Marine on St. Croix; he purchased land cheap, had it surveyed and platted, and named it in honor of Gustaf Vasa (1496–1560), king of Sweden, in order to entice Swedes to move to his town; the village had a sawmill and a post office, which operated, 1857–60, with Register as postmaster. The site did not flourish after the sawmill closed; later the town of Copas developed about two miles north of Marine; see also COPAS; OTISVILLE.

WASHINGTON a platted paper town of 1856 in Oneka Township.

WEST LAKELAND TOWNSHIP named in 1951 when Lakeland Township incorporated.

WILDWOOD a resort village in Grant Township, having many summer homes and noted as a place of picnics and amusements, at the southeast shore of White Bear Lake and extending also north to Mahtomedi, was partly platted in 1883, with additions at later dates.

WILLERNIE a city in Grant Township, established next to Wildwood Amusement Park, the name meaning "wildwood," was incorporated as a village on February 2, 1948; the post office was established in 1916.

WITHROW a village on the border of May and Oneka Townships, named for early settler Thomas Withrow, began with the railroad station and post office in May Township and a general store in Oneka; it had a post office, 1890–1963.

WOODBURY TOWNSHIP organized in 1858, was then called Red Rock, but was renamed in 1859, in honor of Judge Levi Woodbury of New Hampshire, a special friend of John Colby, who was chairman of the board of county commissioners. The fractional area that has the "Red Rock," before noticed, at first forming a part of this township, was annexed to Newport in 1861. Levi Woodbury was born in Francestown, N.H., December 2, 1789; was graduated at Dartmouth College in 1809 and was admitted to practice law in 1812; was a judge of the state supreme court, 1817; removed to Portsmouth, N.H., 1819; was governor of the state, 1823–24; U.S. senator, 1825–31; secretary of the navy, 1831–34, and of the treasury, 1834–41; again U.S. senator, 1841–45; and was a justice of the U.S. Supreme Court, 1846–51; died in Portsmouth, N.H., September 4, 1851. The city of Woodbury was incorporated as a village on March 7, 1967; it had a post office, 1869–93; the first postmaster was Gottfried Hartoung at his home in section 27. The city absorbed the township, which then ceased to exist.

Lakes and Streams

Lake St. Croix and the River St. Croix, bearing their early French name, are noticed in the first chapter. A minor feature of the St. Croix Lake is the Catfish Bar, near the middle of the length of the lake, reaching into it from the east shore, named in allusion to a legend of the Ojibwe, whence their name for this lake is "Gigo-shugumot, Floating Fish lake," as noted by Rev. Joseph A. Gilfillan.

Painted Rock, a ledge of sandstone rising about 30 feet above the St. Croix River in the east part of section 15, Stillwater, has ancient Siouan pictographs, of which 16 are reproduced on a scale of one eighth by Newton H. Winchell in *The Aborigines of Minnesota* (pp. 567–68).

Cedar Bend, a southeastward curve in the St. Croix River about a half mile southwest from the northeast corner of this county, marked the boundary between the country of the Dakota on the south and that of the Ojibwe on the north, named for "an old cedar tree standing on a high bluff," and also for other "cedars that lined the banks of the stream at this turn in its course" (*History of Washington County and the St. Croix Valley*, p. 185). This boundary was agreed to in a treaty at Prairie du Chien, August 19, 1825, defining its course across the area of Minnesota and referring to this place as "the Standing Cedar, about a day's paddle in a canoe above the lake."

Battle Hollow, in the city of Stillwater, tributary to Lake St. Croix at the site of the old Minnesota State Prison, is named from a battle there, July 3, 1839, between the Dakota and the Ojibwe (*History of Washington County and the St. Croix Valley*, p. 103).

From changes in the ownership of the point east of the bay in Baytown, it became known as Mulvey's Point, for James Mulvey, a lumber manufacturer, but was formerly called Kittson's Point.

Belonging to the townships of Newport and Cottage Grove are the large Upper and Lower Grey Cloud Islands of the Mississippi, separated from the mainland by small but permanent channels. Grey Cloud Island was named for Mahkpia-hoto-win, in translation Grey Cloud, a noted Dakota woman, who lived on this island. She was first married to a white trader named Anderson and after his death to the more widely known trader Hazen P. Mooers (MHS Collections 9: 427 [1901]). One of the islands was formerly called Freeborn Island, and before that was Kemp's Island; it commemorated William Freeborn, more fully noticed in the chapter for the county bearing his name. The minor rivercourse along the north side of Grey Cloud Island is commonly called "Grey Cloud slough" or channel.

Medicine Wood, a translation from the Dakota, was a camping place on or near the western end of Grey Cloud Island, occupied for a night by Col. Henry Leavenworth, Thomas Forsyth, and the first troops coming in 1819 for building the fort later named Fort Snelling. Forsyth wrote of it in his journal: "Medicine Wood takes its name from a large beech tree, which kind of wood the Sioux are not acquainted with, and supposing that the Great Spirit has placed it there as a genii to protect or punish them according to their merits or demerits" (MHS Collections 3: 153, 156).

Bolles Creek, in Lakeland and Afton, outflowing from Lake Elmo and Horseshoe Lake, was renowned as the stream on which the first flour mill in Minnesota was built in the winter of 1845–46 by Lemuel Bolles, a farmer in Afton, where he also owned a grindstone quarry. He was a native of New York State and died in Stillwater in 1875.

Other lakes and streams are noted in the following list, in the numerical order of the townships from south to north.

In Denmark are Allibone Lake and Creek and Trout Brook, flowing to Lake St. Croix. The former were named for John Allibone, coming in 1851, whose farm included this lake.

Two lakes on the west part of Grey Cloud Island were mapped by Hon. J. V. Brower as Baldwin and Moore Lakes (Memoirs, vol. 6, *Minnesota*, 1903, p. 42), but the latter was named for the early fur trader of this island, Hazen P. Mooers, and it should therefore be spelled as Mooers Lake. Pine Cooley, named for its tall and old white pines, 20 or more, is a ravine joining the Mississippi a half mile east of the island.

In Woodbury are Colby Lake, named for John Colby, a nearby farmer, who was a member of the board of county commissioners, Powers, Wilmes, and Carver Lakes. The last was named for a farmer who lived beside it, a descendant of Capt. Jonathan Carver.

In Oakdale, with Horseshoe Lake, named for its shape, and Lake Elmo, before noticed, are Eagle Point Lake, having a peninsula on its east side, where eagles nested, Clear Lake, Lake Jane, Lake De Montreville (formerly mapped as Emma Lake), and Long Lake. De Montreville honors a dentist of St. Paul, whose country home was beside this lake.

The city area of Stillwater has McKusick Lake and Lily Lake, the latter having white water lilies. The former was named in honor of John McKusick, who was born in Cornish, Maine, December 18, 1815, and died in Stillwater, October 26, 1900. He came to Minnesota in 1840, settling in this county, built its first sawmill, and was a state senator, 1863–66.

In Stillwater Township is Little Carnelian Lake, having many carnelian pebbles on its shores. Browns Creek, named in honor of Joseph R. Brown, before mentioned as sponsor of a townsite named Dahkotah, flows into Lake St. Croix at the north edge of the city.

Grant Township has Ben's (or Benz) Lake, Mann Lake, Pine Tree Lake, and Echo, Long, and Hamline Lakes, the last three being near Mahtomedi.

White Bear Lake has been noticed for Mahtomedi village and more fully in the chapter on Ramsey County.

May Township has the northern and larger Big Carnelian Lake; Twin Lake, shaped somewhat like a dumbbell; Square Lake, named from its shape; North and South Terrapin Lakes, named for their turtles; East and West Boot Lakes, having bootlike outlines, Bass Lake, and Mud and Long Lakes. Carnelian Creek flowed from Big Marine Lake southward across this township.

Oneka Lake, before noticed, a second Horseshoe Lake, Egg Lake, Rice Lake, having wild rice, Sunset and North and South School Section Lakes, the last lying partly in the school section 36, are in Oneka Township.

New Scandia has Big Lake or Big Marine Lake, Long, Hay, and Sand Lakes, and Fish, Goose, and Bonny or Bone Lakes.

With the large Forest Lake, the township named from it has also Clear and Mud Lakes, whereby the list comprises three Clear Lakes in this county and also three named for their muddy shores and beds.

Watonwan County

This county, established February 25, 1860, was named from the Watonwan River, whose headstreams flow through it. Prof. A. W. Williamson, in his paper on our Dakota geographic names, wrote: "This word might mean 'I see,' or 'he sees,' intransitive; it may have been applied to this branch of the Blue Earth as being a prairie country and presenting a good prospect, but it is uncertain whether this is the meaning on which the appellation was given." Rev. M. N. Adams later stated the significance of this name without doubt, that in being anglicized it was misspelled, and that it should be Watanwan, meaning "fish bait," or "where fish bait abounds," as he had been informed by the Dakota. Our earliest knowledge of the Watonwan River is supplied by Joseph N. Nicollet's report and map, published in 1843. Its accent is on the first syllable; and the first *a* has its sound as in *father*, the last as in *fall*.

Information of the origins and meanings of geographic names has been gathered from History of Cottonwood and Watonwan Counties, *John A. Brown, editor (1916, 2 vols.), pp. 595, 486; and from Fred Church, register of deeds, and Elwin Zillora Rasey, a resident of this county since 1871, each of St. James, the county seat, interviewed during a visit there in July 1916. Mr. Rasey was chairman of the local committee of Watonwan County for compilation of its history in the work here cited.*

ADRIAN TOWNSHIP organized in June 1871, has a name that is borne also by a city in Michigan, villages in New York, Pennsylvania, Georgia, and other states, and also a village in Nobles County of this state.

ANTRIM TOWNSHIP organized in January 1867, has the name of the most northeastern county in Ireland, a county in Michigan, and townships and villages in New Hampshire, Pennsylvania, Ohio, and Louisiana. A post office was located in the township, 1867–99, first in section 17, then in section 20; it was named by George W. Dodge, a settler from Antrim, N.H.

ARCADIA a paper town platted by the St. Paul and Sioux City Railroad in Riverdale Township in 1859, but the route changed, and no buildings were constructed.

ASHIPPUN a post office in section 23, Rosendale Township, 1860–70, with Nels Larsen as the first postmaster.

BILLFRY a post office, 1894–1900, located in the general store of Richard Jones, on Perch Creek in Antrim Township.

BUTTERFIELD TOWNSHIP organized in January 1872, and its city in section 27, which was platted by the St. Paul and Sioux City Railroad on September 13, 1880, and was incorporated February 26, 1895, were named "for William Butterfield, the owner of the townsite and its first settler" (Stennett, *Place Names of the Chicago and Northwestern Railways*, 1908, p. 50). Its post office was established in 1879; most of the early settlers were German-speaking Mennonite immigrants from Austria-Hungary and Russia who came in the mid-1870s.

CEREAL a post office, 1879–1902, in section 23 of Long Lake Township.

DARFUR a city in sections 19, 20, and 29 of Adrian, platted in April 20, 1899, by the Chicago and North Western Railway, and incorporated as a village on December 31, 1903, was named either from a region of Sudan or when two Scandinavian railroad men questioned, "why you stop dar fur?" The townsite was on land owned by farmer Jacob D. Heppner on the east side of the tracks; Heppner, born in Belgium in 1873, was the first postmaster when the post office began in 1900.

ECHOLS a village in section 3 of Long Lake Township, which began as a railroad station, was named by officers of the Minneapolis and St. Louis Railroad company. It is a rare geographic name, borne elsewhere only by a county in Georgia and a village in Kentucky. The village was platted in October 12, 1899, by Harry L. Jenkins, who purchased the land from Moses K. Armstrong.

FIELDON TOWNSHIP organized in March 1868, was then named Wakefield, but was renamed Fieldon in September of that year. Like the foregoing, it is a rare name, found elsewhere only for a village in Illinois.

GODAHL a village in sections 1 and 2 of Nelson Township, whose name is Norwegian for "good valley," Gode Dahl being the Norwegian place from which many of the first settlers had come. The village was never incorporated; the site had a post office, 1894–1907, and a station of the Chicago, St. Paul, Minneapolis and Omaha Railroad; only the cooperative store formed in 1894 remains.

GROGAN a community in section 3, Rosendale Township, "was named in 1890 for Matthew J. Grogan, an early settler" (Stennett, p. 177). The community began as a station on the Chicago, St. Paul, Minneapolis and Omaha Railroad called Lincoln Station; it was platted by B. R. Grogan and Moses K. Armstrong on September 6, 1891; the post office operated 1894–1907.

HOPE a place in section 24, Antrim Township, noted as a post office in the 1886 county atlas.

LA SALLE a city in sections 16 and 17 of Riverdale, platted October 12, 1899, and incorporated as a

village on January 25, 1921, is named like a county and city of Illinois, a county in Texas, and a village on the Niagara River in New York, for the renowned French explorer Robert Cavelier, sieur de la Salle (1643–87). The city was a originally a station of the Minneapolis and St. Louis Railroad; its post office was established in 1900, with John Sundt as postmaster in his general store. The Younger brothers were captured one mile south on September 21, 1876, following their holdup of the Northfield bank.

LEWISVILLE a city in section 4 of Antrim, platted by the Interstate Land Company, May 3, 1899, and incorporated in 1902, was named in honor of Richard, James, and Nelson Lewis, nearby farmers, whose father, Thomas Lewis, a native of Ireland, came here from Ontario, Canada, in 1869, taking a homestead claim that included the site of this village. Richard Lewis was its first postmaster, and James Lewis was president of its Merchants' State Bank. John S. Tilney of New York owned several thousand acres of virgin land, called Tilney Farms, along the railroad right-of-way, which was undeveloped until 1900, when the acreage was divided into half-section units and rented. The post office began in 1899; it had a station of the Chicago, St. Paul, Minneapolis and Omaha Railroad.

LINCOLN a railroad station of the Chicago, St. Paul, Minneapolis and Omaha Railroad in section 3 of Rosendale Township.

LINDEN SETTLEMENT a town with Brown County.

LONG LAKE TOWNSHIP settled in 1857, organized in March 1868, bears the name of one of its three principal lakes.

MADELIA TOWNSHIP organized in 1858, before this county was established, took the name of its city in sections 22, 27, and 28, platted on September 10, 1857, and incorporated as a village on March 8, 1873; it was reincorporated on February 10, 1911, at which time it separated from the township. The name was chosen in honor of the daughter of Gen. Madeline Hartshorn, one of the townsite proprietors. It is "an elision and reconstruction of the name Madeline." The post office was established in Brown County as Wacapa, 1857; its name was changed, and it was transferred to Watonwan County in 1860. This village was the first county seat, from 1860 until it was succeeded by St. James in 1878.

NELSON TOWNSHIP organized in September 1870, had among its pioneer settlers several Swedish families of this name.

NORWEGIAN a post office, 1868–73, in section 18 of South Branch Township.

ODIN TOWNSHIP settled in 1868, organized in January 1872, and its city in Odin and Long Lake Townships, platted by Western Town Lot Company on March 29, 1899, incorporated on July 17, 1902, and separated from the township on March 10, 1903, bear the name of one of the chief gods in the ancient Norse mythology, called Woden by the Anglo-Saxons, for whom Wednesday (Woden's Day) was named. "He is the source of wisdom, and the patron of culture and of heroes." The post office, established in 1880, was first located two miles west of the present site and then one mile north, moving to the village in 1899; it was first known as Aasten's Town.

ORMSBY a city in sections 32 and 33 of Long Lake Township, with Martin County, platted October 14, 1899, and incorporated on September 5, 1902, was named in honor of E. S. Ormsby, of Emmetsburg, Iowa. The north side of Main Street is in Watonwan County, and the south side is in Martin County. The post office was established in 1900.

PERCH a post office, 1885–95, in section 34 of Antrim Township.

RIVERDALE TOWNSHIP organized in November 1869, was named for the Watonwan River, which flows through it.

ROSENDALE TOWNSHIP organized in March 1871, was named by Mrs. Samuel W. Sargeant, who had formerly lived in the township of this name in Fond du Lac County, Wis.

ST. JAMES TOWNSHIP first settled in the spring of 1869, organized in March 1870, received the name of its city in sections 13 and 24, which was platted July 13, 1870. It was planned by the St. Paul and Sioux City Railroad in 1867, although it was not until 1870 that the first lot was purchased. Its post office was established in 1870. The St. Paul and Sioux City Railroad was so far constructed in 1870 that its first passenger train arrived here on November 22, bringing an excursion party from St. Paul, which included Gen. Henry H. Sibley, one of the directors of the railway, and Hon. Elias F. Drake, its president. The name had been selected for the village about three years previously, when

it was designated to be the end of the first division of the railroad. Drake then requested Sibley to name the proposed division point, for which Sibley accordingly recommended a long Dakota name. On the next day, however, neither of them could remember the proposed name, and Sibley said that he would consult papers at his home, "which will help me to think of it again."

"'Never mind, General, never mind,' said the President, 'we will have a name for that town that we *can* think of. I propose that we call it St. James.' Whereupon, by common consent, the point was called St. James by the railroad men some three years before it had any local existence" (Andreas's *Atlas of Minnesota*, 1874, p. 229).

Another version of the name origin says that Drake named the site for James Farrington, the first settler. The village was incorporated in 1871, succeeded Madelia as the county seat in 1878, and received a city charter April 27, 1899. It is the largest place of this name, surpassing villages so named in eight other states.

SOUTH BRANCH TOWNSHIP organized in March 1869, is crossed by the South Branch or Fork of the Watonwan River. The village in section 22 was originally called Drewsville for its location on John Drew's farm; the name was changed for its location on the South Branch of the river. It had a post office, 1875–1907.

SVEADAHL the name of a hamlet on the boundary between Adrian and Nelson Townships, means "Sweden valley or dale." Svealand is one of the three great divisions of Sweden, having its chief city and capital, Stockholm. The village was established about 1868 when immigrants from Sweden arrived; their Lutheran congregation was founded in 1870 and given the name Svea Dal, a form of the name later adopted by the community; the site had a post office, 1892–1907.

TUBERG MILL was established in section 12, Odin Township, in 1877 by Swedish millwright Andrew Tuberg; however, no village was created.

WACAPA see MADELIA.

Lakes and Streams

Nearly all of this county is drained by the Watonwan River and its South Branch or Fork, from each of which a township is named.

Perch Creek flows from Perch Lake in Martin

County, crossing Antrim, and joining the Watonwan River in Blue Earth County.

With Long Lake, the township named from it has also Mary Lake and Kansas Lake. "John Kensie was a scholarly gentleman and of a well-to-do family in England. He had a wife and three or four children and built a log hut on the south side of the grove by the lake, which still bears his name, though in a distorted form, 'Kansas lake.' The original and historic name is Kensie's Lake" (*History of Cottonwood and Watonwan Counties*, p. 436).

In Odin are Irish Lake, School Lake (partly in the school section 16), and Sulem Lake. Residing near the last are farmers named Sulheim. Another family, named Sulem, immigrants from Norway in 1873, lived in Long Lake Township and in Butterfield village.

Rosendale has Bullhead Lake, named for its small species of catfish.

Beside the city of St. James is a fine lake bearing this name.

Madelia has Hopkins, Fedje or Fedji, and Lau Lakes, a group one to two miles northeast from the village, and School Lake, partly in section 16. Emerson Lake, formerly on the north line of Madelia, extending into Brown County, has been drained, as have been Hopkins and Lau.

Adrian has Cottonwood Lake, in section 25, and Wood Lake, named for its adjacent groves.

Wilkin County

This county, established with its present name March 6, 1868, commemorates Col. Alexander Wilkin, who in the Civil War gave his life for the Union, being shot and instantly killed in the battle of Tupelo, Miss., July 14, 1864. He was born in Orange County, N.Y., December 1820; served as a captain in the Mexican War; came to St. Paul in 1849 and entered the practice of law; was U.S. marshal for Minnesota and also secretary of the territory, 1851–53; went to Europe in 1855 and studied the art of war before Sebastopol in the Crimea; afterward again was engaged in law practice in St. Paul; recruited the first company of the First Minnesota Regiment for the Civil War; served also in the Second Regiment and was colonel of the Ninth Regiment. Physically he was of small size and stature, but he stood very high in courage and skill for military leadership.

An earlier county, somewhat corresponding to this in area and likewise having Breckenridge as its county seat but named Toombs County, was established March 8, 1858. It was named for Robert Toombs (1810–85) of Georgia, who had been a member of Congress, 1845–53, and was U.S. senator, 1853–61. He became a leading disunionist, was Confederate secretary of state, 1861, and later was a Confederate general. His disloyalty against the Union so displeased the people of the county that in 1862 they petitioned the legislature to change its name. "In 1863 the act changing the name from Toombs to Andy Johnson became a law. But the subsequent political attitude of Andrew Johnson [succeeding Lincoln as president of the United States] was no less displeasing to the people, and in 1868 the law was again amended and the name changed from Andy Johnson to Wilkin" (*History of the Red River Valley*, 1909, pp. 908–9).

Information of names was learned from History of the Red River Valley *(1909, 2 vols., continuously paged, 1,165 pp.); and from John T. Wells, clerk of the court, and Halvor L. Shirley, president of the First National Bank, each of Breckenridge, the county seat, interviewed during a visit there in September 1916.*

ABERDEEN JUNCTION was a station of the Northern Pacific Railroad in Champion Township.

AKRON TOWNSHIP has a name that is borne by a city in Ohio and villages in nine other states. It is received from the ancient Greek language, meaning the extreme, hence a summit or hilltop. A station of the Great Northern Railway was called Akron, about 1937; location not found.

ALLENS a spur station of the Great Northern Railway in section 8, Wolverton Township.

ANDREA TOWNSHIP is named in honor of Andrea Heider, wife of Philip Heider, a pioneer homesteader here. He died in 1915 and she in 1916.

ATHERTON TOWNSHIP was named for a former extensive landowner of this township, but not a resident. A station of the St. Paul, Minneapolis, and Manitoba Railroad was in sections 15 and 22.

BRADFORD TOWNSHIP was similarly named for an owner of lands along the Red River north of Breckenridge.

BRANDRUP TOWNSHIP was named in honor of Andrew Brandrup, one of its pioneer farmers, who became clerk of the court.

BRECKENRIDGE TOWNSHIP organized May 23, 1857, and its city, the county seat, platted in the spring of 1857, incorporated as a village on May 23, 1857, and as a city on April 5, 1907, are in honor of John Cabell Breckenridge, who was born near Lexington, Ky., January 21, 1821, and died in that city May 17, 1875. He was a member of Congress, 1851–55; vice-president of the United States, 1857–61; general in the Confederate Army, 1861–64; and Confederate secretary of state, January to April 1865.

Early settlement of the city was closely tied to Fort Abercrombie in North Dakota, where the post office was established in Davis County (1858–63), the first in that county; the fort was destroyed by fire in 1872 and reestablished with the coming of railroads to the area; its post office also reestablished in 1873. The city developed with Wahpeton as the first twin towns on the Red River; it had a station of the Great Northern Railway and Northern Pacific Railroad.

BRUSHVALE a village and farm community in section 31 of Nordick, was named for Joseph Brush, on whose farm it was located. It had a post office, 1902–54, and a station of the Great Northern Railway.

BURAU a post office, 1887–1905, in section 35 of Akron Township, with August Burau as first postmaster.

CAMPBELL a city in sections 1 and 2 of Campbell Township, founded in 1871 and incorporated as a village on January 28, 1899, and the township, organized in the fall of 1879, were named by the St. Paul and Pacific Railroad company. This Scottish name is borne by counties in 5 states and by villages of 14 states. The city was a farm community on the stage route to Fergus Falls but developed as a railroad village; the post office began in 1873.

CHAMPION TOWNSHIP was named in honor of Henry Champion, a pioneer homesteader, who during several terms was the county auditor.

CHILDS a village in sections 13 and 14 of Campbell, was named for Job W. Childs, a nearby farmer, who was a member of the board of county commissioners but later removed to California. The village had a station of the Great Northern Railway in section 23, later known as Kutzer and abandoned in 1956; the post office operated 1888–1920.

CONNELLY TOWNSHIP was earliest settled by Edward Connelly, a homestead farmer, who came in 1868 and was a county commissioner.

DEERHORN TOWNSHIP organized November 5, 1881, was named for the creek flowing through its northeast part.

DIBLEY a post office, 1886–1906, first located on C. C. Dibley's poultry farm in section 17, Deerhorn Township, with Johan Martens as postmaster.

DORAN a city in section 5 of Brandrup, was named by James J. Hill in honor of his friend Michael Doran of St. Paul, who was born in County Meath, Ireland, November 1, 1829, and died in St. Paul, February 20, 1915. He came to the United States in 1850 and in 1856 to Le Sueur County in this state, where he engaged in farming and banking; removed to St. Paul in 1877; was a state senator, 1871, 1875, 1876–79, 1883–85; and died in 1915. The city was incorporated as a village on July 8, 1907; the post office opened in 1892.

ELLIOTT a Minneapolis, St. Paul and Sault Ste. Marie Railroad (Soo Line) station in sections 30 and 31 of Champion Township.

ESLEF a post office, 1896–1904, in Bradford Township, first in section 14, then in section 7.

EVERDELL a railway village in sections 1 and 2 of Sunnyside Township, was named in honor of Lyman B. Everdell, an early lawyer in Breckenridge. The village had a post office, 1898–1933.

FOXHOME TOWNSHIP received the name of its city in section 3 from Robert A. Fox, a real estate dealer, who was proprietor of this townsite but removed to Oklahoma. The city was incorporated as a village on January 21, 1902, and reincorporated and separated from the township on June 6, 1913. The post office began in 1896, with Fox as postmaster in his home. The main industry of the community was haying; 400–500 carloads of hay were shipped each year from the Northern Pacific Railroad station.

GRAHAM'S POINT a townsite in section 15 of McCauleyville Township, was platted by surveyor

J. T. M. Barnes, June 1–July 15, 1859, but not developed.

GRENIER a post office, 1903–7, located on section 22 of Roberts Township, on the farm of postmaster Nelson Grenier, who had come to Minnesota from Massachusetts in 1876 and purchased the farm in 1888. The railroad station of the Great Northern Railway was called Romney.

IBSEN a post office, 1893–1905, at the corner of sections 2, 3, 10, and 11 in Wolverton Township.

JACKSVILLE see WOLVERTON.

KENT a city in section 11 of McCauleyville, was named by officers of the Great Northern Railway company. This is the name of a county in England, counties in 5 states of the Union, and villages in 12 states. The city was incorporated as a village on November 22, 1904; the Great Northern Railway track was located one mile east, and many of the first buildings were moved here from McCauleyville; the post office was established in 1888.

LAWNDALE is a village, euphoniously named, in section 33 of Prairie View. It had a station of the Great Northern Railway and a post office, 1892–1953.

MANSTON TOWNSHIP received the name of its former railway village, given by officers of the St. Paul, Minneapolis and Manitoba Railroad. It is the only place known bearing this name. It was once a small townsite known as the Stoneheart Farm, located in sections 20 and 21 of Manston Township, with a station of the Great Northern Railway. A post office called Mauston (1878–79) was changed to Manston (1879–81).

MAUSTON see MANSTON.

McCAULEYVILLE TOWNSHIP and its village on the Red River opposite the site of Fort Abercrombie, were named in honor of David McCauley, sutler of the fort, who later founded this village and was county superintendent of schools for many years. He was born in Merrimack, N.H., July 27, 1825; came to Minnesota in 1858; opened a store here in 1864, which was the beginning of the village. A post office, 1873–1905, was first located in McCauley's general store in section 10.

MEADOWS TOWNSHIP was named for its being a part of a vast area of prairie, having natural hay land.

MILLER/MILLERS STATION see WOLVERTON.

MITCHELL TOWNSHIP organized in 1881, was named in compliment to Charles Mitchell Corliss, a homestead farmer here, a brother of the late Hon. Eben E. Corliss of Fergus Falls and St. Paul.

NASHUA a city in sections 26, 27, 34, and 35 of Champion, was named for its Nash families but took the spelling of a city and river in New Hampshire and of a village in Iowa. The village was incorporated on April 19, 1902; the post office, 1892–1973, operated as a community post office after 1973; the first postmaster was Philip F. Nash.

NILSEN TOWNSHIP the latest organized in this county, has the name of one of its early settlers.

NORDICK TOWNSHIP was named for Barney and Gerhard Nordick, German farmers, who came here from Iowa.

PRAIRIE VIEW the most northeastern township, has from its high eastern part a very extensive view over the flat Red River valley.

REBER a post office, 1901–10, at the border of sections 8 and 9 in Andrea Township, with Charles Reber, postmaster.

ROBERTS TOWNSHIP organized July 19, 1887, was named in honor of Michel Roberts, a French homesteader here, who was a cousin of the widely known Capt. Louis Robert of St. Paul. The old French surname is Anglicized by the addition of *s*.

ROMNEY see GRENIER.

ROTHSAY a city in sections 25 and 36 of Tanberg, governed with Otter Tail County, was named by officers of the railway company for Rothesay, a seaport and watering place about 30 miles west of Glasgow, Scotland. This is the only use of the name in the United States. The city was incorporated as a village on March 5, 1883. The Great Northern Railway came in 1879, and the post office began in 1880 with postmaster Anders B. Pederson.

SUNNYSIDE TOWNSHIP crossed by the Red River, was at first called Riverside, but because that name had been elsewhere used in this state, it was changed, taking this euphonious name. It is borne also by villages and post offices in 16 other states.

TANBERG TOWNSHIP was named in honor of Christian Tanberg, a Norwegian pioneer settler, who was proprietor of its Rothsay townsite.

TENNEY a city in section 28 of Campbell, was named for the owner of its site, lumberman John P. Tenney. It was incorporated on November 30, 1901; the post office began in 1887.

TINTAH a place name in section 19 of Champion Township.

TRENT a village in sections 13 and 14 of Campbell Township, about 1894.

WATOSCO a railroad station on a spur line of the Northern Pacific Railroad, in section 8 of Sunnyside Township.

WOLVERTON the most northwestern township, was organized January 24, 1891, as Nora Township; the name was changed a month later to Wolverton in honor of Dr. William Dilts Wolverton (1834–1922), physician of Fort Abercrombie, who owned much land in this township but removed to the Pacific Coast.

The city of Wolverton was incorporated as a village on April 24, 1913, and separated from the township on March 10, 1936; the townsite in section 28 was platted in 1884. Its post office (1878–81) began at the trading post called Miller's Station operated by Louis M. Miller in his home; it was then changed to Miller in 1881 and to Jacksville, 1881–86; in 1887 the name was changed to the present; it had a station of the Great Northern Railway.

YARMOUTH a station of the Great Northern Railway, in section 18 of Champion Township.

It seems desirable to add two names in North Dakota.

WAHPETON the county seat of Richland County, on the west side of the Red River opposite to the city of Breckenridge, was settled in 1869 and was reached by the construction of the railway crossing the river in 1880. It bears the name of a large division of the Dakota, meaning "leaf dwellers," so named when they lived in the wooded country of Mille Lacs and farther north and east (from *Wakhpe*, "leaf," *tonwan*, "a village").

FORT ABERCROMBIE on the west side of the Red River opposite to McCauleyville, was established in 1858 and was abandoned and dismantled in 1877–78, its buildings being sold and removed or torn down, to be used by settlers for making their homes on the surrounding prairie. It was named in honor of John Joseph Abercrombie, its first commander, who was born in Tennessee in 1802 and died in Roslyn, N.Y., January 3, 1877. He was graduated at West Point, 1822; served in the Florida and Mexican Wars and was brevetted lieutenant colonel; was in this state when the Civil War began, through which he served, being brevetted brigadier general at its close.

Lakes and Streams

One lake of this county, now drained, was crossed by its east boundary two miles east of Foxhome village. It was mapped as Lake Alice but was more commonly known as Shaw Lake, for Thomas Shaw, a nearby farmer. Lake Breckenridge is on the Otter Tail River east of Breckenridge.

The Red River has been noticed in the first chapter and again in part under Red Lake County, and the Bois des Sioux was noted in the chapter of Traverse County.

Deerhorn Creek, for which a township is named, flows northward into Clay County, to the South Branch of Buffalo River. Mushroom Creek is tributary to the Deerhorn from the south. Wolverton has Wolverton Creek.

Whiskey Creek flows ten miles nearly parallel with the Red River, to which it is tributary a mile north of McCauleyville. It was named from unlawful sales of whiskey in dugout huts beside this stream to soldiers of Fort Abercrombie.

Rabbit River, crossing the southern end of the county, is named for its rabbits, like the larger Mustinka River in Traverse County, which is a Dakota word having the same meaning.

Campbell and McCauleyville Beaches

While the Glacial Lake Agassiz flowed south along the valley of Lakes Traverse and Big Stone, its outlet stream, named the River Warren, eroded that remarkable valley, with gradual reduction of the lake level. Five stages of the ancient lake during its southward outflow are shown by so many distinct beaches, each lower than the preceding. In their descending order they are named, from places where they are well developed and were first recognized and mapped, being the Herman and Norcross Beaches, for villages in Grant County, the Tintah Beach for a village in Traverse County, and the Campbell and McCauleyville Beaches in this county. Thence each of these old lake levels, recorded by the successive low beach ridges of sand and gravel, are traced far along each side of the Red River valley in Minnesota and North Dakota and onward in Manitoba.

Winona County

Established February 23, 1854, this county was named for a Dakota woman, Winona, cousin of the last chief named Wabasha, both of whom were prominent in the events attending the removal in 1848 of the Winnebago Indians from Iowa to Wabasha's Prairie (the site of the city of Winona) and thence to Long Prairie in Todd County. This name belonged, said Prof. A. W. Williamson, in any Dakota family, to the "first born, if a daughter, diminutive of wino, woman"; and similarly the name of the "first born child, if a son," was Chaska. In pronunciation, Winona is accented on the middle syllable, and the first and last syllables have the short vowel sounds. The first, however, is often incorrectly given the long sound, as in *wine*; it should be short, as in *win*, or may be quite rightly given the sound of long *e*, as *we*.

William H. Keating gave an impressive narration of the death of a Dakota maiden named Winona, who threw herself to death from the precipice known as "the Maiden's Rock," on the east shore of Lake Pepin, in preference to being married, as her parents requested, to one whom she did not love (*Narrative* of Long's Expedition, 1823, vol. 1, pp. 289–95). With much amplification, including change of the home of the maiden from Wabasha's village of Keoxa to a Dakota village represented to have been near St. Anthony Falls, Hon. Hanford L. Gordon retold this tragedy in a poem bearing her name, "Winona," published in 1881, reprinted in his collected writings (*Indian Legends and Other Poems*, 1910, pp. 43–74).

This name was first applied, about a year before the establishment of the county, to the village of Winona, which became the county seat.

Information of names has been gathered from History of Winona County by Dr. L. H. Bunnell and others (1883, 966 pp.); Winona (We-no-nah) and its Environs on the Mississippi by Lafayette Houghton Bunnell, M.D. (1897, 694 pp.); The History of Winona County, compiled by Franklyn Curtiss-Wedge, editor, assisted by William Jay Whipple (1913, 2 vols., continuously paged, 1,125 pp.); and from interviews with the late Mr. Whipple and Prof. John M. Holzinger, of the State Normal School (Winona State University), each of Winona, during a visit there in April 1916.

ALMON see WARREN.

ALTURA a city in sections 17–20 of Norton Township, was incorporated as a village on August 17, 1906. It was first settled in the 1850s and named for a town in Valencia, Spain, by the Winona and Southwestern Railway when it came in 1889; it was platted in August 1901 by E. C. Burns, proprietor of the land. Early postal service was provided by Frederich Gensmer in 1864 and by Ely Turner, 1866–68, and the official post office began as Norton, 1886–91, with William Simon as postmaster; it was changed to Altura in 1891 and located in the general store of postmaster Herman Hilke.

THE ARCHES a village in section 8, Warren Township, also known as " Arches Waltonia" or "The Valley," named for the large Chicago and North Western Railway culverts or stone-arched underpasses of the creeks.

ARGO a post office, 1860–88, in section 16 of Fremont Township.

ASHTON a post office, 1891–1902, in sections 11 and 12 of Pleasant Hill Township.

BARNESVILLE a post office, 1858–59, with Thomas Barnes, postmaster; location not found.

BEAR CREEK a village in section 15 of Norton Township, with a station of the Chicago Great Western Railroad.

BEAVER a village in section 15 of Whitewater Township, is on the Beaver Creek near its mouth, where it was found obstructed by a beaver dam when the first white settlers came. It was first settled in 1854 by New Englanders and is the oldest village in the Whitewater River valley; it was platted in 1856 by Albert Hopson, Dr. Sheldon Brooks, and William J. Duley as 20 blocks on 40 acres. The post office operated 1857–1906, with Brooks as the first postmaster; Brooks was also the first township chair when the township was organized in May 1858. Many floods devastated the area, settlers moved away, and most of the townsite reverted back to wild countryside.

BETHANY a village in section 33 of Norton, bears the name of a village in Palestine. It is the name of villages or townships in 12 states and of a city in Missouri. The village was organized on July 5, 1867, and developed when the Chicago Great Western Railroad came in 1889; it was platted in 1891 for the Winona Southwestern Improvement Company and named for the Bethanian Moravian Church in the settlement. It had a post office, 1890–1920.

BUNNELLS LANDING see HOMER.

BURNS'S CORNER a place located about one-half mile east of Wyattville, which had a store operated by Percy Gates; it was out of business by 1900.

CATLIN see RICHMOND.

CENTERVILLE is the name of a village in section 35 of Wilson.

CHATTANOOGA a village, was laid out in section 19 of St. Charles Township on land first owned by John Salisbury in 1854 and purchased in 1857 by Joseph Birge; the first addition was platted in 1864 and later incorporated into St. Charles.

CLYDE a village in Saratoga Township, sections 13, 14, and 23, which had a post office, 1873–1902, in section 19 of Fremont Township.

CRESS a post office, 1892–93; location not found.

CROSS ROADS a post office, 1861–64; location not found.

CRYSTAL SPRING a village in sections 13 and 14 of Elba Township.

DAKOTA is a city beside the Mississippi, in section 7 of Dresbach Township and section 12 of New Hartford Township. It was incorporated as a village on May 23, 1951. It was laid out in 1855 and developed in 1859 by Nathan Brown, who came to Minnesota in 1847, had a stockyard, and ran a ferry service to Wisconsin. The post office operated 1855–57 and was reestablished in 1875. Once the center of berry growing, the main industry is now apple growing.

DONEHOWER a village in section 27 of Richmond Township, with a station of the Chicago, Milwaukee and St. Paul Railroad in section 22.

DRESBACH TOWNSHIP organized May 11, 1858, and its village in section 18, were named in honor of George B. Dresbach, who was born in Pickaway County, Ohio, August 27, 1827, came to Minnesota in 1857, founded this village, owned a farm and stone quarries, and was a representative in the legislature in 1868 and 1878. The village was first settled in 1852 by a colony of French settlers; it was purchased by Dresbach (d. 1887) in May 1857 and platted in September. The post office was established in 1858 as Dresbach City, with Abraham L. Weaver as postmaster; the name was changed to Sherwood, 1864–66, with Edgar E. Miner, postmaster, and was changed again in 1866 back to Dresbach, with Caleb Inman, postmaster in his general store. The site had a Chicago, Milwaukee and St. Paul Railroad station, a sawmill, brickyards, lead mines, and limestone and sandstone quarries; much of the village was removed or razed in 1960 because of Highway 90 construction, and only a few of its Victorian homes remain.

DUTCHMAN'S CROSSING a railroad stop at the site of Gottlieb Wulf's lime kiln in Utica Township.

EAGLE BLUFF see GRAY EAGLE.

EAST RICHMOND a station of the Chicago, Milwaukee and St. Paul Railroad in sections 22 and 27 of Richmond Township.

ELBA TOWNSHIP organized May 11, 1858, and its city in sections 3, 9, and 10, founded in 1856, bear the name of an island of Italy, famed for its rich deposits of iron ore. Napoleon was confined there in 1814–15. The city was incorporated as a village on March 9, 1894; the post office operated 1858–1960 and then served as a rural branch until 1965.

ENTERPRISE is a village in section 36 of Utica Township, founded by Alexander Whittier as a stopover for travelers, where he erected three inns. The post office began as Neoca 1858–60, with Luther C. Rice, postmaster in his general store, was changed to Enterprise, 1860–1901, with Nathan B. Ufford the first postmaster at his mill, which was built in 1854 along with the dam. A number of businesses developed, including a lime kiln and match factory, but as Lewiston, four miles north, developed, this site diminished. Neoca was the name of a young Winnebago Indian woman according to an account of the Enterprise history.

FAIRWATER a post office, 1882–1906, in section 5 of Whitewater Township.

FARMERSVILLE a post office, 1857–59; location not found.

FISHER HILL a place name in Whitewater Township, sections 20, 21, 28, and 29, with a school.

FRANK HILL a post office, 1858–93, in section 35 of Warren Township.

FREMONT TOWNSHIP organized May 11, 1858, was named in honor of John Charles Frémont (1813–90), who assisted Joseph N. Nicollet in his expedition through southwestern Minnesota in 1838 and was the first Republican candidate for president of the United States, 1856. The village in sections 9 and 10 had a post office, 1876–1910.

GILMORE a place name in Winona Township, circa 1930–38.

GOODVIEW a city in section 24 of Hillsdale Township, was incorporated as a village on August 8, 1946.

GRAY EAGLE a post office, 1857–61, formerly called Eagle Bluff, 1855–57; location not found.

GROVER a post office, 1886–1902, in section 29 of Fremont Township.

HAMILTON a place name in Winona Township, one mile west of the city of Winona, circa 1930–41.

HAMPTON MILLS a post office, 1873–75, in section 32 of Saratoga Township.

HART TOWNSHIP was organized May 11, 1858. It bears a personal surname, but it is not known for whom. A post office was located in the township, 1867–70 and 1873–1909, first in section 23 and then in section 26.

HILLSDALE TOWNSHIP likewise organized May 11, 1858, was named for its hills or stream bluffs, enclosing dales or valleys.

HOMER TOWNSHIP also organized May 11, 1858, and its village in sections 3 and 4, previously platted in 1855, were named by Willard B. Bunnell, a brother of the historian of this county, for "his birthplace, the village of Homer, New York state." Fourteen states of the Union have villages and townships bearing this name of the early Greek epic poet. The post office began as Bunnells Landing when it was in Wabasha County, 1852–53, was changed to Minneowah, 1853–55, and then to Homer, 1855–60 and 1863–1965, at which time it became a rural branch.

JEFFERSON a post office, 1863–71, in Norton Township.

LAMOILLE a village on the Mississippi, in section 7 of Richmond, platted in May 1860, has the name of a river and county in northern Vermont. The village developed at the point where the stage route crossed the Mississippi River. It had a post office, 1858–1975.

LEWISTON a city in section 14 of Utica, incorporated February 23, 1875, and reincorporated on February 19, 1921, "was named in 1873 for S. J. Lewis, an early settler" (Stennett, *Place Names of the Chicago and Northwestern Railways*, 1908, p. 94). The post office was called New Boston, 1855–72, because postmaster W. H. Dwight was from Boston, Mass., when it was established in Houston County and was transferred to Winona County when the name changed in 1872.

LYNN WALDEN a station of the Chicago, Milwaukee and St. Paul Railroad, one mile south of Minnesota City.

MINNEISKA a city with Wabasha County, which see.

MINNEOWAH see HOMER.

MINNESOTA CITY a city in sections 2 and 11 of Rollingstone Township, was platted in March 1852 for the Western Farm and Village Association, a colony of settlers from New York, this place being named by Robert Pike for the territory. The association was organized in New York City in

October 1851. The city was incorporated as a village on April 12, 1895; it had a station serving the Chicago Great Western Railroad; the post office began in 1852.

MONTEZUMA see WINONA.

MOUNT VERNON TOWNSHIP organized May 11, 1858, is named from the home of George Washington in Virginia, on the Potomac River, commemorating Adm. Edward Vernon (1684–1757). Twenty-one other states have townships and villages or cities of this name. Two post offices of this name were established: the first was called Minneiska, then Mount Vernon, 1852–56, and then was changed back to Minneiska; the second was in Mount Vernon Township, 1858–66 and 1887–1903, moving several times to various sections.

NEOCA see ENTERPRISE.

NEVILLE a post office, 1870–72, with Jepe P. Neville as postmaster; location not found.

NEW BOSTON see LEWISTON.

NEW HARTFORD TOWNSHIP organized in 1858, and its earlier village, in section 19, platted in August 1857, were named by settlers from Connecticut. The village had a post office established three times between 1857 and 1905; it had a station of the Chicago, Milwaukee and St. Paul Railroad.

NODINE a village in sections 9 and 16 of New Hartford Township, which was platted as Rose Hill, but the name was changed, according to the local story, by two government surveyors who could not find a place to eat. The site had a post office, 1896–1905, and a station of the Chicago, Milwaukee and St. Paul Railroad.

NORTH WARREN a post office, 1860–72; location not found.

NORTON TOWNSHIP organized May 11, 1858, at first called Sumner and later Jefferson, bears an honored name of this county. James L. Norton (1825–1904) and Matthew George Norton (1831–1917), brothers who came from Pennsylvania in 1856, were members of the widely known lumber firm of Laird, Norton and Co. in Winona. Daniel S. Norton was born in Mount Vernon, Ohio, April 1829, and died in Washington, D.C., July 14, 1870. He received his education at Kenyon College, Gambier, Ohio; served in the Mexican War and afterward studied law. In 1855, in company with Hon. William Windom, he came to Minnesota and settled in Winona, where he prac-

ticed law ten years. He was a member of the state senate in 1857, 1861, and 1864, and of the U.S. senate from 1866 until his death. See also ALTURA.

OAK RIDGE is a village in sections 29 and 32 of Mount Vernon, which had a post office, 1863–1903.

PICKWICK a village in section 13 of Homer, platted in 1857, was named from the *Pickwick Papers*, published serially by Charles Dickens in 1836–37. The first settler, Thompson Grant, built a sawmill and gristmill combination in 1858 on Big Trout Run Creek. The post office operated 1862–1913; it had a station of the Chicago, Milwaukee and St. Paul Railroad.

PLEASANT HILL TOWNSHIP has many bluffs and ridges, 200 to 300 feet high. Its name originated with the first permanent settler, Joseph Cooper, who, coming in December 1854, "to the ridge at the head of the south branch of Pine creek," exclaimed, "What a pleasant hill!" He immediately took "a claim of 160 acres of land, lying on the ridge and embracing the heads of South Branch and Money Creek valleys" (*History of Winona County*, 1883, p. 582).

PUTNAM a post office, 1857–65, with Sunphronius D. Putnam, postmaster; location not found.

RICHMOND TOWNSHIP organized May 11, 1858, took the name of its village, platted in 1855. "In 1850, a Frenchman named Richmond established a wood-yard on the site of the landing where George Catlin, the noted artist, was forced by obstructing ice to winter his boat, when he was painting his celebrated Indian portraits and pursuing his voyage up the Mississippi in early days. For years, on a conspicuous sand rock in a cove where his boat lay out of danger from running ice, the name of George Catlin could be seen in glaring red, and the landing was well known to steamboat men and pioneers as 'Catlin's Rocks.' Finally, the name of Catlin disappeared by the action of frost and rain, and Richmond's name was given to the landing and perpetuated in village and township" (Bunnell, *Winona and its Environs*, 1897, p. 473). A post office, 1856–1905, which was formerly Catlin, 1855–56, was located in section 21 of the township, with East Richmond in sections 22 and 27; it had a station of the Chicago, Milwaukee and St. Paul Railroad.

ROLLINGSTONE TOWNSHIP organized May 1858, and its city, located on a plateau between two branches of the Rollingstone River, are named from the river or creek. Its Dakota name is "Eyan-omen-man-met-pah, the literal translation of which is 'the stream where the stone rolls'" (*History of Winona County*, 1883, p. 144). The journal of Maj. Thomas Forsyth, with Col. Henry Leavenworth and the troops who came in 1819 for building the fort that in 1825 was named Fort Snelling, called this stream "the Tumbling Rock."

The village was incorporated on August 5, 1892. When the post office was established in 1860, the postmaster was James S. Drew, a member of the Western Farm and Village Association, a group of New Englanders who tried to colonize the site in 1853 but did not succeed because of poor planning as well as illness among the settlers; most were gone by 1854. A group of Luxembourgers came in 1856; the site was developed with sawmills, and the Chicago Great Western Railroad came in 1888.

ROSE HILL see NODINE.

ST. CHARLES TOWNSHIP organized May 11, 1858, and its city founded in 1854 and incorporated as a city February 28, 1870, were named "for St. Charles of Italy, who was born in 1538 and who became cardinal of Milan and secretary to Pope Pius IV" (*The History of Winona County*, 1913, p. 597). The city began in section 19 on land owned by the Lewis H. Springer family, first settlers who had come in 1853; the 1854 plat included 49 blocks and a public park. The first store was built in 1854 by Springer and became a public inn and the first post office when established in 1855. The Winona and St. Peter Railroad came in February 1864. See also CHATTANOOGA.

SARATOGA TOWNSHIP organized May 11, 1858, and the village in sections 18 and 19, were named by settlers from New York, where this is the name of a lake, a county, and a town having famous medicinal springs. It is an Indian word, said to mean "place of miraculous water in a rock" (Gannett, *Place Names in the U.S.*, 1905, p. 275). The village had a post office, 1856–1900, and a station of the Chicago Great Western Railroad.

SHERWOOD see DRESBACH.

SILO a village in Utica Township, section 4, with a post office, 1896–1903, located in the store owned by Emil Kastner, and a station of the Chicago Great Western Railroad.

STOCKTON a city in section 34 of Hillsdale, platted in 1856, was named in honor of J. B. Stockton, who was the proprietor of this townsite. The city was incorporated as a village on August 1, 1947; its post office began in 1855 and became a rural branch in 1959; it had a station of the Winona and St. Peter Railroad.

SUGARLOAF a station of the Chicago Great Western Railroad in section 35 of Winona Township.

TROUT a post office, 1900–1903, in section 17 of Mount Vernon Township.

TROY a village in section 30 of Saratoga, was named from the city in New York, which took this name from the ancient city in Asia Minor, the scene of the Trojan War, narrated by Homer in the *Iliad*. The village had a post office, 1858–1905, and a station of the Chicago Great Western Railroad.

TWIN GROVE a post office, 1856–67; location not found.

UTICA TOWNSHIP organized May 11, 1858, and its city in sections 18 and 19, are named, like Troy, from a city in New York, which, with villages and townships in 14 other states, derived this name from the ancient city of Utica, founded by the Phoenicians in North Africa. The city was incorporated as a village on November 20, 1893; it was platted in 1866 by Benjamin Ellsworth and named by Dr. John W. Bentley, both among the first settlers. Ellsworth had 50 lots, and his elevator was the first building. The post office, begun in 1856, was moved into the platted townsite from Bentley's country home.

WARREN organized May 11, 1858, is thought to have been named in compliment for Warren Wilson, a prominent early settler. A post office called Warren, 1856–61, was in section 27 of Warren Township and was later called Almon, 1891–1902.

WAYLAND a post office, 1857–64; location not found.

WHITEWATER FALLS a village in Whitewater Township, sections 27 and 34; it had a post office, 1856–99.

WHITEWATER TOWNSHIP bears the name of the river flowing through it northward to the Mississippi, derived in translation from two Dakota words, *mini*, "water," *ska*, "white." In Wabasha County this stream has a township and village named Minneiska.

WHITMAN a village in section 17 of Rollingstone Township, which had a Chicago, Milwaukee and St. Paul Railroad station in section 21.

WILSON TOWNSHIP organized May 11, 1858, and the village of Wilson in section 29, are thought to have been named, like Warren Township, in compliment for Warren Wilson, a prominent early settler. The village had a post office, 1872–1928, and a station of the Chicago, Milwaukee and St. Paul Railroad.

WINONA the county seat, platted June 19, 1852, was at first named Montezuma by Ervin H. Johnson, one of the proprietors of the site, for the Aztec war chief of Mexico at the time of the Spanish conquest, who was born in 1477 and died June 30, 1520. It was changed to Winona through request of Henry D. Huff, who in 1853 bought an interest in the townsite and platted an addition. This Dakota name has been fully noticed at the beginning of this chapter. A sobriquet often used is "the Gate City."

"The site of Winona was known to the French as La Prairie aux Ailes (pronounced O'Zell) or the Wing's prairie, presumably because of its having been occupied by members of Red Wing's band." It was latest occupied by Wabasha, the last of the Dakota leaders for whom the county next northward was named, whose village here was called Keoxa, "difficult of translation, but it may be rendered as 'The Homestead,' because in the springtime there was here a family reunion to honor the dead and invoke their blessings upon the land" (*History of Winona County*, 1883, p. 25). Prof. A. W. Williamson spelled and defined this name more correctly that "the name of the band was *Kiyuksan*, breakers in two, or violators, so called because they violated the custom forbidding relatives, however distant, to marry."

Winona Township, at first having a much larger extent than now, was established as an electoral precinct April 29, 1854. The city was incorporated as a village on March 3, 1855, and as a city in 1867. German and Polish immigrants were the majority of the new settlers, and by 1857 Winona was the third largest city in the state. The post office began as Montezuma in Wabasha County, June-August 1852, and was then transferred here.

WISCOY TOWNSHIP bears the name of a creek and a village in Allegany County, New York, "an Indian word meaning 'under the banks,' or, according to another authority, 'many fall creek'" (Gannett, *Place Names in the U.S.*). A post office was in section 16, 1856–1904.

WITOKA a hamlet on the north edge of Wiscoy, platted in 1855, was named for "the daughter of the war chief of Wabasha's band. Witoka was captured by the Sacs (Sauks) near the present site of Witoka, and was rescued by her father's daring dash" (*The History of Winona County*, 1913, p. 549). The village had a post office, 1857–1918, and a station of the Chicago, Milwaukee and St. Paul Railroad.

WOODLAWN a place name in Winona Township, circa 1937.

WORTH a post office, 1857–86, in section 1 of Saratoga Township.

WYATTVILLE a village in section 33 of Warren Township, which had a post office, 1858–1902, begun in mill owner Ed Hall's store, with Hiram Wyatt as postmaster.

Lakes and Streams

Beaver Creek and the Rollingstone and Whitewater Rivers are noticed in the foregoing list, for a village or hamlet and two townships named from them.

The West, Middle, and South Branches of Rollingstone Creek unite in the township of this name; and similarly the North, Middle, and South Branches of Whitewater River unite in Elba.

The presence of brook trout is noted by Trout Creek in Mount Vernon, a second creek so named in Saratoga, and Big and Little Trout Creeks in Homer and Richmond.

White pine and red cedar trees, growing sparingly on stream bluffs, are the source of names of Pine Creek in Pleasant Hill and New Hartford Townships, a second Pine Creek in the southwest part of Fremont, and Cedar Creek in Homer.

Rush and Money Creeks flow south into Fillmore and Houston Counties, there giving names to Rushford and Money Creek Townships.

Other small streams, directly tributary to the Mississippi here, are Gilmore Creek, West and East Burns Creeks, Pleasant Valley Creek, and Dakota Creek, the last having its mouth near Dakota village.

Relatively narrow channels of the Mississippi between its large alluvial islands and the west shore, within a few miles northwest from the city of Winona, are named Crooked Slough and Straight Slough.

Lake Winona, about two miles long, adjoining this city, occupies a part of a former rivercourse, which also was the character of a similarly long but shallow lake three to five miles northwest of the city.

Above the river bottomlands, this county has no lakes, like several other counties in southeastern Minnesota, which belong wholly or partly to an extensive area that was exempt from glaciation. The greater part of this tract lies in Wisconsin, so that it is commonly called by geologists the Wisconsin driftless area.

Sugarloaf Bluff, south of Lake Winona, rises about 550 feet above the lake and river; Minneowah Bluff, in Homer, and Gwinn's Bluff, also called Queen Bluff, in Richmond, have nearly the same height; and the bluffs adjoining the village of Dresbach, including Mineral Bluff, rise 600 feet above the river, or about 1,230 feet above the sea.

State Parks

Whitewater State Park, established in 1919, preserves a deep, nearly level valley surrounded by sheer limestone bluffs.

John A. Latsch State Park, named for the businessman who donated land for the park, features the river bluffs named Faith, Hope, and Charity, used by steamboat captains for navigation on the Mississippi River. It was established as Scenic Highway State Park in 1925; in 1997, after more land was added, it became a state park.

Great River Bluffs State Park was originally established in 1963 as O. L. Kipp State Park on a piece of land several miles downstream of its present location. The park, named for Orin Lansing Kipp, a former state parks administrator, was moved in 1976 and renamed in 1997; it contains the scenically and botannically significant King's Bluff and Queen's Bluff.

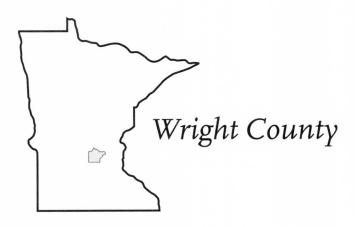

Wright County

Established February 20, 1855, this county was named in honor of a statesman of New York, Silas Wright, who was born in Amherst, Mass., May 24, 1795, and died in Canton, St. Lawrence County, N.Y., August 27, 1847. It is said that the name "was adopted as a compromise after a somewhat animated discussion." Wright had been a personal friend of W. G. McCrory, who was a member of the committee chosen by the citizens of Monticello to go before the territorial legislature and urge the establishment and organization of the county. On their journey to St. Paul the committee discussed several proposed names for it but were unable to agree. Finally, at the suggestion of this member, the name of Wright was adopted. He was graduated at Middlebury College, 1815; studied law and settled for its practice at Canton, N.Y., 1819; was a member of Congress, 1827–29; was comptroller of the state of New York, 1829–33; was a U.S. senator, 1833–44; and was governor of New York, 1845–47. "He refused several offers of cabinet offices and foreign missions. After his term as governor he retired to his farm in Canton, which he cultivated with his own hands." Biographies of Governor Wright have been published in 1847, 1848, 1852, 1874, and 1913.

Information of names has been gathered from History of the Upper Mississippi Valley *(1881), having pp. 483–585 for this county; a series of 35 newspaper articles on the county history by Daniel R. Farnham, published in the* Delano Eagle, *January 6 to September 22, 1881;* History of Wright County *by Franklyn Curtiss-Wedge (1915, 2 vols., continuously paged, 1,111 pp.); and from Oscar J. Peterson, register of deeds, Hon. John T. Alley, formerly county surveyor and judge of probate, and William H. Cutting, attorney, each of Buffalo, the county seat, interviewed during a visit there in October 1916.*

AHLBRECHT see ALBRIGHT.

ALBERTVILLE is a city of the Great Northern Railway in section 1 of Frankfort. Its railway station name during many years was St. Michael, for the village of that name two miles distant to the south. The city was incorporated in 1902; the post office began as St. Michael Station, transferring here in 1909.

ALBION CENTER a village in section 28 of Albion Township had a post office, 1858–87, with farmer Robert S. Holmes, postmaster and justice of the peace; it was incorporated as a village on February 28, 1858, but later unincorporated.

ALBION TOWNSHIP settled in 1855, organized May 11, 1858, bears an ancient name of England, meaning "white land," in allusion to the white chalk cliffs of its south coast.

ALBRIGHT a village in sections 7 and 8 of Middleville Township, on the Crow River. It had a post office known as Ahlbrecht, 1900–1902, Herman Albrecht, postmaster. The site has a county park.

ALLEYVILLE a place name on a 1890 map.

ANNANDALE a Minneapolis, St. Paul and Sault Ste. Marie Railroad (Soo Line) village in section 30 of Corinna, platted in October 1886, was incorporated as a village April 17, 1888, and reincorporated in 1962. It was named for the Annan River and the seaport of Annan at its mouth on the Solway Firth in southern Scotland or, as suggested by Sen. W. D. Washburn, for the showgirl Lizzie Annandale, a minor celebrity of the time. Five other states of the Union have villages of this name. The village was originally established as Abbeyville, but because the name was already in use in the state, it was changed to Annandale. The townsite was platted by James Pratt on a large part of his homestead. The post office began in 1887, with William H. Towle, postmaster.

BEDFORD a post office, 1857–59; location not found.

BERLIN see OTSEGO.

BIANCA see SILVER CREEK.

BIG BEND a post office, 1858–60; location not found.

BIG WOODS a post office, 1867–70; location not found.

BREEZY POINT a village in section 5 of French Lake Township since 1928.

BUFFALO city in sections 30 and 31 of Buffalo Township, the county seat, platted on December 27, 1856, incorporated on May 23, 1857, and as a village on November 22, 1881, and reincorporated on August 25, 1908, took its name, given also to the township, which was first settled in April 1855 and organized May 11, 1858, from their Buffalo Lake, "named by the Indian traders on account of the large numbers of buffalo fish found in its waters." For Kandiyohi County, also named from this species of fish, they are more fully noticed. The city was platted on land owned by Aurasa Ackley; the streets were named for the first settlers, the avenues for trees. The post office was established in 1856 with Ackley as postmaster.

CARLTON a post office, was authorized on March 16, 1892, with Thomas Trepaner to be postmaster, but was not established; location not found.

CASSELL a post office, 1858–74, in section 33 of Franklin Township, with Theodore Jaegler, postmaster.

CENSTOHOWA a post office, 1902–6, in Franklin Township, with Michael Nalewaja, postmaster.

CHATHAM TOWNSHIP part of Buffalo Township until 1866, settled in 1855, organized March 2, 1868, commemorates, with townships and villages so named in 12 other states, the distinguished English statesman William Pitt (1708–78), first earl of Chatham, who was a friend of the American colonies and an opponent of the British policy that brought on the Revolutionary War. A post office was established four times during the period 1860–99 in section 34.

CLEARWATER TOWNSHIP settled in 1854, organized May 11, 1858, and its earlier city in section 35, platted in the spring of 1856, received this name from the Clearwater Lake and River, there tributary to the Mississippi. The city was incorporated as a village on February 26, 1857. A typical New England village, it was settled by Old-Stock Americans; it was platted in 1855 and 1856 for the owners, Simon Stevens, Jonah Talbot, and William Fellows. The Burbank Stage Company came in 1856; the post office began in 1856 with Simon Stevens as postmaster; also known as Clearwater Lake.

COCHRANS MILLS a post office, was first established as Cokato Lake, 1874–78, Charles A. Read, postmaster, and was changed to Cochrans Mills, 1878–92, with Morgan V. Cochran as postmaster at his mill; location not found.

COKATO TOWNSHIP settled in the early spring of 1856, included Middleville Township and was called Middleville when it was first organized; it was reorganized in 1856 with Stockholm Township and called Mooers Prairie Township; it became a separate township in July 1868. The Dakota name Cokato, adopted in 1868, which had been previously borne by the largest lake of the township, signifies "at the middle."

The city of Cokato was incorporated February 16, 1878. The first permanent settler, Josiah P. Mooers, born in Deerfield, N.H., December 27, 1804, came to Minnesota in 1852 and settled here in 1856. The post office was called Mooers Prairie, 1862–78, with Mooers postmaster in his home near Sucker Creek, southwest of the present city; when the name was changed to Cokato in 1878, Marvin R. Lewis served as postmaster in the Great Northern Railway depot.

CORINNA TOWNSHIP was settled in August 1856 by several families from Maine. "The name is said by the late Levi M. Stewart, of Minneapolis, to have been given to the township by Elder

Robinson, a Baptist preacher, who was a boyhood chum of Stewart's, and, like him, a native of Corinna, Maine" (*History of Wright County*, 1915, p. 708). The township was first called Newsport and was organized in 1860 as Delhi, including Southside Township; the name changed to Corinna on June 9, 1864. A post office operated in the township, 1867–87 and 1892.

CROW RIVER/CROW RIVER STATION see DELANO.

DAYTON lying mainly in Hennepin County, for which its name has been explained, reaches also across the Crow River into the most eastern corner of Otsego.

DEAN LAKE a post office, 1862–74, Sylvester H. Dean, postmaster; location not found.

DELANO a city in sections 11–14 of Franklin, platted in 1868 and incorporated February 11, 1876, was at first called Crow River but was renamed in honor of Francis Roach Delano, who was born in New Braintree, Mass., November 20, 1823, and died in St. Paul, February 6, 1887. He came to Minnesota in 1853 and engaged in lumbering in the St. Croix valley; was the first warden of the Minnesota State Prison; settled in St. Paul in 1860 and became general superintendent of the St. Paul and Pacific Railroad; was largely interested in railroad construction in the state and during the later years of his life was right of way agent for the Manitoba (later the Great Northern) Railway. In 1875 he was a representative in the legislature.

The Great Northern Railway came to the city in 1868, and a post office was established in section 11 as Crow River, 1858–59, with Edward Ploudin as postmaster, and was then moved to the section 14 and called Franklin, 1858–61; it was returned to section 11 and named Crow River Station, 1868–70, and was changed to Delano in 1870; it later absorbed the Cassell post office.

DELHI TOWNSHIP see CORINNA TOWNSHIP.

DICKINSON a Soo Line station in section 15 of Rockford Township, was named in honor of A. C. Dickinson, on whose farm it was located.

ENDEAVOR a post office, 1897–1902, in section 1 of Rockford Township.

ENFIELD a village in Silver Creek Township, sections 22 and 23, had a station of the Great Northern Railway in section 22 and a post office, 1910–54.

FAIRHAVEN a village in sections 4 and 9 of South Side Township, was incorporated on March 16, 1858, but later unincorporated.

FRANKFORT TOWNSHIP settled in the summer of 1854, organized May 11, 1858, took the name of its earlier village, platted in January 1857. Many of its pioneer settlers came from Germany, whence they chose this name of an ancient city in Prussia, one of the most important banking cities of the world.

FRANKLIN see DELANO.

FRANKLIN TOWNSHIP settled in 1855 and organized in 1858, was then called Newport, but because that name had been early given to a township in Washington County, it was renamed September 14, 1858, in honor of Benjamin Franklin (1706–90), the American philosopher, statesman, diplomatist, and author.

FRENCH LAKE TOWNSHIP settled in October 1856, organized June 9, 1865, bears the name of its largest lake and of the outflowing creek, given in compliment for French Canadian settlers. The village in section 15 had a post office, 1860–1903, established four times during that period.

GERMANTOWN a post office, 1875–76; location not found.

GRANITE LAKE a post office, 1888–1903, in Albion Township, section 29.

HAMBURG a place in section 36, Otsego Township, shown on a 1901 county map, at St. Michael's Station.

HANOVER a city with Hennepin County in sections 25 and 34–36 of Frankfort on the Crow River, founded in 1877 by the Vollbrecht brothers, was named "in honor of their birthplace in Germany." It was incorporated May 2, 1892; the post office began in 1877.

HASTY a village on the boundary dividing Clearwater and Silver Creek Townships, was platted about 1895 on the farm of Warren Hasty, who later removed to Minneapolis. The post office began as Lund in 1887, was changed to Hasty in 1888, and was discontinued in 1954; it had a station of the Great Northern Railway.

HIGHLAND a village at the intersection of sections 11–14 of Middleville Township; it had a station of the Great Northern Railway.

HOWARD LAKE a city in sections 3 and 4 of Victor, platted in the spring of 1869, incorporated in 1879, "takes its name from the beautiful sheet of water, on the south of which it is located, and which, tradition informs us, was named by the first surveyors who visited this region, in honor of John Howard, the English philanthropist" (*History of the Upper Mississippi Valley*, p. 575). He was born probably at Hackney, London, September 2, 1726; died, at Kherson, Russia, January 20, 1790; was celebrated for his exertions in behalf of prison reform. The first settler, Morgan V. Cochran, came in 1855 to section 3 and laid out a townsite he named Lynden, selling the land in 1863 to Charles Goodsell, who farmed the land until 1869, when the Great Northern Railway came. Goodsell platted the site, and buildings were soon erected, including John F. Pearson's general store, where the post office, transferred from Middlesville, began in 1870 as Howard, changing to Howard Lake in 1892.

KEYSTONE a post office, 1877–1903, in Stockholm Township, section 35.

KJELLBERG PARK a village post office since 1977; location not found.

KNAPP a village in section 32 of French Lake Township. When the post office was requested in 1897, Rev. E. Norsén, pastor of the Swedish Lutheran North Crow River congregation in Wright County, which included this township, suggested it be named in honor of Gustav Knapp, a solder from Östergötland, and his wife, Anna Fredrika Knapp, among the first settlers having come in 1873, and who were active in the Swedish community; the postmaster was August Pearson; the office was discontinued in 1906; it had a station of the Great Northern Railway.

LAKE MARY a post office, 1867–69; location not found.

LAKEVIEW a place in section 21 of Corinna Township, on the southeast point of Clearwater Lake, shown on the 1901 county map.

LILLY POND a post office, 1857–57 and 1861–70; location not found.

LOWER MONTICELLO a village in Monticello Township, was incorporated on May 23, 1857, and annexed to Monticello.

LUDEMANN a post office, 1889–1902, in Frankfort Township, with William F. Ludemann, postmaster.

LUND see HASTY.

MANHATTAN a post office, August-October 1857, in section 18 of Monticello Township, was incorporated as a village on May 23, 1857, but no trace remains.

MAPLE CREST a village in section 4 of Maple Lake Township.

MAPLE LAKE TOWNSHIP first settled in 1856 and organized in 1858, received the name of its largest lake, which is bordered by woodlands of the sugar maple. The city in section 6, bearing the township name, was founded in 1856 and was incorporated on March 20, 1858, December 24, 1890, and February 14, 1913. The post office began in 1858, with Evan B. McCord as postmaster; it had a station of the Soo Line.

MARYSVILLE TOWNSHIP settled in 1855, organized May 14, 1865, was named by its early Roman Catholic settlers.

MELODY LAKE a post office, 1867–69; location not found.

MIDDLESVILLE a post office, 1858–70, which was transferred to Howard; it was established three times during the period 1874–93 as Middleville.

MIDDLEVILLE TOWNSHIP settled in 1856, organized in April 1858, was named by M. V. Cochran, "from his old home in Virginia." When organized, it included Cokato, Stockholm, and Victor Townships.

MONTICELLO TOWNSHIP settled in 1852, organized May 11, 1858, and its city in sections 2, 11, and 12, platted in the autumn of 1854 and incorporated as a village on March 9, 1875, and reincorporated on April 30, 1906, when it separated from the township, were named by Thomas Creighton, one of the townsite proprietors, "from the 'Little Mountain,' a hill of modest proportions, about two miles from the village to the southeast. Previous to this in September [1854] Ashley C. Riggs and Moritzious Weissberger laid out the town of Moritzious." These were respectively the upper and lower parts of the present village of Monticello, being rivals during many years. "Monticello was first incorporated by an act of the Territorial Legislature approved March 1st, 1856. . . . Moritzious was also incorporated by an act of the State Legislature approved August 13th, 1858. . . . In after years, difficulties relating to titles led to some change in the corporation of Monticello, and on the 27th of April, 1861, the present organization was consummated" (*History of the Upper Mississippi Valley*, pp. 537–39). The post office was established in 1855, with D. B. Sutton as postmaster; it had a station of the Great Northern Railway. The home of Thomas Jefferson, in

Virginia, three miles southeast of Charlottesville, bore this name, which thence has been given to townships, villages, and cities in 22 other states of the Union.

MONTROSE a city on the border of Marysville and Woodland Townships, was platted in 1878 in sections 35 and 36 of Marysville Township and was incorporated as a village on February 17, 1881, being named, like villages in 15 other states, from a royal burgh and seaport of Scotland. The city was platted for owners J. F. Miller, T. S. Gunn, and J. N. Haven, partners, who built a grain house and general store; its post office began in 1862; it had a station of the Great Northern Railway.

MOOERS PRAIRIE see COKATO.

MORITZIOUS a village in Monticello Township, was incorporated on August 13, 1858, and annexed to Monticello.

NORMAND a post office, 1874–77; location not found.

NORTHWOOD a village in section 36 of Otsego Township, was incorporated as a village on May 19, 1857, but no trace remains. It had a post office, 1856–59, with Oliver H. Kelley, postmaster on his farm.

OSTER a village in Woodland Township, section 32, had a post office, 1900–1907, and a station of the Great Northern Railway.

OTSEGO TOWNSHIP first settled in October 1852, organized in 1858, and its city in sections 17 and 18, on the Mississippi, were named for a lake, a township, and a county in New York. Henry Gannett notes this name as an Indian word, meaning "welcome water," or "place where meetings are held." The city was platted on 400 acres in May 1857 and incorporated in 1875 as a village. The post office operated 1856–57 as Berling and then as Otsego, 1857–1901.

PELICAN LAKE a post office, 1865–67; location not found.

PULASKI BEACH a place in section 21 of Buffalo Township on the southwest shore of Pulaski Lake, shown on the 1901 county map.

RASSAT a village in Chatham Township, section 32, had a post office, 1900–1903, which was spelled Rasset.

RICE LAKE a village in section 24 of Stockholm Township.

ROCKFORD TOWNSHIP settled in 1855, organized in 1858, received the name of its city in section 29,

with Hennepin County, founded in 1856 at a rocky ford of the Crow River, having its bed strewn with boulders, where a sawmill was built. The city was platted in the spring of 1857 and was incorporated as a village November 21, 1881, and separated from the township on March 25, 1907. The post office began in 1856.

ST. MICHAEL a city in section 36 of Otsego, incorporated February 22, 1890, was named from its Catholic church, which was built in 1856. Three post offices were established: the first was in section 11 of Frankfort Township, 1858–64; the second, 1866–89, was first called St. Michaels and was then changed to St. Michael; the third was called St. Michaels Station, 1866–89, and then St. Michael Station, 1904–9, when it was transferred to Albertville.

SILVER CREEK TOWNSHIP named for its creek, was settled in 1854 and organized in 1858. The village in section 5 had a post office, 1856–63, which was discontinued; the present post office was at Bianca first, 1858–64, and was then transferred here in 1864. A Great Northern Railway siding of this name was located in section 23. It contains Lake Maria State Park, established in 1963 to preserve part of the Big Woods.

SMITH LAKE a village in section 30 of Middleville, platted in July 1869, bears the name of the adjoining lake, beside which Eugene Smith settled in 1858. The first claim was by Smith, who surveyed the first line of the railroad in 1858. A post office operated 1871–1914. The village had a Great Northern Railway depot.

SOUTH HAVEN a village in Southside Township on the Soo Line, which arrived in 1887, was platted in 1888, and was incorporated as a village on May 2, 1902. This name is derived from its township and from Fair Haven Township and village on the north in Stearns County. Adolph G. Lane was postmaster when the post office was established in 1887.

SOUTHSIDE TOWNSHIP formerly part of Corinna Township, named from its relation to the Clearwater River and the series of lakes through which that stream flows, was settled in 1857 and organized on February 19, 1868.

STOCKHOLM TOWNSHIP first settled in 1856, received its first Swedish settlers in 1862 and many more in 1866. It was organized August 15, 1868, being named in compliment to these immigrants. The village in section 8 had a post office, 1897–1903, and a Chicago and North Western Railway station.

VICTOR a post office, 1870–93, in Middleville Township, section 1.

VICTOR TOWNSHIP settled in 1855, organized January 24, 1866, was named at the suggestion of Mark Fosket, an early settler, "in honor of Victor in Ontario county, New York."

WAVERLY a city in section 33 of Marysville, was founded in 1869, when the building of the St. Paul and Pacific Railroad reached this site, and it was incorporated as a village on March 8, 1881. Its name was received from the adjacent Big and Little Waverly Lakes and from an earlier Waverly village platted in 1856 at the outlet of the Little Waverly Lake. The name was originally given by the Colwell brothers, who with others were proprietors of that earlier townsite, for Waverly in Tioga County, N.Y., their former home, which derived it from Sir Walter Scott's Waverley novels, published in 1814–28. The post office began as Zellingen, 1863–69, and was changed to Waverly Mills, 1869–99; it was briefly called Waverly Station, December 12, 1871-January 14, 1872, and became Waverly in 1899.

WEST ALBION a village in sections 18 and 19 of Albion Township, had a Soo Line station.

WHIPPLE a country post office, 1901–5, in Woodland Township and a station of the Great Northern Railway.

WOODLAND TOWNSHIP settled in 1855 and organized in 1858, was named for its originally heavily forested condition, being in the central part of the Big Woods, a large area noticed in the first chapter.

YPSILANTI a post office, 1857–61; location not found.

ZELLINGEN see WAVERLY.

Lakes and Streams

The origin and meaning of the names of the Crow and Clearwater Rivers have been considered in the chapters for Crow Wing and Clearwater Counties. The North and South Branches of Crow River unite on the east side of Rockford.

Buffalo, Clearwater, and Cokato Lakes, French Lake and Creek, Howard Lake, Maple Lake, Silver Creek, Smith Lake, and the Waverly Lakes, are noticed for the townships and villages named from them in the preceding list.

Other lakes and creeks are arranged as follows, in the numerical order of the ranges from east to west, and of the townships from south to north.

Fountain, Cedar, and Rice Lakes, in Franklin, are named respectively for their springs, red cedar trees, and wild rice.

Woodland has Carrigan, Ida, Pooles, and Lauzers Lakes.

Victor has the southern end of Howard Lake, Mud or Milky and Dutch Lakes, close southeastward, and Lakes Ann, Emma, and Mary. Tuey and Little Rice Lakes and Spring Lake, in the northwest part of this township, are scarcely more than marshes during the greater part of the year.

Big Rice Lake or Slough and Shakopee Lake, in Stockholm, have been mostly drained. Butternut Lake, at the south side of Stockholm, reaches into McLeod County; and Collinwood Lake on the west extends into Meeker County, where a township bears this name.

Rockford has Moore, Wagner, Charlotte, and Mary Lakes, crossed by its north line, named for pioneers. Frederick Creek outflowing from Mary Lake, and Dean, Crawford, and Ilstrup Lakes, are also similarly named. Mink and Tamarack Lakes are crossed by the west line of sections 6 and 7.

Marysville has Deer Lake, close southwest of Buffalo Lake, and the Waverly Lakes, adjoining its south line. Twelvemile Creek is the outlet of Little Waverly Lake, and of Lake Ann in Victor and Rice Lake in Stockholm.

In Middleville, besides Howard and Smith Lakes, are also Doerfler and Junkins Lakes.

With Cokato Lake, the township of this name has Brooks and Skifstrom Lakes, named in honor of early settlers. Beaver Dam and Swan Lakes, on the west line of this township, are now mainly dry. Sucker Creek, named for its fish, flows into Cokato Lake.

Frankfort had Lake Foster (drained) in its eastern section 3; Goose, Mud, and School Lakes, the last named (now drained) for its situation in the school section 16; Eulls or Uhl Lake, Williams Lake, Wagner, Beebe, and Schmidt Lakes, each commemorating a pioneer farmer; and the southeastern part of Pelican Lake, the largest of this county.

The west part of Schmidt Lake, extending into

Buffalo Township but now mostly drained, had Crane Island, of 13 acres. This township includes also, with large parts of Pelican and Buffalo Lakes, the beautiful Lake Pulaski, named for the Polish patriot and friend of George Washington in our Revolutionary War; Green Mountain Lake, named by settlers from Vermont; Washington Lake, and Constance and Gilchrist Lakes, the last reaching north into Monticello.

In Chatham, with about half of Buffalo Lake, are Birch Lake, Lakes Abbie and Albert, Cochrane Lake, small Twin Lakes in the northeast quarter of section 22, Lake Mary in section 19, and Rock Lake, on the west line, named from its boulders.

Albion comprises Camp, Granite, Maxim, White, Henshaw, Albion, Edwards, and Swart-watts or Swartout Lakes. The former William and Henry Lakes, on the south sides of sections 5 and 6, have been drained.

In French Lake Township, with its lake and creek so named, are Dans Lake and Lake Francis, also called Hutchins Lake, which extends west into Meeker County.

Otsego has School Lake in the western school section 36.

Monticello, having the northern part of Pelican Lake, includes also the north part of Gilchrist Lake; and farther west it has the series of Black, Cedar, North, Burch or Birch, Bertram, and Long Lakes, outflowing by Otter Creek to the Mississippi. With these are to be noted the little Twin Lakes, in the west edge of this township.

In Maple Lake Township are Maple and Ramsey Lakes, the second being named for Gov. Alexander Ramsey, Light Foot and Angus Lakes, and Lake Mary.

Silver Creek Township comprises Eagle and Ida Lakes, near its southeast corner; Silver (an arm of which is now also known as Lake Maria), Maria (also known as Bjorkland), and Locke Lakes, on Silver Creek; and Ember, Limestone, and Millstone Lakes. Melrose Lake is in the north part of section 36.

Corinna has Sugar Lake, named for its sugar maples, Indian and Mink Lakes, Cedar and Pleas-ant Lakes, Bass Lake, and the greater part of Clearwater Lake, with its Eagle Island.

Southside has Lake John, Goose Lake, crossed by its south line, Lake Sylvia and Twin Lake, connected by a strait, and, along the course of the Clearwater River, forming the northern boundary of this township and of the county, Lakes Louisa, Marie, Caroline, and Augusta.

On the west boundary of Clearwater Township are Grass and Wiegand Lakes, through which the Clearwater River flows; Nixon and Connelly or Cornell Lakes, named for early settlers, are on the east side of sections 22 and 27; Sheldon Lake or Marsh is in section 24; Fish Lake has its outlet by Fish Creek at the south end of an oxbow of the Mississippi, which flows around Boyington Island; and Rice Lake, having wild rice, lies a mile farther east.

Prairies

Relatively small areas of prairie, noteworthy for their occurrence in this mainly well-wooded county, were Clearwater Prairie, nearly adjoining the Mississippi eastward from the Clearwater River; Sanborn Prairie, named for a pioneer farmer, in Silver Creek Township; Monticello Prairie, one to two miles southwest of the village of this name; Winneshiek Prairie, near the Crow River in Frankfort, named "in honor of the Winnebago chief who spent several years in this vicinity," for whom a county in northeastern Iowa is named; and Mooers Prairie in Cokato, for which township it has been more fully noticed.

Winneshiek, previously leader of a band of the Winnebago, was appointed in 1845 by the U.S. War Department to be head chief of this tribe, which had been removed from Wisconsin to northeastern Iowa in 1840. He was thus the head chief while the Winnebago were in Minnesota, from 1848 to 1855 on the Long Prairie Reservation and later in Blue Earth County until 1863, being then removed to a reservation in Dakota. He died after 1880, while making a canoe journey down the Missouri River.

Yellow Medicine County

This county, established March 6, 1871, is crossed by the Yellow Medicine River, whence the name is derived. It is a translation of the Dakota name, which Prof. A. W. Williamson spelled and defined thus: "Pajutazee (Pezhihutazi, abbreviated from Pezhihutazizi kapi),—*peji*, generic name, including grasses and all other erect plants without wood stems; *huta*, root; *zi*, yellow; *kapi*, they dig; diggings of yellow plant root, or yellow medicine diggings; the Dakota name of the Yellow Medicine river, written by Nicollet Pejuta zizi. The name as first spelled was given by Dr. T. S. Williamson to his station, and is found in this form on a number of maps."

The late Dr. Thomas M. Young, who was during several years in charge of the government school for Indian children at the Sisseton Agency, South Dakota, stated that the "yellow medicine" is the long, slender, bitter, yellow root of the moonseed (*Menispermum canadense*), which grows abundantly in thickets in this region. From the root of this plant came thus the name of the river and the county.

It was proposed in 1878–79 to establish a new county, named like the village and city of Canby, in honor of Gen. E. R. S. Canby, whose biography is presented in the notice of that city. The legislative act passed for this purpose, subject to ratification by the people, received the governor's approval February 27, 1879. The proposed county was to comprise the western six townships of Yellow Medicine County, the three most northern of Lincoln County, and three from southwestern Lac qui Parle County. The vote in Yellow Medicine County was 463 yes, 370 no; but the vote in Lincoln County defeated it.

Information of geographic names here, with their meanings, has been gathered from History of the Minnesota Valley *(1882), having pp. 882–912 for this county;* An Illustrated History of Yellow Medicine County *by Arthur P. Rose (1914, 562 pp.); and from George H. Wilson, county auditor, Charles F. Hall, judge of probate, Hon. Ole O. Lende, and Frederic W. Pearsall, each of Granite Falls, the county seat, interviewed during a visit there in July 1916.*

BURR a village in sections 23 and 24 of Florida Township, founded in 1886, was called Stanley until its post office was established in 1894. Because the name Stanley had been given to an earlier post office in this state, the name Burr was adopted at the suggestion of Alfred Froberg, the merchant and grain buyer here, "that being a Froberg family name" (history of the county, 1914, p. 247). An alternate version of the origin of naming of the post office, 1894–1953, is that it was named Burr for early settler Burr Anderson. The first postmaster was Alfred Froberg. He was born in Sweden in 1865 and came to the United States with his parents in 1879, moving to section 35 in

1882 and then to Burr in 1895, where he built a store and did insurance and real estate business; he died in 1924. The village had a station of the Chicago and North Western Railway.

BURTON TOWNSHIP settled in 1877 and organized May 20, 1879, was named "in honor of Burton French, the father of Palmer O. French, a pioneer settler."

CANBY a city in sections 3 and 4 of Norman Township, was platted in the summer of 1876, three years after the building of this line of the Chicago and North Western Railway, was incorporated as a village in January 27, 1879, and as a city March 1, 1905. It was named in honor of Edward Richard Sprigg Canby, as before noted in relation to a proposed county bearing his name. He was born in Kentucky in 1819; was graduated at the U.S. Military Academy, 1839; served during the Mexican War, 1846–48, and the Civil War, 1861–65; was commander in Louisiana and of the U.S. Army departments west of the Mississippi in 1864; captured Mobile, Ala., April 12, 1865; was promoted to major general of volunteers and in 1866 became a brigadier general in the regular army; was killed by the Modoc Indians during a conference in Siskiyou County, northern California, April 11, 1873. The city was established on land owned by John Swenson, who came here in 1872, had a store and trading post, and was the first postmaster in 1874.

CENTERVILLE a village in Minnesota Falls Township, circa 1878, between Granite Falls and Minnesota Falls; no trace remains.

CLARKFIELD a village of the Minneapolis and St. Louis Railroad in sections 4, 5, 8, and 9 of Friendship, platted October 7, 1884, incorporated May 12, 1887, and separated from the township on November 11, 1910, was "named in honor of Mr. [Thomas E.] Clark, who was connected with the railroad company." The post office began in 1883 as Upland, changing to Clarkfield in 1884.

CLEVELAND a village in Minnesota Falls Township near Granite Falls, circa 1884; no trace remains.

DALSTON see PORTER.

ECHO TOWNSHIP first settled in 1869, was organized March 31, 1874, being then named Empire, which was changed in the next month to Rose, "and on July 17, 1874, the name Echo was bestowed upon it. . . . The difficulties encountered

in selecting a name not borne by some other township suggested the final name. This was one case where echo answered" (history of the county, 1914, p. 95). The city in sections 3 and 4, bearing the township name, was founded in August 1884 and was incorporated as a village on May 12, 1893. The city was platted on 26 blocks of land owned by the Minneapolis and St. Louis Railroad, but in 1889 the railroad decided that the original plat was too large and vacated all but nine blocks. The first post office, 1879, was located two miles south of the village on Samuel Mather's farm until he built a store in the village in 1885 and moved the post office there.

FLORIDA TOWNSHIP organized January 27, 1879, is crossed by Florida Lake, which was named for a railway contractor, whose camp was there in 1873, when the railway was built.

FORTIER TOWNSHIP settled in the fall of 1873, was the latest organized in this county, May 30, 1881. "The name of Le Roy was first given to it, but, as there was already a town of that name, Fortier was substituted in honor of Joseph Fortier." He was born in Napierville, Canada, April 12, 1835; came to Minnesota in 1854, and from 1855 to 1862 was employed at the Upper Sioux Agency; was in the battle of New Ulm, the defense of Fort Ridgely, and the battle of Wood Lake, 1862; served also in Henry H. Sibley's and Alfred Sully's expeditions, 1863 and 1864; later was a merchant in Yellow Medicine City and after 1874 at Granite Falls; was sheriff of this county, 1877–87; died at Granite Falls, March 27, 1898.

FRASEVILLE see LORNE.

FRIENDSHIP settled in the spring of 1872, organized March 11, 1879, was named in the petition of its people to the county commissioners for organization.

GARRY a village in Florida Township, 1887–1919.

GORDO a post office, 1886–87; location not found.

GRANITE FALLS a city with Chippewa County, and the county seat, platted May 7, 1872, incorporated as a village March 17, 1879, and as a city on April 24, 1889, received its name from the granite and gneiss outcrops of the Minnesota River here, over which and on boulders in the river bed it falls 38 feet. This county's part of the city is in sections 28, 33, and 34 of Stony Run East Township. George Daniels was the first postmaster at

Palmers Creek, 1868–70, while it was in Chippewa County; the name was changed to Granite Falls, and Daniels continued as postmaster and also served as county surveyor, first judge of probate for the county, and ferry owner. The city had a station of the Great Northern Railway.

HAMMER TOWNSHIP settled in June 1872, organized July 2, 1877, has a name that is borne by villages in Bavaria and Prussia and also by a village in Tennessee.

HANLEY FALLS a city in section 12 of Sandnes Township on the Yellow Medicine River, was founded in the summer of 1884, the Minneapolis and St. Louis Railroad track being laid to this place on August 19, and it was incorporated as a village on November 12, 1894. The city was named for John A. Hanley, general freight agent in Minneapolis for the Minneapolis and St. Louis Railroad. The railroad purchased the land from Svere Norgaard (Samuel Knutson) and platted the townsite in September 1884 in a design based on the plat of Washington, D.C. The post office began as Silliards, one mile west in section 11, with store owner Samuel Knutson as postmaster February-December 1872; Silliards was named for the town of Seljord in Telemarken, Norway. The post office was moved into the village in 1884, the name changing to Hanley Falls in 1887.

HAZEL RUN TOWNSHIP settled in 1871 and organized in 1877, bears the name of its creek, tributary to the Minnesota River. The city in sections 19 and 30, named like the township, was platted in September 1884 and was incorporated as a village on May 22, 1902, and separated from the township on October 4, 1918. Guttorm Halvorson (Ole) Fostvedt served as postmaster, the post office having been established in 1884. The village had a station of the Minneapolis and St. Louis Railroad.

HAZELWOOD a mission station of Revs. T. S. Williamson and S. R. Riggs during the years 1854 to 1862, was in section 15, Minnesota Falls. Here were a mission school and numerous families of Christian Dakota, who were organized under a plan of self-government, called the Hazelwood Republic.

LAC QUI PARLE a place name in Norman Township, section 14, which was a small village on East Lac qui Parle Creek.

LISBON TOWNSHIP settled in June 1871, organized September 20, 1873, has the name of the capital of Portugal, borne also by townships and villages in 19 other states. A post office was in section 22 on postmaster Christian H. Thingelstad's farm, 1878–84.

LORNE a village in section 29 of Minnesota Falls Township, was named in honor of the Marquis of Lorne, a British statesman, the eldest son of the eighth Duke of Argyll. He was born in London, August 6, 1845; represented Argyllshire in parliament, 1868–78; was governor general of Canada, 1878–83; and succeeded to the dukedom in April 1900. He married Princess Louise, fourth daughter of Queen Victoria, in 1871. The Great Northern Railway purchased seven acres in 1898 and laid a siding called Tweed as a flag station; when the post office was established in 1900, the name changed to Fraseville, with farmer August H. Frase as postmaster. The post office name was changed in 1905 to Lorne and was discontinued in 1935.

METZ a post office, 1887–88, 12 miles northwest of Canby.

MINNESOTA FALLS TOWNSHIP settled in October 1865, organized April 5, 1873, and its former village in section 2, platted in 1871, which flourished during a few years, derived their name from the falls of the Minnesota River. At the sawmill and flour mill of Gov. Horace Austin and Park Worden, the utilized fall was 10 feet. The village had a post office, 1872–83, with postmaster George H. Coburn.

NORMAN settled in 1870, was organized April 7, 1874. "The first settlers of this township were Norwegians exclusively, and the name was given in consequence. In Norway a native is referred to as a Norsk or Norman" (history of the county, 1914, p. 94).

NORMANIA TOWNSHIP settled in 1867–68, was organized March 12, 1872, being then named Ree, for "a prominent group of farms in Norway," which was changed in 1874 to the present name, of the same significance as the last preceding. The village in section 28 had a station of the Great Northern Railway.

OMRO TOWNSHIP settled in April 1878, organized January 29, 1880, was named on suggestion of Robert North, the first chairman of the board of supervisors, "after a town in Mr. North's old home county [Winnebago] in Wisconsin" (history of the county, 1914, p. 102).

OSHKOSH TOWNSHIP settled in the spring of 1877 and organized July 19, 1879, was named for the city of Oshkosh in Wisconsin, the county seat of Winnebago County, which commemorates the leader of the Menominee Indians. A map in the 1972 county history shows Oshkosh as a place name in section 3.

OTIS formerly a small fractional township at the west side of Granite Falls, organized October 16, 1873, "named in honor of its first settler, John D. Otis," has been annexed to Stony Run.

PALMERS CREEK see GRANITE FALLS.

PORTER a city in sections 28, 29, 32, and 33 of Wergeland, platted in October 1881 and incorporated February 16, 1898, was named for the L. C. Porter Milling Company, by whom its first grain warehouse was erected. The plat of 4 blocks and 20 warehouse lots was made on a siding of the Winona and St. Peter Railroad. The post office began as Harstad in Lincoln County, June 3, 1875, to November 18, 1881, with W. G. A. Harstad, postmaster on his farm; it was moved to Yellow Medicine County in 1881 and first named Dalston, with store owner Ole Dahl, postmaster; and then changed in 1882 to Porter; it had a station of the Chicago and North Western Railway. The village was also known earlier as Lone Tree for the landmark single tree on Main Street, removed in 1909 for sidewalk construction.

POSEN TOWNSHIP settled in 1868, organized May 17, 1879, received its name "from the province of Posen, formerly belonging to Poland, but now a part of the German Empire, from whence most of the settlers came" (*History of the Minnesota Valley*, p. 908).

ST. LEO a city on the line between Omro and Burton, "was named after the church, and the church was so christened in honor of Pope Leo" (history of the county, p. 247). The church, built in 1896, is commemorative of Saint Leo, the first Pope of this name, A.D. 440–461, who is surnamed "the Great." The city was incorporated on June 6, 1940, as a village. The post office was established in 1880 on Valentine Lenz's farm in section 32 of Omro and moved into the village in 1900.

SANDNES TOWNSHIP settled in 1866, mostly by people from Norway, and organized March 12, 1872, bears the name (with slight change in spelling) of Sandnaes, a seaport town of southwestern Norway, adjoining the Stavanger fjord. The township was called Sennes Township, circa 1874.

SILLIARDS see HANLEY FALLS.

SIOUX AGENCY TOWNSHIP first permanently settled in 1865, "was set apart for organization September 4, 1866," being named Yellow Medicine, and its first township meeting was held April 2, 1867. "In March, 1877, the present boundaries were fixed and the name changed to Sioux Agency" (*History of the Minnesota Valley*, p. 892). The Upper Sioux Agency was on the north side of the Yellow Medicine River and about a mile west of its mouth in the northern part of this township. It was occupied from 1854 to 1862 and, as noted by Rose, "became a place of considerable importance and was virtually the capital of the Indian country." The remains of the agency, which was mostly destroyed in the U.S.-Dakota Conflict of 1862, are now preserved as Upper Sioux Agency State Park, established in 1963.

SORLIENS MILL a hamlet of much business in the pioneer days, had a gristmill and post office on the Yellow Medicine River in the southeast part of Minnesota Falls Township. E. H. Sorlien and brothers erected the mill in 1872. The post office was established in section 35 of the township in 1879, with Ellef H. Sorlien, postmaster at his mill until the post office was discontinued in July 1896.

SPRING CREEK a village in section 36 of Tyro Township.

STANLEY see BURR.

STAVANGER post office named from the fjord, city, and district of this name in southern Norway, was established in 1870 in sections 26 and 27, Ree (afterward Normania), and was discontinued in November 1903. The first postmaster was Ole O. Lende, born in Norway 1839; he came to the United States in 1860 and to Yellow Medicine County in 1866, settling on a farm in section 25; was elected country treasurer in 1875 and moved to Granite Falls for ten years; he held a number of other positions, including state senate, 1886–90, and state house, 1892–94.

STONY RUN TOWNSHIP settled in 1869, organized September 26, 1871, "is named for the creek that courses through it," in many places flowing over drift boulders. A post office was in Stony Run Township, section 8, 1873–83, where Knute E. Neste, postmaster, had a store built in 1871.

SUGAR RIVER see BURR.

SWEDE PRAIRIE TOWNSHIP settled in 1870, was organized January 19, 1878. "The name first given to the town was Green Prairie, but was changed March 12, 1878, to Swede Prairie," in compliment to its many immigrants from Sweden.

TWEED see LORNE.

TYRO TOWNSHIP settled in August 1872, was organized October 25, 1879. This name, meaning a beginner, is borne also by villages or hamlets in Virginia, Mississippi, Arkansas, and Kansas.

TYSONS GROVE a post office, 1872–74; location not found.

UPLAND see CLARKFIELD.

VINELAND a post office, 1873–88, in Sandnes Township, section 30, which was transferred to Cottonwood, Lyon County; postmaster O. P. Reishus was the postmaster the entire time.

WEGDAHL a village in Stony Run Township, 1887–1919.

WERGELAND TOWNSHIP organized April 5, 1879, was then named Union, which was changed on May 1 of that year by request of the many Norwegian settlers, "in honor of one of their native country's poets, Henrik Wergeland." He was born at Christiansand, June 17, 1808, and died at Christiania, July 12, 1845.

WOOD LAKE TOWNSHIP settled in 1868, organized November 1, 1873, was named for its largest lake, fringed with timber, whence the battle fought under General Sibley against the Dakota, about four miles east of this lake, September 23, 1862, has been called the Battle of Wood Lake. That battleground is marked by a monument, on the northwest quarter of section 9, Sioux Agency. The battle was followed by the flight of the Dakota to Dakota Territory and the release of the white captives, September 26, at Camp Release in Lac qui Parle County, opposite Montevideo, likewise marked by a monument. The city of Wood Lake, in section 27, platted on September 8, 1884, was incorporated November 28, 1891. Francis Robson, postmaster in his farm home; the post office moved into the village in 1885.

YELLOW MEDICINE CITY founded in 1866 and platted June 10, 1869, was on the south side of the river of this name, about a mile west of the site of the former Yellow Medicine or Upper Sioux Agency. This village was designated as the county seat early in 1872, but in accordance with the vote of the people in 1874 the county offices were removed in December of that year to Granite Falls, which has since been the county seat. During 1875–80 the area of the Yellow Medicine village site reverted to farming land.

A post office called Yellow Medicine was in section 21 of Sioux Agency Township, 1867–1900, established in Redwood County; John Winter, first postmaster.

The mission station bearing this name, also called Pajutazee, occupied from 1853 to 1862, was in section 24 of the present Minnesota Falls Township, being nearly two miles southeast of the Hazelwood mission school and its Dakota community.

Streams and Lakes

Yellow Medicine River bears this name on the map of Maj. Stephen H. Long's expedition in 1823 and on Joseph N. Nicollet's map, 1843. The latter has also the Dakota name, noted at the beginning of this chapter.

Florida Lake, Hazel Run, and Stony Run, giving their names to townships, and Wood Lake, whence another township is named, are noticed in the preceding pages.

Canby Lake, named from the city, and the East Branch of Lac qui Parle River, crossing the west part of this county, flow northward into Lac qui Parle County.

Mud Creek, flowing eastward across Wergeland and Burton, and Spring Creek, crossing Swede Prairie and the north edge of Normania, are tributary to the Yellow Medicine River.

The lakes of this county, occurring only in its southeastern part, include, with Wood Lake, before noted, Sand and House Lakes (both drained) in the same township, the last being named for a pioneer; three small lakes in sections 8 and 17, Sioux Agency, lying a half mile to one and a half miles south of the Wood Lake battleground and monument, the two northern being named

Highbank and Battle or Lone Tree Lakes; a former Lake of the Woods and another long lake or marsh in Echo Township, both drained; Tyson Lake or Marsh, and an adjoining Twin or Timm Lake, in Posen, the first being named for Joseph Tyson, an early homesteader on its south side; and a group of three lakes in Normania, of which the middle one is called Gullickson Lake, for a pioneer Norwegian farmer beside it.

Index

Elysian c., 324, 611; moraine, 328; t. and v., 324–25

Elysian, l., 324, 613

Elysium p.o., 324–25

Emard p.o., for Pierre Emard, 478

Emardville t., for Pierre Emard, 478

Embarrass/Embarras l., 545; r., 10, 202, 215, 521, 522, 545; t. and sta., 521

Embarrassments, r. of, 215

Ember l., 644

Emco sta., 521

Emerald t., 188

Emerson l., 626

Emerson, l., 76

Emetta p.o., 313

Emily c., 158; cr., 308; l., 158, 362; t., 158

Emily, l., 158, 328, 468

Emma l., 250, 622

Emma, l., 143, 368, 431, 433, 643

Emmaville p.o., 249

Emmert sta., 521

Emmet t., for Robert Emmet, 491

Emmons c., for Henry G. Emmons, b., 203

Empire c., 646; site, 611; t., 168, 646

Empire City v., 168

Encampment id., 314; r., 314

Encampment Island v., 310

Enchanted id., 240

Endeavor p.o., 640

Enderly p.o., 482

Endion v., 521

Enfield v., 640

Eng l., for Erick Pehrson Eng, 184

Engebretson, Sander, for, 437

Engelwood t., 297

England, names from, 34, 194, 199, 219, 232, 249, 253, 256, 292, 445, 448, 553, 593, 629, 638

Engler Mill, 319

Englerville v., 319

Englewood v., 32

English Grove l., 184

Englund v., for Andrew J. Englund, 345

Enok v., 290

Ensign l., for Josiah D. Ensign, 314

Enstrom t., for Louis Enstrom, b., 506–7

Enterprise t., 272; v., 633

Epple l., 110

Epsilon l., 315

Equality t. and v., 478

Erakah r., 551

Erdahl t. and v., for Gullik M. Erdahl, b., 219–20

Erenfight sta., 168

Erhard c. and v., for Alexander E. Erhard, 423

Erhards Grove p.o. and t., for Alexander E. Erhard, 423

Erick, l., 47; p.o., for Magnus Erickson, 14

Erickson, Mandus, for, 508

Erickson p.o., for Peter Erickson, 464; sta., 262

Erickson's ad., 56

Ericksonville p.o., for Lars Erickson, 371

Ericsburg v., 297

Ericson t., for Eric Ericson, 491

Erie, l., 342, 367; t., 32; v., 434–35

Erie Mining Company sta., 521

Erin, l., 565; sta., 496; t., 448, 496

Erskine c., for George Q. Erskine, b., 455; l., 163

Erwin l., for George Erwin, 184

Esba p.o., 386

Esdon p.o., 158

Eshkebugecoshe v., 100

Eshquegumag l., 374

Esko v., 78

Eslef p.o., 628

Espelee, Robert S., for, 345

Espelie t., for Robert S. Espelee, 345

Espelien, Andrew H., for, 281

Espetveh p.o., for James H. Espetveh, 455

Esquagama l., 545

Esquagamah l., 15, 22; t., 15

Essex p.o., 423

Essig v., for John Essig, 73

Esterdy p.o., 94

Estes br., for Israel H. Estes, 370, for Jonathan Estes, 374

Estes Brook v., for Israel H. Estes, 370

Esther t., 455

Estherville p.o., 98

Ethel l., 431

Ethel's id., 371

Etna v., 195

Eton sta., 448

Ettaville p.o., 195

Etter v., for Alexander W. Etter, 168

Euclid t., 455

Euclid Mine sta., 521

Eugene t., 41, 319

Eulls l., 643

Eunice, l., 36; p.o., 33

Eureka p.o., 227; t., 168

Eureka Center sta., 168

Evan v., 73

Evans, David C., n., 67

Evans, Matthew, n., 423

Evansville t. and v., for Albert Evans, 180

Evansville Junction sta., 597

Eveleth c., for Erwin Eveleth, 521

Even's l., 287

Evenson l., 367

Everdell v., for Lyman B. Everdell, 628

Everglade t., 582

Evergreen t., 297; v., 32, 262

Everson l., 613

Everton, Fred, n., 190

Everts t., for Edmund A. and Rezin Everts, b., 423

Ewald p.o., for Henry Ewald, 188

Ewington t., for Thomas C. Ewing, 272

Excel t., 345

Excelsior cr. and t., 227; t. and v. 345

Excelsior Amusement Park, 227

Exmoor sta., 521

Eyota c. and t., 414

Faber sta., 536

Fahlun t., 282

Faille l., 594

Fair Haven t., 568

Fair Hills v., 423

Fair Mount v., 353

Fairbank, D. C., n., 176

Fairbanks l., 36; t. and v., for Charles Warren Fairbanks, b., 521

Fairfax c., 491; t., 455

Fairfield cr., for Fairfield settlers, 183; p.o., 414; t., 158, 587; v., 169, 203, 586

Fairhaven v., 640

Fairland v., 297

Fairlane/Fairlane Taconite sta., 521

Fairmont c., 353

Fairpoint v., 210

Fairview p.o., 196, 291, 392; t., 94, 262, 335, 404; v., 25

Fairwater p.o., 633

Fairy l., 432, 594

Fairy Rock v., 243

Faith v., 409

Falcon Heights c., 470

Falk t., for Erick Falk, 127

Fall l., 310, 314; r., 145

Fall Lake t. and v., 310

Fallon l., 367

Falls cr., 500

Falls Junction v., 297

Falls of St. Louis p.o., 521

False Poplar r., 145

Falun t., 507

Minnesota Place Names was designed at the Minnesota Historical Society Press by Will Powers. Ann Sudmeier set the type in Scala and Scala Sans at Stanton Publication Services, St. Paul. The book was printed by Sheridan Books, Chelsea, Michigan.